Praise for *The Oxford Handbook of the Bible in Early Mode*

'[A] splendid volume . . . This handbook gives us the most far-reaching and detailed picture of the Bible in this place and period ever available . . . [a] masterful collection of scholarly pieces on England's early modern biblical culture. This is a treasure chest resource that more than repays careful and reflective study.'

Donald K. McKim, *Church History*

'[T]his volume contains some of the best examples of the work that global contemporary literary critics, biblical scholars, and historians have produced.'

Ellie Gebarowski-Shafer, *Religious Studies Review*

'[T]he essays in this excellent collection are alert to the complexities and distinctive characteristics of the early modern period and its authors.'

Warren Cernaik, *Milton Quarterly*

'Reading a book such as this in its entirety is a rare pleasure . . . this book provides a more nuanced and better grounded understanding of cultural and religious transformations in early modern England.'

Eyal Poleg, *Journal of Ecclesiastical History*

THE OXFORD HANDBOOK OF

THE BIBLE IN EARLY MODERN ENGLAND, c.1530–1700

The Bible was, by any measure, the most important book in early modern England. It preoccupied the scholarship of the era, and suffused the idioms of literature and speech. Political ideas rode on its interpretation and deployed its terms. It was intricately related to the project of natural philosophy. And it was central to daily life at all levels of society from parliamentarian to preacher, from the 'boy that driveth the plough', famously invoked by Tyndale, to women across the social scale. It circulated in texts ranging from elaborate folios to cheap catechisms; it was mediated in numerous forms, as pictures, songs, and embroideries, and as proverbs, commonplaces, and quotations.

Bringing together leading scholars from a range of fields, *The Oxford Handbook of the Bible in Early Modern England, c. 1530–1700* explores how the scriptures served as a generative motor for ideas, and a resource for creative and political thought, as well as for domestic and devotional life.

Sections tackle the knotty issues of translation, the rich range of early modern biblical scholarship, Bible dissemination and circulation, the changing political uses of the Bible, literary appropriations and responses, and the reception of the text across a range of contexts and media. Where existing scholarship focuses, typically, on Tyndale and the King James Bible of 1611, *The Oxford Handbook of the Bible in Early Modern England, c. 1530–1700* goes further, tracing the vibrant and shifting landscape of biblical culture in the two centuries following the Reformation.

Kevin Killeen is Professor in Renaissance Studies at the University of York.

Helen Smith is Professor in Renaissance Literature at the University of York.

Rachel Willie is Senior Lecturer in English Literature and Cultural History at Liverpool John Moores University.

THE OXFORD HANDBOOK OF

THE BIBLE IN EARLY MODERN ENGLAND, c.1530–1700

Edited by

KEVIN KILLEEN, HELEN SMITH,

and

RACHEL WILLIE

OXFORD
UNIVERSITY PRESS

OXFORD
UNIVERSITY PRESS

Great Clarendon Street, Oxford, OX2 6DP,
United Kingdom

Oxford University Press is a department of the University of Oxford.
It furthers the University's objective of excellence in research, scholarship,
and education by publishing worldwide. Oxford is a registered trade mark of
Oxford University Press in the UK and in certain other countries

Published in the United States of America by Oxford University Press
198 Madison Avenue, New York, NY 10016, United States of America

British Library Cataloguing in Publication Data
Data available

Library of Congress Cataloging in Publication Data
Data available

ISBN 978-0-19-968697-1 (Hbk.)
ISBN 978-0-19-882822-8 (Pbk.)

ACKNOWLEDGEMENTS

THIS volume had its origin in the 2011 Festival of Ideas at the University of York, organized by the late Jane Moody, who helped greatly in its development. We would like to acknowledge and thank the generous support of the British Academy in funding the resulting conference on 'The Bible in the Seventeenth Century: An International Conference', alongside the support of the Society for Renaissance Studies and the Institute of Historical Research. The Department of English and Related Literature at York and the Centre for Renaissance and Early Modern Studies both contributed generously, as did the many postgraduates who helped out. We are grateful not only to our speakers at that event, many of whom subsequently became contributors, but to all of the participants whose comments and questions helped to shape this volume. The conference ran alongside an exhibition at York Minster, and we would like to extend our thanks in particular to Sarah Griffin and Victoria Harrison and the staff of the Minster.

Emma Baldwin provided excellent editorial assistance, and thanks also to Marta Napodano. Help with the chronology was provided by Andrew Willie Sr. Thanks to Tania Demetriou for checking the Greek, and Michele Campopiano and Anna Bernard for their help with Hebrew. Jacqueline Baker has been wonderful to work with from the earliest stages of the book and we thank her and the editorial staff at Oxford University Press. Warm thanks to Hannah DeGroff for her scrupulous patience and imagination in compiling the index. Thanks to Angus McBean and Molly Killeen for advice and ideas, and to Sherlock Bones for her patience in the volume's final stages. Finally, and especially, the editors wish to thank the contributors to the volume, who have been excellent to work with, and endlessly patient with our queries, and whose work—both within and beyond these pages—is an ongoing source of inspiration and excitement.

CONTENTS

List of Illustrations   xv

List of Contributors   xvii

Note to the Reader   xxiii

Introduction. 'All other bookes … are but Notes upon this': The Early Modern Bible   1

KEVIN KILLEEN AND HELEN SMITH

PART I TRANSLATIONS

Introduction to Part I   19

1. 'A day after doomsday': Cranmer and the Bible Translations of the 1530s   23

   SUSAN WABUDA

2. Genevan Legacies: The Making of the English Geneva Bible   38

   FEMKE MOLEKAMP

3. *'A comely gate to so rich and glorious a citie'*: The Paratextual Architecture of the Rheims New Testament and the King James Bible   54

   KATRIN ETTENHUBER

4. The King James Bible and Biblical Images of Desolation   71

   KAREN L. EDWARDS

5. The Roman Inkhorn: Religious Resistance to Latinism in Early Modern England   83

   JAMIE H. FERGUSON

6. Retranslating the Bible in the English Revolution   98

   NIGEL SMITH

PART II SCHOLARSHIP

Introduction to Part II   113

7. The Septuagint and the Transformation of Biblical Scholarship
   in England, from the King James Bible (1611) to the London
   Polyglot (1657)   117
   NICHOLAS HARDY

8. The Apocrypha in Early Modern England   131
   ARIEL HESSAYON

9. Isaiah 63 and the Literal Senses of Scripture   149
   DEBORA SHUGER

10. The 'sundrie waies of Wisdom': Richard Hooker on the
    Authority of Scripture and Reason   164
    TORRANCE KIRBY

11. 'The doors shall fly open': Chronology and Biblical
    Interpretation in England, c.1630–c.1730   176
    SCOTT MANDELBROTE

12. Early Modern *geographia sacra* in the Context of Early Modern
    Scholarship   196
    ZUR SHALEV

13. Milton's Corrupt Bible   209
    NEIL FORSYTH

14. The Commodification of Scripture, 1640–1660: Politics,
    Ecclesiology, and the Cultures of Print   224
    CRAWFORD GRIBBEN

15. Self-Defeating Scholarship? Antiscripturism and Anglican
    Apologetics from Hooker to the Latitudinarians   237
    NICHOLAS MCDOWELL

PART III SPREADING THE WORD

Introduction to Part III   257

16. The Church of England and the English Bible, 1559–1640   261
    LORI ANNE FERRELL

17. 'Hearing' and 'Reading': Disseminating Bible Knowledge and
    Fostering Bible Understanding in Early Modern England   272
    IAN GREEN

18. 'All Scripture is given by inspiration of God': Dissonance and
    Psalmody   287
    RACHEL WILLIE

19. Ornament and Repetition: Biblical Interpretation in Early
    Modern English Preaching   303
    MARY MORRISSEY

20. Preaching, Reading, and Publishing the Word in Protestant Scotland   317
    ALASDAIR RAFFE

21. The Bible in Early Modern Gaelic Ireland: Tradition, Collaboration,
    and Alienation   332
    MARC CABALL

22. 'Wilt thou not read me, Atheist?' The Bible and Conversion   350
    HELEN SMITH

PART IV THE POLITICAL BIBLE

Introduction to Part IV   367

23. Mover and Author: King James VI and I and the Political Use
    of the Bible   371
    JANE RICKARD

24. 'A king like other nations': Political Theory and the Hebrew
    Republic in the Early Modern Age   384
    KIM IAN PARKER

25. Digging, Levelling, and Ranting: The Bible and the Civil War Sects   397
    ANDREW BRADSTOCK

26. A Year in the Life of King Saul: 1643   412
    ANNE LAKE PRESCOTT

27. 'That glory may dwell in our land': The Bible, Britannia, and the
    Glorious Revolution   427
    EMMA MAJOR

PART V   THE BIBLE AND LITERATURE

Introduction to Part V   451

28. The King James Bible in its Cultural Moment   455
    HELEN WILCOX

29. The Noblest Composition in the Universe or Fit for the Flames?
    The Literary Style of the King James Bible   469
    HANNIBAL HAMLIN

30. Epic, Meditation, or Sacred History? Women and Biblical Verse
    Paraphrase in Seventeenth-Century England   483
    SARAH C. E. ROSS

31. Scripture and Tragedy in the Reformation   498
    RUSS LEO

32. 'This verse marks that': George Herbert's *The Temple* and
    Scripture in Context   518
    ALISON KNIGHT

33. 'Blessed Joseph! I would thou hadst more fellows': John
    Bunyan's Joseph   533
    NANCY ROSENFELD

34. *Paradise Lost*, the Bible, and Biblical Epic   546
    BARBARA K. LEWALSKI

PART VI   RECEPTION HISTORIES

Introduction to Part VI   561

35. Donne's Biblical Encounters   564
    EMMA RHATIGAN

36. Domestic Decoration and the Bible in the Early Modern Home   577
    ANDREW MORRALL

37. 'My exquisite copies for action': John Saltmarsh and the
    Machiavellian Bible   598
    KEVIN KILLEEN

38. Unbelief and the Bible   613
     ROGER POOLEY

39. Inwardness and English Bible Translations   626
     ERICA LONGFELLOW

40. Early Modern Davids: From Sin to Critique   640
     YVONNE SHERWOOD

Chronology   659
Bibliography   687
Index   761

LIST OF ILLUSTRATIONS

0.1   Title-page, *The Newe Testament* (with 1611 date), in *The Holy Bible*
(London: Robert Barker, 1613). York Minster Library; HOB Bagby 4.
Reproduced by kind permission of the Chapter of York.   7

0.2   Bible. N.T. Gospels. English. Authorized. 1630. [Little Gidding
concordance] [Little Gidding, 1630.] Houghton Library, Harvard
University, Cambridge, Mass., A 1275.5, p. 10 (seq. 14). Reproduced by
permission of the Houghton Library.   9

3.1   *The Holy Bible, conteyning the Old Testament, and the New* (London,
1611), KJB, A2ʳ. Folger Shakespeare Library, STC 2216. By permission of
the Folger Shakespeare Library.   63

3.2   *The Holy Bible, conteyning the Old Testament, and the New* (London,
1611), KJB, A3ʳ. Folger Shakespeare Library, STC 2216. By permission of
the Folger Shakespeare Library.   65

5.1   Title-page, William Fulke, *The Text of the New Testament of Jesus Christ*
(London: Deputies of Christopher Barker, 1589). YML: OL; I.I.25.
Reproduced by kind permission of the Chapter of York.   87

11.1   Title-page, James Ussher, *Annals of the World* (1658). Reproduced by
permission of the owner.   182

11.2   Frontispiece, Henry Isaacson, *Saturni ephemerides* (1633). By kind
permission of the Master and Fellows of Peterhouse, Cambridge.   187

11.3   A genealogy of the Greek kings, from Robert Cary's *Palaeologia
chronica* (London, 1677). Reproduced by permission of the owner.   188

12.1   Thomas Fuller, *A Pisgah-Sight of Palestine* (London: printed by JF for
John Williams, 1650), 238–9. York Minster Library: OL; XXXVI.B.6.
Reproduced by kind permission of the Chapter of York.   204

18.1   Title-page to *The Psalter or Psalmes of Dauid* (London: in officina
Gulihelmi Seres typographi, 1569). York Minster Library: OL; XI.F.20.
Reproduced by kind permission of the Chapter of York.   300

21.1   Title-page, William Daniel, *Leabhar na nurnaightheadh
gcomhchoidchiond agus mheinisdraldachda na Sacrameinteadh* (Irish
Book of Common Prayer) (Dublin, 1608). York Minster Library: OL;
XI.G.13/2. Reproduced by kind permission of the Chapter of York.   338

22.1   Needlework hanging depicting Faith and Mahomet, Hardwick Hall,
Derbyshire, c.1590s. By permission of National Trust Images.   360

27.1   Robert White, frontispiece to John Nalson's *Impartial Collection of the Great Affairs of State*, 1682 © Trustees of the British Museum.   428

27.2   Commemorative silver medal of Britannia, the Bible, and William III, 1689 © Trustees of the British Museum.   433

27.3   The seven bishops in a pyramid, print by Simon Gribelin, 1688 © Trustees of the British Museum.   440

27.4   The seven bishops, 1688 © Trustees of the British Museum.   441

27.5   *Britannia oppressa per Arausionensium Principem liberata et restaurata*, 1688 © Trustees of the British Museum.   446

36.1   Jörg Breu the Elder, 'Giving Drink to the Thirsty', Design for yellow stained-glass roundel, pen and brush with black ink, with some red tone, 18.3 cm diam. Staatliche Museen, Kupferstichkabinett, Berlin. Photo: Jörg P. Anders. © Staatliche Museen, Kupferstichkabinett, Berlin.   580

36.2   Circle of the Pseudo-Ortkens Group, *Susanna and the Elders*, yellow stained-glass roundel, c.1520–5, diam. 9 ½ in (24.1 cm) with border 13 in (33 cm). New York, The Metropolitan Museum of Art, Cloisters Collection, inv. no. 199.119.1. © The Metropolitan Museum of Art.   581

36.3   Heinrich Sulzer (attrib.), Portrait of the Family of Hans Conrad Bodmer, Landvogt von Greifensee, 1643. Oil on canvas, 73 × 93 cm. Zürich, Schweizerisches Landesmuseum, inv. no. DEP-3721 (on loan from a private collection). © Schweizerisches Landesmuseum.   587

36.4   Fruit Trencher, English, early seventeenth century, Gouache on wood, New York, Metropolitan Museum of Art, inv. no. 64.101.1582. © The Metropolitan Museum of Art.   589

36.5   'David and Abigail', English, third quarter seventeenth century, canvas worked with silk thread, 37 × 44.7 cm. Gift of Irwin Untermeyer 1964, New York, Metropolitan Museum of Art, inv. no. 64.101.1310. © The Metropolitan Museum of Art.   591

36.6   Frontispiece to Genesis, *Geneva Bible* (London, Robert Barker, 1607), woodcut, New York, The Metropolitan Museum of Art, inv. no. 64.101.1291. © The Metropolitan Museum of Art.   593

36.7   Anne Cornwalys, embroidered Bible cover with Adam and Eve (front) and the resurrected Christ (back). English, c.1641. New York, Pierpont Morgan Library, inv. no. PM17197. By permission of the Pierpont Morgan Library.   594

40.1   'Probor', in Daniel Cramer, *Societas Jesu et Roseae crucis vera: Hoc est, Decades quator emblematum sacrorum ex sacra Scriptura, de dulcissimo nomine et cruce Jesu Christi* (Frankfurt: Nicolai Hoffmann, 1617). By permission of Glasgow University Library.   649

LIST OF CONTRIBUTORS

Andrew Bradstock is author and editor of a number of works on religion and politics in seventeenth-century England, including *Faith in the Revolution: The Political Theologies of Müntzer and Winstanley* (SPCK, 1997), *Winstanley and the Diggers 1649–1999* (Routledge, 2000), and *Radical Religion in Cromwell's England: A Concise History from the English Civil War to the End of the Commonwealth* (I. B. Tauris, 2011). He is co-editor, with Christopher Rowland, of *Radical Christian Writings: A Reader* (Wiley-Blackwell, 2002). Currently national secretary for church and society with the United Reformed Church, he was, from 2009 to 2013, Howard Paterson Professor of Theology and Public Issues at the University of Otago, New Zealand. He has lectured in theology and church history at colleges in the UK.

Marc Caball is a historian of early modern Ireland with particular expertise in the cultural history of Gaelic Ireland. He is a senior lecturer in UCD School of History and Archives. A former research scholar of the Dublin Institute for Advanced Studies, he holds a D.Phil. from the University of Oxford and is a fellow of the Royal Historical Society. He is the current chairman of the COST (European Cooperation in Science and Technology) Domain Committee for Individuals, Cultures, Societies and Health (DC ISCH). Among his many publications is *Poets and Politics: Reaction and Continuity in Irish poetry, 1558–1625* (Cork/Notre Dame Press, 1999).

Karen L. Edwards teaches at the University of Exeter and is the author of *Milton and the Natural World: Science and Poetry in* Paradise Lost (Cambridge, 1999), *Milton's Reformed Animals: An Early Modern Bestiary* (2005–9), and a number of articles on seventeenth-century literature, religion, and natural philosophy. She is currently working on a study of abusive epithets in sixteenth- and seventeenth-century religious polemic.

Katrin Ettenhuber is Fellow and Director of Studies in English at Pembroke College, Cambridge, and Newton Trust Lecturer in the Cambridge English Faculty. She is the author of *Donne's Augustine: Renaissance Cultures of Interpretation* (Oxford, 2011), co-editor, with Gavin Alexander and Sylvia Adamson, of *Renaissance Figures of Speech* (Cambridge, 2007), and editor of vol. v of the Oxford edition of the *Sermons of John Donne* (Oxford, 2015). She has published widely on the religious literature and culture of the early modern period, and is currently working on a new project on conceptions of sacred time in seventeenth-century writing.

Jamie H. Ferguson is Assistant Professor of English at the University of Houston. He is completing a book manuscript, *Faith in the Language: the Reformation and English Poetics*, on the convergence of biblical hermeneutics and English literature from Tyndale to Donne. He has recently published 'Miles Coverdale and the Claims of Paraphrase' and has two articles forthcoming: 'Faith in the Language: Biblical Authority and the Meaning of English in the

More–Tyndale Polemics' and 'The Epic and the Prophetic: A Reading of 1 Samuel 15–16 and 2 Samuel 7'.

Lori Anne Ferrell is Professor of Early Modern Literature and History and Director of the Early Modern Studies Program at Claremont Graduate University. She is the author of many recent essays and articles on early modern English religious culture and literature, and the monographs *The Bible and the People* (Yale, 2008) and *Government by Polemic* (Stanford, 1998). Professor Ferrell is currently editing volume xi of the *Oxford Sermons of John Donne: Sermons Preached at St Paul's Cathedral* (forthcoming).

Neil Forsyth is the author of *The Old Enemy: Satan and the Combat Myth* (Princeton, 1989) and *The Satanic Epic* (Princeton, 2003), as well as a recent biography of Milton. His collaborative work on Dickens in Switzerland has just appeared, his essay on films of *Macbeth* has been republished in a new edition of the play, and a brief tribute to the memory of Angela Carter is forthcoming. He is Professeur Honoraire at the University of Lausanne, Switzerland.

Ian Green is Professor Emeritus of Queen's University Belfast, where he taught for thirty years, and Honorary Professorial Fellow in the School of History of the University of Edinburgh. He is author of *'The Christian's ABC': Catechisms and Catechizing in England c.1530–1740* (Oxford, 1996), *Print and Protestantism in Early Modern England* (Oxford, 2000), and *Humanism and Protestantism in Early Modern English Education* (Ashgate, 2009).

Crawford Gribben is Professor of Early Modern British History at Queen's University Belfast. He is the author of *The Puritan Millennium: Literature and Theology, 1550–1682* (Paternoster, 2000), *God's Irishmen: Theological Debates in Cromwellian Ireland* (Oxford, 2007), *Writing the Rapture: Prophecy Fiction in Evangelical America* (Oxford, 2009), and *Evangelical Millennialism in the Trans-Atlantic World, 1500–2000* (Palgrave, 2011).

Hannibal Hamlin is Professor of English at the University of Ohio and researches Renaissance literature and culture. He is the author of *Psalm Culture and Early Modern English Literature* (Cambridge, 2004), as well as editing *The King James Bible After 400 Years: Literary, Linguistic and Cultural Influences* (Cambridge, 2010), and has published articles in *Renaissance Quarterly*, *Spenser Studies*, the *Sidney Journal*, *John Donne Journal*, *Yale Review* , and *Early Modern Literary Studies*.

Nicholas Hardy is a member of the English Faculty and Junior Research Fellow at Trinity College, Cambridge. His principal interests are in the history of scholarship and literary criticism, although he has also worked on the early modern reception of Lucretius. He is currently completing a monograph on the *ars critica* in early modern England.

Ariel Hessayon is Senior Lecturer in the Department of History at Goldsmiths, University of London. He is the author of *'Gold Tried in the Fire': The Prophet TheaurauJohn Tany and the English Revolution* (Ashgate, 2007) and the lead editor of three collections of essays on *Scripture and Scholarship in Early Modern England* (Ashgate, 2006), *Varieties of Seventeenth- and Early Eighteenth-Century English Radicalism in Context* (Ashgate, 2011), and *An Introduction to Jacob Boehme: Four Centuries of Thought and Reception* (Routledge, 2013). He has written extensively on a variety of early modern topics: antiscripturism, book burning, communism, environmentalism, esotericism, extra-canonical texts, heresy, crypto-Jews, Judaizing, millenarianism, mysticism, prophecy, and religious radicalism.

Kevin Killeen is Professor in Renaissance Studies at the University of York. He has edited *Sir Thomas Browne: Twenty-First Century Authors* (Oxford, 2014), and is the author of *Biblical Scholarship, Science and Politics in Early Modern England: Thomas Browne and the Thorny Place of Knowledge* (Ashgate, 2009) and co-editor, with Peter Forshaw, of *Biblical Exegesis and the Emergence of Science in the Early Modern Era* (Palgrave, 2007). He is currently finishing a monograph entitled *The Political Bible in Early Modern England* (Cambridge, forthcoming) and is editing two volumes for *The Oxford Works of Sir Thomas Browne*.

Torrance Kirby is Professor of Ecclesiastical History and Director of the Centre for Research on Religion at McGill University, Montreal. He received a D.Phil. degree in Modern History from Oxford University in 1988. He is a life member of Corpus Christi College, Cambridge, and has been a member of the Princeton Centre of Theological Inquiry since 1996. Recent books include *Persuasion and Conversion: Religion, Politics and the Public Sphere in Early Modern England* (Brill, 2013), *The Zurich Connection and Tudor Political Theology* (Brill, 2007), and *Richard Hooker, Reformer and Platonist* (Ashgate, 2005). He is also the editor of *Mediating Religious Cultures in Early Modern Europe* (Scholars, 2013), *A Companion to Richard Hooker* (Brill, 2008), and *Paul's Cross and the Culture of Persuasion, 1520–1640* (Brill, 2014).

Alison Knight is a research fellow at the University of Cambridge's Centre for Research in the Arts, Social Sciences, and Humanities (CRASSH). She is also a research associate at Emmanuel College, Cambridge. She is currently a member of CRASSH's European Research Council-funded project, 'The Bible and Antiquity in Nineteenth-Century Culture', for which she is developing a project on the history of the English Bible in the nineteenth century. She is also preparing a monograph on the literary use of the book of Job in early modern England.

Russ Leo works in the Department of English at Princeton and is currently completing two projects, one entitled *Enlightenment from Below: Milton, Spinoza and the Resources of Revolution* and a book *Reformation Tragedy: Affect and Necessity*, a work that examines the philosophico-theological purchase of tragedy in early modernity.

Barbara K. Lewalski is Professor of History and Literature at Harvard University, where she has taught for many years. Some publications include: *Protestant Poetics and the Seventeenth-Century Religious Lyric* (Princeton, 1979), *The Life of John Milton: A Critical Biography* (Blackwell, 2000, 2003); *Paradise Lost and the Rhetoric of Literary forms* (Princeton, 1985), and an original spelling/punctuation edition of *Paradise Lost* (Blackwell, 2007). She is co-editor of vol. iii (*Milton's Shorter Poems*) for a multi-volume edition of Milton's Works (Oxford University Press).

Erica Longfellow is Dean of Divinity at New College, Oxford. She is the author of *Women and Religious Writing in Early Modern England* (Cambridge, 2004) and editor of the life writings of Elizabeth Isham. She is currently editing a volume of the Oxford edition of the *Sermons of John Donne* (Oxford, forthcoming).

Emma Major is Senior Lecturer at the Department of English and Related Literature and the interdisciplinary Centre for Eighteenth-Century Studies at the University of York. She has published articles on eighteenth-century women, religion, and national identity. Her monograph is entitled *Madam Britannia: Women, Church, and Nation 1712–1812* (Oxford, 2012).

Scott Mandelbrote is Fellow, Perne Librarian, and Director of Studies in History at Peterhouse, Cambridge, and Sub-Warden of All Souls College, Oxford. He is the author of *Footprints of the Lion: Isaac Newton at Work* (Cambridge, 2001), and *The Garden, the Ark, The Tower, the Temple: Biblical Metaphors of Knowledge in Early Modern Europe* (Oxford, 1998); and has edited *Dissent and the Bible in Britain, c.1650–1950* with Michael Ledger-Lomas (Oxford, 2013); *Nature and Scripture in the Abrahamic Religions* 4 vols, with Jitse van der Meer (Leiden, 2008); and *The Practice of Reform in Health, Medicine, and Science* (Aldershot, 2005). He is editorial director of the Newton Project and his research interests are in early modern intellectual history, particularly the history of religion and the history of knowledge and science.

Nicholas McDowell is Professor of Early Modern Literature and Thought at the University of Exeter. His visiting positions have included Membership of the Institute for Advanced Study, Princeton. He is the author of *The English Radical Imagination: Culture, Religion, and Revolution, 1630–1660* (Oxford, 2003) and *Poetry and Allegiance in the English Civil Wars: Marvell and the Cause of Wit* (Oxford, 2008). He is the co-editor, with Nigel Smith, of *The Oxford Handbook of Milton* (Oxford, 2009) and, with N. H. Keeble, of *The Oxford Complete Works of John Milton*, vol. vi. *Vernacular Regicide and Republican Writings* (Oxford, 2013). An intellectual biography of Milton is forthcoming from Princeton University Press.

Femke Molekamp is a lecturer in Renaissance Literature at the University of Warwick, working on the devotional reading practices of early modern women, female religious literary culture, and the Geneva Bible. She is the author of a number of articles and a monograph entitled *Women and the Bible: Religious Reading and Writing in Early Modern England* (Oxford, 2013).

Andrew Morrall is Professor and Director of Doctoral Studies at the Bard Graduate Center. He specializes in the study of the Reformation and the Arts, and has published widely on the representation of biblical scholarship in artefacts of material culture. He is author of *Jörg Breu the Elder: Art, Culture, and Belief in Reformation Augsburg* (Ashgate, 2002).

Mary Morrissey is Associate Professor in the Department of English Language and Literature, University of Reading. She is author of *Politics and the Paul's Cross Sermons, 1558–1642* (Oxford, 2011) and is editing John Donne's Paul's Cross and Spital sermons for the Oxford edition of the *Sermons of John Donne*. She has published articles on early modern religious culture, preaching rhetoric, and on early modern women's devotional writing.

Kim Ian Parker is Professor of Religious Studies at the Memorial University of Newfoundland. He is the author of *The Biblical Politics of John Locke* (Wilfrid Laurier, 2004), *Wisdom and Law in the Reign of Solomon* (Mellen, 1993), and editor of *Liberal Democracy and the Bible* (Mellen, 1992).

Roger Pooley teaches English at Keele University and researches in Bunyan and the literary cultures of nonconformity. His publications include *English Prose of the Seventeenth Century, 1590–1700* (Longman, 1992) and an edition of *The Pilgrim's Progress* (Penguin classics, 2009).

Anne Lake Prescott is Helen Goodhart Altschul Professor of English Emerita at Barnard College and also teaches at Columbia. She is the author of *French Poets and the English Renaissance* (Yale, 1998) and *Imagining Rabelais in Renaissance England* (Yale, 1978), numerous essays and chapters, and is the editor of *The Norton Critical Edition of Spenser* (Norton,

1993), *Female and Male Voices in Early Modern England: A Renaissance Anthology* (Columbia, 2000), and the *Early Modern Englishwomen* series, published by Ashgate.

Alasdair Raffe is Chancellor's Fellow in History at the University of Edinburgh. He is the author of *The Culture of Controversy: Religious Arguments in Scotland, 1660–1714* (Boydell, 2012) and of articles concerning religious and political culture in early modern Scotland. With Natalie Mears, Stephen Taylor, and Philip Williamson, he co-edited *National Prayers: Special Worship since the Reformation*, vol. i. *Special Prayers, Fasts and Thanksgivings in the British Isles, 1533–1688* (Boydell, 2013).

Emma Rhatigan is Lecturer in Early Modern Literature at the University of Sheffield. She is co-editor of *The Oxford Handbook of the Early Modern Sermon* (Oxford, 2011) and the author of essays and articles on Donne, preaching, and drama. She is currently editing a volume of Donne's Lincoln's Inn sermons for the Oxford edition of the *Sermons of John Donne*.

Jane Rickard is Lecturer in Seventeenth-Century English Literature at the University of Leeds. She is the author of *Authorship and Authority: the Writings of James VI and I* (Manchester, 2007), and co-editor of *Shakespeare's Book: Essays in Reading, Writing and Reception* (Manchester, 2008). She has also published articles and chapters on authors including Ben Jonson, John Donne, and Shakespeare.

Nancy Rosenfeld (University of Haifa, Israel) teaches in the English Studies Unit and in the Humanities Enrichment Program of the Max Stern College of Emek Yizreel (Jezreel Valley), Israel. She is the author of *The Human Satan in Seventeenth Century English Literature: From Milton to Rochester* (Ashgate, 2008), and has published articles on John Milton, John Bunyan, John Wilmot, second Earl of Rochester, John Keats, Robert Graves, and Siegfried Sassoon. Rosenfeld's research interests include the literature of seventeenth-century dissenters and the English soldier-poets of the First World War. She is currently completing a monograph tentatively entitled *John Bunyan's Imaginary*.

Sarah C. E. Ross is a senior lecturer in English at Victoria University of Wellington. She is the author of *Women, Poetry, and Politics in Seventeenth-Century Britain* (Oxford, forthcoming) and numerous articles on early modern women's writing. She is also the editor of *Katherine Austen's Book M: British Library Additional MS 4454* (ACMRS, 2011).

Zur Shalev is a senior lecturer at the University of Haifa. He specializes in early modern European cultural and intellectual history, with particular interest in geographical and religious thought. Currently he is working on geographical Hebraism: a study of the reception of medieval geographical Hebrew texts in early modern Christian Europe. Another research project focuses on early modern learned travel to the Levant and on the real and perceived boundaries of the Republic of Letters. His recent published work includes: *Sacred Words and Worlds* (Brill, 2011), and *Ptolemy's Geography in the Renaissance*, co-edited with Charles Burnett (Warburg Institute, 2011).

Yvonne Sherwood is a professor in the faculty of Theology and Religious Studies at the University of Kent and is the author of *A Biblical Text and its Afterlives: the Survival of Jonah in Western Culture* (Cambridge, 2000), *Sanctified Aggression: Legacies of Biblical and Post-Biblical Vocabularies of Violence* (Continuum, 2004), and *The Prostitute and the Prophet: Reading Hosea in the Late Twentieth Century* (T. & T. Clark, 2004). She has edited *Derrida and*

Religion: Other Testaments (Routledge, 2004) and *Representing the Irreparable: The Shoah, the Bible and the Art of Samuel Bak* (Syracuse/Pucker Gallery, 2008).

Debora Shuger is Professor of Renaissance Studies at UCLA, with interests in Tudor-Stuart devotional poetry and prose, theology and biblical exegesis, legal history, political thought, rhetoric, and life writing. She is the author, among other works, of: *Censorship and Cultural Sensibility: The Regulation of Language in Tudor-Stuart England* (Pennsylvania, 2006); *Political Theologies in Shakespeare's England* (Palgrave, 2001); *The Renaissance Bible* (California, 1994); *Habits of Thought in the English Renaissance: Religion, Politics, and the Dominant Culture* (Toronto, 1990); and *Sacred Rhetoric* (Princeton, 1988).

Helen Smith is Professor in Renaissance Literature at the University of York. She is the author of *Grossly Material Things: Women and Book Production in Early Modern England* (Oxford, 2012; winner of the SHARP DeLong Book History Prize, 2013, and the Roland H. Bainton Literature Prize, 2013), and co-editor, with Louise Wilson, of *Renaissance Paratexts* (Cambridge, 2011). Helen leads the AHRC research network, 'Imagining Jerusalem, c.1099 to the Present Day'. She is currently co-editing, with Simon Ditchfield, *Conversions: Gender and Religious Change in Early Modern Europe*, and completing a monograph on early modern ideas of matter and their material expressions.

Nigel Smith is Professor of English at Princeton. He is the author of *Andrew Marvell: The Chameleon* (Yale, 2010); *Is Milton better than Shakespeare?* (Harvard, 2008); the Longman Annotated English Poets edition of *Andrew Marvell's Poems* (Longman, 2003); *Literature and Revolution in England, 1640–1660* (Yale, 1994); and *Perfection Proclaimed: Language and Literature in English Radical Religion 1640–1660* (Oxford, 1989). He has also edited the *Journal of George Fox* (1998) and the Ranter pamphlets (1983; revised edn. 2012), and co-edited with Nicholas McDowell the *Oxford Handbook to Milton* (Oxford, 2009).

Susan Wabuda is Associate Professor of History at Fordham University and a fellow of the Royal Historical Society. Her specialty is the history and theology of the Reformation. In addition to numerous essays, she is the author of *Preaching during the English Reformation* (Cambridge, 2002).

Helen Wilcox is Professor of English and Head of School at Bangor University, Wales. She has research interests across a range of early modern literature including devotional poetry, autobiographical writings, tragicomedy, women's writing, and the relationship of literary texts to music and the visual arts. Her publications include *Women and Literature in Britain, 1500–1700* (Cambridge, 1996); *Betraying our Selves: Forms of Self-Representation in Early Modern English Texts* (Macmillan, 2000); *The English Poems of George Herbert* (Cambridge, 2007); and, most recently, *1611: Authority, Gender and the Word in Early Modern England* (Blackwell, 2014). She is co-editor of the forthcoming Arden 3 edition of *All's Well That Ends Well* and of the *Oxford Handbook of Early Modern Literature and Religion*.

Rachel Willie is Senior Lecturer in English at Liverpool John Moores University. Her book, *Staging the Revolution: Drama, Reinvention and History, 1647–1672*, is forthcoming from Manchester University Press. She has published on Milton, Charles I and martyrological discourse, and the printing of playtexts in the nascent public sphere.

NOTE TO THE READER

ORIGINAL spelling has been retained, save where noted by contributors. Punctuation and capitalization have generally been preserved as they appear in the sources, although some contractions have been silently expanded. The editors have regularized u/v and i/j, and all English titles have been capitalized in line with house style.

INTRODUCTION

....

'ALL OTHER BOOKES ... ARE BUT NOTES UPON THIS': THE EARLY MODERN BIBLE

....

KEVIN KILLEEN AND HELEN SMITH

WRITING in 1646, the immensely learned Orientalist and linguistic scholar, John Gregory, complained, following Ecclesiastes, that 'in making [books] there is no end, and … reading of them (especially many of them) is a wearinesse unto the flesh'. One book, however, was worthy to 'be meditated in day and night'. The Bible, wrote Gregory, 'is the onely Text we have, all other Bookes, and arts, and men, and the world it selfe are but Notes upon this': the world is merely a marginal commentary on scripture.[1] While there is hyperbole in this, many early modern scholars and divines would have agreed that the purpose of study, whether delving into the intricacies of antiquarianism and the classics, or seeking to understand the world through natural philosophy and geographical enquiry, was to elucidate the scriptures. At the beginning of his address to the reader of his compendious collection of historical and antiquarian questions, Gregory elides the Word as text with the world as the Idea of God, making reference, in the process, to Islamic tradition: 'The Mahumetans say, that the first thing that God created was a Pen: Indeed the whole Creation is but a Transcript. And God when he made the world did but write it out of that Copy which he had of it in his divine understanding from all eternity'. That the first object, prior to the world, was a pen is a beguiling thought, but Gregory's point is the congruity between the Word and the world, each a 'transcript' of God's mind. The Bible mattered in early modern England as the pivot of thought and learning, to which knowledge of all sorts might be directed, and which contained inexhaustible conceptual and intellectual, as well as spiritual, riches.

That the Bible was the most important book in early modern England is more or less a commonplace, but its operative scope remains difficult to conceive. It was important in that it preoccupied the scholarship of the era: historical, geographical, and linguistic thought turned invariably to it. It was important in that political ideas at all levels rode on

---

[1] John Gregory, *Notes and Observations upon Some Passages of Scripture* (1646), A4ʳ; Ecclesiastes 12: 12.

its interpretation and deployed its terms. It suffused the idioms of literature and speech. And of course, it was the pivot, in different ways, to both Protestant and Catholic religious—and hence, daily—experience, from private worship to public sermons. Theological writing from polemic and debate to devotional guides and tracts on godly living referred to, interpreted, and argued about, the Bible and its meanings. The Bible's centrality in the period will be readily granted by almost every scholar working across disciplines from literature to the history of science, art, and music to the history of the book, yet it tends to remain at the periphery of most of them. Political histories have shown that early modern thought was in rich conversation with classical Greece and Rome, but have frequently ignored its attention to the biblical.[2] Our canons of literature (with some important exceptions) have excluded, by default, much that is biblical, and, as a more or less direct consequence, much extant writing by women. The separation of science and the Bible was, until recent decades, almost axiomatic.[3]

Arguing for the marginality of the Bible in our picture of the early modern period might strike some readers as absurd, however. Its translation history has been written again and again and statements of its centrality to European and Anglo-American culture are firmly part of both popular and scholarly history.[4] Many of the authors included in this volume, and numerous others cited in its pages, have written previously and wonderfully on the early modern Bible in its historical moment. Nonetheless, as the chapters in this volume show, the early modern Bible continues to present new possibilities for scholarship, and for a nuanced understanding of the era's biblical culture that moves away from a straightforward narrative of the triumph of the vernacular.

This handbook attends to the diverse and multiple contexts in which the Bible was put to use in the period, its generative role in early modern thought. It ranges across the scholarly, the ecclesiastical, the political, the cultural, the theological, and the devotional, and across a time-frame that goes beyond the immediate concerns of the Reformation or of 1611. It is the sheer diversity of the scriptures and their ability to impinge on all areas of sixteenth- and seventeenth-century life that constituted them as such important texts and concepts. The animating purpose of this book is to trace the knotty practical and intellectual concerns of Bible translation and scholarship, the forms and contexts in which the Bible was seen, heard, and read, its varied uses in political thought and action, and its shaping presence in the literature of the English Renaissance.

---

[2] Quentin Skinner's absenting of the biblical, for instance, has been remarked upon by John Coffey, 'Quentin Skinner and the Religious Dimension of Early Modern Political Thought', in Alister Chapman, John Coffey; and Brad S. Gregory (eds), *Seeing Things Their Way: Intellectual History and the Return of Religion* (Notre Dame, Ind.: University of Notre Dame Press 2009), 46–74.

[3] On which, Peter Harrison, *The Bible, Protestantism and the Rise of Natural Science* (Cambridge: Cambridge University Press, 1998).

[4] See, for instance, Gordon Campbell, *Bible: The Story of the King James Version 1611–2011* (Oxford: Oxford University Press, 2010); David Daniell, *The Bible in English* (New Haven: Yale University Press, 2003); Hannibal Hamlin and Norman W. Jones (eds), *The King James Bible After Four Hundred Years: Literary, Linguistic, and Cultural Influences* (Cambridge: Cambridge University Press, 2010); David S. Katz, *God's Last Words: Reading the English Bible from the Reformation to Fundamentalism* (New Haven: Yale University Press, 2004); David Norton, *The King James Bible: A Short History from Tyndale to Today* (Cambridge: Cambridge University Press, 2011).

I. Which Bible?

But what was the early modern English Bible? During the medieval period, the Bible used in churches, for private reading, or for theological study, was the Latin Vulgate, derived from St Jerome's fourth-century translation from the Hebrew Old Testament and Greek New Testament. Circulating in manuscript, the Vulgate varied in its structure and text until some degree of uniformity was achieved by scholars working at the University of Paris in the thirteenth century. The Bible existed in a variety of written forms, from complete texts to single books or compendia, and from elegant, expensive folios to small volumes mass-produced by rooms full of scribes taking dictation.

With the advent of printing using moveable type, Bibles quickly became a staple of print. The Gutenberg Bible printed in Mainz in early 1455 sold out its first edition of 180 copies almost immediately, admired not only as the word of God but as a technological marvel. Eighty further unglossed editions of the Vulgate followed in print before 1500.[5] Debates surrounding the Bible, in its numerous editions, were central to the European Reformation, and the precise details of translation, annotation, commentary, and presentation, became both weapons and battlefields in the debates surrounding the church. Reformers challenged the authority of the Vulgate, arguing, alongside many humanists, that interpretation should be based on a detailed understanding of the Hebrew and Greek originals. Erasmus's new Latin translation of the New Testament, the *Novum instrumentum* of 1516, not only returned to the Greek original, but printed the Greek text alongside the Latin, allowing the knowledgeable reader to study, and judge, his interpretative choices.

Print and translation projects went hand in hand. At the end of the fifteenth century, vernacular Bibles began to be published across Europe. Despite the popularity of biblical stories, like those in the Franciscan collection *Dives and Pauper* (c.1405–10; first printed 1493), England was far behind most of its continental counterparts in the work of Bible translation and the printing of a vernacular text, not least because of a 1409 ban imposed by Archbishop Arundel in an attempt to quell Wycliffite demands for an English Bible.[6] Nonetheless, during the 1520s, reform-minded translators including William Tyndale demanded, according to the Protestant martyrologist John Foxe, that the Bible, in the vernacular, should be made available even to 'a boye that dryveth the plough', as able as any priest to interpret the scriptures, thanks to the inner guidance of the Spirit.[7]

The history of the Bible in England is connected to but not coterminous with the history of Bible translation into English. The Bible *in English* circulated beyond political and geographic boundaries, reaching across and beyond the four nations, while *in England* (as in Scotland, Wales, and Ireland) the scriptures remained current not only in elite scholarly languages but in a variety of popular pictorial forms. It is nonetheless worth rehearsing briefly the story of the 'Englishing' of the Bible; a story that reminds us not only of the intellectual but of the material European contexts of the scriptures in England. Even

[5] Anthony Kenny, 'Introduction', to Kimberly van Kampen and Paul Saenger (eds), *The Bible as Book: The First Printed Editions* (London and Newcastle: British Library and Oak Knoll Press, 1999), 1–5.
[6] See M. C. A. Bose and J. P. Hornback II (eds), *Wycliffite Controversies* (Turnhout: Brepols, 2011).
[7] John Foxe, *The Unabridged Acts and Monuments Online* or *TAMO* (1563 edn) (Sheffield: HRI Online Publications, 2011). Available from: <http//www.johnfoxe.org>.

after Henry VIII's break with Rome in 1534, the project of Bible translation was regarded with suspicion in many quarters. Tyndale tried and failed to persuade Cuthbert Tunstall, Bishop of London, to print an English Bible. He travelled instead to Cologne, where he commissioned Peter Quentell, a member of a major printing dynasty, to print copies of the New Testament, the first book printed abroad for illegal distribution in England.[8] The remaining sheets of this edition, left incomplete when Tyndale was betrayed and forced to flee, show the overwhelming influence of Luther's 1522 New Testament; it imitates its page layout, paratexts, and order, and translates elements of Luther's commentary and glosses directly.

In Worms, in 1526, Tyndale's New Testament was completed and copies were smuggled into England and Scotland, hidden in bales of cloth. While in Germany, Tyndale learned Hebrew, and in 1530, in Antwerp, he printed the Pentateuch, the first translation from Hebrew into English. Tyndale continued to work on his translation of the Old Testament, but in 1535 was arrested and imprisoned in Vilvorde Castle near Brussels. On 6 October 1536, Tyndale was executed: strangled and then burnt. Many of his phrases and word choices, however, persisted in subsequent translations of the Bible, including the King James Bible of 1611.[9] In 1610, 84-year-old Rose Throckmorton reminisced about her mother's access 'to some light of the gospel' during this period, thanks to 'some English books sent privately to her by my father's factors from beyond the sea'. Throckmorton's mother, she recalled, used to call her daughters into her chamber, and 'read to us out of the same books very privately', a vivid reminder of the dangers of Bible reading, as well as its centrality to domestic life.[10]

The first complete English printed Bible was printed in Cologne in 1535.[11] It was the work of Miles Coverdale, later Bishop of Exeter, and its New Testament, in particular, drew heavily on Tyndale's existing translation. A few months after Tyndale's death, one of his associates, John Roger, gathered his existing printed texts and surviving manuscripts into a complete Bible, using Coverdale's translation to fill the gaps. Already, the religious climate in England had shifted: Archbishop Cranmer and Thomas Cromwell were sympathetic to the project of scriptural translation, and in 1536 Cromwell had set in motion a project to make sure that a copy of the Bible in English could be found in every parish church. Roger's compilation, known as the 'Matthew Bible', following Roger's pseudonym, Thomas Matthew, was licensed by the King, with the result that the reformer's translation began to circulate in print in England only a year after his death. Cromwell and Cranmer commissioned Coverdale to revise the Matthew Bible, and the 'Great Bible' was published, after much delay and wrangling with its Parisian printers, in 1539.

In 1543, Henry drew back from his wary enthusiasm for vernacular scriptures, passing an Act for the Advancement of True Religion, which banned husbandmen, labourers, and women outside the gentry from reading the Bible. The concern about

[8] Peter W. M. Blayney, *The Stationers' Company and the Printers of London, 1501–1557* (Cambridge: Cambridge University Press, 2013), i. 228.

[9] On Tyndale, see David Daniell, *William Tyndale: A Biography* (New Haven: Yale University Press, 1994).

[10] Joy Shakespeare and Maria Dowling, 'Religion and Politics in Mid-Tudor England through the Eyes of a Protestant English Woman: The Recollections of Rose Throckmorton', *Bulletin of the Institute of Historical Research*, 55 (1982): 97.

[11] For an authoritative account, see Blayney, *Stationers' Company*, i. 344–51.

promiscuous interpretation by those deemed insufficiently qualified arose frequently throughout the succeeding decades. Speaking in the House of Lords in 1610, the Archbishop of Canterbury complained about an increasing anti-clericalism among the poor and mean, 'these men who are so hot-brained they condemn the reading of the Fathers and other good authors, and say the scripture is sufficient as the spirit directeth, and so by this means every ignorant ass interpreteth scripture according to his hot humours', adding a little later that he has no need to assert the appropriate scriptural places for his argument: 'You know them as well as I, for we are all doctors and can expound scripture'.[12]

No Bible in English was printed between 1541 and the accession of the reform-minded Edward VI in 1547; the first complete Edwardian Bible entered the market in 1549. Once the Catholic Mary came to the throne, in July 1553, English Bible printing ceased for a further seven years.[13] The market for English printed Bibles expanded rapidly with the publication of the Geneva Bible in England in 1576, sixteen years after its first publication by a group of Protestant exiles working in Calvin's Geneva. Between 1576 and 1644, some 140 editions of the Geneva Bible were printed in England. In 1579, it became the first English Bible to be printed in Scotland. The ongoing influence of this version is suggested by the fact that Archbishop Laud, suspected by many of Catholic leanings, was using the Calvinist Geneva Bible as his source text as late as 1624.[14] From 1579 onwards, black-letter editions of the Geneva Bible, aimed at a less confidently literate audience, instructed their readers to read the scriptures 'everie day, twise at the least', and the Geneva Bible was loaded with reading aids and commentaries designed to guide and enlighten the reader.[15] Elizabeth I never allowed the Geneva Bible to be adopted for official use in English churches, but commissioned her bishops to produce a new translation (the Bishops' Bible, first printed in 1568 and heavily revised in 1572).

The Catholic response to this series of Protestant vernaculars came in 1582, when a Catholic English New Testament appeared, with an initial print run of some 5,000 copies. The Old Testament, translated at around the same time, was not printed until 1609–10. Commissioned by Cardinal William Allen and prepared by Gregory Martin, professor of Hebrew at the Douai seminary, the Douai-Rheims New Testament stimulated a flurry of polemical Protestant response.[16] It circulated widely in England, not least thanks to the refutation published by the Puritan divine, William Fulke, whose massive *The Text of the New Testament of Jesus Christ* reproduced in its entirety the Douai-Rheims translation and

---

[12] *Proceedings in Parliament, 1610*, ed. Elizabeth Read Foster (New Haven: Yale University Press, 1966), i. 72, 30 April 1610.

[13] Blayney, *Stationers' Company*, ii. 674, 676.

[14] Peter White, *Predestination, Policy and Polemic: Conflict and Consensus in the English Civil War* (Cambridge: Cambridge University Press, 2002), 91.

[15] Femke Molekamp, *Women and the Bible in Early Modern England: Religious Reading and Writing* (Oxford: Oxford University Press, 2013), 19. See also Molekamp's chapter in this volume.

[16] Walsham notes: 'The refutation of the "Rhemists translation" was undertaken by some of the outstanding theologians of the age, William Fulke, John Rainolds, and William Whitaker among them, and Sir Francis Walshingham promised the disgraced Presbyterian leader Thomas Cartwright £100 a year to produce a comprehensive refutation of the marginal notes' ('Unclasping the Book? Post-Reformation English Catholicism and the Vernacular Bible', *Journal of British Studies*, 42 (2003): 145–6).

apparatus, with Fulke's energetic confutation inserted between the lines and passages, and running next to them in parallel columns.

In January 1604, King James called together a group of senior church leaders, along with moderate representatives of the Puritan faction who had presented him with the Millenary Petition, a set of requests for further reform. The Hampton Court Conference discussed, and in large part resolved—though not to the satisfaction of its more radical members—a series of doctrinal and practical points. On the second day, the Puritan John Rainolds asked for 'a newe *translation* of the *Bible*, because, those which were allowed in the raignes of *Henrie* the eight, and *Edward* the sixt, were corrupt and not aunswerable to the truth of the Originall'.[17] More than fifty scholars made up six 'companies', two each at the universities of Oxford and Cambridge, and two at Westminster. Each worked to translate a portion of the Bible, and the companies met regularly to read and hear each other's work, ensuring consistency and comprehension. Drawing on existing editions, and with the Bishops' Bible as their base text, the translators claimed they sought not 'to make a new Translation ... but to make a good one better, or out of many good ones, one principall good one'.[18]

Like its predecessors, the King James Bible did not escape controversy. Within a year of its appearance, the Hebrew scholar Hugh Broughton published *A Censure of the Late Translation*, telling the King 'I had rather be rent in pieces by wilde horses, then any such translation ... should bee urged upon poore churches'.[19] Broughton's protests, published from the safety of Middleburg, had little effect, and the King James Bible was widely disseminated, circulating alongside the still-popular Geneva Bible.[20] The KJB did little to lay to rest debates over the scriptures. On the contrary, the plethora of Bibles and increasing linguistic competence to deal with its original languages only added to the complexities of interpretation and the variety of uses to which scripture was put.

In the first part of the seventeenth century, English Bibles were printed by the King's printer: first Robert Barker, and then his former associates Bonham Norton and John Bill (see Figure 0.1).[21] In 1631, Barker and Martin Lucas (Bill's executor) printed an edition of the Bible which resulted in a hefty fine of £300 when the word 'not' was omitted from the seventh commandment in Exodus 20, giving divine support to adultery.[22] As well as the 'wicked Bible', as it came to be known, early modern England could boast, thanks to misprints and idiosyncratic translations, the 'bug Bible' (Coverdale, 1535, in which Psalm 91: 5 tells readers not to be afraid 'for eny bugges by night'); the 'breeches Bible' (Geneva Bible, 1579, in which Genesis 3: 7 suggests that Adam and Eve 'made themselves breeches'); and the 'Judas Bible' (the second edition of the KJB, which prints 'Judas' for 'Jesus' in Matthew 26: 36). Charmingly, in some issues of the 'printers' Bible' from 1612, Psalm 119: 161 offers

---

[17] William Barlow, *The Summe and Substance of the Conference ... at Hampton Court* (London, 1604), G3ʳ.

[18] *The Holy Bible, conteyning the Old Testament, and the New* (London, 1611), B1ᵛ.

[19] Hugh Broughton, *A Censure of the Late Translation for Our Churches* (Middleburg, 1611), n.p. For more on Broughton's and other contemporary responses to the KJB, see the chapter by Hannibal Hamlin in this volume.

[20] The last Geneva New Testament published in the seventeenth century was printed in 1616 (Campbell, *Bible*, 108). Bibles, however, had long reading lives, especially if passed down within families.

[21] On the King's printers, see Graham Rees and Maria Wakely, *Publishing, Politics, and Culture: The King's Printers in the Reign of James I and VI* (Oxford: Oxford University Press, 2009).

[22] For details, see Campbell, *Bible*, 108–10.

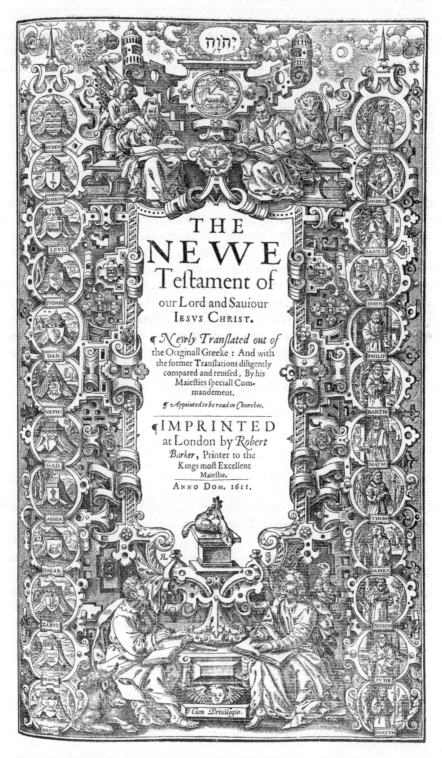

FIGURE 0.1 Title-page of *The Newe Testament* (with 1611 date), in *The Holy Bible* (London: Robert Barker, 1613). Barker reused the title-page from the last (1602) edition of the Bishops' Bible, changing only the text printed in the central cartouche. York Minster Library; HOB Bagby 4.

readers not the Psalmic 'Princes have persecuted me', but 'Printers have persecuted me without a cause', a presumably unintentionally metatextual comment from the scriptures which, contemporaries complained, were often badly treated by their publishers. Looking on the bright side, Charles Wolseley, in 1685, acknowledged:

> we do not say that every *Transcriber*, and every *Printer* of them was, or is infallible; but that 'tis possible (after the utmost of all humane care) in a letter or a word, there may happen to be mistakes (of which no other use can be made, but to quicken and continue our diligence about them;) yet for the whole *body of the scriptures*, we have all the reason to satifie us about the truth of them, that any thing, that we have not actually seen, is possible capable of.[23]

In 1595, the bookseller Andrew Maunsell published the first printed catalogue of English books. The *First Parte of the Catalogue*, dealing with divinity, stretched to 123 pages, whilst the *Second Parte*, concerning 'the Sciences Mathematicall, as Arithmetick, Geometrie, Astronomie, Astrologie, Musick, the Arte of Warre, and Navigation: And also, of Phisick and Surgerie' extended to only twenty-seven. This discrepancy reinforces the popularity and ubiquity of religious reading in early modern England. Maunsell's entry for 'Bible' is revealing: he starts with the major editions, and goes on to list the books of the Bible in order, telling readers where to find commentaries, notes, and explications for each of the scriptures.[24]

The Bible did not simply circulate as a whole volume, or even as individual testaments or books. It was extracted, abridged, and interpreted, not least in commonplace books, whether manuscript compilations of godly sayings or printed collections designed to aid religious study. Under 'C', Maunsell listed a set of printed 'Commonplaces of Divinitie':

> Erasmus *Sarcerius*
> Wolph. *Musculus*
> John *Calvin* his Institutions
> John *Marbecke*
> Peter *Martir*
> Henry *Bullinger*.[25]

Reading like a who's who of influential reformers, Maunsell's list offers a further reminder of the European context of English Bible reading, and is followed by a catalogue of 'Concordances', including a 'Table of the principall matters contained in the Bible, in which the reader may find & practice many common places'. This heading indicates the active engagement demanded of the Bible reader, who was required not simply to locate but to rehearse the 'common places' of scripture. Perhaps no act of biblical interpretation was as intense, or at least as physical, as the work undertaken by female members of the religious community at Little Gidding, who, under the guidance of Nicholas Ferrar, painstakingly cut printed Gospels into their separate parts and then reassembled and glued them together to create a continuous, coherent—and beautifully decorated—gospel narrative (Figure 0.2).[26]

---

[23] Charles Wolseley, *The Unreasonableness of Atheism Made Manifest* (London: for Nathanel Ponder, 1669), B5^r.
[24] On biblical 'how-to guides', see Lori Anne Ferrell, *The Bible and the People* (New Haven: Yale University Press, 2008), ch. 5.
[25] Andrew Maunsell, *The First Part of the Catalogue of English Printed Bookes* (London, 1595), C6^v.
[26] See Adam Smyth, '"Shreds of holinesse": George Herbert, Little Gidding, and Cutting up Texts in Early Modern England', *English Literary Renaissance*, 42 (2012): 452–81.

FIGURE 0.2 Page from a Little Gidding concordance of 1630, showing manuscript rubrication and running head, cut-and-paste biblical text and initials, and illustration. Houghton Library, Harvard University, Cambridge, Mass., A 1275.5, p. 10 (seq. 14).

The variety of interpretive aids, guides, and compendia which circulated during this period reminds us how flexible 'the Bible' was as object and concept. It could be a reassuringly hefty physical resource, a set of abridged themes and stories, or an idea. For the family of Alexander Nyndge, possessed by the devil in 1574, the Bible was a tool for exorcism, laid on the boy's struggling body, and only subsequently read through.[27] Others wore fragments of the Bible as talismans, or used it to predict their fortunes and romantic prospects. For John Knox, it was as much a part of memory as a physical book; recent research shows that his biblical quotations rarely match any existing early modern edition, suggesting that, for Knox, the Bible was a thoroughly familiar part of his mental furniture.[28] Despite Protestant strictures against idolatry, Bible stories were frequently reproduced pictorially, in the elaborate decorative schemes of elite households as well as in cheap and widely circulated prints.[29]

II. WHOSE BIBLE?

The Oxford Handbook of the Bible in Early Modern England, c.1530–1700 explores the history and culture of the scriptures in the two centuries following the Reformation. One historical presupposition that is challenged in the scope and design of this book relates to our understanding of biblical interpretation in and after the Reformation (or, as many scholars now prefer, the Reformations), which is seen as fighting the same fights over and over more or less up until the rise of 'Higher Criticism' in the eighteenth century.[30] The Reformation is generally understood as a sixteenth-century phenomenon, in which the splintering of European Christendom into its Catholic and Protestant constituencies shook the continent in both its geo-political complexity and its seismic intellectual consequences, but had more or less settled into an uneasy and divided status quo by the latter part of the century.[31]

At the level of international politics—the division of the continent into Protestant and Catholic—this may be largely accurate, but the fiercely fought interpretative battles over the use of the Bible, which are central to any account of the Reformation, were by no means settled. There is a continuing sense throughout late sixteenth- and seventeenth-century Protestant thought that the Reformation was still very much under way. The energy of the Counter-Reformation makes it clear that for Catholics too the questions of the earlier

---

[27] Andrew Cambers, 'Demonic Possession, Literacy and "Superstition" in Early Modern England', *Past and Present*, 202 (2009): 3–35.

[28] David Wright, 'John Knox's Bible', in Orlaith O'Sullivan and Ellen N. Herron (eds), *The Bible as Book: The Reformation* (London and Newcastle: British Library and Oak Knoll Press, 2000), 51–64. On Donne's 'virtual Bible', see the chapter by Emma Rhatigan in this volume.

[29] See Tara Hamling, *Decorating the Godly Household: Religious Art in Protestant Britain, c.1560–c.1660* (New Haven: Yale University Press, 2010); on cheap printed pictures, see Tessa Watt, *Cheap Print and Popular Piety, 1550–1640* (Cambridge: Cambridge University Press, 1993).

[30] On the emergence of this mode of critical engagement with the Bible, see Hans Frei, *The Eclipse of Biblical Narrative* (New Haven: Yale University Press, 1974).

[31] On the Reformation, see Eamon Duffy, *Saints, Sacrilege and Sedition: Religion and Conflict in the Tudor Reformations* (London: Continuum, 2012); Diarmaid MacCulloch, *Reformation: Europe's House Divided, 1490–1700* (London: Penguin, 2004); Peter Marshall, *The Reformation: A Very Short Introduction* (Oxford: Oxford University Press, 2009).

period remained current. Debates persisted as to whether in its demi-divine nature the Bible was a uniquely self-interpreting book, at least as far as salvation was concerned; whether it was self-sufficient, and God's word could be discovered through *sola scriptura* (scripture alone, rather than the accumulated traditions of interpretation and revision); or whether it demanded a competent interpretative authority.[32] Attention to the Bible over this longer historical period involves both a set of scholarly questions that had barely been broached in the earlier era and a set of political understandings that arose from new readerships and changing liturgical and homiletic practices.

Those sometimes referred to as the 'magisterial reformers' (in the sense of *magister*, teacher) of the sixteenth century provided a theological and pedagogical ballast—of Christology (the study of the nature and person of Christ), of soteriology (the study of the doctrines of salvation), and of biblical interpretation—on and against which subsequent commentators wrote extensively. The Counter-Reformation too—for all that it is a slippery historiographical notion—prompted an astonishing diversification of the learning brought to the Bible and a shift beyond the theological questions that had prompted the Reformation.[33] Protestant scholars found themselves, more or less against their will, moved to admiration for their confessional opponents. The Jesuit learning of figures such as Benedict Pererius, Robert Bellarmine, and Cornelius à Lapide was widely admired, despite a deep political loathing of the order, in England at least. In similar terms, scholars engaged in unprecedented detail with the learning and traditions of Jewish and Islamic scholars, while remaining hostile to their faith, and hopeful of their eventual conversion.

An emerging body of scholarly thought in the seventeenth century brought a vast array of new contexts for the Bible. When Joseph Scaliger's *De emendatione temporum* (1583), for instance, formulated biblical chronology as an effectively new and complex discipline, or when John Selden produced his account of the pagan gods, *De Diis Syris* (1617), setting new standards of para-biblical anthropology, they set in motion scholarly challenges which were widely taken up. The proliferation and erudition of Arabic, Hebrew, and oriental studies from the Reformation onwards—the works, for instance, of Johannes Buxtorf (1564–1629), Professor of Hebrew at Basel for thirty-nine years, and Edward Pococke (1604–91), the first Professor of Arabic at Oxford, and later, Professor of Hebrew—were instrumental in a range of quasi-historical approaches to the Bible, attending to Semitic and Greco-Roman custom and practice, that dominated the exegetical and commentary traditions of the period.[34]

Vast amounts of scholarship that did not deal with doctrinal or theological issues were nevertheless consummately biblical. The seventeenth century saw the flourishing of sacred geography as a scholarly discipline, in an array of studies on the Levant and Palestine, historical and contemporary, which sought to flesh out the nature of biblical antiquity

[32] See Jean-Louis Quantin, *The Church of England and Christian Antiquity: The Construction of a Confessional Identity in the Seventeenth Century* (Oxford: Oxford University Press, 2009).

[33] See e.g. the essays collected in Alexandra Bamji, Geert J. Janssen, and Mary Laven (eds), *The Ashgate Research Companion to the Counter-Reformation* (Aldershot: Ashgate, 2013).

[34] Anthony T. Grafton, *Joseph Scaliger: A Study in the History of Classical Scholarship* (Oxford: Oxford University Press, 1983–93); G. J. Toomer, *Eastern Wisedome and Learning: The Study of Arabic in Seventeenth-Century England* (Oxford: Clarendon Press, 1995) and *John Selden: A Life in Scholarship* (Oxford: Oxford University Press, 2009), 211–56; Stephen G. Burnett, *From Christian Hebraism to Jewish Studies: Johannes Buxtorf (1564–1629) and Hebrew Learning in the Seventeenth Century* (Leiden: Brill, 1996).

in phenomenal detail, attending to its people, its wars, its agriculture, its economy, and its land.[35] Works such as the Dutch Catholic Christianus Adrichomius's *Theatrum terrae sanctae* (1590), the Reformed French pastor Samuel Bochart's *Geographiae Sacrae* (1646), and the English antiquarian Thomas Fuller's *A Pisgah-Sight of Palestine* (1650) were part of a flood of work that extended to include writings on sacred botany, mathematics, and physics. The linguistic acuity required to deal with the necessary sources is staggering, and a small number of scholars broke new ground in the study of 'exotic' languages, including Chaldee, Coptic, and Aramaic, as well as Arabic and Hebrew. Latin, of course, remained the *lingua franca* of international scholarship throughout our period, even while English became, over time, a more or less respectable interloper in the world of intellectual endeavour.

The Bible was resolutely not the sole preserve of scholarship, nor indeed of theologians, or of primarily ecclesiastical interest. It was important because everybody laid claim to it. As the always invigorating Gerrard Winstanley has it, in announcing a 'New Law of Righteousness', that constituted the taking back of the Bible by the poor, a declaratory spirit:

> shal rise out of the dust, out of the poor people that are trod under foot: For, as the declaration of the Son of man was first declared by Fisher-men, & men that the learned, covetous Scholars despised: so the declaration of the righteous law shal spring up from the poor, the base and despised ones, and fools of the world.[36]

Winstanley's radicalism, the Bible as a manifesto of Levelling, is part of an august tradition of insisting on its plainness, rather than (or in addition to) its complexity. Protestantism, whether that of Luther, Calvin, Hooker, or Perkins, held as one of its basic tenets that the Bible can and should be read, and that, in its essence, the Bible is comprehensible to any and every reader. Many efforts were made to qualify this—in Protestant ecclesiology and catechism as much as in Catholic insistence on the centrality of interpretative tradition—but the Bible was read relentlessly, in public and private, in pulpit and pub, for its politics as much as its Christology. It is this pliability and familiarity that constitutes its importance.

The seventeenth-century historian, Sir Richard Baker, produced a vigorous defence of both reading and exposition of the Bible by non-clerical readers, arguing that 'There are some indeed that allow not Lay men, to read the Scriptures, & think that this *Scrutamini scripturas,* is no Generall precept: but that lay men must take them at second hand: and they, no doubt have reason to tye up Lay mens handes from writing; who close up their Eyes from Reading'. Baker goes on to make the argument that being allowed to read and yet forbidden to write is like being allowed to marry, yet forbidden sex:

> but for men that allow Lay men to Read, and yet Deny them to write; what can be conceaved more Incongruous? much like, as if they would allow men to marry, and not allow them to have children; or if to have Children, yet not to be Legitimate; for, what is their writing, but as it were the Issue and Off-spring of their Reading![37]

[35] See Zur Shalev, *Sacred Words and Worlds: Geography, Religion, and Scholarship, 1550–1700* (Leiden: Brill, 2011). See also Shalev's chapter in this volume.
[36] Gerrard Winstanley, *The New Law of Righteousnes Budding Forth* (London, 1649), E8ᵛ.
[37] Sir Richard Baker, *An Apologie for Lay-Mens Writing in Divinity* (London, 1641), C7ʳ.

Others, more cautiously or conservatively, insisted that Protestant engagement with the scriptures was never meant to include, in unfettered manner, the lower classes. Thus Edward Hyde, Earl of Clarendon, responding to the Catholic convert, Hugh Serenus Cressy, whom he quotes with reluctant approval: 'no Catholick, nor he thinks any other man in his right wits will grant that every Porter, Cobler, or Lawndress is capable to instruct themselves by reading the Scriptures alone'. Hyde insists that Protestantism aims at no such thing: 'In all which I do not know that he hath an adversary'.[38]

Despite Hyde's aversion to the prospect of a laundress reading scripture, women at all levels of the social scale were intimately familiar with their Bibles. Many engaged in a sustained regime of Bible reading and interpretation, like Marie Gunter, who, beset by religious doubt after her childhood conversion from Catholicism,

> vowed that God assisting her, she would every yeare read over the whole Bible in an ordinary course, which course she constantly observed for the space of fifteene yeares together, beginning her taske upon her birth day, and reading every day so many Chapters as to bring it about just with the yeare.[39]

Whilst early criticism on women writers saw religious reading and writing as a disappointingly constrained arena, more recent scholarship has demonstrated the vibrancy of women's biblical engagements, and the creative energies many brought to their encounters with the text.[40] Within the extended household, women organized devotional reading and prayer, influencing the religious habits and understanding of children, servants, and neighbours, as well as their husbands and male relatives. In the turbulent years of the civil wars, women across the spectrum of Christian religion, from Catholics to Protestants, Quakers, and noncomformists, used the Bible to support their doctrinal and devotional positions, and license female speech.[41] With its vivid cast of female characters, Michele Osherow argues, 'the Bible itself negates the requirement—even the desire—for female silence'.[42] In conversation, in writing across a range of genres, and in needlework renderings of biblical stories, women drew on and interpreted the resources of the Bible, and worked to convey them to an audience of both women and men.

Recent work on the history of reading has done much to revise the view that Bible reading by either sex was a passive and straightforwardly receptive activity. In a survey of the early modern Bibles held at the Huntington Library, William H. Sherman discovered that Bibles are annotated at least as frequently as any other class of books from this period, suggesting a sustained textual and intellectual engagement.[43] John Gregory's suggestion, quoted

---

[38] Edward Hyde, Earl of Clarendon, *Animadversions upon a Book Intituled, Fanaticism Fanatically Imputed to the Catholick Church, by Dr. Stillingfleet* (London, 1673), M8^{r-v}.

[39] Thomas Taylor, *The Pilgrims Profession. Or a Sermon Preached at the Funerall of Mris Mary Gunter* (London, 1622), H4^{r-v}.

[40] See esp. Erica Longfellow, *Women and Religious Writing in Early Modern England* (Cambridge: Cambridge University Press, 2004).

[41] See Marcus Nevitt, *Women and the Pamphlet Culture of Revolutionary England* (Farnham: Ashgate, 2006); Hilary Hinds, *God's Englishwomen: Seventeenth-Century Radical Sectarian Writing and Feminist Criticism* (Manchester: Manchester University Press, 1996).

[42] Michele Osherow, *Biblical Women's Voices in Early Modern England* (Farnham: Ashgate, 2009), 4.

[43] William H. Sherman, '"The Book Thus Put in Every Vulgar Hand": Impressions of Readers in Early English Printed Bibles', in Kampen and Saenger, *The Bible as Book*, 125–33.

at the beginning of this introduction, that 'Bookes, and arts, and men, and the world it selfe are but Notes upon [the scriptures]', must have been vivid indeed for his contemporaries, accustomed to seeing the Bible text glossed with both print and manuscript explications and instructions for use. The sheer complexity of the Bible and of its interpretation pushed the technologies of the page to their limits, as authors and editors adopted a range of systems and symbols to mark connections, divide the text, and direct the puzzled reader.

For nearly every early modern English reader, from those who got little further than the Lord's Prayer on their hornbooks to the most advanced, knowing how to read was inseparable from knowing the Bible. Early in the eighteenth century, Susanna Wesley (1669–1742) described her efforts in educating her eldest son, Samuel. She recalled that 'as soon as he knew the letters [he] began at the first chapter of Genesis. He was taught to spell the first verse, then to read it over and over, till he could read it off-hand without any hesitation; so on to the second, etc.'[44] For the Wesley infants, as for so many children in this period, the acquisition of literacy was inseparable from the study of scripture.[45] As Henry Vaughan put it in his poetic address 'To the Holy Bible', 'Thou wert the first put in my hand, / And daily didst my yong eyes lead / To letters, till I learnt to read'.[46]

The lines between reading literacy and other modes of knowing were slippery, and biblical culture incorporated the illiterate as much as the learned and was aural as well as visual.[47] A scriptural 'literacy', a thoroughgoing familiarity with not only the stories, but with the politics, the typologies, and the ethics of the Bible was developed intensively in early modern sermon culture. Sermons as a genre were until recent years almost entirely neglected, but have received some substantial and insightful attention in the work of Peter McCullough, Arnold Hunt, Mary Morrissey, and others.[48] Sermons were popular entertainments in the broadest sense, rivalling the theatre. They might be obstreperous, terrifying, radical, or bullying, but they were, relentlessly and over a long period, the biblical medium of current affairs.[49] The sermons one attended attested to political tastes and there was fierce competition for congregation. In urban areas, people were spoilt for choice and reports of sermon gadding present a picture much like a ratings war, in which disgruntled pastors would bemoan the emptying of the pews for rival churches.[50]

Early modern sermons are very frequently long, complex, and bewilderingly biblical, bewildering in the sense that we necessarily wonder how the congregation could follow

---

[44] Susanna Wesley, *Susanna Wesley: The Complete Writings*, ed. Charles Wallace, jun. (Oxford: Oxford University Press, 1997), 371.

[45] For the importance of catechisms, see Ian Green, *The Christian's ABC: Catechisms and Catechizing in England, c.1530–1740* (Oxford: Clarendon Press, 1996).

[46] Henry Vaughan, 'The Holy Bible', in *Henry Vaughan: The Complete Poems*, ed. Alan Rudrum (Harmondsworth: Penguin, 1976), ll. 5–8.

[47] On the overlaps of oral and literate culture, see esp. Adam Fox, *Oral and Literate Culture in England, 1500–1700* (Oxford: Oxford University Press, 2000).

[48] Peter McCullough, Hugh Adlington, and Emma Rhatigan (eds), *The Oxford Handbook of the Early Modern Sermon* (Oxford: Oxford University Press, 2011); Arnold Hunt, *The Art of Hearing: English Preachers and their Audiences, 1590–1640* (Cambridge: Cambridge University Press, 2010); Mary Morrissey, *Politics and the Paul's Cross Sermons, 1558–1652* (Oxford: Oxford University Press, 2011).

[49] Tony Claydon, 'The Sermon, the "Public Sphere" and the Political Culture of Late Seventeenth-Century England', in Lori Anne Ferrell and Peter McCullough (eds), *The English Sermon Revised: Religion, Literature, and History, 1600–1750* (Manchester: Manchester University Press, 2000), 208–34.

[50] Hunt, *Art of Hearing*, 187–228.

such complexity. This constitutes valuable evidence of the biblicism of early modern culture. We do not doubt that Victorian audiences who read serialized novels were able to understand what they read, and in the same manner should not doubt that congregations more or less followed what they heard. Sermons were also a publishing phenomenon, with works by popular preachers like Henry 'silver-tongued' Smith selling at a remarkable rate.[51] There were often discrepancies between the spoken and written texts of sermons. The preacher John Everard addressed this as a matter of regret and censorship in a 1618 sermon: 'And blame not me, though there be some things *added*, and many things *altered*: The liberty of the *Pulpit* is too litle, but that of the *Presse*, in our affaires, is much lesse'.[52] Nehemiah Rogers must have added substantially to his 1623 sermon, *A Strange Vineyard in Palaestina*, which, coming in at about 120,000 words, would surely have tested the patience of the most avid sermon listener. Much of his text is in fact a meta-commentary on the nature of eloquence in the sermon, and he comments on the ability of scripture to reveal and prise open the true person: 'Thus we see the nature of the Word, which like a Winepresse will make knowne what is within; laying open the poison that lurked in the wicked, and the grace and goodnesse that lay hid in the bosome of the godly'.[53]

As these brief overviews of scholarship, Bible production, and biblical culture show, the 'English' Bible was in many ways an international phenomenon, created by translators who made themselves intimately familiar with the biblical languages; scrutinized by scholars who not only studied sacred geography and history, but sought to understand and appropriate Arabic, Jewish, and classical learning; inspired by the Reformation debates that shaped modern Europe; and regularly published in the great centres of European printing. The essays in this book, whose contents are described briefly in the short introductions that preface each section, explore an array of responses—political, literary, theological—to the fecundity of the biblical text, within a culture that knew the Bible intimately. There is a compelling logic to exploring England (and its neighbours), as a fertile case study. The specificity of its intellectual, political, and social circumstances were such, and its biblicism was of such intensity, that it constituted a unique culture of the book. At the same time, the chapters collected here remain alert to the numerous connections and transactions that brought thinkers and writers across the four nations into contact, and sometimes conflict, with the wider world, through the medium of scriptural scholarship and debate.

Circulating in a staggering diversity of forms and genres, the early modern English Bible informed and was shaped by not only the religious but the social, political, and intellectual currents of the sixteenth and seventeenth centuries. As the chapters collected here show, those currents were inseparable: thanks to the copiousness and malleability of the Bible, it was a tool of devotion, domestic life, political thought, and scholarship in every discipline. Each of those elements finds a home in this volume, whose six sections deal with translation, dissemination, scholarship, the political Bible, literature, and reception histories, shedding new light on the most ubiquitous text, and the most crucial imaginative resource, of the era.

---

[51] Lori Anne Ferrell, 'Sermons', in Andy Kesson and Emma Smith (eds), *The Elizabethan Top Ten: Defining Print Popularity in Early Modern England* (Aldershot: Ashgate, 2013), 193–202.

[52] John Everard, *The Arriereban a Sermon Preached to the Company of the Military Yarde* (London, 1618), A8ʳ.

[53] Nehemiah Rogers, *A Strange Vineyard in Palaestina* (London, 1623), K2ʳ⁻ᵛ.

PART I

TRANSLATIONS

Introduction to Part I

In 1526 William Tyndale's Lutheran-inspired translation of the New Testament, printed at Worms, sparked a revolution. Tyndale's interventions in spreading the word shed light on the contradictory responses to vernacular translations. As Susan Wabuda demonstrates here, six years before Tyndale was denounced, mutilated, and burned, the doctrinally conservative Henry VIII mooted the idea of an English Bible. English evangelicals and senior clerics alike opposed the idea, bringing into focus the ways in which scripture was both disseminated (and forbidden) to the laity. Despite the major biblical translations of the 1530s, in the immediate aftermath of the Reformation, vernacular translations did not so much burst forth as sputter into being.

Tyndale advocated a vernacular Bible on a number of grounds. He was particularly concerned that St Jerome's Vulgate Latin Bible—the Bible of the medieval church—was not widely comprehended by either the laity or members of the priesthood:

> But alas the curates them selves (for the most parte) wote no moare what the newe or olde testamente meaneth then do the turkes. Nether know they of any moare then that they reade at masse matens and evensonge which yet they understonde not … but synge & saye and patter all daye with the lyppes only that which the herte understondeth not.[1]

Jerome's translation had been intended to provide a single, authoritative text in the vernacular language to replace the numerous different Latin translations that had been transcribed (and mistranscribed) after Latin replaced Greek as the common language in the eastern Mediterranean. Yet the manuscript circulation of the Vulgate meant that it too was transmitted in varying forms. Over a thousand years after it had been translated, Tyndale

---

[1] William Tyndale, *The Obedience of a Christen Man and How Christen Rulers Ought to Governe* (1528), B5^{r-v}.

contended that the Vulgate Bible was no longer universal and neither priest nor layperson had the ability to comprehend the scriptures.

Officially, the Catholic Church did not disapprove of translating the word into the vernacular and there were numerous translations in other European languages. Yet, in England, translation and Reformation went hand in glove.[2] As noted in the general introduction, the main English Bible before Tyndale's was John Wycliffe's 1380s translation, which (before the Reformation) became synonymous with heresy and effectively led to an outright ban on translations into English. For Thomas More, translation begat heresy and, in 1532, he applauded Henry VIII's (public) decision to

> prohybyte the scrypture of god to be sufferd in englyshe tonge amonge the peoples hands leste evyll folke by false drawyng of every good thynge they rede in to the colour and mayntenauns of theyr owne fonde fantasyes, and turnynge all hony in to posyn, myght both dedly do hurte vnto theym selfe, and sprede also that infeccyone farther a brode.[3]

Whereas Tyndale argued that the inability to comprehend scripture led uneducated members of the laity and the priesthood to become alienated from God, More retorted that the English were not ready to receive the word in their own language and false biblical translation would infect the populace with heresy.

More's distrust of biblical translation was not shared by Miles Coverdale; in 1535, he dedicated the first full printed English Bible to King Henry who was now publicly supportive of vernacular translation. For Coverdale, far from corrupting the populace, through their very diversity, vernacular translations enhance the unity of faith.[4] Both Catholics and Protestants looked to tradition to assert the veracity of their doctrinal differences and this led to unlikely collaborations across confessional divides. Nicholas Udall's edition of Erasmus's biblical paraphrases (1548) comprised translations from notable Protestants such as Katherine Parr and Coverdale, but even the Catholic Mary Tudor contributed to the volume.[5] Although this would seem to imply that translation could be a way of crossing confessional divides, Catholics frequently emphasized the fragmentary nature of translation and how it could be a way to corrupt the Word.[6] Protestants also expressed anxieties about the 'correct' way to interpret scripture, yet Coverdale reinforced the idea that the various translations enrich scripture. The different translations were not incompatible with *sola scriptura* and become a way to connect the English Reformation with the Reformation in continental Europe.

The transnational quality of translation is examined in Femke Molekamp's chapter, which addresses the most ubiquitous of all sixteenth-century English Bibles. This is the Geneva Bible, first published in 1560 though not published in England until 1576. Molekamp observes the collaborative quality of the Geneva Bible, which was translated by Marian exiles, and traces how it was produced and transmitted from interactions between European Calvinism and English

---

[2] Ian Green, *Print and Protestantism in Early Modern England* (Oxford: Oxford University Press, 2000).

[3] Thomas More, *The Confutacyon of Tyndales Answere Made by Syr Thomas More Knyght Lorde Chauncellour of Englonde* (1532), C1ʳ.

[4] *Biblia the Bible, That Is, the Holy Scrypture of the Olde and New Testament, Faithfully Translated in to Englyshe*, tr. Miles Coverdale (1535).

[5] Nicholas Udall, *The First Tome or Volume of the Paraphrase of Erasmus upon the Newe Testament* (1548).

[6] Tina Krontiris, *Oppositional Voices: Women as Writers and Translators of Literature in the English Renaissance* (London: Routledge, 1992).

Protestantism. The Geneva Bible contained numerous marginal glosses, demonstrating that translating and interpreting the word were two closely related ventures. In tandem with these glosses, prefatory materials directly address the issues of translation and interpretation.

While the Geneva Bible was a collaborative act and earlier Bibles such as the Matthew Bible and the Great Bible drew from various translations, perhaps the most famous of collaborative Bibles was the King James Bible, first published in 1611. Katrin Ettenhuber attends to the way in which Miles Smith's prefatory materials to the KJB justify doctrinal and linguistic principles and how authorization of the word took shape partly as a response to the Catholic Douai-Rheims translations. Gregory Martin, in his preface to *The New Testament Faithfully Translated into English* (1582) uses his translation to reclaim the vernacular for the Catholic Church. Following the lead of German, Flemish, French and Polish 'learned Catholics' who translated the Bible into vernacular tongues as a response to Protestant bibles, Martin translates the Bible 'for the more speedy abolishing of a number of false and impious translations put forth by sundry sectes, and for the better preservation or reclaime of many good soules endangered thereby'.[7] While both Catholics and Protestants claimed doctrinal authority through a connection to the early church, Catholics asserted this authority through the tradition of the church and Protestants through the scriptures. Ettenhuber demonstrates how the King James Bible's assertion of philological meticulousness is presented as a way to negotiate Catholic and Puritan differences.

Yet, unlike the Geneva or the Douai-Rheims Bible, the King James Bible presented largely unannotated scripture. Whereas early Bibles—whether Catholic or Protestant—drew attention to the difficulties of reading scripture through marginal glosses, the King James Bible presents annotation as unnecessary. Individuals are able to understand the word of God without the intervention of (partisan) marginal glosses. Taking the representation of God's vengeance and desolation in Isaiah as a starting point, Karen Edwards reads the minimal glosses of the KJB as themselves politically inflected. Edwards shows how the slender interpretive machinery of the King James Bible became a means to endorse the established church and downplay the strangeness of the Bible. It is to this strangeness that Jamie Ferguson attends when he takes issues of translation and the language of the English Bible as the starting point for defining biblical authority and questioning its relationship to national autonomy and religious identity. Language proved a contentious issue and the Latinate English of the King James Bible was not wholly endorsed.

Finally in this section, Nigel Smith takes Robert Gell's *An Essay Toward the Amendment of the Last English Translation of the Bible* (1659) and its recommendation for close to 500 revisions to the King James Bible as a case study for how people responded to biblical translation in the mid-seventeenth century. Arguing that Gell represents the end of one hermeneutic impulse whilst pre-empting eighteenth-century pietist literalism, Smith shows how translation continued to be contentious throughout the period under discussion. The chapters in this section demonstrate that English vernacular translation was a fraught undertaking. Translating the word of God might attempt to create common understanding through allowing individuals to read scripture in their own language, but debates regarding the appropriateness of biblical translation continued throughout the sixteenth and seventeenth centuries.

---

[7] *The New Testament of Jesus Christ, Translated Faithfully into English … in the English College of Rhemes*, tr. Gregory Martin (1582), A2ᵛ.

CHAPTER 1

···

'A DAY AFTER DOOMSDAY': CRANMER AND THE BIBLE TRANSLATIONS OF THE 1530S[*]

···

SUSAN WABUDA

IF it is true, as Archbishop Thomas Cranmer wrote in his 1540 prologue to the Great Bible, that 'the word of God' is 'the mooste precious Juell, and moste holy relique, that remayneth upon earth',[1] then the history of how, generation by generation, that holy jewel has been possessed and endowed is one of the great stories of the Christian Church. Among the fiercest of the political battles that took place during the Reformation were those over the protocols that governed how scripture was to be withheld, and how it was to be distributed to the laity. To what extent was the Word of God a private gift as well as a common possession to be shared by all believing people?

Although the story may seem familiar, much can still be learned from the struggle to inhibit Bible reading, especially in the 1530s and 1540s. This chapter is concerned with a paradox: how can the most important of all books be given to the laity and withheld from them at the same time?[2] It is one of the great ironies of the Reformation that the translation

---

[*] This chapter is drawn from my forthcoming book, *Hugh Latimer and the Reformation in England: Man and Myth*. In quotations from manuscripts, I have silently expanded common abbreviations and I have modernized punctuation.

[1] Thomas [Cranmer], Archbishop of Canterbury, 'A Prologue or Preface', in *The Bible. In Englyshe*, 2nd edn of the Great Bible (London, 1540), ✠1ʳ–✠3ᵛ, quotation at ✠2ᵛ; and reprinted in *Miscellaneous Writings and Letters of Thomas Cranmer, Archbishop of Canterbury, Martyr, 1556*, ed. John Edmund Cox (Cambridge: Parker Society, 1846), 122.

[2] David Daniell, *The Bible in English: Its History and Influence* (New Haven: Yale University Press, 2003); Lori Anne Ferrell, 'The Preacher's Bibles', in Peter McCullough, Hugh Adlington, and Emma Rhatigan (eds), *The Oxford Handbook of the Early Modern Sermon* (Oxford: Oxford University Press, 2011), 21–33; and Ferrell, *The Bible and the People* (New Haven: Yale University Press, 2008), ch. 3. See also Diarmaid MacCulloch and Elizabeth Solopova, 'Before the King James Bible', in Helen Moore and Julian Reed (eds), *Manifold Greatness: The Making of the King James Bible* (Oxford: Bodleian Library, 2011), 12–39.

of the New Testament that was released under Henry VIII and that was ultimately adopted in the King James Bible was mainly the work of William Tyndale.

I. Rationing the Common Treasure

By 1500, holy writ was understood to be a 'common treasure', yet at the same time it was reserved well away from the laity's touch. As sacred objects, the books that were used during the Mass were kept behind the rood screen in the chancels of parish churches, where they could be glimpsed, but not handled by the worshippers.[3] The mystical sanctity of the Bible meant that it could be compared to the consecrated Host as a numinous treasure that needed to be protected as well as reverenced. Seeing the Host through the rood screen was a daily event for many people. Taking communion once a year at Easter was a communal rite and a public act in every parish.[4] Similarly, the access that the laity was allowed to the Bible was filtered, with the clergy acting as intermediaries between them and the written Word, just as they were also the agents who showed the people the Host. Scriptural teachings were presented to the laity by the clergy in highly ritualized moments: when the verses of the Epistles and Gospel of the day were read or sung; when homilies were read; and when sermons were preached in churches, or outdoors in the pulpit crosses that stood beside cathedrals and religious houses. The people received the Word aurally, in keeping with the understanding from Romans 10: 17 that faith comes by hearing, and hearing by the word of God.[5] The sharing and hearing of the Word was a common or corporate experience, in which the priest or the preacher represented due authority over the people whom he instructed.[6]

Part of the caution that made Bible reading a clerical monopoly before the Reformation stemmed from the fear of Wycliffite heresy. At the end of the fourteenth century, some of the followers of the Oxford theologian John Wyclif collaborated on translations of the entire Bible, which they encouraged the laity to read on their own, privately in their households and without the mediation of priests. To Wyclif and the Lollards, the Bible was the chief source of authority. Their views seemed to threaten a broad range of essential teachings in the church, including the meaning of the eucharist.[7] Authorities moved against Wyclif's followers with a vigorous array of measures. Erring theologians were constrained

---

[3] Margaret Aston, 'Lap Books and Lectern Books: The Revelatory Book in the Reformation', in R. N. Swanson (ed.), *The Church and the Book, Studies in Church History*, 38 (2004): 163–89; and, in the same volume, Susan Wabuda, 'Triple-Deckers and Eagle Lecterns: Church Furniture for the Book in Late Medieval and Early Modern England', 143–52.

[4] Eamon Duffy, *The Stripping of the Altars: Traditional Religion in England 1400–1580* (New Haven: Yale University Press, 1992), 93–102; Arnold Hunt, 'The Lord's Supper in Early Modern England', *Past and Present*, 161 (1998): 60–1, 69.

[5] Arnold Hunt, *The Art of Hearing: English Preachers and their Audiences 1590–1640* (Cambridge: Cambridge University Press, 2010); Matthew Milner, *The Senses and the English Reformation* (Farnham: Ashgate, 2011); Susan Wabuda, *Preaching during the English Reformation* (Cambridge: Cambridge University Press, 2002).

[6] Aston, 'Lap Books', 163–89; Wabuda, 'Triple-Deckers', 143–52.

[7] Anne Hudson, 'Lollardy: The English Heresy?', in *The Lollards and their Books* (London: Hambledon Press, 1985), 149.

as supervision was tightened over scholars at Oxford. Sermons by unlicensed preachers were suppressed. The church, acting in concert with the government, decided that, for the laity, direct access to the Bible in English was not necessary. Three statutes passed by Parliament, as well as church law, forbade the laity from reading the Bible in English. Under the new legislation, the bishops and the secular authorities shared responsibilities for suppressing heretics.[8] Well into the sixteenth century, English bishops continued to hunt for Lollards.

This marked a profound change, for translations of scripture into English had begun during Anglo-Saxon times, as Cranmer noted in his prologue to the Great Bible, for 'the Saxones tonge' was once 'oure mothers tonge'. In 'olde abbeis', as their libraries were being dismantled at the closure of the monasteries, Cranmer noted that manuscript copies had recently been discovered, and they were of 'soch antique maners of writynge and speaking' that few were now able to read and understand them. But as this language had 'waxed olde and out of comen usage', the Bible was again 'translated in the newer language'. He believed that 'it is not moche above one hundredth yeare agoo', from the time that measures were taken against the Lollards, 'sens scripture hath not bene accustomed to be redde in the vulgar tonge within this realme'.[9]

Never completely suppressed nor separated from the church, the Lollards continued to attend Mass in their parishes, and they were able to teach their views in their private 'scoles of heresie',[10] where they could indulge in eccentric ideas as they read to and learned from each other.[11] There may have always been 'an insidious element' in private lay reading of the small, easily concealed books that could encourage 'subversion or heresy'.[12] At the beginning of the sixteenth century, many bishops and theologians remained deeply distrustful that the laity in England could ever approach scripture with the appropriate attitudes of reverence.

Despite all prohibitions, the demand for the Bible in English was strong. Untold numbers of Wycliffite books of scripture in manuscript were confiscated and destroyed, though influential owners, as Margaret Aston has noted, were able to evade prohibitions by reserving their English Bibles for liturgical use. Some great nobles kept a large English Bible on the lecterns of their private chapels in their households. Although their books must have been both expensive and dangerous to possess, evidence suggests many people from a wide

---

[8] Statutes: (1382) 5 Ric. II, st. 2, c. 5; (1401) 2 Hen. IV, c. 15; (1414) 2 Hen. V, st. 1, c. 7. See also Susan Wabuda, 'The Woman with the Rock: The Controversy on Women and Bible Reading', in Wabuda and Caroline Litzenberger (eds), *Belief and Practice in Reformation England: A Tribute to Patrick Collinson from his Students* (Aldershot and Brookfield, Vt.: Ashgate, 1998), 40–59.

[9] Cranmer, 'Prologue', *The Bible* [2nd edn of the Great Bible], ✠1ʳ; Cranmer, *Writings*, 119. A vast literature on the history of the pre-Tyndale Bible has been summarized by MacCulloch and Solopova, 'Before the King James Bible', esp. 14–25.

[10] The confession of Hawisia Moon of Loddon, 1430, printed in Anne Hudson (ed.), *Selections from English Wycliffite Writings* (Cambridge: Cambridge University Press, 1978), 34–7.

[11] Patrick Collinson, 'The English Conventicle', in W. J. Sheils and Diana Woods (eds), *Voluntary Religion, Studies in Church History*, 23 (1986): 229–59; and Collinson, 'Night Schools, Conventicles and Churches: Continuities and Discontinuities in Early Protestant Ecclesiology', in Peter Marshall and Alec Ryrie (eds), *The Beginnings of English Protestantism* (Cambridge: Cambridge University Press, 2002), 209–35.

[12] Aston, 'Lap Books', 164, 167.

social range were willing to obtain them. Approximately 250 medieval English manuscripts still survive for various books of the Bible.[13]

The development of print in the fifteenth century only intensified the desire at all levels of society for devotional books. Withheld though the physical book of the Bible might have been from the majority of people, a large selection of material became available for the laity to enjoy in printed as well as oral and ritual forms, as Eamon Duffy has demonstrated. As many lay people wished to emulate the holiness of monks and nuns by following the round of prayers of the divine office, their primers incorporated important excerpts from the Vulgate in English as well as in Latin. Reading the Gospels or Psalms or Canticles was recognized as being especially appropriate for increasing devotion. The market for macaronic books was almost limitless,[14] though following the readings in a book of hours surely was a different devotional experience than a direct approach to the unabridged text of the New Testament.[15]

II. THE WRITTEN WORD

In the early decades of the sixteenth century, the laity's access to the Bible in the vernacular gained important support from Erasmus and other scholars of the learned languages. In the *Paraclesis*, his introduction to his Greek and Latin New Testament of 1516, Erasmus began to place important new emphasis on Christ. The written Word was his 'living and breathing likeness'. In Erasmus's famous conclusion: the New Testament revealed 'the living image of His holy mind and the speaking, healing, dying, rising Christ himself'. The Gospels 'render Him so fully present that you would see less if you gazed upon him with your very eyes'.[16] Erasmus promoted the written text as a more vital means of understanding God than the visual appeal of contemplating a crucifix or gazing on the Host. His *Paraclesis* came at the same moment that Cardinal Ximénez de Cisneros of Toledo's vast de luxe polyglot edition of the Bible was nearing completion, and they were part of the same trend for the study of biblical languages that English patrons, including Bishop John Fisher of Cambridge, wished that they had the resources to emulate fully. A parallel moment occurred in Europe in the first decades of the sixteenth century: university-educated clergy of the highest stratum could enjoy their exquisite new skills in the learned languages exactly at the same time that Erasmus argued in Latin that men and women of even the lowest echelons of

---

[13] Aston, 'Lap Books', 165–6; Daniell, *Bible in English*, 66; MacCulloch and Solopova, 'Before the King James Bible', 24–5.

[14] Duffy, *Stripping of the Altars*, 53–87, 209–65; and Duffy, *Marking the Hours: English People and their Prayers 1240–1570* (New Haven: Yale University Press, 2006).

[15] Patrick Collinson, 'The Coherence of the Text: How it Hangeth Together: The Bible in Reformation England', in W. P. Stephens (ed.), *The Bible, the Reformation and the Church: Essays in Honour of James Anderson, Journal for the Study of the New Testament*, supplement series, 105 (1995): 84–108.

[16] This is the translation from the Latin by John C. Olin, in *Christian Humanism and the Reformation: Selected Writings of Erasmus*, ed. and tr. Olin (New York: Fordham University Press, 1987), 92–106, esp. 105–6.

society should have the Gospels in their hands and mouths, at least in their books of hours.[17]

The astonishing, even destabilizing, recognition that Erasmus received in his lifetime for his scholarship, not least for his commentaries on St Jerome, and the fresh translation of the New Testament that he made from the Greek in 1519, was problematic. What Erasmus achieved in challenging the primacy of Jerome's Vulgate through his innovative use of critical philology was to create the possibility of a fluid text of scripture, or rather, of translations that could never be fully complete, comprehensive, or fixed in the sense that the Vulgate had set the sacred text for its many uses in the church.[18] Sir Thomas More noted in a rejoinder to John Frith that 'If every man that can fynd out a new fonde fantasye upon a texte of holy scrypture' was believed, even against the orthodoxy of the writings of the holy doctors of the church and the saints, 'than may ye surely se that none article of the christen faith can stand and endure long'.[19]

Erasmus removed some stability from the Christian Church at the same time that he increased the possibility of eccentric readings of scripture that were developed by individuals reading on their own, privately, without guidance. He was heavily criticized for some of the editorial decisions he made as he translated from the Greek. In England, one of his fiercest opponents was Edward Lee, who had been More's friend from their youth. Lee maintained in 1520 that Erasmus did not have the authority to produce what amounted to a new version of holy writ.[20] Now a single translator working alone or almost alone could challenge the primacy of Jerome's text. A decade later, William Tyndale worked directly from the Greek and Hebrew rather than the Vulgate as he translated the New and the Old Testaments into English.[21] In addition to his famous boast that he hoped that 'he would cause a boy that driveth the plough, to know more of the Scripture' than did even learned priests, Tyndale was provocative for his boldness in placing his own name on the title-pages of his translations.[22] In some senses, the translation of scripture by Erasmus or

[17] See Bob Scribner, 'Heterodoxy, Literacy and Print in the Early German Reformation', in Peter Biller and Anne Hudson (eds), *Heresy and Literacy, 1000–1530* (Cambridge: Cambridge University Press, 1994), 255–78.

[18] Margherita Morreale, 'Vernacular Scriptures in Spain', in G. W. H. Lampe (ed.), *The Cambridge History of the Bible*, ii. *The West from the Fathers to the Reformation* (Cambridge: Cambridge University Press, 1969), 465–91; and, in the same volume, Louis Bouyer, 'Erasmus in Relation to the Medieval Biblical Tradition', 492–505.

[19] *A Letter of Syr Tho. More Knight Impugnyge the Erronyouse Writing of John Fryth against the Blessed Sacrament of the Aultare* (London: William Rastell, 1533), C4ᵛ; reprinted in *The Correspondence of Sir Thomas More*, ed. Elizabeth Frances Rogers (Princeton: Princeton University Press, 1947), no. 190, at 446.

[20] *Apologia Edouardi Leei contra quorundum calumnias* and *annotationes Edouardi Leei in annotationes noui testamenti Desiderii Erasmi* (Paris: Egidii Gourmont [1520], CUL Td. 54. 28). For the most recent treatment of their rivalry, see *Controversies: Apologia qua Respondet Invectivis Lei, Responsio Ad Annotationes Lei,* ed. Jane E. Phillips, tr. Ericka Rummel, in *The Collected Works of Erasmus*, lxxii (Toronto: University of Toronto Press, 2005). See also Claire Cross, 'Lee, Edward (1481/2–1544)', *Oxford Dictionary of National Biography (ODNB)*, 2004, <http://www.oxforddnb.com/view/article/16278>.

[21] Patrick Collinson, 'The Bible, the Reformation and the English Language', *Douglas Southall Freeman Historical Review* (Richmond, Va., 1999), 21–2.

[22] Plough boy: John Foxe, *Actes and Monuments* (London: John Day, 1583), 1076. For one example of his title-pages among many: *The Newe Testament, Dylygently Corrected and Compared with the Greke by William Tindale* (Antwerp, 1534). Also included in John Foxe, *Acts and Monuments*, ed. George Townsend, v. 118–19.

Tyndale or Martin Luther represented the triumph of the individual scholar's intellect over the church and its inherited traditions.

To circumvent the manifold dangers that a single translator could impose on his text, for England in the 1530s and afterward into the seventeenth century, a new emphasis was placed on consensus among the divines who worked together on biblical translations. Consensus was the goal for producing fresh translations that were consonant with traditions in the church as they were perceived and interpreted. A common sharing was also the goal for the presentation of scripture in the gathering of the people in worship together. The group in consensus rather than the idiosyncratic reader alone remained one of the goals for public worship.

For England, Luther's appearance only intensified episcopal control over illicit books. Pope Leo X forbade Luther's writings in 1520 and he condemned his views the following year, which precipitated an immediate and sensational response from Henry VIII and Cardinal Thomas Wolsey. The Pope was surprised by the King's spirited defence of the seven sacraments, and for the rest of his life, Henry built his reputation as a scourge of Luther.[23] The threat that Lutheran books posed in England increased the bishops' vigilance against older heretical books and English Bibles. In 1511 and 1521, Archbishop William Warham of Canterbury and Bishop John Longland of Lincoln renewed their efforts against the Lollards they detected in their dioceses.[24] When Tyndale's illicit translation of the New Testament was printed from 1525, first in Cologne, then in Worms, English bishops confiscated every copy that they could find.[25] The Lollards' books, Luther's writings, and Tyndale's New Testament were lumped together as erroneous and dangerous material that deserved to be forbidden.[26] In 1528, the discovery at the universities of heretical books caused Wolsey and Longland great concern. To supply English clergymen with sound material to preach to their audiences, Fisher recommended the *Enchiridion* by one of Luther's greatest opponents, Johann Eck.

III. 1530

In an important episode that deserves to be better known, a paradoxical change in royal policy became evident in 1530.[27] In the previous year, Convocation had begun to examine

---

[23] J. J. Scarisbrick, *Henry VIII* (Berkeley, Calif.: University of California Press, 1968). See also J. J. Scarisbrick, 'Warham, William (1450?–1532)', *ODNB*, 2004; online edition, Jan. 2008, <http://www. oxforddnb.com/view/article/28741>. Susan Wabuda, 'The Reformation of the English Church under Henry VIII', in Arthur L. Schwarz (ed.), *Vivat Rex! An Exhibition Commemorating the 500th Anniversary of the Accession of Henry VIII* (New York: Grolier Club, 2009), 30–44.

[24] Foxe (1583), 973–86; *Acts and Monuments*, iv. 219–46; *Tudor Royal Proclamations*, ed. Paul L. Hughes and James F. Larkin (New Haven: Yale University Press, 1964), i, no. 85; *Lollards of Coventry 1486–1522*, ed. and tr. Shannon McSheffrey and Norman Tanner, Camden 5th ser. 22 (Cambridge: Cambridge University Press, 2003).

[25] John Harryson [*pseud.* for John Bale], *Yet a Course at the Romyshe Foxe* ([Antwerp], 1543), 58ʳ.

[26] See Johann Eck's comprehensive denunciation of heresies in his *Enchiridion locorum communium adversus Lutheranos* (London, 1531) esp. G2ᵛ–G4ʳ.

[27] This remarkable episode was not discussed in David Daniell's *William Tyndale: A Biography* (New Haven: Yale University Press, 1994), nor in any detail in his *Bible in English*, 165. Among the reasons for the meeting at Westminster in May 1530 not receiving adequate attention is the confusing manner in which the

the heretical books that had been discovered at the universities. As Defender of the Faith, Henry was alarmed when he heard that English books 'conteynyng many detestable errours and dampnable opynyons' were being printed 'beyond the see' and brought into England. Now Henry began to position himself all over again as the heroic safeguard of his people, 'like a noble and vertuouse prince', by assuming 'a wider responsibility for the spiritual affairs of his kingdom'.[28]

On 4 May 1530, Henry sent letters to the vice chancellors of the universities, bidding each of them to send a dozen 'of the beste lerned men in divinitye' to London, to arrive within a week so that they could examine the contents of 'certayne printed bokes written in the Englyshe tonge'.[29] In the letter that summoned the Cambridge men to London, Henry announced that he feared the devastating potential of erroneous books to 'perverte and corrupte' the opinions of 'our people', leading to 'division, contention and debate, in the cheif and principall pointes and articles of our faithe and religion' that could bring about 'the dissolution of our common wealthe' through 'totall confusion and destruction'. What Almighty God expected Henry to provide in the governance of the realm were conditions that would encourage 'the unite [unity] and agreement in oone persuasion of faythe and religion'.[30] By the middle of May, a worried Bishop Richard Nixe of Norwich wrote to the Duke of Norfolk to explain that he had done all that he could to suppress 'Arronious bokes in englyshe', but that those he was examining for their heresies were encouraged because they had heard 'that the king's pleasure is the new testament in english shulde go forth, and men shulde have it, and rede it'.[31]

Another urgent reason that drove Henry to assemble the divines was as part of his efforts to discard Katherine of Aragon by establishing that the theological basis of their marriage was unsound. Only two months earlier, the members of the University of Cambridge's Convocation had cast their ballots in a way that supported the legitimacy of Katherine's marriage, but the King, with the contrivance of Hugh Latimer and others, had massaged the results to make them look as if the university supported the King's

material was presented in the Townsend edition of Foxe, where it was divided between volumes v. 569–99 (incompletely) and vii. 499–506. See Louis A. Schuster, 'Thomas More's Polemical Career, 1523–1533', in *The Confutation of Tyndale's Answer, Complete Works of St. Thomas More*, viii/3. 1209–1215 (New Haven: Yale University Press, 1973). For Anne Boleyn's role in persuading Henry towards challenging the papacy through Tyndale's works, see Maria Dowling, 'Anne Boleyn and Reform', *Journal of Ecclesiastical History*, 35 (1984): 30–46; and Eric Ives, *Anne Boleyn* (Oxford: Blackwell, 1986), 160–7.

[28] The National Archives: Public Record Office SP 1/57, 104^r–128^r (LP, vol. 4(3), no. 6401); David Wilkins (ed.), *Concilia Magnae Britanniae et Hibernia* (London, 1737), iii. 717–24. Defender of the Faith: Lambeth Palace Library, Warham's Register, I, 182^r, 185^v. For 'spiritual affairs of his kingdom', see Scarisbrick, *Henry VIII*, 252–4.

[29] The King's letter to Cambridge: CCCC, MS 242, 17^v–18^v printed in John Lamb, *A Collection of Letters, Statutes, and Other Documents, from the MS. Library of Corp. Christ. Coll., Illustrative of the History of the University of Cambridge, during the Period of the Reformation* (London: John W. Parker, 1838), 26–7. Our chief source for events is Archbishop William Warham's Register: LPL, Warham's Register, I, 182^r–186^v, printed in Wilkins, *Concilia*, iii. 736; reprinted in *Acts and Monuments*, vii. 503–4. The 'lerned men': LPL, Warham's Register I, 185^v.

[30] The King's summons: CCCC, MS 242, 17^v–18^v, printed in Lamb, 26–7. Also, *Tudor Royal Proclamations*, i, no. 129.

[31] Bishop Nixe to [the Duke of Norfolk], 14 May 1540: BL, Cotton MS Cleopatra. E. V, 389 (LP, vol. 4(3), no. 6385).

cause instead.[32] Henry thrust himself forward in the matter of heretical books even if his intervention threatened his bishops and the autonomy of the church in England so that he could exert, through them, increased pressure on the papacy to annul his marriage.[33] Like More, Archbishop Warham found himself in an almost impossible predicament. More had defended Erasmus against Lee and probably would have supported a translation of the Bible into English if approved by statute and canon law. But now he and Warham had to decide how to best defend the church's authority against the King's growing cognizance of his own dominion over matters spiritual in his realm.

How were the dozen participants from each university selected? Henry's letter instructed Cambridge's vice chancellor William Buckmaster to 'chose out and apointe' them. Buckmaster had been badly embarrassed when the university voted on the question of the King's marriage, and the selection of those who should go to London was a matter of the greatest sensitivity. We do not know how formally the members of the university met to 'chose out' their delegates, but 'The Names of them whiche I dyd appointe' were recorded on the surviving copy of the King's letter.[34] Among them, John Watson was the most eminent. He was master of Christ's College and he had been one of Erasmus's closest friends during the brief period that the great man had resided in Cambridge. But Watson had examined and denounced Luther's books for Wolsey as long ago as 1521.[35] Latimer was also chosen, and he had already strongly expressed his support for the King in his Great Matter. Buckmaster was present at court when Latimer preached his first sermon there only a few weeks earlier in April.[36] Cranmer was not present to be added to the group, for he had been sent on embassy to Italy at the beginning of the year.[37]

Our most important source for the proceedings is 'a writing' or a 'bill in englisshe' that Warham prepared at Henry's behest as an announcement to be read 'by prechers abroade unto the people'. With some lengthy explanatory material, the bill was recorded in his Register. It was closely related to the royal proclamation that was issued in June 1530, and one borrowed from the other, though the account in Warham's Register is the more revealing of the two.[38] Warham presided over the 'congregacion'.[39] More, as chancellor of England, also took a leading role. In addition to the theologians from the universities, among those who were also called to join the proceedings were 'the cheffe prelates and Clerkes of his Realme':[40] a stellar group of successful career clerics with deep connections to the regime, many of whom were already deeply involved in advancing the King's

[32] CCCC, MS 106, 113–15, printed in Lamb, 20–4. Further details will be found in my forthcoming book, *Hugh Latimer and the Reformation in England*.

[33] Ives, *Anne Boleyn*, 164.

[34] The names of the Cambridge men appointed by Buckmaster were: John Watson, Edward Wigen, Edward Crome, Geoffrey Downes, Nicholas Shaxton, Hugh Latimer, John Thixtell, James Hutton, one Tylson, John Skippe, Nicholas Heath, and Ralph Bayne. CCCC, MS 242, 17ᵛ–18ᵛ; printed in Lamb, 26–7.

[35] *Grace Book B II: Containing the Accounts of the Proctors of the University of Cambridge*, ed. Mary Bateson (Cambridge: Cambridge University Press, 2009), 92.

[36] CCCC, MS 106, 113–15, printed in Lamb, 22–3.

[37] Diarmaid MacCulloch, *Thomas Cranmer: A Life* (New Haven: Yale University Press, 1996), 47–53.

[38] *A Proclamation Made and Divysed by the Kingis Hyghnes / wyth the Advise of his Honorable Counsaile, for Dampning of Erroneous Bokes and Heresies, and Prohibitinge of the Havinge of Holy Scripture* (London: Thomas Berthelet, 1530), printed in *Tudor Royal Proclamations*, i, no. 129.

[39] Congregation: TNA: PRO SP 1/57, fol. 130ʳ (LP, vol. 4(3), no. 6411); LPL, Warham's Register I, 185ᵛ.

[40] LPL, Warham's Register I, 182ʳ, 185ʳ.

marital cause. They included Stephen Gardiner, royal secretary; Richard Sampson, dean of the chapel royal; Richard Wolman, master of the Court of Requests; Nicholas Wilson, confessor to the King, and the Greek scholar William Latimer.[41] Warham was also assisted by Bishop Cuthbert Tunstall, who was about to leave London for his new see at Durham. Tunstall had elicited More's assistance against Wyclif's and Luther's heresies by early 1528. More had begun to write against Tyndale in his *Dyaloge* of 1529.[42] His latest printed work had already denounced one of the confiscated books, Simon Fish's anonymous *Supplicacyon for the Beggars*.[43]

Beginning on 11 May 1530, the divines spent two weeks reading the suspected books to determine whether or not they were 'contagious' and 'whether the oppynyons conteyned in them were agreeable to goddis works and doctrine or noo'.[44] Among them were: Frith's *Revelation of Antichrist*;[45] *The Summe of Scripture*;[46] and several works by Tyndale, as well as his Old and New Testaments.[47] They listed the 'heresies and errours', or the 'Errours blasphemys and heresies' that they found in several of the works. With vehemence (but less detail), they referred to the 'great errours and pestilent heresies' that they observed in the translation of the Bible, which they summed up as having been 'corrupted by William Tyndall'.[48]

The King joined them on 24 May in St Stephen's Chapel in the Parliament house in Westminster, when their discussion turned on the delicate point of royal responsibility as it related to scripture in the vernacular. The potential for division and upheaval in the realm was perceived to be a real threat. Henry told the assembly that he had heard that some of his subjects held the opinion that it was his duty to cause 'the scripture of God' to be translated, and that he and the prelates 'doo wronge in denying' it. He asked every man there present 'freely and frankly' to show what could be proved by scripture itself on this point, and also by the teachings of the ancient fathers of the church. The King 'openly protestid' that he 'might conforme himself therunto, minding to do his dutie towardes his people, as he wolde they shulde' towards him.[49]

Although many of the details are lost to us, the ensuing deliberation was intense and involved. Scripture was sifted for illumination on this point. The opinions of 'holy doctors and auctours' were 'alleged and red'. This process took a long while. In the proclamation that was released in June, the English people were told that the King, 'in his own royal

[41] This William Latymer was not the chaplain of Anne Boleyn. Among the others, as listed in Warham's Register, were John Bell (future Bishop of Worcester) and Richard Dook (Archdeacon of Wiltshire). LPL, Warham's Register I, 186ʳ.
[42] *Correspondence of More*, no. 160. *A Dyaloge of Syr Thomas More ... Wherin be Treatyd Dyvers Maters, as of the Veneration & Worshyp of Ymages* (London, June 1529), reprinted from May? 1530, and answered by Tyndale from Antwerp in 1531. See the comments by J. B. Trapp in More's *Apology* in vol. ix of *The Complete Works of St. Thomas More* (New Haven: Yale University Press, 1979), pp. xxvi–xxviii.
[43] For More: [Simon Fish], *A Supplicacyon for the Beggars* ([Antwerp? 1529?]); answered by More in *The Supplycacyon of Soulys* (London, 1529).
[44] LPL, Warham's Register I, 185ᵛ.
[45] John Frith, *The Revelation of Antichrist* ([Antwerp, 1529]).
[46] Henricus Bomelius, *The Summe of the Holye Scripture*, tr. Simon Fish ([Antwerp, 1529]).
[47] William Tyndale, *That Faith the Mother of all Good Works Justifieth Us (The Parable of the Wicked Mammon)* ([Antwerp, 1528]), and *The Obedience of a Christen Man* ([Antwerp, 1528]).
[48] LPL, Warham's Register I, 182ʳ–183ʳ, 185ʳ.
[49] LPL, Warham's Register I, 185ᵛ.

person', with his primates and divines, 'hath seriously and deeply, with great leisure and long deliberation, consulted, debated, insearched, and discussed the premisses',[50] until 'all thynges sayde might be on both sidys and for bothe partes spoken, deduced and brought furth'.[51]

The release of the Bible in English had its champions: at least three or four of the theologians, Hugh Latimer among them, wanted scripture to be released in English. Latimer was so outspoken that his opinions were widely remarked upon afterward.[52] That Henry made a forceful case in favour of the New Testament in English is hinted in the account of the meeting that Warham released. But the evangelicals were in the small minority, or as Latimer noted later, 'the most part overcometh the better'.[53] After every man had been asked, all authorities consulted, and all things had been said that could be said on the subject, a resolution was reached, or rather, a set of resolutions. The moment of decision was recorded as a defining moment of clarity: 'fynally it appered that the having of the hole [sic] scripture in Englisshe is not necessarye to christen men'. It was not necessary because people could still 'folowe suche leassons as the preacher teachith theym'. They might be as 'lerned by his mowthe' and as edified 'spiritually in their soules' as they would by scripture in written form. Therefore, the Bible in English was not necessary for all men to read. At certain earlier times in the church's history, the fathers had thought that it was 'mete and convenient' for scripture to be 'in the vulgar tongis and in the commen peoples handes', but at other times they had judged it 'not expedient'. Listening to the lessons taught by preachers in their sermons was perfectly adequate for the edification of their audiences. Salvation came from hearing, not reading.[54] The King and his prelates were doing well in carrying out their responsibilities. They were protecting souls by forbidding an imperfect translation.

Perhaps Warham and More now wanted matters to go no further. But this was not the absolute end. Henry seized the opportunity to position himself in the tradition of great Old Testament kings like Hezekiah by promoting scripture. In the midst of their discussion, Henry 'did openlye say and protest, that he wolde cause the newe testament to be by lerned men faithfully and purely translated into [the] englishe tongue' so that he might 'have it in his hands redy to be gevyn to his people' once he was convinced by 'their maners and behavor' that they were 'mete apt and convenient to receyve' it. The onus was on his subjects. They had to demonstrate that they detested pernicious books of the sort that had just been examined. They had to show that they abhorred 'thes hereses and newe opynyons'. The English people had to prove that they were willing to accept the teachings

---

[50] *A Proclamation; Tudor Royal Proclamations*, i, no. 129.

[51] LPL, Warham's Register I, 185[v].

[52] John Clyffe to Edmund Bonner, chaplain to Cardinal Wolsey, 29 May 1530: TNA: PRO SP 1/57r (LP, vol. 4(3), no. 6411).

[53] Hugh Latimer's anonymous and open letter, supposedly to Henry VIII, 1 Dec. 1530: *Sermons and Remains*, ed. George Elwes Corrie (Cambridge: Parker Society, 1845), quotation at 305. Some speculations have been offered about those who shared Latimer's views. He was probably supported by Edward Crome of Cambridge. J. F. Mozley, in *William Tyndale* (London: SPCK, 1937), 161, suggested William Latimer as a third, though he confused this Latimer with Anne Boleyn's chaplain of the same name. In addition to Crome and Thixtell, Allan G. Chester suggested also Nicholas Shaxton as a strong possibility: *Hugh Latimer: Apostle to the English* (Philadelphia: University of Pennsylvania Press, 1954), 58.

[54] LPL, Warham's Register I, 185[v]–186[r].

of their priests rather than pursue their own 'fantasies'. They had to demonstrate that they were 'so sober, quiet, meek and temperate' that they could not be guilty of 'misusing the gift of Scripture'. Only then would the King and his prelates recognize that their duty lay in giving the Word of God in English to the people.[55] But this was a striking promise that Henry uttered, as well as a direct political appeal to good order. It was an early indication that the King intended to take a more direct role in the spiritual lives of his subjects in return for their loyalty.[56]

The next day, 25 May 1530, Henry entered Star Chamber and formally forbade heretical books, though he again promised that he would ask the best learned men of the universities to provide a translation of the New Testament to replace the corrupt version that he was prohibiting.[57] On 22 June 1530, a royal proclamation prohibited books by Tyndale and Fish among others, and also the existing translations of the Old and New Testaments. Copies of the New or Old Testaments in English, being in print, or copied from books in print, were to be surrendered to the local bishop within fifteen days. But the proclamation repeated the King's assertion that he 'intendeth to provide that the Holy Scripture shall by great, learned, and Catholic persons [be] translated into the English tongue, if it shall then seem to his grace convenient so to be'. The only persons allowed to buy, receive, or keep the New or Old Testaments in English were those appointed by the King and the bishops for correcting or amending Tyndale's translation.[58]

Henry's promise was repeated again when Warham released his 'bill' for preachers to read to the laity. His statement incorporated a sensitive rendering of Henry's concern for his people, for it was the King's own 'pleasure and determynation' that his subjects 'be notified by prechers', and especially those theologians who had been called by the King to pass judgement on the heretical books. At the same time, the archbishop ensured that no one would be left in any doubt that the English New Testament would not be released now, or perhaps ever. Warham instructed preachers to declare that the people should not grudge or murmur against the 'very trouthe', which was that they could not 'require or demaunde' for 'scripture to be divulged in thenglishe tonge' unless their superiors thought 'in their conscience it may doo yowe good'. Warham took the idea of disorder that Henry had already conveyed and now he stressed that the risk was far too great to proceed in translating scripture. As the Bible in English had been withheld in ages past, then the King and his prelates were actually doing great good for the realm by withholding it. Warham placed the blame for their decision on the English people themselves, for the people had demonstrated by their appetite for heretical reading matter that they were not ready to take the Word of God into their own hands. If the English New Testament would not benefit the realm, then those authorities would 'doo amysse in sufferyng yowe to have it'.[59]

Not only did Archbishop Warham tune England's pulpits in an attempt to prevent anyone from advocating the release of Tyndale's translation of the Bible, but he affixed a

---

[55] LPL, Warham's Register I, 186ʳ. For Gardiner's view of Henry as another Hezekiah, *The Letters of Stephen Gardiner*, ed. James Arthur Muller (Cambridge: Cambridge University Press, 1933), 313.

[56] Wabuda, *Preaching*, 89–99; Ethan Shagan, *Popular Politics and the English Reformation* (Cambridge: Cambridge University Press, 2002).

[57] Wilkins, *Concilia*, iii. 740.

[58] *Tudor Royal Proclamations*, i, no. 129.

[59] LPL, Warham's Register I, 186ʳ.

formal attestation to the proceedings, certified by his notaries Thomas Ashley, Richard Watkyns, and Mathew Greston, that provided the names of the most notable participants, and declared that they had approved of the decisions that were taken at Westminster. Latimer was embarrassed, for Warham's announcement had the effect of making him publicly endorse a policy that was at odds with his real position that the people should be given the Bible in English as soon as the King allowed. Thus Warham won at least a partial victory over the evangelicals, and perhaps over the King as well. In effect, the archbishop appropriated the victory against Tyndale's New Testament through his own representation of a consensus that did not exist.[60]

Towards the end of 1530, as Henry continued to be absorbed in the struggle to resolve his marital difficulties, he gathered his control over the Church in England. At Michaelmas, the first charges of *praemunire* were made against Fisher and other bishops, and they were followed by a general charge against the entire clergy for infringing on the King's jurisdiction.[61] But there was no immediate sign that Henry thought a 'convienent' time had arrived for a new translation of holy scripture.[62] Wolsey died in disgrace at the end of November 1530, and at that time, Latimer circulated anonymously, among his friends, a satirical letter that he said he had addressed to the King. But it was nothing of the sort. Henry never saw Latimer's letter (nor was he meant to see it). In reality, Latimer shared a clever jest that was meant to hearten those who had been disappointed in the turn that events had taken, and to repair his own reputation, privately, among his friends for seeming to endorse a policy that contradicted his actual intent. The text was a sensational reproof of the King. It warned Henry that his very soul was in jeopardy for not releasing the Bible in English 'even today, before tomorrow'. Those 'mischievous flatterers' who had dissuaded the King from releasing the English New Testament in the summer had pressed forward their own deceitful ideas, 'as they have done many times more'. Henry should not be so confident as 'a defender of his faith' for God would have it defended by no other means than by his Word. Nothing that the King could do that seemed good in his own sight would actually be in keeping with divine commandment 'without the word of God'. The English Bible was essential, and the need for the people to have it was immediate. Henry's initial desire to give the English Bible to his people should be an inseparable element of his kingship.[63]

IV. GREAT LABOUR

In succeeding years, as the terms of the royal supremacy over the English Church were codified, doing as the King wanted became the criterion for all subsequent Henrician Bible translations. Thomas Cranmer succeeded Warham as Archbishop of Canterbury in time to crown Anne Boleyn. Tyndale continued to revise his own work, and his most mature edition of the New Testament was printed in Antwerp late in 1534, the same year that the

[60] LPL, Warham's Register I, 186r–186v.   [61] Scarisbrick, *Henry VIII*, 273–4.
[62] LPL, Warham's Register I, 186r.
[63] Latimer, *Remains*, letter 3. Chester established from the four extant versions of the letter that it was written anonymously and was never meant to be read by the King. *Hugh Latimer*, 61–5.

medieval laws that restricted the Bible in English were repealed by Parliament.[64] In summer 1535, when Fisher and More were going to the block and the King put heavy emphasis on the dangerous 'usurpations' of the Bishop of Rome,[65] the time was more 'convenient' for 'great, learned, and Catholic persons' to see that the New Testament was 'thoroughlie corrected'.[66] Cranmer had it 'devided' into 'ix or x partes', and 'written large', with wide spaces between each line, 'in paper bokes', which he distributed 'unto the best lernyd bishopps, and other lernyd men' so that they could make 'a perfect correction' of the text.[67] Gardiner, now Bishop of Winchester, translated the Gospels of Luke and John, 'wherin I have spent a gret labour', as he informed Thomas Cromwell, in the midst of a full agenda of efforts to promote the royal supremacy.[68] According to the famous story told by Cranmer's secretary Ralph Morice, John Stokesley, Bishop of London (who was a superb scholar, adept in Hebrew as well as Greek), refused to correct the Acts of the Apostles, and returned his portion with the words: 'I mervaile what my lorde of Canterbury meaneth, that thus abuseth the people in gyvyng them libertie to reade the scriptures, which doith nothing else but infect them with heryses'.[69]

Cranmer was able to send 'a new translation' of the Bible in a fresh printed edition to Cromwell in late summer 1537, with a request that Cromwell gain the King's approval for it. This was what has become known as the 'Matthew' Bible, even though the work was mainly Tyndale's, overseen following his execution the previous year by John Rogers and Miles Coverdale, and then issued under a pseudonym. Cranmer admitted that he was only semi-satisfied by the translation: 'so far as I have read thereof, I like it better than any other translation heretofore made; yet not doubting but that there may and will be found some fault therein, as you know no man ever did or can do so well, but it may be from time to time amended'. Cranmer asked that it be licensed to be read of 'every person', with a wry comment about the difficulties involved in correcting the text: 'until such time that we the bishops shall set forth a better translation, which I think will not be till a day after doomsday'.[70] When he learned the King had given his permission to have it sold and read in England, his relief and pleasure, like Latimer's, was unbounded.[71]

Although Cranmer could recommend to Cromwell privately that the Matthew Bible be released for 'every person' to read, his preface to the second edition of the Great Bible of 1540 (Tyndale's work, edited again by Coverdale) was much more cautious. Though the preface was obviously influenced by Erasmus's evocative *Paraclesis*, the potential for

---

[64] For Tyndale's 1534 New Testament, see David Daniell, 'Tyndale, William (c.1494–1536)', *ODNB*, 2004; online edition, May 2011, <http://www.oxforddnb.com/view/article/27947>. 25 Hen. VIII, c. 14. See John Guy, 'The Legal Context of the Controversy: The Law of Heresy' in *The Debellation of Salem and Bizance*, in *Complete Works of St. Thomas More*, x, ed. John Guy (New Haven: Yale University Press, 1987), 47–67.

[65] See my 'Bishop John Longland's Mandate to his Clergy, 1535', *The Library*, 6th ser. 13 (1991): 255–61.

[66] *Tudor Royal Proclamations*, i, no. 129.

[67] British Library, Harley 422, fols. 87ʳ–87ᵛ, printed in 'The Answers of Mr. Thomas Lawney' by Ralph Morice, in *Narratives of the Days of the Reformation*, ed. John Gough Nichols, Camden Society, 77 (1859): 277–8.

[68] Gardiner, *Letters*, no. 49. See also 313.

[69] BL MS Harley 422, fols. 87ʳ–87ᵛ, printed in Morice, 'The Answers of Mr. Thomas Lawney', in *Narratives of the Days of the Reformation*, 277–8.

[70] Cranmer, *Writings*, 344–5; Matthew Bible: *The Byble, which is all the Holy Scripture*, tr. Thomas Matthew [pseud. for William Tyndale and Miles Coverdale] (Antwerp, 1537).

[71] Cranmer, *Writings*, 395–6.

disobedience by members of the laity still concerned the archbishop. The previous year he had sent Lord Lisle in Calais a letter of clarification concerning the manner in which the Bible should be approached. Those who read loudly enough to disturb services 'do much abuse' the King's intent in placing the Bible openly in parish churches. They were not supposed to 'allure great multitudes of people together' to hear them read, nor were they to interrupt worship. The Bible should only be read 'in time convenient', and 'privately' for the 'amendment of the lives' both of the people who read and for 'such hearers as cannot themselves read'. The readers should read only the 'simple and plain text' as it 'lieth printed in the book', and they were not to interpret or expound the text to their listeners unless they had the specific authority to do so, as licensed preachers or other clergymen.[72]

In his preface to the Great Bible, Cranmer argued that those who refused to read the Bible or hear it read, like those who engaged in 'inordinate reading, undiscreet speaking, contentious disputing' through their 'licentious living' did 'slander and hinder the word of God'. By citing long passages from the writings of Sts John Chrysostom and Gregory Nazianzen, Cranmer recommended a seemly restraint. Chrysostom was 'ynough & suffyciente to persuade all' who were not 'perverslye sette in their awne wyllful opinion' that 'it is convenient and good' that the scripture should be read or heard by all sort and kinds of people in the vulgar tongue, especially as the King 'hath approved with his royall assente' its setting forth. And even though the title-page proclaimed that the Old and New Testaments had been translated 'after the veryte of the Hebrue and Greke texts by the dylygent study by dyverse excellent learned men', most of it was the work of William Tyndale.[73]

Take the book in hand, Chrysostom may have advised, but the Great Bible was not meant as a domestic book. Under the terms of the 1538 Injunctions, copies of the Great Bible were placed, somewhat ambiguously, in unfamiliar positions in the naves of churches and cathedrals, chained to desks or lecterns, where churchgoers could read them in loud voices and turn the pages themselves. In 1541, a proclamation again stipulated that English Bibles be set up in every parish church. But Bible reading by the laity in church, by men and especially women, was a conspicuous novelty that disturbed the Mass. The proclamation warned that no one should read the Bible 'with loud and high voices' during the celebration of Mass or other divine services, though the problem proved to be too much for the King to countenance.[74] In 1543 the Act for the Advancement of True Religion forbade all men below the level of yeomanry from reading the Bible, and also all women, except those of the uppermost levels of society, who were permitted Holy Writ only in the strictest seclusion where no one could overhear them as they read.[75] From 1543, most lay people were again excluded from handling the book. They had to learn the teachings of scripture by listening to the clergy as the text was read to them in the lessons, and expounded in homilies and sermons. Once more, the authority of priests and deacons over the people was enhanced. In Edward VI's reign, Gardiner maintained that Cranmer had misrepresented St Gregory's thinking to overemphasize the fact that the laity should read the Bible for themselves. That was not what Gregory meant, Gardiner argued, for poor men could

---

[72] Cranmer, *Writings*, 390–2.
[73] The Great Bible, title-page and ✠2ʳ–✠2ᵛ; Cranmer, *Writings*, 118–25; Aston, 'Lap Books', 180; Wabuda, *Preaching*, 99–106.
[74] *Tudor Royal Proclamations*, i, no. 200; Aston, 'Lap Books', 175–8; Wabuda, 'Woman with the Rock', 54.
[75] *Statutes of the Realm*; Wabuda, 'Woman with the Rock', 40–59.

not leave their other work to spend all of their time in studying scripture. The clergy must present scripture to the people.[76] In the 1540s, Gardiner began plans for a fresh translation which would avoid the errors that he saw in the Great Bible. Another Bible was divided into parts in the Convocation House at Cranmer's direction to be shared out among the bishops and divines.[77] But that work was not completed. The Great Bible remained the most definitive translation for the English under Edward, and it continued in use in Elizabeth's reign until it was revised again as the Bishops' Bible. It informed, once more, the translation that was completed in 1611.[78]

Cranmer understood that true consensus, like a perfect translation, was elusive. So was possession of the treasure. The Bible has always been both a common and a contested jewel. In the sixteenth century bishops discovered that many of the old constraints were defeated. Holy scripture was seized by England's princes to be poured into every ear if not given into every hand. Tyndale's New Testament became the great gift of the English people from its kings.

FURTHER READING

Aston, Margaret. 'Lap Books and Lectern Books: The Revelatory Book in the Reformation', in R. N. Swanson (ed.), *The Church and the Book, Studies in Church History*, 38 (2004): 163–89.
Marshall, Peter, and Alec Ryrie, eds. *The Beginnings of English Protestantism* (Cambridge: Cambridge University Press, 2002).
Lampe, G. W. H., ed. *The Cambridge History of the Bible*, ii. *The West from the Fathers to the Reformation* (Cambridge: Cambridge University Press, 1969).
Hunt, Arnold. *The Art of Hearing: English Preachers and their Audiences 1590–1640* (Cambridge: Cambridge University Press, 2010).
Moore, Helen, and Julian Reid, eds. *Manifold Greatness: The Making of the King James Bible* (Oxford: Bodleian Library, 2011).
Morrissey, Mary. *Politics and the Paul's Cross Sermons 1558–1642* (Oxford: Oxford University Press, 2011).
Nicolson, Adam. *God's Secretaries: The Making of the King James Bible* (New York: Harper Collins, 2003).
Wabuda, Susan. 'The Woman with the Rock: The Controversy on Women and Bible Reading', in Susan Wabuda and Caroline Litzenberger (eds), *Belief and Practice in Reformation England: A Tribute to Patrick Collinson from his Students* (Aldershot: Ashgate, 1998), 40–59.

[76] Gardiner to Cranmer, *Letters*, nos. 124–5, esp. 313, 359.
[77] Gardiner to Cranmer, *Letters*, no. 124, at 313.
[78] Collinson, 'The Bible and the English Language', 20; Daniell, 'William Tyndale', *ODNB*; Adam Nicolson, *God's Secretaries: The Making of the King James Bible* (New York: Harper Collins, 2003), 58–9.

CHAPTER 2

··

GENEVAN LEGACIES: THE MAKING OF THE ENGLISH GENEVA BIBLE

··

FEMKE MOLEKAMP

IN the sixteenth century the Bible in English disseminated Reformation theology, transformed reading practices, and had a profound influence on literary culture. The greatly
increased circulation of the printed Bible in English in the sixteenth century is due particularly to the production of the Geneva Bible. This Bible was far cheaper and more accessible
than any vernacular printed Bible had been so far, and packed with reading aids surrounding the scriptures. It was produced by Protestant exiles in Geneva at Calvin's church during the reign of Queen Mary, where it was first printed in 1560 by the printer Rowland Hall,
and largely sponsored by John Bodley. In 1576, after Archbishop Parker's death, a licence
was obtained to print it England, and it was printed in c.150 editions up until the 1640s. As
William Sherman has observed, the Geneva Bible was, 'in all likelihood, the most widely
distributed book in the English Renaissance', selling more than half a million copies by
the end of the sixteenth century, and continuing in popularity even after the publication
of the King James Bible in 1611.[1] The Geneva Bible greatly extended the possibility for the
application of private reading practices to the scriptures, not only through its lower cost,
but also through the abundance of supplementary material it contained, providing guidance to individual readers. Likewise, it facilitated the growth of domestic Bible-reading
communities.

The history of the Reformation is a textual history and, as Bruce Gordon has stressed,
'the Bible was the central cultural text of the Reformation'.[2] The story of the Geneva Bible
illuminates the reception of continental Protestantism in Britain. This Bible was formed
in a collaborative environment of Reformed scholarship, took material and theological

[1] William H. Sherman, *Used Books: Marking Readers in Renaissance England* (Philadelphia: University
of Pennsylvania Press, 2007), 166.
[2] Bruce Gordon, 'The Changing Face of Protestant History and Identity in Sixteenth-Century Europe',
in Bruce Gordon (ed.), *Protestant History and Identity in Sixteenth Century Europe* (Aldershot: Scholars
Press, 1996), i. 4.

influence from European sources, and transmitted Genevan theology to an English readership.[3] For the first edition (1560) the translators had recourse to the Great Bible as their basic Old Testament text, together with the Latin Old Testaments of Leo Jud (1544), Santes Pagnini (1527), and Robert Estienne (1556/7). For the New Testament they used Tyndale, the Greek New Testament of Erasmus, and Beza's annotated New Testament of 1556/7. The Geneva Bible also relied heavily on various editions of the French Geneva Bible for the host of distinctive paratextual features surrounding the scriptures to guide interpretation. It is a hybrid of English and continental sources, and its cross-cultural origins influence both its theology and the ways in which it offers itself for reading. The narrative of the making, publication, and reception of the English Geneva Bible demonstrates the international scope of Christian humanist scholarship. To gain an understanding of the transmission of European Protestantism in England it is vital to examine the Geneva Bible as a highly influential tool.

Revisionist studies of the English Reformation began some time ago to pluralize the English Reformation and to dismantle older notions of its linearity, while 'postrevisionism' continues to add nuances to what is rightly seen as a complicated set of narratives.[4] Yet despite this opening out of the landscape of religious reform in early modern England, there is further work to be done on the role that continental Protestantism played in shaping it. Peter Marshall has signalled the 'apparent reluctance of much of the historiography of the English Reformation to align itself with the issues and debates of the wider European world', which has led to a certain persistence of the idea of 'English exceptionalism, or at least English particularism'.[5] In 2010, Patrick Collinson asserted that 'no one has yet succeeded in writing a book in which the English Reformation is fully integrated, subsumed and contextualised in the history of the Reformation on a European scale'.[6] Some advances have been made to challenge the insular tendencies of the historiography of the English Reformation. Euan Cameron, Diarmaid MacCulloch, and Philip Benedict have published studies of European Reformations which go some way to situate the English religious landscape within the wider context of European developments.[7] The collection of essays, *The*

---

[3] Reformed theology in Geneva was shaped most influentially by Calvin and Beza. For an introduction to Genevan theology, see Richard Muller, 'John Calvin and Later Calvinism', in David Bagchi and David Steinmetz (eds), *The Cambridge Companion to Reformed Theology* (Cambridge: Cambridge University Press, 2006), 130–49.

[4] Influential revisionist accounts of the English Reformation include Eamon Duffy, *The Stripping of the Altars: Traditional Religion in England, 1400–1580* (New Haven: Yale University Press, 1992); Christopher Haigh, *The English Reformation Revised* (Cambridge: Cambridge University Press, 1987); and J. J. Scarisbrick, *The Reformation and the English People* (Oxford: Blackwell, 1997). Important recent post-revisionist studies include Norman Jones, *The English Reformation: Religion and Cultural Adaptation* (Oxford: Blackwell, 2002); Diarmaid MacCulloch, *Reformation: Europe's House Divided* (London: Penguin, 2004); Ethan Shagan, *Popular Politics and the English Reformation* (Cambridge: Cambridge University Press, 2002); Alexandra Walsham, *Providence in Early Modern England* (Oxford: Oxford University Press, 1999); and Lucy Wooding, *Rethinking Catholicism in Reformation England* (Oxford: Clarendon Press, 2000).

[5] Peter Marshall, '(Re)Defining the English Reformation', *Journal of British Studies*, 48 (2009): 578.

[6] Patrick Collinson, 'The Fog in the Channel Clears: The Rediscovery of the Continental Dimension to the British Reformations', in Patrick Collinson and Polly Ha (eds), *The Reception of Continental Reformation in Britain* (Oxford: Oxford University Press/British Academy, 2010), 27–37, 31.

[7] Euan Cameron, *The European Reformation* (Oxford: Oxford University Press, 1994); MacCulloch, *Reformation: Europe's House Divided*; Philip Benedict, *Christ's Churches Purely Reformed: A Social History of Calvinism* (New Haven: Yale University Press, 2002).

Reception of Continental Reformation in Britain, was an important endeavour to attend more closely to the reception of European Protestantism in Reformation England, and it demonstrates how richly productive this topic can be.[8] I would like to extend that focus by examining the European influences on one of Reformation England's best-selling books: the Geneva Bible.

I. THE TRANSLATORS IN EXILE

The Geneva Bible was a project developed in exile, and while it primarily provided a Bible for the English congregation in Geneva, it eventually also delivered a new kind of Protestant study Bible to readers in England. An estimated 1,000 or so English Protestants left for the continent in Mary's reign, with almost a quarter establishing themselves in Geneva under the protection of Calvin.[9] Of this group of English exiles in Geneva, William Whittingham and Anthony Gilby are the translators who appear to have had the largest role in the making of the 1560 English Geneva Bible, assisted by Thomas Sampson, Christopher Goodman, and possibly others. Whittingham and Gilby had originally been in exile in Frankfurt, where they had become embroiled in disputes over the English liturgy. They were not able to implement their desired reforms to the English prayer book in that congregation, and on 27 August 1554, they left for Geneva together with other discontented members of the Frankfurt congregation, including John Foxe and Christopher Goodman.[10] John Knox, who was to become leader of the English church in Geneva before Whittingham took over this role, had already been forced to leave Frankfurt following the controversy, and had settled in Geneva. By 1555, this group of English exiles had established an English church in Geneva which used a liturgy closely modelled on Calvin's Genevan order, with some modifications.[11] It remained for the exiles to produce a new English translation of the Bible for their congregation.

Geneva was at this time a thriving centre of Protestant Christian humanist scholarship, home to many projects of biblical translation in a rich array of different vernacular languages, in addition to endeavours to produce new biblical commentaries and reformist theological works, including, of course, Calvin's prolific output. In the 1550s, the decade in which the English Geneva Bible was being formed, French, Spanish, and Italian translations of the scriptures were also being completed or revised in Geneva. The English Geneva Bible had its genesis in a multi-lingual, collaborative environment of reformist scholarship. Geneva was also home to various illustrious printers who became well-known for their

---

[8] Collinson and Ha, *Reception*.

[9] Andrew Pettegree, *Marian Protestantism: Six Studies* (Aldershot: Scholars Press, 1996), 3. These figures are a revision of Christina Garrett's original calculations of c.800 refugees made in *Marian Exiles: A Study in the Origins of Elizabethan Puritanism* (Cambridge: Cambridge University Press, 1938; repr. 2010).

[10] Lloyd Berry, 'Introduction' to *The Geneva Bible: The Facsimile Edition of the 1560 Edition* (Madison, Wis.: University of Wisconsin Press, 1969), 6. See also William Whittingham (attrib.), *A Brief Discourse of the Troubles at Frankfort, 1554–1558*, ed. Edward Arber (London, 1908).

[11] These modifications were particularly of the prayers for intercession, which had a strong exilic focus, and on the baptism liturgy, see Charles Martin, *Les protestants anglais réfugiés à Genève au temps de Calvin 1555–1560* (Geneva: Jullien, 1915), 104–5.

editions of bibles and theological works, such as Robert Estienne (Stephanus), Jean Crespin, Conrad Badius, and others. Translators and printers were mutually engaged in the endeavour to produce new, improved editions. Many of the Bibles from these presses are characterized by a diversity of material features such as illustrations, diagrams, and notes. Estienne's 1540 edition of the Vulgate, for example, is a luxurious folio with a critical apparatus explaining his collation of seventeen manuscripts, and many illustrations, including various diagrams that were subsequently borrowed for the English Geneva Bible. These material features had a formative influence upon the English Geneva Bible, which was to contain a host of carefully selected reading aids, such as diagrams, maps, notes, and other paratexts that were new to English printed Bibles, or certainly novel in their sum total.

II. The Making of a Study Bible: French Influences

By 1560, when the first edition of the English Geneva Bible was published, accessible, affordable, smaller-format printed Bibles containing various reading aids had been available in French for use in Geneva and France for some decades. England still lacked these: the Great Bible, officially sanctioned for use in English churches, was a very large folio Bible that could only be consulted chained to the church lectern, or simply heard in church. Like its continental counterparts, the English Geneva Bible was produced in smaller formats, to make it more portable and suitable for private reading; it could be read at home, carried to church, and annotated. It was available in the modern humanist typeface, roman type (although in its later publication life in England editions in the more traditional black-letter, which continued to appeal to some readers, were also printed). It contained a wealth of reading aids in the form of prefaces, diagrams, maps, extensive marginal notes, and prefatory redactions of the 'Argument' of each book of the Bible, along with summaries of individual chapters. These 'Arguments' are a hermeneutic mode of annotation, clarifying the scriptures for readers, and mediating interpretation. They provide Christological interpretations of various Old Testament books of prophecy, for example, equipping the reader with this particular interpretative lens (that focuses upon the deeds and teachings of Jesus) to read the book in question. The summaries of individual chapters work in a similar way, and there are also running headings at the top of each page, picking out a salient theme contained in the scriptures below. All of these paratextual features function as a vehicle for theology, as well as helping to render the scriptures more accessible to the reader.

These features for guiding interpretation all appear in editions of the French Geneva Bible before the publication of its English counterpart, as does the marginal apparatus. The French Geneva Bible, from which the English translators took inspiration, was based on a translation by Pierre Olivetan, first printed in Geneva in 1535 with a Latin preface by Calvin, who produced an entire revision of the translation in 1546. It was later revised by Beza and Viret.[12] The translation of the scriptures themselves was subject to frequent

---

[12] A revision by Calvin together with Beza was published in 1551, and by Viret in 1553.

updating by Genevan scholars, just as the range of supplementary material to guide the reading of the scriptures also proliferated and differed from edition to edition. The printers compiling these editions exerted considerable influence over this variation in the para-texts. Different versions of the French Geneva Bible were produced by a host of Genevan printers including Jean Crespin, Nicholas Barbier & Courteau, Conrad Badius, Philbert Hamelin, and others. These printers actively shaped the presentation of the scriptures and the paratexts. The French Geneva Bible was therefore by no means a single or a stable work, even in the early years of its production in Geneva, before it began to be printed in numer-ous editions in France also (especially in Lyon), and this lack of stability is something the English Geneva Bible was to inherit.

Many of the English paratexts are direct translations of those found in the French Bibles. The 1560 Geneva Bible translates many of the notes produced by Calvin's secretary Nicholas Des Gallars for editions of the French Geneva Bible from 1558. From the 1540s the French Genevan version already contained marginal notes providing exegesis and cross-references, as well as two tables which later appeared in all editions of later French Geneva Bibles, and were adapted for the English Geneva Bible. The first of these tables provides a glossary of unfamiliar words and names appearing in the Bible (from Hebrew, Greek, Chaldean, and Latin) and the second, an 'Index of principal matters contained in the Bible, in which readers may find and effect several common places'.[13] The English Geneva Bible of 1560 likewise contains a glossary of 'strange names' and an index of 'The Principall Things that are Conteined in the Bible'. Both the French and the English Geneva Bibles were designed as personal study Bibles that opened up the meaning of the scriptures to the individual reader. They deliver a programme of reading that is carefully coordinated by the host of paratexts.

The first reading aid in the 1560 English Geneva Bible, the letter to the reader, serves to direct the reader to a variety of the other key paratexts which appear in all editions, such as the 'arguments' prefacing each book and chapter of the Bible, the 'Concordances' and 'two most profitable tables', as well as the marginal apparatus, which is explained again in more detail in a letter from 'The Printer to the Diligent Reader', prefacing the New Testament. The microstructure of the Geneva Bible is designed in this way to be both cohesive and intratextual. The coherence of the scriptures is an important emphasis in the Geneva Bible, in line with Calvin's stress on the 'unity and harmony of the scriptures'.[14] Readers are urged in the prefatory diagram, explaining 'Howe to take profite in reading of the Holy Scriptures', to 'Marke and consider the Coherence of the text, how it hangeth together', as well as 'the agreement that one place of Scripture hath with another, whereby that which Seemed darke in one is made easier in another'.[15] The frequent cross-references printed in the margins of the Geneva Bible emphasize this intratextuality of the scrip-tures themselves. Following the example of Genevan editor and printer Robert Estienne, the makers of the Geneva Bible divided the scripture into numbered verses for the ease

---

[13] My translation. The French title reads: 'Indices des principals matieres continues en la Bible en laquelle les lecteurs pourront trouuer et practiquer plusieurs lieux commune'. All further translations from French are my own.

[14] Richard M. Edwards, *Scriptual Perspicuity in the Early English Reformation in Historical Theology* (New York: Peter Lang, 2009), 88.

[15] On coherence and 'contexture' in Herbert, see Alison Knight's chapter in this volume.

of reading.[16] This was the first English Bible to use numbered verse divisions. The divisions facilitated the possibility of listing and memorizing biblical-cross-references. The individual reader at home could begin to study the scriptures more easily, comparing one passage with another. Marks left in Bibles demonstrate that readers often added to the printed apparatus of their Geneva Bibles with their own cross-references, marginal notes, and emphases (underlining, circling, maniculars), as well as sometimes writing prayers into spaces on the leaves of their Bibles.[17]

The extent to which these Bibles were designed for individual reading and personal study is brought out in the titles of some of the French editions. In 1559, printers Nicolas Barbier and Thomas Courteau produced a version of the French Geneva Bible that incorporated highlights of the paratextual material that had already been published in various different editions of the French Geneva. This Bible was given the lengthy, descriptive title:

> The Bible, that is the complete holy scriptures, comprising the old and new testaments: newly revised, with arguments presented for each book, and new, very useful marginal annotations which permit the reader, without great effort, to access the true meaning of the scripture, through a collection of principle doctrines. There are also some very useful diagrams and maps, the use of which is explained in the prefatory letter.[18]

The title is an advertisement not just for newly revised translations of the scriptures, but for a Bible that is characterized by an elaborate schema of supplementary texts to enable its personal study and true comprehension. It is not the perspicuity of the scriptures themselves that reveal their true meaning ('la vraye intelligence du sens de l'Escriture'), but the additional arguments and annotations. An earlier version of the French Geneva Bible, printed in Lyon in 1550, attests in its title that it contains 'some of the most striking diagrams and illustrations necessary for understanding the meaning of certain passages'.[19] Pictures are used to provide a schema of Noah's Ark, for example, as well as of

[16] Robert Estienne (Stephanus) divided the New Testament into chapter and verses in his 1555 edn. Peter Stallybrass argues that the division of scripture into chapter and verse introduced a discontinuous reading process, in contrast with the continuous reading process involved in reading scrolls; 'Books and Scrolls: Navigating the Bible', in Jennifer Andersen and Elizabeth Sauer (eds), *Books and Readers in Early Modern England: Material Studies* (Philadelphia: University of Pennsylvania Press, 2002), 42–79.

[17] For details of traces of reading left by individual readers in their Geneva Bibles, see Femke Molekamp, 'Using a Collection to Discover Reading Practices: The British Library Geneva Bibles and a History of their Early Modern Readers', *Electronic British Library Journal*, art. 10 (2006): 1–13, <www.bl.uk/eblj/2006 articles/pdf/article10.pdf>; Molekamp '"Of the Incomparable treasure of the Holy Scriptures": The Geneva Bible in the Early Modern Household', in Matthew Dimmock and Andrew Hadfield (eds), *Literature and Popular Culture in Early Modern England* (Farnham: Ashgate, 2009), 121–37; and Molekamp, *Women and the Bible in Early Modern England: Religious Reading and Writing* (Oxford: Oxford University Press, 2013), 34–50.

[18] 'La Bible, qui est Toute la saincte Escriture, ascavoir le vieil et nouveau Testament: De nouveau reveue, avec argumens sur chacun livre, nouvelles annotations en marge, fort utiles: par lequelles on peut sans grand labeur, obtenir la vraye intelligence du sens de l'Escriture, avec recueil de grande doctrine. Il y aussi quelques figures et cartes chorographiques de grande utilité, l'usage desquelles pourrez voir en l'epistre suyvante.'

Francis Higman has drawn attention to this title as suggestive of 'an entire programme' of reading, see '"Without Great Effort, and with Pleasure": Sixteenth-Century Geneva Bibles and Reading Practices', in Orlaith O'Sullivan (ed.), *The Bible as Book: The Reformation* (London: British Library, 2000), 116.

[19] *La sainte Bible, contenant les saintes escritures, tant du vieil, que du nouveau testament; avec aucunes des plus singulieres figures, et pourtraitz necessaires pour l'intelligence de beaucoup de passages* (Lyon: Balthazar Arnoulet, 1550).

details of the Tabernacle and Solomon's Temple. It is through the visual components included in the edition—the diagrams and illustrations—that the sense of various passages of scripture was to be reached. This may seem surprising, given assumptions that are often made about the iconoclastic culture of Protestant reformers. Furthermore, the insistence elsewhere among Protestant translators of the scriptures in the first half of the sixteenth century is upon the perspicuity and self-sufficiency of the plain text of the scriptures. Calvin maintained that, with the help of the inward witness of the Spirit, the scriptures are innately transparent, affording the reader a clear view of God: 'so Scripture, gathering together the impressions of the Deity, which, till then, lay confused in our minds, dissipates the darkness, and shows us the true God clearly'.[20] Tyndale stresses scripture's 'clear and evident texts'[21] which have 'one simple, literal sense, whose light the owls cannot abide'.[22]

These two aims in the production of vernacular study Bibles were not actually as divergent as they might seem. First, it is important to note that that visual culture was not eradicated by early Protestant reformers, as testified by the abundance of pictorial material in early printed Protestant Bibles, and the claim made in the 1550 Bible that such material helps to illuminate the meaning of the scriptures. As Alexandra Walsham has pointed out, scholarship on the long Reformation is increasingly refining 'the relationship between Protestantism and the development of the decorative arts, gradually displacing claims about an extreme and far-reaching iconophobia with a more subtle picture of partial continuity, adaption and change'.[23] Secondly, the pictorial material contained in Geneva Bibles is not simply decorative (although I do not want to entirely exclude that function): those illustrations which end up in the English Geneva Bible in particular are diagrammatic, with the purpose of elucidating what is described in the scriptures, and grounding it in historical reality.

The will to read the scriptures as historical fact appears in the Geneva Bible in the accompanying geographical maps, biblical genealogies, and tables purporting to give a historically accurate representation of time in the Bible. There is a chart, for instance, that sets out 'The order of the yeeres from Pauls conversion shewing the time of his peregrination, and of his Epistles written to the churches' and another that explains 'The Order of Time Whereunto the Contents of this book are to be referred'. As Francis Higman has noted, the supplementary materials included in Geneva Bibles 'draw attention to the literal meaning of the sacred text, encouraging the reader to concentrate on the historical truth of the book, rather than dwelling on allegorical interpretations, as was the case in

[20] John Calvin, *Institutes of the Christian Religion*, tr. Henry Beveridge (Grand Rapids, Mich.: Eerdmans, 1953), 89. Quoted in Edwards, *Scriptural Perspicuity*, 86.

[21] William Tyndale, *Expositions and Notes on Sundry Portions of Holy Scriptures*, ed. Henry Walker (Cambridge: Parker Society, 1849), 240.

[22] William Tyndale, *The Work of William Tyndale*, ed. G. E. Duffield (Philadelphia: Fortress Press, 1965), 31–2. Tyndale is rejecting here the medieval doctrine of the fourfold sense of scripture (the literal, allegorical, moral, and analogical), in favour of 'one simple, literal sense' that shines such a clear light of truth that even those who are spiritually blind may see it. Owls were thought to be blind during the day, hence the choice of this metaphor.

[23] Alexandra Walsham, 'Angels and Idols in England's Long Reformation', in Peter Marshall and Alexandra Walsham (eds), *Angels in the Early Modern World* (Cambridge: Cambridge University Press, 2006), 135.

medieval exegesis'.[24] For Tyndale, it was allegorical interpretation that acted as the corrupting antithesis to 'the plain text', and this was to be avoided above all other hermeneutics. Tyndale felt that vernacular translation of the scriptures elucidated meaning for readers, in contrast to the obfuscating effects of medieval (Latin) scholasticism, which included allegorical interpretation. Glossing was of course also associated with scholasticism, and yet Tyndale's New Testament was furnished with brief annotations, (as was the complete Matthew Bible of 1537, incorporating Tyndale's translation) as an instrument to guide readers and stabilize their responses to 'hard places'.

In the various Geneva Bibles produced in French and English, glosses and other paratexts are not felt to detract from the 'plain text', but are intended rather to shine a light upon it and help the reader get to the literal meaning. Nicholas des Gallars states in his preface to a 1558 edition of the French Geneva Bible that

> Aware of the laudable desire many of us possess to advance the knowledge of the holy scriptures, and to lead others to such knowledge … it was desirable to have some brief explicatory notes in the margin of the New Testament, to provide immediate instruction in the true meaning of some passages.[25]

The translators of the 1560 English Geneva Bible, influenced by the French editions, likewise argue that their marginal apparatus is provided to open up the sense of the scriptures and thereby promote God's glory. They also explain that the notes help to guard against the dangerous risk of heresy:

> considering how hard a thing it is to understand the holy Scriptures, and what errors, sectes and heresies grow dailie for lacke of the true knollage thereof, and how many are discouraged (as thei pretend) because thei can not atteine to the true and simple meaning of the same, we have also indevored bothe by the diligent reading of the best commentaries, and also by the conference with the godly and learned brethren, to gather brief annotations upon all the hard places, aswel for the understanding of such words as are obscure, and for the declaration of the text, as for the application of the same as may moste apperteine to Gods glorie and the edification of his Church.[26]

This Bible, which attempted to communalize a Protestant readership, advertises itself as formed in a collaborative religious environment. At the same time, it invites the reader, through the marginal notes, to participate in the community of interpretative brethren by the experience of reading. The address on the one hand asserts the scholarly 'integritie'of the translation from Greek and Hebrew, where 'the proprietie of the

[24] Higman, 'Sixteenth-Century Geneva Bibles', 117.
[25] 'Cognoissant le bon desir que plusieurs auoyent de s'auancer en la cognoissance des sainctes Letres, & y amener les autres: & que pour ce faire, ils desiroyent auoir quelques briefues expositions a la marge du Noueau Testament, pour ester incontinent instruits du vray sens des passages: i'ay bien voulu obtemperer a vne tant saincte affection, & m'y employer selon la mesure de grace que Dieu m'a departie.' *La Bible, qui est toute la saincte Escriture* (Geneva, 1558).
[26] 'To Our Beloved in the Lord the Brethren of England, Scotland, Ireland &c', in *The Bible and Holy Scriptures conteyned in the Olde and Newe Testament. Translated According to the Ebrue and Greke, and Conferred with the Best Translations in Divers Langages. With Moste Profitable Annotations upon All the Hard Places, and Other Things of Great Importance as May Appeare in the Epistle to the Reader* (Geneva, 1560), ***4^v.

woordes' has been protected. On the other hand, it stresses the accessibility of the meaning of the scriptures in this version, due to the marginal apparatus. The Geneva Bible marginal notes provide an experience of communal consensus, even when the reader is alone with his or her Bible. This Bible was shaping an extensive readership, able to decipher scripture in the act of private reading.

In the Elizabethan period, when the Geneva Bible became popular, books with printed marginal annotations were far from novel. In printed vernacular Bibles, however, marginal notes as a locus of hermeneutic control were met with anxiety and opposition from bishops, monarchs, and sometimes Reformers, alike. The former feared they were politically and or theologically subversive and the latter saw them as obstructing an unfettered, individual communion with the text of the scriptures in reading. Later, and once the heavily annotated Geneva Bible was already flourishing, Archbishop Whitgift voiced a mistrust of marginal annotation to Bibles. In 1583 he presented the Queen with articles requesting 'that no printer set forth any edition of the Bible or New Testament but that allowed by [the Archbishop or Bishop of London], nor add any annotations unless approved by the Archbishop and synod of bishops'.[27] No vernacular Bible in early modern England contained anything like the extensive marginal apparatus of the Geneva Bible, either before or after its production, with the exception of the later Douai Rheims Bible. The 1560 Geneva Bible contains extensive marginal notes to provide 'reason' for their readers, in defiance of Cranmer's warning in the preface to the Great Bible: 'I forbid not to read, but I forbid to reason'. While supplying their own 'reason', the translators were of course limiting the extent to which individual readers can provide their own interpretations.

III. Paratexts as a Vehicle for Theology: French Influences

While the 1560 Geneva Bible borrows heavily from the notes that Calvin's secretary Des Gallars supplied for some editions of the French Geneva Bible, it was also strongly influenced by the 1559 edition produced by Nicholas Barbier and Thomas Courteau for the long 'Arguments' prefacing books of the Bible. These 'Arguments' are important hermeneutic tools. They summarize the contents of the book, and in presenting the prevalent teachings of the book they frequently offer precise theological interpretations. In both the Barbier and Courteau and the English 1560 editions, the 'Argument' to Romans, for instance, is used as a vehicle to highlight the doctrine of predestination, which in the Reformed tradition became very closely linked to Paul's teaching in Romans. In both Bibles, doctrinal emphases, as well as wording, are very similar. The line taken is consistently close to Calvin's teachings. Both intricately connect the new covenant with the doctrine of predestination and justification by faith. Barbier and Courteau argue that

> We are shown here the universal human condition: how every man suffers condemnation and malediction, shut out and banished from the heavenly kingdom, an evil from which

---

[27] W. W. Greg, *A Companion to Arber* (Oxford: Oxford University Press, 1967), 34.

there is no means of escape save by the grace that is given to us in Jesus Christ as preached in the Gospel, that is received by us through faith alone as the only method by which justice and holiness can be extended to us, with all the graces of our Lord Jesus, in order to be justi-fied and sanctified by him.[28]

The 1560 English 'Argument' succinctly distils this teaching in the first line: 'The great mercie of God is declared towarde man in Christ Jesus, whose righteousness is made ours through faith'.

The 'Arguments' in both editions proceed to show that both Christ's mercy and man's faith are dependent on predestination to salvation. The Barbier and Courteau edition explains that God has preordained 'the election of those whom [God] has called to salvation, and the reprobation of those whom he has rejected to damnation, who are called to be vessels for his suffering and vessels for his wrath'.[29] The English 'Argument' tempers the presentation of the doctrine by omitting the metaphor of the vessels for suffering and wrath, although it otherwise uses very similar language to make the same point:

> the very strangers and Gentiles, grafted in by faith, are made heires of the promes [promise]. The cause whereof is the onely will of God: for as much as of his free mercie hee electeth some to be saved, and of his just judgement rejecteth others to be damned.

The emphasis in both 'Arguments' on the relationship between the doctrine of dou-ble predestination to one covenant of grace, enabling justification by faith, is character-istic of Calvin's own teachings. The first biblical commentary written by Calvin was his *Commentary upon Romans* (1540, expanded in 1551 and 1556). Romans occupied an impor-tant place in the development of Calvin's theology, with its treatment of topics such as human depravity, justification by faith, and God's old and new covenants. David Steinmetz has shown that in the last Latin edition of the *Institutes* (1559), Calvin cites Romans 573 times.[30]

Calvin provides a summary 'Argument' of Romans in his commentary, where he states that 'wee are all justified by faith', and that Paul's epistle shows 'what faith that is, and howe wee obteine thereby the righteousnesse of Christe'. He explains that 'the whole must neces-sarily consist and depend' upon the fact that we are called

> unto the election of God ... Againe, seeing this election leaneth onely upon the mercie of God, in vaine is the cause thereof sought for, in the worthiness of men. Reprobation is contrary, which notwithstanding it is most just, yet is there no cause above the will of God.[31]

---

[28] 'Nous est monster en icelle l'estat uniuersal de tout le genre humain, comment tous hommes sont en condemnation & sous malediction, forcloz & banis du royaume celeste: duquel mal-heur il n'ya moyen d'estre retire sinon pargrace qui nou est presentee en Jesus Christ par a predication de l'Evangile, & receve de nous par la foy laquelle est le seul moyen pour appliquer a nous la justice & sainctete avec tous les benifices de nostre Seigneur Jesus, pour ester justifiez & sanctifiez par luy.'

[29] 'L'election de ceux qu'il appelle a salut, & la reprobation de ceux qu'il rejette en condamnation, lesquels il appelle vaisseaux de sa misericorde, & vaisseaux de son ire.'

[30] David C. Steinmetz, *Calvin in Context* (Oxford: Oxford University Press, 2010), 65.

[31] John Calvin, *A Commentarie upon the Epistle of Saint Paul to the Romanes*, tr. Christopher Rosdell (London, 1583), JJ2ʳ; ¶¶ 4ʳ.

Calvin clearly formulates the doctrine of double predestination here, that was to be developed by Theodore Beza, and uses it as the basis to explain how justification by faith can come about: those elected to salvation will be led to faith, and to the receipt of Christ's mercy under the new covenant. While it was Heinrich Bullinger who developed the role of the covenant of grace, Calvin particularly emphasized one covenant of grace, uniting the covenants of the Old and New Testament, through Christ.[32] This leads to a Christological reading of Old Testament prophecy. As Stephen Edmonson points out, the Old Testament prophets are responsible for revealing God's covenant, and so their mediatorial role 'is implicitly Christological for Calvin in all of its aspects; not only is Christ, ultimately, the source of the Law, he is also the head of all the Law's teachers, and he rules the church by their ministry'.[33] The prophets are therefore bound to direct people to Christ; they are substitutes for Christ in his office of priest.

This view of the unity of the scriptures, which rests on the unity of covenant history, comes through in various prefatory 'Arguments' to books of the Old Testament in the 1560 English Geneva Bible. The 'Argument' to the Psalms, for example, proclaims that 'If we would know werein standeth our salvation, and how to attaine to life everlasting, here is Christ our onely redeemer, and mediator most evidently described'. The Barbier and Courteau edition also celebrates the 'glory of the triumphant reign of our Lord Jesus, eternal sacrificial King. Of which we see here many beautiful and excellent prophecies'.[34] Likewise, the chapter summaries to the Psalms in this French edition frequently reference Christ's reign. Psalm 2, for instance, is interpreted as: 'the vain assault of the Jews and Gentiles upon Christ', verse 4 'easily dissipated by the Eternal God, confirming the reign of his son Christ', and verse 10 is summarized as containing a 'very certain and evident prophecy of Jesus Christ and his reign'.[35] This Christological interpretation of Old Testament prophecy runs throughout the paratextual apparatus of editions of the French Geneva Bible and of the English 1560 Geneva Bible. In this way, the English Geneva Bible delivered Calvin's theology to an English readership, via a close relationship with editions of the French Geneva Bible.

IV. Theological Developments: Notes by Tomson and Junius

In 1587, the New Testament translation and accompanying marginal notes were replaced by a revised version undertaken by the Puritan scholar Laurence Tomson. Tomson was an exceptional linguist with twelve languages, who participated in a network of influential

---

[32] John Hesselink, 'Calvin's Theology', in Donald K. McKim (ed.), *The Cambridge Companion to John Calvin* (Cambridge: Cambridge University Press, 2004), 85.

[33] Stephen Edmonson, *Calvin's Christology* (Cambridge: Cambridge University Press, 2004), 67.

[34] 'Gloire au royaume triumphant de nostre Seigneur Jesus, Sacrificateur et Roy eternel. Duquel on voit aussi ici plusieurs belles & excellentes propheties.'

[35] 'Vaine entreprise des Gentils & des Juifs contre Christ, 4 facilement disipée par l'Eternel, 6 confirmant le regne de son Christ. 10 Admoneste les rois & princes a sa crainte. Prophetie tres certaine et evident de Jesus Christ & de son regne.'

Puritans in England, although he avoided controversy. He served as secretary to Frances Walsingham for fifteen years, before eventually coming under the patronage of the Puritan Earl of Huntingdon. He was connected also to Laurence Humphrey, president of Magdalen College, Oxford, where Tomson studied for his BA and MA before becoming a fellow of the college. Magdalen was a hub for Oxford puritanism and Humphrey was at this time an influential leader of Puritan thought. Tomson was also a correspondent of Anthony Gilby, one of the original translators of the Geneva Bible. He may have spent time studying in Geneva; he was certainly interested in reformist scholarship, and spent extensive time travelling on the continent.[36]

Whether or not Tomson was based in Geneva for a period, his contribution to the Geneva Bible has a solid Genevan foundation, being essentially a translation of Theodore Beza's Latin New Testament of 1565. In this way Tomson's translation extends the collaborative Genevan scholarship that went into vernacular biblical translation. As a source, Tomson mostly uses the 1576 edition of Beza (and Beza's notes) prepared by Pierre L'Oiseleur, a Huguenot refugee living in Geneva in the late 1550s and 1560s, who later sought refuge in London.[37] L'Oiseleur mostly translates Beza's notes directly, but does include a few additions of his own, as well as occasionally supplementing notes by the German scholar Camerarius.[38] Tomson follows the same practice, signalling Beza's notes with the use of roman type, and designating other notes with italic typeface, including some of his own notes, and occasionally privileging the 1560 English Geneva Bible over Beza.

Tomson's marginal apparatus is much more extensive than the original 1560 set of marginal notes. In its development, then, the English Geneva Bible became even more of a study Bible over time, with an increase in Calvinist exegesis packed around the biblical text. To return to the doctrine of predestination to illustrate this, we find much more extensive explanation of this doctrine in the Tomson notes than in the 1560 edition. Tomson's notes here are mostly direct translations of Beza, who has often been associated with a harsh, deterministic doctrine of predestination, although some scholars have suggested more continuity with Calvin, especially with regards to a Christological focus.[39] It is clear, however, that Beza developed a supralapsarian emphasis on the matter of election and reprobation.

For Beza, this double predestination always existed in the mind of God and cannot be associated with any human understanding of human merit or demerit. And yet Beza particularly differentiates himself from Calvin in pointing out secondary causes of predestination, which involve the reprobate's voluntary corruption of himself. This point is

[36] Irena Backus, 'Laurence Tomson (1539–1608) and Elizabethan Puritanism', *Journal of Ecclesiastical History*, 28 (1977): 17–27.

[37] Irena Backus, *The Reformed Roots of the English New Testament: The Influence of Theodore Beza on the English New Testament* (Pittsburgh, Pa.: Pickwick Press, 1980), 18.

[38] Johannes Camerarius produced a *Notatio figurarum sermonis* (1572) providing annotations to the New Testament. This was reprinted as the *Commentarius in novum foedus* and published with the Beza New Testament (with separate title-page, register, and pagination) in 1642.

[39] For example, Richard Muller, *Christ and the Decree: Christology and Predestination in Reformed Theology from Calvin to Perkins* (Grand Rapids, Mich.: Baker, 1988), 79–96. For a discussion of these varying positions, see Donald Sinneme, 'Beza's View of Predestination in Historical Perspective', in Irena Backus et al. (eds), *Theodore de Beze (1519–1605)* (Geneva: Librarie Droz, 2007), 219–41.

explained at length in Tomson's note to Romans 9: 18, which translates Beza. The verse reads 'Therefore [God] hath mercy on whom hee will, and whom he will he hardeneth'. The 1560 edition does not gloss this at all. Tomson's note, which in full runs to twenty lines, is centred on the idea that

> there is no injustice in the everlasting councell of God touching the destruction of them whom he listeth to destroy, for that hee hardneth before he destroyeth ... Then follow the fruits of Hardening, to wit, unbeliefe and sinne, which are the true and proper causes of the condemnation of the reprobate. Why doeth he then appoint to destruction? because he will: why doeth he harden? because they are corrupt: why doeth he condemne: because they are sinners.

We see here characteristically Bezean stresses on God's inscrutable will as the primary cause of reprobation, but also on the secondary causes connected with 'hardening'. These ideas were taken up by some Puritan preachers in England, notably by William Perkins. Tomson's notes, following Beza, systematize the biblical text to expound particular doctrines, such as the doctrine of predestination.[40] Unlike the New Testament notes to the 1560 edition, they enact the method of Protestant scholasticism.[41] They are a reflection of developing Protestant thought and method in Geneva, which gained an influential reception amongst English Puritans. Not only puritanism, but wider English theology in the sixteenth century, was strongly coloured by predestinarianism, while positions on the doctrine were varied and contested. The Geneva Bible, as an extensively circulated, popular Bible that emphasized and explained predestination, helped to establish this doctrine in the minds of its English readers.

The Geneva Bible was printed with Tomson's New Testament notes and translations from 1587 until the end of its publication life in the 1640s. In 1599 the annotations to Revelation in the Geneva Bible underwent a dramatic change, when Laurence Tomson's annotations were superseded, in many editions, by those of Franciscus Junius, adapted from his *Apocalypsis, a Brief and Learned Commentarie upon the Revelation of St. John* (1596), written originally in Latin in 1592. Junius was a Huguenot scholar who studied in Geneva from 1562 to 1565. His extensive exegetical notes to Revelation provide a quantity of text which nearly equals the scriptures it surrounds in the Geneva Bible. Following the influential precedent of John Bale's exegesis, Junius's notes decode the vision of St John as revealing 'the Popedome of Rome' as 'the church of the antichrist'; they condemn various popes throughout the history of the Roman Church, as well as identifying the Church of Rome with the Whore of Babylon.[42]

Earlier English commentators on Revelation, notably Bale and Foxe, interpret Revelation historically as a providential map of the world's ages. Prefacing Junius's book of Revelation is a table entitled 'The order of time whereunto the contents of this booke are

---

[40] Peter White, *Predestination, Policy and Polemic: Conflict and Consensus in the English Civil War* (Cambridge: Cambridge University Press, 2002), 15.

[41] Revisionist considerations of Protestant scholasticism have identified continuity between reformed theological traditions, but have placed an emphasis on Protestant scholasticism as a theological method. See esp. Willem J. van Asselt and Eef Dekker (eds), *Reformation and Scholasticism: An Ecumenical Entreprise* (Grand Rapids, Mich.: Baker Academic, 2001).

[42] Junius's note to Rev. 11: 2, *The Bible: That Is, the Holy Scriptures conteined in the Old and New Testament* (London, 1599).

to be referred'. The table provides in one column a chronological list of events described in Revelation; the other column dates these events, but there is a blank space in the second column for some phenomena: the church's defeat of the whore of Babylon, the two beasts, the dragon, and death.[43] The reader can fill in these details, and thus is invited by this table to be a historiographer of the apocalypse. The collaborative dating, shared between Junius and the reader, brings contemporary history into the providential schema of Revelation, as well as allowing a dimension of personal history by enabling the reader to judge when the prophesied events have come to pass, and fill in the dates. The Geneva Bible was formed and reformed by a multiplicity of scholars and influences, with the use of continental as well as English sources. Like its French model, the English Geneva Bible cannot be treated as a single, stable text, since it changes quite considerably over its long publication life, incorporating developments in European and English Protestant theology.

V. Reception in England

The Geneva Bible was not well-received by Elizabeth, who was resistant to Puritan demand for further ecclesiastical reform, and hostile to Genevan scholarship following the publication in 1558 of two texts by Genevan exiles arguing against female rule: John Knox's *The First Blast of the Trumpet against the Monstrous Regiment of Women*, and Christopher Goodman's *How Superior Powers Oght to be Obeyd of Their Subjectes*. Both texts also advocated disobedience to irreligious and tyrannical rulers. In the following year, Elizabeth declined Calvin's gift of a volume of his Latin commentaries on Isaiah, which he had dedicated to her.[44] Elizabeth commissioned the Bishops' Bible (first printed in 1569) as a vernacular Bible to rival the Geneva, to be officially sanctioned for use in churches, which the Geneva never was. Yet the marketplace response was very different from this official disapprobation. The Geneva Bible was affordable and sold in vast numbers. The sheer number of editions produced demonstrates that the reception of the Geneva Bible in England was very successful at a popular level. The breadth of its circulation warns against viewing it exclusively as a Bible of the Puritans, although it certainly was that, too. It is also worth remembering that Archbishop Laud was using the Geneva Bible as late as 1624.[45]

The Geneva Bible was very influential in Scotland, where an edition printed in Edinburgh in 1579 was dedicated by the general assembly to the King, with the suggestion that there should be henceforth a copy of the Bible 'in every parish kirk, to be called the Common Book of the Kirk, as the most meet ornament for such a place'. An Act was passed the same year by the Privy Council in Scotland requiring each 'householder worth three hundred merks of yearly rent', and all yeomen and burgesses possessing over £500 in

---

[43] Crawford Gribben, 'Deconstructing the Geneva Bible: The Search for a Puritan Poetic', *Literature and Theology*, 14 (2000): 7.

[44] Jane Dawson has discussed the consequences of Knox's and Goodman's publications for the exiles returning from Geneva in 'John Knox, Christopher Goodman and the "Example of Geneva"', in Collinson and Ha, *Reception*, 107–35; Andrew Pettegree has discussed Elizabeth's rejection of Calvin's volume in relation to the plight of the returning exiles in 'The Marian Exiles and the Elizabethan Settlement', in *Marian Protestantism: Six Studies* (Aldershot: Scolar Press, 1996), 129–50.

[45] White, *Predestination*, 91.

land and goods, to have a Bible and Psalm Book in the vulgar tongue, 'under the penalty of ten pounds'.[46] In England and Scotland, the readership of this version of the Bible spread rapidly, and it was also to become 'the Bible of … the Ulster Plantation and the Pilgrim Fathers' in the New World.[47]

The success of the Geneva Bible sparked the production of a Catholic English vernacular New Testament: the Rheims, first printed in 1582, which contained extensive marginal notes aimed at refuting those of the Geneva Bible.[48] Although it was essentially an opponent of the Geneva Bible, the Rheims New Testament strikingly followed the Geneva in *mise-en-page* and typography, including the addition of extensive marginal notes; it also relied on much of the Geneva's translations. The Rheims energetically refuted the theology of the Geneva Bible while implicitly advocating the reading practices that the Geneva popularized in early modern England. This legacy of reading practices was also passed on to the King James Bible (via the Bishops' Bible which imitated these features, though produced as a riposte to the Geneva). Like Elizabeth, James I also sought to displace the Geneva by commissioning his own authorized alternative Bible, which was to omit interpretative marginal notes. James particularly objected to several Genevan notes that implied that disobedience to monarchs was permissible.[49] He denounced the notes as 'partial, untrue, seditious and savouring too much of dangerous and trayterous conceits'.[50]

The Geneva continued in popularity, however, for some time after the publication of the King James Bible in 1611, and continued to be printed into the 1640s. The King James Bible was deliberately designed to exclude marginal annotation, except for cross-references and glossing of Hebrew words. However, it actually imitated a variety of interpretative paratexts found in Geneva Bibles (imitated also by the Bishops' Bible), such as the prefatory 'Arguments' and summaries to books and chapters of the Bible, as well as the running headings at the top of each page. Not only did the Geneva Bible bequeath legacies of scholarly translations to English Bibles produced after it, but it also popularized in England a host of distinctive material features which helped to domesticate Bible reading. In these ways, and as a vehicle for European Calvinism, the Geneva played an important role in shaping the landscape of the English Reformation, and it remains one of the most influential Bibles in the history of English printing.

Further Reading

Collinson, Patrick, and Polly Ha, eds. *The Reception of Continental Reformation in Britain*, Proceedings of the British Academy, 164 (Oxford: Oxford University Press/British Academy, 2010).

---

[46] William T. Dobson, *History of the Bassandyne Bible, the First Printed in Scotland* (Edinburgh: William Blackwood, 1887), 120–1.

[47] Dawson, 'John Knox', 115.

[48] The idea for an English Catholic Bible had, however, been around for a few decades.

[49] James objected to the notes to Exod. 1: 19; 2 Chron. 8.15, 16; and Matt. 2: 12 on this basis. See Thomas Fuller, *The Church-History of Britain* (London, 1655), 59.

[50] Peter Heylyn, *Aerius redivivus, the History of the Presbyterians* (Oxford, 1670), 247.

Garret, Christina. *Marian Exiles: A Study in the Origins of Elizabethan Puritanism* (Cambridge: Cambridge University Press, 1938, repr. 2010).

Gordon, Bruce, ed. *Protestant History and Identity in Sixteenth Century Europe*, 2 vols (Aldershot: Scholars Press, 1996).

Gribben, Crawford. 'Deconstructing the Geneva Bible: The Search for a Puritan Poetic'. *Literature and Theology*, 14 (2000): 1–16.

Higman, Francis. '"Without Great Effort, and with Pleasure": Sixteenth-Century Geneva Bibles and Reading Practices', in Orlaith O'Sullivan (ed.), *The Bible as Book: The Reformation* (London: British Library, 2000), 115–22.

Molekamp, Femke. 'Using a Collection to Discover Reading Practices: The British Library Geneva Bibles and a History of their Early Modern Readers'. *Electronic British Library Journal*, art. 10 (2006): 1–13, <www.bl.uk/eblj/2006articles/pdf/article10.pdf>.

Molekamp, Femke. '"Of the Incomparable treasure of the Holy Scriptures": The Geneva Bible in the Early Modern Household', in Matthew Dimmock and Andrew Hadfield (eds), *Literature and Popular Culture in Early Modern England* (Farnham: Ashgate, 2009), 121–37.

Shagan, Ethan. *Popular Politics and the English Reformation* (Cambridge: Cambridge University Press, 2002).

Stallybrass, Peter. 'Books and Scrolls: Navigating the Bible', in Jennifer Andersen and Elizabeth Sauer (eds), *Books and Readers in Early Modern England: Material Studies* (Philadelphia: University of Pennsylvania Press, 2002), 42–80.

CHAPTER 3

....

'A COMELY GATE TO SO RICH AND GLORIOUS A CITIE': THE PARATEXTUAL ARCHITECTURE OF THE RHEIMS NEW TESTAMENT AND THE KING JAMES BIBLE

....

KATRIN ETTENHUBER

THIS chapter traces the Protestant response to the publication of the Rheims New Testament, through the controversial exchanges that followed it, but principally through the Preface to the King James Bible of 1611. I will attend primarily to the ways in which these texts set up fictions and constructions of the past to legitimize their respective approaches to translation. 'The past' in this context is a functionally elastic concept, which encompasses institutional, philological, and hermeneutic traditions: the 'matter' of translation (from the Vulgate or the Greek, in the case of the New Testament) and its 'manner' (a focus on 'the very words' or the 'sense') are deeply imbricated in competing concepts of ecclesiology. In order to win the battle over scripture translation, Protestant divines had to recalibrate their relationship with the history of the early church, and to replace a Catholic narrative of timeless continuity with one of necessary rupture and reinvention.[1] That the translation of scripture is about the place of the church in history may be a commonplace assumption; the urgent demand for a break with the corruptions of medieval Catholicism and a return to primitive tradition was, after all, the constant refrain of Reformed polemic.

---

[1] On the ubiquity of this argument in early modern controversial discourse, see Felicity Heal, 'Appropriating History: Catholic and Protestant Polemics and the National Past', *Huntington Library Quarterly*, 68 (2005): 109–32; John Spurr, '"A special kindness for dead bishops": The Church, History, and Testimony in Seventeenth-Century Protestantism', *Huntington Library Quarterly*, 68 (2005): 313–34; and Katrin Ettenhuber, '"Take vp and read the Scriptures": Patristic Interpretation and the Poetics of Abundance in "The Translators to the Reader" (1611)', *Huntington Library Quarterly*, 75 (2012): 213–32.

More surprising, perhaps, is the profound importance of 'place' and 'time', of scriptural history, chronology, and topography, not simply to the metaphorical furniture of early modern Bible translation, but to its strategies of hermeneutic and linguistic self-legitimation, and to the spatial dynamics of the printed page.[2]

The title quotation of this chapter, 'A comely gate to so rich and glorious a citie', is a tribute from an unidentified admirer to Miles Smith, who composed the Preface to the King James Bible, thereby expertly ushering the reader into the riches of the scripture text.[3] It is also a textbook definition, *avant la lettre*, of Gérard Genette's concept of the paratext, or 'threshold' of interpretation: the idea that the production of meaning depends to a significant degree on the framing or material packaging of a text, through features like prefaces, notes, and indexes. The preface, more particularly, is described in Genette's *Paratexts* as a '"vestibule" that offers the world at large the possibility of either stepping inside or turning back. It is an "undefined zone" between the inside and outside [of the text]'.[4] The key movements outlined by Genette, 'stepping inside' and 'turning back', acquire heightened significance in the textual spaces of the Rheims New Testament and the King James Bible: maps, genealogical charts, indexes, chapter summaries, and various types of annotation provide multiple points of entry into the scriptures, as do the various intertexts embedded in the preface and the margins. But the structure of these textual edifices is also built on pivotal moments of historical recuperation; their different visions of how readers can return to the Christian past determine the shape of the scriptures in the present. The 1611 translation emphasizes the primacy of context—of '*Person, Time*, and *Place*'—in the production and communication of the biblical message, and with it the possibilities and limitations offered by specific moments in history:[5] the Septuagint, for instance, was 'fittest to contain the Scriptures' in an age when the Greek language held the greatest promise of spreading God's word, but 'not so sound and so perfect, but that it needed in many places correction'.[6] In the Rheims Bible, by contrast, change and revision are

---

[2] On the physical presentation of early modern Bibles, see John N. King and Aaron T. Pratt, 'The Materiality of English Printed Bibles from the Tyndale New Testament to the King James Bible', in Hannibal Hamlin and Norman W. Jones (eds), *The King James Bible after 400 Years: Literary, Linguistic, and Cultural Influences* (Cambridge: Cambridge University Press, 2010), 61–99. On early modern attitudes to the early church and to religious history more generally, see Katherine van Liere, Simon Ditchfield, and Howard Louthan (eds), *Sacred History: Uses of the Christian Past in the Renaissance World* (Oxford: Oxford University Press, 2012); and Irena Backus, *Historical Method and Confessional Identity in the Era of the Reformation (1378–1615)* (Leiden: Brill, 2003).

[3] *Sermons of the Right Reverend Father in God Miles Smith, Late Lord Bishop of Gloucester* (London, 1632), 'The Preface' [by 'J.S.'], ¶¶2^r.

[4] Gérard Genette, *Paratexts: Thresholds of Interpretation* (Cambridge: Cambridge University Press, 1997), 2. A recent collection of essays edited by Helen Smith and Louise Wilson offers 'a response to, and an extension of, Genette's wide-ranging taxonomy'; the contributors emphasize 'the importance of investigating the particular paratextual conventions in play in different periods', the need to 'engage with early modern books which are visible as well as legible', and the multi-directional dynamic of paratextual elements. See *Renaissance Paratexts* (Cambridge: Cambridge University Press, 2011), 2–3, 6. On the aesthetic power of liminal spaces more generally, see Subha Mukherji (ed.), *Thinking on Thresholds: The Poetics of Transitive Spaces* (London: Anthem Press, 2011).

[5] *The Holy Bible, conteyning the Old Testament, and the New* (1611), 'The Translators to the Reader', A1^v. Most copies of the 1st edn duplicate signatures across the Preface and the other paratextual material; for clarity's sake, therefore, references to 'Smith' are to the Preface, and 'KJB' references are to other paratexts. The quotation is from the headnote to the KJB's genealogical charts. On the print history of the King James Bible, see further nn. 19 and 20.

[6] Smith, A5^r. On Smith, see John Tiller, 'Smith, Miles (d. 1624)', in the *ODNB*, 2008 <http://www.oxforddnb.com/view/article/25879>. Smith was a member of the first Oxford Company of translators and

associated with the 'windinges and turnings of divers errours'; it follows a different model of history, tracing a direct and continuous 'line of Prophetical and Apostolical interpretation' to the 'most auncient' text, whose lessons are 'delivered unto us as it were from hand to hand'.[7] In both cases, I will suggest, the method and rationale of translation, the treatment of sources and intertexts, and the combination and arrangement of paratextual material, are deeply inflected by constructions of the cultural, ecclesiological, and philological past.

I. 'As neere as is possible, to our text': Constructions of Continuity in the Rheims Translation

In *The Sword of the Spirit: Puritan Responses to the Bible*, John R. Knott observes that '[t]he habit of identifying with the experience of the Israelites, by an essentially ahistorical leap to the truth of the Word, pervades the Geneva Bible'.[8] The embattled Israelites, of course, take centre-stage in the title-page engraving of the first edition of 1560, framed by the scriptural promise that 'The Lord shal fight for you' (Exodus 14: 14). English Protestants in exile, Patrick Collinson has suggested, readily found an analogy with God's chosen people because they viewed the scripture text itself as fundamentally transhistorical, 'of a seamless piece, without caesura or conflict'.[9] This pattern of thought is exemplified by the title-page of a 1602 edition of the Geneva translation, where 'the Twelve Tribes of Israel and the Twelve Apostles, Old Testament and New, form a single continuous frame for the Four Evangelists, each engaged in the writing of his own distinct but harmonious version of the one Gospel. Two open books proclaim: "*Verbum Dei manet in aeternum* [the Word of God endureth forever]"'.[10] Collinson traces this textual philosophy into the seventeenth century, and concludes that the 'motive of protestant expositors and readers, at whatever level, was professedly anti-historicist, making of "Scripture" a text which was not only harmonious but of timeless validity'.[11] The evidence of the Rheims and King James prefaces

---

worked on the prophetic books of the Old Testament. He was appointed Bishop of Gloucester in 1612. The unidentified author of the preface to Smith's *Sermons* notes that Smith was an 'expert in the Chaldie, Syriacke and Arabicke, that he made them as familiar to him almost as his owne native tongue' (¶¶2ʳ) and praises his knowledge of 'the Greeke and Latin Fathers', which rivals that of the most learned 'Professors' (ibid.). On Smith's churchmanship and diocesan activities, see Kenneth Fincham, *Prelate as Pastor: The Episcopate of James I* (Oxford: Clarendon Press, 1990).

[7] *The New Testament of Jesus Christ, Translated Faithfully into English … in the College of Rheims* (Rheims, 1582), b3ʳ, c2ᵛ, c3ʳ, d2ᵛ (hereafter 'Rheims'). On the inception, planning, and execution of the Catholic Bible in English, see Cameron A. MacKenzie, *The Battle for the Bible in England, 1557–1582* (New York: Peter Lang, 2002), esp. chs 4, 7, and 8.

[8] John R. Knott, *The Sword of the Spirit: Puritan Responses to the Bible* (Chicago: University of Chicago Press, 1980), 29.

[9] Patrick Collinson, 'The Coherence of the Text: How it Hangeth Together: The Bible in Reformation England', in W. P. Stephens (ed.), *The Bible, the Reformation and the Church: Essays in Honour of James Anderson* (Sheffield: Sheffield Academic Press, 1995), 92.

[10] Collinson, 'Coherence of the Text', 92–3.

[11] Collinson, 'Coherence of the Text', 96.

suggests, however, that while this 'professedly anti-historicist' stance served the purposes of an English Catholic minority just as much as it had benefited the Geneva exiles twenty years earlier, the King James Bible staged a conscious departure from it, and (paradoxically) sought to establish doctrinal continuity with the early church precisely by recognizing the difference of past writings and cultural practices.

In Gregory Martin's Preface to the Rheims translation, the process of textual transmission is depicted as transparent, continuous, and largely unproblematic: the Vulgate text—'most auncient' and authoritative, in the translators' estimation—is passed down the generations 'from hand to hand', as we have seen; where minor issues have 'crept in', through 'evident corruptions made by the copistes' [sic] or 'faultes now a daies committed by the Printer', they are easily spotted and rectified.[12] The timeless truth of scripture is guaranteed by uninterrupted institutional and spiritual continuity, as Martin's constant appeals to 'the auncient fathers, General Councels, the Churches of al the west part' attest: 'let us in the name of God folow them, speake as they spake, translate as they translated, interprete as they interpreted, because we beleeve as they beleeved' (c2ᵛ). The paratextual architecture of the Rheims translation reinforces the primacy of 'universal' and 'uniforme' consent at every turn (b1ʳ). In the notes appended to the second chapter of St Matthew's Gospel, for instance, historical events are folded into transhistorical cycles of ritual and ceremony. To elucidate the phrase 'behold, there came Sages from the East to Jerusalem' (Matthew 2: 1), the translators initially refer the reader to a marginal note: 'The holy feast of the *Epiphanie* called *Twelfth*-day the 6 of Januarie, upon which day this is the Gospel' (A3ʳ).[13] At the end of the chapter, there is a further note on the word '*Behold*', reminding us that Epiphany also initiates a new phase in the expansion of the church: 'therfore is *Twelfth day* highly celebrated in the Catholike Churche for joy of the calling of us Gentils. His baptisme also and first miracle are celebrated on the same day' (A3ᵛ).[14] What the reader is asked to 'behold' here is not a specific moment in history, but a timeless tableau which unites scriptural past, present liturgical practice, and future narratives of conversion and triumph. As we move from text to margin to end note, guided by asterisks and daggers (stars and crosses of sorts), the Rheims translators encourage us to draw a direct line from the manger at Bethlehem to a sixteenth-century Catholic church. This connection is made explicit by the note on Matthew 2: 11 ('And entring into the house, they founde the childe with MARIE his mother, & falling downe adored him'):

> *Adored him*] This body (*saith S. Chrysostom.*) the Sages adored in the cribbe .... [T]hou seest him not now in the cribbe, but on the altar: not a woman holding him, but the Priest present, and the Holy Ghost powred out aboundantly upon the sacrifice. (A3ʳ⁻ᵛ)

---

[12] Rheims, c1ᵛ. On Martin, see Thomas M. McCoog, 'Martin, Gregory (1542?–1582)', *ODNB*, 2004 <http://www.oxforddnb.com/view/article/18183>. For a bibliographical description of the Rheims New Testament, including a description of the paratexts, see T. H. Darlow and H. F. Moule, *Historical Catalogue of Printed Editions of the English Bible 1525–1961*, rev. and expanded by A. S. Herbert (London: British and Foreign Bible Society, 1968), 95–6 (no. 177; see also no. 258, on the 2nd edn of the New Testament (1600), and no. 300, on the complete Douay Rheims Bible, published in 2 vols in 1609/10).

[13] On scripture marginalia from Tyndale to the KJB, see Evelyn B. Tribble, *Margins and Marginality: The Printed Page in Early Modern England* (Charlottesville, Va.: University Press of Virginia, 1993), ch. 1.

[14] In addition to marginalia and endnotes, the Rheims translators include summaries for each chapter and book of the New Testament (cumulatively, these framing devices create the effect of a pared back, more user-friendly version of the Vulgate with *Glossa Ordinaria*).

The scene of Christ's nativity is made present again in the sacrament, and the translators' note allows us to 'behold' the recapitulation of sacred history in timeless ritual. But just in case anyone should have overlooked this connection, the translators include a further marginal note, and a final reminder that Matthew 2: 11 serves as a proof-text for the 'Adoration of the B. Sacrament' (A3^v).

Perhaps unsurprisingly, the argument for a timeless ecclesiastical and textual tradition is at its most intensely territorial—and least paratextually subtle—in the translators' defence of the Roman canon of scripture. This four-page section consists of a list of books held to be authentic by the church, and a five-point programme establishing its principles of canonicity. 'The discerning of Canonical from not Canonical', emphatically, 'commeth unto us, only by the credite we give unto the Catholike Churche … which even from the most grounded and founded seates of the Apostles, is established until this day, by the line of Bishops succeeding one an other, & by the consent of so many peoples' (d1^v–d2^r). The process of transmission is made explicit in the typographical and spatial structure of this section: rather than using embedded quotations and marginal citations as in the Preface, the five-point checklist on how to establish canonicity is simply a series of glosses on patristic axioms—with the visual effect of having the fathers speak *ex cathedra*, as it were. Once again, this strategy attempts to contain the very idea of a canon that might evolve beyond the wisdom of the primitive church, but it also seeks further ideological retrenchment through a unique (in this book, at least) deployment of the margin. All references except one link ancient heresies combated by the Fathers to contemporary enemies of the Roman faith, and usually in matching numbers. This has the obvious effect of turning the margin into a tool of marginalization, and other faiths into 'heretikes' and 'usurpers' of the promised scriptural land, as the following quotation from Tertullian's *De praescriptionibus adversus haereticos* illustrates (the corresponding 'heretics' in the margin are '*Luther, Zvinglius, Calvin*'):

> Who are you, when, and from whence came you? what doe you in my possession, … by what right (Marcion) doest thou cut downe my wood? who gave the licence (ô Valentine) to turne the course of my fountaines? by what authoritie (Apelles) doest thou remove my boundes? … It is my possession, I possesse it of old, I have assured origins thereof. (d2^r)

Even the manner of questioning (the specifics of 'who', 'when', and 'from whence') relegates doctrinal dissent to the minor and local status of a temporary affliction or parenthesis, unable on principle to compete with the origins of the faith. And by keeping the notion of heresy in a spatial and historical vacuum—the marginal reference allows us to recognize contemporary threats like Calvin and Luther in a lateral move, but not a forward one—the translators also keep alive the hope of permanent containment, with core texts like Tertullian's both the 'principal' and the 'last' line of defence in the battle for 'the most grounded and founded seates of the Apostles' (d2^r). This strategy is replicated in the Preface, which equates 'the Arrian' and 'the Calvinian interpretation' of a passage from 1 Corinthians, for instance (b1^v); and in the 'Table Directing The Reader To Al Catholike truthes', which simply cross-references '*Protestants*' with '*Heretikes*' (DDDDD2^v).

This desire to establish proximity of time and place between contemporary Catholic practice and collective judgement of the early church consistently informs the translators' interpretive and linguistic choices: ecclesiology frequently merges with philology. '[W]e have used no partialitie for the disadvantage of our adversaries, nor no more licence then is sufferable in translating of holy Scriptures', Martin asserts, 'keeping our selves as neere as is possible, to our text & to the very wordes and phrases which by long use are made venerable, though to some prophane or delicate eares they may seeme more hard or barbarous ... lest we misse the sense, we must keepe the very wordes' (b2^{r-v}). The word 'neere' is more than a synonym for 'faithful' here, and powerfully reapplies Martin's topographical and chronological lexicon to the activity of translation. Literalism is understood as a form of time travel, or a means of reopening a direct channel of communication with the sacred past: to come 'near' the original language is to reconnect with the primitive church. But the example of Matthew 2: 11 perhaps also encourages us to understand this insistence on 'the very words' as a linguistic analogy for the real presence. By keeping the phrases of the Vulgate 'word for word, and point for point, for feare of missing, or restraining the sense of the holy Ghost' (c3^{v}), the Rheims translation seeks to co-opt the power of the sacrament, and equates literalism with a notion of embodied speech which is more than a linguistic approximation, or a ghostly memorial of the original scripture utterance.

This is why, in another telling elision of meaning, Martin can claim to be 'very precise and religious in folowing our copie, the old vulgar approved Latin' (c3^{r}). Being precise and being religious are one and the same, in a fully materialized conjunction of doctrine, liturgy, and philology. This approach is designed to preserve the mystery of scripture, but it often sacrifices readability. Where the King James account of Old Testament rites at Numbers 6: 17 clearly prescribes that the priest 'shall offer the ram *for* a sacrifice of peace offerings unto the LORD, with the basket of unleavened bread', the Roman translation is notably less user-friendly: 'the ramme he shal immolate for a pacifique hoste to the Lord, offering withal the baskette of azymes'.[15]

The Rheims translators' focus on timeless and 'uniforme consent' also informs their treatment of sources and proof-texts. Throughout the Preface, individual judgement is pushed into the 'private' sphere of 'Sectaries' and fringe opinion, where it cannot threaten to relativize or subvert authority; the virtuous lay readers of the early church, Martin notes with evident approval, 'referred them selves in all hard places, to the judgement of the auncient fathers and their maisters in religion, never presuming to contend, controule, teach or talke of their owne sense and phantasie, in deepe questions of divinitie' (a3^{v}). By the same token, however, the 'Universal Church' must deliver to 'the good and simple' universal rules of doctrine and religious conduct, as the following exposition of a passage from Augustine's *Contra Cresconium* demonstrates (b2^{v}–b3^{r}).[16] In doubtful points of doctrine

> that in deede are not decided by Scripture, he [Augustine] giveth us this goodly rule to be folowed in all, as he exemplifieth in one. *Then doe we hold* (saith he) *the veritie of the Scriptures, when wee doe that which now hath seemed good to the Universal Church, which the authoritie of the Scriptures themselues doth commend: so that, forasmuch as the holy Scripture can not deceive, whosoever is afraid to be deceived with the obscuritie of questions, let him therein aske counsel of the same Church, which the holy Scripture most certainely and evidently sheweth and pointeth unto.* Aug. li. I. Cont. Crescon. c. 13. (b3^{r})

---

[15] *The Holie Bible Faithfully Translated into English ... By the English College of Doway* (1609), i. 334–5.

[16] The full title of Augustine's treatise is *Contra Cresconium grammaticum partis Donati* (composed 405–6). The Donatists were a schismatic body in the African church who became divided from the Catholics; Augustine's numerous disputations with leading Donatist theologians centre on the sacrament of baptism.

Martin's Augustine is elevated and canonized through the process of citation; he is made to pronounce globally on the relationship between scripture and authority, called not simply to speak for his own time, but adjudicating past practice and laying down laws for future conduct.[17] This attitude towards citation and interpretation, and the view of history that underpins it, comes to be questioned by Protestant controversialists in response to the publication of the Rheims New Testament, in defence of their church, and of their own translations.

II. 'This is your usuall kinde of reasoning, of a particular to inferre an universall': The Particularity of History in the King James Bible

By the time the Protestant controversialist William Fulke arrived at this unflattering summation of Martin's argumentative strategy in 1589, he had been debating his Roman opponent on the subject of Bible translation for some time.[18] Fulke and Martin first locked horns in 1582: Martin had published *A Discovery of the Manifold Corruptions of the Holy Scriptures by the Heretics of our Days, Specially the English Sectaries*, and Fulke responded with *A Defence of the Sincere and True Translations of the Holy Scriptures into the English Tongue against the Manifold Cavils, Frivolous Quarrels and Impudent Slaunders of Gregory Martin*. Seven years later, Fulke published an encyclopedic refutation of the Rheims New Testament, which included a detailed dissection of Martin's Preface. As we will see, this text provides the best point of entry for understanding the rationale behind Smith's Preface to the King James Bible.

In order to gauge the difference between the Roman and Protestant approaches to ecclesiology and translation, we must first attend to Fulke's attempt to redefine the meaning of the terms 'universall' and 'particular'. In the quotation that introduced this section, Fulke uses both terms to describe a form of argument, but they are ultimately inseparable from his broader perspective on church history and doctrine:

> the Popish Church ... is not Catholike, but particular and hereticall, yea Antichristian, and hath no succession in doctrine, from the Apostles and the Bishops of the Primitive Church, whose doctrine it hateth and persecuteth. For it is continuance in the same doctrine, that S. Augustine commendeth, and not sitting in the same place, where the Apostles and auncient Bishops satte. (C6ᵛ)

Once again, the rhetoric gravitates relentlessly towards topographical and chronological discourses, but the positions are now inverted. 'Continuance' and 'succession' appear

---

[17] On the versatile uses of Augustine in early modern religious culture, see Arnoud Visser, *Reading Augustine in the Reformation: The Flexibility of Intellectual Authority in Europe 1500–1620* (Oxford: Oxford University Press, 2011).

[18] Quotation in the section heading is from William Fulke, *The Text of the New Testament of Jesus Christ, Translated out of the Vulgar Latine by the Papists* (London, 1589), C1ᵛ. On Fulke, see Richard Bauckham, Jr., 'The Career and Thought of Dr. William Fulke (1537–1589)', Ph.D. thesis, University of Cambridge, 1973.

not as seamless lines of descent—and ideally the meeting of present and past 'in the same place'—but as more complexly particularized moments of dialogue between different cultures. For Fulke, the desire to rejoin 'the Apostles and auncient Bishops' and sit in their seat only signifies arrogant presumption; past and present, though connected by 'the same doctrine', have distinct identities and require particular forms of analysis and understanding. Thus, paradoxically, it is in the insistence on extrapolating timeless, global meaning from individual cases that the Catholic Church reveals itself as the 'particular and hereticall' Church of Rome, rather than the true, universal embodiment of Christianity. Throughout his response to Martin's Preface, Fulke thinks about the processes of doctrinal and philological transmission in terms of 'place'—their spatial, cultural, and textual situation—and maintains that we cannot determine our relationship with authentic apostolic doctrine without first attending to the local and specific contexts of beliefs and practices.

Fulke's answer to Martin's 'usuall kinde of reasoning, of a particular to inferre an universall', is to proceed 'circumspectly, and advisedly', by 'establishing the scope of the text, and circumstances thereof' (C1ᵛ). These techniques of circumspection are nowhere more apparent than in Fulke's treatment of the patristic topoi—commonplaces or proof-texts—cited by his opponent. Fulke revisits Martin's quotation from Augustine's *Contra Cresconium*, for instance; while his conclusions are entirely unsurprising (the 'Church … hath wisdome to decide questions by Scripture, not auctoritie to determine of points of doctrine, not decided by the Scriptures', B3ʳ), the differences in exegetical method are illuminating. Fulke begins by noting the setting and occasion of the patristic text: Augustine's remarks on the relationship between scriptural and institutional authority were initiated by 'controversie betweene him and the Donatists, that such as were baptized by heretikes might not be rebaptized' (B2ᵛ). He then goes on to argue that Augustine proves the doctrinal case not by appealing to church authority, but by reference to scriptural precept and analogy, citing, first, 'the saying of our Saviour Christ to Peter: He that is once washed, neede not to be washed again', and then 'the example of the Samaritanes, who being circumcised in schisme and heresie, were not circumcised againe, when they were converted to the true Religion of the Jewes' (B2ᵛ).

It is only when his Donatist opponent 'would still urge' the particular example of baptism by heretics that Augustine refers the matter 'to the judgement of the whole Church'; but since the doctrinal gist of the matter has already been decided by scripture, Fulke suggests, this is a minor case of 'particular opinions and practises' (B3ʳ). Fulke has been able to reach this conclusion by close attention to textual and contextual circumstances: he refers the reader to other key moments in *Contra Cresconium* (especially 'the Chapter going before'), evaluates Augustine's use of scripture texts, and sets the debate in the wider context of patristic thought and doctrinal development: '[t]he obscuritie of this question, grew by the contrary judgement and practise of S. Cyprians time, which the whole Church, by auctoritie of the Scriptures, had reformed in S. Augustines time' (B3ʳ). This method seeks to preserve the idea of eternal scriptural verities, but also aims to account for the inevitable impact of cultural change and development.

The project of claiming doctrinal 'continuance' and 'succession' for the Protestant cause continues in Miles Smith's Preface to the King James Bible, 'The Translators to the Reader'. But where Fulke's argument is limited by the parameters of refutation, Smith returns to first principles, and instead of engaging in controversy aims to make a positive case for specifically Protestant forms of historiography and philology. Throughout his introduction to the 1611 Bible, Smith picks up on the connections between doctrine and translation that characterize the Rheims Preface. Furthermore, like their Roman counterparts, the King James translators arrange paratextual furniture in a way that reflects the place of their church in history. One significant addition in this respect is a 34-page section of genealogical charts, '[a]mongst whose manifold uses, this is the chiefest, that by them is prooved how *Christ* was made very man. And therefore in severall Tables they are heere exhibited even from their first roote, and so continued through their spreading branches, so farre as the Scripture giveth them sap'.[19]

At an important level, the concept of continuity exhibited by these charts is timeless and direct: the Spirit or scripture 'sap' runs through every generation and ensures the preservation of the faith. This providential or eschatological reading of human history is reinforced by many of the illustrations that accompany the charts: Adam and Eve, for instance, are depicted at the Tree of Knowledge, and the scene includes an impressive-looking snake, a skeleton in a coffin, and some heavy scriptural hints on the issues of sin, death, and redemption (notably Romans 5: 19, 'As by one mans disobedience many were made sinners'; and Hosea 13: 14, 'O Death I will be thy death'; A2^r) (Figure 3.1). But this is only part of the story. The genealogies are framed by a reminder that 'The Spirit of God in the sacred History, hath laid downe such helps, as are the light and life of all Nations originals. In them the circumstances of *Person, Time,* and *Place,* are the chiefe; else doe wee wander as without a guide' (A1^v). And while the charts cannot be said to articulate anthropological interests in the modern sense, they nevertheless express a composite view of history made up of distinctive societies and cultures, and a Christian world defined by the particular 'circumstances of *Person, Time,* and *Place'.* The King James Bible genealogies contain a system of visual cues that describe different forms of social connections and relationships and record difficult or ruptural moments in the succession narrative: direct descent from parent to child, for instance, is figured as a double vertical line running between names (which are in turn represented in circles or 'rundles'); the names of nations and peoples are represented in rectangular *'Compartiments,* and different letters betwixt direct lines, … and the *Names* next under them, are not inserted as certainly thence descended, but as eminent *Persons* among them' (A1^v).

A crucial watershed, both visually and historiographically, is marked by the representation of God's people before and after the flood. The second and third pages of the genealogical chart juxtapose two different views of humanity: an ante-diluvian version, depicted as a tree growing out of Noah's Ark, faces the much more complex and detailed diagram of lines, 'rundles', and 'compartiments' I have just described. The tree represents the families of Noah and his sons, and is framed on the left by a quotation from Acts 17: 'God that made the world, of one bloud hath made al mankind to dwell upon the face of the earth' (A2^v). To the right of the tree, however, is another quotation which reminds us of the consequences of

---

[19] KJB, A1^v. See Darlow and Moule, rev. Herbert, *Historical Catalogue,* 132: the *Genealogies of Holy Scripture* and a map are inserted before Genesis; both were compiled by the historian John Speed (?1552–1629), 'apparently at the suggestion, and with the assistance of Hugh Broughton (1549–1612)'. Speed 'obtained a patent for ten years, dated 31 Oct. 1610, giving him the right to insert them in every edition of the new version of the Bible'. See further, Francis Fry, *A Description of the Great Bible … also of the Editions, in Large Folio, of the Authorized Version of the Holy Scriptures* (London: Willis & Sotheran, 1865), 32, 40–1. For a full bibliographical description of the *editio princeps* of the King James Bible, see *Historical Catalogue,* Darlow and Moule, rev. Herbert, 131–2.

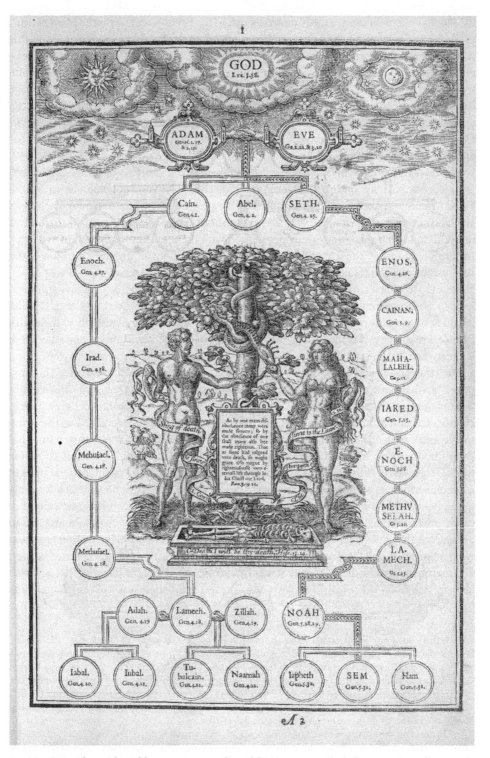

FIGURE 3.1 *The Holy Bible, conteyning the Old Testament, and the New* (London, 1611), KJB, A2ʳ. Folger Shakespeare Library, STC 2216.

the Flood—'out of these were the Nations divided in the Earth'—and forms the point of transition to the genealogical charts proper, beginning with Noah's eldest son Shem. From this moment onwards, 'one blroud' is 'divided' into variegated strands of cultural and religious development: on the first page alone the chart ramifies into Persian, Assyrian, and Aramite tribes. And significantly, as the accompanying illustration of the Tower of Babel on this page suggests, the process of cultural diversification entails linguistic change. In the words of the scripture gloss: 'In this age and at the building of Babel, the language was divided, ... but in Christs Apostles, when the heavenly temple was built, every nation understood their language' (A2ᵛ–A3ʳ; Figure 3.2).

This dual precondition of fallen existence, 'one blroud ... divided' and 'language ... divided', is the starting point for Smith's defence of Protestant ecclesiology and philology. Babel and the Flood (in another paradoxical spin on Christian chronology) divide us from the apostolic past and 'what ever was perfect' then: 'Apostles or Apostolike men' were able to make themselves understood to all because they were 'priviledged with the priviledge of infallibilitie' (A6ᵛ).[20] Instead of 'uniforme' consent and transhistorical communion, Smith offers a vision of the past as radically plural and particular. Those who followed in the tradition of the Apostles, he asserts, were 'men and not God', 'Interpreters, ... not prophets', and 'as men they stumbled and fell' (A5ʳ). One might be tempted to conclude that the past is a different country, but that would be missing the point: the absence of topographical and territorial metaphors in Smith's Preface is itself one way of measuring the distance between Protestant and Catholic models of language and history.

But if the apostolic mission cannot be replicated exactly, if we cannot travel back to 'the same place', in what sense can Smith's church—and its new translation of the scriptures—claim 'continuance' with early Christianity? The answer lies in a continual process of development, change, and accommodation. In order for eternal truth to be communicated as the living word, Smith contends, it must remain responsive to cultural change, 'notwithstanding that some imperfections and blemishes may be noted in the setting foorth of it' (A6ᵛ). At a time when Greek was the 'fittest' means of conversion, for instance, the Septuagint had the effect of a 'candle set upon a candlesticke, which giveth light to all that are in the house', but in contrast to the Roman desire to revert to the 'authentic' text, translation forms a pragmatic point of departure rather than an inviolable point of origin: 'that Translation was not so sound and so perfect, but that it needed in many places correction' (A5ʳ).[21] For Smith, translation has a forward momentum and takes account of institutional and linguistic evolution: 'blessed be they, and most honoured be their name, that breake the yce, and giveth the onset upon that which helpeth forward to the saving of soules' (A6ʳ). The 1611 translation sees itself emphatically as

[20] Smith's preface is now available in an annotated version, *The Translators to the Reader*, ed. Erroll F. Rhodes and Liana Lupas (New York: American Bible Society, 1997). Since Rhodes and Lupas modernize spelling and punctuation, I am citing from the 1611 version of Smith's text (STC 2216, the copy held in Cambridge University Library). Smith's preface was included in the folio edition of the King James Bible (STC 2216), but not in the earliest (1611) separate edition of the New Testament (STC 2909), or in the first quarto (STC 2210; 1612) or octavo (STC 2221; 1612) editions of the KJB. See *Historical Catalogue*, Darlow and Moule, rev. Herbert, 130–5; and Fry, *A Description of the Great Bible*.

[21] On the composition of the King James Bible, see W. S. Allen and E. C. Jacobs, *The Coming of the King James Gospels* (Fayetteville, Ark.: University of Arkansas Press, 1995); E. C. Jacobs, 'Two Stages of Old Testament Translation for the King James Bible', *The Library*, 6th ser. 11 (1980): 16–39; David Norton, *A Textual History of the King James Bible* (Cambridge: Cambridge University Press, 2005).

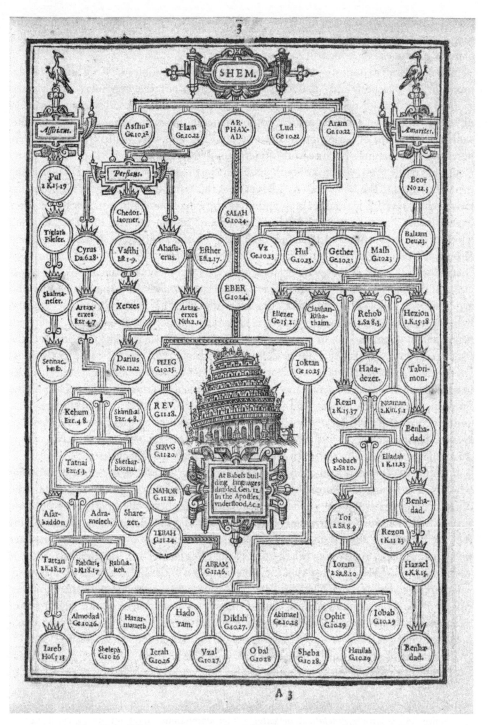

FIGURE 3.2 *The Holy Bible, conteyning the Old Testament, and the New* (London, 1611), KJB, A3ʳ. Folger Shakespeare Library, STC 2216.

part of this ongoing process of reinvention and renewal: 'wee never thought from the beginning, that we should neede to make a new Translation, … but to make a good one better, or out of many good ones, one principall good one' (B1ᵛ).

In their attempt to improve previous English versions of the Bible, the King James translators returned to Hebrew and Greek, 'the two golden pipes, or rather conduits, … fountaines, … [the] precedent, or originall tongues' (B1ᵛ). This means that the Vulgate is regarded as ultimately instrumental, a pragmatic medium of communication, rather than the absolute, 'authentic' standard of perfection invoked by the Rheims Preface. Latin translations were necessary, Smith argues, because 'within a few hundreth yeeres after CHRIST, … very many Countreys of the West, yea of the South, East and North, spake or understood Latine, being made Provinces to the *Romanes*' (A5ʳ). But even at this point in the history of scripture, the movement is towards textual revision and linguistic evolution: Smith notes, with reference to Augustine, that 'the *Latine* translations [of the Old Testament] were too many to be all good, for they were infinite' and that they derived from a 'muddie' '*Greeke* streame'; this is why Jerome, the 'best linguist without controversie, of his age, or of any that went before him', was charged with the task of surveying extant translations and eventually undertook 'the translating of the Old Testament, out of the very fountaines themselves'.[22] And it is Jerome who articulates the philological and historiographical principles that lead Smith to assert that 'to have the Scriptures in the mother-tongue is not a quaint conceit lately taken up … but hath bene thought upon, and put in practise of old' (A5ᵛ); in his Preface to the translation of the Pentateuch, Jerome insists that '*we condemne the ancient … [i]n no case: but after the endevours of them that were before us, wee take the best paines we can in the house of God*'.[23] In order to consolidate his case, and simultaneously counter the Rheims translators' emphasis on the timeless authority of the fathers, Smith highlights the constant patristic drive towards revision and self-correction: 'Saint *Augustine* was not afraide to exhort S. *Herome* to a *Palinodia* or recantation; the same S. *Augustine* was not ashamed to retractate, we might say revoke, many things that had passed him, and doth even glory that he seeth his infirmities' (B1ʳ).

If textual development and change are the working principles of the earliest Christian scholars, Smith suggests, Roman theologians have little justification for objecting to 'the difference that appeareth betweene our Translations, and our often correcting of them' (B1ʳ). By way of adding controversial braces to the belt of principle, however, he also claims that the Catholic Church fails to live up to its own demands of 'uniformity' (another word that resonates richly with the rhetoric of the Rheims Preface): did not Pope Sixtus V 'ordaine by an inviolable decree' that the Bible produced under his reign was the last word, when a mere two years later, Clement VIII, 'his immediate successour, publisheth another edition of the Bible, containing in it infinite differences from that of *Sixtus*, (and many of them waightie and materiall) and yet this must be authentike by all meanes'?[24] And, in a final rhetorical question, he asks, 'what is sweet harmonie and consent, if this be?' (B1ᵛ).

The project of philological re-evaluation is inseparable from the prime goal of effective communication. Smith's continuing connection with those 'that breake the yce' is 'to

---

[22] Smith, A5ʳ⁻ᵛ (invoking another effective polemical trope in the call for a philological return *ad fontes*).

[23] Smith, A6ʳ; see Jerome, *Praefatio … in Pentateuchum*: 'damnamus veteres? minime: sed post priorum studia, in domo Domini quod possumus, laboramus' (PL 28.151A).

[24] The Bible published under the auspices of Sixtus V in 1590 was replaced by his successor Clement VIII in 1592. The Clementine Bible remained the standard Catholic Latin Bible until the publication of the *Nova Vulgata* in 1979. Smith's argument was helped by his own particular time and place in scripture history.

deliver Gods booke unto Gods people in a tongue which they understand' (or, in a more bracing quotation from Augustine's *City of God*, 'A man had rather be with his dog then with a stranger (whose tongue is strange unto him)') (A6^r).[25] '[W]e desire that the Scripture may speake like it selfe, as in the language of Canaan, that it may be understood even of the very vulgar' (B2^v); by contrast, the Rheims approach merely creates stylistic 'obscuritie, ... in their *Azimes, Tunike, Rational, Holocausts, Praepuce, Pasche*, and a number of such like, whereof their late Translation [i.e. Rheims] is full' (B2^v).[26] In order to achieve this aim, Smith argues, the King James translators have committed themselves not to 'the very words', but to a more idiomatic approach that reflects the 'sense and meaning' of 'the spirit', '[f]or it is confessed, that things are to take their denomination of the greater part' (A6^v). However, as Fulke's discussion of the same issues makes clear, the argument about archaic diction and literal translation inevitably feeds back into one about history:

> That in translation of the scriptures, the very words must be kept, as nere as it is possible, and the phrase of the tongue into which we translate wil beare, we do acknowledge ... That the ancient doctors refused not the Barbarismes and the solæcismes of the vulgar Latin translation, which they then had, it was because they did write in Latin, to be understood of the common people, to whom the Latin tongue was vulgar, and that translation familiar: not that those Barbarismes & solaecismes by long use became venerable, or that it is any example for you, to bring in Latine and Greeke words into the English text, neither used before, nor understood now of the English people. (B2^r)

'As nere as it is possible' is a plea for philological accuracy, rather than a testament to the inherent benefits of the ageing process. The fathers tolerated linguistic infelicities when they aided their pastoral mission, Fulke suggests, but would not have expected or tolerated the veneration of Vulgate 'Barbarismes' in the sixteenth century. The presence of 'Latine and Greek words' in the Rheims translation has the same effect as a mock Tudor cottage would on a modern housing estate, neither a faithful echo of the past nor a real conversation with the present. In order to speak effectively to 'the English people', Fulke's ally Smith notes (once again in deliberate reply to Martin's Preface), the translation must reflect the linguistic diversity of lived discourse: 'wee have not tyed our selves to an uniformitie of phrasing, or to an identitie of words, as some peradventure would wish' (B2^v). The translators did 'not varie from the sense of that which we had translated before, if the word signified the same thing in both places'; at the same time, however, 'that we should expresse the same notion in the same particular word; as for example, ... *Journeying*, neuer *Traveiling*, ... wee thought to savour more of curiositie then wisedome' (B2^v).

Smith insists throughout that the word of God must and will withstand some accommodation to linguistic context and cultural change: 'the very meanest translation of the Bible in English, set foorth by men of our profession ... containeth the word of God, nay, is the word of God' (A6^v); in fact, Smith claims, the King James translators' approach finds its

---

[25] See Augustine, *De civitate Dei* 19.7, 'ita ut libentius homo sit cum cane suo, quam cum homine alieno' (PL 41.634).

[26] According to Smith, the Puritans display a similar 'scrupulositie' and 'nicenesse in wordes', albeit for very different reasons: they 'leaue the olde Ecclesiasticall words, and betake them to other, as when they put *washing* for *Baptisme*, and *Congregation* in stead of *Church*' (B2^v). (This is the 'King James Bible' speaking: terms such as 'Baptisme' and 'Congregation' were unlikely to bolster the authority of James I's episcopate and ensure maintenance of 'good order and discipline' in the church (A3^v).)

'patterne for elocution' in 'God' himself, 'using divers words, in his holy writ, and indifferently for one thing in nature' (B2ᵛ). The marginal notes to the Preface constantly rearticulate the 'wisedome' of the translators' method: in addition to citations from scripture and from patristic, classical, medieval, and early modern proof-texts, Smith's margins are populated by Greek words. The corresponding sections in the text are marked off by vertical double lines, and often show consciously idiomatic renderings. Every time this happens, the reader is alerted to the deliberate avoidance of archaism—of words 'neither used before, nor understood now'—and is made to register both the difference of the philological past and Smith's easy expertise in bringing its riches into the present.[27]

The Preface continues its process of linguistic reinvention in its treatment of patristic quotation: Smith notes, as we have seen, that 'S. *Augustine* was not ashamed to retractate, we might say revoke, many things that had passed him' (B1ʳ). Rhetorical strategies such as this one—changing the verb 'retractate' to 'revoke', in order to usher it into the seventeenth century—reaffirm the crucial link between translation and ecclesiology, doctrinal and linguistic choices. To the Rheims translators, the literal rendering of 'retractate' preserves the spirit of Augustine's authority; for the King James translators, Augustine becomes an icon of renewal: were he alive in 1611, the first order of business would be to 'retractate' his allegiance to a 'hereticall and particular' Catholic church and its outdated adherence to contrived Latinity. In Smith's Preface, as we have seen, it is the ancient fathers themselves who reject the idea of dogmatic conservationism and instead insist throughout on the contextual contingency of their work. True 'continuance' with the early church, then, depends on an acknowledgement of cultural and linguistic *discontinuities* (in the same way that scriptural opacity paradoxically facilitates a more profound understanding of its message); the Protestant identity of the King James Bible emerges not simply through a break with the Catholic past, but by emphasizing the tears and seams in the fabric of human history.

These moments of dissonance are foregrounded by the 1611 translators' decision to 'set diversitie of sences in the margin, where there is great probability for each' (B2ʳ).[28] Smith begins by noting the obvious Roman objection to this point: that 'the authoritie of the Scriptures for deciding of controversies by that shew of uncertaintie, should somewhat be shaken' (B2ʳ). He subsequently suggests, however, that such textual difficulties are intentional and productive: they are providentially designed 'to exercise and whet our wits', to encourage us to search the scriptures. In this remark, Smith also affirms what was perceived as the most commonly noted distinction between Protestant and Catholic approaches to the Bible in the early modern period (at least in theory); he reifies the judgement of the individual reader, over and above that of collective authority:

> They that are wise, had rather have their judgements at libertie in differences of readings, then to be captivated to one, when it may be the other. If they were sure that their hie Priest had all lawes shut up in his brest, as *Paul* the second bragged, and that he were as free from errour by special priviledge, as the Dictators of *Rome* were made by law inviolable, it were an other matter; then his word were an Oracle, his opinion a decision. But the eyes of the world

---

[27] For example, Smith, A3ᵛ: 'should be as safe as a Sanctuary, and ‖ out of shot' (from the Greek ἔξω βέλους).
[28] The marginal notes to the King James translation focus on alternative renderings of the original languages and on the citation of parallel scripture passages, in deliberate contrast to the marginalia of the Geneva Bible, which frequently engaged with doctrinal and political issues.

are now open, God be thanked, and have bene a great while, they find that he is subject to the same affections and infirmities, that others be, that his skin is penetrable. (B2ʳ)

Smith's analogy between textual 'uniformitie' and papal infallibility paves the way for another classic trope: the liberation of the Protestant reader from the 'bondage' of the Roman magisterium (B2ᵛ). And once again, this is a topical argument in more senses than one; Smith insists that judgement cannot reside absolutely in a single place—the Pope's 'brest', Rome—and thus replaces the notion of Petrine succession with a more historically supple and particularized notion of doctrinal continuity.

It is worth restating that, in their fundamental positions on scripture reading, Smith's and Martin's prefaces offer few surprises. The chief interest and importance of both pieces resides in the systematic connections they make between doctrinal and textual decisions, and between hermeneutic and historical method. The Rheims and King James Bibles do not simply promulgate ideas about the reader's relationship with scripture in discursive prefaces, but manipulate the book as material object to encourage desired responses in the reader. Through their approach to citation and annotation, and in their use of maps, genealogical charts, and indexes, these two Bibles embody two radically different views of scripture truth and church history. In practice, readers doubtless deviated from the path set out by their guides. But it will be easier to understand the nature and significance of readerly choices—including moments of overt resistance or compliance—if we have a better understanding of the concepts and strategies authors used to direct the textual movements of their audience. The pressure to succeed in this project was nowhere more intense than in a culture that read scriptural topography as a way into the kingdom of heaven.[29]

FURTHER READING

Backus, Irena. *Historical Method and Confessional Identity in the Era of the Reformation (1378–1615)* (Leiden: Brill, 2003).

Collinson, Patrick. 'The Coherence of the Text: How it Hangeth Together: The Bible in Reformation England', in W. P. Stephens (ed.), *The Bible, the Reformation and the Church: Essays in Honour of James Anderson*, Journal for the Study of the New Testament, supplement series, 105 (1995): 84–108.

[29] Peter Stallybrass has drawn attention to the 'discontinuous' reading practices adopted by readers of the Geneva Bible. The use of indexes, concordances, and other aids included in printed (and often customized) Bibles encouraged a non-linear or non-sequential approach to the scriptures; this was perceived, Stallybrass argues, to threaten the coherence of the text. See Stallybrass, 'Books and Scrolls: Navigating the Bible', in Jennifer Andersen and Elizabeth Sauer (eds), *Books and Readers in Early Modern England: Material Studies* (Philadelphia: University of Pennsylvania Press, 2002), 42–79. The rhetorical and material strategies adopted by the Rheims and KJB translators may help to extend our understanding of scriptural 'continuity' and 'discontinuity': the preface and paratextual matter of the Roman translation draw heavily on cyclical, typological, and eschatological concepts of continuity, while the KJB translators emphasize the strategic uses of disruptions and dissonance. Renaissance Bible readers, it seems, were consciously operating within a broad range of chronological and spatial discourses, many of them competing with linear conceptions of continuity and drawing sophisticated connections between doctrinal, textual, and material forms of engagement with scripture.

Ettenhuber, Katrin. '"Take vp and read the Scriptures": Patristic Interpretation and the Poetics of Abundance in "The Translators to the Reader" (1611)'. *Huntington Library Quarterly*, 75 (2012): 213–32.

Genette, Gérard. *Paratexts: Thresholds of Interpretation*, tr. Jane E. Lewin (Cambridge: Cambridge University Press, 1997).

Heal, Felicity. 'Appropriating History: Catholic and Protestant Polemics and the National Past'. *Huntington Library Quarterly*, 68 (2005): 109–32.

King, John N., and Aaron T. Pratt. 'The Materiality of English Printed Bibles from the Tyndale New Testament to the King James Bible', in Hannibal Hamlin and Norman W. Jones (eds), *The King James Bible After 400 Years: Literary, Linguistic, and Cultural Influences* (Cambridge: Cambridge University Press, 2010), 61–99.

Knott, John R. *The Sword of the Spirit: Puritan Responses to the Bible* (Chicago: University of Chicago Press, 1980).

Liere, Katherine van, Simon Ditchfield, and Howard Louthan, eds. *Sacred History: Uses of the Christian Past in the Renaissance World* (Oxford: Oxford University Press, 2012).

Smith, Helen, and Louise Wilson, eds. *Renaissance Paratexts* (Cambridge: Cambridge University Press, 2011).

Spurr, John. '"A special kindness for dead bishops": The Church, History, and Testimony in Seventeenth-Century Protestantism'. *Huntington Library Quarterly*, 68 (2005): 313–34.

Stallybrass, Peter. 'Books and Scrolls: Navigating the Bible', in Jennifer Andersen and Elizabeth Sauer (eds), *Books and Readers in Early Modern England: Material Studies* (Philadelphia: University of Pennsylvania Press, 2002), 42–79.

Tribble, Evelyn B. *Margins and Marginality: The Printed Page in Early Modern England* (Charlottesville, Va.: University Press of Virginia, 1993).

CHAPTER 4

··

THE KING JAMES BIBLE
AND BIBLICAL IMAGES OF
DESOLATION

··

KAREN L. EDWARDS

KING James's dislike of the Geneva Bible is well known.[1] Published in numerous editions between 1560 and 1640, inexpensive, readily available, and filled with aids to help the reader (marginal annotations, chapter summaries, maps, and diagrams), the Geneva Bible, known as the People's Bible, was deeply loved by English Protestants, and not only those of the more zealous sort.[2] James came to regard it as politically subversive. He declared it to be, in William Barlow's account of the Hampton Court Conference of 1604, 'the worst of all' translations, reserving his special animosity for its interpretive annotations.[3] Barlow reports that when the King announced his desire for a new translation of the Bible, he gave 'this caveat':

> that no marginall notes should be added, having found in them which are annexed to the *Geneva* translation ... some notes very partiall, untrue, seditious, and savouring too much of daungerous, and trayterous conceites: As for example, *Exod*. 1.19. where the marginall note alloweth *disobedience to Kings*. And 2. *Chron*. 15.16. the note taxeth *Asa* for deposing his mother, *onely*, and *not killing* her.[4]

This caveat is formalized in the sixth of James's fifteen instructions to the translators: 'No Marginal Notes at all to be affixed, but only for the Explanation of the *Hebrew* or *Greek* Words, which cannot without some circumlocution, so briefly and fitly be express'd in

---

[1] There is thus some irony in the fact that 'it was the first English Bible to be printed in Scotland ... was printed by the king's printer ... was dedicated to King James VI, and displayed the royal coat of arms on its cover', Gordon Campbell, *Bible: The Story of the King James Version 1611–2011* (Oxford: Oxford University Press, 2011), 27.

[2] On the paratexts of the Geneva Bible, see the chapter by Femke Molekamp in this volume.

[3] William Barlow, *The Summe and Substance of the Conference ... at Hampton Court* (London, 1604), 46.

[4] Barlow, *Summe and Substance*, 46–7. Similar warnings are voiced by William Laud thirty years later, with civil war imminent. See *The Works of William Laud* (Oxford: Oxford University Press, 1847–60), iv. 262.

the Text'.[5] The emphatic 'at all' overshadows the qualifying 'but only', and in any case the exception seems devoid of political interest.

James's sensitivity to the political implications of the Geneva's notes is understandable in an era that saw the Bible as the guide to every aspect of human life. One might therefore have expected him to demand notes in the new translation that urge obedience to the monarch and the established church. That is, the use of interpretive glosses would seem to provide an opportunity for impressing obedience to authority upon the Bible-reading English public. However, observing that light annotation is characteristic of the two earlier 'authorized' versions of the English Bible (the Great or Cranmer's Bible of 1539 and the Bishops' Bible of 1568), David Norton points out that marginal notes 'removed the task of interpreting the Bible from the Church' and gave it to the individual reader. The very presence of glosses 'might … be thought of as encouraging independent thought, and therefore dissent and even heresy'.[6] James's exclusion of marginal notes is thus as politically astute as the Geneva translators' inclusion of them.

The King was largely successful in his desire to produce a version of the Bible with uncluttered pages. Indeed, so firmly established is the King James Bible's reputation for dispensing with annotation that scholars have not been much interested in the notes that *do* appear in it, nor indeed in other elements of its editorial apparatus. Yet all of these repay careful study. Its sparse notes, chapter summaries, and page headings provide firm interpretive guidance for readers—guidance which is all the more effective for being almost invisible.[7] It is not amiss, moreover, to call this guidance 'political', as I aim to demonstrate here by considering the King James Bible's annotation of several obscure Hebrew words in Isaiah 13 and 34. These are chapters in which the prophet represents God's punishment of nations and their resulting desolation.[8] The words in which I am interested name creatures that haunt the desolated landscape; their names 'cannot … briefly and fitly be express'd in the Text'.

Oracles of restitution and oracles of desolation, or 'predictions of weal and of woe' alternate in the first thirty-nine chapters of Isaiah.[9] The former were read by early modern Christians as pointing to the coming of the Messiah;[10] the interpretation of the latter was more contentious. Given that post-Reformation England consistently identified itself with ancient Israel and its foes with Israel's foes, biblical prophecies of divinely produced desolation were seen to have significance for the nation and the nation's church.

[5] Alfred W. Pollard (ed.), *Records of the English Bible* (London: Oxford University Press, 1911), 54. Fourteen instructions are given in BL MS Add. 28721, fol. 24[r], and BL MS Harley 750, fols. 1[v]–2[r]; a fifteenth appears in BL MS Egerton 2884, fols. 5[v]–6[r]. The instructions are listed in Pollard, *Records*, 53–5, along with the report to the Synod of Dort, 16 Nov. 1618, possibly written by Samuel Ward, which gives some supplementary rules (336–9).

[6] David Norton, *The King James Bible: A Short History from Tyndale to Today* (Cambridge: Cambridge University Press, 2011), 18.

[7] David Norton suggests that the chapter summaries of the King James Bible were prepared by Miles Smith and Thomas Bilson, perhaps just before printing. As he admits, however, 'just how the last part of the work was done we will probably never know': *A Textual History of the King James Bible* (Cambridge: Cambridge University Press, 2005), 25.

[8] The fact that Matthew Arnold omitted chs 13 and 34 (without comment) from his school edition, *Isaiah of Jerusalem in the Authorized English Version, with an Introduction, Corrections, and Notes* (London: Macmillan, 1883) is another indication (should one be needed) of how troubling the chapters are.

[9] John Barton, *Isaiah 1–39* (Sheffield: Sheffield Academic Press, 1995), 106.

[10] Barton remarks that 'Isaiah has been the most important of the prophetic books for Christians seeking "messianic" prophecies': *Isaiah 1–39*, 115.

The different ways in which that significance was construed are indicated by the summaries that precede the first chapter of Isaiah in the Geneva and the King James Bibles. The Geneva Bible's synopsis of Isaiah 1 begins: 'Isaiah reproveth the Jewes of their ingratitude and stubburnes, that nether for benefites nor punishment wolde amend'.[11] The chapter synopsis in the King James Bible begins: 'Isaiah complaineth of Judah for her rebellion'.[12] Stubbornness versus rebellion: these different constructions of Judah's failings are a subtle reflection of the translators' assumptions about the behaviour of a favoured nation. For the Geneva translators, working in the shadow of the Marian persecutions, the fear is that God will finally lose patience with the hard-hearted ingratitude of the English people if they stubbornly reject, by leaving incomplete, what they have been allowed to witness: 'how' (in the words of John Milton) 'the bright and blissfull *Reformation* (by Divine Power) strook through the black and settled Night of *Ignorance* and *Antichristian Tyranny*'.[13] In contrast, for all those who in the early years of James's reign were at peace with an episcopal ecclesiastical organization, the most grievous sin was to rebel against what they believed to be God's approved settlement for the English Church.

These contrasts in attitude colour the ways in which the translators handle images of desolation in Isaiah. Such images take several forms: the slaughter of armies, earthquake and tempest, deluding dreams, flood, and, of concern to me here, ruined cities inhabited by beasts. The beasts depicted in Isaiah 13 and 34 are very strange beasts indeed, and their identity has been (and continues to be) debated. I will argue that the naming of the beasts in these chapters cannot be separated—any more than the use of 'rebellion' or 'ingratitude' in the chapter summaries can be—from the political and religious conflicts of early modern England. Chapters 13 and 34 of Isaiah are targeted at Babylon and Edom, but there is slippage here between the threatened destruction of Israel's enemies and the threatened destruction of Israel itself.[14] In any case, the lesson is clear: *any* nation that displeases God is liable to punishment.

Miles Smith discusses the problem of animal names explicitly in his preface to the King James Bible, 'The Translators to the Reader'.[15] The discussion occurs as part of Smith's rationale for 'set[ting] diversitie of sences in the margin, where there is great probability for each' (a rationale which itself occurs as a marginal gloss):

> [I]t hath pleased God in his divine providence, heere and there to scatter wordes and sentences of that difficultie and doutfulnesse, not in doctrinall points that concerne salvation, (for in

---

[11] *The Geneva Bible: A Facsimile of the 1560 Edition*, ed. Lloyd E. Berry (Madison, Wis.: University of Wisconsin Press, 1969). All quotations from the Geneva Bible are from this edition. The Geneva Bible translators provide synopses of entire books. These, along with chapter summaries and page headings, are explicitly mentioned in the preface to the reader: they are provided 'that by all meanes the reader might be holpen' (4ᵛ).

[12] For quotations from the King James Bible, I have used *The Holy Bible: Quatercentenary Edition … of the King James Version … Published in the Year 1611* (Oxford: Oxford University Press, 2010), a facsimile of *The Holy Bible, conteyning the Old Testament, and the New* (London: Robert Barker, 1611).

[13] John Milton, *Of Reformation*, in *The Complete Prose Works of John Milton* (New Haven: Yale University Press, 1953–82), i. 524.

[14] John Coggins notes that the material relating to Babylon in ch. 13 may originally have related to Assyria; the material in ch. 34, though apparently relating to Edom, 'goes beyond the historical, so that Edom becomes symbolic of the enemies of God': 'Isaiah', in John Barton and John Muddiman (eds), *Oxford Bible Commentary* (Oxford: Oxford University Press, 2001), 449, 461.

[15] For a detailed account of Smith's preface, see the chapter by Katrin Ettenhuber in this volume.

such it hath beene vouched that the Scriptures are plaine) but in matters of lesse moment, that fearefulnesse would better beseeme us then confidence, and if we will resolve, to resolve upon modestie with *S. Augustine ... Melius est dubitare de occultis, quam litigare de incertis*, it is better to make doubt of those things which are secret, then to strive about those things that are uncertaine. There be many words in the Scriptures, which be never found there but once, (having neither brother nor neighbour, as the *Hebrewes* speake) so that we cannot be holpen by conference of places. Againe, there be many rare names of certaine birds, beastes and precious stones, &c. concerning which the *Hebrewes* [that is, rabbinic scholars] themselves are so divided among themselves for judgement, that they may seeme to have defined this or that, rather because they would say somthing, then because they were sure of that which they said, as *S. Jerome* somewhere saith of the *Septuagint.* Now in such a case, doth not a margine do well to admonish the Reader to seeke further, and not to conclude or dogmatize upon this or that peremptorily? For as it is a fault of incredulitie, to doubt of those things that are evident: so to determine of such things as the Spirit of God hath left (even in the judgment of the judicious) questionable, can be no lesse then presumption. Therfore as *S. Augustine* saith, that varietie of Translations is profitable for the finding out of the sense of the Scriptures: so diversitie of signification and sense in the margine, where the text is not so cleare, must needes doe good, yea, is necessary, as we are perswaded.[16]

There is a defensive undercurrent here, which is understandable in light of the King's stated preferences for the new version. There is also a polemical undercurrent. Our notes, Smith explains, will occasionally acknowledge uncertainty rather than invariably posit meaning—*unlike the Geneva glosses*, he implies. He skirts around the fact that the existence of the Geneva's extensive interpretive apparatus conclusively demonstrates the *need* for interpretation, and that which needs to be interpreted is, by definition, uncertain.

It is worth noting that Smith assumes in the preface that the names of birds and beasts are 'matters of lesse moment'. This is undoubtedly true in terms of 'doctrinall points that concerne salvation'. Yet the naming of creatures (including human creatures) must surely be seen as one of the most political of all cultural activities. Rule brings with it the power to name, and the power to name brings with it the power to reward and the power to kill. At Genesis 2: 19–20, Adam's naming of the animals is the sign and the first manifestation of his dominion over them. The fact that wild animals displace the human population in chapters 13 and 34 of Isaiah hints that the loss of that dominion is one of the catastrophic consequences of God's wrath. The two chapters are linked by their linguistic and structural similiarities; indeed, it has been suggested that the 'eschatological destruction' portrayed in chapter 13 is the model for chapter 34.[17] More specifically, they are linked by the presence in both of the names of creatures mentioned rarely in the Bible, creatures which 'are part of a bestiary rather than those familiar from daily encounters'.[18]

It will be useful to begin the discussion of the naming of these creatures by looking at a modern translation of Isaiah. I have emphasized the names that are to be discussed and have supplied in brackets their transliterated Hebrew original.

---

[16] KJB, B2ʳ.   [17] Coggins, 'Isaiah', 462.
[18] Coggins, 'Isaiah', 462. See H. G. M. Williamson, *The Book Called Isaiah: Deutero-Isaiah's Role in Composition and Redaction* (Oxford: Clarendon Press, 1994), 216–17, for a discussion of the chapters' linguistic similarities.

Isaiah 13
19 And Babylon, the glory of kingdoms,
the splendor and pride of the Chaldeans,
will be like Sodom and Gomorrah when God overthrew them.
20 It will never be inhabited or lived in for all generations;
Arabs will not pitch their tents there,
shepherds will not make their flocks lie down there.
21 But *wild animals* [*ziim*] will lie down there,
and its houses will be full of *howling creatures* [*ohim*];
there ostriches will live, and there *goat-demons* [*sa'ir*] will dance.
22 *Hyenas* [*iim*] will cry in its towers, and *jackals* [*tannim*] in the pleasant palaces;
its time is close at hand, and its days will not be prolonged.

Isaiah 34
9 And the streams of Edom shall be turned into pitch,
and her soil into sulphur;
her land shall become burning pitch.
10 Night and day it shall not be quenched;
its smoke shall go up forever.
From generation to generation it shall lie waste;
no one shall pass through it forever and ever.
11 But the hawk and the hedgehog shall possess it;
the owl and the raven shall live in it.
He shall stretch the line of confusion over it,
and the plummet of chaos over its nobles.
12 They shall name it No Kingdom There,
and all its princes shall be nothing.
13 Thorns shall grow over its strongholds,
nettles and thistles in its fortresses.
It shall be the haunt of *jackals* [*tannim*], an abode for ostriches.
14 *Wildcats* [*ziim*] shall meet with *hyenas* [*iim*],
goat-demons [*sa'ir*] shall call to each other;
there too *Lilith* [*lilit*] shall repose,
and find a place to rest.
15 There shall the owl nest
and lay and hatch and brood in its shadow;
there too the buzzards shall gather,
each one with its mate.[19]

That some of the creatures mentioned in these chapters are unnatural or even supernatural is evident in the modern translation. 'Goat-demons', appearing in both chapters, is a translation of the Hebrew word *sa'ir*, meaning 'hairy one'; it is a standard name for a he-goat, but it may also refer to demons in the form of goats.[20] Isaiah 34 'reminds us', states John Coggins, 'that below the

[19] *The Holy Bible: New Revised Standard Version*, Anglicized edn (Oxford: Oxford University Press, 1995).
[20] Some scholars have found it useful, in this context, to turn to Lev. 17: 7, which restricts animal sacrifices because 'sacrifices in the open fields had been offered to "goat-demons", or "satyrs"': *New Oxford Annotated Bible with the Apocryphal/Deuterocanonical Books*, ed. Bruce M. Metzger and Roland E. Murphy (New York: Oxford University Press, 1991), Isa. 13: 20–2n. and Lev. 17: 4n. Joseph Blenkinsopp argues that the goat-demon or satyr is 'a precursor of Pan, the recipient of cult in the Kingdom of Samaria and perhaps Judah also': *Isaiah 1–39: A New Translation with Introduction and Commentary*, The Anchor Bible (New York: Doubleday-Anchor Bible, 2000), 453. Peter D. Miscall points out that *sa'ir* is a pun on

surface of belief in one God there lurked fears of demons'.[21] He refers not only to goat-demons, but also to Lilith (*lilit*), the Hebrew rendering of a Mesopotamian wind or storm demon (*lilītu*), who is a sexual threat to men and a murderer of children.[22] Other names that are as 'uncertaine' as *sa'ir* and *lilit* are not highlighted in the modern translation. These are the names translated as 'wild animals', 'howling creatures', 'hyenas', 'jackals', and 'wildcats'. Other modern translations render them differently, and many modern commentators hold that all of them signify theriomorphic demons.[23] What modern scholarship makes of these creatures, however, is not my primary interest. Rather, I wish to explore how early modern English translators, and particularly the King James Bible translators, register uncertainty about their identity.

Valuable evidence for the articulating of uncertainty in translations of theses chapters is provided by late fourteenth-century Wycliffite versions of the Bible. These are translated from the Vulgate, which follows here. Again, I have supplied the transliterated Hebrew terms.

> Isaiah 13
> 21 sed requiescent ibi bestiae [*ziim*] et replebuntur domus eorum draconibus [*ohim*]
> et habitabunt ibi strutiones et pilosi [*sa'ir*] saltabunt ibi
> 22 et respondebunt ibi ululae [*iim*] in aedibus eius
> et sirenae [*tannim*] in delubris voluptatis
>
> Isaiah 34
> 13 et erit cubile draconum [*tannim*] et pascua strutionum
> 14 et occurrent daemonia [*ziim*] onocentauris
> et pilosus [*sa'ir*] clamabit alter ad alterum
> ibi cubavit lamia [*lilit*] et invenit sibi requiem[24]

The English versions of Wycliffe and his followers help unfold the full extent of the problem posed by a translation of these verses, revealing it to be as much cultural as linguistic. Indeed, the opaque quality of the English rendering demonstrates that the translators struggled to make sense of the beasts named here. Let us look first at the verses in Isaiah 13, in the later of the parallel versions included in the standard edition of the Wycliffite Bible:

> But wielde beestis schulen reste there, and the housis of hem schulen be fillid with dragouns; and ostrichis schulen dwelle there, and heeri* *beestis* shulen skippe there. And bitouris schulen answere there in the housis therof, and fliynge serpentis in the templis of lust. (Isaiah. 13: 21–2) [25]

Seir, 'Edom's byname', as at Isa. 21: 11: *Isaiah 34–35: A Nightmare/A Dream, Journal for the Study of the Old Testament*, supplement series, 281 (Sheffield: Sheffield Academic Press, 1999), 82.

[21] Coggins, 'Isaiah', 462.

[22] For Lilith, see David Freedman et al. (eds), *Anchor Bible Dictionary* (New York: Doubleday, 1992), iv. 324–5; Karel van der Toorn, Bob Becking, and Pieter W. van der Horst (eds), *Dictionary of Deities and Demons in the Bible*, 2nd edn (Leiden: Brill, 1999), 520–1; *New Oxford Annotated Bible*, Isa. 34: 13–15n. I am grateful to my colleague Siam Bhayro for pointing out that Sumerian *lil* refers to some kind of demon or ghost (probably associated with the wind), and is loaned into Akkadian as *lilû* (masc.) and *lilītu* (fem.). The Hebrew term *lilit* 'Lilith' (fem.) is derived from the feminine Akkadian form. Subsequent folk etymology probably linked Lilith with the Hebrew term for 'night' (*laylā*), hence her role as a succubus.

[23] Compare, for instance, Blenkinsopp's translation (*Isaiah 1–39*, 276, 448–9). For the theory that all of the creatures here are animal demons, see Miscall, *Isaiah 34–35*, 83.

[24] *Biblia sacra iuxta vulgatam versionem*, ed. Robert Weber et al., 5th edn (Stuttgart: Deutsche Bibelgesellschaft, 2007).

[25] *The Holy Bible … in the Earliest English Version … by John Wycliffe and his Followers*, ed. Josiah Forshall and Frederick Madden (Oxford: Oxford University Press, 1850). The editors suggest that the later version was produced soon after 1395.

A marginal gloss explains: '*heery; that is, foxis and wolvys, as sum men seien; ether [i.e. or] heri ben heere wondurful beestis, that in parti han the licnes [likeness] of man and in parti the licnesse of a beeste'. The earlier Wycliffite version of the verse has, instead of 'heeri beestis', 'wodewoses', that is, human or semi-human creatures of wastelands and forests.[26] These renderings of Jerome's pilosi are dependent on the Glossa ordinaria, which adds that pilosi may indicate satyrs or kinds of shaggy, goat-shaped demons.[27] The Glossa ordinaria also provides several meaning for sirens, among them, monstrous serpents, crested and able to fly.[28] By choosing this definition, the Wycliffite translators implicitly reject another possibility raised by the Glossa ordinaria, that the term means creatures who are fish below and women above; they deceive sailors who neglect to block their ears against the sirens' sweet songs. Despite the Wycliffite rejection of this latter meaning, the sense of an unattached, dangerous, tempting sexuality apparently remains (although there are no human inhabitants to be tempted), and the Vulgate's sirenae in delubris voluptatis appears as the mysterious and haunting 'fliynge serpentis in the templis of lust'.

Related problems of language and meaning trouble the later Wycliffite version of Isaiah 34: 13–14, which is similarly dependent on the Glossa ordinaria:

> And fendis and wondurful beestis, lijk men in the hiȝere part and lijk assis in the nethir part, and an heeri schulen meete; oon schal crie to an other. Lamya schal ligge there, and foond rest there to hir silf.

The verses are heavily annotated, 'fendis' being glossed as 'wodewosis', 'wondurful bees-tis' as 'martyn-apis and wielde cattis', and 'Lamya' (the word itself taken directly from the Vulgate) as 'a wondirful beest, lijk a womman above, and hath horse feet bynethe, and sleeth hir owne whelpis'.

What is notable about the Wycliffite versions is the sense of strain with which it renders, for English readers, the Vulgate's translation of verses that seem relatively at home in their Latin garb. Jerome inherited a Christianity that had learned to live within Roman culture, including its indebtedness to the Greeks, and had come to terms with pagan concepts. The clearest expression of this is Augustine's principle that the pagan demi-gods are actually demons. Let us assume that, in translating Isaiah's prophecy, Jerome is reacting to what he has picked up from the Hebrew of the Bible and from the Jewish community with which he was in contact: the suspicion that the image of desolation represented in chapters 13 and 34 is intended to be disgusting as well as terrifying. This impression would

---

[26] See wōde-wōse (n.), sense a, Robert E. Lewis et al. (eds), Middle English Dictionary (Ann Arbor, Mich.: University of Michigan Press, 1952–2001). Online version in Frances McSparran et al. (eds), Middle English Compendium (Ann Arbor, Mich.: University of Michigan Press, 2002–6), <http://ets.umdl.umich.edu/m/med> (2002 release).

[27] Completed in the thirteenth century, and often supplemented with the comments of Jerome and Nicholas of Lyra, the Glossa ordinaria was the standard commentary on the Bible in the Middle Ages. For Wycliffite usage of it, see Mary Dove, The First English Bible: The Text and Context of the Wycliffite Versions (Cambridge: Cambridge University Press, 2007), esp. 83–102. The most convenient way to consult the Glossa ordinaria is via the Lollard Society's online edition <http://lollardsociety.org>, which reproduces the Bibliorum Sacrorum cum glossa ordinaria, 6 vols (Venice, 1603).

[28] This definition is in fact found in Jerome's commentary on Isaiah. Wycliffite translators would also have had Isidore's authority for this rendering of sirens. See Isidore of Seville, Etymologies, ed. Stephen A. Barney et al. (Cambridge: Cambridge University Press, 2006), 257.

have been conveyed by Hebrew words that are obscure and (except for *sa'ir* and *tannim*) extremely rare, possibly because they belong to demotic speech and, if not tabooed, are not commonly written down.

How, not knowing precisely what they mean, is he going to convey this impression to his readers? He draws upon the monsters of the dominant Roman culture that are most frightening in their human-animal hybridity and ferocity and most degraded in their sexuality. Thus *sa'ir* becomes a reference to goat-footed satyrs; *iim*, a reference to onocentaurs (half man, half ass); *lilit*, a reference to Lamia, who is explained as being like one of the Furies, or Erinyes, with the face of a woman and the body of a beast; *ziim*, a reference to demonic, phantasmal wild animals; *tannim*, a reference to sirens, or monstrous, flying serpents or dragons; *ohim*, a reference to Typhon, the gigantic serpentine monster of Greek myth.[29] Yet ironically, because these are known, even literary, monsters, the disgust and fear they engender in readers is limited. One scholar has suggested that the inclusion of such monsters in his text may be part of Jerome's 'characteristically Latin solution to what may be termed the "literary problem"' of the scriptures: that is, that the old Latin Bible was held to be stylistically inferior to classical writers.[30] Jerome's determination to return to the Hebrew (even if he was inconsistent in practice) has among its motives the desire to produce a Latin translation with greater appeal to a sophisticated reading public. This determination, however, limits the ability of his translation to convey the apocalyptic horror of the Hebrew passages, making it difficult, in turn, for Wycliffite translators to make genuine sense of what they are translating. Their translation shows them trying to explain names that they do not entirely understand, not knowing that those names are substitutes for what Jerome himself does not entirely understand.

The Geneva translators undoubtedly avail themselves of the insights offered by Jerome's translation. But they are not as dependent on his Latin—with its cultural entailments—as the Wycliffite translators had been, for European knowledge of Hebrew had grown considerably by the middle of the sixteenth century.[31] Thus, the Geneva translators inform the reader: 'we have in many places reserved the Ebrewe phrases, notwithstanding that thei may seme somewhat hard in their eares that are not wel practised and also delite in the swete sounding phrases of the holy Scriptures'. Their principle, they explain, is to keep 'the proprietie of the wordes, considering that the Apostles who spake and wrote to the Gentiles in the Greke tongue, rather constrayned them to the lively phrase of the Ebrewe, then enterprised farre by mollifying their langage to speake as the Gentils did'.[32] If under

---

[29] Despite his claim to have returned to the Hebrew, Jerome relies heavily here on Greek translations of the Bible. *Lamia*, analogous to Lilith, gets her horse-feet from the Septuagint, where the Hebrew *lilit* is translated *onokentauros*, and her name from the Greek of Symmachos. Jerome's explanations of *lilit, ziim, ohim, iim, tannim*, and *pilosa* are in his commentary on Isaiah: *S. Eusebii Hieronymi stridonensis presbyteri commentariorum in Isaiam prophetam libri duodeviginti*, PL 24.159B–159C (Isa. 13: 21–2) and 372D–373B (Isa. 34: 21–2). See 'Lilith' in Toorn et al., *Dictionary of Deities and Demons*, 520–1, whose editors speculate that the name Lamia 'might ultimately derive from Akkadian Lamashtu' (521).

[30] Adam Kamesar, *Jerome, Greek Scholarship, and the Hebrew Bible: A Study of the 'Quaestiones Hebraicae in Genesim'* (Oxford: Clarendon Press, 1995), 46.

[31] The growth of Hebrew learning and its importance for biblical translations is traced by Basil Hall in 'Biblical Scholarship: Editions and Commentaries', in S. L. Greenslade (ed.), *The Cambridge History of the Bible*, iii. *The West from the Reformation to the Present Day* (Cambridge: Cambridge University Press, 1963), 38–93, esp. 43–8.

[32] Epistle to the Reader, 4ʳ.

'langage' we include the cultural assumptions lying behind choices about translation, then this principle implies rebuke to Jerome. In sharp contrast to his practice, the Geneva translators decline to render into English words that are particularly resistant to 'mollifying', words such as *ohim, ziim,* and *iim,* as we see in their version of Isaiah 13:

> 21 But ᴾZiim shal lodge there, and their houses shalbe ful of Ohim: Ostriches shal dwell there, & the Satyrs shal dance there.
> 22 And Iim shal crye in their palaces, and dragons in their pleasant palaces: and the time thereof is readie to come, & the dayes thereof shal not be prolonged.

This, we might say, is an uncomfortable translation, even at first glance an un-English one, for the 'uncertaine' words are imported into the text. The Geneva translators use the advantage of working from the Hebrew to wrest the passage in Isaiah from its immersion in Roman culture—and 'Roman' applies both to classical Rome and to the Rome of the papacy—and replace Roman superstition with genuine mystery. The inclusion of the transliterated Hebrew words forces readers to confront the strangeness of the passage, which the marginal note at *Ziim* does nothing to lessen, although it casts that strangeness in an English rather than a Roman mould: 'Which were ether wilde beasts, or foules, or wicked spirits, where by Satan deluded man, as by the fairies, gobblins and suche like fantasies'.[33] This stern condemnation of fairies and goblins anticipates the kind of opposition aroused by the publication of the *Book of Sports* in 1618, which was held by zealous Protestants to link old pastimes to folk beliefs and superstitions, and these to an authorized version of Englishness.

The Geneva version adopts for Isaiah 34 a strategy similar to that used for Isaiah 13:

> 13 And it shal bring forthe thornes in [the] palaces thereof, nettles & thistles in [the] strong holdes thereof, and it shalbe an habitacion for dragons and a court for ostriches.
> 14 There shal ⁿmete also Ziim and Iim, and the Satyre shal crye to his fellowe, and the shriche owle shal rest there, & shal finde for her self a quiet dwelling.

The marginal note at verse 14 merely refers the reader to Isaiah 13: 21. Here, in the vicinity of *Ziim* and *Iim,* the satyr loses its classical familiarity, its cry drawing attention away from any associations with lust. Lamia or Lilith has been replaced by a 'schriche owl', a rendering which hints at the scream of storm winds but avoids imputing a demonic personification to them. It also alludes to the unclean fowls of Revelation 19: 18, summoned to prepare for a 'supper' of carrion. At the slaying of the Beast and his followers, says the summoning angel, you may eat 'the flesh of Kings, & the flesh of his Captaines, and the flesh of mightie men, and the flesh of horses, and of them that sit on them, and the flesh of all fre me[n] and bondemen, and of smale and great' (v. 18). When the slaughter comes to pass, 'the foules were filled full with their flesh' (v. 21).

There is no hint of sexual depravity in the Geneva's rendering of Isaiah 13 and 34. What remains is an almost literally unspeakable strangeness. Whatever creatures are going to haunt the ruined cities are too terrible to be imagined, certainly too terrible to be controlled by a familiar or even a new naming. With their strategy of intermixing transliterated and by implication untranslatable Hebrew words, the Geneva translators authenticate readers' contact

[33] *Ohim* and *Iim* are not glossed, presumably because the note on *Ziim* is regarded as sufficient to explain them.

with the Word by showing it in its true awe-fullness. The effect is to make clear that earthly notions of order, rule, and convention are as nothing in the face of the Almighty's wrath.

Let us now turn to the King James translation of the verses in Isaiah 13:

> 21 But †wilde beastes of the desert shall lye there, and their houses shalbe full of †dolefull creatures, and ‖owles shall dwell there, and Satyres shall daunce there.
> 22 And the wilde †beastes of the Ilands shal cry in their ‖ desolate houses, and dragons in their pleasant palaces: and her time is neere to come, and her dayes shall not be prolonged.

The verses bristle with superscripted symbols. F. H. A. Scrivener's comprehensive study of the annotations of the 1611 King James Bible is of little help in analysing the nature of the glosses. There are 6,637 marginal notes in the King James Bible, Scrivener states, of which 4,111 'express the more literal meaning of the original Hebrew or Chaldee'; 2,156 'give alternative renderings (indicated by the word "‖Or")'; sixty-three state 'the meaning of Proper Names'; 240 harmonize 'the text with other passages of Scripture'; and the last sixty-seven 'refer to various readings of the original' (thirty-one of which set the Masoretic revision of the Hebrew against the reading in the text).[34] The kind of marginal notes attached to 'wilde beastes' and 'doleful creatures' is not explicitly mentioned among Scrivener's categories, although perhaps they are to be found among the thirty-six notes remaining after the Masoretic revisions are excluded. The marginal note at the 'wilde beastes' of Isaiah 13: 21 is 'Heb. Ziim'; the note at 'doleful creatures' is 'Hebr. Ochim', and that at the 'wilde beastes' of verse 22 is 'Heb. Iim'. The translation of Isaiah 34 is similarly glossed:

> 13 And thornes shall come up in her palaces, nettles and brambles in the fortresses thereof: and it shalbe an habitation of dragons, and a court for ‖owles.
> 14 The wilde †beasts of the desert shall also meete with the †wilde beasts of the Iland and the satyre shall cry to his felow, the ‖shrichowle also shall rest there, & finde for her selfe a place of rest.

The first 'wilde beasts' of verse 14 is marked as 'Heb. Zijm', the second, as 'Heb Iijm'. 'Schrichowle' is glossed: 'Or, night-monster'. These and the glosses of Isaiah 13: 21–2 are unlike the others categorized by Scrivener; they are 'of a peculiar kind by themselves'.[35] They seem to constitute an admission that the English translation is conjectural, thus conforming to the preference implied by Miles Smith's dictum, that fearfulness better beseems a translator than confidence.

The strategy of the King James Bible translators, in dealing with the difficult names in Isaiah, might be called the opposite of that employed by the Geneva translators. In the King James Bible, the transliterated Hebrew word, or, in the case of lilit, the more frightening meaning, is banished to the margin. Let us ask, first, if these annotations accomplish what Miles Smith states that 'a margine' ought to accomplish. Do they 'admonish the Reader to seeke further, and not to conclude or dogmatize upon this or that peremptorily?' Probably not, unless the reader has enough Hebrew to know that ziim, iim, and ohim are rare and special words, or enough curiosity to try to work out the relationship between a screech owl and a night monster. Surely an ordinary reader—a reader who does not know Hebrew—would glance at the marginal notes and, after perhaps a moment of puzzlement or wonder, pay them no further

---

[34] F. H. A. Scrivener, *The Authorized Edition of the English Bible (1611): Its Subsequent Reprints and Modern Representatives* (Cambridge: Cambridge University Press, 1884), 41–2.

[35] John Ray uses the phrase in his classification of birds that cannot fly, such as the ostrich, emu, and dodo: *The Ornithology of Francis Willughby* (London, 1678), 149.

attention. Where in any case would such a reader go 'to seeke further'? The King James Bible's glosses on the verses in Isaiah do not make the interpretation of its strange words seem more doubtful but rather make them seem more fixed and impervious to alternative readings.

Because the context in which the words occur is the representation of desolation brought about by God's punishment of a sinful nation, one cannot ignore the political dimension of the King James Bible's treatment of *ziim, iim,* and *ohim*. While it would not be altogether accurate to say that these beasts are naturalized, the translation certainly downplays their strangeness. In the most general sense, a reader is discouraged from seeking to experience here a unique confrontation with the overpowering and mysterious word of God. Indeed, the King James Bible's Hebrew glosses impress upon a reader the need to bow to the linguistic expertise of those trained in such things, that is, the clergy—a subtle lesson, perhaps, that a questioning frame of mind (the frame of mind that might lead to rebelliousness) is undesirable and futile. Relegating *ziim, iim,* and *ohim* to the margins considerably reduces the sense of a desolation so overwhelming, to changes so incomprehensible, that our world with its familiar points of reference (including creatures) will have disappeared or been replaced by creatures so 'other' and terrifying that we have no names for them.

Why it would be in the interests of the translators of the royally authorized version to reduce the strangeness of Isaiah's picture of a desolated landscape is fairly plain to see. The Bible in the sixteenth and seventeenth centuries was a mine of divinely sanctioned precedents.[36] Its picture of the possibility of radical, cataclysmic change must necessarily be perceived as dangerous to those with a stake in the status quo. Isaiah's prophecies of such change cannot be made to disappear, but the change itself can be made to seem less threatening. In the King James Bible, the transformed landscape envisioned by Isaiah has the feel of Mercutio's tale of Queen Mab: it is fanciful and familiar at once. The excitement has been excised along with the danger and the mystery, an excising aided by the gentle rhythm of the verses—and we are reminded of the Geneva translators' recognition that apocalyptic horror and 'swete sounding phrases' do not accord. Indeed, the 'pointing' of the King James Bible's verses seems designed to convey a sense of security, which may suggest another dimension to the famous announcement on the title-page: 'Appointed to be read in Churches'.

The King James Bible did not immediately oust the People's Bible from its place in the love and approval of the public. The Geneva version was still being published in the 1640s, and of course copies remained in English households long after this date.[37] As Gordon Campbell notes, 'Puritan distrust of the Authorized Version was deeply rooted', distrust emerging in 1653 in a bill before Parliament 'to enable revision of … its inaccuracies and "prelatical language" '.[38] But after the world turned upside down again at the Restoration,

---

[36] See e.g. the chapters by Andrew Bradstock, Kevin Killeen, Emma Major, Anne Lake Prescott, and Yvonne Sherwood in this volume.

[37] F. F. Bruce points out that '[t]he *Soldier's Pocket Bible*, issued in 1643 for the use of Oliver Cromwell's army, consisted of a selection of extracts from the Geneva Bible': *The English Bible: A History of Translations from the Earliest English Version to the New English Bible*, rev. edn (London: Lutterworth Press, 1970), 92. The last early modern printing of the Geneva Bible in its entirety was in 1644.

[38] Gordon Campbell, 'Fishing in Other Men's Waters: Bunyan and the Theologians', in N. H. Keeble (ed.), *John Bunyan: Conventicle and Parnassus: Tercentenary Essays* (Oxford: Clarendon Press, 1988), 137–51, 139. Campbell observes that Bunyan (1628–88) seems to rely in his early works on the Geneva or other sixteenth-century Bibles, and in his later works, on the KJB, a suggestion that allows us to gauge the acceptance of the latter over the course of the seventeenth century (Campbell, 'Fishing', 138).

the Geneva's crowded margins with their eschatological interest and overt polemical intent came to seem outdated. Without the Geneva's presence as a reminder that the Bible had been and could be treated in a different way, readers came to accept the minimal annotations and editorial aids of the King James Bible as unobjectionable and normal—as, indeed, *the* Bible. The King James Bible's clean margins made the Bible's rough places plain, or apparently plain, which suited a new order that regarded religious fervour as dangerous enthusiasm. It is not too great an exaggeration to say that, by the eighteenth century, the King James Bible had come to function as an English Vulgate.

FURTHER READING

Barton, John. *Isaiah 1–39*, Old Testament Guides (Sheffield: Sheffield Academic Press, 1995).

Betteridge, Maurice. 'The Bitter Notes: The Geneva Bible and its Annotations'. *Sixteenth Century Journal*, 14/1 (1983): 41–62.

Blenkinsopp, Joseph. *Isaiah 1–39: A New Translation with Introduction and Commentary*, The Anchor Bible (New York: Doubleday-Anchor Bible, 2000).

Bruce, F. F. *The English Bible: A History of Translations from the Earliest English Version to the New English Bible*, rev. edn (London: Lutterworth Press, 1970).

Campbell, Gordon. *Bible: The Story of the King James Version 1611–2011* (Oxford: Oxford University Press, 2011).

Dove, Mary. *The First English Bible: The Text and Context of the Wycliffite Versions* (Cambridge: Cambridge University Press, 2007).

Firth, Katharine R. *The Apocalyptic Tradition in Reformation Britain, 1530–1645* (Oxford: Oxford University Press, 1979).

Greenslade, S. L., ed. *The Cambridge History of the Bible*, iii. *The West from the Reformation to the Present Day* (Cambridge: Cambridge University Press, 1963).

Miscall, Peter D. *Isaiah 34–35: A Nightmare/A Dream, Journal for the Study of the Old Testament*, supplement series, 281 (Sheffield: Sheffield Academic Press, 1999).

Muilenburg, James. 'The Literary Character of Isaiah 34'. *Journal of Biblical Literature*, 59/3 (1940): 339–65.

Norton, David. *The King James Bible: A Short History from Tyndale to Today* (Cambridge: Cambridge University Press, 2011).

Porter, J. R., and W. M. S. Russell, eds. *Animals in Folklore* (Cambridge: D. S. Brewer and Rowman & Littlefield for the Folklore Society, 1978).

Slights, William W. E. '"Marginal Notes that Spoile the Text": Scriptural Annotation in the English Renaissance'. *Huntington Library Quarterly*, 55/2 (1992): 255–78.

Toorn, Karel van der, Bob Becking, and Pieter W. van der Horst, eds. *Dictionary of Deities and Demons in the Bible*, 2nd edn (Leiden: Brill, 1999).

Williamson, H. G. M. *The Book Called Isaiah: Deutero-Isaiah's Role in Composition and Redaction* (Oxford: Clarendon Press, 1994).

CHAPTER 5

THE ROMAN INKHORN: RELIGIOUS RESISTANCE TO LATINISM IN EARLY MODERN ENGLAND

JAMIE H. FERGUSON

SIXTEENTH- and early seventeenth-century English is notable for the volume of borrow-ings from other languages.[1] These borrowings served a dual purpose. On the one hand, they added to the supply of concepts (or 'matter') expressible in English, often to fill seman-tic gaps in the language. Richard Sherry's preface to his *Treatise of Schemes and Tropes* (1550) asks rhetorically: 'who hath not in hys mouthe nowe thys worde Paraphrasis, home-lies, usurped, abolished, with manye other lyke? And what marvail is it if these words have not bene used here tofore, seynge there was no suche thynge in oure Englishe tongue where unto they shuld be applied?'[2] The word *paraphrase* is borrowed from the Latin (*paraph-rasis*) in the early sixteenth century to describe a genre of biblical interpretation new to English. The earliest usage of *paraphrase* recorded in the *Oxford English Dictionary* is from Nicholas Udall's English edition of *The First Tome or Volume of the Paraphrase of Erasmus upon the Newe Testamente* (1548), but the word is used already in 1532 in the prologue to Miles Coverdale's version of the Latin paraphrase of the Psalter by Jan van Campen.[3] In the same passage from *The Treatise of Schemes and Tropes* just cited, Sherry describes the other rationale for borrowings: namely, to increase the supply of synonyms in the target lan-guage, in service of the rhetorical ideal of *copia*. Sherry praises 'certayne godlye and well learned men, which by their great studye enrychynge our tongue both wyth matter and

---

[1] Terttu Nevalinen, 'Early Modern English Lexis and Semantics', in Roger Lass (ed.), *The Cambridge History of the English Language*, iii. *1476–1776* (Cambridge: Cambridge University Press, 1999), 336.

[2] Richard Sherry, *A Treatise of Schemes and Tropes: And His Translation of The Education of Children by Desiderius Erasmus*, ed. Herbert W. Hilderbrandt (Gainesville, Fla.: Scholars' Facsimiles and Reprints, 1961), A2ʳ⁻ᵛ.

[3] *A Paraphrasis upon All the Psalmes of David, Made by Johannes Campensis, Reader of the Hebrue Lecture in the Universite of Louvane, and Translated Out of Latine into Englisshe* (London, 1539).

words, have endevoured to make it so copyous and plentyfull that therein it maye compare wyth anye other whiche so ever is the best' (A2ʳ⁻ᵛ). Following the dual track set out by Erasmus's *De duplici copia rerum ac verborum*, Sherry seconds Elyot's and others' projects of 'enrychynge our tongue *both wyth matter and words*' (my emphasis).[4]

The inkhorn represents superfluous—and therefore affected—foreign borrowings (especially from Latin). The inkhorn is a ready figure of comedy in Renaissance England, as elsewhere in Europe: one thinks not only of Shakespeare's Armado and Holofernes, for example, but also of Rabelais's *écolier limousin*. In *Love's Labor's Lost*, the 'peregrinate' Armado, hoping both to demonstrate that he is one of those who has 'eat paper and drunk ink' and to show off his relationship with the king, brags that 'it will please His Grace … sometime to lean upon my poor shoulder and with his royal finger thus dally with my excrement, with my mustachio'.[5] The trouble with the concept of the inkhorn is that the root of the complaint, verbal superfluity, is one of the two basic *raisons d'être* for borrowing. What separates the ridiculous Armado from Erasmus, who comes up with more than one hundred ways to thank someone for a letter in his *De copia*? What is the difference between admirable and laughable verbal superfluity? What renders Armado's *excrement* a crass joke rather than the healthy outgrowth (Latin *excrementum*) of the language? One obvious difference between Erasmus's verbal excess and Armado's is that Erasmus is writing in Latin, while Armado is speaking Latinate English. Erasmus's superfluity represents the harnessing of the full resources of his language, while Armado's demonstrates a subordination of his language to Latin. Armado is laughable because he prefers, or feels he must pretend to prefer, Latin to English: the comedy derives from his use of Latinate words with utter disregard for the meanings these words have taken on in English usage.

The trouble with the inkhorn, then, is not the borrowing of unneeded synonyms but the subordination of English to other tongues. It is a matter of linguistic politics, the status relationships among languages. The relationship between English and Latin is a particular case, largely because of the strong association between the Latin language and the Roman Church. Charles Barber makes the general point that, 'because of the Catholic use of the Vulgate, and insistence on Latin as the liturgical language, there was a tendency to associate Latin with Catholicism, which worked to the disadvantage of Latin in strongly Protestant circles'.[6] Indeed, Protestant resistance to Latinism is easy to document in early modern England: John Rainolds's characterization of Latin as 'the Romish tongue (so to call it) and language of Poperie' is among the most explicit of many such statements.[7] A host of other Protestant writers in the period seek out terms at the Saxon *fontes* of the English language as an alternative to Latinate English. The most uniform application of this principle is likely Sir John Cheke's unpublished version of Matthew (c.1550), where Christ speaks in *biwordes* (parables) and is *crossed* (crucified) prior to his *gainrising* (resurrection).[8] William Fulke, in his *Defense of the*

---

[4] Charles Barber, 'Inkhorn Terms', in Barber, Joan C. Beal, and Philip A. Shaw (eds), *The English Language: A Historical Introduction*, 2nd edn (New York: Cambridge University Press, 2009), 189.

[5] William Shakespeare, *The Complete Works of Shakespeare*, gen. ed. David Bevington, 5th edn (New York: Pearson, 2004), *Love's Labor's Lost*, 4.2.25–6; 5.1.98–101.

[6] *Early Modern English*, rev. edn (Edinburgh: Edinburgh University Press, 1997), 48.

[7] John Rainolds, *The Summe of the Conference betwene John Rainoldes and John Hart: Touching the Head and the Faith of the Church* (London, 1584), 20.

[8] James Goodwin (ed.), *The Gospel according to Saint Matthew, and Part of the First Chapter of the Gospel according to Saint Mark, Translated into English from the Greek, with Original Notes by Sir John Cheke* (London: Pickering, 1843).

Sincere and True Translations of the Holy Scriptures into the English Tongue (1583), draws a connection between the original Greek of the New Testament and older forms of English: 'the etymology [of church] is from the Greek word κυριακη, which was used of Christians for the place of their holy meetings, signifying "the Lord's house"; therefore in the northern, which is the more ancient English speech, is called by contraction *kyrke*, more near to the sound of the Greek word'.[9] However fancifully, Fulke seeks forms of English prior to the influence of Latin usage.

At the same time, of course, any number of 'strongly Protestant' English writers wrote extensively in Latin: William Whitaker, for example, replied to Nicholas Sander's *De visibili monarchia ecclesiae* (1571) with his own Latin polemic, *Ad Nicolai Sanderi demonstrationes quadraginta* (1583). In the preface 'to the Christian reader' of this work, Whitaker includes criticism of the 'unusual and unnatural novelty of words' (*verborum inusitatem & prodigiosam novitatem*) of the Rheims English New Testament (1582).[10] It was only when he was answered in turn, this time in English, by William Rainolds's *A Refutation of Sundry Reprehensions, Cavils, and False Sleightes* (1583) that Whitaker turned to English, in his *An Answere to a Certeine Booke, Written by M. William Rainolds* (1585). The fact that a staunch Protestant like Whitaker could write in Latin against the Latinism of the Rheims New Testament suggests that he was not opposed to Latin but to Latinate English. Whitaker was opposed to writing English as if it were Latin, to subordinating English usage and vocabulary to Latin.

Barber's observation needs to be refined: early modern English Protestants such as Whitaker associated Latinate English, rather than Latin *per se*, with Roman Catholicism. As in the example of Armado, though in a very different context, Latinate English threatens the autonomy of English. According to the *OED*, the first use of *inkhorn* as a description of bookish diction was in an anti-Catholic tract, John Bale's *Yet a Course at the Romyshe Foxe* (1543), where Bale describes the Latin tags *secundum esse* and *exercitium* used by proponents of papal supremacy as 'Ynkehorne termes'.[11] Bale opposes the subordination of English royal power to the papacy; he extends his defence of English ecclesiastical autonomy to apply as well to the integrity of the English language. Characteristically, Bale's accounts of English religion and language converge around a shared preoccupation with English autonomy.

The history of Latinate English in its religious dimension might be said to begin with the list of corrections to the Great Bible that Bishop Stephen Gardiner proposed in 1542: the list included Latinate terms 'that [Gardiner] desired, as far as possible, either retained in their natural state or turned into English speech as closely as possible' (*vel in sua natura retineri, vel quam accommodatissime fieri possit in Anglicum sermonem verti*), both for their inherent and native sense and for the majesty of the thing represented (*pro eorum germano et nativo intellectu et rei majestate*).[12] Gardiner's preference for Latinate neologisms has

---

[9] *A Defence of the Sincere and True Translations of the Holy Scriptures into the English Tongue*, ed. Charles H. Hartshorne (Cambridge: Cambridge University Press, 1843; repr. Eugene, Or.: Wipf & Stock, 2004), 231. For the association between the northern English dialect and English archaism and the literary uses to which this dialect was put in Renaissance England, see Paula Blank, *Broken English: Dialects and the Politics of Language in Renaissance Writings* (London: Routledge, 1996), ch. 4.

[10] *Ad Nicolai Sanderi demonstrationes quadraginta* (London, 1583), **7ʳ.

[11] *Yet a Course at the Romyshe Foxe* (Zurich [i.e. Antwerp], 1543), H3ᵛ.

[12] A. W. Pollard (ed.), *Records of the English Bible: The Documents Relating to the Translation and Publication of the Bible in English, 1525–1611* (Repr. Mansfield Centre, Conn.: Martino, 1974), 273, 274–5n.

nothing to do with increasing the store of English vocabulary; his aim, rather, is to make English pay homage to the special religious significance of the Latin Vulgate. Gardiner at once subordinates the English Church to Rome and the English language to Latin. The English language here acts as a proxy for the English Church: as the language is subordinated to Latin, so the Church of England is subordinated to Rome. Gardiner's brand of Latinism affronts the autonomy both of the English language and of the English Church.

A key element in defining the expressive capacities of early modern English was the establishment of the language's autonomy vis-à-vis Latin. To what extent does English possess its own autonomous semantics and grammar, and to what extent is English subordinate to the more learned languages, such as Latin? Critical accounts of the 'inkhorn controversy' describe an initially impoverished English increased by a stream of borrowings through the early and middle part of the sixteenth century until it reached a kind of fullness or self-sufficiency, at which point the flow of borrowings slowed down.[13] Such accounts imply that this flow and ebb of borrowings reflect the practical needs of vernacular expressiveness and copiousness: they leave out the threat posed by the inkhorn to the linguistic and ecclesiastic autonomy of English—a convergence of language and church out of which the very term emerged and to which much of the early modern English resistance to Latinism refers.

Bishop Gardiner's proposed changes were not incorporated into the Great Bible, but his approach to English Latinism in the translation of the Bible did come to fruition in the Rheims New Testament of 1582. In the same year, the Roman Catholic exile Gregory Martin published a justification of the Rheims version via an attack on the whole line of Protestant English Bibles, the *Discoverie of the Manifold Corruptions of the Holy Scriptures by the Heretikes of our Daies*; Martin's *Discoverie* was answered, paragraph by paragraph, in Fulke's *Defense* in 1583. Also in 1583, as already mentioned, William Whitaker included an attack on the Rheims New Testament in his *Ad Nicolai Sanderi demonstrationes quadraginta*, which William Rainolds answered with *A Refutation*. In 1588 Edward Bulkeley and George Wither published brief attacks on the Rheims New Testament's prefatory remarks and annotations respectively,[14] before Fulke published his comparative volume, *The Text of the New Testament of Jesus Christ, Translated Out of the Vulgar Latine by the Papists of the Traiterous Seminarie at Rhemes. ... Whereunto is Added the Translation Out of the Original Greeke, Commonly Used in the Church of England*, with detailed answers to the Rheims New Testament's entire apparatus, in 1589 (see Figure 5.1); Fulke describes his work as a stopgap in anticipation of a fuller response to the Roman Catholic Bible. He

[13] R. F. Jones, *The Triumph of English: A Survey of Opinions Concerning the Vernacular from the Introduction of Printing to the Restoration* (Stanford, Calif.: Stanford University Press, 1953), 68–141; Barber, 'Inkhorn Terms', 189–90; Veré L. Rubel, *Poetic Diction in the English Renaissance from Skelton through Spenser* (New York: Modern Language Association, 1941), 1–13, 102–18; Alvin Vos, 'Humanistic Standards of Diction in the Inkhorn Controversy', *Studies in Philology*, 73 (1976): 376–96; Matti Rissanen, '"Strange and inkhorne termes": Loan-Words as Style Markers in the Prose of Edward Hall, Thomas Elyot, Thomas More and Roger Ascham', in Håkan Ringbom (ed.), *Style and Text: Studies Presented to Nils Erik Enkvist* (Stockholm: Skriptor, 1975), 250–62; James Sledd, 'A Footnote on the Inkhorn Controversy', *University of Texas Studies in English*, 28 (1949): 49–56.

[14] Edward Bulkeley, *An Answere to Ten Frivolous and Foolish Reasons, Set Downe by the Rhemish Jesuits and Papists in their Preface before the New Testament by Them Lately Translated into English* (London, 1588); George Wither, *A View of the Marginal Notes of the Popish Testament, Translated into English by the English Fugitive Papists Resiant [sic] at Rhemes in France* (London, 1588).

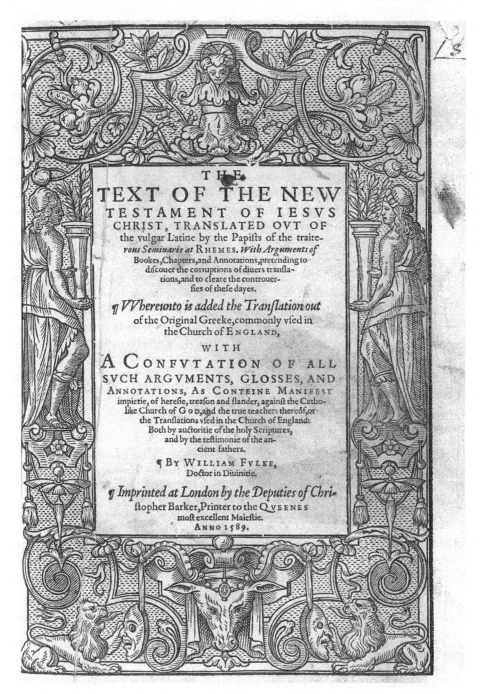

THE
TEXT OF THE NEW
TESTAMENT OF IESVS
CHRIST, TRANSLATED OVT OF
the vulgar Latine by the Papists of the traiterous Seminarie at RHEMES. *With Arguments of*
Bookes, Chapters, and Annotations, pretending to
discouer the corruptions of diuers translations, and to cleare the controuer-
sies of these dayes.

¶ *VVhereunto is added the Translation out*
of the Original Greeke, commonly vsed in
the Church of ENGLAND,

WITH
A CONFVTATION OF ALL
SVCH ARGVMENTS, GLOSSES, AND
ANNOTATIONS, AS CONTEINE MANIFEST
impietie, of heresie, treason and slander, against the Catholike Church of GOD, and the true teachers thereof, or
the Translations vsed in the Church of England:
Both by auctoritie of the holy Scriptures,
and by the testimonie of the ancient fathers.

¶ By WILLIAM FVLKE,
Doctor in Diuinitie.

¶ *Imprinted at London by the Deputies of Chri-*
stopher Barker, Printer to the QVEENES
most excellent Maiestie.
ANNO 1589.

FIGURE 5.1 Title-page of William Fulke, *The Text of the New Testament of Jesus Christ*
(London: Deputies of Christopher Barker, 1589). York Minster Library, OL; I.I.25.

was likely thinking of Thomas Cartwright, who published an *Answere to the Preface of the Rhemish Testament* in 1602, later incorporated into a posthumous volume (1618) answering the annotations as well and reprinting the translation: *A Confutation of the Rhemists Translation, Glosses and Annotations on the New Testament.*[15] The 1582 publication of the Rheims New Testament and Martin's accompanying *Discoverie* thus instigated a flurry of polemics concerning the English Bible. An important subject in these polemics is the Latinate English of the Rheims translation, i.e. the degree to which the English Bible should maintain its autonomy vis-à-vis the Latin Vulgate.

According to Martin's *Discoverie*, the root of the dispute between the Protestants and Roman Catholics is 'the double signification of words'. The Protestants tend to take words in their 'original property', or etymological sense, the Roman Catholics favouring the 'usual taking thereof in all vulgar speech and writing', or derivative sense.[16] Like other Roman Catholic polemicists, Martin emphasizes that the Bible is subject to 'the approved sense of the holy fathers and catholic church'—the church being the one historical institution able to claim divine warrant (*Defense*, 9). For Martin, the 'common use and signification of the word in vulgar speech, and in the holy scriptures [i.e. in English and in the Vulgate]' (*Defense*, 200) alters the 'original property' of biblical words according to 'ecclesiastic use and appropriation'. For example, he writes, '*episcopus*, a Greek word, in the original sense is "every overseer," as Tully useth it, and other profane writers; but among Christians, in ecclesiastical speech, it is "a bishop"; and no man will say, "My lord overseer of London," for "my lord bishop"' (*Defense*, 217).

William Rainolds, in a concurrent exchange with William Whitaker, describes the Protestants' 'common and vulgar kind of disputing, that is, upon the first and original derivation and signification of Ecclesiastic words'.[17] Rainolds illustrates with a parody of a Protestant 'superintendent' speaking to his 'synagoge':

> I that am your *elder* or *surveyer* and *superintendent*, placed in this *synagoge* by the *holy wynd*, for the feeding of your *carcasses*, do denounce unto you in the name of the *Anointed* our *Baal*, that except yow with more devotion come to receave the *thankesgeving*, and performe better your promise made to God in *washing*, you shal be condemned bodie and *carcas* to the *grave*, with the *slaunderers*, I say with the *Lord of a flye* and his *messengers*. (269)

Few of the terms here mocked ever made their way into an English Bible, but several were defended by English Protestant translators as legitimate alternatives to the more usual biblical terms. The substitution of *elder* for *priest* is a central point of contention between

[15] *A Confutation of the Rhemists Translation, Glosses and Annotations on the New Testament* (Leiden, 1618). This volume seems to have gone unfinished by Cartwright; Fulke's answers to the Rheims annotations replace Cartwright at Rev. 16: 6. A preface to the posthumous volume notes also that Fulke has supplied certain 'small defects by Mice' (A2ᵛ). The Roman Catholic translators published their version of the Old Testament in 1609–10; one of their defenders, John Heigham, published *The Gagge of the Reformed Gospell* in 1623, answered by Richard Bernard in 1626 (*Rhemes against Rome*) and by Richard Montagu in 1624 (*A Gagg for the New Gospell? No: a New Gagg for an Old Goose*).

[16] William Fulke, *Defense of the Sincere and True Translations of the Holie Scriptures into the English Tong* (1583) (which reprints Martin's *Discovery* in full), 217. Subsequent references to Martin's *Discovery* are cited from Fulke's *Defense*.

[17] *A Refutation of Sundry Reprehensions, Cavils, and False Sleightes, by Which M. Whitaker Laboureth to Deface the Late English Translation, and Catholike Annotations of the New Testament, and the Booke of Discovery of Heretical Corruptions* (Paris, 1583), 264.

Thomas More and William Tyndale; it forms the subject of chapter 6 in the exchange between Martin and Fulke, but there is little there not already stated in the earlier polemics.

The substitution of 'carcass' and 'grave' for 'soul' and 'hell' does not come up between More and Tyndale, whereas it is a topic of running debate between Martin and Fulke: as Martin points out, Beza's New Testament (1576) renders Acts 2: 27, 'Non derelinques cadaver meum in sepulchro'[18] (in Martin's English, 'Thou shalt not leave my carcase in the grave': *Defense* 280). Both the Geneva Bible and Laurence Tomson's English version of Beza's Latin translation render this line 'thou wilt not leave my soule in grave [sic]', Geneva annotating 'soule', 'Or, life, or, persone'.[19] Beza's version was obnoxious to the orthodox Roman Catholic belief in the passage of Christ's soul through hell following the crucifixion, during which time Christ redeemed the 'godly of the Old Testament', as Fulke calls them, from the *limbus patrum* (*Defense*, 280); on this basis, moreover, were built the doctrines of purgatory and of Christ's bodily ascension to heaven. Martin notes Beza's stated intention to undermine these teachings through his translation (*Defense*, 280).[20] As in the polemics between More and Tyndale, semantics has direct implications for doctrine: the 'original' and 'usual' senses of key theological terms provide justifications of Protestant and Roman Catholic positions respectively.[21]

In line with his Protestant predecessors, Fulke persists in fixing the meaning of scripture at a particular point in textual history: the 'first fountains and springs', the biblical texts in the original languages; he rejects any further historical change, 'any streams that are derived from' these sources (*Defense*, 47). As Cartwright, the last of the Elizabethan polemicists to attack the Rheims New Testament, puts it: 'The true religion being like the heavenly bodies which never change: the Popish religion resembleth the earth, which as the potters clay is readie to receave any forme, according as the wind and weather, times and seasons of the yeare, winter and sommer, spring or fall will set upon it' (*Confutation*, B1ᵛ). Cartwright's allusion to Isaiah ('Wo be unto him that striveth with his maker ... shal the claie saie to him that facioneth it, What makest you?' (45: 9, Geneva version; cf. Isa. 29: 16)) suggests that the subjection of doctrine to historical reception is mere idolatry: the subordination of the divine to the secular.

---

[18] The same language is used at Acts 2: 31.

[19] *The Geneva Bible: A Facsimile of the 1560 Edition* (Madison, Wis.: University of Wisconsin Press, 1969). Subsequent references to this work are included parenthetically in the text. *The New Testament of our Lord Jesus Christ, translated out of Greeke by Theod. Beza*, tr. Laurence Tomson (London, 1576).

[20] Fulke's imperfect defence of Beza and the corresponding English versions refers to the Hebrew words *sheol* and *nephesh* behind the Greek αδης and ψυχη: 'That Beza translated the Greek of the New Testament after the signification of the Hebrew words, although it was true in sense, yet in mine opinion it was not proper in words' (*Defense*, 82). For Fulke the relevant Hebrew words do have the basic sense represented by Beza's translation: it is only by extension that they come to take on the more abstract senses of Christian exegetical tradition. Thus the meaning of the Greek words is essentially the Hebrew words behind them, though Fulke concedes that, as he puts it elsewhere, '[w]ords in derivation and composition do not always signify according to their primitive' (*Defense*, 174). Fulke's diffidence on this point notwithstanding, the distinction between *usual* and *etymological* meaning generally frames the conflict between Roman Catholic and Protestant translators of scripture.

[21] For a reading of the writings between More and Tyndale along these lines, see Jamie Ferguson, 'Faith in the Language: Biblical Authority and the Meaning of English in the More–Tyndale Polemics', *Sixteenth Century Journal*, 43 (2012): 989–1011.

The Roman Catholic entry into the field of English Bible translation in 1582 thus reactivated the fundamental exegetical divide of the Reformation, which plays a central role in the polemics between More and Tyndale in the 1520s and 1530s. Over the course of the sixteenth century, however, control of the language of English religion effectively passed from Roman to Protestant hands, out of the hands of a king (at that time) still loyal to Rome and into those of a queen who—however her more precise critics might accuse her of diffidence—definitely aligned herself with the Protestant movement. Following Henry's vacillations and the violent reversals under Edward and Mary, the Elizabethan establishment consolidated and then extended the Protestant biblical tradition in English.

The Elizabethan phase of this tradition can be conveniently divided into several stages. The first decade of Elizabeth's reign is characterized by the dominance of Genevan versions: an English New Testament was published towards the end of Mary's reign in 1557,[22] a Psalter in the year after Elizabeth took the throne (1559), and a complete Bible in the following year. The Geneva Bible touted itself as the most philologically advanced version available: 'albeit that divers heretofore have indevored to atchieve [the Englishing of scripture]: yet considering the infancie of those tymes and imperfect knollage of the tongues, in respect of this ripe age and cleare light which God hath now reveiled, the translations required greatly to be perused and reformed' (*.4^r). Genevan rigour notwithstanding, English printers continued to issue Coverdale's Great Bible (originally published in 1539), until, at the end of the 1560s, Archbishop of Canterbury Matthew Parker published a new version, the Bishops' Bible, which superseded the Great Bible as representative of an official orthodoxy, more moderate than that coming out of Geneva. Through the better part of Elizabeth's reign, the Bishops' and Geneva Bibles were both printed in many editions, the former typically in massive folio, intended for placement in churches, and the latter in less expensive and more portable formats.[23]

This abundance of Protestant Bibles, and the reversal of political fortunes that it represents, confronted English Roman Catholics with a situation radically different from that of the first three decades of the sixteenth century. The sword More used against Tyndale (customary English ecclesiastic usage) now cut in the other direction, and Elizabethan Roman Catholics were forced to refine and retrench their arguments about the vernacular Bible. Having lost control of biblical English, Roman Catholic partisans returned to a more basic fixture of Roman tradition: the 'true and authentical scripture, ... the vulgar Latin bible, which so many years hath been of so great authority in the church of God' (Fulke, *Defense*, 69, citing Martin). The force of this historical precedent is so powerful, Roman Catholics argue, that the Vulgate should be considered 'not onely better than al other Latin translations, but then the Greeke text itselfe, in those places where they disagree' (268). Where More defends the usual Latin version as *ipso facto* authoritative, however, Elizabethan

---

[22] According to Darlow, this New Testament translation is ascribed to William Whittingham and 'forms the groundwork of the New Testament in the Geneva Bible of 1560': T. H. Darlow and H. F. Moule, *Historical Catalogue of Printed Editions of the English Bible 1525–1961*, rev. and expanded by A. S. Herbert (London: British and Foreign Bible Soc., 1968), 60–1.

[23] See David Norton, *A History of the Bible as Literature* (Cambridge: Cambridge University Press, 1993), i. 117, 120–1. These two Bibles seem to have divided between them public and private functions; they might be taken to represent respectively what Beza calls (in Tomson's English) the 'reformed' and 'transformed' (i.e. proto-Anglican and Puritan) parties within the English Church. *The New Testament*, tr. Tomson (London, 1582), B4^r.

Roman Catholic polemicists justify the Vulgate on historical grounds: they assert that the Latin texts were translated from the Hebrew and Greek prior to the latter texts' corruption by Jewish and Greek heretics.[24]

Roman Catholics extend this charge of corruption to Elizabethan English. More contrasts the novel usages in Tyndale's New Testament with the customary speech of Englishmen, but Elizabethan Roman Catholics were faced with an established English biblical idiom created by Protestants—an idiom that, as Cartwright could justifiably claim in the late 1580s, had 'confirmation, by the common use and practice of our nation for so many yeares together' (F2ʳ). Roman Catholics reject the established biblical usages of Elizabethan England and translate the Bible into an ostentatiously unusual English idiom, one explicitly subordinated to the Latin of the Vulgate. For Elizabethan Roman Catholic translators, the Roman consensus represented by the Vulgate necessarily trumps the (Protestant) Elizabethan consensus around biblical English, meaning that Latinate English trumps the more native idiom of the Protestant English Bibles.

The principle according to which words take on meaning through 'ecclesiastic use and appropriation' is thus applied differently in the Rheims New Testament from the way it is by More. In translating the Bible into English, the Rheims translators condescended to what they called an 'erroneous opinion of necessitie'—namely, that scripture should be available in the vernacular—while maintaining their adherence to the Vulgate.[25] Jerome famously insisted that Cicero's dictum on translation, 'non verbum pro verbo', did not apply to the translation of scripture, where even 'the order of words is a mystery' (*verborum ordo mysterium est*);[26] the Roman Catholic translators used this distinction to justify a new kind of English, which would conform to the Vulgate's Latin 'not only in sense ... but sometimes in the very wordes also and phrases' (279; cf. 263). This practice, the translators admitted, resulted in words that might 'seeme to the vulgar Reader & to common English eares not yet acquainted therewith, rudenesse or ignorance' (279)—words, that is, alien to ordinary English usage. It is 'better', the preface continues, 'that the reader staying at the difficultie of [such words], should take an occasion to looke in the table following, or otherwise to aske the ful meaning of them, then by putting some usual English wordes that expresse them not, so to deceive the reader' (281). In his comparative volume, Fulke gives this glossary of 'explication of certaine wordes ... not familiar to the vulgar reader' more prominence than it has in the Rheims New Testament: Fulke places the table, printed as an appendix to the Rheims New Testament, at the very head of his volume (Cartwright does the same). The table is the only part of the Rheims New Testament that neither Fulke nor Cartwright answers, as if to suggest that examples of 'new fanglednesse of forraine speech' (*Confutation*, F2) such as *contristate, euro-aquilo, prefinition,* and *superedified* spoke for themselves.[27] A modern reader's sympathy with the Protestant position is blunted by

---

[24] The revisionist charge of Hebrew textual meddling had been used much earlier in attacks on Jerome's circumvention of the Greek Septuagint in his new translation of the Old Testament; the analogous charge of Greek meddling was employed in turn by opponents of Erasmus's supplanting of the Vulgate in his retranslation of the New Testament.

[25] The Preface to the Rheims New Testament, repr. in Henry Cotton, *Rhemes and Doway: An Attempt to Shew What Has Been Done by Roman Catholics for the Diffusion of the Holy Scriptures in English* (Oxford: Oxford University Press, 1855), app. 1 (249).

[26] The citation comes from Letter 57 (*c.*396), Jerome's so-called *De optimo genere interpretandi: Lettres,* ed. and tr. Jérôme Labourt (Paris: Société d'Edition 'Les Belles Lettres', 1958), v. 59.

[27] William Whitaker, writing against Reinolds, makes the caustic comment that this glossary would have been a reasonable addition 'if it had been somewhat larger': *An Answere to a Certeine Booke, Written*

the list's inclusion of other words, however, words that have since 'grow[n] to be currant and familiar' (281): *prescience*, for example, *assist, cooperate, issue*, and *victims*.[28]

Elizabethan Protestants also calibrated their positions. In the earlier phase, Tyndale attacked the traditions of the Roman Church as demonstrably corrupt and self-serving and staked the Reformers' exegesis to the unmediated text of scripture; Tyndale argued for a correspondence between the original Greek text of the New Testament—as against the received Vulgate—and the restored etymological (unusual) senses of English words. Because he rejected the traditional Roman Church, Tyndale refused to recognize that biblical language might take on meaning historically within a community of its users, thus exposing himself to More's attacks regarding private language. Elizabethan Protestants, representatives of the dominant religious culture, embraced current English usage, since this usage was a Protestant creation.

Unlike Tyndale, for example, who claimed that biblical language is entirely removed from history, Fulke concedes that the 'first fountains and springs' themselves are to be interpreted in accord with historical conventions; he argues, however, that the convention to be consulted is that of Greek as it stood when the New Testament was written, rather than the Roman, ecclesiastical conventions of later ages: 'there is no better way to know the proper or diverse signification of words, than out of ancient writers, though they be never so profane, who used the words most indifferently in respect of our controversies, of which they were altogether ignorant' (*Defense*, 161).[29] Martin calls this a 'miserable match': the 'unworthy names of Xenophon and Plato, in trial of St Paul's words, against all the glorious doctors' (233). This contextualization of scriptural language in contemporary pagan literature is an acknowledgement of the Protestants' basic aim: that is, to oppose the historical consensus of the Roman Church, rather than the influence of historical consensus in general. Tyndale turns this purpose into a theoretical rejection of any interaction between scripture and historical context; while continuing to give voice to Tyndale's conception, Fulke also refines the argument into a more philologically rational position.

In defence of the unusual English in the Rheims New Testament, the author of the Preface contends that Protestant Bibles include many words more or less transliterated from the Greek and Hebrew: 'if Hosanna, Raca, Belial, and such like be yet untranslated in the English Bibles, why may not we say *Corbana*, and *Parasceue*'; 'if *Pentecost*, Act. 2, be yet untranslated in their bibles, and seemeth not strange: why should not *Pasche* and *Azymes* so remain also ... specially whereas *Passeover* at the first was as strange, as Pasche may seeme now' (280). Within a few years of the publication of the Rheims New Testament, a new Protestant Latin version of the Bible was issued; the translators of the Old Testament for this volume (Immanuel Tremelius and Franciscus Junius) claim in their preface to have 'used Hebraic expressions where it was possible to render them word-for-word without harm to Latin speech' (*Hebraismos ... sine damno latinitatis de verbo ad verbum reddere*

---

by M. William Rainolds Student of Divinitie in the English Colledge at Rhemes, and Entituled, a Refutation of Sundrie Reprehensions, Cavils, &c (London, 1585), 185.

[28] On the impact of Rheims vocabulary on the King James Bible and the language in general, see James G. Carleton, *The Part of Rheims in the Making of the English Bible* (Oxford: Clarendon Press, 1902) and Norton, *History*, i. 127.

[29] Cartwright takes advantage of the same distinction: 'εναγγελια was a Greeke word before the Gospell came into the world' (*Confutation*, F2ᵛ).

licuit, expressimus); more specifically, these translators 'wrote proper names in Hebraic form, to the extent that this could be done' (*Nomina propria … ex Hebraeorum formâ, ut maxime fieri potuit, scripsimus*).[30] William Rainolds calls this tendency a 'most child-ish affectation to seeme somwhat skilful in the hebrew, reduce al sacred names to the old Judaical sound' (*Refutation*, 455) and goes on to critique the principle according to which such practices were justified:

> as though *Petrus, Joannes, Jacobus, Stephanus*, howsoever they be uttered in any other tonge, Hebrew, Greeke, Latin, Spanish, French, or Italian were not truly & exactly expressed in English by *Peter, John, James, Stevin*, but must needes be pronounced, as they are in the first language from which originally they are derived. as [sic] though a man translating some storie out of French or Spanish into English, translated not wel if he said, Frauncis the French King in his warres against the Spaniards, but must needes say, Fransois King of the Fransois in his warres aginst the Espanioulx: or, los Espanoles in such a victorie against los Franceses, in steede of, the Spaniards in such a victorie against the Frenchmen. And why then do they not in the new testament use like noveltie? why for Christ use they not, Jeschua, for our Lady, Miriam, for S. Peter, Cepha, for S. John, Jochannan, and so in the rest of the Apostles, whereas they know that thus were they called in their proper language. (456–7)

While this is an effective attack on what the Rheims preface calls the 'ostentation' (261) of the Protestant translators' 'new names', it would seem no less effective as a critique of the Roman Catholic translation, of which Cartwright complains that 'being translated, it remaineth … as it were un-translated' (*Confuation*, F2). What else is the Roman Catholic English Bible but a deliberate attempt to make English words sound 'as they are in the first language from which originally they are derived [i.e. in the case of the Rheims New Testament, Latin]'? Translators on both sides were ready to adapt their target languages to the lexis and syntax of their sources. The core of the problem was the old argument about source-texts. Protestant English translators were not consistent in defending the 'purity' of their language against the influence of other tongues: they incorporated vocabulary strange to English usage so long as these words were derived from the Hebrew 'first foun-tains and springs', as against Roman Catholic translators' allegiance to the 'old vulgar Latin text' (266).[31] The rise of the English biblical tradition translates this older exegetical question about sources into a question about the relationship between Latin and English, since the subordination of English to Latin norms betokened the subordination of the English Church to Rome.

Each camp was ready to stretch the lexis of English in allegiance to its authoritative text; the differences in allegiance of these translators to English norms are more clearly evident in their approaches to English syntax. The Rheims translation often yields constructions that function much more effectively in Latin than in English. In his *Answere* to William Rainolds, Whitaker cites among the 'goodlie flowers' of the Roman Catholic translation

[30] *Testamenti Veteris Biblia sacra sive libri canonici, priscae Judaeorum ecclesiae a Deo traditi, / Latini recens ex Hebraeo facti, brevibusq[ue] scholiis illustrati ab Immanuele Tremellio & Francisco Junio* (London, 1585), ¶8ʳ.

[31] Norton notes Fulke's objections to Martin's unusual English but does not acknowledge that this was precisely the charge that More levelled against Tyndale (*History*, i. 133); instead Norton calls the potential for biblical translation to reshape English, as illustrated by the language of the Rheims New Testament, 'a real change from More and Tyndale' (i. 133).

the tendency to follow Latin grammar at the expense of intelligibility in English: 'the obscuritie and ambiguitie of sentences, by reason of leaving out the verbs and other words in the English translation, which may in latine more easilie be understood' (185). The Rheims Preface derives this practice from the translators' proper respect for the text: 'we presume not in hard places to mollifie the speaches or phrases, but religiously keepe them word for word, and point for point, for feare of missing, or restraining the sense of the holy Ghost to our phantasie' (282). The Preface cites several examples from the translation where their following of the 'Scriptures phrase' preserves meaningful ambiguities present in the Latin. More often, however, this literal translation has the more straightforward effect of generating English syntax that is difficult to follow:

> He therefore that giveth you the Spirit, and worketh miracles among you: by the workes of the Law, or by the hearing of the faith doeth he it?
> [Vulgate: *qui ergo tribuit vobis Spiritum et operitur virtutes in vobis ex operibus legis an ex auditu fidei*] (Gal. 3: 5)

> But he that of the bond-woman, was borned according to the flesh: and he that of the free-woman, by the promisse.
> [Vulgate: *sed qui de ancilla secundum carnem natus est qui autem de libera per repromissionem*] (Gal. 4: 23)[32]

In each of these passages, Rheims relies on grammatically parallel clauses ('by the workes' coordinated with 'by the hearing'; 'of the bond-woman ... according to the flesh' with 'of the free-woman, by the promisse') to suggest an omitted verb ('doeth' omitted from the first clause, and 'was borned' from the second). The structure of these sentences strains the resources of English grammar, less forgiving than Latin of attenuated syntax. Rheims does 'mollify' the English by interpolating a main clause ('doeth he it') where the Latin assumes that the verbs in the first part of the line ('tribuit', 'operitur') are inferred in the second; generally, however, Rheims treats the English language as if its grammar mirrored that of Latin.

The Bishops' version of these lines shows 13 immediately the greater transparency of less Latinate syntax:

> He therefore that ministreth to you the spirite, and worketh myracles among you, doeth hee it through the deedes of the Lawe, or by hearing of the faith? (Gal. 3: 5)

> But he which was of the bonde woman, was borne after the flesh: but he which was of the free woman *was borne* by promise. (Gal. 4: 23; italics in the original)

In the first of these lines, two individual words seem significant, neither of which has anything to do with syntax: 'ministreth' (for *tribuit*) suggests a more ancillary role for the official than does 'giveth'; 'deedes' for 'workes' (*operibus*) alludes to what William Rainolds dismisses as 'this new solifidian gospel' (*Refutation*, 424). The syntactical differences between the two versions are more subtle: the Bishops' version provides the main clause ('doeth he it') with the first of the two coordinated prepositional phrases rather than with the second and so clarifies the link between them. In the second example, the Bishops'

---

[32] Vulgate cited from *Biblia sacra juxta vulgatem versionem*, ed. Robert Weber et al., 5th edn (Stuttgart: Deutsche Bibelgesellschaft, 2007).

Bible repeats the verb 'was borne' in the second of the two clauses—marking the insertion with roman type in an otherwise italic text. This recalls Coverdale's comment, in the preface to his diglot New Testament, concerning 'the figure called Eclipsis [*sic*], diverse tymes used in the scriptures, the which though she do garnysh the sentence in Latyn, yet wyll not so be admitted in other tunges'.[33] The insertion in Bishops' is clearly intended to compensate for the syntactical difference between Latin and English, differences that the Rheims New Testament ignores.

Fulke's published juxtaposition of the Rheims and Bishops' versions makes explicit a critical awareness of comparative semantics and syntax common to English biblical translators.[34] Similarly, in their polemical texts, both Martin and Fulke treat biblical semantics critically. For both, biblical English was subject to use and abuse, and English religion was therefore subject to what Martin calls 'Machiavel's politic rules' (*Defense*, 172): the caprices of those with the power to determine biblical usage. With regard to the words *priest* and *elder*, for example, Martin contends that the Protestants consciously manipulated the language of the New Testament:

> Because yourselves have them whom you call bishops, the name 'bishops' is in your English bibles; which otherwise by your own rule of translation should be called an 'overseer' or 'superintendent' …. Only 'priests' must be turned contemptuously out of the text of the holy scriptures, and 'elders' put in their place, because you have no priests, nor will none of them, and because that is in controversy between us. (*Defense*, 172)

Fulke in turn accuses the Roman Catholics of 'abusive acception [*sic*] and sounding of the English word "priest" and "priesthood"' (170): 'That "our Christian forefathers" ears were not acquainted with the name of "elders", it was because the name of priest in their time sounded according to the etymology, and not according to the corruption of the papists' (162). Fulke and Martin agree that the assignation of meaning to the Bible is subject to human choice and manipulation.

More and Tyndale advocated respectively historicist and essentialist notions of biblical semantics, based in Roman Catholic and Protestant definitions of biblical authority. Elizabethan polemics rehearse but also revise these positions. Both Martin and Fulke made concessions to changed political circumstances and to each other's positions. Moreover, Fulke's publication of juxtaposed New Testament translations provided readers with a systematic comparison of Protestant and Roman Catholic versions of biblical English. The enormous stakes involved in these textual comparisons induce a correspondingly acute awareness of the capacity of biblical translations to shape the language.[35] From Bishop Gardiner's proposed revisions of the Bishops' Bible forward, English Roman Catholic translators of the English Bible and their defenders pose a challenge to the semantic and grammatical integrity of the

---

[33] *The Newe Testament Both in Latine and Englyshe Eche Correspondente to the Other after the Vulgare Texte, Communely Called S. Jeromes. Faythfullye Translated by Johan Hollybushe* [*sic*] (Southwark, 1538), *3ᵛ. Ironically, in this English sentence about differences between Latin and English, Coverdale uses a feminine pronoun relative to a noun that, in English, is neuter.

[34] The revision of the Wycliffite Bible illustrates the same consciousness of the differences between Latinate and 'natural' English, though in a very different ideological context.

[35] Cf. Norton on Martin's Prologue to the Rheims New Testament and analogous issues in the More–Tyndale polemics: 'English words and phrases were being formed by the language of the [biblical] translators' (*History*, i. 126).

Elizabethan vernacular, and as they subordinate English to Latin, so they would subordinate the English Church to the Roman papacy. The Protestants' consistent rejection of Latinate English, on the other hand, suggests the autonomy of the English from Rome, even as these Protestants qualify this autonomy through a greater openness to the historicity of language.

❧

In 1623, William Lisle published 'an ancient monument of the Church of England', under the title *A Saxon Treatise Concerning the Old and New Testament*, the purpose of which was to establish the integrity of the Christian Church in England prior to the arrival, under the Norman banner, of the Roman Church. Lisle's pseudo-historical attack on the Roman Church joins a tradition of such attacks; Lisle is indebted in particular to John Foxe's preface to *The Gospels of the Fower Evangelistes* (1571).[36] Among Lisle's evidence, in the prologue 'To the Readers', for the prior integrity of the Saxon Church is the expressiveness of the Saxon language, even with regard to highly technical theological vocabulary: the Saxon tongue, Lisle claims, includes equivalents for such terms as 'Trinity, Unity, Deity and Persons thereof; for Coaequal, Coaeternall, Invisible, Incomprehensible; Yea for Incarnation, for Ascension, Descension, Resurrection, for Catholike and all such forraine words as we are now faine to use, because we have forgot better of our owne' (e3ᵛ). The words about which Lisle complains were matched, he insists, by Saxon equivalents prior to their being imported into the language: the new, Latinate terms did not fill semantic gaps but added to the stock of synonyms. While such neologisms should in principle add to the copiousness of English, Lisle finds them offensive for their affront to the autonomy of the language (and, by extension, of the English Church).

Although Lisle laments the unnecessary supplanting of native words for such key theological terms, he is not such an idealist as to dismiss the dictates of current usage: 'I speake not to have them [the Saxon theological terms] recalled into use, now these [the Latinate borrowings] are well knowne; sith I use them and the like my selfe'. As the prologue continues, a more specific target becomes clear: 'the wilfull and purposed obscurity of those other translators', namely, the translators of the Rheims-Douay Bible:

> the Saxon Bibles ... will in many places convince of affected obscuritie some late translators; who to provide for their owne opinions, not otherwise found in the word of God, are faine to stuffe the text with such fustian, such inkehorne termes, as may seeme to favour their parts; or darken at least the true meaning of holy Scripture, and discourage weake readers with doubtfull sense and harshnesse. (e3ʳ)[37]

Where for example the Rheims translators use the Latinate term 'Supersubstantiall bread', which, Lisle suggests, 'no man having but the English tongue onely is able to understand', the Saxon Bible translates the same Greek terms by 'dayly bread'—'plaine ... pure English' (e3ʳ). The difference between 'supersubstantiall' and 'dayly' bread is not merely a matter of linguistic

---

[36] Phillip Pulsiano, 'William L'Isle and the Editing of Old English', in Timothy Graham (ed.), *The Recovery of Old English: Anglo-Saxon Studies in the Sixteenth and Seventeenth Centuries* (Kalamazoo, Mich.: Medieval Institute, 2000), 181–2.

[37] Just prior to this passage, Lisle criticizes both Roman Catholics and Puritans (e2ᵛ), but the reference to 'fustian, ... inkehorne termes' makes it clear that Lisle refers to the Rheims New Testament and Douay Old Testament. Pulsiano cites most of this passage but provides no specific context for Lisle's criticism (205).

transparency, of course: under the guise of attacking Latinate English, Lisle is attacking the Roman doctrine of transubstantiation. As in his historical account, so here Lisle combines religious and linguistic concerns.

The general purpose of Lisle's retrospective is 'to stop the base and beggerly course of borrowing when we need not' (e3^v). Strikingly, Lisle incorporates literary writers into his defence of an English free of Latin influence:

> what tongue is able more shortly and with lesse doubtfulnesse, to give utterance and make way for the cumbersome conceits of our minde, than ours? What more plentifull, than ours might be, if we did use well but our owne garbes, and the words and speeches of our sundry shires and countries in this Iland? Neither is it the least glory of a Nation to have such a language .... Yet our Poetes, I must needs say, have done their part. (e3^v–e4^r)

Lisle's attack on the Roman Catholic versions of the Bible sums up a half-century of Protestant English resistance to the inkhorn. His inclusion of the 'poets' suggests that such religious resistance to Latinism belongs to a broader assertion of the autonomy of English, a project that includes even so light-hearted an example as Shakespeare's lampooning of Armado's peregrinate excrement.

FURTHER READING

Blank, Paula. *Broken English: Dialects and the Politics of Language in Renaissance Writings* (London: Routledge, 1996).

Carleton, James G. *The Part of Rheims in the Making of the English Bible* (Oxford: Clarendon Press, 1902).

Ferguson, Jamie. 'Faith in the Language: Biblical Authority and the Meaning of English in the More–Tyndale Polemics'. *Sixteenth Century Journal*, 43 (2012): 989–1011.

Norton, David. *A History of the Bible as Literature*, 2 vols (Cambridge: Cambridge University Press, 1993).

Rubel, Veré L. *Poetic Diction in the English Renaissance from Skelton through Spenser* (New York: Modern Language Association, 1941).

Sledd, James. 'A Footnote on the Inkhorn Controversy'. *University of Texas Studies in English*, 28 (1949): 49–56.

Vos, Alvin. 'Humanistic Standards of Diction in the Inkhorn Controversy'. *Studies in Philology*, 73 (1976): 376–96.

CHAPTER 6

···

RETRANSLATING THE BIBLE IN THE ENGLISH REVOLUTION

···

NIGEL SMITH

> What in the context, the Translators call *the loynes*, they acknowledge in the margent to be the Thigh, in the Hebrew: as also they do, *Gen.* 46.26. And why then should that be rejected, which the Spirit of God dictates, and that chosen, which seems best to their own humane spirit? When the Scripture saith, *the Thigh*, how dare we say the *Loyns?*[1]

IN the half-century after the appearance of the King James Bible, there were objections and projects for further improvement to the English translation. At least two of these were connected with the triumph of Puritanism after 1640, with the emphasis therein on absolute faithfulness to Hebrew and Greek originals. Robert Gell's *An Essay Toward the Amendment of the Last English-Translation of the Bible* (1659) is usually regarded as the last of these attempts and the most substantial.[2] Beyond an acknowledgement of Gell's interest in rendering a more literal translation, something closer to the sense of the Hebrew or Greek original, nothing else is offered in the standard scholarship.[3] This does a great disservice to a notable work and its author. To rescue Gell and his *Essay* from a compact obscurity, a single short paragraph in the standard work on the English Bibles, is to reveal a series of important cross-currents in scriptural understanding and the development of theology in the period: identities, views, and practices that cut across conventionally understood boundaries. We see in the long-lived Gell's comments on the King James translation the eclectic fomentation of a resistance to Calvinist predestination theology and the seeds of the alternative synthesis of Platonism, Judaic mysticism, perfectionism, enthusiasm, and exceptional Bible learning that would eventually feed into the Pietist

---

[1] Robert Gell, *An Essay Toward the Amendment of the Last English-Translation of the Bible* (1659), 183.

[2] David Norton, *A History of the English Bible as Literature* (Cambridge: Cambridge University Press, 2000), 103.

[3] David Norton, *The King James Bible: A Short History from Tyndale to Today* (Cambridge: Cambridge University Press, 2011), 186–7.

movement of the early eighteenth-century German-speaking world. The interaction of English and German spiritualists in this period, and the role of English personnel and books in the world of north European piety is itself a relatively overlooked and poorly researched subject.

In this chapter Gell's *Essay* is explored and its contents analysed and explained in the context of the events of his life, in particular his circle of patrons, protégés, friends, and associates, including William Laud, Archbishop of Canterbury, the prominent Cambridge Platonist Henry More, the philosopher Anne, Lady Conway, and the Gloucester separatist Robert Bacon. Gell's writings are by no means idiosyncratic, but very much a part of this world of cross-currents. Finally, some account is given of how the translation that Gell preferred might have looked to readers had it been fully assembled.

'And it came to pass, as they were burying a man, that, behold, they spied a band of men; and they cast the man into the sepulchre of Elisha: and when the man was let down, and touched the bones of Elisha, he revived, and stood up on his feet' (2 Kings 13: 21). Thus the King James Bible, quoted quite accurately by Gell in his 1659 *Essay*. He cites the sentence in the preface to his 800-plus page work as an example of what is to come. It exemplifies faulty translation because it introduces a contradiction: the man could have been thrown into the sepulchre or let down gently into it; one or the other but not both.

The Geneva Bible found an elegant solution: 'And as they were burying a man, behold, they saw the soldiers: therefore they cast the man into the sepulcher of Elisha, and when the man was down, and touched the bones of Elisha, he revived and stood upon his feet'. Gell fixes on the phrase 'and when the man was let down', and sees an errant introduction of that which was not really there in the Hebrew original or any other version derived from it (he cites nineteen different versions); the Hebrew merely says 'he went'.[4] There is no judging of a broader context so that the accuracy of the Geneva version can be tested. Instead Gell produces a new sentence for the English Bible: 'And it came to pass, as they were burying a man, that, behold, they spied a band of men; and they cast the man into the sepulchre of Elisha: And the man went and touched the bones of Elisha, he revived, and stood up on his feet'.

But, says Gell, he cannot have been dead in a literal sense. The Bible must be speaking metaphorically: he was spiritually dead through sinfulness and when he touched the bones of Elisha he revived. Gell claims he is for strict literal biblical interpretation but he uses it to derive a 'spiritual' or allegorical meaning. In making the correction and thereby becoming better at translation Gell is sure that mankind will become closer to the nature of God: 'to become one spirit with him', the quality that is held out to those who keep faith. Of the various errors of translation Gell will point in particular to the misunderstanding of metaphor in both senses: taking metaphor as literal and vice versa—taking that which is literal as metaphor. In both senses Gell privileges the literal, by which he means the original sense of the scripture languages.

It is in his view unwise to part company with the metaphorical sense implanted in the Bible in any given instance. In Genesis 3: 1, the serpent might better be described as 'naked'

---

[4] Gell, *An Essay*, A3ᵛ–(a)2ʳ.

rather than 'subtle', the former word better suiting with the sense of Satan as a player—by needing no subterfuge, he actually becomes what he would play as *a Stage-Player*.[5] Gell claims the rendering is most appropriate for the Apostles, because it was in keeping with the early practice of crucifying criminals naked. The Holy Spirit will speak in metaphors and the proper translation of the Bible involves the honouring of them: at Numbers 8: 23, the King James Bible has the Levites 'waiting' on the service of the Tabernacle, but the correct translation, says Gell, is 'warring': the priest fights a battle in his service of the Lord. Part of the point of the metaphor is to force the reader to understand the very qualities of a metaphorical usage, and hence the value of the difference between a signifier and its signified.[6]

Gell claims that far worse crimes involve the actual perversion of the scripture's sense as it is translated. There might be missing words in the originals, but that does not entitle the translator to reconstruct a probable meaning. In some of these places, such as instances of syncategoremata and consignificants, the missing words necessitate that something be supplied in order for meaning to be achieved.[7] The rabbis knew this as conjecture, and Gell is unhappy with the King James Bible translators both adding and taking away words, and for inverting or changing word order. Thus Gell claims that in the King James Bible translation of Matthew 20: 23 Jesus is deprived of the attributes of his majesty:

> And he saith unto them, Ye shall drink indeed of my cup, and be baptized with the baptism that I am baptized with: but to sit on my right hand, and on my left, is not mine to give, but it shall be given to them for whom it is prepared of my Father.

'This Translation makes our Lord absolutely to deny, that he hath any *power* to give the honour of *sitting at his right hand and left*.'[8] Who would follow such a disempowered Jesus, or one so prone to contradiction? The mistranslation also causes a 'foul breach in the deity', Gell revealing himself seemingly as an orthodox trinitarian. He finds that several translations commit the same error when they seek to fill an ellipsis. He prefers to omit these supplements and render the lines in such a way as makes sense of Christ's majesty: 'To sit on my right hand and on my left, is not mine to give, but (or, *unless*) to those for whom it is prepared of my Father'.[9] Jesus offers these places only to the elect.

Here, Gell indicates that not only do several earlier translations agree with this, but also some earlier English versions: Coverdale, the Edward VI Bible (presumably the Great Bible of 1539–41, ordered to be placed in every church), and the English biblical annotations.[10] It could even be translated: 'To sit on Christs right hand and on his left to those for whom it is prepared of my Father'. The supplement itself ('it shall be given') becomes nothing more than a 'superfluous redundancy'.[11] Intrusions in the King James Bible translation exist in many different places. There is no need, Gell argues, for an 'if' in Proverbs 16: 31: 'The

[5] Gell, *An Essay*, (a)3ʳ. Gell is using categories from ancient Greek literary analysis here.
[6] Gell, *An Essay*, 430.   [7] Gell, *An Essay*, (a)3ᵛ.   [8] Gell, *An Essay*, (a)3ᵛ.
[9] Gell, *An Essay*, (a)4ᵛ.
[10] It is unclear whether Gell means marginal annotations, as famously in the Geneva Bible (see Femke Molekamp's chapter in this volume). Most likely the 'English Annotations' are the *Annotations upon All the Books of the Old and New Testament* published first in 1645.
[11] Gell, *An Essay*, (b)2ʳ.

hoary head is a crown of glory, if it be found in the way of Righteousness'. It should read 'The *Hoariness shall be found a crown of glory in the way of righteousness*', and it should be interpreted allegorically: old, grey men are full of wisdom. It is significant, as we shall see, that Gell cites Plato by association in the previous paragraph on Socrates: 'God's gift to the Athenians'.[12]

With a gathering intent that is not merely a matter of insufficient translation, Gell accuses the King James Bible translators of causing depression in the young when they mistranslate 1 John 3: 18–20:

> My little children, let us not love in word, neither in tongue; but in deed and in truth.
> And hereby we know that we are of the truth, and shall assure our hearts before him.
> For if our heart condemn us, God is greater than our heart, and knoweth all things.

In the new translation, the last verse is distinctly modified: 'Because if our heart condemn us, that God is greater then our heart, and knoweth all things, even the present frame and disposition of our heart, *in the truth of love*'.[13] Children may again walk freely about without fear.

Another source of grievance is inversion. Gell gives the example of Hebrews 10: 34: 'For *ye had compassion of me in my bonds, and took joyfully the spoiling of your goods, knowing in yourselves* that ye have in heaven a better and an enduring substance'. The inversion is removed as follows: 'Knowing that ye have in yourselves better wealth in heaven, and that which will endure'.[14] Gell's correction adds a certainty to the nature of the afterlife for believers, and in the possibility that this future begins with a sense of their own substantial worth in this life. Gell is proud of the optimism he finds in the sense of his corrected translations, and claims that this word order is in most Bibles and commentaries he has consulted, so that it is a startling deviation to find the King James Bible translators and all of their English predecessors simply ignoring a well-known piece of verse, denying the good news to English Christians on a matter of faulty word order.

Here Gell for once lashes out at the theological meanness of the translators as they obscure the 'sense of the Holy Spirit': 'for the avoiding and preventing of that (as too many esteem it) execrable error of *inherent righteousness*'.[15] In this respect Gell's critics were right, or at least on the right path, in judging him too close to Luther for Reformed English theology, as we will see. Elsewhere he shows how that which the translators deem legitimate but troubling they put into the margins, never into the main text. Or, where there is a 'true' translation, it is relegated to the margin in preference for 'not a genuine *translation*, but an *exposition*'.[16] In Genesis 22: 24, 'Let the same be the woman whom the Lord hath appointed out for my master's son', Gell finds 'appointed out' to be the least pertinent of three senses of the Hebrew. 'Corrected' and 'prepared to be corrected' have been relegated as possibilities, and Gell fears that the translators made their choice because it 'made for the establishing their opinion of *destiny* and *fatality*'.[17] Once again, what this means will be explained shortly.

---

[12] Gell, *An Essay*, 448–9.   [13] Gell, *An Essay*, 448–9.   [14] Gell, *An Essay*, (b)3ᵛ.
[15] Gell, *An Essay*, (b)3ᵛ–(b)4ʳ.   [16] Gell, *An Essay*, 428.   [17] Gell, *An Essay*, 161.

Omissions and further mistranslations make the Bible fall short of its optimistic message for mankind. Genesis 25: 27 is translated 'Jacob was a plain man', but Gell argues that the Hebrew for 'plain' in fact means 'perfect'.[18] He 'looked' for this reading but did not find it. The words of the Bible each bear many meanings (nothing unorthodox about that), but Gell sees the King James Bible as often denying optimistic readings that should be presented to the studious and godly reader. Thus in Genesis 33: 9, when Esau said 'I have enough', it in fact means 'I have abundance'.[19] Gell uses rabbinic authority to support this reading (he thinks that both translations are true, and that neither should be suppressed); he does not say who his rabbis are. In Genesis 39: 4, 'Joseph found grace in his sight, and he served him', 'served' is denounced as a deviation in the Hebrew words, and should be 'wasted upon him, or ministred unto him', which implies, says Gell, 'a greater neerness unto him unto whom he ministred'. But 'ministred' is used erroneously instead of 'served' in 1 Chronicles 27: 1.[20]

Eight pages later and Gell is showing a political character to his argument: the King James Bible translators were subservient to their political masters who made them stay close to the previous translations for 'reason of state'—so as not to stir up too much disquiet and the allegation that a new translation was in fact a new Bible.[21] But perhaps a new Bible is what Gell himself is promising. It would ideally be a fully annotated text, as opposed to the rigid cast of mind induced by a cost-cutting Bible that excises margins and the Apocrypha.

Gell begins to reveal himself more openly when he refers to allegations that he is unorthodox because he stresses a reading of the Bible as allegorical. His major guides are 'Pagnin' (Sante Pagnini, c.1470–1536, first translator of the Bible into Latin after St Jerome (1527) and influential organizer of texts into chapter and verse), and 'Arius Montanus' (Benito Arias Montano, 1527–98, Spanish orientalist and editor of the 1569 Antwerp Polyglot Bible, printed and published by Plantin), the latter being, Gell acknowledges, considered by some to be too 'curious' and making the Bible nonsensical.[22] Another source is the heavily annotated first German edition of the Hebrew Bible, prepared by Sebastian Münster in 1534–5.[23] Gell himself says he plays up the rusticity of Hebrew, because that is what ancient Hebrew is like. To make the Bible more like 'English sense' is to abandon its own particular meanings. Yet occasionally he refers to an 'antient English Manuscript' translation that he prefers to all later English printed versions.[24]

So who was Gell? He was born on 19 February 1594/5 at Frindsbury in Kent, of the family of Hopton, Derbyshire, and was educated at Westminster School as a King's Scholar, matriculating at Christ's College, Cambridge, as sizar in 1615.[25] He graduated BA 1617/18, MA 1621, BD 1628, and DD 1641, and was a fellow of Christ's from 1623 till after 1638. In all he spent twenty-seven years in the college, and held several college offices in his time. Milton would have known him when he joined the college as a commoner in 1625, and Gell counted the great scholar of biblical chronology Joseph Mede (1586–1639) among his friends. Indeed, it may be that Gell was the fellow appointed to respond to the undergraduate Milton in a verse disputation.[26] More significantly, Gell was the tutor of the great

[18] Gell, *An Essay*, 169.   [19] Gell, *An Essay*, 173.   [20] Gell, *An Essay*, 177.

[21] Gell, *An Essay*, (c)4ʳ.   [22] Gell, *An Essay*, (d)4ʳ.   [23] Gell, *An Essay*, 364.

[24] Gell, *An Essay*, 776.

[25] Louise Hill Curth, 'Gell, Robert (1595–1665)', *ODNB*, 2004; online edition, Jan. 2008, <http://www.oxforddnb.com/view/article/10510>.

[26] Gordon Campbell and Thomas Corns, *John Milton: Life, Work, and Thought* (Oxford: Oxford University Press, 2008), 41.

Platonist Henry More, and nominated More to succeed him.[27] In August 1629 he left a very intelligent and appropriately phrased Latin poem in the *album amicorum* of Johannes Fridericus Wagner of Nuremburg.[28] Later a chaplain to the Archbishop of Canterbury, William Laud, he frequently preached before the University of Cambridge, in 1631 before Charles I, and in 1641 before the lord mayor and aldermen of London in the Mercers' Chapel. He was rector of St Mary Aldermary, London, at his death, which occurred at Pampisford, Cambridgeshire, on 20 March 1665. In 1663, incidentally, Gell would have married Milton to his third wife, Elizabeth Minshull, in this church.[29]

He was, then, a scholarship boy (sizars were nearly the lowest kind of servant-undergraduate) who made good as an academic divine. He clearly had means, not least to equip him with the expensive tomes that made his biblical scholarship possible, and indeed he married a wealthy woman, Elizabeth Laurence of Pampisford, on 7 November 1641, the year he became rector of St Mary Aldermary, itself a very rich London parish. Their daughter, also Elizabeth, had the means to establish a grand altar monument to her parents in Pampisford churchyard in 1674. Her father left books or money to Christ's and Queens' Colleges, and to the King's Scholars of Westminster School. The word that comes to mind is 'establishment': more or less the best education possible in the country in the pre-1640 state of affairs, and a high-flying academic career, before a lucrative posting not to the provinces, but the capital, together with a most appropriate marriage. The poet Andrew Marvell, whose father came from Meldreth, near Pampisford, had to settle for far less: a subsizar at first, ejected from a Trinity College Cambridge scholarship, scraping by as a gentleman's tutor for many years before becoming a civil servant and an MP, but with no great means (no affluent widow for him), and in debt at his death.[30]

Gell was an Arminian perhaps and even, apparently, a Laudian, in London, but a canny one, it would seem, for he managed to hang on to his incumbency despite the objections of some Presbyterian members of his parish in 1645. He argued for the reconciliation of the restored Church of England and the Presbyterians.[31] The Restoration did not present an obstacle to him: on the contrary, he was soon a chaplain for Gilbert Sheldon, the Archbishop of Canterbury. But appearances may deceive. On 24 August 1658, the Presbyterian Matthew Poole reported to Richard Baxter that he had heard Gell preach 'once or twice & I find him run much upon Arminian and some Popish errours & that way of Allegorizing Scripture miserably'. Moreover he had a following: 'divers of them Astrologers, some Seekers others well willers to the Quakers like him'.[32] What of this? It certainly means something, although I think Christopher Hill's picture of Gell as millenarian, Familist, defender of press freedom and religious toleration, and kabbalist (and where Gell's post-Restoration career is confined to a footnote)

---

[27] Anne Conway, *The Conway Letters*, ed. Marjorie Hope Nicolson, rev. Sarah Hutton (Oxford: Clarendon Press, 1992), 540.

[28] BL, MS Add. 15852, f. 49.   [29] Campbell and Corns, *John Milton*, 41, 323–4.

[30] See Nigel Smith, *Andrew Marvell: The Chameleon* (New Haven and London: Yale University Press, 2010).

[31] See Gell, *Eirenikon, or, a Treatise of Peace between the Two Visible Divided Parties … by Irenaeus Philadelphus philanthropus* (1660).

[32] G. F. Nuttall and N. H. Keeble (eds), *Calendar of the Correspondence of Richard Baxter: 1638–1660* (Oxford: Clarendon Press, 1991), i. 335.

sounds exaggeratedly exotic.[33] Nonetheless Poole's letter does contain this intriguing sentence: 'I heare from good hands hee is a familist', by which he means that Gell was alleged to be a member of the Family of Love, the clandestine, dissembling sect of perfectionists, followers of Hendrik Niclaes, which had found its way to eastern and southern England from Emden, Cologne, and Amsterdam in the late sixteenth century.[34] The interest in the esoteric is supported by surviving correspondence of 24 May 1654, from Gell to Lady Conway, as well as the sources in his earlier published sermons. Gell could also appeal to the gathered churches of London when he referred to the importance of the need for *experimental knowledge* of the *living Word*, a clear reference to the theology of experience that was powering the construction of conversion narratives in the Independent churches.[35]

Geoffrey Nuttall had Gell right in his 1954 pamphlet 'James Nayler: A Fresh Approach', a major piece of work explaining 1650s radical theology.[36] He noted that the editor of Gell's *Remains* (1676) was 'R.B.', one Robert Bacon of Gloucestershire, precisely the kind of ecumenical spiritualist that Poole disparages, one happy to have conversations across a broad spectrum of confessional views and practices. In his preface, Bacon praised Gell's exegetical skills, but noted how they were put to a sacred end that was spurned by most:

> that which hath been, is, and will be most objected against this Authour, and his Works, is his way of carrying *home* the sense of the Scripture to its ultimate end, mind, mark and scope, the Divine, Holy and perfect Life: which to effect, he doth often Spiritualize, Allegorize many Scriptures, which almost all others, looking no farther than the Letter, omit, or never fathom or digg into.[37]

Gell was associated and associated himself with Thomas Drayton, Robert Hurt, and William Parker. Gell wrote in the last sermon in the 1659 collection that 'Much more might be written on this subject, had not my worthy friends *Dr. Thomas Drayton*, ὁ μαχαριτης, and *Mr. William Parker* published a Treatise upon the same argument entituled *A Revindication of the possibility of a total mortification of sin in this life*'.[38] Richard Baxter regarded Gell and Parker as 'Sect-makers'; Parker was chaplain to the most mystical Philip Herbert, fifth Earl of Pembroke, great patron of enthusiasts, and Drayton preached two sermons at Pembroke's seat Wilton on 1 March 1657. Jeremy Taylor described this group as 'Perfectionists', and claimed that they were convinced followers of the tolerationist Sebastian Castellio (1515–63); Gell cites Castellio's commentaries and Latin Bible frequently. In the list of relevant scriptures at the end of his sermon on the possibility of

[33] Christopher Hill, *Milton and the English Revolution* (London: Faber & Faber, 1977), 34.

[34] See Alastair Hamilton, *The Family of Love* (Cambridge: James Clarke & Co., 1981); Christopher Marsh, *The Family of Love in English Society, 1550–1630* (Cambridge: Cambridge University Press, 1994).

[35] See Nigel Smith, *Perfection Proclaimed: Language and Literature in English Radical Religion, 1640–1660* (Oxford: Oxford University Press, 1989), pt II.

[36] G. F. Nuttall, *James Nayler: A Fresh Approach* (London: Friends Historical Society, 1954).

[37] R[obert] B[acon], 'A Preface to the Candid and Christian Readers', in Gell, *Gell's Remaines: Or Several Select Scriptures of the New Testament Opened and Explained* (1676), A3ᵛ.

[38] Gell, *An Essay*, 797.

a sinless life, Gell argues that 'perfection' has been masked in several instances of translation: Genesis 25: 27; Job 27: 5; Psalms 15: 2, 18: 21–6; 19: 12–13; 26: 1; and 37: 18. 'Perfectionism',
described by Taylor as the position that it is possible 'to give unto God perfect unsinning
obedience, & to have perfection of degrees in this life' is what Gell means when he refers to
'inherent righteousness'.

In his published *Remaines*, Gell's prayer calls for a complete escape from fleshly
taint: 'thou has made unto us great and precious Promises, *that we should be partak-
ers of thy Divine Nature. But thou requirest, that first* we escape the corruption that
is in the world through lust. *That having received these precious Promises, we should*
purifie our selves from all pollution of flesh and spirit'.[39] Hence the claim for a revised
translation of John 1: 14: not the divine word living 'among us' but 'in us'; 'Happy
Christians—*lona si sua norint!* if they knew their own happiness'.[40] The perfectionists were also regarded as readers of Jakob Böhme, although not very comprehending
of him, but I do not see any evidence for this.[41] Another probable member of Gell's
audience was the wealthy Quaker merchant Robert Rich, a Universalist, and like Gell
hopeful of a coming together of all sects in this spirit.[42] He resisted the authority of
George Fox and was a supporter of the Quaker schismatic John Perrot. Gell's circle of
acquaintance bridged the respectable and the unrespectable: Henry More was happy
to use and to recommend to Lady Conway Gell's rectory in Bow Lane as a place to
leave correspondence.[43] Gell wrote to Lady Conway concerning the Earl of Pembroke's
health.[44]

Readers of Hill's *The World Turned Upside Down* (1972) will be familiar with yet another
picture of Gell. Ariel Hessayon and Leigh Penman note that 'Gell appears to have known
German and at Cambridge had been disliked by some for his "addiction" to Lutheran
notions'.[45] Luther's central tenet of 'imputed righteousness' famously stressed that justification for the believer must come from Christ's atonement, and not from anything in the
believer. Once that primacy of imputed righteousness had been acknowledged, the inherent righteousness in a believer could certainly enhance the manifestation of grace in them,
and the good that they did in the world. Inherent righteousness was understood to come
ultimately from God.[46] But Gell often speaks of inherent righteousness as a wellspring of
divinity in a person, and he allied this optimistic perspective with his confidence in the
beneficent influence of angels and stars upon the sublunary world, together with the high
status he accords occult authorities, such as the kabbalah. This certainly greatly angered
his opponents.

---

[39] Gell, *Remaines*, 711.   [40] Gell, *An Essay*, 363.

[41] Taylor is reported in John Evelyn, *Diary*, ed. Henry Wheatley (London, 1906), iii. 254, 258. For a larger
contextual analysis, see Ariel Hessayon, '*Gold tried in the fire*': *The Prophet TheaurauJohn Tany and the
English Revolution* (Aldershot and Burlington, Vt.: Ashgate, 2007), 321–2.

[42] For Rich, see Nigel Smith, 'Hidden Things Brought to Light: Enthusiasm and Quaker Discourse',
Prose Studies, 18 (1995): 57–69.

[43] Conway, *The Conway Letters*, 54–5.   [44] Conway, *The Conway Letters*, 99.

[45] SUL, HP 25/2/21B–22A; Ariel Hessayon and Leigh Penman, 'Rendering Johann Arndt's *True
Christianity* "into our home-spun habit": Contextualising the 1646 English Edition of Arndt's *Book of
Scripture*', forthcoming.

[46] Martin Luther, *Two Kinds of Righteousness* (1519), in John Dillenberger (ed.), *Martin Luther: Selections
from his Writings* (New York, 1962), 86–96.

Furthermore, on the reverse of the title-page to *Aggelokratia theon: Or a Sermon Touching Gods Government of the World by Angels* (1650), Gell justified astrological speculation by quoting a passage concerning the '*motion of the starres and their great multitude*' from book 4 of Johann Arndt's *Wahres Christenthum*. Elsewhere Gell praised Arndt, 'superintendent of *Luneberg*', as 'a learned, pious, holy man, whose name is honourable among all good men throughout *Germany*'. As for the German version of his 'excellent work called *True Christianity*', the fourth book used the authority of Paracelsus, 'that great Philosopher of *Germany*', to inform readers that: 'the stars are certain treasuries and storehouses, out of which, both to men and beasts, God distributeth His temporal good things wonderfully'.[47]

In keeping with the reading interests of his circle of associates and admirers, much of Gell's *Essay* is a collection of sermons in which new translations are only fitfully offered. Nonetheless we should say that the sources adduced in a series of etymological discussions are inspiringly wide-ranging, as broadly distributed as the interest of his disparate circle. However, the same trends that we have seen elsewhere in *An Essay* continue through its extent. Genesis 1: 20, 'And God said, Let the waters bring forth abundantly the moving creature that hath life, and fowl that may fly above the earth in the open firmament of heaven' becomes 'Let the waters bring forth abundantly the living soul that hath life', in order to make 'familiar' what the King James Bible translators have left as 'uncouth', and Gell cites consistency with French, Spanish, and Italian Bibles, Pagnin, and the Tigurine translation.[48]

In this instance Gell appears to be doubling back on earlier claims of faithfulness to the original: 'living soul' being in his view a more appropriate rendering of the Hebrew original. It is seemingly an act of accommodation to a contemporary readership, as opposed to the faithful rendering of the original. However, where the King James Bible relegates an alternative rendering to a margin, Gell often prefers the margin because that is the literal translation. The literal might make no sense in our words, but it does, he says, if we regard it as an allegory.[49] Thus when Genesis tells readers, 'And the LORD God commanded the man, saying, Of every tree of the garden thou mayest freely eat', the allegory makes more extensive sense of the command: 'thou shalt eat'. Genesis 2: 22: 'And the rib, which the LORD God had taken from man, *made* he a woman, and brought her unto the man' becomes 'And the rib, which the LORD God had taken from man, *built* he a woman, and brought her unto the man'.[50] The mysterious and often-quoted Genesis 3: 15, 'And I will put enmity between thee and the woman, and between thy seed and her seed; it shall bruise thy head, and thou shalt bruise his heel', is so obscure, claims Gell, because poor translation has rendered it so, in addition to false glosses and misinterpretation.[51] But his new translation this time does not arrive, with the exception of the alternative of 'break' for 'bruise'. There is a very large amount of commentary, much of it concerned with the allegorical reading of the verse. Have we reached a point where Matthew Poole's final allegation

---

[47] Robert Gell, *Aggelokratia theon: Or a Sermon Touching Gods Government of the World by Angels* (1650), title-page verso, 34–5.

[48] Whereas Castellio has a different solution, distinguishing between earthbound and aerial creatures. On the 'familiarity' of the King James Bible, see the chapter by Karen Edwards in this volume.

[49] Gell, *An Essay*, 5.   [50] Gell, *An Essay*, 7.   [51] Gell, *An Essay*, 9–25.

makes sense: 'I once went to him & freely declared my dissent & offence: I found him not to bee able to make out what hee had asserted'?[52]

Yet there is the example of Genesis 4: 1: 'AND Adam knew Eve his wife; and she conceived, and bare Cain, and said, I have gotten a man from the LORD'. Gell insists that the last sentence is in fact a piece of Eve's proud deception, because word for word it can only mean 'I have gotten the man the Lord', which many translations render literally, including Luther.[53] (Luther's guides Arias Montano and Castellio quite clearly use Latin 'à', i.e. 'from'.) The King James Bible violates textual integrity, says Gell, in presuming an ellipsis; Eve thinks that Cain is the seed who will bruise the serpent's head, and she could not be more wrong. Suddenly Mosaic narration embraces dramatic irony, and delineates postlapsarian pride in a way that is quite consistent with Milton's portrait of the immediately post-Fall, pre-expulsion period in *Paradise Lost*, books 9 and 10.

'After-gods' in preference to 'other gods' suggests an abandonment of the idea of the idols as conduits for devilry, and indeed Gell's genealogy of the heathen idols urges the reader to see them as inner qualities that hamper believers from seeing the 'face of Christ'.[54] Yet one of these threatening inner qualities is still Antichrist, and when Gell insists that Exodus 26: 7 should translate as 'bearing' rather than 'taking' the Lord's name in vain, he means that the sense is not at all to be taken lightly, but that it carries a genuine charge of perjury in the eyes of God.[55] Likewise, Exodus 22: 8 becomes all the stronger for replacing 'to see' with 'to swear': 'If the thief be not found, then the master of the house shall be brought unto the judges, to see whether he have put his hand unto his neighbour's goods'.

The total effect of reading Gell's *Essay* is of encountering someone with a mind-numbingly relentless method. For a scholar divine with such an impressive pedigree and such illustrious pupils it may be conjectured as to why he did not rise further but was in effect parked in a good living. In the latter part of his life this might have been a strategic decision on the part of a bishop. One imagines a most recalcitrant person, engaged in perpetual quibbles and disputation:

> For the *declining or turning away* of the simple, shall *slay them*, and the *prosperity* [or rather, the ease or rest in sin,] of *fools* shall destroy them, *Prov.* 1. 32, where, (whether it be the *Translators* or the *Printers* fault, I know not, but the marginal reading, [or *ease of the simple*] is misplaced, being directed to the former member of the sentence, unto which it belongs not; not to the latter, unto which word [*ease*] may belong, as answering to [shalom], which they turn, prosperity; but the word there they may simple well be left out, For though [patim], in the former part of the sentence, signifie *simple ones*, such as are *easily persuaded to folly*, yet [kasilim], in the later part, signifies not such simple men, but arrant fools, as being joyn'd with the *brutish person*, and opposed to the *wise*, Psal. 49.10. *troublesome turbulent fools.*[56]

This attitude certainly developed through the 1650s, or was kept from print until 1659: in earlier works Gell's eclectic learning is put in the service of opening up the world of

---

[52] Nuttall and Keeble, *Calendar*, i. 335.   [53] Gell, *An Essay*, 27–30.
[54] Gell, *An Essay*, 225–7.   [55] Gell, *An Essay*, 228.
[56] Gell, *An Essay*, 437.

spiritual beings he discerns, but is not turned towards a revision of Bible translation. In the *Aggelokratia theon*, for example, Gell tells his reader:

> Come we now to the Translation of the *Septuagint*, who read not [sons of Israel], but [sons of the lord], by which commonly we understand the Angels, as *Job* 1.6. and 38.7. and accordingly they render the words words κατ' ἀριθμὸν υἱῶν Ἰσραήλ [according to the number of the sons of Israel].
>
> The authority of this Translation is great; nor do I doubt but I could speak as much for the credit and honour of it, as some learned men have done in disparagement of it; as being that which the *Jews* had in their dispersion; that which in the New Testament is quoted often-times without any notice taken of the Hebrew text, when it much differs from it.[57]

Gell prefers the Septuagint translation but he does not insist on it as part of his own distinct, rectified translation. He always has his eye on translations, but does not push forward to the further stage elaborated in his *Essay*.[58]

Gell's project to rectify the English Bible was unfinished at the time of his death, so we will never see the fullest consequence of his revisionary labours, and there is good evidence to suggest that it was the labour of many years, much of it written perhaps considerably earlier than the late 1650s. Nonetheless, it is possible to locate his work inside the circle of post-Calvinist thinkers we associate with the Cambridge Platonists and the speculative thought that surrounds the Henry More-Anne Conway nexus. One of More's recent biographers regards Gell's influence as crucial when More used 'Platonists and mystical divines' to escape from the hold of predestination theology.[59]

Gell's rich range of reference compasses biblical scholarship, patristic scholarship, rabbinic commentary and kabbalah, ancient and Renaissance poetry and history. In his pages we are in the reading universes of Milton, More, and Mede. More's vision of human potential is only a little short of Gell's, even though his sense of human frailty is significantly stronger than Gell's. In a letter to Lady Conway in which he mentions Gell he writes: 'For the thirst after knowledge is ever dangerous till the divine life has its birth in a man, and so the soul becoming divine, God in man as I may so speake examines his works over againe, and tryes if they sute with the will of that divine Nature which is revived in a man'.[60] More than once in his correspondence with Conway, More makes a reference to Gell immediately after discussing his allegorical reading of Genesis, *Conjectura cabbalistica: or, a Conjectural Essay of Interpreting the Minde of Moses, according to a Threefold Cabbala: viz. Literal, Philosophical, Mystical, or, Divinely Moral* (1653). The literal reading of Genesis, thought More, only encouraged atheism. He must have thought of Gell's work as likeminded, insofar as it pursues allegory in the biblical words that he would render in English as close as possible to the original.[61]

Gell agreed with Lady Conway that miracles of healing were possible in their time, and not only in the time of the early church. To this end, he believed that the touch-healer Matthew Coker was genuine.[62] His thinking and interests are not distant from those of

---

[57] Gell, *Aggelokratia theon*, 9.   [58] Gell, *Aggelokratia theon*, 11, 16.

[59] Robert Crocker, 'Henry More: A Biographical Essay', in Sarah Hutton (ed.), *Henry More (1614–1687): Tercentenary Studies* (Dordrecht: Kluwer Academic Publishers, 1990), 1.

[60] Henry More to Anne Conway, 2 Nov. 1651, in *The Conway Letters*, 54.

[61] Henry More to Anne Conway, 4 Apr. 1653, in *The Conway Letters*, 75–6; Henry More to Anne Conway, 4 July 1653, 82.

[62] Robert Gell to Anne Conway, 26 May 1654, in *The Conway Letters*, 98–9.

Lady Conway's physician, Francis Mercurius van Helmont, if not at all related to the philosophy of Van Helmont's friend, Gottfried Wilhelm von Leibniz. The circle's origins partly lay in early seventeenth-century Christ's College: further investigation into college records would certainly be worthwhile but is beyond the scope of the present chapter. In this company and context, the charge of Familism amounts to little: More read the Familist leader Hendrik Niclaes, and decided the treatises contained some piety but were ultimately shallow. Most with Gell and More's interests would have read and taken something from Familist literature but that is the end of it; familiarity with Familist literature was a facet of learned lay piety and mysticism. The same might be said of Böhme's writings. In one of his 1650s sermons, Gell is careful to condemn the Ranters in detail, explicitly denying the libertine outlook that made Abiezer Coppe state that he was of or sympathetic with the Family of Love.[63] Like More, Gell was fully accommodated to the Restoration Church of England. Yet in the 1640s Gell was regarded as an important preacher and scriptural commentator by those like Edward Howes pursuing Familist and perfectionist agendas.[64]

It is no surprise in this company to find Gell's views on biblical translation the subject of much interest to the German Pietists of the eighteenth century. Although Gell's modes of translation and his hermeneutics are, as I have striven to show, more than strictly speaking literal, the *Essay* was published in Berleburg in 1723 and championed by Johann Heinrich Reitz because of its veneration for the original state of the biblical Hebrew and Greek, and the fidelity of translations to this.[65] The Pietists understood that literalism was the key to a proliferation of biblical meanings, as opposed to the clarity venerated by orthodox Lutherans. In this way Gell 'joined at the hip a strictly objective idea of the biblical text and that spiritual subjectivism so long associated with Pietism'.[66] He might have been the last word against the King James Bible in seventeenth-century England, but he was helping to lay the foundation for a major north European spiritual revival early in the next century.

FURTHER READING

Campbell, Gordon, and Thomas Corns. *John Milton: Life, Work, and Thought* (Oxford: Oxford University Press, 2008).

Hamilton, Alastair, *The Family of Love* (Cambridge: James Clarke & Co., 1981).

Hessayon, Ariel. *'Gold tried in the Fire': The Prophet TheaurauJohn Tany and the English Revolution* (Aldershot and Burlington, Vt.: Ashgate, 2007).

Hill, Christopher. *Milton and the English Revolution* (London: Faber & Faber, 1977).

Marsh, Christopher. *The Family of Love in English Society, 1550–1630* (Cambridge: Cambridge University Press, 1994).

[63] *The Conway Letters*, 39–42.

[64] David R. Como, *Blown by the Spirit: Puritanism and the Emergence of an Antinomian Underground in pre-Civil-War England* (Stanford: Stanford University Press, 2004), 8.

[65] Gell, *Ein Versuch, Muster oder Probe zur Verbesserung der letzten Englischen Übersetzung der Bibel: oder eine … Exempel … dass die letzte Übersetzung der Bibel ins Englische möge verbessert werden; die erste Theil in Pentateuchum …* (Berleburg, 1723); Martin Brecht, 'Die Berleburger Bibel: Hinwiese zu ihrem Verständnis', *Pietismus und Neuzeit*, 8 (1982), 177.

[66] Jonathan Sheehan, *The Enlightenment Bible: Translation, Scholarship, Culture* (Princeton: Princeton University Press, 2005), 68.

Norton, David. *A History of the English Bible as Literature*, 2 vols (Cambridge: Cambridge University Press, 2000).

Norton, David. *The King James Bible: A Short History from Tyndale to Today* (Cambridge: Cambridge University Press, 2011).

Nuttall, G. F. *James Nayler: A Fresh Approach* (London: Friends Historical Society, 1954).

Sheehan, Jonathan. *The Enlightenment Bible: Translation, Scholarship, Culture* (Princeton: Princeton University Press, 2005).

Smith, Nigel. *Perfection Proclaimed: Language and Literature in English Radical Religion, 1640–1660* (Oxford: Oxford University Press, 1989).

Smith, Nigel. 'Hidden Things Brought to Light: Enthusiasm and Quaker Discourse'. *Prose Studies*, 18 (1995): 57–69.

Smith, Nigel. *Andrew Marvell: The Chameleon* (New Haven and London: Yale University Press, 2010).

PART II

SCHOLARSHIP

Introduction to Part II

THE mass of humanist erudition in the sixteenth century that underlay the translation and refinement of the biblical text is hard to overestimate. Scholars fought over the relative authority of Greek, Hebrew, and Latin versions of the Bible, each with their own complex histories of transmission, mistransmission, interpolation, and questionable integrity. Biblical scholarship increased exponentially with the publication of patristic editions, the collation of editions and manuscript witnesses, the increasing familiarity with rabbinic, Eastern and Arabic scholarship, the linguistic acuity of increasing numbers of scholarly centres, and the sheer mass of intellectual resources devoted to exegetical questions. The post-reformation landscape, on its pan-European scale, was one in which scholars pored over not only theologically contentious translations—whether ecclesiastical or eucharistic—but every aspect of both Old and New Testaments. The seventeenth century was no less avid in its biblical scholarship, although the landscape of scholarship changed in quite significant ways.

The essays here make clear that in an important sense, to speak of the 'Bible in English' or other European vernaculars is very much to miss the point. Both the text itself and the commentary traditions around it were conducted in classical tongues. Latin remained the language of such scholarship, conducted in the Republic of Letters (often enough, the republic of poison-pen letters). This Latin had as its object of study the Greek, Hebrew, Syriac, Aramaic, Chaldee, and Coptic languages and traditions, and among its most prestigious outputs were several major polyglot Bibles—all of which, prior to the London Polyglot of 1657, were Catholic scholarly enterprises (see Chronology). Nicholas Hardy's essay on the study of the Septuagint in the seventeenth century demonstrates how complex a matter questions of hermeneutics and philology might remain, tracing the debate on the very nature of theological exposition among scholars who, in the light of emerging manuscript evidence, an expanding patristic corpus, and a renewed focus on the integrity of Vulgate, Septuagint, and Hebrew Bibles, sought to redefine the object of exegetical and textual criticism. Their concerns were stylistic as well as philological; they fought to establish how one should go about the collation, sifting, glossing, and, more controversially, emendation of received texts. Not only the translation, but the canon of the Bible was tussled over, at times furiously, in the era. There was a long history of instability at the edges of the biblical canon, and discussion of the Apocrypha had been a regular feature of patristic and post-patristic debate. Arial Hessayon's essay traces this debate and how the Reformation made it a confessional issue, so that Catholic and Protestant Bibles came to differ quite substantially, in, for instance, the Lutheran excision of the Epistle of James, with its fiery attacks on the rich, or of Maccabees, on the supposition that it was used by Catholics to justify, by turn, 'good works' as a path to salvation and the existence of purgatory. The cumulative oscillations of the Apocrypha in Bibles across the sixteenth century attest to how potent an issue the biblical corpus remained and how, in the English context, the use of apocryphal works in the Book of Common Prayer aroused ire.

Scholarship has become very much aware of how fecund a notion the biblical 'literal' was, as a tool for thinking textually, theologically, and even scientifically. It bears relatively little resemblance to versions of the literal which emerged in the nineteenth century and which equate the literal with the bare surface of the word. In the wake of the widespread Protestant rejection of the *quadriga*—the 'fourfold method' of interpretation in which the multiple levels of meaning, literal, allegorical, anagogical, and moral, were deemed to coexist in the polyvalent biblical word—the burden of interpretation fell on the literal sense. And yet the apparent richness of the post-Reformation scope of the literal leads to the suspicion that the loss of the *quadriga*, with all its interpretative wealth and scope, was not entirely universal, that exegetes regularly smuggled a great deal into the literal sense. Debora Shuger, dealing with this complexity in exegetical sermon writing and commentary, explores how the lineage of Christian allegorical and literal interpretation is complicated by its awareness of, and unease about, Jewish exegetical traditions, that did not allow for the typology whereby Old Testament passages were routinely described as referring 'literally' to Christ. One of most important fault lines dividing Catholics and Protestants was their respective attitudes to the Bible: Protestants insisted upon the sufficiency of the Bible alone, *sola scriptura*, in any part of the essentials of religion, while Catholicism deemed this a disingenuous neglect of interpretative lineage and tradition, pointing out the absence from the Bible of such fundamentals as the Trinity. While both positions were often caricatured and traduced in the polemical literature of the era, they were also subject to complex and sophisticated analysis, perhaps nowhere more so than in the context of scholarship informing Richard Hooker's *Of the Lawes of Ecclesiasticall Politie* (1593), the subject of Torrance Kirby's essay, which explores a superlatively complex hermeneutics of the 'literal' meaning of the Bible.

For all that the turn to the 'literal' might seem to imply that Protestant authors would eschew the non-biblical, the pagan, and the Jewish in their approaches to the Bible, this is resolutely not the case. On the contrary, the impulse to historicize the scriptures, to put them in concert with cognate cultures, was deep set. No previous era had worked quite so intensively to contextualize the Bible, with two disciplines in particular—sacred geography and biblical chronology—coming to characterize this. Zur Shalev's chapter explores how ideas of the fertility of the Holy Land—both past and present—became enwrought in complex theological debates, about the nature of land, covenant, and providence, negotiating the difficult, though contested fact that the Israel which pilgrims encountered and the Palestine that was reported in scholarly map-filled texts seemed curiously arid. Making rich use of classical geographies and historians, early modern scholarship sought to explain, deny, or query how and why this was so. Scott Mandelbrote writes on the importance of sacred chronologies and the extensive intellectual investment in allying the Bible to secular histories in a variety of quasi-scientific endeavours. Both a technical-mathematical and theological discipline that traversed millenarianism and close textual scholarship, chronology, for all its idiosyncratic nature—and it attracted its share of contemporary ridicule—characterizes that most quintessential early modern expectation that all learning, whether natural history, astronomy, or the humanities, might be put to task in understanding the Bible.

It is also the case that early readers, and sometimes surprising ones, developed a degree of scepticism about the intrinsic wholeness and reliability of the biblical text, or at least utilized a hermeneutic that suspended 'mere' certainty. Neil Forsyth's essay on Milton addresses some of the fraught issues around the nature of the biblical text, and, the extent to which Protestant readers came to presume and, within tight parameters, to accept biblical corruption. This was an issue with differing consequences when it was discussed in a scholarly context and when it was the subject of analysis by Goodwin or Hobbes, in a polemical context that was more pressingly political and more fleetingly concerned with learned nuance. The chapter explores Milton the exegete, and how the interpretative protocols in his unpublished theological tract, *De doctrina Christiana,* underlie, though also create exegetical difficulties for, *Paradise Lost.*

The diverse lenses through which the biblical can be seen in the early modern era are, in some respects, difficult to reconcile. Attention to the Hebrew vowel points, or to the legal-contextual minutiae of Deuteronomy seems a long way from the soldiers' catechisms of the Civil Wars, and the ecclesiology of Anglicanism in the 1630s can seem quite distant from the home-spun politics of the radicals and enthusiasts. And yet their distance should not be exaggerated. Crawford Gribben's chapter traverses these apparently alien modes of interest in the Bible, ranging from the concern about the stability of the English text of the Bible in a mass print market, to anxiety about the authenticity of the translation in the context of polyglot projects. The sheer volume of Bibles in circulation is hard to credit, but well attested. The ongoing allegiance to the Geneva Bible and its annotations through the Civil Wars, and the variety of editions and annotative aids to reading the scriptures jostle in importance with the scholarly projects of the interregnum; Gribben's chapter traces the mutual effects of the popular and the elite, neither quite insulated from the other.

Nicholas McDowell's chapter traces a context of 'antiscripturism' that constituted a slowly unfolding panic at the numbers (and social quality) of those whose cynicism about the text of the Bible had appeared in print. Putting politically radical scepticism in dialogue with Latitudinarian and Anglican traditions of sceptical exegesis, McDowell produces an account that refutes the supposition that blunt anti-intellectualism lay at the root of such attitudes, and creates a lineage for such thought out of the surprising resource of pre-Enlightenment orthodox Anglicanism, from Hooker to Chillingworth to Taylor. Scholarship was, then, not cordoned off from other interpretative acts, even if, at times, it found itself engaged in rebarbative dispute, and while its acts of superlative pedantry were open both to mockery and to accusations of contorting the Bible out of simple shape, scriptural scholars were also widely admired and their contributions to early modern culture can hardly be overestimated.

CHAPTER 7

....

THE SEPTUAGINT AND THE TRANSFORMATION OF BIBLICAL SCHOLARSHIP IN ENGLAND, FROM THE KING JAMES BIBLE (1611) TO THE LONDON POLYGLOT (1657)

....

NICHOLAS HARDY

It is a commonplace of religious history that Catholics sought to silence Protestants by asking them: where was your Church before Luther? They might just as well have asked: where was your Bible before your Church? Jews, not Christians, had been responsible for the preservation of the Hebrew Old Testament which the reformers favoured and used in their vernacular translations. Moreover, the earliest extant manuscript witnesses of it were not much more than five hundred years old in the sixteenth century. The Latin translation known to Catholics as the Vulgate, by contrast, was a Christian text whose authority derived from a Christian editor, St Jerome (c.347–420), and whose earliest manuscripts were not much younger than Jerome himself. Ironically, then, the Latin Vulgate might represent a more authentic witness to the original Hebrew text than the Hebrew text that had survived into the early modern period. But there was another version of the Old Testament, ratified by Catholic tradition: the Septuagint. Its history was ambiguous. Almost everybody agreed that it had been translated by Greek-speaking Jews, probably in the third century BC. However, it also seemed to have been used by the earliest Christians, including the authors of the New Testament, and had then been endorsed by many of the fathers of the church, who treated it as divinely inspired. Augustine initially preferred Latin translations made from the Septuagint over those from the Hebrew.[1] While Western Christendom turned to the Vulgate, moreover, the Septuagint continued to be favoured by the Greek Orthodox Church.

---

[1] See in particular Augustine, *Epistulae*, no. 71, to Jerome.

Its surviving manuscripts were even older than those of the Vulgate, providing a further argument for its superiority to the other two versions.

For these reasons, the Septuagint was taken up as a weapon on both sides of the confessional divide. It might be used either to undermine the Hebrew Old Testament, or the Vulgate. The two scholars of the Septuagint on whom this chapter concentrates were not engaged in direct warfare as such, but the course of their work was often determined by their ecclesiastical affiliations. They made significant contributions to the two most important products of biblical scholarship in seventeenth-century England. John Bois (1561–1644) was one of the translators of the King James Bible, and Patrick Young (1584–1652), who served as librarian to James I and Charles I, spent the latter part of his career working on a new edition of the Septuagint.[2] This edition was never completed, but some of Young's notes towards it were published posthumously in the London Polyglot Bible (1657), a colossal collaborative work of biblical erudition in multiple languages.[3] Whereas the King James Bible was a vernacular translation whose scholarly foundations were never publicly exposed, the London Polyglot self-consciously displayed the fruits of well over a century of biblical criticism, all of it communicated in Latin for a learned readership.

This in itself represents a significant shift in the priorities of biblical scholars in England. Comparing the career of John Bois with that of Patrick Young, we can observe the study of the Bible gradually becoming a more technical, specialized discipline. Some of the Church of England's leaders, moreover, were approaching a Catholic position on the text of scripture, according to which the biblical text was so complicated as to demand a highly trained clerical caste to study, preserve, and interpret it for the benefit of lay persons. Indeed, the London Polyglot was the fourth of the great polyglot bibles, but only the first Protestant one.

Patrick Young and John Bois are linked by their shared interest in the Septuagint: indeed, they collaborated with each other directly, and after Bois's death, Young used his unpublished work. These connections give us an unusually clear insight into the way in which intellectual and confessional developments shaped the study of the Septuagint, and the Bible as a whole, over a fifty-year period. Thanks to humanist educational reforms, the philological and historical study of Greek texts, secular as well as sacred, had found a place in university curricula.[4] But as the cases of Bois and Young illustrate, scholars with this humanist training were not necessarily prepared to deal with the questions of profound confessional and theological import that Catholics and Protestants were asking about the different versions and manuscripts of the Bible.

At the beginning of the seventeenth century, John Bois was regarded as one of England's foremost experts on Greek literature, especially in its sacred and ecclesiastical forms. Cambridge provided the foundations for his achievements in that language. His father had been one of the founding fellows of Trinity College in 1546, and his schoolmaster had been a

---

[2] For Bois, see also Ward Allen, *Translating for King James* (London: Allen Lane, 1970); and for Young, the edition of his correspondence with biography: Johannes Kemke (ed.), *Patricius Junius* (Leipzig: M. Spirgatis, 1898).

[3] Henry John Todd, *Memoirs of the Life and Writings of the Right Rev. Brian Walton* (London, 1821); and Peter N. Miller, 'The "Antiquarianization" of Biblical Scholarship and the London Polyglot Bible', *Journal of the History of Ideas*, 62 (2001): 463–82.

[4] Mordechai Feingold, 'The Humanities', in Nicholas Tyacke (ed.), *The History of the University of Oxford*, iv. *Seventeenth-Century Oxford* (Oxford: Clarendon Press, 1997), 211–357.

fellow of St John's. It was at St John's, too, that Bois became the most successful pupil of Andrew Downes, the eventual Regius Professor of Greek.

Having the right ancestors or even schoolmasters was not enough, however. Greek was still relatively new and unfamiliar in the English universities, compared with Latin, which was their first language throughout the period. To reach total mastery of that language took extra effort outside the normal academic curriculum. In Bois's case, this came from Downes, who was in the habit of offering private tuition (for a fee) to students who were interested, and went out of his way to train Bois to deal with particularly difficult texts.[5] When Bois himself became a fellow of St John's, he too provided extra tuition in Greek to willing students, including Thomas Gataker, one of the most celebrated English classicists before Richard Bentley.[6] So while the formal institutional provisions for Greek seem to have been inadequate for advanced scholarship, pupils regarded these extra-curricular arrangements as memorable departures from the normal routine, into a world of recondite but appealing 'matters of learning and criticism'.[7]

Just as serious scholars of Greek were formed outside academic structures, so too were major enterprises that drew on their talents. The King James Bible, for example, may have been executed by university men, but it was conceived by higher political and ecclesiastical authorities. Bois was initially commissioned to work alongside Downes and others on the Old Testament Apocrypha in Cambridge. These books survived mainly in Greek rather than Hebrew, and had not been regarded as canonical by the Jews or the majority of Protestants. Indeed, the King James Bible clearly designated them as extra-canonical, but continental theologians would come to object to the decision to print them at all.[8] As well as working on the Apocrypha, Bois was also involved in the final revision of the whole translation, which took place in London. His extensive notes on the revision of the New Testament epistles and Revelation bear partial witness to this process.[9]

There are several extant sources for Bois's study of the Septuagint, beginning with documents that help us trace his contribution to the King James Bible, and illuminate three subsequent decades of work on the text. One is Bois's copiously annotated working copy of the 1587 Rome Septuagint, which he used both to translate the Apocrypha and during the final revision stage.[10] He was still annotating the book shortly before his death in 1644.[11]

[5] Allen, *Translating*, 133.   [6] Allen, *Translating*, 136.

[7] I quote Simonds D'Ewes, as cited by Elisabeth Leedham-Green and Elisabeth N. G. Wilson, 'Downes, Andrew (c.1549–1628)', *ODNB*, 2004, <http://www.oxforddnb.com/view/article/7972>.

[8] See Anthony Milton (ed.), *The British Delegation and the Synod of Dort (1618–1619)* (Woodbridge: Boydell Press, 2005), 135–7, 140–1, 157.

[9] There are two manuscripts. Corpus Christi College, Oxford, MS 312 was published with translation and introduction by Allen, *Translating*. A second witness was discovered later, in British Library MS Harley 750: see David Norton, 'John Bois's Notes on the Revision of the King James Bible New Testament: A New Manuscript', *The Library*, 6th ser. 18 (1996): 328–46. On the rest of the documentary evidence for the genesis of the KJB, see Norton, *A Textual History of the King James Bible* (Cambridge: Cambridge University Press, 2005).

[10] Bodleian Library, D 1.14 Th.Seld. The hand of the annotator is identical to other documents written and signed by Bois, such as British Library, MS Sloane 118, fols. 24 and 30. My identification is confirmed by Leiden University Library, MS VMI 4, fol. 7ᵛ, where Patrick Young names Bois as the author of the notes. For more on this manuscript, see later in this chapter.

[11] The latest datable references by Bois in this book are to Hugo Grotius's *Annotationes in libros evangeliorum* (Amsterdam, 1641), e.g. 450 and 526. John Selden most likely acquired Bois's Septuagint through Cornelius Bee, who came to publish his *De Synedriis* (London, 1650–5). An anonymous account of Bois's books in

A second is his correspondence with the famous French Protestant scholar Isaac Casaubon (1559–1614), containing detailed discussions of problems of translation in the Apocrypha.[12]

Next, there are sources in which Bois makes considerable use of the Septuagint, even though it is not the primary object of study. He contributed annotations to Sir Henry Savile's monumental edition of the complete works of St John Chrysostom, a church father whose powers of biblical exegesis were highly regarded by Protestants.[13] Later in his career, Bois contributed notes to Patrick Young's *editio princeps* of the sole surviving genuine work of a more ancient father of the church: Clement of Rome's epistle to the Corinthians.[14] He was also prompted by Lancelot Andrewes to write a treatise comparing the ancient Latin translation of the New Testament with modern Latin translations.[15]

Familiarity with the Septuagint was necessary in each of these cases, but for different reasons. Chrysostom and Clement of Rome both quoted the Old Testament in Greek, and the language of Clement in particular seemed to share some of the grammatical and syntactical features of the Septuagint's Greek, even when he did not directly cite it. The *Collatio* written at Andrewes's suggestion was a comparative account of the ancient and modern Latin renderings of the New Testament, assessing them as much for their stylistic qualities as their accuracy in matters of dogma. Here the Septuagint was invoked, from time to time, to illustrate the linguistic background of New Testament Greek and inform its translation into Latin.[16] In the other cases, the Septuagint was cited for all manner of reasons, but particularly often as a parallel for classical Greek turns of phrase.

The miscellaneity of these enterprises is important. They were reactive: Bois undertook them in response to requests for his expertise by a range of different figures. Otherwise, they

Bodleian Library, MS Tanner 278, fol. 3ʳ, records that Bee bought 'ye Library, but whither hee had y m=ss, non constat'.

[12] British Library, MS Burney 363, fols. 101ʳ–105ᵛ. Neither Bois's nor Casaubon's side of the correspondence is dated, but internal evidence shows that it was written after Casaubon had arrived in London in Oct. 1610. On Casaubon, see Mark Pattison, *Isaac Casaubon* (London, 1875); and Anthony Grafton and Joanna Weinberg, '*I Have Always Loved the Holy Tongue*': *Isaac Casaubon, the Jews, and a Forgotten Chapter in Renaissance Scholarship* (Cambridge, Mass.: Harvard University Press, 2010).

[13] *S. Ioannis Chrysostomi opera Graecè* (Eton, 1613). Bois's notes are in vol. viii. On this edition, see Jean-Louis Quantin, 'Du Chrysostome latin au Chrysostome grec: Une histoire européenne (1588–1613)', in Martin Wallraff and Rudolf Brändle (eds), *Chrysostomosbilder in 1600 Jahren: Facetten der Wirkungsgeschichte eines Kirchenvaters* (Berlin: De Gruyter, 2008), 267–346. On Chrysostom's popularity, see Irena Backus, *Historical Method and Confessional Identity in the Era of the Reformation (1378–1615)* (Leiden: Brill, 2003), 102–6; and Anthony Milton, *Catholic and Reformed: The Roman and Protestant Churches in English Protestant Thought, 1600–1640* (Cambridge: Cambridge University Press, 1995), 275.

[14] *Clementis ad Corinthios epistola prior*, ed. Patrick Young (Oxford, 1633). Bois's autograph notes, written originally at the behest of John Williams (1582–1650), then Bishop of Lincoln, are in Bodleian Library, MS Barlow 10, fols. 118ʳ–126ᵛ. Young's commentary repeatedly cites Bois by name.

[15] Published posthumously as *Veteris Interpretis cum Beza aliisque recentioribus collatio* (London, 1655). Bois's autograph manuscript of the work is Bodleian Library, MS Tanner 437. See also the correspondence between Bois and Andrewes in MS Sloane 118, fols. 24 and 30; and in Bodleian Library, MS Smith 73, 1–2 (a copy).

[16] Bois, *Collatio*, 307: 'Unde autem melius discamus quae sit vis multarum dictionum & locutionum in novo Testamento, quàm ex interpretibus illis [scil. the Septuagint], quos constat tanto fuisse in pretio apud Apostolos & Evangelistas, ut in testimoniis ex vetere foedere citandis, ne latum quidem unguem ab illorum verbis & vestigiis discesserint'. (There is no better source from which to learn the force of many words and phrases in the New Testament than the Septuagint. We know that the Apostles and writers of the Gospels valued it so highly that when they cited testimonies from the Old Testament, they did not suffer even the slightest departure from its wording and the precedent it had set.)

were a product of the wide-ranging habits of reading that followed no set course and lasted all of Bois's life. They all drew on a general familiarity with the Septuagint; but they did not lead Bois to do sustained critical work on that text over a long period of time, with a specific purpose in mind. Equally importantly, they did not usually invite him to call the text itself into question. There is very little evidence that Bois ever tried to consult a Greek manuscript of the Old Testament, nor even that he engaged in critical comparison of its various printed versions.

What Bois himself understood by 'criticism' was something quite different from collating manuscripts, or constructing a history of their transmission. In the first place, criticism was, to use an anachronistic distinction, literary as well as historical. This is demonstrated most clearly by his *Collatio*, which defended the ancient Latin version of the New Testament as a superior translation to any modern one.[17] In doing so, Bois treated the ancient translators as colleagues in a modern-day enterprise. The *vetus Latina* was superior, moreover, on the level of style as well as fidelity to the original: Bois praised its *elegantia* as well as its accuracy.[18] Although his commentary was not overwhelmingly aesthetically orientated, he does seem to have considered stylistic superiority and philological accuracy as parts of a whole. When the Flemish Hebraist, Johannes Drusius, quoted on Bois's title-page, described this ancient translation as 'a lot better than is commonly believed', Bois may well have taken him to mean that it was 'better' on both of these levels.

Bois, then, was essentially arguing that the ancient authors of the Latin translation were better grammarians than their modern counterparts, in terms both of their linguistic facility and factual awareness. This conviction was founded on a common humanist principle, applied to Christian antiquity: 'the older, the better'.[19] He also emphasized the interpenetration of pagan, Jewish, and Christian culture. He glossed his copy of the Septuagint with historical, rhetorical, and linguistic parallels from classical authors, as well as Jewish and Christian ones.

It is also worth noting how rarely Bois cites professional theologians in the margins of his Septuagint. Such references can be counted on the fingers of both hands. They take in Luther, Melanchthon, Martin Chemnitz, Peter Martyr, and William Whitaker (Master of St John's, Cambridge, Bois's own college), but not a single Catholic theologian.[20] Most of the passages Bois cites from their works, moreover, are concerned on a scholarly level with grammatical issues, rather than dogma or doctrine *per se*. On the other hand, he repeatedly cites modern grammarians and critics, whether Protestant (such as Scaliger, Casaubon, Drusius, Johannes Buxtorf the Elder, and Daniel Heinsius) or Catholic (Erasmus, Guillaume Budé, Andreas Masius, Angelo Canini, and Barnabé Brisson). His use of biblical editions

---

[17] I use the term 'ancient Latin translation' because Bois himself avoided referring to the 'Vulgate' or 'Jerome's version', preferring to speak of the *vetus interpres* ('ancient translator'). Bois was refusing to accord the Latin New Testament the same status which Catholics had given it after the Council of Trent, as well as hinting at the fact that Jerome seemed to have revised the ancient Latin translations of the New Testament less thoroughly than he had revised those of the Old Testament, and therefore that the Latin New Testament did not deserve to be called his. See e.g. Jerome, *Praefatio in quatuor evangelia*.

[18] See for instance, Bois, *Collatio*, 8 (on Matt. 5: 12).

[19] As he put it to Andrewes, 25 Oct. 1621, in MS Smith 73, 2: 'ὁ παλαιός χρηστότερος ἐστι'.

[20] For Bois's reminiscence of Whitaker, see his diary: Cambridge University Library, MS Add. 3856, fol. 156ʳ. Bois praised the notorious Catholic theologian Robert Bellarmine in private, but for his learning, not for his piety or orthodoxy: see his letter to John Williams, 23 Sept. 1630, in MS Smith 73, 9.

and translations is equally multi-confessional, covering not only the Roman Septuagint of 1587, but also the Complutensian Polyglot printed in 1514–17, as well as the Latin translations of the Old Testament by Immanuel Tremellius and Franciscus Junius (1597), and of the Apocrypha by the German reformer Petrus Cholinus (1543).

In short, Bois's approach to the Septuagint was that of a Christian humanist rather than an academic theologian. Nor was it that of a textual editor: his erudition was extensive, but diffuse, jumping from one interesting or obscure passage to another without immersing itself in thorny questions of manuscript transmission or the relative canonical authority of individual translations. But it took more than contextualizing glosses and linguistic parallels to edit the text of the Septuagint. The case of Patrick Young, a Greek scholar of the generation after Bois's, illustrates this distinction.

Bois and Young's interests first directly overlapped when the former contributed to the latter's edition of Clement of Rome in the early 1630s. Clement's Epistle to the Corinthians had never been published because the first manuscript witness had only recently come to the West, as a gift to the King of England from the Greek Orthodox Patriarch of Constantinople, Cyril Lucaris. This fifth-century uncial manuscript, later known as Codex Alexandrinus, also contained a near-complete text of the entire Bible in Greek.[21] This text of the Bible would become crucial to Young's editorial work on the Septuagint. For now, however, Young focused on producing the *editio princeps* of Clement. Since Codex Alexandrinus contained the only surviving text of the author, Clement posed different editorial problems from the Old Testament. Young needed to restore damaged or otherwise illegible sections by pure conjecture, rather than consulting other manuscripts, but his use of conjectural emendation overstepped these bounds. He often suggested alternatives to words which were perfectly legible, and regularly did so on stylistic and rhetorical grounds. Bois's notes took a similar approach. Both scholars' commentaries, moreover, glossed the text with passages from classical authors, as well as later ecclesiastical ones and the Bible. Young's edition of Clement was an exhibition of humanistic learning and critical acumen.

Once he had published Clement, Young moved on to a different project: a new edition of the Septuagint based on Codex Alexandrinus. In editing the Septuagint, however, Young confronted a set of problems with which neither he nor Bois had been trained to deal. These problems were largely technical and methodological, revolving around the questions outlined at the beginning of this chapter: might a translation reflect the original Old Testament better than the extant Hebrew text? Could the surviving manuscripts be used to show this? And did it matter whether a version was divinely inspired or not?

In part, these were problems for the scholars to ponder. However, technical advances were often the result of confessional warfare. Before 1650, the most important developments in Septuagint scholarship had been made by Catholics, and we cannot make sense of Young's work without first considering their positions. The principal editions of the Septuagint published during this period were not Protestant products. They include the Complutensian Polyglot, printed at Alcalá de Henares in Spain between 1514 and 1517; the Aldine Septuagint, published in 1518; and the Roman Septuagint, published, as we have seen, in 1587. The last of

---

[21] Scott Mandelbrote, 'English Scholarship and the Greek Text of the Old Testament, 1620–1720: The Impact of Codex Alexandrinus', in Ariel Hessayon and Nicholas Keene (eds), *Scripture and Scholarship in Early Modern England* (Aldershot: Ashgate, 2006), 77–83; and Matthew Spinka, 'Acquisition of the Codex Alexandrinus by England', *The Journal of Religion*, 16 (1936): 10–29.

these had been commissioned by Pope Sixtus V himself, and was enshrined as the authoritative text of the Septuagint, just as Sixtus intended the Vulgate text published at the same time to serve as the official Latin version.[22] To these three we must also add the Antwerp Polyglot of 1568–73; Jean Morin's republication of the Roman Septuagint in Paris in 1628; and, eventually, the Paris Polyglot of 1645. These were Catholic projects. They all contained new paratextual material in varying quantities, and amounted to expensive statements that the Septuagint was an extremely important witness to the Old Testament, and document of Christian antiquity. In light of this Catholic background, the acquisition of Codex Alexandrinus by a Protestant nation was potentially disruptive. How different was it from the major published texts of the Septuagint? Might it trump them all, or even be used to show that the Hebrew text was superior?

These questions never received satisfactory answers in the seventeenth century. The arrival of new manuscripts only increased their complexity. Accordingly, Codex Alexandrinus failed to have much impact on the study of the Septuagint because critics were growing disillusioned with the notion that it was possible for a single manuscript to offer an uncorrupted version of the Bible. Textual criticism had simply become too sophisticated, and its practitioners too 'cautious and critical' or 'serious and broad-minded' to countenance such a possibility.[23] However, this explanation needs to be supplemented by an account of what was old-fashioned, rather than progressive, in Young's approach. Although he managed to transcend his dogmatism about individual manuscripts by means of new critical methods, Young's progress continued to be hampered by his struggles to reconcile the traditional tools of humanist erudition with the rigours of a historical study of the Bible and its different versions.

In order to advance a serious argument about the importance of Codex Alexandrinus, Young needed to do more than publish a transcription of it. He had to collate it with other manuscripts of the Bible, or printed editions where those were not available. In addition to this, he would have to collate his manuscript with citations of the Septuagint preserved in early Christian texts, from the New Testament to the Greek fathers. This question of the relative value of biblical and patristic citations for the text of the Old Testament introduced an entirely new set of difficulties. Many of the extant Greek fathers' writings predated the earliest Septuagint manuscripts, even if the manuscripts of those writings did not. One father in particular presented a further problem: as well as citing the Septuagint, Origen had edited it. The most famous of these editions was known as the Hexapla, for the six different versions it placed alongside each other.[24] By Origen's time, the Septuagint was not the only available translation into Greek: and Origen's editions served as the tools with which these competing translations, as well as the Hebrew text, could be compared. In Origen's own work, the various translations were carefully distinguished from each other. Usually, he placed them in separate columns, with one exception: when the Septuagint lacked a passage which the Hebrew text contained, he filled in the gap with the later Greek translation by Theodotion.

---

[22] On the authority of the Septuagint upheld by the Council of Trent, see Jared Wicks, 'The Decrees of the Council of Trent on the Old Testament Canon, the Vulgate and Biblical Interpretation', in Magne Sæbø (ed.), *Hebrew Bible/Old Testament: The History of its Interpretation* (Göttingen: Vandenhoeck & Ruprecht, 2008), ii. 617–48 (ii. 627–8 and 634–6 on the eventual publication of the Vulgate and Septuagint in Rome).

[23] Mandelbrote, 'English Scholarship', 87, 92.

[24] See *Brill's New Pauly*, s.v. 'Septuagint'.

Whenever the Septuagint differed from the Hebrew text in this way, however, or if it contained something which the Hebrew text did not, Origen took care to mark the discrepancy using critical sigla.

Later on, however, when Origen's texts were copied, these critical sigla and distinctions into columns were not always preserved. As a result, the work of Theodotion in particular, but also the other Greek translators, came to be confused with the Septuagint. Origen was therefore an unavoidable obstacle for any modern editor of the Septuagint, and so were the other Greek translators whose work had become incorporated into and confused with the Septuagint via his multi-text editions.[25] Young knew he had to glean as much information as he could about the other versions by Aquila, Symmachus, and Theodotion, but he did not know how to go beyond them and isolate the work of the Seventy in every verse of the Old Testament. Finally, Young confronted the question of whether he needed to go beyond the manuscript evidence, and how far: whether he could restore the original text by conjectural emendation. He still wished to assess the Septuagint using the tools of grammatical, rhetorical, and stylistic evaluation as well as the more sober study of manuscripts.

Some of these challenges are encapsulated in Young's first publication that concerned itself with the text of the Septuagint: his edition in 1637 of a selection, or *Catena*, of patristic commentaries on the Book of Job which had originally been compiled by Nicetas, the eleventh-century Bishop of Heraclea.[26] Young accompanied this with a text of Job taken from Codex Alexandrinus, which the title-page advertised as representative of the 'the true and genuine translation of the Seventy Elders' and as the 'oldest and most important' manuscript in the whole world. For Young, however, the text alone was not enough: its accuracy was confirmed by the patristic citations of the Septuagint in the commentaries he had published, as well as by the fragment of a famous letter by Origen which he had placed just before the text of Job. These supposedly showed that Codex Alexandrinus was 'absolutely unblemished by any mingling of other translations'.[27]

Young's *Catena* was the first real sample of his work on the edition, and the uses he planned to make of patristic sources as well as Codex Alexandrinus. Soon after its publication, he received a letter from Jean Morin (1591–1659), an oratorian who had studied at Leiden before his conversion to Catholicism.[28] As we have seen, Morin had republished the Roman Septuagint of 1587 in Paris, in 1628. Morin's work, followed up by full-scale academic dissertations on the Septuagint and counterblasts aimed at his critics, became the key reference point for any budding biblical critic in the following decades, including Young.

---

[25] See Scott Mandelbrote, 'Origen Against Jerome in Early Modern Europe', in Silke-Petra Bergjan and Karla Pollmann (eds), *Patristic Tradition and Intellectual Paradigms in the Seventeenth Century* (Tübingen: Mohr Siebeck, 2010), 105–35.

[26] *Catena Graecorum patrum in beatum Iob, collectore Niceta Heracleae metropolita . . . accessit ad calcem textus Iobi στιχηρῶς*, ed. Patrick Young (London, 1637).

[27] *Catena*, ¶4ʳ.

[28] See the biography (by Richard Simon) and selected correspondence in *Antiquitates ecclesiae orientalis* (London, 1682); Paul Auvray, 'Jean Morin (1591–1659)', *Revue Biblique*, 66 (1959): 397–414; François Laplanche, *L'Ecriture, le sacré et l'histoire: Erudits et politiques protestants devant la Bible en France au XVIIe siècle* (Amsterdam: APA-Holand University Press, 1986), esp. 315–17; and Peter N. Miller, 'Making the Paris Polyglot Bible: Humanism and Orientalism in the Early Seventeenth Century', in Herbert Jaumann (ed.), *Die Europäische Gelehrtenrepublik im Zeitalter des Konfessionalismus* (Wiesbaden: Harrassowitz, 2001), 59–85, esp. 71–84.

Morin's publications argued that the Greek version of the Old Testament (especially that embodied in Codex Vaticanus, the manuscript on which the Roman edition had been based) was textually more authentic than the Hebrew original. Not only were the surviving manuscripts much older (Codex Vaticanus dates to the fourth century AD; the oldest complete Hebrew manuscripts to the tenth), but the manuscript transmission of them was demonstrably more stable. Predictably, Morin provoked almost exclusively hostile responses from Protestant scholars, while his work divided Catholics.[29] Nonetheless, he played an important role in determining Young's approach to the task: unlike Bois, he had actually edited the Septuagint, rather than simply deploying it in learned commentaries or other miscellaneous projects. But their correspondence shows that the ground of textual criticism was shifting under Young's feet. Morin was offering new standards by which to assess the value of a particular manuscript, edition, or translation.

It is significant that Morin seems to have waited until after Young published the *Catena* to write to him directly. He had shown little interest in Young's edition of Clement. His own work specialized in the textual history of the Bible, and he had no time for the kind of multifarious philological commentary Young and Bois had practised in that book. His response to Young's first venture into Old Testament criticism, however, was a devastating rebuttal.[30] Morin's letter argued that it was highly unlikely that any single extant manuscript reflected the genuine text of the Septuagint, free from the corruptions of later translators; and that in any case, Codex Vaticanus had a much better claim to such a status than Codex Alexandrinus.

Although Morin's letter arrived in 1638, when Young was just beginning to work seriously on the edition, he never advanced a substantial counter-argument in the remaining fourteen years of his life. He did, however, take elements of Morin's criticism on board. For instance, Morin advised that he look at Procopius of Gaza's commentary on Isaiah. Procopius was a father of the fifth and sixth centuries whose commentaries preserved many details about how later Greek translations differed from the original Septuagint. At the same time, Morin also recommended a book by a modern Catholic scholar: Andreas Masius's Greek edition of the Book of Joshua.[31] Masius had used a Syriac translation of the Septuagint column in Origen's Hexapla, which preserved the sigla Origen had used to mark interpolations in the Septuagint from the Hebrew or the other Greek versions. This made his work an extremely valuable source for establishing a purer text of the Septuagint. Young followed Morin's advice.[32]

---

[29] See Arnold Boate and Francis Tayler, *Examen praefationis Morini* (Leiden, 1636); and, for a critique by a Catholic Hebraist, Siméon de Muis, *Assertio veritatis Hebraicae* (Paris, 1631). For more on the controversial status of Morin's work within Catholicism, see Miller, 'Making the Paris Polyglot Bible', 76.

[30] The letter of Morin to Young of 26 Aug. 1638 published by Kemke (ed.), *Patricius Junius*, 138–9, is abridged from fifteen pages to two. For a full printed edition, see *Antiquitates ecclesiae orientalis*, 273–88. In 1634 Morin had already seen a sample of Codex Alexandrinus, communicated to him by Young via Fr Robert Philip, the Scottish confessor to Queen Henrietta Maria (and an oratorian, like Morin himself): *Antiquitates*, 236, 242–3.

[31] See Theodor Dunkelgrün, 'The Hebrew Library of a Renaissance Humanist: Andreas Masius and the Bibliography to his *Iosuae Imperatoris Historia* (1574), with a Latin Edition and an Annotated English Translation', *Studia Rosenthaliana*, 42–3 (2010–11): 197–252.

[32] See Trinity College, Cambridge, MS O.10.33, fols. 15^r–27^r for Procopius; and British Library, MS Harley 1328, fol. 67 for Masius. Young managed, at one point, to use Procopius against Morin, to correct the 1587 Roman edition of the Septuagint: see the note on p. 563 of his copy, Bodleian Library, Radcl. c. 8.

In doing so, however, Young became acutely aware of a new difficulty: that of studying the Greek text independently from its Hebrew antecedent. After he had begun collecting fragments of the other Greek translations from Procopius, he noticed that there was already an edition of these fragments, compiled by Johannes Drusius, the Protestant Hebraist whose work on the Septuagint John Bois had admired and often cited.[33] But Young decided to carry on compiling his own list of fragments, because Drusius failed to make clear which parts of Theodotion and the other translators had been added to the Septuagint and which parts had been left out:

> I undertook and finished most of this task before laying eyes on Drusius's *Supplement*. But I don't consider my work to have been done entirely in vain, above all because Drusius makes no mention whatsoever of the asterisks [with which Origen marked passages of other translations inserted into the Septuagint]. Without them, it is impossible to understand what kind of translation the Seventy Elders originally published, and what was subsequently added from Theodotion and the other translators. In his collection, Drusius seems to have paid more attention to the Hebrew text than to the Greek.[34]

Young was right. Drusius's book had not promised a pure text of the Septuagint, free from any other versions. He had a different purpose in mind. What mattered to Drusius was whether the Greek of Theodotion offered an alternative gloss on, or even reading for, the Hebrew Bible, one not offered by the extant Hebrew manuscripts or other sources—not whether Origen had used it to interpolate the Septuagint. The broader problem Young was gesturing at was that previous Protestant scholars had studied the Septuagint as a means to an end, to understand and perhaps improve the Hebrew text. They had not made much of an effort to disentangle the different Greek versions from each other, because for them, those Greek versions all emanated from a single, original, authoritative, and still extant Hebrew source. No Greek version had any authority by comparison with the Hebrew: all were to be embraced or discarded according to whether their translation of it was helpful or unhelpful.

Young tacitly acknowledged that Morin's approach was much more responsive than Drusius's to the possibility that one Greek version might have more authority, on account of its historical position, than the others. Origen's role was vital. Morin argued that rather than doing anything innovative, he was simply trying to reconstruct Origen's work on the Septuagint.[35] Both had made the unusual step of deciding that a pure text of the Septuagint needed to be published, independent from any interpolations made with reference to any existing or hypothetical Hebrew version.[36] Morin presented Origen as a skilful textual critic who had intervened at a particular moment in the history of the church in order to

---

[33] Trinity MS O.10.33, fol. 15ʳ. The book in question is Drusius's *Veterum interpretum Graecorum in totum vetus testamentum fragmenta* (Arnhem, 1622; published posthumously).

[34] 'Priusquam oculos in supplementum Drusij coniecissemus, laborem hunc suscepimus, et maximam partem absoluimus; neq*ue* planè inutiliter à nobis operam collocatam esse arbitramur: praecipuè cùm Drusius asteriscorum nullam omnino mentionem faciat, sine quibus qualem versionem 70 Seniores primùm ediderint, et quid à Theodotione et aliis deinceps additum sit, intelligi nequeat, et ad hebraicum textum potius quam ad graecum in collectione sua respexisse videatur.'

[35] See esp. his *Exercitationes biblicae* (Paris, 1633), 6.1. 156–9, and 9.1. 389–90.

[36] See Morin's preface to his 1628 Greek Bible, sig. *6ᵛ. In his letter to Young he questioned the value of Codex Alexandrinus on the grounds that it seemed to have been corrected according to a Hebrew text (or one of the other Greek versions, which in turn had been corrected using the Hebrew).

preserve the text of the Septuagint. His hexaplaric edition was the result of an autonomous decision-making process and scholarly method which was knowable and might stand up under critical scrutiny. Morin's perspective on the Septuagint was a patristic one, focused on a moment in ecclesiastical tradition, and in that sense it was characteristically Catholic.

Young, on the other hand, effaced this vision of Origen as a conscious, intelligent, and authoritative editor. The sole conceivable source of authority was the Hebrew text, whether extant or hypothetical (inferred from translations or other sources). The next best source was a perfect, original Septuagint text. For precisely this reason, Young rarely spoke about Origen's active role in establishing the text of the Septuagint. Instead, he reduced Origen to the same status as all the other fathers whose writings he adduced in his work. They yielded up lists of testimonies whose value was to be assessed according to whether they matched the available Greek manuscripts.[37] For Young, to follow Origen would have been to attribute too much authority to a father, and to reduce the preservation of the biblical text to a matter of human traditions. He had adopted some of the methods and tools of Catholic scholarship on the Septuagint, without adopting the notion of ecclesiastical tradition on which they depended. For Young, all of the fathers, Origen included, had to be judged by other, deeper criteria.

Young never stated definitively what those criteria were, but he felt that they ultimately had to have something to do with the bedrock of the Hebrew text. He could not abandon his faith in the 'Hebraica veritas', to which he often appealed in his notes comparing the Hebrew and Greek versions.[38] This faith manifested itself in two ways: sometimes it relied on textual criticism, but at other times it formed part of a literary-critical approach to the relationship between Hebrew original and Greek translation. The haphazard combination of these two approaches helps to explain why Young never formulated a serious argument about the history and text of the Septuagint.

As far as textual criticism was concerned, Young compared different manuscripts of the Septuagint in order to show not simply that Codex Alexandrinus was closest to the Greek text edited by Origen, but also that it was closest to the Hebrew text—although in some cases he had to acknowledge that other versions were closer.[39] This ran counter to his stated aim of treating the traditions of the Greek text more independently than Drusius, who had assimilated them with the Hebrew. He wanted the study of the Septuagint to become more specialized than it had been for an earlier generation of Protestant scholars, but not so specialized as to detach itself entirely from consideration of the Hebrew text.

His reliance on the Hebrew original also manifested itself in the literary-critical inclinations of his notes. Throughout his manuscripts, as well as the notes which were printed in the London Polyglot, Young resorts to grammatical, stylistic, or rhetorical judgements about the quality of certain renderings of the Hebrew text into Greek, or sometimes Latin. His note on Genesis 1: 2 offers a striking example. Young conjectures that ἀόρατος ('invisible', describing the earth) should be replaced by ἄωρος, which, he contends, could mean 'shapeless' as well as 'untimely' or 'unripe'. The latter 'seems to come closer to the *Hebraica veritas*: but such a daring alteration should not be made when it

---

[37] For instance, Origen was treated as simply one of many commentators who had cited the Old Testament in *Catena*, ed. Young.

[38] For example, British Library, MS Harley 1328, fols. 51ᵛ, 52ᵛ; Leiden University Library, MS VMI 4, fol. 2ᵛ.

[39] Such as the Complutensian, in the case of Exodus 36–9: see MS Harley 1328, fols. 49ʳ–50ᵛ.

opposes the faithful testimony of all the manuscript copies and the unanimous agreement of the whole body of fathers'.[40] Young repeatedly vacillates between a conjecture which improves the quality of the translation from the Hebrew, and the evidence offered by manuscripts and patristic citations. We can also observe the way in which he used the fathers: rather than treating any one father as particularly authoritative, he tended to pile up patristic testimonies until he felt that they tipped the scales in favour of a particular reading. This is equally true of his use of manuscripts. But the most surprising feature of Young's annotation is the proposal of a conjecture which Young himself admitted was baseless and had to be rejected. He was clearly reluctant to be constrained by the form of the text-critical commentary he was supposed to be writing, and wanted to venture further towards the kind of work he had done on Clement: not pursuing any one conclusion, but branching out from the text in multiple directions. After one particularly long exegetical note, he had to rein himself in, observing that he was supposed to be writing 'scholia, not commentaries'.[41]

The value of the Hebrew text for Young, then, was partly that it allowed him to indulge his speculative, literary-critical tendencies, and correspondingly abandon the rigours of textual criticism—precisely because he could not suffer the Hebrew text to be historically constructed like any other. This is not to say that Young behaved like an enthusiastic literalist in his use of the Hebrew text: his appeals to it are casual, diffuse, and unpremeditated. Rather than beginning with a clear, dogmatic defence of *Hebraica veritas*, he invokes it on an occasional basis. The Hebrew text did not lay the foundation of Young's textual criticism. It would be better to describe it as filling a void. This void had been left by the absence of a Catholic account following the example set by Morin: an account of the formation of the competing versions at different moments in the history of the church, with different kinds of ecclesiastical authority and scholarly input affecting them.

We have already seen how Young's surviving papers demonstrate his uncertainty about the nature of the text-critical enterprise he was undertaking. There is one further example of this, which returns us to the scholar with whom this chapter began. In the 1640s, when his edition was already well under way, Young copied out many of John Bois's marginal annotations on the Roman Septuagint and used several of them in his own notes.[42] What Bois's notes gave him were occasionally illuminating, but disjointed, comments on individual passages of the Greek text. They did not provide an overarching theory about the history or value of the Septuagint, because the translators of the King James Bible were not looking for one: like Drusius, they wanted a new perspective on the Hebrew text. Despite Morin's partial success in forcing Young to reconsider his approach to editing, Young's continuing interest in Bois's work suggests that he was reluctant to abandon the quite different model of biblical scholarship which it represented.

---

[40] See *Biblia sacra polyglotta*, ed. Brian Walton (1657), vi/1 of Young's notes; MS Harley 1328, fol. 1ʳ 'ad veritatem hebraicam propius accedere videtur: sed contra fidem omnium exemplarium & unanimem [*sic*] universorum Patrum consensum nihil ausu temerario mutandum est'.

[41] *Biblia sacra polyglotta*, vi/10 of Young's notes (on Gen. 36: 6).

[42] Leiden MS VMI 4, fols. 6ʳ–10ʳ. For an instance of Young's use of these marginalia, see p. 8 of his notes in the London Polyglot (discussing Gen. 29: 27), where he repeats the identification of 'Boeotian' verb forms on 153 and 230 of Bois's Septuagint (Bodleian Library, D 1.14 Th.Seld). Young must have borrowed the book in the 1640s or 1650s (his copy includes the aforementioned references to Grotius's 1641 Gospel commentaries), after Bois had died and Selden had acquired it.

Young's hopes for Codex Alexandrinus had been downgraded by Morin's response to his *Catena*, and his plans for the edition had been disrupted, if not thrown into disarray. As Morin had pointed out, no serious critic could believe that a single manuscript offered a pristine text of the Septuagint.[43] He freely admitted that this was not even true of Codex Vaticanus, which was occasionally inferior to Young's manuscript.[44] Young's subsequent work tacitly accepts this point, as demonstrated by his willingness to offer conjectures not found in Codex Alexandrinus, and his willingness to note the value and importance of other manuscripts or patristic citations which presented alternative readings to it, especially when those conjectures or alternative readings brought the Septuagint and Hebrew texts closer together. Since Young was not prepared to become an ecclesiastical historian of the biblical text in the manner of Morin, he ended up oscillating between the twin poles of conjectural emendation and raw collation, uninformed by any historical context or narrative. Young probably realized that neither of these modes of criticism could compete with Morin's account of the text of the Septuagint. At best, they could embarrass the champions of Codex Vaticanus as far as specific passages were concerned, without ever showing that it was fundamentally corrupt.

This chapter has compared the career of John Bois with that of Patrick Young; and, by extension, the culture that produced the King James Bible with the culture that produced the London Polyglot Bible, almost half a century later. Within this story, several interesting trends can be highlighted. First of all, there was no movement away from Latin as the language of biblical scholarship, towards the vernacular: if anything, scholars were going in the opposite direction. Partly because its learned culture remained Latinate, England became more open to direct engagement with continental biblical scholarship, Catholic as well as Protestant. What is more, this scholarship became more intimately linked to vexed questions of confessional identity, not less. Finally, the need for technical specialization became increasingly apparent the more scholars confronted the complexity of the transmission of the Old Testament. The availability of new manuscript evidence, along with the need to uphold specific denominational positions on the authority of the Latin, Greek, or Hebrew texts, forced scholars to concentrate their attention on textual editing, rather than simply translation or commentary; but not every scholar was equally prepared to make this change, or fully able to reconcile the demands of editorial problems with those of confessional identity. In an age of intense debate and anxiety about the text of the Bible throughout Christendom, a French Catholic, Jean Morin, managed these demands more successfully than his English counterparts.[45]

---

[43] *Antiquitates ecclesiae orientalis*, 275: 'Quis adeo istarum rerum rudis est, aut fatue supersitiosus, ut tam insanam opinionem de quo libuerit Codice Graeco, Hebraeo, Latino in animum suum inducat?'

[44] *Antiquitates*, 285.

[45] I would like to thank Kevin Killeen, Scott Mandelbrote, Theodor Dunkelgrün and Karen Collis for their advice regarding various versions of this chapter. Mr Mandelbrote also allowed me to see an advance version of his piece on 'Isaac Vossius and the Septuagint', in Eric Jorink and Dirk van Miert (eds), *Between Scholarship and Science: The Wonderful World of Isaac Vossius* (Leiden: Brill, 2012), 85–117. I would like to thank my audiences at the 2011 conferences on the King James Bible at Oxford and York. The issues covered in this chapter are treated in greater depth in my D.Phil. thesis, 'The *ars critica* in Early Modern England' (Oxford University, 2012).

Further reading

Allen, Ward. *Translating for King James* (London: Allen Lane, 1970).

Auvray, Paul. 'Jean Morin (1591–1659)'. *Revue Biblique*, 66 (1959): 397–414.

Feingold, Mordechai. 'The Humanities', in Nicholas Tyacke (ed.), *The History of the University of Oxford*, iv. *Seventeenth-Century Oxford* (Oxford: Clarendon Press, 1997), 211–357.

Grafton, Anthony, and Joanna Weinberg. *'I have always Loved the Holy Tongue': Isaac Casaubon, the Jews, and a Forgotten Chapter in Renaissance Scholarship* (Cambridge, Mass.: Harvard University Press, 2010).

Kemke, Johannes, ed. *Patricius Junius* (Leipzig: M. Spirgatis, 1898).

Laplanche, François. *L'Ecriture, le sacré et l'histoire: Erudits et politiques protestants devant la Bible en France au XVIIe siècle* (Amsterdam: APA-Holand University Press, 1986).

Malcolm, Noel. 'Hobbes, Ezra and the Bible: The History of a Subversive Idea', in *Aspects of Hobbes* (Oxford: Clarendon Press, 2002).

Mandelbrote, Scott. 'The Authority of the Word: Manuscript, Print, and the Text of the Bible in Seventeenth-Century England', in Julia Crick and Alexandra Walsham (eds), *The Uses of Script and Print, 1300–1700* (Cambridge: Cambridge University Press, 2004), 135–53.

Mandelbrote, Scott. 'English Scholarship and the Greek Text of the Old Testament, 1620–1720: The Impact of Codex Alexandrinus', in Ariel Hessayon and Nicholas Keene (eds), *Scripture and Scholarship in Early Modern England* (Aldershot: Ashgate, 2006), 74–93.

Miller, Peter N. 'The "Antiquarianization" of Biblical Scholarship and the London Polyglot Bible'. *Journal of the History of Ideas*, 62 (2001): 463–82.

Norton, David. 'John Bois's Notes on the Revision of the King James Bible New Testament: A New Manuscript'. *The Library*, 6th ser. 18 (1996): 328–46.

Norton, David. *A Textual History of the King James Bible* (Cambridge: Cambridge University Press, 2005).

Pattison, Mark. *Isaac Casaubon* (London: Longmans, Green, & Co., 1875).

CHAPTER 8

....

THE APOCRYPHA IN EARLY MODERN ENGLAND

....

ARIEL HESSAYON

Q. Are the Apocrypha Books to be owned as Gods Word?
A. *No. Every word of God is pure: add thou not unto his words, least he reprove thee, and thou be found a lyar.* (Proverbs 30:5–6)[1]

PROTESTANTISM is a religion based on an anthology: the Bible. English Protestants, how-ever, generally accepted fewer holy books than Catholics. Scripture alone, rather than the papacy or church councils, was paramount. Yet which scriptures were to be accepted and which rejected was no straightforward matter. This chapter begins with a brief account of how and why certain Jewish writings came to be regarded as apocryphal, highlighting the crucial contribution Jerome's contentious canonical theory would play. It also underscores the fact that the Apocrypha was a Protestant construction, one moreover that reflected the privileging of Jewish texts available in Hebrew over those then extant in Greek. For the gradual evolution of the Apocrypha as a distinct corpus was partially a by-product of the humanist return to the sources—specifically Hebrew.

Previous studies of the Apocrypha in early modern England have tended to stress two points: first, that the removal of these books from the Old Testament was unauthor-ized, lacking explicit royal and ecclesiastical sanction; secondly, that their influence was greater than commonly recognized. Here I want to suggest that in addition the Apocrypha was important because of its inherent potential to exacerbate religious conflict—not just between Catholics, Lutherans and Calvinists, but also between moderate churchmen and Puritans. Thus, to take an emotive example, the controversial Hebraist Hugh Broughton urged printers to omit the Apocrypha from the Bible, dismissing these 'unperfect histories' as nothing better than trifling Jewish fables and 'meane wittes' work:

> A Turky leprous slave might as seemly be placed in seat, cheek by cheek, betwixt two the best Christian Kings; as the wicked Apocrypha betwixt both testaments. And no monster of many legges, armes, or heades can be more ugly.[2]

---

[1] Anon., *A Protestant Catechisme for Little Children* (1673), 3–4.
[2] Hugh Broughton, *Principle Positions for Groundes of the Holy Bible* (1609), 4–5, 21, 27.

I. Historical Background and Definitions

Apocrypha is a Latin neuter plural noun (singular: *apocryphon*). It has a Greek etymology, derived from an adjective meaning hidden away, kept secret. The word occurs several times in the Septuagint (Deut. 27: 15; Isa. 4: 6; Psalms 17: 12, 27: 5), a Greek version of the Hebrew scriptures originally written on papyrus or leather scrolls and compiled, according to the legendary *Letter of Aristeas*, in the third century BC by seventy—or seventy-two—translators for the benefit of Alexandrian Jews. Initially the Greek adjective, when applied to books, was occasionally used in an approving manner to describe writings containing mysterious wisdom too profound or holy to be communicated to any save the initiated (cf. Daniel 12: 4; 2 Esdras 14: 45–6; 1 Enoch 108: 1). The Greek-speaking Origen, however, subsequently employed the term to distinguish between writings read in public worship and those of questionable value which were studied privately. Yet Origen also used the word negatively to describe something false, while his contemporary Clement of Alexandria employed it with reference to dubious secret works possessed by heretics—especially Gnostics. This last, pejorative sense eventually became prevalent among Latin speakers. Accordingly, when from the mid-fourth century the church began the process of establishing a uniform canon by drawing up authoritative lists of books regarded as sacred scripture, the adjective was applied to texts deemed heretical or spurious.

Jerome was the first to designate a particular corpus of writings as apocryphal because of their exclusion from what had by then become a closed Jewish canon. These were Jewish compositions omitted from the Hebrew Bible but with the exception of 2 Esdras nonetheless found in certain versions of the Septuagint preserved in codices, and hence generally included in the canon being defined by the church. In 382 and with the likely approval of Pope Damasus, Jerome undertook a new Latin version of the scriptures to supersede variants of what we now call an Old Latin version based on the Greek. In his much cited *Prologus galeatus* ('helmeted preface', c.392) to Samuel and Kings, Jerome asserted that books which he did not list as constituting the Hebrew Bible must be classed as apocryphal writings—specifically disbarring Wisdom of Solomon, Sirach, Judith, Tobit, the Shepherd of Hermas, and 1 and 2 Maccabees from the canon.[3]

There is still debate in modern scholarship as to whether or not Jerome maintained this position consistently. Elsewhere, for example, his pronouncements accorded with contemporary usage; 'beware of all apocrypha' he advised, 'they were not written by those to whom they are ascribed ... many vile things have been mixed in ... they require great prudence to find the gold in the filth'.[4] All the same, for our purposes what is important is that Jerome's Bible translations, which were ultimately underpinned by his faith in the 'Hebrew verity', became increasingly authoritative, at least until the advent of sophisticated

[3] Jerome, 'Prologus Galeatus', tr. W. H. Fremantle as 'Preface to the Books of Samuel and Kings' in Philip Schaff and Henry Wace (eds), *Nicene and Post-Nicene Fathers*, 2nd ser. 6 (New York, 1893), 489–90, <http://www.tertullian.org/fathers2/NPNF2-06/Npnf2-06-21.htm>.

[4] Jerome, *Epistles*, 107.12, quoted in A. S. Jacobs, 'The Disorder of Books: Priscillian's Canonical Defense of Apocrypha', *Harvard Theological Review*, 93 (2000): 157.

humanist criticism.[5] From the 1520s, they were being referred to as the *vulgata editio*, or, as the English exile translators of the Douay Old Testament (1609–10) first called them, the Vulgate Latin edition.[6] Moreover, Jerome's unheeded call for the church to reject the Septuagint in favour of the Hebrew Bible as the basis of the Old Testament, together with his criteria for determining which books should be considered apocryphal, would provide vital ammunition in the polemical battles waged between Protestant reformers and their Catholic adversaries.

Following the Romano-Jewish historian Flavius Josephus and Athanasius of Alexandria, Jerome held that the twenty-two books in the Hebrew Bible corresponded to the number of letters in the Hebrew alphabet (the twelve minor prophets counting as one book). Although, as Jerome acknowledged, some reckoned there were twenty-four books (corresponding to the twenty-four elders of Revelation 4: 4), this discrepancy mattered less than the tripartite division of the Hebrew Bible that he adopted: namely the Pentateuch, Prophets, and Hagiographa (five, eight, and nine books respectively). Here too Jewish precedent was crucial, for the dominant strain of rabbinic Second Temple Judaism divided its Bible into three sections: the Laws (*Torah*), Prophets (*Nevi'im*), and Writings (*Ketuvim*). Furthermore, whereas Athanasius in his 39th Festal epistle (367) had distinguished three types of writings—canonical (twenty-two Old Testament and twenty-seven New Testament books), non-canonical (suitable to be read by new converts 'for instruction in the word of godliness', including Wisdom of Solomon, Sirach, Esther, Judith, and Tobit), and the apocrypha (which were the 'invention of heretics')—Jerome designated the non-canonical books apocryphal while likewise recognizing their didactic rather than doctrinal value: 'The Church reads [these] books … for the edification of the common people, but not as authority to confirm any of the Church's doctrines'.[7] This again significantly contributed towards establishing the boundaries of what became highly contested theological territory during the Reformation and its aftermath.

Here my definition of the Apocrypha reflects early modern English Protestant usage. They are taken to be the books designated as such in sixteenth- and seventeenth-century English printed Bibles. Adhering to the sixth of the Thirty-Nine Articles of the Church of England (1571), the King James Bible (1611) named and ordered fourteen books, giving the number of chapters in each; 1 Esdras (9), 2 Esdras (16), Tobit (14), Judith (16), the rest of Esther (6), the Wisdom of Solomon (19), the Wisdom of Jesus the son of Sirach, or Ecclesiasticus (51), Baruch, with the epistle of Jeremiah (6), the Song of the Three Holy Children (1), the History of Susanna (1), Bel and the Dragon (1), the Prayer of Manasses king of Judah (1), 1 Maccabees (16), and 2 Maccabees (15). Previously 3 Maccabees had also been included in Edmund Becke's 1549 Bible, while 4 Maccabees and Psalm 151 were consistently omitted despite having been preserved in some Septuagint manuscripts.

---

[5] Jerome translated the Hebrew Bible, Tobit, Judith, and the four Gospels into Latin, but not Acts, the New Testament epistles, or Revelation.

[6] The English word vulgate, as in vulgar or common tongue, had however been in use since at least the 1520s.

[7] Jerome, 'Preface to Proverbs, Ecclesiastes, and the Song of Songs', in Schaff and Wace, *Nicene and Post-Nicene Fathers*, 492.

II. The Reformation: Karlstadt, Luther, and the First Printed English Bibles

Although numerous and widely used Latin translations of the Apocrypha were made before the Reformation, Jerome's acerbic views also circulated through prefatory epistles appended to his translations. Indeed, compiling a list of those influenced to varying degrees by Jerome's canonical theory is a straightforward exercise, because a Protestant royalist exile did just that in a publication of 1657, so as to emphasize the chasm separating the Church of England from Rome. Among them were Gregory the Great, Bede, Alcuin, Hugh of St Victor, Peter of Cluny [the Venerable], Peter Comestor, John of Salisbury, Hugh of Saint-Cher, the Franciscans Nicholas of Lyra and William Ockham, and the English translators of the Wycliffite Bible. Hence in the prologue to the Old Testament commonly but dubiously attributed to the heretic John Purvey, the authority of Jerome's *Prologus galeatus* was used to consign books such as Wisdom of Solomon, Sirach, Judith, and Tobit 'among apocrifa, that is, with outen autorite of bileue'.[8] In the same vein Alonso Tostado, Bishop of Ávila, declared that the Apocrypha had been 'set without the canon' because 'even though they are read among the other books of the Bible, and read in the Church' none were of 'so great authority that the Church argues from it to maintain any truth'.[9] Likewise, in a prologue to the Complutensian Polyglot (Alcalá, 1514–17) Cardinal Francisco Ximénes placed Old Testament books not then extant in Hebrew outside the canon, reiterating Jerome's remarks concerning their edificatory worth.

The German Thomistic theologian Andreas Bodenstein von Karlstadt, who had sided with Martin Luther in the Leipzig disputations of 1519 against Johann Eck, issued his ground-breaking *De canonicis scripturis libellus* (Wittenberg, 1520), against a backdrop of, first, renewed interest in Hebrew pioneered successively by Johannes Reuchlin and his nephew Philip Melanchthon; secondly, hostility within reformist circles towards unpalatable aspects of the church fathers' teachings—in particular Jerome's views on fasting, monasticism, relics, virginity, and the Virgin Mary; and thirdly, resentment of papal corruption, notably the sale of indulgences. Here and in a subsequent German epitome Karlstadt drew heavily on Jerome and Augustine to justify his contention that theological disputes should be resolved by appeal to the highest authority, specifically the Bible rather than church councils, thereby confirming his adoption of the principle of *sola scriptura* ('by scripture alone'). Karlstadt then took the bold step of diverging from Augustine and subdivided the Apocrypha into two categories. On the one hand were books outside the Hebrew canon yet still *agiographi* (i.e. classed among the third and lowest rank of sacred scripture: Wisdom of Solomon, Sirach, Judith, Tobit, and 1 and 2 Maccabees). These were 'not to be despised' immediately but could be consulted if leisure permitted. On the other were plainly apocryphal books worthy of condemnation (1

---

[8] *The Holy Bible … Made from the Latin Vulgate by John Wycliffe and His Followers*, ed. John Forshall and Frederic Madden (Oxford: Oxford University Press, 1850), i. 1–2. It is noteworthy that the Wycliffite Bible did not include an English translation of 2 Esdras.

[9] Quoted in Brooke Foss Westcott, *The Bible in the Church*, 2nd edn (London: Macmillan, 1866), 201.

and 2 Esdras, Baruch, the Prayer of Manasses, and the additions to Daniel—Three Holy Children, Susanna, and Bel).[10]

Luther was even more extreme, circumventing in his disputation with Eck a proof-text for the doctrine of purgatory (2 Maccabees 12: 45) adduced at the Council of Florence (1438–43) by excising the inconvenient book from his canon. This belligerent former Augustinian monk became convinced that justification was to be attained through faith alone. So he scorned the Epistle of James, dismissing it as a worthless unapostolic letter of straw. In his vernacular translation of the New Testament (Wittenberg, 1522) Luther separated this epistle along with that to the Hebrews (spuriously attributed to Paul), Jude (canonicity questioned by some church fathers), and Revelation (deemed neither apostolic nor prophetic) from the undisputed works, placing these *antilegomena* unnumbered at the end.

For his incomplete German Old Testament (1523–4) Luther embraced Jerome's principle of the 'Hebrew verity', distinguishing between the canon and Apocrypha with the intention—as the contents indicate—of consigning the latter to the conclusion. This radical arrangement was first implemented in the third book of a four-volume Greek Septuagint edited by Luther's collaborator Johannes Lonicerus (Strasbourg, 1524–6). Similarly, in a two-volume Dutch Bible largely based on Luther's translation and published by Jacob van Liesveldt (Antwerp, 1526), the Apocrypha were placed separately after Malachi and introduced with a disclaimer: 'the books which are not in the canon, that is to say, which one does not find among the Jews in the Hebrew'. Finally, having been assisted by Melanchthon and others, a complete two-volume folio edition of Luther's German Old Testament with accompanying woodcuts designed by the workshop of Lucas Cranach was printed by Hans Lufft and issued at Wittenberg in 1534. Here, after Malachi and an interval of two blank pages, most of the Apocrypha appeared in a unique sequence with their own title-page and a caveat: 'books that are not held equal to Holy Scripture, yet they are useful and good to read'. Thus, despite its historical inaccuracies, Judith, if regarded as a divine allegory, was 'a fine, good, holy, useful book'; Wisdom of Solomon had 'very much that is good in it'; Tobit when read as a poem was 'right beautiful, wholesome, profitable'; while Sirach, which was suitable for instilling household discipline, was 'a profitable book for an ordinary man'. Luther, however, had been reluctant to translate the Greek additions to Esther and Daniel, likening them to uprooted cornflowers that he had chosen to preserve by planting them 'in a kind of special little spice garden'. He was more contemptuous of 2 Maccabees: it should be 'thrown out, even though it contains some good things'. 1 and 2 Esdras fared worse. They were omitted and slighted as inferior to Aesop's fables.[11]

According with echoes of Jerome's criteria for canonicity, heard most notably in reservations expressed by Desiderius Erasmus, Sanctes Pagninus, and Cardinal Tommaso Cajetan, these important Lutheran precedents were swiftly adopted by certain continental reformers. For example, the Zürich Bible (1524–9) which was translated into Swyzerdeutsch and Oberdeutsch by Huldrych Zwingli and his fellow preachers included a separate volume for

---

[10] Andreas Bodenstein von Karlstadt, *De canonicis scripturis libellus* (Wittenburg, 1520), K2ʳ–K3ʳ.

[11] Martin Luther, 'Prefaces to the Apocrypha' (1533–4), in *Luther's Works*, ed. Jaroslav Pelikan and Helmut Lehmann (Philadelphia and St Louis: Concordia Publishing House, 1955–86), xxxv; Westcott, *Bible in the Church*, 259–63. In conversation Luther was if anything even more hostile, reportedly wanting to throw 2 Esdras into the River Elbe, while loathing 2 Maccabees so much that he wished it had never survived.

the Apocrypha based on both the Septuagint and Vulgate prepared by Leo Jud. Its title-page affirmed: 'these are the books which are not reckoned as biblical by the ancients, nor are found among the Hebrews'. Likewise, Pierre Robert Olivétan's French Bible (Neuchâtel, 1535), which included an address by his cousin Jean Calvin, had after the last book in the Hebrew canon a distinct title-page for 'The volume of all the Apocryphal books, contained in the common translation, which we have not found in Hebrew or Chaldean'. This translation resembled that of an earlier French Bible by Jacques Lefèvre d'Étaples with some minor amendments.

In Henrician England there was antipathy by Catholic traditionalists towards issuing Bibles in the vernacular which meshed with a desire to maintain a clerical monopoly on interpretation. Accordingly, copies of William Tyndale's complete English translation of the New Testament (Worms, 1526) were seized and publicly burned, his body eventually meeting the same fate at Antwerp in October 1536. Significantly, although Tyndale followed Luther's treatment of New Testament *antilegomena* (Hebrews, James, Jude, and Revelation), his incomplete Old Testament (Antwerp, 1530–1) suggests he did not intend excluding the Apocrypha from the canon. That unauthorized initiative was undertaken by Miles Coverdale, whose translation of the entire Bible was based on a medley of five sources, although none were in the original Hebrew or Greek: the Vulgate and another Latin version by Pagninus together with vernacular renderings found in Luther, Tyndale, and the Zürich Bible. Completed at Antwerp, where the enterprise was sponsored, and probably printed at Cologne—though the place of publication has been hotly contested by scholars—Coverdale's Bible was soon reprinted with minor amendments by James Nicolson in England (Southwark, 1535 and 1537).

Undoubtedly the most important of these changes was the addition of a dedication to Henry VIII, who had dramatically reversed his opposition to vernacular Bibles. Here the Apocrypha, which were mainly translated from the Zürich Bible and to a lesser extent the Vulgate and Luther, were introduced by an illustrated title-page with a caveat derived from the Zürich Bible: 'the bokes and treatises which amonge the fathers of olde are not rekened to be of like authorite with the other bokes of the byble, nether are they fou[n]de in the Canon of the Hebrue'. Invoking Jerome, Coverdale justified this extraordinary move by explaining that there were many passages in the Apocrypha which seemed repugnant and contradictory to the 'manyfest treuth' found in other biblical books. Even so, he had not gathered the Apocrypha together so that they might be despised or undervalued. As he could not prove they were false writings, Coverdale simply warned that:

> These & many other darck places of scripture have bene sore stered and myxte with blynde and cuvetous opynions of men, which have caste soch a myst afore the eyes of ye symple, that as longe as they be not co[n]ferred with the other places of scripture, they shall not seme other wyse to be understonde, then as cuvetousnes expoundeth them.[12]

After Tyndale's execution, his associate John Rogers, who was then based in Antwerp, helped perpetuate his legacy by preventing the seizure of Tyndale's unfinished manuscript translation of the Old Testament. Together with Coverdale's version of the Old Testament and material drawn from the French Bibles of Lefèvre d'Étaples and Olivétan,

---

[12] *Biblia the Bible, That Is, the Holy Scripture*, tr. Miles Coverdale ([Cologne], 1535).

this provided the basis for Rogers's own edition of the Bible. Known as Matthew's Bible because of its spurious attribution to Thomas Matthew, it appears to have been printed by Matthew Crom at Antwerp and was published by Richard Grafton and Edward Whitchurch in 1537. This too was dedicated to the King and unlike Coverdale's Bible issued with a prized royal licence. Again, the Apocrypha constituted a discrete part with their own illustrated title-page and admonition: 'the volume of the bokes called Apocripha: Contayned in the comen transl[ation] in Latyne, whych are not founde in the Hebreue nor in the Chalde'. The translations were those of Coverdale, with the addition of the Prayer of Manasses done by Rogers. The one-page apologetic address to the reader was taken directly from Olivétan who, as was becoming standard, had cited Jerome; since these books were not taken as legitimate and lawful either by the Jews or the whole church, men might read them to edify the people, but not to confirm and strengthen the doctrine of the church.

In 1539 the evangelical reformer Richard Taverner, a Greek scholar noted for his translation of Erasmus as well as propagandizing on behalf of Henry VIII's chief minster Thomas Cromwell, issued a revision of Matthew's Bible. Presumably with Cromwell's sanction he drew the sting from Rogers's controversial renderings. As before, the Apocrypha were separated from the Old Testament but for the first time without explanation. Taverner's Bible, however, was quickly superseded by a more thorough revision of Matthew's Bible also supported by Cromwell. This was undertaken by Coverdale, initially at Paris, because of its superior printing presses. Despite serious obstacles which delayed the process, a first printing was completed at London in April 1539. Called the Great Bible because of its size rather than the superior quality of its translation, this 'authorized' version used Sebastian Münster's annotated Latin translation of the Hebrew (1534–5) to correct the Old Testament. It also departed from the arrangement of New Testament books in Matthew's Bible, thus abandoning Luther's *antilegomena* in favour of the Vulgate's sequence. Again the Apocrypha were separated and preceded with a translation of Olivétan's prologue. The text was essentially the same with one significant difference: the word Hagiographa was substituted for Apocrypha and used synonymously rather than, as we would expect, in Jerome's sense as signifying the third part of the Hebrew Bible.

A second folio edition with a preface by Thomas Cranmer, Archbishop of Canterbury, was issued in April 1540 and appointed to be read in churches. Its title-page for the Hagiographa (i.e. Apocrypha) was new, featuring sixteen woodcuts largely illustrating scenes from the text. Subsequent editions of the Great Bible contained variations, the most significant being the erasure of Cromwell's arms from the title-page following his execution in July 1540, while one 1541 edition omitted Olivétan's introduction to what was described as neither Apocrypha nor Hagiographa but simply the fourth part of the Bible. This suggests a pragmatic decision—perhaps taken by traditionalist Catholic prelates then in ascendancy—to restore these books to the Old Testament canon without incurring the expense of printing a new edition of the Bible.

Although no further editions of the Great Bible were printed from 1542 until after Henry's death in January 1547, it is noteworthy that Coverdale's version of four books attributed to Solomon (Proverbs, Ecclesiastes, Song, Wisdom), together with Sirach, were frequently reprinted as a collected volume between 1540 and 1551. Furthermore, an anonymous translation of Jeremiah's epistle dissuading people from idolatry, ordinarily appended to Baruch in the Apocrypha, was issued separately (Southwark, 1539?) with a warning against the superstitious veneration of saints' images.[13]

By the end of Henry VIII's reign the Apocrypha had been separated from the Hebrew Bible. This initiative had been taken without royal or ecclesiastical approval but was nonetheless partially facilitated by Cromwell's reformist agenda. It followed a radical Lutheran model, presenting a discrete text for the edification of readers that was essentially an English version of a Swiss-German cum French translation of the Greek. These books, moreover, were shortly preceded by an apology written by a French reformer. Yet if thus far English Protestants had merely followed the precedents of their continental brethren, the most extreme among them would, by the turn of the seventeenth century, disparage the Apocrypha in hitherto almost inconceivable ways.

III. From Trent to Hampton Court, and Beyond

On 8 April 1546, after three months of debate and disagreement, the Council of Trent following the example of orthodox church fathers as well as conciliar decisions taken at Laodicea (363–4), Hippo (393), Carthage (397), and Florence (1438–43), approved what it determined to be all the books of the Old and New Testaments as the Bible of the Roman Catholic Church. With the exception of the Prayer of Manasses and 1 and 2 Esdras, texts judged apocryphal by Jerome but forming part of the 'old Latin Vulgate edition' were decreed 'sacred and canonical ... in their entirety and with all their parts'—with an anathema pronounced on anyone believing the contrary.[14]

In the wake of this Tridentine judgement, Sixtus of Siena, possibly a converted Jew and certainly a former heretic, produced *Bibliotheca sancta ex præcipuis Catholicæ Ecclesiæ auctoribus collecta* (1566). Drawing on patristic precedent, Sixtus advocated a tripartite division of biblical books: the protocanonical, deuterocanonical, and apocryphal. While the protocanonical writings were universally accepted, the deuterocanonical—which included Esther, Tobit, Judith, Baruch with the epistle of Jeremiah, Wisdom of Solomon, Sirach, the additions to Daniel and 1 and 2 Maccabees as well as several New Testament texts—were considered problematic, since they 'were not generally known till a late period'.

This distinction between proto- (i.e. first) and deutero- (i.e. second) canonical was, Sixtus emphasized, one of 'cognition and time, not of authority, certitude, or worth, for both orders received their excellency and majesty from the same Holy Spirit'.[15] The Jesuit Robert Bellarmine reiterated the distinction while continuing to defend both the second category

---

[13] This translation of Jeremiah's epistle differs from Coverdale's version which was printed without alteration in Coverdale's Bible, Matthew's Bible, Taverner's Bible, and the Great Bible.

[14] R. H. Charles has suggested that the exclusion of 1 Esdras may have been based on a misunderstanding. Also omitted was 3 Maccabees. R. H. Charles, *The Apocrypha and Pseudepigrapha of the Old Testament in English* (Oxford: Clarendon, 1913), i, pp. vii, ix–x.

[15] Quoted in J. H. Hayes, 'Historical Criticism of the Old Testament Canon', in Magne Sæbø (ed.), *Hebrew Bible, Old Testament: The History of its Interpretation*, ii. *From the Renaissance to the Enlightenment* (Göttingen: Vandenhoeck & Ruprecht, 2008), 985–1005, 991.

of books, whose 'authority was not always equally clear and confirmed', and the accuracy of the Vulgate itself, declaring 'there is no error in this translation in matters pertaining to faith and morals'.[16] Afterwards a critical three-volume edition of the Vulgate was issued under the patronage of Pope Sixtus V. Known as the Sixtine Bible (1590), it was superseded by a heavily amended version sponsored by Clement VIII, the Clementine (1592). These Bibles incorporated most of what Protestants regarded as the Apocrypha within the sequence of Old Testament books; Judith and Tobit, for example, succeeded Nehemiah; Wisdom and Sirach came after the Song of Solomon; with the Maccabees concluding the Old Testament. The Prayer of Manasses and 1 and 2 Esdras, however, were scorned by Sixtus and omitted from the Bible bearing his name. In the Clementine revision these texts were restored but still deemed apocryphal. Consequently they were printed in smaller typeface and without marginal notes as an appendix after the New Testament, in case they should perish altogether.

English Protestants in the meantime generally continued to regard the Apocrypha as edifying if subordinate to other biblical books. Thus in the preface to *The Volume of the Bokes Called Apocripha* (1549), which formed the fourth part of Edmund Becke's revision of Taverner's Bible, the translator explained that, although they lacked the same authority, these texts still contained 'moste godly examples and preceptes of the feare and loue of God and our neyghboure'. Accordingly, he recommended that they be diligently read and 'the learning in them earnestly' followed.[17] In the same vein, the lectionary prefixed to the Book of Common Prayer (1549) contained 108 prescribed daily lessons from Tobit, Judith, Wisdom of Solomon, Sirach, and Baruch that were to be read between 5 October and 27 November. The revised lectionaries contained in amended prayer books issued during the reigns of Edward VI and Elizabeth (1552, 1558, 1561) even added to the number of lessons taken from the Apocrypha at the expense of Old Testament verses. Similarly, the books of Homilies (1547, 1562, 1571) cited all the apocryphal books except 2 Maccabees and 1 and 2 Esdras (echoing Luther) in homilies mainly written by Cranmer and Bishop John Jewel concerning subjects such as swearing, excess of apparel, idolatry, and giving alms.

Although the status of the Apocrypha had not been established as ecclesiastical dogma in either the Ten Articles (1536) or the Forty-Two Articles (1552), this omission was rectified in both the original Latin and slightly enlarged English version of the sixth of the Thirty-Nine Articles of the Church of England (1563, 1571). Here Jerome's authority was once more invoked. Regarding these 'other bookes'—that is, those whose canonical status had previously been doubted: 'the Church doth reade for example of life, and instruction of maners: but yet doeth it not applye them to stablishe any doctrine'. This sixth article drew on the phraseology of the Protestant Württemberg Confession of Faith (1552), and also resembled the sixth article of the Belgic confession (1561) penned by the Walloon pastor and martyr Guy de Brès. Yet as scholars long ago observed, it formulated a definition of the canon that was ambiguous. Moreover, its provisions appeared to contradict the thirty-fifth article which declared that second book of Homilies contained 'godly and wholesome doctrine'

---

[16] Quoted in Alastair Hamilton, *The Apocryphal Apocalypse* (Oxford: Clarendon Press, 1999), 90–1; Eugene Rice, *Saint Jerome in the Renaissance* (Baltimore, Md.: Johns Hopkins University Press, 1985), 187.

[17] *The Volume of the Bokes Called Apocripha* (1549), A2^{r-v}. It has been suggested that 1 Esdras, Tobit, and Judith were new translations commissioned for this Bible. H. Howorth, 'The Origin and Authority of the Biblical Canon in the Anglican Church', *Journal of Theological Studies*, os 8 (1906): 17. 3 Maccabees also appeared here for the first and only time in a printed English Bible.

even though the message of these homilies was sustained by more than forty references to the Apocrypha.[18]

The prevailing, albeit far from uniform, view of the Apocrypha within the Elizabethan church can be usefully compared with contemporary attitudes towards Jewish law. Thus the seventh of the Thirty-Nine Articles reaffirmed the conventional Christian division of Mosaic Law into three categories—the moral, judicial, and ceremonial. The moral law was derived from the Ten Commandments (Exodus 20: 1–17) and regarded as inviolate by all but a handful of Christians. Its authority can be considered analogous to that of the Old Testament canonical books. It was generally agreed, on the other hand, that the judicial laws had been annulled by the coming of Christ. Yet like the Apocrypha they too could serve as non-binding exemplars.

Returning to the Apocrypha's place in various editions of the English Bible, the Geneva version was the first to be printed in roman type and the first to subdivide the text by incorporating verses as well as chapters. Produced by English exiles in the heartland of Calvinism, a city idealized as 'the patron and mirrour of true religion & godlines',[19] this reader-friendly Bible with its prefaces, helpful if sometimes provocative marginalia, woodcut illustrations, maps, and indexes was originally issued in quarto in May 1560 and remained extremely popular among Protestants until eventually supplanted by the King James Bible.[20] Here the Apocrypha came after Malachi (with the noteworthy exception of the Prayer of Manasses, which was appended to 2 Chronicles). Lacking a separate title-page they were preceded by a caveat which implicitly challenged the Book of Common Prayer's provisions for reading daily lessons taken from these texts while nonetheless acknowledging that private study of the Apocrypha would promote understanding of Jewish history:

> These bokes … were not received by a com[m]une consent to be red and expounded publikely in the Church, nether yet served to prove any point of Christian religion, save in asmuche as they had the consent of the other Scriptures called Canonical … but as bokes proceding from godlie men, were received to be red for the advancement and furtherance of the knowledge of the historie, & for the instruction of godlie maners.[21]

By contrast the home-grown black letter Bishops' Bible (1568), a revised translation initiated by Archbishop Matthew Parker and collectively undertaken mainly by bishops, respected the arrangement of some later editions of the Great Bible in designating the Apocrypha as the fourth part of the Bible. The relevant books were assigned to the Bishops of Norwich and Chichester, John Parkhurst and William Barlow. But, instructed to intervene only when correcting significant deviations in meaning from the original Greek, they barely amended the text of the Great Bible. Notwithstanding a separate title-page and the adoption of Genevan chapters and verses, Olivétan's introduction was again discarded.

Following a suggestion made at the Hampton Court conference of January 1604 by John Rainolds, a distinguished Greek scholar, Puritan theologian, and then President of Corpus Christi College, Oxford, a new translation was commissioned by James I. This so-called

---

[18] *Articles Whereupon It Was Agreed by the Archbishoppes and Bishoppes* (1571), 6, 21.
[19] 'To the Reader Mercy and Peace through Christ Our Saviour', *The Newe Testament of our Lord Jesus Christ* (1575), ¶2ᵛ.
[20] On the interpretive machinery of the Geneva Bible, see the chapter by Femke Molekamp in this volume.
[21] *The Bible and Holy Scriptures Conteyned in the Olde and Newe Testament* (Geneva, 1560), 386.

King James Bible (1611) was built on the solid foundations laid by its predecessors. The work was split into six companies, with the second of two Cambridge groups in charge of revising the Apocrypha. Chiefly selected for their skill in Greek and headed by John Duport, Master of Jesus College, the other members were John Bois (whose notes on some of the discussions survive in manuscript copies), William Branthwaite, Andrew Downes, Jeremiah Radcliffe, Robert Ward, and Samuel Ward.[22] Although criticized for apparent carelessness, inelegance, and use of colloquialisms, not to mention their reluctance to depart from inferior renderings in the Bishops' Bible (Tobit excepted),[23] the translators were diligent, making use of an extensive range of then available sources: principally the Complutensian Polyglot (1514–17), Aldine Bible (1518–19), and Roman Septuagint (1586), as well as Latin manuscripts and a paraphrase by Franciscus Junius for 2 Esdras. In addition, they supplied an estimated 1,018 marginal notes that dealt primarily with variant readings, the exact sense of the original, or alternative forms of proper names, citing, among others, Herodotus, Pliny, and especially Josephus as authorities. No apology was given, however, for separating these books from the Old Testament and the Apocrypha followed immediately after Malachi, lacking both a distinct title-page and prefatory remarks. Doubtless these were deliberate omissions, their absence replicating the corresponding page layout of the Geneva Bible apart from an innocuous ornamental woodcut replacing the Genevan eleven-line introduction.

The Apocrypha's treatment in the King James Bible differed markedly, as might be expected, from its Catholic competitor the Douai Old Testament (1609–10). Adhering to post-Tridentine orthodoxy, this professedly literal version depended first and foremost upon the Vulgate and it followed the Clementine Bible in declaring the Prayer of Manasses and 1 and 2 Esdras apocryphal (they were placed after 2 Maccabees, considered the last historical book of the Old Testament). Here justification for distinguishing between canonical and apocryphal books was provided by a brief prefatory note which maintained that only the Catholic Church, guided by the Holy Spirit, could affirm which books were divine scriptures.

Finally notice needs to be taken of the last and most comprehensive of the Polyglot Bibles. Beginning with the Prayer of Manasses and then following the sequence in the King James Bible, volume 4 of the London Polyglot Bible (1653–7) reproduced each book of the Apocrypha in most of the languages in which it was then known to be extant. Thus besides the Septuagint and Vulgate there were, for example, Syriac versions of 1 Esdras, Tobit, Judith, and Wisdom of Solomon; two forms of a Hebrew text of Tobit; and Arabic renderings of Wisdom and Sirach. Even so, 2 Esdras was reproduced only in Latin despite John Gregory's discovery of an important Arabic manuscript witness in the Bodleian Library.

IV. A Patchwork of Human Invention

Within the wider context of the rise of Elizabethan puritanism, the Apocrypha became a renewed source of religious controversy from the early 1570s. Partly this was an aspect

---

[22] On Bois's scholarship, see the chapter by Nicholas Hardy in this volume.
[23] The KJB version of Tobit clearly depended upon the Geneva Bible translation.

of Calvinist responses to the Council of Trent, partly a feature of growing opposition within Presbyterian circles to the Book of Common Prayer. The orthodox Calvinist position was that the primitive church had been pure. Built on the foundation of the Prophets and Apostles it had subsequently become corrupted over the generations by intermeddling popes and councils. Among the godly, canonical scripture was sufficient for establishing rules of faith and virtuous conduct in daily life. Knowledge of extra-canonical texts—including the Apocrypha—was deemed unnecessary for attaining salvation, while certain unwritten traditions were judged contrary to God's immaculate word. Although some traditions were, as the Calvinist theologian William Perkins conceded, 'true and profitable', Protestants consistently objected against their use by the Catholic Church to supplement scripture.[24] As with the Apocrypha, these 'unwritten verities' were superfluous for confirming doctrine. To quote a preacher fulminating against post-Tridentine apologetics: 'Traditions are gathered of an evill egge: digge the Papists never so deep, they shall not find the myne nor spring of them in the Primitive Church'.[25]

Meanwhile 'popish abuses' embedded within the Prayer Book, including lessons taken from the Apocrypha, had proved a flashpoint in the major controversy between John Whitgift, future Archbishop of Canterbury, and Thomas Cartwright, 'true progenitor of English Presbyterianism'.[26] The religious separatist Henry Barrow was yet more extreme, denouncing the Book of Common Prayer as a pregnant idol full of abominations and bitter fruit. Fuming against the Apocrypha's customary presence in church worship (a relic of Popery), he demanded if it were ever read, reverenced, and received as God's sacred word? For these writings, Barrow insisted, swarmed with 'unsufferable forgeries, lies and errors'.[27] He was not alone. Indeed, at the Hampton Court conference, John Rainolds voiced the concern of Puritan delegates that by subscribing to the Thirty-Nine Articles they would be endorsing the Prayer Book, and with it the lectionary and its chapters drawn from the Apocrypha—some of which, such as Sirach 48: 10, contained 'manifest errors, directly repugna[n]t to the scripture'.[28] King James somewhat agreed with this position, observing, in an unwitting endorsement of the Geneva Bible's marginalia, that although the books of Maccabees' account of Jewish persecution was instructive, their teaching on praying for the dead and seeking death in battle was mistaken.[29] Accordingly, a revised edition of the Prayer Book was issued (1604) to accommodate Puritan sensibilities. This measure, however, failed to stifle criticism and despite the amendments dissenters protested that the Book of Common Prayer still gave 'too much honour' to the Apocrypha: about 104 of 172 chapters continued to be read publicly in church compared with only 592 of 779 canonical chapters of the Old Testament.[30]

[24] William Perkins, *A godlie and learned exposition upon the whole Epistle of Jude* (1606), 111.
[25] Samuel Otes, *An Explanation of the Generall Epistle of Saint Jude* (1633), 309–11.
[26] Patrick Collinson, 'Cartwright, Thomas (1534/5–1603)', *ODNB*, 2004 <http://www.oxforddnb.com/view/article/4820>.
[27] Henry Barrow, *A Collection of Certaine Sclaunderous Articles Gyven out by the Bishops* (1590), F3ᵛ; Henry Barrow, *A Brief Discoverie of the False Church* (1590), 65–6, 76.
[28] William Barlow, *The Summe and Substance of the Conference* (1605), 59–63.
[29] Cf. Geneva Bible annotations to 2 Maccabees 12: 44, 14: 37–46.
[30] *An Abridgement of that Booke Which the Ministers of Lincolne Diocese Delivered to His Majestie* (1617), 6–8; Samuel Hieron, *A Defence of the Ministers Reasons* (Amsterdam?, 1607), part 2, 115–17.

Rainolds himself had from the late 1580s frequently lectured at Oxford on the Apocrypha, directing his ire at the Jesuit Bellarmine. These 250 lectures were published posthumously as *Censura librorum apocryphorum veteris testamenti* (Oppenheim, 1611), a monumental work of erudition whose central arguments influenced various shades of Protestant thinking on the subject throughout the seventeenth century. Other contemporaries repeated Rainolds's complaint that these books sometimes contradicted both scripture and each other. Their grievances, moreover, were reminiscent of Jerome and Luther. Both 1 and 2 Esdras were dismissed as creditless works 'stuffed full of vayne fables, fitter to feede curious eares, then tending to edification'.[31] The History of Susanna was a 'lying story', Bel and the Dragon a fable, while the presence of Tobias's dog together with the exorcism of the evil spirit Asmodeus by means of burning a fish's heart and liver made Tobit an outlandish tale. Indeed, in the words of the separatist John Canne, these *'false, wicked,* and *abominable'* books contained a number of *'shamefull lies, horrible blasphemies, vaine vanities, plaine contradictions, ridiculous fooleries',* impieties, and fables that made them fitter for pagans than God's people.[32] Furthermore, since divinely inspired prophecy was believed to be absent from the Apocrypha there was nothing in them—with the crucial exception of 2 Esdras—that might be interpreted as prophesying Christ's coming and his kingdom. To quote John Rogers, renowned Puritan preacher of Dedham, Essex, 'we finde no Testimony of our Savior Christ, Evangelist or Apostle, cited out of them'.[33]

It was the pseudonymous Puritan pamphleteer Martin Marprelate, suspected to be either Job Throckmorton or his accomplice John Penry, who in 1589 appears to have first demanded that the Apocrypha be removed from the rest of the Bible. Despite Archbishop Whitgift's retort calling for such 'giddy heads' to be bridled (Penry was executed),[34] a 1599 edition of the Geneva Bible was bound without the Apocrypha between the Old and New Testaments. Then in December 1608, it was reported that some Puritan bookbinders in Fetter Lane, London, were leaving the Apocrypha out of the Bible.[35] The practice must have spread for in 1615 Archbishop George Abbot threatened any stationer caught excising the Apocrypha from a published Bible with a year's imprisonment. Yet the risk was taken. Between 1616 and 1633 several editions of the King James Bible were printed lacking the Apocrypha, probably due to the growing demand for inexpensive, less cumbersome Bibles. And in December 1634 an apprentice London stationer denied, when questioned by ecclesiastical commissioners, that he had sold editions of the bible without the Apocrypha.[36]

Henry Burton would doubtless have welcomed these developments. An Independent minister famously persecuted by the Laudian church (his ears were cut off for libel and sedition) he likened the binding of the Apocrypha between the two Testaments to a blackamoor *'placed between two pure unspotted Virgins'.*[37] For the Hebraist John Lightfoot, inserting the Apocrypha between Malachi and Matthew placed an earthly barrier between two cherubim whose wings—unlike those inside the innermost room of the Jerusalem Temple

---

[31] Andrew Willet, *Synopsis Papismi … Now This Second Time Perused and Published* (1594), 8.

[32] John Canne, *A Necessitie of Separation from the Church of England* (Amsterdam, 1634), 108–9.

[33] John Rogers, *A Godly & Fruitful Exposition upon All the First Epistle of Peter* (1650), 100.

[34] Thomas Cooper, *An Admonition to the People of England* (1589), 49.

[35] *The Letters of John Chamberlain*, ed. Norman McClure (Philadelphia: American Philosophical Society, 1939), i. 276 n. 1.

[36] John Bruce (ed.), *Calendar of State Papers Domestic: Charles I, 1634–35* (London: Longman, 1864), 355.

[37] Henry Burton, *A Replie to a Relation* (1640), 196–7.

(1 Kings 6: 27)—were prevented from touching. Preaching a fast sermon before the House of Commons in March 1643 he expressed his wish to see the Old and New Testaments joined 'sweetly and neerely' together. Thus 'divinely would they kisse each other', but 'the wretched *Apocrypha* doth thrust in betweene'. Not for him the typical contemporary recognition that these books, while ranking below the indisputable messianic truths of the Old Testament, still had edificatory value. Rather, Lightfoot insisted that this 'patchery of humane invention' was a direct precursor to the superstitious fables found in the Talmud (hitherto frequently burned at the behest of Popes and Inquisitions), written before an unsuspecting world became better acquainted with the vanity of Jewish learning and its impieties.[38] Similarly, in a tract provocatively entitled *Unholsome Henbane between Two Fragrant Roses* (1645) John Vicars marvelled at the 'ill misplacing' of the most vile, vicious, erroneous, and unholy apocryphal writings in English Bibles. Comparing them to the noxious weed darnel infesting a wheatfield, he urged the Westminster Assembly of Divines to expunge this 'uncomely and corrupt' piece of '*patcherie*' from the Bible.[39] More moderate in tone if not Puritan sentiment, Edward Leigh, biblical exegete and MP for Stafford, also hoped in a work dedicated to Parliament and licensed June 1646 that the Apocrypha would be expurgated from the Bible and no longer read in church; an appeal shortly answered.[40]

In 1640 a Geneva Bible had been printed at Amsterdam, probably for members of the English Reformed church there, which deliberately omitted the section dedicated to the Apocrypha (the Prayer of Manasses, however, was retained since it was appended to 2 Chronicles). It contained after Malachi an admonition 'to the Christian reader' explaining that these were neither divinely inspired books nor accepted as such by Jews and hence uncanonical. This justification was translated from an introduction to the Apocrypha in a recently published Dutch Bible (Amsterdam, 1637), a preamble itself sanctioned by proceedings at the ninth and tenth sessions of the Synod of Dort (November 1618). Such a bold step would have been hazardous in England during the Laudian ascendancy. Yet with the parliamentary dissolution of the ecclesiastical Court of High Commission (July 1641) and then the abolition of episcopacy (October 1646), the Westminster Assembly, which had been initially commissioned by Parliament in June 1643 to revise doctrine, liturgy, and church government, confronted the issue. Their Confession of Faith was drafted by committee, debated, amended, and approved, presented to the House of Commons (September 1646), discussed there, and the Assembly's advice licensed for publication (December 1646). A final version incorporating scriptural proofs in the margins was eventually authorized by both Houses of Parliament (21 June 1648). Replacing the Thirty-Nine Articles with Thirty-One Articles of Christian Religion, the first chapter concerning 'Holy Scripture' resolved that:

> The Books commonly called Apocrypha, not being of Divine inspiration, are no part of the Canon of the Scripture; and therefore are of no authority in the Church of God, nor to be any otherwise approved, or made use of, than other humane Writings.[41]

[38] John Lightfoot, *Erubhin* (1629), 116–17; John Lightfoot, *Elias Redivivus* (1643), 5–6.
[39] John Vicars, *Unholsome Henbane* (1645), 1, 8.
[40] Edward Leigh, *A Treatise of Divinity* (1646), 83–91, 90.
[41] *Articles of Christian Religion* (1648), 4; *The Confession of Faith and Catechisms* (1649), 4. It is noteworthy that a 1648 edition of the King James Bible printed for the London Stationers' Company purposefully omitted the Apocrypha.

Another of the Westminster Assembly's significant outputs was a Directory for Public Worship, which replaced the Book of Common Prayer in January 1645. First proposed, like the Confession of Faith, by the General Assembly of the Church of Scotland, the Directory decreed that the Apocrypha was not to be read publicly. At a stroke the smouldering resentment Puritan ministers had felt at being obliged to deliver what they considered a number of unscriptural daily lessons to their congregations, was extinguished. But in the wake of the restoration of the monarchy came a restored prayer book. Following the Savoy Conference a revised Book of Common Prayer (1662) was issued which added more readings from the Apocrypha to the lectionary, spanning from 28 September to 24 November. Many nonconformist ministers balked at this prospect, objecting especially to the stories of Tobias's dog, Bel and the Dragon, and Judith and Baruch, 'which they found the most celebrated bishops and doctors of the church owning to be false and fictitious'.[42] All the same, in a spirit of accommodation Richard Baxter suggested that, while it was not ordinarily lawful to read lessons from the Apocrypha, it was still permissible—with certain provisos—to draw upon these manifestly untruthful and fabulous books publicly. After William III's accession revisions to the prayer book were mooted as one of the means of reconciling Protestant dissenters to the new regime. These would have included substituting the apocryphal lessons with chapters chiefly from Proverbs and Ecclesiastes. But nothing came of this proposal and substantial alterations were not undertaken until 1867, when the number of apocryphal daily lessons was drastically reduced.

V. CONCLUSION

Unfortunately lack of space does not permit a full discussion of the Apocrypha's wider impact on early modern English literature, drama, art, music, and indeed religious culture. Still, it is worth mentioning in passing that various apocryphal books were rendered into English or Latin verse by, among others, the preacher and reputed Geneva Bible collaborator John Pulleyne, the clergyman James Calfhill, the surgeon John Hall, the playwright Anthony Munday, the poet Robert Whitehall, and another clergyman Thomas Warton, while John Milton alluded to Tobit when writing of 'Asmodeus with the fishy fume' and describing Raphael as a 'sociable spirit', the 'affable archangel' (Paradise Lost, 4.166–71, 5.220–3, 7.40–1). On stage, much as the apocryphal Gospel of Nicodemus (c.600) had provided the basis for the fourteenth-century mystery play the Harrowing of Hell (Corpus Christi cycle), so Judith's encounter with Holofernes was performed at Derby (1572) and Bartholomew Fair (c.1721).[43] Then there is William Shakespeare, whose two daughters Susanna and Judith shared their names with figures from the Apocrypha. Evidently he used a Bible bound with these books since his plays contain numerous allusions to them: Portia's 'The quality of mercy is not strain'd / It droppeth as the gentle rain from heaven', for example, and Shylock's exclamation

---

[42] Edmund Calamy, The Nonconformist's Memorial, ed. Samuel Palmer (London: Button & Son, 1802–3), i. 42.

[43] Judith and Holofernes also inspired dramatic treatments by Guillaume de Salluste Du Bartas (c.1574) as well as several German playwrights, notably, Georg Wickram (1539); Cornelius Schonaeus (1592); Martin Behm (1618); and Friedrich Hebbel (1840).

'A Daniel come to judgment!'; referencing first, Sirach 35: 20, and second, young Daniel's rescue of the virtuous Susanna from false witnesses (*Merchant of Venice*, 4.1.184–6, 223–4).

As one of the female Jewish worthies Judith—along with Deborah, Esther, and Jael—was a model of courage in adversity, a heroine who resisted tyranny by seducing and then decapitating Holofernes. Queens were compared to her: Mary of England, Mary of Guise at her funeral, and Elizabeth, notably in John Aylmer's defence of government by a woman, and at a pageant on entering Norwich in August 1578. 'Judith with the head of Holofernes' was also portrayed by continental Protestant artists such as Hans Baldung (c.1525) and Lucas Cranach the elder (1530), yet in England, besides sixteenth-century tapestries woven at various workshops, the subject seems to have received little attention until William Hogarth depicted it as the frontispiece to William Huggins's *Judith: an Oratorio; or, Sacred Drama* (1733).

Likewise, scenes from Tobit inspired works by Adam Elsheimer, Wenceslaus Hollar, Rembrandt, and Titian, but not their English Protestant contemporaries. The same can be said of Flemish representations of 1 Esdras, which lacked an English counterpart. Again, whereas Edward I's Painted Chamber in the royal palace at Westminster had featured a cycle of murals (1292–7) devoted to the Maccabees—imagery which probably mirrored the King's aspiration for another crusade—the extremely rare references to the Maccabees as holy war-riors in the rhetoric of Parliamentarian Civil War sermons or indeed the absence of appo-site quotations from these books in *The Souldiers Pocket Bible* (1643) is noteworthy. There is a similarly silent interlude when it comes to the Apocrypha and music. Although verses 35–66 of the Song of the Three Holy Children were converted into a canticle ('Benedicite, omnia opera') sung at morning prayers, it was not until the Hanoverian period that compos-ers began returning to the Apocrypha for inspiration.

Just as the Apocrypha began receiving renewed cultural attention in Hanoverian England so it is equally significant that critical commentaries on the majority of these books were not published until the mid-eighteenth century. Hitherto, they had been treated summarily in introductions to the Bible, had been belatedly incorporated in concordances, and had also been selectively paraphrased. As might be expected, the Apocrypha were occasionally cited and quoted in sermons and a variety of other works by moderate churchmen throughout the sixteenth, seventeenth, and early eighteenth centuries. What is striking, however, is their near total disappearance from the texts of religious radicals; unless it was to repudiate con-tent, caution against misuse, or draw historical parallels.

Hence John Bunyan was unusual in deriving spiritual comfort from a passage in the unca-nonical Sirach, while Diggers and Ranters appear to have shown little familiarity with the Apocrypha.[44] Moreover, Quakers seldom referred to these books: there are only scattered mentions of Wisdom of Solomon, Sirach, Bel and the Dragon, and Maccabees, as well as an untypical citation of 2 Esdras foretelling the suffering of the Lord's chosen people. Indeed, several notable Quakers seemed ostensibly more interested in other extra-canonical texts such as the book of Enoch and the forged Pauline epistle to the Laodiceans. Among them were James Nayler (who provocatively wore his hair long and centre-parted in imitation of Publius Lentulus' spurious description of Christ) and the controversialist Samuel Fisher. Fisher defended Quakers from the calumny that they slighted the scriptures by highlighting

---

[44] John Bunyan, *Grace Abounding* (1666), 17–18.

at enormous discursive length the Bible's inherent flaws, stressing that the creation of the biblical canon had been an arbitrary process. Suggestively, the Irish freethinker John Toland later adopted a similar polemical strategy.

Yet there was one apocryphal book that received consistent attention, a work that neither Jews, post-Tridentine Catholics, nor the Church of England accepted as canonical, namely 'the *Apocrypha* of the *Apocrypha*', 2 Esdras.[45] This Jewish apocalypse was extensively studied by Catholics, Lutherans, Calvinists, Anabaptists, and Familists alike, its central vision of an eagle rising from the sea with twelve feathered wings and three heads variously understood as a portent of the destruction of the Roman Empire, the Holy Roman Empire, the Ottoman Empire, or the papacy. Other verses concerning the whereabouts of the ten tribes of Israel were interpreted as foretelling the conversion of the Jews to Christianity and the deliverance of the church from Antichrist. But as the reception of this composite text with its Christian additions and interpolations has been thoroughly documented, it is best now to conclude.[46]

Broadly speaking, in Protestant England the 'Hebrew verity' ultimately triumphed over both unwritten verities and the Septuagint. Consequently, the Apocrypha's influence when compared with that of the canonical books of the Old Testament was marginal. Nevertheless, that is not where its importance lies. For in addition to its wider religious and cultural impact, the Apocrypha's presence in the Bible and the lectionary prefixed to the Book of Common Prayer was a perennial grievance for dissenters from the Elizabethan Reformation to the Glorious Revolution.

FURTHER READING

Bredenhof, W. 'Guy de Brès and the Apocrypha'. *Westminster Theological Journal*, 74 (2012): 305–21.

Cadbury, H. J. 'Early Quakerism and Uncanonical Lore'. *Harvard Theological Review*, 40 (1947): 177–205.

Champion, J. A. I. 'Apocrypha, Canon and Criticism from Samuel Fisher to John Toland 1650–1718', in A. P. Coudert, Sarah Hutton, R. H. Popkin, and G. M. Weiner (eds), *Judaeo-Christian Intellectual Culture in the Seventeenth Century: A Celebration of the Library of Narcissus Marsh (1638–1713)* (Dordrecht: Kluwer, 1999), 97–124.

Charles, R. H., ed. *The Apocrypha and Pseudepigrapha of the Old Testament in English*, 2 vols (Oxford: Clarendon Press, 1913; repr. 1973).

Gallagher, E. L. 'The Old Testament "Apocrypha" in Jerome's Canonical Theory'. *Journal of Early Christian Studies*, 20 (2012): 213–33.

Goodman, Martin, John Barton, and John Muddiman, eds. *The Apocrypha* (Oxford: Oxford University Press, 2012).

Greenslade S. L., ed. *The Cambridge History of the Bible*, iii. *The West from the Reformation to the Present Day* (Cambridge: Cambridge University Press, 1963).

Hamilton, Alastair. *The Apocryphal Apocalypse: The Reception of the Second Book of Esdras (4 Ezra) from the Renaissance to the Enlightenment* (Oxford: Clarendon Press, 1999).

---

[45] Thomas Fuller, *A Pisgah-Sight of Palestine* (1650), v. 192.
[46] See Hamilton, *The Apocryphal Apocalypse*.

Hayes, J. H. 'Historical Criticism of the Old Testament Canon', in Magne Sæbø (ed.), *Hebrew Bible, Old Testament: The History of its Interpretation*, ii. *From the Renaissance to the Enlightenment* (Göttingen: Vandenhoeck & Ruprecht, 2008), 985–1005.

Howorth, H. 'The Origin and Authority of the Biblical Canon in the Anglican Church'. *Journal of Theological Studies*, OS 8 (1906): 1–40.

Howorth, H. 'The Origin and Authority of the Biblical Canon According to the Continental Reformers: I. Luther and Karlstadt'. *Journal of Theological Studies*, OS 8 (1907): 321–65.

Howorth, H. 'The Origin and Authority of the Biblical Canon According to the Continental Reformers: II. Luther, Zwingli, Lefèvre, and Calvin'. *Journal of Theological Studies*, OS 9 (1908): 188–232.

Howorth, H. 'The Canon of the Bible among the Later Reformers'. *Journal of Theological Studies*, OS 10 (1909): 183–232.

Jacobs, A. S. 'The Disorder of Books: Priscillian's Canonical Defense of Apocrypha'. *Harvard Theological Review*, 93 (2000): 135–59.

Metzger, Bruce. *An Introduction to the Apocrypha* (New York: Oxford University Press, 1957).

Rice, Eugene. *Saint Jerome in the Renaissance* (Baltimore, Md.: Johns Hopkins University Press, 1985).

Signori, Gabriela, ed. *Dying for the Faith, Killing for the Faith: Old Testament Faith-Warriors (1 and 2 Maccabees) in Historical Perspective* (Leiden: Brill, 2012).

Turner, H. L. 'Some Small Tapestries of Judith with the Head of Holofernes: Should they be called Sheldon?' *Textile History*, 41 (2010): 161–81.

Westcott, Brooke Foss. *The Bible in the Church: A Popular Account of the Collection and Reception of the Holy Scriptures in the Christian Churches*, 2nd edn (London and Cambridge: Macmillan & Co., 1866).

Zeitlin, S. 'Jewish Apocryphal Literature'. *Jewish Quarterly Review*, NS 40 (1950): 223–50.

CHAPTER 9

....

ISAIAH 63 AND THE LITERAL SENSES OF SCRIPTURE

....

DEBORA SHUGER

PROTESTANT reformers affirmed and Reformation scholarship has long remarked the discarding of medieval allegorical exegesis in favour of what Luther called scripture's 'one, simple, stable, and certain literal sense'.[1] However, although sixteenth-century Protestants may have understood well enough what they meant by 'literal sense', in current Reformation scholarship the term often seems to shoot at a moving target. One notes this even in the very best scholarship: for example, Peter Harrison's 1998 *The Bible, Protestantism and the Rise of Natural Science*, whose thesis is that by insisting 'on the primacy of the [Bible's] literal sense', sixteenth-century Protestants 'found themselves forced to jettison traditional concepts of the world'.[2] Harrison tends to identify literal with factual: to read Genesis literally is to read it as a factual account of what happened. Yet at moments he also associates the literal with a passage's obvious, commonsense meaning; with the grammatical sense of the words on the page; with the 'simple gospel message'; with attention to the 'historicity of the biblical text' and 'circumstances of its human authors'; with that which these original authors meant to communicate; with that which the Holy Ghost meant to communicate.[3] It is hard to see how these partial definitions might cohere; perhaps the literal sense is itself fourfold, or perhaps Harrison's various glossings of 'literal' do not pick out distinct facets of a single (albeit fuzzy) concept, but rather point to the existence of competing post-Reformation versions of the literal sense.

What follows is an attempt to recover, at least in part, the literal sense or senses of scripture as understood in the century following the Reformation. Early modern biblical exegesis fills, of course, a vast field, so that from the distance required for a bird's-eye view, one sees only a haze of generalizations. This essay, therefore, will instead descend to a single passage

[1] Frederic Farrar, *History of Interpretation: Eight Lectures Preached before the University of Oxford in the Year MDCCCLXXXV* (London: Macmillan, 1886), 327. Translation mine.

[2] Peter Harrison, *The Bible, Protestantism and the Rise of Natural Science* (Cambridge: Cambridge University Press, 1998), 4.

[3] Harrison, *The Bible*, 108–15, 124.

in order to explore the literal at close range. The chosen passage is Isaiah 63: 1–3, which in the King James translation reads:

> 1 Who is this that cometh from Edom, with dyed garments from Bozrah? this that is glorious in his apparel, travelling in the greatness of his strength? I that speak in righteousness, mighty to save.
> 2 Wherefore art thou red in thine apparel, and thy garments like him that treadeth in the winefat?
> 3 I have trodden the winepress alone; and of the people there was none with me: for I will tread them in mine anger, and trample them in my fury; and their blood shall be sprinkled upon my garments, and I will stain all my raiment.

The passage was not a proof-text for any contested Reformation dogma, nor does the Hebrew present unusual difficulty. I chose these verses because they provide the pericope (set of verses) for Lancelot Andrewes's 1623 Easter sermon, a sermon that struck me as a powerful, albeit surprisingly late, example of medieval allegoresis. I had thought I would begin research with an instance of old-style allegory because, although I was not sure what the literal sense of scripture was, I thought I knew what it was not, and inquiry starts from the known.

As the passage quoted next makes clear, Andrewes reads Isaiah 63: 1–3 as taking place out of time, in an undefined visionary space where the Prophet encounters a figure coming from Edom in red garments, whom Andrewes informs us at the outset is Christ.

> And Christ when? Even this day of all days. His coming here from Edom will fall out to be his rising from the dead. His return from Bozrah, nothing but his vanquishing of hell ....
> The prophets use to speak of things to come as if they saw them present before their eyes. That makes their prophecies be called visions. In his vision here, the Prophet being taken up in spirit sees one coming. Coming, whence? From the land or country of Idumaea or Edom. From what place there? From Bozrah, the chief city in the land, the place of greatest strength ....
> With joy then, but not without admiration, such a party sees the Prophet come toward him. Sees him, but knows him not ... and not knowing, is desirous to be instructed concerning him. Out of this desire asks, *Quis est*? Not of himself, he durst not be so bold, 'Who are you?' but of some stander by, 'Whom have we here? Can you tell who this might be?' The first question.
> But before we come to the question, a word or two of the place where he had been, and whence he came. Edom and Bozrah, what is meant by them? ...
> I will give you a key to this, and such like Scriptures. Familiar it is with the prophets, nothing more ... than to express their ghostly enemies, the both mortal and immortal enemies of their souls, under the titles and terms of those nations and cities as were the known sworn enemies of the commonwealth of Israel ....
> Now then have we the Prophet's true Edom, his very Bozrah indeed. By this we understand what they mean: Edom, the kingdom of darkness and death; Bozrah, the seat of the prince of darkness, that is, hell itself. From both which Christ this day returned. His soul was not left in hell; his flesh saw not (but rose from) corruption.
> For over Edom, strong as it was, yet David cast his shoe over it (that is, after the Hebrew phrase), set his foot upon it and trod it down. And Bozrah, as impregnable a hold as it was holden, yet David won it, was led into the strong city, led into it, and came thence again. So did the Son of David this day from his Edom, death, how strong soever, yet swallowed up in victory, this day. And from hell, his Bozrah ... Christ is got forth, we see. How many souls soever were there left, his was not left there.
> And when did he this? when *solutus doloribus inferni*; he loosed the pains of hell, trod upon the serpent's head, and all to bruised it; took from death his sting, from hell his victory—that

is, his standard, alluding to the Roman standard that had in it the image of the goddess Victory … and triumphantly came thence with the keys of Edom and Bozrah both, of hell and of death, both at his girdle, as he shews himself (Apoc.1). And when was this? if ever, on this very day. On which, having made a full and perfect conquest of death, and of him that hath the power of death, that is the devil (Heb. 2), he rose and returned thence, this morning, as a mighty conqueror, saying as Debora did in her song, O my soul, thou hast trodden down strength, thou hast marched valiantly![4]

I turned to this sermon assuming that it exemplified the power and the glory of medieval allegoresis and would therefore provide a luminous foil to the post-Reformation literal sense, highlighting the latter's secularization and historicization of the real. Andrewes's reading of Isaiah 63 as a vision of the risen Christ, victorious over death and hell, was, I assumed, not conceivably the literal sense.

As the alert reader has already sensed, these assumptions turned out to be false. To see the actual relation of Andrewes's sermon to post-Reformation biblical hermeneutics, we can turn to two of the period's most influential exegetical works, both widely used in England. The first, the massive (c.2200 folio pages) *Clavis scripturae sacrae* of the Lutheran polymath, Matthias Flacius Illyricus (1520–75), dates from 1567 with further editions coming out every twenty years or so until 1719;[5] often considered the first important treatise on hermeneutics, it served (according to McKim's 2007 *Dictionary of Major Biblical Interpreters*) 'as the anchor of much Protestant exegesis for two centuries.'[6] The second is the 1622 *Commentaria in quatuor prophetas maiores* of the Flemish Jesuit, Cornelius à Lapide (1567–1637),[7] part of his multi-volume commentary long beloved of English Protestant clergymen despite its Catholic provenance: John Donne purchased the individual volumes as they came out; Andrewes used à Lapide, as did George Herbert, Sir Thomas Browne, and Jeremy Taylor, along with 'a number of Puritan divines', and, over a century later, John Wesley.[8]

The two works are of particular value to the present inquiry since both explicitly confine their attention to the literal sense: à Lapide on the grounds that earlier exegetes had discussed the spiritual senses at length (63); Flacius, more polemically, on the grounds

---

[4] Lancelot Andrewes, *A Sermon Preached before the King's Majesty at Whitehall, on the xiii of April … 1623* (published in *XCVI Sermons*, 1629), quoted from *Documents of Anglophone Christianity: Early Stuart England*, ed. Debora Shuger (Waco, Tex.: Baylor University Press, 2012), 323–6.

[5] Quotations from the Basel edition of 1607; all citations are given parenthenthetically in the text, prefixed by an 'F' where needed to avoid confusion. Translations mine.

[6] Donald McKim, *Dictionary of Major Biblical Interpreters* (Downers Grove, Ill.: InterVarsity Press, 2007); he describes the *Clavis* as a *summa* of the 'principles that Luther, Melanchthon and other evangelical theologians had been employing in the revolution in exegesis that accompanied the Reformation' (438, 441). See also Richard Muller, 'Biblical Interpretation in the Sixteenth and Seventeenth Centuries', in McKim, *Dictionary*, 33, <http://www.ivpress.com/title/exc/2927-1.pdf>. Debora Shuger, *Sacred Rhetoric: The Christian Grand Style in the English Renaissance* (Princeton: Princeton University Press, 1988), 73–98 *et passim*.

[7] Page numbers for à Lapide refer to vol. xi of *Commentaria in Scripturam Sacram*, ed. Augustinus Crapon, 23 vols (Paris, 1881). Here and throughout, the 'v' and 'r' specifications refer to the left and the right side of the *opening*, not to the sides of the *leaf*. Citations will be parenthetical in the text, prefixed by an 'L' where needed to avoid confusion. Translations mine.

[8] *The Sermons of John Donne*, ed. George Potter and Evelyn Simpson (Berkeley, Calif.: University of California Press, 1953–62), ix. 369–74; David Jeffrey, *A Dictionary of Biblical Tradition in English Literature* (Grand Rapids, Mich.: Eerdmans, 1992), 518a, 599, 909.

that scripture has only a literal sense (22). Yet their readings of Isaiah 63: 1–3 (and of Old Testament prophecy more generally) seem remarkably close to Andrewes's sermon. Both take Isaiah's visionary passages as actual visions; the Prophet *sees* things hidden or to come. Moreover, for both Flacius and à Lapide, Christ is the scope, the true subject, of all the Prophets (F172; L57ᵛ). Both treat the prophetic language of conquest, vengeance, and slaughter as figuring a *literal* spiritual warfare; those who read such images of worldly power *ad verbum*, Flacius observes, 'have strayed very far indeed from the true sense', which has to do with the kingdom of Christ, not temporal rule (30). Thus according to its literal sense, à Lapide writes, Isaiah 63 'concerns the victory of Christ: not that the devil really has blood, which Christ sheds, or that he slays heathen nations'; the Prophets use military images 'because Christ trod down his enemies, namely the devil, sin, the flesh, death; and because he subjected the faithless and sinful to himself, killing in them their unbelief and sin' (78ᵛ). For à Lapide, the figure Isaiah saw coming from Edom was the risen Christ, victorious over the infidels (Edomites), who were now captives to the Gospel (730ᵛ–732ʳ).

The literal sense, it would seem, has enlarged its scope to include much of what a medieval exegete would have considered allegory. Instead of an historicist-humanist reading, one finds a thoroughgoing spiritualization. For Flacius and à Lapide, Christological meaning does not rest on the Prophet's literal sense; it *is* the literal sense of his prophecy. Nor is their traditionalism anomalous; Richard Muller's broad survey of post-Reformation hermeneutics comes to the like conclusion: namely, that throughout this period 'the doctrinal, moral and eschatological dimensions of the *quadriga* (medieval four-fold allegory) were not lost but rather were found more precisely lodged in the literal sense'.[9] This, however, raises the obvious question of why early modern biblical commentaries expand the literal sense in this manner? What was the objection to the multiple senses of patristic and medieval exegesis?

To grasp the objection, some account of this traditional hermeneutic will be requisite. The key text for our purposes turns out to be Augustine's earliest foray into the principles of scriptural interpretation, the *De utilitate credendi*, written in 391 to a Manichaean friend who thought that a religion grounded on belief rather than certainties was poor stuff. As part of his response, Augustine notes three common errors in reading: readers may be deceived by an author's lies; or misled by the author's own errors; or a reader may mistake the author's meaning, but his mistaken interpretation, although not what the author meant, is nonetheless true—so, for example, a reader might wrongly think Epicurus held that virtue is the highest good. This third sort of misreading, Augustine argues, is both natural to and worthy of good people: for, given that we cannot know a writer's actual thoughts, we should read generously, taking his words in the best sense possible. If readers find a good meaning in a text, even if not the intended meaning, they have gained something of solid value; grasping authorial intent is not essential to profitable reading, and indeed Augustine thinks that readers seldom do grasp the original intent of difficult works. Moreover, if the author is dead or otherwise unavailable for questioning, how could we ever know whether or not we had rightly grasped it? What matters, Augustine argues, is that readers find a truth, an insight. But what readers find in a text cannot but be shaped by their own desires and expectations; thus precisely *because* boys love Virgil, they credit interpretations that disclose his

⁹ Muller, 'Biblical Interpretation', 26. See also G. Sujin Pak, *The Judaizing Calvin* (Oxford: Oxford University Press, 2010), 19. Modern scholarship usually associates this absorption of the spiritual senses into the literal with Faber Stapulensis (d. 1536), but it would seem to be of far wider extent.

poems' depth and beauty. *Credo ut intelligam*; one has to believe in order to understand. Yet, although belief and love can lead to understanding, the generous interpretation may not in fact be what the author meant. Interpretation for Augustine thus *hovers* between the discovery of the author's meaning and making meaning out of the words, between seeking the intent of a passage and seeking a truth from it.[10]

As even this brief summary makes evident, the premises of Augustinian hermeneutics underwrite the characteristic procedures of patristic and medieval exegesis. That the same words can be taken in different senses and yield different truths allows for the multiple interpretations of the *quadriga*. Subsequent exegesis likewise bears the print of Augustine's view that neither historical context nor the author's intent matters very much—that what matters is finding truth, not what some dead person thought. Finally, Augustine's recognition that a found truth may or may not be an intended one stands behind the hovering character of much traditional exegesis: that is to say, its overarching vagueness as to whether meaning resides in the words on the page, in the intent of the human author, or the intent of the Holy Spirit; whether the reader, like a Barthian scriptor, at least in part creates that which he perceives.[11]

As I shall try to show in what follows, à Lapide and Flacius largely retain these Augustinian premises. First, however, we need to return to the question of why post-Reformation exegetes disown the traditional framework of spiritual senses and multiple levels? Why do they insistently identify their (often ahistorical and spiritualized) reading of scripture with its literal sense? The answer would seem to be implicit in the claim that motivates and grounds Augustinian exegesis: the claim that misreading—misconstruing the author's intent—is nigh inevitable. For Augustine, for whom the mediate object of faith was *traditio*, broadly understood, rather than the text *per se*, such misreading presented no great difficulty. Once scripture became the sole rule of faith—as it did for Reformation Protestants, but also earlier in the Christian–Jewish disputations of the Middle Ages—the problem becomes acutely serious. Flacius is explicit on this point: to serve as a rule of faith, scripture must possess a single, clear sense, since a text that has no determinate meaning is but 'a nose of wax' and cannot teach with either certainty or authority (65–7, 172).[12] The Catholic à Lapide, however, also identifies scripture's meaning with its literal sense, and moreover holds that this literal sense must include the Old Testament prophecies of Christ (57ᵛ)—a position he defends on the grounds that if one were to restrict the literal sense to matters within the Prophets' own temporal horizon, with all that pertains to Christ relegated to the allegory, this would effectively abandon the fort to the Jews, since they simply dismiss this so-called spiritual sense as Christian fairy-tales (64ʳ).[13]

I shall take up this Jewish critique in the second half of this essay. It relates to the present discussion because it helps explain why in the Catholic à Lapide (and going back to the high Middle Ages) one finds a turn from the spiritual to the literal sense, and yet a turn that

---

[10] *De utilitate credendi*, sect. 10–13, On the Profit of Believing, tr. C. Cornish, *Nicence and Post-Nicene Fathers*, 1st ser. 3, ed. Philip Schaff (1887), <http://www.newadvent.org/fathers/1306.htm>.

[11] See Henri de Lubac, *Exégèse médiévale* (Paris, 1959–64), iv. 86–90.

[12] 'Nose of wax', i.e. easily twisted any way one likes. On this phrase, which goes back to the twelfth century, see Timothy George, *Reading Scripture with the Reformers* (Downers Grove, Ill.: InterVarsity Press, 2011), 107–9.

[13] 'a Christianis confictum.'

pivots on the spiritualization of the letter—the letter which, in à Lapide's words, now 'tells of both mystery and history' (68ʳ). Hence, while Flacius and à Lapide lay claim to the literal sense to avoid the charge that scripture is a 'nose of wax', they reclassify a good deal of traditional exegesis, including its Augustinian substructure, under that rubric. To see how this works—to see how two cutting-edge early modern exegetes understand the literal sense of scripture—we can return to their reading of Old Testament prophecy in general and Isaiah 63: 1–3 in particular.

The Augustinianism hermeneutic betrays itself, first, in an almost total lack of *interest* in the historical circumstances of prophetic books. Both Flacius and à Lapide note that such information can at times be crucial for understanding a passage—not, however, because the prophetic writers (generally) engage their own historical circumstances, but because they use local knowledge to trope spiritual realities; even the clearly historical parts of the Old Testament have also a spiritual referent (F5, 30, 92–3, 185, 194). À Lapide adds the striking suggestion that the Prophets used an obscure, involuted, and heavily figurative style in order to block historicist readings; the style itself, so different from that of the Bible's historical books, signals that the prophecies swing back and forth across time; like 'a ceremonial tunic embroidered with gold', the prophetic writings 'cut off the narrative thread in order to weave Christ into and through the design of history' (67ʳ; see 71ʳ).[14]

If Flacius and à Lapide give little weight to the Prophets' historical moment, they have even less interest in them as historical persons. They do not see them as historical persons but as instruments of the Holy Spirit to convey the eternal things of God (F8, 21–2; L53ᵛ). À Lapide explains that the prophetic narratives move abruptly between the immediate future and the distant coming of Christ because the Prophets, 'carried aloft by divine light, beheld all things, however temporally remote and far apart they appear to us … as simultaneously visible in all their interconnectedness' (67ʳ). So too for Flacius, the books of scripture form an intricately interrelated structure (22–3), coupled together into a coherent whole by the single Spirit informing them, 'like a necklace made of interconnected circles, where whichever link you pick up, the rest hang from it in a single loop' (176).

This understanding of holy scripture as an integral single-author text stands behind the pervasive early modern exegetic (and homiletic) practice known as *collatio locorum* (conferring of places), a practice that à Lapide explicitly designates as an interpretation of the literal sense (63ʳ). Citing Augustine's *De doctrina Christiana*, Flacius praises the *collatio locorum* as the single best method for discovering the scriptures' true sense (15, 160), for 'by the marvelous providence and wisdom of God, they have been so written that similar expressions occur in the most diverse books and passages' and these 'reciprocally illuminate each other in a most wondrous fashion' (36). Thus 'there can be no better way to understand what is being said to God [in Psalm 35: 2], "Take hold of arms and shield [*scutum*]: and rise up to help me", than from that place where we read "thou, Lord, hast crowned us, as with a shield of thy good will [*scuto bonae voluntatis*]"'.[15]

The *collocatio locorum*, as this suggests, should not be confused with proof-texting; the places collocated do not contain doctrinal statements but shields. To see the theological

---

[14] 'quasi in cyclade variegata et auro intertexta praecidunt saepe historiae filum, ut Christum historiae attexant et intertexant.'

[15] F160, quoting Ps. 5: 13. I am following the Douai-Rheims translation, with slight modifications to align the wording with Flacius's Latin, which is not that of the Vulgate.

power of this exegetical method—and, again, how little it resembles our own notion of literal interpretation—we may once again turn to Andrewes's Easter sermon, which reads Isaiah 63: 3 ('I have trodden the winepress alone') via an interlaced collocation of widely scattered oenopoetic images.

> Out of these pressures ran the blood of the grapes of the true vine, the fruit whereof (as it is said in Judg. 9) *cheereth both God and man*. God, as a *libamen* or drink-offering to him; man, as *the cup of salvation* to them. But, to make this wine, his clusters were to be cut; cut, and cast in; cast in, and trodden on; trodden and pressed out; all these, before he came to be wine in the cup ....
>
> But, to return to the winepress, to tell you the occasion or reason, why thus it behoved to be. It was not idly done. What need then was there of it, this first pressing? We find (1 Cor. 10) *calix daemoniorum*; the devil hath a cup. Adam must needs be sipping of it; *eritis sicut Dii* went down sweetly, but poisoned him, turned his nature quite. For Adam was by God planted a natural vine, a true root, but thereby, by that cup, degenerated into a wild strange vine, which, instead of good grapes, brought forth *labruscas, wild grapes, grapes of gall, bitter clusters*; Moses calls them *coloquintida*; the Prophet, *mors in olla*, and *mors in calice*; by which is meant, the deadly fruit of our deadly sins.
>
> But (as it is in the fifth chapter of this prophecy), where God planted this vine first, he made a winepress in it; so the grapes that came of this strange vine were cut and cast into the press; thereof came a deadly wine, of which, saith the Psalmist, *in the hand of the Lord there is a cup; the wine is red, it is full mixed, and he pours out of it; and the sinners of the earth are to drink it, dregs and all* [Ps. 75: 8]. Those sinners were our fathers, and we. It came to *bibite ex hoc omnes* [Matt. 26: 27]; they and we were to drink of it all, one after another round. Good reason, to drink as we had brewed, to drink the fruit of our own inventions, our own words and works we had brought forth.
>
> About, the cup went; all strained at it. At last, to Christ it came. He was none of the sinners, but was *found among them*. By his good will, he would have had it pass; *transeat a Me calix iste*,—you know who that was. Yet, rather than we, than any of us should take it—it would be our bane, he knew—he took it; off it went, dregs and all.

The *collatio locorum* has Augustinian roots, but, in Andrewes's hands, it also resembles nothing so much as the New Criticism of the mid-twentieth century with its studies of water-imagery in Milton's *Lycidas* that disclosed the poem's deep structure by collocating allusions to tears, fountains, seas, and streams. The new-critical character of this post-Reformation exegesis rests, in turn, on its understanding of scripture as a single-author divine poem, and hence, as literary critics of an earlier generation used to say, an organic unity; or as Flacius says, a 'single body', whose parts manifest 'an agreement, harmony, and proportion among themselves, as likewise in relation both to the body as a whole and, above all, to its Head' (22).[16]

Lastly, both Flacius and à Lapide preserve the 'hovering' character of Augustinian exegesis: that is, their interpretations of scripture retain the pervasive ambiguity explored in *De utilitate credendi* as to whether exegesis renders the meaning intended by the original author, the sense of the Holy Spirit, the grammatical sense of the words on the page, or some insight the words have suggested to the exegete—in which case what matters is the truth

---

[16] See also George Herbert's 'The H. Scriptures (II)'; and John Donne's *Devotions on Emergent Occasions* (1624), expostulation 19.

of the insight, not whether it represents a successful mind-meld with Moses. Flacius and à Lapide hover between these possibilities, at one point or another affirming each option.

Two sequential paragraphs from à Lapide provide a fairly typical example.[17] The forty-fifth of his canons for interpreting the prophetic books states that whatever the Prophets promise or threaten the Jews can 'by a simple name change be applied to Christians'. According to this canon it is evidently we—the Christian reader, scholar, preacher—who make the updated application. However canon 46 maintains, citing Isaiah 63, that the Prophets 'typically depict the redeeming work of Christ as a military victory in which he destroys his enemies … because Christ both trampled upon his foes—namely, the devil, sin, the flesh, and death' (78ᵛ⁻ʳ). According to this canon, the Old Testament prophecies of triumphant slaughter are metaphors, whose literal sense foretells 'how Christ, the world's redeemer, as a victor won the day'.[18] Canons 45 and 46 stake out opposite positions on the Christian *sensus literalis* of the Old Testament, the contrast highlighted by their proximity. Yet the tension is neither resolved nor even acknowledged; meanings, like Schrodinger's cat, hover between two incompatible states, and, until the box is opened at the Last Judgement, that appears to be the best one can do.

By this point it seems clear that there existed an influential and sophisticated post-Reformation biblical hermeneutics that, although committed to the primacy of the literal sense, preserved a deep continuity with the spiritual exegesis of the patristic and medieval church. The chapter could end here, were it not that, thus far, Reformed exegesis has been conspicuous only by its omission.

The survival of traditional exegesis seems less amazing once one sees the alternative. For there was an alternative by the mid-sixteenth century, and one far closer to what we normally think of as literal interpretation. Here at last we encounter the focus on authorial intention and socio-political context, with attendant 'restrictions on christological exegesis of the Old Testament', that herald modern biblical criticism.[19] Here is Calvin, whose commentary on Isaiah 63: 1–3 catapults one into a different world.

> 1. *Who is this that cometh from Edom?* This chapter has been violently distorted by Christians, as if what is said here related to Christ, whereas the Prophet speaks simply of God himself; and they have imagined that here Christ is red, because he was wet with his own blood which he shed on the cross. But the Prophet meant nothing of that sort. The obvious meaning is, that the Lord comes forth with red garments in the view of his people, that all may know that he is their protector and avenger; for when the people were weighed down by innumerable evils, and at the same time the Edomites … freely indulged in wickedness, which remained unpunished, a dangerous temptation might arise, as if these things happened by chance, or as if God did not care for his people ….
>
> The Prophet meets this very serious temptation by representing God the avenger as returning from the slaughter of the Edomites, as if he were drenched with their blood ….

---

[17] For a similar example of hovering, see canons 3 and 4 in Flacius, *Clavis*, 30.

[18] The quotation comes from Fortunatus's sixth-century hymn, *Pange, lingua*, tr. John Mason Neale, *Mediæval Hymns and Sequences* (1851), 1–5.

[19] Pak, *Judaizing*, 139. On the fundamental difference between Reformation and modern exegesis, whatever their similarities, see David Steinmetz, 'The Superiority of Pre-Critical Exegesis', *Theology Today*, 37 (1980): 27–38.

Beautiful in his raiment ....To impress men with reverence for God's righteous vengeance, he pronounces the blood with which God was sprinkled by slaying and destroying the wicked to be highly beautiful ....

...

3. *Alone have I pressed the wine-press*. The Prophet now explains the vision, and the reason why the Lord was stained with blood. It is because he will take vengeance on the Edomites and other enemies who treated his people cruelly. It would be absurd to say that these things relate to Christ because he alone and without human aid redeemed us; for it means that God will punish the Edomites ....

In my wrath. He shews that this is of itself sufficient for destroying the Edomites, that the Lord is angry with them .... Hence we may infer that the destruction of men proceeds from nothing else than the wrath of God.[20]

The erasure of references to Christ is typical of Calvin's commentaries, a position he defends by appeal to 'the human author's intention' or the passage's 'simple and natural' meaning.[21] For Flacius and à Lapide, scripture's literal sense was mysteriously meant. Calvin will have none of this. The surface meaning is the real meaning. Hence, as his commentary on Isaiah 63: 1–3 makes evident, the violence is real violence, with all the trappings: a wrathful deity, a longing for vengeance on one's enemies, an exulting in their destruction. This is the Protestant literalism that James Simpson calls the 'new allegorization': the reading of the Hebrew scripture as a template for and foreshadowing of the here-and-now of God's people, such that 'the divine violence' visited on the heathen of the Old Testament 'legitimates, if not demands' the same against the Catholic idolator.[22]

But where is this coming from? There is nothing remotely equivalent in the medieval glosses to Isaiah 63, nor Nicholas of Lyra's postils, nor Luther.[23] As should be evident, Calvin's reading differs sharply from other strands of mainstream post-Reformation exegesis. However, a 1593 Lutheran tract attacking precisely those aspects of Calvin's exegesis conspicuous in his Isaiah 63 gloss suggests a possible answer. The tract's title, *Calvinus Judizans*, gives the basic thesis—a thesis corroborated by G. Sunjin Pak's far more sympathetic recent study, *The Judaizing Calvin*. In both works Calvin's 'Judaizing' refers specifically to his debt to the new school of Jewish exegesis that flourished in Spain and northern France during the long twelfth century, an exegesis whose focus on scripture's literal sense (*peschat*) broke sharply with the allegorical, homiletic, and mystical strains of earlier rabbinic exegesis.[24] The leading figures of this new school include

---

[20] Calvin, *Commentary on the Book of the Prophet Isaiah*, tr. William Pringle (Edinburgh: Calvin Translation Society, 1850–3), iv. 339, <http://www.ccel.org/ccel/calvin/calcom16>.

[21] Pak, *Judaizing*, 8, 81–2, 99. À Lapide, citing Hugo of St Victor rather than Calvin, notes that Isa. 63: 1–3 could refer to an an actual massacre, but dismisses the reading as 'frigidum et Judaicum' (730ʳ).

[22] James Simpson, *Burning to Read: English Fundamentalism and its Reformation Opponents* (Cambridge, Mass.: Harvard University Press, 2007), 217–18. Reading Old Testament history as prefiguring subsequent historical events is, properly speaking, typology, not allegory. Standard typology, which goes back to St Paul, reads Old Testament events as types of New Testament ones, whereas Calvin tends to read the former as types of the still-unfolding history of God's church. De Lubac traces this presentist typology to Joachim of Fiore (d. 1202) (*Exégèse médiévale*, iv. 326ff.).

[23] Martin Luther, *Vorlesung ueber Jesaia*, in *D. Martin Luthers Werke: Kritische Gesammtausgabe* (Weimar: Hermann Boehlaus, 1902), xxv. 376–7. R. Gerald Hobbs suggests that Calvin took his cue from Martin Bucer: 'How Firm a Foundation: Martin Bucer's Historical Exegesis of the Psalms', *Church History*, 53 (1984): 484–6. Pak, however, argues that Bucer's exegesis remains largely within a traditional Christian framework: *Judaizing*, 95.

[24] Frederick Greenspahn, 'The Significance of Hebrew Philology for the Development of a Literal and Historical Jewish Bible Interpretation', 56; Stephen Garfinkel, 'Clearing *Peshat* and *Derash*', 132; G. R. Evans,

Ibn Ezra (1192–1267), Rashi (1040–1105), and Kimhi (1160–1235). By the mid-sixteenth century, their principal commentaries were easily available to Christian scholars: the 1517–18 Bomberg Rabbinic Bible included Kimhi's Isaiah commentary; the 1525 second edition added the commentaries of Ibn Ezra and Rashi. Calvin's Old Testament commentaries use both Rashi and Kimhi: for the Isaiah commentary, principally Kimhi, his favourite among the Jewish exegetes.[25]

From the early sixteenth century on, all serious biblical scholarship used the philological and grammatical insights of this twelfth-century school. Calvin's startlingly distinctive approach to Isaiah 63, however, also draws on three further hallmarks of their commentaries, the first of which forms the probable prototype for Simpson's new allegorization: namely, the reading of biblical sacred history as prefiguring latter-day sacred history. This is precisely how Ibn Ezra reads Isaiah 63:

> The prophecy contains the decree made against Edom, that is, against the empire of Rome and Constantinople, who are called Edomites, because they adopted the Edomite religion—that is, the Christian religion—which was first established among the Edomites .... 3. *I have trodden*, etc. This prophecy refers to the destruction of Edom, and the overthrow of the dominion of his religion .... 4. *For the day of vengeance*, etc. For I will wreak vengeance against my enemies, and I will redeem my friends.[26]

For Ibn Ezra, Edom is a type of Rome: that is, of Christianity. The prophecy concerns Israel's captivity under Christian yoke, which God will avenge. For Kimhi likewise the Edomites of Isaiah 63 prefigure Christians; and the principal consolation Kimhi has to offer the diaspora is that in the end the Jews will be restored to own land, the 'Kingdom of Rome' destroyed.[27] Both commentators read Isaiah 63 as eschatalogical prophecy, but one whose fulfilment brings no metaphoric transfiguration of violence; rather the vision foretells a historical bloodbath in which God saves us and destroys our enemies.

The Ibn Ezra and Kimhi glosses to Isaiah 63 likewise illustrate the second hallmark of the twelfth-century commentaries: the frequent rejection of traditional messianic readings (these were, rather obviously, *Jewish* messianic readings). Commenting on Psalm 2, Rashi thus observes that 'our rabbis expound it as relating to King Messiah, but according to the plain meaning it is proper to interpret it in connection with David'. Kimhi's commentary takes a similar position: 'Some interpret this psalm of Gog and Magog' (who wage war against the Messiah) 'but the better explanation is that David uttered it concerning himself .... He composed and recited this psalm at the beginning of his reign, when the nations gathered against him'.[28]

'Masters and Disciples: Aspects of Christian Interpretation', 254—all three in Magne Sæbø (ed.), *Hebrew Bible/ Old Testament: The History of its Appropriation*, i/2. *The Middle Ages* (Göttingen: Vanderhoeck & Ruprecht, 2000), hereafter cited as 'Sæbø'.

[25] E. A. de Boer, *John Calvin on the Visions of Ezekiel* (Leiden: Brill, 2004), 93; Amy Pauw, 'Becoming a Part of Israel', in Claire McGinnis and Patricia Tull (eds), *'As Those Who Are Taught': The Interpretation of Isaiah from the LXX to the SBL* (Atlanta, Ga.: Society of Biblical Literature, 2006), 214–15; Mordechai Cohen, 'The Qimhi Family', in Sæbø, 388–415 (389, 414). From this point on, I am dependent on secondary sources, since I cannot read the Hebrew to see whether the 'historicism' of these medieval Jewish commentaries really prefigures Calvin's exegesis.

[26] *The Commentary of Ibn Ezra on Isaiah*, tr. and ed. M. Friedlaender (London, 1873), i. 285–7.

[27] Frank Talmage, *Apples of Gold*, ed. Barry Dov Walfish (Toronto: Pontifical Institute of Medieval Studies, 1999), 208–9.

[28] Quoted in Raymond Apple,<http://www.oztorah.com/2010/02/david-kimhis-response-to-christianity-in-his-psalm-commentary>.

Both accounts of Psalm 2 also make apparent the link between rejection of messianic reading and a new historicism, the third hallmark of this Jewish exegetic school. For Rashi and Kimhi the psalm concerns not a future redeemer but David's own time and circumstances. Although Jewish commentators had always denied that the Christians' Old Testament proof-texts referred to Jesus of Nazereth, not until the twelfth century do they argue that such passages had 'to be understood in their historical context'.[29] Rashi, who regularly bases his interpretations 'on the historical background of the prophets' times', sees Isaiah 1–39 as concerned throughout with the rise of Assyria and Sennacherib's defeat at Jerusalem.[30] Kimhi reads Isaiah along similar lines, arguing, for example, that Isaiah 7: 14 ('a virgin shall conceive', etc.) must refer to the birth of Ahaz's son, Hezekiah, since the sign is for Ahaz, and 'how could he be encouraged by something which did not happen in his own time?' The prophets speak to and of their historical moment; the passage has nothing to do with a messiah.[31]

Isaiah 7: 14 is, of course, the prophecy quoted by Matthew and Luke at the beginning of their respective Gospels. Kimhi's point in rejecting a messianic reading in favour of a local-historical one is that the passage has nothing to do with Jesus. One would hardly expect him to have done otherwise, yet prior to the 1950s, no one seems to have connected this literal-historical method with the period's Jewish–Christian public disputations or realized that it had been fashioned for the purposes of anti-Christian polemic.[32] Medieval Jewish scholars, Avraham Grossman explains, felt that traditional rabbinic exegesis lent support to Christian allegorization, whereas 'adherence to the literal meaning of the text' presented major difficulties for their Christian counterparts. The demands of Jewish–Christian polemic, Grossman continues, leave 'a considerable imprint' on Rashi's commentaries, although the polemical point is usually left implicit. Yet scattered comments make it clear that his commitment to the literal sense 'was meant, *inter alia*, to hinder efforts on the part of Christian adversaries to offer their Christological, allegorical version of the text'.[33] Most contemporary scholars reach conclusions similar to Grossman's. David Berger thus considers it 'beyond question that the desire to refute Christian interpretation' led Jewish exegetes to develop a 'type of exegesis' that made allegedly Christological passages instead refer to persons and events of the biblical author's own historical moment. Guenter Stemberger similarly finds 'polemical anti-Christian interpretations … in many Jewish Bible commentaries of this period'. So too Frederick Greenspahn concludes that the twelfth-century Jewish exegetes evolved a historicist-literalist approach to scripture because it 'served Jewish purposes best in their confrontation with Christianity'.[34]

---

[29] Günter Stemberger, 'Elements of Biblical Interpretation in Medieval Jewish-Christian Disputation', in Sæbø, 578–90 (582, 587).

[30] Avraham Grossman, 'The School of Literal Jewish Exegesis in Northern France', in Sæbø, 321–71 (341).

[31] Stemberger, 'Elements', 587; Talmage, *Apples*, 191–2.

[32] Yitzhak Baer, 'Rashi and the Historical Reality of his Time', *Tarbiz*, 20 (1950): 320–32 (in Hebrew); my comments are based on Grossman, 'The School', 325. See also Daniel Lasker, 'Jewish-Christian Polemics at the Turning Point', *Harvard Theological Review*, 89 (1996): 161–73.

[33] Grossman, 'The School', 330, 339, 361–2.

[34] David Berger, 'The Jewish–Christian Debate in the High Middle Ages', in Jeremy Cohen (ed.), *Essential Papers on Judaism and Christianity in Conflict* (New York: NYU Press, 1991), 490; Sternberger, 'Elements', 579; Greenspahn, 'Jewish Bible Interpretation', 62; see also Talmage, *Apples*, 192.

Moreover, as the same scholars point out, these historicized readings often had little historical basis, nor is it clear that their authors believed them. While the author of the *Sefer nizzahon vetus,* a thirteenth-century compendium of anti-Christian exegesis, 'apparently understood that chapter [Isaiah 11] messianically', he also suggested 'that it could be referred to Hezekiah and Sennacherib', since showing that purportedly messianic texts in fact had local referents 'perfectly suited the needs of disputation with Christians'.[35] Yet, as noted, in most of the commentaries associated with Rashi and his school, the polemical intent remains implicit. In general, the readings are presented as historicist philology, as defending the literal sense against wishful thinking, and were presumably understood as such by Calvin (and by most post-Enlightenment scholars, Christian and Jewish alike, into the twentieth century).

All three hallmark features of twelfth-century Jewish exegesis reappear in Calvin's commentaries. However, the first—that is, presentist typology or what Simpson calls the 'new allegorization'—entered mainstream Christian hermeneutics via the great Christian Hebraist of the fourteenth century, Nicholas of Lyra. The early sixteenth-century commentaries of the Protestant Hebraist Sebastian Münster and his Benedictine counterpart Isidore Clarius both echo Ibn Ezra's reading of Isaiah 63: 1–3, reversing its anti-Christian spin by the simple expedient of identifying Edom as synagogue rather than church.[36] The same flexibly polemical typology informs the pervasive tendency in Calvin, and in Reformed exegesis generally, to read Hebrew scripture as foreshadowing the church of the present age: the persecution of God's true Israel by bloodthirsty oppressors, etc.[37] Often Reformed controversialists simply took over the Jewish exegetes' anti-Christian identification of Edom with Rome for their own anti-Catholic readings.

That Calvinists enlisted a militantly presentist typology to attack the Romish Antichrist is well-known. In Calvin, however, this presentism is yoke-fellow to a historicist literalism that privileges local context over Christological-messianic allegory. He assumes that, on the whole, biblical writers spoke to and about their own historical moment—and hence that the literal sense of a passage concerns its local context—although a local context often deeply relevant to the church of Calvin's day; in her study of Calvin's Isaiah commentary, Pauw thus notes that 'Calvin generally portrayed Isaiah as thoroughly enmeshed, as he was himself, in the historical realm, trusting God even when the promised redemption seemed nowhere in sight'.[38] The presentist typology, suspicion of Christian back-formations, and preference for local-historical readings are all visible in his commentary on Isaiah 63: 1–3 quoted in this chapter.[39] But these are also, of course, the hallmarks of twelfth-century Jewish exegesis. As Pak's *Judaizing Calvin* argues, albeit with different emphases, Calvin's hermeneutics betray a striking debt to medieval Hebrew scholarship.

Moreover, with respect to the second and third of these hallmark features, the debt would appear to be Calvin's own; at least I cannot find evidence of similar indebtedness in the Christian Hebraists of the earlier sixteenth century. In his annotations to Isaiah 63, published in the mid-1530s, Sebastian Münster identifies the figure in blood-stained garments

[35] Sternberger, 'Elements', 590; Berger, 'Jewish-Christian Debate', 484.
[36] Both repr. in *Critici Sacri,* ed. John Pearson (London, 1660), iv, cols 5413, 5415.
[37] Pauw, 'Becoming', *passim.*   [38] Pauw, 'Becoming', 206.
[39] Pak notes the same features in Calvin's Psalm commentaries: *Judaizing,* 8, 78–9, 100.

as 'Christ who most justly battles & conquers ... the Edomites & Moabites, making ceaseless war against the blood-thirsty Synagogue, in order to free those who are his'.[40] This is, for Münster, the literal sense, but it is scarcely historicist; indeed, its reading of Isaiah is closer to Andrewes, since presumably Christ's battles do not take place on the killing fields of temporal history. Rather, it would seem—and Pak's *Judaizing Calvin* amasses considerable evidence in support[41]—that it was Calvin's signal innovation to Christianize, as it were, a hermeneutic originally intended to disable the Christian appropriation of the Hebrew Bible.

Thus whereas Luther reads Isaiah 44: 23 Christologically, Calvin makes 'no mention of Christ, focusing instead on the original context'; that is, he sees Isaiah as exhorting the Jews to give thanks to God. For Luther, Isaiah 44: 28 is a prophecy of Christ; for Calvin, of Cyrus.[42] On Isaiah 14: 12, 'how art thou fallen from heaven, O Lucifer', Calvin declares that the traditional exposition of the passage as referring to Satan 'has arisen from ignorance; for the context plainly shows that these statements must be understood in reference to the king of the Babylonians'.[43] So too, as we have seen, in Calvin's reading of Isaiah 63, Edom is Edom, not hell or death; and the blood-stained figure Isaiah sees is a God who does not forgive those who persecute him. It is the historicist literalism of the Geneva Bible's gloss to Isaiah 63:

> This prophecy is against the Idumeans, and enemies which persecuted the Church, on whom God will take vengeance, and is here set forth all bloody after that he hath destroyed him in Bozrah, the chief city of the Idumeans; for these were their greatest enemies .... God answereth them that asked this question, Who is this, etc., and sayeth, Ye see now performed in deed the vengeance, which my prophets threatened.[44]

Apart from replacing 'Israel' with 'Church', this is close to twelfth-century Jewish exegesis, and also to *modern* biblical scholarship.[45] For Calvin's hermeneutic surely does feel more modern—may have shaped the modern sense of the literal: our gut reaction is that Calvin's reading is faithful to Hebrew scripture *because* it is not Christian. Calvin would not appreciate my putting it this way, yet this is not altogether the wrong way to put it, since the hermeneutic Calvin adopted—one suspicious of reading the New Testament back into the Old and inclined to equate the literal sense with authorial intention and local context—was initially forged as a weapon against Christian exegesis.[46]

It is worth underscoring that this adoption was not the inevitable consequence of Christian Hebraism. Nicholas of Lyra (d. 1349) was a fine Hebraist and deeply indebted to Rashi, yet his reading of Isaiah 63 is far closer to Lancelot Andrewes, also a fine

---

[40] *Critici Sacri*, iv, col. 5413.

[41] Pauw similarly concludes that Calvin's readings, although repeatedly departing from 'the mainstream of Christian biblical interpretation', are 'not infrequently in line with Jewish interpretations': 'Becoming', 214–16; also 212.

[42] Pauw, 'Becoming', 206–7; see Pak, *Judaizing*, 33, 46, 78–9.

[43] Calvin, *Commentary on Isaiah*, i. 442, <http://www.ccel.org/ccel/calvin/calcom13.xxi.i.html>. Calvin does defend a Christological reading of Isa. 7: 14.

[44] *The Bible and Holy Scriptures conteyned in the Olde and Newe Testament* (Geneva, 1560). Spelling modernized.

[45] Although acknowledging the pre-critical nature of all sixteenth-century exegesis, Pak makes the same point: *Judaizing*, 133–9.

[46] On the complex interplay between Jewish and Christian, medieval and modern exegesis, see Joel Rembaum's amazing essay, 'The Development of a Jewish Exegetical Tradition Regarding Isaiah 53', *Harvard Theological Review*, 75 (1982): 289–311.

Hebraist—indeed, one of the King James translators—than to Calvin. Nor was it the inevitable result of Christian Hebraism plus Renaissance humanism, although the coupling of historicist and presentist foci characterizes humanist reading practices as well as Calvinist exegesis. Of the leading sixteenth-century Christian Hebraists whose Isaiah commentaries were reprinted in the great compendium of humanist biblical scholarship, the *Critici sacri* of 1660, only Vatabulus rejects the identification of the one coming from Edom with Christ, and all spiritualize the violence.[47] In his Latin Bible of 1580, the Jewish convert and eminent Calvinist biblical scholar, Immanuel Tremellius, reads Isaiah 63 as an Easter dialogue between Christ and a congregation of the Jews (*ecclesia Judaeorum*).[48] For none of these scholars, no more than for Flacius and à Lapide, was it self-evident that the local-historical hermeneutic of twelfth-century Jewish exegesis held the key to the literal sense.

Hence, although one can perhaps trace some sort of trajectory from the school of Rashi to Calvin to modern biblical hermeneutics, the major biblical commentaries of the Reformation and post-Reformation do not chart a linear transition from medieval Catholic spiritualization to a proto-modern Protestant literalism. Of this, the King James Bible provides an elegantly concise illustration, which may serve for a conclusion. The truism that the KJB has no substantive annotations is not quite true, since from its first printing in 1611 brief headnotes preface every chapter of every book. We do not know who wrote them;[49] studies of the KJB rarely mention their existence. Chapter headnotes were a standard feature of early modern Bibles, Protestant and Catholic, and generally ignored as mere summaries of the literal sense. Yet as evidence for what the literal sense might mean in the post-Reformation era they are most enlightening. The Geneva Bible's headnote for Isaiah 63 reads as one might expect: 'God shall destroy his enemies for his Churches sake'.[50] Fifty-one years later the KJB substitutes its own precis. Andrewes (as far as we know) was not the author, but this headnote gives the same ancient reading of Isaiah 63: 1–3 as his Easter sermon: '1. Christ sheweth who he is. 2. What his victory over his enemies'.[51] In 1611, this was the literal sense.

Further Reading

Baer, Yitzhak. 'Rashi and the Historical Reality of his Time'. *Tarbiz*, 20 (1950): 320–32.
Berger, David. 'The Jewish-Christian Debate in the High Middle Ages', in Jeremy Cohen (ed.), *Essential Papers on Judaism and Christianity in Conflict* (New York: NYU Press, 1991).
Boer, E. A. de. *John Calvin on the Visions of Ezekiel* (Leiden: Brill, 2004).

[47] In Vatabulus, God promises to take vengeance on the enemies of the human race; in Clarius, the promised vengeance extends to the hostile powers and angels of Satan; Forerius reads the threatened violence as a metaphor for Christ's spiritual victory—the subjection of the Gentiles to the obedience of faith. See *Critici Sacri*, iv, cols 5414–17.

[48] *Testamenti Veteris Biblia Sacra ... Latini recens ex Hebraeo facti ... ab Immanuele Tremellio & Francisco Junio* (London, 1580).

[49] Alexander McClure credits Miles Smith and Thomas Bilson, but without explanation or evidence: *The Translators Revived* (New York: Scribner, 1853), 214.

[50] The Geneva Bibles of 1560 (see n. 44), 1583, and 1602; all have the same headnote.

[51] *The Holy Bible, conteyning the Old Testament, and the New* (London, 1611).

George, Timothy. *Reading Scripture with the Reformers* (Downers Grove, Ill.: InterVarsity Press, 2011).

Harrison, Peter. *The Bible, Protestantism and the Rise of Natural Science* (Cambridge: Cambridge University Press, 1998).

Hobbs, Gerald R. 'How Firm a Foundation: Martin Bucer's Historical Exegesis of the Psalms'. *Church History*, 53 (1984): 484–6.

Lasker, Daniel. 'Jewish-Christian Polemics at the Turning Point'. *Harvard Theological Review*, 89 (1996): 161–73.

Lubac, Henri de. *Exégèse medievale*, 4 vols (Paris: Aubier, 1959–64).

Pak, Sujin G. *The Judaizing Calvin* (Oxford: Oxford University Press, 2010).

Pauw, Amy. 'Becoming a Part of Israel', in Claire McGinnis and Patricia Tull (eds), *'As Those Who Are Taught': The Interpretation of Isaiah from the LXX to the SBL* (Atlanta, Ga.: Society of Biblical Literature, 2006), 201–21.

Rembaum, Joel. 'The Development of a Jewish Exegetical Tradition Regarding Isaiah 53'. *Harvard Theological Review*, 75 (1982): 289–311.

Sæbø, Magne, ed. *Hebrew Bible/Old Testament: The History of its Interpretation*, i/2. *The Middle Ages* (Göttingen: Vanderhoeck & Ruprecht, 2000).

Shuger, Debora. *Sacred Rhetoric: The Christian Grand Style in the English Renaissance* (Princeton: Princeton University Press, 1988).

Simpson, James. *Burning to Read: English Fundamentalism and its Reformation Opponents* (Cambridge, Mass.: Harvard University Press, 2007).

Steinmetz, David. 'The Superiority of Pre-Critical Exegesis'. *Theology Today*, 37 (1980): 27–38.

Talmage, Frank. *Apples of Gold*, ed. Barry Dov Walfish (Toronto: Pontifical Institute of Medieval Studies, 1999).

....

CHAPTER 10

THE 'SUNDRIE WAIES OF WISDOM': RICHARD HOOKER ON THE AUTHORITY OF SCRIPTURE AND REASON

....

TORRANCE KIRBY

Wisdom reacheth from one end to another mightily, and sweetly doth she order all things.[1]

IN the second book of his treatise *Of the Lawes of Ecclesiastical Politie* (1593), Richard Hooker addresses the definition and limits of the authority of scripture. The ways of Wisdom are

of sundrie kindes, so her maner of teaching is not meerely one and the same. Some things she openeth by the sacred bookes of Scripture; some things by the glorious works of nature: with some things she inspireth them from above by spirituall influence, in some thinges she leadeth and trayneth them onely by worldly experience and practise. We may not so in any one speciall kind admire her that we disgrace her in any other, but let all her waies be according unto their place and degree adored.[2]

He affirms the magisterial reformers' doctrine of *sola scriptura*, that the Bible contains all things 'necessary to salvation'. Tradition and human authority cannot add anything

---

[1] Wisdom 8: 1. See also the Advent antiphon 'O Sapientia', in the Almanack of the Book of Common Prayer (1559), quoted by Hooker in *Of the Lawes of Ecclesiasticall Politie* (c.1593), I.2.3; *The Folger Library Edition [FLE] of the Works of Richard Hooker* (Cambridge, Mass.: Harvard University Press, 1977), 1.60.27–61.6. All references to the *Lawes* cite book, chapter, and section, followed by volume, page, and line numbers in *FLE*. The modern critical edition comprises books I–IV in *FLE*, vol. 1, ed. Georges Edelen (1977), book V in vol. 2, ed. W. Speed Hill (1977), and books VI–VIII in vol. 3, ed. P. G. Stanwood (1981). David Neelands has shown that this passage is quoted by Thomas Aquinas, esp. in the *Summa theologica*, e.g. in discussions of divine government (I, q103. a8), grace (Ia IIæ q110. a2), charity (IIa IIæ q23. a2), the temptation of Adam and Eve (IIa IIæ q165. a1), Christ's miracles (IIIa q44. a4), the passion of Christ (IIIa q46. a9), and the resurrection (IIIa q55. a6). See Neelands, 'Predestination', in Torrance Kirby (ed.), *A Companion to Richard Hooker* (Leiden and Boston: E. J. Brill, 2009), 209.

[2] *Lawes*, II.1.4; 1:147.23–148.6.

to God's written word for this purpose. At the same time, God the creator of the world speaks through nature 'whose voice is his instrument' and is manifest to the eye of reason in the glorious works of creation. Whereas scripture alone is to be followed in the formulation of the 'rule of faith', reason, custom, and human authority—especially the authority of the perennial philosophy manifested in the works of Plato, Aristotle, the Stoics, and Neoplatonists—are necessary to sustain the *external* ordering of religion. It is not the purpose of the revealed law to provide prescriptions for the political structures of the church. The chief aim of this chapter is to explore Hooker's contribution to the Reformation treatment of the boundaries between the authority of scripture and that of reason, and to consider the distinctive manner of his uniting of these two 'waies of wisdom' in the context of a sapiential theology.

In the peroration to his wide-ranging consideration of the nature of law and its various kinds at the end of the first book of his treatise *Of the Lawes of Ecclesiasticall Politie* (1593), Hooker summarizes his argument in a striking passage evocative of the hymns to Holy Wisdom in the scriptures:

> Of lawe there can be no lesse acknowledged, then that her seate is the bosome of God, her voyce the harmony of the world, all things in heaven and earth doe her homage, the very least as feeling her care, and the greatest as not exempted from her power; both Angels and men and creatures of what condition so ever, though each in different sort and manner, yet all with uniforme consent, admiring her as the mother of their peace and joy.[3]

As Rowan Williams has pointed out, Hooker's use of the feminine pronoun 'would alert any scripturally literate reader to the parallel with the divine *Sophia*'—indeed, what Hooker claims on behalf of Law, the sapiential books of Proverbs, Job, and particularly the Wisdom of Solomon identify with the very Wisdom of God:[4] 'The LORD possessed me in the beginning of his way, before his works of old. I was set up from everlasting, from the beginning, or ever the earth was'.[5] For Hooker the sapiential theologian, 'the being of God is a law to his working. For that perfection which God is, geveth perfection to that he doth'.[6] Indeed for Hooker God *is* law:

> a law both to himself, and to all other things besides … All those things which are done by him have some end for which they are done; and the end for which they are done is a reason of his will to do them … They err, therefore, who think that of the will of God to do this or that there is no reason besides his will.[7]

---

[3] *Lawes*, I.16.8; 1:142.9.

[4] Rowan Williams, 'Hooker: Philosopher, Anglican, Contemporary', in Arthur Stephen McGrade (ed.), *Richard Hooker and the Construction of Christian Community* (Tempe, Ariz.: Medieval & Renaissance Texts & Studies, 1997), 370). Prov. 8: 22–31; Job 28; Wisdom 6: 12–9:18; and Romans 11: 33. See *Lawes*, I.2.5; 1:62.2–6.

[5] Prov. 8: 22, 23.

[6] *Lawes*, I.2.2; 1:59.6. On the character of sapiential theology and its applicability to Hooker, see Williams, 'Hooker', in McGrade, *Richard Hooker*.

[7] *Lawes*, I.2.5; 1:60.17–18. Compare Aquinas, *ST*, Ia IIæ q91. a1: 'The law implies order to the end actively, in so far as it directs certain things to the end; but not passively—that is to say, the law itself is not ordained to the end—except accidentally, in a governor whose end is extrinsic to him, and to which end his law must needs be ordained. But the end of the Divine government is God Himself, and His law is not distinct from Himself. Wherefore the eternal law is not ordained to another end'.

Hooker's reference to the theological 'error' of an extreme voluntarism can be read as a swipe at the strong proclivity among disciplinarian Puritans of the stripe of Thomas Cartwright and Walter Travers in favour of the position staked out by Petrus Ramus.[8] In corroboration of this sapiential *nomos* theology, Hooker cites the authority of the New Testament—both the Epistle to the Ephesians: God acts in all things in accordance with 'the Counsel of his own will', and Paul's Letter to the Romans: 'O the depth of the riches both of the wisdom and knowledge of God! How unsearchable are his judgements'[9]—together with an eclectic assortment of ancient philosophers, as well early church fathers and medieval scholastic theologians. Hooker's appeal to the principles of sapiential theology with their defining emphasis on the yoking together of wisdom, both natural and revealed, constitutes the mainstay of his apologetic throughout his great treatise.

Much of Hooker's (1554–1600) career was spent in theological controversy concerning the constitutional provisions of the Elizabethan Settlement of 1559.[10] In his capacity as Master of the Temple in the Inns of Court in the mid-1580s, nearly a decade prior to publication of the initial four books of the *Lawes*, Hooker preached a series of sermons on themes of Reformation soteriology and ecclesiology. In *A Supplication Made to the Privie Counsell*, the disciplinarian Puritan divine Walter Travers (1548?–1635) challenged the orthodoxy of Hooker's sustained appeal to reason and natural law in religious and ecclesiastical matters as inconsistent with the tenets of reformed doctrinal orthodoxy with respect to the pre-eminent authority of scripture.[11] Hooker's formal *Answere* to Travers's objections in the *Supplication* laid the groundwork of the sapiential theology which he would later expound in considerably greater detail in his treatise of the 1590s, *Of the Lawes of Ecclesiasticall Politie*.[12]

The *Lawes* is a complex polemical argument and consists of a lengthy preface and eight books, usually published in three separate volumes.[13] The first four books address what Hooker describes as 'general meditations' concerning the nature of law in its essence as well as in its principal 'kindes and qualities'; the proper uses of natural reason and supernatural revelation as pre-eminent genera of law; the proper application of both to the government of the church; and objections to religious practices judged by critics of the Elizabethan Settlement to be inconsistent with the continental 'reformed' example. The final four books address the 'particular decisions' established under the Acts of Supremacy and Uniformity of 1559 concerning public religious duties as laid out in the liturgy of the Book of Common Prayer; the power of spiritual jurisdiction exercised by ministers in holy orders; the

---

[8] Steven J. Reid and Emma A. Wilson (eds), *Ramus, Pedagogy, and the Liberal Arts: Ramism in Britain and the Wider World* (Farnham: Ashgate, 2011).

[9] Eph. 1: 11; Rom. 11: 33. *Lawes*, I.2.5; 1:62.

[10] For a recent account of Richard Hooker's career, see Lee W. Gibbs, 'Life of Hooker', in Kirby, *Companion*, 1–26.

[11] *A Supplication Made to the Privy Counsel by Mr Walter Travers* (Oxford, 1612). See Egil Grislis, 'Introduction to Commentary on Tractates and Sermons: § iv. The Controversy with Travers', in *The Folger Library Edition of the Works of Richard Hooker*, vol. v, ed. Laetitia Yeandle and Egil Grislis (Cambridge, Mass., and London: Belknap Press of Harvard University Press 1990), 641–8.

[12] *The Answere of Mr. Richard Hooker to a Supplication Preferred by Mr Walter Travers to the HH. Lords of the Privie Counsell* (Oxford, 1612).

[13] Books I–IV were published in 1593, book V in 1597, and books VI and VIII posthumously in 1648, and the first complete edition, including VII, ed. John Gauden, was published following the Restoration: *The Works of Mr. Richard Hooker* (London, 1662).

jurisdiction and authority of bishops; and finally the supreme authority of the civil magistrate over both church and commonwealth, and hence their unity in a unified Christian state.

Throughout the *Lawes* Hooker's express aim is to explicate systematically the principles underlying the religious settlement of 1559 in such a manner as to secure conscientious obedience and conformity by means of all the instruments of persuasion:

> my whole endevour is to resolve the conscience, and to shew as neare as I can what in this controversie the hart is to thinke, if it will follow the light of sound and sincere judgement, without either clowd of prejudice or mist of passionate affection.[14]

The treatise is framed as a sustained response to Thomas Cartwright who had been John Whitgift's formidable adversary in the Admonition Controversy of the 1570s.[15] The preface is addressed specifically 'to them that seeke (as they tearme it) the reformation of lawes, and orders ecclesiasticall, in the Church of England', that is to disciplinarian Puritans who, like Cartwright and Travers, sought closer conformity to the pattern of the 'best reformed churches' on the continent, especially Calvin's Geneva.[16] The preface sets the tone of the work and announces Hooker's main apologetic intent. There is a significant difference between Hooker's rhetorical approach and that of previous contributions to Elizabethan polemics. He abandons the usual recourse to ridicule and personal abuse which was so characteristic of the vast majority of tracts contributed by both sides of the controversy—by such as John Bridges, for example, on behalf of the establishment, or Martin Marprelate on the other part—and speaks irenically to the fundamental theological assumptions with the professed aim of securing conscientious acceptance of the settlement. To this end he sets out to persuade by an appeal to mutually acceptable theological assumptions and authorities: 'wee offer the lawes whereby wee live unto the generall triall and judgement of the whole world'.[17]

Hooker's starting point is to accept unconditionally the disciplinarian premise that the doctrinal tenets and the pastoral aspirations of the Reformation had to be fulfilled in the polity of the Church of England. Chief among these was the affirmation of the primacy of the authority of scripture—*sola scriptura*—as containing 'all things necessary to salvation'.[18] The rhetorical slant is intended to serve the main apologetic aim of the treatise, namely to justify the Elizabethan Settlement as consistent with the principles of reformed doctrinal orthodoxy. Thus the grand cosmic scheme of laws set out in book I is intended to place the particulars of the controversy within the foundational context of a sapiential theology:

> because the point about which wee strive is the qualitie of our *Lawes*, our first entrance hereinto cannot better be made, then with consideration of the nature of lawe in generall and of that lawe which giveth life unto all the rest which are commendable just and good, namely the lawe whereby the Eternall himselfe doth worke. Proceeding from hence to the lawe, first of nature, then of scripture, we shall have the easier access unto those things which come after to be debated, concerning the particular cause and question which wee have in hand.[19]

---

[14] *Lawes*, pref. 7.1, 2; 1:34.20–35.2.

[15] See Peter Lake, *Anglicans and Puritans? Presbyterianism and English Conformist Thought from Whitgift to Hooker* (London: Unwin Hyman, 1988).

[16] *Lawes*, pref. title; 1:1.1.   [17] *Lawes*, I.1.3; *FLE* 1:58.5–6.

[18] See Article VI of the Thirty-Nine Articles of Religion.   [19] *Lawes*, I.1.3; *FLE* 1:58.11–19.

The rhetorical aim is to persuade opponents of the settlement to conscientious conformity by demonstrating the coherence of the 'particular decisions' embodied in the institutions of the 1559 settlement—the liturgy of the Book of Common Prayer, hierarchy, episcopacy, royal supremacy, and thus ultimately 'Ecclesiastical Dominion', with certain 'general meditations' on the metaphysics or first principles concerning the nature of law—i.e. the 'waies of wisdom'. In Renaissance humanist fashion Hooker adduces broadly eclectic support for his affirmation that Law is the very substance of the life of God by referring to the *logos* theology of the Hellenic philosophers.[20] He cites the example of the *demiourgos* of Plato's *Timaeus* who, as an '*intellectual* worker', brings the cosmos into being according to a plan or pattern (*paradeigma*). Operating as an 'Agent, which knowing what and why it worketh, observeth in working a most exact order or law', the divine craftsman is made known through the intelligent design manifest in his work.[21]

Hooker further cites Mercurius Trismegistus, who had continued to be regarded in the sixteenth century as the ancient Egyptian teacher of a universal philosophy and who held in his discourse on the 'mixing bowl' that 'the world was made not with hands, but by Reason'.[22] Cicero's definition of Law as 'something eternal which rules the whole universe by its wisdom in command and prohibition' also receives mention.[23] And finally, Hooker appeals to the early sixth-century Christian philosopher Boethius, for whom 'the counsel of God', being one, is defined as a thing 'unchangeable', 'nor is the freedom of the will of God any whit abated, let, or hindered, by means of this; because the imposition of this law upon himself is his own free and voluntary act'.[24] This self-limiting of the divine will is illustrated by Hooker with a reference to Homer who, in the opening lines of the *Iliad*, invokes the Muse to sing of the accomplishment of the 'counsel' of Zeus—'Διὸς δ᾽ ἐτελείτο βουλή';[25] so also, for Hooker, God freely submits to the constraint imposed upon his operation by his own divine nature as *Logos*.

According to Hooker's sapiential iteration of the doctrine of participation, all creatures are the 'offspring' of God and are therefore '*in him* as effects in their highest cause, he

---

[20] *Lawes*, I.2.3; 1:59.33–60.14 'the wise and learned among the verie Heathens themselves, have all acknowledged some first cause, whereupon originallie the being of all things dependeth. Neither have they otherwise spoken of that cause, then as an Agent, which knowing *what* and *why* it worketh, observeth in working a most exact *order* or *lawe* .... all confesse in the working of that first cause, that *counsell* is used, *reason* followed, a *way* observed, that is to say, constant *order* and *law* is kept, wherof it selfe must needs be author unto itselfe'. See Torrance Kirby, *Richard Hooker, Reformer and Platonist* (Aldershot: Ashgate, 2005), 45–56.

[21] *Lawes*, I.2.3; 1:60.4–11. See *Timaeus*, 37d, tr. Benjamin Jowett, in *The Collected Dialogues of Plato*, ed. Edith Hamilton and Huntington Cairns (Princeton: Princeton University Press, 1961), 1167: 'The nature of the ideal being was everlasting, but to bestow this attribute in its fullness upon a creature was impossible. Wherefore [the demiourgos] resolved to have a moving image of eternity, and when he set in order the heaven, he made this image eternal but moving according to number, while eternity itself rests in unity, and this image we call time .... Time and the heaven came into being at the same instant'.

[22] *Lawes*, I.2.3; 1:60. 'Τὸν πάντα κόσμον ἐποίησεν ὁ δημιουργὸς οὐ χερσὶν ἀλλὰ λόγῳ'. See *Hermetica*, IV.1, 'A discourse of Hermes to Tat: the Mixing Bowl or the Monad', in Brian P. Copenhaver (ed. and tr.), *Hermetica: the Greek 'Corpus Hermeticum' and the Latin 'Asclepius'* (Cambridge: Cambridge University Press, 1992), 15. On Hooker's use of the *Hermetica*, see Wayne Shumaker, *The Occult Sciences in the Renaissance: A Study in Intellectual Patterns* (Berkeley, Calif.: University of California Press, 1972), 238–9.

[23] Cicero, *De legibus*, 2.6., tr. C. W. Keyes, Loeb Classical Library (Cambridge, Mass.: Harvard University Press, 1988), 379–81.

[24] Boethius, *De consolatione philosophiae*, lib. 4, prosa 5. Qu. *Lawes*, I.2.6; 1:62.

[25] *Iliad* 1.5; qu. *Lawes*, I.2.3; 1:60.4.

likewise actually is *in them*, the assistance and influence of his Deity is *their life*.[26] The order-
liness of causality and the purposiveness of the cosmos derive from and indeed presuppose
that the divine activity is itself law-like, and therefore God is encountered not simply as arbitrary will and command but makes himself known in the very intelligibility of the world.
Moreover, for Hooker this encounter with the divine understood as Law or Wisdom is inextricably bound up with the very act of interpreting this relation of causality.[27]

> But if we wil give judgement of the laws under which we live, first let that law eternall be
> alwayes before our eyes, as being of principall force and moment to breed in religious minds
> a dutifull estimation of all lawes, the use and benefite whereof we see; because there can be
> no doubt but that lawes apparently good, are (as it were) things copied out of the very tables
> of that high everlasting law, even as the booke of that law hath said concerning it selfe, *By me
> Kings raigne, and* by me *Princes decree justice.* Not as if men did behold that booke, and accord-
> ingly frame their lawes; but because it worketh in them, because it discovereth and (as it were)
> readeth it selfe to the world by them, when the lawes which they make are righteous.[28]

The eternal law is the fount and origin of all derivative species of law which for Hooker are
divided into two primary divisions, namely the supernatural law revealed in the scriptures
and the natural law manifest in the rational order of the cosmos and accessible to the faculty
of human reason. Both are manifestations of one and the same divine wisdom. Scripture
attests to the common source of these *summa genera* of law in God himself: 'Doth not the
Apostle term the law of nature even as the Evangelist doth the law of Scripture, Δικαίωμα
τοῦ Θεοῦ, Gods own righteous ordinance?'[29]

Further on in book V of the *Lawes*, in his comprehensive summary of orthodox patristic
Christology as defined by the ecumenical councils of the fourth and fifth centuries, Hooker
proceeds to identify this divine Wisdom with Christ.[30] What the scriptures and the Greek
philosophers claim for Wisdom, *Logos*, and Law, the church claims on behalf of Christ who,
as man, participates in the divine providential governance:

> The Father as Goodness, the Son as Wisdom, the Holy Ghost as Power do all concur in every
> particular outwardly issuing from that one only glorious Deity which they all are. For that
> which moveth God to work is his Goodness, and that which ordereth his work is Wisdom, and
> that which perfecteth his work is Power. All things which God in their times and seasons hath
> brought forth were eternally and before all times in God, as a work unbegun is in the artificer
> which afterward bringeth it unto effect.[31]

By Hooker's account, Christ the 'Wisdom of God' is 'by three degrees' a receiver: first, as
son of God, that is by virtue of his full participation in the divine substance as co-equal with
his heavenly Father, whatsoever Christ possesses as the divine *Logos* he holds naturally and
eternally in common with the Father. Secondly, Christ's human nature has the honour of
union with the Deity bestowed upon it; and thirdly, by virtue of hypostatic union of the two

---

[26] *Lawes*, V.56.5; 2:237.24–5.
[27] On this, see Williams, 'Hooker', in McGrade, *Richard Hooker*.
[28] *Lawes*, I.16.2; 1:4–15.
[29] Rom. 1: 32 and Luke 1: 6. See *Lawes*, VII.11.10; 3:211.12. Earlier in the same passage Hooker's purpose is
to justify the discourse of reason in determining the polity of the church. See further VII.11.10; 1:210.27–211.6.
[30] Kirby, *Richard Hooker*, 79–90.   [31] *Lawes*, V.56.5; 2:236.

natures, there is a mystical communication of effects from the divine nature into the human nature.[32] Consequently,

> The light created of God in the beginning did first by itself illuminate the world; but after that the Sun and Moon were created, the world sithence hath by them always enjoyed the same. And that Deity of Christ which before our Lord's incarnation wrought all things without man, doth now work nothing wherein the nature which it hath assumed is either absent from it or idle. Christ as man hath all power both in heaven and earth given him. He hath as Man, not as God only, supreme dominion over quick and dead, for so much his ascension into heaven, and his session at the right hand of God do import.[33]

Through this filtering of Wisdom theology through a Christological prism we can begin to apprehend the logic underpinning Hooker's account of the relationship between scriptural authority and his epistemology. As in the orthodox Chalcedonian definition of the hypostatic union of the divine and human natures in Christ, 'there are but fower thinges which concurre to make compleate the whole state of our Lord Jesus Christ, his deitie, his manhood, the conjunction of both, and the distinction of the one from the other beinge joyned in one'. Hooker's sapiential approach to the definition of law follows an analogous logical pattern in seeking to avoid the 'fower principall heresies there are which have in those thinges withstood the truth'. The full account of the manifestation of law thus requires affirmation of the authority of revealed law, the distinct authority of the natural and human law, and the preservation of their unity in one eternal law without collapsing their generic distinction.[34]

Back in the second book of the *Lawes*, he sought to define the authority of scripture by explicit reference to the terms of sapiential theology:

> Whatsoever either men on earth, or the Angels of heaven do know, it is as a drop of that unemptiable fountaine of wisdom, which wisdom hath diversly imparted her treasures unto the world. As her waies are of sundrie kinds, so her maner of teaching is not meerely one and the same. Some things she openeth by the sacred bookes of Scripture; some things by the glorious works of nature: with some things she inspireth them from above by spirituall influence, in some thinges she leadeth and trayneth them onely by worldly experience and practise. We may not so in any one speciall kind admire her that we disgrace her in any other, but let all her wayes be according unto their place and degree adored.[35]

Once again we detect prominent traces of the hymn to *Sophia* in the Wisdom of Solomon. Here in the second book of the *Lawes*, however, the argument has taken a polemical turn. Hooker addresses the 'maine pillar', as he puts it, of Puritan objections to the Elizabethan Settlement which rested upon the claim '*That Scripture is the onely rule of all things which in this life may be done by men*'.[36] In the context of Elizabethan religious polemics, Hooker's immediate practical concern was to establish the limits of scriptural authority in order to determine the acceptability of the structures of both civil and ecclesiastical government as defined by the Acts of Supremacy and Uniformity of 1559.[37] In effect, the debate between the

---

[32] *Lawes*, V.54.1; 2:220. See also Hooker's brilliant summation of the Chalcedonian definition in *Lawes*, V.54.10; 2.226.22–227.15.
[33] *Lawes*, V.55.8; 2:232.   [34] *Lawes*, V.54.10; 2.226.22–227.15.
[35] *Lawes*, II.1.4; 1:147.23–148.6. See Wisdom of Solomon 11: 20.
[36] *Lawes*, II.title; 1:143.
[37] 1 Eliz., c. 2, *Statutes of the Realm*, vol. 4, 355–8.

critics and defenders of the settlement turned decisively on the question of what it meant to adhere to the 'sole' authority of the scriptures. Hooker argues that the perfection of the authority of scripture must be interpreted strictly with respect to 'that end whereto it tendeth'.[38] He affirms the magisterial Protestant reformers' claims concerning the sole authority of scripture, namely the assertion that the canonical scriptures contain a complete account of all things 'necessary to salvation':

> albeit scripture do professe to conteyne in it all things which are necessary unto salvation; yet the meaning cannot be symplye of all things that are necessarye, but all things that are necessarye in some certaine kinde of forme; as all things that are necessarye, and eyther could not at all, or could not easily be knowne by the light of naturall discourse; all thinges which are necessarie to be knowne that we might be saved; but known with presupposal of knowledge concerning certain principles whereof it receiveth us alreadie persuaded, and then instructeth us in all the residue that are necessarie. In the number of these principles one is the sacred authoritie of Scripture [itself]. Being therefore persuaded by other means that these Scriptures are the oracles of God, themselves do then teach us the rest, and lay before us all the duties which God requireth at our hands as necessarie to salvation.[39]

While the text of the divine word 'revealed' by God is not of human creation, scripture is not on this account self-authenticating: 'it is not the worde of God which doth or possiblie can assure us, that wee doe well to thinke it his worde'.[40] There is a critical 'presupposal' of natural knowledge. On the matter of authenticating the sacred text it is necessary to be 'perswaded by other meanes that these scriptures are the oracles of God' and 'by experience we all know, that the first outward motive leading men so to esteeme of the scripture is the authority of Gods Church'.[41] Indeed 'the scripture could not teach us the thinges that are of God, unless we did credite men who have taught us that the wordes of scripture doe signifie those things'.[42]

While Hooker affirmed that the scriptures contained an 'infinite varietie of matter of all kinds'—including the knowledge of diverse arts and sciences as well as many different sorts of laws, including laws cosmic, angelic, natural, positive, political, criminal, civil, domestic, and economic—'the principal intent of scripture is to deliver the lawes of duties supernaturall'.[43] Reason, tradition, and human authority exercised through the church cannot add anything to God's word written for this purpose, yet belief in such crucial doctrines as the Trinity, the co-eternity of the Son of God with the Father, the double procession of the Spirit, the duty

---

[38] *Lawes*, II.8.5; 1.

[39] *Lawes*, I.14.1; 1:125.32–126.5. For a recent insightful discussion of Hooker's approach to the authority of scripture, see Egil Grislis, 'Scriptural Hermeneutics', in Kirby, *Companion*, 273–304. Anthony Lane argues that the technical term 'sola scriptura' is nowhere to be found in the writings of the first-generation magisterial reformers. See his essay 'Sola Scriptura? Making Sense of a Post-Reformation Slogan', in P. E. Satterthwaite and D. F. Wright (eds), *A Pathway into the Holy Scripture* (Grand Rapids, Mich.: Eerdmans, 1994), 297–327.

[40] *Lawes*, II.4.2; 1:153.17–18.

[41] *Lawes*, I.14.1; 1:126.10–11. See also III.8.13; 2:231: 'Scripture teacheth us that saving truth which God hath discovered unto the world by revelation, and it presumeth us taught otherwise that itself is divine and sacred'. *Lawes*, III.8.14; 1:231.20–2.

[42] *Lawes*, II.7.3; 1:177.31–3.

[43] *Lawes*, I.14.1; 1:124.31–2 and I.14.3; 1:127.21–7: 'The severall bookes of scripture having had each some severall occasion and particular purpose which caused them to be written, the contents thereof are according to the exigence of that speciall end whereunto they are intended. Hereupon it groweth, that everie booke of holy scripture doth take out of all kinds of truth, naturall, historicall, forreine, supernaturall, so much as the matter handled requireth'.

of baptizing infants, is nowhere to be found in the scripture 'by express literal mention'. Hooker concludes, 'It sufficeth therefore that nature and scripture doe serve in such full sort, that they both joyntly and not severallye eyther of them be so complete, that unto everlasting felicitie wee neede not the knowledge of any thing more then these two [and] may easily furnish our mindes with on all sides'.[44] Moreover, 'the unsufficiencie of the light of nature is by the light of scripture so fully and so perfectly herein supplied, that further light then this hath added there doth not neede unto that ende'.[45]

In a recent article Nigel Voak addresses the disputed question of Hooker's adherence to the primacy of scriptural authority in matters of Christian doctrine.[46] Along with such sixteenth-century reformers as Luther, Calvin, and Bullinger, Hooker plainly affirms the magisterial view that scripture is alone sufficient for knowledge of saving doctrine, and is thus the *principium cognoscendi theologiae*.[47] While Hooker plainly regards scripture as a higher infallible authority than demonstrative reason, Voak argues that his position cannot ultimately be reconciled with the magisterial reformers' position on *sola scriptura*. 'Crucially', Voak maintains, Hooker 'makes the authority of the former evidentially dependent on the authority of the latter, in that Holy Scripture must be authenticated as divine revelation by demonstrative reasoning. In addition, some Christian doctrines, such as the Trinity, must be deduced from Scripture, and so are dependent for him on such reasoning'.[48] In Voak's view, Hooker appears to step beyond the boundaries of Reformed orthodoxy in his argument regarding the authentication of scripture.

> We all beleeve that the Scriptures of God are sacred, and that they have proceeded from God; our selves we assure that wee doe right well in so beleeving. We have for this point a demonstration sound and infallible. But it is not the worde of God which doth or possibilie can assure us, that wee doe well to thinke it his worde.[49]

I am persuaded, however, contrary to Voak's reading of this passage, that Hooker's claim to a 'demonstration sound and infallible' that the scriptures have 'proceeded from God' actually corresponds to arguments for scripture's authentication based on the inner testimony of the Spirit, such as one finds, for example, in Calvin's *Institutio*.[50] Hooker's 'infallible demonstration' is, in fact, the inner testimony of the Spirit.

At the same time, there is for Hooker a decisive role for a 'ratiocinative account' (to borrow Voak's terminology) of the marks and objective authenticity of the revealed word: 'Scripture teacheth us that saving truth which God hath discovered unto the world by revelation, and it presumeth us taught otherwise that it self is divine and sacred'.[51] For Hooker the sapiential theologian, claims regarding the respective authorities of scripture and reason are not to be construed in binary opposition, in 'zero-sum' fashion. Rather he views these two sources as

---

[44]   *Lawes*, I.14.5; 1:129.10–14.

[45]   *Lawes*, II.8.3; 1:188.4–7.

[46]   Nigel Voak, 'Richard Hooker and the Principle of *Sola Scriptura*', *Journal of Theological Studies*, 59 (2008): 96–139.

[47]   See Voak, 'Richard Hooker', 123.   [48]   Voak, 'Richard Hooker', 97.

[49]   *Lawes*, II.4.2; 1:153.13–25.

[50]   Calvin, *Inst.* I.7.4. On this point I find myself in agreement with Ranall Ingalls, 'Richard Hooker on the Scriptures: Saint Augustine's Trinitarianism and the Interpretation of Sola Scriptura' (Ph.D. thesis, University of Wales Lampeter, 2004), 220.

[51]   *Lawes*, III.8.13; 1:231.12–15.

simultaneously both presupposing and participating in a higher, unifying principle which is present in both as a cause in its effects.[52] On this point it is worth quoting Hooker at length:

> Because we maintaine that in scripture we are taught all things necessary unto salvation, here-upon very childishly it is by some demaunded, what scripture can teach us the sacred authori-tie of the scripture, upon the knowledge wherof our whole faith and salvation dependeth. As though there were any kind of science in the world which leadeth men into knowledge with-out presupposing a number of thinges already knowne. No science doth make knowne the first principles whereon it buildeth, but they are alwaies either taken as plaine and manifest in them selves, or as proved and graunted already, some former knowledge having made them evident. Scripture teacheth al supernaturally revealed truth, without the knowledge wherof salvation cannot be attayned. The maine principle whereupon our beliefe of all things therin contayned dependeth is, that the scriptures are the oracles of God him selfe. This in it selfe wee cannot say is evident. For then all men that heare it would acknowledge it in hart, as they do when they heare that every whole is more then any parte of that whole, because this in it selfe is evident. The other we knowe that all do not acknowledge when they heare it. There must be therefore some former knowledge presupposed which doth herein assure the hartes of all believers. Scripture teacheth us that saving truth which God hath discovered unto the world by revelation, and it presumeth us taught otherwise that it self is divine and sacred.[53]

Whereas 'scripture alone' is to be followed in the formulation of the 'rule of faith', rea-son, custom, and human authority are necessary in order to avoid 'infinite perplexities, scrupulosities, doubts insoluble and extreme despaires' in the *external* ordering of reli-gion.[54] It is not the purpose of the divine law as revealed in the scriptures to provide pre-scriptions for the political structure of the church; to this end Wisdom provides the 'law of nature' which Hooker defines as 'an infallible knowledge imprinted in the minds of all the children of men, whereby both general principles for directing of human actions are comprehended, and conclusions derived from them; upon which conclusions groweth in particularity the choice of good and evil in the daily affairs of this life'.[55] In order to con-strue Hooker's reconciliation of the 'inner testimony' with the 'ratiocinative account', it is necessary to probe further into the underlying Neoplatonic assumptions of his sapiential approach.

Hooker's scheme of the generic division of law by way of a graduated, hierarchical disposi-tion systematizes the 'sundrie waies of Wisdom' in decidedly Proclean fashion.[56] The eternal law contains all derivative forms of law as 'effectes' within itself as 'cause'. This primordial law 'which God hath eternallie purposed himself in all his works to observe' is the 'highest welspring and

---

[52] *Lawes*, V.56.5; 2:237.15–25: 'All things which God in their times and seasons hath brought forth, were eternally and before all times in God, as a work unbegun is in the Artificer, which afterward bringeth it unto effect. Therefore whatsoever we do behold now in this present World, it was inwrapped within the Bowels of Divine Mercy, written in the Book of Eternal Wisdom, and held in the hands of Omnipotent Power, the first Foundations of the World being as yet unlaid. So that all things which God hath made, are in that respect the Off-spring of God, they are in him as effects in their highest cause; he likewise actually is in them, the assistance and influence of his Deity is their life'.

[53] *Lawes*, III.8.13; 1:230.25–231.15.   [54] *Lawes*, II.8.6; 1:190.18–19.

[55] *Lawes*, II.8.6; 1:190.11.16.

[56] See e.g. Proclus, *Elements of Theology*, tr. E. R. Dodds (Oxford: Oxford University Press, 1963), prop. 23, 27: 'all that is unparticipated produces out of itself the participated; and all participated substances are linked by upward tension to existences not participated'.

fountaine' of all species of law. Hooker speaks of this source as 'one, or rather *verie Onenesse*, and meere unitie, having nothing but it selfe in it selfe, and not consisting (as all things do besides God) of many things'.[57] Of this First Eternal Law in its original divine simplicity, says Hooker:

> our soundest knowledge is to know that we know him not as in deed he is, neither can know him: and our safest eloquence concerning him is our silence, when we confesse without confession that his glory is inexplicable, his greatnes above our capacitie to reach. He is above, and we upon earth, and therefore it behoveth our wordes to be warie and fewe.[58]

Yet Hooker's theological purpose is to demonstrate the derivation of all law from this unparticipated 'Onenesse', 'even to shew in what maner as every good and perfect gift, so this very gift of good and perfect lawes is derived from the father of lightes'.[59]

The manifold variety of the derivative species of law comprise a 'Second Eternal Law', that is to say, the eternal law as 'participated' which 'receyveth according unto the different kinds of things which are subject unto it different and sundry kinds of names'.[60] In its primary and comprehensive disposition it consists of two *summa genera*, namely the law of nature and the revealed law of scripture. While the eternal law as unutterable 'verie Onenesse' remains within itself beyond participation, nonetheless it communicates itself in a 'one–many', i.e. a Second Eternal Law, from which all order proceeds 'reaching from one end to another mightily' and to which all ultimately reverts. As Proclus maintained, 'all procession is accomplished through a likeness of the secondary to the primary; all that is immediately produced by any principle both remains in the producing cause and proceeds from it; all that proceeds from any principle reverts in respect of its being upon that from which it proceeds'.[61] Scripture itself attests to the common source of these two *summa genera* of the eternal law in God himself, Hooker maintains: 'Doth not the Apostle term the law of nature even as the Evangelist doth the law of Scripture, δικαίωμα τοῦ θεοῦ, Gods own righteous ordinance?'[62]

These two 'waies of Wisdom' together account for both the 'outward procession' of the entire created order from the original divine unity and its final redemptive return by a 'way mystical and supernaturall' back to its source.[63] Speaking to justify the institution of episcopacy as being as divine in origin as civil government, Hooker maintains that:

> of all good things God himself is author, and consequently an approver of them … If therefore all things be of God which are well done, and if all things be well done which are according to the rule of well-doing, and if the rule of well-doing be more ample than the Scripture: what necessity is there, that everything which is of God should be set down in holy Scripture?

Thus episcopacy for Hooker is not an institution to be construed as immediately *jure divino*, but rather divine sanction derives from the antiquity of practice and constitutional

---

[57] *Lawes*, I.3.1; 1:63.7; *Lawes*, I.2.2; 1:59.20–2.
[58] *Lawes*, I.2.2; 1:59.14–19.   [59] *Lawes*, I.16.1; 1:135.11–13.
[60] *Lawes*, I.3.1; 1:63.16. Compare Aquinas, *ST* Ia IIæ q. 93. a.1: 'But things that are diverse in themselves are considered as one according to their ordination to something common. There, the Eternal Law is one, that is the exemplar of this ordination'.
[61] Proclus, *Elements*, props. 29, 30, and 31, 35.
[62] See Rom. 1: 32 and Luke 1: 6. Qu. *Lawes*, VII.11.10; 3:211.12.
[63] Cp. *Lawes*, I.16.1; 1:135.11–13 and III.11.3; 1:248.23–6.

tradition. As with kings so also with bishops: human ordinances are 'many times presup-
posed as grounds in the statutes of God'.[64]

Thus for Hooker to uphold the doctrine of *sola scriptura* is not in any sense to denigrate
the authority of the light of reason.

> Injurious we are unto God, the Author and giver of humane capacity, judgement and wit, when
> because of some things wherein he precisely forbiddeth men to use their own inventions, we take
> occasion to disauthorize and disgrace the works which he doth produce by the hand, either of
> nature or of grace in them. We offer contumely, even unto him, when we scornfully reject what
> we list without any other exception then this, 'the brain of man hath devised it'. Whether we look
> into the church or commonweal, as well in the one as in the other, both the ordination of officers,
> and the very institution of their offices may be truly derived from God, and approved of him,
> although they be not always of him in such sort as those things are which are in Scripture.[65]

Thus sweetly governing the constitution in church and commonwealth, Wisdom works decorously through the natural law and its derivative forms of positive law and human tradition
to bring to the political cosmos a peaceable order. Although such laws are mutable, through
them Wisdom directs human institutions in history to enable our participation of a higher
justice and to direct human nature to fulfilment of both our natural and our supernatural
ends. Of such a law and holy wisdom

> there can be no lesse acknowledged, then that her seate is the bosome of God, her voyce the
> harmony of the world, all things in heaven and earth doe her homage, the very least as feeling
> her care, and the greatest as not exempted from her power; both Angels and men and creatures
> of what condition so ever, though each in different sort and manner, yet all with uniforme con-
> sent, admiring her as the mother of their peace and joy.[66]

FURTHER READING

Atkinson, Nigel. *Richard Hooker and the Authority of Scripture, Tradition and Reason: Reformed
    Theologian of the Church of England?* (Carlisle: Paternoster Press, 1997).
Hankey, Wayne. 'Augustinian Immediacy and Dionysian Mediation in John Colet, Edmund
    Spenser, Richard Hooker and the Cardinal de Bérulle', in Dominique Courcelles (ed.),
    Augustinus in der Neuzeit: Colloque de las Herzog August Bibliothek de Wolfenbüttel
    (Turnhout: Brepols, 1998), 125–60.
Kaye, Bruce N. 'Authority and Interpretation of Scripture in Hooker's of the Laws of
    Ecclesiastical Polity'. *Journal of Religious History*, 21 (1997), 80–109.
Kirby, Torrance. 'Richard Hooker's Theory of Natural Law in the Context of Reformation
    Theology'. *Sixteenth Century Journal*, 30 (1999): 681–703.
Kirby, Torrance. *Richard Hooker, Reformer and Platonist* (Aldershot: Ashgate, 2005).
McGrade, Arthur Stephen, ed. *Richard Hooker and the Construction of Christian Community*
    (Tempe, Ariz.: Medieval & Renaissance Texts & Studies, 1997).
Neelands, David. 'Predestination', in Torrance Kirby (ed.), *A Companion to Richard Hooker*
    (Leiden and Boston: E. J. Brill, 2008), 185–220.

---

[64] *Lawes*, VIII.3.; 3:335.22–336.4.   [65] *Lawes*, VII.11.10; 3:210.27–211.6.
[66] *Lawes*, I.2.3; 1:60.27–61.6.

CHAPTER 11

···

'THE DOORS SHALL FLY OPEN': CHRONOLOGY AND BIBLICAL INTERPRETATION IN ENGLAND, C.1630–C.1730

···

SCOTT MANDELBROTE

> What then shall we say of those who think to clear up the Sacred Text, and the Sacred Chronology, by its own Light? Truly they may be likened to a sort of Men, who coming to make their entry into a House fast locked, and seeing in the Yard or Porch a bunch of Keys lying fit for their purpose, yet not knowing how to use them, or perhaps misapplying them otherwise than to their proper Locks, do therefore resolve to throw away all, and to try whether they can put the Bolts back with their Finger, or else expect that at their appearance the Doors shall fly open ...[1]

WHEN the Devonian antiquary, Robert Cary (1615–88), wrote these words, his purpose was to outline errors in contemporary approaches to biblical history. He wished to defend the practice of what has come to be called scientific chronology, that is the use of 'Secular History and Chronology', consisting of the records of ancient history tempered by the evidence of astronomy and calculation, in making sense of the Bible.[2] Cary believed that errors in the standard accounts of biblical history, which relied too closely on the apparent chronology of the Hebrew text, had opened up a space for attacks on the integrity and truth of the Bible. His ire was directed against those who sought to determine future dates from the fulfilment of prophecy in order to justify recent events (for example, the readmission of the Jews to England in December 1655 or the political upheavals of the Civil Wars) as having providential causes. He was critical of those who wanted to use apparent technical problems in biblical chronology to cast doubt on doctrinal certainties. 'Licentious Brains' needed to be kept 'from their wild-goose chase

---

[1] Robert Cary, *Palaeologia chronica* (London, 1677), a2ᵛ.
[2] See Anthony Grafton, *Joseph Scaliger: A Study in the History of Classical Scholarship* (Oxford: Clarendon Press, 1983–93), ii.

of Prophesying upon Prophecies' and Jews, fanatics, millenarians, sceptics, and 'another sort of late Discoverers, who seem to be of the race of the *Aborigines*, namely the *Pre-Adamites*, who have taken occasion to infer their Proposition from such Principles which our Chronology doth not only not own, but professedly refutes', had to be shown the error of their ways.[3]

The keys that Cary believed that he had found to open up biblical history and to clear the minds of his opponents consisted of alternative sources, in particular the rival dates and longer periods of chronology offered by the Hellenistic Greek translation of the Old Testament, the Septuagint. Cary was just one of many English writers, almost all of them orthodox church-men, whose developing sense of the complexity of the history of the transmission of the Bible led them to be suspicious of the actions and motives of the Jewish redactors who had worked on the Hebrew Bible since the time of Christ. For Cary, one of the major discoveries of the 1650s, with which biblical chronology had to be made consistent, was that of the appar-ent antiquity of the dynasties of the Chinese emperors. By contrast, the argument that most impressed Cary's contemporary and fellow enthusiast for the Septuagint chronology, Edward Stillingfleet (1635–99), was the consideration that the biblical Flood need not have been uni-versal.[4] Stillingfleet justified his appeal to the longer chronology of the Septuagint by look-ing beyond the horizon of contemporary controversy to the authority of Sir Walter Ralegh's *History of the World*, which indicated that an extended span of time between Noah and Abraham was more consistent with what could be known about the growth of human society in the ancient world.[5]

Many sources and techniques were necessary to disentangle the past, and contempo-rary discoveries were still developing or refining these. Even the founder of the approach that Cary was emulating, the Leiden scholar Joseph Scaliger (1540–1609), whose inven-tion of the Julian period had established the role of astronomy in providing an external and determined series of dates to which the events of sacred and secular history could be calibrated and whose textual discoveries had also helped to sort genuine from forged accounts of ancient history, was not immune to error. Despite praising Scaliger, Cary argued that he had not always been properly faithful to his sources and attacked him for 'dressing *Eusebius* in the Vestments of *Syncellus*'.[6] Along with several of his contem-poraries, Cary felt that Scaliger's work, which 'broke the Ice for us of later Times' might compare unfavourably at times with that of the Jesuit critic, Denis Petau (1583–1652),

[3] Cary, *Palaeologia chronica*, a2ʳ–b2ʳ; David S. Katz, *Philo-Semitism and the Readmission of the Jews to England, 1603–1655* (Oxford: Clarendon Press, 1982), 89–157. One aspect of such debate concerned the nature of the divine covenant with the Jews, which, for the French libertine, Isaac La Peyrère, might be understood in the light of a radical reinterpretation of the limits of biblical history: *Men before Adam* (London, 1655–6); Andreas Pietsch, *Isaac La Peyrère. Bibelkritik, Philosemitismus und Patronage in der Gelehrtenrepublik des 17. Jahrhunderts* (Berlin: De Gruyter, 2012), 89–106, 141–95.

[4] Cary, *Palaeologia chronica*, 161–2, 259–60; Edward Stillingfleet, *Origines sacrae* (London, 1662), 539–41, 557–8. See also Rhoda Rappaport, *When Geologists were Historians, 1665–1750* (Ithaca, NY: Cornell University Press, 1997), 78; William Poole, *The World Makers* (Oxford: Peter Lang, 2010), 27–44. The ultimate source concerning Chinese chronology was Martino Martini, *Sinicae historiae decas prima* (Munich, 1658).

[5] Walter Ralegh, *The History of the World* (London, 1614), 226–8.

[6] Cary, *Palaeologia chronica*, b2ʳ, whose criticism relates to Scaliger's reconstruction of Eusebius and other early Christian chronicles in his *Thesaurus temporum* (Leiden, 1606), and derives from perceived errors in his use of a manuscript of the Byzantine chronicler, Georgius Syncellus. See also Grafton, *Joseph Scaliger*, ii.

and was attracted by the simpler and tabular presentations of chronological conclusions that he associated with the Giessen professor and follower of Scaliger, Christoph Helwig (1581–1617).[7]

Interest in handbooks such as those of Helwig reflected the comparatively limited status accorded to chronology in the education of general readers. Chronology formed part of the education of undergraduates at Oxford and Cambridge, which might be encountered in the context of learning in astronomy, and also in the teaching of professors of history. Thus, in a series of lectures that began in October 1635, Degory Wheare (1573–1647), the first holder of the chair of history at Oxford endowed by William Camden, surveyed the field of biblical, ancient, and modern authors of history, and the epochs that they described. Although aware of the work of Scaliger, Petau, and others, Wheare was not concerned with the technical practice of chronology.[8] Much later in the century, Isaac Newton regarded education in the 'principles of Geography & Chronology' as part of the reading that an undergraduate might undertake with his tutor.[9] General histories such as that by Ralegh or the widely recommended compendium of Johann Sleidan (1506–56) considered biblical chronology as part of a wider account of humanity.[10]

The complexity of scientific chronology, in terms of astronomy, mathematics, and textual studies, tended to restrict its appeal to successive and overlapping coteries of highly learned men: the circle of John Dee, which shaded into the associates of Ralegh; the friends of Archbishop James Ussher (1581–1656), who included Camden and John Selden, as well as Thomas Lydiat and John Bainbridge.[11] As Savilian Professor of Astronomy at Oxford, Bainbridge (1582–1643) included chronology in his lectures. Others at the university in the first half of the seventeenth century, notably John Gregory (1607–46) of Christ Church, produced successful general introductions to chronological learning. The conjunction of mathematical skill and knowledge of oriental languages that they embodied continued to mark out the practice of prominent figures in post-Restoration

---

569–91; Alden A. Mosshammer, *The 'Chronicle' of Eusebius and Greek Chronographic Tradition* (Lewisburg, Pa.: Bucknell University Press, 1979).

[7] Cary, *Palaeologia chronica*, b1^r–2^v; for Helwig's innovations in the tabular presentation of the passage of time, see Daniel Rosenberg and Anthony Grafton, *Cartographies of Time: A History of the Timeline* (New York: Princeton Architectural Press, 2010), 76–9. Helwig's work was widely available in England and recommended to beginners in chronology; see Barrett Kalter, *Modern Antiques: The Material Past in England, 1660–1780* (Lewisburg, Pa.: Bucknell University Press, 2012), 37. This was largely thanks to an edition prepared for students by the young Christopher Wren and his contemporaries at Wadham College, Oxford, in 1651 (repr. 1662, and tr. into English in 1687): see C. S. L. Davies, 'The Youth and Education of Christopher Wren', *English Historical Review*, 123 (2008): 300–27.

[8] Degory Wheare, *The Method and Order of Reading both Civil and Ecclesiastical Histories*, tr. Edmund Bohun (London, 1685), esp. 32–43.

[9] See *Unpublished Scientific Papers of Isaac Newton*, ed. A. R. Hall and Marie Boas Hall (Cambridge: Cambridge University Press, 1962), 369–70, perhaps written c.1690. Newton echoed the advice of successful tutors such as James Duport (1606–79), see C. D. Preston and P. H. Oswald, 'James Duport's Rules for his Tutorial Pupils: A Comparison of Two Surviving Manuscripts', *Transactions of the Cambridge Bibliographical Society*, 14 (2008–11): 351.

[10] Johann Sleidan, *A Briefe Chronicle of the Foure Principall Empyres*, tr. Stephan Wythers (London, 1563); Sleidan, *The Key of Historie* (London, 1627). These are both much reprinted versions of the author's *De quatuor summis imperiis* (London, 1584 [cf. Strasbourg, 1556]), itself often reprinted.

[11] Lesley B. Cormack, *Charting an Empire: Geography at the English Universities, 1580–1620* (Chicago: University of Chicago Press, 1997), 124–7.

Oxford, such as Edward Bernard (1638–97), Savilian Professor of Astronomy and editor of Josephus.[12] By the late seventeenth century, however, there is evidence for considerable interest in chronology by lay readers of the Bible. Printers of English Bibles began to accompany the text of scripture with a system of marginal dates that allowed readers to give it historical meaning.[13] A succession of lay writers from Ralegh to Newton contributed to discussion of chronology in print, and many others dabbled in it without ever thinking of publication.[14]

The rebarbativeness of the scientific practice of chronology, and the relatively simplistic references to it in most English-language works, have led some historians to doubt its intellectual currency and importance. Mordechai Feingold argues that 'the circumscribed role of chronology within English learned culture arose as much from the subordinate position of the discipline with respect to sacred and civil history as from the composition of the English scholarly community—predominantly divines'.[15] Certainly, chronology (like the study of languages) was meant to assist its practitioners to higher things rather than to be an end in itself. Even professional members of the clergy might therefore be content that a little might go a long way: 'some skill in Chronology will be necessary for a Divine after a convenient knowledge of the Tecknical part of Chronology', as Thomas Barlow (1607–91) put it. Yet, as Barlow's recommendations for the reading to be undertaken by advanced students indicated, chronology was recognized as an international field of study, which engaged theologians regardless of confession in a collaborative as much as a competitive enterprise.[16] Lutheran divines, in particular pupils or associates of Philip Melanchthon, shared a vision of history with writers like Sleidan who were closer to the Reformed or Calvinist Churches.[17] Jesuit authors such as Petau were worth consulting despite their criticism of Scaliger, a convert to the Reformed religion. English students of chronology like the Regius Professor of Hebrew at Cambridge, Edward Lively (c.1545–1605), or Camden's sometime pupil Edward Simpson (1578–1651), contributed to such scholarship by writing or publishing their own work in Latin and engaging with the arguments of Scaliger, Petau, or the Huguenot Professor of Hebrew at the Academy of Sedan, Jacques Cappel (1570–1624), in the process.[18]

---

[12] See Dublin, Trinity College, MS. 382, fols 9–10, 88–99 (papers of John Bainbridge); John Gregory, *Gregorii posthuma*, ed. John Gurganie (London, 1649), 125–255.

[13] See T. H. Darlow and H. F. Moule, *Historical Catalogue of Printed Editions of the English Bible 1525–1961*, rev. A. S. Herbert (London: British and Foreign Bible Society, 1968), 217.

[14] For example, Henry Paget, first Earl of Uxbridge (c.1663–1743), whose study of history and biblical chronology, probably composed in the mid–late 1680s, may be found in a private collection in Cambridge.

[15] Jed Z. Buchwald and Mordechai Feingold, *Newton and the Origin of Civilization* (Princeton: Princeton University Press, 2013), 111.

[16] Thomas Barlow, *The Genuine Remains*, ed. P. Pett (London, 1693), 28. Barlow recommended reading Petau, Paulus Crusius, and Helwig for chronological terms of art and the use of Helwig, Ussher, Edward Simpson, and Carion, Melanchthon, and Peucer more generally.

[17] See Alexandra Kess, *Johann Sleidan and the Protestant Vision of History* (Aldershot: Ashgate, 2008); Heinz Scheible, 'Melanchthons Verständnis des Danielbuchs', in Katharina Bracht and David S. du Toit (eds), *Die Geschichte der Daniel-Auslegung in Judentum, Christentum und Islam* (Berlin: De Gruyter, 2007), 293–321.

[18] See Dublin, Trinity College, Mss. 125–6 (copies of Lively's 'Chronologia seu notitia temporum', the second one with Ussher's notes); Edward Simpson, *Chronicon historiam catholicam complectens, ab exordio mundi ad nativitatem D.N. Iesv Christi* (Oxford, 1652). Ussher's work was originally issued in Latin: *Annales veteris testamenti* (London, 1650–4), as was William Beveridge, *Institutionum chronologicarum libri II* (London, 1669).

For most Christian writers, the purpose of biblical chronology was to serve the interests of the church. It could do so by helping to indicate the date of Christ's nativity or of Easter (thus settling or justifying disputes within the church or between Christians and Jews).[19] In tackling these issues, chronology dealt inevitably with matters that connected with the fulfilment of biblical prophecy. For many English divines, the main function of chronology lay in the assistance that it gave to the interpretation of the hardest biblical texts, in particular the book of Daniel in the Old Testament and that of Revelation in the New. Protestant historians, notably Sleidan or Matthieu Béroalde (d. 1576), offered a reinterpretation of world history based on the idea of four monarchies (Babylon, Persia, Greece, and Rome) to be found in Daniel, chapters 2 and 7. The history of these monarchies could be traced through the fulfilment of prophecy, and intertwined with the history of the Jewish and later the Christian church.[20] Although ridiculed by humanist critics such as Jean Bodin, English scholars like the Hebraist Hugh Broughton (1549–1612) were happy to endorse these ideas.[21] They did this in part to help to sustain the continuity of the witness of the Old and New Testaments. This was one reason why it was difficult for learned divines to resist tackling the issue of the progressive fulfilment of prophecy, despite the recognition that to do so risked dangerous speculation. For both Thomas Lydiat (1572–1646) and Joseph Mede (1586–1638), the possibility that better understandings of the evidence of pagan historians would allow a closer alignment of the testimony of prophecy with recorded history was one of the essential attractions of the study of chronology.[22] The method that Mede, a convert to millenarianism, developed for synchronizing the prophecies of Daniel and Revelation into a common sequence represented an essential advance in techniques for interpreting the Bible and identifying events that foretold the birth of Christ and the future history of the Christian church.[23]

[19] C. Philipp E. Nothaft, *Dating the Passion* (Leiden: Brill, 2012); Joanna Weinberg, 'Invention and Convention: Jewish and Christian Critique of the Jewish Fixed Calendar', *Jewish History*, 14 (2000): 317–30; Robert Poole, *Time's Alteration: Calendar Reform in Early Modern England* (London: UCL Press, 1998); Carl Philipp Emanuel Nothaft, 'From Sukkot to Saturnalia: The Attack on Christmas in Sixteenth-Century Chronological Scholarship', *Journal of the History of Ideas*, 72 (2011): 503–22. Cf. John Selden, *[Theanthropos]: Or, God made Man. A Tract Proving the Nativity of Our Saviour to be on the 25. of December* (London, 1661), a work composed to placate James VI and I in 1618 or 1619 whose orthodox conclusions (as contemporary readers noted) clashed with the scepticism expressed elsewhere by Selden: see G. J. Toomer, *John Selden: A Life in Scholarship* (Oxford: Oxford University Press, 2009), i. 306; John Butler, *[Christologia]. Or a Brief (but True) Account of the Certain Year, Moneth, Day and Minute of the Birth of Jesus Christ* (London, 1671), which used astrology as well as chronology to prove its point.

[20] See Arno Seifert, *Der Rückzug der biblischen Prophetie von der neueren Geschichte* (Cologne: Böhlau, 1990); H. H. Rowley, *Darius the Mede and the Four World Empires* (Cardiff: University of Wales Press, 1935); Barbara Pitkin, 'Prophecy and History in Calvin's Lectures on Daniel (1561)', in Bracht and du Toit (eds), *Geschichte der Daniel-Auslegung*, 323–47.

[21] Hugh Broughton, *Daniel His Chaldie Visions and His Ebrew: Both Translated after the Original: And Expounded Both* (London, 1596); cf. Anthony Grafton, *What was History? The Art of History in Early Modern Europe* (Cambridge: Cambridge University Press, 2007), 167–81.

[22] Kristine Louise Haugen, 'Thomas Lydiat's Scholarship in Prison: Discovery and Disaster in the Seventeenth Century', *Bodleian Library Record*, 25 (2012): 183–216; Henning Graf Reventlow, 'The Saints of the Most High und die Rätsel der Chronologie—Danielrezeption in England im 17. und 18. Jahrhundert', in Mariano Delgado, Klaus Koch, and Edgar Marsch (eds), *Europa, Tausendjähriges Reich und Neue Welt* (Stuttgart: Kohlhammer, 2003), 306–25; Katharine R. Firth, *The Apocalyptic Tradition in Reformation Britain 1530–1645* (Oxford: Oxford University Press, 1979), 204–41.

[23] Jeffrey K. Jue, *Heaven upon Earth: Joseph Mede (1586–1638) and the Legacy of Millenarianism* (Dordrecht: Springer, 2006), 89–107. Mede's chronological interests are not especially apparent in the work

Following Scaliger, Lively and other scholars were critical of Broughton and of some of the assumptions common in apocalyptic chronologies. Despite his friendship with Mede, Ussher did not endorse millenarian interpretations of biblical history.[24] Yet neither Ussher nor Simpson, for example, wished entirely to abandon the prophetic structure provided for the history of Israel (as a forerunner to the church) and the significance to Christ's nativity that a stress on the providential succession of monarchies, in particular those of Cyrus and Alexander the Great, provided.[25] Later writers, such as Ralph Cudworth (1617–88), joined Ussher in rejecting Lydiat's redating of the Hellenistic rulers of Egypt and Palestine in part in order to preserve the significance of prophecy for the 'Confirmation of Religion ag[ains]t [th]e Jews' and to buttress Protestant criticisms of Catholic ecclesiastical history. In so doing, Cudworth (unlike Mede) preferred the work of Johann Funck (1518–66) to that of Scaliger because it helped him to argue that Jesus had been the Messiah expected by the Jews.[26] Disputes about the correct application of chronology to the interpretation of prophecy were not settled by the acceptance that the Pope might not be equivalent to the apocalyptic Antichrist or that biblical prophecies might have been fulfilled in their entirety in the first centuries of the Christian era.[27] Indeed, the radical interpretations of prophecy and chronology offered respectively by the Dutch Arminian lay theologians, Hugo Grotius (1583–1645) and Isaac Vossius (1618–89), provided the immediate context for Cary in his re-examination of the structures of biblical time.[28]

English authors fretted about the legacy of Scaliger. They could never quite forget his vicious mockery of their countryman, Thomas Lydiat. Lydiat had criticized his rival's textual learning and proposed an alternative great period of 592 years in an attempt to reconcile the divergent chronologies of solar and lunar months used in ancient sources.[29] Then,

that briefly set out his millenarian ideas, *Clavis apocalyptica* (Cambridge, 1627); they are made much clearer in his *Works*, ed. John Worthington (London, 1664).

[24] Dublin, Trinity College, Ms. 125, fols 17–26; Alan Ford, *James Ussher* (Oxford: Oxford University Press, 2007), 77–84; cf. Hugh Broughton, *An Apologie in Briefe Assertions Defending That Our Lord Died in the Time Properly Foretold to Daniel* (London, 1592).

[25] Simpson, *Chronicon*, esp. part vii, 52–8; Ussher, *Annales*, i. A6ʳ.

[26] London, British Library, MS Add. 4987, fols 81–186, at 181ʳ; cf. Thomas Lydiat, *Canones chronologici* (Oxford, 1675), 27–109, Johann Funck, *Chronologia* (Nuremberg, 1545). See Marilyn A. Lewis, '"The Messiah Promised in the Sacred Scripture Came a Long Time Ago": the Cambridge Platonists' Attitudes towards the Readmission of the Jews, 1655–56', *Jewish Historical Studies: Transactions of the Jewish Historical Society of England*, 45 (2013): 41–61.

[27] Johannes van den Berg, *Religious Currents and Cross-Currents*, ed. Jan de Bruijn, Pieter Holtrop, and Ernestine van der Wall (Leiden: Brill, 1999), 83–115; William M. Lamont, *Richard Baxter and the Millennium* (London: Croom Helm, 1979), 27–75; Warren Johnston, *Revelation Restored: The Apocalypse in Later Seventeenth-Century England* (Woodbridge: Boydell, 2011), 23–66.

[28] Cary, *Palaeologia chronica*, 135–46, 202–7.

[29] Thomas Lydiat, *Tractatus de variis annorum formis* (London, 1605); Lydiat, *Defensio tractatus de variis annorum formis* (London, 1607). Lydiat's writings were given currency in the 1670s by the desire of the refounded Oxford University Press to put locally available works of scholarship into print. The Camden Professor of History at Oxford, John Lamphire, edited Lydiat's *Canones chronologici* from manuscripts in his possession (cf. Oxford, Bodleian Library, Ms. Bodley 666, containing copies of drafts in English and Latin), and Humphrey Prideaux included Lydiat's notes on the Parian Chronicle (cf. copies at Oxford, Bodleian Library, Mss. Auct. F. 6. 22, fols 23ʳ–93ʳ; Bodley 670, fols. 21ʳ–92ʳ; Dublin, Trinity College, Ms. 388) in his edition of *Marmora Oxoniensia* (Oxford, 1676). See Haugen, 'Thomas Lydiat's Scholarship in Prison'.

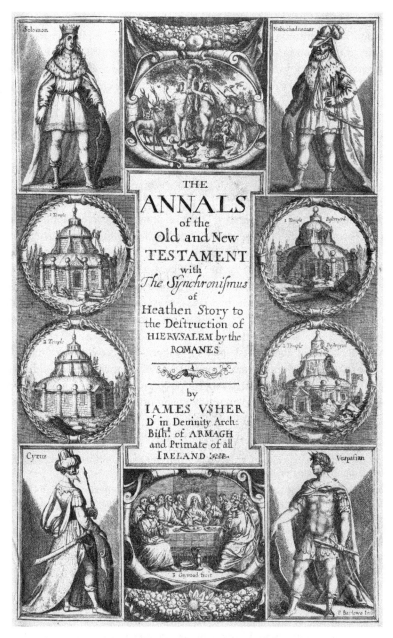

FIGURE 11.1 The title-page, engraved by Francis Barlow and Richard Gaywood, of Ussher's *Annals of the World* (1658), illustrating, in synchrony, scenes from the Old and New Testament. From top to bottom: Adam and Eve in the Garden of Eve, flanked by Solomon and Nebuchadnezzar (builder and destroyer of the first Jewish Temple respectively); the first Temple and its destruction; the second Temple and its destruction; and, flanking a scene of the Last Supper, Cyrus and Vespasian (facilitator and destroyer of the second Temple respectively). Solomon, Nebuchadnezzar, Cyrus, and Vespasian stand also for Jewish, Babylonian, Persian, and Roman monarchy. (By permission of author.)

there were doubts about Scaliger's commitment to the received text of the Old Testament and about his debts to other authors. The use made of the Julian period by Ussher, however, helped to establish the authority of Scaliger's method, even though it modified some of his conclusions.

Ussher's contribution to the development of biblical chronology in England was critical in a number of ways. His work seemed to bring a greater degree of certainty to chronology than many practitioners were happy with. A paradoxical result of this was that Ussher's conclusions had the potential for a more widespread readership than many other works of chronology. More immediately, his writings gave support to a chronology derived from the Hebrew Bible and intimately bound up with orthodox readings of that text. They did so at a time when chronology had become one of the most important determinants in a serious debate about the transmission and authority of the text of the Old Testament that raised many questions about the relationship of the past described in the Bible to the present. Ussher was one of the first writers to be fully aware of the variety of the manuscript witnesses for biblical history and the discrepancies in ancient testimony regarding the chronology of the Old Testament (Figure 11.1). He was confronted with similar problems of reconciling divergent texts and coping with the apparent evidence for the existence of ancient civilisations beyond the knowledge of the Bible that had crowded in on Scaliger. His solution lay in an assertion of the authority of Hebrew Bible that was not based on dogma but on the conclusion of extensive inquiries into the transmission and preservation of alternative textual witnesses, in particular the Samaritan Pentateuch and the Septuagint.[30]

Ussher's conclusions about the reliability of these versions were quickly echoed in mainstream English biblical criticism. Commenting on Genesis 5, therefore, John Richardson (1579/80–1654), who had assisted Ussher as a preacher in Dublin and at Trinity College, remarked:

> Of the LXX-Chronology in this Chapter. They extend the age of *Methuselah* beyond the flood, contrary to Scripture, and adde almost 1600 yeares, to the true Chronology, in this and the eleventh chapters. Haply out of some considerations touching the Heathens, for whom that Greek Translation was made. But the LXX now is no where extant, but patched infinitely.[31]

The solution that Ussher provided to the problem of competing authorities was not at first uncontroversial. This chapter began with a quotation from one of his critics, Robert Cary. Cary's work was by no means as well known (or perhaps notorious) as that of the author on whom he often relied, Isaac Vossius (of whom Charles II was said to have remarked that he would believe anything so long as it was not in the Bible). Isaac Vossius's father, Gerardus Joannes Vossius (1577–1649), had noted the possibilities

---

[30] Bodleian Library, Oxford, Mss. Rawlinson C 850, D 280, and D 1290; Richard Parr (ed.), *The Life of the Most Reverend Father in God, James Usher, Late Lord Arch-Bishop of Armagh, Primate and Metropolitan of all Ireland. With a Collection of Three Hundred Letters* (London, 1686), 2–11 (*Letters*); James Ussher and William Eyre, *De textus hebraici veteris testamenti variantibus ad Ludovicum Cappellum epistola* (London, 1652); Bodleian Library, Ms. Rawlinson C 849, fols 262–3; James Ussher, *De graeca septuaginta, interpretum versione syntagma* (London, 1655).

[31] John Richardson, *Choice Observations and Explanations upon the Old Testament* (London, 1655), B4r; cf. Ussher, *De graeca septuaginta.*

provided by the longer chronology of the Septuagint for resolving some of the difficulties posed by the variant genealogies for Christ given in the Gospels. His careful conclusions were edited and published by his son in 1659, the same year that Isaac Vossius printed his own *Dissertatio de vera aetate mundi*.[32] The younger Vossius argued that, contrary to first impressions, the text of the Hebrew Bible was not as close to the events that it described as that of the Septuagint. Some of the most important evidence that he presented for this view derived from the testimony of first-century Jewish historian, Josephus.

The chronologies provided in Josephus's *Antiquities* had often featured in discussions of the variant chronologies of the Bible. However Vossius's use of them was novel in two respects. First, he claimed that the numbers given by Josephus represented the genuine tradition of the Old Testament. Secondly, he suggested that the time at which Josephus had been writing had constituted a watershed in in the history of the Jews, after which the original Hebrew codices of the Bible had been corrupted. Josephus had had access to these manuscripts, from which the Septuagint had initially been translated.[33] The argument about the supposed corruption of the text of the Hebrew Bible by Jews of a later period was one to which Vossius returned when he extended his treatment of the chronology of the Septuagint in *De septuaginta interpretibus* (The Hague, 1661). He was not content to allege that the circumstance of the sack of Jerusalem and the destruction of the Temple had dislocated the record preserved by the Jews. Instead he returned to the familiar claim that the text had been deliberately changed in order to obscure the messiahship of Christ. A key witness here was provided by the early third-century Christian historian Julius Africanus, who gave evidence that the early church had believed that Christ's incarnation had followed some 5,500 years after the Creation. Vossius quietly ignored the fact that Julius had thought himself to be living not much more than a hundred years before the last days. He was thus able to deploy Julius's work to discredit the traditional Jewish notion of a world divided into three ages, each of which would last 2,000 years. Elements of this interpretation had certainly animated Ussher, who had taken care to argue that the nativity of Christ had occurred four thousand years after the creation.[34]

In the place of such orthodox interpretations, Vossius used the Septuagint chronology, as amended by Josephus, to construct an original messianic reading of the prophecy of the seventy weeks from the book of Daniel. He showed the relevance of the prophecy not only for the advent of Christ but also as a prediction of the destruction of the Temple and the apostasy of the Jews. This was a considerable act of ingenuity, since these interpretations had usually been offered as alternatives by critics, and it nicely illustrates Vossius's desire to have his cake and eat it. One might detect a similar slipperiness in his reformulation of what was meant by following the chronology of the

[32] G. J. Vossius, *Dissertatio gemina* (Amsterdam, 1643); G. J. Vossius, *Chronologiae sacrae isagoge*, ed. I. Vossius (The Hague, 1659).

[33] Isaac Vossius, *Dissertatio de vera aetate mundi* (The Hague, 1659), 9–10.

[34] Isaac Vossius, *De septuaginta interpretibus eorumque tralatione & chronologia dissertationes* (The Hague, 1661), 168–72; Ussher is both praised and blamed throughout the defences of Vossius's work appended to this volume. Ussher, *Annales*, ii. 531–2.

Septuagint, and in his fierce criticism of the work of the Catholic editors of the Sixtine edition of that text.[35]

Vossius's work was not without virtue. As already noted, it offered a way to deal with the evidence that supported even more heterodox conclusions about biblical chronology. For example, the lengthened timescale that it provided allowed for the successful rein-corporation of the early history of the Chinese dynasties into the story of the dispersion of peoples after the confusion of tongues at the Tower of Babel. Moreover, Vossius's broad learning and the extensive contacts that he had formed meant that he had had access to sources that had even eluded Scaliger. Thus one of Vossius's English sympathizers, the late seventeenth-century Master of Peterhouse, Thomas Richardson, was able to collate a manu-script of Eusebius's canon from Vossius's library and to use the readings that it provided to correct those given by Scaliger, entering them as notes in his own copy of the *Thesaurus temporum*.[36]

Despite the self-confidence of Vossius, most early modern authors accepted that chro-nology was a conjectural business. Chronologies were principally concerned with some-thing that continues to occupy modern historians and theologians. This is the problem of the relationship between a variety of sources that purport to describe the history of the ancient Near East, but which mention different places and different people and seem to date similar events to different times. Even Ussher, who believed that he had so improved on the work of Scaliger and of Petau as to be able to suggest that he could number the days as well as the years of sacred history, was careful in the way in which he phrased his conclusion concerning the date of creation: 'I encline to this opinion, that from the even-ing ushering in the first day of the World, to that midnight which began the first day of the Christian æra, there was 4003 years, seventy dayes, and six temporarie howers'.[37]

Cary was similarly cautious about the value for chronology of the consideration of the age of the world: 'For this I know, that the *Æra* of the World's Creation, is the most used by Writers of all sorts: but am well perswaded, the least understood of any'.[38] Such caution needs to be viewed in the context of contemporary reactions to the work of biblical chro-nologists. The attacks of the radical millenarians, sceptics, and pre-Adamites to whom Cary himself referred, should be placed alongside the concern of more mainstream churchmen about the usefulness of biblical chronology. The anxiety of the orthodox focused on the problem of 'how wavering and unconstant these learned men are', and on the tendency of writers of biblical chronology to be 'not only at variance with others, but often times also with [themselves]'.[39] The invention of the Julian period appeared to some to offer the chance

[35] Vossius, *De septuaginta interpretibus*, a4ᵛ–c2ᵛ; David S. Katz, 'Isaac Vossius and the English Biblical Critics, 1670–1689', in R. H. Popkin and A. J. Vanderjagt (eds), *Scepticism and Irreligion in the Seventeenth and Eighteenth Centuries* (Leiden: Brill, 1993), 142–84; Anthony Grafton, 'Isaac Vossius, Chronologer', in Eric Jorink and Dirk van Miert (eds), *Isaac Vossius (1618–1689) between Science and Scholarship* (Leiden: Brill, 2012), 43–84.

[36] Joseph Scaliger (ed.), *Thesaurus temporum*, 2nd edn (Amsterdam, 1658): Cambridge, Peterhouse, Perne Library, shelfmark H.4.31.

[37] James Ussher, *The Annals of the World* (London, 1658), A5ʳ (cf. Ussher, *Annales veteris testamenti*, A5ʳ); James Barr, 'Why the World was Created in 4004 B.C.: Archbishop Ussher and Biblical Chronology', *Bulletin of the John Rylands University Library of Manchester, 67* (1984–5): 575–608.

[38] Cary, *Palaeologia chronica*, 91.

[39] John Milner, *A Defence of Arch-Bishop Usher against Dr Cary and Dr Isaac Vossius, Together with an Introduction concerning the Uncertainty of Chronology* (Cambridge, 1694), 29.

of certainty in chronology.[40] Subsequent disagreement about the age of the earth and the length of the period to Christ's nativity reignited disagreement.

Henry Isaacson (1581–1654) conceded that 'insomuch as when two men be irreconcileable, they are ... compared to *Chronologers*'. Nevertheless, his book, *Saturni Ephemerides* (London, 1633), and the poem that was composed as an explanation for its frontispiece (Figure 11.2), reveal something about contemporary attitudes to the relationship of the evidences provided by creation, human history, and chronology in the context of divine providence:

> *Creation* is *Gods Booke*, wherein he writ
> Each Creature, as a Letter filling it.
> *History* is *Creations* Booke; which showes
> To what effects the *Series* of it goes.
> *Chronologie*'s the Booke of *Historie*, and beares
> The just account of *Dayes, Moneths*, and *Yeares*.
> But *Resurrection*, in a Later Presse,
> And *New Edition*, is the summe of these.[41]

Isaacson acted as amanuensis to the avant-garde bishop, Lancelot Andrewes, and was a committed disciple of Scaliger's methods in chronology. This commitment manifested itself most clearly in his assertion that the Julian period, as defined by Scaliger, was the necessary foundation for any certainty in chronology. Chronology was essential to enable people to find their way through history, to identify the stories of the past from which they would profit most, and to provide a context for the teaching of those stories: 'the very *Load-star*, which directeth a man, out of the sea of *History* into the wished for *Haven* of his Reading'.[42] Moreover, it might be linked to the natural world, understood as the book of God's creatures, as well as to prophecy. A full understanding of each would only be revealed with the completion of the divine plan for creation, at the resurrection which would follow the dissolution of the created world and the last judgement of those who had been its inhabitants.

A good deal of the uncertainty concerning biblical chronology in the late seventeenth century derived from questions relating to the coherence of the text of the Bible that were not strictly relevant to the application of Scaliger's method. It would be fair to suggest that, although several of those who wrote about biblical chronology were at least competent as mathematicians or astronomers, theological debate had overwhelmed technical competence in chronology. Yet there is a sense in which such an argument loses sight of the purpose of chronology. The application of astronomy to biblical chronology was one way in which the book of creation could be used to make the history of the Bible tell appropriate moral lessons. Those moral lessons were also very apparent when critics considered the history of the fulfilment of prophecy, itself an area in which chronological and astronomical data and arguments played an important role. The writers who presented the strongest opposition to the ideas of Vossius were those who also had a clear idea of what the biblical past implied for future ages.

---

[40] William Holder, *A Discourse concerning Time* (London, 1694), 48–52.

[41] Attributed in the seventeenth century to Richard Crashaw (*Steps to the Temple* (London, 1646), 128), this poem was probably written by Edward Rainbow, Fellow of Magdalene College, Cambridge and later Bishop of Carlisle: see [Jonathan Banks], *The Life of the Right Reverend Father in God, Edw. Rainbow, D.D.* (London, 1688), 84–8.

[42] Henry Isaacson, *Saturni ephemerides* (London, 1633), A4$^{r–v}$.

FIGURE 11.2 The frontispiece, engraved by William Marshall, of Henry Isaacson's *Saturni ephemerides* (1633). History and chronology flank Cronus devouring his children at the top; celestial and terrestrial globes top pillars constructed of works of learning, at the foot of which tableaux of the creation of Adam and the Last Judgment flank an image of the building of the Tower of Babel. (By kind permission of the Master and Fellows of Peterhouse, Cambridge.)

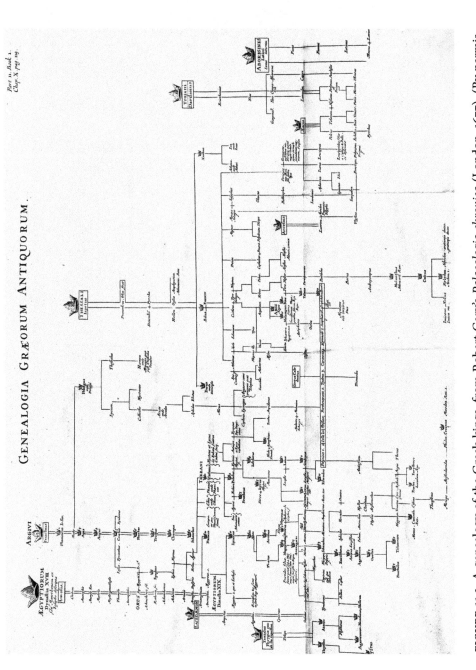

FIGURE 11.3 A genealogy of the Greek kings, from Robert Cary's *Palaeologia chronica* (London, 1677). (By permission of author.)

Alternatives to Vossius's chronology took a variety of forms. One, represented by Cary, was a more carefully apologetic restatement of some elements of Vossius's arguments (Figure 11.3). Another was the work of the Kentish antiquary and royalist, Sir John Marsham (1602–85), whose earliest excursion into biblical chronology had largely been concerned with the fulfilment of the prophecy of the seventy weeks in Daniel, which he interpreted primarily in the context of the desecration of the Temple by Antiochus IV Epiphanes. Marsham was remarkably straightforward about the difficulties of writing biblical chronology from a comparison of ancient sources. He was conscious of the criticism that writers on chronology in the early church had directed at the inconsistencies of the Hebrew Bible. He wished to take seriously the range of sources concerning ancient history that had been available to Scaliger, as well as the evidence of inscriptions (especially those of the Arundel marbles) that had been discovered more recently.

Influenced by the astronomer and traveller John Greaves, to whom he dedicated *Diatriba chronologica* (London, 1649), Marsham was principally concerned with the problem of reconciling the long chronology for the Egyptian kings provided by Manetho with the other records of the ancient Near East. Although, following Scaliger, he used information grounded in astronomy to reconcile series of dates that depended on differing interpretations of the length of the year, Marsham's work engaged primarily in the textual comparison that had become the principal method for chronological debate. He dismissed entirely the possibility that one might identify the true date of creation and began his work after the end of the biblical Flood. Marsham's conclusions were in a sense the opposite of those of Vossius, although they also rested heavily on use of techniques and information to be found in Josephus. By identifying the Egyptian figure of Sesostris with the biblical Sesac, and dating him to the time of Solomon and his sons, Marsham was able to abbreviate Egyptian chronology and bring it into the scope of that part of biblical chronology that seemed to him reliable.[43] Isaac Newton (1642–1727) later followed several of Marsham's suggestions, although there were important differences in some of his eventual conclusions. Newton's method, however, differed from Marsham's in the attention that it paid to the external evidence of astronomy for adjudicating between otherwise simply incompatible historical sources.[44]

Newton was not the only English writer of the late seventeenth century to see the value of the living historical testimony of the heavens for putting flesh on the bones of biblical chronology. For example, Richard Allin, whom the Cambridge natural philosopher, William Whiston, consulted about chronology between 1699 and 1707, was certain that astronomical evidence could settle a series of disputed points in contemporary chronology. Allin was an attentive reader of Scaliger and was critical of Ussher's claim that the antediluvian months had all begun at the full moon. He attempted to correct parts of Whiston's own account of the cause of the deluge in the passage of a comet near to the earth with reference to lunar tables and, later, wondered whether Newton's theory of the moon's motion or calculations of the eccentricity of the earth's orbit over time might

---

[43] John Marsham, *Chronicus canon Ægyptiacus Ebraicus Græcus* (London, 1672), 12, 22, 54–5, 352–89; Marsham, *Diatriba chronologica* (London, 1649); Maidstone, Kent History and Library Centre, Mss. U1121/ Z 22, 23/1–2, 25/1–3; Zur Shalev, 'Measurer of All Things: John Greaves (1602–1652), the Great Pyramid and Early Modern Metrology', *Journal of the History of Ideas*, 63 (2002): 555–75.

[44] See Buchwald and Feingold, *Newton and the Origin of Civilization*; Frank E. Manuel, *Isaac Newton: Historian* (Cambridge: Cambridge University Press, 1963). Newton's own copy of Marsham's *Chronicus canon* (Leipzig, 1676) may be found at Kansas City, Mo., Linda Hall Library, shelfmark D59. M36 1676.

enable the more accurate computation of the relationship between dates given in solar and in lunar years.[45]

Allin's correspondence with Whiston also reveals the extent to which the discussion of ancient written sources, the evaluation of both ancient and modern evidence regarding the geography of the Near East, the evidence of the heavens (as understood by contemporary observation and theorizing), and knowledge (some of it derived from collecting, some from experiment) of the natural world jostled for attention in chronological discussion. The assumption was that the evidence of the senses ought to be compatible with the events of biblical history and should support an accurate biblical chronology. The acceptance that astronomical data might provide a means to determine issues of biblical chronology was thus a first step in a much broader programme of inquiry that sought to make physical sense of what had happened in the world through the period of biblical time. The answers that were given in this inquiry often suggested that keys to open the locks of time could be found in the experience and understanding of the present and that the traces of the past in the contemporary world provided the clues necessary to sort out the puzzles of biblical history.

The book that really set off the search for evidence of biblical history in the contemporary world was Thomas Burnet's *Telluris theoria sacra* (1681). Burnet's work was widely read, not least at Cambridge, where it converted Whiston to an interest in biblical chronology. There were also many published criticisms of Burnet's work, whose number increased as the author completed the second part of his theory, which discussed the completion of the sacred history of the earth. This would come about with the conflagration of the world, prophesied in the New Testament, and the creation from it of a new heaven and a new earth, similar in form to the original, pristine world, which would last for a thousand years during which the saints would practise devotion to and contemplation of the divine. After the Day of Judgement, the earth's final state would be that of a star, like the sun. Despite the stirring times in which he was writing, Burnet did not attempt to set any clear timetable for the arrival of the millennium, remarking that:

> the difference there is betwixt the Greek, Hebrew, and Samaritan Copies of the Bible, makes the Age of the World altogether undetermin'd: ... Seeing therefore we have no assurance how long the World hath stood already, neither could we be assur'd how long it hath to stand.[46]

Burnet later supported his treatment of the natural evidence for sacred history with a consideration of the written evidence for the biblical account of creation, *Archaeologiae philosophiae* (1692). This work also reconstructed a history of the progress of human knowledge about divine moral teaching. Thus, Burnet moved from an interpretation of Moses the historian to one of Moses the lawgiver. He discussed the transmission through the gentile world of the precepts of morality which had been known to Noah and his children, as well as the Mosaic account of the fall. In this account, he argued for the importance of Egyptian civilization as a vector for the transmission of knowledge about nature and morality, from which both the Israelites and the Greeks had learned. He suggested similarities between the

---

[45] Leicester, Leicestershire Record Office, Conant Mss., Barker Correspondence, vol. 2, nos. 90, 92, 94; cf. William Whiston, *A New Theory of the Earth* (London, 1696), 123–54.

[46] Thomas Burnet, *The Theory of the Earth* (London, 1690), 31; on the Burnet controversy, see Poole, *The World Makers*.

account of the origin of morality given by Moses and the fables told by other lawgivers, for example Orpheus, in order to establish their authority. He also maintained that knowledge of the original principles of Noah had been preserved best among northern peoples, in the teachings of the druids. These ideas of Burnet chimed very well with those of a variety of late seventeenth-century English critics, most of them orthodox churchmen and many with a Cambridge connection, whose growing anxieties about the stability of the Hebrew text of the Old Testament encouraged them to maintain a belief in the truth of ancient wisdom and in the communication to Moses of secrets about nature and worship by the priests of the Egyptians.[47]

For others who proved influential in advancing the argument that natural artefacts provided a kind of living history that supported biblical chronology, however, such beliefs seemed to undermine the very things that they sought to preserve. The natural historian, John Woodward (1665/8–1728), thus attacked Burnet's views about the Egyptians as part of a broader attempt to associate biblical history with what could be observed in the natural world. Although Woodward's work again attracted a good deal of controversy, it would be wrong to conclude, from the often vitriolic attacks mounted on particular parts of the argument or the vicious responses of an especially bad-tempered author, that the main point of his argument did not command widespread assent. Woodward summarized this in a letter to Thomas Baker, written in 1699. Baker (1656–1740), a Cambridge non-juror, had been so exasperated by the rival claims recently made for the authority of ancient or of modern learning that, in *Reflections upon Learning* (1699), he sought to underline the frailty of human knowledge and the consequent necessity of trust in revelation. He was particularly harsh on the faults of chronology, attacking both Vossius and Marsham, and suggesting that modern chronological works were no better than the ancient forgeries that they often sought to expose.[48] In reply, Woodward suggested:

> my Argument was, if History be *insufficient* & *uncertain*, we have no way left to prove *Revelation* is realy *Revelation*. 'Tis demonstrable we could have no reasonable satisfaction in [th]e Affair. The best we could do would be to have recourse either to Rome or Enthusiasm: & take our information from Oral Tradition; or [th]e Light within …. Take away [th]e Certainty of History, & Natural Philosophy, which likewise [God] attempts, & ye destroy all means of evinceing his Existence.[49]

Baker's response recognized both the originality and the difficulty of the approach that Woodward was trying to maintain. He argued that in the *Reflections*:

> he has purposely forborn reflecting upon Ecclesiastical History from w[hi]ch the Canon of Scripture may be prov'd, by as universal a consent as can be had for any Truth. Nor can you but know, that both the French & Dutch Churches do insist chiefly upon other Reasons viz.

---

[47] See Dmitri Levitin, 'From Sacred History to the History of Religion: Paganism, Judaism, and Christianity in European Historiography from Reformation to "Enlightenment"', *Historical Journal*, 55 (2012): 1117–60; Daniel Stolzenberg, 'John Spencer and the Perils of Sacred Philology', *Past and Present*, 214 (2012): 129–63; Dmitri Levitin, 'John Spencer's *De Legibus Hebraeorum* (1683–85) and "Enlightened" Sacred History: A New Interpretation', *Journal of the Warburg and Courtauld Institutes*, 76 (2013): 49–92.

[48] Thomas Baker, *Reflections upon Learning* (London, 1699), 125–37.

[49] Cambridge University Library, Ms. Add. 7647, letter 34.

Internal Arguments from the Intrinsic evidence of the Books themselves &c (as appears by their Confessions ...)[50]

Yet, in spite of the problems that Woodward and others who sought to construct arguments about biblical history from natural history faced, it was Baker, not they, who was swimming against the stream.

The providential argument to which he appealed (the preservation of scripture) had been a theme in natural theology for many years, but was now quaking before anxieties about the true history of the text.[51] The alternative providential argument to which Woodward and others looked, however, was being constantly verified by discoveries that were being newly placed before people's eyes.[52] These discoveries not only gave general proofs of the truth of scriptural history, they also provided specific revisions to biblical chronology. For example, in October 1730, the antiquary and divine William Stukeley reflected on the discovery of what appeared to be petrified hazelnuts in a quarry at Aynho, near Oxford. These fossils, he believed provided evidence that Scaliger, Ussher, and other writers of chronology had been wrong in their estimates of the start of the biblical deluge. They noted that the Bible stated that the Flood had begun on the seventeenth day of the second month and claimed that, because the first month had started at the autumnal equinox, the deluge had commenced in a period bounded by the dates 17 November (Scaliger) and 17 December (Ussher). In doing so they were mistaken, 'as if Moses reckon'd time by exact Julian years', since, Stukeley argued, with the support of the hazelnuts, the Flood had occurred when the grain and the fruit were newly ripe: that is, on or about the day of the equinox itself (12 October).[53]

By no means everyone was so enthusiastic about the value of evidence from the natural world. Isaac Newton's initial doubts about Burnet's ideas are well known.[54] Less frequently cited is evidence provided by the notes of Henry Wharton (1664–95), who had been one of the few young men at Cambridge to benefit from private tuition from Newton. Wharton criticized a number of aspects of Burnet's approach, some of which were common features of biblical chronology. He doubted the validity of linking the chronology of the antediluvian earth to the equinoxes. More specifically, he applied his understanding of the working of gravity to dismantle aspects of Burnet's physical system, in particular his suggestions regarding the shape of the primitive earth and the effects of the dissolution of its original crust.[55] Among his many accomplishments as a historian, Wharton edited Ussher's posthumous *Historia dogmatica* (1690), which included further reflections on the text of the Bible. He was also a friend of one of Ussher's most enthusiastic supporters, William Lloyd (1627–1717).

[50] Cambridge University Library, Ms. Add. 7647, letter 35.

[51] For two different sources of anxiety about the self-interpreting nature of scripture, see George H. Tavard, *The Seventeenth Century Tradition: A Study in Recusant Thought* (Leiden: Brill, 1978), 12–106; J. Samuel Preus, *Spinoza and the Irrelevance of Biblical Authority* (Cambridge: Cambridge University Press, 2001).

[52] See Rappaport, *When Geologists were Historians*; the argument to which Baker appealed is, for example, a critical part of John Wilkins's natural theology in *Of the Principles and Duties of Natural Religion* (London, 1678).

[53] London, British Library, Ms. Sloane 4051, fols 123–5; cf. London, Royal Society, Ms. Register Book 15, 101–4.

[54] *The Correspondence of Isaac Newton*, ed. H. W. Turnbull et al. (Cambridge: Cambridge University Press, 1959–77), ii. 319, 321–7, 329–34.

[55] London, Lambeth Palace Library, Ms. 592, fols 118–20.

Lloyd's public commitment to chronology is clearest in the numbers that he provided for the margins of folio Bibles printed in London from 1701. There, the nativity took centre stage in a system of dates reckoned not from Ussher's date of creation but calculated as being years before or after Christ.[56] Lloyd was not simply interested in popularizing Ussher's chronology, he also worked hard to understand and defend it, as well as to show its usefulness for determining the true date of ecclesiastical feasts, such as Easter. For example, he consulted Newton about the evidence for ancient usage of lunar calendars.[57] Lloyd's revisions of Ussher's chronological tables were eagerly awaited from the 1690s, and were published by his chaplain, Benjamin Marshall, in 1712.[58] Similar expectation surrounded Lloyd's exposition of Daniel's prophecy of the seventy weeks, part of which was printed in 1690 and which Marshall revised after Lloyd's death.[59] The interest expressed in Lloyd's work was exaggerated by his role as a public figure, intimately involved with the events of the Revolution of 1688. It was not always friendly. One of the prebends of Lloyd's final Diocese of Worcester, for example, preached a sermon in the cathedral attacking 'Fanatical Prophets in our Age; such as Pretend to interpret Daniel's weeks', and calling for their punishment 'whether B[isho]ps or others'. In response to this brazen act of disloyalty, Lloyd sheepishly admitted to one of his fellow bishops that, although he had not spoken of the depostion of the French King or the destruction of the papacy, 'yet I confess I have spoke of [th]e fall of French Empire in this Age, & Rome's being burnt within a very few yeers after'.[60]

It is difficult to know what to make of a figure like Lloyd, who was at the same time immensely respected and openly ridiculed, in both cases partly on account of his attitude to biblical chronology. Certainly, it is not enough to write him off as an enthusiast. Lloyd displayed considerable technical chronological learning in identifying and seeking to correct William Whiston's dating of the Passion, which was partly intended to invalidate the orthodox interpretation of the prophecy of the seventy weeks.[61] Although Lloyd's conclusions did not always agree with those of Humphrey Prideaux (1648–1724), the work of these two men did help to establish a consensus that the prophecy of the seventy weeks was fulfilled in Christ.[62] The correspondence between Lloyd and Prideaux showed very clearly the ongoing importance of chronological learning, and of the tradition of Scaliger, for leading English divines. The popularity of Prideaux's work and of others like it that appeared to demonstrate that the historicity of the biblical past provided proof of the value of chronology to lay readers as well.[63]

---

[56] Darlow and Moule, Historical Catalogue, rev. Herbert, 233–4.

[57] London, British Library, Ms. Add. 6489, fols 67–8.

[58] Benjamin Marshall, Chronological Tables (Oxford, 1712–13).

[59] [William Lloyd], An Exposition of the Prophecy of Seventy Weeks ([London, 1690]); Benjamin Marshall, A Chronological Treatise upon the Seventy Weeks of Daniel (London, 1725).

[60] Gloucester, Gloucestershire Record Office, Lloyd Baker Mss D 3549, box 77, bundle O, no. 23 (Lloyd to John Sharp, 27 Feb. 1710).

[61] London, British Library, MS. Add. 24,197; Northampton, Northamptonshire Record Office, Finch Hatton Mss. 2623–5; see also A. Tindal Hart, William Lloyd, 1627–1717 (London: SPCK, 1952).

[62] Humphrey Prideaux, The Old and New Testament Connected (London, 1716–18), i. 262–307; Prideaux and Lloyd exchanged letters about the correct interpretation of the prophecy in 1710: The Life of the Reverend Humphrey Prideaux (London, 1748), 237–66.

[63] Thomas R. Preston, 'Biblical Criticism, Literature, and the Eighteenth-Century Reader', in Isabel Rivers (ed.), Books and their Readers in Eighteenth-Century England (Leicester: Leicester University Press, 1982), 97–126.

Such consensus formed part of the argument against Newton's chronological work mounted by the Bristol divine and moral reformer, Arthur Bedford (1668–1745). Bedford developed a wide interest in astronomy, calendrical calculation, and chronology, and, during the early 1720s, began in earnest his *Scripture Chronology Demonstrated by Astronomical Calculations*, a vast work 'recommended by Archbishop Usher in his Annals, but never attempted 'til then; the Consequence of which was the Establishing the Authority of the Hebrew Chronology'.[64] It was published by subscription in 1730, in an edition remarkable both for its physical size and the interest that it generated. Bedford was highly critical of Newton's chronology, and also printed extensive objections to it in the *Animadversions* that he published in 1728. He correctly noticed the heretical implications of some of Newton's alterations to traditional biblical chronology and associated them with the revival of anti-trinitarian theology.

Bedford's concern with the 'Mahometanism' of Newton's chronology might appear to be evidence of Thomas Hearne's belief that he was 'a crazed man'.[65] The Scottish annalist, Robert Wodrow certainly thought the whole business of the English addiction to squabbles over biblical chronology rather silly. He commented on one of Bedford's principal differences from Newton that 'He endeavours to prove the Sabbath first to have been institute in the wildernes; and the change of the Christian Sabbath, and some other singularitys, as most part of the English writers, who mix all their writtings with whims'.[66] Yet Bedford ended his days as chaplain to the Prince of Wales and collected an exceptional list of subscribers for his work that included noblemen as well as bishops, the President of the Royal Society as well as low-church clerics, many of the most prominent figures in the Society for the Promotion of Christian Knowledge, and most of the major London and provincial booksellers. Of course, his book had pictures as well as tables, but these served also to make its historical message more immediate.

Despite the efforts of Ussher and his adherents, there can be no doubt that chronology remained a difficult subject to an English audience, and one with uncertain conclusions. Nevertheless chronology might reach out beyond controversy and use the evidence of nature to construct a more immediate sense of the presence of biblical history, in the process tying the past more firmly to the contemporary world and even to its future. Chronology puzzled numerous commentators, but the edge to their ridicule hinted that others indeed took seriously what it taught. That they did so had something to do with the appeal of the esoteric, but also owed much to contemporary ideas about how to read and make sense of history, particularly biblical history. As Cary noted, to set dates for events such as 'the precise Year of the World's Creation' was 'an Audacious Resolution'. Nevertheless, he maintained, chronology properly done might be 'in so near Consent with the Ancient Churches, walking by the same Rule of the Holy Scriptures, and in perfect Agreement with the most Justifiable Memorials of the World'.[67]

[64] Trowbridge, Wiltshire Record Office, Ms. 1178/631.
[65] *Remarks and Collections of Thomas Hearne*, ed. C. E. Doble et al. (Oxford: Oxford Historical Society, 1885–1921), x. 7.
[66] Robert Wodrow, *Analecta*, ed. Matthew Leishman (Glasgow, 1842–3), iii. 428.
[67] Cary, *Palaeologia chronica*, 270.

FURTHER READING

Bennett, Jim, and Scott Mandelbrote. *The Garden, the Ark, the Tower, the Temple* (Oxford: Bodleian Library, 1998).

Buchwald, Jed Z., and Mordechai Feingold. *Newton and the Origin of Civilization* (Princeton: Princeton University Press, 2013).

Ford, Alan. *James Ussher* (Oxford: Oxford University Press, 2007).

Grafton, Anthony. *Joseph Scaliger: A Study in the History of Classical Scholarship*, 2 vols (Oxford: Clarendon Press, 1983–93).

Jorink, Eric, and Dirk van Miert, eds. *Isaac Vossius (1618–1689) between Science and Scholarship* (Leiden: Brill, 2012).

Lamont, William M. *Richard Baxter and the Millennium* (London: Croom Helm, 1979).

Levitin, Dmitri. 'From Sacred History to the History of Religion: Paganism, Judaism, and Christianity in European Historiography from Reformation to "Enlightenment"'. *Historical Journal*, 55 (2012): 1117–60.

Nothaft, C. Philipp E. *Dating the Passion* (Leiden: Brill, 2012).

Poole, William. *The World Makers* (Oxford: Peter Lang, 2010).

Rappaport, Rhoda. *When Geologists Were Historians, 1665–1750* (Ithaca, NY: Cornell University Press, 1997).

Rosenberg, Daniel, and Anthony Grafton. *Cartographies of Time: A History of the Timeline* (New York: Princeton Architectural Press, 2010).

CHAPTER 12

....

EARLY MODERN *GEOGRAPHIA SACRA* IN THE CONTEXT OF EARLY MODERN SCHOLARSHIP

....

ZUR SHALEV

'PERUSING the nine last Chapters of Ezekiels prophesie', confessed the Anglican Thomas Fuller, 'in stead of a literall sense I found the *Canaan* by him described no Geography, but Ouranography, no earthly truth, but mysticall prediction'. Rather than trying to bring Ezekiel's visionary geography down to (a mappable) earth, Fuller was resigned to the impossibility of the project: 'Yea, God may seem of set purpose to have troubled, and perplexed the text, imbittering the Nibbles thereof with inextricable difficulties, meerly to wean us from the milke of the letter, and make us with more appetite seek for stronger meat therein'.[1] Fuller's short public reflection on his difficulties in localizing scripture encapsulates the themes, methods, and dilemmas of early modern sacred geography—the subject of this chapter.

The notions of sacred geography and sacred space are central in current studies of religion, history, and society.[2] Scholars often refer to sacred space as a product of the human effort to imbue a locale—whether a single structure, a city, or a wider region—with religious meaning. Humans, it has been argued, distinguish the sacred from the profane by several means, both material (expressed in shrine architecture and liturgical practice) and spiritual (symbols, representations, and cosmologies shared by a community). This scholarly attention to religious spatialities takes part in a broader preoccupation with space and place as useful research categories in the human sciences, often referred to as 'the spatial turn'. Space is now understood as a malleable human construct, continually created and negotiated.[3]

---

[1] Thomas Fuller, *A Pisgah-sight of Palestine and the Confines thereof* (London, 1650), book 5, 189, 191.

[2] This overview is based on the introduction to my *Sacred Words and Worlds: Geography, Religion, and Scholarship, 1550–1700* (Leiden: Brill, 2012).

[3] The literature on the subject is vast and growing. For two recent overviews see Charles W. J. Withers, 'Place and the "Spatial Turn" in Geography and in History', *Journal of the History of Ideas*, 70 (2009): 637–58; Santa Arias, 'Rethinking Space: An Outsider's View of the Spatial Turn', *GeoJournal*, 75 (2010): 29–41.

Thus sacred space is used to understand topics as varied as church architecture and history, magic and landscape, within numerous critical fields.

The term sacred geography, however, has a rich and long heritage, which goes back to the early modern period, when it was coined, and to the sphere of biblical scholarship, within which it was first developed. *Geographia sacra* in the sixteenth and seventeenth centuries denoted the systematic study of biblical and ecclesiastical geography. This was not, even then, a new field of inquiry. In the early fourth century, Eusebius of Caesarea listed the components of sacred geography in the preface to his *Onomasticon*. Eusebius planned to produce a list of the people of the world, a map of Judaea and the twelve tribes, a map of Jerusalem and the Temple, and an alphabetical list of scriptural place-names.[4] Following Eusebius, Jewish and Christian scholars continued to elucidate the geographical elements in the Bible, such as natural features, settlements, peoples, and boundaries, often representing their work on a map. The centrality of the sacred text in this pursuit guaranteed a strong continuity in the genre, from its inception until today. Modern archaeology, philology, and cartographic techniques have not dramatically changed this basic aim. Yet despite this continuity, sacred geography is never a technical arrangement of place-names in map or list form, but an exegetical and interpretative act. The history of sacred geography therefore belongs with the wider and rocky history of biblical scholarship.

Within this longer tradition, the early modern period is uniquely significant for several reasons. First, the geographical culture of the period had been transformed by humanist methods and practices in general, and particularly by the revival of classical geography. While early modern geography began to develop and rely on scientific and empirical methods, it was at the same time a historical-philological enterprise, dealing with translation and interpretation of ancient texts. The study of biblical geography was part of this broader trend. References to sacred geography feature prominently in the general geographical literature of the time. The study of the earth, of measurements and distances, was seen as crucial to a fuller understanding of scripture and religion. William Cuningham (*c*.1531–86) explained in the introduction to his *Cosmographical Glasse* that geography, 'as touching the study of divinitie, it is so requisite, and neadfull, that you shall not understa[n]d any boke, ether of th' old law or Prophets … being in this Art ignoraunt'.[5]

The humanist and philological aspects of early modern biblical scholarship, too, made their mark on sacred geography. Students of scripture increasingly insisted that valid interpretation must be based on correct geography and chronology.[6] A whole set of study aids emerged to facilitate the correct literal reading of the holy text. Both Catholics and Protestants approached the Bible armed with greater knowledge of Oriental languages and texts, and produced detailed place-name indices, maps, and textual geographical accounts relating to biblical landscapes. These were often printed in major Bible editions, or in separate treatises.[7]

---

[4] See the English translation: *Palestine in the Fourth Century A.D.: The* Onomasticon *by Eusebius of Caesarea*, ed. Joan E. Taylor, tr. G. S. P. Freeman-Grenville (Jerusalem: Carta, 2003), 11. Of all the proposed items in Eusebius' plan only the list of biblical place-names, commonly known as the *Onomasticon*, has reached us.

[5] William Cuningham, *The Cosmographical Glasse Conteinyng the Pleasant Principles of Cosmographie, Geographie, Hydrographie, or Nauigation* (London, 1559), sig. A4ᵛ–A5ʳ.

[6] On biblical chronology, see the chapter by Scott Mandelbrote in this volume.

[7] For example, Jacob Ziegler and Wolfgang Wissenburg, *Terrae Sanctae, quam Palaestinam nominant, … descriptio* (Strasburg, 1536); Robert Estienne, *Hebraea & Chaldaea nomina virorum, mulierum, populorum, idoloru[m], … , quae in Bibliis leguntur* (Paris, 1549).

The broader and dynamic contexts of *geographia sacra* call upon us to adopt flexible definitions that match early modern usage. In terms of sources, *geographia sacra* as biblical geography used scripture as both its main source and object of study. However, for most early modern scholars, extra-biblical (e.g. Josephus) and pagan (e.g. Ptolemy, Pliny) sources were essential tools in the reconstruction of biblical lands. Works in this genre were not limited to the eastern Mediterranean, the traditional theatre of biblical stories. The title *geographia sacra* often referred to ecclesiastical subject matter—dioceses, provinces, and shrines—thus enabling any region to have its own sacred geography. Moreover, some scholars adopted a global approach. Indeed, the term 'geographia' was often used in its Ptolemaic sense, that is, a treatment of the whole earth, or vast areas at least, as opposed to the particular and local 'chorographia'.

Sacred geography during the age of discovery and global expansion faced new challenges. Like medieval *mappaemundi*, early modern sacred geography was genuinely global in scope, but it had to contend with and explain previously unaccounted for regions and peoples that could not fit easily within the traditional frame. The Bible maintained its status among scholars as a valid and complete record of human history and geography, well into the seventeenth century. The impact of the new discoveries on biblical geography was therefore not necessarily a secularizing one. Some authors incorporated the Americas and other regions into the framework of scriptural space. The Spanish theologian and orientalist, Benito Arias Montano (1527–98, of whom more later), following Columbus and Guillaume Postel, located *Ophir*, the biblical gold-bearing region (1 Kings 9: 28), in Peru. Montano employed his philological skill to reaffirm that the Hebrews and other ancient peoples reached the New World, and more importantly, that the authority of scripture remained intact.[8] Others dismissed such views or at least kept silent on the issue. The admirably learned Huguenot pastor, Samuel Bochart (1599–1667), deciphered, so he presumed, the dispersion of Noah's descendants (Genesis 10) and provided numerous etymological proofs for the Hebraic origins of languages and cultures, propagated by Phoenician navigations. Significantly, Bochart left the New World out of his ethnic map of antiquity. Nevertheless, to Bochart as to many orthodox Calvinists at the time, scripture was the most reliable and most ancient record of humanity's origins.

Another point that ties sacred geography to a broader intellectual history of the time is the emergence of biblical antiquarianism. Following the immense interest in classical antiquities and material culture, early modern scholars attempted to create a fully blown image of biblical societies, especially that of the ancient Hebrews in the Holy Land during the time of Christ. Sacred antiquarianism stood at a meeting point between traditional exegesis and the study of classical antiquities.[9] Churchmen and pilgrims in Jerusalem (and other sites) devoted considerable efforts to visual and textual documentation of monuments and traditions. The Franciscan Bernardino Amico, for example,

---

[8] Giuliano Gliozzi, *Adamo e il nuovo mondo* (Florence: La nuova Italia editrice, 1977); James Romm, 'Biblical History and the Americas: The Legend of Solomon's Ophir, 1492–1591', in Paolo Bernardini and Norman Fiering (eds), *The Jews and the Expansion of Europe to the West, 1450 to 1800* (New York: Berghahn Books, 2001), 27–46.

[9] Arnaldo Momigliano, 'Ancient History and the Antiquarian', *Journal of the Warburg and Courtauld Institutes*, 13 (1950): 285–315; Peter N. Miller, 'The "Antiquarianization" of Biblical Scholarship and the London Polyglot Bible (1653–57)', *Journal of the History of Ideas*, 62 (2001): 463–82.

drew elegant views and carefully measured architectural plans of the sacred sites in Jerusalem.[10]

Maps, too, played a central role in this antiquarian culture, as the example of Abraham Ortelius (1527–98) clearly (but not uniquely) shows.[11] Maps of the Holy Land, or views of Jerusalem and the Temple, presenting measured, visual documentation, as well as being antiquarian products, aimed at a growing cartographically literate curious public. Early modern biblical maps, even if still closely tied to scripture, quickly adopted the new representational ideals of Renaissance cartography. They were now regional maps that showed north at the top and had gridded borders and a scale. Scholars used these newly designed maps to argue questions in sacred geography, such as the itineraries of the Apostles, or the location of the terrestrial Paradise.[12]

Confessional strife in the wake of the Reformation also distinguished early modern sacred geography, although it is hard and at times futile to draw clear lines and arguments separating the Catholic and Protestant camps. The study of geography was often coloured and energized by the tense amalgam of erudition and devotion that characterized biblical and ecclesiastical scholarship as a whole. Franciscan publications, such as Amico's and other Franciscan-inspired publications, not only documented the sacred topography of Jerusalem, but also defended the authenticity of the holy sites and the traditions related to them, against severe Protestant critics.[13] Similarly, especially during the seventeenth century, the Jesuits, Augustinians, and other monastic orders created atlases that portrayed their global reach. Together with lavish map murals, such as the Vatican's *Galleria delle carte geographiche*, these works presented a continual, well-ordered, and global Catholic space.[14]

On the other hand, Protestant geographical-historical studies doubted this alleged continuity. For example, the Genevan scholar Jacques Godefroy (1587–1652) attacked the expansive territorial presumptions of the Bishop of Rome by scrutinizing the fourth-century limits of the Pope's jurisdiction. Needless to say, according to Godefroy, that jurisdiction was very limited.[15] In terms of methods and reasoning, however, these geographical battles raged on common antiquarian ground. We certainly cannot point to literal-minded Protestant geography arguing against allegorical Catholic readings.[16] Sacred geography clearly captivated scholars on both sides of the confessional divide. All employed their erudition in

---

[10] Bernardino Amico, *Trattato de sacri edificii di Terra Santa* (Rome, 1609; Florence, 1620).

[11] Tine L. Meganck, 'Erudite Eyes: Artists and Antiquarians in the Circle of Abraham Ortelius' (Ph.D. thesis, Princeton University, 2003). George Tolias, 'Ptolemy's *Geography* and Early Modern Antiquarian Practices', in Zur Shalev and Charles Burnett (eds), *Ptolemy's 'Geography' in the Renaissance* (London: Warburg Institute, 2011), 121–42; Adam Beaver, 'Scholarly Pilgrims: Antiquarian Visions of the Holy Land', in Katherine van Liere, Simon Ditchfield, and Howard Louthan (eds), *Sacred History: Uses of the Christian Past in the Renaissance World* (Oxford: Oxford University Press, 2012), 267–83.

[12] Alessandro Scafi, *Mapping Paradise: A History of Heaven on Earth* (Chicago: University of Chicago Press, 2006).

[13] Franciscus Quaresmius, *Historica theologica et moralis Terræ Sanctæ elucidatio* (Antwerp, 1639); Heinrich Bünting, *Itinerarium et chronicon ecclesiasticum totius sacræ scripturæ* (Magdeburg, 1597).

[14] Francesca Fiorani, *The Marvel of Maps: Art, Cartography and Politics in Renaissance Italy* (New Haven: Yale University Press, 2005); François de Dainville, *Cartes anciennes de l'église de France: Historique—répertoire—guide d'usage* (Paris: J. Vrin, 1956).

[15] Simon Ditchfield, 'Text Before Trowel: Antonio Bosio's *Roma sotterranea* Revisited', in R. N. Swanson (ed.), *The Church Retrospective, Studies in Church History*, 33 (1997): 343–60.

[16] Cf. Frank Lestringant, Introduction to André Thevet, *Cosmographie de Levant* (Geneva: Droz, 1985), pp. lxi–lxiv.

creative ways, whether to argue a historical-theological point, or to find spiritual meaning in geography and cartography. Especially in the seventeenth century, we can find examples of mutual respect and citation among Catholic and Protestant scholars.[17]

Geographia sacra was a rich scholarly genre in which many central figures of the European republic of letters engaged. As such it was deeply embedded in the learned humanist, antiquarian, and scientific culture of the time, while in constant dialogue with exegetical traditions. It was a major tool, or even mode of thinking, for biblical and ecclesiastical scholars, who in a sense had taken the spatial turn long before us. The church was the primary patron of geographical learning, both sacred and secular, as far as the two could be separated. The revival of classical geography together with the new discoveries gave a new impetus to sacred geography as a powerful interpretative tool for the global role of Christianity.[18]

In the following section I shall illustrate the uses and scope of early modern sacred geography by looking a little more closely at one typical question that attracted the attention of many authors at the time: the fertility of Palestine. The Promised Land, a fertile land of milk and honey, embodies ideas of election and providence. The rich land stands at the centre of God's troubled relations with the Israelites, His chosen people. It is promised to the Patriarchs and to Moses as a reward, then ungratefully rejected by the people in the desert, given to another generation, then taken away and made desolate. Let us be reminded of some representative biblical expressions of the theme:

> And I am come down to deliver them out of the hand of the Egyptians, and to bring them up out of that land unto a good land and a large, unto a land flowing with milk and honey.[19] (Exodus 3: 8 (the burning bush))

> And they told him, and said, We came unto the land whither thou sentest us, and surely it floweth with milk and honey; and this is the fruit of it. Nevertheless the people be strong that dwell in the land, and the cities are walled, and very great: and moreover we saw the children of Anak there. … But the men that went up with him said, We be not able to go up against the people; for they are stronger than we. (Numbers 13: 27–32 (the spies))

> Behold, the day of the LORD cometh, cruel both with wrath and fierce anger, to lay the land desolate: and he shall destroy the sinners thereof out of it. (Isaiah 13: 9)

Such references to a promised land, 'God's land', or the 'good land', pervade the whole biblical corpus. Not surprisingly, this theme drew the attention of exegetes from antiquity to our own age. Babylonian rabbis, for example, both challenged and exaggerated the privileged status of the Land of Israel (*Eretz Israel*). Voltaire and Gibbon in the eighteenth century took several shots at the Promised Land and described it as less fortunate than Mesopotamia or Wales, respectively.[20] Even today's religio-political discourse both in and outside Israel/

---

[17] For example, the Jesuit Jacques Bonfrère's work on the geography of the Holy Land was included in Walton's *London Polyglot*.

[18] David Livingstone, 'Science, Magic, and Religion: A Contextual Reassessment of Geography in the Sixteenth and Seventeenth Centuries', *History of Science*, 26 (1988): 269–94.

[19] All biblical citations are taken from the 1611 KJB.

[20] Dan Ben Amos, 'Talmudic Tall Tales', in Linda Dégh, Henry Glassie, and Felix J. Oinas (eds), *Folklore Today: A Festschrift for Richard M. Dorson* (Bloomington, Ind.: Research Center for Language and Semiotic

Palestine is heavily laden with notions of promise, cultivation, and fertility, which serve a whole spectrum of political motivations. Here I focus on the early modern manifestations of the debate on the land's physical fertility. By debate I mean the range of expressed views on the question, and not necessarily a pointed exchange between specific individuals, although, as we shall see, some such cases are also to be found.

The divine promise and its fulfilment in the land was one of the central questions that preoccupied early modern scholars well into the late seventeenth century. On the one hand, travellers and pilgrims often (although not always) described the harsh and barren terrain of the area. On the other hand, such reports were at times ignored, refuted, or contended with in creative and therefore revealing ways. The question, as developed at the time by biblical scholars and geographers, presents a mix of exegetic, providential, political, and natural-historical concerns that is unique to early modern sacred geography and to biblical culture as a whole.

The large literary corpus of pilgrimage and travel narratives supplied important eye-witness reports about the physical reality of the land of promise qua contemporary Palestine. During the early modern period, travel accounts, including pilgrimage, increasingly valued detailed descriptions based on personal visual observation and testimony (autopsy) over mere repetition of textual authorities. Early fifteenth-century antiquarians who travelled the Mediterranean described natural landscapes and human monuments with growing attention to historical precision and on-site measurement.[21] Pilgrims to Jerusalem, too, enriched their written accounts—now widely circulating in printed editions and in multiple languages—with rich textual and visual testimonies. However, in the context of Holy Land pilgrimage, witnessing often meant looking for another kind of evidence. Pilgrims who followed Christ's path were witnesses to biblical truths and events. They were at times engaging the sacred text rather than the land itself, and they used their sight and their mind's eye to remember and re-enact, as it were, the heightened scenes of sacred history.[22] This textual/territorial duality manifested itself both on-site, as part of the pilgrims' devout routine, and later, during the composition of the narrative. In other words, we cannot read any pilgrim pronouncement on the fertility of the Promised Land as direct evidence regarding crops, streams, and climate conditions.

This basic tension surfaces already in Burchard of Mt. Sion, a Dominican who had extensively travelled the region in the 1280s and left a detailed and widely circulated description that was still influential well into the seventeenth century.[23] Burchard's account strongly confirmed the Promised Land's fertility:

> Now, you must know that, as a matter of fact, the whole of the Holy Land was, and is at this day, the best of all lands, albeit some who have not carefully regarded it say the contrary. It is very fertile in corn, which is tilled and grown with scarce any labour ....

Studies, Indiana University, 1976), 25–43; Voltaire, *Dictionnaire philosophique* (1764), s.v. Abraham. Edward Gibbon, *The History of the Decline and Fall of the Roman Empire*, i (London: William Strahan & Thomas Cadell, 1776), 1.

[21] For example, Francesco Scalamonti, *Vita viri clarissimi et famosissimi Kyriaci Anconitani*, ed. Charles Mitchell and Edward W. Bodnar, Transactions of the American Philosophical Society, 86/4 (Philadelphia: American Philosophical Society, 1996).

[22] On late antiquity see Georgia Frank, *The Memory of the Eyes: Pilgrims to Living Saints in Christian Late Antiquity* (Berkeley, Calif.: University of California Press, 2000).

[23] For example, Kaspar Peucer, *De dimensione terrae* (Wittenberg, 1554), which appended Burchard's description.

> The wine of the Holy Land is very good and noble, especially round about Bethlehem, in the Valley of Rephaim, and so on, from whence the children of Israel bore the branch on a staff.[24]

Burchard highlights his status as a careful observer and collector of facts in order to substantiate his report and justify his praise of the land's richness. Indeed Burchard is regarded today as one of the most factually valuable written sources on medieval Palestine. At the same time, for the modern historian, it reveals that the fertility of the land was an open question during the later years of the crusader Kingdom of Jerusalem—the land had its detractors. Moreover, it is crucially important to note Burchard's reference to the biblical spies sent by Moses to survey the land. The spies function not only as an ancient model for the observer-traveller, but also as humans who mistrusted God's promise despite their first-hand experience which proved it. Burchard, as a travelling sacred geographer, paid close attention to the physical reality of the land, but at the same time experienced it as a question of faith.

The Lutheran physician and botanist Dr Leonhard Rauwolf, who travelled widely in the Levant in the 1570s, mainly in pursuit of medicinal herbs, was no less acute an observer than Burchard.[25] However, he pronounced differently on the question. In the context of his visit to Jerusalem, Rauwolf remarked that the land had the natural features and potential to be very fertile:

> This holy Land … was … a most fruitful and rich Country, abounding with Corn, Fruits, Wine and all that is required to the maintenance of Man's Life. So the Lord himself saith, *That he will give them a Land, that still floweth with Milk and Honey.* For it hath rich Valleys, Hills, Fields, and Gardens, richly adorned with Fountains and Trees, so that it was very well chosen to be the worldly Paradise, wherein Adam and Eve did live, honor and serve God ….
>
> But when they [the Israelites] would not acknowledge his merciful Visitation, nor receive his Messengers … , God did reject and disperse them … and reduced their fruitful country into barren Deserts, and a desolate Wilderness … , which the holy Prophet Esaiah did foretel them (Isaiah 13: 9).[26]

Rauwolf unusually suggested that the Terrestrial Paradise was located in Canaan and not in Mesopotamia. However, the model he proposed—a fertile land which turned sterile by God's punishment—was not unique at all. It was, as the quote from Isaiah demonstrates, embedded in scripture itself. Near Jerusalem, Rauwolf's botanical expedition changed its tone into a sermon-like oration on providence and faith.

Similar remarks are found in the account of the Flemish Catholic pilgrim Jean Zuallart, who undertook a 'most devout voyage' to the Holy Land a few years later. Zuallart observed desolation all around him. Unlike Burchard and Rauwolf, Zuallart spent a very short time in the region, mainly in the area of Jerusalem. His published narrative, however, augmented by materials from the Franciscan keepers of the holy sites, proved to be very influential and its rich illustrations were pillaged by later pilgrims.

---

[24] Burchard of Mt. Sion, *Description of the Holy Land*, tr. Aubrey Stewart (London: Palestine Pilgrims' Text Society, 1897[6]), 99.

[25] See the comprehensive monograph by Karl H. Dannenfeldt, *Leonhard Rauwolf: Sixteenth-Century Physician, Botanist, and Traveler* (Cambridge, Mass.: Harvard University Press, 1968).

[26] Leonhard Rauwolf et al., *A Collection of Curious Travels & Voyages* (London, 1693), 276–7. The original (in German dialect) was published in 1582.

For Zuallart, nothing remained of the land's former fertility but stones, useless herbs, and poisonous snakes. This, Zuallart said, was the Lord's punishment to the opinionated and ungrateful Jews.[27]

Pilgrims and travellers, then, provide a set of conflicting reports. While they claimed authority by appealing to their direct testimony, their judgements were predetermined by, and served to validate scripture. If eye-witness accounts often discussed the fertility of the Promised Land as a moral rather than empirical issue, it is not surprising that those who did not travel at all employed the same approach. A broad range of authors, from exegetes and theologians to political commentators and geographers addressed the issue in various genres: in Bible-related literature, such as commentaries, sermons, and specialized treatises, as well as in general geographical, historical, and political texts.

The above-mentioned Arias Montano, for example, discussed the qualities of Canaan in a special treatise appended to the Antwerp Polyglot Bible.[28] The Polyglot—a major scholarly collective enterprise undertaken at Christophe Plantin's printing house under the auspices of Philip II—included an extensive three-volume *Apparatus* of linguistic, historical, and geographical surveys and reading aids. Montano's treatise on Canaan, which included a large and nicely executed map, emphasized the unusual power of nature in the land. Despite its humble size, Montano argued, it was able to support thirty-one kingdoms. Canaan's uneven mountainous landscape, he conjectured, significantly enlarged its land surface and enabled the procreation of animals and plants. Canaan, continually under God's caring eyes (Deut. 11: 12), was meant for pleasant life defined by worship and love of God. Its inhabitants, however, first the Canaanites and then the Israelites, did not appreciate their blessings.[29] Thus, as opposed to Rauwolf and Zuallart, Montano implies that the land itself never lost its divine powers. Only its inhabitants fell out of God's favour. Despite Montano's semi-naturalistic explanations of the fertility of the Promised Land, his main goal was to encourage joint textual-visual reflection on the Holy Land as an emblem of providence and faith. The prolific Thomas Fuller (1608–61), a popularizer of sacred geography, repeated Montano's view in *Pisgah-Sight of Palestine*: '[T]he land may passe for the quintessence of fruitfullnesse it self. So that what it lacked in length and breadth, it had in depth, as if nature had heaped on acre upon another in the matchlesse fertility thereof' (Figure 12.1).[30]

By insisting on the land's perpetual fertility Montano was indirectly arguing against the views expressed by another Spanish scholar, Michel Servetus, who had ended his life at the stake (27 October 1553), after a notorious heresy trial in Calvin's Geneva. Among many demonstrations of Servetus's unorthodox views during his trial was a short comment he had printed in an edition of Ptolemy's *Geography* (Lyons, 1535), next to a map of the Holy Land:

---

[27] Jean Zuallart, *Le tresdeuot voyage de Jerusalem* (Antwerp, 1608), book 1, ch. 7, 49: 'Et ne faict rien si la susdite terre de promission, n'est tant feconde & fertile, comme au temps passé, ains sterile, pierreuse, & abiecte, les Citez desertes, & les champs ne produisans que chardons, & herbes inutiles, des Serpens & animaux nuisibles: car tout cela provient de la malediction que Dieu à donnee aux Iuifz, peuple rebelle, opiniastre & ingrate'.

[28] The most recent comprehensive work on Montano and the Polyglot is Theodor W. Dunkelgrün, 'The Multiplicity of Scripture: The Confluence of Textual Traditions in the Making of the Antwerp Polyglot Bible (1568–1573)' (Ph.D. thesis, University of Chicago, 2012).

[29] See reprint in Benito Arias Montano, *Antiquitates Judaicae* (Leiden, 1593), 52–4.

[30] Fuller, *Pisgah-Sight*, 6.

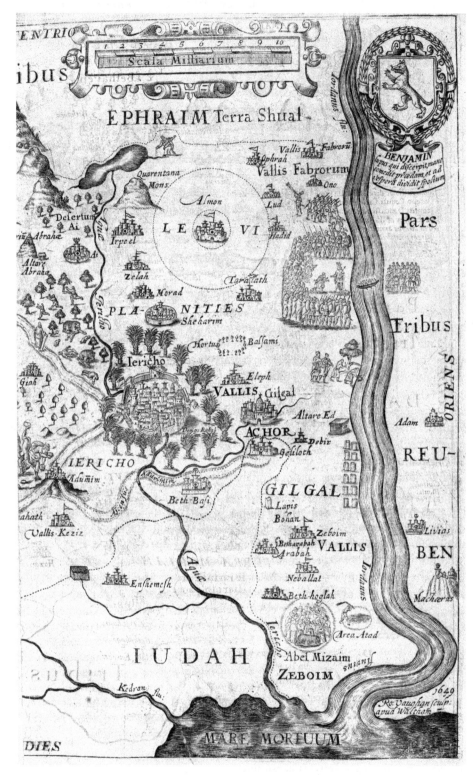

FIGURE 12.1 The 'Map of Benjamin' from Thomas Fuller, *A Pisgah-Sight of Palestine* (London, printed by JF for John Williams, 1650), 238–9. Note the verdant vegetation surrounding the walls of Jericho. York Minster Library: OL; XXXVI.B.6.

Nevertheless be assured, reader, that it is sheer misinterpretation to attribute such excellence to this land which the experience of merchants and travellers proves to be barren, sterile and without charm, so that you may call it in the vernacular 'the promised land' only in the sense that it was promised, not that it had any promise.[31]

In his defence Servetus rightly insisted that these were not his own words but those of a previous editor; that in his second Ptolemy edition (Vienne, 1541) the paragraph was omitted; and that it did not refer to biblical times but to contemporary Palestine. The accusation was eventually dropped from the final sentence, which had enough other items to rely on. However, this unusually dramatic clash over a seemingly minor, half-humorous, and quite common remark calls to our attention first the broader and grave political context of biblical scholarship, *geographia sacra* included. Secondly, a closer look demonstrates that this was not simply a case of Genevan literalism in defence of scripture. The casual note in Ptolemy hints at a more complex picture, that has yet to be fully elaborated. A partial answer could be found in Calvin's *Sermons on Deuteronomy*, delivered three years after the execution of Servetus.

Calvin read the Promised Land's fertility in the context of God's grace and the obligation of believers to acknowledge His gifts. It would seem that Calvin was minimally interested in the land's actual fertility as a natural phenomenon, whether past or present. Rather, he emphasized what it stood for. In his sermon on Deuteronomy 27 he says:

> We know that at this day it is not so fruitfull a land, neither was it so fertill before their coming thither, and that is a wonderful thing.[32]

And again in the sermon on Deuteronomy 32:

> And no doubt but he [Moses] meant here to magnifie Gods goodnes, by declaring that he passed the common order of nature when he had such a care to sustaine his people so welthily in that lande which a man woulde never have thought able to do it.[33]

Calvin required no naturalistic explanation that had to do with particular features of the Land. The improbable richness of this dry region during its Israelite phase was, in other words, an ongoing miracle. Servetus's error, much like that of the spies before him, who witnessed at first hand God's favour and rejected it, was mockery of the actual promise:

> And yet notwithstanding the wicked have taken occasion here upon, to blaspheme, as that wicked heritike which was punished here, mocked both Moses and the prophets saying, that when they praised the land of Chanaan, they did but fable. Yea but he sheweth himselfe (as all

---

[31] 'Scias tamen lector optime, iniuria aut iactantia pura, tantam huic terrae bonitatem fuisse adscriptam, eo que ipsa experientia, mercatorum & peraegre profiscentium, hanc incultam, sterilem, omni dulcedine carentem depromit. Quare promissam terram pollicitam, & non vernacula lingua laudantem pronuncies.' *Claudii Ptolemaei Alexandrini geographicae enarrationis libri octo* (Lyons, 1535), TAB. TER. SANCTAE. I use the translation of Roland H. Bainton, *Hunted Heretic: The Life and Death of Michael Servetus, 1511–1553* (Boston: Beacon Press, 1960), 95, ch. 10. For more documents from the trial see Robert M. Kingdon and Jean-François Bergier (eds), *Registres de la Compagnie des pasteurs de Genève au temps de Calvin*, Travaux d'humanisme et Renaissance, 55 (Genève: Droz, 1962), ii. 3–54.

[32] Jean Calvin, *The Sermons of M. Iohn Calvin Upon the Fifth Booke of Moses Called Deuteronomie*, tr. Arthur Golding (London, 1583), 920.

[33] Calvin, *Sermons*, 1124.

despisers of God & such enraged folke whom Satan possesseth use to do) to skorne Gods benefits which men may see with their eyes.[34]

Like the stubborn Israelites, who had rejected God's grace, Servetus was contemptuous of it. The sermon on Deuteronomy 32, again:

> [T]hat cursed heretike which was executed heere among vs; was not ashamed to write in one of his books that the land of Chanaan is indeede spoken of, howbeit over favourablie, and that they which have so spoken thereof, have made us to beleeve many things unadvisedly. And what caused him so to do, but that he was a worldly man and a despiser of God, seeking by all meanes to skorne God, and to abolish his grace, and that men might no more knowe how to worship him?

Calvin, in other words, probably realized that Servetus, like himself, placed the Promised Land and its fruitfulness within a larger theological framework. As G. H. Williams showed half a century ago, Canaan, as Paradise, played an important role in Servetus's problematic baptismal theology.[35] Alessandro Scafi suggested that Calvin's insistence that Paradise was located in Mesopotamia may have been in response to Servetus's formulation. Ironically perhaps, Calvin probably used Servetus's Ptolemy edition for his geographical reconstruction of Eden.[36] The factual reality of Canaan was less significant than what it represented in a broader scheme of faith, grace, and salvation. Indeed the biblical-promise topos in itself (especially in the story of the spies, Numbers 13, Deuteronomy 1) is construed around the question of God's relations with His people. In other words, while these passages in Calvin's sermons on Deuteronomy may reflect a post-factum justification of Servetus's execution, they also disclose that more was at stake around the question of promise and fertility than literal-empirical analysis.

Another editor of Ptolemy, Sebastian Münster (1488–1552), also addressed the question. Münster, the prolific Hebraist and cosmographer, added to his fourth edition of the *Geography* (1552) a geographical appendix. The appendix described the inhabitants, customs, rites, as well as the natural qualities of various kingdoms and provinces. Discussing his native Germany, Münster argued for what we might call *translatio fertilitatis*—natural elements, he explained, obey God's word, which blesses and punishes lands and peoples. The once plentiful land of promise has turned into a barely habitable desert of thorns and briars. Germany on the other hand, whose past had been barbarous and infertile, was now a large, fertile land, inhabited by resourceful people.[37] Münster's use of 'thorns and briars' (*spinis et tribulis*) alludes to Gideon's punishment of the elders of Succoth, who had refused him help and mistrusted God's promised victory over Midian.[38] As Matthew McLean has

---

[34] Calvin, *Sermons*, 920–1.

[35] George H. Williams, *Wilderness and Paradise in Christian Thought* (New York: Harper, 1962), 71–2.

[36] Alessandro Scafi, 'After Ptolemy: The Mapping of Eden', in Zur Shalev and Charles Burnett (eds), *Ptolemy's Geography in the Renaissance* (London: Warburg Institute, 2011), 187–206.

[37] 'Sic enim videmus mutatam fertilitatem terrae promissionis propter peccata populi, ut hodie vix sit habilis spinis & tribulis ferendis. Et contra, Germania quae scribitur olim fuisse barbara, horrida & infoecunda, semper aüt bellicosa aliisque populis fortior, ut solet esse gens laboribus indurata et exercitata, parumque civilibus imbuta moribus, visitata a domino universae terrae ex gratia eius talis facta est regio, ut vix unquam alia fuerit, vel fertilior magisque habilis ad omne genus fructus producendos, vel felicior ingeniorum animorumque bonitate, magnitudine et praestantia.' *Geographiae Claudij Ptolemæi Alexandrini* (Basel, 1552), Appendix geographica, 169.

[38] Judges 8: 7, 16. Cf. Matt. 7: 16 and parallels (thorns will not bear fruit).

shown, Münster's *Cosmography*, his more famous and widely read publication, presents a panorama of human history and geography which is governed by this providential principle. Empires rise and fall, once famous cities disappear, and fertile lands become arid.[39]

Following Münster's lead, the literary genre of cosmography in the later sixteenth and in the seventeenth centuries enabled discussion of fertility as a category in a variety of political, economic, natural historical, as well as religious contexts. The analysis of kingdoms in terms of cultivation and population, the call to colonize new promised lands across the ocean, or the theology of improvement and husbandry—all inherited elements that had developed earlier in the context of biblical scholarship and *geographia sacra*, though these broader contexts are beyond the scope of this chapter.[40]

The discourse around the fertility of the Promised Land in early modern Europe was varied and not easily reduced to clear groupings. Both travellers and stationary scholars, both Catholics and Protestants, both Spanish and English authors, pronounced on the subject in different ways and genres that are not always related to these epithets. The discussion on fertility during the early modern period was at times reliant on direct observations or naturalistic conjectures, and made use of the most advanced tools a geographer could employ at the time. Ultimately, however, it aimed at a moral interpretation. This was embedded in the biblical narrative itself, and eagerly adopted by scholars who operated in religiously charged environments. The debate was thus less about the factual veracity of the biblical text—there were no real affronts to its authority at the time, Servetus included. Rather, it was more involved in promoting a certain vision of the Promised Land as an emblem of divine promise more generally.

In the later seventeenth century and during the eighteenth, typical questions in sacred geography—the location of Paradise, the route of the Israelites in the desert, the itineraries of the Apostles—still occupied biblical scholars and geographers. Biblical maps were printed in ever increasing numbers and diverse formats, alongside weighty tomes of compilations on sacred geography. Scholars, including Gibbon, relied on the scholarship of earlier workers in the field. However, by that time, sacred geography has lost some of its polemical edge, a characteristic that was so prominent in the age of fresh geographical and theological discoveries.

FURTHER READING

Blair, Ann. 'Mosaic Physics and the Search for a Pious Natural Philosophy in the Late Renaissance'. *Isis*, 91 (2000): 32–58.

Büttner, Manfred. 'The Significance of the Reformation for the Reorientation of Geography in Lutheran Germany'. *History of Science*, 17 (1979): 151–69.

---

[39] Matthew McLean, *The Cosmographia of Sebastian Münster: Describing the World in the Reformation* (Aldershot: Ashgate, 2007). On the tradition of patriotic German humanism, see Gerald Strauss, *Sixteenth-Century Germany: Its Topography and Topographers* (Madison, Wis.: University of Wisconsin Press, 1959).

[40] John M. Headley, 'Geography and Empire in the Late Renaissance: Botero's Assignment, Western Universalism, and the Civilization Process', *Renaissance Quarterly*, 53 (2000): 1119–55; Perry Miller, *Errand into the Wilderness* (Cambridge, Mass.: Belknap Press, 1956); J. A Bennett and Scott Mandelbrote, *The Garden, the Ark, the Tower, the Temple: Biblical Metaphors of Knowledge in Early Modern Europe* (Oxford: Museum of the History of Science in association with the Bodleian Library, 1998).

Edson, Evelyn. *Mapping Time and Space: How Medieval Mapmakers Viewed their World* (London: British Library, 1997).

Johnson, Trevor. 'Gardening for God: Carmelite Deserts and the Sacralisation of Natural Space in Counter-Reformation Spain', in Will Coster and Andrew Spicer (eds), *Sacred Space in Early Modern Europe* (Cambridge: Cambridge University Press, 2005), 193–210.

Karrow, Robert W., Jr. *Mapmakers of the Sixteenth Century and their Maps: Bio-Bibliographies of the Cartographers of Abraham Ortelius, 1570* (Chicago: Speculum Orbis Press, 1993).

Melion, Walter S. '*Ad ductum itineris et dispositionem mansionum ostendendam*: Meditation, Vocation, and Sacred History in Abraham Ortelius's "Parergon"'. *Journal of the Walters Art Gallery*, 57 (1999): 49–72.

Nice, Jason A. '"The Peculiar Place of God": Early Modern Representations of England and France'. *English Historical Review*, 121/493 (2006): 1002–18.

Noonan, Thomas F. *The Road to Jerusalem: Pilgrimage and Travel in the Age of Discovery* (Philadelphia: University of Pennsylvania Press, 2007).

Rubin, Rehav. *Image and Reality: Jerusalem in Maps and Views* (Jerusalem: Hebrew University Magnes Press, 1999).

Shalev, Zur. *Sacred Words and Worlds: Geography, Religion, and Scholarship, 1550–1700* (Leiden: Brill, 2012).

Smith, Catherine Delano, and Elizabeth M. Ingram. *Maps in Bibles, 1500–1600: An Illustrated Catalogue* (Genève: Droz, 1991).

Spicer, Andrew, and Sarah Hamilton, eds. *Defining the Holy: Sacred Space in Medieval and Early Modern Europe* (Aldershot: Ashgate, 2005).

Watts, Pauline Moffitt. 'The European Religious Worldview and its Influence on Mapping', in David Woodward (ed.), *The History of Cartography*, iii. *Cartography in the European Renaissance* (Chicago: University of Chicago Press, 2007), 382–400.

....

CHAPTER 13

MILTON'S CORRUPT BIBLE

....

NEIL FORSYTH

LIKE most other serious Christians of the early modern period, Milton knew quite well that the text of the Bible was untrustworthy. That was why Catholics argued for a parallel church tradition alongside the holy word. As Thomas More pointed out in his argument with the Bible translator, William Tyndale, some of the scripture has been lost, and we cannot know how much; parts of what we have are 'corrupted with mysse wrytynge'.[1] This argument generated a lot of heat and strength of feeling. Thomas More is often given credit for being the more polished writer, but he rather loses his polish when attacking Tyndale in less-than-saintly mode: 'Judge, good Christian reader, whether it be possible that he be any better than a beast, out of whose brutish beastly mouth cometh such a filthy foam of blasphemies against Christ's holy ceremonies and blessed sacraments'.[2] The reason for More's venom is evidently Tyndale's distrust of priests as transmitters of the Gospel and consequent insistence on *sola scriptura*, that only the written word of the Bible has any authority. For More, the faith of Christ came to the Apostles by preaching: it was written by his holy hand in men's hearts, or 'rather . . . written in the lyvely myndes of men/than in ye dede skynnes of bestes'. That part of Christian faith was not in question, he argued, but what had come down as 'the Bible' certainly was. It needed a priesthood to explain it.[3]

One only had to open a Bible to recognize how much corruption there was. Bibles were soon being printed on cheap paper, with the result that many errors were mass-produced: a notorious example is the 1631 King James Bible known as 'The Wicked Bible' because it made the seventh commandment 'Thou shalt commit adultery'. Another, also sometimes known as the Wicked Bible, omits a 'not' before the word 'inherit', making 1 Corinthians 6: 9 read 'Know ye not that the unrighteous shall inherit the kingdom of God?'[4] Edward Leigh, an

---

[1] Thomas More, 'Dialogue Concerning Heresies', ed. Thomas M. C. Lawler, Germain Marc'hadour, and Richard C. Marius, in *Complete Works of St Thomas More* (New Haven: Yale University Press, 1963–97, 1981), vi. 115. See further R. I. Lakowski, 'The Dialogue Concerning Heresies', *Interactive Early Modern Literary Studies* (1995), <http://extra.shu.ac.uk/emls/iemls/work/chapters/heresy1.html#BT4>; and Matthew DeCoursey, 'The Thomas More/William Tyndale Polemic', *Early Modern Literary Studies*, Texts Series, 3 (2010), <http://purl.org/emls/moretyndale.pdf>.

[2] More, 'The Confutation of Tyndale's Answer' (1532–3), ed. Louis A. Schuster, Richard C. Marius, and James P. Lusardi, in *Complete Works* (1973), viii. 38.

[3] More, 'Dialogue', vi. 144.

[4] These and similar examples are quoted in Gordon Campbell, *Bible: The Story of the King James Version 1611–2011* (Oxford: Oxford University Press, 2010), 3.

MP and lay theologian, worries about all this in his 1646 *A Treatise of Divinity Consisting of Three Books* where he says that because of this sort of thing 'the Papists stile the Scripture … the black Gospell, inky Divinity'.[5] Protestants, that is, following the doctrine of *sola scriptura,* turn the Bible into an idolatrous divinity made of ink. Leigh was aware that many doubts about the authority of scripture persist 'till we be taught it of God, till the Holy Spirit of God have inwardly certified and sealed it'.[6]

Conservative churchmen like Thomas Edwards in his venomous *Gangraena,* also of 1646, denounced such statements, although in practice many of his opponents were even more radical. Puritans like William Walwyn, Gerrard Winstanley, George Fox, Samuel Fisher, and Clement Writer exemplified a crisis of confidence in the scriptural basis of faith.[7] The revolutionary ferment of mid-seventeenth-century England encouraged radical ideas to flourish and circulate. Isaac La Peyrère, for example, claimed that 'men had existed for countless aeons before Adam' and that the Bible story was just about Jews.[8] Stephen Nye, a Socinian, was soon arguing that the God represented by the creation narrative has 'the *just* Character of an Almighty Devil. For if the Devil had Supream Power, what worse could he do?'[9]

There are many contemporary instances of such anxiety about the text of the Bible. A friend of Milton's, John Goodwin, in his *Divine Authority of the Scriptures Asserted* (1648), attacked 'Antiscripturism' for destroying the faith of many. Yet he stood by the claims made in his *Hagiomastix or the Scourge of the Saints* (1647) that the scriptures were not the foundation of Christian religion: neither English translations nor the extant Greek and Hebrew manuscripts were the word of God, 'great benefactours unto the world' though they were. The translations differed among themselves and so must also differ from the original texts, no longer extant. The impeccable Word of God could not be identified with imperfect texts, although they might, he suggested in a brilliant phrase, be considered as the cup that contained the wine of the Gospel. 'The true and proper foundation of Christian Religion' was not 'inke and paper' but the substance of the Gospel.[10]

---

[5] Edward Leigh, *A Treatise of Divinity* (London, 1646), 23–4, G4ᵛ. The phrase is quoted in Joshua Calhoun, 'The Word Made Flax: Cheap Bibles, Textual Corruption, and the Poetics of Paper', *PMLA* 126 (2011): 331.

[6] Quoted in John Coffey, *John Goodwin and the Puritan Revolution* (Woodbridge: Boydell & Brewer, 2006), 157.

[7] Clement Wrighter e.g. was 'an anti-Scripturist, a Questionist and Sceptick, and I fear an Atheist': Edwards, *Gangraena* (London, 1646), i. 96, quoted in Coffey, *John Goodwin,* 154.

[8] Isaac La Peyrère, *A Theological Systeme upon That Presupposition, That Men Were before Adam* (London, 1655), 2.10.112–17, quoted in Jeffrey L. Morrow, 'Pre-Adamites, Politics and Criticism: Isaac La Peyrère's Contribution to Modern Biblical Studies', *Journal of the Orthodox Center for the Advancement of Biblical Studies,* 4 (2011): 9–11. La Peyrère's work was circulating in manuscript in 1640s, and may have influenced Hobbes. He writes in a similar vein: 'Moses is there read to have died. For how could Moses write after his death? They say that Josuah added the death of Moses to Deuteronomie. But, who added the death of Josuah to that book which is so call'd; and which, being written by Josuah himself, is reckon'd in Moses his Pentateuch?' *Theological Systeme,* 4.1.205. La Peyrère also anticipated the theory that there were two creation stories in Genesis: see Philip C. Almond, 'Adam, Pre-Adamites, and Extra-Terrestrial Beings in Early Modern Europe', *Journal of Religious History,* 30/2 (2006): 166–8; and *Adam and Eve in Seventeenth-Century Thought* (Cambridge: Cambridge University Press, 1999), 53. Many such opinions are collected in William Poole, *Milton and the Idea of the Fall* (Oxford: Oxford University Press, 2005), this one on 4–5.

[9] Stephen Nye, *The Trinitarian Scheme of Religion Concerning Almighty God; and Mankind Considered Both before and after the (Pretended) Fall* (London, 1692), quoted in Poole, *Milton,* 17.

[10] Goodwin, *The Divine Authority of the Scriptures Asserted* (London, 1648), a4ᵛ, quoted in Coffey, *John Goodwin,* 156–7. Coffey shows that Goodwin was relatively orthodox in his own views: he did not doubt the authorship of the Pentateuch, nor the great age of the Patriarchs, nor the young age of the earth. He thought

The most far-reaching of these critiques was that of Thomas Hobbes. He shows in chapter 33 of *Leviathan* (1651) that the five books of Moses, the Pentateuch, could not have been written by Moses. Hobbes queries, for example, how Moses could write that his own tomb had not been found, as he does in the last chapter of Deuteronomy, 'wherein he was yet living'. Genesis 12: 6 says that Abraham passed through when 'the Canaanite was then in the land; which must needs bee the words of one that wrote when the Canaanite was not in the land; and consequently, not of Moses, who dyed before he came into it'.[11]

Milton knew but did not like Hobbes, and as usual went his own way. If its introductory epistle to the reader is to be believed, he spent much of his adult life writing at various times an immense theological treatise, *De doctrina Christiana*. Although he never makes the more radical kind of Hobbesian argument questioning the authorship of the biblical narratives, he was clearly aware of the controversy. He shows for example that, because of the mention of the Sabbath at Genesis 2: 2–3, Moses must have written the book of Genesis long after the giving of the law on Sinai.[12] Elsewhere in *De doctrina*, he writes as follows: 'Apparently not all the instructions which the apostles gave the churches were written down, or if they were written down they have not survived', and he then goes even further, to argue that scripture, 'particularly the New Testament, has often been liable to corruption and is, in fact, corrupt ("saepe corrumpi potuit, et corrupta est"). This has come about because it has been committed to the care of various untrustworthy authorities, has been collected together from an assortment of divergent manuscripts, and has survived in a medley of transcripts and editions'.[13]

This is the process that leads to transcription errors: one amusing passage in the 1612 Bible, Psalm 119: 161, which ought to read 'Princes have persecuted me without a cause', is made to read 'Printers have persecuted me without a cause'. Or there is another (in a 1611 printing) in which, in Gethsemane, it is Judas, not Jesus, who says 'Sit ye here while I go yonder and pray'.[14] So Milton had good reason to be aware of textual muddle. He refers explicitly to the textual irregularities and corruptions uncovered by Erasmus or Théodore de Bèze. Heretic that he was, Milton was ready to exploit such textual problems against the orthodox view of the Trinity, or to show that the soul is subject to death.[15] He was also ready to offer his own Latin versions, rather than the standard Junius-Tremellius translation, of the biblical proof-texts he used, as when he demonstrated that Elohim, the plural word for *God*, can be

Matthew had begun writing his Gospel just eight years after Christ's ascension, and defended the Trinity and the torments of hell.

[11] Noel Malcolm discusses this emerging critical scholarship on the Bible, including Isaac La Peyrère, Baruch Spinoza, and Richard Simon, in 'Hobbes, Ezra, and the Bible: The History of a Subversive Idea', *Aspects of Hobbes* (Oxford: Oxford University Press, 2002), ch. 12.

[12] *De doctrina Christiana*, ed. Maurice Kelley, in *The Complete Prose Works of John Milton*, gen ed. Don M. Wolfe (New Haven: Yale University Press, 1953–82), vi. 354 (I x). Hereafter *CPW*. For a full discussion, see Jason Rosenblatt, *Torah and Law in 'Paradise Lost'* (Princeton: Princeton University Press, 1994), 71–135.

[13] *CPW* vi. 586–8. In the Latin text printed in *The Works of John Milton*, general ed. Frank Allen Patterson (New York: Columbia University Press, 1931–40), this remark occurs in vol. xvi, ch. 30, pp. 270–4.

[14] Campbell, *Bible*, 3, 112.

[15] For Milton's Latin of Lev. 21: 11, 'animas mortuas' (dead souls) the first translator, Charles Sumner, substituted 'dead body', which is the KJB reading, making nonsense of Milton's point. The Sumner translation is the one reproduced in the Columbia Milton (and now in the recent Oxford edition of Milton's prose), whereas the Yale edition prints the more dependable version by John Carey. For Milton's 'mortalism', see Norman T. Burns, *Christian Mortalism from Tyndale to Milton* (Cambridge, Mass.: Harvard University Press, 1972).

given to angels in scripture, and cited Psalm 8: 5 as *minorem diis*, less than gods, even though Tremellius has *minorem angelis*, and the King James Bible also reads 'lower than the angels'.[16] Recognizing these irregularities, Milton, like many other Protestants, was driven to argue for 'a double scripture', to distinguish the external scripture of the written word from the internal scripture of the Holy Spirit engraved upon the hearts of believers.[17] This separation will produce in the reader of scripture both great confidence, and gnawing anxiety, probably in equal measures.[18] It helps to account for the poet's complex relationship to his Heavenly Muse ('May I express thee unblam'd?'[19]), it allows for Eve's rereading and misreading of what became scripture, and it establishes the gap between meaning and significance[20] that Satan fills, or exploits.

Milton arrived quite early at this view of the Bible. His first extant poem is 'A Paraphrase of *Psalm* 114', composed, he says, at the age of 15. This may be seen as prophetic in that he was later to write the great poems which are, in a sense, paraphrases or extrapolations from the Bible, not only *Paradise Lost,* but *Paradise Regained* and *Samson Agonistes*.[21] Like his fellow Protestants he always scrupulously followed the doctrine of *sola scriptura*, but he put special emphasis on 'the right and responsibility of every Christian to read and interpret scripture for himself'.[22] In his early anti-prelatical tracts, Milton confidently asserted that the scriptures protest 'their own plainness, and perspicuity', so that not only the wise but 'the simple, the poor, the babes', can be usefully instructed.[23] Soon, however, he came to see that this principle encouraged readers to think that unexamined interpretations were 'clear' just because they were 'commonplace'.[24] When he came to write his tracts in favour of divorce in the years 1643 to 1645, he faced a major problem: at Matthew 19: 3–9, Christ appears to forbid divorce except for fornication.[25] And, even worse, Christ appears to argue that the Law of Moses, which was less rigid, has been surpassed: a man who remarries is now said to commit adultery himself. How was Milton to get round this prohibition?

His strategy in *The Doctrine and Discipline of Divorce* is to put the particular text in what he regards as the context, that is to say, the whole Bible read with one principle in mind—charity, 'called the *new Commandment* by St John' (*CPW* ii. 331).[26] If you read the

---

[16] Harris Francis Fletcher, *The Use of the Bible in Milton's Prose* (New York: Haskell House, 1929), 76–7, prints the two versions side by side. Carey calls attention to the verse in his 'Translator's Preface', *CPW* vi. 15.

[17] 'De doctrina', *CPW* vi. 587–90, quoting 2 Cor. 3: 3.

[18] William Kerrigan, *Prophetic Milton* (Charlottesville, Va.: University of Virginia Press, 1974), 125–61, discusses some of these anxieties.

[19] *Paradise Lost*, 3.3. *Paradise Lost* (*PL*) is quoted from *The Riverside Milton*, ed. Roy Flannagan (Boston: Houghton Mifflin, 1998) throughout.

[20] For these terms, see E. D. Hirsch, *The Aims of Textuality* (Chicago: University of Chicago Press, 1976), 1–13, 79–81; for a critique, Frank Lentricchia, *After the New Criticism* (Chicago: University of Chicago Press, 1980), 256–80.

[21] James H. Sims, 'Milton and the Bible', in William B. Hunter et al. (eds), *A Milton Encyclopedia* (Lewisburg: Bucknell University Press, 1978–83), i. 147.

[22] Barbara Lewalski 'Milton, the Bible and Human Experience', *Topoi*, 7 (1988): 221–9.

[23] 'Of Reformation', *CPW* i. 556.

[24] Dayton Haskin, *Milton's Burden of Interpretation* (Philadelphia: University of Pennsylvania Press, 1994), 184.

[25] On this word, as Haskin shows (69), Milton in a later divorce tract, *Tetrachordon*, turns philologist, moving across Hebrew, Latin, and Greek, arguing that it means not only trespass of body but 'any notable disobedience, or intractable carriage of the wife to the husband' (*CPW* ii. 672).

[26] See Regina M. Schwartz, 'Milton on the Bible', in Thomas N. Corns (ed.), *A Companion to Milton* (Oxford: Blackwell, 2001), 42.

prohibition on divorce in the light of Christ's overriding principle of charity, it can't mean what it says. 'There is scarce any one saying in the Gospel, but must be read with limitation and distinction, to be rightly understood; for Christ gives no full comments or continu'd discourses, but scatters the heavenly grain of his doctrin like pearle heer and there, which requires a skilful and laborious gatherer' (*CPW* ii. 338). So although Christian liberty means that Christ 'frees us from the slavery of sin and thus from the rule of the law', that is, the Law of Moses, he cannot have meant to rescind the Mosaic permission to divorce and remarry, which is 'a grave and prudent Law, full of moral equity, full of due consideration toward nature' (*De doctrina, CPW* vi. 537). Comparing the two texts makes clear that one is to be read in the light of the other. And the words 'grave and prudent' are obviously designed to appeal to his Puritan readers. The Mosaic law of Deuteronomy 24: 1 ('let him write her a bill of divorcement, and give it in her hand, and send her out of the house'), far from being abrogated by Christ, becomes the central focus of the argument. God even becomes a precedent, in that his method of creation was to make the world rise out of chaos 'by a divorcing command' ('Doctrine and Discipline', *CPW* ii. 272).

Milton's radical interpretation of Christian liberty here allowed him to adopt a variant of what was called the 'experimental' method.[27] The emotional impact of the knowledge acquired from the scriptures was given great importance: it is a serious misinterpretation of scripture by an obstinate *literality* (*CPW* ii. 279) to imagine that it requires us to endure loveless sex, what he calls, with characteristically frank language, a grinding 'in the mill of an undelighted and servil copulation' (ii. 258). What Milton calls earlier in the treatise 'the spur of self-concernment' (ii. 226) has prompted him to reconsider what others still argued were 'the statutes of God'. In fact Christ had often been required by the close-mindedness of his Pharisaic auditors 'to perplex and stumble them with contriv'd obscurities', so that the biblical text became 'not so much a teaching as an intangling'.[28]

Milton continued to put this method into practice, so that in the theological treatise, he constantly compares texts with texts. He called *De doctrina Christiana* 'my dearest and best possession' ('quibus melius aut pretiosius nihil habeo'), and he seems to have worked on it a lot while composing *Paradise Lost* (from 1658).

Like its models among Reformation theologies *De doctrina* is in Latin, and thus addressed to a learned and European audience. Every argument is supported by scriptural citation, sometimes copiously, though often slanted to fit Milton's own heterodox views. His method as he prepared the work was 'to list under general headings all passages from the scriptures which suggested themselves for quotation' (*CPW* vi. 127). And that is also the final form of the treatise. The effect is to disrupt the reading of the Bible, for citations are listed all together as having the same weight and not usually referred to their context (except when it suits him, as in the part about divorce). Those 'general headings' give chapter titles such as 'Of God' or 'Of Predestination' or 'Of the Special Government of Angels'. As he gained confidence, he tells us in the epistle, he read many longer works of theology and was seriously disappointed. Often they defended as truth what was manifestly false, and ignored the arguments of their

---

[27] Haskin, *Milton's Burden*, 15–24; Karen Edwards, *Milton and the Natural World* (Cambridge: Cambridge University Press, 1999), 68–71.
[28] *Tetrachordon, CPW* ii. 642–3. The phrase is the title of the first chapter in one of the most influential books on Milton: Stanley Fish, *Surprised by Sin* (London: Macmillan, 1967; 2nd edn, Cambridge, Mass.: Harvard University Press, 1997).

opponents. So whenever Milton finds himself in disagreement with his models among the many Reformation theologians who wrote similar treatises, he produces long and elaborate arguments to persuade us (for he did intend to publish the book) that his heterodox views are correct. The longest section of all is book 1, chapter 5, 'Of the Son of God', for this is where he contests the Trinity. It even gets its own little 'Preface'. He takes far less space to defend polygamy, however unorthodox it may be, since it is much less important.

Given this experimental, even personal, attitude towards the Bible, it is not surprising that Milton could permit himself to develop it so radically in *Paradise Lost*. Any doubt he might have about retelling the story so thoroughly can be resolved by the device, several times repeated, of calling upon the Holy Spirit to be his Muse. And the retelling is major. The story of Adam and Eve is tersely told in three chapters of Genesis with little exploration of character or theological complication. Adam names all the creatures in Genesis 2: 19–20, and Milton follows suit, but then gives Eve the role of naming the flowers (11.273–9). It is not clear in Genesis where Adam is when Eve takes the fruit and eats it: Milton invents an elaborate scene, a kind of marital tiff, to separate Eve from Adam before the serpent makes his approach. And in a sharp break from orthodox Christian tradition, Adam and Eve have a kind of sanctified sex before the Fall.[29]

Indeed the story of Adam and Eve was potentially subversive as soon as anyone began to examine it seriously. Take Genesis 3: 22: 'Behold the man is become as one of us to know good and evil'. If God was not being sarcastic here, as many, including Luther, were forced to argue, then he admits the force and truth of the serpent's discourse. The fruit did indeed contain real wisdom. So why was it banned? One justification, common in the Eastern Church, is that Adam and Eve were still like children, not yet ready for the knowledge contained in the fruit. Milton rejected such a view, following Augustine, on the grounds that it makes Adam an 'idiot'. And yet an originally perfect, or even a mature, adult Adam, raises the problem of how he fell at all. Augustine had great difficulty with this, given his exalted conception of Adam and Eve, and eventually found himself insisting on an inherent weakness of the will, predating the serpent's temptation. Here is the origin of Raphael's warning to Adam in *Paradise Lost* that 'God made thee perfet, not immutable' (5.524). Augustine's followers before Milton did not find the problem any easier to solve. No wonder Gibbon could later describe the Western Church's adoption of Augustine's views as conducted 'with public applause and secret reluctance'.[30] Milton's brilliant solution to the problem was to insist on what is traditionally called 'uxoriousness', that is, to make Adam too much in love.

In *Paradise Lost* there are many places where Milton subtly alters the text. Genesis 3: 22, for example, following on from the words just quoted, 'Behold the man is become as one of us to know good and evil', continues (in the King James Bible): 'and now, lest he put forth his hand, and take also of the tree of life, and eat, and live for ever: Therefore the lord God sent him forth from the garden of Eden'. The narrative logic of this is inescapable. Before he reaches out and eats the other tree as well, and lives for ever, we must get him out of there! Generations of theologians had tried to cope with this, and many decided, like Luther, that God was being ironic. Milton's God, though capable of irony, is less subtle at this point. Here is what he says:

---

[29] See Achsah Guibbory, 'Bible, Religion, Spirituality in *Paradise Lost*', in Angelica Duran (ed.), *A Concise Companion to Milton* (Oxford: Blackwell, 2007), 128–43.

[30] Edward Gibbon, *The History of the Decline and Fall of the Roman Empire*, ed. J. B. Bury (London: Methuen, 1896–1902), iii. 407.

> Lest therefore his now bolder hand
> Reach also of the tree of life, and eat,
> And live for ever, dream at least to live
> For ever, to remove him I decree. (11.93–6)

God, and the text of Genesis, is thus saved by a few extra words—'dream at least to live for ever'—from what would otherwise appear to be a hastily contrived and theologically unacceptable afterthought.

Another example, less overtly transformative, is the words associated with the creation of hell. Most scholars recognize that Milton's hell, if not its chief inhabitant, is a Vergilian place (with some Dantesque additions). But where does this hell come from? That is not a question Vergil asks, or needs to, but Milton does, and answers it. In doing so he faces the key theological question of whether the Christian God creates evil: in *Paradise Lost* he does, but in a subordinate clause. The important (and famous) passage follows the council scene in book 2, when the more adventurous devils take off to explore hell, their new habitation, and do not much like what they see:

> through many a dark and drearie Vale
> They pass'd, and many a Region dolorous,
> O'er many a Frozen, many a fiery Alpe,
> Rocks, Caves, Lakes, Fens, Bogs, Dens, and shades of death,
> A universe of death, which God by curse
> Created evil, for evil only good,
> Where all life dies, death lives, and Nature breeds,
> Perverse, all monstrous, all prodigious things,
> Abominable, inutterable, and worse
> Than Fables yet have feign'd, or fear conceiv'd,
> *Gorgons* and *Hydra's*, and *Chimaera's* dire. (2.619–29)

The key line about 'evil' ('Created evil, for evil only good'), in which the word is repeated, and which seems a bit short, visually at least, is actually, as Flannagan points out, too long by one syllable and requires an elision across the repetition in 'for evil'. That means that the final word, 'good', is supernumerary: 'good' is the word that is 'extra' in Hell.

The whole passage is suitably dotted with unpleasant bits of the natural world, including those oddly fiery alps, but also the classical monsters, Gorgons, Hydras, and Chimaeras, who threatened Aeneas during his underworld journey.[31] But the most important allusion by far is not to Vergil but to a biblical text that attributes evil to God, Isaiah 45: 7. In the King James Bible it reads: 'I form the light and create darkness; I make peace and create evil. I the Lord do all these things'.

Now Christians have generally wanted to avoid the conclusion that their God is directly responsible for evil. In his Latin theological treatise, Milton cites this unsettling Isaiah text in the Latin of the Protestant Tremellius-Junius Bible: *facientem pacem et creantem malum*.[32] He then explains it as follows: 'that is, what afterwards became and is now evil; for whatever God created was originally good, as he himself testifies, Gen. i'.[33] So the stark statement of the biblical text is avoided, partly by a further citation, partly by introducing a narrative time

---

[31] *Aeneid* 6.288–9.
[32] *The Works of John Milton*, xv. 66; *CPW* vi. 330.
[33] The translation is that of John Carey, *CPW* vi. 330.

scheme—'afterwards' (*postea*). This is indeed the orthodox Christian narrative, as developed by Origen and Augustine: good and evil are not coeval principles, but evil comes into being only afterwards, once the Devil, and then man, decide to sin. And the passage from Milton's *De doctrina* shows how useful that invented narrative could be. Of course, the narrative is not there at all in Isaiah, where God is the one who creates evil, and in the present tense at that. Indeed he sounds proud of it.

Commentators on Isaiah tie themselves in knots over this language, but the most common move is to argue that God is asserting his omnipotence, and in the most persuasive way he can. Given that the addressee of this claim is Cyrus the Persian, some have seen a buried polemic against Zoroastrian dualism, since the passage begins: 'I am the Lord, and there is no other; besides Me there is no God' (Isaiah 45: 5). Milton justifies his *postea* by quoting other biblical texts than Isaiah, and making the assumption that they all tend in the same direction, as is clear to a properly reading spirit. Of course, if one assumes, as most commentators still did, that God was the ultimate author of the Bible, then all such problem texts could be interpreted in the light of others less problematic.

That 'afterwards' idea is important for Milton. He repeats it, for example, when explaining why the tree of knowledge of good and evil is so called: *ab eventu*, 'in the event', 'because of what happened afterwards'.[34] Milton argues for a reversed time-scheme in this passage: we know good only by the later evil, but also, by a twist of divine logic, God brings good out of that evil. 'For where does virtue shine, where is it usually exercised, if not in evil?' (*CPW* vi. 353). Curiously, in view of his own heresy, Milton also cites here Paul's words about tolerating heresies, 1 Corinthians 11: 19: 'There must be heresies among you, that those who are righteous among you may be clearly shown'.

Elsewhere in *De doctrina Christiana*, the grounds on which Milton defends God become more explicit. It has to do with freedom, with Milton's Arminian arguments against Calvin.

> It is sufficiently clear that neither God's decree nor his foreknowledge can shackle free causes with any kind of necessity. There are some people, however, who, struggling to oppose this doctrine through thick and thin, do not hesitate to assert that God is himself the cause and author of sin …. If I should attempt to refute them, it would be like inventing a long argument to prove that God is not the Devil. (*CPW* i. 3, 166)

Witty or casual as that may sound, it is in fact deadly serious: it is what *Paradise Lost* sets out to do, though all it actually claims is 'to justifie the ways of God to man'. Milton knew that a God who needed to be justified might seem very like the Devil.[35]

The King James translation of that key Isaiah verse 'make peace and create evil' has usually been avoided by more recent English-language versions. The Hebrew word *ra* does in fact cover most of what the English word 'evil' means. In the Hebrew Bible *ra* occurs 663 times, and 431 times it is translated in the King James Bible as 'evil'. The Hebrew word can refer to moral evil, and often does have this meaning in the Hebrew scriptures. The primary meaning of *ra* is worthless or useless, hence bad or ugly. As a metaphysical entity there is not much about *evil* in Judaism, except for a brief flurry in the intertestamental or Second

---

[34] *Works*, xv. 114, *CPW* vi. 352.
[35] I have discussed these texts at greater length in *The Satanic Epic* (Princeton: Princeton University Press, 2003), 8–9; and *John Milton: A Biography* (Oxford: Lion, 2008), 141. See n. 9 of this chapter for the Socinian view of Stephen Nye.

Temple period. And there is no entry for *evil* in the *Encyclopedia Judaica*. All the more recent translators of the Isaiah verse choose a word like 'calamity', 'disaster', or 'woe' (as in the RSV). It has been precisely that kind of issue that generates the call for new translations. The Greek Old Testament, the Septuagint, has *kaka*, the most common Greek equivalent. So neither of the original languages makes the distinction between moral and natural evil that the later translators settle on to avoid the issue.

Milton clearly does not avoid the issue in *De doctrina Christiana*, although he introduces a narrative time-scheme in order to explain it, but his solution in *Paradise Lost* is different. Of course in a sense the whole of the epic is a narrative to include the 'afterwards' that Milton adds in his theological treatise, but when he repeats the Isaiah phrase 'create evil' in the poem (2.624, in the long passage already quoted), he sails much closer to the wind. He makes the important grammatical modification that *evil* is an adjective in the phrase 'which God by curse created evil', and only then becomes an abstract noun in the extension through apposition, 'for evil only good'. The first use of the word is a predicative adjective agreeing with the pronoun 'which', and so referring to 'a universe of death'. No question, then, but that God himself creates this dreadful place, and by curse at that. Milton's language game with *good* and *evil* makes the theological relation of good to evil quite muddy. We may well have to read twice to see that these syntactic niceties do not actually make God directly responsible for evil, at least not evil as a nominal and metaphysical abstraction. But he clearly makes something—hell—that is itself unequivocally called evil.

There is no biblical text Milton can cite which confirms God's creation of hell. In the section on the Special Governance of Angels, 1.9 of *De doctrina Christiana*, Milton cites the various passages which announce the punishment of the bad angels, including 2 Peter 2:4, 'he thrust them down to hell and chained them in dark chains, to be kept for damnation'; Jude 6, which more or less repeats those words; Revelation 20: 10, 'they shall be tortured for ever and ever', as well as Revelation 20: 2–3, 'he seized the dragon and bound him, he threw him into hell (*abyssum*) and closed it up' (*CPW* vi. 348–9). Hell is already there. Matthew 25: 41 comes closest to having God make hell, yet the verb is passive: 'into the eternal fire which is prepared for the devil and his angels'. Yet God's making hell follows logically from Milton's insistence, in citing the Isaiah 45 passage, on the supremacy and uniqueness of God. 'I am the Lord, there is no other … I the Lord do all these things'. In the poem, Milton can have his God curse to create hell; as a poet he allows himself much more freedom than he can in a treatise that is so strictly tied to the method of Bible quotation.

Plato, we may recall, had condemned Homer and the tragic poets in the *Republic* 2.379–82, and argued (in the mouth of Socrates) that the gods were good and thus could not be responsible for evil.[36] Milton appears implicitly to be taking the side of the narrative poets in that quarrel with philosophy, and thus increasing the moral ambivalence of his God. The unforgettable impact of hell in the poem is partly because that is where Milton makes the narrative begin. It is linked to what is perhaps the most radical change from the text of

---

[36] Plato's various and naïvely optimistic discussions of evil (or evils) are at *Gorgias* 477e, *Theaetetus* 176a, *Politikos* 269c–d, 273b–c, *Lysias* 221a–c, *Cratylus* 403e–f, *Timaeus* 42d, 48a, 53b, 86b–c, *Laws* 10.903b–905d. His general solution is that either evils are not the work of god, or they are not really evils but deserved punishments. We call things evil, runs the argument in *Laws* 10, out of ignorance. For further discussion, see Neil Forsyth, '*Paradise Lost* and the Origin of Evil', *International Journal for the Classical Tradition*, 6 (2000): 516–48.

Genesis, though anticipated by centuries of commentary: the serpent is an instrument for the overwhelmingly powerful character of Satan.

A key moment in Milton's retelling of the Genesis story comes when, during the temptation scene in book 9, Satan, disguised as the serpent, teaches Eve to read the Bible—or rather, how to interpret the spoken words that would later form part of the written Bible.[37] In particular he shows her that the apparently stark prohibition against eating the fruit of the tree of knowledge is actually more complicated: he explains what it really means. There are several things about the serpent that attract Eve during their meeting. He is very beautiful, for example, even sexy, but what impresses Eve above all is that the serpent talks. He imposes his own language on the text.

Milton's treatment of this necessary theme is interesting in several ways. Adam and Eve have been warned to beware of Satan—they have been told all about the rebels' war in heaven, but they have not been told to look out for talking snakes. An explicit warning would spoil the story. Earlier interpreters had tried to explain why the Eve of Genesis is not suspicious of a snake that speaks. All the animals could talk before the Fall, ran one Jewish line of thought, but this was not popular among the church fathers, since there is no biblical evidence for it.[38] More hesitantly, Thomas Browne, among others, suggested that Eve might still be so new to life in Eden that she 'might not yet be certain only man was privileged with speech' (*Pseudodoxia Epidemica*, 5.4). Calvin, however, had argued that, although Genesis doesn't mention Eve's surprise, no doubt she perceived this speaking serpent to be extraordinary—and 'therefore she greedily received that whereat she wondered'.[39]

Milton adopted Calvin's version, as he often did, but with a clever variation. When she hears him address her, Eve is amazed and asks:

What may this mean? Language of Man pronounc't
By Tongue of Brute, and human sense exprest?
The first at least of these I thought deni'd
To Beasts, whom God on their Creation-Day
Created mute to all articulate sound. (9.553–57)

Satan manages to turn this surprise to his advantage. Eve asks him how he learned speech— and to do so she uses a new word in the English language—'How camst thou *speakable* of mute?'(9.563). Satan responds, with typical cunning, by telling a mini-narrative, a little myth on its own, about how he acquired the new power, remarkably enough from eating the fruit of one of the trees hereabouts. Once she asks 'where grows the Tree, from hence how far?' (9.617), Satan 'blithe and glad' (9.625) knows she is hooked. He offers in his elaborately formal language to show her: 'the way is readie, and not long / … if thou accept / My conduct, I can bring thee thither soon' (9.626–30). She agrees to follow him.

[37] Dayton Haskin has shown how these terms could be virtually interchangeable: 'even in Paradise Adam and Eve were living under an injunction to increase and multiply the knowledge of God's proliferating writing' (*Milton's Burden*, 229). That writing was not scripture yet, but rather what was widely known as the Book of the World. See further Joanna Picciotto, *Labors of Innocence in Early Modern England* (Cambridge, Mass.: Harvard University Press, 2010).

[38] 'The Book of Jubilees', 3: 28, in *The Old Testament Pseudepigrapha*, ed. James H. Charlesworth (New York: Doubleday, 1985), ii. 60. For this argument, see J. M. Evans, *'Paradise Lost' and the Genesis Tradition* (Oxford: Clarendon Press, 1968), 31, 275.

[39] *A Commentarie of John Calvin upon the First Booke of Moses, Called Genesis*, tr. Thomas Tymne (1578), 3.3, quoted in Evans, 'Paradise Lost', 276.

When they reach the tree, Eve says, showing herself as capable as Satan of an appropriate pun, 'Serpent, we might have spar'd our coming hither, / Fruitless to mee, though Fruit be here to excess' (9.647–8). She explains that they are not allowed to eat just that particular tree. Her disappointed and personal 'fruitless to me' is quickly followed by an implied accusation against nature: the tree has fruit 'to excess'.[40] So the serpent's command of human language is the key to the whole temptation. Eve is already, because of Satan's wily words, in a state of frustrated expectation, ready to listen further to his discourse.

Milton's Eve has heard peculiar voices before, so we can understand her confusion: not only did Satan tempt her in a dream with a seductive speech ('I rose as at thy call, but found thee not', 5.48), but her first experience of language was hearing a mysterious voice, warning her to turn away from her own image in the lake and seek him 'whose image thou art', that is, Adam.[41] The voice had told her, like the serpent's now, to 'follow me,' and she commented at that time: 'what could I doe, / But follow strait, invisibly thus led?' (4.467–76). The source of this voice is not explicitly identified at that point, and Eve clearly does not know to whom it belongs. The poem is equally cagey about the serpent's voice and where it comes from: he speaks either 'with Serpent Tongue / Organic, or impulse of vocal Air' (9.529–30). Biblical commentators indeed frequently discussed the problem of how it was possible for the serpent to speak.[42] No wonder Eve can be so easily led by a mysterious voice.

Indeed the poem itself is uncertain not only about the serpent's voice but also about the source of that first voice she hears, with its directive to 'follow me'. Later in the poem, at 8.485–6, Adam somehow knows the voice belongs to 'her Heavenly Maker', but at 4.712, it is explicitly a 'genial angel' that brings Eve to Adam for the first time, 'More lovely than Pandora'. This is one of those discrepancies of which there are surprisingly few in a poem composed by a blind man. It is interesting to note, nonetheless, that one of the others, even more important for the outcome of the story, also concerns what Eve hears: did she or did she not hear Raphael's story about Satan's rebellion and the war in heaven, a story that is told with the sole intention of warning Adam and Eve that they have a serious enemy? At 9.275–8, she says she knew about the enemy both from Adam himself and from overhearing the conversation with the 'parting angel' as she returned from her flowers. Yet at that point, the end of book 8, Raphael said nothing about Satan, and more to the point, Eve was in fact present during the whole story of the war in heaven in book 6: 'He with his consorted Eve / The story heard attentive' (7.50–1).

Why then does Raphael feel he has to say 'Warn / Thy weaker' (6.908) in summarizing the story, as if he is speaking only to Adam? How strange that there should be these discrepancies, even contradictions, around what Eve actually heard, given how everything that is to happen supposedly turns on this warning! It is the reason for Raphael's descent in the first place, to

[40] For discussion of the pun, see Christopher Ricks, *Milton's Grand Style* (Oxford: Clarendon Press, 1963), 73–4; and R. A. Shoaf, *Milton, Poet of Duality*, 2nd edn (Gainsville, Fla.: University of Florida Press, 1993), 144–53.

[41] See esp. Diane McColley, *Milton's Eve* (Urbana, Ill.: University of Illinois Press, 1983), 77, on Eve at the lake.

[42] N. P. Williams, *The Ideas of the Fall and of Original Sin* (London: Longman, 1927), 116–17. In the Christian tradition, quite often, the Devil occupied the serpent or spoke through his mouth rather in the way that demons might speak through a possessed man—one among many instances of how the New Testament affected reading of the Old. On the scientific options for the 'serpent tongue / Organic', see Edwards, *Milton and the Natural World*, 25.

warn mankind and so liberate God from any responsibility: they know the story of Satan, and they are free to do as they will within that knowledge (5.235–45). Yet even at that moment, God speaks to Raphael only of conversing with Adam. Perhaps this is because, in the end, everything depends on whether Adam himself will eat. Yet surely, in Milton's version of the story at least, it also turns on whether Eve has grounds to resist the serpent's voice. Satan knows quite well that Adam will eat once Eve has done so, and does not wait to see what happens.

Satan first gets the idea of using reason and knowledge to tempt Adam and Eve when he overhears them discussing the prohibition on the tree and learns it is 'One fatal Tree ... of Knowledge call'd'. He reacts with apparently genuine indignation (in soliloquy):

> Knowledge forbidd'n?
> Suspicious, reasonless. Why should thir Lord
> Envie them that? can it be sin to know,
> Can it be death? and do they onely stand
> By Ignorance ...?
>   ... Hence I will excite thir minds
> With more desire to know. (4.514–23)

And he does not change that part of his strategy on finding Eve alone. She is assumed, like Adam, to be eager for knowledge.

The means of Satan's temptation is rhetorical persuasion, a logical argument including but by no means limited to flattery, not (as it was in other versions) sexual seduction. Eve says to Adam afterwards that he could not

> have discernd
> Fraud in the Serpent, speaking as he spake;
> No ground of enmitie between us known,
> Why hee should mean me ill, or seek to harme. (9.1149–52)

This is a serious point. Indeed it is Satan who teaches her to *discern*, as the course of the scene shows. True, he uses some of the weapons of magic, such as the tradition of forbidden knowledge—to tempt her—but notice how he puts it: the tree gives power, he claims, to 'discern things in their causes' (681–2). This impresses Eve—as her own musing confirms. Watch for the word 'discern' in the following passage, at the climax of a rising series:

> ... In the day we eat
> Of this fair Fruit, our doom is, we shall die.
> How dies the Serpent? hee hath eat'n and lives,
> And knows and speaks and reasons and discerns,
> Irrational till then. (9.762–6)

So what has most impressed her is the serpent's ability to develop rational arguments, in particular rational arguments about words, to *discern* or *discriminate* their meanings. God said, 'In the day ye eat thereof ye shall surely die'—and by showing Eve he is not dead himself, though he has supposedly eaten it, Satan has propelled her to think about the terms of the prohibition (as so many biblical commentators had already done), to interpret and divide its meanings, to rewrite it.

> So shall ye die perhaps, but putting off
> Human, to put on Gods, death to be wisht,
> Though threat'nd, which no worse than this can bring. (9.713–15)

She now refers the power of the word to Satan rather than God—or reads God's word via Satan's interpretation.

So Satan as serpent teaches Eve to use language in a new way, for herself. She thinks through the sacred injunction and makes it mean something different from what it had originally seemed to mean. Yet the fault for these discrepancies is not entirely Satan's. Look at the original text in Genesis. There God says, in the King James Bible: 'But of the tree of the knowledge of good and evil, thou shalt not eat of it: for in the day that thou eatest thereof thou shalt surely die' (2: 17). Commentators had long had difficulty with this text, especially with the word 'day', since clearly in the Genesis narrative, neither Adam nor Eve dies on the day they eat. But there were other problems. For one thing, the pronoun is singular. God is addressing only one person, Adam. Eve in fact is not there yet. She is actually created only in the subsequent verses (2: 18–25).

Nonetheless she somehow hears about the prohibition, since she repeats it to the serpent, but with minor variations.[43] Not only does she turn it into a plural form of address, thus including herself, but she exaggerates it. 'God hath said, Ye shall not eat of it, neither shall ye touch it, lest ye die'. Some misogynist commentators, including St Ambrose, the medieval rabbi Rashi, and Thomas Browne, thought that in Genesis 3: 3 she was unwarrantably adding to God's precept: 'We can't even touch it'.[44] Many also thought that with her phrase 'lest ye die' Eve was hedging. God had said to Adam, after all, 'Ye shall surely die'. At this point the Vulgate has *ne forte moriamini*, 'lest by chance you should die', an even more striking variation.[45] Fowler's excellent note on 9.663 adds that her phrase about the 'fruit of the tree which is in the midst of the garden' was also seen as an evasion of that 'morally definitive "tree of the knowledge of good and evil"'. She is simply pointing to the position of the tree rather than announcing its properties.

What does Milton do with the ambiguities of this verse (Genesis 3: 3) that generations of theologians had pored over? First of all, as often in the poem, he resists the misogyny. He is not using these two Genesis versions of the prohibition to undermine Eve: at 9.925 Adam too speaks of the 'ban to touch' (when it is too late), and so does the epic voice at 7.46 ('Charged not to touch the interdicted Tree'). But Milton does seize the opportunity of the biblical variation to make the focus of Eve's attitude clear. In saying she must not even touch the tree, repeating her exact words from Genesis, Eve is temporarily reinforcing her determination, but she is also admitting the attraction.

[43] On the basis of these variations, some rabbis deduced that when Adam told Eve about the command he deliberately exaggerated the terms, and thus unwittingly caused Eve's downfall. Having heard that the prohibition includes touching the tree, not just tasting it, the serpent 'took her and thrust her against it. "Have you then died?" he said to her'. Thus 'by proving that one part of the command as transmitted by Adam was unfounded, [the serpent] led her to believe that the prohibition as a whole was groundless': Evans, *'Paradise Lost'*, 49.

[44] Browne accuses her of 'two mistakes, or rather additional mendacities', and adds that 'therefore although it be said, and that very truly, that the Devil was a liar from the beginning, yet was the woman herein the first express beginner: and falsified twice before the reply of Satan', *Pseudodoxia Epidemica*, 1.1, in *Thomas Browne: Twenty-First-Century Oxford Authors*, ed. Kevin Killeen (Oxford: Oxford University Press, 2014), 100–3. Cheryl Fresch, 'Milton's Eve and the Problem of the Additions to the Command', *Milton Quarterly*, 12 (1978): 83–91, explores the commentators on this discrepancy, citing the rabbi Rashi as also accusing Eve of lying.

[45] Fresch, 'Milton's Eve', 84, shows that while Ambrose believed Eve added to God's words in order to express her hatred and disgust by exaggerating the rigours of life in Eden ('ex taedio et odio ... , itaque invidiose exaggerasse duritiem praecepti'), Cornelius's *Commentaria in Pentateuchum*, the most frequently printed Catholic commentary of its kind in the seventeenth century, argued her stipulation against touching evidenced her respect and reverence for God.

By the time she does eat the fruit, however, God's word has lost its authority for Eve. She has been talked into believing that the words cannot possibly mean what they say: how could God be so cruel? No, rather he will praise your 'dauntless virtue'—a word which etymologically contains the Latin for 'man' (*vir*), and which may thus refer more specifically to courage or manliness. As Empson puts it, Eve 'feels the answer to this elaborate puzzle must be that God wants her to eat the apple, since what he is testing is not her obedience but her courage'.[46] If the first variation on the prohibition is in the text of Genesis itself, the Miltonic Satan's further variation is much more radical. 'Death' does not mean death, but rather putting off the old life to put on a new, just as he has in becoming a talking snake. And besides, knowledge is good. How could it not be? Be bold and taste. Milton's Satan is so impressive not simply because he challenges the authenticity of God's word, but because he builds on the discrepancies in Genesis itself, and he does so on rational grounds: Eve finds his arguments 'impregn'd / With Reason, to her seeming, and with Truth' (9.737–8). Even 'if what is evil / Be real', he says (a major concession), 'why not known, since easier shunnd?' (9.698–9).

Christianity is the religion of the word, and so Satan's subversive strategy is to put distance between the key terms, the relationship of God to word. In so doing, he has undermined the word itself. The text may be God's, but, as we have seen even for non-Satanic interpreters, it can shift its meaning, and so is not always to be trusted. Milton, in his role as the narrator, fears that, without the constant and sustaining presence of the Heavenly Muse, he may fall (a vital word throughout the poem) from his flying steed, 'Erroneous ... to wander and forlorn' (7.19–20). The anxiety is obvious, and necessary if you separate the word from the spirit. Yet it is also what allowed for the kind of creative freedom from textual dogma to which we owe *Paradise Lost*.

FURTHER READING

Almond, Philip C. 'Adam, Pre-Adamites, and Extra-Terrestrial Beings in Early Modern Europe'. *Journal of Religious History*, 30 (2006): 163–74.
Calhoun, Joshua. 'The Word Made Flax: Cheap Bibles, Textual Corruption, and the Poetics of Paper'. *PMLA*, 126 (2011): 327–44.
Coffey, John. *John Goodwin and the Puritan Revolution* (Woodbridge: Boydell & Brewer, 2006).
Edwards, Karen L. *Milton and the Natural World* (Cambridge: Cambridge University Press, 1999).
Empson, William. *Milton's God* (London: Chatto & Windus, 1961; rev. edn 1965).
Evans, J. M. *'Paradise Lost' and the Genesis Tradition* (Oxford: Clarendon Press, 1968).
Fish, Stanley. *Surprised by Sin* (London: Macmillan, 1967).
Fletcher, Harris Francis. *The Use of the Bible in Milton's Prose* (New York: Haskell House, 1929).
Forsyth, Neil. *The Satanic Epic* (Princeton: Princeton University Press, 2003).
Forsyth, Neil. *John Milton: A Biography* (Oxford: Lion, 2008).
Fresch, Cheryl. 'Milton's Eve and the Problem of the Additions to the Command'. *Milton Quarterly*, 12 (1978): 83–91.
Guibbory, Achsah. 'Bible, Religion, Spirituality in *Paradise Lost*', in Angelica Duran (ed.), *A Concise Companion to Milton* (Oxford: Blackwell, 2007), 128–43.

[46] William Empson, *Milton's God* (London: Chatto & Windus, 1961; rev. edn 1965), 159.

Haskin, Dayton. *Milton's Burden of Interpretation* (Philadelphia: University of Pennsylvania Press, 1994).

Lewalski, Barbara K. 'Milton, the Bible and Human Experience'. *Topoi*, 7 (1988): 221–9.

McColley, Diane. *Milton's Eve* (Urbana, Ill.: University of Illinois Press, 1983).

Milton, John. *Paradise Lost*, ed. Alastair Fowler (Harlow: Pearson Longman, 2007).

Poole, William. *Milton and the Idea of the Fall* (Oxford: Oxford University Press, 2005).

Rosenblatt, Jason P. *Torah and Law in Paradise Lost* (Princeton: Princeton University Press, 1994).

Schwartz, Regina M. 'Milton on the Bible', in Thomas N. Corns (ed.), *A Companion to Milton* (Oxford: Blackwell, 2001), 37–54.

Sims, James H. *The Bible in Milton's Epics* (Gainsville: University of Florida Press, 1962).

CHAPTER 14

....

THE COMMODIFICATION OF SCRIPTURE, 1640–1660: POLITICS, ECCLESIOLOGY, AND THE CULTURES OF PRINT

....

CRAWFORD GRIBBEN

In 1650, an anonymous pamphlet, *Humble Proposals concerning the Printing of the Bible*, appealed for clarity in the debate about the reliability of available copies of scripture. The pamphlet addressed the fear of some English Bible readers that they were consuming something less than the inspired text, and reflected concern that the increasing quantity of English Bibles did not also correspond to their increasing quality. The *Humble Proposals* suggested that 'a fair Copie of the last Translation of the BIBLE, ingrossed either in Parchment or Vellam, in a full Character', with its accuracy guaranteed by a committee of clergymen, should be kept in Sion College, London, 'that so all people, upon any doubt, may have recours to the Original, to prove whether their Printed Copies varie, or not'.[1]

The *Humble Proposals* encoded a series of foundational assumptions about the reception of the Bible in early modern England. The pamphlet's notion of a manuscript 'original' in the vernacular language was indicative of the extent to which the Bible, for many of its readers, had become a normatively and natively English text: the author of the proposals was suggesting that an appeal for accuracy should not be made to Hebrew, Aramaic, or Greek manuscripts, but to a 'fair Copie' in English which would correspond as closely as possible to the first printed edition of the King James Bible (1611). In making this appeal, the *Humble Proposals* was elevating the King James Bible to a status corresponding to that of the Latin Vulgate, which, Catholic theologians at the Council of Trent had agreed, was *authentica*,

---

[1] *Humble Proposals concerning the Printing of the Bible* (1650), single sheet. For a general survey of Bible usage in early modern England, see Christopher Hill, *The English Bible and the Seventeenth-Century Revolution* (London: Allen Lane, 1993), 1–44; Peter Burke, *Popular Culture in Early Modern Europe* (1978; 3rd edn Aldershot: Ashgate, 2009), 315–21.

an authoritative translation which was to become the final court of appeal in all matters biblical.

But the *Humble Proposals* also indicated the extent to which manuscript 'originals' retained their value and status, even as the production of print increased. The idea of an authentic textual 'original' was a troubling concept in early modern criticism, of course, but the growing popularity of the King James Bible, and awareness of the shortcomings of the production values of those editions of its text which were being made available in the mid-seventeenth century, presented a different set of problems. After all, the pamphlet's appeal for a certified manuscript 'original' of the King James Bible was being made only six years after the last publication in England of the Geneva Bible, and may have reflected an enduring sense of unease among the more radical promoters of the Reformation of church and state that the annotated translation which had been so useful to their project was now going out of print, and that its replacement betrayed a quite different set of social and political values.[2] And what if the new translation was also unreliable in its printing? The *Humble Proposals* emanated out of and reflected the turmoil of the mid-seventeenth-century market for English Bible translations.

But this market turmoil was occurring in a larger context. The *Humble Proposals* bear witness to the fact that the ecclesiastical authority which had attempted to supervise Bible production was breaking down in the mid-seventeenth century. Its displacement allowed the extra-ecclesiastical commodification of the Bible to accelerate, while also providing for an ensuing acceleration in the provision of Bible-reading helps for 'simple readers' as well as scholarly and popular discussion of structural problems in the Bible's textual basis, translation, production, dissemination, and consumption.[3] Since the sudden explosion of print, in the early 1640s, English Bible readers had been faced with a growing literature concerned to identify and address the difficulties of the sacred text.

Some of these difficulties were textual, and involved complex appeals to critical apparatus in multiple languages in an effort to establish an authentic text. Others related to the politics of translation, centring, for example, on the suitability of 'bishop' over 'elder', or 'church' over 'congregation'. Other difficulties were theological, requiring those readers wishing to maintain assumptions about the coherence, even infallibility, of the biblical text to reconcile its apparent contradictions. But perhaps the most pressing set of difficulties were technical, as English Bible readers began to realize that the texts of scripture which were coming to market were often unreliable representatives of the translations they purported to represent. Since the Reformation, the printing and publication of English Bibles had been a commercial as well as an ecclesiastical activity: it is not the case, as some scholars have argued, that the Bible moved from being an 'ecclesiastical text' to become an unregulated and fetishized commodity in and after early print capitalism.[4] But it is certainly the case that the problems of production, which illustrated structural issues in the emerging marketplace of print as well as the difficulties faced by individual entrepreneurs

---

[2] Naomi Tadmor, *The Social Universe of the English Bible: Scripture, Society, and Culture in Early Modern England* (Cambridge: Cambridge University Press, 2010), 119–64.

[3] Michael Jensen, '"Simply" Reading the Geneva Bible: The Geneva Bible and its Readers', *Literature and Theology*, 9 (1995): 30–45.

[4] I borrow this term from Theodore Letis, *The Ecclesiastical Text: Text Criticism, Biblical Authority and the Popular Mind* (Philadelphia: Institute for Renaissance and Reformation Biblical Studies, 1997).

operating within it, became most marked in the middle part of the seventeenth century, as political and ecclesiastical structures broke down, with the acceleration in the commodification of scripture, as well as in increasingly vocal debates about its intellectual and technical credibility.

This mid-seventeenth-century crisis in biblical production and reception may have represented the beginnings of the critical reduction of scripture in the popular imagination, and a crucial moment of early 'enlightenment', but it also had demonstrable political consequences. Paradoxically, the crisis in popular biblical reception occurred alongside the maturation of the most determined attempts to refashion English society and institutions along Hebraic lines: it was in this period, for example, that Fifth Monarchist theorists developed complex accounts of the immediate relevance of the Mosaic legal and penal codes, while covenanting Presbyterians on both sides of the border pushed a raft of legislation which criminalized an extensive and growing catalogue of sins.[5] But the biblical scholars to whom both Fifth Monarchists and Covenanters appealed were increasingly aware of the tensions in their position caused by the advance of textual criticism, as well as the criticism of the available published texts. Two of the most robust Reformed theologians of the period, the Scottish Presbyterian Samuel Rutherford and the English Independent John Owen, both acknowledged the presence of difficulties—and, in Rutherford's case, even errors—in the available editions of scripture, while simultaneously arguing for the infallibility of the inspired text.

'The Bible only' may well have been 'the religion of Protestants'—but mid-seventeenth-century Protestants were faced with questions of which text-critical tradition, in which translation, from which printer—and for how long? For while legal theorists and theologians appealed to scripture to justify a variety of policy positions, attempting to refashion the legal and political institutions of England along Hebraic lines, the crisis in popular biblical reception undermined simple appeals to the letter of the biblical text. The issues at stake in these high-level debates found their counterpart in the populist concerns evidenced in the *Humble Proposals concerning the Printing of the Bible*. From straightforward concerns about the accuracy of available copies of the King James Bible to the complex and multidisciplinary debates between Brian Walton and John Owen about the antiquity of the Hebrew vowel points, the intense concern in the mid-seventeenth century with the textual verity of special revelation and its vernacular translations drove the commodification of the English Bible and illustrated some of the complex relationships between politics, ecclesiology, and the developing cultures of print.

I

The Bible, for perhaps the majority of its readers from the middle of the sixteenth to the later seventeenth century, was a translation into English made by refugees from Mary Tudor's

---

[5] See e.g. John Young, 'The Covenanters and the Scottish Parliament, 1639–51: The Rule of the Godly and the "Second Scottish Reformation"', in Elizabethanne Boran and Crawford Gribben (eds), *Enforcing Reformation in Ireland and Scotland, 1550–1700* (Aldershot: Ashgate, 2006), 131–58; Crawford Gribben, 'Samuel Rutherford and Liberty of Conscience', *Westminster Theological Journal*, 71 (2009): 355–73.

England.[6] This 'Geneva' Bible actually referred to several distinct editions of the text, which offered a choice of translations, different sets of annotations, and an expanding body of interpretive helps, variously including, alongside the biblical texts, maps, illustrations, concordances, glossaries, chronologies, tables of prophetic fulfilment, guidelines for devotion and study, as well as text-critical, linguistic, and theological annotations.[7] These annotations themselves evolved, and in eschatological terms grew more radical, as the Geneva Bible project was picked up by different sets of publishers and contributors to editorial matter. Many examples of these differing texts continued to circulate in the mid-seventeenth century, even after the last edition of a Geneva Bible was published, in 1644. It was this translation which continued to be the translation of choice for many of the most influential writers, preachers, and institutions of the period: the Parliamentary army issued its soldiers with extracts from the translation in *The Souldiers Pocket Bible* (1644), even as preachers and scholars, such as John Owen and John Milton, routinely drew upon its familiar expressions.

The first English translation of the New Testament to be published in Geneva, and recognizably as part of the 'Geneva Bible' project, appeared in 1557, under the supervision of William Whittingham, who may have been the brother-in-law of Calvin's wife. The first full Bible appeared within the same community of exiles in 1560, the fruit of collaboration between Whittingham, Miles Coverdale, and Christopher Goodman. This was to become the most popular of the Geneva translations, continuing to be published into the early seventeenth century, and, presumably, to be sold thereafter: it was the only Bible to be published in Scotland before 1610, where the established church insisted that a copy should be purchased by and displayed in every parish, and where the Scottish Parliament decreed that copies should be purchased by higher value householders, in the first instance of (compulsory) subscription publishing in the literary history of these isles.[8] A third variety of Geneva Bible, though still recognizably part of the Geneva Bible tradition, appeared in 1576, when a new translation of the New Testament, by Laurence Tomson MP, was bound with the earlier version of the Old Testament. And a fourth major edition appeared in 1599, combining the original Old Testament with Tomson's New Testament and a new set of annotations on Revelation, culled from expository work by the French Huguenot scholar Franciscus Junius (1545–1602), and reflecting the new interest in apocalyptic thinking in the context of geopolitical tensions at the end of Elizabeth's reign.[9] With its developing range of interpretive helps, the Geneva Bible offered a library of texts for an increasingly radical Protestant everyman.

This translation's dominance of the marketplace for Bibles is well known. Between 1560, when the first full Geneva Bible was published, and 1611, when the first edition of the King James Bible was published, there appeared five editions of Tyndale's New Testament, seven editions of the Great Bible, and twenty-two editions of the Bishops' Bible. Both the Great Bible and the Bishops' Bible were ecclesiastically 'authorized'—the only English Bibles

---

[6] Crawford Gribben, *The Puritan Millennium: Literature and Theology 1550–1682* (Dublin: Four Courts, 2000), 57–79; Tom Furniss, 'Reading the Geneva Bible: Notes towards an English Revolution?' *Prose Studies*, 31 (2009): 1–21.

[7] On the paratexts and reading aids of the Geneva Bible, see the chapter by Femke Molekamp in this volume.

[8] David Daniell, *The Bible in English: Its History and Influence* (New Haven: Yale University Press, 2003), 295. On the Reformation in Scotland, see the chapter by Alasdair Raffe in this volume.

[9] Gribben, *Puritan Millennium*, 68–70.

to have been accorded this status. But none of these translations could compete with the extraordinary popularity of the first Bible to be successfully mass-marketed in early modern cultures of print. For in the same period, over 120 editions of the Geneva Bible were published to respond to—and simultaneously to consolidate—the demands of the 'simple reader'.[10] One hundred and forty editions of the most popular Geneva Bible were published in England between 1560 and 1644, at least one new edition of the Geneva Bible was published every year between 1575 and 1618, and over sixty editions of the Geneva Bible appeared between 1611 and 1644.

In 1644, after almost one century of production, the last edition of the Geneva Bible was published in England.[11] But this translation didn't simply dominate the marketplace—it also invented the format of the text which was to become that of the English biblical tradition. For, in addition to the chapter divisions which by the mid-sixteenth century had been firmly established, the Geneva Bible was the first English translation to include divisions into verse-paragraphs. And by popularizing this new method for making particular citations, even allowing readers to identify parts of sentences by means of a simple system of numerical references, the Geneva Bible revolutionized the manner in which the Bible was being formatted, read, imagined, and, increasingly, used. It was this feature of its presentation of the text that allowed for the development of an acute, urgent, and precise culture of interpretive debate, supported by the new concordances offering a scientific data-mining of scripture, by the middle of the seventeenth century.

And yet, for all of its enduring popularity, the Geneva Bible was not an ecclesiastically sanctioned project. Its original translation team had included Miles Coverdale, a serial translation entrepreneur, whose background included work on the Matthew Bible (1537) and the Great Bible (1538). But its earlier printings appeared anonymously, with no indication of the personnel involved or even the locations of the printers. Due to the hostility of English bishops, who forbade production in London, early texts were imported into England well into Elizabeth's reign, with the first Geneva Bible being printed in England only in 1576. As textual production moved into England, editions of the Geneva Bible were published by Christopher Barker, 'printer to the Queen's most excellent majesty', as later title-pages declared (1583). But James VI, dedicatee of the Scottish edition of the Geneva Bible, the 'Bassandyne Bible' (1579), was not an enthusiastic exponent of its virtues, and, in his new guise as James I, took advantage of his accession to the English throne and English Puritan pressure for ecclesiastical change to sponsor an entirely new translation of scripture. In its status as an 'ecclesiastical text', James's flagship religious project was intended, among other things, to locate the authority for the production of scripture within proper political and ecclesiastical boundaries appropriate to his increasing sense of monarchy's divine rights. The new translation was not offered to the range of printers then involved in the production of the various Geneva Bibles. Instead, James created a royal monopoly which ensured, among other things, that the text remained free of the marginal annotations which, in the case of the Geneva Bible, he felt had such a corrosive effect on the body politic.[12]

But James's granting of a monopoly for the production of the text also safeguarded its future. Bible publishing had for many years been a risky business. Gutenberg, after all,

---

[10] For the editors' use of this term, see Jensen, '"Simply" Reading', 30–45; Gribben, *Puritan Millennium*, 67.
[11] Gribben, *Puritan Millennium*, 67.
[12] On the remaining marginal annotations in the KJB, see the chapter by Karen L. Edwards in this volume.

had gone bankrupt, and the undercapitalized nature of so much early printing, as well as the difficulty in securing access to markets, did not make his experience unique.[13] Similar challenges faced Bible publishers in mid-seventeenth-century England. Publishers were being challenged to continue to sell a text which was already circulating in vast numbers. There were corresponding lulls in the production of Bibles, as for example during the 1630s. But these lulls in production continued while the market for Bibles valued the text as the single most important object in the material world. And so, in the choppy seas of mid-seventeenth-century print capitalism and ecclesiastical and constitutional change, the royal monopoly on Bible production broke down, while foreign-based printers continued to supply English readers with imported copies of their sacred text. Inevitably, the new conditions of production drove down the quality of the sacred texts. And inevitably English Bible readers were faced with a crisis in their reception of scripture.

Nevertheless, slowly but surely, the King James Bible overtook the Geneva Bible in the marketplace for scripture. Some readers continued to prefer the older translation, with its venerable tradition of anti-absolutist marginal annotations, and in the 1640s the Geneva Bible was again taken up by the new administrations of the Civil Wars. And the audience for the annotations appears to have endured: in the latter third of the seventeenth century, publishers in overseas locations, especially Amsterdam, would continue to produce editions of the King James text with the annotations of the Geneva Bible—a phenomenon which continued until 1715. Nevertheless, despite the flurry of interest in producing copies of the Geneva Bible during the Civil Wars, and the odd habit of combining the Geneva annotations with King James's biblical text, the general trend was clear. King James's translation was entering its long period of market dominance, in which it would move from being an untrusted innovation to become the translation of choice, and then, simply, the translation, later being identified as a foundational text in the English literary tradition: for the King James Bible came to acquire its literary value as its theological credibility was being undermined.[14] Throughout the middle third of the seventeenth century, scholars would work to codify a standard text of scripture—producing, for example, the first great wave of concordances and harmonies—while also making that standard text problematic. The King James Bible came to dominate the market for English Bibles as challenges to its credibility were becoming more frequent and more substantial.

II

One of the most marked consequences of the decreasing production of Geneva Bibles was an attempt by publishers to meet new demands for helps for 'simple readers'. The standard editions of the new translation lacked many of the features which readers of the Geneva Bible had found so valuable, including explanatory annotations, concordances, psalters, glossaries of names, maps, and illustrations. Throughout the 1640s, and into the 1650s, therefore, publishers began to multiply helps for lay Bible reading. Some of the aids which

---

[13] Andrew Pettegree, *The Book in the Renaissance* (New Haven: Yale University Press, 2010), 22–42.
[14] This is, broadly, the argument of David Norton, *A History of the English Bible as Literature* (Cambridge: Cambridge University Press, 2000).

had been provided by the Geneva Bibles found their own place in the new literature of Bible-reading assistance, for, as we have already noted, a number of editions of the King James Bible appeared with annotations from the old Geneva Bible in their margins until the early eighteenth century. But whatever the reasons for its rise, this new literature of hermeneutical assistance was designed to promote a sacred 'science of order',[15] in which knowledge about scripture was being produced and organized to reflect assumptions about its divine origin and character. One of the most impressive texts in this regard was Robert Wickens's *A Compleat & Perfect Concordance of the English Bible Composed after a New, and Most Compendious Method, Whereby May Be Readily Found Any Place of Canonicall Scripture* (Oxford, 1655).

Wickens's massive scholarly apparatus offered a key to the text of scripture which the trend towards verse divisions had made possible, an early gesture towards the 'data-mining' method of Bible reading, in which readers could create meanings for the text outside of its culture and context, using rather than reading the text. This new and rapidly expanding library of Bible-reading helps included commentaries, chronologies, daily Bible reading plans, and spiritual directions for how to read the biblical texts, as well as apologetic material designed to confront the new challenges to the textual, theological, or ethical integrity of the text. Other texts dealt with challenges in translation, including (perhaps ironically) Robert Codrington's translation of Jean d'Espagne's *Shibboleth, or The Reformation of Severall Places in the Translations of the French and of the English Bible* (1655), as well as Robert Gell's *An Essay toward the Amendment of the Last English-Translation of the Bible, or, a Proof, by Many Instances, That the Last Translation of the Bible into English May Be Improved* (1659)—the 'many instances' being so numerous as to justify 800 pages of text.[16] But in some respects this attempt to defend the integrity of scripture only acknowledged the scale of the difficulties involved. Joannes Thaddaeus's *The Reconciler of the Bible* (1655), for example, might have more effectively achieved its goals if its subtitle had not advertised its merits in reconciling 'above two thousand seeming contradictions throughout the Old and New Testament'.

But the commodification of scripture continued despite growing awareness of the difficulties associated with the biblical text. In the 1630s and 1640s, London printers contested whether they could produce reliable editions of the Bible at prices which the market could support. The earlier overproduction of the Geneva Bible had in some respects dampened the mid-century market, for while Geneva Bibles were not continually being produced, they did continue to circulate: the evidence from many later seventeenth-century writers, including John Bunyan, indicates that copies of the Geneva Bible continued to be used, and numerous copies in archives illustrate the extent to which, and the extended period over which, these Bibles were being passed through friendship networks and families.[17] In the mid-1640s, concerns about the quality and price of available Bibles were expressed by members of the Westminster Assembly of Divines, the ecclesiastical talking-shop established by the London Parliament and supported by the Scottish Parliament to hammer out new catechisms and a new confession of faith to guide the future thinking of the church in the

---

[15] Michel Foucault, *The Order of Things: An Archaeology of the Human Sciences*, tr. A. M. Sheridan Smith (London: Tavistock, 1970).

[16] On Gell, see the chapter by Nigel Smith in this volume.

[17] William H. Sherman, *Used Books: Marking Readers in Renaissance England* (Philadelphia: University of Pennsylvania Press, 2007), 71–86.

three nations. Members of the Assembly campaigned to ensure the production of cheap and reliable editions of the King James Bible—a campaign which ironically was to provide thousands of 'Bentley' Bibles to the English army which invaded Ireland, and then Scotland, in 1649–50—and which may have done more than has been recognized to flood some of the most radical religious networks of period, already provided with the Geneva-based text, *The Souldiers Pocket Bible*, with a government-sponsored edition of the King James translation. In July 1649, the Essex clergyman Ralph Josselin paid 3s 2d for a Bible for his son: 'this booke is now very cheape,' he considered.[18]

The intervention of the Westminster divines in some senses represented an attempt to identify the production of Bibles as a matter appropriate to ecclesiastical jurisdictions. But their consultation with a series of London printers served only to indicate the extent to which the church had lost control of its most important material object. For cheap and reliable Bibles were not to be produced under the oversight of the Assembly—though it did oversee the production of a new metrical version of the Psalms designed for public worship. Instead, the Assembly recognized in its tense and diffident dealings with the London printers that control of the Bible had passed from the established church. In the mid-seventeenth century, the always tenuous relationship between the church and the Bible was broken.

III

This fear that the church had lost control of the Bible concerned many of the more conservative theologians of the period, among them Brian Walton, churchman, royalist sympathizer, and future Bishop of Chester. Walton operated at the opposite end of the theological spectrum from the divines of the Westminster Assembly, and illustrates Richard Muller's claim that, if the Reformation 'derailed the movement toward pure philology and textual criticism by drawing the study and revision of the text of scripture into the theological battles of the age, it is also the case that the humanistic interests in philology and criticism grew and expanded toward the great age of text criticism and orientalism that was to come'.[19] In the early 1650s, therefore, Walton consolidated a network of political and scholarly acquaintances to advance the most ambitious work of biblical scholarship in early modern Europe. With the support of the Cromwellian administrations, enthusiastic endorsements by leading biblical linguists and historians such as James Ussher and John Selden, and modest state sponsorship, Walton set about a research project the output of which was the most impressive textual product published in the period: the London Polyglot Bible (1654–7). The London Polyglot was a triumph of technology, simultaneously presenting in its volume on the New Testament the Greek, Syriac, Ethiopic, Arabic, Persian, and two Latin texts.[20] It was a triumph of learning, demonstrating the extraordinary scholarly capacity of the members of the production scheme. And it was a triumph in terms of the organization of print

---

[18] Ralph Josselin, *The Diary of Ralph Josselin 1616–1683*, ed. Alan Macfarlane (Oxford: Oxford University Press), 173.

[19] Richard A. Muller, *Post-Reformation Reformed Dogmatics: The Rise and Development of Reformed Orthodoxy, ca. 1520 to ca. 1725*, 2nd edn (Grand Rapids, Mich.: Baker Academic, 2003), ii. 61.

[20] Daniell, *The Bible in English*, 510.

capital, representing an early example of the trend towards subscription publication which would become so familiar in later decades, and demonstrating that a technically complex multi-linguistic text could be sold for a fraction of the price of the Paris Polyglot (1645) with which it was intended to compete.

The London Polyglot project indicated the value that was being attached to the study of scripture in its original languages in the middle third of the seventeenth century. This interest in the Hebrew language and its religious and political significance developed across the theological and political spectrum. A number of Civil Wars radicals had argued that Hebrew was the original language of Eden; others, like John Rogers, in *Ohel or Beth-Shemesh* (1653) had begun to put Hebrew characters on title-pages; and others, like TheaurauJohn Tany, had moved from this linguistic interest to imagine that they were in fact Jews with a distinctive role in the drama of the last days.[21] A number of items in the period were published to explore the possibilities of greater knowledge of Hebrew in particular. Some of these enthusiasts—scholarly and populist—would have benefited from the study of such works as William Robertson's *Safer tehilim usafer eykhah sepher tehilim u-sepher echam: The Hebrew Text of the Psalmes and Lamentations, but Published (for to Encourage and Facilitate Beginners in Their Way) with the Reading Thereof in Known English Letters, excepting only the Letter `, Which Because of the Incertainty of Its Genuine Pronunciation is Left Either to Be Read or Not, According as the Reason of the Reader Shall Judge Most Convenient* (1656). But Walton and his colleagues represented an alternative discursive community—royalist, high church, and utterly learned. And so the publication of the London Polyglot did not provoke the consternation of unlettered radicals, so much as the scholarly opponents of the political and ecclesiastical assumptions upon which the polyglot project had been founded. For the project had advanced upon the basis of a number of presuppositions about the nature of the biblical text, and the relationship between the Bible and the church. And these presuppositions were clarified in the vociferous debate which followed upon the publication of the project—a debate about the pointing of the Hebrew vowels joined most memorably by the Vice-Chancellor of the University of Oxford, John Owen.

The controversy about the pointing of vowels in the Hebrew text, though apparently abstruse, was closely related to the political and theological debates of the revolutionary decades. The debate illustrated the extent to which the London Polyglot was an ecclesiastical project, and demonstrated that its technically brilliant, simultaneous representation of multiple translations underscored the survival of Laudian assumptions about ecclesiology and the church's formation of scripture. Owen, who by the later 1650s was being recognized as the pre-eminent theologian of the Cromwellian establishment, had long argued that the church should be controlled by the Bible, operating in government, and worship should be under the final authority of scripture. But Walton's juxtaposition of multiple and competing texts of scripture entirely undermined this argument—offering competing texts without attempts to reconcile their differences—as did his decision to print Hebrew characters without the pointing marks which had long been used to indicate the appropriate accompanying vowels.

---

[21] Nigel Smith, 'The Uses of Hebrew in the English Revolution', in Peter Burke and Roy Porter (eds), *Language, Self and Society: A Social History of Language* (Cambridge: Polity Press, 1991), 51–71; Ariel Hessayon, *'Gold Tried in the Fire': The Prophet TheaurauJohn Tany and the English Revolution* (Aldershot: Ashgate, 2007).

Owen objected that the vowel pointing had to be original—otherwise God would have inspired a Hebrew text which was capable of ambiguity. But Walton, following a Jewish scholarly tradition, argued that the pointing had come late into the Hebrew textual tradition, and that God had in fact inspired a text which in many important elements was capable of multiple meanings. The consequences of the debate were shocking, for Walton was arguing both that one manuscript tradition need not be preferred above others, and that even individual manuscript traditions could bear multiple meanings. Walton's point was ecclesiological: as an ex-Laudian, who would after the Restoration again sport his high church leanings, he was insisting that the church created the meaning of scripture, and that the multiple and competing biblical texts could only be recognized as being *authentica* by the decision of the church. Owen himself was no text-critical slouch: he could recognize in another context that the Synoptic Gospels had made decisions about the arrangement of certain pericopes which indicated that their intentions were not to provide a straightforward chronological account of the life of Christ.[22] But what he could not stomach was the supposition that the Bible was created by the church. Walton's *Biblia sacra polyglotta complectentia textus originales, Hebraicum, cum Pentateucho Samaritano, Chaldaicum, Graecum: versionumque antiquarum, Samaritanae, Graecae LXXII interp., Chaldaicae, Syriacae, Arabicae, Æthiopicae, Persicae, Vulg. Lat., quicquid compari poterat* (1657) was thus much more than a demonstration of technical brilliance and scholarly ingenuity in Cromwellian England, and insisted that the church was constitutive of the Bible.

IV

In the 1640s and 1650s, the expansion of study helps underscored the popularity of Bible reading, even as it called attention to the difficulties of establishing and circulating credible texts and translations of scripture. Ironically, the unique and sacred qualities of scripture were being undermined in the period in which the case for its political utility was most successfully being argued. For Owen and his allies in Cromwellian government, the quest for an authentic text of scripture preceded and paralleled the quest for an authentic church and godly government: politics and ecclesiology were intimately bound up with the scholarly enterprise of establishing, translating, circulating, promoting, and defending reliable editions of scripture, in an age in which scripture was being read, used, and, increasingly, interrogated. But the Bible, its Puritan advocates argued, was constitutive of church and formative of the state.

Of course, the Bible exercised an almost ubiquitous influence in early modern England: its influence was virtually co-extensive with culture, popular or high, and its relevance to politics was pervasive, immediate, and widely recognized. The annotations of the Geneva Bible had developed an influential critique of the claims of absolute monarchy.[23] Simultaneously, the confessions of the Reformed churches emphasized that the functions of the civil magistrate should be controlled by scripture. The Scots Confession (1560) described

[22] John Owen, *The Works of John Owen*, ed. William H. Goold (Edinburgh: Johnstone and Hunter, 1852), XV. 13.
[23] Furniss, 'Reading the Geneva Bible', 1–21.

civil magistrates as 'lieutenants of God, in whose seats God himself doth sit and judge'.[24] The Second Helvetic Confession (1564), a statement of faith which was adopted by churches from Scotland to Poland, defined the task of the civil magistrate as being to 'advance the preaching of the truth, and the pure and sincere faith ... For indeed we teach that the care of religion doth chiefly appertain to the holy magistrate', who should 'hold the word of God in his hands' while pursuing 'all those whom God hath commanded him to punish or even to execute'.[25] One century later, in the period of high orthodoxy, the Westminster Confession of Faith (1647) likewise insisted that it was the duty of the civil magistrate to ensure that 'Unity and Peace be preserved in the Church, that the Truth of God be kept pure and entire, that all Blasphemies and Heresies be suppressed, all corruptions and abuses in Worship and Discipline prevented, or reformed, and all the Ordinances of God duly setled, administred, and observed'.[26]

The affirmation of the Westminster Confession reflected the expectations of the most advanced of the English Puritans, whose sermons to Parliament in the earlier 1640s had returned to the theme of the divine responsibility of the Commons. The fast sermons of the early 1640s articulated a radical critique of current political trends advanced by preachers with clear sympathies for the emerging Parliamentary cause. Stephen Marshall hailed the Commons in Hebraic terms as representing 'the chosen men of your tribes',[27] while Jeremiah Burroughs reminded members of their holy duty: 'You came together by prayer, you stand by prayer, your successe hitherto is a blessed fruit of prayer. The blessings of the prayers of thousand thousands of the Saints, are daily upon you', that the members should continue the 'great publike work ye are called unto'.[28] And these conclusions reflected the expectations of a wide range of political radicals. As Britain and Ireland entered the vortex of civil war, the political use of scripture drove a series of revolutions, from the Covenanters' theocratic remodelling of the Scottish legal system to the attempts by Fifth Monarchists to reshape English law and political institutions along Old Testament lines.[29] The 'revolution' of the mid-seventeenth century was grounded in assumptions about the political utility of scrip-ture. This kind of religious ferment was entirely typical of the period. For, as Christopher Hill memorably put it, 'to say that the ... revolution was about religion is tautologous; it took place in the seventeenth century'.[30]

---

[24] Peter Hall (ed.), *Harmony of the Protestant Confessions* (London: J. F. Shaw, 1842), 482.

[25] Hall, *Harmony*, 473–4.

[26] *The Humble Advice of the Assembly of Divines, Now By Authority of Parliament Sitting at Westminster, concerning a Confession of Faith* (London, 1647), 23.3 (F1^{v}).

[27] Stephen Marshall, *A Sermon Preached Before the Honourable House of Commons ... November 17. 1640* (1641), 29.

[28] Jeremiah Burroughs, *Sions Joy: A Sermon Preached to the Honourable House of Commons ... September 7. 1641* (1641), A2^{v}–A3^{r}.

[29] On the political interpretation of scripture in early modern Britain and Ireland, see Lee W. Gibbs, 'Biblical Interpretation in Medieval England and the English Reformation', in Alan J. Hauser and Duane F. Watson (eds), *A History of Biblical Interpretation* (Grand Rapids, Mich.: Eerdmans, 2009), ii. 372–402; John Coffey, *Politics, Religion and the British Revolutions: The Mind of Samuel Rutherford* (Cambridge: Cambridge University Press, 1997), 146–87; David George Mullan, *Scottish Puritanism, 1590–1638* (Oxford: Oxford University Press, 2000), 244–84; Alan Ford, 'James Ussher and the Godly Prince in Early Seventeenth-Century Ireland', in Hiram Morgan (ed.), *Political Ideology in Ireland, 1541–1641* (Dublin: Four Courts, 1999), 203–28.

[30] Hill, *The English Bible*, 34.

Nevertheless, throughout the mid-seventeenth century, biblical tropes and language proved sufficiently plastic to support a competing variety of political positions, English and Scottish, royalist and parliamentarian, radical and conservative. Even members of a single new religious movement, the Baptists, could be associated both with the 'democratic secularism' and 'theocratic millennialism'.[31] But, the new criticism suggested, it was not only that biblical rhetoric was plastic—so too was the biblical text.

In mid-seventeenth-century England, Bible reading was increasingly being impacted by the new consequences of historicism: the effort to establish a critical text of the Bible scuttled hopes that its various and ambiguous textual base could mandate any kind of successful earthly polity. If scripture had no inherent authority, it could not be used to establish any kind of authority—unless, of course, the locus of authority was the church, and only then the 'ecclesiastical text' it sanctioned.

Thus the challenge to the English Bible intensified in the mid-seventeenth century. The challenge was not from the market, but from scholars concerned about its textual base and translation decisions. Throughout the 1640s and 1650s, scholars would work simultaneously to codify a standard text—producing the first great wave of scholarly concordances—and to make that standard text problematic. The commodification of scripture in the mid-seventeenth century worked, paradoxically, to devalue the biblical text, as its infallibility was critically undermined by changing contexts in politics, ecclesiology, and the cultures of print.

Further Reading

Daniell, David. *The Bible in English: Its History and Influence* (New Haven: Yale University Press, 2003).

Furniss, Tom. 'Reading the Geneva Bible: Notes toward an English Revolution?' *Prose Studies*, 31 (2009): 1–21.

Gibbs, Lee W. 'Biblical Interpretation in Medieval England and the English Reformation', in Alan J. Hauser and Duane F. Watson (eds), *A History of Biblical Interpretation* (Grand Rapids, Mich.: Eerdmans, 2009), ii. 372–402.

Gribben, Crawford. 'Deconstructing *the* Geneva Bible: The Search for a Puritan Poetic'. *Literature and Theology*, 14 (2000): 1–16.

Gribben, Crawford. 'Reading the Bible in the Puritan Revolution', in Robert Armstrong and Tadhg O'Hannrachain (eds), *Early Modern Bibles*, St Andrews Studies in Reformation History (Aldershot: Ashgate, forthcoming).

Hill, Christopher. *The English Bible and the Seventeenth-Century Revolution* (London: Allen Lane, 1993).

Muller, Richard A. *Post-Reformation Reformed Dogmatics: The Rise and Development of Reformed Orthodoxy, ca. 1520 to ca. 1725*, 4 vols (Grand Rapids, Mich.: Baker Academic, 2003).

Norton, David. *History of the English Bible as Literature*, 2 vols (Cambridge: Cambridge University Press, 1993; rev. edn 2000).

---

[31] Mark Bell, 'Freedom to Form: The Development of Baptist Movements during the English Revolution', in Christopher Durston and Judith Maltby (eds), *Religion in Revolutionary England* (Manchester: Manchester University Press, 2006), 181.

Pettegree, Andrew. *The Book in the Renaissance* (New Haven: Yale University Press, 2011).

Sherman, William H. *Used Books: Marking Readers in Renaissance England* (Philadelphia: University of Pennsylvania Press, 2007).

Tadmor, Naomi. *The Social Universe of the English Bible: Scripture, Society, and Culture in Early Modern England* (Cambridge: Cambridge University Press, 2010).

CHAPTER 15

SELF-DEFEATING SCHOLARSHIP? ANTISCRIPTURISM AND ANGLICAN APOLOGETICS FROM HOOKER TO THE LATITUDINARIANS

NICHOLAS MCDOWELL

THE term 'antiscripturism', meaning 'the doctrine or practice' of 'one who denies the truth and authority of Scripture', is unique, according to the *OED*, to Robert Boyle's *Some Considerations Touching the Style of the H. Scriptures* (1661). It is worth quoting Boyle's typically ornate sentence in full:

> Wherefore, as in Infectious Times, when the Plague reigns, Physicians use more strictly to forbid the smaller Excesses and Inordinancies of Dyet, and the uses of Meats of ill Digestion, or apt to breed any Distemper; because every petty Feaver becomes through the Malignity of the Air, apt to turn into a Plague: so now, that Antiscripturism grows so rife, and spreads so fast, I hope twill not appear Unseasonable to advise those, that tender the Safety and Serenity of their Faith, to be more than ordinarily shy of being too Venturous on any Books, or Company, that may derogate from their Veneration of the Scripture; because by the Predominant and Contagious Profanenesse of the Times, the least Injurious Opinions Habor'd of it, are prone to degenerate into Irreligion. (146–7)

The metaphor of infection to describe the outbreak of irreligious belief recalls the title of the most notorious heresiography of the 1640s, Thomas Edwards's *Gangræna* (3 parts, 1646). Indeed Boyle may have derived the term 'Antiscripturism' from *Gangræna*, in which the Presbyterian cleric Edwards warned the Independents, rivals of the Presbyterians to religious ascendancy in the 1640s and generally more tolerant of sectarianism, to

> Stay no longer in the way of Schisme and Separation wherein thou art, but upon all these dis-
> coveries of the Errours, Heresies, Blasphemies, &c. of the Sectaries leave them lest God be
> provoked to leave thee to go a great way further, then yet thou art, from Independency and
> Anabaptisme, to a Seeker, to Arrianisme, Antiscripturisme, yea, Blasphemy, and Atheisme.[1]

'Antiscripturism' is here the penultimate stage in a sliding scale of irreligion which begins
with Independency and ends with blasphemy and atheism.

For Edwards, one particular heretic called Clement Writer (fl.1627–58), a clothier from
Worcestershire, personified this sliding scale and Edwards devotes several pages in the
first part of *Gangræna* to discussion of this 'arch-Heretique and fearfull Apostate'. First
an Independent, then a Baptist and Arminian, Writer 'fell to be a Seeker, and is now an
Anti-Scripturist, a Questionist and Sceptick, and I fear an Atheist'. The opinion ascribed to
Writer, that the text of scripture 'whether in Hebrew, Greek, or English [is] unsufficient and
uncertain', is one of the first heresies listed by Edwards as gaining ground in England in the
absence of a Presbyterian church discipline.[2] As with dozens of other heresies catalogued in
Gangraena, antiscripturism is presented not merely as one belief among others that an individual might adopt, but as the characteristic heterodoxy of a specific sect. Ephraim Pagitt's
Heresiography (1646), another of the great Presbyterian catalogues of the sectarian heresy
allegedly sweeping Civil War England, claims the existence of an 'Antiscriptuarian' sect, who
'denyeth the Scriptures both of the old and new Testament' (149).

The etymological record for 'antiscripturism', 'antiscripturist', and their variants corresponds with long-standing historiographical assumptions that scepticism about the truth
and authority of the Bible first became a part of public discourse in Britain with the proliferation of radical ideas during the 1640s and 1650s, when the established structures of political and religious authority, the court and the Church of England, had disintegrated. In the
narrative developed by Christopher Hill, still influential in shaping perceptions of the role of
the Bible in seventeenth-century Britain, scepticism about biblical authority had always circulated at an underground level among the 'common' people but in the 1640s it became public and visible: 'Discussion, both verbal and in print, was suddenly liberated. Ideas that had
long been muttered in alehouses could now be freely aired; and as they were aired they were
themselves modified and refined by discussion, and other novelties suggested themselves'.[3]

A figure such as Writer exemplifies not only hostile contemporary claims about the
spread of popular heresy in the Civil Wars but also the sympathetic historiographical narrative of the relation between Civil War radicalism and modernity developed by Hill in
his many books.[4] In one of the most powerful of these books, *The English Bible and the
Seventeenth-Century Revolution* (1993), Hill sought to show not only how central the Bible
was to the conflicts of the Civil Wars but also how the Bible was 'dethroned' by those conflicts as a consequence of the radical and sceptical criticism to which it was widely subjected

---

[1] Thomas Edwards, *Gangræna, or, A Catalogue and Discovery of Many of the Errors, Heresies, Blasphemies
and Pernicious Practices of the Sectaries of this Time* (1646), ii. 170.

[2] Edwards, *Gangræna*, i. 18, 113–16.

[3] Christopher Hill, 'Freethinking and Libertinism: The Legacy of the English Revolution', in Roger D. Lund
(ed.), *The Margins of Orthodoxy: Heterodox Writing and Cultural Response, 1660–1750* (Cambridge: Cambridge
University Press, 1995), 55.

[4] For further discussion, see Nicholas McDowell, *The English Radical Imagination: Culture, Religion, and
Revolution, 1630–1660* (Oxford: Oxford University Press, 2003), esp. 1–21.

by 'mechanic' or formally uneducated sectarians. Consequently Hill drew a straight histo-riographical line from the popular, anticlerical radicalism of the 1640s to the radical Whigs, deists, freethinkers, and libertines of the late seventeenth and early eighteenth centuries: 'There was no English Enlightenment in the eighteenth century because the job had been done in the seventeenth century: the ideas of the European (and Scottish) Enlightenment derive from the biblically inspired discussions of the English Revolution'.[5] The Bible, in other words, was the engine not only of religious Revolution in the seventeenth century but of secular Enlightenment in the eighteenth.

The simplifications and misrepresentations of Hill's paradigm have been much criticized over the years, with some justification, but there have also been related and more refined arguments for the connections between the philosophical free-thought of the 1700s and the native sectarian and anticlerical movement of the 1640–60 period. As Justin Champion puts it:

> historians of the seventeenth century should not (just like the Church men of the period could not) underestimate the impact and cultural consequences of the 1650s in determining many of the intellectual and literary problems that confronted the pillars of political orthodoxy ... the cultural crisis of the 1650s did in some sense redefine the mental and cultural landscape which enabled later writers to think and argue in new ways.[6]

For Champion, the English Enlightenment is a radical movement, the intellectual and cul-tural origins of which can be traced back to the turmoil of the mid-seventeenth century. Other scholars, most prominently J. G. A. Pocock, have regarded the English Enlightenment quite differently, as an essentially conservative and clerical movement linked to latitudinar-ian rationalism in the Restoration and defined in opposition not only to Roman Catholicism but more immediately to the twin but opposed extremes of the 1650s, popular sectar-ian enthusiasm and the sceptical materialism embodied in the 'civil science' of Thomas Hobbes: 'The historical situation was such that the Church of England had to steer its way between three menacing figures: Giant Pope, Giant Hobbes and Giant Enthusiast, the last a many-headed figure to be identified with no individual in particular, but with the individual himself or herself'.[7]

The purpose of this chapter is twofold. First, to show that there is a current of scepticism about the authority of the Bible as a sufficient rule of faith *within* the 'Anglican' tradition as that tradition was retrospectively constructed as intellectual and religious orthodoxy at the Restoration. This current can be followed back to Richard Hooker (1554–1600) and through

[5] Hill, 'Freethinking and Libertinism', 67. Cf. Hill, *The English Bible and the Seventeenth-Century Revolution* (London: Allen Lane, 1993), 413–35.

[6] J. A. I. Champion, 'Apocrypha, Canon and Criticism from Samuel Fisher to John Toland, 1650–1718', in A. P. Coudert et al. (eds), *Judaeo-Christian Intellectual Culture in the Seventeenth Century* (Dordrecht: Kluwer, 1999), 104. See also the introduction to *John Toland's 'Nazarenus' (1718)*, ed. J. A. I. Champion (Oxford: Voltaire Foundation, 1999).

[7] J. G. A. Pocock, 'Within the Margins: The Definitions of Orthodoxy', in Lund, *Margins of Orthodoxy*, 43. Compare Champion, '"May the last king be strangled in the bowels of the last priest": Irreligion and the English Enlightenment', in Timothy Morton and Nigel Smith (eds), *Radicalism in British Literary Culture, 1650–1830* (Cambridge: Cambridge University Press, 2002), 29–44; with Pocock, 'Post-Puritan England and the Problem of Enlightenment', in Perez Zagorin (ed.), *Culture and Politics: From Puritanism to the Enlightenment* (Berkeley, Calif.: University of California Press, 1980), 91–112.

the writings of the mid-seventeenth-century bishop Jeremy Taylor (1613–67) into the latitudinarian rationalism of the latter half of the century and the early 1700s.[8] It emerges and develops in reaction to the rise, or perceived rise, of puritanism and enthusiasm, and its major figures sought to press the claims of reason, probability, and historical scholarship against biblical literalism and assertions of inspired interpretation. As Pocock has observed, to this extent a degree of scepticism had long 'reinforced [the Church of England's] authority and [became] part of its orthodoxy'.[9] Yet this chapter will also show how scholarship which demonstrated the historicity of the biblical texts, although intended to bolster orthodoxy and as a polemical response to claims for the self-sufficiency of the Bible or the authority of inspired interpretation, also provided intellectual resources for critiques of the authority of the Bible and of clerical claims to privileged interpretation which are more usually associated with the 'radical Enlightenment'.

Intellectual and cultural historians have increasingly come to regard the relationship between orthodoxy and heterodoxy in the pre-1750 period as dynamic and symbiotic rather than static and oppositional.[10] At the same time it has become clear that radicalism in the seventeenth century was produced by an interaction between elite and popular cultures and was not simply the consequence of lower order revolt and anti-intellectualism.[11] This relationship or process of interaction is exemplified by the ways in which attempts to buttress orthodoxy could in fact furnish and generate heterodox antiscripturist argument. Anglican intellectuals would eventually find themselves ensnared in a double-bind concerning the textual authority of the Bible as they sought to combat 'Giant Pope' on one side and 'Giant Enthusiast' on the other, and the way out could take them perilously close to the path which led to 'Giant Hobbes'.

I. A Space Mediated by Reason: Richard Hooker and William Chillingworth

Richard Hooker's *Of the Laws of Ecclesiastical Polity* is a work that has been seen since Izaak Walton's *Life* of Hooker (1665) as having defined and even invented Anglican identity.[12] The first four of its eight books were published in 1593, in the midst of a church and government

---

[8] For an impressive recent account of the emergence of an 'Anglican' identity which explores disjunction as much as continuity between Hooker and the Restoration, see Jean-Louis Quantin, *The Church of England and Christian Antiquity: The Construction of a Confessional Identity in the Seventeenth Century* (Oxford: Oxford University Press, 2009).

[9] Pocock, 'Within the Margins', 50.

[10] See in particular the essays in Lund, *Margins of Orthodoxy*, and more recently, with specific reference to the significance of biblical scholarship, in Ariel Hessayon and Nicholas Keene (eds), *Scripture and Scholarship in Early Modern England* (Farnham: Ashgate, 2006).

[11] See McDowell, *English Radical Imagination, passim.*

[12] For influential views on the role of Hooker's *Laws* in the development of Anglicanism, see Peter Lake, *Anglicans and Puritans? Presbyterianism and English Conformist Thought from Whitgift to Hooker* (London: Unwin Hyman, 1988); Patrick Collinson, 'Hooker and the Elizabethan Establishment', in Arthur Stephen McGrade (ed.), *Richard Hooker and the Construction of Christian Community* (Tempe, Ariz.: Medieval & Renaissance Texts & Studies, 1997), 149–81.

crackdown on Presbyterian and separatist activists which included the imprisonment of Thomas Cartwright and the execution in 1593 of Henry Barrow, John Greenwood, and John Penry. Richard Bancroft's *Daungerous Positions and Proceedings, Published and Practiced within This Iland of Brytaine, Under Pretence of Reformation, and for the Presbiteriall Discipline* (1593) sought polemically to elide the Presbyterian movement with sectarian claims to prophetic inspiration, as embodied in the sensational episode of the attempted uprising in 1591 led by William Hackett, the self-proclaimed prophet of the Second Coming, to present Presbyterianism as a fanatical and treasonous threat to the Elizabethan church and state.[13] Hooker's *Laws*, for all its stylistic elegance and elevated tone, should be read in the context of this concerted anti-Puritan campaign. The lengthy preface to the *Laws* is, after all, addressed to 'them that seek (as they term it), the reformation of the laws and orders ecclesiastical in the Church of England' and Hooker dedicates the second book of the *Laws* to 'sifting', as he puts it, the alleged Presbyterian claim that 'Scripture is the only rule of all things which in this life may be done by men'.[14]

The polemical purpose of the *Laws* comes into sharper focus towards the end of the preface, when Hooker adopts the same strategy as Bancroft of eliding Elizabethan Presbyterian activism with enthusiastic sectarianism by dwelling on the episode of the Münster Anabaptists, slaughtered after their rebellion and occupation of the city in 1534–5 and led by itinerant lay preachers including the notorious John of Leiden. It was, according to Hooker, private reading of the Bible by ignorant 'mechanics' that was at the root of the awful events at Münster: 'When they and their Bibles were alone together, what strange fantastical opinion soever at any time entered into their heads, their use was to think the Spirit taught it to them' (i. 135). The Münster rebellion illustrates for Hooker how clerically unsupervised encounters between the biblical texts and the weak minds of the common people can lead to heresy and violence which is subversive both of Christian morality (evident in their introduction of polygamy) and civil and social order (evident in their 'overturning of the seats of magistracy' and 'bringing in community of goods'). In the second book of the *Laws*, Hooker declares his purpose is to demonstrate that men should not seek 'to exact at our hands for every action the knowledge of some place of scripture out of which we stand bound to deduce it … but rather as the truth is, so acknowledge, that it sufficeth if such actions be framed according to the law of Reason'.

Hooker's argument concerning biblical interpretation is that, since revelation has ceased, the authority of Puritan arguments from scripture must rest upon the 'ordinary' illumination of reason; not upon 'the fervent earnestness of their persuasion, but the soundness of those reasons whereupon the same is built, which must declare their opinion in these things to have been wrought by the holy Ghost, and not by the fraud of that evil Spirit which is even in his illusions strong' (i. 102). In other words, the Bible retains its infallibility as the Word of God but, in the absence of revelation, all human readers are fallible: 'we all believe that the Scriptures of God are sacred, and that they have proceeded from God … We have for this point a demonstration sound and infallible. But it is not the word of God which doth or possibly can assure us, that we do well to think it his word' (i. 242). Hooker challenges

---

[13] See Alexandra Walsham, '"Frantick Hacket": Prophecy, Insanity and the Elizabethan Puritan Movement', *Historical Journal*, 41 (1998): 27–66.

[14] Richard Hooker, *Of the Laws of Ecclesiastical Polity*, ed. Christopher Morris (London: J. M. Dent, 1963), i. 122, 233. All references to Hooker's *Laws* are to this edition and cited parenthetically within the text.

Puritan biblicism by identifying a space, as Debora Shuger puts it, between 'divine meaning and human reading—a space mediated by reason but therefore almost always productive of probabilities and conjectural inferences rather than certain knowledge'.[15] In the absence of the certainty of prophetic revelation, the 'credit' of any biblical interpretation is crucial, and that credit is secured by 'learned men's judgments in opening that truth' (i. 272). A rejection of 'human authority' in biblical interpretation meant that 'a man whose capacity will scarce serve to utter him five words in sensible manner blusheth not in any doubt concerning matter of Scripture to think his own bare *Yea* as good as the *Nay* of all the wise, grave, and learned judgments that are in the whole world' (i. 273). Hooker justified the existence of a university-educated clerical caste by insisting that arguments from scripture become more probable as they are based on specialized historical and linguistic learning: 'Scripture could not teach us the things that are of God, unless we did credit men who have taught us that the words of Scripture do signify those things' (i. 267).

Hooker opposed pretended inspiration (Giant Enthusiast) not straightforwardly to ecclesiastical tradition, which would have brought him uncomfortably close to Roman Catholic apology (Giant Pope), but to rational exposition of the Bible, which he in turn identified with the demonstrable, quantifiable learning of clerical ordination.[16] However the Jesuit controversialist Thomas Thorold cited precisely this sentence from the *Laws* ('Scripture could not teach us the things that are of God, unless we did credit men who have taught us that the words of Scripture do signify those things') as evidence that the logical consequence of Hooker's argument that the Bible could not authenticate itself was that the authority of an infallible church was required to do so:

> Now seeing *Hooker* affirms, that this *sound and infallible Demonstration* that Scripture proceeds from God, is *not the word of God,* or Scripture it self, he must either settle no *infallible* ground at all … or must say, that the Tradition of the Church is *that ground.* For seeing he assigns no other save *the Authority of man* (which, as the Bishop here acknowledges, is *the name he gives to Tradition*) it must necessarily follow, that either we have no *infallible ground* at all to believe Scripture to be the word of God, or it is Tradition.[17]

Although Thorold's work was first published in 1658, he was writing in response to William Laud's use of Hooker in disputation with the Jesuit John Fisher in the 1620s and more specifically to the publication of the record of that disputation by Laud in 1639 as *A Relation of the Conference Between William Laud … and Mr. Fisher the Jesuit.*

As we shall see, the Laud–Fisher debate was one of the most significant religious disputations of the seventeenth century. One man whose confessional history was entwined with the debate was William Chillingworth (1602–44), who was converted to Rome by Fisher in 1628 but remained close to his godfather Laud and soon returned to the Church of England, spending much of the mid-1630s in religious and philosophical conversation at the estate of Lucius Cary, Viscount Falkland, at Great Tew in Oxfordshire. While always opposed to the

---

[15] Debora Shuger, *Habits of Thought in the English Renaissance: Religion, Politics, and the Dominant Culture* (Berkeley, Calif.: University of California Press, 1990), 35. See also W. David Neelands, 'Hooker on Scripture, Reason and "Tradition"', in A. S. McGrade (ed.), *Richard Hooker and the Construction of Christian Community* (Tempe, Ariz.: Medieval & Renaissance Texts & Studies, 1997), 75–94.

[16] Cf. Quantin, *Church of England,* 92–4.

[17] Thorold, *Labyrinthus Cantuariensis, or, Doctor Lawd's Labyrinth* (Paris, 1658), 93, 95.

Calvinist doctrine of predestination, Chillingworth also became anxious that Laudianism was placing too much emphasis on clerical ritual at the expense of the personal encounter with the Bible that was at the heart of Protestantism. *The Religion of Protestants a Safe Way to Salvation* (1638), the most influential work to emerge from the intellectual context of the Great Tew circle, is a response to another Jesuit controversialist, Edward Knott, who sought to appropriate Hooker's inheritance for Roman Catholicism. Chillingworth recognizes that bits and pieces of Hooker can be made to justify aspects of the Roman Catholic assertion of the supremacy of ecclesiastical tradition over the doctrine of *sola scriptura*, but this was due to the polemical context in which Hooker was writing:

> For M. *Hooker,* if writing against Puritans, he had said something unawares that might give advantage to Papists it were not inexcusable: seeing it is a matter of such extreme difficulty, to hold such a temper in opposing one extreme opinion, as not to seem to favour the other … M. *Hooker* is as far from making such an Idol of Ecclesiasticall Authority, as the Puritans whom he writes against.[18]

Chillingworth emphasizes rather Hooker's insistence on both the infallibility of the Bible and the fallibility of human interpretation, and he regards the keystone of Hooker's thought to be his appeal to reason and probability as the surest guide to religious truth. So in response to Knott's argument that the Bible can provide no infallible demonstration of its own divine status, for which Knott summons Hooker as an authority from within the Church of England's own camp, Chillingworth asserts the place of reasonable supposition and probability based upon historical scholarship, textual comparison, and linguistic expertise:

> For first, the Question *whether such or such a book be Canonicall Scripture,* though it may be decided negatively out of Scripture, by shewing apparent and irreconcileable contradictions between it and some other book confessedly Canonicall; yet affirmatively it cannot but only by the testimonies of the ancient Churches: any book being to be received as undoubtedly Canonicall, or to be doubted of as uncertain, or rejected as Apocryphall, according as it was received, or doubted of, or rejected by them. Then for the Question, *of various readings which is the true,* it is in reason evident and confessed by your own Pope, that there is no possible determination of it, but only by comparison with ancient Copies. And lastly for controversies about different translations of Scripture, the learned have the same meanes to satisfy themselves in it, as in the Questions which happen about the translation of any other Author, that is, skill in the language of the Originall, and comparing translations with it. (63)

To the Jesuit argument that only the Roman Catholic Church could rule authoritatively on the meaning of the biblical books because they are subject to historical and textual process as well as interpretatively uncertain, Chillingworth does not insist on the greater accuracy of Protestant translations but accepts the fallibility of any translation and argues for the mediating role of comparative scholarship in arriving at a probable meaning:

> In which way if there be no certainty, I would know what certainty you have, that your *Doway* old, and *Rhemish* new Testament are true translations? And then for the unlearned those on your side are subject to as much, nay the very same uncertainty with those on ours. Neither is there any reason imaginable, why an ignorant English Protestant may not be as secure of

---

[18] William Chillingworth, *The Religion of Protestants a Safe way to Salvation* (Oxford, 1638), 309, 311.

the translation of our Church, that it is free from errour; if not absolutely, yet in matters of moment, as an ignorant English Papist can be of his Rhemist Testament, or Doway Bible. The best direction I can give them is to compare both together, and where there is no reall difference (as in the translation of controverted places I believe there is very little) there to be confident, that they are right; where they differ, there to be prudent in the choice of the guides they follow. Which way of proceeding, if it be subject to some possible errour, yet is it the best that either we, or you have; and it is not required that we use any better then the best we have. (63–4)

Chillingworth here characteristically emphasizes the element of doubt surrounding all theological and doctrinal readings of scripture given the post-apostolic cessation of direct divine revelation; but he does so only to emphasize the fundamental beliefs common to all Christian confessional identities—beliefs which for Chillingworth were accessible to human reason through scripture. It was on this basis that he argued for a comprehensive national church which would encompass all those who subscribed to the common fundamentals of Christianity.

While Chillingworth's arguments for widespread toleration extending to Roman Catholics and his emphasis on personal rational encounter with the scriptures appear quite distinct from the Laudians' sacerdotalism and vision of a compulsory national church government, his rejection of the possibility of direct revelation and insistence on the essential role of academic training in increasing the probability of scriptural exegesis provided a rationale, as they did for Hooker, for an established clergy and episcopal Church of England. The Presbyterian Francis Cheynell, however, accused Chillingworth of rejecting the Protestant principle of the self-sufficiency of the scriptures with the intention of seeking both to introduce Roman Catholicism to England through Laudian reform ('an Accommodation between Rome and Canterbury') and promote Socinian heresy, according to which human reason was allegedly given pre-eminence over the revealed Word of the Bible as the rule of faith.[19]

So against Roman Catholic claims that the Bible could not serve as an infallible rule of faith because its nature as a textual object meant it was subject to historical process, human error, and interpretative doubt, Caroline defenders of the Church of England could find in Hooker an assertion of the interpretative role of reason, manifest in practice as formal learning, in ascertaining the probable meaning of scripture. At the same time, against Presbyterian and sectarian claims (which they tended polemically to elide) for the sufficiency of the Bible and the authority of lay and prophetic readings, 'Anglican' apologists could exploit aspects of the Roman Catholic argument about the uncertainty of the Bible as a rule of faith to insist both on the relevance of historical consensus derived from ecclesiastical tradition and the necessity of formal historical and linguistic training, such as was demanded of clerical ordination, to arrive at reasonable conclusions about the sense of scripture.

We can see here the outline of the ideal projected by Newman, Keble, and the Oxford Movement in the nineteenth century of the Church of England as a *via media* between

---

[19] Cheynell, *The Rise, Growth, and Danger of Socinianisme* (London, 1643), 7. See also Warren Chernaik, 'Chillingworth, William (1602–1644)', *ODNB*, 2004; online edition, Jan. 2010, <http://www.oxforddnb. com/view/article/5308>. On the role of Socinian thought in the ideas which emerged from Great Tew, see Sarah Mortimer, *Reason and Religion in the English Revolution: The Challenge of Socinianism* (Cambridge: Cambridge University Press, 2010).

persecutory 'Papists' on one side and Puritan and sectarian 'fanatics' on the other—an ideal that the movement regarded as having originated in Hooker and having inspired key monuments of collaborative biblical scholarship in the seventeenth century, from the King James Bible of 1611 to the Polyglot Bible of 1654–7 and beyond. This notion of the Church of England as *via media* would seem to be encapsulated by the title that the future Restoration bishop Jeremy Taylor gave in 1657 to his *Polemical and Moral Discourses Wherein the Church of England in Its Worst as Well as More Flourishing Condition is Defended in Many Material Points, against the Attempts of the Papists on One Hand, and the Fanaticks on the Other*. Yet in the preface to this collection, Taylor felt he had to defend himself against the charge that in his Civil War writings he had not only 'wholly destroyed the Topick of Ecclesiastical Antiquity' but actually 'arm'd the *Anabaptists*'. It was the experience of the Civil Wars and of the triumph of Presbyterianism and Independency during the 1640s and 1650s which led Taylor to fuse Chillingworth's arguments for toleration based upon the fundamental uncertainty of theological knowledge with a full-blown rejection of the Bible as a rule of faith on historical and textual grounds. Yet in seeking to employ scholarly method to undermine Puritan biblical literalism in a fashion similar to Jesuit arguments against the Protestant doctrine of *sola scriptura*, Taylor, a protégé of Laud and a defender of episcopacy, did indeed arm the antiscripturists.

II. JEREMY TAYLOR, TEXTUAL SCHOLARSHIP, AND THE RESOURCES OF THE ANTISCRIPTURISTS

The name of Jeremy Taylor was long synonymous with mid-seventeenth-century Anglicanism, although familiarity with Taylor and his works has declined sharply even since T. S. Eliot's confident declaration of 1926 that 'to the ordinary observer the English Church in history means Hooker and Jeremy Taylor'.[20] Taylor's reputation as a preacher at Cambridge brought him to the attention of Laud, who recommended him to a fellowship at All Souls, Oxford, and made him a chaplain in ordinary to Charles I. In 1642 Taylor presented Charles I with the manuscript of his *Of the Sacred Order, and Offices of Episcopacy* (1642), which the King appreciated so much that he ordered that Taylor should be made doctor of divinity at Oxford. The publication of this work may have led to the Parliamentary sequestration of Taylor's church living at Uppingham in Rutland. Taylor retreated to south Wales, where he set up a school close to Golden Grove, the home of Richard Vaughan, second Earl of Carbery, who had led the King's forces in Wales until 1644. Carbery appointed Taylor his chaplain and Taylor spent the next decade at Golden Grove, where he composed many of the devotional texts for which he is best known, including *The Rule and Exercises of Holy Living* (1650) and *The Golden Grove, or, a Manual of Daily Prayers and Litanies* (1654).

---

[20] 'Lancelot Andrewes' (1626), in *Selected Prose of T. S. Eliot*, ed. Frank Kermode (London: Faber & Faber, 1975), 180.

These texts develop a quietist but defiant mode of Anglican survivalism by offering the private reader a set of devotional forms by which to live in the absence of the external structures and community of the Church of England. In the preface to *The Golden Grove*, addressed to the 'Pious and Devout Believer', Taylor encourages Anglican survival and envisages restoration: 'We must now take care that the young men who were born in the Captivity, may be taught how to worship to the God of Israel after the manner of their fore-fathers, till it shall please God that Religion shall return into the Land, and dwell safely and grow prosperously' (A3ᵛ). Taylor seems in fact to have been imprisoned for his comments about Independency in this preface, although his friend John Evelyn records that Taylor was also conducting illegal Prayer-Book services in London at this time. However he was soon released and left for the north of Ireland in 1658 to act as chaplain to Lord Conway; after the Restoration he became Bishop of Down and Connor. He died in 1667 after several years of conflict with both Presbyterians and Roman Catholics in County Down. Taylor's writings are chiefly celebrated today for their ornate prose style, which preserved in language his keen sense of the beauty of devotional ritual and forms.[21]

So why did Taylor feel he had to apologize for his orthodoxy in 1657? The charge that Taylor 'armed the *Anabaptists*' derives immediately from a disputation between two Oxford graduates in Folkestone, Kent, on 10 March 1650. The Calvinist cleric John Reading had travelled to debate with Samuel Fisher, formerly a respected Puritan minister who now led a General Baptist congregation in Ashford, over the question of whether 'all Christians indefinitely were equally and eternally obliged to preach the Gospel without ecclesiastical ordination, or contrary to the demands of the civil magistrate'. Fisher, Wood tells us, took 'most of his argument from Jer. Taylor's *Discourse of the Liberty of Prophesying*. After the debate was ended, our Author Reading thought himself obliged to answer several passages in the said book of Dr. Taylor, which gave too great a seeming advantage to fanaticism and enthusiasm'.[22] Reading's book, *Anabaptism Routed … With a Particular Answer to All That is Alledged in Favour of the Anabaptists, by Dr. Jer. Taylor, in his Book, Called, The Liberty of Prophesying*, appeared in 1655. The text in question, ΘΕΟΛΟΓΙΑ ἘΚΛΕΚΤΙΚΗ: *A Discourse of the Liberty of Prophesying* (1647), was conceived, Taylor tells us, in the midst of 'this great Storm [of the Civil Wars] which hath dasht the Vessell of the Church to pieces'; he wrote it 'with as much greedinesse as if I had thought it possible with my Arguments to have perswaded the rough and hard handed Souldiers to have disbanded presently' (1–3). Taylor effectively set out to abolish the religious conflict which had provoked civil war by defining Christian belief in terms of ethics rather than theology and by establishing the validity of toleration on the basis of the uncertainty of religious knowledge. His arguments are indebted to Chillingworth, with whom he had been acquainted at Oxford, and they anticipate the principal ideas that came to be associated with the latitudinarians, on whom Taylor was an acknowledged and respected influence.[23] But on one crucial religious and political question, the divine authority of the biblical texts, Taylor went beyond them both.

[21] C. J. Spranks, *The Life and Writings of Jeremy Taylor* (London: SPCK, 1952), 139, 290; see also John Spurr, 'Taylor, Jeremy (*bap.* 1613, *d.* 1667)', *ODNB*, 2004; online edition, Oct. 2006, <http://www.oxforddnb.com/view/article/27041>; Nicholas McDowell, 'Jeremy Taylor', in Garrett Sullivan, Jr., et al. (eds), *The Encyclopedia of English Renaissance Literature* (Oxford: Blackwell, 2012), iii. 947–8.

[22] Anthony Wood, *Athenae Oxonienses*, ed. Philip Bliss (Oxford, 1813–20), iii. 796.

[23] Isabel Rivers, *Reason, Grace, and Sentiment: A Study of the Language of Religion and Ethics in England, 1660–1780*, i. *Whichcote to Wesley* (Cambridge: Cambridge University Press, 1991), 25–6, 35–6.

Taylor insists that the moral fundamentals of Christian conduct, as laid down in the Apostles' creed, are clear and in accord with natural reason, and any person who follows them lives the Christian life. However, reason also tells us that there is no possibility of certainty in matters of religion beyond these fundamentals and no external authority sufficient to settle issues of speculative theology. Taylor specifically considers and rejects the claims to absolute authority of scripture, of all methods of expounding scripture, of tradition (including the decisions of ecclesiastical councils), and of the Pope. In the absence of certainty, all religious beliefs and practices that are not opposed to the essential articles of Christian morality or pose no threat to the security of the state should be tolerated. Taylor is emphatic not only in replacing theology with ethics as the basis of Christian doctrine but also external authority with personal reason as the rule of faith. Heresy thus becomes a matter of uncertain opinion rather than certain error:

> I am certain that a Drunkard is as contrary to God, and lives as contrary to the lawes of Christianity, as a Heretick; and I am also sure that I know what drunkennesse is, but I am not sure that such an opinion is Heresy, neither would other men be so sure as they think for if they did consider it aright, and observe the infinite deceptions, and causes of deceptions in wise men, and in most things, and in all doubtfull Questions, and that they did not mistake confidence for certainty. (38–9)

While human beings must be directed by their own reason and judgement in the absence of external sources of certain knowledge, subjective reason is of course fallible—'even when a man thinks he hath most reason to bee confident, hee may easily bee deceived'—so no individual or group has the authority to impose their beliefs, or rather opinions, on another individual (45).[24]

Taylor was evidently reacting to Presbyterian demands for an enforced national church discipline and hoping to convince the Presbyterians, the dominant party in 1647, to allow Church of England services to continue alongside their own: he says as much in the preface to the 1657 reissue of the tract in *Polemical Discourses*. However as one biographer has rather condescendingly observed, 'Taylor's subjects always carried him away'; or, as Samuel Taylor Coleridge, who regarded Taylor as the greatest English prose writer alongside Francis Bacon and who extensively annotated Taylor's works, more perceptively observed, Taylor was a man whose allegiances were split between the heterodox conclusions that he reached by inexorably following his reason and his instinctive, emotional allegiance to episcopal order and hierarchy.[25]

While Hooker and Chillingworth maintained the infallibility of the Bible but stressed the uncertainty of human interpretation, in *The Liberty of Prophesying* Taylor explicitly questions the very status of the biblical texts as the infallible Word of God. While he does maintain, as had Chillingworth, that the fundamentals of Christian doctrine as laid down in the

---

[24] For further discussion of the place of reason and scepticism in Taylor's thought, see Nicholas McDowell, 'The Ghost in the Marble: Jeremy Taylor's *Liberty of Prophesying* (1647) and its Readers', in Hessayon and Keene (eds), *Scripture and Scholarship in Early Modern England* (Aldershot: Ashgate, 2006), 176–91, from which several of the following paragraphs derive.

[25] Spranks, *Jeremy Taylor*, 85. Coleridge's fascinating marginal notes on Taylor could be profitably edited; but for now, see R. Florence Brinkley, 'Coleridge's Criticism of Jeremy Taylor', *Huntington Library Quarterly*, 13 (1950): 313–23.

Apostles' creed are plainly evident in scripture, he argues on historical and textual as well as hermeneutical grounds that the Bible can provide no decisive answers concerning speculative theology.[26] It was probably the pressure to respond to the rise of enthusiasm in the 1640s that led Taylor to this position. The orthodox Protestant doctrine that revelation had ceased, shared by Laudians, Presbyterians, and the more conservative Independents, was the basis of the claim that only an educated and trained ministry was qualified to make an authoritative interpretation of scripture. This claim was now furiously denied and indeed inverted by 'mechanic' preachers such as the cobbler Samuel How, who declared that 'such as are taught by the Spirit, destitute of human learning, are the learned ones who truly understand the Scriptures'.[27] Of course Taylor, like Chillingworth before him and the latitudinarians who followed him, ultimately envisaged religious difference as encompassed within an inclusive national church administered by a tithe-funded clerical caste and headed by an episcopal government. Yet if he hoped to undermine enthusiastic lay interpretation of scripture by denying the authority of the text itself beyond the creedal essentials, he also provided radical readers with a powerful argument for the abolition of the clergy. John Reading recognized this when he accused Taylor of conveying 'ammunition' to 'known and professed enemies' of the Christian church.[28] Clement Writer, the infamous 1640s heretic, was one such unlearned reader who found in *The Liberty of Prophesying* a scholarly basis for his radically antiscripturist and anticlerical arguments.

In *Fides divina: The Ground of True Faith Asserted* (1657), Writer set out to demonstrate the insufficiency of scripture as a rule of faith, citing 'some few modern English Protestant Authors of most eminent learning whose concurrent Testimony herein [is] ... back't with such Arguments and Reasons as are evident to our own understanding and experience' (2). Pride of place amongst these authors is given to 'Jer. Taylor Dr. in Divinity, and a great Schollar, [who] in his Discourse of Liberty of prophesying pag. 61, 62, 63 shews, and by many Reasons proves that which in effect amounts to an impossibility for any man to find out a true Copy or Translation, or right sense of Scripture' (9). Writer refers to section 3 of *The Liberty of Prophesying*, in which Taylor surveys 'considerations taken from the nature of Scripture it selfe' for the 'difficulty and uncertainty of arguments from Scripture'. Here Writer found a comprehensive series of historical, linguistic, and textual arguments against the authority of the biblical texts.

First, Writer quotes Taylor on the issue of the 'many thousands of Copies that were writ by persons of severall interests and perswasions'. Taylor himself at this point offers what amounts to a brief historical analysis of the possible priestly corruptions of the text. For example he cites the claim of Justin Martyr that Jewish scribes excised phrases relating to Christ from the Psalms, specifically 'from the tree' from the end of the tenth line of Psalm 96 ('Say among the heathen that the Lord reigneth'); as the phrase had only ever been included in Justin Martyr's Bible, either one of the fathers was at fault or all of our editions and translations of the Bible are incorrect. This is not to say that the New Testament is any more trustworthy, for some Greek copies of St Mark's Gospel have a verse 'thought by some to savour of

[26] H. R. McAdoo emphasizes that Taylor does not reject the authority of scripture in fundamentals in *The Spirit of Anglicanism: A Survey of Anglican Theological Method in the Seventeenth Century* (London: A. & C. Black, 1965), 70.
[27] Samuel How, *The Sufficience of the Spirits Teaching without Humane Learning* (1640), 12–13.
[28] Reading, *Anabaptism Routed*, A2r.

Manichaisme' and so these copies were rejected by the Catholic Church as inauthentic: 'Now suppose that a Manichee in disputation should urge this place, having found it in his Bible, if a Catholike should answer him by saying it is Apocryphall, and not found in divers Greek copies, might not the Manichee ask how it came in, if it was not the word of God, and if it was, how came it out?' If a verse from St Mark's Gospel can be excised simply on the grounds that it does not agree with theological orthodoxy, 'is there not as much reason for the fierce Lutherans to reject the Epistle of S. James for favouring justification by works?' The existence of so many different versions of scripture undermines the very concept of orthodox and heterodox exegesis: conventional conceptions of the Trinity are defended on the basis on 1 John 5: 7—'For there are three that bear record in heaven, the Father, the Son, and the Holy Ghost: and these three are one'—but antitrinitarians can simply respond by 'saying the Syrian translation, and divers Greek copies have not that verse in them, and therefore being of doubtfull Authority, cannot conclude with certainty in a Question of Faith'.[29]

Taylor's own linguistic learning is deployed in his subsequent discussion in *The Liberty of Prophesying* of how in the original languages 'there are some words so neer in sound, that the Scribes might easily mistake' (62). He demonstrates how a small error such as the mistranscription of a single Greek letter can change completely the meaning of a passage, and speculates how such an error proceeding from the 'negligence or ignorance of the Transcribers' might become the basis of a bitter theological dispute or the origin of a sect (63). While Anglican intellectuals such as Meric Casaubon and Edward Stillingfleet reacted in the 1650s to the rise of the enthusiastic interpretation of scripture by emphasizing that the authority of the Bible rested on the use of historical and philological scholarship to recover the original meaning of the texts, Taylor is emphatic that 'the knowledge of such circumstances and particular stories is irrevocably lost'.[30] The treacherous textual history of the Bible means that it can only be regarded as a human and thus fallible document; besides all the various modes of hermeneutical method are hopelessly subjective: 'Scriptures look like Pictures, wherein every man in the roome believes they look on him only, and that wheresoever he stands, or how often so ever he changes his station' (80). Taylor implicitly suggests here that to treat the Bible as a certain source of religious authority is to worship a false idol.

Writer concludes his summary of Taylor's arguments by reiterating that the 'many pregnant instances and reasons' listed by the 'learned and ingenious Doctor' prove that argument from scripture, whether advanced by 'Councels, Fathers, Traditions ... Churches, Pope and pretenders to have the Spirit', can never be used to justify the imposition of religious uniformity (14). While he makes no mention of the Apostles' creed, Writer echoes Taylor in arguing that scripture should be treated as an ethical rather a theological guide and valued for 'such practical points as are evident to every rational mans understanding and conscience' (24). Taylor's Arminian insistence on the efficacy of reason and the liberty of every man to work out his own salvation clearly appealed to Writer, who derived from his contact with General Baptists—he was a member of Thomas Lamb's General Baptist church in London in the early 1640s—the conviction that redemption is granted to all and that damnation is the result of individual choice and action in this life. Writer fuses General

---

[29] Taylor, *Liberty of Prophesying*, 61–2, 64; quoted by Writer, *Fides Divina*, 10–11.

[30] *Generall Learning: A Seventeenth-Century Treatise on the Formation of the General Scholar by Meric Casaubon*, ed. Richard Serjeantson (Cambridge: RTM Publications, 1999), 19–20; Taylor, *Liberty of Prophesying*, 82, quoted in Writer, *Fides Divina*, 11–12.

Baptist soteriology with a Leveller-influenced conception of natural rights: no external authority can be allowed to deprive 'men of that natural native Right which God hath given to every man, being born a rational Creature, to be saved by his own Faith, and therefore must have that liberty in Matter of Religion and Worship, as to be led by the result of his own understanding, and not of any other mans' (15–16).[31]

Crucially, however, Writer then uses Taylor's learned demonstration of the myriad uncertainties and contradictions of biblical scholarship as the basis of his refutation of Richard Baxter's argument in *The Unreasonableness of Infidelity* (1655) that the spiritual and temporal authority of the clergy is justified by their communication to 'the illiterate', in the sense of those without Latin and Greek, of the saving knowledge obtained from scriptural exegesis (35–6). In other words, Writer rejects the relevance of clerical scholarship to spiritual knowledge—indeed he accuses priests throughout the ages of having corrupted the scriptural text, whether 'through negligence, ignorance or design'—but at the same time he deploys learned clerical argument to prove the rational validity of this rejection (2). Jeremy Taylor, royal chaplain and Restoration bishop, thus confirmed the fears of his Calvinist critics by providing the intellectual resources for the extreme antiscriptural statements of a 'mechanick' preacher.[32]

John Reading believed that Taylor's scepticism about the scriptural texts would have the effect not of undermining enthusiasm but of encouraging claims that the Spirit within was the only true source of spiritual knowledge. Writer's use of *The Liberty of Prophesying* raises the possibility that Samuel Fisher (1605–65), the sectarian whom Reading claimed took his arguments from Taylor's book in disputation in 1655, was also influenced by Taylor's scholarly criticism of scripture when Fisher came to declare the inner light as the only infallible rule of faith. For within months of the Restoration, Fisher, who had been converted to Quakerism in 1655, published the most strident and comprehensive rejection of the Bible as a framework for understanding man and the universe written in early modern England. Stretching to some 1,000 quarto pages, *Rusticus ad Academicos* (1660) subjects the Bible to rigorous historical and textual criticism while brilliantly satirizing the futility of the clerical application of logical, philological, and rhetorical skill to biblical exegesis.[33]

Fisher's argument is grounded upon the epistemological fallacy of identifying God's Word with a material object which is subject to physical change and corruption. The seventeenth-century texts are but 'the Remote issue and Product, at the hundredth hand perhaps of God's voice in the Prophets, yea but Remote Transcripts of fallible men from the handy-work or manuscripts of the first Penmen … the Letter is changeable, alterable, flexable, passing, perishing, corruptible at mans will, who may mis-transcribe, turn, tear, change, alter, burn it'. This material plasticity of the biblical texts is contrasted with the infallible inner light of the resurrected Christ: 'but the Voice and Word of the Son in the heart … this is permanent, lasting, stable, sure, stedfast'. If the Bible is 'yielded to be as Alterable in

---

[31] On Writer's biography, see the entry in R. L. Greaves and R. Zaller (eds), *A Biographical Dictionary of British Radicals in the Seventeenth Century* (Brighton: Harvester Press, 1982–4).

[32] Christopher Hill often discusses Writer but nowhere mentions that most of Writer's arguments are taken directly from Taylor; see e.g. *The World Turned Upside Down: Radical Ideas during the English Revolution* (1972; Harmondsworth: Penguin, 1991), 261–8.

[33] For a full account of the rhetorical strategies of *Rusticus ad Academicos*, see McDowell, *English Radical Imagination*, 137–70.

the very Greek, and Hebrew Copies of it, as the Letters, Vowels, Accents and Iotaes of it, are Lyable to be Chang'd in Sound or Shape, at the Wills of Criticks', then it must be treated as a historical rather than a divine document.[34]

In *Rusticus ad Academicos* and another, briefer work of 1660, the anonymous *Something Concerning Agbarus, Prince of Edesseans*—in which he presented as canonical transcriptions taken from Eusebius of apocryphal letters between Agbar and Christ, with the implicit intention of casting doubt on the authority of the biblical canon—Fisher appropriated philological and textual materials originally produced by scholars in defence of orthodoxy to destabilize, in their own terms and with their own weapons, arguments for special clerical access to divine truth through learning. It was a method of ironic mimicry of scholarly conventions to undermine the claims to truth of biblical scholarship that would be adopted by later radicals and freethinkers such as the Irish deist John Toland (1670–1722).

While Toland opposed sceptical reasoning to Christian orthodoxy and Fisher placed divine truth in a supra-rational inner light, they both challenged Anglican biblical scholarship, and thus the authority of the Church of England in early modern society, 'not by rejecting revelation but by extending the textual basis for what revelation was on to uncertain grounds'.[35] Yet the tendency to such extension was already a latent strain within defences of the Church of England against puritanism and sectarianism stretching back to Hooker. In *The Liberty of Prophesying*, Jeremy Taylor's arguments against scripture as a sufficient rule of faith lead him into discussions which anticipate Spinoza, Richard Simon, and Pierre Bayle later in the century in explicitly challenging through historical and textual analysis the revealed status of the biblical texts. The use of Taylor's arguments by Writer and Fisher suggests that the Independent John Owen had some grounds for his horrified reaction to the publication of Brian Walton's Polyglot Bible, with its lists of thousands of textual variants; Owen indeed tells us that he was spurred into action against the Polyglot by the appropriation of such philological information in the cause of antiscripturism in Writer's *Fides Divina*:

> I dare not mention the desperate consequences that attend this imagination [of the proliferation of textual variants in the prolegomena to the Polyglot], being affrighted among other things, by a little Treatise lately sent me (upon the occasion of a discourse on this subject) by my worthy and learned friend *Dr. Ward*, intituled *fides divina*, wherein its Author, who ever he be, from some principles of this Nature, and unwary Expressions of some learned men amongst us, labours to eject and cast out as uselesse the whole Scripture or word of God.[36]

The 'unwary expressions' of the learned Jeremy Taylor must be the target of Owen's criticism here. Robert Boyle may have had books like *Fides Divina* and *Rusticus ad Academicos* in mind when he urged his readers in 1661 to avoid 'any Books ... that may derogate from their Veneration of Scripture'; yet his warning that even books containing the 'least Injurious Opinions Habor'd of [the Bible] are prone to degenerate into Irreligion' also echoes the

[34] Samuel Fisher, *Rusticus ad Academicos* (London, 1660), 'To the Reader', sig. d4ᵛ; 'The Third Apologetical, and Expostulary Exercitation', 149, in *The Testimony of Truth Exalted*, ed. William Penn (London, 1679), 49, 521.

[35] Champion, 'Apocrypha, Canon and Criticism', 115.

[36] John Owen, *Of the Divine Originall, Authority, Self-evidencing Light, and Power of the Scriptures* (Oxford, 1659), A3ʳ⁻ᵛ.

controversy of the late 1650s over the dangers of applying the full apparatus of philological scholarship to scripture.

III. RESTORATION CODA: EDWARD STILLINGFLEET AND 'RATIONAL INFALLIBILITY'

The sceptical, rationalistic treatment of scripture that this chapter has traced in defences of the Church of England—an approach that might be described as Erasmian in its emphasis on the place of humanist scholarship in biblical matters, but which nonetheless employed that scholarship polemically to subvert the contrasting claims for infallibility which came from both Roman Catholic and Calvinist opponents—continued into the Restoration among those Anglican churchmen pejoratively called latitudinarians. One of the most prominent and learned of these, Edward Stillingfleet (1635–99), responded in *A Rational Account of the Grounds of Protestant Religion* (1665) to Roman Catholic objections that the scriptures were too uncertain to be taken as the ultimate rule of faith by championing philological scholarship as the tool to establish what Stillingfleet called the 'rational Infallibility' of the Bible. Stillingfleet returned to Laud's disputations with Fisher in the 1620s and to the invocations of the authority of Hooker by both sides to insist, echoing Chillingworth, that Hooker's famous statement that the scriptures could not authenticate themselves as revelation was not a justification of the supremacy of ecclesiastical tradition but an acknowledgement of our reliance as readers on philological and historical learning:

> For his sense is plain and obvious, *viz.* that men cannot come to the natural sense and importance of the words used in Scripture, unless they rely on the authority of men for the signification of those words. He speaks not here then at all concerning Church-Tradition properly taken, but meerly of the authority of man, which he contends must in many cases be relyed on, particularly in that of the sense and meaning of the words which occurr in Scripture. Therefore with his Lordships leave and yours too, I do not think that in this place Hooker by the authority of man doth understand Church-Tradition, but if I may so call it Humane-Tradition, viz. that which acquainteth us with the force and signification of words in use.

'[A]ll the difficulty lies', adds Stillingfleet, 'in understanding what [Hooker] means by Infallible; which he takes not in your [i.e. the Roman Catholic] sense for a supernatural, but only for a rational Infallibility; not such a one as excludes possibility of deception, but all reasonable doubting'.[37] Yet, '[a]s many Restoration controversialists came to learn, "reason" was a double-edged weapon in religious debate, and when wielded against an opponent it might well injure the very cause it was intended to defend'.[38]

---

[37] Stillingfleet, *A Rational Account of the Grounds of Protestant Religion Being a Vindication of the Lord Archbishop of Canterbury's Relation of a Conference, &c., from the Pretended Answer by T.C.* (London, 1665), 233–4.

[38] John Spurr, '"Rational Religion" in Restoration England', *Journal of the History of Ideas*, 49 (1988): 584. Cf. Joseph M. Levine, 'Deists and Anglicans: The Ancient Wisdom and the Idea of Progress', in Lund, *Margins of Orthodoxy*, 219–39.

If philological scholarship could be used to argue against both Roman Catholic claims for the incoherence and uncertainty of scripture and Calvinists' claims for its sufficiency and transparency, antiscripturists, Quakers, and deists could appropriate this same scholarship to assert the supremacy of natural reason or the 'inner light' over any mere textual object which, by virtue of its very materiality, was inevitably subject to corruption. Critics of the latitudinarians repeatedly accused them of providing a nurturing soil for deist and other heterodox principles, both in their principles of rational religion and in the policy of comprehending nonconformity which they derived from those principles.[39] The use made in the cause of antiscripturism of the writings of Jeremy Taylor, one of the intellectual forebears of the latitudinarian outlook, suggests these critics may have had a point.[40]

FURTHER READING

Champion, J. A. I. 'Apocrypha, Canon and Criticism from Samuel Fisher to John Toland, 1650–1718', in A. P. Coudert et al. (eds), *Judaeo-Christian Intellectual Culture in the Seventeenth Century: A Celebration of the Library of Narcissus Marsh (1638–1713)* (Dordrecht: Kluwer, 1999), 91–117.

Hessayon, Ariel, and Nicholas Keene, eds. *Scripture and Scholarship in Early Modern England* (Farnham: Ashgate, 2006).

Hill, Christopher. *The World Turned Upside Down: Radical Ideas during the English Revolution* (1972; Harmondsworth, Penguin 1991).

Hill, Christopher. *The English Bible and the Seventeenth-Century Revolution* (London: Allen Lane, 1993).

Lund, Roger D., ed. *The Margins of Orthodoxy: Heterodox Writing and Cultural Response, 1660–1750* (Cambridge: Cambridge University Press, 1995).

McAdoo, H. R. *The Spirit of Anglicanism: A Survey of Anglican Theological Method in the Seventeenth Century* (London: A. & C. Black, 1965).

McDowell, Nicholas. *The English Radical Imagination: Culture, Religion, and Revolution, 1630–1660* (Oxford: Oxford University Press, 2003).

McGrade, Arthur Stephen, ed. *Richard Hooker and the Construction of Christian Community* (Tempe, Ariz.: Medieval & Renaissance Texts & Studies, 1997).

Mortimer, Sarah. *Reason and Religion in the English Revolution: The Challenge of Socinianism* (Cambridge: Cambridge University Press, 2010).

Morton, Timothy, and Nigel Smith, eds. *Radicalism in British Literary Culture, 1650–1830* (Cambridge: Cambridge University Press, 2002).

Pocock, J. G. A. 'Post-Puritan England and the Problem of Enlightenment', in Perez Zagorin (ed.), *Culture and Politics: From Puritanism to the Enlightenment* (Berkeley, Calif.: University of California Press, 1980), 91–111.

[39] W. M. Spellman, *The Latitudinarians and the Church of England, 1660–1700* (Athens, Ga.: University of Georgia Press, 1993), 11–32.

[40] Joseph Glanvill cites Taylor alongside Henry Hammond and Hugo Grotius as men whose books can particularly serve as an antidote to enthusiasm and sectarianism in the section on 'Anti-Fanatical Religion and Free Philosophy', in *Essays On Several Important Subjects in Philosophy and Religion* (London, 1676), 'Essay 7', 6.

Quantin, Jean-Louis. *The Church of England and Christian Antiquity: The Construction of a Confessional Identity in the Seventeenth Century* (Oxford: Oxford University Press, 2009).

Rivers, Isabel. *Reason, Grace, and Sentiment: A Study of the Language of Religion and Ethics in England, 1660–1780*, i. *Whichcote to Wesley* (Cambridge: Cambridge University Press, 1991).

Shuger, Debora. *Habits of Thought in the English Renaissance: Religion, Politics, and the Dominant Culture* (Berkeley, Calif.: University of California Press, 1990).

Spellman, W. M. *The Latitudinarians and the Church of England, 1660–1700* (Athens, Ga.: University of Georgia Press, 1993).

Spurr, John. "'Rational Religion' in Restoration England'. *Journal of the History of Ideas*, 49 (1988): 563–85.

PART III

SPREADING
THE WORD

Introduction to Part III

DEDICATING *The Seconde Parte of the Catalogue of English Printed Bookes* (1595) to Robert Devereux, second Earl of Essex, Andrew Maunsell boasted that he had already shown in *The First Parte* 'that in *Divine* matters necessarie to salvation, no Nation hath better or more plentifull instructions in their owne tongue then wee.'[1] Alongside translations of the scriptures, whether as whole Bibles or individual books, biblical knowledge was disseminated, received, and reshaped in a plethora of forms and venues. Hornbooks, used to teach basic literacy, followed the alphabet (usually begun with a small cross upon which users were asked to meditate) with the Lord's Prayer. Catechisms used a question and answer format to teach Bible stories and godly principles, primarily to children but also to the unlettered, potential converts, and even sailors.[2] Commonplace books, concordances, and abridgements offered easy access to the scriptures. The first known 'Thumb Bible', directed at children, John Weever's versified *An Agnus Dei* was printed in 1601, measuring 3.3 by 2.7 cm.

For the majority of men, women, children—and dogs, if complaints about canine bad behaviour in church are to be believed—sermons formed the primary means to access and understand the scriptures. The skill of preachers was variable: particularly in the early years of Elizabeth's reign, parochial clergy were frequently described as barely literate, ignorant of the scriptures, and poorly equipped to cater to the spiritual needs of their cure. Campaigns for a learned ministry urged the ordination of graduates, and propagated a variety of schemes for the training and scrutiny of ministers. Elements of that scrutiny survive in printed copies of the Articles of Inquiry that bishops prepared before visiting the parishes in their dioceses: a series of questions posed to ministers and church officials on subjects from the physical cleanliness of the church to the spiritual cleanliness of parishioners. In her chapter, Lori Anne Ferrell draws on these suggestive sources, whose frequent annotation attests to the extent of their use, to track the English Church's official position on scripture during the reigns of Elizabeth I, James I, and,

---

[1] *The Seconde Parte of the Catalogue of English Printed Bookes* (London, 1595).
[2] John Flavel, *Navigation Spiritualized: or, A New Compass for Seamen* (London, 1677).

briefly, Charles I. She argues that, whilst the Church of England, in 1559, worked hard to promote Bible reading in domestic as well as ecclesiastical settings, attitudes had changed significantly by the mid-seventeenth century, when the visitation articles insisted instead upon the importance of the spoken word in sermons delivered by qualified preachers.

Ian Green explains which parts of the Bible were read in churches, and the fixed rotas of readings, communal worship, and set prayers that constituted most worshippers' experience of the Bible in England throughout the sixteenth and into the seventeenth centuries. The congregation heard God's word read aloud to them, and had its meaning elaborated and explained in sermons that sought to make scripture directly applicable to the lives of its hearers. More than that, the church service, Green shows, was structured to provide numerous opportunities for the congregation to speak and sing parts of the Bible aloud, entering into an experience of communal worship, and learning the terms and attitudes of devotion and praise.

It is the controversial subject of singing, and particularly of the Psalms, that Rachel Willie takes as her subject. Understood as the Bible in miniature, the Psalms taught individuals how to converse with God; communal singing allowed them to perform that conversation in ways that were both public and intensely personal. Whilst the musicality of the Psalms was understood to create a pleasing harmony, not only between the soul of the individual believer and God, but between members of the congregation and the larger Christian community, debates around the genre of the Psalms, the propriety of singing, and the politics of reproduction introduced notes of dissonance into post-Reformation discussions of liturgical practice and godly living. Willie's chapter explores these controversial subjects, paying particular attention to the bodily and social forms of psalm reading and singing.

The best preachers were celebrities, admired for the passion and eloquence of their performances: performances which could be intensely dramatic, provoking urgent and deeply felt responses in their hearers.[3] Though handbooks of preaching urge the need to make the scriptures relevant to the particular circumstances of the audience, they give little sense of how preachers achieved their effects, or of which approaches and interpretative techniques were most appreciated by audiences hungry for novelty as well as edification. Mary Morrissey sheds new light on this question by turning to the evidence of rehearsal sermons, preached annually in London and Oxford, which gave abbreviated accounts of previous sermons before concluding with a new sermon composed by the rehearser. In the terms rehearsers use to describe (and occasionally to satirize) the techniques of their seniors, we begin to understand how preachers thought about the biblical texts they represented to their hearers, and how they achieved the difficult combination of communicating sound doctrine and engaging an audience through skilful embellishment and inventive interpretation. Rehearsal sermons emphasize the need for the repetition of doctrine, but also the importance of the ability to 'ornament' scripture and expand the interpretative possibilities of the text. Treading a perilous line between literal sense and figurative reading, preachers searched out ways to reveal new meanings to their hearers, prompting anxieties about the relationship between the charisma of preaching and the learning of the clergy.

Whilst Green and Morrissey focus primarily on the English case, and Willie counterpoints that example with reformed practices in Geneva and elsewhere, Alasdair Raffe and Marc Caball offer accounts, respectively, of the dissemination of the scriptures in Scotland and in Ireland. The highly varied experiences of England's near neighbours—with the Reformation

---

[3] See esp. Arnold Hunt, *The Art of Hearing: English Preachers and their Audiences, 1590–1640* (Cambridge: Cambridge University Press, 2010).

gaining a firm hold in Scotland and only a precarious one in Gaelic Ireland—open up new perspectives on how the scriptures were understood and on attempts to expand their reach and reception. The full implementation of the Scottish Reformation, Raffe argues, depended upon decades of ecclesiastical innovation, but also upon the instruction and conversion of worshippers from a wide range of backgrounds. His chapter explores the ways in which the Bible was disseminated and consumed by Scottish Protestants in the century and a half after 1560. Like Green, Morrissey, and Ferrell, Raffe is particularly concerned with the role played by the scriptures in public worship. He contrasts the practice of public reading with the interpretative preaching preferred by leading Scottish Protestants, a tendency that became more marked after the covenanting revolution of 1638–41. In time, Raffe argues, the Bible was rarely read aloud in the context of public worship, but was, increasingly, studied in domestic and personal contexts, transforming Scots' engagement with the Word.

Caball, in contrast, attests to the evangelical spirit that motivated those who worked to print the scriptures in Irish Gaelic, but notes that more research is needed to fully under-stand the partial and often hostile reception of the fruits of their labours among Irish Catholics, as well as their adoption and appropriation by Protestant converts. Though pro-jects to print an Irish translation began as early as the 1560s, no complete Irish Bible was published until 1685. As late as the printing of the Irish Book of Common Prayer in 1608, Caball demonstrates, Gaelic Irishmen, often members of elite bardic families, were central to the project of evangelization through print. Yet ironically the printed scriptures were essentially an expression of state authority which privileged the use of English. Caball takes us through the first printings of the New and Old Testaments in Gaelic, and reveals the cen-tral role played by the philosopher Robert Boyle in the republication of the New Testament in 1681 and Old Testament in 1685. Boyle's support for the distribution of the Gaelic Bible in Scotland neatly complements the very different religious climate described by Raffe.

The final chapter in this section, by Helen Smith, is centrally concerned with questions of conversion. Smith explores, on the one hand, the ways in which the Bible was used as a tool for personal transformation, and, on the other, how it was deployed in attempts to achieve the conversion of others, not least in missionary efforts to establish Christianity in the New World. This chapter illustrates the ways in which influential accounts of conversion informed, and helped to shape, the approach of early modern readers to their Bibles, and emphasizes the transformative effects scripture was understood to possess. Smith explores the material charge of the Bible as a devotional object, and the physical—as well as intensely imaginative—ways in which readers experienced and used their Bibles. The second part of Smith's chapter follows the English Bible across the seas, charting the centrality of the Bible to debates around conversion, but also exploring the challenges to evangelization faced by Protestants and Puritans who insisted upon the necessity of scriptural knowledge gained through reading to the full realization of the conversion experience.

Read, spoken, or sung; heard (almost) in its entirety over the course of a year; condensed in the form of a favourite Psalm or meaningful and often-meditated verse; repeated verbatim or explored and expanded by inventive preachers, the Bible was a flexible and varied resource across and beyond the four nations in the early modern period. Taken together, the chapters in this section reveal the massive administrative efforts that lay behind the dissemination and interpretation of the scriptures, and alert us to the variety of responses provoked by biblical encounters, and to the resistance and hostility that faced those who wished to impose the Bible, or a particular version of the scriptures, onto an unwilling population.

CHAPTER 16

THE CHURCH OF ENGLAND AND THE ENGLISH BIBLE, 1559–1640

LORI ANNE FERRELL

'THE Bible only', the English churchman William Chillingworth wrote in 1638, 'is the religion of Protestants'.[1] Whether it was also the religion of England's Protestant Church is the question that prompts this chapter. It is a question rarely asked. Students of the early modern period are well educated in the English Bible's literary influence, reception, and modes of translation. Bibliographic, print-historical, and materialist studies of the sixteenth- and seventeenth-century Bible abound. Fuelled by recent, ambitious text-editing projects, scripture as filtered through the medium of early modern preaching has been a subject of intense scholarly interest since the 1990s.[2] Those who work on early modern English religion, in fact, do almost nothing but investigate the social consequences and cultural impact of the Word: on worship and doctrine; on education, rhetoric, poetry, and politics; on post-Reformation England's nascent Protestantism and its lingering Catholicism. They rarely take, however, a simple look at the Church of England's formally articulated attitudes towards the Bible.

This chapter tracks a different course: the English Church's official position on scripture as promulgated in the reigns of Elizabeth I, James I, and, briefly, Charles I.[3] The survey will

---

[1] William Chillingworth, *The Religion of Protestants a Safe Way to Salvation* (London: 1638), 375.

[2] Peter McCullough, *Sermons at Court: Politics and Religion in Elizabethan and Jacobean Preaching* (Cambridge: Cambridge University Press, 1998); Lori Anne Ferrell, *Government by Polemic* (Stanford: Stanford University Press, 1998); *Lancelot Andrewes: Selected Sermons and Lectures*, ed. Peter McCullough (Oxford: Oxford University Press, 2005); Jeanne Shami, *John Donne and Conformity in Crisis in the Late Jacobean Pulpit* (Cambridge: D. S. Brewer, 2003); Mary Morrissey, *Politics and the Paul's Cross Sermons, 1558–1642* (Oxford: Oxford University Press, 2011); Peter McCullough, Hugh Adlington, and Emma Rhatigan (eds), *The Oxford Handbook of the Early Modern Sermon* (Oxford: Oxford University Press, 2011).

[3] An earlier version of this chapter appeared as 'The King James Bible in Early Modern Political Context', in David G. Burke, John F. Kutsko, and Philip H. Towner (eds), *The King James Version at 400: Asserting its Genius as Bible Translation and its Literary Influence* (Atlanta, Ga.: Society of Biblical Literature, 2013), 31–42. © Society of Biblical Literature. Used by permission.

show that the Church of England's statements about scripture shifted markedly between the Protestant Settlement of 1559 and the Long Parliament of 1640, revealing, I will argue, a national church increasingly intent upon downplaying or even countering the reliance on *sola scripturalism* that had animated its early Reformation. In the end, this created subjects so alarmed by a perceived decline in reformed principles that they became politically radicalized.

My claim is based on a single essential source: the acts and injunctions dispensed by a legislatively minded church increasingly intent between the 1560s and 1630s on keeping its local parishes under effective control by means of episcopal visitation and oversight. Diocesan and parish visitation was 'the linchpin of effective ecclesiastical government' in England's polity, something that did not change with the Reformation but which did make the changes demanded by wholesale protestantization easier to implement and oversee.[4] Here the long arm of church law reached all the way to parish pews, altars, and churchyards. Almost all bishops were required to visit their sees within eighteen months of translation or elevation by the monarch.[5] After that, they were supposed to visit their region every three years (and amazingly, many did; even archbishops visited all the dioceses in their provinces as soon as possible after consecration and returned to individual dioceses when a see was vacated). The questions these august individuals planned to ask—about how the church was run, what it owned, and the spiritual condition and habits of its personnel and laity—were pre-circulated to local churchwardens, who were charged with providing answers to dozens of searching questions: whether, for example, 'curates and ministers be of that conversation of living, that worthily they can be reprehended of no man?', or 'there be any images in your church?', or any members of the congregation who 'speaketh against baptism of infants?'[6]

By the beginning of the seventeenth century, these articles were routinely printed so churchwardens could provision themselves with pre-test study guides, thereby bequeathing to historians of the Church of England a treasure-trove of illuminating evidence about how the generalized values of the church translated into the material costs of Reformation and the degree to which any church, whether parish or cathedral, was willing to comply with them. The Reformation first made itself known at the parish level by changes in church fabric and the purchase of new books, the Bible among them, which made a singular impact. The Church of England housed, after all, a transitionally literate laity; surely people in its pews noticed the new books before they could all spell out the new words within them.

Visitation articles are some of the most heavily hand-annotated of any early modern printed pages in the research library: proof of their having been read, and carefully. This was for good reason. Churchwardens were required to speak fully and truthfully when presenting; their oath was printed inside the title-page of the articles.[7] They had much to answer for in a religiously and politically perilous age. There are only a few, mostly reissued,

[4] Drawn from Kenneth Fincham's *Visitation Articles and Injunctions of the Early Stuart Church* (Woodbridge: Boydell Press, 1994–8), i, p. xvi.

[5] In England, archiepiscopal authority could be unusual or untoward: York, for example, did not, generally speaking, visit Durham. Archbishop Abbot never conducted a London visitation nor Laud an Oxford one. For the process itself, see Kenneth Fincham, *Pastor as Prelate* (Oxford: Clarendon Press, 1990), 112–23.

[6] Questions 1, 48, and 59 from Nicholas Ridley's *Articles for London Diocese*, 1550, repr. in W. H. Frere and W. M. Kennedy (eds), *Visitation Articles and Injunctions of the Period of the Reformation*, ii. *1536–1558*, Alcuin Club Collections, 15 (London: Longmans, Green & Co., 1910), 231, 238, 240.

[7] Many thanks to Kenneth Fincham for pointing this out.

injunctions and articles in printed form for Elizabeth's reign. But many published versions of the Jacobean and Caroline articles—most of these variations on a theme set by Richard Bancroft's articles for the Diocese of London in the late sixteenth century—are extant in seventeenth-century copies. With these pamphlets (usually printed in quarto format and containing around fourteen pages, though with significant variations in length—the 1571 York articles were forty-four pages), we can trace an ecclesiastical message from the top down that is fairly clean and straightforward. This chapter is, therefore, about the language of official policy—not the manner or efficacy of its enforcement, nor lay and clerical response to that policy.[8] The English people, the English clergy, even the English episcopate never responded to the canons of the English Church in a uniform way. Nonetheless, if we track the church's official voice across three reigns, we can discern a trajectory, an unmistakable narrative of change over time, as the church's stated attitude towards the English Bible moved from promotion, to increasing suspicion, to select disavowal. This trend, I will finally suggest, led the more godly-minded of English lay people increasingly to view their Bibles as personal rather than corporate scripts: a development that would eventually become the characteristic aspect of the Bible's reception and dissemination in America.

What was the English Church's policy on the Bible and on Bible reading? After much vacillation, Henry VIII finally ensured in 1539 that humanist translating energy would be channelled into the creation of an official, public version of scripture: a 'Great Bible' that, by royal injunction, was required to be purchased by all churches.[9] Henry came to repent of his decision and, later, in 1543, his Parliament explicitly restricted the bounds of lay reading.[10] But Bible production increased markedly under the regent governments of Edward VI; given the early death of the evangelical boy king, however, this had limited cultural impact. Although the Catholic government of Mary I did not succeed in eradicating the vernacular Bible it burnt people suspected of printing or promulgating the now-illegal English scriptures. Nor were English Bibles printed in her reign.[11]

Elizabeth I's visitation articles, and the injunctions of 1559 from which they derived, offer, then, a piercing look into what it took to restore a Protestant Church that presented itself in official print as diminished and badly traumatized by its recent past. At first, her government sounds far more concerned with getting the Bible back into the churches than it is with restoring the liturgy, something that makes sense when we consider just how radical most of her ecclesiastical establishment, returning from an enforced exile on the continent during Mary's reign, had to be. The Church of England's obsession with its liturgical traditions—exemplified in a Book of Common Prayer that was, in effect, a cautious revision of England's traditional Catholic Mass—was not much in evidence in 1558–9.

Its obsession with the Bible was. To read the official language of the church at the very beginning of Elizabeth's reign is suddenly to apprehend just how radically scripture-oriented the culture of the religious settlement would seem to contemporary observers a scant fifty

---

[8] For new approaches to questions of dissemination and enforcement, see the other chapters in Part III of this volume, especially by Marc Caball, Ian Green, and Alasdair Raffe.

[9] On the Bible translation projects of the 1530s, see the chapter by Susan Wabuda in this volume.

[10] The Act restricted lay reading to public reading only by licence. The right to read privately was restricted to the well-off, the well-educated, and the male of the species. See David Daniell, *The Bible in English* (New Haven: Yale University Press, 2003), 228–9.

[11] This brief narrative account is drawn from my recent work. See Lori Anne Ferrell, *The Bible and the People* (New Haven: Yale University Press, 2008), esp. ch. 3. See also Daniell, *The Bible in English*, 245, 263.

years later. In 1558, Protestant martyrdom was not only so recent as to seem ever-present; it was also inextricably bound up with the struggle for a vernacular Bible. William Tyndale and others had died for this cause, and even those who went to the flames for reasons other than translating had arrived at their fatal doctrinal positions after reading the translated Bible.[12]

A stark tone of biblical witness characterizes items 46 and 49 of the *Articles to Be Inquired of in the Visitation of the Church*, first printed in 1559, which not only ring an extraordinary variation on any bureaucratic church's ongoing concerns with inventory, but also bind together, in inseparable union, English Bibles and England's true believers. Elizabethan bishops were required to ask of parish churchwardens the following: 'Item, what bokes of Goddes Scripture you have delivered to be burnt, or otherwise destroyed, and to whom ye have delivered the same',[13] and, 'Item how many persones for religion have dyed by fyer, famine, or otherwise, or have ben imprysoned for the same'.[14] The sober checklist reminds us that, by the time of Elizabeth's accession, many churches in England had been depleted of two essential and intimately related resources: their Bibles, and their people.

Bibles were more easily procured and reinstated in the Church of England than were martyrs (it would take the many lurid woodcuts in John Foxe's *Actes and Monuments* to effect the latter). Within three months of an initial visitation and (of course) at parish expense, 'one book of the whole Bible of the largest volume in English' was to be reinstalled in the church. By the end of the year, Erasmus's paraphrases were also to be purchased, and both books were to be set up in a central location where parishioners could consult the scriptures at any time except during the service. The 1559 Injunctions specifically, and at great length, commanded clergy to 'discorage no man from the readyng of any parte of the Byble, eyther in Latin or in Englyshe, but … rather exhorte every person to reade the same', and they went on to endorse the scriptures as 'the verye lyvely woorde of God, and the specyal fode of mans soule, which all Christian persones are bounde to embrace, beleve, and followe, yf they looke to be saved: wherby they maye the better knowe their dueties to God, to theyr Soveraigne Lady the Quene, and [to] theyr neyghbour'.[15]

For their part, parishioners of the insistently Protestant sort—the kind who later would be called 'Puritans'—were to be reminded that not all clergy currently beneficed in the Church of England had instantly become Bible enthusiasts when Elizabeth took over the church. These more godly lay people were enjoined to think charitably rather than censoriously about priests who 'of long time favored fond fantasies rather than Gods truth'. Notwithstanding, churchwardens were to be asked whether their parish minister was a 'letter', or hinderer, of Bible reading by others in private or in church, or a hinderer of 'sincere' preaching of biblical texts; they were also urged to report any clergyman who spent his time off idling rather than learning his chapters and verses. These admonitions on both sides were early warning systems. The Bible often brought not peace but a sword to the uneasily reforming parish churches of late Elizabethan England, torn as they were between traditional practices of liturgy and Latin prayers and new demands that the people be edified with scripture and preaching in their own tongue. For now, though, Elizabethan 'Parsons,

---

[12] This was, in large part, the work of John Foxe's *Actes and Monuments*: see Daniell, *The Bible in English*, 131.
[13] *Articles to be Enquyred in the Visitacion* (London: 1559), B1ᵛ–B2ʳ. In the margin is the simple word 'Bokes'.
[14] *Articles*, B2ʳ. In this margin we find, simply, 'Howe many burnt'.
[15] *Injunctions Geven by the Quenes Majestie* (London, 1559), A3ʳ⁻ᵛ.

Vicars, and Ministers of Churches' were commanded to 'painfully be occupied in scripture', and to memorize Bible passages in English so as to have the right words at the tips of their tongues when parishioners sought spiritual counsel and comfort. They were therefore explicitly commanded to undertake active reading: to purchase for their own private use copies of the New Testament in Latin and English and to work through them, comparing them and taking notes.[16]

This explicitly articulated privileging of the Word was the foundation on which the Elizabethan Church was first reconstructed. The *Book of Certaine Canons*, which covered the specific responsibilities of every member of an episcopal polity from archbishops on down and was published by royal decree in 1571, opened: 'All Bishops shall diligently teach the Gospel ... principally they shall exhort their people to the reading, and hearing, of the holy scriptures'. Bishops were to ordain only any 'who hath been well exercised in the holy scriptures'. By this time, every bishop was expected to own both a Bible and a copy of *Actes and Monuments* and place them 'either in the hall, or in the great chamber that they may serve to the use of their servants and to strangers'. Deans of cathedral churches were ordered also to have 'the very same books we spoke of last ... in such convenient place that the vicars and petty canons, and other ministers of the church, as also strangers and foreigners can easily come unto them and read thereon'. All deans, cathedral residents, and archdeacons were to 'buye the same bookes every one for his owne familye, and ... lay them in some fit place, either in the hall or in the chamber'. Moving these concerns with biblical teaching out from the private chamber to the visible congregation, the *Canons* then enjoined all licensed ministers not only to preach 'the word of God' but also to ascertain that any statutes of the church 'not contrary to the word of God' were preached diligently.[17]

Just how diligently was spelled out in further injunctions and articles. Preachers were to 'take heed, that they teach nothing in their preaching, which they would have the people to believe, but that which is agreeable to the doctrine of the Old Testament or the New'. They were to teach that the 'articles of Christian religion, agreed upon by the Bishoppes, in ... convocation [and commanded by the Queen], undoubtedly are gathered out of the holy bookes of the olde, and new Testamente, and in all pointes agree with the heavenly doctrine conteyned in them ... also [that] the booke of common prayers, ... conteyne nothing repugnant to the same'.[18] This is Reformation by scripture, the Bible as the religion of Protestants. These injunctions and national articles, such advocates of the Bible and for Bible reading—lay and clerical, private and public—appeared in at least five editions between 1559 and 1600 without alteration, while the governmental attitude on further reform on the model set by the Calvinist churches on the continent, and the outspoken people who so hotly clamoured for it, was cooling to lukewarm. And so, ironically, the long reign that finally ensured England's Protestantism after a century of Tudor confessional vacillation also created the conditions—a church but 'halfly reformed'; the retention of traditional worship practices

---

[16] *Articles*, A2ᵛ (in the margin: 'Reading the Scriptures'); and A4ʳ (in the margin: 'Letters of the worde or preachinge'.

[17] *A Booke of Certaine Canons, concerning Some Parte of the Discipline of the Church of England* (London, 1571), A2ʳ–A4ʳ. This abbreviated set of canons outlined the duties for each level of church governmental officer from archbishops to patrons.

[18] *Certaine Canons*, C4ʳ.

and church government leading to the rise of indignant and demanding parishioners called 'Puritans' within this same church—that spelled the end of an era of *sola scriptura*.[19]

Or, perhaps better said, allowed it to fade away ('time out of mind' seems always to have arrived ahead of schedule in post-Reformation England). For first- and second-generation Protestant reformers, *sola scriptura* seems to have carried a capacious and active meaning: that the Bible was not merely sufficient to the simple doctrine of salvation by faith, which would establish the church invisible, but was also the literal standard against which the visible church, its doctrines and practices, was to be judged. Here recall the words of the injunction that described the Bible as a book all Christians were to 'embrace, believe, and follow if they look to be saved', but also that 'they may the better know their duties to God, Queen, and their neighbor', these last three, when compounded, making a nicely succinct definition of a national church.

The relatively late date (1600) of the final Elizabethan reissue of the articles thus makes the near disappearance of explicit Bible policy at the beginning of the reign of James I all the more striking. In the Jacobean articles, the Bible appears as little more than another furnishing to be procured and purchased and inventoried by churchwardens. The assertive tone of the 1559 *Injunctions* and the 1571 *Canons*, their many stated provisions for biblical reading and displaying and instruction, their plethora of approving references to holy scripture, are hardly to be found in the canons of 1604. Silence can, admittedly, be misleading evidence of decline. And perhaps after fifty years of Protestantism in England, with the secure establishment of the Church of England under the Supreme Governorship of the monarch by 1603, we could simply say that a passionate defence of the Bible was no longer necessary and was in fact assumed. But instead let us recall that the turn of the century, and with it the end of the Tudors, and the accession of their Stuart cousins to the throne, was a particularly unstable time in early modern England, especially in matters of religion.[20] And let us also recall who scripted those 1604 canons: Richard Bancroft, Bishop of London, hammer of the Puritans and the author of a set of visitation articles for London in 1598 that, in their range and comprehensiveness, set the template for and, arguably, the tone of policy in the Church of England until that church was dismantled, violently, in the 1640s.

A reading of 1604 in the light of 1598 and against 1559 thus yields the following suggestive if not definitive insights: where 1559 was concerned with the circulation and reading of the Bible, 1604 is centrally concerned with preaching. 1559 aims to discover whether curates 'discourage any person from readying of any parte of the Byble, eyther in latyn or englysh', expecting them instead to 'exhort every person to read the same at convenyent tymes, as the very lyvley worde of god and the speciall fode of mans soule'.[21] In contrast, 1604 inquires 'Whether any of your parishioners hauing a Preacher to their Parson, Vicar, or Curate, do absent themselues from his Sermons, and resort to any other place to heare other preachers?'[22]

[19] Patrick Collinson identified 'Puritanism' as a non-sectarian phenomenon within the Church of England—a kind of 'leaven in the loaf'—in 1967, and this model continues to inform all treatments of early modern English Protestantism: *The Elizabethan Puritan Movement* (London: Jonathan Cape, 1967); the 'leaven' remark comes from his Ford Lectures of 1979 at the University of Oxford, later published as *The Religion of Protestants: The Church in English Society 1559–1625* (Oxford: Clarendon Press, 1982).
[20] Ferrell, *Government by Polemic*, 64–109.
[21] *Articles*, A2ᵛ.
[22] *Articles, to be Enquired of Within the Dioces of London* (London, 1604), B2ᵛ.

And where we now find the word 'preaching' it is not always in tones of unalloyed approval. Article 15, for example, asks 'Whether is there any man in your parish, being neither your Parson, Vicar, nor Curate, that taketh upon him to preach or read Lectures eyther in private houses, or publikely in your church or chappell, who is not licensed to preach or read there'.[23] The Church of England's ongoing defence of its other authoritative text, the Book of Common Prayer, becomes more apparent and focused as a result.[24] Article 24, for example, asks 'Whether there be any in your parish who will come to heare the Sermon, but will not come to the publike prayer appoynted by the booke of Common prayer, making a schisme or division (as it were) betweene the use of publike prayer and preaching?'[25] A dichotomy is established between 'preaching' and 'praying', and so the Prayer Book becomes the Bible's chief competitor—and not the Bishop's Bible of 1568, discredited on all sides, but the populist and instructive Geneva Bible first published in England in 1560.

Take, for example, the 57th canon of 1604, titled 'The Sacraments not to be refused at the hands of unpreaching Ministers': 'forasmuch as the doctrine both of Baptism and of the Lords Supper is so sufficiently set downe in the booke of Common Prayer … as nothing can be added unto it that is material and necessary: We doe require and charge every such person seduced as aforesaid, to reforme … their willfulness, and to submit himselfe to the order of the Church'.[26] There is no real equivalent to this in the 1559 *Injunctions*. The authoritative text has, arguably, shifted; sacramental doctrine is to be judged relative to its articulation in the Book of Common Prayer, not scripture. The 1559 command that only statutes 'not contrary to the word of God' could be preached had been pressed into busy service in Elizabeth's reign, and we see here the effect such service had on cultural notions of preaching versus prayer—of scripture versus liturgy. Like bishops, like the ring in marriage, like any ceremony that was no longer adjudged sacrament (penance, for example) or never had been but required a service nonetheless (the 'churching' of post-partum women, for example[27]), common prayer was protected under what we might call the 'not contrary' clause. This concept soon expanded the range and reach of adiaphora. As the category of 'things indifferent' expanded and contracted under the pressure of religious debates over the official apparatus of the church, the Prayer Book lost interpretive elasticity. The importance of *sola scriptura* dwindled; what we might call *sola liturgia* took its place.

This realization might prompt us to pay attention for the first time to a throwaway line at Hampton Court in 1604. On day two of the conference called by the King to discuss the state of religion in his new realm, John Rainolds, who headed the delegation of moderates assigned to present the Puritan cause for reform to the King and his bishops, brought that case compiled under four heads: (1) 'that the doctrine of the Church might be preserved in purity *according to God's word*'; (2) 'that good pastors be planted in the Church *to preach the same*' (i.e. God's word); (3) 'that the Church's government be sincerely administered

---

[23] *Articles* (1604), B2ʳ.

[24] See Fincham, *Visitation Articles*, p. xxii. For recent critical accounts of the Book of Common Prayer, see esp. Charles Hefling and Cynthia Shattuck (eds), *The Oxford Guide to the Book of Common Prayer: A Worldwide Survey* (New York: Oxford University Press, 2006); and Judith Maltby, *Prayer Book and People in Elizabethan and Early Stuart England* (Cambridge: Cambridge University Press, 1998).

[25] *Articles* (1604), B3ʳ.

[26] *Constitutions and Canons Ecclesiastical, Treated upon by the Bishop of London* (London, 1604), K4ᵛ.

[27] See David Cressy on the controversial practice of churching: *Birth, Marriage and Death: Ritual, Religion, and the Life-Cycle in Tudor and Stuart England* (Oxford: Oxford University Press, 1997), 197–232.

according to God's word'; and (4) 'that the Book of Common Prayer *might be better fitted to more increase of piety*'. Alas for Rainolds, Richard Bancroft—who not only loathed Puritan petitioners but also loathed, even more, any man who did *not* loathe Puritan petitioners— was present. The request appears to have amused Bancroft and his King. Laughing, James remarked that, if everything the Puritans wanted better explained in the liturgy were to be added to the liturgy, that the Prayer Book would 'swell into a volume as big as the Bible, and confound the reader'. Rainolds, heedless of the warning encoded in the King's joke, then shifted gears and asked for something that, to most observers (then and now) has seemed entirely uncontroversial: a new and improved translation of the Bible. The King readily and heartily agreed. In so doing, he dealt a real and lasting deathblow to conformist puritanism in the Church of England.[28]

It is clear that James I and others (including the infamous chronicler of this exchange, the anti-Puritan William Barlow) thought Rainolds was advocating for the Geneva Bible that he—and most people, many far more conservative than he—preferred to England's current state Bible, the justly maligned 'Bishops' Bible'. But for all its widespread popularity, and for all that it could easily be obtained in official-looking folio, the Geneva was a book without official status in the Church of England. It was thus a Bible inevitably associated with private reading—if by 'private' we do not mean 'individual', or even 'never bought nor used in any parish church in England', but, simply, 'not commanded to be read in the churches during worship'. This portentous misunderstanding at Hampton Court, then, may well have had everything to do with the difference between Bibles for private use and Bibles for public use—more, even, than it did with the Calvinist glosses in its marginal notes. Both the King and his Puritan clergy wanted a new Bible for a public Church; James I, however, did not want that Bible to be one that famously had been designed along private lines.

In historical hindsight the decision at Hampton Court to commission the 1611 or 'King James' Bible signalled the end of a century of biblically oriented reform in the Church of England. At the very moment James I acceded to the wishes of his Puritan loyalists, the bedrock assumption of their reforming hopes—that the principle of *sola scriptura* did not simply mean the Bible was sufficient to salvation, but that this sufficiency extended to form a 'measuring rod' for orthodoxy, the 'chief cornerstone' of the church—was, effectively, doomed. With its Latinate cadences and lack of explanatory marginal notes, the 1611 Bible, that masterpiece of English prose, was not designed to be a Bible for study and instruction but a text aimed at supporting the Church of England's Book of Common Prayer. It became a sacred companion piece to sacralized worship and has remained in that supporting role ever since.

This is not to claim there is no Bible in the Prayer Book. There is, in fact, a lot of Bible in the Prayer Book. The language of common prayer surely sounds scriptural (which accounts for why so many parishioners, then and now, can be excused for forgetting which was, and is, which). The Book of Common Prayer also reprints an impressive array of scriptural passages, but in doing so it effectively organizes and redacts those passages to complement a national liturgy. In short, the Book of Common Prayer acts as a curb to individual scriptural interpretation—which, of course, is exactly what a state church's liturgy is meant

---

[28] The account is taken from Bishop William Barlow's *The Summe and Substance of the Conference ... at Hampton Court. January 14. 1603* (London, 1604).

to do: express a corporate, not private, religious culture. It did its job well, then. Brian Cummings has pointed out that Cranmer's proposal for a truly reformed liturgy, preserved in a 1530s Latin manuscript at the British Library, called for an ambitious programme of Bible reading to accompany common prayer: every book, every verse, every jot and tittle of both testaments—'entire and unbroken', as Cranmer put it—to be read at service, so congregants would have heard it all, in order, by year's end, with all the Psalms covered monthly.[29]

Cranmer was ambitious for his laity. His preface to the first Book of Common Prayer opened historically and optimistically:

> [I]f a manne woulde searche out by the auncient fathers, he shall finde that … [divine service] was not ordeyned, but of a good purpose, and for a great advauncement of godlines: For they so ordered the matter, that all the whole Bible (or the greatest parte thereof) should be read over once in the yeare … and further, that the people (by daily hearynge of holy scripture read in the Churche) should continuallye profite more and more in the knowledge of God.[30]

But the devil is in the details here. The Psalter was not bound into the Book of Common Prayer until Elizabeth's reign. And somewhere between the manuscript plan of the 1530s and its published execution in 1549, Cranmer redrafted 'entire and unbroken' to read 'greatest parte thereof'. While this may seem a small point, parish compliance with diligent scriptural reading has been harder to document than parish compliance (or lack thereof) with rubrics and communion language, altar positioning and churching practices.[31] This may indicate how unimportant concerns about a certain kind of diligent lay hearing and reading had become. In any case, the prayer book was designed to be the hammer of the scripture, its lectionary a discipline in official exegetical connection, bypassing less comprehensible (or, to be fair, less interesting) passages.

And that was just the problem. In the 1640s and 1650s, loyalists met privately to read the prayer book, not the Bible, to keep the established church alive in an age of public directories and Cromwellian independency.[32] By the 1630s, however, William Laud had already anticipated this division of purpose, an antagonistic split between 'prayer' (for which read: liturgy) and 'preaching' (for which read: the Bible) in his own visitation articles for London,

---

[29] *The Book of Common Prayer: The Texts of 1549, 1559, and 1662*, ed. Brian Cummings (Oxford: Oxford University Press, 2011), 690 n. On the rota of readings fixed by Cranmer and his supporters, see the chapter by Ian Green in this volume.

[30] Cited in *Book of Common Prayer*, ed. Cummings, 4.

[31] For stimulating uses of the evidence of visitation articles, see Laura Feitzinger Brown, 'Brawling in Church: Noise and the Rhetoric of Lay Behavior in Early Modern England', *The Sixteenth Century Journal*, 34 (2003): 955–72; David Cressy, 'Purification, Thanskgiving and the Churching of Women in Post-Reformation England', *Past and Present*, 141 (1993): 106–46; Kenneth Fincham, 'The Restoration of Altars in the 1630s', *The Historical Journal*, 44 (2001): 919–40; Mary Fissell, 'The Politics of Reproduction in the English Reformation', *Representations*, 87 (2004): 43–81; and Susan Wabuda, 'Bishops and the Provision of Homilies, 1520 to 1547', *The Sixteenth Century Journal*, 25 (1994): 551–66.

[32] Judith Maltby, 'Suffering and Surviving: The Civil Wars, the Commonwealth, and the Formation of "Anglicanism", 1642–60', in Christopher Durston and Judith Maltby (eds), *Religion in Revolutionary England* (Manchester: Manchester University Press, 2006), 158–80. It is probably worth noting—but not placing undue significance on—the fact that 'scripture', as an indexed subject, seems only to appear in the essays there that cover religious practices and beliefs outside those held by this remnant of a proto-Anglican, once-and-future 'established' church.

asking the following: 'Whether have any affirmed, preached, or taught, that the forme of making and consecrating Bishops, Priests, and Deacons, or any thing therein contained, is repugnant, or not agreeable to the Word of God? ... Or that the government of the Church by Archbishops, Bishops, or others that beare any Office therein, is Antichristian, or not agreeable to the word of God?'[33] By the reign of Charles I, the Bible had become the church's problem: the potentially unruly text which, studied privately and with bias, could be used to challenge the governmentally sanctioned practices of the Church of England and even monarchical authority itself. (A quick survey of the more exuberant political pamphlets published in the interregnum attests to what kind of creative work some men and women could do with unvarnished, unmediated scripture in its entirety.[34])

Returning to the Elizabethan official instructions regarding the Bible we find, then, that the later sixteenth-century church either felt it unnecessary or, perhaps had no particular opinion yet on whether it had to distinguish between types of reading. The early Elizabethan directives on the Bible were downright promiscuous: they speak of public and private reading—lay and clergy, in halls, in houses, and on stands; in churches and from the reading desk—mixed together. The Hampton Court Conference did not establish a single Bible in English; it did establish two ways of Bible reading. One way would best flourish in a national church, bounded, organized, and channelled through the liturgy. This is the Bible we should call, simply, *King James's Version*. James's other Bible—same text, different context—would need to come westward, across an ocean and athwart a continent, to thrive in America, where private reading established a multitude of visible denominations, each claiming public status for their singular and eccentric takes on Holy Writ. This is what happens when a Church, and its Bible, are privatized.

FURTHER READING

Collinson, Patrick. *The Religion of Protestants: The Church in English Society 1559–1625* (Oxford: Clarendon Press, 1982).

Cressy, David. *Birth, Marriage and Death: Ritual, Religion, and the Life-Cycle in Tudor and Stuart England* (Oxford: Oxford University Press, 1997).

The Book of Common Prayer: The Texts of 1549, 1559, and 1662, ed. Brian Cummings (Oxford: Oxford University Press, 2011).

Daniell, David. *The Bible in English: Its History and Influence* (New Haven: Yale University Press, 2003).

Ferrell, Lori Anne. *Government by Polemic* (Stanford, Calif.: Stanford University Press, 1998).

Ferrell, Lori Anne. *The Bible and the People* (New Haven: Yale University Press, 2008).

Fincham, Kenneth. *Prelate as Pastor: The Episcopate of James I* (Oxford: Clarendon Press, 1990).

Fincham, Kenneth, ed., *Visitation Articles and Injunctions of the Early Stuart Church*, 2 vols (Woodbridge: Boydell Press, 1994–8).

Frere, W. H., and W. M. Kennedy, eds. *Visitation Articles and Injunctions of the Period of the Reformation*, ii. *1536–1558*, Alcuin Club Collections, 15 (London: Longmans, Green & Co., 1910).

---

[33] *Articles to be Enquired of Within the Dioces of London* (London: 1631), B6^r.

[34] On the political uses of the early modern Bible, see the chapters collected in Part IV of this volume.

Lake, Peter. *Anglicans and Puritans? Presbyterianism and English Conformist Thought from Whitgift to Hooker* (London: Unwin Hyman, 1988).

Maltby, Judith. 'Suffering and Surviving: The Civil Wars, the Commonwealth, and the Formation of "Anglicanism", 1642–60', in Christopher Durston and Judith Maltby (eds), *Religion in Revolutionary England* (Manchester: Manchester University Press, 2006), 158–80.

CHAPTER 17

....

'HEARING' AND 'READING': DISSEMINATING BIBLE KNOWLEDGE AND FOSTERING BIBLE UNDERSTANDING IN EARLY MODERN ENGLAND

....

IAN GREEN

In the early 1530s Henry VIII was still undecided about permitting lay access to vernacular translations of the Bible. The product of a humanist education and an active patron of humanist scholars and scholarship, Henry was well aware of the calls for reform of the Latin 'Vulgate' and for making a vernacular version available to the people, but he was still surrounded by bishops who, while not hostile to the Bible in the hands of suitable readers, were convinced that the clergy could convey to the laity as much scriptural knowledge as was necessary for their salvation.[1] By the mid-1530s, however, Henry saw himself as a divinely appointed, reforming ruler who would purge the English Church of its errors and abuses without breaking with many of its traditional doctrines and practices, and he accepted proposals from budding Protestants such as Cranmer and Cromwell for the licensing of new translations of the Bible into English and the placing of a copy in every parish church for laity as well as clergy to read.[2] One set of royal injunctions ordered the clergy to 'discourage

---

[1] Lucy Wooding, *Henry VIII* (London: Routledge, 2009), 19–24, 76–9; Richard Rex, *Henry VIII and the English Reformation* (Basingstoke: Palgrave Macmillan, 1993), ch. 4; Christoper Haigh, *English Reformations: Religion, Politics, and Society under the Tudors* (Oxford, Clarendon Press, 1993), 56–7, 60, 64–5, 125.

[2] Lucy Wooding, *Rethinking Catholicism in Reformation England* (Oxford: Clarendon Press, 2000), chs 2–3; Wooding, *Henry VIII*, 54–6, 58–9, 182–90; George Bernard, *The King's Reformation: Henry VIII and the Remaking of the English Church* (London: Yale University Press, 2005), ch. 3.

no man privily or apertly [openly] from ... reading or hearing' the Bible in English, but rather to 'expressly provoke, stir and exhort every person to read the same'.[3]

Progress was slow. Producing enough copies of the expensive folio for the 10,000 churches and chapels in England, and ensuring each parish purchased one and had it chained to a lectern, took years.[4] While a number of the clergy, and apparently not a few of the laity, needed convincing of the need to abandon the traditional ways of handling the Bible, others interpreted its text in ways that Henry found heretical or seditious, and he soon took steps to try to limit access to those readers who could be relied on to interpret the Bible in the way he wished. Nevertheless, for the last ten years of his reign, he continued to support two related campaigns: one to ensure that the laity were taught and understood key passages of the Bible in English, in particular the Ten Commandments and the Lord's Prayer, and the other to provide the clergy with handbooks like the *Bishops' Book* and the *King's Book* to help them explain these and other basic formulae to their flocks.[5] Moreover, although all church services remained in Latin, Henry's regime continued to license a variety of 'primers' (handbooks for the laity that supplied both devotional needs and basic instruction) which incorporated English translations of frequently recited groups of psalms, such as the Penitential Psalms, and of selected 'Bible prayers' and pivotal passages from the Gospels that were declaimed in church on major feast days.[6] And from 1537 the regime also permitted the publication of many editions of a short work, the *Pistles and Gospels*, which helped clergy and literate laity find the English versions of the 'Epistles' and 'Gospels' (the specially selected readings declaimed during celebrations of the mass throughout the year) that were to be read 'out of the English Bible, plainly and distinctly'.[7]

Major breakthroughs in ensuring wider exposure of the laity to the English Bible were initiated during the reign of Edward VI and fully implemented during the reign of Elizabeth I. In 1547 the remaining restrictions on lay reading of the Bible were soon removed, and each church had to make available, for laity as well as clergy to read, a 'Great Bible' and a copy of the court-sponsored translation of Erasmus's *Paraphrases upon the New Testament*.[8] But whereas in 1538 'every person' was to be encouraged to 'read' the Bible or 'hear' it if he or she was not literate, in the first of *The Homilies Appointed to be Read in Churches* (1547) the order was reversed: 'Christian man' should 'reverently hear and read holy Scriptures, which is the

[3] Issued in 1538: W. H. Frere and W. M. Kennedy (eds), *Visitation Articles and Injunctions of the Period of the Reformation* (London: Longmans, 1910), ii. 36.

[4] Bernard, *King's Reformation*, ch. 6; Haigh, *English Reformations*, 129–30, 134–5, 150–1, 156–61, 165–6; Ian Green, *Print and Protestantism in Early Modern England* (Oxford: Oxford University Press, 2000), 45–6, 50–3, 56–7, 61–4.

[5] Bernard, *King's Reformation*, ch. 6; Ian Green, *Word, Ritual and Image in Early Modern English Protestantism* (Oxford, forthcoming).

[6] Green, *Word, Ritual and Image*; and also STC[2] 15986–16057; Edgar Hoskins, 'Horae Beatae Virginis' or Sarum and York Primers (London: Longmans, 1901); and Charles C. Butterworth, *The English Primers (1529–1545): Their Publication and Connection with the English Bible and the Reformation in England* (Philadelphia: University of Pennsylvania Press, 1953).

[7] Butterworth, *English Primers*, 149–63; STC[2] 2964.5–2982; Frere and Kennedy, *Visitation Articles*, ii. 46-7, 53-4, 61; Green, *Word, Ritual and Image*. Details of these readings were also listed in the calendar section of some almanacs in the 1540s: *An Almanack and Prognostication for 1544* (STC[2] 394); and Bernard Capp, *Astrology and the Popular Press: English Almanacs 1500–1800* (London: Faber, 1979), 28.

[8] Frere and Kennedy, *Visitation Articles*, ii. 117–18, 122–3 (and see iii. 10, 13–14).

food of the soul'.[9] The reality was that the majority of English parishioners were, and for some time would remain, illiterate, and so more likely to hear the Bible than read it.

This 'hearing' was effected in various ways. The royal injunctions of 1547 insisted that 'Epistles' and 'Gospels' at what was then still called 'high mass' should all be read 'in English and not in Latin'.[10] In the *Homilies* of 1547, scores of scripture texts were carefully deployed and expounded to ensure lay comprehension of the misery of all mankind through sin, and salvation through faith in Christ. To judge from the dearth of preaching clergy and the thirty editions of this work published between 1547 and 1587 (and the sixteen of volume ii from 1563 to 1587), these homilies must have been widely and regularly used for much of Edward's and Elizabeth's reigns.[11] In 1549 there appeared the first officially approved question-and-answer catechism, designed to ensure that the next generation of believers, whether literate or not, would not only learn the complete texts of the Decalogue and Lord's Prayer (and Creed) in English, but also master a brief account of their meaning and significance in trying to lead a Christian life. Whether linked to the 'Confirmation' section of the Book of Common Prayer, or combined with abecedaries or primers, this short catechism was reproduced in millions of printed copies in the early modern world.[12] At about the same time, the practice began of replacing medieval iconography on church walls with selected scripture texts in English, so that those with at least basic literacy would be able to learn them.[13]

Above all dissemination of Bible knowledge was widened and reinforced through the way the Word was deployed in the most commonly performed services of the new Protestant liturgy of 1549, as revised in 1552 and 1559–61. Inspired by their respect for many aspects of the ancient, medieval, and Lutheran liturgies which they had encountered, and convinced of the unanswerable case for the Bible being presented to the faithful in their own language, Cranmer and his supporters decided not to abolish the elaborate patterns of readings used in late medieval religious communities and to a lesser extent in parish churches, but to purge them of unsuitable additions and replace the Vulgate texts with their 'Great Bible' equivalents. They provided fixed rotas of readings in English that at appropriate points of the calendar year reflected the seasons and major feast days of the medieval church—Advent, Christmas, the Circumcision of Christ, Epiphany, Lent, Easter week, Ascensiontide, Whitsuntide, and Trinity, and a score of red-letter saints' days—but which also within that structure prescribed readings from Old and New Testaments and the book of Psalms for every service on every day of the year.

In addition to these two rotas, Cranmer and his supporters persisted with two other practices. One was to embed in the appropriate point of each service clutches of sentences or specific psalms, canticles, or other passages of the Bible that provided authentic forms of confession, exhortation, praise, or thanksgiving. By this means regular attenders were exposed to scripture passages that liturgists of different eras considered to be of particular

---

[9] Probably the work of Thomas Cranmer: *The Two Books of Homilies Appointed to be Read in Churches*, ed. J. Griffiths (Oxford: Oxford University Press, 1859), pp. xxvii, 7.

[10] Frere and Kennedy, *Visitation Articles*, ii. 123.

[11] Green, *Print and Protestantism*, 209–10, 630; Luc Borot, 'The Bible and Protestant Inculturation in the *Homilies* of the Church of England', in Richard Griffiths (ed.), *The Bible in the Renaissance* (Aldershot: Ashgate, 2001), 150–75.

[12] Ian Green, *The Christian's ABC: Catechisms and Catechizing in England c.1530–1740* (Oxford: Clarendon Press, 1996), index under 'Prayer Book catechism'.

[13] Margaret Aston, *England's Iconoclasts*, i. *Laws Against Images* (Oxford: Oxford University Press, 1988), 361–2, 368.

value in communal worship. The second was to compose set prayers, collects, and responses that as far as possible consisted of phrases or sentences taken directly from the 'very pure Word of God … or that which is evidently grounded upon the same … in the English tongue'. As a result of these various devices, the congregation was led orally through a series of readings, psalms, sentences, canticles, prayers, and responses which were either taken straight from the Bible or were paraphrases inspired directly by it.[14]

By comparison with the practice of most Protestant churches abroad, which by the late 1540s had abandoned fixed rotas of readings, and permitted their preaching clergy to choose the lessons and psalms which they felt would best match the sermon and extempore prayers that dominated each service,[15] the English system appears very conservative. Cranmer's successors in 1559–61 had the opportunity to start anew, but, unlike the clergy in Scotland in 1560 who abandoned festivals such as Christmas and Easter and all saints' days and rotas of set readings, their English counterparts decided not only to resume where Cranmer had left off, but to reinforce medieval principles.[16] Thus they added another rota, of Old Testament readings for Sundays, and allowed the number of saints' days to recover from a low in the Second Prayer Book of 1552 to a new high in 1561.[17] Let us examine these features in turn.

Cranmer's decision to retain a fixed sequence of Bible readings for each day of the year was influenced by the revision of the Catholic Breviary carried out in the early 1530s at the request of Pope Clement VII by Cardinal Francesco de Quiñones, General of the Franciscans. This is evident in a preface Cranmer probably drew up about 1538, but used with only minor alterations in both Edwardian Prayer Books.[18] In order that 'the people (by daily hearing of holy scripture read in the church) should continually profit more and more in the knowledge of God, and be the more inflamed with the love of his true religion', the ancient fathers had instituted a system that 'all the whole Bible (or the greatest part thereof) should be read over once in the year'. But

> this godly and decent order of the ancient fathers hath been so altered, broken and neglected, by planting in uncertain stories, Legends, Responds, Verses, vain repetitions, Commemorations and Synodals, that commonly when any book of the Bible was begun, before three or four chapters were read out, all the rest were unread.

---

[14] See later in this chapter, and my *Word, Ritual and Image*. Still invaluable are F. Procter and W. H. Frere, *A New History of the Book of Common Prayer* (London: Macmillan, 1925), quotation at 52; and G. J. Cuming, *A History of Anglican Liturgy* (London: Macmillan, 1969), and *The Godly Order: Texts and Studies relating to the Book of Common Prayer* (London: Alcuin Club, 1983). Most up-to-date are Diarmaid MacCulloch, *Thomas Cranmer: A Life* (New Haven: Yale University Press, 1996), index under 'Book of Common Prayer'; and *The Book of Common Prayer: The Texts of 1549, 1559 and 1662*, ed. Brian Cummings (Oxford: Oxford University Press, 2011), Introduction and Explanatory notes.

[15] Cuming, *Anglican Liturgy*, 37–44.

[16] On developments in post-Reformation Scotland, see the chapter by Alasdair Raffe in this volume.

[17] See n. 15, and later in this chapter. The Prayer Books of 1549 and 1552 and 1661 can be compared in F. E. Brightman, *The English Rite* (London: Rivingtons, 1915–22), i. 78–125. The 1559 text is reproduced in *Liturgical Services … Set Forth in the Reign of Queen Elizabeth*, ed. W. K. Clay (Cambridge: Parker Society, 1847), together with the 1561 Kalendar, 435–55; and also in *The Book of Common Prayer 1559*, ed. J. E. Booty (Charlottesville, Va.: University Press of Virginia, 1976); and *Book of Common Prayer*, ed. Cummings.

[18] *Book of Common Prayer*, ed. Cummings, pp. xxi–xxiii, 689; and Cuming, *Anglican Liturgy*, 47–8, 52, 54, 69–71.

Moreover, 'there hath been great diversity in saying and singing in churches within this realm, some following Salisbury use, some Hereford use', and so on. Cranmer set out to remove non-scriptural elements from the sequence, and to provide a single 'Kalendar' based on 'certain rules … plain and easy to be understood' that were compatible with the Fathers' aims but 'a great deal more profitable and commodious than that which of late was used'.[19] Various rotas were countenanced between c.1538 and 1549: some were based on three readings at Morning Prayer and three at Evensong every day; another on a single chapter in turn of the New Testament and then of the Old, every Sunday and holy day—a form of the *lectio continua* found in some Protestant churches abroad, including Geneva, which provided a free-standing sequence of readings not tied to particular days of the year.[20]

The rota chosen in 1549 consisted of two lessons each for Morning Prayer and Evensong. The morning lessons started in early January with one from the Old Testament, Genesis 1, and one from the New, Matthew 1, and those in the evening with an Old Testament reading from Genesis 2 and a New from Romans 1.[21] With minor alterations in 1559 and more substantial ones in 1561, the result was that the Old Testament and Apocrypha were read through once a year, with the exception of 'certain books and chapters which be least edifying, and might best be spared, and therefore are left unread'.[22] The omissions included Jewish legal matters in the Pentateuch, the duplications in 1 and 2 Chronicles, and the easily misunderstood Song of Solomon. Depending upon the recension, omissions included 9 or 10 chapters from Exodus, 24 or 25 from Leviticus, 9 from Numbers (rising to 17 in 1561), 12 from Joshua (from 1561), 38 or 39 from Ezekiel, and the whole of 1 and 2 Chronicles and the Song of Solomon.[23] There was also one major deviation from the canonical sequence for the Old Testament: following on medieval tradition, the reading of the 'Gospel Prophet' Isaiah was switched to last place in the sequence, to coincide with Advent (the weeks during which the birth of Christ was anticipated).[24] By contrast the New Testament was read daily in parallel streams in such a way that each book was read right through three times every year between January and December. There was one exception: the whole of the 'Apocalypse' (the Revelation of St John the Divine), the sixth-largest book of the New Testament, was excluded. The comments made by the Edwardian and Elizabethan authorities about the 'profit' and good 'example' that the laity derived from hearing Bible readings, and the order to Parker, Grindal, and other ecclesiastical commissioners in 1561 to remove a few 'chapters or parcels of less edification' and replace them with 'others more profitable', tend to confirm that Revelation was not deemed 'edifying', especially at a time when there was a dearth of preaching clergy to expound it wisely, and few reliable commentaries available in print to guide the Bible studies of the literate minority.[25]

---

[19] Brightman, *English Rite*, i. 34–9.

[20] Cuming, *The Godly Order*, 1–125; Cuming, *Anglican Liturgy*, 38, 40; MacCulloch, *Cranmer*, 221–6, 332–4; *Book of Common Prayer*, ed. Cummings, pp. xxii–xxxiv; Frere and Kennedy, *Visitation Articles*, ii. 123; T. H. L. Parker, *Calvin's Preaching* (Edinburgh: Clark, 1992), ch. 9 and *passim*.

[21] Procter and Frere, *Book of Common Prayer*, 319–21, 341–3; Brightman, *English Rite*, i. 78–125; *Book of Common Prayer 1559*, ed. Booty, 36–47; and *Liturgical Services*, ed. Clay, 444–55.

[22] On the reception of the Apocrypha, see the chapter by Ariel Hessayon in this volume.

[23] Brightman, *English Rite*, i. 48–51.

[24] Procter and Frere, *Book of Common Prayer*, 342 n., 378; Brightman, *English Rite*, i. 34–5.

[25] Griffiths, *Two Books of Homilies*, 7, 10; Brightman, *English Rite*, i. 50–1; Procter and Frere, *Book of Common Prayer*, 109.

This 365-day cycle remained in place for centuries, and was deployed in whole or in part in institutions where daily worship was the norm, such as the Chapel Royal, cathedrals, college chapels, inns of court, and many schools, almshouses, and hospitals, and in theory in parishes too where the incumbent or his curate was supposed to read service daily.[26] In an appendix to the 1564 edition of his *Apologie* (written to rebut criticisms of the English church), Bishop Jewel stated it as a fact that 'in our churches', the Old and New Testaments were 'read over' so many times a year in English. Drawing on his own experience of conducting worship in Essex and London in the 1570s, William Harrison used very similar terms to describe normal church practice.[27] In the early 1660s there were reports of the laity pressing for the restoration of daily prayer book services that had been proscribed for a decade and a half; a few decades later, there was sufficient demand in some urban churches for four services on weekdays.[28]

That the 365-day rota was widely followed is also suggested by the ongoing friction between conformists and nonconformists over the use of the Apocrypha. The irony of reading from the non-canonical books of the Apocrypha on fifty days of the year while excluding canonical material was not lost on the first critics of the official liturgy, but Article 6 of the Thirty-Nine Articles justified it on the grounds that 'as Jerome saith, the Church doth read [the Apocrypha] for example of life and instruction of manners' rather than to establish doctrine. At the Savoy Conference in 1661, the nonconformists still urged a total ban on readings from the Apocrypha, but in the Convocation of 1662 supporters outnumbered opponents. One member of Convocation who emerged from a fraught meeting on this topic was heard to exclaim 'with great joy, that they had carried it for *Bel and the Dragon*'.[29]

While encouraging the laity to attend church on weekdays, the Edwardian and Elizabethan authorities decided to *insist* on lay attendance on Sundays only, and by the last quarter of the sixteenth century most of the laity seem to have cooperated.[30] But owing to the vagaries of the lunar calendar that provided the basis for the new 'Kalendar', those who attended church regularly on Sundays under Edward and in the opening years of Elizabeth's reign would have heard a different set of lessons each year over a six- or seven-year cycle. In the case of the Old Testament, which was rehearsed only once a year and was harder to grasp because of its pre-Christian character, this must have weakened its potential impact on the laity. The solution adopted in the Elizabethan Prayer Book of 1559 was to specify a new set of Old Testament readings for each Sunday which would be the same every year. This ran *alongside* the 365-day Kalendar which was still used on weekdays and still provided the New Testament readings for Sundays.[31]

[26] Frere and Kennedy, *Visitation Articles*, iii. 97–8, 165.

[27] John Jewell, *An Apologie or Answere in Defence of the Churche of Englande* (1564), Q8ʳ–R2ʳ; *The Description of England by William Harrison*, ed. G. Edelen (Washington, DC: Folger Shakespeare Library, 1994), 33–4.

[28] J. Wickham Legg, *English Church Life from the Restoration to the Tractarian Movement* (London: Longmans, 1914), 78–110.

[29] Procter and Frere, *Book of Common Prayer*, 139, 149, 153, 159, 173–4, 200, 207–9, 378; Cuming, *Anglican Liturgy*, 161; *Articles Whereupon It Was Agreed . . . in the Convocation Holden at London in . . . 1562* (1571), 6.

[30] Brightman, *English Rite*, i. 16; Frere and Kennedy, *Visitation Articles*, 166, 266, 288; Christopher Marsh, *Popular Religion in Sixteenth-Century England* (Basingstoke: Macmillan, 1998), 45–6.

[31] Procter and Frere, *Book of Common Prayer*, 109–10; *Book of Common Prayer 1559*, ed. Booty, 27–9.

There are again reasonably good grounds for believing that from an early date this Sunday sequence was also widely deployed in church. *A Brief Exposition of Such Chapters of the Old Testament as Usually Are Read in the Church at Common Prayer on the Sundays*, published in 1573 by Thomas Cooper, a leading educator promoted to the Diocese of Lincoln under Elizabeth, was probably intended to help less well educated clergy, but was also described as being 'for the better help and instruction of the unlearned' and for 'the good and modest Christian that delighteth in reading and hearing of the worde of God, and lacketh those ordinarie helps, whereby he may the sooner attaine to the understanding of it'.[32] It was perhaps not a coincidence that the books of the Old Testament which occurred most often in this sequence, such as Genesis, Isaiah, and Proverbs, were also among the books on which there were soon a number of commentaries and sermons circulating in print.[33] With only minor changes in 1661–2, this Sunday sequence represents one of most frequently heard series of Bible readings of Elizabethan and Stuart times, and is worth a closer look.

In all, 110 chapters of the Old Testament were chosen to be read as first lessons of Morning and Evening Prayer on fifty-five Sundays (thus catering for the slight variation from year to year in the number of Sundays in Advent, after Epiphany, in Lent, or in Trinity).[34] These were taken from eighteen books of the canonical Old Testament, and represented just over a fifth of their contents, or one seventh of the whole Testament if we include the twenty books from which no readings were selected. The main omissions were perhaps predictable: technical material on Jewish law and ritual in Leviticus, and an entire chunk of genealogy and narrative in the historical books from 1 Chronicles to Esther from which it was harder to draw prophecies of Christ's mission. The omission of some of the Wisdom literature and poetry in Job, Ecclesiastes, and the Song of Solomon is perhaps more surprising, though the Psalms featured prominently elsewhere in the liturgy. By comparison, the books that provided the largest numbers of readings, over half in all, were just four: Isaiah (24 chapters), Genesis (15), Proverbs (11), and Deuteronomy (9).[35] Isaiah has sometimes been called the 'Fifth Gospel' because it contains what Christians thought were the clearest prophecies in the Old Testament canon of the coming of Christ;[36] Genesis records not only God's immense creative powers, but also the Fall of Man and its consequences; Proverbs lists many virtues to follow and contrary vices to avoid; while the relevant chapters of Deuteronomy record the calls to obedience and faith that Moses made to the people and a restatement of the Law given at Sinai.

Unlike the 365-day sequence, which began in January, the Sunday sequence was designed to begin in early December, and so follow the church's liturgical year from Advent to Trinity. Thus the chapters selected from Isaiah for Advent began with God's anger at the corruptions of His people, but moved on to His readiness to forgive them and the joys that awaited the righteous. This sequence also cleverly spanned the passages from Isaiah which had already

---

[32] Thomas Cooper, *A Brief Exposition of Such Chapters of the Old Testament as Usually Are Read in the Church at Common Prayer on the Sundays* (London, 1573), title-page; A4^{r-v}.

[33] See next paragraph, and for relative numbers of commentaries and sermons, see Green, *Print and Protestantism*, 112–18.

[34] In addition, one reading had two chapters and one chapter was used twice (Genesis 1 on Advent 1 and Trinity Sunday): *Book of Common Prayer 1559*, ed. Booty, 27–9.

[35] Statistics from the 1561 table: *Liturgical Services*, ed. Clay, 437.

[36] J. F. A. Sawyer, *The Fifth Gospel: Isaiah in the History of Christianity* (Cambridge: Cambridge University Press, 1996).

been selected in 1549 for use on Christmas Day: Isaiah 9: 1–8 (which includes 'For unto us a child is born') and 7: 10–17 (which includes 'Behold, a virgin shall conceive and bear a son'). Readings from Isaiah continued on Sundays throughout Epiphany, providing further assurances from God to His Church, and also passages such as Isaiah 53 which was held to foretell Christ's sufferings ('He is despised and abhorred of men … a man … full of sorrows').[37] Next, in Lent, selected chapters from Genesis and Exodus described the Fall of Man, God's judgements on Adam and Eve and on subsequent evil-doers, Abraham's readiness to sacrifice his son, and signs that God was about to deliver His people from bondage. The latter coincided quite closely with the readings from Exodus that had already been specified in 1549 for use on Easter Day: on the initiation of the Passover (chapter 12), and the escape of the Children of Israel through the Red Sea (chapter 14), which was considered a 'type' (a prophetic similitude) of Christians' deliverance from the death of sin by baptism.

On Sundays after Easter, readings from Numbers and Deuteronomy were organized so that the story of Moses, and his receipt of the Ten Commandments and exhortations to the people to obey them, led to the reading already fixed for Whitsunday, from Deuteronomy 16. This stipulated solemn yearly commemorations of the Jews' delivery from slavery, which was regarded as a type of Christians' delivery from bondage to sin through the sending of the Holy Ghost to illumine their way.[38] There followed the very long Trinity season occupying nearly half the church's calendar year. During the summer and early autumn Sunday lessons consisted of selections from some of the historical books and the prophets on God's terrible judgements on those who did not worship Him in the way He had indicated, and the need for believers to repent sins and love and obey God if they hoped to be delivered from their enemies. But in the late autumn, selected chapters from the book of Proverbs, deferred from its canonical position *before* the prophets, described what virtues to cultivate and what vices to avoid in obeying God. Thus the Sunday readings not only represented a selection of chapters which Elizabeth's bishops appear to have regarded as especially informative and edifying for those attending on a weekly basis, but were integrated into an older sequence of readings which climaxed at the major festivals that had been carried over into the new church's liturgy.[39]

The shift within the Sunday Old Testament readings—from the anticipation of the coming of a Messiah to deliver God's people (in the first half), to warnings on the need to behave in such a way as to avoid God's anger (in the second)—in many ways echoed that of another sequence of Bible readings, this time from the New Testament: the 'Epistles and Gospels, to be used at the celebration of the Lord's Supper and Holy Communion through the year'. Again, many of the texts chosen in 1549 were the same as those that had been specified in the Sarum Missal, which itself derived from a sequence, the *Comes*, originally drawn up in the fifth century.[40] From 1549 the Sarum Rite and the Latin Mass were abandoned, but most of the same pairs of readings, in the 'Great Bible' translation, were used regularly in the new 'Lord's Supper', one of the two sacraments still recognized by English Protestantism.

---

[37] Citations from the 'Great Bible' version.   [38] Cooper, *Briefe Exposition*, fols 7ᵛ, 94ᵛ, 129ʳ.

[39] Surprisingly little has been written on the Sunday sequence since Procter and Frere's brief account in *Book of Common Prayer*, 343, 378–9.

[40] Procter and Frere, *Book of Common Prayer*, 465–6, 522–3, 525–50.

Moreover, each pair was preceded by a 'collect' or short prayer that turned the message in each reading into collective petitions for divine help to lead better lives. While most of these were based in their Latin precursors, they were pruned of unacceptable references to non-scriptural figures and practices, and expanded by the addition of many quotations from the Bible.[41] The 'Collects, Epistles and Gospels' were from the outset printed in full in most copies of the Book of Common Prayer, where they not only occupied a third of the printed space, but provided all those who could read and afford a copy with a reservoir of key New Testament passages and related forms of prayer.

The 'Epistles' and 'Gospels' had didactic as well as liturgical value. From Advent to Whitsunday the readings chosen from the Gospels drew lessons from events in Christ's life: his birth, childhood, ministry, trial and death, and appearance to the disciples to assure them that a Comforter would come; while those from the Epistles described the benefits the faithful received through Christ's mediation and atonement for their sins. During Trinity, however, the lessons chosen from the Epistles were a relatively continuous series of readings taken from Romans to Colossians that contained exhortations on the practice of Christian virtues, while the chapters chosen from the Gospels included parables, miracles, and sayings of Christ which in many cases illustrated the teaching of the Epistle for the day.[42]

Apart from those adults who attended cathedrals and those churches and chapels where regular communion was the norm, few of the Edwardian and Elizabethan laity took communion more than a handful of times each year; indeed, most probably communicated only once a year. Moreover, although monthly communions had been established in some urban parish churches by the late sixteenth century, it was not until the early or late seventeenth century that we can be reasonably confident that monthly and even weekly communions took place in other churches.[43] However, this did not mean that congregations did not hear at least part of the Epistle and Gospel sequences regularly in the Elizabethan period. Where a congregation had gathered, but communion was not possible or anticipated, the authorities seem to have encouraged the practice of following Morning Prayer immediately with the reading of the 'ante-communion service': the opening part of the communion service that included the Ten Commandments, the Collect, Epistle and Gospel and Nicene Creed, but not the consecration or distribution of the sacrament (hence the nicknames of 'dry communion' or 'half communion' given the practice by its critics).

That ante-communion was being performed reasonably often from the 1560s to the 1630s is suggested by the objections to the 'half-Communion' in the 'godly' *Admonition to the Parliament*, by Harrison's testimony that it was a regular practice, and by Laud's efforts to move the reading of ante-communion from the reading-pew in the nave to the communion table.[44] Moreover, as celebrations of the complete service became more frequent, so those who received communion whenever it was celebrated, or who attended church when it was

---

[41] Brightman, *English Rite*, i. 200–ii. 637; Procter and Frere, *Book of Common Prayer*, 522–6; James A. Devereux, 'Reformed Doctrine in the Collects of the First *Book of Common Prayer*', *Harvard Theological Review*, 58 (1965): 48–68; *Book of Common Prayer*, ed. Cummings, 763–8.

[42] Procter and Frere, *Book of Common Prayer*, 522–3, 525–50.

[43] J. P. Boulton, 'The Limits of Formal Religion: The Administration of Holy Communion in Late Elizabethan and Early Stuart London', *London Journal*, 10 (1984): 140–1, 146–9, 152–4; F. C. Mather, 'Georgian Churchmanship Reconsidered: Some Variations in Anglican Public Worship 1714–1830', *Journal of Ecclesiastical History*, 36 (1985): 269–75.

[44] Procter and Frere, *Book of Common Prayer*, 498–9; Harrison, *Description of England*, 34; Cuming, *Anglican Liturgy*, 128–9, 133, 142, 156.

others' turn to communicate (the practice in very large parishes of staggering admission from Passion or Palm Sunday to Whit or Trinity Sundays was fairly widespread), would have been exposed to the 'Epistles' and 'Gospels' on all those days.[45]

There is also plenty of evidence that from an early stage reforming bishops like Hugh Latimer and John Jewel selected for their sermon texts part of the Epistle or Gospel that was read on that day; and there are also the striking sales (given its size) of the translation into English of Neils Hemmingsen's *A Postill, or Exposition of the Gospels*—five editions between 1569 and 1585. Drawn up to help fellow clergy, this work consisted of a brief introduction, summary, and exposition of seventy different passages from the Gospels used in the Lutheran Church, nine-tenths of which were the same as those used in Protestant England. The translation into English was sponsored by two stationers, and became required reading for less educated clergy in the northernmost Diocese of Durham in the 1570s and 1580s. In the next few decades we also find the Calvinist conformist Toby Matthew routinely, and the moderate Anthony Higgin and conservative Mark Frank often, opting to preach on the Epistle or Gospel specified for that day. In the early 1610s John Boys made his own notes available to less educated clergy, and since the *Exposition of the Dominical Epistles and Gospels* passed through successive editions, and as late as 1646 binders in London were still expecting demand for bound copies of 'Boyses works', it may well have provided the basis for homilies or sermons in many early Stuart parishes.[46]

There are at least two other sets of readings prescribed for prayer book services that are worth a mention. One was for the saints' days carried over into the Protestant calendar as 'sanctified' to the worship of God and the edification of his congregations. What parishioners would have heard at Morning Prayer or Evening Prayer on a typical red-letter saint's day would have been lessons not from the 365-day calendar, but for the first lesson an edifying text from Wisdom and Ecclesiasticus in the Apocrypha or from Proverbs or Ecclesiastes, and for the second a chapter from the Acts of the Apostles or a Gospel that demonstrated the significance of some aspect of the saint's life. If there was a communion or ante-communion service then there was also a special collect, 'Epistle', and 'Gospel' too.[47] While few parishioners would have attended the services held on all these days, they might well have attended on a day with strong local associations, such as the saint to whose memory their own parish church was dedicated. Long after he had left his curacy at Wye in Jacobean Kent, the upwardly mobile preacher Thomas Jackson returned there every 30 November to preach on St Andrew's day. The dedicatee's day was also the occasion for lively festivities (especially for the young), known as 'wakes', which long outlived their medieval origins.[48] The selection of appropriate readings and drafting of

[45] Boulton, 'Limits of Formal Religion', 135–54.

[46] Green, *Print and Protestantism*, 113–15; Green, *Continuity and Change in Protestant Preaching in Early Modern England* (London: Dr Williams's Trust, 2009), 32, 42; and Green, 'Preaching in the Parishes', in Peter McCullough et al. (eds), *The Oxford Handbook of the Early Modern Sermon* (Oxford: Oxford University Press, 2011), 143–4.

[47] David Cressy, *Bonfires and Bells: National Memory and the Protestant Calendar in Elizabethan and Stuart England* (Stroud: Sutton, 2004), 4–8; *Liturgical Services*, ed. Clay, 438–9; *Book of Common Prayer*, ed. Cummings, 220–1; Brightman, *English Rite*, ii. 553–637; Procter and Frere, *Book of Common Prayer*, 335–8, 528–52; Cuming, *Anglican Liturgy*, 122–3.

[48] Green, 'Preaching in the Parishes', 149; R. W. Malcolmson, *Popular Recreations in English Society 1700–1850* (Cambridge: Cambridge University Press, 1973), 16–19, 52–6, 146–50.

suitable prayers for these saints' days served as a template for the new 'Protestant Calendar' days such as Elizabeth's accession and 5 November—services that were probably also reasonably well attended prior to the associated celebrations.[49]

The other set of readings featured the book of Psalms. Cranmer admired the Psalms as a sacred text especially suited to both public worship and private devotions, and as a useful teaching tool containing many prophecies of Christ, and was adamant that for all these functions the Psalms had to be in English, not Latin. To this end he devised a new rota for the whole book to be read through regularly in church in the 'Great Bible' version. Of the different permutations open to him, Cranmer opted for a rota in which an average of five psalms a day, shared between Morning and Evening Prayer, were 'said' by the minister or clerk, or 'sung' if there was a choir or musically literate members of the congregation. In this way, the whole book was repeated out loud no less than twelve times every year.[50]

The helpful instructions in the prayer book on 'The order how the Psalter is appointed to be read' and a 'table for the order of the psalms' resolved problems of coping with the massive Psalm 119, and months with more or less than thirty days. And to facilitate these frequent repetitions, a prose psalter was published, usually as the last third of the hundreds of editions of the Book of Common Prayer published in the early modern period. Pointing was added to the text of the Psalms to aid chanting, as also were headers to indicate on which day and at what time of day of the month each psalm was to be said.[51] In those parish churches where choirs and organs persisted, often into the 1570s and in the case of organs much later, there was probably a regular 'sung' performance of the daily quota of psalms, at least on Sundays and holy days during the second half of the reign of Edward and the first of Elizabeth's.[52] Elsewhere they were probably 'said': in the mid-1570s William Harrison described the psalms and prayers for the day being declaimed from 'a little tabernacle of wainscot'—a reading desk—'by which means the ignorant ... learn divers of the Psalms and usual prayers by heart'.[53]

In time, the rota of prose psalms was first supplemented and then (in parishes but not cathedrals) overtaken by the singing of metrical psalms, at least for a century, until the chanting of the prose psalter started to make a comeback at parish level after the Restoration.[54] Even before then, however, there had been a smaller group of psalms which the rubrics in the prayer book ordered to be read or sung during specific church services. Over thirty 'proper' psalms were specified for use on half a dozen major festivals—initially Christmas, Easter, Ascension and Whitsunday, to which in 1661 were added special psalms for Ash Wednesday and Good Friday. In addition, half a dozen psalms were embedded in four prayer book services: Morning and Evening Prayer, marriages, and funerals, and these too were probably heard by the laity much more often than the others.[55]

---

[49] *Liturgical Services*, ed. Clay, 463–4; Cuming, *Anglican Liturgy*, 124–6; Cressy, *Bonfires and Bells*, passim.

[50] Brightman, *English Rite*, i. 46–9; Procter and Frere, *Book of Common Prayer*, 52, 311–19.

[51] STC² 2378–2413; Ian Green, 'L'utilisation protestante des psaumes en Angleterre (1530–1740)', *Bulletin de la Société de l'Histoire du Protestantisme Français*, 158 (2012): 354.

[52] On reformist debates surrounding psalm-singing, see the chapter by Rachel Willie in this volume.

[53] Green, 'L'utilisation protestante des psaumes', 354–6; Harrison, *Description of England*, 36. But see also John Craig, 'Psalms, Groans and Dog-Whippers: The Soundscape of Sacred Space in the English Parish Church, 1547–1642', in Will Coster and Andrew Spicer (eds), *Sacred Space in Early Modern Europe* (Cambridge: Cambridge University Press, 2005), 104–23; and Christopher Marsh, *Music and Society in Early Modern England* (Cambridge: Cambridge University Press, 2010), 394–405, 422–5, 450–2.

[54] Marsh, *Music and Society*, 405–52; Ruth Mack Wilson, *Anglican Chant and Chanting in England, Scotland and America, 1660 to 1820* (Oxford: Clarendon Press, 1996).

[55] Brightman, *English Rite*, i. 50–65, 134–5, 145, 159, 161; ii. 849–53, 860–6.

The embedding of selected texts in church services brings us to the wider adoption of this practice in Protestant England. If a significant proportion of the time spent in church by a moderately frequent attender was devoted to listening to chapters and psalms taken directly from the Bible—perhaps as much as half the time when both chapters and psalms were above average in length—much of the rest of the time was spent listening to or joining in the repetition of passages lifted whole from the Bible or closely paraphrasing a passage of it. Direct citations included Exodus 20 (the Ten Commandments, used from 1552 at the start of Holy Communion), Matthew 6 or Luke 11 (the Lord's Prayer, used in all regularly performed services and rites of passage), Mark 10: 13–16 ('Suffer little children to come unto me' in the Baptism service), Luke 1–2 (for the *Benedictus, Magnificat,* and *Nunc dimittis*—canticles said or sung during Morning or Evening Prayer), 1 Corinthians 11 (in the Lord's Supper), 1 Corinthians 15: 20–58 ('As by Adam all die, even so in Christ shall all be made alive' in the Burial of the Dead), and (from 1662) 2 Corinthians 13: 14 ('The grace of our Lord Jesus Christ … be with us all evermore', used at the very end of Morning and Evening Prayer).[56] In addition, there were also clusters of sentences with a specific purpose, to exhort to repentance, to encourage charitable giving, or to provide comfort for the bereaved; and there were many prayers, responses, and collects that contained either single words, such as 'Amen', or whole phrases or sentences taken from the Bible, for example, Psalm 51: 15, 'O Lord, open thou my lips, and my mouth shall show forth thy praise', which was used in the plural as a response.[57] That the Stuart clergy were well aware of the provenance of the texts and phrases thus deployed in the Book of Common Prayer, and not only appreciated their value but were prepared to use some of them occasionally as the basis for a sermon is evident from the publication and sales of John Boys's *An Exposition of Al the Principal Scriptures Used in Our English Liturgie Together with a Reason Why the Church did Chuse the Same* (1609), and from the various guides to the prayer book that sold well in the later seventeenth and eighteenth centuries.[58]

Taken together, the oral mechanisms adopted in the middle third of the sixteenth century to disseminate Bible knowledge among the laity probably occupied a larger proportion of service time than in most other Protestant churches. At this stage, the printing press was used mainly to reinforce these mechanisms: large format copies of the Bible, Book of Common Prayer, and official Homilies, and smaller format copies of primers and catechisms, a growing number of which were soon being provided with scriptural proof-texts for each answer.[59] It was only in the last quarter of the sixteenth century and especially the first half of the seventeenth century that print was at last used to provide increasing numbers of complete Bibles for the laity.

[56] Brightman, *English Rite,* ii. 641–6; i. 132–3, 146–7, 156–7, ii. 732, 810–11, 872–3, 730–1; i. 142–5, 158–61; ii. 650–1, 866–71; i. 151, 169.

[57] *Book of Common Prayer,* ed. Cummings, 690–720; Brightman, *English Rite,* i. 129, 153–5, ii. 658–63, 848–9; *passim*; and i. 132–3, 157.

[58] STC² 3455–56.7; Green, *Print and Protestantism,* 347–50.

[59] Green, *Christian's ABC,* 50–2, 62–79; Ian Green, 'The Bible in Catechesis, c.1500–c.1750', in Euan Cameron (ed.), *The New Cambridge History of the Bible,* iii (Cambridge, forthcoming).

These were characterized by formats which were easier to use in the pew, schoolroom, or parlour than the large 'church bibles', and by typeface, apparatus, and prices that were better suited to the needs of those anxious to acquire their own copy. Rising literacy, growing prosperity, and increased commitment to the Protestant cause among the upper and middling ranks created an enlarged market for such copies; and belated increases in the number of presses and skilled operatives and growing self-confidence among leading members of the English print trade meant that by 1575 a number of them were competing for a share in what had been until then a closely guarded monopoly.[60] Setting up and selling complete Bibles remained a very expensive business, and not without risks. But considerable progress was made between the 1580s and the 1600s in the production of quartos in the Genevan translation, many still in black-letter type for householders, and of octavos in the Bishops' version in roman type for students.

The Genevan quartos had a number of features that made them attractive to the laity: summaries at the start of each chapter, notes (which, as Thomas Fuller put it, were like a pair of spectacles in helping them see 'the sense of the scripture'), maps, and from the 1580s Herrey's concordance.[61] The decades after the publication of the King James Bible in 1611 witnessed even higher production—both more repeat editions, and from the 1630s longer print runs than before—so that as many copies of the King James Bible may have been printed in the thirty years after its appearance as of all translations in the previous seventy years. Moreover, in these decades many more octavos were published, and duodecimos appeared on a regular basis. These smaller formats cost half the price of a quarto, and were often published in tandem with new editions of the Book of Common Prayer and 'Sternhold and Hopkins', so that purchasers could buy matching copies of each in sheets and have them bound together.[62] In the late seventeenth and early eighteenth centuries, duodecimos came to dominate production, as charitable societies tried to ensure a complete Bible or New Testament was found in the homes of all who regarded themselves as sound English Protestants.[63]

It is tempting to believe that during the seventeenth century the laity had the skills and the confidence to fulfil the clerical and 'godly' ideal of every literate adult reading the Bible voraciously and studying it critically in search of spiritual enlightenment and comfort. In well-known cases like Grace Mildmay, Nehemiah Wallington, and Sarah Savage, this was clearly the case.[64] But outside the households of the clergy and the most pious laity, it is far from evident that this was the norm. One substantial category of Bible owners—students—used their Bibles for a variety of exercises in handwriting, memorization, and translation, as well as to follow readings during assemblies; and children who were taught at home were often guided towards Bible 'stories' or what were regarded as easier or

---

[60] Green, *Print and Protestantism*, chs 2, 3, and 10.

[61] Thomas Fuller, *The Church History of Britain* (London, 1655), Hhh1ᵛ. Green, *Print and Protestantism*, 73–9. On reading aids in the Geneva Bible, see the chapter by Femke Molekamp in this volume.

[62] Green, *Print and Protestantism*, 50–62.

[63] Green, *Print and Protestantism*, 53, 62, 92–3, 99, and 102 n. 8.

[64] Andrew Cambers, *Godly Reading: Print, Manuscript and Puritanism in England, 1580–1720* (Cambridge: Cambridge University Press, 2011); Kate Narveson, *Bible Readers and Lay Writers in Early Modern England* (Farnham: Ashgate, 2012); Jeremy Schildt, "'In my private reading of the scriptures": Protestant Bible-Reading in England, c.1580–1720', in Jessica Martin and Alec Ryrie (eds), *Private and Domestic Devotion in Early Modern Britain* (Farnham: Ashgate, 2012), 189–210.

safer books, such as Genesis, the Psalms, and the Gospels, which in some cases remained their preferred reading later in life.[65] When adults were involved, what we find in many households was a routine of Bible readings that reflected the practice in church. Lady Anne Clifford 'had three or four chapters read to her by some of her women daily', 'as much as one of the Gospels every week', while Lady Frances Hobart read 'the psalms monthly, the New Testament thrice each year, and the Old once'—one of the many recorded cases where a lay householder adapted the rotas specified in the Book of Common Prayer to their needs.[66]

For those of the laity who wished to break out of these routines or obtain deeper understanding than mere recitation could generate, there were the textual analyses and applications in the sermons of the better educated clergy, and the growing range of aids to Bible study designed to help the inexperienced navigate their way round a long and often difficult text. Initially many of these aids were targeted at less educated clergy and better educated, leisured lay readers, but increasingly during the seventeenth and early eighteenth centuries they became shorter and simpler, for those householders who had only recently purchased or been given a Bible and had limited time for study.[67] That there remained large numbers of men and women who found the Bible hard to understand without clear guidance helps explain two contrasting publishing phenomena from the 1680s to the 1740s. One was the growing number of paraphrases, expositions, and helpful tips targeted at the average reader rather than the scholar, prepared by both conformist and dissenting clergy, like Simon Patrick, David Collyer, Matthew Henry, and Philip Doddridge. The other was the growing fashion for 'histories of the Bible'—scripture stories made familiar through the Prayer Book but now lavishly illustrated or in verse—which it was hoped would attract lay readers who might reject a conventional copy of the Bible.[68]

The supporters of the initiatives taken in the 1530s had aimed high: 'every person' should be encouraged to read the Bible in English. But the harsh realities of mass illiteracy and a dearth of copies meant that the focus had to switch to using oral means to disseminate a carefully interlocking range of 'edifying' and 'profitable' texts, designed to teach those who attended church reasonably often the main duties of Christian life during each season of the Christian year. Once literacy levels improved and supplies of affordable Bibles increased, the numbers of the laity who were in a position to pursue spiritual enlightenment, and even challenge the official interpretations backed by crown and clergy, increased markedly. But for the significant minority of the laity who were still illiterate, the passages of the English Bible declaimed regularly in church continued to be the primary source of their scriptural knowledge, and among the more cautious of those who could read and owned a Bible, there were probably many who mimicked that pattern rather than striking out on their own.

---

[65] Ian Green, *Humanism and Protestantism in Early Modern English Education* (Farnham: Ashgate, 2009), index under 'Bible' and 'biblical material'; Ian Green, 'Lay Responses to the Bible in Early Modern England', paper given at a symposium in Trinity College, Dublin; and Green, *Word, Ritual and Image*.

[66] R. T. Spence, *Lady Anne Clifford* (Stroud: Sutton, 1997), 221; Edward Rainbowe, *A Sermon Preached at the Funeral of … Anne Countess of Pembroke* (1677), 62; Elizabeth Allen, 'Hobart, Lady Frances (1603–1664)', *ODNB*, 2004, <http://www.oxforddnb.com/view/article/66725>; Green, 'Lay Responses'.

[67] Green, *Print and Protestantism*, ch. 3.

[68] Green, *Print and Protestantism*, 118–24, 150, 154, 160–2.

FURTHER READING

The Book of Common Prayer: The Texts of 1549, 1559 and 1662, ed. Brian Cummings (Oxford: Oxford University Press, 2011).

Boys, John. *An Exposition of Al the Principal Scriptures Used in Our English Liturgie Together with a Reason Why the Church did Chuse the Same* (London, 1609).

Boys, John. *An Exposition of the Dominical Epistles and Gospels* (London, 1610–14).

Brightman, F. E. *The English Rite: Being a Synopsis of the Sources and Revisions of the Book of Common Prayer*, 2 vols (London: Rivingtons, 1915–22).

Cooper, Thomas. *A Brief Exposition of Such Chapters of the Old Testament as Usually Are Read in the Church at Common Prayer on the Sundays* (London, 1573).

Cuming, G. J. *A History of Anglican Liturgy* (London: Macmillan, 1969).

Cuming, G. J. *The Godly Order: Texts and Studies Relating to the Book of Common Prayer* (London: Alcuin Club, 1983).

Frere, W. H., and W. M. Kennedy, eds. *Visitation Articles and Injunctions of the Period of the Reformation*, 2 vols, Alcuin Club Collections (London: Longmans, 1910).

Green, Ian. *Print and Protestantism in Early Modern England* (Oxford: Oxford University Press, 2000).

Green, Ian. *Humanism and Protestantism in Early Modern English Education* (Farnham: Ashgate, 2009).

Hemmingsen, Niels. *A Postill, or Exposition of the Gospels* (London, 1569).

MacCulloch, Diarmaid. *Thomas Cranmer: A Life* (New Haven: Yale University Press, 1996).

Procter, F., and W. H. Frere. *A New History of the Book of Common Prayer* (London: Macmillan, 1925).

The Two Books of Homilies Appointed to be Read in Churches, ed. J. Griffiths (Oxford: Oxford University Press, 1859).

CHAPTER 18

'ALL SCRIPTURE IS GIVEN BY INSPIRATION OF GOD': DISSONANCE AND PSALMODY

RACHEL WILLIE

IF the Bible was believed to comprise the word of God disseminated to the people, psalms taught individuals how to converse with God, while at the same time containing axioms that epitomized biblical truths.[1] As David Norton notes, 'As both essential teaching and as poetry, the Psalms were central to early English literary ideas of the Bible in ways that the prose Bible could not be'.[2] Psalms were often regarded as the Bible in miniature: each psalm contributed to a paraphrase of biblical teachings and consequently they were much translated and discussed.

The Bible was fundamental to early modern culture, but the Psalms underpinned devotional practice: from 1559, the Book of Common Prayer enjoined parishioners to read through the entire Old Testament annually, the New Testament three times a year, and the Psalms once a month. The reading of the psalter was to begin afresh on the first of each month, regardless of how many days the month comprised: for February, the final psalms in the psalter would be left unread and in months containing thirty-one days, the psalms read on the 30th of the month would be repeated the next day.[3] This repetition imposed a fixed, cyclical pattern on church worship, which ran parallel with the emphasis Protestants placed upon *sola scriptura* and the dissemination of divine authority through Bible reading. Yet psalms are a generically unstable form, operating at the margins of oral and literate cultures and between music and poetry. They were widely published and in varying forms. As we will see, the various psalm translations and their transmission in textual and aural/oral form meant that the enduring and perpetual cycle of psalmody articulated in the Book

---

[1] Timothy 3: 16.

[2] David Norton, *A History of the Bible as Literature*, rev. edn (Cambridge: Cambridge University Press, 2000), 115.

[3] *The Book of Common Prayer: The Texts of 1549, 1559 and 1662*, ed. Brian Cummings (Oxford: Oxford University Press, 2011), 217. On the rota of public readings, see the chapter by Ian Green in this volume.

of Common Prayer was challenged by the ways in which early modern people engaged with the psalter.

Over the last thirty years, scholarship has afforded much critical attention to the relationship between words and music and the reception history of the psalms. Rivkah Zim's 1987 study established the psalms as a literary and devotional form, while Robin A. Leaver examined church music and the relationship between the psalms and hymnody.[4] More recently, the turn to material culture has led to some insightful interdisciplinary studies on the relationship between the psalms' devotional, literary, and musical functions; their utility in attempting to assert congregational unity through the practices of performing and printing; and their role in domestic settings.[5] Beth Quitslund has endeavoured to rescue the most ubiquitous of metrical psalm translations—Sternhold and Hopkins—from the late seventeenth century's derisory view of the volume, and to show the practices of making and unmaking that afforded the psalter so prominent a place in early modern culture.[6]

These insights locate the psalms at the centre of Protestant and Reformation debates about the use of vernacular language and music in church worship, and illustrate how they functioned as a means of disseminating biblical teachings in a Protestant domestic setting. Yet the psalms were, of course, not the sole property of Protestants; Catholics also read, sang, and translated the holy songs.[7] Drawing upon these studies, this chapter focuses upon how the psalms were used. It first examines the distinctive position of the psalms, understood as both poems and devotions, and the conditions under which psalms were translated into the vernacular in England, before addressing their use in worship and the relationship between music, text, and the body. Finally, I explore the material practices of printing the psalms. While psalm-singing was presented as a means of creating unity, the ways in which the psalms were transmitted meant that they became a site of discord.

Translating and paraphrasing the psalms appears not to have been as contentious as the translation of the Bible into vernacular languages (at least not until the Reformation rendered all forms of intervention in the scripture delicate). The earliest psalms in English can be dated back to King Alfred: the Paris psalter contains Old English translations running parallel to their Latin counterparts and it was widely copied. An extant Middle English psalter comprising rhymed quatrains dates to the early fourteenth century.[8] Translating the psalms into the vernacular was for both pre- and early modern writers an act of piety, and the sixteenth-century reader understood the psalm as both a pleasurable piece of

[4]   Rivkah Zim, *English Metrical Psalms: Poetry as Praise and Prayer, 1535–1601* (Cambridge: Cambridge University Press, 1987); Robin R. Leaver, *'Goostly Psalms and Spirituall Songes': English and Dutch Metrical Psalms from Coverdale to Utenhove, 1535–1566* (Oxford: Oxford University Press, 1991).

[5]   See e.g. Linda Phyllis Austern, Kari Boyd McBride, and David L. Orvis (eds), *Psalms in the Early Modern World* (Farnham: Ashgate, 2011); Hannibal Hamlin, *Psalm Culture and Early Modern English Literature* (Cambridge: Cambridge University Press, 2005); Christopher Marsh, *Music and Society in Early Modern England* (Cambridge: Cambridge University Press, 2010).

[6]   Beth Quitslund, *The Reformation in Rhyme* (Aldershot: Ashgate, 2008).

[7]   An example of both female and Catholic translation is Laura Battiferra's Florentine translation of the penitential psalms, *I sette salmi penitentiali profeta Davit* (Florence, 1566), which were dedicated to Vittoria, Duchess of Guidobaldo, the granddaughter of Pope Paul III; for an English translation and commentary, see *Laura Battiferra and her Literary Circle: An Anthology*, ed. and tr. Victoria Kirkham (Chicago: University of Chicago Press, 2006).

[8]   For an overview of pre-Sternhold psalms, see Quitslund, *Reformation in Rhyme*, 11–18.

versification and a piece of devotional writing that instilled doctrinal truths in those who experienced it.

In the mid-sixteenth century, the conceptual distinction between the psalms as devotional acts and as literary productions was further blurred by the appearance of what Quitslund has termed 'Tower Psalms'. Composed by those incarcerated in the Tower of London, these psalms are intensely topical. Courtly poets such as Thomas Wyatt and Henry Howard may have developed this form of metrical psalmody as an act of piety, but in so doing, they appropriated scripture to comment upon their own plight.[9] Poetry and prophecy are both central to Sir Philip Sidney's reading of the psalms in his *Defense of Poesy*:

> And may I not ... say that the holy David's Psalms are a divine poem? If I do, I shall not do it without the testimony of great learned men both ancient and modern. But even the name of 'Psalms' will speak for me, which being interpreted, is nothing but 'songs'; then, that is fully written in metre, as all learned Hebreians agree, although the rules be not yet fully found; lastly and principally, his handling his prophecy which is merely poetical. For what else is the awaking his musical instruments ... but a heavenly poesy, wherein almost he showeth himself a passionate lover of that unspeakable and everlasting beauty, to be seen by the eyes of the mind, only cleared by faith?[10]

Sidney thus insists upon the status of the psalms as poetry: he focuses upon the stresses and patterns that are generated by the length of the syllables and in so doing implies that there is musicality in the production of words. Musical metaphors focus Sidney's discussions upon the role of the psalms as divine poems.[11] Although early modern scholars were uncertain about the textures and shape of Hebrew poetry, it seems evident that Sidney's insistence upon the psalms being poetry follows a pattern of thought regarding how the psalms operated. The psalms, difficult to categorize generically, serve two purposes for Sidney: they disseminate scripture, but they also entertain and delight. Sidney presents the psalms as a form of biblical exegesis, and the praise that was subsequently given to his collaborative translations appears to endorse this view.

Mary Sidney completed the psalter after her brother's death in 1586 and is responsible for the majority of the translations that make up the Sidney psalter. Despite the obvious literary and rhetorical flourishes of the poems, they were celebrated not only as a literary form but also as a mode for religious devotion.[12] Mary Sidney's psalm translations, as Danielle Clarke and others have demonstrated, offer insights into early modern authorship and female agency.[13] Women were involved in the manuscript circulation of devotional texts throughout the sixteenth and seventeenth centuries.[14] Whereas women reading Bibles was seen by

---

[9] Quitslund, *Reformation in Rhyme*, 15–16.

[10] Gavin Alexander (ed.), *Sidney's 'The Defense of Poesy' and Selected Renaissance Literary Criticism* (London: Penguin, 2004), 7.

[11] Early modern scholars followed the lead of St Jerome in identifying versification and classical metres in the construction of psalms; later critics have found similar patterns present in prose sections of the Hebrew scriptures. See Hamlin, *Psalm Culture*, 5.

[12] Margaret P. Hannay, 'Re-revealing the Psalms: Mary Sidney, Countess of Pembroke, and her Early Modern Readers', in Austern et al., *Psalms in the Early Modern World*, 219–33.

[13] Danielle Clarke, *The Politics of Early Modern Women's Writing* (Harlow: Longman, 2001), esp. 127–47.

[14] For a case study of three seventeenth-century devotional manuscripts, see Victoria E. Burke, '"My Poor Returns": Devotional Manuscripts by Seventeenth-Century Women', in Sarah C. E. Ross (ed.), 'Early Modern Women and the Apparatus of Authorship', *Parergon*, 29/2 (2012): 47–68.

some as contentious, there was a long tradition of women reading, singing, and translating psalms, as well as using the psalms within a domestic setting as a form of religious instruction, material object, devotional writing, and as a way to legitimize their writing.[15]

The Sidney psalms blur the lines between religious and poetic concerns, but also draw familial bonds into their discourse. In Mary Sidney's prefatory poem, 'To th'Angell spirit', courtly poetry and religious meditation conjoin:

> How can I name whom singing sighs extend,
> And not unstop my tears' eternal spring?
> But he did warp, I weaved this web to end;
> The stuff not ours, our work no curious thing,
> Wherein yet well we thought the Psalmist King,
> Now English denizened, though Hebrew born,
> Would to thy music undispleasèd sing,
> Oft having worse, without repining worn;[16]

As Margaret Hannay notes, Mary Sidney uses the common metaphor of translation clothing text, first as a way to weave together the psalms' dual authorship and then to explicate the scriptural genesis of the psalms.[17] However, the metaphor also becomes a way of weaving together divine authority, kingship, and scripture. In referencing 'singing sighs', Mary Sidney draws attention to her brother's absence. The translation becomes a means of memorializing and monumentalizing Philip Sidney and of drawing male and female translator together with the voice of David; at the same time, it focuses attention upon the court and upon vernacular language—'English denizened'—as a form of harmonious music. Claiming that her translations shy away from intricate detail ('no curious thing'), Mary Sidney's statement chimes with the notion that translating the psalms should lack art as a means to focus upon the divine word, but also gestures towards translating in English as a form of nationalism. In a second dedicatory poem, addressed to Elizabeth, Mary Sidney further emphasizes the relationship between court, language, and nation. Thirty years later, William Loe (chaplain to James I), would take this notion to the extreme by publishing psalm translations written entirely in monosyllables, 'It being a received opinion amo[n]gst many … that heretofore our english [sic] tongue in the true idiome thereof consisted altogether of Monasillables, until it came to be blended, and mingled with the commixture of Exotique languages'.[18] For Loe, Psalm translation becomes not just a means of devotion, but a way to purify the English language.

For these writers, the psalms were written texts that could be translated and appropriated to suit particular contexts and directed towards certain audiences. Whereas Sidney presents David 'awakening his musical instruments' as a metaphor invoking the musicality of poetic metre, some Reformists praised the psalms as sung forms. Despite this appreciation of the

[15] Margaret P. Hannay, '"So May I With the *Psalmist* Truly Say": Early Modern English Women's Psalm Discourse', in Barbara Smith and Ursula Appelt (eds), *Write or Be Written: Early Modern Women Poets and Cultural Constraints* (Aldershot: Ashgate, 2001), 105–27.

[16] *The Sidney Psalter: The Psalms of Sir Philip and Mary Sidney*, ed. Hannibal Hamlin, Michael G. Brennan, Margaret P. Hannay, and Noel J. Kinnamon (Oxford: Oxford University Press, 2009), 5–6.

[17] Hannay, 'Re-vealing the Psalms', 222–3.

[18] [William Loe], *Songs of Sion for the Joy of Gods Deere Ones, Who Sitt Here by the Brookes of this Worlds Babel, & Weepe When They Thinke on Jerusalem Which Is on Highe* ([Hamburg, 1620]), A3[r].

psalms' virtue as song, psalm setting was the topic of heated debate, especially in the English context.

In the epistle to the reader of his 1542 French translation of the psalter, John Calvin asserts the importance of music in church worship:

> And in truth we know by experience that song has great force and vigor to move and inflame the hearts … to invoke and praise God with a more vehement and ardent zeal. It must always be looked to that the song be not light and frivolous but have weight and majesty, as Saint Augustine says, and there is likewise a great difference between the music one makes to entertain men at table and in their homes, and the psalms which are sung in the Church in the presence of God and his angels.[19]

Calvin thus advocates the use of song in church on the grounds that, by appealing to the senses, music aids devotion: the combined aural and oral sensation of singing speaks directly to the heart and soul of the congregation and in so doing causes people to praise God more fully. Group singing connects individuals to a wider religious community, and within the space of the church a symbiotic relationship is established where members of the congregation feed off each other's fervour. Communal prayer becomes a form of nourishment for the soul, which is enhanced through the use of music.

Earlier, Calvin asserts that 'Saint Paul speaks not only of praying by word of mouth, but also of singing'.[20] Chapter 14 of Paul's first epistle to the Corinthians bursts with allusions to singing and praying. The Geneva Bible (1560) states, 'For if I pray *in* a *strange* tongue, my spirit praieth: but mine understading [*sic*] is without frute. What is it then? I wil praye with the spirit, but I wil pray with the understanding also; I wil sing with the spirite, but I wil sing with the understanding also' (1 Corinthians 14: 14–15). The King James Bible alters the conjunctive to read, 'For if I pray in an unknown tongue, my spirit prayeth, and my understanding is unfruitful. What is it then? I will pray with the spirit and I will pray with the understanding also: I will sing with the spirit, and I will sing with the understanding also'. While these may seem like minor textual variants, the shift in tone heralded by the alteration in conjunctive is telling. In the Genevan version, the abrasive 'but' cuts through the connection that has been established between the processes of praying and the need to understand devotional practices. Employing parataxis (the rhetorical strategy most commonly associated with the King James Bible), the more gentle 'and' turns prayer and understanding into a collective undertaking where the one necessitates the other. Wycliffe and Tyndale used the word 'mind' instead of the word 'understanding', which further alters the resonances of the passage and gestures to a dualistic view of mind and body and how the soul connects to God. In each instance, the need for comprehension is brought to the fore. In order to participate in church worship, the congregation needs to understand what is going on.

Yet Paul's main focus is not upon the rights or wrongs of singing in church; instead he discusses the relative merits of speaking in tongues. Calvin appropriates and reinvents Paul's teachings to endorse psalmody and advocate singing in churches and vernacular worship. However, the presence of St Augustine in these discussions complicates the relationship between prayer, music, and language. In alluding to St Augustine's remarks regarding the

---

[19] Oliver Strunk (ed.), *Strunk's Source Readings in Music History*, ed. Leo Trietler, rev. edn (New York and London: Norton, 1978), 365. Calvin is referencing Augustine's *Epistola* 55.18.34.

[20] *Strunk's Source Readings*, 365.

need for church music to have 'weight and majesty', Calvin draws attention to some of the perceived perils of music: in being able to affect the senses and move the spirit to godliness, there is also the danger that music could drive a person to vice. For this reason, not all reformers were in favour of using music in church worship.

Augustine's views regarding music were not limited to the comment to which Calvin alludes. When considering the place and function of music in church worship, Augustine oscillates between acknowledging that it offers earthly pleasure and contending that it enhances religious devotion:

> Thus floate I betweene peril of pleasure, and an approved profitable custome: enclined … to allow of the old usage of singing in the Church, that so by the delight taken in at the eares, the weaker minds may be rowzed up into some feeling of devotion. And yet againe, so oft as it befalls me to be more mov'd with the *voyce* then with the *ditty*, I confesse myselfe to have grievously offended.[21]

Music aids devotion, but only when used correctly: if the hearer is more delighted with the beauty of the apparatus that produces the music, the listener has erred. The pleasure of music can thus be tempered with remorse. Despite these qualms, Augustine ultimately conforms to orthodox patristic beliefs that advocated music in early Christian church worship.

The combinations of sounds and harmony allure, but this ability to attract individuals was not universally endorsed. Despite the practice of psalm-singing in some churches, the apparent accord achieved through music hides the tensions elicited by psalm-singing. The Reformed Church in Geneva initially followed the practice of their counterparts in Berne (who in turn followed the practice that Zwingli had implemented in Zurich) and banned music in church worship. As more Protestants who feared persecution fled Catholic countries and settled in Geneva, the prohibition of music in all churches ceased. In January 1537, Calvin convinced the Genevan council to permit psalm-singing in church worship.[22]

In England, as Quitslund notes, one translation from the 1530s demonstrates an indebtedness to the hymnological tradition that influenced continental psalmody. This is Miles Coverdale's *Goostly psalmes and spirituall songes* (c.1535). This was one of four psalters that Coverdale published between 1534 and 1540; as Jamie Ferguson deftly observes, it 'manifests a pluralistic conception of scriptural truth'.[23] Scriptural truth is not fixed; it is fluid and open to reappraisal, despite Protestantism's allegiance to *sola scriptura*. What sets *Goostly psalmes* apart from the other psalters is that it is the first English psalter to be published with music. This might suggest that *Goostly psalmes* could be used in church worship, but officially England was still married to a Latin liturgy and would not have its first vernacular prayer book for another fourteen years; Coverdale asserts that his psalter is intended for domestic use.

Denouncing profane music, in his epistle to the reader, Coverdale expresses a desire that:

[21] *Saint Augustines Confessions Translated*, tr. William Watts (1631), Gg3r.
[22] For a study that examines the varying Protestant attitudes to church music, see Jonathan Willis, *Church Music and Protestantism in Post-Reformation England: Discourses, Sites and Identities* (Farnham: Ashgate, 2010).
[23] Jamie H. Ferguson, 'Miles Coverdale and the Claims of Paraphrase', in Austern et al., *Psalms in the Early Modern World*, 137–54, 138.

our mynstrels had none other thynge to playe upo[n], nether oure carters & plowmen other thynge to whistle upon, save Psalmes, hymnes, and soch godley songes as David is occupied with all. And yf women syttynge at theyr rockes, or spynnynge at the wheles, had none other songes to passe theyr tyme … they shulde be better occupied, then with hey nony nony, hey troly loly, & soch lyke fantasies.[24]

Coverdale weaves psalm-singing into all aspects of everyday life: not only men, but women from all social groupings are considered as fit audiences to consume and disseminate the psalms through song.

Coverdale seeks to replace popular tunes and ballads with psalm-singing. Such a desire demonstrates an anxiety regarding the place and function of both music and scripture in early modern England. Fearful that secular music can only lead to profane conduct, Coverdale views the singing of psalms as a way to heighten spirituality. This view is manifested in a text that was translated by Coverdale and reprinted frequently throughout the sixteenth century. Here, Heinrich Bullinger advises against allowing daughters to read romances and suggests they should sing psalms instead:

> Bookes of Robin hood, Bevis of Hampton, Troilus & such like fables, do but kyndel in lyers like lyes and wanton love, which ought not in youth with their first spittle to be drunken in, least they ever remayne in them. If ye delight to sing songs, ye have the Psalmes and many goodly songes and books in English, right fruitful & sweete.[25]

The potential for books to be a corrupting influence—as well as a source for good—means that the psalms ought to be the only texts that are digested.

While Coverdale's psalms marked an important intervention in the paraphrasing of scripture, the shifts in royal authority in the mid-sixteenth century contributed to the psalms not being widely used in church worship. Coverdale hints at psalm-singing being connected to private and public devotion, but biblical reading and church worship were far from private acts. In 1547, Edward VI and his advisers (more sympathetic to reformist measures in continental Europe) permitted Archbishop Thomas Cranmer to draw up a liturgy in English. However, with Mary's accession, in 1553, many prominent Protestants fled to Geneva, and other Protestant states, taking with them the psalms that had been translated in or around 1547 by Thomas Sternhold, groom to Edward's bedchamber, and augmented by John Hopkins around 1549. During the five-year suspension of Protestant worship in England, these psalms would be developed into a complete psalter overseas, published in various formats and with different paratextual materials from 1562.[26] While Coverdale's psalms would be added to the 1662 Book of Common Prayer, the Sternhold and Hopkins psalter would become the dominant psalter in domestic and church settings for the next one hundred and fifty years.

With popularity came derision. Part of the controversy lay in the psalm settings. Most of the Sternhold and Hopkins psalms are in ballad metre. This rhythmic affinity

---

[24] *Goostly Psalmes and Spirituall Songes Drawen out of the Holy Scripture, for the Co[m]forte and Consolacyon of Soch as Love to Rejoyse in God and his Worde* ([London: 1535]), *2ᵛ.

[25] Heinrich Bullinger, *The Christian State of Matrimony, Wherein Husbands & Wyves May Learne to Keepe House Together wyth Love*, tr. Miles Coverdale (London, 1575), M7ʳ.

[26] Beth Quitslund, 'The Psalm Book', in Andy Kesson and Emma Smith (eds), *The Elizabethan Top Ten: Defining Print Popularity in Early Modern England* (Farnham: Ashgate, 2013), 203–11.

meant that, despite Coverdale envisaging the psalms as replacing ballads, they could be, and were, set to ballad tunes. However, the title-page of the 1560 edition of the—as yet incomplete—Sternhold and Hopkins *Psalmes of David in English Metre* states clearly how they are to be read:

> VERY METE TO BE USED of all sorts of people privately for their godly solace and confort, laying aparte all ungodly songs and ballads, which tend only to the nourishing of vice, and corrupting of youth.[27]

From the earliest editions of *The Whole Booke of Psalms*, the holy songs were presented as the opposite of ballads. The title-page emphasizes that psalms are a form of spiritual nourishment. Feeding the soul, the psalms present a counterbalance to the corrupting influence of ballads: the content of the words rather than their metrical patterns mean that the psalms aid private devotion.

By 1566, the title-page declares the psalms to be 'Newly set forth and alowed to me [*sic*] song in all churches, of all the people together … & moreover in private houses, for their godly solace and comfort'.[28] Within six years, the text becomes universal, operating at the borders of private and public devotion and at the hinterland of secular and sacred pastime. Such ubiquity allowed the psalms to become a means of solace and of pleasure, yet they still met with hostility. Catholics attacked Protestant worship through references to 'Genevan psalms':

> their service is nought, because they have divers false and blasphemous things therein: and that which is yet worse, they so place those things, as they may seem to the simple, to be very scripture. As for example, in the end of a certain *Geneva* Psalme, they pray to God to keepe them from Pope, Turke, and Papist, which is blasphemous.[29]

Thus claimed *A Briefe Discourse Containing Certaine Reasons Why Catholicks Refuse to Goe to Church* (1601). However, it is not clear which of the psalms is being referenced; by prefacing 'psalme' with 'Genevan', the author distances translations of the psalms from their roots in the Bible and instead suggests that the mode of translation is an act that conflates political and confessional differences as a way of deceiving a naïve audience. The psalms may be the Bible in miniature, but this reading demonstrates ongoing concerns regarding the exigencies of translation: rather than being a means of disseminating the divine word and unifying the audience, translating the psalms provokes hostility and suspicion.

Protestants may have been reforming church worship from the sixteenth century, but so too were Roman Catholics. This highlights ways in which Catholics and Protestants reconceptualized church worship in the wake of the Reformation. Amongst some Protestants, congregational psalm-singing was actively promoted: stylistically different to the Catholic Mass, metrical psalm-singing represented a novel interjection in the soundscape.[30] At the

---

[27] *Psalmes of David in Englishe Metre, by T. Sterneholde and Others* (London, 1560), title-page.

[28] *The First Part of the Psalmes of David in English Meter by T. Sternhold and Others* (London, 1566), title-page.

[29] Robert Parsons, *A Briefe Discourse Containing Certaine Reasons Why Catholikes Refuse to Goe to Church* (Doway [i.e. England], 1601), E7ᵛ.

[30] For a discussion of psalm-singing in church, and the noisiness of the English church, see John Craig, 'Psalms, Groans and Dog-Whippers: The Soundscape of Sacred Space in the English Parish Church,

same time, recusant Catholics retained the material objects of devotion—books, rosaries and sacred items—and married these with pilgrimages to sacred sites and private devotion at home.[31] Yet Catholics also invested in the religious soundscape and Protestants were in possession of commodities that brought religious imagery into the domestic setting, thereby enhancing their doctrinal refutation of sacred space being fixed in particular religious places.[32] This interrelationship of the materiality of faith is mirrored by the lack of consensus regarding whether psalms should be sung. Not all Protestants encouraged the singing of psalms; although Sternhold and Hopkins's *Whole Booke of Psalms* was bound frequently with Bibles and the Book of Common Prayer, the place and function of the psalms in reformed church worship continued to be contentious. Far from demonstrating Protestant unity against Catholicism and vice versa, the material practices of devotion were pliable.

Although the psalms were translated into numerous vernacular languages, the Genevan melodies were adopted and appropriated across language divides.[33] This was due to how the music was composed and the development of metrical psalmody across Europe. There was a fluid interplay in the use of music, and composers borrowed from plainsong used in the Catholic liturgy as well as from popular tunes, vernacular hymns, and the psalter used in reformist churches in France and Germany.[34] This musical interplay emphasizes that it was not just Protestants who were using psalms in early modern Europe, and also reveals the extent to which the relative syllabic and rhythmic unity of the metrical psalms ensured that they could be sung easily to existing tunes. This would seem to imply that the psalms are a way to disseminate the divine word and inspire euphony through the use of music.

Perhaps erroneously attributed to John Case, *The Praise of Musicke* (1586) enforces the connection between word, space, and congregation:

> Musick with the concinnitie of her sound, and the excellency of harmony, doth as it were knit & joyne us unto God, putting us in mind of our maker and of that mutuall unitie & consent, which ought to bee as of voices so of mindes in Gods church and congregations …. if there were no other reason, yet this were of sufficient force to perswade the lawful use of Musicke: in that as a pleasant bait, it doeth both allure men into the church which otherwise would not come, & … continue till the divine service bee ended.[35]

Music thus becomes a means of creating unity, not just in the church or congregation, but also between an individual and God. It boosts attendance at church and encourages people

---

1547–1642', in Will Coster and Andrew Spicer (eds), *Sacred Space in Early Modern Europe* (Cambridge: Cambridge University Press, 2005), 104–23.

[31] See Alexandra Walsham, 'Beads, Books and Bare Ruined Choirs: Transmutations of Catholic Ritual Life in Protestant England', in Benjamin J. Kaplan, Bob Moore, Henk van Nierop, and Judith Pollmann (eds), *Catholic Communities in Protestant States: Britain and the Netherlands c.1570–1720* (Manchester: Manchester University Press, 2009), 103–22.

[32] Tara Hamling, 'Reconciling Image and Object: Religious Imagery in Protestant Interior Decoration', in Hamling and Catherine Richardson (eds), *Everyday Objects: Medieval and Early Modern Material Culture and its Meanings* (Farnham: Ashgate, 2010), 321–34; Craig, 'Psalms, Groans and Dog-Whippers', 104–5.

[33] Andreas Marti and Bert Polman, 'Reformed and Presbyterian Church Music', Oxford Music Online, <http://www.oxfordmusiconline.com/subscriber/article/grove/music/48535>.

[34] 'Introduction', in Austern et al., *Psalms in the Early Modern World*, 1–33, 20.

[35] *The Praise of Musicke: Wherein besides the Antiquitie, Dignitie, Delectation, & Use Thereof in Civill Matters, is also Declared the Sober and Lawfull Use of the Same in the Congregation and Church of God* (1586), K4^r.

to be receptive to the words that are sung. However, as we have seen, psalm-singing was not limited to church worship. While Calvin supported the singing of psalms in church, the preface to Claude Goudimel's 1565 four-part harmonization of the psalms asserts that his settings are intended for a different venue: 'To the melody of the psalms we have, in this little volume, adopted three parts, not to induce you to sing them in Church but that you may rejoice in God, particularly at home'.[36] Through psalm-singing, secular space is rendered sacred. The psalms become a means of bringing musical devotion into the domestic realm, and transforming the household into a congregation.[37] But the addition of harmonization acknowledges the household may have greater musical skill and levels of literacy than the average congregation. It also demonstrates how ubiquitous psalm-singing was in early modern culture: it was designed not only to enhance church worship, but also to entertain and as a means to inspire spirituality in the home.

Roger Bray argues that psalm settings composed for domestic use by the recusant William Byrd could be palatable to Catholics and Protestants alike, implying a unity across confessional divides.[38] However, the material practices of performance mean that domestic singers might be more focused upon the demands of playing than of praying. As Richard Wistreich tellingly observes, notation 'constantly reminds the reader of the inherent provisionality of music's textual authority'.[39] The retranslating of text into oral/aural form means that the performer's immediate attention may be on the production of sound rather than the godly content of the words being sung. This leads to discussions over what the place and function of music is in relation to scripture, and points again to Augustine's fears that the sensory experiences of music both enhance and potentially corrupt devotion.

In 1619, the poet and later Parliamentarian radical, George Wither, commented at length on the perils present in the relationship between words and music:

> I would advise touching the *Musicke* of these divine *Hymnes* … that men should be carefull to let it bee such as were grave, & suitable to the qualitie of those Songs. For, *Musicke* hath many *Species*, and is of very different operations: insomuch, as if that been not observed, and the qualitie of the subject well considered, with what Straines it most naturally requires; the *Song* and the *Tune* will as improperly sute together, as a Clownes habit, upon a grave Stateman. Yea, the inarticulate sounds have, in themselves, I know not what secret power, to move the very affections of mens soules, according to the qualitie of their Straines … And if they would remember themselves, they could truely say, that when they have been exceedingly merrily disposed, one deepe solemne Straine hath made them, suddenly and extremely melancholy: And that, on contrary againe, at another time, when they have been oppressed with sadnesse, a touch or two of sprightly *Musicke*, hath quickly raised their hearts to a pitch of jollity.[40]

Echoing Calvin and Coverdale, Wither notes the transformative effects of music, but suggests more clearly the connection between music and humoral imbalances in the body. Hearing serves a medicinal purpose, but this relationship between body and sounds also

---

[36] *Strunk's Source Readings*, 368.

[37] Beth Quitslund, 'Singing the Psalms for Fun and Profit', in Jessica Martin and Alec Ryrie (eds), *Private and Domestic Devotion in Early Modern Britain* (Farnham: Ashgate, 2012), 237–58.

[38] Roger Bray, 'William Byrd's English Psalms', in Austern et al., *Psalms in the Early Modern World*, 61–75.

[39] Richard Wistreich, 'Musical Materials and Cultural Spaces', *Renaissance Studies*, 26 (2012): 1.

[40] George Wither, *A Preparation to the Psalter* (London, 1619), H1ᵛ–H2ʳ.

means that music can be dangerous.[41] Rather than emphasizing the elevated spiritual nourishment that the words of the psalms can afford the listener, inappropriate settings render sacred texts profane:

> As our praises of God, and holy invocation ought to bee made with such reverent heede, and in such grace, modest and decent tunes as become them, whether they bee the *Psalmes of Davide*, or other holy *Hymns*, invented for the honour of God, and our spirituall comfort: So, in whatsoever subject it bee, we ought to have a care, that Jesus, or any other name of God, be never used in any song, but where the voice may be lifted up with unfained reverence .... I have heard in foolish, and ridiculous Ballads ... the name of our blessed Saviour, invocated and sung to these roguish tunes, which have formerly served for prophane Jiggs ... : and yet use hath made it so familiar, that we now heare it, and scare take notice that there is ought evill therin .... to offer a Prince wine in the uncleanest vessel, were no greater indignity, then to present the great King of heaven with his praises, & the devotions of our soules, in such tunes as have bin formerly dedicated, to some loose Harlot, or used in expression of our basest and most wanton affections. Nor do I recon it little better then Sacriledge, for any man to use those tunes with a profane subject, which have beene once consecrated unto the service and honour of God. (I2ʳ)

Wither's attack on 'improper' settings is long, but worth quoting at length. Not only the psalms, but hymns and anthems need to be presented in the appropriate register. 'Decent' tunes may supply the words with a suitably modest setting, but the use of the word 'grace' points to both earthly elegance (the graceful tone of the words and the music) and the inner grace through which the elect were believed to gain salvation. The sensual experience of listening provides spiritual comfort, but only when the words are set to appropriate music.

Yet Wither's insistence upon 'unfained reverence' suggests a more qualified sense of spirituality and the comfort that can be gained from singing sacred texts. In her spiritual autobiography (c. 1639), Elizabeth Isham wrote of the delight she took in learning to sing psalms, and recorded the nourishment that they provided her mother during a time of sickness: 'in the night she would call for Suppings that thereby she might refressh her selfe ... after when somthing better she could give care to reading she called for Psalmes of David, which were often read over to her'.[42] After receiving bodily nourishment, Isham's mother gains spiritual nourishment, though she is only healed when Mr Dod comforts her by explicating the later verses of Isaiah 28.[43] The combined attention to the needs of the body and the soul become a healing ritual, which enforces Helen Smith's contention that reading is a 'bodily and an embodied practice' and emphasizes the complexities of the relationship between text and setting.[44]

Wither's condemnation of ballad tunes being used for psalmody centres around their relationship to the ballad text. However, his impassioned critique of praising God through songs that had previously adored prostitutes is not without qualification. Aghast at the

---

[41] For a reading of the relationship between sounds, hearing, and the 'green' passions of desire, see Bruce Smith, 'Hearing Green', in Gail Kern Paster, Katherine Rowe, and Mary Floyd-Wilson (eds), *Reading the Early Modern Passions: Essays in the Cultural History of Emotion* (Philadelphia: University of Pennsylvania Press, 2004), 147–68.

[42] NjP, Robert Taylor Collection, MS RTCO1, fol. 11ʳ, cited in Femke Molekamp, *Women and the Bible in Early Modern England: Religious Reading and Writing* (Oxford: Oxford University Press, 2013), 153. Transcribed at <http://web.warwick.ac.uk/english/perdita/Isham>.

[43] NjP, Robert Taylor Collection, MS RTCO1, fols 11ᵛ–12ʳ.

[44] Helen Smith, '"More swete vnto the eare / than holsome for ye mynde": Embodying Early Modern Women's Reading', *Huntington Library Quarterly*, 73 (2010): 414.

intertextual resonances that are created through recycling music, and believing this will lead people to connect the spiritual with the earthly and thereby fail to place their sights on higher matters, Wither ends with a curious concession:

> So I beleeve, that he who applies, unto vaine songs, those tunes which are once appropriated to Divine Subjects (especially the holy *Psalms*) doth that which is abominable unto the Lord. This is my opinion: If I erre, pardon it, for the Zeale I have unto Gods honour, is the cause of this error. (I2r)

After decreeing that vain songs and divine subjects are not to be mixed, Wither includes the caveat that this is his opinion only. Zeal may have caused him to commit an error, but admitting the potential for (theological) error casts doubt upon Wither's narrative. What has previously been decreed as sacrilege could be a means of enhancing spirituality by setting new words to familiar tunes: memory, text, and music conjoin to purge the music of its previous, profane utterances. The words and music of the psalms thus have a destabilizing effect, with some who criticized the use of popular tunes unclear over why their appropriation should be an abomination to God's honour.[45]

These distinctions become blurred further when we consider the material practices of printing: under James I's patronage, in 1623, Wither was granted a patent for his *Hymnes and Songs of the Church* to be bound with all metrical psalm-books. This overruled earlier, lucrative patents for printing Sternhold and Hopkins.[46] The right to print the psalms was hotly contested.[47] In 1575, the composers Thomas Tallis and William Byrd were granted a monopoly to print music, which included the printing of music paper and music importation. From 1588 to 1593, Byrd had sole ownership of the monopoly and appears to have focused upon printing his own, Catholic music.[48] However, from 1592, Byrd's assignee, Thomas East, was printing editions of *The Whole Booke of Psalms* that included musical notation. Such an enterprise was not without its controversies, given that the patent for printing the psalms was a source of vehement dispute, and East certainly lacked authority to print the words.

Printing music blurs the distinctions between the textual and musical transmission of the psalms in print. In a dedication to Sir John Puckering, East presents the printing of words and tunes as providing the whole psalm and suggests that through experiencing the psalms in their entirety, a restorative pleasure is bestowed on the body: 'The word of God (Right honourable) delighteth those which are spiritually mynded: the Art of Musick recreateth such, as are not sensually affected: wher zeal in the one, and skill in the other doe

---

[45] Wither seeks to separate sacred from secular words and music, though, Tessa Watt notes, it was in the middle of Elizabeth's reign that ballads began to be seen as an immoral and scandalous means of spreading the word. This presents the interesting possibility that the ballad metre of the psalm translations may have been a residual echo of this popular inheritance. Tessa Watt, *Cheap Print and Popular Piety* (Cambridge: Cambridge University Press, 1993).

[46] David Norbrook, *Poetry and Politics in the English Renaissance*, rev. edn (Oxford: Oxford University Press, 2002), 216.

[47] Jeremy L. Smith, *Thomas East and Music Publishing in Renaissance England* (Oxford: Oxford University Press, 2003), 22–8 and 71–5.

[48] Smith, *Thomas East*, 58. See also Jeremy L. Smith, 'Turning a New Leaf: William Byrd, the East Music-Publishing Firm and the Jacobean Succession', in Robin Myers, Michael Harris, and Giles Mandelbrote (eds), *Music and the Book Trade from the Sixteenth to the Twentieth Century* (Newcastle and London: Oak Knoll Press and British Library, 2008), 25–43.

meet, the whole man is revived'.[49] Words and music conjoin to aid spirituality. The assertion that those of a spiritual mind gain solace from the words of scripture seems to be an early modern commonplace, but East's observation that music 'recreateth such, as are not sensually affected' is intriguing. The *Oxford English Dictionary* tells us that 'Recreateth' can mean 'to restore to a good or normal physical condition from a state of weakness or exhaustion', or alternatively it could mean, 'to refresh or enliven (the spirits or mind, a person) by means of sensory or purely physical influence'.[50] Yet again, we are presented with the ability of sounds to affect the emotions, understood in this period as both psychological and physical.[51] In this reading, *The Whole Booke of Psalmes* needs to include musical notation as a way to complete the text and to allow the words to be sung. Through the combined sensory experience of hearing skilful music and zealous scripture, an individual is restored. In the paratexts to psalms, sound is often brought into focus (Figure 18.1).

In making these claims, East asserts that 'the hart rejoicing in the word, & the eares delighting in the Notes & Tunes, both these might joyne together unto the praise of God' (A2r). The page becomes a textual space where utterances can be stored prior to performance. These 'complete' texts do not just rival the psalter monopoly, but, due to the presence of notation on the page, become superior to other textual forms. However, East's other textual engagements complicate this representation of Protestant accord. As has been noted, Byrd used his patent and East's press to publish his own works. While East delayed entering some of these works in the Stationers' Company Register and published some as 'hidden' works, which makes their dating ambiguous, he saw through the printing press volumes of Catholic music, including Byrd's *Cantiones* and *Gradualia*, which were designed for Catholic worship.[52] In April 1600, recusants met at East's house in Aldersgate to discuss the succession of the crown.[53] East's printing press (and home) brings into focus the fraught relationships between different faith communities and emphasizes that, while psalm-singing is presented as a way to inspire euphony and make an individual whole (and Byrd produced psalm-settings that could be appreciated by both Catholics and Protestants), the multiple ways in which the psalms were disseminated meant that the processes of psalm-singing often highlighted discord.

This discord is further emphasized when we reconsider East's dedicatory letter, part of which has been quoted. East's use of the word 'sensually' is striking. In the late sixteenth century, 'sensually' means 'with subservience to the senses or lower nature; with undue indulgence of the physical appetites: lustfully, licentiously' and it was not until 1624 that 'sensually' came to mean 'in a manner perceptible to the senses'.[54] In 1592, East appears to be using 'sensually' in this later sense, but 'recreateth' could also have a secondary meaning. The word both connotes 'mental or spiritual comfort or consolation', but also 'the action or fact of refreshing or entertaining oneself through a pleasurable or interesting pastime, amusement, activity'.[55] 'Pleasurable, or interesting' pastimes need not be licentious, but this

---

[49] *The Whole Booke of Psalmes with Their Wonted Tunes, as They Are Song in Churches, Composed into Foure Parts* (London, 1592), A2r.

[50] 'recreate, v.1', *OED Online*, Mar. 2014.

[51] See Gail Kern Paster, *Humoring the Body: Emotions and the Shakespearean Stage* (Chicago: University of Chicago Press, 2004), 1–24.

[52] Smith, *Thomas East*, 96–102.   [53] Smith, *Thomas East*, 103–5.

[54] 'sensually, adv.', *OED Online*, Mar. 2014.   [55] 'recreation, n.1', *OED Online*, Mar. 2014.

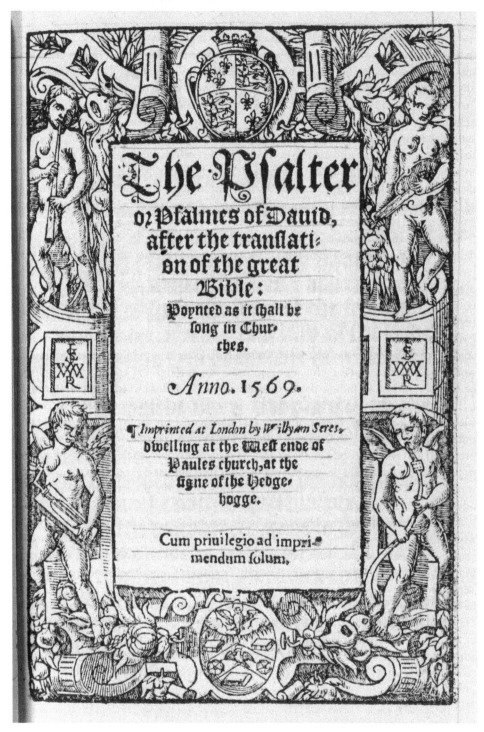

FIGURE 18.1 Title-page to *The Psalter or Psalmes of Dauid* (London: in officina Gulihelmi Seres typographi, 1569). Featuring books (in the lower cartouche), and cherubim playing instruments, the title-page speaks to the Psalms as both read and sung texts. York Minster Library: OL; XI.F.20.

blurring of the spiritual with the sensual through singing psalms is striking. East may assert that, for those who are not spiritually minded, music can restore balance in the humours and in so doing restore the senses and thereby allow the individual to receive the word of God, but the language that he employs brings to the fore tensions between the word and music-setting.

While neither Catholics nor Protestants would question the authority of the Bible, the principle of *sola scriptura* implies that the Bible conveys a fixed divine authority that can be deciphered by the lay reader without the intervention of the church. However, if the psalms represented the Bible in miniature, we see that *sola scriptura* quickly became fragmented as individuals battled over the 'correct' way to transmit them. Due to translators' use of ballad metre, the most ubiquitous of Protestant psalm translations in late sixteenth- and seventeenth-century England could be sung to ballad tunes. The distinctions between sacred and secular were further compromised by the marketplace of print, where the lucrative and legally contested patent for printed psalmbooks would eventually be taken into the ownership of the Worshipful Company of Stationers.[56] Psalm-singing was not only undertaken by Protestant communities, but also by Catholics, and the singing of the psalms took place within formal church worship and in a domestic setting. The unregulated and confessional nature of psalm-singing meant that psalmody often exposed religious contentions. As with the early modern Bible, translating the word would prove a controversial task. Printing, disseminating, and singing psalms only enhanced this dissonance.

FURTHER READING

Austern, Linda Phyllis, Kari Boyd McBride, and David L. Orvis, eds. *Psalms in the Early Modern World* (Farnham: Ashgate, 2011).

Craig, John. 'Psalms, Groans and Dog-Whippers: The Soundscape of Sacred Space in the English Parish Church, 1547–1642', in Will Coster and Andrew Spicer (eds), *Sacred Space in Early Modern Europe* (Cambridge: Cambridge University Press, 2005), 104–23.

Hamlin, Hannibal. *Psalm Culture and Early Modern English Literature* (Cambridge: Cambridge University Press, 2004).

Marsh, Christopher. *Music and Society in Early Modern England* (Cambridge: Cambridge University Press, 2010).

Molekamp, Femke. *Women and the Bible in Early Modern England: Religious Reading and Writing* (Oxford: Oxford University Press, 2013).

Norton, David. *A History of the Bible as Literature*, rev. edn (Cambridge: Cambridge University Press, 2000).

Quitslund, Beth. *The Reformation in Rhyme* (Aldershot: Ashgate, 2008).

Smith, Barbara, and Ursula Appelt, eds. *Write or Be Written: Early Modern Women Poets and Cultural Constraints* (Aldershot: Ashgate, 2001).

[56] Smith, *Thomas East*, 28.

Smith, Jeremy L. *Thomas East and Music Publishing in Renaissance England* (Oxford: Oxford University Press, 2003).

Targoff, Ramie. *Common Prayer: The Language of Public Devotion in Early Modern England* (Chicago: University of Chicago Press, 2001).

Temperley, Nicholas. *The Music of the English Parish Church* (Cambridge: Cambridge University Press, 1979).

Watt, Tessa. *Cheap Print and Popular Piety* (Cambridge: Cambridge University Press, 1993).

Willis, Jonathan. *Church Music and Protestantism in Post-Reformation England: Discourses, Sites and Identities* (Farnham: Ashgate, 2010).

CHAPTER 19

ORNAMENT AND REPETITION: BIBLICAL INTERPRETATION IN EARLY MODERN ENGLISH PREACHING

MARY MORRISSEY

BECAUSE it simultaneously enunciated scripture and expounded its meanings, the sermon was a powerful vehicle for advancing particular interpretations of the Bible. The interpretative element of early modern preaching cannot be emphasized enough: the sermons of the period between the Elizabethan Settlement and the English Civil War were essentially exercises in literary interpretation that were then 'applied' to the circumstances of the sermon's hearers. Preachers and preaching handbooks often tell us that preaching was, in the words of John Brinsley, 'an action of the Minister of the Word, soundly interpreting and opening the sense of the Scriptures by the Scriptures, with Application of them to the use of the Church'.[1] While preachers and preaching handbooks often prescribe correct approaches to this task, few offer much insight into the pitfalls of any particular method, or the relative prestige of different interpretative approaches. We do find such comments in a particular kind of sermon: the annual 'rehearsal' preached at Paul's Cross and in Oxford on the Sunday after Easter. This chapter will examine surviving rehearsal sermons to see what we can learn about the ways that preachers thought about the biblical texts that they represented to their hearers. Two concerns about preaching can be discerned in what preachers say in these sermons: a deep intellectual engagement with the multiple interpretative possibilities of Scripture, and an acknowledgement of the need to repeat the fundamentals of the faith to an audience who have heard it before. There is an evident tension between these goals, and the rehearsal sermons suggest that it was not resolved.

---

[1] John Brinsley, *The Preachers Charge, and Peoples Duty about Preaching and Hearing of the Word* (London, 1631), B3ʳ.

The rehearsal sermon is one that repeats, in summary form, a sermon by another preacher. The origins of the custom are unknown. In London, the Paul's Cross Good Friday sermon and the three Easter sermons preached at St Mary's Spital (Spitalfields) were repeated in summary form in a rehearsal sermon that took place on 'Low Sunday', the Sunday after Easter, at Paul's Cross. The annual series was described by John Stow as an ancient one, and a 'laudable custom' that involved sermons by 'some especial learned men'. The Oxford series is much less well documented, and appears to have added to pre-existing arrangements in order to create a copy of the London series. The Laudian statutes, for example, tell us that a sermon in English on Good Friday was to be preached in Christ Church Cathedral. An Easter Sunday morning sermon was to be preached at St Peter's in the East 'as was the custom of old'; 'two sermons in English' were to be preached in St Mary's on the 'two holidays next following Easter Sunday', under regulations governing 'extraordinary sermons' on holidays like 5 November. No mention is made of a rehearsal sermon in the statutes, but given that there was to be an English sermon every Sunday morning, in and out of term, in St Mary's, it seems likely that this sermon on Low Sunday was used for the rehearsal sermon.[2]

In both Oxford and London, these sermon series were prestigious events. It was the highpoint of the London Corporation's formal religious observance, and the Lord Mayor and aldermen processed to the pulpit crosses at St Paul's and St Mary's Spital in their livery. Senior churchmen took their turn preaching in the Easter series at both places, and there was a clear hierarchy for the sermons. The Passion sermon was one of the Oxford sermons preached 'by the heads of colleges, by the dean and prebendaries of Christ Church, by the two divinity professors, and by the professor of the Hebrew tongue' according to a set rota. The other three Easter sermons were preached by men appointed by the vice-chancellor.[3] In London, the appointment of the Good Friday sermon and the rehearsal sermon lay with the Bishop of London, who was also consulted by the Corporation of London about the appointment of the three Spital preachers. The Monday sermon was reserved for the most senior cleric, where possible a bishop or a dean. The Tuesday sermon was usually assigned to someone equal to the Monday preacher or a little less senior, a dean or archdeacon if a bishop had preached on Monday. Wednesday was the day where younger members of the clerical elite first appeared: episcopal or aristocratic chaplains or men recently instituted to lucrative benefices.[4]

The rehearser's task was particularly noteworthy, as he critiqued as well as summarized the other four sermons, as Stow put it: 'either commending or reproving them' and then making 'a sermon of his own study, which in all was five sermons in one'.[5] Records from early in Elizabeth's reign indicate that the task was assigned to particularly able preachers: Thomas Sampson preached the rehearsal sermons of 1559, 1560, and 1562, and John Strype later reported that Sampson was chosen for the task 'in regard of his excellent elocution and memory'.[6] In spite of this, few rehearsal sermons have been preserved in manuscript or

---

[2] *Oxford University Statutes*, tr. G. R. M. Ward (London, 1845), i. 167–71. My thanks go to Ms Anna Petre, Assistant Keeper of the Archives at Oxford University, for her help.

[3] *Oxford University Statutes*, tr. Ward, i. 167–8, 170.

[4] The names of those who had agreed to preach a Spital sermon are recorded annually in the minutes of the Court of Aldermen Repertories. The minutes record who had been assigned to which day, and the hierarchy becomes apparent when the appointments are viewed chronologically.

[5] John Stow, *A Survey of London by John Stow*, ed. Charles Lethbridge Kingsford (Oxford: Clarendon Press, 1908), i. 167.

[6] John Strype, *Annals of the Reformation*, i (1709; new edn Oxford, 1824), pt 1, 408.

print. This may be because it was a rather odd sermon, being made up in effect of the summaries of four other men's labour with only the introduction and the conclusion composed
by the rehearser. John Hoskins published only the conclusion to the rehearsal sermon he
delivered in 1614; John Boys merely put a marginal note in his sermon for the Second Sunday
of Lent (on 1 Thessalonions 4: 1), to say that 'these observations I delivered in my rehearsal
at *Paul's anno* 1603'.[7] Hearers' notes by Richard Newdigate from the rehearsal sermon of 1627
survive but they are quite cursory.[8] There are only two surviving copies of full rehearsal sermons (with the rehearser's introduction and conclusion along with his summary of the four
sermons) from Paul's Cross: that preached by Ralph Barlowe in 1605 (extant in manuscript)
and one printed sermon preached in 1618 by Daniel Featley.[9] For the Oxford series, we have
Daniel Featley's 1610 rehearsal sermon printed in full in *Clavis Mystica* (the same collection that contains his London 1618 rehearsal sermon) and two manuscript sermons (a full
rehearsal sermon from 1632 and some notes from the rehearser's introduction from the 1633
sermon), extant in a collection of Oxford sermons transcribed in 1633.[10]

Even though Stow's account of the London sermon suggests that the rehearser might
critique the sermons he summarized, surviving evidence suggests that elaborate compliments to the preachers were at least as common.[11] This may be partly explained by the fact
that the the rehearser was often junior to some of the men whose sermons he summarized. In *The Spouse Her Precious Borders*, Daniel Featley rehearses the sermons of Joseph
Hall. Featley had served as household chaplain to the English ambassador in Paris (Sir
Thomas Edmondes) and had recently been made chaplain to Archbishop Abbot. But in
1618, Joseph Hall was Dean of Worcester and a scholar whose reputation gained him a
seat at the Synod of Dort; he was also a writer of very popular books of piety and various
works of church apologetics.[12] Whatever the motives for these compliments, they nonetheless reveal many of the qualities that were admired in early modern English preachers.
Oratorical skill, zeal in teaching, and scholarly understanding of the Bible were admired,
particularly when combined. The anonymous rehearser heard by Richard Newdigate
described the preacher of the Passion sermon as having 'strength of wit and reason'.
Ralph Barlowe described Roger Fenton, preacher of the Passion sermon in 1605, as 'a
man meeke like Moses, and spoken like Moses: his doctrine dropt as the rayne, and his
speeches stilled as the dew'. Of Dr John King's sermon, he declared it 'impossible for me,

---

[7] John Hoskins. 'The Conclusion of the Rehearsal Sermon at Pauls Crosse, Anno 1614', *Sermons Preached
at Pauls Crosse and Elsewhere* (London, 1615), E2^r–G^v; John Boys, *Workes* (London, 1622), X^v.

[8] Warwickshire County Record Office, MS CR 136/A/12. I would like to thank Mary Ann Lund for alerting
me to the existence of these notes.

[9] Huntington Library, San Marino, California, Ellesmere MS 1172; Daniel Featley, 'The Spouse Her
Precious Borders', in *Clavis Mystica* (1636), M6^r–QQ5^r.

[10] Featley, 'Foure Rowes of Precious Stones', in *Clavis Mystica*, VV3^v–ZZ4^v; Bodleian MS Eng.th.e.14,
88–136; 408–11.

[11] Daniel Featley denounces rehearsers who criticize others at the start of his 1618 sermon (*Clavis Mystica*,
NN2^v–NN3^r), and his revision of Francis White's sermon is very gentle criticism by Featley's standards. More
robust criticism evidently did happen: Thomas Goffe accuses the rehearser of his sermon of making up 'with
malice' whatever in Goffe's sermon he forgot or failed to understand: *Deliverance from the Grave* (London,
1627), A2^{r-v}.

[12] Arnold Hunt, 'Featley, Daniel (1582–1645)', *ODNB*, 2004; online edition, Jan. 2008, <http://www.
oxforddnb.com/view/article/9242>; Richard A. McCabe, 'Hall, Joseph (1574–1656)', *ODNB*, 2004; online
edition, Jan. 2008, <http://www.oxforddnb.com/view/article/11976>.

to attayne either to the strong or to the sweete therof' (while punning on Samson's riddle); Mr Ireland, the youngest preacher who took the Wednesday, gave a sermon that was 'comely and orderly'.[13] A concern for preaching that combined soundness of doctrine with effective communication (words that were 'sweet' and persuasive) is mentioned repeatedly. Barlowe said that his preachers 'sought to find out pleasant wordes' (paraphrasing Ecclesiastes 12: 10; the phrase is usually translated 'acceptable words'), and 'such as thy soule would desire and delight to heare', and gave 'the right sense of scriptures', and 'the wordes of truth, whether for proofe or reproofe' (Ellesmere 1172, fol. 36ᵛ). In the rehearsal sermon of 1632, Mr Robinson of Pembroke College spoke of his preachers as disciples, like those in his text (Luke 24: 14, which he interprets as referring to the seventy-two disciples sent out by Jesus); they are men 'tutor'd in the schoole of Christ', and 'as their doctrine argues them schollars, so doth their life bespeake them travellours in the holy pilgrimage journeying towards Jerusalem'. Their preaching was not of 'any sophisticall and deceitfull thinge', or 'any frivolous, or vaine thing, noe empty airy speculations void of satisfaction and solidity'.[14]

Metaphors appropriate for the preachers as a group were sought from Scripture, and those that came in fours were favoured. The 1627 rehearser appears to have taken divine love as his theme (Newdigate notes, he 'sounds on love as if his hand would strike on noe other string'), and compares the preachers to the four cherubim on the Ark of the Covenant: 'each part answers one another as the faces of cherubims'.[15] Daniel Featley in his 1610 Oxford sermon shows how overly elaborate such attempts could become. His text is Exodus 28: 15–21, a description of the twelve gems (four rows of three) that were fitted on the high priest's breastplate, part of the *ephod*. The twelve stones were engraved with the names of the twelve tribes, and Featley offers a lengthy account, with ostentatious displays of learning, into the qualities of the individual gemstones. These he eventually compares to the doctrine in the preacher's sermons: 'these judicious and methodical Sermons, foure in number, are the *foure rows in* Aarons *breast-plate of judgement*, the jewels are their precious doctrines, the *embossments* of gold, in which these jewels are set, were their *texts* of Scripture'.[16]

In his 1618 Paul's Cross rehearsal sermon, *The Spouse Her Precious Borders,* Featley jokes about the overuse of these comparisons in fours, complaining that they have all been used: the *'foure rivers of Paradise* have been *drawne dry',* and his predecessor in the role the year before 'with whose praises the Crosse yet rings' had chimed '*the Rehearsers knell* with foure Bells in this place, where there was never yet any one hung'.[17] So Featley exercises his ingenuity in finding a comparison of four in his text: Canticles 1: 11, 'We will make thee borders of gold, with studs of silver'.[18] He explains that the friends of the Bride represent preachers and the 'borders of gold' are compared to their sermons 'in a foure fold respect'.[19] Ralph

---

[13] Ellesmere MS 1172, fols 3ᵛ, 12ʳ, 29ʳ.   [14] Bodl. Eng.th.e.14, 90, 91.

[15] Warwickshire CRO MS CR 136/A/12, fol. 77ʳ. The temptation to use the pun offered by the name of the preacher for Good Friday ([Richard?] Love) must have been hard to resist.

[16] *Clavis Mystica,* XXʳ.   [17] *Clavis Mystica,* NN3ᵛ.

[18] As preachers do not always use particular translations of the Bible faithfully when rendering their text (cf. the chapter by Emma Rhatigan in this volume), the version of the preacher's text given here is that found in the copy of the sermon being quoted.

[19] *Clavis Mystica,* NN3ᵛ–NN4ʳ.

Barlowe also took a text that would provide him with means to compliment his preachers in four ways: Ecclesiastes 12: 11, 'The wordes of the wise are like goades and like nayles fastned, the words I saie of the masters of assemblies which are given by one pastor'. Unlike Featley's almost metaphysical comparison, Barlowe offers a simple simile by which the words of the preacher are compared to the nails in the biblical text in four ways:

> *Sicut clavi*, like nayles, for matter; not like weak wooddén pinnes, but like strong iron nayles, … Squar'd with a 4 fold squar'dnes, whereby thei passe the more currantly, and take the better hold, in that they do *quadrare*, Fitt, 1, the person that speakes. 2. the persons that are spoken to. 3. the scripture whereupon they are spoken 4 the time and place when and where they are spoken, headed with summary and capitall pointes with pithy recapitulations.[20]

Why would preachers of the rehearsal sermon go to such trouble to find biblical metaphors and similes of four? Finding a fitting metaphor for the four preachers obviously demonstrated both knowledge of the Scriptures and wit in creating the comparison. But there was something particular about a simile or metaphor built around four points: such figures were set to 'quadrate', and so were considered the most firm, 'four squared' as Barlowe says.[21] If a preacher was to compare things in his text with things in the world, he wanted the comparison to be as watertight as possible, especially when discussing the duty of the preacher. The rehearsal sermon was not just an event in which preachers commented publicly on each others' skill (although that might give sufficient grounds for anxiety); it was also a sermon that required the preacher to address the duty of the preacher to God and his hearers. Two themes emerge from the rehearsal sermons extant. One is taken up by Ralph Barlowe in his very effective sermon of 1605, and that is the necessity to drive home the message of the Gospel through repetition. Barlowe's plainer style, and his use of a perspicuous simile to compare preachers with the 'nails' in his text, suits this theme. Daniel Featley's 1618 sermon is preached on an enigmatic phrase from the Bible with no overt connection to preaching. It requires a metaphorical reading to connect the text to the theme of preaching, and the connection that Featley creates is through the idea of ornament. For Featley, and for some of his contemporaries, the preacher's task was not merely to repeat doctrine with catechetical plainness but to 'ornament' Scripture with homiletic skill. That ornament might, however, impede the hearers' understanding, and this created a conflict between the preacher's duty to his text and his duty to his hearers.

Featley's sermon is unusual because of its ostentatious use of allegorical interpretation; his choice of a questionable method for a sermon on the duties of the preacher suggests that the sermon was designed to be provocative. Although it is not heterodox in what it says, its use of a suspect method of interpretation merits our attention. The text from Canticles makes an allegorical reading not altogether surprising, however; the Song of Songs had been interpreted metaphorically before Christian exegetes began working on it, and ever since. The literal sense (the love song) was usually thought to be inadequate, and so was assumed

---

[20] Ellesmere 1172, fol. 39[v].

[21] These texts suggest that the use of the term 'quadrate' to refer to metaphors and allegory that are thought to 'fit' was common at the time, but it is not recorded in the *OED*. J. A. Burrow shows that it was well known in the late eighteenth century: 'Allegory: The Literal Level', in *Essays on Medieval Literature* (Oxford: Clarendon Press, 1984), 192–212, 204–6.

to be a 'veil' or 'shell' for the more spiritually nourishing themes that could be found by decoding the metaphor.[22] A principle established by Augustine and contradicted by no one determined that everything in Scripture was designed for the building up of charity, and so any individual text that did not appear to do this must have another meaning: the text used metaphor. By comparison with other more perspicuous texts, the transferred sense (and the real meaning intended by the Holy Ghost) could be established. This is 'the analogy of faith'.[23]

Allegory is an interpretative method that is sometimes treated as a medieval phenomenon disavowed by the Reformers. But the Reformers did not abandon allegory, because it was necessary to the interpretation of problematic biblical texts like Canticles.[24] Rather, they treated metaphor as a rhetorical figure, and so defined it as part of the grammar of the text. This figurative approach explained the apparent obscurities of words in Scripture by referring to the use of metaphors, allegories, and parables (all rhetorical figures) by the author of the sacred text. By employing ordinary grammatical procedures (examining these rhetorical figures in the context of the passage) and by comparison with less ambiguous parts of Scripture, metaphors could be interpreted within the limits set by the analogy of faith and the fundamentals of doctrine. So there were no various senses of a text in Scripture; there was a single sense which might need to include the vehicle and transferred sense of a metaphor or parable. As Brian Cummings writes: the 'protestant method' 'accepts allegory only when it can be shown to work intrinsically; when Scripture itself intends the allegory. We could call this allegory as an extension of the literal sense: indeed, the literal meaning *is* an allegorical one'.[25]

This was certainly the position that the Reformers advanced in theory; in practice, however, things became more complicated. Even Melanchthon, with whom this figurative method is often associated, may have been less strict in avoiding transferred senses than we suppose. On occasion when interpreting the Psalms, he suggested that the 'primary' sense of the text referred to Christ even though a literal explication referring to David might be offered unproblematically.[26] Melanchthon, like others, did not abandon the idea that the Bible had historical and typological meanings which were mapped out over time and not merely in words. Because Scripture is about the fulfilment of God's promise in time, a single text may be applicable to the ancient Israelites and to modern Christians, as followers of the

---

[22] On the debates surrounding the literal sense of Scripture, see the chapter by Debora Shuger in this volume.

[23] Augustine, *On Christian Doctrine*, 1.35–7, 2.9–12, ed. and tr. R. P. H. Green (Oxford: Clarendon Press, 1995), 48–53, 70–5.

[24] G. R. Evans traces the impact of debates over authority to scriptural exegesis in the Reformation: *Problems of Authority in the Reformation Debates* (Cambridge: Cambridge University Press, 1992), esp. 57–77. On the ways in which English Reformed writers adapted to, and engaged with, the textual and historical problems of the text of the Bible, see Alison Knight, 'Pen of Iron: Scriptural Text and the Book of Job in Early Modern English Literature' (Ph.D. thesis, University of Cambridge, 2012), esp. ch. 1.

[25] Brian Cummings, 'Protestant Allegory', in Rita Copeland and Peter T. Struck (eds), *The Cambridge Companion to Allegory* (Cambridge: Cambridge University Press, 2010), 179.

[26] On Melanchthon's typological reading of the Psalms, see R. Gerald Hobbs, 'Pluriformity of Early Reformation Scriptural Interpretation', in Magne Sæbø (ed.), *Hebrew Bible/Old Testament: The History of its Interpretation*, ii. *From the Renaissance to the Enlightenment* (Gottingen: Vandenhoeck & Ruprecht, 2008), 501–2.

same God. The text can have several referents, and so different readings, even when there is no obvious metaphor that needs to be deciphered.

We see how this complicates a purely figurative approach to interpretation in William Perkins *Commentary on Galatians*. Perkins begins with a standard, Reformed statement of the simplicity of Scripture's meaning:

> there is but one full and intire sense of every place of Scripture, and that is also the literal sense, sometimes expressed in proper, and sometimes in borrowed or figurative speeches. To make many senses of Scripture, is to overturne all sense, and to make nothing certaine. As for the three spirituall senses (so called) they are not senses, but applications or uses of Scripture.[27]

But he then goes on to explain that this text, while not a metaphor, has another sense that was also intended by the Holy Ghost. St Paul declares in Galatians 4: 22–5 that Abraham's two children by his two wives represent the two dispensations (law and gospel), and Perkins has to explain how Paul can read Abraham's history allegorically in this way. [28] Perkins does not deny that Abraham's two wives represent the two testaments or covenants; rather, he denies that these two meanings are separate. The history signifies something beyond itself, and that meaning is part of the full 'sense' intended by the author of Scripture:

> It may be said, that the historie of *Abrahams* family here propounded, hath beside his proper and literall senses, a spiritual or mystical sense. I answer, they are not two senses, but two parts of one full and intire sense. For not onely the bare history, but also that which is therby signified, is the full sense of the holy Ghost. (298)

Protestant exegetes like Perkins extended the range of meanings that they included in the literal sense of the biblical text to include metaphors (like the love songs of Canticles), and to include typological readings (the psalms referring to Christ). They also allowed for a moral interpretation, where events in the biblical narrative were thought to speak to present conditions, detailing the moral and religious duties demanded of Christians (the threat of punishment for sin, for example, referring not merely to the Israelites). As we find with Perkins on Galatians, they do not always insist that these interpretations be treated in isolation, as if only *one* captured the literal sense.

Something interesting happens when these interpretative methods are used in the context of a sermon (rather than a scriptural commentary): in sermons, the latitude to make use of multiple figurative readings of the Bible gave rise to practices that look a lot like allegorical exposition: different 'senses' or readings of the text are offered without any of them being given priority as the 'one full and intire sense'. This does not involve a change of theory, but rather it arose out of the method of sermon composition used in England in the sixteenth and seventeenth centuries. Preachers were taught to 'apply' the teachings that their biblical text contained to the life and manners of their hearers; sometimes the biblical text might contain different teachings for different parts of the congregation, and so there were often different 'applications' in a sermon (for example, to householders and then to servants, or

---

[27] William Perkins, *A Commentarie upon the Epistle to the Galatians*, in *Works* (1631), ii. 298.
[28] The Greek uses the word *allegoroumena* ('allegorizing') in Gal. 4: 24. Perkins follows the Geneva Bible, which translates the verse as 'by which thing another thing is meant', while the KJB translates it more straightforwardly as 'which things are an allegory'.

to wives and then to husbands, and so on). Even the hard-line Puritan writer William Ames allows that allegories 'invented by mans study' may be used in this part of a sermon, the application of doctrine to the hearers' lives. He writes, 'if it be lawful to use a Metaphore, it is lawfull to continue the same'.[29] John Donne uses this method in his sermon on Psalm 38: 4, delivered at Lincoln's Inn, probably in 1618: 'First then, all these things are *literally* spoken of *David*; By *application*, of us; and by *figure*, of Christ. *Historically, David; morally,* we; *Typically,* Christ is the subject of this text'.[30]

Other strategies for expanding the interpretative possibilities of the text that fell just short of allegorical 'multiple senses' were far from uncommon in prestigious pulpits like Paul's Cross. Indeed, the sort of linguistic competence that the humanists considered essential for uncovering the literal meaning of the text became the grounds for such extensions, as the variety of translations available provided alternative readings, all of which might be explicated. Varying translations do not, of course, complicate the stability of the 'literal sense' in the original languages. And so we find early seventeenth-century preachers making use of the various readings available to them to expand the interpretative range of their biblical texts. In *Loves Complaint, for Want of Entertainment,* William Holbrooke considers the 'general' and 'restrained' sense of the word *adikia,* meaning both 'sin' and 'injustice'. Rather than use only the meaning that best translates the passage (1 Corinthians 13: 6), he uses both, and explains why:

> Now wee see the acceptation of this word in the Scripture, the Question is, how it is to be taken in this place, unto which I Answere, though I take the second sense, to be especially meant in this place, yet I see no reason why it may not carie both the senses here, both which doe set out the nature of Love the better, and therefore I wil take it in both senses (but specially in the latter) it being the safest way to construe Scripture, and take it in the largest sense, when both the drift of the holy Ghost, the sense of the originall words, and the Analogie of Faith, gainesay it not.[31]

For Holbrooke, Scripture is full of meaning, and so the 'safest' way to interpret it is the one that allows the greatest range of interpretations, 'the largest sense'. The same approach is taken by Richard Sibthorpe, in a sermon preached in 1617. The first word of his text (Jeremiah 5: 7, 'How shall I pardon thee for this?' etc.) is variously translated into Latin (*ubi, quomodo,* and *super quo*), and Sibthorpe declares that all offer instruction in the different shades of meaning that they capture: 'And all these Readings, as they may be borne without any repugnancy, or the Texts rackt exension: So will every one of them not unaptly affoorde us matter of instruction'.[32]

Where ambiguities in translation did not provide opportunities to extend the meanings of the scriptural text, interpretative differences might. Thomas Aylesbury preached at Paul's Cross in 1622 on a text whose translation offered no problems but whose interpretations varied dramatically, Luke 17: 37 ('Wheresoever the body is, thither will the eagles gather

[29] William Ames. *Conscience with the Power and Cases Thereof* (Leiden and London, 1639), KK2ʳ.
[30] *The Sermons of John Donne,* ed. E. M. Simpson and G. R. Potter (Berkeley, Calif.: University of California Press, 1953–62), ii, no. 3, 97. On Donne and the literal sense, see Jeanne M. Shami, 'Donne on Discretion', *ELH* 47 (1980), 57–9.
[31] William Holbrooke, *Loves Complaint, for Want of Entertainement* (London, 1610), B2ᵛ–B3ʳ.
[32] Robert Sibthorpe, *A Counter-Plea to an Apostates Pardon* (London, 1618), B2ʳ.

together'). Aylesbury describes this enigmatic text as a 'parabolicall proverb'; although recorded twice in Scripture, it is not 'illuminated by any divine exposition', and so 'the bread thereof, that is, the meaning, is to be eaten in the sweat of our studies'. [33] This is obviously a text whose literal sense contains metaphors that need to be decoded, but Aylesbury does not explicate his text in order to arrive at a single, simple 'literal' sense that explains these metaphors. Instead, he structures his sermon around four very different interpretations offered by the church fathers; the sequence of interpretations provides the argument of the sermon, beginning with a discussion of authority and scriptural interpretation and ending with '*Gregories* analogical sense' (H1ᵛ): the saints congregating around Christ in the world to come. Similarly, in his Gunpowder Plot sermon of 1622, John Donne uses the different possible historical referents for his text in combination, in order to reach the approved lesson on political obedience. Whether the king lamented in the text refers to good King Josiah or bad King Zedekiah does not matter:

> we argue not, we dispute not now; we imbrace that which arises from both, That both good Kings, and bad Kings, *Josiah*, and *Zedekiah*, are the *anointed* of the Lord, and the *breath of the nostrills*, that is, The life of the people; and therefore both to be lamented.[34]

Examples like Donne's show how skilfully preachers could use the exegetical tradition to extend the meaning of their text. Other preachers made similar use of multiple readings cumulatively, so that the combined readings of the text point to doctrines that individual translations would not contain. We see a very good example in Ralph Barlowe's 1605 sermon. The phrase he translates as 'masters of Assembles' could mean several things, Barlowe explains: the original word signifies 'either popular assemblyes, *scholarlik collections or Ecclesiasticall synods*' and has been translated in all three ways.[35] Rather than choose one, however, Barlowe uses all three. His preachers have been masters of 'populous judicious and discreet Auditoryes', a compliment to the hearers at Paul's Cross and St Mary's Spital. Their mastery of popular assemblies derives partly from their learning: they are masters of 'scholarlik collections' who, by their 'reading and hearing', have 'gather'd much skill and knowledge'.[36] Such learning fits them for positions of authority in the church: they are 'the Lordes and masters of Ecclesiastical synods'. So the three preachers are 'masters of the assembly' according to all three possible interpretations of the word, and each meaning is added to the previous, not offered as alternatives, so that 'masters of Assembles' ends up meaning senior clerics. Barlowe ends his sermon with an exhortation to obedience towards the ecclesiastical authorities, and particularly to ecclesiastical synods, and this reading of 'master of assemblies' becomes pertinent here. Christ may be the one pastor, but he has deputed responsibility to these 'masters of assembles'. Barlowe has combined the different translations of his text so that he can reconfigure the text in order to make it carry a very particular interpretation (that obedience is due to bishops) that was not obviously contained in the literal sense.

Such examples show how an interpretative approach that was intended to help explain the 'dark' texts of Scripture had been extended into a method for multiplying the ways in which

---

[33] Thomas Aylesbury, *A Sermon Preached at Paules-Crosse* (London, 1623), B2ʳ⁻ᵛ.

[34] John Donne, 'A Sermon upon the Fift of November 1622: Being the Anniversary Celebration of our Deliverance from the Powder Treason', in *Sermons*, ed. Simpson and Potter, iv. 239.

[35] Ellesmere 1172, fol. 43ᵛ.   [36] Ellesmere 1172, fol. 44ʳ.

a single text from the Bible could be handled. English Reformed preachers of the early seventeenth century did not merely look for figurative readings when the literary sense seemed incompatible with the rule of faith. They began to *look for* figurative readings, historical, moral, or typical, as a way of extending the range of 'applications' of the text, a way of saying more about Christian doctrine from the same text, 'mining' deeper into the word, to borrow their metaphor, while remaining tied to a notional commitment to the primacy of the literal sense.

Daniel Featley goes further than Barlowe and Donne, however, in that he explicitly advocates an allegorical reading of Scripture. In his introduction to *The Spouse Her Precious Borders*, he stresses that Scripture generally contains a 'varietie of senses'. He insists on the layering of meaning throughout Scripture and compares the hidden meanings to the incarnate Word: the divine nature of Christ lay hidden under the human nature and both inspired and incarnate Word were 'conceived by the Holy Ghost, and brought forth in sacred sheets'. From this he alleges that 'the deeper we dig' in the text 'by diligent meditation, the veine of precious truth should prove still the richer'.[37] He implies that it is the hidden, invisible senses which generally contain the 'substance', the 'spiritual' meanings of the words. He also emphatically disagrees with those who maintain that there is a single sense in Scripture: such divines 'affect an opinion of judgement' that there is 'no sense of Scripture, nor doctrine from thence, except that which the text itselfe at the first proposing offereth to their conceit'.[38] This explicit espousal of allegorical methods in scriptural interpretation is unusual. The only other statement like this in a sermon that I have found is by John Boys, an equally ostentatious preacher (although otherwise far closer to the Laudian camp than the determinedly Calvinist Featley). Near the end of his *Exposition of the Last Psalme,* Boys declares: 'The word of God is a two edged sword, sharp in a literal, and sharp in an allegoricall exposition. Hitherto you have heard the history, now there remaineth a mistery', and he offers several metaphorical readings of his text.[39]

What prompted English preachers to adopt such methods of extending the meaning of their text in various directions? The vastness of the riches of Scripture was a commonplace from the beginning of biblical exegesis, but the problems of preaching were different to those of commentary. The preacher had not only to explain the words; he had to represent them to an auditory that had probably heard them before, and were doubtless familiar with the more commonplace interpretations. Preachers in Oxford and London addressed hearers who were accustomed to learned preaching, and who required a preacher who was capable of 'mining' through the senses of Scripture to find new lessons in familiar biblical texts. Novelty was not, however, treated as a virtue in preaching. From the rehearsal sermons extant, it is clear that the rehearsers juggled the teacher's need to insist on the reiterating of fundamental doctrine with the orator's fear of boring his audience. Given the task assigned to him, it is not surprising that many rehearsers described the preacher's role as the continual repetition of the same fundamental points, not the hunting out of new meanings. John Boys delivered the following 'observations' in his rehearsal sermon in 1603:

---

[37] *Clavis Mystica*, MM6ᵛ, NNʳ.   [38] *Clavis Mystica*, NNʳ.
[39] John Boys, *An Exposition of the Last Psalme* (London, 1613), B5ʳ.

And in truth, all our Sermons are nothing else, but *rehearsals* of that old *Spittle Sermon*, (as it were) preached by God himselfe to decayed *Adam* and *Eve*, Genesis. 3.15. For first, all that is said by Christ and his blessed Apostles in the New Testament, is summarily nothing else, but a repetition and explanation of that one prophecie, *Semen mulieris conteret caput serpentis*.[40]

Similarly, John Hoskins, in the conclusion to his rehearsal sermon of 1614 on the text Isaiah 62: 6 ('You that be the Lord's Remembrancers, be not silent') writes that the preacher's duty is to repeat the fundamentals of faith. Preachers are remembrancers because the doctrine delivered by Christ is a 'treasury', delivered fully and perfectly. And so 'after Christ, there is no further need of curiositie, after the Gospell, no use of further inquisition', and so preaching requires the reiteration of a revelation already fulfilled. Since the ascension, 'all Psalmes ensuing were like the 105.6.7 rehearsall Psalmes. All prayers like the Levites, *Nehem.* 9. rehearsal prayers, and all Sermons like *Stephens, Act 7*, rehearsall sermons'.[41] Scripture itself is full of examples of doctrine repeated. In his 1610 Oxford rehearsal sermon, Daniel Featley offers 'the Gentiles at Antiochia, *who besought the Apostles to preach unto them the same words the next sabbath*' in Acts 13: 42 as an example.[42] This text was taken by the preacher of the 1633 rehearsal sermon in the same place. Mr Lawford of Oriel College begins his rehearsal sermon of 1633 by placing the rehearsal sermon in the tradition of liturgies commemorating Christ's death and he commends the 'wisdome of this place' in determining to have 'a vocall repetition of those seasonable words'.[43] Unfortunately our note-taker does not give us more than Lawford's introduction to the theme, which gets embroiled in various textual problems when the note-taker leaves off.

The previous year, Mr Robinson opened his rehearsal sermon by saying that the retelling of the Passion and Resurrection of Christ is a natural response to such a miracle, 'joy and wonder both conspire to make the matter knowne'.[44] Such repetition, from the first to the last revelation, is the task of every preacher, Robinson claims:

> You finde noe new thinge: the cognisance of there doctrine is that same with St John concerninge that which was from the beginninge the same doctrine which was preached in paradise to relapsed Adam in the beginning of the world; the same which was preached in publike to the ingrafted gentiles in the beginninge of the Church, the sure accomplishment of that antient hidden promise the bruising of the serpents head was the latitude of their selected argument.[45]

It is only 'misaffected auditors' who 'thirst after such pleasing interdicted waters' as deceitful learning or frivolous, vain teaching.

Preachers of the rehearsal sermons in London and Oxford are, of course, themselves repeating doctrine: that delivered by the men whose sermon they summarize. It is partly due to the 'modesty topos' that expressions of uncertainty about the value of such repetition are made in their sermons. Also evident, however, is a more systemic anxiety about the effectiveness of repeating second-hand doctrine to a jaded audience. In his 1610 Oxford sermon, Daniel Featley defends his repetition of the Easter sermons as a necessary, if inferior, recital of useful doctrine, because 'it is not once plowing, but the often breaking up of the

---

[40] John Boys. *Workes* (London, 1622), Xᵛ.   [41] 'Conclusion', 29, 31.   [42] *Clavis Mystica*, VV6ᵛ.
[43] Bodl. Eng.th.e.14, 408.   [44] Bodl. Eng.th.e.14, 90.   [45] Bodl. Eng.th.e.14, 91.

earth which maketh it fruitfull; nor is it the incident, but the reflected beame of the Sunne that giveth the greatest heate'. His sermon does not offer such 'reflected beames'; the sermons previous heard are refracted rather, 'cast backe from my fluid and waterish memory, and so they 'cannot but lose much of their light and grace'.[46] Featley goes on to complain of the thanklessness of the rehearser's task, because no glory can be gained from simply repeating other men's discoveries. Featley says, 'if the Rehearser acquit himself never so well, what can he expect for all his pains but the bare commendation of a good memory? but if he faile, not only his memory, but his judgement and discretion are called into question'.[47]

Ralph Barlowe's sermon is more focused on the idea of repetition than Featley's. Unlike Featley, he is a more traditional 'rehearser' in that he puts the usefulness of repetition at the centre of his explication of his text. But Barlowe too sounds a note of uncertainty as to the actual success of the preacher's repetition of Scripture and doctrine:

> And sure as there is *no end making many bookes as Ecclesiastes* tells me in the next verse and *much reading is but a wearines to the flesh*: no more is there of multipying sermons and much preaching is no better. Sermons I doubt are like nailes in this that as *clavus clavum pellit* according to the proverb. One naile drives out another: so sermon thrustes out sermon.[48]

Barlowe uses an acknowledgement of the different audiences that his sermon will have in order to suggest that, through repetition in various media, his sermon might stand a better chance of success. Those that were absent, and readers of the sermon, will gain 'knowledge', as Christ 'rehearsed to Thomas that had bene absent at the first his resurrection sermon'. Those that were present will gain 'better remembrance' of what was said, because 'nailes are not *fastned* at the first: no not without often beating upon them'.[49] Nonetheless, Barlowe explains in his rehearser's conclusion that the effectiveness of the preacher's sermon depends not only on his skill and zeal, but also on the disposition of the hearers, and the operation of the Holy Spirit:[50]

> Howbeit that Caution which we added to the effect of the goad, we must likewise to this of the nayles. They may miss their effects through the misdisposition of the subject. If men be either too soft of nature, too fickle of fancy, too unstable of judgment: If againe too loose of memory, or which is worse, too loose of life that nayles can take no more hold of them then if they were driven into sapp. Againe if men have either too hard heartes through synne, or too hard conceites through prejudice either of thinges or persons, that the nayles cannot pierce, enter nor fasten upon them; or that they will sooner burst them then fasten them: as the Jews brast for anger at St Stevens sermon Acts 7: 54. But let the auditors or readers be fitt as those that brought honest and good hartes to receive the seed sowne, luk 8: 8.15, and then are they like nayles indeed.[51]

For John Hoskins, the obligations on preachers are also balanced with a sense of the impossibility of converting the hearers by rhetoric alone. Repetition is an inevitable consequence of the finiteness of necessary doctrine. It would be possible, Hoskins opines, to teach 'the fundamentall Articles of faith … within lesse then the terme of a Preachers life', if he avoided idle speculations and digressions, 'either he must preach the same againe,

---

[46] *Clavis Mystica*, VV6ᵛ.   [47] *Clavis Mystica*, XXʳ⁻ᵛ.   [48] Ellesmere 1172, fol. 2ʳ.
[49] Ellesmere 1172, fol. 2ᵛ.
[50] On the role of the Holy Spirit in English Reformed theories of preaching, see my 'Scripture, Style and Persuasion in Seventeenth-Century English Theories of Preaching', *The Journal of Ecclesiastical History*, 53 (2002): 686–706.
[51] Ellesmere 1172, fol. 41ʳ.

and be a *Remembrancer*, or be silent, and be no Preacher, which the execution of our office, the second part of my division now succeeding, by no means will permit'. The preacher is obliged to 'be not silent', and therefore he must repeat doctrines formerly delivered; otherwise, he shares the punishment attendant on sin and connivance with sin: 'Every day we kill as many as we suffer to die, by the coldnesse of our zeale & silence'.[52] This does not make the preacher solely responsible for the salvation of his hearers, because a duty rests with the hearers, and Hoskins ends his sermon with an appeal to them: that they listen for more than the skill of the orator and with a mind disposed towards the preacher's message:

> I grant that men of these latter times have eares judicious inough, I heare them praising voices, magnifying the learning, extolling the gifts of teachers. Nay, you would soone confute me, would I deny that many painefull labourers are in the highest places in the Church: But (beloved men and brethren) there is one preferment yet behind: and that most proper unto preaching, a preferment in the hearts of the hearers. If Preachers were at your hearts, all your works would prove effectuall examples, and your examples would prove a second kind of preaching.[53]

His exhortation ends: 'Howsoever answerable to the degrees of your Regeneration bee the degrees of your attention, likenes causeth liking'.[54]

Ultimately, the success of the preacher rests with the Holy Spirit and the hearers; their success as exegetes who 'mined' the Scripture might be measured in scholarly terms, and their preaching styles could be applauded by the standards of formal oratory (melodious voices, 'finding out acceptable words', impressive displays of learning in biblical commentary and translation, vehemence and affective rhetoric). Such praises the rehearser could bestow on the preachers whose sermons he repeated. But the fundamental purpose of the preacher, to bring people to repentance, required little art beyond patience and repetition, and success was beyond the preacher's art to deliver, depending as it did on the cooperation of the hearers and the Holy Spirit. The elaborate metaphors and complex explications of the rehearsal sermons betray, I suggest, an anxiety about the exact relationship between the charisma of preaching and the learning of the clergy, a debate that would rage far more visibly in the 1650s. English preachers of the late sixteenth and early seventeenth centuries celebrated the polysemous and yet simultaneously autopistic quality of their biblical text, but they were unsure if their demonstrations of these qualities were what their hearers needed most.

FURTHER READING

Burrow, J. A. 'Allegory: The Literal Level', in *Essays on Medieval Literature* (Oxford: Clarendon Press, 1984), 192–212.

Collinson, Patrick. 'The Coherence of the Text: How it Hangeth Together: The Bible in Reformation England', in W. P. Stephens (ed.), *The Bible, the Reformation and the Church: Essays in Honour of James Atkinson*, Journal for the Study of the New Testament, supplement series, 105 (1995), 84–108.

[52] 'Conclusion', 33, 34, 37.   [53] 'Conclusion', 40–1.   [54] 'Conclusion', 31.

Copeland, Rita, and Peter T. Struck, eds. *The Cambridge Companion to Allegory* (Cambridge: Cambridge University Press, 2010).

Cummings, Brian. *The Literary Culture of the Reformation: Grammar and Grace* (Oxford: Oxford University Press, 2002).

Evans, G. R. *Problems of Authority in the Reformation Debates* (Cambridge: Cambridge University Press, 1992).

Green, Ian. *Print and Protestantism in Early Modern England* (Oxford: Oxford University Press, 2000).

Hunt, Arnold. *The Art of Hearing: English Preachers and their Audiences, 1590–1640* (Cambridge: Cambridge University Press, 2010).

McCullough, Peter. 'Donne as Preacher', in Achsah Guibbory (ed.), *The Cambridge Companion to John Donne* (Cambridge: Cambridge University Press, 2006), 167–81.

McCullough, Peter, Hugh Adlington, and Emma Rhatigan, eds. *The Oxford Handbook of the Early Modern Sermon* (Oxford: Oxford University Press, 2011).

Morrissey, Mary. 'Scripture, Style and Persuasion in Seventeenth-Century English Theories of Preaching'. *The Journal of Ecclesiastical History*, 53 (2002): 686–706.

Muller, Richard A., and John L. Thompson, eds. *Biblical Interpretation in the Era of the Reformation* (Grand Rapids, Mich.: Eerdmans, 1996).

CHAPTER 20

PREACHING, READING, AND PUBLISHING THE WORD IN PROTESTANT SCOTLAND

ALASDAIR RAFFE

THOUGH it was born in a revolution, Protestant Scotland was formed by gradual cultural change. As Jane Dawson has put it, the country's brief 'Reformation by the sword' was followed by a longer 'Reformation by the Word'.[1] The upheavals of 1559–60—the revolt against the regent Mary of Guise and the adoption of Protestantism by the Reformation Parliament—were of immediate political and diplomatic significance.[2] But implementing the Reformation required decades of ecclesiastical innovation, as well as the instruction, conversion, and edification of the people. Institutional change and debates about church government have been examined in great detail, most recently by James Kirk, David Mullan, and Alan MacDonald.[3] Local studies continue to deepen our understanding of the church's structural and administrative reforms.[4] Scholars have now turned to questions about the Reformation's cultural impact. David Mullan has examined theological ideas, their social and psychological implications, while Margo Todd and John McCallum have used the plentiful local church records to chart the effects of reformed worship and discipline on ordinary Scots.[5] As a result of this research, we now think of the Scottish Reformation as a long-term process, but one with a high degree of success.

---

[1] Jane E. A. Dawson, *Scotland Re-formed, 1488–1587* (Edinburgh: Edinburgh University Press, 2007), chs 9–10.

[2] See, most recently, Clare Kellar, *Scotland, England, and the Reformation, 1534–1561* (Oxford: Oxford University Press, 2003); Alec Ryrie, *The Origins of the Scottish Reformation* (Manchester: Manchester University Press, 2006).

[3] James Kirk, *Patterns of Reform: Continuity and Change in the Reformation Kirk* (Edinburgh: T. & T. Clark, 1989), esp. chs 5–6, 9–10; David George Mullan, *Episcopacy in Scotland: The History of an Idea, 1560–1638* (Edinburgh: John Donald Publishers, 1986); Alan R. MacDonald, *The Jacobean Kirk, 1567–1625: Sovereignty, Polity and Liturgy* (Aldershot: Ashgate, 1998).

[4] Linda J. Dunbar, *Reforming the Scottish Church: John Winram (c.1492–1582) and the Example of Fife* (Aldershot: Ashgate, 2002); Mary Verschuur, *Politics or Religion? The Reformation in Perth, 1540–1570* (Edinburgh: Dunedin Academic Press, 2006).

[5] David George Mullan, *Scottish Puritanism, 1590–1638* (Oxford: Oxford University Press, 2000); David George Mullan, *Narratives of the Religious Self in Early-Modern Scotland* (Farnham: Ashgate, 2010); Margo

By the mid-seventeenth century, then, the Reformation had transformed Scottish society. Foremost among its effects was the marginalization of Catholics. In 1680, there were perhaps 24,000 Catholics in Scotland, equivalent to 2 or 2.5 per cent of the national population.[6] Indeed, recusancy had been almost eradicated in south and central Scotland, and the Catholic population was largely concentrated in parts of the north-east and the western Highlands. For the great majority of Scots who recognized the Protestant Church, daily life itself had been reformed by the imposition of Calvinist discipline. The constant surveillance of morals, church attendance, domestic and social life was a menace to some, but perhaps welcome to many.[7]

Compared to the widespread public acceptance of the Kirk's discipline, it is more difficult to assess what proportion of Scots understood Reformed theology. We have quite extensive evidence of the most godly Protestants, but know little about their less pious and literate neighbours. Perhaps relatively few men and women mastered the catechism, appreciated doctrinally sophisticated sermons, and enjoyed emotionally fulfilling spiritual lives. But though Scots differed in their comprehension of Protestant ideas, and their enthusiasm for its practices, the Kirk was long able to contain this diversity. Before the late seventeenth century, moreover, doctrinal controversies did not permanently rupture the country's shared Protestantism. Only after 1660 did a lasting divergence among Protestants begin to evolve, as Presbyterians and Episcopalians came to disagree fundamentally over theology and worship, as well as about church government.[8] In its first century, the religious culture of Protestant Scotland was able to accommodate varying levels of personal commitment, while keeping ideological and political tensions in check.

This chapter examines the ways in which the Bible was disseminated and consumed by Scottish Protestants in the century and a half after 1560. Its main focus is on the scriptures in public worship, rather than domestic and private reading of the Bible.[9] To provide a fuller account of ordinary Scots' engagement with the Bible, it would be necessary to tackle the difficult subject of early modern literacy. R. A. Houston showed that the ability to sign one's name was correlated with social rank and gender, and that, well into the eighteenth century, more than half of male labourers and servants in lowland Scotland were unable to write.[10] But it is now generally accepted that many early modern people could read without having learned to write. Anecdotal evidence—including well-known statements by the English visitors Daniel Defoe and George Whitefield—suggests that, by the eighteenth century, the Bible was ubiquitous and widely read, at least in lowland Scotland.[11]

Todd, *The Culture of Protestantism in Early Modern Scotland* (New Haven: Yale University Press, 2002); John McCallum, *Reforming the Scottish Parish: The Reformation in Fife, 1560–1640* (Farnham: Ashgate, 2010).

[6] John Watts, *Scalan: The Forbidden College, 1716–1799* (East Linton: Tuckwell Press, 1999), 4.

[7] Cf. Jenny Wormald, 'Reformed and Godly Scotland?', in T. M. Devine and Jenny Wormald (eds), *The Oxford Handbook of Modern Scottish History* (Oxford: Oxford University Press, 2012), 204–19.

[8] Alasdair Raffe, 'Presbyterians and Episcopalians: The Formation of Confessional Cultures in Scotland, 1660–1715', *English Historical Review*, 125 (2010): 570–98.

[9] For evangelical Presbyterians' Bible reading, see Mullan, *Narratives*, ch. 6.

[10] R. A. Houston, *Scottish Literacy and the Scottish Identity: Illiteracy and Society in Scotland and Northern England, 1600–1800* (Cambridge: Cambridge University Press, 1985), 33.

[11] T. C. Smout, 'Born Again at Cambuslang: New Evidence on Popular Religion and Literacy in Eighteenth-Century Scotland', *Past and Present*, 97 (1982): 123.

I begin with some reflections on the Bible's publication and distribution. Turning to the uses of the Bible in church, I argue that leading Scottish Protestants, like the English Puritans studied by Arnold Hunt, favoured preaching over public reading.[12] The tendency to prioritize preaching became more marked after the Covenanting revolution of 1638–41, and in time reading the Bible was almost entirely removed from the Church of Scotland's public worship. By re-examining familiar records, I attempt to cast new light on these developments. But I also indicate where more research, especially in manuscript ecclesiastical registers, might identify local and regional diversity, and illustrate the mundane patterns of religious life as much as its hard-fought controversies. And though I focus on the Bible's uses in church, I conclude by suggesting that, at the end of the period, personal reading increasingly shaped Scots' engagement with the Word.

The early Reformers expected the Bible to play a central role in Protestant Scotland. According to their confession of faith, approved by the Reformation Parliament in 1560, the 'trew preaching of the Worde of God' was one 'note' 'be the quhilk [by which] the trewe kirk is decernit fra the false'.[13] This principle of ecclesiology had practical consequences for public worship. The *First Book of Discipline*, a programme for reform drawn up by Protestant ministers in 1560, called for every church to have a copy of the Bible 'in English'. Congregations were to 'be commanded to convene and heare the plaine reading and interpretation of the Scripture'. '[F]requent reading', the *Book* argued, would help to counteract the 'grosse ignorance' that, because of 'cursed Papistry', had 'overflowed all'.[14] In an address to King James VI, prefixed to the first Scottish edition of the Bible in 1579, the general assembly reiterated the expectation that every church should have a copy. The Bible was to be 'made patent to all the people of everie congregation as the only richt rule to direct & governe thame in materis of religio[n]', 'to co[n]ferme thame in the trueth receavit and to reforme and redresse corruptiones'.[15]

Behind these oft-quoted statements lie various complications. For a start, the Scottish Reformation did not achieve the Protestant objective of making the Bible available in the vernacular languages of the people. The 1579 Bible was the Genevan translation into English. The assembly's letter acknowledged that the translators were 'men of the nation of England for the maist part'. But the assembly did not comment on the differences between the 'common Scottis language' of its address and the English of the scriptural text itself.[16] That the translation was intelligible to Scots speakers was partly a result of the linguistic adjustments made by preachers and public readers of the Bible.[17] But the situation was rather different

---

[12] Arnold Hunt, *The Art of Hearing: English Preachers and their Audiences, 1590–1640* (Cambridge: Cambridge University Press, 2010), ch. 1.

[13] *Scots Confession, 1560 (Confessio Scoticana) and Negative Confession, 1581 (Confessio negativa)*, ed. G. D. Henderson (Edinburgh: Church of Scotland, Committee on Publications, 1937), 73, 75.

[14] *The First Book of Discipline*, ed. James K. Cameron (Edinburgh: St Andrew Press, 1972), 184–5.

[15] *The Bible and Holy Scriptures Conteined in the Olde and Newe Testament* (Edinburgh, 1579), (∴)2r–v.

[16] *The Bible and Holy Scriptures*, (∴)2r.

[17] For example, David Fergusson, *Ane Sermon Preichit befoir the Regent and Nobilitie, Upon a Part of the Third Chapter of the Prophet Malachi, in the Kirk of Leith, at the Tyme of the Generall Assemblie on Sonday the 13. of Januarie* (St Andrews, 1572), A4r–v, where the text is stated in Scots. See also McCallum, *Reforming the Scottish Parish*, 88. The Psalter adopted by the Scottish Reformers was also in English: Jamie Reid Baxter, 'Metrical Psalmody and the Bannatyne Manuscript: Robert Pont's Psalm 83', *Renaissance and Reformation*, 30 (2007): 44–5.

in Gaelic-speaking regions. The first Gaelic translation of the New Testament appeared in 1602, and a full Gaelic Old Testament was not published until 1685. These translations were produced in Ireland and used Classical Gaelic, which differed from the language spoken in Scotland.[18] It remained difficult, more than a century after Scotland adopted the Reformation, for ministers in Gaelic areas to communicate the contents of the Bible. As Bishop James Ramsay of Ross put it in 1688, ministers were 'at the pains to translate' passages of scripture to read in their churches, and yet 'I have heard some of them complain that they could not get words to Express In Irish some passages of holy writ'.[19]

Other problems arose from the small scale of the Scottish printing industry. The limited capacity and resources of Scottish publishers explain why the first domestic Bible edition did not appear until 1579. This edition was funded by a campaign, ordered by the General Assembly and approved by the Privy Council, to raise subscriptions in advance of publication. When copies appeared, Parliament passed an Act requiring wealthy householders to possess a Bible and Psalter. And there is evidence of attempts to enforce this law, at least in Edinburgh.[20] That the second Scottish Bible edition was published only in 1610, again prompting the church courts to canvass for buyers, is further indication that printing the Bible was a risky undertaking for Scottish publishers.[21] Moreover, the Bibles of 1579 and 1610 were folio editions, and it was not until the 1630s that the scriptures were printed in the smaller and cheaper octavo and duodecimo formats. Consequently Scotland relied throughout the period on imports of Bibles printed in the Dutch republic and England. Indeed, the presses of Amsterdam and Leiden deliberately aimed to capture from publishers in London part of the Scottish market.[22] It is difficult to estimate the scale of the imports. In Edinburgh, the bookseller Henry Charteris had fewer than 100 Bibles in stock at his death in 1599, though the numbers available for sale increased in subsequent decades.[23] Given the problems of supply and distribution, it is unsurprising that the General Assembly, district-level presbyteries, and parochial kirk sessions continued in the 1640s and 1650s to urge churches and households to purchase Bibles.[24]

The size of the domestic printing industry relates to another issue: the slow adoption of the King James Bible in preference to the Geneva translation. Though it was published in the

[18] Donald Meek, 'The Gaelic Bible', in David F. Wright (ed.), *The Bible in Scottish Life and Literature* (Edinburgh: St Andrew Press, 1988), 9–23. On the Irish Gaelic Bible, see the chapter by Marc Caball in this volume.

[19] *The Correspondence of Robert Boyle*, ed. Michael Hunter, Antonio Clericuzio, and Lawrence M. Principe (London, 2001), vi. 352.

[20] *Acts and Proceedings of the General Assemblies of the Kirk of Scotland* (Edinburgh: Bannatyne Club, 1839–45), i. 327–9; *The Register of the Privy Council of Scotland*, 1st ser., ed. John H. Burton (Edinburgh, 1877–98), ii. 544–6; *Records of the Parliaments of Scotland to 1707*, ed. Keith M. Brown et al., <http://www.rps.ac.uk>, 1579/10/25; Alastair J. Mann, *The Scottish Book Trade, 1500–1720: Print Commerce and Print Control in Early Modern Scotland* (East Linton: Tuckwell Press, 2000), 37–8, 19–20.

[21] Mann, *Scottish Book Trade*, 38.

[22] Mann, *Scottish Book Trade*, 91–3, 122–3.

[23] Michael Lynch, 'Preaching to the Converted? Perspectives on the Scottish Reformation', in A. A. MacDonald, Michael Lynch, and Ian B. Cowan (eds), *The Renaissance in Scotland: Studies in Literature, Religion, History and Culture Offered to John Durkan* (Leiden: Brill, 1994), 330.

[24] G. D. Henderson, *Religious Life in Seventeenth-Century Scotland* (Cambridge: Cambridge University Press, 1937), 4–5; Christopher R. Langley, 'Times of Trouble and Deliverance: Worship in the Kirk of Scotland, 1645–1658' (Ph.D. thesis, University of Aberdeen, 2012), 133–4. Further research in local church records would produce a more complete picture of the challenges of bringing the Bible to the people.

year of the new version, the Scottish Bible of 1610 used the Geneva text. The next Scottish printing of the Bible adopted the King James translation, but this edition appeared only in 1633. The delay is one reason why the translation was not officially specified for use in Scottish churches until the canons of 1636.[25] It is possible that James VI was reluctant simply to impose the new Bible on the Scottish Church, given that in 1601 proposals for revising the Geneva Bible were a matter for discussion in a General Assembly.[26] Moreover, the canons promoted by his more authoritarian son, Charles I, were swept away in the Covenanting revolution. Thus the King James Bible was 'authorised' in the Church of Scotland for less than three years. In the 1640s, Dutch-printed Geneva Bibles, which in contrast to English editions lacked the Apocrypha, continued to be imported to Scotland.[27] This did not prevent the King James Bible from gradually superseding its predecessor. But some evidence suggests that Presbyterians were critical of the King James translation. As late as 1695, a minister censured the approach of the translators, 'alledging that they were a company of men set to please King James'. Unsurprisingly, one of his objections was to the frequent use of the word 'bishop', which the minister saw as a deliberate strategy 'to countenance Episcopacy'.[28]

The Scottish Reformers' enthusiasm for the Bible masked a significant tension in the balance between its different functions in public worship. There were three ways in which congregations experienced the scriptures: singing metrical psalms, hearing passages from elsewhere in the Old and New Testaments read, and listening to sermons that analysed shorter biblical excerpts. Scotland's Reformers promoted the three practices, but attached particular importance to preaching. According to the *First Book of Discipline*, it was 'utterly necessarie' that 'the word be truly preached'. It was 'profitable' but not essential that psalms were sung and 'that certain places of Scripture be read when there is no sermon'.[29] The distinction between reading and singing the scriptures, on the one hand, and preaching about them, on the other, was reflected in the distribution of responsibilities in the Kirk's worship. Until the mid-seventeenth century, Sunday morning services were partially conducted by readers, laymen sufficiently literate to say prayers, lead psalm-singing, and read biblical passages.[30] In towns, readers also conducted weekday services at which there was no preaching. Some readers eventually became ministers or secured the intermediate office of exhorter. But readers were of significantly lower status than ordained clergy, and received much smaller stipends. Indeed, the reader's office was intended to be a temporary expedient, and the *Second Book of Discipline* (1578) did not mention readers.[31] Nevertheless, the *Second Book* maintained a clear distinction between ministers—who preached—and other officers (doctors, elders, and deacons) who did not.[32]

To think about the relationship between reading and preaching the Word, we need to understand public worship in the Church of Scotland. Several contemporary

---

[25] *The Anglican Canons, 1529–1947*, ed. Gerald Bray (Woodbridge: Boydell & Brewer, 1998), 546–7.

[26] *Acts and Proceedings of the General Assemblies*, iii. 970.

[27] Mann, *Scottish Book Trade*, 91–2.

[28] National Records of Scotland [NRS], GD1/649/1, Copy of George Home of Kimmerghame's diary, 1694–6, 37–8.

[29] *First Book of Discipline*, 180.   [30] *First Book of Discipline*, 105–6.

[31] Lynch, 'Preaching to the Converted?', 310–12; *The Second Book of Discipline*, ed. James Kirk (Edinburgh: St Andrew Press, 1980), 83–4.

[32] *Second Book of Discipline*, 184, 187–9, 193, 207.

descriptions, some written by English visitors to the country, together give a clear picture of weekly church services.[33] Scholars including Margo Todd and John McCallum have supplemented this evidence with detailed scrutiny of references to public worship in kirk session and presbytery records.[34] Collectively, the sources show that Sunday morning services in most parishes were structured by three rings of the church bell. The first, heard perhaps half an hour before the service began, was to call the people to church. A second ring accompanied the start of worship, a service of sung psalms and public prayers usually led by a reader. Only at a third sound of the bell would the minister enter the pulpit, pray, and preach a sermon.[35]

Well into the 1590s, however, a shortage of ministers dictated that their services were often shared between parishes. Not every church had the phases of worship before and after the third bell each Sunday morning.[36] As a result, the Reformed Church's early successes in winning over the people depended to a considerable extent on the parts of worship led by readers. Psalm-singing, directed by the reader acting as a precentor, was distinctive in being a congregational activity. The first complete Scottish Psalter was published in 1564, appended to the Book of Common Order, the text that indicated the structure and substance of Scottish worship until the 1640s.[37] Though congregations found it easiest to master the unison 'common tunes', used with psalms in 'common metre', in some Scottish churches harmonized psalmody persisted for a few decades after the Reformation.[38] Recent work by Jamie Reid Baxter, Jane Dawson, and colleagues has drawn attention to this brief post-Reformation flowering, especially in the illustrated part-books produced by Thomas Wode in St Andrews.[39] An older literature deplored the subsequent fall in musical standards, emphasizing that the Psalter published in 1635 with harmonized and fugal melodies had no successor. When in 1650 a revised translation of the Psalms was published, it was without music. The twelve common tunes published in 1666 for use with the new Psalter dominated psalmody into the eighteenth century.[40] But the music historians' narrative of decline misses the crucial point of recent scholarship: metrical psalms, whatever the quality of the translation and music, were popular with congregations. The singing of particular psalms (notably numbers 76 and 124) became associated with the kingdom's delivery from trouble, and thus with the view that God peculiarly favoured Scotland. In short, psalmody

[33] William D. Maxwell, *A History of Worship in the Church of Scotland* (London: Oxford University Press, 1955), 93–7, 124–5; William McMillan, *The Worship of the Scottish Reformed Church, 1550–1638* (London: James Clarke, 1931), 128–30.

[34] Todd, *Culture of Protestantism*, esp. chs 1–2; McCallum, *Reforming the Scottish Parish*, ch. 3.

[35] Sunday afternoon services followed a different pattern, typically combining public catechizing with a further sermon: McMillan, *Worship*, 133–5.

[36] Todd, *Culture of Protestantism*, 67; McCallum, *Reforming the Scottish Parish*, ch. 1.

[37] Millar Patrick, *Four Centuries of Scottish Psalmody* (London: Oxford University Press, 1949), 45–75. On debate surrounding psalm-singing, and on the use of the Psalms in the English service, see the chapters by Rachel Willie and Ian Green in this volume.

[38] Patrick, *Four Centuries*, 59–61; *The Perth Kirk Session Books, 1577–1590*, ed. Margo Todd (Woodbridge: Scottish History Society, 2012), 264.

[39] Jamie Reid Baxter, 'Thomas Wode, Christopher Goodman and the Curious Death of Scottish Music', *Scotlands*, 4 (1997): 1–20; Jane Dawson et al., Wode Psalter Project, <http://www.ed.ac.uk/schools-departments/divinity/research/projects/wode-psalter>.

[40] Patrick, *Four Centuries*; David Johnson, *Music and Society in Lowland Scotland in the Eighteenth Century* (London: Oxford University Press, 1972), ch. 9.

was a Protestant success, and an important dimension of early modern Scots' experience of the Bible.[41]

The other way in which readers communicated the Bible's contents to parishioners—by reading the text—has been studied in less detail. The Scottish Reformers, by insisting that the Bible be read in order, made a cleaner break with the Catholic past than did the early English Protestants. Abandoning the lectionary, with its 'skipping ... from place to place of Scripture', the *First Book of Discipline* explained, would make Bible reading more edifying for congregations.[42] In small rural parishes, where services took place on Sundays only, sequential reading of the Bible may have entertained parishioners, but it is questionable whether the practice led many to a detailed knowledge of such a long book, served to them in so many short portions.[43] It is also unclear what standards were expected of readers. Men doing the job were accountable to kirk sessions and presbyteries, the latter established in the 1580s. In September 1583, for example, the presbytery of Stirling deprived from office one reader, Robert Fogo, in part 'becaus he reidis nocht distinctlie, keipis na point in his reiding nor undirstandis nocht quhat [i.e. what] he reidis'. How widespread were such complaints? In the previous March, the presbytery recorded its dissatisfaction with the performance of another reader, who had written out his text and committed it to memory.[44] Was this practice, used by ministers when preparing their sermons, common among readers? Was reading made difficult by a shortage of Bibles? Some readers chafed at the limitations of their role. John Coiss, reader at Gogar near Edinburgh, was repeatedly warned by the presbytery not to preach or administer the sacraments.[45] Did long-standing readers in parishes without ministers, such as Gogar, commonly seek extra responsibilities? A thorough survey of the local courts' records would be required to examine how readers exercised their functions, and how often their abilities were found wanting.

The third bell, if a minister was present, marked the transition from 'profitable' to essential parts of worship: from reading to the preaching of the Word. In large towns, as envisaged by the *First Book of Discipline*, there were by the late sixteenth century sermons on one or more weekdays, as well as twice on Sundays.[46] As with reading, preaching was to follow the order of the biblical text. The minister advanced incrementally through his chosen book, often preaching a sermon or more on every verse. The text was referred to as the minister's 'ordinary'. Like most other matters, however, the order of ministers' sermons was subject to the church courts' oversight. In 1586, Perth's minister agreed to a suggestion of his elders that he abandon his ordinary for a scriptural passage likely to move the congregation to

[41] Jane Dawson, 'Patterns of Worship in Reformation Scotland', in Duncan B. Forrester and Doug Gay (eds), *Worship and Liturgy in Context: Studies and Case Studies in Theology and Practice* (London: SCM Press, 2009), 143; Todd, *Culture of Protestantism*, 70–3; James Porter, '"Blessed spirits, sing with me!" Psalm-Singing in Context and Practice', in James Porter (ed.), *Defining Strains: The Musical Life of Scots in the Seventeenth Century* (Oxford: Peter Lang, 2007), 299–322; Alec Ryrie, 'The Psalms and Confrontation in English and Scottish Protestantism', *Archiv für Reformationsgeschichte*, 101 (2010): 114–37.

[42] *First Book of Discipline*, 185. Cf. W. R. Owens, 'Sequential Bible Reading in Early Modern England', *Bunyan Studies*, 15 (2011): 64–74.

[43] Maxwell, *History of Worship*, 57.

[44] *Stirling Presbytery Records, 1581–1587*, ed. James Kirk (Edinburgh: Scottish History Society, 1981), 95, 172, 173 (quotation).

[45] NRS, CH2/121/1, Presbytery of Edinburgh minutes, 1586–93, 23; CH2/121/2, Presbytery of Edinburgh minutes, 1593–1601, 243. I am grateful to Norah Carlin for these references.

[46] *First Book of Discipline*, 180–1; Todd, *Culture of Protestantism*, 30.

donate funds for the upkeep of the Church.[47] In 1651, the presbytery of Fordyce heard a complaint that David Abercrombie dwelt too long on each text, preaching for ten days on part of Psalm 94.[48] Abercrombie's painful analysis may well have encompassed numerous theological issues and topical applications. But perhaps the sequential use of the Bible sometimes obstructed the Church's objective of building up Christians' knowledge and understanding.

What was the nature of Scottish sermons after the Reformation? Here it should be recognized that the printed and manuscript sermons to which historians have access do not provide straightforward evidence of what was said in the pulpit. Manuscript copies were often made by hearers, sometimes transcribing from shorthand notes. Even when the printing of a sermon was the responsibility of its preacher, there was sometimes revision between preaching and publication.[49] Nevertheless, we can detect in the period's sermons common characteristics. Some traits were relatively constant across the century and a half after 1560, while others exhibited change in this period.

Among the sermons' lasting characteristics was a closely analytical engagement with a scriptural verse, or part of a verse. Ministers examined each verse in fine detail, while also placing the text in the context of scripture as a whole, drawing parallels and making allusions to other parts of the Bible. The most allusive sermons are presumably easier to follow on the page than they were in church, especially when printed editions provide marginal references or indicate quotations with italics. To take an extreme example, a printed sermon of 1629 by the Glasgow minister Zachary Boyd contained in its first five pages (or approximately 750 words) references to the sermon text (Psalm 73: 24), the preceding verse, on which Boyd had previously preached, and seventeen other Old and New Testament verses.[50] The view that difficult passages were to be interpreted in the light of clearer biblical texts, as expressed in the Westminster Confession (1646), called into question the use of non-scriptural authorities in preaching. But the extent to which ministers' range of reference changed over time, or became a matter of controversy, calls for more systematic research. The printed sermons of David Fergusson (1572) and Robert Pont (1599) drew on various ancient and patristic sources.[51] Whereas pagan philosophers and the church fathers remained of interest to Restoration Episcopalians,[52] Presbyterian preachers of the late seventeenth and early eighteenth centuries seem to have avoided much reference to texts other than the Bible.[53] Perhaps different hermeneutical strategies and styles of preaching contributed to the late seventeenth-century divergence between Presbyterian and Episcopalian cultures.

---

[47] *Perth Kirk Session Books*, 353.   [48] Langley, 'Times of Trouble', 60.

[49] Crawford Gribben, 'Preaching the Scottish Reformation, 1560–1707', in Hugh Adlington, Peter McCullough, and Emma Rhatigan (eds), *The Oxford Handbook of the Early Modern Sermon* (Oxford: Oxford University Press, 2011), 271–86, 277.

[50] Zachary Boyd, *Two Orientall Pearles, Grace and Glory* (Edinburgh, 1629), 7–11.

[51] Fergusson, *Sermon Preichit befoir the Regent*, B2^r, B6^v; Robert Pont, *Against Sacrilege, Three Sermons* (Edinburgh, 1599), B5^r–B6^r. See also Jamie Reid Baxter, 'Mr Andrew Boyd (1567–1636): A Neo-Stoic Bishop of Argyll and his Writings', in Julian Goodare and Alasdair A. MacDonald (eds), *Sixteenth-Century Scotland: Essays in Honour of Michael Lynch* (Leiden: Brill, 2008), 395–426.

[52] Alexander Monro, *Sermons Preached upon Several Occasions* (London, 1693), e.g. 42, 83, 212, 451, 466–8; John Cockburn, *Fifteen Sermons Preach'd upon Several Occasions, and on Various Subjects* (London, 1697), e.g. 11–12, 387, 390, 495, 496, 502.

[53] For example, Edinburgh University Library, MS. La. III 116, Sermons of Robert Wodrow, 1703–23 (in the preacher's hand).

Scottish sermons were generally plain in style. Recent studies of Robert Rollock, the late sixteenth-century principal of Edinburgh University, and Zachary Boyd emphasize that their sermons were clearly structured and used only simple rhetorical devices. Rollock employed 'discourse markers', including phrases instructing the congregation to remember important points, and he used conversational passages to vary his presentation. Boyd was fond of anaphora, the repetition of words or phrases in successive clauses. Both preachers posed questions, perhaps intended to elicit muttered responses from the congregation, drawing worshippers into the sermon.[54] Features such as numbered lists, and the stating of the 'heads' under which the sermon was organized, reflected the influence of Ramist logic and helped listeners follow what was preached. These structuring devices also enabled ministers to remember what they were to say: by the late seventeenth century, if not before, most Presbyterians wrote their sermons in advance but preached from memory.[55] Yet the stating of 'heads' and the practice of distinguishing between 'doctrines' and 'uses' (the applications of a sermon's message) were abandoned by an increasing number of Presbyterian ministers from the 1640s onwards.[56]

This development, combined with the long-standing belief that the Holy Spirit assisted ministers in the pulpit, may have changed the balance in Presbyterian sermons between methodical exposition and affecting eloquence. Some Episcopalians, especially in the late seventeenth century, mocked what they perceived as the canting and ignorant preaching of their Presbyterian rivals.[57] But we know too little about the Episcopalians' preaching methods to judge whether they adopted the new type of 'plain style', based on principles of classical rhetoric, which Mary Morrissey has identified in Anglican sermons of the Restoration period.[58]

How did listeners respond to the preached Word? No doubt some were guilty of the 'private whisperings, conferences, salutations … gazing, sleeping, and other undecent behaviour' that the authors of the Westminster Directory for Public Worship (1645) felt the need to forbid.[59] Yet numerous godly Scots were convinced that preaching had helped them to experience conversion. This was partly a result of study: the shorthand scribes who took down their ministers' words could read and discuss the doctrines with family and friends.[60] More fundamentally, sermons awakened hearers to the enormity of their sins, and the necessity of divine grace for their salvation. Ministers examined the numerous ways in which their parishioners were in breach of the moral law, and were thus worthy of damnation, a manner

---

[54] Mark Garner, 'Preaching as a Communicative Event: A Discourse Analysis of Sermons by Robert Rollock (1555–1599)', *Reformation and Renaissance Review*, 9 (2007): 45–70; David W. Atkinson, 'Introduction', in *Selected Sermons of Zachary Boyd*, ed. Atkinson (Aberdeen: Scottish Text Society, 1989), xxxi–xxxiv; Todd, *Culture of Protestantism*, 53–4.

[55] Henderson, *Religious Life*, 197–8; Donald Meek, 'The Pulpit and the Pen: Clergy, Orality and Print in the Scottish Gaelic World', in Adam Fox and Daniel Woolf (eds), *The Spoken World: Oral Culture in Britain, 1500–1850* (Manchester: Manchester University Press, 2002), 101–3.

[56] Gribben, 'Preaching the Scottish Reformation', 280.

[57] Alasdair Raffe, *The Culture of Controversy: Religious Arguments in Scotland, 1660–1714* (Woodbridge: Boydell Press, 2012), 146–7.

[58] Mary Morrissey, 'Scripture, Style and Persuasion in Seventeenth-Century English Theories of Preaching', *Journal of Ecclesiastical History*, 53 (2002): 702–5.

[59] *A Directory for the Publike Worship of God Throughout the Three Kingdoms of Scotland, England, and Ireland* (Edinburgh, 1645), 10–11.

[60] Mullan, *Narratives*, 117–18.

of preaching known as 'law-work'.[61] But to coax parishioners to conversion, it was necessary to balance such horrifying messages with more optimistic teachings about God's grace.
Again, these generalizations apply principally to Presbyterian ministers' preaching. As late
seventeenth-century Episcopalians became increasingly hostile to models of piety centred
on conversion, the goals of their preaching shifted. Influential Episcopalians called for sermons to become briefer, simpler, and less dogmatic.[62]

It is now time to discuss the mid-seventeenth-century changes that displaced scriptural
reading from its important place in public worship. A new practice known as 'lecturing'
evolved in the 1640s and came to be used before the sermon on Sunday mornings, the interval formerly occupied by readings. The lecture was an analysis of a biblical passage by the
minister. In most respects it resembled a sermon, though longer scriptural texts might be
chosen for lectures. To examine the origins of lecturing, it will be necessary to consider the
balance between three trends affecting Scottish worship after 1638, the year of the National
Covenant and the revolt against episcopacy in the Church. First, there was a general reaction against ceremonies and set forms of prayer in public worship. The Covenant was the
culmination of protests against Charles I's attempt to impose an Anglican-style Prayer Book
on the Scottish Church. Covenanting ministers such as Robert Baillie denounced the Prayer
Book, but more radical Presbyterians called for reforms to worship beyond the mere rejection of the book. Some ministers stopped saying the Lord's Prayer and discountenanced the
doxology, a sung address to God added to the end of psalms. Though controversial in the
early 1640s, these changes were gradually adopted across the Church, and the absence of
set forms became characteristic of Presbyterian worship. Presbyterians justified their use
of extemporary prayer by emphasizing the Holy Spirit's role in inspiring both the tone and
some of the words of their prayers.[63]

It is unclear whether opposition to public reading of the Bible was initially part of the
radical Presbyterians' reaction against set forms of prayer. It is plausible that innovators in
prayer would have changed other parts of public worship. Andrew Cant of Aberdeen, one
of the radicals, reportedly 'cryit out' against scriptural reading, and introduced a 'lecture
lesson' or 'ordinar lector' in place of afternoon prayers three or four times per week.[64] Yet
the experimentation in worship of the 1640s is difficult to explain. Contemporaries used the
very imprecise term 'Brownism' to blame the changes on the influence of English sects.[65]
Certainly Scots who knew of the proliferating and diverse separatist groups in England had
reason to worry. Robert Baillie, who as a commissioner to the Westminster Assembly gained
first-hand knowledge of religious developments in London, claimed that the 'Brownists'
refused to read scripture publicly without explanation.[66] But this and other sources written

[61] Louise A. Yeoman, 'Heart-work: Emotion, Empowerment and Authority in Covenanting Times'
(Ph.D. thesis, University of St Andrews, 1991), 9–11.
[62] Raffe, 'Presbyterians and Episcopalians', 582.
[63] David Stevenson, 'The Radical Party in the Kirk, 1637–45', Journal of Ecclesiastical History, 26 (1974),
135–65; Gordon Donaldson, 'Covenant to Revolution', in Duncan B. Forrester and Douglas M. Murray (eds),
Studies in the History of Worship in Scotland, 2nd edn (Edinburgh: T. & T. Clark, 1996), 52–64; Raffe, Culture
of Controversy, ch. 5.
[64] John Spalding, The History of the Troubles and Memorable Transactions in Scotland and England, from
M.DC.XXVI. to M.DC.XLV (Edinburgh: Bannatyne Club, 1828–9), ii. 56, 114; Extracts from the Council
Register of the Burgh of Aberdeen, 1625–1642 (Edinburgh: Scottish Burgh Records Society, 1871), 279.
[65] Stevenson, 'Radical Party in the Kirk', esp. 135.
[66] Robert Baillie, A Dissuasive from the Errours of the Time (London, 1645), 30.

by the opponents of English sects cannot account for what was happening in Scotland. Given the vagueness of the label 'Brownist', and the difficulty of providing evidence of English sects' influence before the Cromwellian invasion of Scotland in 1650–3, it is misleading to parrot contemporary polemicists on this point.[67]

A second and probably more decisive factor influencing Scottish church services was the introduction in 1645 of the Directory for Public Worship, which had been devised by the Westminster Assembly. The Directory made clear that 'Reading of the Word in the Congregation' is 'part of the publike Worship of God', and indicated that reading should take place before the sermon. In these respects, the Directory accorded with previous Scottish practice. But there were two ways in which the Directory encouraged change in Sunday morning services. First, it specified that reading was to be 'performed by the Pastors and Teachers'. Though the Directory most often used the term 'minister' to refer to a clergyman, both in the section 'Of Publike Reading of the holy Scriptures' and elsewhere in the text, the words 'Pastors' and 'Teachers' seem likewise to have been used of ordained ministers. The Directory allowed for someone other than the minister to 'line out' the psalms (to read each line before the congregation sang it), but there was no mention of an office resembling the Scottish reader. The Directory's second departure from Scottish practice—to which I will return below—was to allow ministers to 'expound any part of what is read'.[68] The Directory's instructions were based on the patterns of worship in some English churches. Robert Baillie, reporting in late 1643 on the assembly's discussions of public worship, wrote that ministers 'of best note about London are now in use, in the [reader's] desk, to pray, and read in the Sunday morning four chapters, and expone some of them, and cause sing two Psalms, and then to goe to the pulpit to preach'.[69]

By specifying an English model of worship, the Directory called into question the existing Scottish arrangements, particularly the distribution of responsibilities between ministers and readers. As well as mandating the use of the Directory, the General Assembly of 1645 ordered that 'for regulating' the reading and expounding of scripture in Sunday services, ministers and congregations should 'repair to the Kirk half an hour before that time at which ordinarily the Minister now entreth to the publick worship'.[70] In effect, ministers were told to perform the reader's service. This may have had the welcome effect of reducing parish expenditure on readers. In some large towns, moreover, weekday services conducted solely by readers were phased out. In 1645 in Edinburgh, the diarist John Nicoll claimed, 'the reiding of chapteris in the kirk by the commoun reidar, and singing of psalmes wer dischargit'.[71] Enquiring about these events seventy years later, the historian Robert Wodrow was informed that some ministers had doubted the legitimacy of scriptural reading by the reader, thinking that 'an act of publick worship' should not be undertaken 'by one who was not a Church Officer'. This opinion was presumably justified with reference to the Directory. In Edinburgh, it seems that there was no public reading for a period in the 1640s, and that

[67] See e.g. Maxwell, *History of Worship*, 97–8.
[68] *A Directory for the Publike Worship of God*, 11–12 (quotations), 65.
[69] *The Letters and Journals of Robert Baillie* (Edinburgh: Bannatyne Club, 1841–2), ii. 122.
[70] *Acts of the General Assembly of the Church of Scotland, M.DC.XXXVIII.–M.DCCC.XLII.* (Edinburgh, 1843), 115–16, 120 (quotations).
[71] John Nicoll, *A Diary of Public Transactions and other Occurrences, Chiefly in Scotland, from January 1650 to June 1667* (Edinburgh: Bannatyne Club, 1836), 114–15.

this was followed by an interval in which the ministers took turns to read and explain the Bible.[72]

The introduction of the Directory left readers with little to do. In the long term, their residual function of leading the congregation in sung psalms was often performed by the parish schoolmaster or session clerk. But we should acknowledge a third trend shaping the evolution of Scottish worship: a scepticism about readers and reading that had been present since 1560. As we have seen, the early Reformers attached more importance to preaching than to reading. After adopting the *Second Book of Discipline*, which envisaged a polity without readers, the General Assembly attempted to phase out the office. In July 1580, the assembly concluded that the reader was 'no ordinar office within the Kirk of God', and called for an examination of readers' abilities. In the following year, the assembly resolved that no more readers were to be appointed.[73] This decision, though it had little practical effect, accords with the concerns about readers' competence soon to be expressed by Stirling presbytery. And the assembly's attitude reflected the rise, at least among a vocal minority of clergy, of dogmatic Presbyterian ideas of church government. Generally there was frustration at the slow supply of preaching ministers to parts of Scotland.[74] The Covenanting revolution brought back to prominence many of the attitudes of late sixteenth-century Presbyterians. Thus while in 1642 the General Assembly recommended that each parish should have a reader, there is little evidence of discontent when the office lost its most significant function.[75] Perhaps the re-establishment of Presbyterianism after 1638 revived a latent hostility towards readers, prompting calls for ministers to take more complete control of public worship.

The Directory, in line with this strain of clericalism in Scottish Presbyterian thought, insisted that it was the minister's special function to communicate biblical messages to his congregation. All agreed that it was the clergy's gift to draw out the meaning of the sacred text. Thus the Directory gave ministers the option of explaining what they had read. Yet they were supposed to do this only after reading a whole chapter or psalm. It is this aspect of the Directory's instructions that came to be disregarded when extended lectures were given on shorter scriptural passages.[76] Perhaps some worshippers objected to sermon-like discussions of a whole biblical chapter, rather than a shorter section. When in 1644 the minister of the Scots Kirk in Rotterdam adopted the practice, he was criticized by members of the congregation.[77] On the other hand, Wodrow's account of developments in Edinburgh suggests that the ministers there found daily reading onerous, and thus they introduced in its place Sunday morning lectures.[78] It is unclear from the scattered evidence how quickly, and for what reasons,

---

[72] Robert Wodrow, *Analecta: Or, Materials for a History of Remarkable Providences* (Edinburgh: Maitland Club, 1842–3), ii. 291 (quotations), 368; Nicoll, *Diary*, 5. In the 1640s, the Edinburgh ministers' roles in national religious politics limited their time for duties in the town: Laura A. M. Stewart, *Urban Politics and the British Civil Wars: Edinburgh, 1617–53* (Leiden: Brill, 2006), 86–7.

[73] *Acts and Proceedings of the General Assemblies*, ii. 455 (quotation), 456–7, 460, 513; *Second Book of Discipline*, 83–4.

[74] Lynch, 'Preaching to the Converted?', 310–11.

[75] *Acts of the General Assembly*, 63.

[76] *Directory for the Publike Worship of God*, 12.

[77] William Steven, *The History of the Scottish Church, Rotterdam* (Edinburgh: Waugh & Innes, 1833), 8–11.

[78] Wodrow, *Analecta*, ii. 291, 368.

Presbyterians across Scotland adopted the standard pattern of lecturing before the sermon on Sunday mornings.

Whether as a result of slow change or conscious decisions, the minister's explanation of his readings became the focal point of worship between the second and third bells. In 1652, the General Assembly felt the need to recommend that ministers' comments on each chapter of the Old Testament be sufficiently brief to allow time for a New Testament chapter to be read.[79] By this point, the Church had split into two parties: the Resolutioners and Protesters. Protesters, who did not recognize the 1652 assembly, were more inclined than their rivals to experiment in worship. Perhaps it was Protesters who first made reading and expounding resemble a sermon. More generally, it is likely that ministers steadily increased the length and doctrinal content of their commentaries, and the biblical passages chosen were necessarily shorter. But even in the Restoration period, when lecturing remained part of dissenting Presbyterian worship, some ministers analysed quite long extracts. Though a published lecture by John Welsh began with his reading only 'two or three Verses', Richard Cameron lectured on (and presumably read to the congregation) as many as seventeen verses at a time. Even so, Cameron's discussion was much longer than his scriptural text.[80] The practice of lecturing, therefore, subordinated the words of the Bible to the doctrines of Calvinism. The introduction of lectures increased the clergy's control over popular understanding of the scriptures, at a time when ministers gained considerable political influence and social status. It was not just the Westminster Directory that led ministers to start lecturing, but the clericalist tendency that had long been part of Scottish Presbyterianism.

The re-establishment of episcopacy in 1661–2 led to coordinated attempts to abolish lecturing and restore reading to Scottish church services.[81] In autumn 1662, resolutions to this effect were adopted at the diocesan synods of Moray, Aberdeen, Dunblane, St Andrews, and probably others whose records are missing. Aberdeen and Dunblane synods ordered that readers again be appointed.[82] Together with scriptural reading, the synods reinstated the Lord's Prayer, Apostles' Creed, and the doxology. These reforms were clearly intended to reverse changes made by the Covenanters, whose revolution had been repudiated by much of the ruling elite. This context ensured that the use of the Bible in public worship had considerable political significance: according to one source, the Archbishop of St Andrews 'declared it was the King's will that' ministers should stop lecturing.[83] It seems that some ministers were slow to implement the reforms, which were regularly restated at synod meetings. Bishop Robert Leighton of Dunblane, renewing his criticisms of lectures in 1665,

[79] *Acts of the General Assembly*, 1151.

[80] John Welsh, *A Preface, Lecture, and a Sermon* (1686), 10; John Howie (ed.), *A Collection of Lectures and Sermons, Preached upon Several Subjects, Mostly in the Time of the Late Persecution* (Glasgow, 1779), 330–40.

[81] The English naturalist John Ray, visiting Scotland in 1661, reported that the minister 'reads and expounds in some places, in some not': P. Hume Brown (ed.), *Early Travellers in Scotland* (Edinburgh: D. Douglas, 1891), 239.

[82] NRS, CH2/271/2, Synod of Moray records, 1646–68, 374; *Selections from the Records of the Kirk Session, Presbytery, and Synod of Aberdeen* (Aberdeen: Spalding Club, 1846), 262–3; *Register of the Diocesan Synod of Dunblane, 1662–1688*, ed. John Wilson (Edinburgh, 1877), 2, 7; William Row, *The Life of Mr Robert Blair, Minister of St Andrews*, ed. Thomas M'Crie (Edinburgh: Wodrow Society, 1848), 425–6. See also the Act of Oct. 1664 in *The Register of the Synod of Galloway, from October 1664 to April 1671* (Kirkcudbright, 1856), 9.

[83] Row, *Life of Mr Robert Blair*, 425.

warned his clergy against fomenting 'in people's myndes the foolish prejudice and proude disdain they have taken against the Scriptures read without a superadded discourse'.[84]

As we have noted, dissenting Presbyterians continued to lecture in the Restoration period. And when Presbyterianism was re-established in the revolution of 1688–90, the practice of lecturing returned to parish churches. There was evidently some concern that lectures were given on excessively short passages of scripture, and that this was contrary to the Directory's instructions. In 1694, the General Assembly ordered that in their lectures ministers should 'read and open up to the people some large and considerable portion of the Word of God', so that 'the old custom introduced and established by the Directory may by degrees be recovered'. But the balance between reading and 'opening up' remained unsatisfactory: the assembly reiterated its Act in 1704; two years later, the assembly reported that its instructions concerning lecturing were 'much neglected in many places'.[85] Long lectures had become a standard part of Scottish Presbyterian worship, and they continued into the nineteenth century.

The replacement of public reading by lecturing was an important, and so far insufficiently understood, result of the triumph of Presbyterian clericalism in the Covenanting revolution. It is tempting to agree with Bishop Leighton and conclude that, like Catholics, lecturing Presbyterians denied the people unmediated access to the Bible.[86] But we should remember that the mid-seventeenth-century developments in public worship took place at a time when the distribution of the Bible was improving, allowing more Scots to read for themselves. Perhaps some Presbyterians had a higher regard for the doctrines communicated in sermons than for the scriptural text itself. Yet it would probably be fairer to suggest that though, at the start of our period, the Bible was most frequently read aloud in churches, by the early eighteenth century, it was more often enjoyed domestically or privately. Elizabeth Breehom, a 25-year-old converted in the Cambuslang revival of 1742, was strongly influenced by her minister's sermons and popular devotional literature. Yet she did not lack direct access to scripture: she would sit 'spinning on my wheel, with my bible on my knee'. Another young female convert, 'at home reading a Chapter, at the fire side', was 'persuaded that it was the Lord who was thereby speaking to me'.[87] In the eighteenth century, more than ever before, Scots encountered the Bible both through preaching and reading. They heard their ministers' interpretations, and cultivated personal relationships with the scriptural text. The Word was experienced in multiple ways, and its lessons could be put to many purposes.[88]

FURTHER READING

Dawson, Jane. 'Patterns of Worship in Reformation Scotland', in Duncan B. Forrester and Doug Gay (eds), *Worship and Liturgy in Context: Studies and Case Studies in Theology and Practice* (London: SCM Press, 2009), 136–51.

---

[84] *Register of the Diocesan Synod of Dunblane*, 34.
[85] *Acts of the General Assembly*, 238, 327, 394.
[86] *Register of the Diocesan Synod of Dunblane*, 34.
[87] *The McCulloch Examinations of the Cambuslang Revival (1742)*, ed. Keith Edward Beebe (Woodbridge and Rochester, NY: Scottish History Society, 2013), i. 336–7, 338, ii. 237.
[88] For helpful comments, I am grateful to the audience of the Scottish History research seminar at the University of Edinburgh, and especially to Norah Carlin, Chris Langley, Jamie Reid Baxter, and Laura Stewart.

Donaldson, Gordon. 'Covenant to Revolution', in Duncan B. Forrester and Douglas M. Murray (eds), *Studies in the History of Worship in Scotland*, 2nd edn (Edinburgh: T. & T. Clark, 1996), 52–64.

Gribben, Crawford. 'Preaching the Scottish Reformation, 1560–1707', in Hugh Adlington, Peter McCullough, and Emma Rhatigan (eds), *The Oxford Handbook of the Early Modern Sermon* (Oxford: Oxford University Press, 2011), 271–86.

Lynch, Michael. 'Preaching to the Converted? Perspectives on the Scottish Reformation', in A. A. MacDonald, Michael Lynch, and Ian B. Cowan (eds), *The Renaissance in Scotland: Studies in Literature, Religion, History and Culture Offered to John Durkan* (Leiden: Brill, 1994), 301–43.

McCallum, John. *Reforming the Scottish Parish: The Reformation in Fife, 1560–1640* (Farnham: Ashgate, 2010).

Mann, Alastair J. *The Scottish Book Trade, 1500–1720: Print Commerce and Print Control in Early Modern Scotland* (East Linton: Tuckwell Press, 2000).

Meek, Donald. 'The Gaelic Bible', in David F. Wright (ed.), *The Bible in Scottish Life and Literature* (Edinburgh: St Andrew Press, 1988), 9–23.

Mullan, David George. *Narratives of the Religious Self in Early-Modern Scotland* (Farnham: Ashgate, 2010).

Raffe, Alasdair. 'Presbyterians and Episcopalians: The Formation of Confessional Cultures in Scotland, 1660–1715'. *English Historical Review*, 125 (2010): 570–98.

Raffe, Alasdair. *The Culture of Controversy: Religious Arguments in Scotland, 1660–1714* (Woodbridge: Boydell Press, 2012).

Smout, T. C. 'Born Again at Cambuslang: New Evidence on Popular Religion and Literacy in Eighteenth-Century Scotland'. *Past and Present*, 97 (1982): 114–27.

Todd, Margo. *The Culture of Protestantism in Early Modern Scotland* (New Haven: Yale University Press, 2002).

CHAPTER 21

THE BIBLE IN EARLY MODERN GAELIC IRELAND: TRADITION, COLLABORATION, AND ALIENATION

MARC CABALL

THE history of the Gaelic Bible in the early modern period is reflective of broader patterns of political, religious, and cultural evolution in Ireland in the late sixteenth and seventeenth centuries when the island was progressively rendered subject to the centralizing jurisdiction of the English state. Moreover, the translation of the New and Old Testaments into Irish is a remarkable example of beneficial interchange between English and Gaelic cultures while concurrently illustrating a progressive ethno-religious dissonance in the fractured meeting between the cultural dynamism of Gaelic Ireland and the predominantly English Protestant ethos of the island's political and religious elites. The story of the translation of the Irish Bible, a protracted process marked variously by a triumph of scholarship, the power of technology, official indifference, occasional or more often latent Protestant hostility, and evangelical fervour, is in many respects a parable for the failure of the Protestant Reformation to nurture indigenous roots in Irish soil. The history of the Irish Bible is also the story of the multi-faceted encounter between English and Gaelic societies which was simultaneously tense, aggressive, and mutually dismissive, and also complementary and mutually enriching across a range of social, cultural. and linguistic interaction.

In other words, the extended and episodic production of a complete Irish translation of the Bible from the tentative origins of the project in the 1560s to its final completion in 1685 is emblematic of the complexity of the political, religious, and cultural history of early modern Ireland. Fundamentally, the history of the Irish Bible is indicative of an evolving cleavage between Protestantism and Gaelic culture in seventeenth-century Ireland. Gaelic Irish Protestants were centrally involved in the translation and production of the New Testament, while the key role of English Protestants such as William Bedell, Narcissus Marsh, and Robert Boyle in the translation and publication of the Old Testament is symptomatic of a progressive and enduring alienation of the Gaelic literati from the established church of the Anglo-Irish Protestant elite.

As the story of the Bible in Irish was essentially determined by an often abrasive though creative encounter between two cultures, English and Gaelic Irish, it is appropriate to begin the following account by locating the origins of its religious and cultural lineage in two institutions which were critical influences on its evolution. The first was Emmanuel College, Cambridge, founded by a royal charter granted in 1584 to Sir Walter Mildmay (d. 1589), Elizabeth's Chancellor of the Exchequer, a member of her Privy Council, and a staunch Protestant. Laurence Chaderton became the first Master of the college and would remain in the post for the next thirty-six years. Mildmay's political and financial skills were an important factor in the early consolidation of the new foundation which by the beginning of the seventeenth century enrolled more students than any other Cambridge college except Trinity. Mildmay and Chaderton envisaged Emmanuel as a seminary, marked by a definite Puritan inflection, committed to the supply of a teaching ministry. Although never institutionalized as such, puritanism and its adherents were broadly characterized by a commitment to removing surviving Roman Catholic teachings and practice from the Reformed Church and by an emphasis on the importance of access to the scriptures in the vernacular. The Puritan emphasis on the provision of university-educated preachers for every parish is reflected in Mildmay's original statutes which stipulated that no fellow of Emmanuel could remain in the college for more than ten years after receiving his MA or more than one year after the award to him of his DD. This requirement ensured that Emmanuel provided a steady supply of clergymen committed to an active pastoral ministry.

During its first fifty years, the college produced a distinguished cohort of prominent churchmen, scholars, colonists. and, to a lesser extent, politicians. Among its former students were two clergymen, one an Irishman and the other an Englishman, who would prove pivotal to the translation of the Bible into Irish. William Bedell, who enabled the translation of the Gaelic Old Testament, entered Emmanuel among its first students in 1584, graduated BA in 1588 and MA in 1592, and became a fellow of the college in 1593.[1] Uilliam Ó Domhnuill, who saw to completion the translation and printing of the Gaelic New Testament, matriculated at Emmanuel in 1586 and graduated BA in 1590 and MA in 1593.[2] The presence of Ó Domhnuill's 1602 New Testament (Tiomna Nuadh) in the library of Emmanuel College shortly after its publication in Dublin and Bedell's gift to the college library of a copy of Erasmus's New Testament in Greek and Latin, published in Basle in 1570, are emblematic of the impact of Emmanuel's intellectual milieu on the story of the Gaelic Bible.[3]

If the immediate evangelical background to the Irish Bible can be traced to Emmanuel, its cultural and linguistic pedigree was considerably more antique. Such influences derived from a venerable canon of medieval Gaelic literary scholarship centred in the main on the composition of praise poetry in syllabic metres by a largely hereditary caste of bardic poets. Drawing on a codified repertoire of themes and tropes and composing in a grammatically

---

[1] Aidan Clarke, 'Bedell, William (1571–1642)', in James McGuire and James Quinn (eds), *Dictionary of Irish Biography* (Cambridge: Cambridge University Press, 2009), i. 411–12.

[2] Terry Clavin and Judy Barry, 'Daniel (Ó Domhnuill, O'Donnell), William (1570–1628)', in McGuire and Quinn, *Dictionary of Irish Biography*, iii. 37–9.

[3] Sargent Bush and Carl J. Rasmussen, *The Library of Emmanuel College, Cambridge, 1584–1637* (Cambridge: Cambridge University Press, 1986), 24, 55, 66.

standardized form of the Irish language, bardic poets, whose formal institutional origins are to be traced to the thirteenth century, were intimately linked to the ruling elites of Gaelic Ireland and Scotland on the basis of the communal ideological function of their poetry. The greater part of the extant corpus of poetry in the bardic idiom is professional in nature, in so far as praise poems were composed in honour of affluent or high-status patrons whose dynastic position and aspirations were endorsed by means of imagery which resonated culturally and socially among the Gaelic and gaelicized Anglo-Norman elites. Paradoxically, although the Gaelic world was politically fragmented and lacked a university, it was characterized by a considerable level of cultural unity among its dynastic elites and professional classes. Indeed, the generic nature of bardic composition enabled some poets to respond in a coherent and strategic way to the cumulative consolidation of English political authority in Ireland in the late sixteenth and early seventeenth centuries.[4] Invested with a considerable measure of cultural authority and exponents of sanctioned linguistic usage, praise poets were deemed important collaborators by evangelical translators.

I. Reformation, Print, and Gaelic Culture in Ireland and Scotland

Given the contemporary importance accorded print as a means of encouraging acquiescence in political and religious authority, the engagement of the Tudor state with print in Irish was both relatively late in date and limited in scope. However, it is known that early in Elizabeth's reign the authorities authorized a payment to Adam Loftus, Archbishop of Armagh, and Hugh Brady, Bishop of Meath, for the production of type to enable the printing of the New Testament in Irish.[5] By 1567, repayment of the sum of £66 13s 4d was sought from the defaulting prelates in the absence of imminent publication of the New Testament.[6] The evidence of the primer of Irish specifically composed for her use by Christopher Nugent suggests that Elizabeth was nominally sympathetic to Gaelic culture. Possibly presented to the monarch during a visit to Cambridge in 1564, Nugent's preface praised both her linguistic ability and her desire to understand the language of her Irish subjects.[7]

Nonetheless, the sovereign was publicly reminded of the failure to disseminate scripture in Irish during a visit to Woodstock near Oxford in 1575. In the course of an address of welcome, Laurence Humphrey, President of Magdalen College and Vice-Chancellor of the university, presented Elizabeth with a tattered manuscript of the Bible in Irish apparently translated by Richard Fitzralph, a famous Archbishop of Armagh in the fourteenth century. Emphasizing the potency of God's word, he expressed the hope that the Queen would promote holy scripture among her subjects with a view to strengthening the English and

---

[4] Marc Caball, *Poets and Politics: Reaction and Continuity in Irish Poetry, 1558–1625* (Cork: Cork University Press, 1998).

[5] Charles McNeill (ed.), 'Fitzwilliam Manuscripts at Milton, England', *Analecta Hibernica*, 4 (1932): 300.

[6] Hans Claude Hamilton (ed.), *CSP Ireland, 1509–1573* (London: Her Majesty's Public Record Office, 1860), 356.

[7] Pádraig Ó Macháin, 'Two Nugent Manuscripts: The Nugent *duanaire* and Queen Elizabeth's Primer', *Ríocht na Midhe*, 23 (2012), 121–42.

reforming the 'wild' Irish.[8] It is possibly not entirely coincidental that Humphrey's former student, Sir William Herbert, arranged for the translation into Irish of the Lord's Prayer, the Ten Commandments, and the Articles of Faith shortly after arriving in 1587 at the Kerry estate granted him under the auspices of the Munster plantation.[9] There is no indication that these translations were printed, and their apparent scribal and oral dissemination serves as a corrective to assumptions of the communicative primacy of the printed word in Ireland as elsewhere in early modern Europe.

The first printed book in Gaelic was published in Scotland in 1567, reflecting both the initially limited impact of the Reformation in Ireland and the comparatively late launch of print technology in Ireland as a result of unfavourable cultural, demographic, political, and economic factors.[10] John Carswell (c.1522–72), superintendent of Argyll and Bishop of the Isles, translated the Book of Common Order under the title *Foirm na n-urrnuidheadh*. A Gaelic-speaking native of Argyll, Carswell was an ecclesiastical and political supporter of the powerful Campbell dynasty, Earls of Argyll, whose early commitment to religious reform enabled him to rise steadily within the ranks of the church in Scotland.[11] The Book of Common Order, first printed in Edinburgh in 1564, was a revised version of the Geneva Book, also known as John Knox's Liturgy, which had been printed in Edinburgh in 1562.[12] Although Carswell's translation was largely faithful to the 1564 edition, his confident deployment of classical literary Irish, commonly used by the Gaelic learned elites of late medieval Ireland and Scotland, is significant for its presentation of an innovative religious message by means of an authoritative and prestigious linguistic medium. Carswell appended a highly informative poem in bardic metre to his translation. Addressed to the book, this composition of five quatrains summarizes Carswell's ambitions for the work and in its allusion to the Gaelic bardic cohort touches on questions of cultural authority which were also critical considerations in Protestant efforts to provide the scriptures in Irish.

The volume is advised first to present itself to Archibald Campbell (c.1530–75), Earl of Argyll, and subsequently to tour Scotland. Since it will serve no practical function in England, the book must then travel overseas to circulate in Ireland where it is advised to anticipate hostility from the friars. With a strategic eye to the future, the book is encouraged to engage intimately with poets and chroniclers who respect intellectual integrity and truth.[13] Carswell's acknowledgement of the cultural authority of the learned elite is significant in so far as it envisages implicit legitimation of evangelical objectives and teaching

---

[8] John Nichols (ed.), *The Progresses and Public Processions of Queen Elizabeth* (London: John Nichols, 1823), i. 598; William Herbert, *Croftus sive de Hibernia liber*, ed. Arthur Keaveney and John A. Madden (Dublin: Irish Manuscripts Commission, 1992), 160–1; Felicity Heal, 'Mediating the Word: Language and Dialects in the British and Irish Reformations', *Journal of Ecclesiastical History*, 56 (2005): 277–8.

[9] Hans Claude Hamilton (ed.), *CSP Ireland, 1586–1588, July* (London: Her Majesty's Public Record Office, 1877), 331, 533; Brian Ó Cuív, *Irish Dialects and Irish-Speaking Districts* (Dublin: Dublin Institute for Advanced Studies, 1971), 13–14; Heal, 'Mediating the Word', 278.

[10] Niall Ó Ciosáin, 'Print and Irish, 1570–1900: An Exception among the Celtic Languages?' *Radharc: A Journal of Irish and Irish-American Studies*, 5–7 (2004–6): 73–106.

[11] Donald E. Meek, 'The Reformation and Gaelic Culture: Perspectives on Patronage, Language and Literature in John Carswell's Translation of "The Book of Common Order"', in James Kirk (ed.), *The Church in the Highlands* (Edinburgh: Scottish Church History Society, 1998), 37–62.

[12] *Foirm na n-urrnuidheadh: John Carswell's Gaelic Translation of the Book of Common Order*, ed. R. L. Thomson (Edinburgh: Scottish Gaelic Texts Society, 1970), 59.

[13] *Foirm na n-urrnuidheadh*, 13.

by means of mutual recognition and engagement. Moreover, in the case of Ireland, the essentially external intrusion of the Reformation as the religious ancillary of the Tudor programme of consolidation rendered the need for some degree of domestic ideological validation even more acute. As with Carswell previously, a handful of Irish-born and Cambridge-educated clergymen confronted a strategic and practical challenge in regard to the presentation of the message of reform in a Gaelic linguistic and cultural format. This challenge became even more pronounced as the personnel and culture of the established church became increasingly anglocentric towards the close of the sixteenth century. Indeed, the Protestant Church in Ireland was in many respects an English colonial phenomenon by the 1620s in terms of its cultural and linguistic orientation, clerical personnel, and membership.[14] Four Irish evangelicals who undertook their theological formation in Cambridge from the 1560s to the 1580s, namely, Seaán Ó Cearnaigh, Nicholas Walsh, Fearganainm Ó Domhnalláin, and Uilliam Ó Domhnuill, were evidently conscious both of the practical challenge of communicating devotional and doctrinal innovation in a manner intelligible to the Gaelic Irish as well as responding to a core precept of the Reformation: the provision of the scriptures in the local vernacular.

Ó Cearnaigh is best known for his central role in the publication of the first book printed in the Irish language in Ireland. He was born around 1545 and was possibly a native of Leyney in Sligo. It has been suggested that he was initially educated at a bardic school, on the basis of a short description of Irish letters included in his 1571 catechism.[15] Awarded a sizarship at Magdalene College in 1561, he graduated from Cambridge with a BA degree in 1565. Having taken holy orders, Ó Cearnaigh was treasurer of St Patrick's Cathedral in Dublin when he was reimbursed in October 1570 by the authorities for expenses (£22 13s 4d) defrayed by him in relation to the manufacture of an Irish type and the printing of 200 catechisms in Irish.[16] It has been proposed that the appearance of Carswell's *Foirm na n-urrnuidheadh* in 1567 raised the possibility of the dissemination of Calvinist doctrine in Ireland and that this unwelcome prospect encouraged the authorities in Dublin to expedite the publication of devotional material in Irish.[17] Therefore, it may not be a coincidence that Ó Cearnaigh's catechism was printed just four years later in June 1571 with the financial support of alderman John Ussher, a member of an old Dublin merchant family and fervent evangelical.[18]

The *Aibidil* is a concise primer of religion and consists of an epistle, an overview of the Gaelic alphabet, a catechism which is essentially a translation of the equivalent text in the Book of Common Prayer as revised in 1559, ten prayers (four of which are based on texts in

[14] Aidan Clarke, 'Varieties of Uniformity: The First Century of the Church of Ireland', in W. J. Sheils and Diana Wood (eds), *The Churches, Ireland and the Irish* (Oxford: Basil Blackwell, 1989), 117–19; Colm Lennon and Ciaran Diamond, 'The Ministry of the Church of Ireland, 1536–1636', in T. C. Barnard and W. G. Neely (eds), *The Clergy of the Church of Ireland 1000–2000: Messengers, Watchmen and Stewards* (Dublin: Four Courts Press, 2006), 46.

[15] *Aibidil Gaoidheilge & Caiticiosma: Seaán Ó Cearnaigh's Irish Primer of Religion Published in 1571*, ed. Brian Ó Cuív (Dublin: Dublin Institute for Advanced Studies, 1994), 3–4.

[16] Ó Cearnaigh was reimbursed for the 'full furnishing of stamps, formes and "matrises" necessary for the printing in the Irish tongue of CC (200) catechisms': McNeill (ed.), 'Fitzwilliam Manuscripts', 300.

[17] Nicholas Williams, *I bprionta i leabhar: na protastúin agus prós na Gaeilge 1567–1724* (Dublin: An Clóchomhar, 1986), 21.

[18] *Aibidil*, 6; William Ball Wright, *The Ussher Memoirs; or Genealogical Memoirs of the Ussher Families in Ireland* (Dublin: Sealy, Bryers & Walker, 1889), 121–6; Colm Lennon, *The Lords of Dublin in the Age of Reformation* (Blackrock, Co. Dublin: Irish Academic Press, 1989), 137.

Carswell's book), and a translation of a proclamation on the principles of religion promulgated by Lord Deputy Sir Henry Sidney at Dublin in 1566. It concludes with a number of Irish translations of biblical quotations and details of corrigenda.[19] Unlike Carswell's volume which was produced using a roman font, the 1571 catechism was printed using a hybrid font consisting of roman and distinctively Gaelic letters (known by later scholars as Queen Elizabeth's Irish type) which was designed by someone with a knowledge of Irish scribal conventions.[20] The symbolic and practical implications of such visual and material acknowledgement of Gaelic cultural heritage complemented Ó Cearnaigh's acquiescence in the literary authority of the bardic cohort in his short commentary on the Gaelic alphabet. Further manifestation of such deference to Irish scholarship is evident in the selection of a devotional bardic poem by the fifteenth-century Franciscan Pilib Bocht Ó hUiginn (d. 1487) for inclusion on a broadsheet from 1571, which is usually considered a printer's trial piece undertaken in advance of printing the catechism.[21] Of course, it is also possible that this item was intended as an inaugural publication in a series of religious broadsheets which might be produced inexpensively and distributed easily.

The publication of the 1571 catechism is relevant to the composite history of the Irish Bible in so far as it was evidently intended as a preliminary stage in a broader programme of translation culminating in the provision of the scriptures in Irish. Crucially, it also entailed the launch of the technology, the Gaelic font in particular, required for hand-press printing. It is not known who served as pressmen for the project nor who designed and cut the hybrid Gaelic type used to print the catechism, the New Testament in 1602/3, the Irish Book of Common Prayer in 1608 (Figure 21.1), and other texts in Irish printed as late as 1652. Since it is unlikely that the university-educated Ó Cearnaigh had the technical expertise necessary to design and produce the font, it is possible that either Humphrey Powell or William Kearney, the only printers recorded as working in Dublin in the sixteenth century, played a role in its manufacture.

Unlike Powell, who is remembered for printing the English Book of Common Prayer in Dublin in 1551, Kearney's capacity in printing Gaelic material is attested. He was described as a kinsman of Ó Cearnaigh in a 1587 letter from the Privy Council to the Lord Deputy and Council in Dublin and it was also stated in this letter that he had a copy of an Irish translation of the New Testament by Ó Cearnaigh and Nicholas Walsh in his possession. Kearney was described as having mastered the art of printing over the previous fourteen years both in London and on the continent. The Privy Council communication claimed also that the Gaelic New Testament remained unprinted because of a lack of suitable Irish characters and for want of skilled printers versed in the language. Kearney, subject to the provision of funding, was ready to make available his knowledge of both printing and the Irish language to expedite the publication of the Gaelic New Testament.[22] The reference to Kearney's printing

[19] *Aibidil*, 11–16; Tomás de Bhaldraithe, 'Leabhar Charswell in Éirinn', *Éigse*, 9 (1958): 61–7.

[20] Dermot McGuinne, *Irish Type Design: A History of Printing Types in the Irish Character* (Blackrock, Co. Dublin: Irish Academic Press, 1992): 4–22; *Aibidil*, 4.

[21] *Aibidil*, 1, 191.

[22] John Roche Dasent (ed.), *Acts of the Privy Council of England*, NS 15 (*A.D. 1587–1588*) (London: Her Majesty's Stationery Office, 1897), 201–2; E. R. McC. Dix, 'William Kearney, the Second Earliest Known Printer in Dublin', *Proceedings of the Royal Irish Academy*, 28 (1910): 157–61; D. B. Quinn, 'John Denton Desires William Kearney to Print Books for Use in Down, *circa* 1588: A Sidelight on Printing in Ireland', *Irish Booklore*, 3 (1977): 87–90; M. Pollard, *Dublin's Trade in Books 1550–1800* (Oxford: Clarendon Press, 1989), 2; McGuinne, *Irish Type Design*, 4–22.

FIGURE 21.1 Title-page, William Daniel, *Leabhar na nurnaightheadh gcomhchoidchiond agus mheinisdraldachda na Sacrameinteadh* [Irish Book of Common Prayer] (Dublin, 1608). York Minster Library: OL; XI.G.13/2.

experience of fourteen years' duration, dating back to c.1573, would not preclude him from having assisted, perhaps as an apprentice, in the printing of the catechism two years previously and it is possible that he subsequently left Ireland to pursue his craft in London and on the continent.

Ó Cearnaigh, in his prefatory epistle to the reader in the *Aibidil*, emphasized his commitment to further religious publications in Irish.[23] William Kearney's claim in 1587 that he possessed a copy of the Irish New Testament indicates that Ó Cearnaigh continued his programme of translation in collaboration with Nicholas Walsh. Like his fellow translator, Walsh had studied at Magdalene in Cambridge and was in 1571/2 appointed Chancellor of St Patrick's Cathedral in Dublin and Bishop of Ossory in 1577/8. It was perhaps when they worked together at St Patrick's that they embarked on the translation of the New Testament.[24] Certainly, their capacity to preach in Irish was recognized by the authorities in 1572 when Ó Cearnaigh was proposed as candidate for the western archbishopric of Tuam and Walsh was proposed for the bishopric of Kilmacdaugh within the same archdiocese.[25] However, it seems unlikely that they completed the translation fully, contrary to the assertion in the 1587 Privy Council letter that William Kearney was in possession of a manuscript copy of the Irish New Testament. It is known that Ó Cearnaigh served as treasurer of St Patrick's up to 1578 at least and it is assumed that he was dead by 1587.[26] Walsh was murdered in his house in Kilkenny in 1585 by an individual he had accused of adultery and against whom he had launched a court case to recover episcopal lands.[27] The demise of both men resulted in the abandonment of the Gaelic New Testament project until its revival in the mid-1590s by two other Irish graduates of Cambridge, Fearganainm Ó Domhnalláin and Uilliam Ó Domhnuill.

II. THE IRISH NEW TESTAMENT (1602)

Notwithstanding its protracted and at times uncertain gestation, the Irish New Testament was finally published in Dublin in 1602 with financial support from Sir William Ussher, Clerk of the Council and son of John Ussher who had subvented the publication of Ó Cearnaigh's catechism.[28] The work was printed in folio by John Franckton in Ussher's house on Bridgefoot Street in Dublin. In his epistle dedicatory to James VI of Scotland and I of England, composed after the death of Queen Elizabeth on 23 March 1603 and prefixed to printed copies of the work which he had originally planned to present to the Queen in person at London, Uilliam Ó Domhnuill acknowledged the contribution of several individuals

---

[23] *Aibidil*, 55.

[24] Richard Butler (ed.), *The Annals of Ireland* (Dublin: Irish Archaeological Society, 1849), 41.

[25] Hamilton, *CSP Ireland, 1509–1573*, 481, 486.

[26] Hugh Jackson Lawlor, *The Fasti of St Patrick's, Dublin* (Dundalk: W. Tempest, 1930), 70.

[27] Cosslett Quin, 'Nicholas Walsh and his Friends: A Forgotten Chapter in the Irish Reformation', *Journal of the Butler Society*, 2 (1984): 294–8; Anthony M. McCormack and Terry Clavin, 'Walsh, Nicholas (Nicolás Bhailis) (1538?–1585)', in McGuire and Quinn, *Dictionary of Irish Biography*, ix. 751.

[28] An early nineteenth-century source claimed that 500 copies of the Irish New Testament were printed: Christopher Anderson, *Historical Sketches of the Native Irish and their Descendants* (Edinburgh: Oliver & Boyd, 1828), 183.

to the translation and described how he had managed the project to completion and publication.

A native of Kilkenny, Ó Domhnuill was educated at Emmanuel College where he was awarded an MA in 1593. An early scholar and fellow of Trinity College, which was founded in 1592 to promote religious and political conformity in Ireland, Ó Domhnuill was dispatched by the Lord Deputy and his Council in the mid-1590s to Galway to preach the Gospel to the town's inhabitants in both the Irish and English languages.[29] Writing to Lord Burghley in 1596, he reported that, while he had been initially hopeful of success, his mission in Galway had quickly encountered entrenched resistance which he attributed to the malevolence of local Catholic clergy. However, his response to the hostile reception accorded him seems disingenuous in light of his pride in the destruction of 'idols' in the town.[30]

Although there is no reason to doubt the sincerity of his evangelical fervour, especially given the singularity of his achievement in seeing the New Testament through the press, it is tempting to speculate that Ó Domhnuill's commitment to the translation was partly motivated by a desire to escape Galway for a more congenial professional appointment. Indeed, his position as a preacher to the army in Ireland and the fact that he is known to have preached before Lord Deputy Russell suggests that Ó Domhnuill was ambitious to advance in the crown's service.[31] In any case, by 1602 he had assumed the Treasurership of St Patrick's Cathedral in Dublin and it seems likely that his elevation was in part or in whole by way of recognition for his work in relation to the publication of the New Testament.[32] Richard Boyle, later created Earl of Cork, an English settler in Ireland distinguished by his avidity for land, wealth, and influence, provided Ó Domhnuill with a letter of introduction to Sir Robert Cecil in late 1602 informing him of the bearer's translation of the New Testament and his journey to London to present it to the Queen. Boyle also claimed that he had provided Ó Domhnuill with a prebend at St Patrick's which was in his gift and that this was the Irishman's sole source of financial support.[33]

Ó Domhnuill sketched a brief history of the Irish translation of the New Testament in both the epistle dedicatory and in his address to the reader ('Do chum an leughthora') which he composed in Irish unlike the epistle for James I in English.[34] In the epistle addressed to James, Ó Domhnuill praised the late Queen's interest in making the Gospel available to the Irish in their own language, especially through her support for the provision of 'Irish characters and other instrumentes for the presse, in hope that God in mercy would raise up some to translate the Newe Testament into their mother tongue'.[35] He summarized previous

[29] K. W. Nicholls, *The Irish Fiants of the Tudor Sovereigns* (Dublin: Éamonn de Búrca, 1994), iii, fiant 5718; Alan Ford, *The Protestant Reformation in Ireland, 1590–1641* (Dublin: Four Courts Press, 1997), 106–7.

[30] Ernest George Atkinson (ed.), *CSP Ireland, 1596, July–1597, December* (London: Her Majesty's Stationery Office, 1893), 121.

[31] J. S. Brewer and William Bullen (eds), *Calendar of the Carew Manuscripts, Preserved in the Archiepiscopal Library at Lambeth: 1589–1600* (London: Longmans, Green, & Co., 1869), 241; Ernest George Atkinson (ed.), *CSP Ireland, 1599, April–1600, February* (London: Her Majesty's Stationery Office, 1899), 360.

[32] Lawlor, *Fasti of St Patrick's, Dublin*, 71.

[33] Alexander B. Grosart (ed.), *The Lismore Papers (Second Series) viz. Selections from the Private and Public (or State) Correspondence of Sir Richard Boyle, First and Great Earl of Cork* (London: Chiswick Press, 1887), i. 39–40.

[34] Marc Caball, 'Gaelic and Protestant: A Case Study in Early Modern Self-Fashioning, 1567–1608', *Proceedings of the Royal Irish Academy*, 110 (2010): 191–215.

[35] *Tiomna Nuadh*, tr. Uilliam Ó Domhnuill (Dublin, 1602), 1ᵛ.

efforts to translate the New Testament by noting that Nicholas Walsh, Bishop of Ossory, Seaán Ó Cearnaigh, and Fearganainm Ó Domhnalláin (d. c.1609), Archbishop of Tuam, had successively worked on the translation. However, their endeavours 'were notwithstanding untimely cut off in Gods secret judgement' and the full weight of the task fell on Ó Domhnuill. He proceeded to outline how he had translated directly from the original Greek text or *Textus Receptus* in as faithful a fashion as possible.[36] Moreover, further to the reference to his support on the work's title-page, William Ussher who 'following the steps of his religious father, willingly undertooke the greatest part of the charges of this impression' is once more acknowledged for his largesse.[37]

In the address in Irish to the reader, Ó Domhnuill provides a more detailed account of the long-awaited translation's genesis and progress. Mentioning previous efforts by Ó Cearnaigh, Walsh, and Ó Domhnalláin, Ó Domhnuill elaborates on the preceding text in English by acknowledging the contribution of the latter in particular and that of two praise poets to the project.[38] Ó Domhnalláin who was educated at Cambridge was a member of a south-east Galway bardic family some of whose members embraced Protestantism.[39] On returning to Ireland, he served as a divine in the Diocese of Ossory and, in due course, he was appointed coadjutor to the elderly Archbishop of Tuam whom he succeeded in 1595. In the writ of his appointment to Tuam, it was noted that Ó Domhnalláin had been assiduous in his efforts to translate to Irish both the New Testament and the Book of Common Prayer.[40] He and Ó Domhnuill were assisted in their work on the New Testament by the poet Maoilín Óg Mac Bruaideadha who was described as an expert in the Irish language at Trinity College ('duine iúlmhar sa teanguidh Ghaoidheilge, sa gcoláisde nuádh láimh ré Baile Átha Cliath'). Apparently, by 1597 the Gospels as far as the sixth chapter of St Luke had been typeset with the financial support of Sir Richard Bingham, President of Connaught.[41] The rest of the Gospel of St Luke and the Gospel of St John were still in manuscript form. The texts initially translated were printed in Trinity College in the mid-1590s by William Kearney, who had returned home around 1592 with a warrant from the authorities to travel to Ireland to print Bibles.[42] The evidence of Protestant works printed by Kearney in London between 1590 and 1592 suggests that he was a committed evangelical.[43] With

---

[36] Fearghus Ó Fearghail has argued persuasively that the translators worked from the Greek text of the New Testament as well as being influenced by the 1556 Latin translation of Theodore Beza and the 1557 Geneva English translation: 'The Irish New Testament of 1602 in its European Context', *Proceedings of the Irish Biblical Association*, 31 (2008): 90–101. Ó Domhnuill remained informed of developments in biblical translation in England after the publication of the Gaelic New Testament. David Norton, *The King James Bible: A Short History from Tyndale to Today* (Cambridge: Cambridge University Press, 2011), 91.

[37] *Tiomna Nuadh*, 2ʳ.

[38] *Tiomna Nuadh*, 'Do chum an leughthora'.

[39] Nicholas Canny, 'Why the Reformation Failed in Ireland: Une question mal posée', *The Journal of Ecclesiastical History*, 30 (1979): 442.

[40] James Morrin (ed.), *Calendar of the Patent and Close Rolls of Chancery in Ireland*, ii (Dublin and London: Her Majesty's Stationery Office, 1862), 401.

[41] Archbishop Loftus reported to Burghley in 1595 that Ó Domhnalláin had translated the Irish New Testament and that it was being printed. Hans Claude Hamilton (ed.), *CSP Ireland, 1592, October–1596, June* (London: Her Majesty's Stationery Office, 1890), 308.

[42] John Roche Dasent (ed.), *Acts of the Privy Council of England*, ns 22, *A.D. 1591–2* (London: Her Majesty's Stationery Office, 1901), 26; E. R. McC. Dix, *Printing in Dublin Prior to 1601* (Dublin: At the Sign of the Three Candles, 1932 edn), 27–31.

[43] For instance, Kearney printed work by Henry Smith (d. 1591), clergyman and renowned preacher, and Hugh Broughton (d. 1612), divine and Hebraist.

the assistance of the poet Domhnall Óg Ó hUiginn in matters of Irish usage and style, Uilliam Ó Domhnuill completed the translation subsequent to Ó Domhnalláin's retirement from the project in the mid-1590s to take up his appointment as Archbishop of Tuam.[44]

The epistle in English to the monarch in Whitehall and the preface to the reader in Irish signed respectively 'William Daniell' and 'Uilliam O Domhnuill' are suggestive of the cultural and religious ambivalence which characterized the entire Reformation project in Ireland. Given the hostility of the English authorities in Ireland to the status and dynastic influence of Gaelic praise poets, it is significant that neither Mac Bruaideadha nor Ó hUiginn are mentioned in the epistle to James which was evidently intended for consumption by an establishment readership in London and Dublin. A prayer in Irish which is placed at the end of the translation strikes both an intimate and candid note in attributing Irish misfortune to divine punishment for contemporary and ancestral sin. Providentially, scripture now offered a pathway to temporal beneficence and eternal salvation.[45] However, notwithstanding the tensions inherent in the production of a translation by Gaelic Irishmen which was sponsored by the crown, the publication of the New Testament in Irish, as in other European vernacular languages, was a radical act of religious and cultural agency.

The printing of the work in Dublin was considered a major logistical and technological challenge.[46] Osborn Bergin faulted Ó Domhnuill and Ó hUiginn for a lack of consistency in their observation of the orthographic and stylistic conventions of learned classical Irish and the supposedly intrusive influence of the original Greek on the translation. More recently, Nicholas Williams has praised its natural and fluent style.[47] Although clearly mindful of the cultural authority of poets in Gaelic society, Ó Domhnuill was surely less concerned to comply with the exacting linguistic standards of the Gaelic learned elite than with communicating the divine word as widely and effectively as possible. Indeed, both Ó Domhnuill and Ó hUiginn may have consciously attempted to cultivate a somewhat more accessible style untrammelled by prescriptive usage. Appointed Archbishop of Tuam in 1609, Uilliam Ó Domhnuill's Puritan beliefs mellowed over the years and he died in disillusioned obscurity in 1628.[48] He was in many respects Gaelic Ireland's equivalent to the great English biblical translator and scholar, William Tyndale (d. 1536). However, the effective failure of the Reformation to implant itself other than superficially in Irish soil means that Ó Domhnuill's name and extraordinary achievement in respect of the Irish New Testament and the Gaelic Book of Common Prayer (1608) have gone largely unrecognized in the narrative of Ireland's cultural history.[49]

---

[44] Williams, *I bprionta*, 30; McGuinne, *Irish Type Design*, 14.

[45] *Tiomna Nuadh*, 215.

[46] John Rider, *A Friendly Caveat to Irelands Catholickes* (Dublin, 1602), A4ʳ.

[47] William Bell and N. D. Emerson (eds), *The Church of Ireland A.D. 432–1932* (Dublin: Church of Ireland Printing and Publishing Co., 1932), 162–3; Williams, *I bprionta*, 34.

[48] British Library, Sloane MS 3827, fol. 69ʳ⁻ᵛ (William, Archbishop of Tuam to Lord Deputy Falkland, 27 Feb. 1625); John Lynch, *The Portrait of a Pious Bishop; or, the Life and Death of the Most Reverend Francis Kirwan, Bishop of Killala*, tr. C. P. Meehan (Dublin: James Duffy, 1848), 69–71; Arthur Vicars (ed.), *Index to the Prerogative Wills of Ireland, 1536–1810* (Dublin: Edward Ponsonby, 1897), 122. For Ó Domhnuill's funeral entry as recorded by Ulster's Office, see British Library, Additional MS 4820, fol. 92ʳ; National Library of Ireland, MS GO 68, fol. 80.

[49] Fearghus Ó Fearghail, 'Uilliam Ó Domhnaill's Irish Version of the *Book of Common Prayer* (1608) and his Old Testament Translations into Irish', *Proceedings of the Irish Biblical Association*, 32 (2009): 99–130.

III. WILLIAM BEDELL AND THE IRISH TRANSLATION OF THE OLD TESTAMENT

Although the Irish Old Testament was published in 1685, the genesis of the translation dated as far back as the late 1620s. William Bedell, whose experience as chaplain during the years 1607–10/11 to Sir Henry Wotton, English ambassador to Venice, refined his appreciation of cultural and linguistic diversity, conceived and funded the project for the Irish translation of the Old Testament. While in Venice, Bedell had learned Italian as well as taking lessons in Hebrew in the Venetian ghetto from the famous Jewish scholar, Leon Modena.[50] Anticipating his later work among Irish speakers, Bedell translated the prayer book and other devotional works into Italian for the benefit of friends and those disposed to convert to Protestantism. Somewhat unexpectedly, Bedell, who had ministered in relative obscurity in East Anglia after his return from Venice, was appointed Provost of Trinity College Dublin in 1627. Spending just two years at Trinity, during which period he promoted lectures and prayers in the Irish language at the college, Bedell was appointed to the combined bishoprics of Kilmore and Ardagh in 1629. Resigning Ardagh in 1632 in line with his opposition to pluralism, Bedell is best remembered in the historical record for his sympathetic attitude to the Gaelic Irish of Kilmore and for his sponsorship of the Irish Old Testament which was emblematic of a relatively benign and enlightened approach to the evangelization of the Gaelic Irish.

As early as 1628, Bedell had enlisted the expertise of Muircheartach Ó Cionga, a member of a midlands bardic family, first to translate the Psalms and afterwards the rest of the Old Testament and Apocrypha. Bedell later ordained Ó Cionga and provided him with a living in Kilmore Diocese. In 1630, Bedell was contemplating printing the Psalter and he noted that he had been advised by James Nangle, also ordained a clergyman in Kilmore, to publish a prose rather than metrical translation of the Psalms. By 1634, Bedell reported that the translation of the Old Testament was in hand and that he was having a fair copy of the text compiled.[51] The Irish translation was made from the King James Bible of 1611 and complemented by revisions to the text made by Bedell based on comparative readings of the original Hebrew text, the Septuagint, and Giovanni Diodati's Italian translation of the Bible.[52] However, the contribution of Ó Cionga was central to the translation process. Bedell, writing in 1637 credited him with having 'translated the psalms into Irish first and after all the Old Testament'.[53]

[50] Marc Caball, '"Solid Divine and Worthy Scholar": William Bedell, Venice and Gaelic Culture', in James Kelly and Ciarán Mac Murchaidh (eds), *Irish and English: Essays on the Irish Linguistic and Cultural Frontier, 1600–1900* (Dublin: Four Courts Press, 2012), 43–57.

[51] Nicholas Bernard, *Certain Discourses ... unto Which is Added a Character of Bishop Bedel* (London, 1659), 352; Henry Jones, *A Sermon of Antichrist, Preached at Christ-Church, Dublin, Novemb. 12. 1676* (London, 1686), unpaginated epistle dedicatory; Pádraig de Brún and Máire Herbert, *Catalogue of Irish Manuscripts in Cambridge Libraries* (Cambridge: Cambridge University Press, 1986), 118–19.

[52] Terence McCaughey, *Dr. Bedell and Mr. King: The Making of the Irish Bible* (Dublin: Dublin Institute for Advanced Studies, 2001), 2–3.

[53] E. S. Shuckburgh (ed.), *Two Biographies of William Bedell* (Cambridge: Cambridge University Press, 1902), 342; Brendan Scott, 'Accusations against Murtagh King, 1638', *Archivium Hibernicum*, 65 (2012): 76–81.

With a view to printing the translation, Bedell apparently decided to have a new Irish type prepared and, according to his son-in-law and biographer Alexander Clogie, had 'all things made ready for the carrying on so good a work'.[54] However, the translation was not printed. A manuscript copy survived the conflagration of the 1641 rising, when Bedell's house was occupied by rebels, thanks apparently to the intervention of Denis Sheridan, a local man ordained by Bedell, who managed to salvage some of the bishop's books and papers.[55] Bedell died of fever in Sheridan's house in early 1642. The manuscript was acquired by Bedell's executor, Henry Jones, Dean of Kilmore (1637) and Bishop of Clogher (1645), possibly from Sheridan or his son Thomas, later Bishop of Kilmore and godson of Bedell.

IV. ROBERT BOYLE AND THE IRISH NEW TESTAMENT (1681) AND OLD TESTAMENT (1685)

The republication of Ó Domhnuill's New Testament in 1681 and the publication of Bedell's Old Testament in 1685 were made possible by the financial support and evangelical commitment of Robert Boyle (1627–91), a remarkable figure in seventeenth-century new science. Son of Richard Boyle, first Earl of Cork, Robert was born at Lismore castle in County Waterford and left Ireland permanently (with the exception of a sojourn on the island between 1652 and 1654) in 1635 to attend Eton. Deeply pious from an early age, Boyle developed an interest in the biblical languages and scholarship relating to biblical and classical history in the years around 1650. He also became actively involved with missionary projects and, convinced of the power of print, he contributed financially to the publication of a Turkish New Testament and catechism as well as supporting the evangelization of North American Indians.[56] In 1662, for instance, he was appointed governor of the Company for the Propagation of the Gospel in New England. A grant to Boyle from Charles II of impropriations of one-time monastic lands in Ireland, possibly originally intended to support his scientific research, was instead used by him to support the church in Ireland and missionary programmes in New England. Boyle's interest in making devotional material available in Irish is evident in his possession of a list of objectives drafted in 1675 by Sir William Petty that were 'fit to be done in the Kingdom of Ireland', including the publication of Irish translations of the Bible and Book of Common Prayer.[57]

[54] Shuckburgh, *Two Biographies*, 135.

[55] It has been suggested that the presence of interlinear corrections and variants in the surviving 3-volume manuscript (vols 1–2 [Genesis to the Song of Songs] are in Marsh's Library, Dublin, and vol. 3 [Prophets and Apocrypha] is in Cambridge University Library) indicate that it is not Bedell's fair copy and the dominant hand may be that of Ó Cionga or Denis Sheridan. De Brún and Herbert, *Catalogue*, 120.

[56] Miles Ogborn, *Indian Ink: Script and Print in the Making of the English East India Company* (Chicago: University of Chicago Press, 2007), 18; Michael Hunter, 'Robert Boyle and the Uses of Print', in Danielle Westerhof (ed.), *The Alchemy of Medicine and Print: The Edward Worth Library, Dublin* (Dublin: Four Courts Press, 2010), 110–24. On the Bible and English attitudes to conversion, see the chapter by Helen Smith in this volume.

[57] R. E. W. Maddison, 'Robert Boyle and the Irish Bible', *John Rylands Library Bulletin*, 41 (1958): 81–2; Michael Hunter, 'Robert Boyle, Narcissus Marsh and the Anglo-Irish Intellectual Scene in the Late Seventeenth Century', in Muriel McCarthy and Ann Simmons (eds), *The Making of Marsh's Library: Learning, Politics and Religion in Ireland, 1650–1750* (Dublin: Four Courts Press, 2004): 61.

With a view initially to having the 1602 New Testament reprinted, Boyle engaged the assistance of Andrew Sall (d. 1682), member of a Tipperary Old English family and a former Jesuit, who, encouraged by Thomas Price, Church of Ireland Archbishop of Cashel, controversially converted to Anglicanism in 1674. Sall lived in Oxford between 1675 and 1680 where he enjoyed the patronage of John Fell, Bishop of Oxford and a former Dean of Christ Church. Fell, who in his capacity as Vice-Chancellor of Oxford revived its university press, had also collaborated with Boyle on the publication of the Gospels and the Acts of the Apostles in Malay and he may have introduced Sall to Boyle. In any case, Sall was both committed to worship in the vernacular and an Irish speaker who was anxious to assist Boyle with the publication of religious texts in that language.[58]

By 1680, Sall was in Dublin seeking support from the influential for Boyle's plans. The recently appointed Provost of Trinity, Narcissus Marsh (1638–1713), a distinguished scholar immersed in Oriental and Classical languages, and Henry Jones, now Bishop of Meath, enthusiastically supported the initiative. However, as the project developed it became apparent that no Irish printing type was available. Jones alleged, possibly fancifully, that the Queen Elizabeth type had been spirited away to the continent by Jesuits.[59] Accordingly, Boyle funded the casting of a new font of Irish type, produced by the printer and globe maker Joseph Moxon in London and modelled on the type produced by the Irish Franciscans in Louvain.[60] The Moxon Irish type was first used in 1680 to print a short catechism, *An teagasg Criosduighe*. Sponsored by Boyle and his sister Katherine Jones, Viscountess Ranelagh, this slim octavo volume was printed by Robert Everingham in London.[61] A translation of the catechism from the Book of Common Prayer, it consists of fourteen pages containing a concise Gaelic grammar and the fundamentals of the faith. Probably a trial piece in advance of printing the New Testament the following year, the work was possibly seen through the press in London by the obscure Hugh O'Reilly, who also prepared the copy and supervised the printing of the New Testament in quarto by Everingham.[62]

Sall, in his preface to the New Testament, paid a warm tribute to Boyle's generous support for the publication of 500 copies and indicated that it was also planned to publish imminently the Irish Old Testament and other pious works. Sall urged those able to do so to read the holy book frequently. Clergymen were requested to read it aloud to their Irish-speaking congregations, while pious fathers were instructed to have it read to their households 'in lieu of Romances, and other idle or noisom Divertisements'. Moreover, foreigners in Ireland who wished to learn the country's language could do so by comparing the Irish New Testament with the equivalent in their own language. Finally, it was incumbent on those student

[58]   Andrew Sall, *A Sermon Preached at Christ-Church in Dublin, before the Lord Lieutenant and Council, the Fifth Day of July, 1674* (Dublin, 1674), preface, 94–101; Andrew Breeze, 'Andrew Sall (†1682), Andrew Sall (†1686), and the Irish Bible', *Éigse*, 28 (1994–5): 100–2; Terence P. McCaughey, 'Andrew Sall (1624–82): Textual Editor and Facilitator of the Irish Translation of the Old Testament', in Cathal G. Ó Háinle and Donald E. Meek (eds), *Léann na Tríonóide Trinity Irish Studies* (Dublin: School of Irish, Trinity College, 2004), 167.

[59]   Maddison, 'Robert Boyle', 83–4.

[60]   Adrian Johns, *The Nature of the Book: Print and Knowledge in the Making* (Chicago: University of Chicago Press, 1998), 79–83.

[61]   Betsey Taylor Fitzsimon, 'Conversion, the Bible and the Irish Language: The Correspondence of Lady Ranelagh and Bishop Dopping', in Michael Brown, Charles Ivar McGrath, and Thomas P. Power (eds), *Converts and Conversion in Ireland, 1650–1850* (Dublin: Four Courts Press, 2005), 157–82.

[62]   McGuinne, *Irish Type Design*, 52–3. Regarding O'Reilly see de Brún and Herbert, *Catalogue*, 122.

divines seeking to minister in Ireland 'to procure such Knowledge in the Language of the Natives, as may enable them to help and instruct the Souls committed to their Charge, and of which they are to give an Account to God'. Knowledge of Irish on the part of the clergy was essential as there were 'many Parishes, Baronies, and whole Counties, in which the far greater number of the Common People do understand no other Language but Irish'.[63] Sall's preface was translated to Irish by O'Reilly and was printed directly following the original English text. Nicholas Williams has demonstrated that O'Reilly also revised Ó Domhnuill's text in matters of vocabulary and spelling, and in order to align the translation to the text of the King James Bible of 1611.[64]

Henry Jones provided Sall with the surviving manuscript of Bedell's Old Testament in 1681. Sall in a letter to Boyle described the manuscript as a 'confused heap, pitifully defaced and broken' and mentioned that he was being assisted in reordering it correctly by the Trinity Irish lecturer, Pól Ó hUiginn.[65] As the transcription process progressed, it also became evident that some revision of the Irish text was necessary. Criticism of the copy was a collaborative affair and involved Sall, Ó hUiginn, Marsh, and a divine called Mullan, possibly the John Mullan who was later appointed to a benefice in the Diocese of Ossory. The work of transcription was undertaken by the Gaelic scribe Uilliam Ó Duinnín, first in Sall's house and later Marsh arranged to have a room allocated him in Trinity. The death of Sall in April 1682 slowed progress and this situation was further compounded by the appointment of Ó hUiginn to his livings in the Diocese of Cashel. However, the work of transcription and revision continued and sheets were forwarded to Boyle in London for printing and were seen through the press by Hugh O'Reilly who was quick to express to Boyle his dissatisfaction with inaccuracies in the transcription, notwithstanding the editorial interventions of Sall and Ó hUiginn.

Although it had been planned to publish the Old Testament by public subscription, ultimately Boyle appears to have funded the entire project. The first sheet of Genesis was printed in 1682 and the Psalms were being printed by early 1685. The remaining work, with the exception of the Apocrypha which Boyle decided not to print, was completed by the end of 1685, the imprint date of the quarto Old Testament.[66] The book was published without a preface and while the title-page makes no mention of its printer, it is assumed that it was printed by Robert Everingham. Nicholas Williams has argued that, notwithstanding various editorial interventions during the preparation of the Old Testament for publication, the printed text is essentially that translated under Bedell's supervision.[67] Of course, the instability of print and the impossibility of a literal translation from one language to another were inherent in all such processes and in turn implicitly rendered unstable the

[63] *Tiomna Nuadh* (London, 1681), unpaginated preface; *Robert Boyle by Himself and his Friends*, ed. Michael Hunter (London: William Pickering, 1994), 107. Maddison states that, although Boyle had contracted for a print-run of 500 New Testaments, at least another 180 were also printed: 'Robert Boyle', 92, 98.

[64] Williams, *I bprionta*, 76–80. Cf. T. K. Abbott, 'On the History of the Irish Bible', *Hermathena*, 17 (1913): 36–7.

[65] Tomás Ó Fiaich, 'Pól Ó hUiginn', *The Maynooth Review*, 2 (1976): 42–51; Williams, *I bprionta*, 80–8; de Brún and Herbert, *Catalogue*, 121–2.

[66] *Leabhuir na Seintiomna ar na ttarruing go Gaidhlig* (London, 1685). See Maddison, 'Robert Boyle', 94–5; Cosslett Ó Cuinn (ed.), *Scéalta as an Apocrypha* (Dublin: Oifig an tSoláthair, 1971). On the status of the Apocrypha, see the chapter by Ariel Hessayon in this volume.

[67] Williams, *I bprionta*, 92.

assumption that print, unlike script, maintained the integrity of doctrine established by scripture.[68]

V. Robert Boyle and the Bible in Gaelic Scotland

Apparently unaware that Gaelic was spoken in the north and west of Scotland, Boyle responded favourably to overtures from a Scottish clergyman living in England for assistance in rectifying 'the sad state of religion in the Highlands of Scotland, where they had neither Bibles nor catechism in their own language.'[69] James Kirkwood, an exiled Episcopalian clergyman resident in Bedfordshire, and a member of the English Society for Promoting Christian Knowledge, arranged with Boyle for the dispatch to Scotland in 1688 of 207 copies of Bedell's Bible, and afterwards some copies of the 1681 New Testament. Ironically, the distribution of the books was curtailed as a result of hostility to episcopacy on the part of the established church in Scotland, particularly after 1690 when Presbyterianism was re-established. It is recorded that eighty Old Testaments were still in Edinburgh in 1710.[70] Boyle also funded the printing of catechisms and prayer books in Gaelic for Scotland.[71] However, the use in the Old and New Testaments of the Gaelic type which preserved scribal contractions further diminished their accessibility in Scotland where the use of roman script for Gaelic in print had been underwritten by Carswell in 1567 and the second printed book in Gaelic which was a version of Calvin's Geneva catechism published in c.1630.[72]

With partial financial support from Boyle, a project was inaugurated to transliterate the Irish Bible into roman characters and subscriptions were solicited.[73] The transliteration was undertaken by Robert Kirk (1644–92), a Gaelic scholar and minister of Aberfoyle in Monteith, who also compiled a glossary of unfamiliar words to render it more intelligible to Gaelic speakers in Scotland. Kirk had previous experience of translation and print through his publication of a Gaelic metrical Psalter in Edinburgh in 1684.[74] Robert Everingham printed 3,000 copies in duodecimo, of which Boyle subsidized 100 copies, of this edition in 1690.[75] Apart from an enthusiastic response to it from the Synod of Argyll, which

[68] Scott Mandelbrote, 'The Authority of the Word: Manuscript, Print and the Text of the Bible in Seventeenth-Century England', in Julia Crick and Alexandra Walsham (eds), *The Uses of Script and Print, 1300–1700* (Cambridge: Cambridge University Press, 2004), 138.

[69] George P. Johnston, 'Notices of a Collection of MSS. Relating to the Circulation of the Irish Bibles of 1685 and 1690 in the Highlands and the Association of the Rev. James Kirkwood Therewith', *Papers of the Edinburgh Bibliographical Society*, 6 (1901–4): 5.

[70] Victor Edward Durkacz, *The Decline of the Celtic Languages* (Edinburgh: John Donald, 1983), 19; Donald Meek, 'The Gaelic Bible', in David F. Wright, ed. *The Bible in Scottish Life and Literature* (Edinburgh: St Andrew Press, 1988), 10–11; *Robert Boyle*, ed. Hunter, 107.

[71] Maddison, 'Robert Boyle', 98.

[72] *Adtimchiol an chreidimh*, ed. R. L. Thomson (Edinburgh: Scottish Gaelic Texts Society, 1962).

[73] *An Account of the Design of Printing about 3000 Bibles* (London? 1690?).

[74] Donald Maclean, 'The Life and Literary Labours of the Rev. Robert Kirk, of Aberfoyle', *Transactions of the Gaelic Society of Inverness*, 31 (1922–4): 328–66.

[75] *An Biobla Naomtha* (London, 1690).

significantly had sponsored the publication in Gaelic of the first fifty Psalms in 1659, the circulation of the 1690 Bible was also protracted and limited, yet in due course it was considered to have 'rooted itself deeply in the affections of the people'.[76]

VI. CONCLUSION

If the framework narrative of the Protestant Reformation and the Bible in Irish has been established in broad outline, it is also clear how little is known of the cultural and intellectual aspects of this rich and complex encounter between Gaelic culture, Protestantism, and print. Reflecting a shift in emphasis in the history of the book from the text to the reader, it is no longer adequate to focus on the study of publishers' output and on networks of distribution and trade at the expense of understanding how books were read and how texts were contemporaneously interpreted and activated by their readers.[77] However, such is the present dearth of information in relation to the Bible in Irish that it is necessary to approach the reconstruction and exploration of this obscure chapter in Irish cultural history from a diversity of thematic angles and sources. If the Reformation and print have traditionally been linked to increased intellectual prestige for vernacular languages in early modern Europe, the intrusion of the Reformation into Ireland raised issues of hegemony and agency. As late as the printing of the Irish Book of Common Prayer in 1608, it is arguable that Gaelic Irishmen were central to the propagation and execution of the larger project of evangelization through print. Yet notwithstanding such indigenous commitment, the deployment of print in early modern Ireland was essentially an expression of state authority which privileged the use of English. Emblematically, while William Kearney was engaged to print the New Testament, in 1595 he printed a government proclamation in English and in Irish declaring Hugh O'Neill a traitor in rebellion.[78]

Print was frequently an instrument of control and authority in early modern Ireland. The dynamics of distribution, readership, and orality require extended consideration. There was apparently no trade in Irish Bibles and catechisms equivalent to the vibrant market for the texts in English evident from late seventeenth-century Dublin booksellers' advertisements.[79] Moreover, Gaelic literature had been transmitted for centuries in script and verbally. As late as the early nineteenth century, Bedell's Bible was being read aloud and copied scribally from a printed exemplar in Cork.[80] Indeed the remarkably late publication of a complete Irish Bible, in contrast to a complete Bible in Algonquian printed in 1663 for use in New England, arguably reveals the limits of Anglo-Irish cultural interaction and highlights English Protestant fears of the disruptive potential of Gaelic culture.

[76] Donald MacKinnon, *The Gaelic Bible and Psalter* (Dingwall: Ross-shire Printing and Publishing Co., 1930), 5–6, 53.

[77] Jean-François Gilmont, 'Protestant Reformations and Reading', in Guglielmo Cavallo and Roger Chartier (eds), *A History of Reading in the West* (Cambridge: Polity Press, 1999), tr. Lydia G. Cochrane, 224–5; Raymond Gillespie, 'Reading the Bible in Seventeenth-Century Ireland', in Bernadette Cunningham and Máire Kennedy (eds), *The Experience of Reading: Irish Historical Perspectives* (Dublin: Rare Books Group of the Library Association of Ireland, 1999), 10–38.

[78] Dix, *Printing in Dublin*, 12.

[79] Raymond Gillespie, *Seventeenth-Century Dubliners and their Books* (Dublin: Dublin City Public Libraries, 2005), 22–5.

[80] Pádraig de Brún, *Scriptural Instruction in the Vernacular: The Irish Society and its Teachers 1818–1827* (Dublin: Dublin Institute for Advanced Studies, 2009), 23.

As elsewhere in Europe, manuscripts continued to play a central role in cultural and intellectual expression and communication. Therefore, it is important to stress that the inchoate nature of print in Irish is in no way commensurate with broader cultural stasis. On the contrary, Gaelic literature in the late sixteenth and seventeenth centuries experienced a remarkable creative transformation. This renaissance was enabled by a dynamic scribal culture. Undoubtedly, there were also readers of printed texts in Irish. Closer scrutiny of readers' inscriptions and marginalia will shed light on ownership, distribution, and readership patterns. It is possible that such books were more often presented as gifts than seen as readily saleable.[81] Indeed, the unexpected ownership of a combined 1681/85 Bible by Nicholas Foran, Catholic Bishop of Waterford (1837–55), and the possession of the 1602 New Testament by the Logan family of Staverton in England or the use of a copy of Carswell's 1567 work by eighteenth-century Scottish schoolboys to practise their written English suggests that the history of the Protestant books in Irish forms part of intersecting narratives of identity, culture, and religion in Ireland and Britain down to the nineteenth century.[82]

FURTHER READING

Aibidil Gaoidheilge & Caiticiosma: Seaán Ó Cearnaigh's Irish Primer of Religion Published in 1571, ed. Brian Ó Cuív (Dublin: Dublin Institute for Advanced Studies, 1994).

Black, Ronald. 'Gaelic Religious Publishing 1567–1800', in Colm Ó Baoill and Nancy R. McGuire (eds), *Caindel Alban: fèill-sgrìobhainn do Dhòmhnall E. Meek*, Scottish Gaelic Studies, 24 (Aberdeen: University of Aberdeen, 2008), 73–85.

Caball, Marc. 'Gaelic and Protestant: A Case Study in Early Modern Self-Fashioning, 1567–1608'. *Proceedings of the Royal Irish Academy*, 110 (2010): 191–215.

Caball, Marc. '"Solid Divine and Worthy Scholar": William Bedell, Venice and Gaelic Culture', in James Kelly and Ciarán Mac Murchaidh (eds), *Irish and English: Essays on the Irish Linguistic and Cultural Frontier, 1600–1900* (Dublin: Four Courts Press, 2012), 43–57.

McCaughey, Terence. *Dr. Bedell and Mr. King: The Making of the Irish Bible* (Dublin: Dublin Institute for Advanced Studies, 2001).

Meek, Donald. 'The Gaelic Bible', in David F. Wright (ed.), *The Bible in Scottish Life and Literature* (Edinburgh: St Andrew Press, 1988), 9–23.

Ó Ciosáin, Niall. 'Print and Irish, 1570–1900: An Exception among the Celtic Languages?' *Radharc: A Journal of Irish and Irish-American Studies*, 5–7 (2004–6): 73–106.

Williams, Nicholas. *I bprionta i leabhar: na protastúin agus prós na Gaeilge 1567–1724* (Dublin: An Clóchomhar, 1986).

---

[81] For example, an inscription on a British Library copy (1003 b 8) of Kirk's 1690 Bible records that it was given as a gift from the Revd Mr Bailie, minister of Inverness, to John Chamberlayne on 28 Feb. 1710/11. Inscriptions in a New York Public Library copy (*KC 1690 Bible) state it was owned in 1716 by Robert McFarlane, minister at Buchanan, and that when he died in 1758, he left the book to Duncan McFarlane, minister at Drumin.

[82] Foran's Bible is in the Newberry Library, Chicago (Bonaparte 7126); Victor Collins, *Attempt at a Catalogue of the Library of Late Prince Louis-Lucien Bonaparte* (London: Henry Sotheran & Co., 1894), i. 367. The Logan family copy of the 1602 New Testament is in the Newberry Library, Chicago (Case X 8285.108) and *Foirm na n-urrnuidheadh* is in the British Library, London (C 36.a.16).

CHAPTER 22

....

'WILT THOU NOT READ ME, ATHEIST?' THE BIBLE AND CONVERSION

....

HELEN SMITH

IN a printed sermon concerning 'The use and benefit of Divine MEDITATION', William Fenner refers to the French Reformed writer and Bible translator, Franciscus Junius (1545–1602). As a young man, Junius studied for two years in Lyons, where his love of the Classics threatened to undermine his Protestant faith. Fenner encourages his doubting reader:

> Deal with thy heart as Junius his father dealt with him: he seeing his son was Atheisticall, he laid a Bible in every room, that his son could look in no room, but behold a Bible haunted him, upbraiding him, Wilt thou not read me, Atheist? Wilt thou not read me? And so at last he read it, and was converted from his Atheisme.[1]

In the decades following the Reformation, continued religious controversy, along with the growing mercantile and political might of the Ottoman Empire and encounters with indigenous faiths, lent questions of conversion a new force. Variously experienced as the revelation of divine grace, an intensification of religious feeling, or a change between confessions or religions, conversion was, for controversialists and polemical writers, at once a means to win souls on the theological battleground and a persistent reminder of the mutability of belief, and the threat of heresy, schism, and apostasy.[2]

It was, in the end, an act of reading (the Gospel of John) that secured Junius's conversion. This chapter explores the role that books and reading (or, sometimes, not reading) played in conversion in early modern England and its colonies. I begin with a conversion 'by the book' that underpinned and informed many accounts of bibliographic transformation, before going on to explore the use of books as technologies of conversion both in a domestic milieu

---

[1] William Fenner, *A Divine Message to the Elect Soule* (London, 1647), D4ʳ.

[2] See e.g. Anthony Grafton and Keith Mills (eds), *Conversion: Old Worlds and New* (Suffolk: Boydell & Brewer, 2003), Michael Questier, *Conversion, Politics and Religion in England, 1580–1625* (Cambridge: Cambridge University Press, 1996).

and within the broader context of mercantile and missionary projects.[3] Brought into dialogue with 'the anecdote of the "speaking paper" or "talking book" [which] became one of the tales almost reflexively told about the "illiterate primitives" of the New World', Fenner's hectoring scriptures undermine the recurrent distinction made between literate Europeans and painfully literal 'savages'.[4] Fenner's fantasy resituates, for example, the assumed superiority of Samuel Purchas, who, writing of the Americas in 1625, complained that 'Want of letters hath made some so seely as to thinke the Letter it selfe could speak'.[5] Both text and object, script and voice, the Bible was understood as affective and transformative, able to provoke real change in its readers and users, though doubts about the efficacy and force of bookish conversions shadow many accounts. The chapter aims to contribute both to the history of the Bible as a tool of evangelical transformation and identity-formation, and to the history of reading, offering a taxonomy of the kinds of inspirational, polemical, and ritual engagements through which readers effected—or hoped to effect—religious change.[6]

As the translators of the 1611 King James Bible reminded readers: 'Tolle, lege; Tolle, lege, Take up and read, take up and read the Scriptures … it was said unto S. Augustine by a supernaturall voyce'.[7] Augustine, fourth-century Bishop of Hippo, tells the story of his conversion in book 8 of the *Confessions*. Wracked with fear and doubt, the would-be Christian rushes into the garden of his lodgings in Milan, followed by his friend Alypius. There, he hears a voice, 'as if it had been of some boy, or girle from some house not farre off' repeating 'tolle lege'. Augustine

> rose up, conceaving that I was only required from heaven, to read that Chapter which the first opening of the booke should lead me to. For I had heard of Antony, that by reading of the Ghospell (to the hearing whereof he came once by accident) he held himselfe to be admonished, as if that which was read, had beene particularly meant to him ….
>
> Therefore I went hastily thither, where Alipius sate, for there I had laid the Apostolicall booke. I tooke it quickly into my hand; I opened it, and I read of that Chapter in silence, which first mine eies were cast upon. *Not in surfetting and drunkenes not in carnality and uncleanes; not in strife and emulation but put you on the Lord Iesus Christ, and take not care to fullfill the concupiscences o[f] the flesh ….* [I]nstantly with the end of this sentence, as by a cleere and constant light infused into my hart, the darkenes of all former doubtes was driven away.[8]

Augustine's conversion is framed within the tradition of the *sortes virgilianae*, a bibliomantic technique for predicting the future or directing action. In a moment of book use that highlights the utility of the codex, adopted by early Christianity as 'its privileged form' (in place

[3] Frederick V. Russell, 'Augustine: Conversion by the Book', in James Muldoon (ed.), *Varieties of Religious Conversion in the Middle Ages* (Gainesville, Fla.: University Press of Florida, 1997), 13–30.

[4] James Kearney, *The Incarnate Text: Imagining the Book in Reformation England* (Philadelphia: University of Pennsylvania Press, 2009), 194.

[5] Samuel Purchas, *Purchas his Pilgrimes in Five Bookes* (London, 1625), Q4ᵛ.

[6] The history of reading has become a major strand in early modern studies in the past decade. See esp. Jennifer Andersen and Elizabeth Sauer, *Books and Readers in Early Modern England: Material Studies* (Philadelphia: University of Pennsylvania Press, 2001); Heidi Brayman Hackel, *Reading Material in Early Modern England* (Cambridge: Cambridge University Press, 2005); and William H. Sherman, *Used Books: Marking Readers in Renaissance England* (Philadelphia: University of Pennsylvania Press, 2007).

[7] *The Holy Bible, Conteyning the Old Testament, and the New* (London, 1611), A4ʳ.

[8] Augustine, *The Confessions of the Incomparable Doctour S. Augustine*, tr. Tobie Matthew (St Omer, 1620), Bb6ᵛ–Bb7ʳ.

of the scroll),[9] Augustine places his finger, 'or some other such thing', between the leaves and tells Alypius of his conversion. Alypius reads the next verse, and is, in turn, converted.

Augustine's account is structured by the parallel turnings of Alypius and Antony, demonstrating the extent to which conversion could be modelled on existing narrative frames. The *Confessions'* first English translator, Tobie Matthew, a Catholic convert, and son of the Protestant Archbishop of York, drew the reader's attention to this exemplary parallelling with a marginal instruction: 'Note this of S. Anthony'. Embedded within Augustine's own conversion is the story of another convert, Saul/Paul, who wrote the evangelical words ('the Apostolicall booke') which catalysed Augustine's change of heart. Augustine's narrative became exemplary for later readers, perhaps most famously in the self-determining pilgrimage the Tuscan poet Petrarch made to the summit of Mont Ventoux in April 1366. After a symbolically digressive climb, Petrarch produced Augustine's *Confessions* from his pocket, and followed the saint's example by selecting a passage at random: an act which, predictably enough, inspired his own conversion.

By the Reformation, Augustine's example was widely known in England as well as on the continent.[10] During the 1520s, Miles Coverdale, later translator of the first complete English printed Bible, was influenced by the example of Robert Barnes, prior of the Augustinian house at Cambridge. Barnes's own conversion to the reformist cause was suspected when he began to 'read openly in the house, Paules Epistles, and put by Duns & Dorbel'.[11] Barnes's change in reading matter was a symptom of confessional practice, reflecting the Reformation move from scholasticism to scriptures. During the same decade, the Abbot of the Augustinian house at Inchcolm, in dispute with his monks, commanded them to retire to their cells and study the works of the order's patron. For Thomas Forret, the experience of reading about Augustine's revelatory reading was transformative: he moved towards a life of active preaching as Vicar of Dollar, promoted lay study of the scriptures, and began to criticize clerical abuses, including the purchase of pardons. Forret's conversion to the Reformist cause involved a change of reading technique: he is alleged to have begun learning Paul's epistle to the Romans—the text which converted Augustine—by heart, repeating three chapters each evening to his servant.[12] The decision to read Paul's Epistles may have been prompted in part by the text's evangelical purpose, but it is telling that both Barnes and Forret effected their own conversions through a willed repetition of Augustine's spontaneous reading act.

In the 1570s, Archbishop Whitgift reminded his own readers that 'divers [Reformers] in the beginning came to the light of the gospel only by reading and hearing the new testament in English read'.[13] Sir Nicholas Carew, for example, was reported to have been converted to the Reformist cause whilst awaiting execution in March 1539, having been given a Bible by Thomas Phelips, Keeper of the Tower. According to Hall's *Chronicles*, Carew gave 'god most

---

[9] Peter Stallybrass, 'Books and Scrolls: Navigating the Bible', in Andersen and Sauer, *Books and Readers*, 43.

[10] For the reception of Augustine in this period, see Arnoud S. Q. Visser, *Reading Augustine in the Reformation: The Flexibility of Intellectual Authority in Europe, 1500–1620* (Oxford: Oxford University Press, 2011).

[11] John Foxe, *The Unabridged Acts and Monuments Online* (1570 edn), VIII.1403 (Sheffield: HRI Online Publications, 2011), <http//www.johnfoxe.org>.

[12] David Calderwood, *The History of the Kirk of Scotland* (Edinburgh: for the Wodrow Society, 1842), i. 127–8.

[13] John Whitgift, *The Defense of the Aunswere to the Admonition* (London, 1574), Bbb6ʳ.

hartie thankes that ever he came in the prison of the tower, where he first savored the life & swetenes of Goddes most holy word meanyng the Bible in English'.[14] The idea that scripture might be tasted and savoured was not confined to Carew; in 1576, George Gascoigne instructed readers: 'Even as the mouth doth discerne and taste everie morsell or peece of the bodily sustenance … even so the inwarde taste of the soule ought in prayer and singyng of Psalmes to marke and taste the sence of everye worde and sentence'.[15] At least in Hall's report, Carew's conversion clearly contributes to the polemical presentation of Protestantism as the religion not simply of scripture but of the *Englished* book.

For Katrin Ettenhuber, Augustine's conversion, followed as it is by an allegorical interpretation of Genesis, encourages us 'to rethink key categories in the history of reading'. Where influential accounts of commonplacing and reading 'for action' encourage us to understand early modern reading as a technique of selection and application, Augustine demands that his readers understand the text 'not in parts but in wholes', meditating and reflecting upon its 'broader moral and spiritual purposes'.[16] By the mid-seventeenth century, however, the verse encountered by Augustine had become a by-word for scriptural study as a tool for the confirmation of faith, often read, or certainly cited, in splendid isolation. In 1653, the evangelical Christopher Love told his readers that 'S. Austin' 'was converted not by hearing a Sermon, but by opening the Bible, and reading that place. *Rom* 13.13. Let us walk honestly as in the day time, not in rioting and drunkennesse, not in chambering and wantonnesse: and the reading of this verse wrought upon him'.[17]

In 1664, the ejected minister Samuel Crossman warned of the dangers facing a young man entering 'the dangerous season of his life', and offered a model for self-preservation: 'he goes to Gods Armory, he takes up his Bible, and often reads the Fathers conversion-Scripture, praying the Lord that it may prove his also … *Not in chambering, and wantonness: but in putting on the Lord Christ*'.[18] A marginal note again directs the reader to Romans 13: 13. The obscurity of Crossman's reference to Augustine, named neither in the text nor in the margin, suggests the ubiquity of his example, and the extent to which an Augustinian model of transformative bibliomancy lay behind many early modern encounters with scripture.

Where Augustine quoted 'a section' of Paul's epistles and, notably, proved himself ignorant of what came next (he and Alypius go on to discover it together, along with, implicitly, Augustine's own reader), Crossman, thanks to the division of the text into chapter and verse, an innovation introduced in England by the Geneva Bible, can extract it confidently by a tightly abbreviated reference, turning Augustine's bibliomantic moment into a reassuring textual resource. By 1694, even the animal kingdom could cite the Bible by chapter and verse, at least according to Alexander Clogie's *Vox Corvi: Or, the Voice of a Raven*. In this 'incredible Relation', Clogie tells of a family gathering during which a child left the house and returned repeating 'Look in the Third of the *Colossians*, and the Fifteenth'. Asked to explain himself, the boy 'answered with great Ardency of Spirit, That a Raven had spoken

---

[14] Edward Hall, *The Union of the Two Noble and Illustre Famelies of Lancastre [and] Yorke* (London, 1548), Qqq6ʳ.

[15] George Gascoigne, *The Droomme of Doomes Day* (London, 1576), R8ʳ.

[16] Katrin Ettenhuber, *Donne's Augustine: Renaissance Cultures of Interpretation* (Oxford: Oxford University Press, 2011), 21.

[17] Christopher Love, *A Treatise of Effectual Calling and Election* (London, 1653), Q2ᵛ.

[18] Samuel Crossman, *The Young Mans Monitor* (London, 1664), K8ᵛ.

them Three times from the Peak [*sic*] of the Steeple'. His grandfather, a minister, reached for his Bible and found the place, 'Upon reading whereof, the Child was fully satisfied and his Countenance perfectly composed agen'. The raven's irenic message both resolved a family quarrel and became the subject for Clogie's printed sermon.[19]

Crossman's advice to the reader brings together in striking ways a discontinuous and aphoristic mode of biblical reading, and the meditative devotional techniques described by Ettenhuber.[20] For Crossman, as for many of his contemporaries, the application of scripture is not a straightforward act of personal agency, with the would-be believer deploying the right verse like a spiritual sticking plaster; instead the reader must embrace and meditate upon the text in the hope that, through divine agency, he or she may fully experience grace.[21] The search for a particular scriptural verse which might prompt conversion and form a basis for reflection was a tenet of nonconformist belief. Throughout *Spirituall Experiences, of Sundry Beleevers*, a monumental collection of conversion narratives published in 1653, converts note the verse which first inspired their change of heart. One woman, M.W., after a perilous physical and spiritual journey during the Civil Wars, recalled huddling in a barn with 'my wounded Childe, and a little daughter … having gotten a peece of an old Bible; and then and since I have found much setlednesse in my faith from severall Promises of the Lord, revealed in his holy Word'.[22] She goes on to cite, as testimony, the key scriptural passages which effected her transformation: John 15: 7, Matthew 5: 6, and Matthew 11: 28. 'I.I.', in similar terms, cites 'those severall places of Scripture, in which I chiefly found comfort from the Promises of God'.[23]

Accounts of conversion were themselves understood to possess an evangelical force. 1601 witnessed the publication of the stories of *Eight Learned Personages Lately Converted (in the Realm of France)*, a text which was followed that same year by an enlarged edition, *Ten Learned Personages*, and, in 1602, by *The Confession and Publike Recantation of Thirteene Learned Personages*, with additions of Dutch examples.[24] The first edition expresses the translator's hope that, upon reading these examples, 'the adversarie Papist will be confuted, the wavering Protestant confirmed, the carnall professor rouzed and awaked, & the godly Christian comforted & encouraged, cheerefully & zealously to go on, in the holy profession of Christ'.[25] 'A Table of the Principall points handled in this treatise', reiterates the polemical divide between Protestant scripture and Catholic idolatry, with entries describing Catholic tenets including 'Forbidding of Scripture', 'Insufficiencie of Scriptures', and 'Pope above the Scriptures' (A2^v). The conversion of one 'Signeur Melchior' aligns his lack of scriptural understanding with his Spanish upbringing: 'For so long as I conversed at home in my contry,

---

[19] Alexander Clogie, *Vox Corvi: or, the Voice of a Raven* (London, 1694), A3^v–A4^r.

[20] See Kevin Killeen, '"Chopp'd and Minc'd": Reading the Old Testament in Early Modern England', in Jennifer Richards and Fred Schurink (eds), 'The Textuality of Reading in Early Modern England', *Huntington Library Quarterly*, 73 (2010): 491–506.

[21] As Thomas Luxon observes of Bunyan's obsessive search for his own Bible verse: 'The words of Scripture must be interpreted, but truly saving knowledge of God's Word involves more than interpretation; it must be experienced in the heart', 'Calvin and Bunyan on Word and Image: Is there a Text in Interpreter's House?' *English Literary Renaissance*, 18 (1988): 449. Nancy Rosenfeld explores Bunyan's intense engagement with individual words and verses in her chapter in this volume.

[22] Vavasour Powell, *Spirituall Experiences, of Sundry Beleevers* (London, 1653), B7^v–B8^r.

[23] *Spirituall Experiences*, C11^r.

[24] STC 1073–1074.5.

[25] Anon., *Eight Learned Personages Lately Converted* (London, 1601), A3^r.

I never knewe ought else saving a companie of traditions and humane inventions … : but so soone as I conveyed my selfe to the Gospell, under the wings of grace, farre from my familiars, I learned more in a day, than in my life before' (D2ᵛ).

The 'myth of Protestant bibliocentricity' propagated in the sixteenth century 'lingers on in modern historical thinking' and exists in parallel with the idea 'that Roman Catholicism was inherently hostile' to print technology.[26] Alexandra Walsham rebuts this paradigm, describing the project to produce a Catholic English Bible that resulted in the Douai-Rheims New Testament of 1582, and Old Testament, translated at around the same time, but not printed until 1609–10. Commissioned by Cardinal William Allen and prepared by Gregory Martin, professor of Hebrew at the Douai seminary, the Douai-Rheims New Testament appeared in a large initial print-run of some 5,000 copies, and stimulated a flurry of polemical Protestant response.[27] The work's full title emphasizes the post-Reformation context of the translation, explaining that the summary arguments and copious marginal annotations are designed 'for the better understanding of the text, and specially for the discoverie of the corruptions of divers late translations, and for cleering the controversies in religion, of these daies'. Using the language of clarity and revision, rather than of conversion, the Douai-Rheims New Testament—and especially the paratextual features that shape the reading experience—is presented as a necessary clearing away of dangerous novelty.[28]

At least one entrant to the Jesuit College in Rome, James Rosier, ascribed his conversion to reading the Douai-Rheims Bible, alongside Frans de Costere's influential account of religious controversy, *Enchiridion controversiarum præcipuarum nostri temporis de religione*, which was published in Cologne in 1585, 1587, 1589, and 1593, revised and enlarged in 1596, 1605, and 1608, and translated into several languages.[29] Evidence of Rosier's reading can be found in the *Responsa scholarum*, a set of detailed questions used to examine each entrant to the Jesuit College to ascertain his reasons for leaving England, vocation, mental and physical health, and the status of his family. Numerous entrants cite reading as part of their conversion experience. As well as the Douai-Rheims Bible and Costere, Rosier described reading Robert Persons's *A Book of Christian Exercise, Appertaining to Resolution*, also known as the *Directory* or *Resolutions*, and first published in Rouen in 1582. In a manuscript account of his mission to create English converts, the Jesuit Father John Gerrard reminisced about meeting Persons as he was seeing the *Directory* through the press, calling it: 'a most useful and wonderful book which I believe has converted more souls to God than it contains pages'.[30] Numerous college entrants attest to the book's power. Thomas Pulton (alias Brooke), in particular, recorded that reading the *Resolutions* caused him to 'weep copiously each day, to

---

[26] Alexandra Walsham, 'Unclasping the Book? Post-Reformation English Catholicism and the Vernacular Bible', *Journal of British Studies*, 42 (2003): 143.

[27] Walsham, 'Unclasping the Book?', 145–6.

[28] On the paratexts of the Rheims New Testament, see the chapter by Katrin Ettenhuber in this volume.

[29] *The Responsa Scholarum of the English College, Rome*, ed. and tr. Anthony Kenny (London: Catholic Record Society, 1962–3), i. 207. Rosier, son of a Church of England clergyman, converted around 1602, and went on to join George Waymouth's 1605 voyage to explore the coast of Maine. For an analysis of the *Responsa*, see Lucy Underwood, 'Youth, Religious Identity, and Autobiography at the English Colleges in Rome and Valladolid, 1592–1685', *The Historical Journal*, 55 (2012): 349–74.

[30] John Gerard, *John Gerard: The Autobiography of an Elizabethan*, tr. Philip Caraman, with an introduction by Graham Greene (London: Longmans, 1951), 2.

care little for food and sleep, to spend nights in prayer and fortunes in alms, and to read Bede and Stapleton and other books of the conversion of England'.[31]

Despite the evident contemporary force and instrumentality of the *Directory*, Persons presents his exercises as techniques intended to prompt the spiritual conversion that would bring his readers closer to God (rather than the confessional conversion that would make them Catholic). He laments the procrastination of those who 'will convert them selves to God at the evenyng'.[32] Augustine again offers a key model: Persons describes at length the saint's struggle to convert, and his final full resolution, and culminates in an explicit recommendation to imitate Augustine: 'by reading of good bookes, frequenting of good companie, & the lyke: whiche thou oughtest also (good reader) to doe when thou feelest thy selfe inwardlie moved'.[33] The *Resolutions* was so popular that the Anglican Edmund Bunny converted the book itself, producing a version for English Protestant readers in 1584. The reworked text went through twenty-four editions before 1600, and became the grounds for a legal battle amongst printers desperate to keep possession of 'the moste vendible Copye that happened in our Companie theis many yeeres'.[34]

In a manuscript account of his conversion, the serial convert, and poet, William Alabaster recounted his reading experiences. Until the age of 28, he claimed, he hated Catholicism, but then began to believe that Catholics and Protestants were members of the same church. Alabaster explicitly invokes the Augustinian parallel, again raising the question of how far this powerful narrative framed and prompted the conversion experience, as well as providing a useful means to describe it:

> fynding one daye a certayne Inglish booke lying upon the ... table (which I hope was put ther by the providence of Allmightie God for my confersion, as St. *August* reconteth the booke of St. *Antony* the monke his lyf was in Trevers for the present conversion of two that lighted upon it), I asked Master Wright what booke it was, and hee told me Master William Reynals [Rainolds] against one Master Whitakers, in defence of the Inglish translation of the new testament by the Inglish Catholiques in Rhemes.[35]

In a moment of paratextual clarity, Alabaster was converted before he had finished the preface:

> I had not read for the space of a quarter of a howre (if I remember well) but as if those squames [scales] that fell from St. Paules boddylye eyes at his ... and understandinge so was I lightned upon the suddene, feeling my selfe so wonderfully and sencybly chaunged both in iudgment and affection as I remaned astonished at my trewe state. I fownde my minde wholie and perfectly Catholique in an instante.[36]

Again the two archetypal converts—Paul and Augustine—are brought together. Though Alabaster elsewhere makes clear that he had for some years been seeking the means of his

---

[31] *Responsa Scholarum*, 236.
[32] Robert Parsons, *The First Booke of the Christian Exercise Appertayning to Resolution* (Rouen, 1582), S5ʳ.
[33] Parsons, *Christian Exercise*, L10ᵛ.
[34] 'Memorial of Edmund Bollifant and his Partners in the Matter of E. Bunney's Work *The resolution*', in Edward Arber, *A Transcript of the Registers of the Company of Stationers of London, 1554–1640 A.D.* (London, 1875–94; repr. New York: Peter Smith, 1950), ii. 793.
[35] William Alabaster, *Unpublished Works by William Alabaster (1560–1640)*, ed. Dana F. Sutton (Salzburg: Salzburg Poetry, 1997), 114. The manuscript is Venerable English College Rome, Liber 1394.
[36] Alabaster, *Unpublished Works*, 118.

conversion, his description emphasizes both the suddenness of the change, and the trans-formative effects of his reading experience. Describing his conversion as 'sensible', Alabaster insists that it is a physiological experience—perceptible by the senses—and one in which the text works upon both his reason and his emotions (his 'affection').[37]

Many of the accounts cited thus far call our attention to the physical presence of the Bible, whether in Augustine's marking of his place, or M.W.'s 'peece of an old Bible'. Instances like these insist upon the material charge of the book, and its utility as a tool of personal transformation. Several converts describe the physicality of the reading experi-ence, demonstrating that 'particularly intense experiential engagements with books' were central to the processes of conversion.[38] In his account of his own turn to Catholicism, Alabaster describes Rainolds's prior conversion: '[Rainolds] dyd so much detest Mr Jewels falsehood in his wrytynge and was so angry with it as for revenge he was wont to pull out the leafe where he founde it'.[39] As Molly Murray drily notes, 'once he found himself carrying a book without pages, Rainolds realized that he had become a Catholic'.[40] In a counter-story of attempted conversion, the Chancellor of Ely, John Fuller, gave William Wolsey and Robert Pygot a book of sermons written by Dr Watson, designed to win them to the Protestant faith. Wolsey read the book, and used a pen to draw through all the pas-sages with which he disagreed. These were evidently numerous, as 'Fuller declared Wolsey "an obstinate hereticke" and expressed his outrage at his acts of textual vandalism, saying he "hath quite marred my booke"'.[41]

Like Junius's father, cited at the beginning of this chapter, Mary Rich, Countess of Warwick, hoped that the physical presence of the Bible might stir the conscience and prompt a godly reading encounter. According to Anthony Walker, who delivered her funeral sermon in 1678, Rich reshaped her household as a pathway to Christian practice, 'scattering good Books in all the common Rooms and places of attendance, that those that waited might not lose their time, but well employ it, and have a bait laid of some practical, useful Book, and fitted to their capacity, which might catch and take them'.[42] The language of bait and snare establishes Rich as a fisher for souls within a rich biblical and icono-graphic tradition, and reminds us of women's evangelical role within the household and larger community.[43]

Other biblical encounters were presented as providential accidents, setting the endan-gered soul on the right path. Christopher Love reminded his readers that not only Junius but Cyprian was converted by reading, whilst 'the Eunuch was converted by reading *Isa.* 53.7'. 'The Eunuch' leads us to a peculiarly self-referential New Testament moment in which

---

[37] On the bodily effects of reading, see Katharine A. Craik, *Reading Sensations in Early Modern England* (Basingstoke: Palgrave Macmillan, 2007); and Elizabeth Spiller, *Reading and the History of Race in the Renaissance* (Cambridge: Cambridge University Press, 2011).

[38] Molly Murray, *The Poetics of Conversion in Early Modern English Literature: Verse and Change from Donne to Dryden* (Cambridge: Cambridge University Press, 2009), 47.

[39] Alabaster, *Unpublished Works*, 116.

[40] Murray, *Poetics of Conversion*, 47.

[41] Andrew Cambers, *Godly Reading: Print, Manuscript and Puritanism in England, 1580–1720* (Cambridge: Cambridge University Press, 2011), 224.

[42] Anthony Walker, *Eureka, Eureka* (London, 1678), G3ʳ; cited in Cambers, *Godly Reading*, 88.

[43] See Helen Smith, '"The needle may convert more than the pen": Women and the Work of Conversion in Early Modern England', in Simon Ditchfield and Helen Smith (eds), *Conversions: Gender and Religious Change in Early Modern Europe* (Manchester: Manchester University Press, forthcoming, 2015).

'a man of Ethiopia, an eunuch of great authority' (Acts 8: 27) sits in his carriage reading the Old Testament book of Isaiah. The apostle Philip demands 'Understandest thou what thou readest?' (8: 30) and helps the eunuch to interpret Isaiah 53: 7–8, quoted again in Acts (a book centrally concerned with evangelization). Converted, the eunuch seeks a place to be baptized.[44]

Ensconced within Love's ancient and biblical examples is a contemporary anecdote concerning a 'famous Minister, that going by a Book-binders shop, he was converted by reading a Sermon of Repentance that cost but two pence; & hath bin a famous Minister since for the conversion of many hundreds to Jesus Christ'.[45] Here, it is not Bible but sermon reading that effects conversion. Love is uneasy about the efficacy of scriptural reading, insisting that it is sermons that God prefers as 'a means instrumental to convert souls'.[46] Indeed, if Love's reader followed the tale of the eunuch, and read forward in his or her Bible, they would discover that it was not the word read but the word heard that effected his conversion, as 'Philip opened his mouth, and began at the same scripture, and preached unto him Jesus' (Acts 8: 35). As Arnold Hunt has recently pointed out, many Protestants, particularly those of more extreme positions, were wary of conversion through scriptural reading, preferring the soul to be stirred by the persuasions of an informed preacher.[47]

For the ejected minister Richard Baxter, conversion 'by the book' might be allowed, but only overseas. Disputing the necessity of adult baptism, he argued that 'entring into the Covenant of God, doth make a man a Christian even without baptism it self. As if a Bible or good book or speech convert a man among Infidels where there is no one to baptize him'.[48] Where the Douai-Rheims Bible addressed itself specifically to European confessional divisions, remarking that 'since Luthers revolt ... divers learned Catholikes, for the more speedy abolishing of a number of false and impious translations put forth by sundry sectes, and for the better preservation or reclaime of many good soules endangered thereby, have published the Bible in the several languages of almost all the principal provinces of the Latin Church', the translators of the King James Bible offered an imperial vision of the Anglican faith.[49] Urging James 'to goe forward with the confidence and resolution of a man in maintaining the trueth of CHRIST, and propagating it farre and neere', the dedicatory address announces that the King's zeal 'doth not slacke or goe backward, but is more and more kindled, manifesting it selfe abroad in the furthest parts of Christendome'.[50] In the subsequent address from 'The Translators to the Reader',

---

[44] Though the Bible offers numerous examples that contemporary audiences understood as conversions, its language is ambiguous. The Hebrew and Greek of the Old and New Testaments contain a variety of terms that can be translated as 'conversion' or 'to convert', though their meaning is complex. The Hebrew *shubh* literally means 'return', but is often glossed as 'repent', and the Greek *epistrefein* and *metanoein* are most often translated as meaning, respectively, to turn oneself towards a person or God, and 'to repent'. In the King James Bible, the term 'conversion' appears once in the New Testament and once in the Apocrypha, 'convert' once in each of the Old and New Testaments, 'converteth' once in the New Testament, and 'converting' and 'converts' once each in the Old Testament. 'Converted' appears twice in the Old Testament and seven times in the New.

[45] Love, *Treatise*, Q2ᵛ.

[46] Love, *Treatise*, Q2ᵛ. Love acknowledges that 'God sometimes hath blessed the reading of the Word to be a means of converting souls likewise'.

[47] Arnold Hunt, *The Art of Hearing: English Preachers and their Audiences, 1590–1640* (Cambridge: Cambridge University Press, 2010), 22–42.

[48] Richard Baxter, *The True and Only Way of Concord of All the Christian Churches* (London, 1680), O4ʳ.

[49] *The New Testament of Jesus Christ* (Rheims, 1582), A2ᵛ.

[50] *The Holy Bible*, A2ʳ⁻ᵛ; A3ʳ.

the link between translation, the physical Bible, and the propagation of faith is reinforced: towards the end of a global history of biblical translation, designed to deflect charges of novelty, the translators note 'most nations under heaven did shortly after their conversion, heare CHRIST speaking unto them in their mother tongue, not by the voice of their Minister onely, but also by the written word translated' (A5ᵛ).

The conversion of 'the infidel' loomed large in the early modern imagination. The military and mercantile might of the Ottoman Empire brought Islam into the national consciousness, raising at once the spectre of English men 'turning Turk' and fantasies that members of this monotheistic religion might be persuaded to embrace Protestantism.[51] An appliqué hanging at Hardwick Hall, Derbyshire, completed in the 1590s, builds on but reworks the iconographic tradition of 'True Faith' overwhelming 'Mahomet' (Mohammed). Where earlier versions of this theme depict Mahomet crushed beneath the foot of Faith, here Faith (looking suspiciously like Elizabeth I) clasps a Bible and proffers the cup of true religion to her dejected counterpart, playing out an unlikely fantasy of the conversion of the powerful Ottoman Empire (Figure 22.1).[52]

Those fantasies took textual as well as textile forms. As early as 1529, Erasmus, in the English translation of William Roye, wished that 'all women shuld reade the gospell and Paules epistles / and I wold to god they were translated in to the tonges of all men / So that they might not only be reade / and knowne of the scotes and yryshmen / But also of the Turkes & saracenes'.[53] Given his conflation of women, the Celtic fringe, and the Near East, Erasmus might have been surprised that it was a woman, the Quaker Margaret Fell, who in 1656 attempted to set his evangelical ambitions in motion, publishing a short pamphlet *For Manasseth Ben Israel* and the lengthier *A Loving Salutation to the Jews*. Both are densely packed with scriptural quotation, reminding us that the Bible circulated not just as complete text, but as extract and citation. The former urges Menasseh ben Israel, a rabbi working for the readmission of the Jews, who had come to England in the previous year, to 'let this be read and published among thy Brethren, and to goe abroad among them where they are scattered', in order to ensure their conversion.[54] In 1657–8, John Stubbs and Samuel Fisher left England with the avowed aim of converting the Pope and the Ottoman Sultan to Christianity. In the Netherlands, they had Fell's two tracts translated into Hebrew, before continuing to Venice and Rome.

As the seventeenth century progressed, the New World increasingly became the focus for attempts at 'the converting of Infidels'.[55] The Massachusetts Bay Trading Company, granted a royal charter in 1628, took as its emblem a bare-chested figure clad in a skirt of plant fronds pleading 'Come over and help us': a quotation of Acts 16: 9 in which the Macedonians appear to Paul in a dream and beg him to convert them. Granting the company a royal charter, Charles I emphasized its missionary role, insisting that its members must work to 'wynn and incite the natives of [the] country to the knowledge and obedience of the onlie

[51] See Nabil Matar, *Islam in Britain 1558–1685* (Cambridge: Cambridge University Press, 2008); Gerald MacLean and Nabil Matar, *Britain and the Islamic World* (Oxford: Oxford University Press, 2011).

[52] For a discussion of this image, see Matthew Dimmock, *Mythologies of the Prophet Muhammad in Early Modern English Culture* (Cambridge: Cambridge University Press, 2013), 74–6.

[53] Desiderius Erasmus, *An Exhortation to the Diligent Studye of Scripture* (Antwerp, [1529]), ¶4ᵛ–¶5ʳ.

[54] Margaret Fell, *For Manasseth Ben Israel: The Call of the Jewes out of Babylon* (London, 1656), C3ʳ.

[55] Thomas Fuller, *Two Sermons the First, Comfort in Calamitie* (London, 1654), I1ʳ.

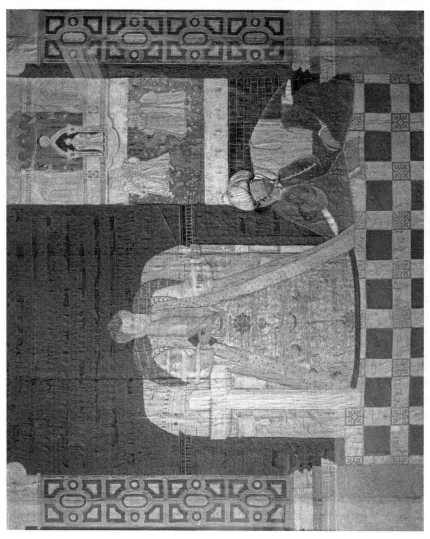

FIGURE 22.1 Needlework hanging depicting Faith and Mahomet, Hardwick Hall, Derbyshire, c.1590s.

God and Savior of mankinde'.[56] The blending of commercial and conversionary interests was remarked by Morgan Godwyn, who railed against the Protestant habit of preferring trade before religion. For Godwyn, his compatriots lacked the evangelical zeal of European Catholics, who, he claimed, were 'indefatigable Missioners' compared to their Protestant neighbours who 'like lazy Drones, sit at home not daring to wet a Foot'.[57]

One important aspect of the Catholic Counter-Reformation was the renewed evangelism of the Roman Church. By the time their founder, Ignatius Loyola, died in 1556, the Jesuits had reached the Americas, Africa, and Asia.[58] In 1622, Pope Gregory XV formally established the Sacra Congregatio de Propaganda Fide (Sacred Congregation for the Propagation of the Faith), and in 1627, Urban VIII established a training college for missionaries. Given the Catholic emphasis on retaining the scriptures in Latin, and in treating the Bible through its constituent parts, particularly the Psalter and Gospel readings, there was no sustained effort to translate the Bible wholesale for missionary use. Equally, however, there was no Protestant translation of any part of the Bible into a non-European language until 1629, when Albert Cornelius Ruyl, an agent of the Dutch East India Company, translated the Gospel of St Matthew into Malay.[59] Nonetheless, David Black argues, writing of the Upper Amazon Missions, that the Bible and Missal were understood to be crucial 'tools of the missionary's trade'.[60] Despite a polemical Protestant insistence that Spanish missions relied on violence and coercion (the sword rather than the word) and that the French cheerfully baptized indigenous peoples who possessed no knowledge of the Gospel, Jesuit translation efforts ranged from rendering hymns, the Pater Noster, and other liturgical texts into the Huron language in what is now French Canada, to a Vietnamese-Latin catechism, produced by Alexandre de Rhodes in 1658.[61] At the initiative of Jeronimo Nadal, an illustrated life of Christ, *The Annotations and Meditations on the Gospels*, was compiled for Jesuit study, and labelled in Latin. The accessibility of the text's illustrations as a tool for conversion was quickly recognized, and the images were adapted and circulated as far afield as China.[62]

Each of these examples highlights the flexibility of the Bible as object and concept, as Jesuits frequently prioritized the preaching of the Word and establishment of forms of worship over translation or dissemination of the Bible itself. In his *Naturall and Moral Historie of the East and West Indies* (1590; English translation 1604), the Jesuit José de Acosta commended the

[56] Nathaniel B. Shurtleff (ed.), *Records of the Governor and Company of the Massachusetts Bay in New England* (Boston: William White, 1853–4), i. 17.

[57] Morgan Godwyn, *Trade Preferr'd before Religion and Christ Made to Give Place to Mammon Represented in a Sermon Relating to the Plantations* (London, 1685), D4ᵛ.

[58] Eric Fenn, 'The Bible and the Missionary', in S. L. Greenslade (ed.), *The Cambridge History of the Bible*, iii. *The West from the Reformation to the Present Day* (Cambridge: Cambridge University Press, 1963), 384.

[59] Fenn, 'The Bible and the Missionary', 385. Ruyl later added the Gospel of St Mark, and in 1646 Jan van Hasel, also a merchant, translated Luke and John. The Psalms and Acts were translated into Malay in 1652.

[60] David Black, *Mission Culture in the Upper Amazon: Native Tradition, Jesuit Enterprise and Secular Policy in Moxos, 1660–1880* (Lincoln, Neb.: University of Nebraska Press, 1994), 117.

[61] Increase Mather jokes about a Franciscan missionary who wrote to a friend in Europe boasting of having converted thousands of Indians and asking him to send 'a book called the *Bible*, for he heard there was such a book in *Europe*; which might be of some use to him'. *A Brief History of the War with the Indians in New-England* (Boston, 1676), A3ʳ⁻ᵛ. See also John L. Steckley, 'The Warrior and the Lineage: Jesuit Use of Iroquoian Images to Communicate Christianity', *Ethnohistory*, 39 (1992): 478–509.

[62] Gerónimo Nadal, *Annotations and Meditations on the Gospels*, ed. and tr. Frederick A. Homann, with an introductory study by Walter S. Melion (Philadelphia: St Joseph's University Press, 2003–5).

Peruvian substitution of indigenous technologies of repetition and memorization for the books of the Bible and the catechism: he described seeing 'a handfull of … strings, wherein an Indian woman carried written a generall confession of all her life, and thereby confessed her-selfe, as well as I could have done it in written paper'. Acosta further celebrated 'a kind of writing with small stones', exclaiming 'It is a pleasant thing to see the olde and the impotent (with a wheele made of small stones) learne the *Pater noster*, with another the *Ave Maria*, with another the Creede; and to remember what stone signifies, *Which was conceived by the holy-ghost*, and which, *Suffered under Pontius Pilate*'.[63] According to Acosta, the Bible had been translated into a native memory system and a series of practical devotions; the italicized typography of Acosta's text seems to imitate the materiality of spiritual accounting, stone by stone.

Godwyn's mingled envy and ire was not reserved solely for Catholics; he noted the energy of the English sects, arguing that the Church of England had failed to imitate the 'great Industry of our People in New-England … , their converting of Nations, turning the whole Bible into the Indian Tongue; their Colledg built and endowed, for the Education of Indian Youth: Their Missioners sent forth, and Lands purchased for their Maintenance'.[64] Written in 1685, Godwyn's assessment of the success of colonial conversions seems optimistic: the massive native uprising known as King Philip's War or Metacom's Rebellion that began in 1675 had revealed the tenuous nature of early conversion efforts and decisively altered relations between the colonists and indigenous peoples.[65] What Godwyn's naïve statement does reveal is the effectiveness of the 'lively promotional correspondence' the early settlers maintained with their supporters in England; these accounts were frequently printed to reach a wider audience.[66]

For those settlers, and especially for John Eliot, who joined the Massachusetts Bay Colony in 1631, the Bible was central to evangelization. The Bible and catechism, Eliot argued, 'are general helps to all parts and places about us, and are the ground-work of Community amongst all our Indian-Churches and Christians'.[67] Eliot's emphasis upon the catechism—a set of model questions and answers concerning the events, character, and places of the Bible—reminds us of the centrality of catechizing to the dissemination of biblical knowledge.[68] In 1650, Caspar Sibelius published an account *Of the Conversion of Five Thousand and Nine Hundred East-Indians, in the Isle Formosa, neere China … with a Post-Script of the Gospels Good Successe Also amongst the West-Indians in New England*. Marvelling at the reported successes of the Dutch missionary Robert Junius, Sibelius noted that on his return to Holland Junius 'hath endeavoured to instruct a young man in their Language … and hath Printed some Catechismes in that Tongue, to send over unto them'.[69]

In a set of dialogues, written by Eliot, and designed to teach Christian Indians how to proselytize, one would-be convert laments 'we cannot Pray, nor Reade, how shall we keep

[63] José de Acosta, *The Naturall and Morall Historie of the East and West Indies*, tr. E.G. (London, 1604), Gg2ᵛ.

[64] Godwyn, *Trade Preferr'd before Religion*, D4ᵛ.

[65] See esp. Jill Lepore, *The Name of War: King Philip's War and the Origins of American Identity* (New York: Vintage Books, 1999).

[66] Kathleen Lynch, *Protestant Autobiography in the Seventeenth-Century Anglophone World* (Oxford: Oxford University Press, 2012), 156.

[67] John Eliot, *A Brief Narrative of the Progress of the Gospel amongst the Indians in New-England* (London, 1671), B1ᵛ.

[68] For the English case, see Ian Green, *The Christian's ABC: Catechisms and Catechizing in England, c.1530–1740* (Oxford: Clarendon Press, 1996).

[69] Caspar Sibelius, *Of the Conversion of Five Thousand and Nine Hundred East-Indians* (London, 1650), A3ʳ.

a Sabbath?'[70] His Christian friend instructs him to 'learn the word of God by heart; and … meditate upon the same night and day' but also to 'pray God to teach you [to read], and to open your heart to learn'. By learning to read the catechism, he concludes, 'you will learn to reade and understand the whole Bible'.[71] Yet what were naturalized technologies of reading to English missionaries were alien to Indian converts: Eliot noted that even those who were biblically literate 'doe not know the Booke, Chapter, or Verse, but distinguish my Lectures by the first materiall word in it'.[72] In the face of Indian cynicism that the rules of the Bible had been created by the English as a means of subjection, the colonists insisted upon its status as the word of God, translated into many languages and in circulation for thousands of years.

As well as teaching English to the Indians, Eliot composed a primer in logic, whose title-page asserts the connection between education and evangelization: 'The use of this Iron Key is to open the rich Treasury of the holy Scriptures'.[73] Eliot's most ambitious scheme, however, was the translation of biblical and devotional texts into Algonquian. By 1663, with the help of two Indian translators, Job Nesutan and John Sassamon, and an Indian typesetter, James Printer, Eliot had produced two editions of an Algonquian primer, two books of psalms, and the entire Bible: the first Bible to be printed in North America, composed entirely in Eliot's newly invented written system to represent the Algonquian language.[74] Eliot's activities were supported in part thanks to the Act for the Promoting and Propagating the Gospel of Jesus Christ in New England passed in 1649 by the Commonwealth Parliament, and the efforts of the Corporation then established to support and promote missionary activity. In 1662, the natural philosopher Robert Boyle, who had a long-standing interest in the study of biblical languages, was appointed as chair of the corporation. Boyle not only supported the distribution of the Bible in New England, he paid for the printing of Edward Pococke's Arabic translation of Grotius's *De veritate religionis Christianae*, contributed to the cost of publishing a Turkish catechism and New Testament, assisted the exiled Samuel Chylinski in getting his Lithuanian Bible published, and was instrumental in the printing of both Old and New Testaments in Irish Gaelic.[75]

The colonists' insistence upon literacy and Bible reading as conditions for grace provoked anxiety among aspirant converts: one of Eliot's Bibles, owned by a Christian Indian from Martha's Vineyard bears the poignant marginal inscription: 'I am forever a pitiful person in the world. I am not able clearly to read this, this book'.[76] During King Philip's War, the Bible became a potent symbol both of the colonists' ambitions and of their vulnerability: in June 1675, English soldiers pursuing Indian troops near Swansea, Massachusetts, passed some recently burned houses and discovered 'a Bible newly torn, and the Leaves scattered about',

[70] John Eliot, *Indian Dialogues for their Instruction in that Great Service of Christ* (Cambridge, 1671), D2^v.

[71] Eliot, *Indian Dialogues*, E4^r.

[72] William Gouge (ed.), *Strength out of Weakness: Or a Glorious Manifestation of the Further Progresse of the Gospel amongst the Indians in New-England* (London, 1652), C4^v.

[73] John Eliot, *The Logick Primer* (Cambridge, Mass., 1672).

[74] On the centrality of Eliot's 'Indian Library' to early printing in New England, and the subsequent development of Anglo-American literary culture, see Matthew P. Brown, *The Pilgrim and the Bee: Reading Rituals and Book Culture in Early New England* (Philadelphia: University of Pennsylvania Press, 2007), 179–207.

[75] Michael Hunter, 'Boyle, Robert (1627–1691)', *ODNB*, 2004; online edition, May 2006,<http://www.oxforddnb.com/view/article/3137>. For Boyle's Irish Bibles, see the chapter by Marc Caball in this volume.

[76] Lepore, *Name of War*, 32.

followed by a grisly scene of 'Heads, Scalps, and Hands cut off from the Bodies of some of the English, and stuck upon Poles near the Highway'.[77] In this new context of colonization, the Bible once again occupied an uneasy zone between textual resource and symbolic object. Yet the totemic power of the Bible could itself be appropriated and reworked in new contexts. Within the grave of an 11-year-old girl in a seventeenth-century Mashantucket Pequot cemetery in Connecticut, archaeologists discovered a bear paw and a page from a small-format Bible, folded and rolled together with a piece of fabric.[78] The girl's body was buried in a foetal position, facing south-west towards the Algonquian creator Kiehtan. No longer a Christian object, the Bible page may be a spoil of war; its repurposing as a grave good suggests something of the power the physical page possessed, in different ways, for both indigenous Americans and their English colonizers.

Experienced as a symbolic, providential, or directive object; read as a text, heard as a sermon, or recited in the form of a catechism; broken into chapter and verse, or meditated upon as part of a structured regime of devotional reading, the Bible was a potent and a flexible tool for conversion and identity-formation, both willed and coerced. Bible reading was understood and experienced as a profoundly affective and potentially transformative activity, offering a complex series of models for the relationship between reading, experience, and the self. The numerous accounts of early modern biblical conversions prompt us to ask how far conversion is inherently an act of reception and interpretation, at the same time as resistant uses of the Bible converted the Europeans' holy text to new purposes.

FURTHER READING

Cambers, Andrew. *Godly Reading: Print, Manuscript and Puritanism in England, 1580–1720* (Cambridge: Cambridge University Press, 2011).
Ettenhuber, Katrin. *Donne's Augustine: Renaissance Cultures of Interpretation* (Oxford: Oxford University Press, 2011).
Kearney, James. *The Incarnate Text: Imagining the Book in Reformation England* (Philadelphia: University of Pennsylvania Press, 2009).
Lepore, Jill. *The Name of War: King Philip's War and the Origins of American Identity* (New York: Vintage Books, 1999).
Lynch, Kathleen. *Protestant Autobiography in the Seventeenth-Century Anglophone World* (Oxford: Oxford University Press, 2012).
Murray, Molly. *The Poetics of Conversion in Early Modern English Literature: Verse and Change from Donne to Dryden* (Cambridge: Cambridge University Press, 2009).
Visser, Arnoud S. Q. *Reading Augustine in the Reformation: The Flexibility of Intellectual Authority in Europe, 1500–1620* (Oxford: Oxford University Press, 2011).
Walsham, Alexandra. 'Unclasping the Book? Post-Reformation English Catholicism and the Vernacular Bible'. *Journal of British Studies*, 42 (2003): 141–66.

---

[77] William Hubbard, *A Narrative of the Troubles with the Indians in New-England* (Boston, 1677), D2ʳ.
[78] For a bibliographical quest to identify the Bible fragment, see Hugh Amory, 'The Trout and the Milk: An Ethnobibliographical Talk', *Harvard Library Bulletin*, NS 7 (1996): 50–65.

PART IV

....

THE POLITICAL
BIBLE

....

Introduction to Part IV

THE Bible was political in every sense: it was the object of political battles in its translation and dissemination; it was a source of political thought and legitimacy; it was a model for how one should govern and, equally, for political opposition. For some, its authority could trump secular power; for others, policing its misuse was among the most troubling tasks of governance. It is also the case that the political nature of the Bible changed drastically across the period covered in this book. In the sixteenth century, many of the 'political' issues surrounding the Bible were facets of its place in the life and liturgy of the country. The tensions between the established Anglican Church, its Puritan edges, and the survival of Catholicism were at the very centre of English political life in the century following the break from Rome, and the Bible was very frequently at issue, either directly or indirectly. Fierce disputes over idolatry, church decoration, and the role of preaching in religion were all dependent on diverse scriptural readings. The doctrinal fissures between Rome and the Protestantisms of Europe devolved upon the claims to interpretative authority, whether, as Catholics argued, interpretation had to be rooted in a centuries-old mediating tradition, to tether how the Bible was understood, or, as Protestants often claimed, that the scriptures were plain and perspicuous, containing the tools for understanding within their own pages. The Bible was read as a significant source of authority in discerning the rights and duties of ruler and ruled, along with matters of sovereignty and the relationship between ecclesiastical and secular government.

In many ways, the seventeenth century in England was still more heavily dominated by scriptural interpretation as a way of figuring questions of state. A culture of politically inflected sermons was one of the dominant features of English life in the era, in court, urban parish, and print. Biblical literacy—familiarity with its stories and their political import—was unparalleled, and the Bible became, it is no exaggeration to say, the quotidian language of political thought. It can mean a wide variety of things to say that a particular

piece of writing is 'political'. A good deal has been written, for example, on the ecclesiastical politics of church and state, on the politics of doctrine, of Calvinism and Arminianism,
Presbyterianim and Anglicanism. But the role of the Bible in the politics of the era goes
beyond its theology and ecclesiology. In a culture that knew its Bible so thoroughly, that
could expect its readers and listeners to be familiar with what seem to us obscure scriptural
references, sermons and tracts that consist of biblical exegesis were often pointedly political,
even before any direct 'application'.

Jane Rickard explores one of the key sources of and models for political interpretation, James VI and I, an inveterate exegete, who from early in his Scottish reign to late in
his English kingship, produced learned scriptural annotations. James engaged in lengthy
polemical and political readings of the Bible. These were widely read and genuinely
admired, even among those who could not countenance the absolutist political positions
he drew from the scriptures. The seventeenth century in England saw battles over the constitutional weight of King, Parliament, and people more vehement than any previous era.
Though inadvertently, James's political exegesis provided an impressive prototype for those
many who subsequently transposed questions of biblical polity forward to the seventeenth
century. It is often a mistake to attribute too much of a country's politics to a monarch, if it is
at the expense of the multiple currents of political thought. However, in both his championing of preaching and in his own Protestant model of non-clerical exegesis—his books were
produced in both affordable and lavish editions—James had a significant influence on the
diffusion of biblical-political practice. That this practice bore terrible fruit has become one
of the truisms of seventeenth-century historiography, which has often seen overwrought
interpretation of the Bible as, if not a cause, then at least a contributory factor to the radical-
isms and fanaticisms of the Civil Wars.

Anne Lake Prescott's chapter produces a micro-history of biblical-political interpretation
of King Saul, the first Israelite king, in a single year, 1643, to show just how varied a set of
interpretations might accrue around a biblical figure. Demonstrating the multidimension-
ality of such exegetical histories, Prescott's chapter traces the cornucopia of different readings and political wrangles around this most flawed monarch, who might be seen as either
sacrosanct in his anointing, or as a king deposed by the subsequent anointing of David.
The array of constitutional thought that arose from this—whether the people had in effect
elected their king, whether David, pursued by the increasingly incapacitated and demented
Saul, exemplified legitimate self-defence—is counterbalanced by an array of related matter,
on, for instance, what the story had to say about the nature of music or the nature of witchcraft. Early modern readers derived vast amounts from the minutiae of the Bible and in no
sphere was this more apparent than when it was being used to create the vibrant language of
politics.

That certain verses of the Bible were particularly fraught is illustrated in a number of
tracts and essays touching on the electric ambiguity of 1 Samuel 8, in which kingship was
inaugurated. Readers debated—and we might say went to war over—the constitutional
implications of this story, how far it licensed or limited a king. It was a text that generated much comment, from tyrannicidal and Jesuit writings of the later sixteenth century,
to the radical republicans and absolutist royalism of the Civil Wars. This first and tainted
grant of kingship is the subject of Kim Ian Parker's chapter, which traces across a number
of writers what Samuel meant for early modern politics, and demonstrates a vibrant movement of ideas across writers who produced radically inconsistent readings of a single text.

Proceeding from early modern understandings of the 'Hebrew Republic', Parker explores the ambiguities around the idea of a monarch, and the interpretative uncertainty about whether the scripture endorsed or repudiated kingship.

Alongside constitutional debate that sought to define the relative merits of monarchy, the Civil War era also gave rise to new forms of radicalism that drew heavily on the Bible, none more troubling than the communism of the Levellers, whose argument, in large part, was premised on a vexed question of biblical authorship. Leveller writers, as Andrew Bradstock's chapter shows, made the case very seriously that the scriptures were the work of fishermen and shepherds, of herdsmen and husbandmen, that the inspiration that prompted the writers of the Bible was the same Holy Spirit that properly animated its interpretation. In such a reading, the elaborate scholarship that gathered around the Bible was a terrible ruse to lock away its liberating message, in the same way that the complexity of the *quadriga*, in early Reformation thought, was seen as a Roman ruse to retain interpretative control of the scriptures. Protestant thought across the sixteenth and seventeenth centuries remained entangled in its insistence that the Bible was self-interpreting—that obscurity in one place would be clarified in another—and the contrary position that interpretation of the Bible was complex, demanding scholarly acumen and certainly not something that anyone untutored or untrained was fit to take upon themselves. Enthusiasm—the notion that the interpretation of the Bible was first a matter of the infused spirit, with bookish learning either secondary or a positive hindrance to understanding—remained a problem for the established church and, not surprisingly, there was often a political dimension to such untrammelled readings.

It remains an entrenched belief that the radical Bible of the Civil War era lost its political bite at the Restoration, and that, as the nation recoiled from the incendiary and regicidal uses to which it had been put, the country's political language became more or less secular. However, it is quite wrong to suppose that this happened in any rapid fashion. Emma Major's chapter describes the continuing currency of the Bible in political affairs up to and beyond the end of the century. Exploring the turmoil that engulfed the monarchy and country around the Exclusion Crisis and invasion by the Dutch King, William of Orange, she traces the role of scripture in the acrimonious disputes by which the country resisted the Catholic direction imposed by James II and how the Bible emerged again as a political resource, in the widely held supposition that matters of state and that the providential hand of God in events could be discerned in its pages.

....

CHAPTER 23

MOVER AND AUTHOR: KING JAMES VI AND I AND THE POLITICAL USE OF THE BIBLE

....

JANE RICKARD

'THERE are infinite arguments of this right Christian and Religious affection in your MAJESTIE', the translators of the Bible that was to become known as the King James Bible announce in their 'Epistle Dedicatorie'. '[B]ut none is more forcible to declare it to others', they continue, 'then the vehement and perpetuated desire of the accomplishing and publishing of this Worke'. The new Bible translation, as this assertion renders explicit, constituted a public statement about James's religious commitment. The translators identify another of the 'infinite arguments' for the King's 'right Christian and Religious affection' as his own anti-Catholic publications, implicitly aligning royal authorization and royal authorship, the divine word and the royal word. The dedication also presents James as 'author' in the sense of 'creator', stating that his subjects bless him as 'that sanctified person, who under GOD, is the immediate authour of their true happinesse'. The King is beneath God, but reflects the divine in his ability to originate, to create. These different but interconnected conceptions of royal authorship inform the translators' more well-known assertion that the King is 'the principall moover and Author' of the translation.[1]

These prefatory comments reflect the fact that James's sponsorship of the translation early in his English reign was no one-off act of religious devotion but an extension of a highly politicized project of moving, authoring, and authorizing. These were endeavours which he had pursued since the 1580s when he was a young King of Scotland, and which he would continue to pursue throughout his reign. James's political use of the Bible took three main forms. His employment of scriptural interpretation in his own publications, including those anti-Catholic works highlighted by the Bible translators, was the first. The second was his interventions in the work of his preachers, which in various ways sought to shape what was

---

[1] *The Holy Bible, Conteyning the Old Testament, and the New* (London, 1611), A2ᵛ.

preached and when. Sponsoring the Bible translation was the third and most ambitious dimension of James's attempts to mediate and direct the access of his subjects to the Word of God. This direct and visible royal participation in scriptural interpretation, preaching, and Bible translation reflects James's political shrewdness. These activities also, however, put the King in some awkward and exposed positions.

There has been some important work on sermons in recent years, and the King James Bible attracted more critical attention than ever around the quartercentenary of its publication.[2] Yet there still has not been sufficient recognition of how sermons and translation were for the King only parts of a larger project in which his own publications were vital. The present chapter explores James's writings alongside some of his other interventions in the work of the church in Scotland and England, and highlights how central his role as an interpreter of scripture was to his conception and exercise of his authority. The chapter also considers how James's self-construction as scriptural interpreter was greeted by his English subjects. It argues that contemporaries such as John Donne subtly articulated reservations about and challenges to the King's political use of the Bible.

James's early experiences in Scotland emphasized the important role of the church and the Bible in determining the fate of the monarchy. James was crowned in 1567 (aged thirteen months) following the forced abdication of his Catholic mother, Mary Queen of Scots. The Kirk (the Protestant Scottish Church) had helped to authorize this action.[3] The treatment of Mary was, moreover, underpinned by resistance theory which—like other political theories in the period—participated in debates about the interpretation of scripture. Theories of resistance to royal authority, which developed across Europe in the 1570s, argued that it was legitimate for subjects to depose their ruler in certain circumstances. The main proponent of resistance theory in Scotland, George Buchanan, was James's boyhood tutor. Buchanan wrote his *De Jure Regni apud Scotos* just after Mary's forced abdication. This work was published in Edinburgh in 1579, with a dedication in which Buchanan ominously warned his King and pupil that this work will 'advise you of your duty towards your subjects'.[4]

Buchanan's treatise highlighted the extent to which scriptural interpretation could pose a direct challenge to monarchical authority. It is less concerned to ground its arguments in scriptural precept than other works of resistance theory, appealing more often to classical authorities. But the exception to this is a section in which Buchanan comments at length on biblical passages invoked by Maitland, the other speaker in the dialogue, to support the view that obedience is owed to even the most tyrannical of rulers. These are 1 Samuel

[2] On early modern sermons, see, in particular, Peter E. McCullough, *Sermons at Court: Politics and Religion in Elizabethan and Jacobean Preaching* (Cambridge: Cambridge University Press, 1998); Lori Anne Ferrell and Peter E. McCullough (eds), *The English Sermon Revised: Religion, Literature and History 1600–1750* (Manchester: Manchester University Press, 2000); Mary Morrissey, *Politics and the Paul's Cross Sermons, 1558–1642* (Oxford: Oxford University Press, 2011); and Peter E. McCullough, Hugh Adlington, and Emma Rhatigan (eds), *The Oxford Handbook of the Early Modern Sermon* (Oxford: Oxford University Press, 2011). Publications marking the quartercentenary of the King James Bible include Gordon Campbell, *Bible: The Story of the King James Version, 1611–2011* (Oxford: Oxford University Press, 2010); David Crystal, *Begat: The King James Bible and the English Language* (Oxford: Oxford University Press, 2010); and Adam Nicolson, *When God Spoke English: The Making of the King James Bible* (London: HarperPress, 2011).

[3] For the position of the Kirk in the years 1567–85, see Alan R. MacDonald, *The Jacobean Kirk, 1567–1625: Sovereignty, Polity and Liturgy* (Aldershot: Ashgate, 1998), ch 1.

[4] George Buchanan, *A Dialogue on the Law of Kingship among the Scots*, ed. and tr. Roger A. Mason and Martin S. Smith (Aldershot: Ashgate, 2004), 3.

8: 9–20 and Romans 13: 1–8, texts which were 'widely debated in the polemical literature of the Reformation era' and which proponents of resistance theory were 'obliged' to attempt to counter.[5] Buchanan gives 1 Samuel 8, in which the people of Israel ask Samuel for a king to rule over them, short shrift. He affirms that 'it is readily apparent that it is a tyrant, not a king, who is described here'—and for Buchanan a tyrant may justifiably be killed, even by an individual acting alone.[6] 1 Samuel 8 was, as we shall see, to be of particular importance to James, and, in turn, to some of his readers. For Buchanan did not succeed in simply imposing his views on his pupil; his teaching and example also helped to equip the King with the ability to respond.

The year 1584 saw the crown take a number of significant steps. The so-called 'Black Acts' asserted royal power over the still troublesome Kirk, while an Act against 'slanderers of the King, his progenitours, Estait and Realme' censored the now dead Buchanan's *De Jure Regni*.[7] James also published his first book: *The Essayes of a Prentise, in the Divine Art of Poesie*. While claiming poetry itself as a 'divine art', this collection of original poems, poetic translations, and poetic theory is largely secular in its concerns. The collection does, however, include one important exercise in scriptural interpretation: a translation of Psalm 104. Translating psalms aligns James with King David, a biblical poet-king who afforded 'an Old Testament precedent for royal authorisation of Bible translation'.[8] James's rendering of Psalm 104 presents him as an aspiring religious writer, beginning 'O Lord inspyre my spreit and pen, to praise / Thy Name'.[9] The 18-year-old King was beginning to suggest that part of his role would be to produce religious literature. And Psalm 104 was a pointed choice with which to make this claim. This psalm existed in a Latin version, famous across Europe, produced by none other than Buchanan.[10] James was beginning to utilize scriptural interpretation as a site for political contest.

James seems to have planned to produce a Psalter for use in churches but he was never to complete this major undertaking.[11] His translation of Psalm 104 did pave the way for the scriptural prose works that he produced next. After *The Essayes of a Prentise*, he wrote a paraphrase of all twenty-two chapters of Revelation. This ambitious and extensive work would not be printed until many years later, but a complementary piece formed James's second publication: *Ane Fruitfull Meditatioun* (1588), a commentary on Revelation 20: 7–10.

---

[5] Buchanan, *Dialogue*, Introduction, pp. xlvi–xlvii. These biblical texts would also feature prominently in the pamphlet wars of the mid-seventeenth century; for a detailed discussion, see Warren Chernaik, 'Biblical Republicanism', *Prose Studies*, 23 (2000): 147–60. On 1 Sam. 8, see also the chapter by Kim Ian Parker in this volume.

[6] Buchanan, *Dialogue*, 111.

[7] For the Act against slander, see T. Thomson, and C. Innes (eds), *The Acts of the Parliaments of Scotland* (Edinburgh, 1814–75), iii. 296. On the 'Black Acts' and the opposition they met, see MacDonald, *Jacobean Kirk*, 26–9.

[8] John N. King, 'James I and King David: Jacobean Iconography and its Legacy', in Daniel Fischlin and Mark Fortier (eds), *Royal Subjects: Essays on the Writings of James VI and I* (Detroit: Wayne State University Press, 2002), 430.

[9] James, *The Essayes of a Prentise, in the Divine Art of Poesie* (Edinburgh, 1584), N3ʳ.

[10] James Doelman, 'The Reception of King James's Psalter', in Fischlin and Fortier, *Royal Subjects*, 455.

[11] The British Library Royal MS 18 B.16, contains thirty psalms by the King, but 104 was the only one to be printed in his lifetime. *The Psalms of King David* was authorized and attributed to James by King Charles in 1631, but seems to have been largely written by William Alexander. For further discussion, see Doelman, 'Reception of King James's Psalter'.

This was quickly followed by *Ane Meditatioun* (1589), on 1 Chronicles 15: 25–9. Though these three scriptural works were for a long time critically neglected, some recent scholars have recognized their combined political and literary significance.[12]

The two printed meditations serve immediate political aims. These include placating the Kirk by emphasizing the King's support of the 'true' religion and rejection of Catholicism. Revelation was a particularly contested text, and an important one for Protestant propagandists who identified the Pope with the Antichrist.[13] James follows this established Protestant interpretation, even suggesting in *Ane Fruitfull Meditatioun* that any 'indifferent man' may judge that the Pope bears the marks of the Antichrist.[14] Both meditations include commendatory prefaces by the minister Patrick Galloway, exemplifying and encouraging cooperation between Kirk and crown.

Writing in the aftermath of the defeat of the Spanish Armada, James is also concerned to stress his support for England and to present the Scottish and English as joint defenders of a single land against a single enemy. '[W]e may', he writes in *Ane Fruitfull Meditatioun*, 'concur ane with another as warriouris in ane camp and citizenis of ane belovit citie' (B4^r). *Ane Meditatioun* draws an analogy between the biblical story of the Philistines attacking Israel and the Catholics attacking 'this Ile', and highlights the role of King David.[15] James had already identified himself with this biblical king through psalm translation, but what is especially significant here is David's holding together what were to become, under his grandson, the unhappily divided kingdoms of Israel and Judah. These emphases not only seek to strengthen diplomatic relations in the present but also point towards James's hoped-for future role as a king uniting Scotland and England.

Beyond these particular aims, James's early scriptural works serve more fundamental purposes, enabling him to emphasize the divinely ordained hierarchy by which he is king by divine right, with a unique position of proximity to God, and therefore a special ability to interpret God's word. *Ane Fruitfull Meditatioun* states on its title-page that it is 'in forme of ane sermon'. James goes on to explain that he will first 'expone or paraphrase the hardnes of the wordis, nixt interpreit ye meaning of them, and thridlie note quhat [what] we sould learne of all' (A3^v). He is asserting his ability to penetrate the difficulty of the text and reveal its true meaning, which he will then deliver to his readers as a lesson. He goes even further in his *Paraphrase upon the Revelation*, speaking on behalf of John in the first person as

---

[12] See in particular Daniel Fischlin, '"To Eate the Flesh of Kings": James VI and I, Apocalyse, Nation and Sovereignty', in Fischlin and Fortier, *Royal Subjects*, 388–420; Jane Rickard, 'The Word of God and the Word of the King: The Scriptural Exegeses of James VI and I and the King James Bible', in Ralph Houlbrooke (ed.), *James VI and I: Ideas, Authority, and Government* (Aldershot: Ashgate, 2006), 135–49, and *Authorship and Authority: The Writings of James VI and I* (Manchester: Manchester University Press, 2007), ch. 2; Astrid J. Stilma, 'King James VI and I as a Religious Writer', in Crawford Gribben and David George Mullan (eds), *Literature and the Scottish Reformation* (Aldershot: Ashgate, 2009), 127–41, and '"As Warriouris in Ane Camp": The Image of King James VI as a Protestant Crusader', in Kevin J. McGinley and Nicola Royan (eds), *The Apparelling of Truth: Literature and Literary Culture in the Reign of James VI* (Cambridge: Cambridge Scholars Publishing, 2010), 241–51. There is still no modern edition of these three scriptural works.

[13] See Bernard Capp, 'The Political Dimension of Apocalyptic Thought', in C. A. Patrides and Joseph Wittreich (eds), *The Apocalypse in English Renaissance Thought and Literature: Patterns, Antecedents, Repercussions* (Manchester: Manchester University Press, 1984), 93–124 (esp. 93–4, 97).

[14] James, *Ane Fruitfull Meditatioun* (Edinburgh, 1588), B2^r.

[15] James, *Ane Meditatioun upon the First Buke of the Chronicles of the Kingis* (Edinburgh, 1589), B3^v.

though he were the prophet to whom God has chosen to 'reveale … certaine things'.[16] James was trying to draw to himself the authority of the exegete, the preacher, and the prophet, identifying himself as having a special role in interpreting and disseminating God's word.

This identity is exploited in the political treatises that James began to write in the 1590s, by which time his hold on power was more secure. The exemplary text here is *The True Lawe of Free Monarchies* (1598). This treatise offers a controversial defence of divine right kingship in reaction to theories of resistance. The main argument is structured around a reading of 'the wordes of SAMUEL, dited by Gods spirit'.[17] 1 Samuel 8 was, as we have already seen, a key text in debates about monarchical rule. James maintains that its true meaning is singular and self-evident: 'will ye consider the very words of the text in order, as they are set downe, it shall plainely declare the obedience that the people owe to their King in all respects' (B8^r). Thus claiming that the biblical text speaks for itself and that his own procedure as interpreter is transparent, James quotes in full 'the very words of the text' (B5^r). The words he has selected are verses 9–20, the very verses Buchanan's *De Jure Regni* had considered.

James's claims are disingenuous: the text is not allowed to speak for itself but is analysed line by line. That analysis highlights and expands upon particular details. Verse 20, for example, reads 'our King shall judge us, and go out before us, and fight our battels' (B6^r). In his discussion, James, we might be unsurprised to find, has little to say about battles and a lot to say about judgement. He brings in apparently corroboratory evidence from Exodus 22: 28, 'Thou shalt not rayle uppon the Judges, neither speake evill of the ruler of thy people', and concludes in his own words that the people should acknowledge their King 'a Judge set by GOD over them, having power to judge them, but to be judged onely by GOD' (C4^r–C5^v). James is clearly interpreting the text to fit his political needs and beliefs. Indeed, there are, as James Craigie has pointed out, several discrepancies between *True Lawe*'s biblical references and the words of the scriptural texts in question.[18] *True Lawe* highlights both the centrality of scripture to political debate and the fine line between interpreting and rewriting.

James's two meditations on scripture and *The True Lawe of Free Monarchies*, along with the other prose works he had published in Edinburgh, were reprinted in London upon his accession to the English throne. His new English subjects were quick to praise him for his religious learning. His coronation sermon, given by Thomas Bilson, affirms that James is 'a religious and learned King, who both by penne and practise these many yeeres hath witnessed to the world, how well acquainted he is with christian and godly government'. This sermon is also, however, careful to use scripture to advise James on his princely duty and to underline the King's accountability to God.[19] James's handbook on kingship, *Basilikon Doron* (1599, 1603) attracted particular comment in the early years of his English reign, but there was praise too for his other works, including *True Lawe*. Francis Bacon's *The Advancement of Learning* (1605) offers in its opening pages fulsome praise for James's erudition: 'there hath not beene since Christs time any King or temporall Monarch which hath ben so learned in

---

[16] James, *A Paraphrase upon the Revelation of the Apostle S. John*, in *The Workes of the Most High and Mighty Prince, James* (London, 1616), 7.

[17] James, *The True Lawe of Free Monarchies* (Edinburgh, 1598), B5^r. Subsequent references are to this edition and given in parentheses in the text.

[18] *Minor Prose Works of King James VI and I*, ed. James Craigie (Edinburgh: William Blackwood & Sons, 1982), notes, 128–9, 132.

[19] Thomas Bilson, *A Sermon Preached at Westminster before the King and Queenes Majesties, at their Coronations* (London, 1603), C3^{r-v}.

all literature & erudition, divine & humane'. But later in the work Bacon makes more pointed comments on the King's books, observing that 'in your book of a free Monarchy, you do well give men to understand, that you know the plentitude of the power and right of a King, as well as the Circle of his office and duty'.[20] This is praise that functions as counsel; like Bilson, Bacon emphasizes that the King must know the limits as well as the extent of his power.

James's reputation for scriptural learning was reinforced by one of the first major events of his English reign, the Hampton Court conference of early 1604. This conference brought Puritans, the King, his bishops, and others together to discuss matters of doctrine and worship. Some of those present had already helped to present James as a man of religious learning: Patrick Galloway, assisting the Puritan spokesmen, had contributed prefaces to the first editions of James's meditations, and Thomas Bilson had recognized James as a religious writer in his coronation sermon. Others would later assist the King as mover and author: William Barlow and Lancelot Andrewes would both write on James's behalf in the Oath of Allegiance controversy; James Montague would help to edit James's folio collection of *Workes*; and George Abbot would help to circulate James's *Directions for Preachers*. According to the official account of the proceedings, the conference gave all of these learned, important, and influential men the opportunity to witness first-hand the King's practice as a reader of the Bible.

William Barlow was the bishop commissioned to write the official account of the conference and he is careful to ensure he gives the new King as much credit as possible. By the end of the first day, he writes, he and his fellows were astonished that the King 'should, in points of Divinity shew himselfe as expedite and perfect as the greatest Schollers, and most industrious Students, there present, might not outstrip him'.[21] By the end of the second day, the Lords were so impressed that 'one of them sayde, hee was fully perswaded, his Majestie spake by the instinct of the spirite of God'. The King is, Barlow adds, 'a Living Library, and a Walking Study' (83–4). James is not merely as learned as any great scholar, but a mouthpiece for God and a repository of knowledge upon which others might draw. As well as this general praise, Barlow cites instances of James displaying his interpretive skills during discussions. At one point the King resolves a disagreement over Ecclesiastes: he called for a copy of the Bible, analysed the chapter in question, and 'so exactly and divinelike, unfolded the summe of that place' (61–2). Debate as to the accuracy of Barlow's account has raged since its publication.[22] It seems likely that the instances of James calling for a Bible and publicly interpreting it are not entirely fabricated, emphasizing his determination to present himself as a mediator of God's word for his people. Whether or not those present were anything like as impressed by this performance as Barlow claims, the account creates a powerful impression of James's biblical learning for other readers.

Beyond the Hampton Court conference, James made full and careful use of his divines. One of the outcomes of the conference was, of course, the decision to produce the new

---

[20] Francis Bacon, *The Twoo Bookes of Francis Bacon: Of the Proficience and Advancement of Learning, Divine and Humane* (London, 1605), A3ᵛ, Vv3ᵛ.

[21] William Barlow, *The Summe and Substance of the Conference ... at Hampton Court* (London, 1604), 20.

[22] For a recent discussion of Barlow's account in relation to other contemporary reports, which argues that many of the account's statements can be corroborated, and that James himself was pleased with how it represented events, see Alan Cromartie, 'King James and the Hampton Court Conference', in Houlbrooke, *James VI and I*, 61–80 (esp. 67–71).

Bible translation. Barlow records instructions which James laid down at the outset, including his insistence that there should be no marginal notes (the copious marginal notes in the Geneva Bible were, in his view, anti-monarchist).[23] James's involvement in the translation seems to have extended beyond the conference, the rules that Bancroft circulated to the translators noting points on which 'his Majesty is very carefull'.[24] At the same time, the King began to enjoy a degree of influence over preaching that he had never been able to achieve in Scotland. He increased the numbers of court sermons and deployed court preaching for political ends, associating himself with selected preachers and commanding certain court sermons into print for reasons of policy.[25] He also made innovative and consistent use of the public pulpits. The government's support for sermons on political anniversaries such as the Gunpowder Plot led to a dramatic increase in the number of political sermons preached and printed in the Jacobean period. James even helped to determine the content of some of these sermons.[26]

The controversy surrounding the Oath of Allegiance, which James introduced following the Gunpowder Plot, involved the King in a fresh wave of moving and authoring. This controversy hinged precisely on the question of the relationship between religion and politics. James required his subjects to sign an oath affirming that their primary allegiance was to him not the Pope, and that the Pope did not have the authority to depose him or release his subjects from that allegiance. The Pope and his followers attacked the Oath and urged English Catholics not to sign it. James counterattacked with *An Apologie for the Oath of Allegiance* (1607), published anonymously. When this work met further hostile response from the Catholic side, James republished it under his name in a revised, extended, and still more virulently anti-Papist version (1609). He also commissioned works including William Barlow's *Answer to a Catholike English-Man* (1609) and Lancelot Andrewes's *Tortura Torti* (1609). He even, according to Donne, inspired voluntary contributions. Donne's *Pseudo-Martyr* (1610) claims in its dedication to the King that 'The influence of those your Majesties Bookes … exhaled from my poore Meditations, these discourses'.[27] Donne was to be, as we shall see, a penetrating reader of the King's books.

Like James's earlier polemical works, *An Apologie for the Oath of Allegiance* grounds its argument for the obedience subjects owe to their King in scripture. At the same time, James implies that his adversaries are making assertions not based on scripture:

> how the profession of the naturall Allegiance of Subjects to their Prince, can be directly opposite to the faith and salvation of soules, is so farre beyond my simple reading in Divinitie, as I must thinke it a strange and new Assertion … I reade indeede, and not in one, or two, or three

---

[23] Barlow, *Summe and Substance*, 46–7. For James, this plan built on steps he had begun to take in Scotland: in the General Assembly of 1601 he introduced his idea of a revised Book of Common Order and metrical Psalter, and the assembly decided to begin a correction of the Geneva Bible. See James Doelman, *King James I and the Religious Culture of England* (Woodbridge: D. S. Brewer, 2000), 14–15. On the political function of the remaining notes in the King James Bible, see the chapter by Karen Edwards in this volume.

[24] 'Bishop Bancroft's Rules for the Revisers' are reproduced in full in *King James Bible: A Selection*, ed. W. H. Stevenson (London and New York: Longman, 1994), 497–510.

[25] McCullough, *Sermons at Court*, 117, 138.

[26] See Mary Morrissey, 'Presenting James VI and I to the Public: Preaching on Political Anniversaries at Paul's Cross', in Houlbrooke, *James VI and I*, 107–8, 115.

[27] Donne, *Pseudo-Martyr* (London, 1610), A3ʳ.

places of Scripture, that Subjects are bound to obey their Princes for conscience sake, whether they were good or wicked Princes.[28]

James then quotes a series of biblical texts (Joshua 1: 17, Jeremiah 27: 12, Exodus 5: 1, Ezra 1: 3, and Romans 13: 5). The arch, wry tone of the passage, and its employment of the rhetorical tactic of false modesty, suggests increased confidence in his identity as a scriptural interpreter. This was an identity he was now promoting on an international stage, against fierce opponents and with high stakes.[29]

The appearance in 1611 of a new translation of the Bible, sponsored by and dedicated to the King, helped to reinforce the impression of royal devotion to (Protestant) biblical scholarship that had long been cultivated. James must have been delighted that his desire for a new translation, without the Geneva Bible's troubling marginal notes, had finally been realized. He must have been pleased too with some of the comments made about him in the dedication. He has not only displayed 'right Christian and Religious affection' but is 'learned and judicious' with 'deepe judgement'. He also cares for the church 'as a most tender and loving nourcing Father'. This phrase echoes Isaiah 49: 23, which had been evoked in Bilson's coronation sermon.[30] Bilson, along with the scholar Miles Smith, had undertaken the final revision of the translation and, particularly since we know that Smith wrote the preface to the readers, it seems likely that Bilson took responsibility for the dedication. The dedication also reflects the recent theological controversy and it is in this context that James's literal authorship is acknowledged: the King has manifested his religious zeal abroad 'by writing in defence of the Trueth, (which hath given such a blow unto that man of Sinne, as will not be healed)'. The translators' work is presented as an extension of this royal assault on popery: they too are attempting to 'make GODS holy Trueth to be yet more and more knowen unto the people' and may be 'traduced by Popish persons at home or abroad'.[31] Even the King James Bible—now renowned above all for the grandeur of its language—situated itself in a conflict that was political as well as theological.

The King may have been pleased, but he was not satisfied. He continued to furnish his subjects with his own scriptural interpretations; the production of an authorized version did not change the fact that, for James, the Bible did not really speak for itself. His early meditations were reprinted, along with the previously unprinted *Paraphrase upon the Revelation*, in a folio edition of his prose works, *The Workes of the Most High and Mighty Prince, James* (1616). James Montague's preface draws particular attention to the paraphrase and to James's special ability in interpreting the notoriously difficult book of Revelation: 'GOD hath given him an understanding Heart in the Interpretation of that Booke, beyond the measure of other men ... this Paraphrase ... leades the way to all the rest of his Majesties Workes'. This formulation suggests that scriptural interpretation is the foundation of all of James's works. The preface also, like the dedication to the King James Bible, recalls the Oath of Allegiance controversy. It asserts triumphantly that James's adversaries 'are not safe from being blasted

[28] James, *Triplici nodo, Triplex cuneus: Or an Apologie for the Oath of Allegiance* (London, 1607), C3ᵛ.
[29] For a detailed account of this European-wide and long-lived controversy, see W. B. Patterson, *King James VI and I and the Reunion of Christendom* (Cambridge: Cambridge University Press, 1997), 75–123.
[30] Bilson, *A Sermon Preached at Westminster*, B5ᵛ. The same verse had also been evoked in one of Galloway's prefaces (see James, *Ane Meditatioun*, A2ʳ).
[31] *Holy Bible*, A2ᵛ.

by the breath of his Majesties Bookes'. But it also acknowledges other views of James's publishing activities, including that 'Little it befitts the Majesty of a King to turne Clerke, and to
make a warre with the penne, that were fitter to be fought with the Pike'.[32] The preface thus
registers some of the concerns about James's style of rule that would become more widespread in the following years.

    The outbreak of the Thirty Years War in Europe in 1618 left James under mounting pres-
sure to take military action against Catholic Spain. James refused to take this step, preferring to negotiate for a Spanish marriage for Prince Charles as a means of securing peace.[33]
He also continued to write, publishing *A Meditation upon the Lords Prayer* in 1619 and *A
Meditation upon St. Matthew. Or a Paterne for a Kings Inauguration* in 1620. These scriptural
meditations draw on the Bible to support James's defending of his authority and extolling of
the virtues of peace. In *A Meditation upon St. Matthew*, for example, he cites Matthew 26:
52: Christ 'had no use of a sword then, nay, he found fault with S. Peters using it, telling him,
He that striketh with the sword shall perish by the sword'.[34] The immediate political import
of such material is obvious. These late works also find James reflecting self-consciously on a
long career as a scriptural interpreter which was now drawing to a close: he has come from
'wading in these high and profound Mysteries in the Revelation, wherein an Elephant may
swimme; to meditate upon the plaine, smoothe and easie Lords Prayer … the reason is, I
grow in yeeres'.[35]

    Some of James's subjects also recalled his earlier works in the late Jacobean period, but
they did so as a means of opposing his current policies. To many, it seemed incomprehensible that a King who had denounced the Pope as Antichrist in print was now seeking a
Catholic marriage for his son and heir. The Puritan minister Robert Bolton, for example,
gave a sermon in Northampton in 1621 which made repeated reference to the words that
came 'from King *James* his noble pen'. Bolton pays particular attention to the anti-papal
and polemical works, encouraging his auditory to 'heare King *James*' and quoting or
paraphrasing parts of those works. Bolton was ostensibly praising James for his defence
of the Reformed religion, but in 1621 this implied criticism of his current stance towards
Catholicism.[36] James's religious writings had not only incensed Catholic opponents abroad
but also given his own subjects a subtle means of questioning and contesting his actions.

    By 1622, public discussion and criticism of James's pursuit of the Spanish match and
refusal to make a military intervention in Europe had reached its height. Parliament had
been dissolved but many preachers, particularly on the Puritan wing of the church, were
defiantly continuing in such discussion.[37] In an attempt to impose order, James issued a set
of *Directions for Preachers*, which included instructions that preachers should not 'meddle

---

[32] James, *Workes*, D3^v, C4^v, B2^v. Though the collection has the date 1616 on its title-page, it seems to have
appeared early in what we would term 1617.

[33] For a useful discussion of the political context, see Thomas Cogswell, *The Blessed Revolution: English
Politics and the Coming of War, 1621–1624* (Cambridge: Cambridge University Press, 1989).

[34] James, *A Meditation upon St. Matthew: Or A Paterne for a Kings Inauguration* (London, 1620), E12^v.

[35] James, *A Meditation upon the Lords Prayer* (London, 1619), A2^v–A3^r.

[36] Robert Bolton, *Two Sermons Preached at Northampton* (London, 1635), esp. 13–14, 30–2 (quotations
13, 31).

[37] For an overview of sermons arguing for intervention in Europe in 1622, and a list of the preachers who
were reprimanded in this year, see Cogswell, *Blessed Revolution*, 27–31.

with … matters of state' or rail against either Papists or Puritans.[38] To help circulate and defend the directions, James called upon George Abbot, now Archbishop of Canterbury. He sent the *Directions* to Abbot in August, with a letter explaining that he should pass them on to the bishops, who were to transmit them to the rest of the clergy. The *Directions* were then printed, along with two letters of support from Abbot.[39] When it came to explaining and defending the *Directions* to a large audience at Paul's Cross, however, the preacher to whom James turned was John Donne. This commissioned sermon, given in September 1622, was surely one of the most difficult Donne ever had to preach, but it satisfied the King who reviewed it in manuscript and ordered it printed.[40]

Just two months later, Donne gave another Paul's Cross sermon, and commented to a friend that this time he had been 'left more to mine own liberty', a comment which suggests how much pressure he had been under in September.[41] This Gunpowder Plot anniversary sermon was also submitted to the King in manuscript, but was not then printed. The manuscript submitted to the King appears to be the one still held in the British Library.[42] What Donne does in this sermon with the greater 'liberty' he felt he had is to offer *his* commentary on the *King's* role as scriptural interpreter. The sermon remains within the boundaries of political acceptability—it may not have pleased the King enough to see print, but Donne did not get into trouble over it. Yet within those boundaries it offers one of the most searching and challenging contemporary responses to the identity as scriptural interpreter that, as we have seen throughout this chapter, James was so concerned to sustain.

The sermon is based on Lamentations 4: 20, 'The breath of our nostrils, the anointed of the Lord, was taken in their pits', and centres on two Old Testament kings, the 'good king', Josiah, and the 'bad king', his son Zedekiah. Its central argument was appropriate for a sermon given on the anniversary of the Gunpowder Plot: all kings, even bad kings, must be preserved, and it should be left to God to pass judgement over them. This argument not only accords with the theory of kingship James had expounded at most length in *The True Lawe of Free Monarchies*. It is also made with reference to 1 Samuel 8, the text on which James's treatise had been based. The manuscript copy of the sermon highlights this use of Samuel through several marginal references. Donne seems to be inviting comparison between his sermon and his King's earlier treatise.

[38] Kenneth Fincham (ed.), *Visitation Articles and Injunctions of the Early Stuart Church* (Woodbridge: Boydell Press, 1994–8), i. 211–14.

[39] For the complicated publication history of the *Directions*, see Joseph Marshall, 'Reading and Misreading King James 1622–42', in Fischlin and Fortier, *Royal Subjects*, 488–9.

[40] Donne, *A Sermon upon the XV Verse of the XX Chapter of the Booke of Judges* (London, 1622). See also Jeanne Shami, *John Donne and Conformity in Crisis in the Late Jacobean Pulpit* (Cambridge: D. S. Brewer, 2003), ch. 4. For further discussion of how Donne's 1622 sermons and other works engage with James as scriptural interpreter and writer, see my *Writing the Monarch in Jacobean England: Jonson, Donne, Shakespeare, and the Works of King James* (Cambridge: Cambridge University Press, 2015).

[41] Letter to Sir Thomas Roe in *The Life and Letters of John Donne*, ed. Edmund Gosse (London: William Heinemann, 1899), ii. 174.

[42] BL MS Royal 17.B.XX is a scribal manuscript of this sermon corrected in Donne's own hand. Unsigned and lacking a title-page, this manuscript was only recently identified by Jeanne Shami, whose *John Donne's 1622 Gunpowder Plot Sermon: A Parallel-Text Edition* (Pittsburgh, Pa.: Duquesne University Press, 1996), includes a facsimile and transcript. All subsequent references to this sermon are to this edition and given in parentheses in the text.

Such a comparison reveals that beyond this shared central argument there are subtle but important divergences. James, as noted earlier, quotes and discusses only verses 9–20 of 1 Samuel 8. Donne emphasizes two of the verses that James chose to omit. He quotes part of verse 7, in which Samuel, unhappy that the people he rules have asked for a king, is comforted by God: 'he says to Samuel, They have not rejected thee, Thou wast not king, but they have rejected me; I was' (73). For Donne this passage shows that people should trust in God: a king was 'a good thing, and intended' for the people of Israel, but, he stresses, they 'would not trust gods meanes, there was their first fault' (75). The verse also, however, suggests that to desire to serve a king is not necessarily to serve God and may even constitute a rejection of the divine. Moreover, God's speech to Samuel in this verse begins 'Hearken unto the voice of the people in all that they say unto thee'. Little wonder that James did not wish to include the verse in his discussion of the divine right of kings. Though Donne leaves the instruction to listen to the people out of his discussion, by quoting part of the verse he subtly calls the whole verse to mind.

Later in the sermon Donne turns more directly to the people who appealed to Samuel, quoting verse 4. This verse, less often cited in discussions of 1 Samuel 8, in the Bible reads simply 'Then all the elders of Israel gathered themselves together, and came to Samuel unto Ramah'. This time Donne is the one who expands significantly upon the biblical text:

> The elders of Israel gatherd togeather, So far they were in theyr way; for this was no popular, no seditious assembly of light and turbulent Men; but the elders: and then they came to Samuel; so far they were in theyr right way too. for they … came to the right place, for redresse of greivances … when they were then lawfully met, they forbear not to lay open unto him, the injustices of his officers … and thus far they kept within convenient limitts. (89)

While Donne goes on to emphasize that in pressing Samuel to accept their remedy—that is, to give them a king—the elders were wrong, here he is carefully maintaining that it is lawful for certain people to present their grievances to their ruler. The topical resonance of this passage is heightened by the qualification 'this was no popular, no seditious assembly of light and turbulent Men'. This recalls language James had recently used: in a letter, reproduced in his *Declaration* on the dissolution of Parliament, he attacks those 'fiery and popular spirits in Our House of Commons' who discussed mysteries of state, and adds that if good laws are not made the blame will lie upon 'such turbulent spirits'.[43] Donne seems to be suggesting that the very scriptural text through which James had defended his authority also teaches that the people should be ready to present grievances to their ruler in an ordered way, and that such representation from the people is lawful, not seditious. The apparent echoing of James's *Declaration* raises the possibility that Donne was, more specifically, supporting the desire of many others for James to call a Parliament.[44]

---

[43] James, *His Majesties Declaration, Touching his Proceedings in the Late Assemblie and Convention of Parliament* (London, 1621 [1622]), B2ᵛ–B4ʳ.

[44] The pressure James was under at this time to call a parliament is evident in the manuscript poem 'The wiper of the Peoples teares', written in late 1622 or early 1623 and attributed to James. This poem, written in response to a libel, asserts 'The parliament I will appoint / When I see thyngs more out of joynt', *The Poems of James VI of Scotland*, ed. James Craigie (Edinburgh and London: William Blackwood & Sons, 1955–8), ii. 182–90, lines 60–1.

As familiar a text as 1 Samuel 8 was in the period, Donne seems in these ways to be making particularly pointed use of it. The sermon balances the notion that the people should not judge or think ill *of* their king with the notion that the people should be able to speak *to* their king. Donne responds to the prevailing conditions of popular discontent and royal censorship, showing how the Bible encourages both the people to revere their rulers and rulers to listen to their people. In the process, the sermon hints that James's use of Samuel in *True Lawe* is rather selective, and that the biblical text also has challenging implications to which he should give further consideration.

This implicit concern with the King as a scriptural interpreter becomes explicit in the sermon's conclusion. Here Donne compliments his King, describing him as 'a most perfit text Man in the booke of god'. Taken out of context this might seem like mere flattery and at odds with the argument made here about the rest of the sermon. If we read on, we see that this is the kind of praise that presents its object with an ideal to aspire towards. Donne continues by imagining how the King, *as* 'a most perfit text Man in the booke of god', would respond if asked whether the souls of his subjects belong to him:

> I know he would cite *Daniel*, though our god do not deliuer us, yet know, O king that we will not worshipp thy gods; I know he would cite *Saint Peter*, we ought to obey god rather then men; And he would cite Christ himselfe, fear not them (for the soule) that cannot hurt the soule. (139)

This anticipating of royal speech is a bold move on Donne's behalf. Where two months earlier James had put his words—the *Directions* and his reasons for them—into Donne's mouth, Donne in effect puts God's words into James's mouth. Donne is not simply praising the King's scriptural learning as many of his contemporaries had done but pursuing the logic that James's use of the Bible had set in motion: he who exploits the Bible is also answerable to the Bible. Specifically, Donne is reminding the King that his knowledge of scripture should lead him to recognize that the first obedience of his subjects is to God, not to him. The Bible might exalt his power but it also limits it.

Donne's November 1622 sermon thus engages in complex ways with James as scriptural interpreter and political theorist. Donne is in effect reading James's reading of the Bible. He draws out the further implications of biblical texts James had exploited for political ends, emphasizing in particular that some of these texts might give scriptural licence for kinds of speech James seemed to be trying to censor. In its defence of representation from the people, the sermon is implicitly self-legitimizing; it enacts the ideal it presents of being able, reverently but directly, to address the King. In the process, the sermon is itself of course selectively reading the Bible to serve particular ends. Yet what it advocates is listening to many voices, not one, and showing humility before God's word and those who speak it. Donne even boldly notes, paraphrasing 2 Chronicles 36: 12, that one of the things that made Zedekiah an evil king was 'That he humbled not him selfe to gods prophets' (107). This assertion is particularly pertinent to James in the climate of the early 1620s and might be interpreted as part of a defence of preaching itself, but its emphasis on humbly listening to more than one voice also has a wider application. The sermon—unlike, say, *The True Lawe of Free Monarchies*—presents itself as simply one part of an ongoing conversation.

This idea of ongoing conversation suggests the further implications of, and poses a particular challenge to, James's self-construction as biblical interpreter. Donne highlights how scriptural interpretation, rather than allowing James to close down debates about the nature of his authority, fuelled and multiplied those debates. The authority the King himself accorded scripture in his works gave his readers, who could bring their own interpretations of scripture to bear, a way of challenging his claims. It also empowered others to presume to specify what he would, and implicitly *should*, say on particular topics. Above all, Donne's sermon emphasizes that the Bible itself is resistant to singular, fixed interpretations—that the debates it generates can never be definitively resolved.

All of the individuals considered in this chapter, from Buchanan writing a political treatise in Scotland in the 1560s to Donne preaching in England in 1622, used the Bible to support particular viewpoints or serve particular needs. King James's use of the Bible was in this sense not exceptional. Yet the extent of James's engagement in the activities of the scholar and the preacher was unprecedented in a monarch. As much as he made use of the clergy, he remained unwilling entirely to rely on others to translate, interpret, and disseminate God's word. His self-construction as an interpreter of scripture in his own right garnered him praise, even adulation, but it also left him exposed to scrutiny and attack. Most of the commentators considered here seem simply to have judged James's interpretations according to whether or not those interpretations agreed with their own theological or political position, or according to what response best served their own interests. What Donne offers, however, is a more searching assessment of the merits, limitations, and implications of James's political use of the Bible, considering how far the King really was what he sought to appear: 'a most perfit text Man in the booke of god'.

FURTHER READING

Buchanan, George. *A Dialogue on the Law of Kingship among the Scots*, ed. and tr. Roger A. Mason and Martin S. Smith (Aldershot: Ashgate, 2004).

Doelman, James. *King James I and the Religious Culture of England* (Woodbridge: D. S. Brewer, 2000).

Donne, John. *John Donne's 1622 Gunpowder Plot Sermon: A Parallel-Text Edition*, ed. Jeanne Shami (Pittsburgh, Pa.: Duquesne University Press, 1996).

Fischlin, Daniel and Mark Fortier, eds. *Royal Subjects: Essays on the Writings of James VI and I* (Detroit: Wayne State University Press, 2002).

Houlbrooke, Ralph, ed. *James VI and I: Ideas, Authority, and Government* (Aldershot: Ashgate, 2006).

James VI and I. *The True Lawe of Free Monarchies* (Edinburgh: Robert Waldegrave, 1598).

James VI and I. *The Workes of the Most High and Mighty Prince, James* (London: Robert Barker & John Bill, 1616).

McCullough, Peter E. *Sermons at Court: Politics and Religion in Elizabethan and Jacobean Preaching* (Cambridge: Cambridge University Press, 1998).

Rickard, Jane. *Authorship and Authority: The Writings of James VI and I* (Manchester: Manchester University Press, 2007).

Shami, Jeanne. *John Donne and Conformity in Crisis in the Late Jacobean Pulpit* (Cambridge: D. S. Brewer, 2003).

Stilma, Astrid J. 'King James VI and I as a Religious Writer', in C. Gribben and D. George Mullan (eds), *Literature and the Scottish Reformation* (Aldershot: Ashgate, 2009), 127–41.

CHAPTER 24

....

'A KING LIKE OTHER NATIONS': POLITICAL THEORY AND THE HEBREW REPUBLIC IN THE EARLY MODERN AGE

....

KIM IAN PARKER

If the study of the Bible's influence on the political thought of the early modern period was all but ignored until the last three decades of the twentieth century, the study of political Hebraism has been off the political map until the first decade of the twenty-first.[1] This is all the more remarkable given the frequency of biblical citations in virtually all political discussion in the seventeenth century; indeed, the seventeenth century is unprecedented in the quantity and the quality of its biblical scholarship, outstripping all others before it. This outpouring of biblical activity should not be all that surprising for, as many others have pointed out, the Reformation, with its emphasis on *sola scriptura*, placed the Bible squarely in the centre of culture, and political culture in particular.[2]

Interest in biblical and Jewish texts by largely Christian scholars in England and Scotland came to be an integral part of the political landscape in the seventeenth century. This in turn led to a rereading of the biblical sources themselves in order to see what kind of political order God had decreed. As might be expected, there were almost as many constitutions proposed as there were interpreters but, undoubtedly, one of the main points of contention was whether or not God ordained a divinely constituted monarchy. The exegetical cruxes rested on how one interpreted Deuteronomy 17 and 1 Samuel 8 and, depending on which

---

[1] Fania Oz-Salzberger, 'The Political Thought of John Locke and the Significance of Political Hebraism', *Hebraic Political Studies*, 1 (2006): 569–70.

[2] Michael C. Legaspi, *The Death of Scripture and the Rise of Biblical Studies* (Oxford: Oxford University Press, 2010); Jonathan Sheehan, *The Enlightenment Bible: Translation, Scholarship, Culture* (Princeton: Princeton University Press, 2005); Adam Sutcliffe, *Judaism and Enlightenment* (Cambridge: Cambridge University Press, 2003).

side of the political divide one stood, one could favour monarchical absolutism or republican exclusivism. Early in the century these two texts entered into the debate between the so-called 'monarchomachs' (Protestant and Catholic defenders of the people's right actively to resist a tyrant) and their opponents, such as William Barclay (1546–1608, who coined the term 'monarchomachs') and King James I of England. James, in fact, has an extended discussion of 1 Samuel 8 in *The Trew Law of Free Monarchies* (1598), and understood the passage to 'plainely declare the obedience that the people owe to their King in all respects'.[3]

In what follows, I want to discuss briefly the idea of the Hebrew Republic and follow the biblical discussion of Deuteronomy 17 and 1 Samuel 8 in the work of four seventeenth-century English political thinkers: John Maxwell and his opponent Samuel Rutherford during the English Civil War, and Sir Robert Filmer and his opponent Algernon Sidney during the Exclusion Crisis. While there are many seventeenth-century political thinkers who could exemplify this strategy (such as John Selden, 1584–1654; John Milton, 1608–74; Thomas Hobbes, 1588–1679; James Harrington, 1611–77; John Locke, 1632–1704; and many others),[4] these four have been chosen not only because of the ease with which we can see their biblical argument, but also because their battle, in part, represents the transition from a political order based on the divine right of kings to one where the republican principle of limited government becomes the new political reality. I will argue that biblical interpretation played a formative role in the development of early modern political thought in the West, especially as transmitted through the idea of the rebirth of the Hebrew Republic.

For the most part, the revival of the study of Hebrew and interest in Hebraic texts began in the fifteenth and early sixteenth centuries. It was initially conducted by humanists who wanted to establish a more reliable text.[5] After the Reformation, the study of Hebrew was a particular concern for Protestants who, responding to Luther's and the Reformers' rallying cry of *sola scriptura*, wanted to read the biblical texts in their original languages.[6] Since the Council of Trent (1545–63) had sanctioned the Latin Vulgate as the official Bible of the Church, Catholics were slower to respond to the advances made in Hebraic study over the next two centuries. Protestants in general found the political and historical readings of the Bible to be a subject of intrinsic value in themselves.[7] Other important factors in the revival of Hebrew learning were the discovery of new manuscripts, the quantity of accessible texts now that the printing industry was well under way, and the establishment of professorships of Hebrew at major universities. Alongside the interest in reading the Old Testament was an emphasis on translating and studying Judaica. Hebrew grammars, midrashic works, parts of the Talmud, and medieval Jewish rabbinical commentaries were all beginning to be

---

[3] *The Political Works of James I*, ed. C. H. McIlwain (New York: Russell & Russell, 1965), 58. On James's use of the scriptures to political ends, see the chapter by Jane Rickard in this volume.

[4] Eric Nelson, *The Hebrew Republic: Jewish Sources and the Transformation of European Political Thought* (Cambridge, Mass.: Harvard University Press, 2010); Sutcliffe, *Judaism and Enlightenment*; Annette Weber-Möckl, *Das Recht des Königs, der über euch herrschen soll: Studien zu I Samuel, 11ff. in der Literatur des frühen Neuzeit* (Berlin: Duncker & Humblot, 1986).

[5] Legaspi, *Death of Scripture*, 3–26.

[6] Kalman Neuman, 'Political Hebraism and the Early Modern "Respublica Hebraeorum"': On Defining the Field', *Hebraic Political Studies*, 1 (2005): 57–70; Stephen G Burnett, *From Christian Hebraism to Jewish Studies: Johannes Buxtorf (1564–1629) and Hebrew Learning in the Seventeenth Century* (Leiden: Brill, 1996); G. Lloyd Jones, *The Discovery of Hebrew in Tudor England: A Third Language* (Manchester: Manchester University Press, 1983).

[7] Sutcliffe, *Judaism and Enlightenment*, 43–4.

translated into Latin in the late sixteenth century and, by the end of the seventeenth century, most of the major Jewish sources were available to a wider public.[8]

What is so interesting about this Protestant apotheosis of the Bible is the interest generated in reading it politically. While political readings of biblical narratives had been around since the patristic period, it was Protestant hermeneutics that played a major role in the renewed interest in the discussion of biblical narratives. If the Old Testament was no longer thought of as the old dispensation, rendered null and void by the new, neither was it seen as only 'a prefiguration of eternal truths';[9] it was viewed, rather, as God's revealed word on a host of matters, especially politics. The laws of the Old Testament were, therefore, not anachronistic features of a primitive and outdated religion, but vibrant living laws relevant to contemporary times. If the Hebrew polity was not subject to historical obsolescence, it could be analysed like any other government in antiquity for its moral and political worth. Therefore, how and why ancient Israel decided to have a king was extremely important for a society which wanted to emulate its biblical forebears.[10] If God had been responsible for building a state, then it was incumbent on every political thinker to determine just what went into the making of the commonwealth. Indeed, it was the goal of political thinkers to duplicate what God had in mind in the *respublica Hebraeorum*.[11] In order to understand this, Christian political thinkers began to turn to the wealth of Jewish texts that were now becoming available. As we shall see, there was a wholesale shift during the seventeenth century in how the ancient Hebrew Republic was viewed politically. In 1609 James I could write, 'for Kings are not onely GODS Lieutenants upon earth, and sit upon GODS throne, but even by GOD himselfe they are called Gods'.[12]

The two key biblical texts around which the monarchy/republic battle was staged were Deuteronomy 17: 14–20 and 1 Samuel 8. The text in Deuteronomy is the first place where an Israelite form of kingship is mentioned, and the passage in 1 Samuel is where Israel becomes a monarchy. The passage in Deuteronomy is embedded in a narrative concerning Moses's speech to the Israelites on the plains of Moab prior to their entrance into the Promised Land:

> When thou art come unto the land which the LORD thy God giveth thee, and shalt possess it, and shalt dwell therein, and shalt say, I will set a king over me, like as all the nations that are about me; Thou shalt in any wise set him king over thee, whom the LORD thy God shall choose: one from among thy brethren shalt thou set king over thee: thou mayest not set a stranger over thee, which is not thy brother. But he shall not multiply horses to himself, nor cause the people to return to Egypt, to the end that he should multiply horses: forasmuch as the LORD hath said unto you, Ye shall henceforth return no more that way. Neither shall he multiply wives to himself, that his heart turn not away: neither shall he greatly multiply to himself silver and gold. And it shall be, when he sitteth upon the throne of his kingdom, that he shall write him a copy of this law in a book out of that which is before the priests the Levites: And it shall be with him, and he shall read therein all the days of his life: that he may learn to fear the LORD his God, to keep all the words of this law and these statutes, to do them: That his heart be not lifted up

[8] Nelson, *Hebrew Republic*, 7–16; Sutcliffe, *Judaism and Enlightenment*, 23–41.

[9] Neuman, 'Political Hebraism', 61.

[10] Frank E. Manuel, *The Broken Staff: Judaism through Christian Eyes* (Cambridge, Mass.: Harvard University Press, 1992), 116.

[11] Christopher Hill, *The English Bible and the Seventeenth Century Revolution* (London: Allen Lane, 1993), 3–44.

[12] *Political Works of James I*, ed. McIlwain, 307.

above his brethren, and that he turn not aside from the commandment, to the right hand, or
to the left: to the end that he may prolong his days in his kingdom, he, and his children, in the
midst of Israel.

Deuteronomy 17: 14–20 specifies that a king can only be introduced by popular demand
and the demand is somewhat tainted since Israel would become 'like all the nations that are
around' (17: 14). Permission is given to appoint a king, but he must be chosen by God, and he
must be an Israelite. This is followed by a list of restrictions, principally devoted to limiting
the king's ability to accumulate horses, wealth, or wives.

Another issue that concerned biblical political commentators was whether the passage
in Deuteronomy was a prediction of what may happen when the Israelites entered the
Promised Land (i.e. '*if* you say I will set a king over me') or whether the passage should
be rendered more forcefully (i.e. 'you *shall* say I will set a king over me'). This was not just
an idle distinction, for it makes a difference whether God was merely predicting that the
Israelites might establish a monarchy like other nations or whether God was telling them to
establish a monarchy like other nations and, if the latter, why would God get so angry at the
Israelites for doing so? Thus, while God was not in favour of a tyranny, or a 'king like other
nations', he may not have been against a monarchy.

The problem is even more complicated when Israel actually gets a king. In fact, 1 Samuel
8–12 presents two parallel accounts of the establishment of the monarchy. One is hostile to
the very idea, and the other tacitly accepts it.[13] Depending on one's political stance, therefore, one could easily support or reject monarchy. For instance, while Samuel warns the people of the tyrannical excesses to which a monarchy is prone, he also anoints Saul as king and
appears to approve of him. Saul in fact saves the people from the Ammonites and unifies the
tribes in an anarchic period.[14]

In any event, the main point of contention is to determine why, if God sanctioned kingship in Deuteronomy, would he condemn it in 1 Samuel 8? Early medieval and Renaissance
commentators resolved this problem by arguing that (a) the Israelites selected a king who
did not meet the criteria set out in Deuteronomy 17, i.e. he was tyrannical rather than
godly or (b), that in asking for a regime change from the rule by the charismatic judges, the
Israelites were rebelling against God's established order. This, as we shall see, is a similar
argument to the one that underlies the theory of the divine right of kings. In both cases,
however, the legitimacy of a monarchy is not the issue, as monarchs or their designates are
chosen by God.[15]

John Figgis argued in his pioneering study of *The Divine Right of Kings* (1896) that
the theory of divine right was not a hastily cobbled together one, but a coherent doctrine emerging from medieval times to deal with the real political problems posed in
the aftermath of the Reformation. According to Figgis, the doctrine of the divine right
of kings was 'a necessary transition stage between medieval and modern politics'.[16] The

---

[13] This is something of a *locus classicus* for source division of the Hebrew Bible. The common division is a
pro-monarchic source in 9: 1–10: 16, 11: 1–15, and an anti-monarchic one in 8: 1–22, 10: 17–27, 12: 1–25.

[14] On the political uses of Saul in the Civil War period, see the chapter by Anne Lake Prescott in this
volume.

[15] See Nelson, *Hebrew Republic*, 31.

[16] John N. Figgis, *The Divine Right of Kings* (Gloucester, Mass.: Peter Smith, 1970), 258. First published as
The Theory of the Divine Right of Kings (Cambridge: Cambridge University Press, 1896).

idea that secular political power was given by God was perhaps so common in the early seventeenth century that the doctrine hardly needed restating, though it did take many forms.[17] Some believed that it was based on a patriarchal pattern in nature where the ruler was like a father, whereas others believed that it derived from human consent.[18] Thus a government might hold power by election but still rule by divine right as, for instance, we see in James I's paraphrase of God's promise to the Israelites in 1 Samuel 8: 'although you shall grudge and murmure, yet it shal not be lawful to you to cast it [kingship] off, in respect it is not only the ordinance of God, but also your selves have chosen him unto you, thereby renouncing for ever all priviledges, by your willing consent out of your hands'.[19]

Part of the appeal of the divine right of kings is that it mirrors what E. W. M. Tillyard called 'The Great Chain of Being'.[20] This is a doctrine of order and harmony in nature in which everything has its proper place in a divinely created, hierarchically ordered universe. The chain starts with God and progresses downward to the angels, kings, princes, nobles, men, women, children, and then the animals, plants, and minerals. Indeed, the main point about this harmonious order was that it originated from God and to upset it in any way, shape, or form was to disturb the balance of the order and sin against God. Although kings wielded considerable power in this hierarchy, sitting at the top of the human order, they still had to be accountable to some sort of divine law. As Peter Wentworth wrote in the early seventeenth century, 'it is necessarie for princes as well as for others, to doe those thinges that are pleasing and acceptable to god, and therefore when they shall sit upon the throne of their kingdomes they are commanded, to have the booke of God and to studye it, and not to departe therefrom either to the righte hand, or the lefte'.[21] In what follows I want to show the degree to which political commentators of various stripes felt kings were accountable to divine law, particularly through their readings of Deuteronomy 17 and 1 Samuel 8.

One of the more forceful advocates of the absolute power of the king based on a reading of the Hebrew Republic was the Scottish royalist John Maxwell. In his *Sacro-sancta regnum majestas* (1644), Maxwell argued that kingly authority was from God and that what was required of the people was passive obedience to the king. He argued against the Puritan and Catholic view (notably of Suarez and Bellarmine) that the king's power derives from the people. For Maxwell, this doctrine was nonsensical as the people do not have any innate power in the first place and cannot, therefore, transfer it to anyone. If political authority rested with the people (and since the nature of the people was always to be in a state of flux), then the people could not be held accountable by any constitutional arrangements. This was anarchy for Maxwell. Bellarmine and Suarez had used the passage in Deuteronomy 17 to

[17] See Owen Chadwick, who writes that 'the dogma that Kings rule by divine right was common ground to everyone who used the Bible', *The Reformation* (Harmondsworth: Penguin, 1964), 391.
[18] See Conrad Russell, 'Divine Rights in the Early Seventeenth Century', in John Morrill, Paul Slack, and Daniel Woolf (eds), *Public Duty and Private Conscience in Seventeenth-Century England* (Oxford: Oxford University Press, 1993), 103.
[19] In *Political Works of James I*, ed. McIlwain, 59.
[20] E. M. W. Tillyard, *The Elizabethan World Picture* (Cambridge: Cambridge University Press, 1943), *passim*.
[21] Cited in Russell, 'Divine Rights', 110.

argue for the inherent power of the people but, for Maxwell, this was a patent violation of scripture:

> say they [Suarez and Bellarmine], the Constitution is the Peoples, the Election of the Person is Gods. It is a lame Consequence; for the words *Constitues super te*, Thou shalt set over thee, are not to be understood of Constitution by collating, or transferring from them to the King, Majesty and Sovereignty: but of Constitution by way of Approbation, or of accepting of him as King, acknowledging him as a King, reverencing and obeying him as King, whom God hath both designed and constituted by himself King.[22]

When dealing with the passages in Samuel where the Israelites actually get a king in the person of Saul, Maxwell turns his attention to the pro-monarchic passages (1 Samuel 9, 10) and glosses over the passages dealing with the tyrannical behaviour of the king (1 Samuel 8, 12). Maxwell claims that it is God who ordains and sets a king over the people, not the people who transfer their power over to a king. Samuel's anointing of Saul in 10: 1 is proof, for Maxwell, that God desires a king (32). Maxwell also uses the chapters in 1 Samuel to indicate that 'Disobedience to sovereign Power is not only Violation of Truth, Breach of Covenant, but also high Disobedience and Contempt' (48). This time, Maxwell focuses on 1 Samuel 11 and interprets Saul's call for arms to fight the Ammonites as a divine sanction to obey the king. As Maxwell later argues, God 'left no other act to his People but to admit him [Saul], which was not left to their voluntary determination to admit or reject him at pleasure' (93).

Maxwell further understands the chapters in 1 Samuel to indicate a shift from a political order where God *was* the sovereign to a political order where God *sets up* the sovereign. There is no indication, for Maxwell, that God had placed any power in the community; Moses and the judges merely act as God's temporary regents, but it is only with the ascension of Saul as king that the political structure changes. In other words, Maxwell sees the ancient Hebrew Republic go from a unique political order under God to a divinely appointed monarchy. Maxwell points to the passage in 1 Samuel 11 where 'the spirit of God' came mightily upon Saul as an indication of God's bestowal of favour on monarchy as an institution (93–4). In sum, Maxwell uses the passages in Deuteronomy 17 and the chapters on the origin of kingship in 1 Samuel 8–12 to argue against the claims made by Suarez, Bellarmine and the Puritans, making the case that God sets up and approves of monarchy and that any act of resistance to the king is tantamount to rebellion against God. Treason, for Maxwell, is a form of blasphemy.

Maxwell's work was published in 1644, a time when England was in the midst of a bloody civil war as royalist forces were actively engaged in warfare against parliamentary ones from 1642 to 1649. As such, it was inevitable that Maxwell's *Sacro-sancta* would get a response. It did perhaps most famously by Samuel Rutherford (1600?–1661) in a work titled *Lex, Rex* (1644), a lengthy treatise in the scholastic form of questions and answers. Rutherford's work also gained a good deal of notoriety in the years following the restoration of the Stuart monarchy under Charles II in 1660. Rutherford himself was summoned by the court in Edinburgh to appear on a charge of high sedition but died in 1661 before he could be tried. *Lex, Rex* figures prominently in *The Judgment and Decree of the University of Oxford … against Certain Pernicious Books and Damnable Doctrines* (1683), a document written to strengthen the absolutist and divine right principles of the Stuart monarchy in the aftermath of the failed Rye

---

[22] John Maxwell, *Sacro-sancta regnum majestas* (Oxford, 1644), 32.

House Plot (1683). The decree required books named in it to be burned, and Rutherford's *Lex, Rex* appears in four of the twenty-seven articles, more than any other named book.[23]

In *Lex, Rex*, Rutherford does concede that the power of the King derives from God. The main authority that Rutherford invokes to show this claim is the Bible, particularly Deuteronomy 17.[24] As John Coffey and others point out, Deuteronomy 17 is Rutherford's favourite passage and he returns to it often in his attack on Maxwell.[25] It is important to note in this regard that Rutherford's argument from Deuteronomy is not an argument against kingship *per se*, but an argument which, in many instances, actually supports kingship. The king, however, must abide by the laws and statutes; thus although God may establish kingship as a legitimate political regime, there lies something beyond kingship.[26] In this sense Rutherford makes a distinction between the office of the king (which is divinely sanctioned) and the person of the king (who is not necessarily so sanctioned). Thus the people can appoint a king, but the people's choice is to be guided by divine law. If God instructs the people how to act in this regard, they can choose anyone for a king as long as it falls within the specifications of divine law. As Rutherford writes, 'the first king is a king by election, not by birth, Deut. 17.15' (80). The king cannot rule according to his own will, but must act according to God's law. In other words, the office is bound by the laws of God and the office of the king is there by divine right, not through a transferring of the right from the people (as in Hobbes for instance).

Interestingly enough, Rutherford also uses the passage in Deuteronomy to argue in favour of the separation of powers. He writes:

> nor ought the King to contend for sole power in himself, of ministring justice to all; for God layeth not upon Kings, burdens unpossible, and God by Institution hath denied to the King, all power of doing all good, because it is his Will that other Judges be sharers with the King in that power, Num. 14.16; Deut. i.14, 15, 16, 17; 1 Pet. 2.14; Rom. 13.1, 2, 3, 4. And therefore the Duke of Venice to me cometh nearest to the King, moulded by God, Deut. 17 in respect of power, *de jure*, of any King I know in Europe (259).

The separation of powers is important for another reason. For given the fallen condition of humanity, the dangers of one man acting tyrannically with absolute power are worse than if many wield power and if there is an external law to hold the king in check. In fact 'the Fall' is the reason why humans need government in the first place—since humans are sinful by nature they need a strong government to control their actions and activities. As Rutherford states, 'if there had not been sin, there should not have been need of a King ... but because sinne is entered into the world, God devised, as a remedy of violence and unjustice, a living rationall, breathing Law called a King, a Judge, a Father'.[27]

In dealing with the passage in 1 Samuel, Rutherford is keen to show that a king is not above the law and that a king does not have absolute powers. Question 18 in *Lex, Rex* gives

[23] See David Wootton (ed.), *Divine Right and Democracy: An Anthology of Political Writing in Stuart England* (Harmondsworth: Penguin, 1986), 92–3 and 120–6.

[24] Samuel Rutherford, *Lex, Rex* (London, 1644), 6, 7, 8.

[25] John Coffey, *Politics, Religion, and the British Revolution: The Mind of Samuel Rutherford* (Cambridge: Cambridge University Press, 1997), 165. See also Richard Flinn, 'Samuel Rutherford and Puritan Political Theory', *Journal of Christian Reconstruction*, 5 (1978–9): 72.

[26] Rutherford, *Lex, Rex*, 35, 140, 176. See also Coffey, *Politics Religion, and the British Revolution*, 152, 171–2.

[27] *Lex, Rex*, 213; cf. 215.

an extended discussion of the problem, a discussion in which Rutherford shows his virtuosity in dealing with both the Hebrew and Greek biblical sources. Rutherford's opponent in this section is William Barclay (1546–1608) who argued in favour of an absolute monarch in his *Contra monarchomachos* (1600). Barclay distinguishes between the king's office (as specified in Deuteronomy 17) and the king's power (as specified in 1 Samuel 8) and argued that the list of crimes that kings would commit as detailed in 1 Samuel 8: 11–18 were an indication of the absolute power of the king. Rutherford counters by saying that the king cannot transgress the law of God (as in Deuteronomy 17) and behave like a tyrant (81). Among others, Rutherford uses a rabbinical source, Rabbi Levi Ben Gersom (in a Latin translation) to support his point, indicating an early awareness of rabbinical sources for the Hebrew Republic (74). Indeed, for Rutherford, the passage in 1 Samuel 8 does not give licence for a king to act tyrannically, but is a warning of what might happen if a king does not obey the law of God.[28] Rutherford continually hammers home the point that no king is above God's law.

In sum, Rutherford's position is that, although God may have granted Israel (and by analogy, Scotland or England) the right to have a king, the king must be bound to the law of God as specified in Deuteronomy 17 and not act tyrannously. The king does not have absolute power but the power is shared between the magistrates and the law. The king is bound by a covenant between himself and the people and between himself and God and cannot act as he wishes. Numerous biblical citations are mustered to show this is the case, but the text in Deuteronomy 17 is the one that Rutherford cites most often.

Another Civil War writer who was interested in biblical politics was Sir Robert Filmer (1588–1653). Unlike Maxwell and Rutherford, however, Filmer's works did not attract immediate attention when they were published anonymously in 1648, but a manuscript text published posthumously in 1680 did attract considerable attention. Indeed, the timely posthumous publication of *Patriarcha* (even though it was written no later than 1642), in the middle of the 'Exclusion Crisis' (1679–81, i.e. the attempt by the Earl of Shaftesbury and the newly formed Whig Party to exclude James, the Catholic brother of Charles II, from succeeding to the throne), gave the royalist Tory Party an ideological weapon to combat Shaftesbury and the Whig exclusionists: here was a political work whose biblical base justified hereditary succession and the absolute power of kings.

In terms of the intellectual history of the seventeenth century, Filmer is probably best known for his attempt to establish the absolute dominion of Adam on the basis of the first few chapters of the book of Genesis. In so doing, Filmer argues that all kings rule by divine right 'because they are, or are reputed to be, the natural heirs of Adam'.[29] His opponent, John Locke, devoted the first of his *Two Treatises on Government* (1690) to tearing down Filmer's argument and establishing his own liberal principles of freedom and equality on the same biblical passages in Genesis.[30] Less well known, perhaps, is Filmer's exegesis of Deuteronomy 17 and 1 Samuel 8 in which he argues in favour of the absolute power of the king over his subjects.

[28] *Lex, Rex*, 76–7, 100.

[29] *Patriarcha and Other Writings*, ed. J. P. Sommerville (Cambridge: Cambridge University Press, 1991), 61–2.

[30] Kim Ian Parker, *The Biblical Politics of John Locke* (Waterloo, ON: Wilfrid Laurier University Press, 2004), 95–122.

In *Patriarcha*, Filmer uses Deuteronomy 17 to support the idea that the Israelites did not have the power to choose a king, only a power to set a king over them. It is the Lord who chooses the king, not Israel, and Filmer quotes a lengthy passage from Richard Hooker's biblical argument to help make the distinction between *eligere* (choose) and *constituere* (set up) clearer.[31] If the Israelites had the power to choose whatever king they wanted, they never would have chosen boy kings (as, for instance, Josiah). Filmer also cites the Jewish historian Flavius Josephus as saying that the law concerning the duty of the king in Deuteronomy was not the same as the law that Samuel wrote. If it was the same, asks Filmer, why did he need to write it again? Secondly, the audience is different—the law in Deuteronomy was addressed to the king, whereas the law in 1 Samuel is read to the people. Thirdly, the law in Deuteronomy is not a law as such, but only a few precepts inveighing against multiplying wealth, horses, and marrying foreign women. Finally, the laws are only laws to Jews as a unique people—not laws to all kings.[32]

When Filmer discusses the passage in 1 Samuel in *Patriarcha*, he suggests that, even prior to the establishment of the monarchy under Saul, Israel was 'governed by a kingly power'. Although the priests and the judges were not called kings, they were deputed to be such by God himself. For Filmer, 'the patriarchs, Dukes, judges, and kings were all monarchs'. The Israelites, therefore, did not want a king 'by deputation, but desired one by succession like all the other nations'. Thus, Samuel governed the people in the manner of a king as appointed by God and the desire of the Israelites to have a king 'like other nations' only referred to a hereditary monarchy—in other words, the prayer of the Israelites was not to choose a king in an election but to have one through inheritance (23).

Samuel's job, moreover, was to teach the people the unlimited monarchy of their sovereign. As Filmer writes, 'for as Kingly power is by the law of God, so it hath no inferior limit to it' (26). The list of possible consequences of a kingship reported at the end of 1 Samuel 8 such as conscription, expropriation of land, and taxation, does not necessarily give kings the right to indulge in all these practices and crimes. It merely means that kings cannot be held accountable by the people if such injuries are committed. Thus, the question of whether Samuel is describing a king or a tyrant is irrelevant, as the people must obey either. Even if the words of Samuel do describe the actions of a tyrant (which Filmer does not concede), there is no remedy against a tyranny but to pray to God. Citing Ralegh, Filmer argues that one could easily give a more charitable interpretation to 1 Samuel 8, and that the 'inconveniences' described by Samuel are not necessarily all that onerous and may be borne lightly. In fact, Filmer argues that what is being described is quite ordinary and may even be deemed 'mild' (37–8).

According to Filmer, the people did not ask for a tyrant and Saul himself did not by any means act tyrannically. Indeed, Saul was never punished or blamed for doing those things that Samuel suggested a king would do in 1 Samuel 8. As Filmer reasonably argues, Saul was certainly punished, but the punishment was for sparing King Agag's life, that is, for being too merciful, not for being too tyrannical (cf. 1 Samuel 15). Furthermore, the Israelites themselves never complained about the conditions proposed by Saul, but accepted them. They

---

[31] Filmer, *Patriarcha*, 22.   [32] *Patriarcha*, 66.

do complain, however, about the conditions imposed by Solomon, who was no tyrant (cf. 1 Kings 12).[33]

In sum, Filmer's use of Deuteronomy and 1 Samuel in *Patriarcha* to support his views on the absolute power of the monarch closely resembles that of his contemporary John Maxwell.[34] Both are keen to use scripture to prove that the original form of government was a divinely ordained monarchy and that some form of monarchical rule existed in ancient Israel from Adam until its dissolution at the Babylonian exile. The monarchy, moreover, has unlimited powers, as the passage in 1 Samuel 8 indicates. To rebel against a king was tantamount to upsetting God's divine order. *Patriarcha* was probably one of the last works to make a strong biblical case for the divine right of kings and its argument would not go unnoticed.

Algernon Sidney (1622–83) wrote his *Discourses concerning Government* (1698, originally written around 1683) as a lengthy rebuttal to Filmer's biblically based argument in *Patriarcha*. Like Locke's *Two Treatises* (1690, written 1682–3), and James Tyrrell's *Patriarcha non monarcha* (1681), Sidney's work dealt with Filmer's claim that government originates from Adam and that kings have absolute power over their subjects. Sidney, however, expands his exegetical net to include the passages in Deuteronomy and 1 Samuel which Filmer had also used. Sidney's work is especially instructive in showing the transition from monarchical absolutism to republican exclusivism. It should be noted, too, how volatile these arguments were in the early 1680s. Sidney's unpublished *Discourses* was used as evidence against him in the prosecution's case on the charge of sedition, for which Sidney was convicted and hanged in 1683.

The first chapter of the *Discourses* attacks Filmer's claim that God had ordained a monarchical government because he gave sole dominion to Adam. Sidney's argument here largely parallels that of Locke's. In chapters 2 and 3, however, Sidney sets forth his argument for republican exclusivism largely based on the passages in Deuteronomy 17 and 1 Samuel. Sidney sought to demonstrate that kingship was a sin in the eyes of God and that Israel had committed the sin of idolatry.[35] Like Locke, Sidney takes great delight in ridiculing the absurdities of Filmer's position. And while Sidney brings in much more historical evidence to back up his position than does Filmer (or Locke for that matter), his work is replete with scriptural citations.[36]

If Filmer had used Deuteronomy 17 to distinguish between *eligere* (choose) and *constituere* (set up), Sidney argues that Deuteronomy does not make such a distinction—that *eligere* and *constituere* are the same—one cannot be elected without having the institution in place

---

[33] *Patriarcha*, 37–8.

[34] Maxwell, *Sacro-sancta*, 64–5, 76, 147–8.

[35] Algernon Sidney, *Discourses concerning Government*, ed. Thomas G. West (New York: Liberty Fund, 1996), 48. See also Jonathan Scott, *Algernon Sidney and the English Republic, 1623–1677* (Cambridge: Cambridge University Press, 1988), 198.

[36] In spite of a flurry of substantial work on Sidney in the 1990s, there are relatively few works which deal with Sidney's biblical argument. Neither Jonathan Scott, *Algernon Sidney and the Restoration Crisis* (Cambridge: Cambridge University Press, 1991), nor Alan Craig Houston, *Algernon Sidney and the Republican Heritage in England and America* (Princeton: Princeton University Press, 1991), pay much attention to Sidney's scriptural argument, but see Nathan R. Perl-Rosenthal, 'The "Divine Right of Republics": Hebraic Republicanism and the Debate over Kingless Government in Revolutionary America', *William and Mary Quarterly*, 66 (2009): 535–64.

and those who are so instituted are elected. Sidney argues that God allows the people to choose a king *if they want*, the choice being the people's in the first place; the only stipulation is that the king they choose should 'abide by the rules prescribed by Moses his servant'.[37] In Sidney's analysis, there is no monarchical institution in place or necessarily ordained by God; it is a matter for the people to decide. The fact that the Israelites did not have a king for 300 years indicates that kingship was not a necessity.

Filmer had also argued that the only legitimate king was a king who had absolute power. But, as Sidney points out, the limitations to the king set out by God in Deuteronomy 17 ensure that the king's powers cannot be absolute. Sidney quotes Josephus's paraphrase of this passage, that is, 'He shall do nothing without the advice of the Sanhedrin; or, if he do, they shall oppose him'.[38] In the lengthy third chapter, Sidney goes further in his exegesis of Deuteronomy 17, and summons both the aid of the medieval Jewish philosopher Moses Maimonides and Hugo Grotius to suggest that the Sanhedrin is a powerful political body. In fact, the Sanhedrin's power to keep the kings in check and its right to call the people together for assemblies 'were the foundations of their liberty; and being added to the law of the kingdom prescribed in the seventeenth of Deuteronomy (if they should think fit to have a king) established the freedom of that people upon a solid foundation' (335). If Filmer had also made the point that it is right and proper for kings to be powerful and have riches, Sidney does not hesitate to point out that it is against the law of the kings in Deuteronomy 17 for kings to multiply silver and gold for themselves.[39] Sidney's king, as prescribed in Deuteronomy 17, is limited by the law of God and cannot do whatever he pleased.

Sidney understood the passage in 1 Samuel to mean that God had condemned monarchy in total. For Sidney, the government originally decreed by God was kingless, and kingship only started after a rejection of God. There is no evidence of kings in Israel's early history, and people like Gideon, who refuses kingship, and Abimelech, who accepts it, are respectively praised and blamed. Sidney also suggests that, in asking for a king, the Israelites were being proud and haughty and not humbly seeking good governance (130). Sidney ridicules Filmer's position that Israel was governed until the time of Samuel as if it were a kingdom. Indeed, as Sidney legitimately asks, why would the Israelites ask for a king if they already had one?[40]

If Filmer had argued that the list of oppressions mentioned in 1 Samuel 8 indicated the power of the monarch, Sidney countered by saying this passage indicated the horrible things that might happen to the people under a tyranny. The passage, moreover, was a strong indictment of monarchy, deeming it a punishment from a God so angry that he would not listen to the Israelite's prayers for deliverance. Far from the king being above the law as Filmer claims, Sidney argues that God abrogates Saul's dynasty because Saul had violated divine law and turned the kingdom into a tyranny.[41]

Sidney also points out that the establishment of a kingship in 1 Samuel was not a command but only a possibility, and if the Israelites decided to have a king, the monarchy would bring about the misery which both Moses and Samuel had foretold. Far

---

[37] Sidney, *Discourses*, 109, cf. 125, 290.
[38] *Discourses*, 289, cf. 312.
[39] *Discourses*, 349 (cf. *Patriarcha*, 37).
[40] *Discourses*, 324.
[41] *Discourses*, 328–33.

from being a free choice of a monarchy as Filmer had argued, monarchy was a rejection of God's divine rule (337). To help prove this, Sidney invokes the help of Jewish
authorities:

> Josephus says, that Saul's first sin by which he fell, was, *that he took away the aristocracy*; which
> he could not do if it had never been established. Philo imputes the institution of kingly gov-
> ernment, as it was in Israel, neither to God nor his Word, but to the fury of the sinful People.
> Abravanel says, it proceeded from their delight in the idolatry to which their neighbours were
> addicted, and which could be upheld only by a government, in practice and principle contrary
> to that which God had instituted. Maimonides frequently says the same thing, grounded upon
> the words of Hosea, *I gave them a king in my wrath.* (124)

For Sidney, this is not a *description* of the absolute power of a king (so Filmer), but a *condemnation*, listing the sufferings that the people must endure. In his unpublished dialogue *Court
Maxims*, Sidney's mouthpiece, Eunomius, says that 'monarchy is in itself an irrational, evil
government'.[42] God foretold the misery that would follow if the Israelites persisted in their
wickedness, and brought upon themselves the deserved punishment thereof. Sidney elaborates this point in the *Discourses*, explaining that 1 Samuel 8 reveals 'how strict a union there
is between idolatry and tyranny'.[43]

From the early to the mid-seventeenth century, therefore, political writers such as
James I, William Barclay, John Maxwell, and Robert Filmer used the Bible to bolster and
prove the argument that kings rule by divine right, whereas by the mid- to late seventeenth
century political theorists such as Rutherford, Milton, Harrington, Tyrrell, Locke, and
Sidney used the Bible to tear down biblically based monarchic absolutism and to establish their own republican principles based on biblical texts. By the eighteenth century,
however, biblical politics all but disappears in England, and theorists no longer evoked
sacred scripture to support or inveigh against monarchy. Hebraic politics did, however,
find a home in the Atlantic world mainly due to its being kept alive in Puritan circles.[44]
Sidney's works were especially popular in colonial America during the Revolutionary
War, though, ironically enough, they were sometimes used to support the idea of a limited
monarchy. Many sermons in New England in fact quoted from the *Discourses* to sum-
mon support for the king.[45] And although political Hebraism in the Atlantic world has
not been studied until recently, these studies have exposed the extent to which colonial
America in particular was coming to grips with how ancient Israel provided a political
model for the emerging polity.

The thesis that the availability of biblical and Judaic sources in the seventeenth century
was a deciding factor that helped swing the political tide from a pro-monarchic divine right
of kings regime to a republican exclusivist one has much to recommend it. As we have seen,
a biblical argument that concerns the regime to which God gives His approval is certainly
central to the political dialogue in seventeenth-century England. It seems evident from the
brief sampling of the thinkers presented here that the summoning of biblical evidence, especially from Deuteronomy and 1 Samuel, played an important role not only in framing the

---

[42] Algernon Sidney, *Court Maxims*, ed. Hans Blom, Eco Haitsma-Mulier, and Ronald Janse (Cambridge:
Cambridge University Press, 1996), 65; cf. 42–3, 47.
[43] Sidney, *Discourses*, 86.   [44] Manuel, *Broken Staff*, 117–18.
[45] See Perl-Rosenthal, 'Divine Right', 544–5.

questions, but in coming up with the solutions as well. Whether or not the interpretation pointed one in the direction of monarchical absolutism or republican exclusivism depended on how one interpreted Deuteronomy 17 and 1 Samuel 8, not whether or not the Bible was relevant to the political discussion. And, given the tense polarized political climate of the times—the Civil Wars, the execution of King Charles I, the Exclusion Crisis, the Glorious Revolution—this discussion was not insignificant. The modern political landscape in all its complexity developed from a biblically saturated culture in which political theorists tried to discern what kind of government God had ordained.

FURTHER READING

Hill, Christopher. *The English Bible and the Seventeenth Century Revolution* (London: Allen Lane, 1993).

Legaspi, Michael C. *The Death of Scripture and the Rise of Biblical Studies* (Oxford: Oxford University Press, 2010).

Manuel, Frank E. *The Broken Staff: Judaism through Christian Eyes* (Cambridge, Mass.: Harvard University Press, 1992).

Nelson, Eric. *The Hebrew Republic: Jewish Sources and the Transformation of European Political Thought* (Cambridge, Mass.: Harvard University Press, 2010).

Neuman, Kalman. 'Political Hebraism and the Early Modern "*Respublica Hebraeorum*": On Defining the Field'. *Hebraic Political Studies*, 1 (2005): 57–70.

Perl-Rosenthal, Nathan R. 'The "Divine Right of Republics": Hebraic Republicanism and the Debate over Kingless Government in Revolutionary America'. *William and Mary Quarterly*, 66 (2009): 535–64.

Sheehan, Jonathan. *The Enlightenment Bible: Translation, Scholarship, Culture* (Princeton: Princeton University Press, 2005).

Sutcliffe, Adam. *Judaism and Enlightenment* (Cambridge: Cambridge University Press, 2003).

CHAPTER 25

....

DIGGING, LEVELLING, AND RANTING: THE BIBLE AND THE CIVIL WAR SECTS

....

ANDREW BRADSTOCK

'THE Scriptures of the Bible', wrote the Digger leader Gerrard Winstanley in 1650, 'were writ-ten by the experimentall hand of Shepherds, Husbandmen, Fishermen, and such inferiour men of the world'.[1] It was a direct challenge to the learned and tithe-funded clergy of his day, who jealously guarded their right to determine the meaning of the biblical text and preach it to the people. For Winstanley, these were 'false Prophets', men who did not know the scriptures by experience and who spoke only 'from their imagination'.[2] The ability truly to discern the meaning of scripture lay with 'inferior' people like himself, the equivalents of the original authors, who knew the truth 'purely and experimentally' having 'received it of the Father' rather than 'from man, and by man'.[3] For Winstanley it was the Spirit's teaching, not that to be found in universities, that enabled a reader to discern the mind of God.

The principle that the scriptures derived from and spoke to ordinary people was funda-mental for Winstanley and others who resented the clergy's role in preaching up a system in which economic and political power lay with a small elite. One of the Leveller leaders, William Walwyn, also noted that God did not choose the learned to be his 'Prophets and publishers of the Gospell; but Heards-men, Fisher-men, Tent-makers, Toll-gatherers, etc'; and Walwyn shared Winstanley's concern that, although the people now had the scriptures in their own tongue, they were still being warned by the clergy not to trust their own under-standing. 'What are you the better for having the Scripture in your own language … [if] … you must have an university man to interpret the English', Walwyn asked; 'Let me prevail with you to free yourselves from this bondage'.[4] Like Winstanley, Walwyn argued that lay

---

[1] Gerrard Winstanley, *Fire in the Bush* (1650) in *The Complete Works of Gerrard Winstanley*, ed. Thomas N. Corns, Ann Hughes, and David Loewenstein (Oxford: Oxford University Press, 2009), hereafter *CW*, ii. 200.

[2] Winstanley, *Truth Lifting up his Head above Scandals* (1648), *CW* i. 432.

[3] Winstanley, *Fire in the Bush*, *CW* ii. 200.

[4] Cited in Brian Manning, 'The Levellers and Religion', in J. F. McGregor and B. Reay (eds), *Radical Religion in the English Revolution* (Oxford: Oxford University Press, 1984), 66, and Christopher Hill, *The English Bible and the Seventeenth-Century Revolution* (London: Allen Lane, 1993), 200.

people could 'come to a good and right understanding' of the Bible themselves without the aid of a priest; just as they were perfectly able to understand and participate in politics if they were given the opportunity, so they could comprehend the Bible themselves if they 'would but take boldnes to themselves and not distrust their own understandings'.[5]

The point about encouraging lay people to interpret scripture for themselves was that the clergy used it to maintain their dominance over them, preaching a gospel suited to their 'covetous, ambitious, and persecuting spirit', as Walwyn put it.[6] Winstanley was clear that the university-educated divines had deliberately overlain the 'plaine language' employed by the original writers 'with their darke interpretation, and glosses', not just to make a show of their learning but to ensure that their rich benefactors continued to enjoy their privileged access to the land. Whereas the Bible spoke of the earth and its fruits having been created for all to enjoy in equal measure, the 'beneficed clergy', by obscuring the straightforward meaning of the text, 'deceive the simple, and makes a prey of the poore, and cosens them of the Earth, and of the tenth of their labors'.[7]

We should see the mid-seventeenth century, then, as a period when the Bible became a site of class struggle, with the counterparts of its original 'inferior' authors vying with the learned and scholarly for ownership and control of the text. At stake for the Levellers was the question of whether scripture sanctified the existing system of land ownership and government, or advocated measures to bring about radical change. As long as biblical exposition remained in the hands of the university-educated clergy—a situation which successive monarchs and bishops of the Anglican Church sought to preserve—a degree of consistency regarding its 'meaning' could be maintained and heretical opinions, at least to some extent, kept in check.[8] As Charles himself recognized, 'people are governed by the pulpit more than the sword in times of peace'.[9] Since the breakdown of censorship and abolition of the church courts in the early 1640s, however, the heretical and subversive ideas which two centuries of popular Bible reading had generated could be discussed and preached more freely. Passages relating to God having 'put down the mighty from *their* seats, and exalted them of low degree' (Luke 1: 52) might well now be used by unlettered preachers to encourage a re-enactment of such revolutionary upheavals. Winstanley is unlikely to have been alone, in the months leading up to Charles's execution, in understanding God's promise in Haggai 2: 7 to 'shake all nations' to have contemporary relevance. God, Winstanley wrote, 'will yet shake, Kings, Parliaments, Armies, Counties, Kingdomes, Universities, humane learnings, studies, yea, shake rich men and poore men, and throwes down every thing that stands in his way opposing him in his work'.[10]

---

[5] Cited in Manning, 'The Levellers and Religion', 65–7.

[6] Cited in Manning, 'The Levellers and Religion', 84.

[7] Winstanley, *Fire in the Bush, CW* ii. 200.

[8] It is worth noting that the practice of separating from the established church may have begun as far back as the 1530s, and Dutch Anabaptists were known to be meeting in England in the reigns of Henry VIII, Edward VI, and Mary. The ideas which Diggers, Ranters, and others promulgated openly in the 1640s and 1650s were not unknown to previous generations of English people, as we know from accounts of John Ball, Lollards, the Family of Love, and others. See my *Radical Religion in Cromwell's England: A Concise History from the English Civil War to the End of the Commonwealth* (London: I. B. Tauris, 2011) for a fuller discussion of this.

[9] Cited in Pauline Gregg, *King Charles I* (Berkeley, Calif.: University of California Press, 1984), 409. On fears surrounding popular reception of scripture in the 1530s, see the chapter by Susan Wabuda in this volume.

[10] Winstanley, *The Breaking of the Day of God* (1648), *CW* i. 180.

As Christopher Hill observes, the political upheaval of the 1640s and its consequences 'shattered the universal acceptance of the Bible as an infallible text whose pronouncements were to be followed implicitly';[11] this was a period, as Nigel Smith suggests, when 'the Bible was stretched to uses and interpretations with a density which had not occurred before in England'.[12] The Geneva Bible, first published in 1560 but printed as late as 1644, spelt out for its readers the subversive implications of various texts in its marginal notes, although the King James Bible was plain enough when it spoke of the fate of corrupt rulers or the eventual triumph of the saints. Texts such as 'where the Spirit of the Lord is, there is liberty' (2 Corinthians 3: 17) or 'Stand fast therefore in the liberty wherewith Christ hath made us free, and be not entangled again with the yoke of bondage' (Galatians 5: 1) would have had an immediate political relevance for uneducated men and women, as Hill has argued.[13] And it was not only the lower orders who found insurrectionary impulses supported in scripture: among the passages that Oliver Cromwell studied in the months leading up to the trial of Charles was the account in Judges 6–8 of Gideon, a farmer called by God to shake up and lead the armies of Israel to overcome their foes and execute their kings.[14]

I need hardly labour the point that, throughout the Civil War period, the Bible was the go-to source for wisdom concerning the drift of events. Widely available to laity and clergy alike in the vernacular, it shaped thinking and manners in all areas of life. People turned to scripture to validate positions and settle arguments, citing chapter and verse to convince an opponent or persuade a sceptic. Even political theorists of the period usually thought of as 'secular', like Thomas Hobbes and James Harrington, cited scripture frequently. 'Biblical reference helped authors of every sort of treatise to communicate with their readers to an extent inconceivable to most modern readers', writes Elizabeth Tuttle.[15] In fact, so widespread was knowledge of the Bible that a preacher or writer need only refer to the name of a character or episode to make their point—a distinct advantage when it might be thought wise not to make one's point too explicitly!

The Bible 'was everywhere in the lives of men, women and children' in the 1640s, Christopher Hill has written.[16] It was not simply a book to be read or listened to; its messages continually confronted people, not only in the church services they were required to attend but on the walls of homes and taverns and in the words of ballads and plays. By the middle of the seventeenth century, asserts Hill, English men and women had become so used to an 'emphasis on the sovereignty of the Scriptures as the unique source of divine wisdom on all subjects' that, when caught in the midst of unprecedented political and constitutional upheaval, and forced to 'improvise' in the absence of ideological treatises such as were available to people in 'revolutionary' situations in later centuries, '[t]he Bible in English was the book to which they naturally turned for guidance. It was God's Word, whose authority no one

---

[11] Hill, *English Bible*, 39.

[12] Nigel Smith, *Literature and Revolution in England, 1640–1660* (New Haven: Yale University Press, 1994), 117.

[13] Hill, *English Bible*, 179–80.

[14] John Morrill, *Oliver Cromwell* (Oxford: Oxford University Press, 2007), 44–5.

[15] Elizabeth Tuttle, 'Biblical Reference in the Political Pamphlets of the Levellers and Milton, 1638–1654', in David Armitage, Armand Himy, and Quentin Skinner (eds), *Milton and Republicanism* (Cambridge: Cambridge University Press, 1995), 64.

[16] Hill, *English Bible*, 38.

could reject'.[17] Certainly those who came together to promote particular causes or challenge the established order, like Levellers, Diggers, and Ranters, drew heavily on scripture, finding support for their core ideas throughout both testaments. These ideas included, in the case of the Levellers, extending the franchise and enshrining freedom of religion, and, for Diggers, encouraging the landless to work together communally on the common land in order to make the earth once more a 'common treasury'. The writings of Levellers, Diggers, and Ranters proved the case for those keen to outlaw discussion of the Bible in homes and taverns.

If the Bible was both the principal source of political ideas and provider of the grammar for their articulation, it also supplied the key to the grander purpose towards which a political project might be directed. As David Katz has argued, men and women in the mid-seventeenth century believed themselves to be caught up in a sophisticated divine plan which was more or less complete, and thus they took it for granted 'that God was continuously intervening in worldly affairs, sowing small clues directing mankind's attention to His pleasure. Apart from conspicuous and meaningful signs and "providences", the largest single collection of clues was to be found in God's last words, His legacy to mankind—the Bible'.[18] Certainly Cromwell was not alone in concluding, as he surveyed events in the months immediately before the trial and execution of the King, that 'these things that have lately come to pass have been the wonderful works of God, breaking the rod of the oppressor as in the day of Midian' (a reference to Isaiah 9: 4). The Lord, Cromwell affirmed, 'will yet save His people and confound His enemies as in that day'.[19]

Belief that God was bringing history to its end was widespread, with two biblical books in particular, Daniel in the Old Testament and the Revelation of John in the New, being understood to describe figuratively the denouement of history. Both were read with particular interest amid the tumult of the 1640s and 1650s, with many who fought for Parliament being encouraged to see the war against the King in apocalyptic terms, the struggle between Christ and Antichrist. John Milton reflected a widely held view when he spoke in 1641 of Christ as 'the eternal and shortly-expected King' who would 'open the clouds to judge the several kingdoms of the world'.[20] Perhaps only the Fifth Monarchists actually built a political movement around an expectation that the thousand-year reign of Christ on earth, the millennium, was imminent (the execution of Charles, with his connections to the Church of Rome, signalling that the last of the four kingdoms mentioned in the book of Daniel had been overthrown); but a sense that Christ would presently come to reign through, with, or even within his saints, informed most of the sects and movements in the years of the Civil War and Interregnum. For many, the Bible proved an indispensable guide both to the *meaning* of contemporary events and the way in which they would unfold.

∾

Winstanley was clear that the scriptures were an aid to understanding the present since they 'do but declare the sending downe of the spirit and how he shall rule in the earth

---

[17] Hill, *English Bible*, 38–9, 18, 8.
[18] David S. Katz, *God's Last Words: Reading the English Bible from the Reformation to Fundamentalism* (New Haven: Yale University Press, 2004), 52.
[19] Letter to Sir Thomas Fairfax dated 28 June 1648; cited in Morrill, *Oliver Cromwell*, 44.
[20] John Milton, *Of Reformation* (1641) in *Complete Prose Works of John Milton*, gen. ed. Don M. Wolfe (New Haven: Yale University Press, 1953–82), i. 616.

in the latter dayes'.[21] Like many of his contemporaries, Winstanley was concerned less to ascertain the original 'intention' of the biblical writers, or the precise meaning of the words, than how the text can become a catalyst for discerning the divine purpose in the present. He was also convinced that, if the divine will was to be observed on the pages of scripture, it was necessary for the reader to experience, as did the original writers themselves, the presence of Christ within. Winstanley was deeply distrustful of scholars who attempted to create a distance between text and reader, stressing the centrality of 'experimental knowledge' in contrast to abstract reflection on the Bible and secondary application of it.[22] The scriptures 'were writ not from imagination of flesh, but from pure experience, and teachings of the Father', Winstanley affirms, and 'we are taught thereby to waite upon the Father with a meek and obedient spirit, till he teach us, and feed us with sincere milk, as he taught them, that wrote these scriptures'.[23] To have an obedient spirit was to be prepared to act in accordance with the divine will: the very work of digging the commons, Winstanley tells us in the Diggers' first manifesto, was undertaken in obedience to the Spirit's instruction: 'Work together, Eat Bread together, Declare this all abroad'.[24] Action was central to Winstanley's whole understanding of scripture: as he put it a few months after the digging commenced, 'action is the life of all, and if thou dost not act, thou dost nothing'.[25]

Ordinary people should therefore not rely upon so-called 'learned' divines to teach them, for it is the Spirit who will lead them into all truth. When you have 'a teacher within your selves (which is the Spirit) … you shall not need to run after men for instruction', Winstanley argued in one of his pre-Digging tracts.[26] Like Ranters, Winstanley held that book learning was as nothing compared to what one could receive by experience or revelation, and he considered the historical accounts in the Bible no substitute for the indwelling of the living 'word' within. The Bible was written by ordinary people recounting their experiences, and readers should know God and Christ 'experimentally' themselves.

Winstanley's latest editors, Tom Corns, Ann Hughes, and David Loewenstein, describe their subject as '[a] self-proclaimed prophet inspired by the spirit within and moved "by Vision, Voyce, and Revelation"', a writer who 'makes idiosyncratic use of the Bible and its potent myths throughout his works'.[27] Winstanley is certainly a master of allegory (perhaps second only to his contemporary, John Bunyan), seeing the great dramas of scripture—the Garden of Eden and its aftermath, the Exodus from Egypt, the visions of Daniel and Revelation—in original and inspiring ways. Scripture, for Winstanley, becomes a tool for discerning both the 'external' struggle, between the forces of oppression seeking to uphold the status quo and those in bondage to the system, and the (inextricably linked) struggle within the individual as he or she seeks to overcome their consciousness of sin (which Winstanley called 'Imagination' and which was deliberately generated by the clergy's teaching). Winstanley encouraged his readers to overcome this by gaining an awareness that

---

[21] Winstanley, *Truth Lifting up His Head*, *CW* i. 435.
[22] See Christopher Rowland, *Blake and the Bible* (New Haven: Yale University Press, 2011), 166.
[23] Winstanley, *Truth Lifting up His Head*, *CW* i. 435.
[24] Winstanley, *A Declaration to the Powers of England* (1649), *CW* ii. 14.
[25] Winstanley, *A Watch-Word to the City of London, and the Armie* (1649), *CW* ii. 80.
[26] Winstanley, *The Saints Paradice* (1648), *CW* i. 314.
[27] Thomas N. Corns, Ann Hughes, and David Loewenstein, 'Introduction', to Winstanley, *CW* i. 60.

they have the creator dwelling within them and are each perfect creatures of themselves, able to judge all things by their own experience.

Winstanley was critical of approaches to the Bible which do not get beyond reading it purely as history, since for him the biblical narrative continues to be lived out in the present as the rich and the powerful struggle to subjugate the poor and the oppressed: Cain is still murdering Abel, Esau still seeking Jacob's birthright, Ishmael still at odds with Isaac. For Winstanley and his short-lived Digger movement, which had an active commitment to seeing that all, not just the wealthy and powerful, could have access to the land, identification with the 'younger brother' was a powerful motivating factor. Winstanley (like Levellers and others) used the Exodus narrative powerfully; his final tract, addressed to Cromwell, noted how the General was head of a people 'who have cast out an Oppressing Pharaoh'.[28] Walwyn likened his fellow Leveller leader John Lilburne, when imprisoned by the authorities, to Abel persecuted by Cain, and the Levellers collectively to Abel.[29]

Even more frequently, Winstanley invoked 'Adam' who, though he 'lived upon earth many thousand years ago', was also to be seen 'every day before our eyes walking up and down the street' in the form of those who live 'upon the objects of the creation, and not in and upon the spirit that made the creation'.[30] Adam was symbolic of that hypocrisy, subtlety, 'lying imagination', and self-love that leads to 'all unrighteous outward acting' in humanity: 'he sits down in the chair of Magistracy, in some above others', giving rise to tyranny. He was 'the first power that appears to act and rule in every man' and, like Esau, gets the birthright which 'by the Law of equity was more properly Jacob's'. But the point for Winstanley was that, just as Jacob in the end prevails, so the 'Adam' that dwells in each person will be overcome by the rising of the second Adam, 'the power of Christ', 'the Son bringing honour and peace'; and '[t]his second man is the spirituall man, that judges all things according to the law of equity and reason'.[31]

Other biblical figures and images epitomize the present human condition: Judas represents the 'power of covetousnesse'; Ahab's eagerness to acquire Naboth's vineyard symbolizes landlords desiring possession of the common land; the Garden of Eden is the human spirit or heart.[32] 'Winstanley's allegorizing imagination', writes John R. Knott, 'transmuted historical figures—Cain, Jacob and Esau, Abraham—into actors in a cosmic struggle between the forces of the flesh and those of the Spirit, between covetousness and love, that he saw raging in the world and in the soul of man'.[33] It is almost as if, as David Loewenstein has argued, 'from Winstanley's visionary perspective, all of biblical history can be discerned within the self'.[34] As Winstanley himself put it, 'whether there was any such outward things or no, it

[28] Winstanley, *The Law of Freedom in a Platform* (1652), CW ii. 279. See John Coffey, *Exodus and Liberation: Deliverance Politics from John Calvin to Martin Luther King Jr* (Oxford: Oxford University Press, 2014), ch. 1, for a discussion of the use of the Exodus motif during the Civil War period and beyond.

[29] Hill, *English Bible*, 207.

[30] Winstanley, *Truth Lifting up His Head*, CW i. 427.

[31] Winstanley, *The New Law of Righteousnes* (1649), CW i. 481, 499–502.

[32] Winstanley, *Fire in the Bush*, CW ii. 205 (cf. i. 538); *An Appeal to the House of Commons* (1649), CW ii. 71–2; *Fire in the Bush*, CW ii. 172–3.

[33] John R. Knott, *The Sword of the Spirit: Puritan Responses to the Bible* (Chicago: University of Chicago Press, 1980), 88.

[34] David Loewenstein, 'Gerrard Winstanley and the Diggers', in Laura Lunger Knoppers (ed.), *The Oxford Handbook of Literature and the English Revolution* (Oxford: Oxford University Press, 2012), 338.

matters not much, if thou seest all within, this will be thy life'.[35] Other writings with which Winstanley may or may not have been associated—the attribution of Digger and Leveller writings is not always clear—also adopted this approach, the tract *More Light Shining in Buckingham-shire* deducing from the character of Nimrod that 'the whole Scriptures declare Kings to be no better then Tyrants and Usurpers',[36] and the Iver Diggers' 1650 'broadside' asserting that 'Cain is still alive in all the great Landlords'.[37]

Winstanley's writings are saturated with biblical references, all painstakingly reproduced in full by Corns, Hughes, and Loewenstein in the endnotes to their Oxford University Press collection. It was vital for Winstanley that the Diggers' central task of bringing the earth once more into common ownership be shown to be thoroughly grounded in scripture—not least because his opponents once challenged him on that very point[38]—hence his invitation to those who preached but did not live the Gospel to 'search the Scriptures, you that stand up to be Teachers, that say I deny the Scriptures, and let them judge me, whether I deny them or no'.[39] On one occasion in *A Declaration to the Powers of England* (more commonly known as *The True Levellers Standard Advanced*) he backed up this claim about the Diggers' work being scriptural by citing no fewer than sixteen biblical passages drawn from fourteen different books (thirteen from the Old Testament and one from the New).[40] Earlier in this tract he showed his project to be rooted in the Creation narrative in Genesis, asserting that

> In the beginning of time, the great Creator Reason, made the Earth to be a common Treasury, to preserve Beasts, Birds, Fishes, and Man, the Lord that was to govern this Creation ... but not one word was spoken in the beginning, that one branch of mankind should rule over another.[41]

Expanding upon this in *The Fire in the Bush*, Winstanley argued that, originally when 'the whole Earth was common to all without exception', the stronger helped the weaker by working harder.[42] What ended this idyllic early arrangement was 'the Fall', but, taking a characteristically unorthodox approach to the biblical texts, Winstanley sees the original desire by the strong to fence off portions of the land for themselves, and deny others access to it, not as a *consequence* of Adam's sin but the first step of the Fall—to be followed by the second, the 'outward action', in which the desire becomes actualized.[43]

It was Winstanley's singular interpretation of the Fall which compelled him to believe that common ownership of the earth was again possible. Greed, envy, and selfishness were not hard-wired in human beings as a consequence of the Fall, rather human nature was largely shaped by the prevailing social conditions—the 'inward bondages of the minde ...

---

[35] Winstanley, *Fire in the Bush*, *CW* ii. 188.

[36] Anon., *More Light Shining in Buckingham-shire* (1649), in George H. Sabine (ed.), *The Works of Gerrard Winstanley* (New York: Cornell University Press, 1941), 629.

[37] Anon., *A Declaration of the Grounds and Reasons* (1650), in Andrew Hopton (ed.), *Digger Tracts 1649–50* (London: Aporia Press, 1989), 31.

[38] Winstanley mentions a challenge by the local lord of the manor, Parson John Platt, in the preface to *An Humble Request* (1650), *CW* ii. 256; cf. John Gurney, *Gerrard Winstanley: The Digger's Life and Legacy* (London: Pluto Press, 2013), 82.

[39] Winstanley, *The New Law of Righteousnes*, *CW* i. 487.

[40] Winstanley, *Declaration*, *CW* ii. 14.

[41] Winstanley, *Declaration*, *CW* ii. 4.

[42] Winstanley, *Fire in the Bush*, *CW* ii. 215.

[43] Winstanley, *Fire in the Bush*, *CW* ii. 215–16.

are all occasioned by the outward bondage, that one sort of people lay upon another', as he puts it in his last tract.[44] Hence, once private property was abolished, and God—or 'Reason', the term Winstanley preferred for God—reigned once more in the human heart, so the prelapsarian community might again be realizable.

Woven into this vision is the biblical promise of the Second Coming of Christ, the overpowering of the 'first Adam' by the second. For Winstanley, though, Christ would not appear in a sudden or dramatic way 'in the clouds', or even as an individual person at all, but 'rise up' in men and women, reawakening them to the rule of Reason within and leading them to embrace the principle of community lost since the Fall. Thus Winstanley can equate the Second Coming with the gradual transformation of humanity—and, in another unorthodox twist, with Christ's resurrection. To expect Christ to 'come in one single person' is to 'mistake the resurrection of Christ ... you must see, feel and know from himself his own resurrection within you'. Christ 'is now rising and spreading himself in these his sons and daughters, and so rising from one to many persons, till he enlighten the whole creation'.[45]

Like many in his day, Winstanley looked to the apocalyptic visions in Daniel and Revelation to shed light upon the power struggle unfolding before him. Thus the four beasts which Daniel saw rise out of the sea were those forces which, for Winstanley, were united in oppressing the poor and landless: 'Kingly power', 'selfish Lawes', 'the thieving Art of buying and selling, the Earth with her fruits one to another', 'the Imaginary Clergy-Power'. However, while these may appear to flourish for a time, oppressing and burdening the creation, they will 'run into the Sea againe, and be swallowed up in those waters; that is, into Mankinde, who shall be abundantly inlightned' at the glorious appearance of Christ.[46]

Again like many of his contemporaries, Winstanley found biblical allusions to the figurative period '42 months', '1260 days', and 'a time, times, and dividing of time' (which appear in both Daniel and Revelation and which were held to signify three and a half years) helpful in confirming his understanding that he was living in the last days. This period of time, that during which the Beast will be allowed to exercise power before the reign of Christ (Revelation 13: 5), appears in a number of Winstanley's writings, though unlike many other millenarians of his day he is never to be found offering a precise date or time by when he imagines the millennium will be instituted. But that all would once more be able to enjoy the land he was in no doubt: 'all the Prophesies, Visions, and Revelations of Scriptures, of Prophets, and Apostles, concerning the calling of the Jews, the Restauration of Israel, and making of that people, the Inheritors of the whole earth, doth all seat themselves in this work of making the Earth a Common Treasury'.[47]

While biblical language features often in Leveller writings, Levellers' propensity to argue the case for political rights from natural law has convinced many commentators that its inclusion was largely rhetorical. Thus H. N. Brailsford, author of a seminal history of the

---

[44] Winstanley, *Law of Freedom*, *CW* ii. 296.

[45] Winstanley, *Saints Paradice*, *CW* i. 356.

[46] Winstanley, *Fire in the Bush*, *CW* ii. 190–2.

[47] Winstanley, *Declaration*, *CW* ii. 14. In his very first tract, *The Mysterie of God* (1648), Winstanley links his conception of the millennium to a 'dispensationalist' view in which history is divided into seven stages. However, his interest in this particular schema appears to have waned thereafter.

movement, feels able to offer what he calls a summary of the 'whole philosophy of liberal democracy' promulgated by John Lilburne in the form of a substantial extract from his *The Free Man's Freedom Vindicated* (1646), '[s]tripped of ... all its Biblical quotations'.[48] Yet Leveller spokespeople like Lilburne and Richard Overton suggest in their writings that they had much more than a passing interest in religion, and appear to see no necessary contradiction in arguing for the essential rationality of human beings and the implanting of that rationality in them by God. As Overton argued in his *An Appeale from the Degenerate Representative Body* (1647), 'God is not a God of irrationality ... Therefore all his communications are reasonable and just, and what is so, is of God';[49] and William Bray thought a person could claim to have been treated unjustly if he or she were handled 'contrary to Law, Reason, or Christianity', that any law made 'contrary to Law and Scripture' and to 'the Laws of God, or Nature' was a 'meer nullity ... unjust in it self, and voyd'.[50]

Colin Mason has suggested that, influenced by their reading of Luther, Levellers developed a concept of individual rights and freedom rooted in the doctrine that Christ died to redeem humanity. Unlike Calvinists, who held to some notion of rule by an 'elect', Levellers believed in the potential of all people to become believers, such that 'no-one has the right to rule and no-one is to be treated as irredeemably "lost" and unfree'. All are made free in Christ because Christ died for all, and this freedom in Christ becomes the basis of *political* freedom.[51] Equality under the law was rooted for Levellers in our equality in Christ: as the Leveller women's petition of 1649 puts it, 'we are assured of our creation in the image of God, and of an interest in Christ equal unto men, as also of a proportionate share in the freedoms of this Commonwealth'.[52] As Brian Manning points out, Levellers did not segregate the sphere of nature from the sphere of religion but thought 'natural law embraced much of the moral law of the Bible'.[53]

Christ's death also freed us from the claims of the Old Testament, in particular the demands of the Mosaic law, Levellers argued. For Walwyn, all were 'justified freely by [God's] grace through the redemption that is in Jesus Christ',[54] a grace that freed us from the old law to follow Christ's new commandment to love. This approach to the Old Testament also informed Leveller thinking on toleration. The traditional view, held by those who defended the concept of a national church, was that practices found in the Old Testament were forerunners or 'shadows' of practices followed by the church—so circumcision prefigured baptism, and the state of Israel, the church. Thus as Israel had been governed by kings charged with maintaining holy living by compulsion, so the church had a similar task to ensure that true religion was adhered to in the present age. To Levellers, however, many of

[48] H. N. Brailsford, *The Levellers and the English Revolution* (Nottingham: Spokesman Books, 1976), 118–19.
[49] Richard Overton, *An Appeale from the Degenerate Representative Body* (1647), in Don M. Wolfe (ed.), *Leveller Manifestoes of the Puritan Revolution* (New York: Thomas Nelson, 1944), 158.
[50] William Bray, *Innocency and the Blood of the Slain Souldiers* (1649), 9; cited in Colin Mason, 'Political Theology and the Levellers: A Discussion of the Theological Sources of the Political Thought of the Levellers and of Some Implications for Modern Understandings of Political Liberalism' (Ph.D. thesis, University of Durham, 2009), 185.
[51] Mason, 'Political Theology and the Levellers', 116.
[52] *A Petition of Women* (1649), in A. S. P. Woodhouse (ed.), *Puritanism and Liberty: Being the Army Debates (1647–49) from the Clarke Manuscripts* (London: J. M. Dent, 1938), 367–9.
[53] Manning, 'The Levellers and Religion', 80.
[54] William Walwyn, *The Power of Love* (1643), in Jack McMichael and Barbara Taft (eds), *The Writings of William Walwyn* (Athens, Ga.: University of Georgia Press, 1989), 89–90; cited in Mason, 'Political Theology and the Levellers', 109.

whom were or had close links to Baptists, this typology could not be maintained since the church was essentially a voluntary, self-governing assembly; and in arguing against compulsion by the state in matters of belief and religious practice Levellers even went so far as to promote religious toleration for Jews, Muslims, and people accused of atheism and idolatry. This was a radically consistent position at a time when Catholicism was still illegal.

At Putney, where Levellers debated their case with Cromwell, Ireton, and other army leaders in 1647, Thomas Collier drew an argument for the civil powers having no power over religious matters from the New Testament account of the woman taken in adultery (John 7: 53–8: 11). In this narrative, Christ, by suggesting that only those of the woman's accusers who are 'without sin' should stone her death, appears to give priority to a new ethic over the law of Moses.[55] The Leveller leader John Wildman argued quite directly at Putney that nothing can be found in the word of God regarding 'what is fitt to bee done in civill matters'.[56] It was but a short step to argue that church and state should have different spheres of competence and that it was not the duty of the magistrate to compel or restrict in matters of religion.

Walwyn thought scripture contained much of value, insights that the Apostles have left us regarding 'the mind and will of God'.[57] He titled a tract denying a charge of atheism *A Still and Soft Voice from the Scriptures, Witnessing Them to be the Word of God*, and claimed that 'All those passages therein that declare the nature of God, viz. his grace and goodness to men, I believe are the Word of God'—though 'the Scripture is plainly and directly contradictory to itself'.[58] Overton also used biblical texts to testify to his faith: 'I know that my Redeemer liveth' (Job 19: 25), 'I know my life is hid in Christ' (Colossians 3: 3). But primarily Levellers thought scripture showed Christianity to be *practical*: the Bible 'plainly set forth' the works which were 'most pleasing to God', and these included 'Feeding the hungry, Cloathing the naked, visiting and comforting of the sicke', tending to the fatherless, widows, and the aged, 'supporting of poore families', and 'delivering of Prisoners'.[59] In one of his many ripostes to his harshest critic, *A Whisper in the eare of Mr Thomas Edwards, Minister* (1646), Walwyn emphasizes the practical nature of scripture: 'I carry with me in all places a touch-stone that tryeth all things, and labours to hold nothing but what upon plain grounds appeareth good and usefull'.[60]

As Manning has argued, '[t]he principle which linked the religious beliefs of the Levellers to political action was the "golden rule"',[61] which is found in a number of sources including Jesus' Sermon on the Mount: 'all things whatsoever ye would that men should do to you, do ye even so to them' (Matthew 7: 12). Lilburne affirmed that God had engraved this rule upon his heart as a younger man, but the point for the Levellers was that it did not apply to believers only but was the basic principle that made civil society possible.[62] As John Wildman puts it in his

---

[55] William Clarke, *The Clarke Papers: Selections from the Papers of William Clarke, Secretary to the Council of the Army, 1647–1649, and to General Monck and the Commanders of the Army in Scotland, 1651–1660*, ed. C. H. Firth (London: Camden Society, 1891–1901), ii. 126.

[56] *Clarke Papers*, i. 384.

[57] William Walwyn, *A Whisper in the Eare of Mr Thomas Edwards, Minister* (1646), 6; cited in J. F. McGregor, 'Seekers and Ranters', in McGregor and Reay, *Radical Religion*, 125.

[58] Cited in Brailsford, *The Levellers and the English Revolution*, 69–70.

[59] Cited in Manning, 'The Levellers and Religion', 72–3.

[60] Cited in McGregor, 'Seekers and Ranters', 125.

[61] Manning, 'The Levellers and Religion', 71.

[62] Manning, 'The Levellers and Religion', 72.

Truths Triumph (1648), it is the command of God 'that every man should seek the good of his neighbour'.[63] Two tracts often associated with the Levellers, *Light Shining in Buckingham-shire* (1648) and *More Light Shining in Buckingham-shire* (1649), both highlight the importance of 'that golden rule or law, which we call equitie', 'that excellent Rule of right Reason'.[64]

Despite their nomenclature—which they did not choose themselves—Levellers did not share the Diggers' enthusiasm to see the land commonly owned; indeed, in their third 'Agreement of the Free People of England' (1649) they explicitly state that no representative of the people should have any power to 'level mens Estates, destroy Propriety, or make all things Common' (Article 30).[65] Walwyn recognizes that the New Testament records the first Christians selling their possessions, distributing the proceeds, and having 'all things in common' (Acts 2: 44–5) but argues that this was a voluntary act rather than a duty or 'the Injunction of any Constitution', was short-lived, and occurred 'in but two or three places'.[66]

Mason estimates that, alongside Magna Carta and Coke's *Institutes of the Laws of England*, the Bible is the most quoted source in Levellers' writings.[67] If the Levellers were—as they acknowledge themselves in their writings—frequently attacked as atheists and deniers of scripture, their frequent citation of biblical texts at least places the burden of proof with their detractors, as does Walwyn's assertion that 'we have no Preacher of the Gospel but the Scriptures ... the infallible word of God'.[68]

Ranters shared with Diggers and Levellers a disdain for the so-called wisdom of the formally educated priesthood: 'better scholars they, that have their lessons without book, and can read God (not by rote) but plainly and perfectly ... within book, and without book, and as well without book, as within book', wrote the most notorious of the Ranters, Abiezer Coppe, early in 1649.[69] Like Winstanley, Coppe stressed the importance of an experience of God in order to understand God's communication, even if he was concerned primarily with God's presence within *himself* rather than within people in general. Coppe explicitly claims authority for interpreting and preaching the Word of God, asserting in various places 'the word of the Lord came expressly to me' and employing the expression 'thus saith the Lord' with notable frequency. The subtitle of his major tract *A Fiery Flying Roll* (1649) reads 'A Word from the Lord to all the Great Ones of the Earth' and he is not averse to using terms such as 'excellent majesty' and 'almightiness' self-descriptively.[70] Richard Coppin, whose 1649 treatise *Divine Teachings* boasted a preface by Coppe, also argued that scripture was secondary to

[63] Cited in Manning, 'The Levellers and Religion', 70.

[64] *The Works of Gerrard Winstanley*, ed. Sabine, 611, 627.

[65] A. L. Morton (ed.), *Freedom in Arms: A Selection of Leveller Writings* (London: Lawrence & Wishart, 1985), 276.

[66] William Walwyn, *A Manifestation* (1649), *The Writings of William Walwyn*, 338; cited in Mason, 'Political Theology and the Levellers', 226–7.

[67] Mason, 'Political Theology and the Levellers', 8, 204.

[68] William Walwyn, *The Vanitie of the Present Churches* (1648/9), in William Haller and Godfrey Davies (eds), *The Leveller Tracts, 1647–1653* (New York: Columbia University Press, 1944), 261; cited in Mason, 'Political Theology and the Levellers', 106.

[69] Abiezer Coppe, *Some Sweet Sips of Some Spirituall Wine* (1649); cited in Rowland, *Blake and the Bible*, 173.

[70] Abiezer Coppe, *A Fiery Flying Roll* (1649) in *Abiezer Coppe: Selected Writings*, ed. Andrew Hopton (London: Aporia Press, 1987), 15–16.

that which could be learned from those 'indwelt' by Christ. 'God now comes forth from the great and learned of the world, and exalts himself in the poor and ignorant', Coppin writes.[71]

As Coppe's terminology suggests, he is less concerned than either Winstanley or the chief Leveller writers with seeking biblical support or validation for his claims. While Winstanley went to great lengths to demonstrate how his project of digging the commons fulfilled various injunctions in scripture, Coppe, as Chris Rowland has written, 'being indwelt by God, did not need to refer back to any divine sanction in the Bible. Coppe's theological treatise *is* the divine word'.[72]

'Ranter language', Smith says in his introduction to a collection of their writings, 'comes almost entirely from the Bible'.[73] Certainly Coppe's writings are saturated with biblical allusions, but the purpose of these is to demonstrate how the Bible is 're-worked' in the writer's own spiritual experience. In a detailed exegesis of the preface to *A Fiery Flying Roll*, Ariel Hessayon powerfully shows how each of the experiences described is echoed in scripture itself. As Hessayon writes, Coppe in this chapter describes how

> he lay 'trembling, sweating, and smoking (for the space of half an houre)' [Revelation 8: 1] before the immanent presence of the Lord. At length Coppe entreated the Lord: 'what wilt thou do with me; my most excellent majesty' [Daniel 4: 36] and eternall glory (in me) [cf. 2 Timothy 2: 10] answered & sayd, Fear not, I will take thee up into mine everlasting Kingdom [Psalm 145: 13]. But thou shalt (first) drink a bitter cup, a bitter cup, a bitter cup; whereupon (being filled with exceeding amazement) I was throwne into the belly of hell [Jonah 2: 2].[74]

As Rowland observes of Coppe's writing, while

> there is hardly a line which does not have some biblical allusion ... the biblical words have been woven into something new, a new word of God in which the received words mutate in a kaleidoscopic way, just as the prophetic words are digested and reappear in different combinations in the Book of Revelation.[75]

Ranters were antinomian, though to describe them as such is to tell only half the truth. Among their contemporaries to whom the term was sometimes (critically) applied (such as Particular Baptists), most held that the Mosaic law was no longer binding upon men and women because, if a person were among those 'elected' by God for salvation, no sin they might commit could undermine that transaction; and furthermore, being among 'the elect' did not free a person from obedience to the law, rather it impelled them to observe it more keenly. Ranters, however, argued that the law was redundant, because every man and woman had God dwelling within them and therefore need no longer consider any actions

[71] Cited in Thomas N. Corns, *Uncloistered Virtue: English Political Literature 1640–1660* (Oxford: Oxford University Press, 1992), 187.

[72] Rowland, *Blake and the Bible*, 174.

[73] Nigel Smith, *A Collection of Ranter Writings from the Seventeenth Century* (London: Junction Books, 1983), 23.

[74] Ariel Hessayon, 'The Making of Abiezer Coppe', *Journal of Ecclesiastical History*, 62 (2011): 54. For a discussion of the rabbinic reading practice 'midrash' as a clue to understanding Coppe's biblical allusions, see Noam Flinker, 'The Poetics of Biblical Prophecy: Abiezer Coppe's Late Converted Midrash', in Ariel Hessayon and David Finnegan (eds), *Varieties of Seventeenth- and Early Eighteenth-Century English Radicalism in Context* (Farnham: Ashgate, 2011), 113–27.

[75] Rowland, *Blake and the Bible*, 174.

they committed 'sinful'. If God 'indwelt' a person, Ranters claimed, then it was impossible for him or her to commit sin; sin was an entirely imaginary and humanly created concept.

Lawrence Clarkson claimed to find this teaching in scripture, noting in his autobiography *The Lost Sheep Found* (1660) how on one occasion he 'pleaded' in support of his position the words of Paul (in Romans 14: 14),

> That I know, and am perswaded by the Lord Jesus, that there was nothing unclean, but as man esteemed it, unfolding that was intended all acts, as well as meats and drinks, and therefore till you can lie with all women as one woman, and not judge it sin, you can do nothing but sin: now in Scripture I found a perfection spoken of, so that I understood no man could attain perfection but this way ...[76]

Clarkson cited another of St Paul's aphorisms, 'To the pure all things are pure' (Titus 1: 15) in defence of his position, arguing that 'if Reason were admitted, and thereby Scripture interpreted, then they should observe in that Act they call Honesty, to be Adultry, and that Act so called Adultry, to have as much honesty as the other, for with God they are but one, and that one Act holy, just, and good as God'.[77] 'What act so-ever is done by thee in light and love', Clarkson concluded, 'is light and lovely, though it be that act called adultery ... No matter what Scripture, saints or churches say, if that within thee do not condemn thee, thou shalt not be condemned'.[78] Clarkson appears to have lived consistently with his beliefs, finding no shortage of women anxious for his services; and contemporary reports by their many detractors positively ooze with tales of the Ranters' sexual immorality—to the extent, as Hill wryly notes, that the counterattack was almost as threatening to orthodoxy as anything the Ranters themselves wrote![79] Operating on the premise, articulated by Clarkson, 'till acted that so called Sin, thou art not delivered from the power of sin',[80] Ranters showed no restraint in indulging whatever their particular calling, often to the horror of those observing.

Ranters took to extremes, not only their antinomianism, but their licence to interpret the Bible as they liked. Abiezer Coppe was adept at using strange or unwholesome stories in scripture to suit his purpose, speaking approvingly of Hosea 'who went in to a whore',[81] and expressing a preference for seeing 'the spirit of Nehemiah (in any form of man, or woman) ... making others fall a swearing' to hearing a zealous minister 'pray, preach, or exercise'.[82] Coppe's take on Christ's promise to come as a 'thief in the night'—when he will command the rich to give his money to the poor and the outcast—is both highly creative and an arguably more striking example than even Winstanley can offer of using scripture to challenge the legitimacy of the socio-economic order.[83]

---

[76] Lawrence Clarkson, *A Lost Sheep Found* (1660), cited in Norman Cohn, *The Pursuit of the Millennium: Revolutionary Millenarians and Mystical Anarchists of the Middle Ages*, rev. edn (London: Paladin, 1970), 310.

[77] Lawrence Clarkson, *A Single Eye All Light, no Darkness* (1650) in Cohn, *Pursuit of the Millennium*, 312.

[78] Lawrence Clarkson, *A Single Eye*; cited in Christopher Hill, *The World Turned Upside Down: Radical Ideas during the English Revolution* (Harmondsworth: Penguin, 1975), 215.

[79] Christopher Hill, *A Nation of Change and Novelty: Radical Politics, Religion and Literature in Seventeenth-Century England* (London: Routledge, 1990), 184.

[80] Clarkson, *A Single Eye*, in Cohn, *Pursuit of the Millennium*, 315.

[81] Coppe, *A Second Fiery Flying Roule*, in *Abiezer Coppe*, ed. Hopton, 42.

[82] Coppe, *A Fiery Flying Roll*, in *Abiezer Coppe*, ed. Hopton, 27.

[83] Coppe, *A Second Fiery Flying Roule*, in *Abiezer Coppe*, ed. Hopton, 37.

Coppe used passages like Mary's Magnificat (Luke 1: 46–55), the account of the Jerusalem church holding all things in common in Acts, and James's fulminations against the rich (in chapter 5 of his Epistle), to similar effect. Both Coppe and Clarkson based their highly libertarian sexual ethic on passages in the Bible as well as on direct revelations from on high, Clarkson admitting in *The Lost Sheep Found* that passages from the Song of Solomon were 'the original of my filthy lust'.[84] Some Ranters went so far as to say that there would be no peace until all Bibles were burned, a few putting this opinion into practice.[85] In the highly charged atmosphere of the early 1650s it is little surprise that Parliament sought to rein in Ranterish activities and suppress their writings.

∾

Much ink has been spilt debating the significance of biblical references in the writings of the Levellers, Diggers, and others. For several decades following the Second World War there was a tendency among scholars of the seventeenth century to see Winstanley and other 'radicals' as essentially 'secular' and 'modern' in their attitude, driven only to cite scripture by the conventions of the day and tending to move, over time, from using a biblical frame of reference to a 'political' one. Had these people lived fifty years later than they did, the argument went, they would probably have expressed their ideas in the language of rational deism, saving us the trouble of having to penetrate through their religious verbiage in order to discover the 'real' ideas they wished to communicate beneath.

In one sense this was always a sterile debate, since, as I have observed, this was an age when the Bible was central to intellectual and moral life and provided the measure of all things: it necessarily informed people's thinking and language. The argument that political ideas could somehow be separated from the language in which they are expressed was also problematic, and the possibility that sincere religious convictions might underlie the biblical citations of the Levellers and Diggers is now more seriously entertained and the fusing of (as we define them) 'religious' and 'political' principles in their writings acknowledged without demur. Thus Winstanley's understanding of the alienation of the 'poor oppressed people of England' (as he described the Diggers) can be understood as at the same time economic, political, and spiritual, and the Levellers' employment of, for example, both natural law and the creation narratives of Genesis to develop their ideas about liberty, accepted as coherent and adding to the richness and depth of their writers' thought.

John Coffey has argued that, when people in the 1640s spoke of the Civil War as 'England's Exodus' and Cromwell as the 'new' Moses to lead them to the 'promised land', they saw that event, like the editors of the Geneva Bible, both as a metaphor for their experience, and themselves also, like the Israelites of old, under the delivering hand of God. 'Crucially', as Coffey argues, this was a biblical story 'that could capture the imagination and put fire in the belly'.[86] It was by no means alone.

[84] Clarkson [Claxton], *The Lost Sheep Found* (London: for the author, 1660), 26.
[85] Christopher Hill, 'Irreligion in the "Puritan" Revolution', in McGregor and Reay, *Radical Religion*, 199; cf. Hill, *The World Turned Upside Down*, 262. Quakers were known to adopt this practice on occasions too.
[86] John Coffey, 'England's Exodus: The Civil War as War of Liberation', paper given at conference 'The Last of the Wars of Religion: A Salute to John Morrill', University of Hull, 12 July 2008.

FURTHER READING

Bradstock, Andrew. *Faith in the Revolution: The Political Theologies of Müntzer and Winstanley* (London: SPCK, 1997).

Bradstock, Andrew. *Radical Religion in Cromwell's England: A Concise History from the English Civil War to the End of the Commonwealth* (London: I. B. Tauris, 2011).

Corns, Thomas N. *Uncloistered Virtue: English Political Literature 1640–1660* (Oxford: Oxford University Press, 1992).

Davis, J. C. 'The Levellers and Christianity', in Brian Manning (ed.), *Politics, Religion and the English Civil War* (London: Edward Arnold, 1973), 225–50.

Durston, Christopher, and Judith Maltby, eds. *Religion in Revolutionary England* (Manchester: Manchester University Press, 2006).

Hill, Christopher. *The Religion of Gerrard Winstanley* (Oxford: Past and Present Society, 1978).

Hill, Christopher. *The English Bible and the Seventeenth-Century Revolution* (London: Allen Lane, 1993).

Katz, David S. *God's Last Words: Reading the English Bible from the Reformation to Fundamentalism* (New Haven and London: Yale University Press, 2004).

Keeble, N. H., ed. *The Cambridge Companion to Writing of the English Revolution* (Cambridge: Cambridge University Press, 2001).

Knoppers, Laura Lunger, ed. *The Oxford Handbook of Literature and the English Revolution* (Oxford: Oxford University Press, 2012).

Knott, John R. *The Sword of the Spirit: Puritan Responses to the Bible* (Chicago: University of Chicago Press, 1980).

McGregor, J. F., and B. Reay, eds. *Radical Religion in the English Revolution* (Oxford: Oxford University Press, 1984).

Mason, Colin. 'Political Theology and the Levellers: A Discussion of the Theological Sources of the Political Thought of the Levellers and of Some Implications for Modern Understandings of Political Liberalism' (Ph.D. thesis, University of Durham, 2009).

Sharp, Andrew, ed. *The English Levellers* (Cambridge: Cambridge University Press, 1998).

Smith, Nigel. *A Collection of Ranter Writings from the Seventeenth Century* (London: Junction Books, 1983).

Smith, Nigel. *Perfection Proclaimed: Language and Literature in English Radical Religion 1640–1660* (Oxford: Oxford University Press, 1989).

Tuttle, Elizabeth. 'Biblical Reference in the Political Pamphlets of the Levellers and Milton, 1638–1654', in David Armitage, Armand Himy, and Quentin Skinner (eds), *Milton and Republicanism* (Cambridge: Cambridge University Press, 1995), 63–81.

Walwyn, William. *The Writings of William Walwyn*, ed. Jack McMichael and Barbara Taft (Athens, Ga.: University of Georgia Press, 1989).

Winstanley, Gerrard. *The Complete Works of Gerrard Winstanley*, ed. Thomas N. Corns, Ann Hughes, and David Loewenstein (Oxford: Oxford University Press, 2009).

CHAPTER 26

A YEAR IN THE LIFE OF KING SAUL: 1643

ANNE LAKE PRESCOTT

KING David, it hardly needs saying, was of supreme importance in Renaissance literature, both as psalmist and political figure, his dramatic career narrated in the two Books of Samuel. Translated, imitated, the star of many poems and plays, he was both pitied for his courage when young and admired as a ruler. Despite his adultery with Bathsheba and his murder of her husband Uriah, sins he repented in compelling song, he was both a prophet and a 'type' of Christ, his words in the Psalter often read in terms of Jesus' life and speech. Because he was chosen by God, moreover, and anointed as Israel's future king by the prophet Samuel, he and his career had political meaning as a model (or, sometimes, a warning). No wonder that rulers such as François Ier, Elizabeth I, and Charles I, to cite only three, were called Davids, like him anointed as rulers and like him suffering griefs as well as triumphs.

What, though, of David's father-in-law and Israel's first king, Saul? His reputation in early modern England was mostly dark: although God's choice as ruler of the Israelites, although anointed by the prophet Samuel, he made a number of missteps, not least his maltreatment of David but also his crimes while on the throne. Not a prophet, not a poet, he was for most of the English a negative example and yet, said many, because he was anointed he was (or should have been) untouchable by anyone longing to remove him. It was just this complexity that made him useful to political debate and polemic as Britain slid into civil war in the early 1640s. David and Saul were not merely historical examples, to be cited as one might cite Caesar or Hannibal. When Samuel anointed Saul he initiated a system of monarchy that was more than a precedent—it was a divinely instituted tradition not to be violated, or so royalists argued. Did David violate it when taking up arms against Saul? Or did he in fact do so *against* the king? Was he not acting in self-defence? And what of those who resorted to violence against Charles I? To those involved in the Civil Wars, David and Saul were models, types, their lives and words unavoidable. The story of Saul in early modern Britain, then, makes part of a larger story in which biblical texts formed a necessary system of reference, not least for those who imagined that

Britain might yet be the new Israel. If not the full story of Saul's role in early modern times, his political relevance is a major part of that role.

To trace the story of Saul's utility to those engaged in the Civil Wars would be a valuable exercise.[1] Here, rather, as an experiment in tracking a biblical figure's reputation and utility, I will offer a close-up, a snapshot or survey, of one year in the 'life' of an anointed but often wicked monarch, hoping to make even more visible the poignant complexity of biblical precedents at a time when remembering such figures was a spiritual, political, and emotional necessity. I have chosen the year 1643, both because so many allusions to Saul during those twelve months are in themselves intriguing and because by that time the arguments over legitimacy—royal or parliamentarian—were so painfully unavoidable. Britain's political and religious atmosphere had been darkening for decades, but by the start of 1643 those supporting Parliament's rebellion had joined open warfare to their protests, not least at the Battle of Edgehill in 1642.

Rather than moving chronologically through the months of 1643, I will structure my description in terms of Saul's career, starting with his anointing by Samuel (1 Samuel 10). The prophet had earlier warned the Israelites that, whatever their desire to have a king and thus more closely resemble their gentile neighbours, a monarch can bring injustice and anguish. Samuel was right, for Saul was a melancholic and jealous ruler and, from a divine viewpoint, a disobedient one. That very fact, however, makes his life during Britain's Civil Wars all the more poignant. Saul was an *anointed* monarch, raised by God from tending to his father's asses to ruling men. That anointing—particularly if we ignore the popular ratification that some said both he and David had needed for full kingship—was a challenge for anyone claiming that, because David had resisted Saul's persecutions with force, Parliament likewise had the right to resist tyrannical actions by King Charles, and with the sword if necessary. Thinking about the divine anointment of British monarchs required thinking also about the relevance of scripture to the unwritten British constitution and its perhaps mixed monarchy. Above all, Samuel's anointing, first of Saul and then of David while Saul still lived—an heir and a spare, so to speak—required manoeuvring around David's refusal to harm his king when he had the chance. I might add that here it is not always clear which biblical translation the authors I quote use, and yet it would be good to know if it made a difference to them that the King James Bible lacks the tendentious and at times quasi-republican marginal notes on the Geneva version's Psalms that read David as the victim of a king and his cruel minions.[2]

Any British subject who had forgotten the darker moments of Saul's life could turn to a prefatory chronology, with many of them in the anonymous *A Parallel between the Israelites Desiring of King Saul, and Englands Desiring of a Parliament* (a long subtitle notes Samuel's warning to Israel about the dangers of monarchy). Saul, we read, overreached by taking upon himself a priestly office, failed to kill the pagan King Agag, refused Samuel's subsequent rebuke, envied others, tried to kill David even after that harpist had driven away the demon possessing him, broke his oath to David and the neighbouring Gibeonites, was treacherous, murderous, killed priests, and towards the end consulted a witch.[3]

---

[1] On the debates surrounding David and kingship, see the chapter by Kim Ian Parker in this volume.

[2] See e.g. my 'Evil Tongues at the Court of Saul', *Journal of Medieval and Renaissance Studies*, 12 (1991): 163–86. Here I cite the King James Bible. Unless otherwise indicated, texts cited were printed in London and date of publication is 1643.

[3] *A Parallel between the Israelites Desiring of King Saul, and Englands Desiring of a Parliament*, A2ʳ; 1 Sam. 15–28.

Like that anonymous author, then, I will take up Saul's missteps in biographical order. His life was exploited in various ways, but the most important may be its service to political discourse, the biblical texts wielded as swords and shields in arguments now bloodied by war.

I. Killing Jonathan

Charles I may or may not have been a constitution-defying tyrant who provoked armed resistance or, some claimed, who was rescued from evil advisers, but nobody doubted in 1643 that Saul was a bad king. His wickedness began conspicuously at Gilgal when he disobediently offered a sacrifice without waiting for Samuel (1 Samuel 13) and was confirmed horribly when he ordered the Israelite soldiers to kill his own son Jonathan, who had innocently broken a foolish royal decree (1 Samuel 14). The Israelites refused to obey: 'the people rescued Jonathan, that hee died not'. As the chapter's summary in the King James Bible puts it, Jonathan 'is saved by the people'. Few would accuse the King James Bible of overt republicanism, but in 1643 such phrasing could have political resonance. The passage gave those resisting the King an argument that royalists had to dismiss or refute. A significant issue was whether or not 'the people' used force, or at least would have done so had necessity urged it. Henry Ferne, claiming with some justice in his *Resolving of Conscience*—here as elsewhere, the default date is 1643—to argue from both 'Scripture and Reason', asserted that Parliament's army, like new Wat Tylers and Jack Cades, would 'boast themselves Reformers of the Commonwealth, overthrow King and Parliament, fill all with rapine and confusion, draw all to a Folkmoot, and make every Shire a severall Government'. David, as indeed many in 1643 agreed, is all the more to be praised for not laying a violent hand on his king when protecting himself against Saul's 'cut throats'.[4] Ferne's appeal to *both* 'Scripture and Reason' is itself interesting as yet another reminder not to make too smooth what we too often see as a straight path of increasing secularization in the seventeenth century.[5]

Unsurprisingly, Ferne denies the modern relevance of the scene, arguing in this same text that 'the people drew not into Armes of themselves, but being [there] at *Sauls* command, did by a loving violence and importunitie hinder the execution of a particular and passionate unlawfull command'.[6] Ferne's *Reply unto Severall Treatises* (Oxford) says more or less the same: Saul's people merely showed 'a loving importunate violence by way of intercession, set off with a Souldierly boldnesse'—and Saul's order to kill his own son was likewise 'but a Souldierly boldnesse of speech'.[7] As for fantasies of ancient democracy, says Ferne

[4] Henry Ferne, *The Resolving of Conscience* (Oxford), D4^{r-v}, B3^v.
[5] See Kevin Killeen, 'Hanging up Kings: The Political Bible in Early Modern England', *Journal of the History of Ideas*, 72 (2011): 549–70, and 'Chastising with Scorpions: Reading the Old Testament in Early Modern England', *Huntington Library Quarterly*, 73 (2010): 491–506. Cf. Eric Nelson, *The Hebrew Republic: Jewish Sources and the Transformation of European Political Thought* (Cambridge, Mass.: Harvard University Press, 2010); N. H. Keeble (ed.), *The Cambridge Companion to Writing of the English Revolution* (Cambridge: Cambridge University Press, 2001); and Nigel Smith, *Literature and Revolution in England, 1640–1660* (New Haven: Yale University Press, 1994).
[6] Ferne, *Resolving of Conscience*, B3^v.
[7] Henry Ferne, *A Reply unto Severall Treatises* (Oxford), H3^v.

sarcastically in *Conscience Satisfied*, there could have been no popular establishment of royal sovereignty on 'this island' unless its 'rude' early inhabitants had been 'brought together by some Orpheus his pipe', for they were not 'politique' enough to 'contrive a Government'.[8] The image of Orpheus plying his mystic lyre to round up primitive but 'politique' proto-Britons has a number of contradictions, but it is a curious reminder that David's harp, so often associated with Orpheus' lyre, had political significance thanks to his power to soothe Saul's demonic melancholy. At least Ferne concedes that subjects can, however, deploy petitions, reproofs, intercessions, and denial of funds. He is not an utter absolutist, and indeed his compelling royalist voice can be worthy of Edmund Burke (one might nominate William Prynne as Tom Paine).

With depressing touches of racism, the anonymous author of *The Un-Deceiver*, will have none of this biblical interpretation: the Israelites *did* resist, he says, and we too will rescue any of 'our Jonathans', that is, any 'good Parliament-man, or Common-wealths-man', from illegal execution, and this despite a king who employs foreigners, Papists, 'Cavaliers, Negro's, Welsh and Irish, &c'.[9] Such distaste for alien others shows elsewhere, too. In a passage citing Saul's order to kill God's priests and the 'unnaturall rage' behind Saul's filicidal order, Henry Parker's *Accommodation Cordially Desired* says that the situation might have accelerated to war had Saul possessed 'as many Idumeans in his service as King Charles now has'.[10] Not all foreigners were a threat, of course. The Israelites indeed set a good example, says Philip Hunton's pro-parliamentarian *Treatise of Monarchie*—and so did the United Provinces.[11] Hunton, who did not put his name on this treatise, was hardly alone in citing the Dutch Revolution, and others sometimes also mention the Huguenots, leading Ferne to ask ironically in his *Reply unto Severall Treatises* whether in that case we should support Catholic rebels in Ireland.[12] Stephen Marshall's *Plea for Defensive Armes* is less paradoxical but likewise observes that both 'Papists and Protestants, when they have been put to it, have borne defensive Armes against the unlawfull violence of their mis-led Princes'.[13] Indeed, the threat of popery colours a number of texts that name Saul. Do you dislike Puritans? Then you would not like the Papists into which they have turned, says Dr David Owen in *Puritano-Jesuitismus*. They both have 'concord in the matter' of their sedition, but 'discord in the manner', says the title-page. Jesus himself told us to obey Caesar, and whatever the provocation David was similarly submissive; nor did either state or priesthood ever punish the 'monster' Saul for his many misdeeds. And yet, says Owen, there is no respect for anointed monarchs in either Rome or Geneva.[14]

---

[8] Henry Ferne, *Conscience Satisfied* (Oxford, i.e. London), B1^r.

[9] *The Un-Deceiver*, A4^r, A2^v.

[10] Henry Parker's *Accommodation Cordially Desired*, B2^v; admirers of Philip Sidney would enjoy Parker's comparison of cavalier polemic to the flowery style of *The Lady of May*'s pretentious Rombus (A1^v).

[11] Philip Hunton, *Treatise of Monarchie*, C1^v.

[12] Ferne, *Reply*, E2^v. Herbert Palmer, *Scripture and Reason*, cites the Dutch (K2^r; on Jonathan, see C1^v–C2^r). For more on Jonathan, see William Prynne's *The Third Part of the Soveraigne Power*, L1^r; and John Saltmarsh, *Examinations, or, a Discovery of Some Dangerous Positions*, A4^v, an objection to Thomas Fuller's *A Sermon of Reformation*.

[13] Stephen Marshall, *A Plea for Defensive Armes*, B2^r; Marshall also speculates, on the next page, that the same Israelites, had they been nearby, might have stopped Saul from killing priests.

[14] David Owen, *Puritano-Jesuitismus*, B1^v–B2^r, on Geneva, citing both Beza and Buchanan.

II. Sparing Agag

If Saul was too violent in ordering his troops to kill Jonathan, what of God's anger at his failure to obey the divine command, in 1 Samuel 15, to slay the Amalekite king, Agag? Jehovah can reject a monarch, not least one also responsible for slaying dozens of priests, and turn his divine favour elsewhere. Mercy is a virtue, of course, but rulers must also avoid misplaced leniency.[15] Richard Baker's *Chronicle of the Kings of England* thus recalls how Elizabeth's counsellors, when urging her to execute Mary Stuart, reminded her of Saul's crime in not killing Agag.[16] Similarly, Charles Herle, author of a reply to Ferne, in a sermon to Parliament urges the members to show more grit than had Saul when he failed to kill Agag.[17] On the other hand, Henry Killigrew's sermon before Charles says exactly the same thing but in reverse: do not spare parliamentary Agags. Evidently Agagness is in the eye of the beholder. Many joined this debate. In a sermon preached before Parliament, Herbert Palmer (a stern opponent of stageplays) reminds his listeners that God punished King Agag anyway.[18] Arthur Jackson's *Help for the Understanding of the Holy Scripture* is more moderate, and so is John Ellis, a Cambridge preacher whose *Sole Path to a Sound Peace* argues against extremism on either side and also observes that Saul was wrong to think a sacrifice sufficient to assuage God's wrath for the sparing of Agag.[19]

Can the hapless Agag also serve comedy? John Booker's *No Mercurius Aquaticus*, a send-up of John Taylor the 'Water Poet' that gives Venus a messenger named 'Morbus Gallicus' and suggests that a bucket or two of Irish Protestant blood makes a good royal cordial, asks why, if Saul was indeed seeking his father's asses when Samuel found him, he later chose to 'play the Asse and lose his Kingdome? Was it not for saving Agag the King of the Amalekites …?'[20] Booker was a moderate but was said to have a face that would 'fright a razor'.[21] Agag's murder could also be allegorized: the learned Puritan William Greenhill says in a parliamentary sermon, *The Axe at the Root*, that 'It was an Argument of wickednesse in Saul that he spared Agag, of righteousnesse in Samuel in that he hewed him to pieces'. Kill your own inner Agag, he urges us, that is to say your inner lusts—and also protect Magna Carta against royalists.[22] More chilling is George Wither, his temper perhaps darkened by recent service in the parliamentary army, who writes in *Campo-Musae*, a poem remarkable for narcissism and numerology, that we, like Saul, 'those Amalakites have spared, / Whose preservation may become our Fall; / If his commands, no better we regard'. Thus 'Those bloody executions must be done, / Which both defile and purge, a sinfull Land', all too familiar a claim

---

[15] Some who note the Israelite refusal to kill Jonathan also mention Saul's priest-slaying (1 Sam. 22). Cf. *Davids Three Mighties* (Oxford), E1^r, and Prynne's *Third part*, H4^r.

[16] Richard Baker, *A Chronicle of the Kings of England*, Iii4^r; Elizabeth was unimpressed.

[17] Charles Herle, *Davids Song* (Oxford), E1^r.

[18] Henry Killigrew, *A Sermon Preached before the Kings Most Excellent Majesty*, C1^v.

[19] Arthur Jackson, *A Help for the Understanding of the Holy Scripture* (Cambridge), Dd6v; John Ellis, *The Sole Path to a Sound Peace*, D3^r.

[20] John Booker, *No Mercurius Aquaticus*, A3^r; dated 1644, but as an almanac doubtless printed before 25 March, then the customary new year's day

[21] Cited in Bernard Capp, 'Booker, John (1602–1667)', *ODNB*, 2004, <http://www.oxforddnb.com/view/article/2865>.

[22] William Greenhill, *The Axe at the Root*, E4^v, F4^r.

about necessary violence, if one at least admitting to the paradox that letting blood can be both a dirty job and a curative procedure.[23]

Now God rejects Saul 'from reigning over Israel' (1 Samuel 16: 1) and Samuel goes in search of David to anoint, even if will be some years before the latter ascends the throne.

III. THE DEMON

Christian views on David's harping away the evil spirit that God sent Saul (1 Samuel 16) had varied for centuries, prompting debates on how to understand demons, for example, and on the legitimacy of church music. There was a large body of evidence that music can, for instance, cure gout, abash drunks, manipulate conquerors, and even make babies stop crying. Angels sing, after all. But, others held, demons have no bodies with which to respond to music; if David's harmonious goodness alone cured the king, then his example allows no excuse for having organs in church.[24] The anonymous *Holy Harmony: Or, a Plea for the Abolishing of Organs and other Musick out of the Protestant Churches of Great Britain* thus observes that David chose 'the stillest instrument among the Jewes' with which to cure Saul, and that he later granted his people a little music only because they were not yet 'fully reduc'd to civility'.[25] Indeed, in his *Sole Path to a Sound Peace* the Yorkshire-born preacher John Ellis reads this same scriptural passage as merely Saul's effort to deafen the 'clamour' of his conscience through 'company' and 'mirth'.[26] The eloquent William Fenner, an Essex minister, might agree: Saul's demon, he asserts in his posthumously reprinted *Soules Looking-Glasse ... with a Treatise of Conscience*, was really his bad conscience: 'No musick, mirth, or jovializing can calm conscience, but it will play the devil to a wretched soul for all that. What was the evil spirit of melancholy that came upon Saul, but conscience? He thought to allay it with instruments of musick; but it still came again'.[27] No exorcism was needed: the demon *is* melancholy, black bile, guilt, inward wretchedness.

On the one hand, then, a single-page advertisement for music teachers entitled *By Heavens Decree* can show an actual demon fleeing Saul; David is shown harping, with St Cecelia—whom the godly might call the subject of Papist fictions—seated below at the organ. On the other hand, John Spencer's *Votivae Angliae*, a collection of petitions, is sceptical about music's inherent power. After all, says Spencer, if Saul's problems had been physical he would have needed 'material drugges' that 'might rectifie the humour'; if truly possessed, no natural music or companionable mirth could help him. His must have been 'an absolute madnesse or melancholy fury with some intermission, in which time he could hear advice, and do mischief—and hence was punishable'. In other words: guilty by reason of intermittent sanity. 'I cannot conceive', says Spencer, 'what naturall power musick or melodie can

---

[23] George Wither, *Campo-Musae*, B1^v–B2^r.

[24] See my '"Formes of Joy and Art": Donne, David, and the Power of Music', *John Donne Journal*, 25 (2006): 3–36.

[25] *The Holy Harmony: or, a Plea for the Abolishing of Organs and Other Musick out of the Protestant Churches of Great Britain*, B2^v, A1^v.

[26] Ellis, *Sole Path*, E1^r; although condemning the rich, Ellis says the fickle 'people with Mole-like earthiness' would betray David to 'secure themselves'.

[27] William Fenner, *Soules Looking-Glasse ... with A Treatise of Conscience* (Cambridge), C4^v.

have for the profligation or repulsion of devils'. Music cured Saul 'not as music, but as Davids musick', and had the king merely wanted something to listen to he had other musicians to send for.[28]

Is Saul's demon relevant to political resistance? It certainly added resonance to the king's tragedy. In *Englands Second Alarm to War* the king of Israel 'hugges [it] as his best friend, though the worst enemy to Saul, next to himselfe'. The demon is both self and other, a demonic 'frenemy', inner and outer. Even more relevant, the anonymous *Englands Third Alarm to Warre* sees Saul as a great man with a will corrupted by the devil. David was no rebel and neither are the parliamentary forces, for Charles is both wickedly advised and demonically possessed. If he will not do his duty, we subjects must do ours—liberate our king from his inner devil. If he were not possessed, he would even thank us.[29] Joseph Caryl, a moderate Independent, asks in *An Exposition … upon the Three First Chapters of the Book of Job*, 'how was it an evill spirit if it were from the Lord? can the Lord send forth any evill …?' He replies: 'In that [the demon] was evill that was from [Saul's] own will, but that he had power to trouble Saul that was from the Lord'.[30] A complicated matter.

IV. Goliath and Foreskins

An intermittently cured Saul remained subject to murderous jealousy. Inevitably appearing on my survey of Saul's role in the discourse of 1643 is Goliath, for it was on the king's behalf that David—young but already anointed—took on the Philistine giant. Not all comments concern Saul's envy. We read in *A Discovery of the Rebels by J. V., Prisoner* (identified by the ESTC, improbably, as the radical John Vicars) that Saul's offer of tax relief to anyone killing Goliath is further evidence that kings have the right to extract money from subjects.[31] For the royalist G. D[ownham] of Durham, the giant represents whatever is overbearing but vulnerable to attack from below. If our rebels look in their hearts, he says in the ambiguously titled *Rex meus est deus*, their consciences will tell them that they 'live in prophane and wicked courses'. For 'what can cast a man downe if conscience be upright? Or what can raise man up, if conscience once deject him?' Goliath, after all, was felled by a mere pebble: 'Conscience in wicked men like a bandogge, barkes at them' while they are alive and then, when they are dead, 'teares out the throat of their soules, and makes a full end of them'.[32] Edmund Calamy's *The Noble-Mans Patterne Of True and Reall Thankfulnesse* takes a different tack: when the head is at fault, God can punish the body's members, and thus when Goliath fell the Philistines fled. God, then, helped David kill Goliath, just as he has rescued the English from the Armada, the Gunpowder Plot, and war with Scotland. But have no fear, Calamy says reassuringly in this sermon preached before the House of Lords, we want no 'popular equality'.[33] True, his tact did not save Calamy from a sneer in Samuel

---

[28] John Spencer, *Votivae Angliae*, M2^{r-v}. Spencer's text was first published in 1624.

[29] *Englands Second Alarm to War*, B1^v; *Englands Third Alarm to Warre*, Preface and A1r-C1v; cf. *A Parallel between the Israelites …* , A2^r, which cites Saul's ingratitude.

[30] Joseph Caryl, *An Exposition … upon the Three First Chapters of the Book of Job*, T2^r.

[31] *A Discovery of the Rebels by J. V., Prisoner*, B3^v.

[32] G. D[ownham], *Rex meus est deus*, B2^r, C1^v.

[33] Edmund Calamy, *The Noble-Mans Patterne of True and Reall Thankfulnesse*, H3^v, G2^v.

Butler's *Hudibras*: that "'Tis He who taught the Pulpit and the Press / To mask Rebellion in a Gospel-dress'.[34]

More overtly 'Puritan' in rhetoric is Thomas Wilson's *Jerichoes Down-Fall*. In a passage on Saul's evil counsellors, Wilson urges his readers to stop trying to 'convert Papists with May-poles and Morris-dances' and prays that there may be no 'frogs' or 'croakers' from the 'mouth of the Dragon' to creep into royal chambers and incite war. Yet he says much the same as others: David defeated Goliath without a sword. Why would Saul, with plenty of swords, envy a young man with five pebblestones?[35] In his sermon *The Parliaments Commission*, James Durham asks the same question, and replies that 'the people sung after that Goliah was slain, that *Saul had killed a thousand, and David his ten thousand*: which was as much to say as they thought that David was a mightier man than Saul, and meeter to be king'.[36] Exactly so. Did Saul suffer from sling-envy? David had at least five stones, not counting his other two, and popular opinion behind him to hint, whatever his innocence, that kings, like fathers, can be replaced.

Saul's response was to make David his son-in-law and then try to kill him by demanding he bring home a hundred Philistine foreskins. The year 1643, though, shows a mere scattering of such grisly trophies. Squeamishness? The biblical exegete Arthur Jackson merely notes in his *Help for the Understanding* that the king's request shows that in those days both sexes provided dowries.[37] Jeremiah Burroughs, though, who took Parliament's side in *The Glorious Name of God* and tangled manfully with the royalist Ferne, understandably calls gathering foreskins 'a work of difficulty and hazard'—after all, it was Saul's hope that one of the threatened Philistines would kill David—and he cites the episode as evidence of the latter's courage.[38] One can also imagine all those dying enemies of Israel clutching their bleeding crotches. It was perhaps such a thought that inspired Ferne himself to say in his *Camp at Gilgal*, possibly with some irony, that his pamphlet might 'sometimes prove as sharpe as the Circumcisers knife or the Baptists language'.[39]

V. PERSECUTION AND RESISTANCE

In 1643, although without the intensity produced by debates before Charles's execution in 1649, Saul's treatment of David was interpreted with profoundly different assumptions and conclusions. Jealousy soon led Israel's king into violent persecution, first hurling a javelin at the young man who was now his son-in-law and later seeking him out with armed force and making him, as he laments to the king in 1 Samuel 26: 20, run on the hills like a hunted partridge. David's other bird was the dove. In his *Vanity of Self-Boasters* (a funeral sermon with a subtitle calling such arrogant men 'tyrannnizing Sauls' who 'atheistically' glory in their

[34] Sharon Achinstein, 'Calamy, Edmund (1600–1666)', *ODNB*, 2004; online edition, Sept. 2013, <http://www.oxforddnb.com/view/article/4355>.

[35] Thomas Wilson, *Jerichoes Down-Fall*, F1v, G2v.

[36] James Durham, *The Parliaments Commission*, A2r.

[37] Jackson, *Help for the Understanding*, F1v.

[38] Jeremiah Burroughs, *The Glorious Name of God*, O2v.

[39] Henry Ferne, *The Camp at Gilgal* (Oxford), A6r.

mischief), Edward Hinton wittily recalls Noah's bird, calling David 'an innocent persecuted Dove' who 'willingly would have returned with an Olive branch in his mouth, for *hee sought peace, but they would have warre*'. As for the 'Sauls' of his subtitle, Hinton blames that king's tyranny on flatterers.[40] Over and over, those who comment on Saul's treatment of David, often with an eye on Charles and in passages far too numerous to describe here, mention the king's angry injustice in pursuing a man whose behaviour had given him no cause (for thus the assumption had to be, granted God's love for David, a love that would continue despite his various sins). The issue was not what David had done to deserve this cruelty, but rather how he was forced to defend himself in ways that did, or did not, justify the much later rebellion in Britain. Aside from jealousy, what would drive Saul to such impolitic behaviour? Many, especially those nervous over their own defiance of Charles, had an answer: wicked advice.

VI. Evil Counsel

Ever since his failure to kill Agag, ever since his first efforts to kill David, Saul's rule had gone downhill. In 1643 some argued that evil counsel had hastened his slide into tyranny. This is of course an old story, rendered fresh by Parliament's strategic need to claim that its proclamations and soldiers aimed not at the King himself but at his advisers, and merely in the hope of rescuing Charles from Saulhood. 'Here is no taking up of Arms against the King', writes Samuel Clarke in *Englands Covenant Proved Lawfull*, when commenting on David's punishment of the Amalekite who claimed to have killed Saul, but rather 'against his evill Counsellours who have imbittered his spirit against his Counsell and doe still captivate his person amongst them'.[41] Many said the same. More specifically, Saul was 'seduced by Edomites', and so too nowadays oceans of blood cry from the ground, from Bristol and from Oxford, or so claims *Englands Second Alarm*.[42] The likewise anonymous author of *A Parallel* agrees: just as Saul had his Edomites, Charles 'takes Atheists and Papists to him now', even though 'the SUPREME LAW' is 'the *welfare of the People*'.[43] We cannot even take the King's words as his own, for they are the work of those around him. Over and over one reads the same. William Bridge, whose *Truth of the Times Vindicated* draws on both biblical and classical texts and figures, counters Ferne's objection that David had in fact spared his anointed ruler by insisting that David's real military object was the gang of advisers around Saul. So too, Parliament is trying 'to deliver the Prince out of the hands of Malignants'.[44]

Royalists of course rejected such comparisons. Ferne's *Conscience Satisfied*, not unexpectedly, claims that unlike the badly counselled Saul, Charles had shown a tender regard for Parliament's reputation, and the distinguished Peter Heylyn offered more such royalist argument in his *Rebells Catechism*.[45] Probably the most eloquent dissent from rebellion,

---

[40] Edward Hinton, *Vanity of Self-Boasters*, A4^r; E3^r; the annotations on Psalms in the Geneva Bible say the same.

[41] Samuel Clarke, *Englands Covenant Proved Lawfull*, B4^r.

[42] Clarke, *Englands Covenant*, B3^r.

[43] *A Parallel between the Israelites ...* , C1^{r-v}.

[44] William Bridge, *The Truth of the Times Vindicated*, E4^v.

[45] Ferne, *Conscience Satisfied*, K4^v; Peter Heylyn, *Rebells Catechism* (Oxford), C1^r.

though, is *A Letter from a Scholler in Oxenford to his Uncle a Merchant in Broad Street*, in one edition printed continuously with *The Loyal Citizen Revived* by Henry Garraway, Lord Mayor of London. The scholar argues passionately against 'The Replyer', who 'hath the face to compare the Kings making Warre upon his Parliament to Sauls hunting of David'. But had David 'ever given Saul any cause to feare him by spreading Declarations, or raising and encouraging Tumults, against him and the established Lawes? ... Did he invade Sauls Privileges, and deny him a Negative voyce? ... Did hee raise an Armie to fetch those Evill Counsellours from about Saul who had perswaded him to seeke his life?' No, and his heart smote him for 'cutting but the lapp of his Garment?' Thus there is 'a wide difference between what the King did, and what was done to him; and Sauls provocations of David, and Davids returns towards Saul. And who ever had waited on the King this last yeare from place to place would easily conclude, whether he or the Parliament were hunted most like the Partridge'.[46] In this role-reversal the King, not the Commons, plays David.

VII. THE CAVE

A major issue was thus how we should read David's armed but defensive resistance and yet his refusal to hurt the Lord's anointed. This dilemma led to another question: what was the origin of kingship itself? Did Samuel, who had warned his people against monarchy, institute it (with God's help)? But was not his anointing of Saul ratified by the Israelites? Is such ratification a part of legitimate monarchy? Indeed, in his massive *Fourth Part of the Soveraigne Power of Parliaments*, a work with many allusions to David's story, Prynne calls Saul 'elected and made King by Samuel and the people'.[47] What then of other Israelite kings, or even gentile ones, and what was the relevance of all this to the ancient British or Saxon constitutions, if these last were in fact real?

I have no space for a full description of 1643's many allusions to David's restrained but armed resistance to his king, so let me take, briefly, one image exploited over and over that year—that of David hiding in the cave when the king enters it to relieve himself ('to cover his feet') and does not see the lurking object of his chase. David will not touch the Lord's anointed, and a number of texts cite his subsequent repentance for silently cutting off the hem of an inattentive Saul's garment. Not everyone was impressed by the argument that David's showed respect for Saul's anointed kingship, and sceptics attacked royalist exegesis and reasoning. William Bridge, among those stressing that Samuel's anointment was ratified by popular voice, observed that although David regretted cutting Saul's garment, the Bible also reports that he nevertheless 'went out against Saul'.[48] Moreover, if Ferne was right that David's resistance was not a model because David was 'extraordinary', then we can retort that his refusal to lay hands on Saul was likewise 'extraordinary'.[49] Prynne of course mentions the scene, arguing that, because Saul was unaware of David's presence, it is 'Non-sence' to say that David was unwilling to touch him.[50] By that logic, we must conclude that, if Saul and

---

[46] *A Letter from a Scholler in Oxenford to his Uncle a Merchant in Broad Street*, B4^v–C1^r; cf. 1 Sam. 26: 20.

[47] William Prynne, *Fourth Part of the Soveraigne Power of Parliaments*, T21^r.

[48] Bridge, *Truth*, B3^r.   [49] Bridge, *Truth*, D2^v, F1–F1^v.

[50] Prynne, *Third Part*, Mm4^r.

the men Prynne elsewhere scoffingly and anachronistically calls his 'cut-throate Cavaleers' and 'Popish depopulating Cavaleers' had seen David and assaulted him, the latter would not have had the right to fight back.[51] And David Hume's posthumous *History of the Houses of Douglas and Angus* objects to the royalists' very logic when demanding full obedience to the King: 'David *did not slay* Saul, therefore no man should lay hands on a Tyrant how loose is it [i.e. the reasoning]?'[52]

Indeed, there were difficulties for those citing David's restraint. For example, the anonymous royalist's *Davids Three Mighties* (i.e. Luther, Calvin, and Tyndale) claims both that David was right not to touch the Lord's anointed *and* that God did 'break the bloudy Scepters of proud Kings, and overthrew their intolerable governments'.[53] But did not God in such cases often use mortals as his instruments, allowing them to touch an anointed ruler? Are those who dethrone bad kings, even if God so wills, themselves guilty? Are there kings who do not have royal rights? How do we tell? The cave is a fine symbol for such perplexities—dark, bristling with hidden soldiers, a refuge for hunted prey, and if useful as a privy then that very fact is resonant with the knowledge that even kings have innards. Does the body politic have to take a bathroom break? It certainly has secrets, and James I once compared prying into royal matters to Pantagruel's doctors descending in bathyspheres to cleanse his lower colon.[54] A cave, moreover, well represents mental inwardness, a place of retreat but also of conscience; understandably, Fenner's discussion of such introspection in *Looking-Glasse* mentions David's repentance for cutting Saul's garment.[55] No wonder then, that the image of Saul in the dark, more vulnerable than he knew as he crouched there with his skirts covering his feet and his young enemy nearby with a knife, struck more people than did David's parallel sparing of Saul when in the open.

In a vigorous paragraph on cosmic hierarchy and harmony worthy to set next to Ulysses's great speech in *Troilus and Cressida*, G. Downham asks in his *Rex meus*, 'shall we admit of no Order among reasonable men?' David knew Saul to be 'a bloudy, Butcherly barbarous Prince' and yet he, himself an anointed future king, 'was so farr from hurting him' in 'the Cave, that his heart smote him when hee had but cut off the skirt of his garment'.[56] Remember that, 'You fire-brands of strife, you trumpets of sedition, you red horses', whose sitters have taken peace from the earth, you furies of hel ...'.[57] Not, he adds hastily, that Charles is like Saul. Sir John Spelman, soon to die of camp fever, took the same position in his *Case of Our Affaires ... Presented to the Conscience*: David 'did but lay his hand upon Sauls garment to cut off the lap for a testimonie of his loyaltie and innocent intention towards Saul, and yet even for that saith the Text, *his heart smote him*'.[58] The Anabaptist John Tombes will have none of this. Yes, he points out, in *Jehova Iireh*,

[51] Prynne, *Third Part*, L3ᵛ.
[52] David Hume, *History of the Houses of Douglas and Angus* (Edinburgh, 1644), Hh3ᵛ. Hume's comments appear in *The Second Part of the History of the Douglasses, containing the House of Angus*, which has continuous pagination and register, but a separate title-page dated 1643.
[53] *Davids Three Mighties*, C2ʳ–C3ʳ.
[54] *His Majesties Declaration concerning ... Conradus Vorstius* (1612), G4ᵛ.
[55] Fenner, *Looking-Glasse*, G2ʳ.   [56] Downham, *Rex meus*, C3ᵛ.
[57] Downham, *Rex meus*, D1ᵛ.
[58] Sir John Spelman, *Case of our Affaires ... Presented to the Conscience* (Oxford?), D1ᵛ.

'Davids heart smote him when he cut off the lap of Sauls garment, yet we reade not that he repented his gathering a band of men to him, his getting into strongholds for defence of himselfe against Saul'.[59]

One more example. According to Philip Hunton, political disorder can be medicinal: it 'may for the time disturbe, as Physick while it is working disturbes the naturall bodie, if the peccant humors make strong opposition: but sure it tends to health, and so doth this resistence of disorder to Order'.[60] Without the right to resist, moreover, and should prayer and petition fail, we are left with 'absolute subjection, that is servitude: for the end of all constitution of moderated forms is not that the supreme power might not lawfully exorbitate, but that it might have no power to exorbitate'.[61] What of David in the cave? He took up arms only 'to secure his person against the cut-throats of Saul', and although he did not aim at the king's person, he would have been justified using violence against 'Saul himself' if the king had accompanied his 'cut-throats'.[62] Is this relevant? Of course. David was not really 'extraordinary', being at the time a mere subject and his anointment just a 'designation'.[63] Or, rather, there is no relevance. Ferne's arguments are pointless, for these Israelite kings were 'of Gods particular designation'.[64] Many argued for David's status as 'extraordinary' (and hence not exemplary as a rebel) or 'ordinary' and still 'private' (and hence useful to arguments for resistance). Here we see, though, that David can be, for the same author, both model and non-model.

In sum, rebels could point out that, even if David did not assault Saul in the cave or on the field, he might have done so if pushed. Complexities remained, however. If Saul had gone out with his own army and been killed by a now more aggressive David, would that have been suicide? Regicide? If the latter, is it by the ordinary soldier David or by the anointed heir David? The answer depends on how one reads the effects of that holy oil *and* how one reads might-have-been history. When arguing in his *Serpent Salve* that we cannot serve both King and Parliament, Archbishop John Bramhall asks what, if a stray arrow could kill Ahab, king of Israel, 'shall secure King Charles from a bullet?' True, we must obey God first, which is why Saul's guard 'refused justly to slay the Priests of the Lord'.[65]

VIII. The Witch of Endor

Just before the end of his life an embattled Saul visited the Witch of Endor so he could consult the shade of his deceased mentor Samuel. The scene had attracted interest in this time of witch trials, James I's book on demonology, and an established church asserting that the dead cannot return. For some, such as the sceptical Reginald Scot writing two generations earlier in his lively *Discoverie of Witchcraft* (1584), the witch was a charlatan and 'Samuel'

[59] John Tombes, *Jehova Iireh*, C1ᵛ.

[60] Hunton, *Treatise of Monarchie*, I2ʳ, a deployment of the body–state analogy that more often served royalism.

[61] Hunton, *Treatise of Monarchie*, H3ᵛ.   [62] Hunton, *Treatise of Monarchie*, H2ʳ.

[63] Hunton, *Treatise of Monarchie*, H3ʳ.   [64] Hunton, *Treatise of Monarchie*, I1ʳ.

[65] John Bramhall, *The Serpent Salve*, K4ᵛ; cf. 1 Kings 22.

her mortal assistant, but for many others in early modern England she was indeed friendly with the dark powers and the figure she summoned up was a demon. In his *Exposition* of Job, the erudite Caryl at least leaves the question open: this supposed prophet is perhaps 'the Devill in the appearance of Samuel'.[66] Giovanni Diodati, in *Pious Annotations*, agrees with the sceptics: the demon persuades Saul that all souls 'as well good as bad go to the same place' precisely so as to 'blot out' the king's 'knowledge and apprehension of eternall life'.[67] In any case, Saul receives evil counsel. True, the swaggering royalist weekly, *Mercurius Aulicus*, edited by Peter Heylyn and important in the early history of the press, merely reports in the issue for 6–12 August that some say to 'vote for peace' is 'like the plot of the *Trojan horse*, and like Saul, to fly in distresse to the Witch of Endor'.[68] Troy and Endor? Their juxtaposition is another reminder that scripture and classics merged in Civil War polemic. Indeed, the author follows this nose-thumbing by complaining that 'the Printed Newes-men are this weeke turn'd Preachers, using Scripture (in place of Newes) … yet ever and anon sprinkling a lye' (examples follow). Some allusions to the witch can be puzzling. In his *Solemn Discourse upon the Grand Covenant*, John Saltmarsh mystifyingly compares a reliance on laws to Saul at Endor summoning 'Aron'. Irony, error, or misprint? He goes on to say that anti-Reformers would call up 'the whole Hierarchy, and bring us back again to the Law', drawing a curtain 'before the light of the Gospel'.[69] The accusation—that anti-Reformers would ignore the New Testament—is a reminder, if in this case an odd one, that the Revolution energized both a desire to enforce the Hebrew Bible's injunctions and a quasi-mystical distaste for ancient, if biblical, rules.

Perhaps the most entertaining fragment of the Endor area in my survey is from Thomas Jordan's verse *Piety, and Poesy*. In an 'Eclogue' starring Saul and the Witch, a panicked king calls 'For Wizards, Witches, and his Fate refers / No more to Prophets but to Sorcerers'. So have I seen, says Jordan, a 'fawning Parasite' become a malcontent. Thus 'Saul's resolved, since Heaven denies to tell / What he would know, makes his next means to Hell'. He flatters the witch, who is puzzled, for Saul had once tried to get rid of witches. Thanks to the king's own rules, after all, she must now live in darkness and 'converse with nought, but Batts and Owls'. At least she can produce a fiend who resembles Samuel and offers wisdom: good kings are gods, bad ones devils. Saul will lose his crown; David will have it. The distraught Saul advises posterity: 'Ye Princes, that successfully shall Reign ["successfully" must mean in succeeding times] / After my haplesse End, with care and pain, / Peruse my pitied Story, do not be / Too confident of your frail Sov'reignty'. He should have listened to the real Samuel, confesses Saul, and says in lines doubtless aimed at Charles: 'All you that stand, be wary lest you fall, / And when ye think you're sure, Remember Saul'.[70] True enough, and to this survey of allusions one should add *Obedience Active and Passive Due to the Supream Power* by W.J. The author argues, he says, from scripture, theology, and reason that we must obey kings, for '*Rebellion is as the sinne of Witch-craft*, as Samuel saith to Saul from God, 1 *Sam.* 15.23. *And Thou shalt not suffer a Witch to live*, saith God him selfe'.[71] He does not say what to

---

[66] Caryl, *An Exposition*, Fff2r.
[67] Giovanni Diodati, *Pious Annotations*, Y2v.
[68] *Mercurius Aulicus*, 32nd week (Oxford, 12 Aug. 1643), 3Q4v.
[69] John Saltmarsh, *A Solemn Discourse upon the Grand Covenant*, C3r.
[70] Thomas Jordan, *Piety, and Poesy*, C3v–C6v.
[71] W.J., *Obedience Active and Passive Due to the Supream Power*, C1r.

do with kings who consult witches. He does, though, admire David, to whom he compares Henri de Navarre when praising the latter for not instantly exacting revenge for the 1572 St Bartholomew massacre of Huguenots.[72]

IX. SUICIDE

And now, as my scan of Saul's career in 1643 Britain nears its end, comes Saul's messy suicide. One issue had long troubled the charitable: may we pray for Saul? (Indeed, whether we may pray for any of the dead was something on which Catholic and Protestant might disagree.) On the whole, texts in 1643 ignore the matter, although William Slatyer's *Compleat Christian* says we should not pray for God's enemies, such as Saul.[73] In his *Noble-Mans Patterne*, Calamy observes merely that 'when Saul fell upon his Sword, his Armourbearer seeing the King to doe so, fell also upon his Sword and killed himselfe. When great men fall into sinne, they fall as men that fall in a croud, drawing many others downe with them'.[74] Prynne's view in *The Third Part* not unexpectedly reads the armour-bearer's refusal to kill Saul when asked to do so as yet another legitimate refusal to obey kings. A few, such as *Davids Three Mighties* and Caryl in his *Exposition*, note the vivid scene (2 Samuel 1) in which David's weeps over Saul's death, rends his garments, and orders the Amalekite claiming to have killed him put to death.[75] And yet, as Fenner's *Souls Looking-Glasse* notes, the biblical text is not without ambiguity.[76]

Indeed, some might reflect quietly to themselves, David was in any case too politic to rejoice openly, and it is easy to believe that he felt an ambivalence not unlike that of Elizabeth imagining the head of Mary Stuart: relieved, but alert to troubling implications. The death of Saul relieved Israel of a tyrant but also raised intriguing questions, ones not unrelated to the theory of the king's two bodies, and indeed to how the *name* 'king' relates to the king's person(s). Samuel Clarke's *Englands Covenant* explicitly raises the issue when mulling over the murder of Saul's purported assassin, saying that David ordered the killing as a king, not as David.[77] In a related argument, the anonymous author of the royalist *Worse & Worse*, a tract against the oath of the New Covenant, objects that 'our learned Schismaticks think to dawbe up mens consciences with their untempered mortar, by distinguishing between the Naturall and Politique Person of the King. The most of England can now laugh at their fond subtilty, knowing that he who killed Saul, the then King of Israel, did thereby kill the same King named Saul'.[78] One sees the point, and yet ... the aim of the two-bodies theory is precisely to distinguish between 'the Naturall and Politique' persons. When Richard III died, one body died with him, but the other continued in Henry VII. These are subtle

---

[72] W.J., *Obedience*, D3ʳ; he fails to mention that Navarre later warred against Henri III.
[73] William Slatyer, *The Compleat Christian*, Llʰ1ʳ.
[74] Calamy, *Noble-mans Patterne*, E2ʳ.
[75] Prynne, *Third Part*, H4ᵛ; *Davids Three Mighties*, E1ʳ; Caryl, *Exposition*, Aa2ᵛ.
[76] Fenner, *Souls Looking-Glasse*, C4ᵛ.
[77] Clarke, *Englands Covenant*, B4ʳ.
[78] *Worse & Worse*, B2ᵛ.

matters: how do Saul's 'name' and the 'name' of king relate to the identity of that poor dead body? Or is it 'bodies'? How does *verbum* relate to *res*, or 'Saul' to '*rex*'?

What to conclude? First that the story of Saul—if less often than that of David, for Saul wrote no psalms that allow us entry into his mind—facilitates a focus on inwardness, on how political and military action relates to conscience, for example, or to repentance over a cut garment. I do not myself fully agree with claims that the early modern period saw an increased subjectivity, but the extent of interest in a sinner's inwardness and the exhortations to self-examination remain striking. The material I have collected for my survey, moreover, shows an intermittent but keen attention to cultural and linguistic differences. Did an opponent read the biblical text correctly? If Israel had anointed kings, did Rome? Need we? Must we translate Israelite culture to Stuart times in a *translatio regum*, or is Israelite kingship, like the Ten Commandments, transcultural?

Such debates suggest something deeper. Even Protestants, with a little nudging, could agree with Thomas More when he argues against Luther that words are arbitrary and shifty creatures as they slither from one language to another, and we must not identify them with the Word.[79] What Jesus spoke in Hebrew or Aramaic was written down in Greek, but even Jerome would agree that the *Logos* itself is not Latin. This puts the burden of interpretation on us, and as any English professor knows, it takes minimal ingenuity to wrest and wrestle biblical words into supporting popular sovereignty or royal absolutism. Words matter. But so do force, money, land ownership, and trade; so do armies and the axe of 1649. Whether Charles was another Saul or another David, or Cromwell a David who became Saul in 1660, or Charles II the true David if with Achitophel for a son: all this was debated. The life of Saul did not fade from political discourse even as Davidhood shifted from ruler to ruler to ruler—but that is yet another story.

Further Reading

Keeble, N. H., ed. *Cambridge Companion to Writing of the English Revolution* (Cambridge: Cambridge University Press, 2001).

Killeen, Kevin. 'Chastising with Scorpions: Reading the Old Testament in Early Modern England'. *Huntington Library Quarterly*, 73 (2010): 491–506.

Killeen, Kevin. 'Hanging up Kings: The Political Bible in Early Modern England'. *Journal of the History of Ideas*, 72 (2011): 549–70.

Nelson, Eric. *The Hebrew Republic: Jewish Sources and the Transformation of European Political Thought* (Cambridge, Mass.: Harvard University Press, 2010).

Prescott, Anne Lake. '"Formes of Joy and Art": Donne, David, and the Power of Music'. *John Donne Journal*, 25 (2006): 3–36.

Prescott, Anne Lake. 'Evil Tongues at the Court of Saul'. *Journal of Medieval and Renaissance Studies*, 12 (1991): 163–86.

Smith, Nigel. *Literature and Revolution in England, 1640–1660* (New Haven: Yale University Press, 1994).

[79] Thomas More, *Responsio ad Lutherum*, ed. John M. Hadley (New Haven: Yale University Press, 1969), e.g. 241.

CHAPTER 27

'THAT GLORY MAY DWELL IN OUR LAND': THE BIBLE, BRITANNIA, AND THE GLORIOUS REVOLUTION

EMMA MAJOR

IN 1682, the Anglican Tory cleric John Nalson published the first volume of his ambitious but never-to-be-completed *An Impartial Collection of the Great Affairs of State from the Scotch Rebellion in the Year MDCXXXIX to the Murther of Charles I.*[1] Keen to make plain his arguments from the beginning, he glossed his opening image (Figure 27.1) with a poetic summary of 'The Mind of the Frontispiece':

> See the World's Glory once, here sits forlorn.
> Expos'd to Foreign, and Domestick Scorn;
> *Britannia* who so many Foes withstood,
> Her Bowels torn, by her own Viperous Brood:
> Her Sons, most damnably Religious grown,
> Canted the Diadem and Mitre down,
> And Zealously usurpt both Church, and Crown:
> Look on that Axe embru'd in Royal gore,
> A Crime unknown to Pagans heretofore;
> Whence they their own Fanatick Zeal applaud[.][2]

Having described the recent Civil Wars and killing of Charles I, Nalson drew the reader's attention to the Janus figure of 'Rome and Geneva', urged on by the Devil whose cloven foot tramples the Bible. Yet Britannia's woes had not ended with the return of the monarchy, despite Nalson's post-Restoration complacency. The proximity of the Bible and the

---

[1] The quotation in the chapter title is from Ps. 85: 9. I am grateful to Kevin Killeen and Richard Rowland for their comments on drafts of this chapter, and to Frances Dann and Emilie Morin for helping me to decide on its focus.

[2] John Nalson, *An Impartial Collection of the Great Affairs of State from the Scotch Rebellion in the Year MDCXXXIX to the Murther of Charles I* (1682), frontispiece.

FIGURE 27.1 Robert White, frontispiece to John Nalson's *Impartial Collection of the Great Affairs of State*, 1682.

Magna Carta, and the tumbled crown and mitre, were to prove a continued source of anxiety through the 1680s, the nation haunted by the spectres of Civil War. The eye of providence beaming down upon Britannia in the frontispiece was less easily perceived by Protestants with the accession of the Catholic James II in 1685, when once again the relationship between church, crown, and people came under pressure. For many contemporary commentators—both Whig and Tory—an identifiably beneficent providence was only to return in 1688, when according to the Bishop of St Asaph, William Lloyd, 'God made the Winds his good Angels for our Deliverance' and blew William of Orange's ships safely to shore on 5 November, that most propitious date in the national calendar for the overturning of Papist plots.[3]

Lloyd's sermon, preached on 5 November 1689 before William and Mary, took as its text Psalm 57 and read David's rescue from the pit as Britain's deliverance from the Catholics. In choosing Psalms, Lloyd revisited a book that had provided much comfort during James's reign to Protestants of all denominations: Psalms, Exodus, Isaiah, Revelation, and St Paul had in particular consoled, harrowed, and inspired, and generated many sermons during years when Protestantism was under threat at home and abroad. Lloyd's choice of Psalms and his discussion of David's plight were powerful reminders of the religious persecution suffered by Protestants. The combination of biblical texts about persecution and salvation in the sermon he preached to the new monarchs is typical of the ways in which the King James Bible was used to legitimate the Glorious Revolution and affirm Britain's status as the new Israel, both punished and blessed.[4]

In this chapter, I will explore some of the ways in which the Bible was used between 1685 and 1689 to empower Protestants under a Catholic king and then to validate the replacement of James II with William III and Mary II. The changes in church and government prompted by James II's Catholic faith, the presence of his unpopular Jesuit advisers at court, rumours—from Easter 1687—that James himself was an affiliate of the Society of Jesus, and, in 1688, the unexpected arrival of a male heir to the throne, meant that loyalties to king, faith, and nation were often divided or at the very least under pressure. There was widespread suspicion of the queen consort Mary of Modena's child-bearing abilities; many thought that the baby had been smuggled in to secure the Catholic succession, and according to Burnet, 'The pretended birth made them reckon that Popery and Slavery would be entailed on the Nation'.[5] Questions of authority were raised in church and in government: some asked if James II could even be regarded as a legitimate office-holder, when dissenters (all non-Anglicans) were technically excluded from public posts.

---

[3] William Lloyd, *A Sermon Preach'd before Their Majesties at Whitehall, on the Fifth Day of November, 1689* (London, 1689), 31.

[4] On the Glorious Revolution, see Tony Claydon, *William III and the Godly Revolution* (Cambridge: Cambridge University Press, 1996); William Gibson, *James II and the Trial of the Seven Bishops* (Basingstoke: Palgrave Macmillan, 2009); Tim Harris, *Revolution: The Great Crisis of the British Monarchy, 1685–1720* (Harmondsworth: Penguin, 2007); Harris and Stephen Taylor (eds), *The Final Crisis of the Stuart Monarchy: The Revolutions of 1688–91 in their British, Atlantic and European Contexts* (Woodbridge: Boydell, 2013); Scott Sowerby, *Making Toleration: The Repealers and the Glorious Revolution* (Cambridge, Mass.: Harvard University Press, 2013).

[5] Gilbert Burnet, *Bishop Burnet's History of His Own Time*, i (London, 1724), 755. On Mary of Modena, see Rachel J. Weil, 'The Politics of Legitimacy: Women and the Warming-Pan Scandal', in Lois G. Schwoerer (ed.), *The Revolution of 1688–9: Changing Perspectives* (Cambridge: Cambridge University Press, 1992), 65–82.

Given the established nature of the church, there were legal dimensions to the obvious difficulties entailed by having a Catholic head of a Protestant national church.[6] These arguments later formed part of William's justification for invading Britain.[7] Such debates meant that by 1687–8 even Tory bishops, those least likely rebels, were forced to choose between their conscience and their king. Proverbs 14: 34—'Righteousness exalteth a Nation, but sin is a reproach to any people'—became a popular text for sermons, though not all those who spoke to it could share the nonconformist John Shawe's cheerful separation of God and King in his *Britannia Rediviva* (1649), when he asked his audience 'how much more excellent, and honorable is it, to be Gods Town, to be Christs Town, then *Kings Town* upon *Hull*?'[8] Memories of regicide made the possibility that being the king's town might not be the same as being God's or Christ's town particularly fraught, but for Protestants of all denominations it became an increasingly urgent question as James II's plans to establish the Catholic Church in Britain began to take form.

I will begin by looking at the relationship between the church, Bible, and history and exploring the questions of loyalty and authority that dogged James II's rule. These debates reached a crisis in the summer of 1688, when the refusal of the seven bishops to subscribe to the king's Declaration of Indulgence gratified so many Protestants of all denominations that, as Patrick Collinson drily observes, 'The Church of England now briefly enjoyed the greatest popularity in its entire history'.[9] In the final section of the chapter I return to the book of Revelation and argue that the Bible and Britannia were central to interpretations of the Glorious Revolution as an event that supported rather than threatened patriarchal structures.

I. 'A Church of England Loyalty': The Bible and Britannia

On the accession of James II, William Sherlock, then one of the king's chaplains, told the House of Commons that 'next to having our King of the Communion of the Church of *England*, we can desire no more, than to have a King, who will defend it'.[10] Emphasizing his

---

[6] On James II and authority in the Church of England, see Jacqueline Rose, *Godly Kingship in Restoration England: The Politics of the Royal Supremacy, 1660–1688* (Cambridge: Cambridge University Press, 2011), 237–74. The Corporation Act of 1661, and the Test Acts of 1673 and 1678 in England and Wales (1681 in Scotland), prevented all those who were not members of the Church of England from taking public office. (Women of all denominations and the poor were already excluded.) James had resigned his position as Lord High Admiral in 1673 because he could not legally hold the post as a Roman Catholic. He initially kept his conversion secret, but had converted by 1669. W. A. Speck, 'James II and VII (1633–1701)', *ODNB*, 2004; online edition, Oct. 2009, <http://www.oxforddnb.com/view/article/14593>.

[7] See e.g. [William Henry, Prince of Orange], *The Prince of Orange His Declaration: Shewing the Reasons Why he Invades England* (London, 1688), 4–9, and [William III or William Lloyd], *Utrum Horum; Or, God's Ways of Disposing of Kingdoms: And Some Clergy-Men's Ways of Disposing of Them* (London, 1691), 6 and passim.

[8] John Shawe, *Britannia Rediviva: Or the Proper and Sovereign Remedy for the Healing and Recovering of These Three Distracted Nations* (London, 1649), 9.

[9] Patrick Collinson, *From Cranmer to Sancroft* (London: Hambledon Continuum, 2006), 190.

[10] William Sherlock, *A Sermon Preached at St Margarets Westminster, May 29, 1685. Before the Honourable House of Commons* (London, 1685), 26.

personal admiration of James II, his argument nevertheless depended rather on the logic of a monarch's protection of an institution that safeguarded his throne, rather than on the king's status or honour:

> Loyalty and Obedience is a powerful Obligation on Princes to rule well; for Princes must value Obedience and Subjection as they do their Crowns. To this we owe the present Security and Protection of the Church of *England*; for if there were nothing else to be liked in it, yet a gener-ous Prince cannot but like and reward its Loyalty; and it would seem very harsh for any Prince to desire that religion should be turned out of the Church, which secures him in a quiet pos-session of his Throne.[11]

Instead, then, of seeking parliamentary loyalty to a Catholic king, Sherlock urged them to 'a Church of *England* Loyalty', 'for there is no such lasting and immoveable Loyalty, as that of the Church of *England*'.[12] By taking as his text Ecclesiastes 10: 17, 'Blessed art thou, O Land, when thy King is the Son of Nobles', Sherlock had set a conditional tone to the sermon, which, rather like the sombre Ecclesiastes 10 itself, combined warnings against foolish rulers with exhortations not to curse the king. James II could be assured of 'lasting and immove-able Loyalty' as long as he protected the Church of England, as of course he would do if he acted with wisdom, as 'the Son of Nobles'. There was a clear and menacing undercurrent to Sherlock's logic, which made the security of the throne dependent on the safety of the church. Sherlock concluded with a prayer:

> God grant the whole Nation may follow the Example of this Honourable Senate, to be Loyal to their Prince, Zealous for the Service of the Crown, and true to the Religion of the Church of England, as dearer to them than their Lives.[13]

Such faithfulness to the church, Sherlock argued, proved the value of these subjects, for, as many after him were to tell James II, 'the English man may be Loyal, but not the Papist', whose allegiance lay with the Pope in Rome.[14] James threw the term back at the church when he clashed with it over his attempts to open Oxford up to Catholics and appoint the Catholic Anthony Farmer as President of Magdalen College in early 1687; accusing the fellows of the college of behaving 'very uncivilly' to him, he said they should 'know I am your King and will be obeyed', and asked, 'Is this your Church of England loyalty?'[15]

'The Protestant Church of England, our Holy Mother, admits of no other Rule for Faith and practice than the Holy Scriptures, which according to the Apostles are able to make us wise unto Salvation', argued Burnet in *The Protestant's Companion* (1685).[16] Burnet's pugna-cious booklet was not only concerned with outlining Protestant doctrine, however: as its full title makes clear, it was specifically an assertion of the superiority of Protestantism over Roman Catholicism. *The Protestant's Companion, or, an Impartial Survey and Comparison of the Protestant Religion as by Law Established, with the Main Doctrines of Popery wherein*

---

[11] Sherlock, *Sermon Preached at St Margarets*, 30.

[12] Sherlock, *Sermon Preached at St Margarets*, 31.

[13] Sherlock, *Sermon Preached at St Margarets*, 32.

[14] Sherlock, *Sermon Preached at St Margarets*, 32.

[15] Quoted in Gibson, *James II and the Trial of the Seven Bishops*, 67. James's Ecclesiastical Commission was later to expel the Magdalen Fellows for having omitted to act in accordance with the Anglican doctrine of passive obedience.

[16] Burnet, *The Protestant's Companion* (London, 1685), 1.

is Shewn that Popery is Contrary to Scripture, Primitive Fathers and Councils was part of a wave of anti-Catholic publications and sermons that followed James II's accession to the throne. Such attacks had been forbidden by James II, who in 1686 repeatedly instructed the Archbishop of Canterbury, William Sancroft, to forbid his clergy preaching on controversy; but the increasing power of Roman Catholics at court meant that there was an urgent sense of the Church of England being under attack, and anti-Roman Catholic arguments continued to proliferate from pulpits and presses.[17] Burnet's opening statement included three strands which were to become key in the defence of the Church of England: she was 'our Holy Mother'; her only rule was the 'Holy Scriptures'; and her authority for her reliance on the Bible derived from the Apostles themselves.

The Church of England was commonly personified as a woman of unimpeachable virtue, one who taught a 'Religion, which robs neither God of his Honour, nor the King of his due; a Religion, whose venerable Rites keep a just *medium* betwixt vain Popish Pomp, and Fanatical Indecency'.[18] Increasingly, this figure was depicted as one whose loyalty to the king was unappreciated to the point of martyrdom. Burnet's 1687 defence of the church emphasized her obedience to James II, arguing that the '*Church of England* may justly expostulate when she is treated as Seditious, after she has rendred [*sic*] the highest Services to the Civil Authority, that any Church now on Earth has done'; never lacking in a sense of his own worth, he noted that '[s]he has beaten down all the Principles of Rebellion, with more Force and Learning, than any Body of men has ever yet done', and pointed out

> *She* knew well what were the Doctrines and Practices of those of the *Roman Church*, with Relation to *Hereticks*; and yet *She* was so true to her *Loyalty*, that *She* shut her eyes on all the Temptations, that so just a fear could raise in her: and *She* set her self to support His *Majesties* Right of Succession, with so much Zeal, that *She* thereby not only put her self in the power of her Enemies; but *She* has also exposed her self to the Scorn of those who insult over her in her Misfortune[.][19]

This injured figure, depicted as bravely facing the infamous methods of the Inquisition rather than betray her Catholic monarch by supporting the Duke of Monmouth's Protestant uprising in 1685, was ripe for rescue, and was to play an important and powerful role in legitimating the revolution of 1688.

In his *History*, Burnet admitted that 'A new eighty eight raised new expectations': in a fusion of history and faith evident in commentators from clerics to diarists like Evelyn, Elizabeth I and her providential triumph over the Spanish Armada in 1588 was conjured up to support the ailing church she had established.[20] References to the church under Elizabeth and James I opposed historical monarchs to the current one, while celebrations of anniversaries such as Elizabeth I's accession or Guy Fawkes became annual opportunities for popular resentment of James II's Catholic rule to be expressed in apparently legitimate guise.[21]

---

[17] Gibson, *James II*, 56–9.

[18] Burnet, *Protestant's Companion*, A4[v]. On the personified Church of England, see Emma Major, *Madam Britannia: Women, Church, and Nation, 1712–1812* (Oxford: Oxford University Press, 2012), 1–37.

[19] Gilbert Burnet, *An Answer to a Paper Printed with Allowance, Entitled, a New Test of the Church of England's Loyalty* ([London?], 1687), 3 and 1.

[20] Burnet, *History*, 728.

[21] Harris, *Revolution*, 95, 209–10; Gibson, *James II*, 73.

FIGURE 27.2 Commemorative silver medal of Britannia, the Bible, and William III, 1689.

(Indeed, Elizabeth I would dog James II, appearing at the most inconvenient moments, including at the firework spectacular held on 17 July 1688 to celebrate the birth of the royal prince: the mechanical figures of fecundity, loyalty, and Bacchus were sabotaged and transformed into Elizabeth I, Anne Boleyn, and Henry VIII, and the rumour spread that James II would blow these up as a mark of Catholic defiance.[22])

The image of the Church of England became the site of contested histories and possible loyalties, much like that of Britannia. In the figure greeting William of Orange on the commemorative medal struck in 1689 (Figure 27.2), Britannia is church, queen, and nation as she takes the centre position (the other side depicted William alone). She is flanked by the figures of Liberty and Religion. Dedicated to the Restorer of Britain, the medal claims 'Te servatore non servimus', 'under your protection we are not slaves'. Between William and Britannia's heads is an open Bible with a text from Isaiah 40: 8 asserting in Latin that 'The word of God stands forever'. It is ironic, given the emphasis placed by Protestants of the time on the possession of the vernacular King James Bible in Britain, that the biblical text should appear in Latin; but it is also a reminder, as Steve Pincus has cogently argued, that the Glorious Revolution was a European event.[23] Sermons by influential clergy such as Sancroft

[22] Harris, *Revolution*, 270.
[23] Steve Pincus, *1688: The First Modern Revolution* (New Haven: Yale University Press, 2011).

and Burnet were translated into Dutch and French, while Dutch and Huguenot artisans were involved in the production of many of the prints and carvings commemorating the Protestant succession.[24] The Church of England and Britannia were central to the depiction of William's advent as rescue, not invasion, and their asserted possession of the Bible was essential in validating the change of monarch by appeal to the highest power of all.

Despite the triumphant international claims of Britain's contemporary freedom, commentators of the time were also concerned to establish the historic independence from Rome of the British Bible, church and Britannia. The extent to which the histories of the three were imbricated is evident in the writings of Lloyd and his friend Edward Stillingfleet (Bishop of Worcester from 1689). In their church histories, which were partly inspired by the controversies that followed the Popish Plot of 1678, origin myths were re-examined and biblical authorities sought in preference to classical sources. The famous Trojan lineage, whereby Brutus, great-grandson of Aeneas, gave Britain its name, was rejected by Lloyd as 'a prank' executed by Romans upon gullible Saxons.[25] He preferred a more biblical origin myth for the British: 'Namely, that they were so called from one Brito, that was the son of Hysichion, the son of Alanus, of the Progeny of Japhet', who was himself the son of Noah.[26] Signs of the British being favoured by God were read into the early nurturing of Christianity in their isles, and the notion that the 'Gospel was Providentially planted among the English or Saxons by a British Ministry, and not by Romish' was central to Anglican publications of the period as the clergy fought to publicize and establish a narrative of church and nation which was allied to the Bible in its faith, not to Rome.[27]

Stillingfleet's main objective was to emphasize the antiquity and authority of native Christianity by establishing 'that there was a Christian Church planted in Britain during the Apostles times'.[28] He drew on an impressive range of classical and medieval historians to prove that St Paul came to Britain after he went to Spain.[29] His conclusion that 'from this undoubted Testimony of Clemens it follows, not onely, That the Gospel was preached in Britain in the times of the Romans, but, That St Paul himself was the Preacher of it' proved to be very influential and was believed long into the nineteenth century.[30] Claiming St Paul as the source of Christianity in Britain not only refuted the Catholic Church as the mother church, but also asserted a direct apostolic link between Britain, the era of Jesus, and the Bible. This connection was strengthened by the notion, curiously persistent today, that there was a pure native strain of Britons. Lloyd insisted that

> We live still in that Country of which our Ancestors were the first Inhabitants .... And we have this to say more, which few can say elsewhere: that we keep still the same Language, which was spoken first in this Country: and ... as one of our Ancestors told a great King that invaded us, God will have an account for this Country in no other Language but ours at the day of Judgment.[31]

[24] Antony Griffiths, *The Print in Stuart Britain 1603–1689* (London: British Museum Press, 1998), 297.

[25] William Lloyd, *An Historical Account of Church-Government as It Was in Great-Britain and Ireland, When They First Received the Christian Religion* (London, 1684), a1ᵛ.

[26] Lloyd, *Historical Account*, a1ʳ. For Japheth, see Gen. 5: 32, 9: 18, and 10: 1.

[27] William Lloyd, *Papists no Catholicks, and Popery no true Christianity* (1677; London, 1686), 7.

[28] Edward Stillingfleet, *Origines Britannicae, or, the Antiquities of the British Churches* (London, 1685), 35.

[29] Stillingfleet, *Origines Britannicae*, 37–9.

[30] Stillingfleet, *Origines Britannicae*, 39. On the continued influence of Stilllingfleet's ecclesiastical histories, see Barry Till, 'Stillingfleet, Edward (1635–1699)', *ODNB*, 2004; online edition, Jan. 2008, <http://www.oxforddnb.com/view/article/26526>.

[31] Lloyd, *Historical Account*, a6ᵛ–a7ʳ.

Despite the fact that the native language had changed considerably, and would continue to do so, the very language of the King James Bible was thus historically sanctified. Although it was a translation, according to those who believed Britain had received the Word directly from St Paul himself, the translation of the Bible was in a sense a translation back into the sounds of the original apostolic instruction that had converted the nation.

Such ownership of the Bible was central to the debates of the late 1680s. In his 1687 sermon *Scripture and Tradition Compared*, Stillingfleet's arguments in favour of the primacy of the Bible as Christian authority emphasized its divine authority. For 'That which the Apostles did in common deliver to the Churches planted by them, was the Genuine Doctrine of Christ', and that which they left in their writings can be relied upon, because 'no disagreement is ever so much as mention'd, as to what the Apostles themselves taught; They had one Body, one Spirit, one Lord, one Faith, one Baptism, one God and Father of all'.[32] By contrast, he claimed, church traditions were fallible and liable to corruption, and the Catholic Church placed too much importance on these human and inconsistent sources of doctrine. For the Church of England, Protestant emphasis on the Bible and on worship in the vernacular was not a sign of rebellion against the true church, but evidence of its faithfulness to the original teachings of Christ. Like many fellow Anglican anti-Catholic polemicists, Stillingfleet repeatedly argued that charges of schism should be laid not against the Church of England, but against the Church of Rome.

The advent of a Catholic king to the throne prompted fundamental questions about church authority: how far should the Church of England obey a king who had refused to include communion as part of the coronation ceremony performed by Sancroft, Archbishop of Canterbury? There was a long Anglican tradition of passive obedience and non-resistance, but this was a king who saw himself as possessing a divine mission to establish the Church of Rome in Britain alongside the Church of England. Texts exhorting obedience, such as 1 Peter 2: 13–14, 'Submit your selves to every Ordinance of Man for the Lord's sake, whether it be to the King, as supreme, or unto Governours' became ambivalent, as duty to church and king was fissured and Sherlock's 'Church of England Loyalty' seemed, as James II's reign unfolded, to involve acting against royal demands.[33] As with criticism of Charles I, debates focused on the threats represented by the excessive influence exerted over the monarch by misguided or malicious advisers, rather than criticizing the king himself. (Even William of Orange's self-justification for invasion repeatedly blamed James's 'Evil Councellors' rather than the king's own policies.[34]) By 1688, Burnet claimed that James II 'was in all points governed by the Jesuits, and the French Ambassador'.[35] Old prejudices and suspicions of the Jesuits centred on the Privy Councillor Father Edward Petre, James's close confidant, who it was rumoured the king wanted to see made both Archbishop of York and Cardinal.[36] Jesuit influence was particularly galling to those Protestants who prided themselves on belonging to a nation which,

---

[32] Edward Stillingfleet, *Scripture and Tradition Compared in a Sermon Preached at Guild Hall Chapel, November 27th, 1687* (London, 1688), 7–8. He is referring to Eph. 4.

[33] Sherlock, *Sermon Preached at St Margarets*, 31.

[34] [William], *The Prince of Orange His Declaration*, 5 and *passim*.

[35] Burnet, *History*, 733.   [36] Burnet, *History*, 733.

they claimed, had never, even before the Reformation, fallen under papal jurisdiction; Burnet was one of many clergy who quoted Catholic authorities 'allowing the Bishop of Rome to have Supremacy elsewhere; yet [admitting] the Pope hath no Supremacy in Britain'.[37]

As its title suggests, Burnet's *Protestant Companion* was aimed at a broad Protestant readership. Although the cleric Richard Coulton voiced the residual prejudices of many Anglicans when he warned against 'the Enthusiastical Dream' of the dissenters, and fumed that the 'Presbyterians ... (and the other unclean Beasts that herd together with them) lay as great a Claim to the Scepter of Jesus Christ, as the Pope does to the Keys of St Peter', nevertheless there was a distinct and fascinating strand of anti-popery writing that invited participation in a national Protestant community which shared histories and loyalties.[38] It is to this readership that Lloyd appeals when he argues that:

> no English or British Christian Subject (of what Perswasion soever) can with any Conscience, or thankfulness to God, renounce his Mother Christian Church of Britain to own a foreign, later, and besides Apostate Church of Rome: or desert his Colours from under Christ, to list and throw himself under the slavery of that Popish Antichrist, to act against his own Church and Countrey, without being apparently convict before God, the World and his Conscience, of being a *Renegado* to his Church and false unnatural to his Country[.][39]

A century later, when they were still being regularly demonized as regicidal, anarchic pursuers of an 'Enthusiastical Dream', dissenters were to envy this moment of national Protestant community.

There was an increasing practical necessity to placate dissenters under James II, as they were joint beneficiaries with the Catholics of the royal Declarations of Indulgence of spring 1687 and then 1688 that lifted some of the penalties imposed by the Corporation Act of 1661 and the Test Acts of 1673 and 1678 against all those who worshipped outside the Church of England. Native familiarity with the Bible was central to appeals to the shared national Protestantism that issued from pulpits and presses, prompted for some by expediency and others by genuine latitudinarian churchmanship. Burnet reiterated 'how contrary the Popish Religion is to our Church, and how inconsistent with Scripture', asserting that 'Her greatest defendants reject the Scripture' in favour of tradition, and that 'not only the Popish Laity, but even the Priests themselves are very ignorant in the Holy Scriptures'.[40] Lloyd went further, arguing in *Papists no Catholicks, and Popery no True Christianity* (1679) that 'the Pope and his Creatures forbid Christians to read the Holy Scriptures: therefore they directly and formally oppose JESUS CHRIST and his Apostles'.[41] The implied contrast between Catholic believers and British Protestants was both flattering—the latter were able to read the word of God for themselves—but also portentous, warning dissenters not to become too closely allied to a Catholic king who might initially offer toleration but might later deprive them of their Bibles.

---

[37] Burnet, *Protestant's Companion*, C2ᵛ.

[38] Richard Coulton, *The Loyalty of the Church of England* (York, 1685), 10.

[39] Lloyd, *Papists no Catholicks*, 9.

[40] Burnet, *Protestant's Companion*, B1ᵛ, B3ʳ, 2 n. 12.

[41] Lloyd, *Papists no Catholicks*, 3.

II. Daughters of Zion: Isaiah 40: 8, 'The word of our God shall stand for ever'

Anti-Catholic polemic under James II meant that Isaiah 40: 8, 'The word of our God shall stand for ever', possessed particular resonance in a country whose Bible was putatively under threat from Catholic censorship. For dissenters who had suffered for their interpretations of the Word, it was a text for which they continued to do battle. British Protestants had the King James Bible in common, but those who did not subscribe to the Thirty-Nine Articles of the Church of England had already suffered for their readings of it. They, more than those in the established church, could and did read and write themselves into the sufferings of the persecuted Israelites long before James II's accession.[42] The biblical texts that featured so regularly in Anglican defences of the church had a different history within Protestant dissent. William Tyndale had been immortalized by John Foxe as 'the apostle of England' whose 'godly zeal' led him to defy the Pope and bring the Gospels in English to the common people; his famous cry—'Lord, open the king of England's eyes'—before being executed and burnt at the stake resonated with particular force amongst dissenters before and after the Glorious Revolution.[43]

The Baptist Elizabeth Gaunt was among those who supported the Duke of Monmouth's rebellion in the summer of 1685, and as a commoner woman found guilty of treason she was sentenced to be burnt at the stake. She used the Bible as her authority for having acted as she did in providing hospitality to those in need of shelter; she referred to it precisely and authoritatively in her final speech to ask her auditors, 'now who to Obey, Judge ye', man or God:

> And I bless his holy Name, that in all this, together with what I was Charged with, I can approve my Heart to him, that I have done his Will, though it does cross Man's Will: and the Scriptures that satisfie me are Isa. 16. 4. Hide the Outcasts, bewray not him that wandereth: And Obad. 13, 14. Thou shouldst not have given up those of his that did escape in the day of his distress: But Man says, you shall give them up, or you shall dye for it; now who to Obey, Judge ye: So that I have cause to rejoyce and be exceeding glad, in that I suffer for righteousness sake, and that I am accounted worthy to suffer for well doing[.][44]

Gaunt's confidence that she understood God's will better than James II came from her familiarity with the Bible and her ability to quote 'the Scriptures that satisfie me'. Melinda S. Zook has shown that Gaunt was a respected figure amongst Whig dissenting circles in Britain and Holland, and argues persuasively that this remarkable woman was pursued by the government because they believed she was in possession of secret intelligence about key figures

---

[42] See Scott Mandelbrote and Michael Ledger-Lomas (eds), *Dissent and the Bible in Britain, c.1650–1950* (Oxford: Oxford University Press, 2013); and Michael Watts, *The Dissenters: From the Reformation to the French Revolution* (Oxford: Oxford University Press, 1985).

[43] John Foxe, *Foxe's Book of Martyrs: Select Narratives*, ed. John N. King (Oxford: Oxford University Press, 2009), 13, 15, 20.

[44] 'Mrs Gaunt's Speech, Written the Day before her Sufferings', in *The Dying Speeches, Letters and Prayers, & c. of those Eminent Protestants who Suffered … under the Cruel Sentence of the Late Lord Chancellour* (London, 1689), 11.

in exile or rebellion.[45] She refused to pass on any information, however, and gained lasting fame as one of the victims of the Bloody Assizes, her final speech published in various collections of the death speeches of those sentenced by Judge George Jeffreys, and her story told in various Whig martyrologies. Her calm resolve at the stake was remarked upon by witnesses such as William Penn, whose account was a key source for Burnet's recounting of Gaunt's fate in his history. She died forgiving her persecutors, but warned them—and James II—that:

> as it is done in an implacable mind against the Lord Christ, and his righteous Cause and Followers, I leave it to him who is the avenger of all such wrongs, who will tread upon Princes as upon mortar, and be terrible to the Kings of the Earth: ... and therefore O that you would be wise, instructed and learn, is the desire of her that finds no Mercy from you[.][46]

She held the Bible up as she delivered her final speech to vindicate her opposition to earthly law.

Gaunt's use of the Bible to oppose her king was read variously as the courageous championing of Protestantism against an oppressive Catholic monarch, or as the rebellious behaviour only to be expected from such a 'Conventicle-bidding-Bell-Woman', a type attacked by Coulton and satirized by Aphra Behn.[47] Her identification with 'poor desolate Sion', the personification of Jerusalem, was similarly ambivalent: she could be specifically speaking as a dissenter identifying with Zion against the worldly powers of the established church, or as a Protestant refuting Catholic might.[48] Dissenters saw Protestantism and biblical Christianity as defining the New Jerusalem, and read themselves into the narrative of national providential rescue by William III, though they were to gain fewer rights under William than they would have under the unsuccessful Monmouth.

Timothy Cruso, preaching to his Presbyterian congregation on 31 January 1689, the day of public thanksgiving for the rescue of the nation by William, urged his audience to take courage from providence and, emulating the Daughter of Sion, defy the seemingly insuperable powers of Babylon; for, he asked, 'What hath God wrought, and how hath he defeated every Divination against the English Israel?'[49] Taking as his text Numbers 23: 23, and drawing parallels throughout the sermon between the idol-worship of Balaam and the putative idolatry of the Jesuits, he paraphrased Exodus 19: 4 to argue that, like the Israelites, the English had been borne on divine eagles' wings and secured 'the most marvellous Salvation upon the cheapest terms, [of] any People in the World'.[50] Cruso was known for his effective preaching, and he concluded this section on a rousing note: 'Let us not be seduced to weaken the Protestant Interest, and uphold the contrary, by unnecessary and uncharitable separations from our Holy brethren'.[51] Yet Cruso's invitation to other Protestant denominations to join

[45] Melinda S. Zook, *Protestantism, Politics, and Women in Britain, 1660–1714* (Basingstoke: Palgrave Macmillan, 2013), 48–56.

[46] 'Mrs Gaunt's Speech', 12.

[47] Coulton, *Loyalty*, A2ʳ. On Behn and female Dissenters, see Zook, *Protestantism, Politics, and Women*, 119–22.

[48] 'Mrs Gaunt's Speech', 11. Zion was the holy hill of God's temple; it came to represent Jerusalem and God's chosen people.

[49] Timothy Cruso, *The Mighty Wonders of a Merciful Providence* (London, 1689), 19.

[50] Cruso, *Mighty Wonders*, 12, 14.

[51] Cruso, *Mighty Wonders*, 20.

together like the tribes of Israel met with limited success. The Archbishop of Canterbury might urge his bishops to encourage dissenting brethren 'to joyn with us in daily fervent Prayer to the God of Peace, for an Universal Blessed Union of all Reformed Churches ... against our common Enemies', but the rhetoric of solidarity against the Catholics was not sufficiently deep-rooted and widespread to banish the spectres and prejudices of the sectarian past.[52]

The dissenter John Hickes's final speech, collected with that of Gaunt, pointed to the nineteenth of the Thirty-Nine Articles of the Church of England and argued, using its definition of the church as 'a congregation of faithful men, in which the pure Word of God is preached', for a more biblical understanding of a church untrammelled by 'Ecclesiastical Government', where 'a pure and undefiled Religion doth flourish, and that which contains and really practices Holiness'.[53] This was to be famously but again fruitlessly repeated a century later by theologians such as Richard Price and Joseph Priestley, after a hundred years which saw the popular spread of the concept of the British Israel but not much growth in Protestant ecumenicism: the parliamentary Acts excluding dissenters from public office were not repealed until 1828 (and 1829 for Catholics).[54]

III. Revelations: Bishops, Trinity Sunday, and the Glorious Revolution

For the moment, however, such dissenting and latitudinarian disappointments lay ahead. In the summer of 1688, fears of James II's plans to establish the Catholic Church in Britain meant that hostility to Rome and shared interpretations of key biblical books fostered the growth of a fragile and contingent idealized Protestant—as opposed to specifically Anglican—nation. The king's imprisonment of the seven bishops who refused him meant that Protestants in Britain and abroad gained a set of unlikely heroes. Although, as Mark Goldie has argued, the rebellion of the bishops was in itself an Anglican revolution separate from the Glorious Revolution, the two are woven closely together when examined in terms of Protestantism, national identity, and arguments about whether the Church of Rome or the Church of England was the true guardian of Christianity.[55] Protests against the Catholic king took the form of celebrations of the seven bishops, and as can be seen from the examples in Figures 27.3 and 27.4, the book of Revelation was a key interpretative lens through which to see the bishops' heroism and the king's iniquity. In this final section, I will argue that the Bible was central to the clash over the bishops, and that this exegetical battle helped

---

[52] William Sancroft, *The Articles Recommended by the Arch-Bishop of Canterbury to All the Bishops within His Metropolitan Jurisdiction, the 16th of July, 1688* ([London?], 1688), 4.

[53] See Article XIX in the Book of Common Prayer. 'Of the Church. The visible Church of Christ is a congregation of faithful men, in which the pure Word of God is preached, and the Sacraments be duly ministered according to Christ's ordinance, in all those things that of necessity are requisite to the same. As the Church of Jerusalem, Alexandria, and Antioch, have erred, so also the Church of Rome hath erred, not only in their living and manner of Ceremonies, but also in matters of Faith'.

[54] 'John Hickes' last speech', *Dying Speeches, Letters and Prayers*, 15.

[55] Mark Goldie, 'The Political Thought of the Anglican Revolution', in Robert Beddard (ed.), *The Revolutions of 1688* (Oxford: Oxford University Press, 1991), 102–36.

FIGURE 27.3 The seven bishops in a pyramid, print by Simon Gribelin, 1688.

FIGURE 27.4 The seven bishops, 1688.

popularize readings of the book of Revelation which would be fundamental to the legitimation of the Glorious Revolution.

The bishops' refusal to support James II's Declaration of Indulgence in May 1688 meant that royal and religious powers were brought into explicit conflict. On 4 April 1687 the king had issued the English Declaration of Indulgence, using his royal prerogative to grant indulgence to those who wished to worship outside the Church of England. Penalties were lifted, and public office then became available to Catholics. Now, in the wake of the public thanksgivings he had ordered be held in all churches to celebrate his wife's pregnancy, he not only reissued the Declaration, but demanded, on 4 May 1688, that bishops should ensure they and their clergy read it from their pulpits on two successive Sundays. Sancroft and six bishops petitioned the king to be excused reading the petition. James II met with general resistance from the rest of the clergy. Only four of the London clergy read the Declaration out; in the rest of the country, clergy either did not read it out, or read it to empty churches, having suggested to their congregation that they did not have to listen.[56] In some cases, when the Declaration was read out, the congregation marched out in protest. Unable to persuade the bishops to follow his orders, James sent the seven bishops to the Tower on 8 June 1688.

Evelyn noted when he visited them in the Tower that 'The action of the Bishop[s] universally applauded, and reconciling many adverse parties, Papists onely excepted'.[57] Like other contemporary observers, he was impressed by the crowds they attracted as they made their way down the Thames to the Tower: 'Wonderfull was the concerne of the people for them, infinite crowds of people on their knees, beging their blessing and praying for them as they passed out of the Barge; along the Tower wharfe etc'.[58] The scene was depicted in paintings and prints, and circulated in France and Holland as part of anti-Catholic propaganda.

Yet these were in many ways awkward heroes for Whiggish and dissenting anti-Catholics. Opposition to James II's religious policies did not mean support of the Glorious Revolution, and five of the seven bishops refused to take the new Oath of Allegiance to William and Mary. With four other bishops, they lost their posts in the Church of England and became leaders of the 400 non-juror clergy, very few of whom had offered James unconditional loyalty but who felt allegiance to the new monarchs could not be reconciled with divine right theology and the doctrine of non-resistance.[59] There were, thus, different definitions of Church of England loyalty, and the non-juring version created a schism that was to endure to the end of the following century with the death of the last Stuart successor to James II. The publication of the bishops' response to James II, swiftly achieved by a propitious leaking of the document (probably by the bellicose Henry Compton), meant that they were swept into a broader print debate.[60] In May and June 1688 the bishops' differences from the majority of those who claimed them as Protestant champions were not important: they had become the

---

[56] Gibson, *James II*, 64–150; Harris, *Revolution*, 258–72.

[57] John Evelyn, *The Diary of John Evelyn*, ed. John Bowle (Oxford: Oxford University Press, 1985), 358, 25 May 1688.

[58] Evelyn, *Diary*, 358, 8 June 1688.

[59] On the non-jurors, see Robert D. Cornwall, *Visible and Apostolic: The Constitution of the Church in High Church Anglican and Non-Juror Thought* (Newark, Del.: University of Delaware Press, 1993); for a summary of the different ways in which subjects reconciled themselves to the changed succession, see Harris, *Revolution*, 356–63.

[60] On the publication of the response, see Gibson, *James II*, 90–2.

'seven men of honest report, full of the Holy Ghost and wisdom' (Acts 6: 3) who were to fight the Catholic king.

The dates of the bishops' trial and the birth of the royal prince were so close they appeared portentous: the bishops were sent to the Tower on 8 June, and the Stuart heir was born on 10 June. The Catholic baby's advent had already been regarded with some fear and suspicion by many of James II's subjects, but after the bishops' stand against the king it became, in Sir Walter Scott's words, 'a distinguishing mark of a true Protestant' to doubt the parentage of the infant and regard it as a Catholic imposition on the people.[61] More bonfires appeared in support of the bishops' acquittal and release than could be rustled up by royalists in celebration of the infant prince.[62] Heaven and the Devil appeared to be engaging in pitched battle in London, and interpreters on both sides turned to the book of Revelation, drawing on a long millenarian tradition.[63] Revelation was in its very origin hostile to the Roman Empire.[64] Its opposition of the forces of the Roman Empire to those of heaven made it a text readily translated by Protestants into the battle between the Church of Rome and Protestantism, which as we have seen, for many Anglican commentators, in fact meant the Church of England or—for those of latitudinarian tendencies—a British Church. Revelation's powerful story, with its rich symbolism of dragon, whore, and mysterious seven-sealed scroll, combined with its eschatological plenitude to enable Protestants to interpret it as prophesying the condition of Britain in 1688.

The number seven, which appears repeatedly in Revelation, became a key element of the bishops' depiction.[65] Popular prints that appeared in Holland and France as well as Britain drew on the book of Revelation by accompanying the portrait medallions with the seven stars and seven candlesticks referred to in Revelation 1: 20: 'The mystery of the seven stars which thou sawest in my right hand, and the seven golden candlesticks. The seven stars are the angels of the seven churches: and the seven candlesticks which thou sawest are the seven churches'. According to this reading of Revelation, James II's persecution of the bishops was ushering in the apocalypse. In most prints, the allusions went unglossed, but in Gribelin's pyramidical celebration (Figure 27.4) it is not only glossed but given in English and French.[66] In Figure 27.3, the seven candlesticks and stars are joined by the eye of providence, as in Figure 27.1 watchful of the Church of England. The specific biblical textual references combine with an all-encompassing providence both to validate a Protestant reading of the prophecies and to affirm the apostolic powers of the Church of England. Providence was to become increasingly important in explaining the events of 1688; along

[61] Quoted by Anne Barbeau Gardiner in 'Dryden's "Britannia Rediviva": Interpreting the Signs of the Times in June 1688', *Huntington Library Quarterly,* 48 (1985): 261.

[62] Harris, *Revolution*, 270; Gibson, *James II*, 135–6.

[63] See Frances E. Dolan, *Whores of Babylon: Catholicism, Gender and Seventeenth-Century Print Culture* (Notre Dame, Ind.: University of Notre Dame Press, 1999); and Esther Gilman Richey, *The Politics of Revelation in the English Renaissance* (Columbia, Mo.: University of Missouri Press, 1998).

[64] Richard Baukman, *The Theology of the Book of Revelation* (Cambridge: Cambridge University Press, 1993), 35–44, and Elisabeth Schüssler Fiorenza, 'The Words of Prophecy: Reading the Apocalypse Theologically', in Stephen Moyise (ed.), *Studies in the Book of Revelation* (London: T. & T. Clark, 2001), 9–19.

[65] For British readers, the seven bishops may also have recalled Richard Johnson's *The Most Famous History of the Seaven Champions of Christendome* (1596), a popular text on national saints which went through many editions through the seventeenth and eighteenth centuries.

[66] Other versions of the same print omitted the text: see the British Museum Catalogue for examples.

with James II's flight from the throne, it enabled Williamite participants in the Glorious Revolution to claim theirs was a divinely sanctioned rebellion rather than a treasonous uprising.

'The time is at hand', the book of Revelation repeatedly claims (1: 3, 22: 10). For some, this meant it was the time of the bishops and then William of Orange, the time to affirm Britain as a Protestant nation. For others, however, the times belonged to James II: John Dryden's 'Britannia Rediviva' and Aphra Behn's 'Congratulatory Poem' on the birth of the Prince of Wales offered royalist exegeses that suggested the infant might be a sign of the parousia, and would unite a fragmented Britain. Both interpreted the royal birth having taken place on Trinity Sunday as a sign of great divine favour. 'No MONARCH's Birth was ever Usher'd in / With Signs so Fortunate as this has been. / The Holy Trinity his BIRTH-DAY claims', argued Behn, who, 'Inspir'd by Nothing but *Prophetick Truth*', saw the infant's birth foretold in Matthew 3: 12 along with that of the Messiah.[67] Dryden suggested that the divided nations of England (and Wales as its principality), Scotland, and Ireland, might be united by the prince:

> So great a Blessing to so good a King
> None but th' Eternal Comforter cou'd bring.
>   Or did the Mighty Trinity Conspire,
> As once, in Council to Create our Sire?
> It seems as if they sent the New-Born Guest
> To wait on the Procession of their Feast;
> And on their Sacred Anniverse decree'd
> To stamp their Image on the promis'd Seed.
> Three Realms united, and on One bestow'd,
> An Emblem of their Mystick Union show'd[.][68]

James II's promotion of religious toleration, Dryden implies, will bear fruit in a Britain united under the Stuart prince, so that the Trinity Sunday birth had brought James's subjects a 'Blessing' of such divine greatness that 'Your self our Ballance hold, the Worlds, our Isle'.[69]

The significance of dates could change, however. As we saw earlier, James II had battled with varying success against the Protestant celebration of the 5 November and 17 November (the date of Elizabeth I's accession). By 1688, on 14 October, the king's birthday was marked by active rebellion in Norwich where a thousand-strong mob attacked a Roman Catholic chapel.[70] Evelyn noted the date in his diary in sober and prophetic mood:

> The Kings Birth-day, no Gunns from the Tower, as usualy: The sunn Eclips'd at its rising: This day signal the Victory of William the Conqueror against Herold neere Battel in Sussex: The wind (which had hitherto ben West) all this day East, wonderfull expectation of the Dutch fleete.[71]

---

[67] Aphra Behn, *A Congratulatory Poem to His Most Sacred Majesty on the Happy Birth of the Prince of Wales* (London, 1688), 2 and 5.

[68] John Dryden, *Britannia Rediviva: A Poem on the Birth of the Prince* (London, 1688), 3.

[69] Dryden, *Britannia Rediviva*, 20.

[70] Harris, *Revolution*, 293.   [71] Evelyn, *Diary*, 360–1.

Looking back beyond the birth of the current monarch, Evelyn saw another, William III's namesake and precursor, like the Dutch prince a foreign invader who would be transformed by the telling into a native champion of liberty. When Charles Petre, brother of James II's Jesuit adviser, preached against the King James Bible on 30 September 1688, a crowd gathered where he was preaching in Lime Street, London, pulled him from the pulpit, and only mayoral intervention prevented the chapel being completely destroyed.[72] The Bible, and by extension, the church and Protestant nation, needed to be liberated. Burnet's later account of William's invasion neutralized the aggression by describing him as an instrument of divine providence, recounting that William 'did not know how God might dispose of him: To his providence he committed himself'.[73] The 'Protestant wind' blowing from the east, the delayed landing taking place on 5 November, and various other events were all such powerful signs of God's favour that Burnet, presenting himself as a reluctant reader of portents, concluded that he 'would never forget that providence of God, which had appeared so signally on this occasion', and recounted that 'as we were now happily landed, and marching, we saw new and unthought of characters of a favourable providence of God watching over us'.[74]

By foregrounding Britannia and the Bible, as in Figures 27.1, 27.2, and 27.5, the providential narrative, whereby God defended his Word in the form of the King James Bible and his new Israel, Britain, was affirmed. The battle between James II and William III for male royal supremacy, and difficult questions of loyalty to Anglican tenets of passive obedience and non-resistance, were sidelined in favour of a rescue narrative. As I have argued elsewhere, in *Britannia Oppressa* (Figure 27.5) William appears in full biblical glory to rescue Britannia and the Bible from her Jesuit oppressors, and this print is representative of the celebrations of William and Mary's arrival.[75] Wherever he appears on prints, commemorative medals, and coins, Britannia and the Bible are there to confirm this as a Glorious Revolution, not a successful invasion.

'Shall I call this our Birth-Day?' asked Lloyd in his Glorious Revolution anniversary sermon on 5 November 1689,

> or rather the day of our Resurrection? It is a Day that brought us new Life from the dead. It brought nothing but Life: There was no man dyed for it …. [It was] a Conquest without Blood … a Perfect decisive Deliverance; such as that of Israel was from the Egyptians, when Moses said, you shall see them no more for ever, Exod. 14.13.[76]

Lloyd's triumphant assertion of the significance of the Glorious Revolution caught a powerful national sentiment, one that was to be fostered by subsequent generations keen to prove the worthiness of the British as the new Israelites. This concept became a key part of national mythology, popularized through its inclusion in Handel's magnificent *Messiah* (1742), in which Britain was celebrated as the New Jerusalem (ignoring the assertions within Isaiah 40 that nations did not matter to God). Charles Jennens described his text for the *Messiah* as a 'Scripture Collection'; it is unusual in that it is a collection of biblical verses

---

[72] Harris, *Revolution*, 291.   [73] Burnet, *History*, 782.
[74] Burnet, *History*, 784–9.   [75] Major, *Madam Britannia*, 1–10.
[76] Lloyd, *A sermon preach'd before their Majesties*, 32.

FIGURE 27.5 *Britannia oppressa per Arausionensium Principem liberata et restaurata*, 1688.

from the KJB and the Myles Coverdale translation of the Psalms in the Book of Common Prayer, but Jennens was being modest, for the libretto creates a new text.[77] His selection of biblical texts shows the continued importance to concepts of nation and worship, in 1735, of the battles of the late 1680s. The same texts reappear: Isaiah and the Book of Revelation dominate, with lines from the Psalms and Luke. It is perhaps appropriate that the *Messiah*, embraced so enthusiastically by eighteenth-century Anglicans, should have had its libretto drawn from the King James Bible by one of the few remaining non-juring Jacobites, and the music composed by a German Protestant who became a naturalized Briton. The heterogeneity and complexity of the relationship between the Bible and the Glorious Revolution, and its continuing importance, are woven into the 'new song' (Revelation 5: 9) which concludes so triumphantly with lines from Revelation 5: 13: 'Blessings and Honour, Glory, and Power, be unto him that sitteth upon the Throne, and unto the Lamb, for ever and ever. Amen.'[78]

FURTHER READING

Baukman, Richard. *The Theology of the Book of Revelation* (Cambridge: Cambridge University Press, 1993).

Claydon, Tony. *William III and the Godly Revolution* (Cambridge: Cambridge University Press, 1996).

Collinson, Patrick. *From Cranmer to Sancroft* (London: Hambledon Continuum, 2006).

Cornwall, Robert D. *Visible and Apostolic: The Constitution of the Church in High Church Anglican and Non-Juror Thought* (Newark, Del.: University of Delaware Press, 1993).

Dolan, Frances E. *Whores of Babylon: Catholicism, Gender and Seventeenth-Century Print Culture* (Notre Dame, Ind.: University of Notre Dame Press, 1999).

Gibson, William. *James II and the Trial of the Seven Bishops* (Basingstoke: Palgrave Macmillan, 2009).

Harris, Tim. *Revolution: The Great Crisis of the British Monarchy, 1685–1720* (Harmondsworth: Penguin, 2007).

Harris, Tim, and Stephen Taylor, eds. *The Final Crisis of the Stuart Monarchy: The Revolutions of 1688–91 in their British, Atlantic and European Contexts* (Woodbridge: Boydell, 2013).

Major, Emma. *Madam Britannia: Women, Church, and Nation, 1712–1812* (Oxford: Oxford University Press, 2012).

Mandelbrote, Scott, and Michael Ledger-Lomas, eds. *Dissent and the Bible in Britain, c.1650–1950* (Oxford: Oxford University Press, 2013).

Monod, Paul Kléber. *Jacobitism and the English People, 1688–1788* (Cambridge: Cambridge University Press, 1993).

Pincus, Steve. *1688: The First Modern Revolution* (New Haven: Yale University Press, 2011).

Richey, Esther Gilman. *The Politics of Revelation in the English Renaissance* (Columbia, Mo.: University of Missouri Press, 1998).

---

[77] Charles Jennens, quoted in Donald Burrows, *Handel: Messiah* (Cambridge: Cambridge University Press, 1991), 11. On Jacobites after 1688, see Paul Kléber Monod, *Jacobitism and the English People, 1688–1788* (Cambridge: Cambridge University Press, 1993); on Jacobitism and non-jurors, see 138–46. On the *Messiah*, see Ruth Smith, *Handel's Oratorios and Eighteenth-Century Thought* (Cambridge: Cambridge University Press, 1995), 32–9, 147–52.

[78] Charles Jennens, libretto, *Messiah: An Oratorio* (Dublin: James Hoey, 1745), 8.

Rose, Jacqueline. *Godly Kingship in Restoration England: The Politics of the Royal Supremacy, 1660–1688* (Cambridge: Cambridge University Press, 2011).

Sowerby, Scott. *Making Toleration: The Repealers and the Glorious Revolution* (Cambridge, Mass.: Harvard University Press, 2013).

Watts, Michael. *The Dissenters: From the Reformation to the French Revolution* (Oxford: Oxford University Press, 1985).

Zook, Melinda S. *Protestantism, Politics, and Women in Britain, 1660–1714* (Basingstoke: Palgrave Macmillan, 2013).

PART V

THE BIBLE AND LITERATURE

Introduction to Part V

THROUGHOUT the early modern period, the Bible proved a fruitful source for authors. The influential tradition of biblical paraphrase allowed writers to extemporize upon scripture, merging scriptural narratives with their own. In discussing the 'religious turn' of scholarship, Ken Jackson and Arthur Marotti demonstrate that it is imperative to understand individual spirituality and the ethics that underpin religion as a lived experience in the early modern period. 'Religion', Jackson and Marrotti write, 'is not just another field for anthropological investigation or political decoding. There are ethical and philosophical issues at stake'.[1] While critics have long taken seriously the complex religious poetics of texts such as Edmund Spenser's *The Faerie Queene* (1590–6) and John Donne's *Holy Sonnets*, the chapters collected here demonstrate how thoroughgoing the early modern weaving of the scriptural into the literary was, taking in drama, poetry, and prose; considering the Bible as a direct and a pervasive cultural influence; and examining the multiple ways in which writers engaged with, took on, and appropriated scriptural and religious content to a variety of ends.

Over the last twenty years, important scholarship has unearthed the enormous contribution that women made to biblical paraphrase, which could be blunt and uncompromising in its political stance.[2] In 1589, Anne Dowriche printed *The French History*, a lengthy and impassioned account of the St Bartholomew's Day Massacre of 1572 where, in Paris, after a series of assassinations of prominent Protestant Huguenots, other Huguenots were slaughtered by a Catholic mob. Appearing in print a year after the defeat of the Spanish

---

[1] Ken Jackson and Arthur Marotti, 'The Turn to Religion in Early Modern English Studies', *Criticism*, 46 (2004): 181.

[2] See e.g. Kate Narveson, *Bible Readers and Lay Writers: Gender and Self-Definition in an Emergent Writing Culture* (Farnham: Ashgate, 2012); Michele Osherow, *Biblical Women's Voices in Early Modern England* (Farnham: Ashgate, 2009).

Armada's attempted invasion of England, Dowriche's text interweaves biblical narrative and contemporary politics to produce a powerful attack on the Catholic Church and militant Catholicism.

Women's engagement in devotional writing has been the subject of intense focus, challenging orthodoxies that once presented such writing as a 'safe' and marginal activity.[3] Perhaps most notably, Mary Sidney, Aemelia Lanyer, and Anne Southwell all contributed to a culture of women's writing that, as Sarah Ross shows in this volume, is the genesis of women's writerly engagement with scripture—an engagement that continued throughout the seventeenth century. The description that first appeared in print in 1591 of Katherine Stubbes as a virtuous—if not compulsive—reader of the Bible shows that women also engaged in biblical culture as readers:

> [Stubbes's] whole delight was to be conversant in the Scriptures, and to meditate upon them day and night inasmuch as you could seldome or never have come into her house, and have found her without a Bible or some other good book in her hands. And when she was not reading, she would spend the time conferring, talking and reasoning with her husband of the word of God and of Religion: asking him what is the sense of this place and what is the sense of that.[4]

As noted in the general introduction, Henry VIII may have banned women from reading the Bible, but by the late sixteenth century, Bible reading had become central to female domestic and public life. While the account of Stubbes's life and death asserts that she deferred to her husband when seeking explication of parts of the Bible, it emphasizes that women could and did read and interpret scripture and this reading of the Bible led some women to write their own biblically informed literature. Regardless of the levels of reading literacy in the early modern period, biblical literacy was high.

This post-Reformation familiarity with the Bible allowed writers to weave the biblical together with their non-biblical narratives. Helen Wilcox examines the cultural and literary impulses current in the year that the King James Bible was published. By locating the King James Bible in its cultural moment, Wilcox makes us aware of the ways in which its vocabulary is part of a wider cultural nexus that accommodates other literary forms. Following on from this appreciation of its literary context, Hannibal Hamlin addresses the literary style of the King James Bible, relating it to various cognate prose styles in the seventeenth century. Early modern translators of the Protestant Bible translated word for word; rather than trying to translate the thoughts or idioms of the text, they focused upon the language and created a distinct style. The reception history of the King James Bible shows that its language seemed strange to seventeenth-century readers, but despite this strangeness, the King James Bible influenced literature over the next three centuries.

The remaining chapters in this section examine the various ways in which writers appropriated and reworked scripture. Sarah Ross examines women's writerly engagements with the genre of biblical verse paraphrase. Starting with Lucy Hutchinson's *Order and Disorder* and the uneasy relationship this biblical epic has with the epic genre, Ross

---

[3] Erica Longfellow, *Women and Religious Writing in Early Modern England* (Cambridge: Cambridge University Press, 2004).

[4] *A Christal Glasse for Christian Women* (1591), A2[v].

resituates the text within a framework of seventeenth-century women's literary engagements that use biblical verse paraphrase to reflect on British society and politics.

The cultural importance of the Bible was not, of course, new to the post-Reformation period. Medieval Mystery Plays drew heavily on biblical narrative, but it is commonly accepted that these public, communal, and guild performances more or less died out in the sixteenth century. The Reformation did not, however, bring about the complete demise of exegetical and heuristic uses of drama and the Bible. Among the rich stock of classical texts rediscovered with the fall of Constantinople in 1453 was Aristotle's *Poetics*. Russ Leo argues that the *Poetics* became a means by which scripture could be read. With this came the emergence of biblical comedy and tragedy, which, performed and published in Latin, crossed confessional divides and national boundaries. Leo attends to a range of largely forgotten biblical tragedies, the theological questions they pose, and attempts to comprehend the scripture in dramatic terms.

The sheer volume of literary responses to the Bible would seem to be at odds with Protestantism's adherence to *sola scriptura*, taken strictly, especially biblical paraphrasing and quotations that cut through the biblical text. Devotional writers incorporated scriptural phrasing into their poetry and in doing so frequently quoted the Bible out of context. Alison Knight argues that early modern devotional writers understood *sola scriptura* within a framework of *coherence* and *contexture*. Focusing upon the poetry of George Herbert, Knight shows how text is woven together; scriptural verse becomes connected to the phrasing that encloses it, thereby mediating and conflating the meanings of the different texts. This blending creates an interplay between the scriptural and profane phraseology of devotional writers.

Nancy Rosenfeld explores how John Bunyan used the Bible to construct narratives of his personal suffering and redemption, refiguring the biblical narrative in a manner that paved the way for the kinds of literary representation that later would typify the construction of characters in the novel. Consequently, Bunyan implicitly pushes towards a mode of engagement with the Bible that moves beyond *sola scriptura* and towards a literary response to biblical exegesis. Such a practice was perhaps most fully and brilliantly developed by Milton. Finally, Barbara Lewalski turns to the most famous of all seventeenth-century biblical epics, Milton's *Paradise Lost* and the freedoms that it takes with scripture. Milton may have drawn heavily from scripture in composing his biblical epic, but it is also clear that he takes ample and at times disconcerting liberties in his amplification of the Bible.

Collectively, these essays emphasize the rich and varied literary responses to the Bible and how a culture so concerned with authenticity of biblical reference, and with the sanctity of the unmediated text, regularly augmented, expanded on, and mediated scripture in many different literary forms. The scriptures were important to men's and women's literary and domestic writing throughout this period: whether in literature or as literature, the Bible and biblical poetics was central to early modern literary culture.

CHAPTER 28

....

THE KING JAMES BIBLE IN
ITS CULTURAL MOMENT

....

HELEN WILCOX

> After that, [Dr Reynoldes] moved his Majestie, that there might be a newe *trans-*
> *lation* of the *Bible*, because, those which were allowed in the raignes of *Henrie*
> the eight, and *Edward* the sixt, were corrupt and not aunswerable to the truth of
> the Originall.[1]

The intervention of Dr John Rainolds at the Hampton Court Conference in 1604,
pressing James VI and I to commission a 'newe *translation*' of the Bible 'aunswerable to
the truth of the Originall', led to the publication seven years later of what has become
known as the King James or Authorized Version of the Bible (KJB).The subsequent
fortunes of the KJB across the centuries and continents have been charted in detail
in book-length studies by Gordon Campbell, Alister McGrath, and David Daniell,
among many others.[2] The particular concern of this chapter is neither to investigate
the origins of the KJB nor to trace its later impact, but to place it specifically in its
early Jacobean literary environment. My purpose is to identify the ways in which the
KJB was very much a part and product of its cultural moment, setting it in conversation with a range of other texts and writings that emerged at the same time and from a
similar milieu.

In the following pages, I focus on five key aspects of the KJB. Each of these is introduced by reference to statements from the translators' prefatory material, after which
I discuss the highlighted feature alongside other texts published or performed in the
same year as the KJB. This landmark version of the Bible will thus be read in the company of works that shared with it the same gestation period, the same political and
religious contexts, and a common readership or audience. It may be safely claimed
that the Bibles of post-Reformation England not only shaped but were also *shaped*

---

[1] William Barlow, *The Summe and Substance of the Conference ... at Hampton Court* (London, 1604), 45.
[2] Gordon Campbell, *Bible: The Story of the King James Version, 1611–2011* (Oxford: Oxford University
Press, 2010); David Daniell, *The Bible in English: Its History and Influence* (New Haven: Yale University
Press, 2003); Alister McGrath, *In the Beginning: The Story of the King James Bible* (London: Hodder &
Stoughton, 2001).

by the literary and creative cultures of their day. The KJB was no exception to this rule and was embedded in, and responsive to, early Jacobean practices of writing and performance.

I. TRANSLATION

The six companies of scholars who worked on the production of the KJB between 1604 and 1611 were taking part in an activity that was fundamental not only to the principles of the Reformation but also to those of humanist education: making the textual materials of past ages and modern learning available to readers in their own language.[3] As is stated by Miles Smith with visionary confidence in his prefatory epistle to the KJB, given the communal title of 'The Translators to the Reader',

> Translation it is that openeth the window, to let in the light; that breaketh the shell, that we might eat the kernel; that putteth aside the curtain, that we may look into the most holy place.[4]

Translation is celebrated here as a means of illumination and revelation, enlightening the mind and pulling back the curtains that otherwise smother understanding. It is not seen as a subsidiary task but one with the primary goal of making accessible the 'kernel' or heart of the matter. In order to achieve this in the case of the KJB, the team of over fifty translators required more than their already formidable biblical and linguistic scholarship: they asserted their freedom to use the target language, English, creatively, refusing to be 'tied' to any 'uniformity of phrasing' (p. lxviii). Instead of consistently matching each word of the original with just one equivalent in English and using that word throughout, the translators awarded themselves the liberty to choose the most appropriate and beneficial word in each individual instance. In 'The Translators to the Reader', Smith defends this apparently bold method—potentially tampering with the Word of God—in a series of rhetorical questions:

> For is the kingdom of God become words or syllables? Why should we be in bondage to them, if we may be free? use one precisely, when we may use another no less fit as commodiously? (p. lxviii)

Ironically, of course, the process of translation does indeed temporarily reduce the larger matters of the Bible to 'words' and 'syllables' as the translators pore over the detail of their work. However, Smith's point is that those preparing the new biblical version should not be bound or limited in ways that would reduce the power of the divine word; their text can

---

[3] There were two 'companies' of translators based in Oxford, two in Cambridge and two in Westminster, each responsible for a designated section of the translation, though regularly brought together to maintain consistency. For a clear account of their work, see Campbell, *Bible*, 32–64, and for an appendix supplying their names and other details, 276–93.

[4] 'The Translators to the Reader', *The Bible: Authorized King James Version*, ed. Robert Carroll and Stephen Prickett (Oxford: Oxford University Press, 1997), p. lxvii. All further biblical references are to this edition. See the chapters by Katrin Ettenhuber and Jamie Ferguson in this volume.

express spiritual matters and achieve its impact through their exercise of discriminating linguistic taste. Mere precision of language is set against the greater value of 'fit' words and the choice of 'commodious' English vocabulary—that is, those words most likely to profit the reader's soul.

Not all works of translation in early seventeenth-century England—and there were many—were concerned with the spiritual welfare of their readers.[5] However, what the Jacobean translators did have in common was a lively, though often debated, sense of the virtues of the vernacular language into which they were converting a foreign-language original. Perhaps surprisingly, the scholars working on the KJB claimed the freedom to exploit the full variety of possibilities in the English language for the expression of God's word. This belief in the potential of the language was echoed and extended in the prefatory poem to the second great English translation brought to completion in 1611, Chapman's verse rendering of Homer's *Iliad*:

> And, for our tongue, that still is so empayr'd
> By travailing linguists; I can prove it cleare,
> That no tongue hath the Muses utterance heyr'd
> For verse, and that sweete Musique to the eare
> Strooke out of rime, so naturally as this;[6]

While the translators of the KJB defended their linguistic freedom against the likely accusation that they were corrupting the scriptures with their own favoured vocabulary, Chapman felt the need to defend the language *itself* against the abuses of uninspired or 'travailing linguists' (a word that might refer to translators as well as to students of language).

Refuting the inelegancies of linguistic innovation, Chapman praises the language's 'natural' ability to form itself into verse with the beauty of 'sweete Musique'. In lines which themselves flow with the natural rhythms of speech across the constraints of metre and rhyme, Chapman proves his point with ease. His claim is typified in the expressive double sense of the verb he associates with rhyming verse, 'Strooke', which suggests both 'struck' (the firmness of a poet's craft) and 'stroke' (the sensuous effect of poetic sound). Chapman goes on to celebrate the harmonious relationship between individual words in English: he suggests that his rhyme-sounds 'meete' as if 'they did kisse', whereas French and Italian multi-syllabic words crash into one another 'in harsh Collision', jarring unmusically as though 'they brake their necks' (A1ᵛ). The superiority of English is expressed in and through its 'tongue', but the allegory is also political. Chapman represents the language and, by extension, the people of England as a locus of harmonious relationships—precisely the peace-making model promoted by James in this period and similarly upheld by the project of the KJB itself as proposed at the Hampton Court Conference.

Chapman's unashamed linguistic chauvinism drives and justifies his huge long-term project to produce an English verse translation of Homer. The humanist principle of

---

[5] See Sara K. Barker and Brenda M. Hosington (eds), *Renaissance Cultural Crossroads: Translation, Print and Culture in Britain, 1473–1640* (Leiden: Brill, 2013).

[6] George Chapman, 'To the Reader', *The Iliads of Homer Prince of Poets* (London, 1611), A1ᵛ. All further Chapman references are to this text. Chapman published his translation of the *Iliad* in instalments from 1598 onwards, and *The Whole Works of Homer*, including the *Iliad* and the *Odyssey*, in 1616.

making texts accessible in the vernacular is emblematized in English versions of two works of incalculable classical and spiritual importance, translated during the same period and published almost simultaneously. Both texts were of such communal significance that they had the capacity to be adopted and absorbed by readers as their own. Chapman anticipated this relationship when writing his prefatory poem:

> Thus having rid the rubs, and strow'd these flowers
> In our thrice sacred *Homers* English way;
> What rests to make him, yet more worthy yours? (A1ᵛ)

Making the Bible and the *Iliad* 'yours'—capable of being possessed, understood, taken to heart, and applied by their readers—was the common aim of the KJB translators and Chapman, despite the differences between their original texts, their methods, and the ensuing translations. As Smith asked bluntly in 'The Translators to the Reader', 'how shall men meditate in that which they cannot understand? How shall they understand that which is kept close in an unknown tongue?' (pp. lvi–lvii). Both Chapman and the KJB translators responded to and participated in contemporary controversies about the purpose, the aims, and indeed the desirability of translation. Presenting their works as revelatory of the original, the translators tread a fine line between innovation and tradition, engaging with the techniques of translation in order to clear away the distance between past writing and modern readers.

II. TRADITION OR INNOVATION

At the turning point of Shakespeare's *The Winter's Tale*, first performed in 1611, the aged shepherd comments to his son: 'Thou met'st with things dying, I with things new-born'.[7] Shakespeare complicates the simple opposition of death and life by associating the optimistic, forward-looking attitude with the older generation while assigning to the younger man the 'things dying'. This paradox is completely in keeping with the Janus-like sense of looking in both directions that characterizes the beginning of the seventeenth century and clearly marks the KJB project. The era in which this Bible was translated and published was one of transition between ancient and new languages, between long-established and newly reformed religious practices, between the extended period of Elizabeth's reign and the unfamiliar rule of James, and between the old century and the new.

Despite the title given to their prefatory epistle, 'The Translators to the Reader', and the boast on the title-page that the Bible was 'Newly Translated out of the Originall tongues', the scholars who oversaw the translation preferred to be known as 'revisers'.[8] They publicly represented their work as the next step in a long sequence of translations: the title-page

---

[7] William Shakespeare, *The Winter's Tale* in *The Arden Shakespeare Complete Works*, gen. ed. Richard Proudfoot (Walton-on-Thames: Nelson, 1998), 3.3.111–12. All further Shakespeare references are to this edition.

[8] See Helen Moore and Julian Reid (eds), *Manifold Greatness: The Making of the King James Bible* (Oxford: Bodleian Library, 2011), 87–114.

description adds that the 'former Translations' have been 'diligently compared and revised'. As Smith goes on to explain in the preface,

> Truly, good Christian Reader, we never thought from the beginning that we should need to make a *new* translation, nor yet to make of a bad one a good one; ... but to make a good one *better*, or out of many good ones one principal good one, not justly to be excepted against; that hath been our endeavour, that our mark. (p. lxv; emphasis added)

This was a shrewd move by the 'revisers', smoothing the way for acceptance of the new, potentially unifying but inevitably controversial English Bible by indicating that it was not a conversion from 'bad' to 'good' but an improvement from 'good' to 'better'. Their language here also upholds an eminently scriptural principle by unifying the 'many' into the 'one' as previous translations are brought together into a 'principal good one'. This Bible was new and at the same time not new, presented as the sacred word for the future and yet full of deliberate archaisms and links with previous versions. The KJB's compromise between the given past and the ordained future may be seen in the detail of the revisers' choices: the voices of Tyndale and Coverdale, the tones of the Roman Catholic Douai Bible, and phrases of the Protestant Geneva Bible are all to be heard within the verbal echo-chamber of the KJB, yet it has its own distinctive cadence and blend of vocabulary, particularly in areas of Jacobean theological controversy such as priesthood and the church.[9] Ironically yet typically, the engraved title-page of the New Testament in the KJB is actually borrowed from the last edition of the old Bishops' Bible (1602), asserting visually as well as verbally the new Bible's acknowledged line of inheritance.

In its mingling of tradition and innovation, the KJB is utterly in keeping with the self-consciously transitional atmosphere of the period of its creation and publication. John Donne's first printed poem, 'The Anatomy of the World' (later known as 'The First Anniversary'), which memorialized the young Elizabeth Drury in 1611, repeatedly makes the claim that the world is damaged or ruined, a state of affairs expressed most vividly in the death of the young woman mourned in this extravagant elegy: 'Shee, shee is dead; shee's dead: when thou knowst this, / Thou knowst how lame a cripple this world is'.[10] The centrepiece of the poem's ruthless dissection of the crippled condition of the world is the well-known passage in which the radical modes of thinking that marked the new century are shown to unsettle all familiar certainties:

> And new Philosophy cals all in doubt,
>   The Element of fire is quite put out;
>   The Sun is lost, and th'earth, and no mans wit
>   Can well direct him, where to looke for it.
>   And freely men confesse, that this world's spent,
>   When in the Planets, and the Firmament
>   They seeke so many new; (ll. 205–11)

---

[9] In Archbishop Richard Bancroft's 'Rules' for the translators (BL Harley MS 750), the application of certain crucial terms was made absolutely clear. For example, a gathering of the early Christians was to be referred to as a 'church' rather than the more radical term 'congregation', and 'priest' was preferred to 'minister' (1ᵛ).

[10] John Donne, 'An Anatomy of the World', ll. 237–8, *The Complete English Poems*, ed. C. A. Patrides (London: Dent, 1985), 336. All further Donne references are to this edition.

The challenge of these lines lies in their daring analysis of the consequences of new knowledge and the culture of 'doubt' necessary to scientific enquiry. Donne vividly conveys the restless mood of his era, searching for new worlds—the very adventurousness which animates his own 'wit'—even while lamenting the loss of a secure and familiar world:

> 'Tis all in pieces, all cohaerence gone;
> All just supply, and all Relation:
> Prince, Subject, Father, Sonne, are things forgot,
> For every man alone thinkes he hath got
> To be a Phoenix, and that there can bee
> None of that kinde, of which he is, but hee. (ll. 213–18)

Donne's metaphor of the phoenix reveals the paradox of his thinking: a phoenix is unique, suggesting the potentially destructive individualism of this new and incoherent society anatomized by Donne, but it is also the bird which can rise again from the ashes, suggesting hope in rebirth and newness.

Donne's intense awareness of old and new worlds side by side may be likened to the conscious overlapping of the past and the present, tradition and newness, integral to the KJB. Many other writers contemporary with the production and publication of the newly authorized Bible were also fascinated by the interrelatedness of preceding and current experience. The second of Shakespeare's plays to receive its initial performances in 1611, *The Tempest*, is a good example of this preoccupation, beginning as it does with Prospero's narrative of Miranda's past and predicating its dramatic development on the assumption that 'what's past is prologue' (2.1.254). The ambiguous nature of change, which recognizes the past but allows it to undergo a metamorphosis into something enriching in its newness, is summed up in Ariel's song to the grieving Ferdinand:

> Full fadom five thy father lies;
> Of his bones are coral made;
> Those are pearls that were his eyes:
> Nothing of him that doth fade,
> But doth suffer a sea-change
> Into something rich and strange.
> Sea-nymphs hourly ring his knell. (1.2.399–405)

In the transforming vision of Ariel's lyric, Ferdinand's father, Alonso, is depicted as lost at sea—his death-knell is being tolled and his whole being will 'fade'—but he is simultaneously metamorphosing into 'something rich and strange'. According to the song, Alonso's bones and eyes have become the precious substances coral and pearl: past mortality has yielded to the materiality of a beautiful future. The dramatic irony of the song is that Alonso has not drowned at all, though he is indeed undergoing a metaphorical 'sea-change' as a result of Prospero's art. The interplay of security and insecurity, familiar and unfamiliar worlds, old certainties and new opportunities, defines the play just as much as it does the project of the KJB. The play's conclusion specifically questions what newness is: the 'brave new world' of Miranda's experience is only 'new' to her and not to her world-weary father (5.1.183–4). The first audiences of *The Tempest*, like those who heard the KJB read in church for the first time, were challenged to reassess the meanings of newness as well as the newness of meanings.

III. Interpretation

All translation, whether old or new, is inevitably an act of interpretation: new meanings necessarily emerge from a pre-existing text when it is given expression in another language. In the case of the KJB, while the Protestant principle that the Bible should be readily available in the vernacular led to the sacred text being 'Newly Translated' and thus reinterpreted, the project also fed into the equally Protestant practice of individual response to the scriptures. The KJB was thus both the *result* of an interpretative process and the *means* to continuing reinterpretation by others. Both the translation and its spiritual use were acts of interpretation, the second dependent upon the first. This sequence of events would have come as no surprise to the translators: in 'The Translators to the Reader', Miles Smith specifically encouraged the reader's active engagement with the biblical text. 'Happy is the man that delighteth in the Scripture', he wrote, 'and thrice happy that meditateth in it day and night' (p. lvi). This was the era of powerful scripturally based preaching such as that by Bishop Lancelot Andrewes, himself a prominent member of the team of translators of the KJB as chair of the first Westminster Company of biblical scholars.

In the publication year of the KJB, Andrewes preached at least twice before King James and, as was his customary method, insisted upon teasing out the interpretative possibilities of each individual word of his chosen text. In the sermon delivered at Whitehall on Easter Sunday 1611, Andrewes uses the brief but telling phrase, 'We weigh the word', aptly conveying a sense of the painstaking exegesis of the scriptural text on which his preaching was built. As he added in explanation of his purpose, 'Three senses then, there are of the Text: and (to do it right) we touch them all three'.[11] The practice of squeezing every conceivable meaning out of the biblical original is summed up in the title of a work also published in 1611, James Forester's *The Marrow and Juice of Two Hundred and Sixtie Scriptures*.[12] By implication, the biblical text is to be tasted or sucked in order to yield the rich spiritual nourishment it contains. The interpretative processes inherent in the KJB project were inspired by, and in turn fed into, this emphasis on detailed textual engagement that formed such an important aspect of early modern intellectual and devotional culture.

The prefatory epistle to the KJB encouraged the ordinary Christian's active experience of scriptural interpretation. The practice of constant 'meditating' on the Bible seems to have coincided with growing evidence of women as independent consumers of the biblical text.[13] In January 1611, Lancelot Langhorne preached the funeral sermon of one Mistress Mary Swaine at the church of '*Saint Buttolphs* without *Aldersgate*'.[14] The printed sermon takes its evocative title, *Mary Sitting at Christs Feet*, from the biblical passage in Luke 10: 38–42 describing how Jesus visits the home of the sisters Martha and Mary where, while

---

[11] Lancelot Andrewes, *A Sermon Preached Before His Majestie at White-Hall, On the 24 March last, being Easter day* (London, 1611), 5, 4. On the literal sense, see the chapter by Debora Shuger in this volume; on the use of the Bible in sermons, see the chapters by Mary Morrisey and Emma Rhatigan.

[12] James Forester, *The Marrow and Juice of Two Hundred and Sixtie Scriptures* (London, 1611).

[13] See Femke Molekamp, *Women and the Bible in Early Modern England: Religious Reading and Writing* (Oxford: Oxford University Press, 2013).

[14] Lancelot Langhorne, *Mary Sitting at Christs Feet: A Sermon preached at the Funerall of M^ris Mary Swaine* (London, 1611), title-page. All further Langhorne references are to this text.

Martha is busy with household tasks, Mary is absorbed in listening to Jesus. Langhorne draws parallels between the Jacobean Mary and her several biblical namesakes, particularly the attentive Mary who sits 'at Christs feet' hanging onto every word spoken by her saviour.

Mistress Swaine is said to have presented herself, metaphorically, at Christ's feet 'all the daies of her life':

> How often did she fall at Christs feet to pray unto him? Shee praied, not three times a day, with *Daniel*, but *Continually*. I have often observed her, that all the time she was not imployed in houshold businesse, she spent it in meditation and praier ... Her whole care and desire was (with *Mary*) to sit at *Christs feet*, to heare God speaking unto her, or else to speake unto God by praier: And the oftner she fell downe and kist her *Saviours feet*, the more desirous she was. (16–17)

This sermon is not only another instance of the interpretation of a biblical text by the preacher himself, but also establishes, despite the idealizing tone and nature of the funeral sermon, that the centre of Mary Swaine's pious life was her prayerful and meditative use of the Bible. The yardsticks for her possible practices of prayer are biblical: she did not limit herself to praying three times a day, as 'with *Daniel*', but her desire was, 'with *Mary*', constantly to 'heare' and understand the words of God. According to Langhorne she achieved this by listening attentively to Christ, thus modelling herself on the biblical Mary, and there is little doubt that the words received and meditated upon by Mary Swaine were themselves scriptural. 'Let us learne to humble our selves at the feet of *Jesus Christ*', he urges in his 'application' of the scriptural text in the light of Mary Swaine's life, 'and then we shall profit by his word *to the saving of our soules*' (20). It is possible that Mary was unable to read the Bible for herself—like so many early modern men and women—and the reference to her desire to 'heare God speaking unto her' is certainly a timely reminder that for the majority in this period their experience of the biblical text was aural. From 1611 onwards it was the KJB, newly reinterpreted in the process of translation, which provided the officially sanctioned biblical readings heard week by week in the churches.[15]

Although Langhorne warmly commends Mary Swaine as an example of biblically inspired piety, his sermon remains a male-authored and didactic account of a virtuous woman's engagement with the text of scripture. By contrast, Aemilia Lanyer's volume of poetry, *Salve Deus Rex Judaeorum*, published in 1611, is a defiantly female-focused work addressed to contemporary women and closely interested in biblical women such as the falsely maligned Eve and the visionary wife of Pontius Pilate. It is significant that the first dedicatory poem of *Salve Deus* is addressed to James's wife Anna, that 'Renowned Empress, and great Britaines Queene, / Most gratious Mother of succeeding Kings' (3), offering the Queen a female reading of certain biblical events in the same year as the male translators completed their text for the King. In her poem to Anna, Lanyer also reveals her consciousness of the interpretative freedom brought to the text by the woman reader as well as its female author. Being all too aware that *Salve Deus* is in itself a rarity—something 'seldome seene, / A Womans writing of divinest things' (3)—Lanyer invites Her Majesty to cross-check the poem's contents against their biblical sources.

---

[15] On the weekly readings, see the chapter by Ian Green in this volume.

These multiple layers of interpretation are encapsulated in the following stanza from the dedicatory poem to Anna:

> Behold, great Queene, faire *Eves* Apologie,
> Which I have writ in honour of your sexe,
> And doe referre unto your Majestie,
> To judge if it agree not with the Text:
> And if it doe, why are poore Women blam'd,
> Or by more faultie Men so much defam'd? (6)

The poet submits herself to the critical judgement of her anticipated royal reader, 'referring' her work for consideration and (she trusts) approval by the Queen. Contrary to what we might expect of an inexperienced female poet, Lanyer does not ask for Anna's confirmation of the technical quality of her poetry but, rather, seeks reassurance as to the accuracy of her biblical rereadings. The Queen is firmly instructed to 'judge if it agree not with the Text'. Clearly, the skilful biblical interpretation in her poetry is what matters to Lanyer. There is a symbiotic interpretative partnership in *Salve Deus* between the poetic text written 'in honour' of women, the poet who radically interprets familiar scriptural passages within the poem, and the reader who is to test the accuracy of Lanyer's biblical exegesis. In the last two lines of the stanza, it becomes clear that nothing less than a visionary interrogation of social structures will be sufficient. If the Queen or any other reader accepts the outcome of Lanyer's poetic debate, then the constrained roles of women are rendered unstable and opened up to new questioning. Their position in life is no longer universally to be 'blam'd' and 'defam'd' by men who are like Adam in being 'more faultie'. The culture of biblical interpretation which inspired and at times threatened the KJB was alive and well among its earliest readers, too—of both sexes.

IV. Patronage and Authority

Lanyer's dedicatory poem to Queen Anna serves as a reminder that the textual cultures of the early modern period were premised upon the need for writers to find patrons to authorize, honour, and support their work. A significant proportion of Lanyer's own book is taken up with poems addressed to the prominent aristocratic and literary women of 1611 in the hope that, upon receiving the volume, they will 'grace both It and Mee' (3). The backing of a gracious patron was never in doubt for the KJB. Indeed, the fact that it has been traditionally known in Britain as the 'Authorized Version' is indicative of its pre-eminent status with regard to royal patronage. Although the paratextual materials of the KJB do not actually refer specifically to 'authorization', the new translation is described on the title-page as having been prepared 'by his Majesties speciall Commandement' and James is later described as 'the principal Mover and Author of the work' (p. lxxii).

The prefatory matter makes this debt to the King's patronage abundantly clear. Immediately after 'The Translators to the Reader', which concludes with a prayer to the 'living God', the KJB prints a fulsome dedication to James, the almighty's representative on earth:

> To the Most High and Mighty Prince JAMES, by the grace of God King of Great Britain, France and Ireland, Defender of the Faith, &c., the Translators of the Bible wish Grace, Mercy, and Peace through Jesus Christ our Lord. (p. lxxi)

The opening phrase refers to James by the generic early modern title for a monarch, 'Prince', a choice of vocabulary that anticipates the repeated use of this one word by the translators throughout the KJB whenever the original text featured any of the fourteen different Hebrew words for a monarch. Their royal patron is, as it were, woven into the fabric of the text as they have rendered it. Each time a biblical ruler is referred to as a 'Prince' there is an implicit recollection of that 'Most High and Mighty Prince' who caused the translation to be made. James is explicitly praised for fulfilling his role as 'Defender of the Faith, &c'—a splendid use of the throw-away 'etcetera' drawing attention to the phrase that precedes it and reaffirming the King's spiritual responsibilities. The epistle asserts that, as a result of James's commissioning of the translation, the English Church has been well defended and steered with care between the two extremes that threaten it: 'Popish Persons at home or abroad' and 'selfconceited Brethren, who run their own ways' (p. lxxii). It is no doubt the latter group, the Calvinist or Puritan faction in the Church, that the translators had in mind when requesting the 'powerful protection' of their patron against the 'bitter censures' of others. Indeed, the translators' discourse of patronage, conventional though it may seem, reveals a surprisingly high level of insecurity in spite of the royal 'approbation' with which they knew they were blessed. The dread of 'uncharitable imputations' (p. lxxii) is very close to the surface. Having begun by wishing the King 'grace', it is not long before the epistle is requesting that very same gift from the King for the protection of its authors.

The KJB was known to be the King's Bible by all who used it, and this work may be said to be the epitome of the Jacobean culture of textual authorization.[16] It was in tune with the textual and social practice of its day, not only in requiring the support of a patron but also in making the matter of its patronage central to its identity as a work. The complex culture of praise and authorization is also clearly to be seen in the experience of Thomas Coryate, whose account of his adventurous journeys across Europe, *Coryats Crudities*, was published in 1611. In addition to the customary dedications written by the author, Coryate's book is prefaced by an enormous amount of paratextual material written by Coryate's witty acquaintances—assuring the reader that the author is, among other things, a great wit and the 'travelling *Wonder* of our daies'.[17] These texts turn out to be almost entirely satirical. The parody of the processes of patronage in *Coryats Crudities* was so extensive that this collection of pseudo-panegyrics was also published separately in the same year under the title of *The Odcombian Banquet*. The dependence of authors upon the support of patrons and well-wishers had evidently become such a familiar feature of the literary landscape that it was legitimate fare for inspired mockery—and by notable writers including Ben Jonson and John Donne.

It is little wonder, then, that Coryate's own dedication of his work to James's son Henry is paradoxically both hyperbolic and tentative. The volume is presented to 'the High and Mighty Prince Henry, Prince of Wales, Duke of Cornwall and Rothsay, Earle of Chester, Knight of the most noble Order of the Garter, &c'. (a4ʳ), with another well-placed 'etcetera', in this case coming at the end of a long list and implying the even greater extent of the young prince's realms. However, Coryate's subsequent tone is hesitant, embellishing

---

[16] See Jane Rickard, *Authorship and Authority: the Writings of James VI and I* (Manchester: Manchester University Press, 2007).

[17] Thomas Coryate, *Coryats Crudities* (London, 1611), c7ʳ. All further Coryate references are to this text.

the expected language of modesty before a patron with a marked anxiety about 'carping criticks':

> Though I am very confidently perswaded (most gracious Prince the Orient Pearl of the Christian world) that I shall expose myself to the severe censure at the least, if not to the scandalous calumniations of divers carping criticks, for presuming to dedicate to your Highnesse the greene fruits of my short travels ... yet there are some few reasons that have emboldned and encouraged me. (a4^{r-v})

In explaining why he feels 'bold' enough to dedicate his work to Prince Henry—particularly citing the positive impact the young prince's approval would have on 'many noble and generose yong Gallants'—Coryate chooses a powerful simile with which to express his assumptions about the role of a patron. If Henry will 'deigne to protect' Coryate's work with 'favourable and gracious Patronage', it will be as though the book were being defended by 'the seven-fold shield of Ajax' (a4^v).

Jacobean authors' ostentatious displays of their dependency on powers higher than their own—both the original divine 'author' and the authorizing patron—are by no means limited to the dedicatory poems and epistles framing their works. Frequent indicators of patronage are also to be found within the main text of works contemporary with the KJB, particularly the masques written for performance at court. New Year 1611 was celebrated at Whitehall with Jonson's masque *Oberon, The Faery Prince*, whose subtitle clearly announces the source of its patronage: *A Masque of Prince Henries*. Jonson's allegorical scheme is unmistakable: Oberon is Henry's *alter ego* in the kingdom of the faeries, and all compliments paid to the faery prince are intended for his flesh-and-blood equivalent. The hyperbole of the songs fulfils the idealizing purpose of the masque, as when the rough satyrs are given a description of Oberon:

> *Satyres*, he doth fill with grace,
> Every season, ev'ry place;
> Beautie dwels, but in his face:
> He'is the height of all our race.[18]

Jonson's elaborate stage-directions for Henry's triumphant entry (naturally in the role of Oberon) vividly construct the relation of the text to this patron, in whom grace and beauty have reached their 'height'.

At the climax of the masque's first and only performance, Oberon's palace, elaborately designed by Inigo Jones, was revealed to the audience's view, and the stage directions inform us that the faery prince's subjects were also on display, 'some with instruments, some bearing lights; others singing'. Beyond them, within the glorious palace though significantly 'a farre off in perspective', Henry's own 'knights masquers' were displayed 'sitting in their severall sieges', symbolic of the royal power they represented. Finally, Oberon himself was made visible, resplendently distant 'at the further end of all', seated 'in a chariot, which to a lowd triumphant musique began to move forward' (ll. 291–6). These detailed stage-directions confirm how Prince Henry was centrally present in the text and its

---

[18] Ben Jonson, *Oberon, The Faery Prince*, ll. 62–5, *Ben Jonson*, ed. C. H. Herford, Percy and Evelyn Simpson (Oxford: Clarendon Press, 1941), vii. 343. All further Jonson references are by line number from this edition.

envisaged performance, as befitted his function as patron. Through the technique of perspective, shown to its full advantage in masque scenery, the audience saw the Prince 'far offe'—a politically expedient arrangement—yet they could not fail to notice that he was at the heart of the verbal, visual, and musical symbolism of the masque. Patrons could thus be enshrined within performance as well as responsible for the commissioning of a work, influential in a writer's aspirations, or evoked through elaborate parody. In these multiple ways, patronage formed an integral part of textual production in the era of the KJB.

V. Performance and the Discovery of Wonder

The example of *Oberon* has brought into the foreground the ingenuity and vitality of performance in Jacobean culture. The London theatres were growing in number and flourishing (apart from when outbreaks of the plague led to their temporary closure) and the influence of several royal patrons ensured a steady series of performances at court. The intellectual and social interests of young trainee lawyers fostered plenty of dramatic activity at the Inns of Court, while the settings of popular sermons, particularly those preached out of doors as at Paul's Cross in the City of London, gave a theatrical aspect to some of the best preaching of the day. The KJB fits well into this early modern culture of performance, not because it was in any sense a work of drama, but because it was specifically intended to be declaimed rather than read quietly or individually. The title-page of the KJB announces this unequivocally in its final clause:

> The Holy Bible, Conteyning the Old Testament, and the New: Newly Translated out of the Originall tongues: & with the former Translations diligently compared and revised by his Majesties speciall Commandement. Appointed to be read in Churches.

As these words remind us, the KJB was a translation bringing together new and already familiar material in a diligent reinterpretation realized through royal patronage—but above all it was specifically intended 'to be read in Churches'. It was to be performed, read *aloud* for the congregation to absorb, listened to by all but particularly by those who could not read for themselves. The kind of language chosen for the KJB reflects this purpose: the sentences are mainly short with few subclauses; the narrative style maintains the repetitive syntax appropriate to an oral tradition, and the oratory fulfils the translators' express desire for a 'majestic' manner.[19] In a year boasting at least a dozen new plays in London, theatrical tours to provincial cities, court masques, Lord Mayors' pageants and rhetorically charged preaching, the KJB was both an example to and a reflection of its performative cultural environment.

The KJB was the product of collaborative work on a very significant scale, with six companies of scholars entrusted with the task of producing a coherently translated whole. Though never on the same scale as the massive collaborative efforts that produced the KJB,

---

[19] John Bois, notes on the translation process of the KJB, Corpus Christi College, Oxford, MS 312, 73ᵛ.

other literary texts—and perhaps especially drama—were equally the products of collaboration and revision, in ways that have only recently been recognized by scholars.[20] Creative
partnerships of 1611 included Jonson and Jones, who also collaborated with the composers Alfonso Ferrabosco and Robert Johnson in masques such as *Oberon*, and the playwright duos of Beaumont and Fletcher, and Middleton and Dekker. The latter pair worked
together on the cross-dressing comedy *The Roaring Girl*, based on the contemporary
real-life character of Mary Frith, also known as Moll Cutpurse. The play's published text is
preceded by a self-reflective prologue raising the concept and pitfalls of performance:

> A play expected long makes the audience look
> For wonders:—that each scene should be a book,
> Composed to all perfection; each one comes
> And brings a play in's head with him: up he sums
> What he would of a roaring girl have writ;
> If that he finds not here, he mews at it.[21]

Since the play had been 'expected long' and the story of the 'roaring girl' was already familiar,
Middleton and Dekker were well aware that their audience would come with preconceptions.
The tendency of an audience to anticipate 'perfection' is apparently a worry for the playwrights,
as is the idea that each member of the audience will already come with 'a play in's head', comparing their own version with that of *The Roaring Girl* itself. The clash between private imagination and the shared experience of a performance is fascinatingly touched upon here.

If the danger of performance is the possibility of disappointment or disapproval among
the audience, its concomitant excitement is the potential for surprise and the thrill of discovery. Middleton and Dekker's prologue admits that the audience will 'look / For wonders', and they were fully aware that they were writing at a time dominated by the search
to discover new worlds.[22] Shakespeare's 1611 plays both share this emphasis on the need to
search and the consequent power of revelation. *The Winter's Tale* concludes its many journeys with the statue scene in which all those watching Hermione's transformation from
death to life are struck with 'marvel' (5.3.100). *The Tempest* not only presents its characters
with new worlds but also focuses its hopes on a character whose name, Miranda, means
admirable or wonderful, and who herself considers the 'goodly creatures' around her as a
'wonder' (5.1.181).

In the same year, John Davies's poems on *The XII Wonders of the World* were published
for performance in musical settings by John Maynard. One of the so-called 'Wonders' is a
merchant who 'discovers unknown coasts'.[23] In fact, Davies's 'wonders' are ironic and his
poetic sequence treats the trend for amazement satirically—a sure sign of the ubiquity of
the phenomenon. The words of 'The Translators to the Reader' link closely with this spirit
of enquiry and discovery: defending the benefits of access to the Bible in the vernacular,
Smith insists that Christians are 'commanded to search' the scriptures (p. lv). The biblical

---

[20] See e.g. Heather Hirschfeld, *Joint Enterprises: Collaborative Drama and the Institutionalization of the
English Renaissance Theater* (Amherst, Mass.: University of Massachusetts Press, 2004).

[21] Thomas Dekker and Thomas Middleton, 'Prologus', *The Roaring Girl* (1611), ed. Elizabeth Cook
(London: Methuen, 1997), ll. 1–6.

[22] On 'wonder' as an epistemological category in this period, see Lorraine Daston and Katharine Park,
Wonders and the Order of Nature, 1150–1750 (New York: Zone Books, 1998).

[23] John Davies, *The XII Wonders of the World* (London, 1611), D1ʳ.

text is presented as a site of exploration with the potential for life-changing discoveries and the prospect of spiritual wonders. Thus the KJB is, once again, in line with a dominant feature of the cultural moment in which it was published, aware of its own processes as a journey to be 'travelled' (p. lxi) and encouraging its readers to trust to the power of the Holy Spirit to take them 'further than we can ask or think' (p. lxviii).

The KJB is in many ways a paradoxical work: a translation that claims to be accurate and yet free from linguistic constraints; a work which is both old and new, steeped in tradition but also innovative; a task of precise scholarly interpretation that sets its readers free to interpret for themselves; a text of divinely inspired authorship whose proclaimed 'author' is the royal patron himself, and a work for communal performance that encourages private spiritual discovery. In these paradoxes, as in so many other details of its conception and execution, the KJB is mirrored in the texts with which it was contemporary. Perhaps the greatest paradox of all is that this landmark biblical text is at once unique and yet typical of its literary and cultural moment.

FURTHER READING

Campbell, Gordon. *Bible: The Story of the King James Version, 1611–2011* (Oxford: Oxford University Press, 2010).

Daniell, David. *The Bible in English: Its History and Influence* (New Haven: Yale University Press, 2003).

Doelman, James. *King James I and the Religious Culture of England* (Woodbridge: D. S. Brewer, 2000).

McCullough, Peter. *Sermons at Court: Politics and Religion in Elizabethan and Jacobean Preaching* (Cambridge: Cambridge University Press, 1998).

McGrath, Alister. *In the Beginning: The Story of the King James Bible* (London: Hodder & Stoughton, 2001).

Molekamp, Femke. *Women and the Bible in Early Modern England: Religious Reading and Writing* (Oxford: Oxford University Press, 2013).

Moore, Helen, and Julian Reid, eds. *Manifold Greatness: The Making of the King James Bible* (Oxford: Bodleian Library, 2011).

Nicolson, Adam. *Power and Glory: Jacobean England and the Making of the King James Bible* (London: Harper Collins, 2003).

Rees, Graham, and Maria Wakely. *Publishing, Politics and Culture: The King's Printers in the Reign of James I and VI* (Oxford: Oxford University Press, 2009).

Shuger, Debora K. *The Renaissance Bible: Scholarship, Sacrifice, and Subjectivity* (Berkeley, Calif.: University of California Press, 1994).

Tadmor, Naomi. *The Social Universe of the English Bible* (Cambridge: Cambridge University Press, 2010).

Wilcox, Helen. *1611: Authority, Gender and the Word in Early Modern England* (Oxford: Wiley Blackwell, 2014).

CHAPTER 29

THE NOBLEST COMPOSITION IN THE UNIVERSE OR FIT FOR THE FLAMES? THE LITERARY STYLE OF THE KING JAMES BIBLE

HANNIBAL HAMLIN

My title quotes two critical assessments of the King James Bible, about a hundred and fifty years apart. The first, that it is the 'noblest composition in the universe', is from Samuel Jackson Pratt's *The Sublime and Beautiful of Scripture* (1777).[1] Few critics of the Bible have matched the extent of Pratt's hyperbole, in which the beauties of scripture surpass not only all earthly literature but that of other galaxies. Nevertheless, an only slightly more modest hyperbole characterized attitudes to the literary pre-eminence of the King James Bible for the next two centuries. Thomas Babington Macaulay, poet, historian, and Whig politician, described the King James Bible as 'a book which if everything else in our language should perish would alone suffice to show the whole extent of its beauty and power'.[2] Other nineteenth-century accolades came from Matthew Arnold, John Ruskin, and Cardinal Newman, a group whose diversity testifies to the unanimity of feeling for what had become the Bible of all Englishmen. For early twentieth-century Harvard professor John Livingstone Lowes, it was 'the noblest monument of English prose'.[3] George Saintsbury called it 'the best words of the best time of English, in the best order, on the best subjects'.[4] Even the otherwise sceptical H. L. Mencken called the King James Bible 'probably the most

---

[1] Cited in David Norton, *A History of the English Bible as Literature* (Cambridge: Cambridge University Press, 2000), 256. Pratt published his two-volume work under his usual pseudonym Courtney Melmoth. He was first a clergyman and preacher, then (after a scandalous love affair) an actor, then a poet and novelist.

[2] Norton, *History*, 302.

[3] John Livingston Lowes, 'The Noblest Monument of English Prose', *Essays in Appreciation* (Boston and New York: Houghton Mifflin Co., 1936), 3–31.

[4] George Saintsbury, *A History of English Prose Rhythm* (London: Macmillan & Co., 1912), 157.

beautiful piece of writing in all the literature of the world'.[5] The Dante scholar Charles Allen Dinsmore went so far as to suggest that the King James Bible was 'finer and nobler literature than the Scriptures in their original tongues'.[6] Many of these gushing accolades have become familiar, especially due to David Norton's work on the literary reception of the English Bible, and contemporary versions are easy to find too. Harold Bloom, for instance, follows Dinsmore in arguing that, at least for the New Testament, English translations from William Tyndale's to the King James Bible surpass the Greek originals.[7] Melvyn Bragg writes of the King James Bible that 'There has never been a book to match it'.[8]

By contrast, the second quotation in my title is from the ornery English Hebraist Hugh Broughton. Broughton had urged the retranslation of the Bible into English in his 1597 *Epistle to the Learned Nobilitie of England*, and himself published translations of Daniel (1596), Lamentations (1606), and Job (1610), as well as a commentary on Ecclesiastes and studies of biblical language, chronology, and genealogy. As one of England's most learned Hebraists, and as an outspoken advocate of a new Bible translation, Broughton would have been an obvious choice to serve on one of the King James Bible companies, but he was not included, probably because of his fierce impatience with scholarly disagreement. In 1611, while the King James Bible was still hot off the press, Broughton printed from the safety of Middleburg *A Censure of the Late Translation for our Churches*. For his opening salvo, Broughton wrote 'It is so ill done. Tell his Majest. that I had rather be rent in pieces with wilde horses, then any such translation by my consent should bee urged upon poore Churches'. 'The New edition crosseth me', he complained, 'I require it to be burnt'.[9]

Yoking Broughton together with Pratt is misleading, however, since they are not talking about the same thing. Broughton's criticisms have nothing to do with literary style, beauty, or power, but focus on what he perceives as specific errors of translation, as is evident in the following passages:

> Abraham bought no sepulchre in Sichem [Gen. 33: 19].[10] And the sepulchre there was bought for sheep. Thrise the term Keshita is used, and still in the Chaldie and Greeke for sheepe. The margent note for sheepe burneth the hart of the Translatours: who bade them put the errour in the text, and right in the margent?
>
> Sadik and Ain in Chaldea had one forme and sound, as in Daniels Chaldie: the Ebrew S. is expressed by ain. and so Saint Peter calling Balaam the sonne of Bosor [2 Pet. 2: 15], sheweth that he was then in Chaldea: where ain was expressed by an S. as Thalmud Jerusalemy in Megilah and R. Azarias in a learned treatise noteth.[11]

---

[5] H. L. Mencken, *Treatise on the Gods* (New York: Alfred A. Knopf, 1930, repr. 1946), 205.

[6] Charles Allen Dinsmore, *The English Bible as Literature* (London: Allen & Unwin, 1931), cited in Norton, *History*, 401.

[7] Harold Bloom, *The Shadow of a Great Rock: A Literary Appreciation of the King James Bible* (New Haven and London: Yale University Press, 2011), 245–7.

[8] Melvyn Bragg, *The Book of Books: The Radical Impact of the King James Bible 1611–2011* (Berkeley, Calif.: Counterpoint, 2011), 5.

[9] Hugh Broughton, *A Censure of the Late Translation for Our Churches* (Middleburg, 1611), n.p.

[10] The KJB text of Gen. 33: 19 reads, 'And he bought a parcel of a field, where he had spread his tent, at the hand of the children of Hamor, Shechem's father, for a hundred pieces of money'. The marginal note reads 'Or, lambes'. Broughton's reference to Abraham is curious, since it is Jacob who is described in this verse. Abraham builds an altar at Sichem at Gen. 12: 6–7, and he buys a tomb from Ephron in Gen. 23, but he pays with 400 shekels of silver; the Hebrew word 'Keshita' is not used with reference to Abraham.

[11] Broughton. 'Sadik' and 'Ain' are Hebrew letters.

Other seventeenth-century references to the King James Bible were similarly concerned with the word choices of the translators. Among the dozens of references to the 'new translation' in sermons, commentaries, and other scholarly works, not a single one is interested in any quality we might call literary.[12] All of them concern the King James Bible's rendering of specific words or phrases, in most cases simply noting that they are citing the 'new translation'. John Boys, for instance, himself one of the translators, in *An Exposition of the Last Psalme*, a sermon preached at Paul's Cross on the anniversary of the Gunpowder Plot (5 November) 1613, noted that '*Luther, Calvin, Vatablus,* your *English-Geneva* bibles, and our new translation have praise God in his *sanctuarie* [Psalm 150: 1], the which in holy scripture signifieth either heaven, or the temple'.[13] Similarly, Nicholas Larke, in *The Practice of Thankefulnesse*, supports his reading of Psalm 148: 11-12 with the witness of 'the learned Translatours of the New Translation'.[14] Samuel Page, in *Nine Sermons upon Sun[drie] Texts of Scripture*, writes of Proverbs 9: 5, 'Come eate of my Bread, and drinke of the Wine, which I have drawne':

> In the beginning of this chapter, *Wisedome buildth her an house,* that is, Christ, a church, and it is not like to our great houses, without hospitalitie: here are three rooms expressed in it: a Slaughter-house: For she hath *killed her beasts:* the *Oxen and Fatlings* in the Parable: heere is her Wine-presse: for shee hath mingled her Wine, saith the new translation, it is the phrase of Scripture, to express the making of wine of the juice of many grapes commixed: or it is her cellar, for the olde reading was, that shee hath *drawne the wine.*[15]

These and similar comments confirm the argument made by David Norton that the early reception of the King James Bible was at best lukewarm and that readers were entirely unconscious of what were later praised as its superlative literary merits.[16] This argument requires some qualification, however. How does one distinguish between the literary qualities of the Bible in Hebrew and Greek and those of an English translation of it? Writers since St Jerome had recognized the Bible as a great literary work. Jerome compared the writing of the Old Testament to Horace and Pindar, suggesting that the Hebrew poetry, like the Greek and Latin, 'now flows in iambs, now rings with Alcaics, swells to a Sapphic measure or moves along with a half-foot'.[17] Jerome also cites Josephus and Origen, who, he claims, praise the hexameters and pentameters of Deuteronomy, Isaiah, and Job. These comments were widely known and cited in the Renaissance. Sir Philip Sidney, John Harington, George Puttenham, and John Milton were among the many who praised the biblical writers for their literary pre-eminence, preceding and surpassing, they believed, the achievements of classical poets.[18] The translation of the Bible

---

[12] The nicknames 'King James Bible' and 'Authorized Version' appear quite late, the former from the late seventeenth or early eighteenth centuries, the latter from only 1824. See Norton, *The King James Bible: A Short History from Tyndale to Today* (Cambridge: Cambridge University Press, 2011), 133–5.

[13] John Boys, *An Exposition of the Last Psalme* (London, 1613), 9.

[14] [Nicholas Larke], *The Practice of Thankefulnesse: or Davids choyse directions how to prayse God* (London, 1622), 72–3.

[15] Samuel Page, *Nine Sermons upon Sun[drie] Texts of Scripture* (London, 1616), 23–4.

[16] Norton, *History*, ch. 5.

[17] Jerome, 'Preface to Eusebius', cited in James Kugel, *The Idea of Biblical Poetry: Parallelism and its History* (New Haven and London: Yale University Press, 1981), 152.

[18] Hannibal Hamlin, *Psalm Culture and Early Modern English Literature* (Cambridge: Cambridge University Press, 2004), 85–8; and Israel Baroway, 'The Bible as Poetry in the English Renaissance: An Introduction', *Journal of English and Germanic Philology*, 32 (1933): 447–80.

into Latin by Immanuel Tremellius, mentioned in Sidney's *Defence of Poesy*, and read by John Donne, Milton, and countless other educated readers, included notes on the literary forms, genres, and rhetorical figures of scripture.[19] Seventeenth-century Bible readers were aware of its literary qualities, whether they were reading it in English, Latin, Greek, or Hebrew. Moreover, some of the literary qualities of the original Hebrew and Greek texts translated readily into English. The parallelism of Hebrew poetry, for instance, was largely translatable and therefore graspable by seventeenth-century English readers, even if the formal scholarly definition of this stylistic device was only pronounced by Bishop Robert Lowth in the next century.[20]

Tropes and schemes like metaphor, simile, anaphora, and the like are also possible to translate. When Eliphaz says in the book of Job, 'man is born unto trouble as sparks fly upward' (5: 7), is the power of this simile owing to the original Hebrew writer or to the English translators? Robert Alter's recent translation from the Hebrew opts for 'wretchedness' instead of 'trouble', and inverts the word order of the first clause, but the simile is basically the same: 'But man is to wretchedness born like sparks flying upward'.[21] Similarly, the metaphor at the opening of John's Gospel—'In the beginning was the Word' (John 1: 1)—is rich and meaningful in English as well as in Greek, even though the full range of *logos* is diminished. *Logos*, translated since the Wycliffite Bible as 'word' (the initial capital first appears in the 1560 Geneva Bible), signifies everything from 'word' to 'saying', 'decree', 'speech', 'discourse', 'doctrine', 'reason', 'mind', or even the organizing principle of the universe.[22] The English 'word' (even capitalized) does not have quite this range. However, it figures Christ as language and speech, and, in conjunction with Genesis 1, the words with which and (signified by the capital) by which God speaks the universe into being.[23] 'Word' may also signify Jesus's words, the teaching of the Gospel (literally in Anglo-Saxon, 'good word'). Most of the scope of the Greek metaphor is available in translation.

A further complication for the study of the King James Bible's reception derives from the nature of post-Reformation English Bible translation. As Miles Smith famously put it in his prefatory 'Translators to the Reader' in the King James Bible,

> Truly (good Christian Reader) wee never thought from the beginning, that we should neede to make a new Translation, nor yet to make of a bad one a good one ... but to make a good one better, or out of many good ones, one principall good one, not justly to be excepted against; that hath bene our indeavor, that our marke.[24]

---

[19] Kenneth Austin, 'Immanuel Tremellius' Latin Bible (1575–79) as a Pillar of the Calvinist Faith', in David Adams and Adrian Armstrong (eds), *Print and Power in France and England, 1500–1800* (Aldershot: Ashgate, 2006), 27–38.

[20] Robert Lowth, *Lectures on the Sacred Poetry of the Hebrews*, tr. George Gregory (London, 1787); first published as *De Sacra Poesi Hebraeorum Praelectiones* (Oxford, 1753).

[21] Robert Alter (tr.), *The Wisdom Books: Job, Proverbs, and Ecclesiastes, A Translation with Commentary* (New York and London: W. W. Norton & Co., 2010), 28.

[22] 'λόγος', according to James Strong's *Exhaustive Concordance of the Bible*, as cited in *Blue Letter Bible*, <http://www.blueletterbible.org/lang/lexicon/lexicon.cfm?Strongs=G3056&t=KJV>.

[23] The connection with Genesis is clear enough from John's opening 'in the beginning', but Christ's presence at the Creation is made in conjunction with the description of Wisdom being with God 'in the beginning of his way, before his works of old' in Proverbs 8. As John Meyendorrf writes, 'the Jewish tendency to personalize Wisdom in Proverbs led directly to the doctrine of the Logos in the Gospel of John'. 'Wisdom-Sophia: Contrasting Approaches to a Complex Theme', *Dumbarton Oaks Papers*, 41, Studies in Art and Archaeology in Honor of Ernst Kitzinger on his Seventy-Fifth Birthday (1987), 392.

[24] [Miles Smith], 'The Translators to the Reader', *The Holy Bible* (London, 1611), B^v.

Bible translation was a process of ongoing revision: John Rogers combined and revised Tyndale and Miles Coverdale in the Matthew Bible (1537); Coverdale revised the Matthew Bible into the Great Bible (1539); the Geneva Bible (1560) translators revised the Great Bible; the Bishops' Bible (1568) translators revised the Great and the Geneva; and the King James Bible companies revised all of the above, as well as the Rheims New Testament (1582).

The reason for the deafening silence with which the King James Bible was received may be partly because many did not think of it as anything especially new. (Even Broughton, as quoted, referred to it as the 'New edition', suggesting that the King James Bible was simply a revision of the Bishops', which is indeed just what King James intended it to be.) For many readers, the only notable difference between the King James Bible and its predecessor translations would have been its relative lack of interpretive marginal notes. There are still marginal notes, but they are confined to cross-references and problems of translation as opposed to doctrine and exegesis. It takes careful reading, with half a dozen English versions side by side, to recognize what is new in the King James translation, and even then it is often not new but simply a choice made among various pre-existing options. Consider the following translations:

> How is the gold become so dim? the most fine gold is changed, and the stones of the Sanctuary are scattered in the corner of every street.
> The noble men of Zion comparable to fine gold, how are they esteemed as earthen pitchers, even the work of the hands of the potter!
> Even the dragons draw out the breasts, and give suck to their young, but the daughter of my people is become cruel like the ostriches in the wilderness.
> The tongue of the sucking child cleaveth to the roof of his mouth for thirst: the young children ask bread, but no man breaketh it unto them. (Lamentations 4: 1–4, Geneva)

> How is the gold become dim! how is the most fine gold changed! the stones of the sanctuary are poured out in the top of every street. The precious sons of Zion, comparable to fine gold, how are they esteemed as earthen pitchers, the work of the hands of the potter! Even the sea monsters draw out the breast, they give suck to their young ones: the daughter of my people is become cruel, like the ostriches in the wilderness.
> The tongue of the sucking child cleaveth to the roof of his mouth for thirst: the young children ask bread, and no man breaketh it unto them. (Lamentations 4: 1–4, KJB)

The differences between these translations are small, and, while arguments might be made about their relative accuracy, they have little qualitative effect on the passage's style. The King James Bible expands a little—'how is the most fine gold changed' and 'they give suck to their young ones'—and substitutes 'poured out' for 'scattered' and 'sea monsters' for 'dragons', but the reader will likely find the translations equally effective in conveying the lament.

With these major caveats in mind—that the literary qualities of original and translation overlap, and that the literary qualities of the King James Bible are often inseparable from those of earlier translations—it is still possible to talk about the style of the King James Bible. Defining the 'literary' is notoriously difficult, but it includes at least formal matters of diction, syntax, tropes and schemes, and rhythm. The King James Bible actually exhibits various styles. Stephen Prickett has written about what he calls the 'King James steamroller', the way in which the King James translators homogenized and flattened out the stylistic differences among the many biblical writers.[25] The point is well taken, but the homogeneity of the King James Bible can be overstated. Even without recourse to the original languages, readers can recognize that the evangelists Mark and John have different narrative styles.

> And straightway in the morning the chief priests held a consultation with the elders and scribes and the whole council, and bound Jesus, and carried *him* away, and delivered *him* to Pilate. And Pilate asked him, Art thou the King of the Jews? And he answering said unto him, Thou sayest *it*. And the chief priests accused him of many things: but he answered nothing. And Pilate asked him again, saying, Answerest thou nothing? behold how many things they witness against thee. But Jesus yet answered nothing; so that Pilate marvelled. (Mark 15: 1–5)

> Then Pilate entered into the judgment hall again, and called Jesus, and said unto him, Art thou the King of the Jews? Jesus answered him, Sayest thou this thing of thyself, or did others tell it thee of me? Pilate answered, Am I a Jew? Thine own nation and the chief priests have delivered thee unto me: what hast thou done? Jesus answered, My kingdom is not of this world: if my kingdom were of this world, then would my servants fight, that I should not be delivered to the Jews: but now is my kingdom not from hence. Pilate therefore said unto him, Art thou a king then? Jesus answered, Thou sayest that I am a king. To this end was I born, and for this cause came I into the world, that I should bear witness unto the truth. Every one that is of the truth heareth my voice. Pilate saith unto him, What is truth? And when he had said this, he went out again unto the Jews, and saith unto them, I find in him no fault *at all*. (John 18: 33–8)

Mark is terse, plain, abrupt, all action with minimal dialogue. John is discursive, expansive, less interested in action than thought; his dialogue not just functional but philosophical. Mark's Pilate would never pause to consider 'What is truth?' Similarly, in a different comparison, few readers could fail to perceive the different styles of the Old Testament books of Leviticus and the Song of Solomon, even in the English of the King James Bible. The Song of Songs is thick with metaphor and simile, tactile, luxuriant, odorous, tasty: 'His cheeks are as a bed of spices, as sweet flowers: his lips like lilies, dropping sweet smelling myrrh' (Song 5: 13). Leviticus is arid legal code: 'And all thy estimations shall be according to the shekel of the sanctuary: twenty gerahs shall be the shekel' (Leviticus 27: 25).

Those who celebrate the general sublimity of the King James Bible also tend to be selective, focusing on certain passages rather than others: Isaiah's 'Arise, shine, for thy light is come' (60: 1), for instance, or Paul's 'For now we see through a glass darkly', from 1 Corinthians (13: 12). Richard Chenevix Trench, Archbishop of Dublin as well as philologist and poet, praised the King James Bible's '*delectus verborum* on which Cicero insists so earnestly ... All the words used are of the noblest stamp, alike removed from vulgarity and pedantry'.[26] He was not likely thinking of Isaiah 36: 12, 'But Rabshakeh

[25] Stephen Prickett, 'Language within Language: The King James Steamroller', in Hannibal Hamlin and Norman W. Jones (eds), *The King James Bible After 400 Years: Literary, Linguistic, and Cultural Influences* (Cambridge: Cambridge University Press, 2010), 27–44.

[26] Richard Chenevix Trench, *On the Authorized Version of the New Testament* (New York: Redfield, 1858), 20.

said, Hath my master ... not sent me to the men that sit upon the wall, that they may eat their own dung, and drink their own piss with you?' On the other hand, passages like this have their own power, based on visceral detail and colloquial diction. In 1936, Livingston Lowes argued that the biblical style was characterized not just by 'a singular nobility of diction and by a rhythmic quality which is ... unrivalled in its beauty' but by 'phrases of homely vigour or happy pregnancy'.[27] Tyndale and Coverdale had been masters of this homely or even gutter vocabulary, though in the case of Isaiah 36 the King James translation is actually identical to the Bishops' Bible. (Coverdale has 'stale' instead of 'piss'.) There is quite a bit of piss and dung in the King James Bible, as also vomit and other bodily emissions. Ezekiel 23: 19–20 is especially indecorous, almost pornographic:

> Yet she multiplied her whoredoms, in calling to remembrance the days of her youth, wherein she had played the harlot in the land of Egypt.For she doted upon their paramours, whose flesh is as the flesh of asses, and whose issue is like the issue of horses.[28]

For the most part the translators recognized that such diction was deliberately coarse and in its own way effective, and, most importantly, reflected accurately the diction of the original passages. However, in a few instances, the physicality seems too much for them and they resort to euphemism, as in Deuteronomy 25: 11: 'When men strive together one with another, and the wife of the one draweth near for to deliver her husband out of the hand of him that smiteth him, and putteth forth her hand, and taketh him by the secrets: Then thou shalt cut off her hand, thine eye shall not pity her'. Instead of the mysterious 'secrets' modern translations have 'private parts' (New International Version) or even 'testicles' (New Living Translation). 'Secrets' persisted, though, through the English Revised Version of 1881 and the American Standard Version of 1901. The ultimate source, surprisingly, is Tyndale, who uses 'secrets' throughout his Pentateuch to translate everything from general nakedness to male and female genitals. In Genesis 9: 23, for example, 'Sem and Japheth toke a mantell and put it on both there shuldere and went backward / and covered there fathers secrets'.[29] Tyndale is not being coy, however, since contemporary usage allowed 'secrets', like 'privates', to mean genitals (OED s.v., 6).[30] Edward Topsell, for instance, in his Historie of Foure-Footed Beastes (1607), writes about a badger 'much troubled with lice about his secrets'.[31] The retention of 'secrets' in Deuteronomy 25 of the King James Bible is unusual, though, since none of the other naughty 'secrets' are retained. But in this the translators were simply following their base text, the 1602 edition of the Bishops' Bible. Here again, we think we have found something singular about the King James Bible, only to discover that it is not original after all.

[27] Lowes, 'Noblest Monument', 4–5.

[28] The New English Bible helpfully clarifies for the modern reader: 'whose members were like those of asses and whose seed came in floods like that of horses'.

[29] The Pentateuch ([Antwerp, 1530]), fol. xii[r].

[30] Tyndale's use of 'secrets' is earlier than the OED's first citation from the 1535 Coverdale Bible (Deut. 25: 11).

[31] Edward Topsell, The Historie of Foure-Footed Beastes (London, 1607), 34.

Other passages in the King James Bible are neither singularly noble nor happily pregnant, but just puzzling, as in Ezekiel 13: 20:

> Wherefore thus saith the Lord God. 'Behold, I am against your pillows, wherewith ye there
> hunt the souls to make them fly, and I will tear them from your arms, and will let the souls
> go, even the souls that ye hunt to make them fly'.

The point seems to have something to do with styles of sleeve (in Ezekiel 13: 18 God says, 'Woe
to the women that sew pillows to all arm-holes'), but the text is obscure at best. The King
James translators cannot really be blamed, however, for a passage that is simply obscure in
the Hebrew, nor for the sense of God as interior decorator that results from the modern connotations of pillows. Once again, moreover, the 'pillows' are not original in 1611 but come ultimately from the Coverdale Bible of 1535 and are retained in the Bishops'. As is often the case,
it is impossible to distinguish the King James Bible from the translations that came before it.

The book of Revelation is full of puzzling passages (early exegetes called them 'hard
places'), like the description of the beast out of the sea:

> And I stood upon the sand of the sea, and saw a beast rise up out of the sea, having seven
> heads and ten horns, and upon his horns ten crowns, and upon his heads the name of blas-
> phemy. And the beast which I saw was like unto a leopard, and his feet were as the feet of a
> bear, and his mouth as the mouth of a lion: and the dragon gave him his power, and his seat,
> and great authority. (Revelation 13: 1–2)

The next verse notes that 'all the world wondered at the beast', which hardly seems surprising. How are the ten horns distributed among the seven heads, and is 'blasphemy' written on each of the heads or somehow across all of them? The bizarre amalgam of animal
body parts is derived from the apocalyptic prophecy in Daniel 7, which is more bizarre
still. Four beasts come out of the sea, the first 'like a lion, and had eagle's wings', the second
'like to a bear', the third 'like a leopard' but with 'four wings of a fowl', and the fourth with
'great iron teeth'. The last also has 'ten horns':

> I considered the horns, and, behold, there came up among them another little horn, before
> whom there were three of the first horns plucked up by the roots: and, behold, in this horn
> were eyes like the eyes of man, and a mouth speaking great things. (Daniel 7: 8)

This description defies visualization, though an interpretation is given to Daniel by a man
standing by in his dream:

> And the ten horns out of this kingdom are ten kings that shall arise: and another shall rise after
> them; and he shall be diverse from the first, and he shall subdue three kings. And he shall speak
> great words against the most High, and shall wear out the saints of the most High, and think to
> change times and laws: and they shall be given into his hand until a time and times and the divid-
> ing of time. But the judgment shall sit, and they shall take away his dominion, to consume and
> to destroy it unto the end. And the kingdom and dominion, and the greatness of the kingdom
> under the whole heaven, shall be given to the people of the saints of the most High, whose king-
> dom is an everlasting kingdom, and all dominions shall serve and obey him. (Daniel 7: 24–7)

By contrast, the interpretation of John's vision in Revelation is left to the reader; the obscurity of the passage actually makes it highly adaptable. According to William Hicks, 'all
interpreters of the Reformation do harmoniously accord that by the Beast of seven heads

and ten horns, *Rev.* 13 1. must be meant the Romish Empire divided into ten Kingdoms'.[32] But for John himself, the Rome symbolized by the seven heads (corresponding to the city's seven hills) was the imperial Rome of the first century, and for one recent interpreter, the beast is England's Prince Charles (the ten horns correspond to the ten nations that will be left in the European Union sometime in the future).[33] T. Chase, on the other hand, suggests that the ten horns will be the ten nations belonging to the Shanghai Cooperation Organization (currently Russia, China, Tajikistan, Uzbekistan, Kazakhstan, and Kyrgyzstan; Vladimir Putin, according to Chase, is the 'little horn' from Daniel).[34] The obscurity of the prophecies in Daniel or Revelation, however conducive to apocalyptic prophecy, and however distinctive as one of the King James Bible styles, cannot be blamed on the translators.

Many stylistic features of the King James Bible, and this is true of English Bibles since Tyndale, are accidental by-products of the translators' efforts to follow the original literally. In the terminology of the modern Bible translator Eugene Nida, sixteenth-century translators aimed for formal rather than dynamic or functional equivalence, translating word for word rather than thought for thought, or idiom for idiom.[35] The resulting effect was a weird hybrid of English with Hebrew and Hebraized Greek. That this seemed odd in the sixteenth and seventeenth centuries is clear from one of the few contemporary responses to the King James Bible other than Broughton's. In his *Tabletalk*, the polymathic scholar John Selden expressed his sense of the oddity of the King James Bible's style:

> There is no book so translated as the Bible. For the purpose, if I translate a *French* book into *English*, I turn it into *English* phrase and not into *French English*. [*Il fait froid*] I say 'tis cold, not it makes cold; but the Bible is rather translated into *English* Words than into *English* phrase. The *Hebraisms* are kept, and the Phrase of that Language is kept: As for Example, [He uncovered her Shame] which is well enough, so long as Scholars have to do with it; but when it comes among the Common People, Lord what Gear do they make of it![36]

And yet, despite Selden's learned objections, it is surely the Hebraic English of the King James Bible that its readers have found so distinctive and which over the next several hundred years became naturalized as biblical English. Indeed, some Hebraisms—'the skin of my teeth' (Job 19: 20), for instance, or 'the apple of my eye' (Psalm 17: 8)—have become idiomatic in English to the extent that most who use them today are unaware of their biblical origins, or indeed their original meaning.[37]

---

[32] William Hicks, *Apokalypsis apokalypseos, or, The Revelation Revealed Being a Practical Exposition on the Revelation of St. John* (London, 1659), C1ᵛ.

[33] On Revelation in its original context, see Elaine Pagels, *Revelations: Visions, Prophecies, and Politics in the Book of Revelation* (Harmondsworth: Penguin, 2012). On Prince Charles, see Monte Judah, 'The Prince Who is to Come' (Nov. 2001) *Lion and Lamb Ministries*, <http://lionlamb.net/v3/YAVOHArchives/Volume7/11>.

[34] <http://www.angelfire.com/zine2/Number666/index.html>. Chase writes in parentheses 'note Putin's small size'.

[35] See Paul C. Gutjahr, 'From Monarchy to Democracy: The Dethroning of the KJV in the United States', in Hamlin and Jones, *KJB After 400 Years*, 164–78.

[36] John Selden, *The Table-Talk of John Selden*, ed. Samuel Weller Singer (London: Reeves & Turner, 1890), 6.

[37] See David Crystal, *Begat: The King James Bible and the English Language* (Oxford: Oxford University Press, 2010). The first English Bible to use both 'skin of my teeth' and 'apple of the eye' was the 1560 Geneva

The most obvious feature of the King James Bible's style is parataxis, reflecting the tendency of both Hebrew and Greek to favour coordinating over subordinating conjunctions.[38] The King James translators link clauses and sentences with 'and' far more often than other English versions before or since, as in this passage from 2 Kings:

> *And* [Elisha] went up from thence unto Beth-el: *and* as he was going up by the way, there came forth little children out of the city, *and* mocked him, *and* said unto him, Go up thou bald-head, go up, thou bald-head. *And* he turned back, *and* looked on them, *and* cursed them in the name of the Lord. *And* there came forth two she bears out of the wood, *and* tore forty and two children of them. *And* he went from thence to mount Carmel, *and* from thence he returned to Samaria. (2 Kings 2: 23–5; emphasis added)

The strangeness of the narrative is intensified because it is left up to the reader to determine the precise relationship between one clause or sentence and another. Biblical Greek also favours parataxis, as was recognized in the 1520s by Robert Wakefield, Cambridge University's first lecturer in Hebrew.[39] This paratactic style is very different from the complex syntaxis of most seventeenth-century prose. John Donne, Thomas Browne, and Robert Burton quote and allude to the Bible constantly, but their prose style owes more to the Latin classics (whether Cicero or Seneca) than the Old or New Testaments.

Other Hebraisms in the King James Bible include the preference for 'noun + of + noun' constructions rather than using the genitive apostrophe 's': as in the 'flower of the field' (Psalm 103: 15), rather than 'field's flower', or the 'generations of Esau' (Genesis 36: 1) or the 'valley of the shadow of death' (Psalm 23: 4). Another is the use of 'even' to introduce a parallel clause that extends the meaning of the preceding one: 'For the day is near, even the day of the Lord is near, a cloudy day' (Ezekiel 30: 3). The use of 'thereof' as a possessive comes into English through Bible translations, starting with the Wycliffite Bibles in the fifteenth century. They are far more common in the King James Bible: 'and the door of the ark shalt thou set in the side thereof' (Genesis 6: 16), rather than 'the ark's side' or 'in the side of it'; 'The leaves thereof were fair, and the fruit thereof much' (Daniel 4: 12). There are more Hebraisms employed by the Bible translators. Selden and his contemporaries would have found them strange or innovative, though there is no evidence that common people really 'made gear [jeer]' of them, as Selden feared. With time, however, such usage became naturalized. It is still biblical English, a special idiom, but it is English nonetheless, and has been imitated and exploited by non-biblical writers: we hear it in Bunyan and Melville, in Blake and Whitman, and in the oratory of John Bright and Martin Luther King.[40]

Another notable feature of the King James Bible style, at its most successful, is the rhythm of its prose. In one of the few detailed analyses of this style, early in the twentieth century, George Saintsbury suggested that the style's effectiveness lies in its simultaneously

---

Bible, though the phrases, or versions of them, were used as early as the Anglo-Saxons. Here too their ultimate origins are biblical.

[38] The best study of the King James Bible's Hebraic English is Gerald Hammond, *The Making of the English Bible* (Manchester: Carcanet, 1982).

[39] See Gerald Hammond, 'The Sore and Strong Prose of the English Bible', in Neil Rhodes (ed.), *English Renaissance Prose: History, Language, and Politics* (Tempe, Ariz.: Medieval & Renaissance Texts & Studies, 1997), 26. Wakefield termed the New Testament language *hebraicograecum*.

[40] See Hamlin and Jones, *The King James Bible After 400 Years*; Robert Alter, *Pen of Iron: American Prose and the King James Bible* (Princeton: Princeton University Press, 2010).

tending towards and yet ultimately resisting the regularity of metre.[41] The rhythms of biblical prose have a nearly metrical consistency, but enough variety is maintained to avoid monotony:

> And there were in that same country shepherds abiding in the field, keeping watch over their flock by night. And lo, the angel of the Lord came upon them, and the glory of the Lord shone round about them, and they were sore afraid. (Luke 2: 8–9)

The rhythm of these lines is not quite metrical, but it is persistently rising (i.e. iambs and anapests as opposed to trochees and dactlys), with a swing of often two, sometimes one or three, unstressed syllables toward a stressed one ('and there *were*', 'keeping *watch*', 'over their *flock*', 'by *night*'). Similar loose patterning can be seen in the often-quoted song from Isaiah 60:

> Arise, shine; for thy light is come, and the glory of the Lord is risen upon thee.
> For, behold, the darkness shall cover the earth, and gross darkness the people: but the Lord shall arise upon thee, and his glory shall be seen upon thee.
> And the Gentiles shall come to thy light, and kings to the brightness of thy rising.
> (Isaiah 60: 1–3)

Despite its old-fashioned aestheticism and linguistic nationalism, Saintsbury's analysis of this passage is still valuable, since it attempts to explain the phenomena of sound behind its rhetorical power:

> In the very opening we have the benefit of that glorious vowel *i* which, in perfection (though the Germans have something of it in their *ei*) belongs only to English. Its clarion sound is thrice repeated in five words ('thy' has it slightly modified and muffled in note) with indifferent consonants preceding and following in each case, and contrasted in the strongest and most euphonious manner possible with the long *o*'s of 'Glory of the Lord', while the vigour of the contrast shades off into the duller resonances of '*ri*sen *u*pon th*ee* ...'. The opening clause, 'Arise, shine; for thy light is come', is a possible verse; but it is not an obtrusive one, and any suggestion of it being verse at all is at once quenched by the cadence of the second half. It is the same with the next, and throughout; that inevitable nisus [i.e. tendency] towards metre which the ancient critics had noticed being invariably counteracted, neutralised, and turned into 'the other harmony' by succeeding phrases which achieve the prose suggestion and negative the poetic.[42]

C. S. Lewis, in his grumpy critique of the notion of the Bible as Literature, claimed that its rhythms were simply 'unavoidable in the English language'.[43] He surely knew better. All one needs for counterproof are the same passages from the flatter, 'dynamic equivalence' Bible translations of the last century. The Good News Bible is representative:[44]

> Arise, Jerusalem, and shine like the sun; The glory of the Lord is shining on you! Other nations will be covered by darkness, But on you the light of the Lord will shine; The

---

[41] Saintsbury, *English Prose Rhythm*, ch. 6.

[42] Saintsbury, *English Prose Rhythm*, 145–6.

[43] C. S. Lewis, *The Literary Impact of the Authorized Version* (Philadelphia: Fortress Press, 1963), 20.

[44] See Eugene Nida, *Toward a Science of Translating, with Special Reference to Principles and Procedures Involved in Bible Translating* (Leiden: E. J. Brill, 1964).

brightness of his presence will be with you. Nations will be drawn to your light, And kings to the dawning of your new day. (Isaiah 60: 1–3)[45]

Whether the King James translators were conscious of the prose rhythms of their translation is impossible to know. It is perhaps telling that demonstrable sound effects, which have nothing to do with the Hebrew or Greek originals, do suggest the translators were at some level concerned with more than sense alone. The King James Bible passage from Isaiah 60, for instance, as Saintsbury notes, uses assonance to create a clarion call of repeated bright 'eye' sounds: arise, shine, thy, light, Gentiles, brightness, rising. These bright vowels are perfectly suited to Isaiah's prophecy of light (and the vowel of 'light' itself may have inspired the translators to find words to match it). These vowels contrast with the darker, covered vowels of 'For behold, darkness shall cover the earth'. Looking at earlier translations of this passage reinforces the argument for the King James Bible translators' deliberate use of assonance:

> Get thee up betimes, and be bright, O Hierusalem, for thy light cometh, and the glory of the Lord is risen up upon thee.
> For loe, while the darknesse and cloud covereth the earth and the people, the Lord shall shew thee light, and his glory shall be seene in thee.
> The Gentiles shall come to thy light, and kings to the brightnesse that springeth forth upon thee. (Isaiah 60: 1–3, Bishops' 1602)

> Arise, O Jerusalem: be bright, for thy light is come, and the glorie of the Lord is risen upon thee.
> For beholde, darkenes shal cover the earth, and grosse darkenes the people: but the Lord shal arise upon thee, and his glorie shalbe sene upon thee.
> And the Gentiles shal walke in thy light, and Kings at the brightnes of thy rising up. (Isaiah 60: 1–3, Geneva 1560).

In this case, the King James Bible translators (for Isaiah the first Oxford Company, including John Rainolds and Miles Smith) followed the Geneva over the Bishops', but they added still more assonance and further condensed the prose in verses 1 and 3.

Many of the effects of the King James Bible's language are not original, but the translators seem to have known what was worth keeping. Coverdale's wonderful Psalm 22: 20, for instance, they did not touch: 'Deliver my soul from the sword: my darling from the power of the dog'. Or rather they did not touch the Bishops' translation, which kept Coverdale's 'darling' as opposed to the Geneva's 'desolate soule'.[46] The opening of Isaiah 60 in the King James Bible is not only more densely alliterative, with four 'eyes' in the first five words, but the rhythm is more intensely rising without the polysyllabic slackening of 'Jerusalem' and the auxiliary verb 'be' (though 'be bright' has its own alliterative effect). The final 'rising' also seems an improvement on 'rising up', one that again depends on concision. The only surviving evidence of the translation process focuses entirely on capturing the Hebrew words as literally as possible. Perhaps the translators unconsciously shaped the prose

---

[45] Good News Bible, at <www.BibleStudyTools.com>.

[46] The Geneva translators seem to have wanted to preserve Coverdale's alliteration (deliver/darling/dog) but rejected his choice of 'darling'. The Hebrew word here can mean 'solitary' but it is also used poetically to mean 'life' or 'soul'. Geneva recognizes the latter sense as best, but tucks in 'desolate' as well, which maintains the 'd' sound. Robert Alter has the differently alliterative 'Save from the sword my life, from the cur's power my person', *The Book of Psalms*, tr. Robert Alter (New York: W. W. Norton & Co., 2007), 74.

rhythms according to their experience of reading and hearing the Bible in church. Or perhaps they worked at this deliberately, but it didn't get recorded in the documents that survive. However they came to be, the rhythms of the best prose of the King James Bible can be demonstrated critically, as can other features of its literary style or styles.

Many passages from Paul, for instance, work against the King James Bible norm, admitting more complex parataxis and a more Latinate vocabulary:[47]

> And we know that all things work together for good to them that love God, to them who are the called according to his purpose. For whom he did foreknow, he also did predestinate to be conformed to the image of his Son, that he might be the firstborn among many brethren. Moreover whom he did predestinate, them he also called: and whom he called, them he also justified: and whom he justified, them he also glorified.
>
> What shall we then say to these things? If God be for us, who can be against us? He that spared not his own Son, but delivered him up for us all, how shall he not with him also freely give us all things? Who shall lay any thing to the charge of God's elect? It is God that justifieth. Who is he that condemneth? It is Christ that died, yea rather, that is risen again, who is even at the right hand of God, who also maketh intercession for us. (Romans, 8: 28–34)

Along with three 'ands', there are the subordinating conjunctions 'for', 'that', 'but', and 'rather', as well as the conjunctive adverb 'moreover'. The diction of the passage is dominated by Latin polysyllables: 'predestinate', 'conformed', 'justified', 'glorified', 'elect', 'condemneth', 'intercession'. As a result of the translators' linguistic decisions, the style of Paul's theological exposition is recognizably distinct from other kinds of biblical writing. The King James translation is also even more Latinate than Tyndale, who has 'ordained before' instead of 'predestinate', and 'chosen' instead of 'elect'.[48] 'Predestinate' comes from the Bishops' Bible, and 'elect' from the Catholic Rheims New Testament.[49] Matthew's Jesus has a much homelier style than Paul's, especially when speaking to a broad audience, as in the Sermon on the Mount:

> Ye are the salt of the earth: but if the salt have lost its savour, wherewith shall it be salted? It is thenceforth good for nothing, but to be cast out, and to be trodden under foot of men. Ye are the light of the world. A city that is set on a hill cannot be hid. Neither do men light a candle, and put it under a bushel, but on a candlestick, and it giveth light unto all that are in the house. Let your light so shine before men, that they may see your good works, and glorify your Father which is in heaven. (Matthew, 5: 13–16)

Of these 106 words, only 20 are polysyllables, with 'glorify' the only trisyllable. 'Glorify' is also the only word which is notably Latinate. ('City', 'candle', and 'salt' are ultimately Latin borrowings too, but they were imported into English in the Anglo-Saxon period.) The simplicity of diction matches the ordinariness of the metaphors: salt, candle, bushel, house. Paul's language is more abstract, Jesus's (in Matthew) more concrete.

C. S. Lewis was surely right to argue that the main influence of the Bible has been religious rather than literary. It is also important to recognize that the centuries-long

---

[47] As noted, biblical Greek is significantly Hebraized and more paratactic than the classical language, as Wakefield (and perhaps Tyndale?) recognized in the 1520s. See n. 39.

[48] William Tyndale, *Tyndale's New Testament*, ed. David Daniell (New Haven and London: Yale University Press, 1989), 233.

[49] *The Holy Bible* (London, 1602). *The New Testament of Jesus Christ*, tr. Gregory Martin (Rheims, 1582).

dominance of the King James translation among English-speaking Christians depended on printing monopolies and British cultural imperialism as much as on its style or literary qualities.[50] And yet, even if it is difficult to prove it the noblest composition in the universe, it does contain some powerful English prose, in a variety of styles. The same, however, can be said of Tyndale's and Coverdale's translations and the Geneva Bible's. The work of the King James companies was fine-tuning, or one further draft in an ongoing process of revision. That there was no further substantial revision for nearly three centuries would have surprised and perhaps appalled the translators. Whatever the validity of Broughton's specific criticisms of the King James Bible translation, the translators would no doubt have agreed that legitimate improvements to the English Bible should continue to be made, though probably not that their whole work should be burned. In any case, more important than the originality of the prose style of the King James Bible is its influence on the English language and on literature in English, because it was the translation that most English speakers knew for over three centuries: from Milton and Bunyan to Allen Ginsberg and Toni Morrison, it is the specific language of the translation as much as the Bible's content or ideology that marks that influence.

Further Reading

Adams, David and Adrian Armstrong, eds. *Print and Power in France and England, 1500–1800* (Aldershot: Ashgate, 2006).

Baroway, Israel. 'The Bible as Poetry in the English Renaissance: An Introduction'. *Journal of English and Germanic Philology*, 32 (1933): 447–80.

Bloom, Harold. *The Shadow of a Great Rock: A Literary Appreciation of the King James Bible* (New Haven and London: Yale University Press, 2011).

Crystal, David. *Begat: The King James Bible and the English Language* (Oxford: Oxford University Press, 2010).

Hamlin, Hannibal. *Psalm Culture and Early Modern English Literature* (Cambridge: Cambridge University Press, 2004).

Hamlin, Hannibal, and Norman W. Jones, eds, *The King James Bible after 400 Years: Literary, Linguistic, and Cultural Influences* (Cambridge: Cambridge University Press, 2010).

Hammond, Gerald. *The Making of the English Bible* (Manchester: Carcanet, 1982).

Hammond, Gerald. 'The Sore and Strong Prose of the English Bible', in Neil Rhodes, ed., *English Renaissance Prose: History, Language, and Politics* (Tempe, AZ: Medieval & Renaissance Texts & Studies, 1997), 19–34.

Lewis, C.S. *The Literary Impact of the Authorized Version* (Philadelphia: Fortress Press, 1963).

Lowes, John Livingston. 'The Noblest Monument of English Prose', *Essays in Appreciation* (Boston and New York: Houghton Mifflin Company, 1936), 3–31.

Norton, David. *A History of the English Bible as Literature* (Cambridge: Cambridge University Press, 2000).

Norton, David. *The King James Bible: A Short History from Tyndale to Today* (Cambridge: Cambridge University Press, 2011).

[50] See e.g. R. S. Sugirtharajah, 'Postcolonial Notes of the King James Bible', in Hamlin and Jones, *KJB After 400 Years*, 146–63.

....

CHAPTER 30

EPIC, MEDITATION, OR SACRED HISTORY? WOMEN AND BIBLICAL VERSE PARAPHRASE IN SEVENTEENTH-CENTURY ENGLAND

....

SARAH C. E. ROSS

IT is almost axiomatic that the Bible 'lay at the heart' of women's reading and writing practices in early modern England.[1] *Women* is a category of enquiry that encompasses enormous social, educational, and geographical diversities, but it is safe to say that early modern culture encouraged a particular intimacy between the Bible and female literacy at all social levels and in all doctrinal spheres. Conduct books and treatises on women's education focused heavily on the reading and repetition of religious texts and sentences; and the commonplace books and meditational diaries, manuscripts and publications of women across the sixteenth and seventeenth centuries reflect their predominantly religious educations.[2] Women's Bible-centric reading practices in early modern England also informed their generic engagements as writers of theological works, prayers and meditations, psalm versifications, spiritual diaries, and sermon paraphrases, genres that have been 'marginal to early modern literary criticism', in the words of Micheline White.[3] Recent scholarship has done much to redress this critical marginality: to foreground the

---

[1] Femke Molekamp, *Women and the Bible in Early Modern England: Religious Reading and Writing* (Oxford: Oxford University Press, 2013), 1.

[2] See e.g. Kenneth Charlton, *Women, Religion and Education in Early Modern England* (London: Routledge, 1999).

[3] Micheline White, 'Introduction: Women, Religious Communities, Prose Genres, and Textual Production', in White (ed.), *English Women, Religion, and Textual Production, 1500–1625* (Farnham: Ashgate, 2011), 1.

importance of women's religious writing to the intellectual experience and lives of early modern women and men, and to emphasize its level of public engagement.[4] Early modern women, from Anne Askew, Katherine Parr, and Anne Lock at the Reformation, to Mary Astell and Elizabeth Singer Rowe at the end of the seventeenth century, engaged in the social, doctrinal, and political debates of their world through their religious writings.

If the intimacy of early modern women readers with the Bible informs the genres, contexts, and material forms in which they wrote, however, the relationship of these textual practices to the 'high' poetic genres favoured in modern literary canon-formation is more complex. Women's poetry in the sixteenth and seventeenth centuries is heavily focused in religious genres of psalm paraphrase (Mary Sidney), the dream vision (Sidney, Elizabeth Melville, Rachel Speght), the Passion poem (Aemilia Lanyer, 'Elizabeth Middleton', Constance Aston Fowler), and the devotional occasional lyric (Jane Cavendish, An Collins, 'Eliza'). Katherine Philips and Margaret Cavendish, whose secular poetry was published in the mid-seventeenth century, are commonly celebrated as instigating a newly *literary* engagement on the part of women poets, with the literary often defined in explicit contradistinction to the religious.[5] So while it is clear that early modern women's engagement with the Bible facilitated their interpretative and religio-political authority, its effect on the development of women's literary writing is more contested. Exploring women writers' use of the Song of Songs, Elizabeth Clarke wonders whether self-expression via the biblical book in fact obstructed authorship in 'self-consciously literary genres like poetry'.[6] The recovery of early modern women's texts in recent decades has engendered a positive re-evaluation of religious genres, but it is difficult to escape an ongoing sense of critical disappointment at the paucity of high-status female-authored poetry to emerge out of the archive and the period.

Such critical predilections, and early modern women writers' generic choices and preferences, provide the background to this chapter's focus on one particular poetic genre exploited by early modern women that is to date little explored: the biblical verse paraphrase. Lucy Hutchinson's *Order and Disorder* (1679) and its fifteen-canto continuation in manuscript have been much-celebrated in recent years, and can serve to bring the genre into focus. The poem is a retelling of Genesis, including the Fall of Adam and Eve and their exclusion from Paradise; its focus and narrative scope enable direct comparison with Milton's *Paradise Lost*, and the poem has persistently been read and marketed as 'Eve's version of Genesis' and as 'the first epic poem by an Englishwoman'.[7] Such a comparison is on very many levels warranted: like Milton, Hutchinson is a republican writing after the demise of the Good Old Cause and using the Christian story of humanity's fall

[4] Important contributions include Erica Longfellow, *Women and Religious Writing in Early Modern England* (Cambridge: Cambridge University Press, 2004); Kimberly Anne Coles, *Religion, Reform, and Women's Writing in Early Modern England* (Cambridge: Cambridge University Press, 2008); and Elizabeth Clarke, *Politics, Religion and the Song of Songs in Seventeenth-Century England* (Basingstoke: Palgrave Macmillan, 2011).

[5] Hero Chalmers, for example, describes Cavendish's works as inaugurating 'an avowedly literary author moving beyond the notion of religion as a prime motivating force; the birth of the modern woman author': *Royalist Women Writers 1650–1689* (Oxford: Oxford University Press, 2004), 1–2.

[6] Clarke, *Politics*, 161.

[7] David Norbrook, 'A Devine Originall: Lucy Hutchinson and the "Woman's Version"', *TLS* 19 Mar. 1999, 13–15; and the back cover to Lucy Hutchinson, *Order and Disorder*, ed. Norbrook (Oxford: Blackwell, 2001).

as 'an analogy for troubled times'.[8] At the same time, however, Hutchinson's preface and the invocation to her first canto explicitly differentiate her poem not only from Milton's but from the elite culture of poetic invention that epic epitomizes. Several discussions of *Order and Disorder*, including David Norbrook's first notice of it, have exhibited unease about the 'epic' designation of the poem, focusing on its subtitle, 'Meditations upon the Creation and the Fall' and the poem's discursive qualities.[9] Norbrook describes the subtitle's 'Meditations' as implying 'a secondary form of writing, one whose main aim is not to tell a story but to summarise it'; Robert Mayer suggests that the poem is 'not an epic … but … a summary and an interpretation of Genesis'; and Robert Wilcher describes it as a 'verse redaction', suggesting that Francis Quarles's sacred histories, penned in the 1620s, are an important generic precedent.[10]

In this chapter, I suggest that we can shed light on the generic affiliations of Hutchinson's poem if we read it more explicitly in terms of seventeenth-century women's writerly engagements with the Bible. Anne Southwell penned biblical verse paraphrases in the 1620s and 1630s that announce themselves as meditations, as do those of Guillaume de Saluste du Bartas and Francis Quarles, on whom Southwell drew. Each of these texts, like Hutchinson's, uses a meditational mode of biblical verse paraphrase to enter into a digressive poetic retelling of the Bible narrative, encompassing analogous reflections on contemporary British society and politics. Reading *Order and Disorder* in light of Southwell and her models in Du Bartas and Quarles, as well as in conversation with the Christianized Virgilian epic attempted by Abraham Cowley and exemplified in *Paradise Lost*, allows us to identify a 'tradition' of biblical verse paraphrase penned by seventeenth-century women that is not identical with epic—and which, perhaps not coincidentally, frequently exists only in manuscript. There is no evidence that Hutchinson read Southwell—indeed, it seems unlikely that she would have—but reading *Order and Disorder* in relation to Southwell's poems reveals striking commonalities in their generic engagements, extending our understanding of the Bible's position in the gendered writing cultures of early modern England, and of the relationship between religion, the epic and high poetic culture, and other less glamorous literary modes.

The emergence of Lucy Hutchinson's *Order and Disorder* out of the archives itself reflects dominant critical narratives of the Bible, gender, and the status of literary genres. *Order and Disorder: Or, the World Made and Undone. Being Meditations Upon the Creation and the Fall; As It Is Recorded in the Beginning of Genesis* was published anonymously in 1679, and was until 1999 attributed to Hutchinson's brother Sir Allen Apsley—to the extent that any notice was taken of it at all. Reference to a 'very small poem' inspired by Milton's 'very great one' echoes the dismissive critical evaluation that clusters around the biblical verse paraphrases of Frances Quarles ('pious light reading') or the Scots poet-pastor

[8] Back cover to *Order and Disorder*, ed. Norbrook.

[9] Norbrook suggests that the subtitle's description of the poem as meditations 'accords better with the poem's generic affiliations than the Miltonic epic': 'A Devine Originall', 15.

[10] *Order and Disorder*, ed. Norbrook, p. xxv; Robert Mayer, 'Lucy Hutchinson: A Life of Writing', *The Seventeenth Century*, 22 (2007): 317; Robert Wilcher, '"Adventurous song" or "presumptuous folly"': The Problem of "utterance" in John Milton's *Paradise Lost* and Lucy Hutchinson's *Order and Disorder*', *The Seventeenth Century*, 21 (2006): 304, 312 n. 314; and Wilcher, 'Lucy Hutchinson and Genesis: Paraphrase, Epic, Romance', *English*, 59 (2010): 25–42.

James Melville ('religio-literary flatulence').[11] It is only with the poem's attribution to Lucy Hutchinson that critical discussion has become particularly invested in a more positive comparison with Milton. *Order and Disorder* has become Judith Milton's *Paradise Lost*. This reclamation and celebration is well deserved, but I contend in this chapter that the prevalent comparison with Milton's epic is determined by a narrowly canonical view of seventeenth-century biblical poetry, and that it obscures Hutchinson's nuanced engagement with a rather different biblical poetic mode.

Certainly, the five cantos printed as *Order and Disorder* in 1679 are directly comparable to *Paradise Lost* in the structural parallels that they suggest between mankind's undoing of God's created world and the loss of the republican cause.[12] These cantos end, as does *Paradise Lost*, with Adam and Eve's exclusion from Paradise, and Hutchinson 'wind[s] up' the printed poem with a series of 'most certain truths' on God's arrangement of the world's affairs and the providential benefit of suffering (5.675).[13] She describes, 'We cease t'admire a Paradise below, / Rejoice in that which lately was our loss, / And see a crown made up of every cross' (5.696–8), in lines that connote not only Adam and Eve's late loss of Paradise, but her own and republican England's late losses of personal and political kinds. Hutchinson is likely to have begun composing her poem around 1664, making it broadly contemporaneous with Milton's years of composition, and it is entirely possible that the poets knew each other's work in manuscript: both had connections to the Earl of Anglesey and his important private library.[14]

If *Order and Disorder* has much in common with *Paradise Lost*, however, there are also sharp divergences in its frame, content, structure, and style; and it seems very likely that Hutchinson explicitly differentiates her poem from Milton's. She picks up on the 'Meditations' of her second subtitle in the first sentence of her preface, explaining:

> These meditations were not at first designed for public view, but fixed upon to reclaim a busy roving thought from wandering in the pernicious and perplexed maze of human inventions; whereinto the vain curiosity of youth had drawn me to consider and translate the account some old poets and philosophers give of the original of things. (3)

Her consideration of the old poets and philosophers is that of Lucretius's *De rerum natura*, which she translated in her youth; she goes on vehemently to disavow 'those heathenish authors I have been conversant in', and this preface is an explicit recantation of that work.[15] But her insistence on the meditational nature of her poem and her denial of the 'perplexed

---

[11] C. A. Moore, 'Miltoniana (1679–1741)', *Modern Philology*, 24 (1927): 321; Karl Josef Höltgen, 'Quarles, Francis (1592–1644)', *ODNB*, 2004; online edition, Jan. 2008, <http://www.oxforddnb.com/view/article/22945>; Maurice Lindsay, *History of Scottish Literature* (London: Hale, 1977), 109.

[12] The title *Order and Disorder* is given only to the five cantos printed in 1679; the twenty-canto manuscript version of the poem has no title, and it is arguably less applicable to the long version of the poem. For ease of reference, however, I have followed the convention of giving the title to the poem in both its printed and extended versions.

[13] All quotations from Hutchinson's poem are from *Order and Disorder*, ed. Norbrook.

[14] See Annabel Patterson and Martin Dzelzainis, 'Marvell and the Earl of Anglesey: A Chapter in the History of Reading', *Historical Journal*, 44 (2001): 703–26; and Elizabeth Scott-Baumann, *Forms of Engagement: Women, Poetry, and Culture 1640–1680* (Oxford: Oxford University Press, 2013), 175.

[15] See *Lucy Hutchinson's Translation of Lucretius: De rerum natura*, ed. Hugh de Quehen (Ann Arbor, Mich.: University of Michigan Press, 1996); *Order and Disorder*, ed. Norbrook, pp. xvii–xviii.

maze of human inventions' also bear directly on her conception of divine poetry, one that she seems to articulate against Milton's ambitious, inventive epic. She protests that those who read her poem 'will find nothing of fancy in it; no elevations of style, no charms of language'; and she asks in the invocation to the first canto, 'Let not my thoughts beyond their bounds aspire' (1.42), in striking contrast to Milton's invocation of 'aid to my adventurous song, / That with no middle flight intends to soar / Above the Aonian mount' (I.13–15). In what appears to be a direct attack on Milton's extensive imagining of the war in heaven, she says, 'what hath been / Before the race of time did first begin, / It were presumptuous folly to inquire' (1.39–41). Hutchinson reiterates throughout her poem an aversion to 'gross poetic fables' (4.49), and to the ambitious poetics that Milton seeks to embrace in his soaring opening lines.[16]

Hutchinson's prefatory discourse is one of rhetorical modesty and unadorned scripturalism; it is also emphatically one of female *contemplation*. She insists that 'all the language I have, is much too narrow to express the least of those wonders my soul hath been ravished with in the contemplation of God and his works' (p. 5); she approaches her theme in 'endless admiration' (1.15); and she describes her explicitly female soul's 'imperfect strugglings' and 'rude conceptions' (1.28–9). Such expressions of poetic passivity and conceptual weakness can, of course, be read as gendered and conventional modesty tropes, of the kind that Patricia Pender has recently warned against reading in literal terms. Pender argues compellingly against the gynocritical impulse to ascribe autobiographical 'truth-value' to women's disavowals of authorship. As she points out, when Milton presents himself as 'Not skilled nor studious' (*PL*, IX.42), 'the image that we get is not one of Milton's deep-seated insecurity. Instead, it is one of his colossal ambition'.[17]

Pender's emphasis on the rhetorical nature of women's modesty tropes is timely; but we need also to sift from the conventionalities of Hutchinson's preface and invocation the assertions of poetic genre that are present in it, and attend to them. Just as we afford enormous respect to Milton's paratextual engagements in questions of genre and topical decorum—his delineation of *Samson Agonistes* as a Senecan closet drama, his elaboration on the verse style of *Paradise Lost*, and his invocatory declaration of the poem's theodicy—so we need to consider the literary-critical 'truth-value' in Hutchinson's declaration of her poem's genre, and its bearing on the work that follows.

What, then, does Hutchinson mean when she describes her poetic posture as one of contemplation, and her poem as 'Meditations'? Her subtitle and invocation align her poem with a model of divine poetry that derives from the writings of the French Protestant poet Guillaume de Saluste du Bartas: a divine poetry that is relatively unambitious in literary terms, that is discursive, and that is not identical with Milton's Christianized epic.[18] Du Bartas's biblical verse paraphrases were enormously popular in Scotland and England. James VI translated *L'Uranie* and published it in *The Essayes of a Prentise, in the Divine Art of Poesie* (1584), and Josuah Sylvester translated *La semaine ou création du monde* (1578)

---

[16] Robert Wilcher offers a detailed outline of Hutchinson's differentiations, in '"Adventurous song" or "presumptuous folly"', and 'Lucy Hutchinson and *Genesis*'.

[17] Patricia Pender, *Early Modern Women's Writing and the Rhetoric of Modesty* (Basingstoke: Palgrave Macmillan, 2012), 3, 7.

[18] The classic study of divine poetry in the period is Lily B. Campbell, *Divine Poetry and Drama in Sixteenth-Century England* (Cambridge: Cambridge University Press, 1959).

and *La seconde semaine* (1584) as *Bartas: His Devine Weekes and Workes* in 1605, a text that became a favourite of English readers, female and male.[19] Susan Snyder has enumerated the English imitators and followers of Du Bartas, from Drayton, Aylett and Quarles to Cowley and Milton; as she makes clear, these poetic imitations were not only multitudinous but, crucially, generically diverse.[20] All divine poetry in seventeenth-century Britain owes something to Du Bartas's harnessing of secular verse forms to sacred subject matter, but the inheritances of Southwell, Quarles, and Hutchinson are not identical to those of Cowley and Milton. Critical precision is vital in delineating the 'Bartasian' traces and influences in any given text.

Du Bartas's *L'Uranie* (in James VI's translation) sets out a manifesto for the writing of a divine poetry that differentiates itself from the classical tradition. Du Bartas casts aside the muses of secular arts, and numerous and elaborated modes of secular writing—'Princes flattry', the 'honnie' of Pindar, Virgil's efforts as Homer's disciple, and 'verse prophane'— declaring that 'man from man must wholly parted be, / If with his age, his verse do well agree'.[21] He invokes instead Urania, the muse of divine poetry, and in the first of his *Weeks*, he also sets out his poetic enterprise with a declared focus on the divine:

> My heedfull *Muse*, trayned in true Religion
> Devinely-humane keepes the middle Region:
> Least, if she should too-high a pitch presume,
> Heav'ns glowing flame should melt her waxen plume. (1.1.135–8)[22]

Du Bartas's divine poetry is not, of course, entirely modest, but he claims neither the epic tradition nor the language of extreme poetic ambition that marks Milton's later poem. His insistence on keeping the 'middle region' is a precedent for Lucy Hutchinson's insistence that her thoughts must not 'beyond their bounds aspire', and it is representative of a more democratic and demotic poetic. This poetic is less attractive to modern readers than the poetically canonical works of Milton (indeed, Du Bartas rapidly fell out of fashion as the seventeenth century progressed), but it was clearly enabling for women writers, enjoined to be 'silent but for the word' and relatively uneducated in classical rhetoric or literature.[23]

If Du Bartas eschews the ambitious poetics of classical epic, his divine poems are also explicitly discursive, defined against the structural principles of epic and its focus on a hero. Du Bartas countered those who '*accuse me … that I have neglected the Rules which Aristotle and Horace prescribe as proper to heroicke Poets*' with the defence that '*my second Weeke is not (no more then my first) a worke purely Epique or Heroique*', and he expands:

> *Heere I simply set down the History, there I move affections: Heere I call upon God, there I yeeld his thankes: heere I sing a Hymne unto him, & there I vomit out a Satyre against the*

---

[19] Du Bartas's *La muse Chrestiene* comprised *L'Uranie, La Judit,* and *Le triomfe de la foi* (Bordeaux, 1574). Philip Sidney translated *La Première Semaine* in manuscript in the 1580s, but the translation is lost (Alan Sinfield, 'Sidney and Du Bartas', *Comparative Literature,* 27 (1975): 8–20).

[20] *The Divine Weeks and Works of Guillaume De Saluste, Sieur Du Bartas, Translated by Josuah Sylvester,* ed. Susan Snyder (Oxford: Clarendon Press, 1979), i. 79–80.

[21] James VI and I, 'The Uranie or heauenly Muse translated', in *The Essayes of a Prentise, in the Divine Art of Poesie* (Edinburgh, 1584), D4ʳ and E1ʳ.

[22] *Divine Weeks and Works,* ed. Snyder, i. 115.

[23] Anne Lake Prescott, 'The Reception of Du Bartas in England', *Studies in the Renaissance,* 15 (1968): 144–73.

Vices of mine Age; Heere I instruct men in good manners, there in piete: Here I discourse of naturall things and other-where I praise good spirits.[24]

This unfortunate admission of verbal vomiting notwithstanding, Du Bartas's description of his own poetic is accurate. The *Devine Weekes* (and Sylvester's translation of them) are famously digressive, capacious, and various in their retelling of the creation of the world and the history of mankind; as Susan Snyder describes, the Bartasian 'aesthetic instinct was compendious rather than selective'.[25] This aesthetic contrasts sharply with the genealogy of epic heroism that runs from Virgil's *Aeneid* through Cowley's *Davideis* to Milton's *Paradise Lost*; as Cowley describes of his own epic poem, 'I designed [it] … after the *Patern* of our Master *Virgil*'.[26]

One woman reader of Du Bartas who composed biblical verse paraphrases according to his model is Anne Southwell, whose two manuscripts of the 1620s and 1630s include extended verses on the Ten Commandments.[27] These Decalogue verses evoke precisely the language of Du Bartas, whose *Devine Weekes* in Sylvester's translation is named (as 'Salust his history in English') in her booklist.[28] She opens her verse on the first commandment, 'Thou shalt have no other Gods before me', with an invocation of an exclusively sacred muse:

> Raise vp thy ffacultyes my Soule ti's time
> to Wake ffrom Idleness the Childe of death
> Mount to the heauens, and ther thy wings subblime
> wheare bodies liue, not bound to hassard breath
> And being dipt in heauens Selestiall Springes
> My penn shall portrait Supernaturall thinges. (1–6)

Southwell asks that 'fayth, hope, loue, zeale, assist my limber winges' so that she 'with reuerence shall ascend gods bower', but she is eager to insist that the attempt of heavenly flight is not an ambitious one:

> Presumptuous knowledge was the angells fall
> presumptuous knowledge wrought poore Adams woe
> O sacred wisdome, iudge and guide of all
> true limiter, how farre ech witt should goe
> with mediocritye asist my flight
> as free from fogges, as farre from winges to light. (43–8)[29]

[24] 'The Advertisement of William of Salust, Lord of Bartas, upon the first and second Weeke', in Simon Goulart, *A Learned Summary upon the Famous Poeme of William of Saluste, Lord of Bartas*, tr. Thomas Lodge (1621), ¶10ʳ; and see Chloe Wheatley, *Epic, Epitome, and the Early Modern Historical Imagination* (Farnham: Ashgate, 2011), 72.
[25] *Divine Weeks and Works*, ed. Snyder, i. 2.
[26] This epic genealogy is explored by Sue Starke in '"The Eternal Now": Virgilian Echoes and Miltonic Premonitions in Cowley's "Davideis"', *Christianity and Literature*, 55 (2006): 195, 199. See Cowley, 'The Preface', *Poems* (1656), (b)1ᵛ.
[27] Folger Library, MS V.b.198 and British Library, Lansdowne MS 740, both edited in *The Southwell-Sibthorpe Commonplace Book: Folger MS V.b.198*, ed. Jean Klene, Renaissance English Text Society, 7th ser. 20 (Tempe, Ariz.: Medieval & Renaissance Texts & Studies, 1997).
[28] *Southwell-Sibthorpe Commonplace Book*, ed. Klene, 99. All quotations are from this edition.
[29] *Southwell-Sibthorpe Commonplace Book*, ed. Klene, 44–6.

Southwell's insistence on 'mediocritye' is in part a modesty trope (later, she refers to the 'waxen plewmes' of the 'weake female'), but more importantly, it explicitly echoes Du Bartas's sense of 'keep[ing] the middle Region'.[30] Her invocation then moves into an image of her subject matter which again derives from the opening of Du Bartas's long verse. For Du Bartas, the world is 'A paire of Staires, whereby our mounting Soule / Ascends by steps above the Arched Pole' (1.1.159–60); for Southwell, the Decalogue, the 'tenne precepts by Iehouah spoken', are 'tenne steppes to this high throne', the throne of heaven (89, 85).[31] Du Bartas's subject matter is the creation of the world, and Southwell delimits hers, in theory at least, to the Decalogue, but a vital Bartasian influence and commonality of mode is intimated in Southwell's opening stanzas.

In a letter to her friend Cicely, Lady Ridgeway, celebrating 'devine Poesye', she describes her biblical verse paraphrases in meditational terms.[32] She is 'affected vnto rime / but as it is a help to memorye', and because it 'gives wittes fire more fuell / & from an Ingott formes a curious Iewell', descriptions evocative both of the brief occasional meditation modelled by Joseph Hall and of Lucy Hutchinson's reclamation of a 'busy roving thought'.[33] And her rhetoric of exclusive piousness notwithstanding, Southwell's meditations are also distinctly discursive, exhibiting a tendency to 'wheel away from the particular to the general', as Danielle Clarke puts it in describing her elegies.[34] Her stanzas on the fourth commandment in the Folger manuscript, for example, move into a lengthy moralizing diversion which, at face value, is only loosely connected to the biblical precept that 'Thou shalt keep holy the sabbath day'. 'Thy children modelize thyself', she declares, before proffering advice across twenty-two stanzas on keeping sons from drink and the court, daughters from dancing, cosmetics, and 'the stamp of fashions'; this precipitates a further, fifteen-stanza section on the arts—metaphysics, philosophy, music, astronomy, poetry—which are the accomplishments and weapons of God's soldiers.[35] These are extraordinary, meandering poetic structures that shed light on Hutchinson's later poetic discursions. Southwell's meditational poetic structure offers her, it seems, a large degree of freedom to speculate on moral and social affairs—a freedom that takes its lead in part from Du Bartas himself, for whom 'The World's a Schoole, where (in a generall Storie) / God alwayes reades dumbe Lectures of his Glorie'.[36]

Southwell's Decalogue verses echo Du Bartas, but her closest influence is likely to have been a poet in his image: Francis Quarles, another favourite of the woman reader, who published several biblical verse paraphrases in the 1620s. A Feast for Wormes: Set Forth in a Poeme of the History of Jonah (1620), Hadassa: Or, The History of Queene Ester: With Meditations thereupon, Divine and Morall (1621), Job Militant: With Meditations Divine and Morall (1624), and The Historie of Samson (1630) are almost entirely overlooked

[30] Southwell-Sibthorpe Commonplace Book, ed. Klene, 72.
[31] The Divine Weeks and Works, ed. Snyder, i. 115–16; Southwell-Sibthorpe Commonplace Book, ed. Klene, 47.
[32] Southwell-Sibthorpe Commonplace Book, ed. Klene, 5.
[33] Southwell-Sibthorpe Commonplace Book, ed. Klene, 130, 152; for Hall, see Frank Livingstone Huntley, Bishop Joseph Hall and Protestant Meditation in Seventeenth-Century England (Binghampton, NY: Medieval & Renaissance Texts & Studies, 1981).
[34] Danielle Clarke, The Politics of Early Modern Women's Writing (Harlow: Longman, 2001), 174.
[35] Southwell-Sibthorpe Commonplace Book, ed. Klene, 62–9.
[36] The Divine Weeks and Works, ed. Snyder, i. 115.

in critical explorations of Quarles himself, let alone the writers he influenced, no doubt because they extend Du Bartas's model in a pious and popular, rather than an avowedly literary way.[37] Quarles describes these poems as 'periphrases' of 'sacred history', and they are digressive, meditative, and outspokenly political.

Quarles evokes Urania as his sacred Muse, but he sets out in several prefaces to his readers what he describes as a new poetic 'manner' (or method) *consisting in the Periphrase, the adjournment of the Story, and interposition of Meditations*.[38] Quarles's meditations evolve out of and interrupt the sacred history being retold: each meditation is explicitly demarcated from the poem's main text by a decorative band, and generalities are extrapolated from the thrust of the main text. Quarles divides his moral meditations into three kinds: ethical (*'the Manners of a private man'*), political (*'Publike Society'*, including *'the behaviour of a Prince, to his Subject* and of *the Subject to his Prince'*), and *oeconomicall* in the sense of household management (*'Private Society'*, including *'the carriage of the Wife, to her Husband*, and *of the Husband, to his Wife, in ruling'*).[39] Quarles insists on direct parallels between the sacred and the contemporary, instructing: *'I have gleaned some few* Meditations, *obvious to the* History; *Let me advise thee to keepe the* Taste *of the* History, *whilest thou readest the* Meditations, *and that will make thee* Rellish *both, the better'*.[40]

Anne Southwell's admiration for Francis Quarles is declared in an ingenious, interlinking acrostic poem in her Folger manuscript, where she describes him as 'Quaintest of all the Heliconian traine'.[41] Her admiration must be based on Quarles's early works, as his more famous *Emblemes* were not published until 1635, the year before Southwell's death; and as the Folger manuscript has been compiled, the acrostic's placement emphasizes its material connection to her own biblical verse paraphrases. It occurs on folio 17, interposed between (on the one hand) her first scriptural paraphrase on the Decalogue and a brief and witty lyric on the creation of Adam (fols 12–16), and (on the other) a 122-line poem on the creation of Adam, addressed to Bishop Adams of Limerick (fols 18–19ʳ). Her acrostic is therefore positioned amidst her own biblical verse paraphrases, in what may be a deliberate act on the part of the manuscript's compiler, and even the witty lyric on the creation of Adam later reappears, integrated into a rewritten version of her poem on Genesis, this time addressed to her neighbour and parish curate in Acton, Roger Cox. Southwell's propensity to rewrite and readdress biblical poetry to social affiliates is a topic for discussion elsewhere, but her acrostic and its location in the Folger manuscript suggest a direct relationship between her biblical verse paraphrases and those of Francis Quarles.[42]

Southwell's poem on Genesis to Roger Cox—another author of biblical verse paraphrase—includes commentary on the 'oeconomicall' arrangements between husbands and wives that may respond directly to Quarles, and not entirely in slavish

---

[37] The exceptions are Wilcher, 'Lucy Hutchinson and *Genesis*', 29–32; and Adrian Streete, 'Frances Quarles' Early Poetry and the Discourses of Jacobean Spenserianism', *Journal of the Northern Renaissance*, 1 (2009): 88–108.

[38] See Quarles's prefaces to the reader, *A Feast for Wormes* (1620), *Hadassa: Or, the History of Queene Ester* (1621), and *Job Militant* (1624).

[39] Quarles, *Hadassa*, 'A Preface to the Reader', A3ᵛ.

[40] Quarles, *A Feast for Wormes*, 'To the Reader', ¶2ʳ.

[41] *Southwell-Sibthorpe Commonplace Book*, ed. Klene, 20.

[42] I discuss these poems in more detail in *Women, Poetry, and Politics in Seventeenth-Century Britain* (Oxford: Oxford University Press, 2015).

admiration. Southwell adds a number of starkly polemical lines to the opening of her poem, remonstrating with her addressee on his 'resolved' and wilfully heretical views 'In thinking ffemales haue so little witt / as but to serue men they are only fit' (5–6).[43] She continues her defence of Eve in the lines that follow:

> [God] brought her vnto Adam as a bride
>   the text saith shee was taken from his syde
> A symbolle of that syde from whence did flowe
>   Christ's spouse (the Church) as all wise men doe knowe
> But Adam slept, as saith the historie,
>   vncapable of such a mistarie
> And they sleepe still that doe not vnderstand
>   the curiouse ffabrick of th'almighties hand. (15–22)[44]

These lines are a version of the brief, witty lyric that is self-standing on folio 16[r]; both versions are in keeping with combative texts of the *querelle des femmes*, providing an acerbic indictment of men's assumption of women's subordinacy.

Southwell's willingness to engage in contemporary social questions through biblical verse paraphrase and its modification is manifest; quite what she is responding to is less obvious. Cox's own biblical paraphrase contains no clear provocation but, curiously, Quarles's *Hadassa* does: a meditation on the creation of Eve, prompted by Queen Vashti's disobedience, in which Quarles (via King Assuerus's vice-regent Memucan) at length 'propound[s] the height of her offence'. Memucan pronouces, '*Since of a Rib first framed was a Wife, / Let Ribs be Hi'rogliphicks of their life*', and he extracts numerous misogynist morals from the hieroglyph; for example, '*Ribs are firmely fixt, and seldome moue: / Women (like Ribs) must keepe their wonted home, / And not (like Dinah that was rauish't) rome*'.[45] The passage ends with a lengthy insistence that husbands must command and wives obey, the very principle to which Southwell turns in argument after her lines on Eve's creation out of Adam's rib: 'God made a helper meete and can you think / a fool a help, vnless a help to sink'.[46] There seems to be little question that the lines on folio 26 are addressed to Cox—a reference to their 'noble neighbour' Featley appears to tie it to the Acton community in which they all lived—but it is tempting to believe that Southwell has Quarles in mind as she presents her defence of Eve. Even if this defence is not a direct riposte to Quarles, a generic debt is manifest in her rewritten lines on Genesis, which interrupt sacred history as Quarles's meditations do to make explicit social comment and, indeed, to enter into controversy with the 'oeconomicall' views that Quarles presents.

Quarles's description of his poems as 'periphrases of sacred history' provides another productive generic category for thinking about his own work and Southwell's: it reflects a focus on a broad sweep of biblical history rather than on one particular hero with Christian epic potential, and both he and Southwell use their retelling of biblical history to

---

[43] Jonathan Gibson has demonstrated that the leaf on which this poem has been written has been tipped into the Folger manuscript the wrong way around, meaning that the poem needs to be read from recto to verso ('Synchrony and Process: Editing Manuscript Miscellanies', *SEL* 52/1 (2012): 85–100, 90–3.

[44] *Southwell-Sibthorpe Commonplace Book*, ed. Klene, 42.

[45] Quarles, *Hadassa*, D3[r-v].

[46] *Southwell-Sibthorpe Commonplace Book*, ed. Klene, 42. Memucan's disquisition is an expansion of Esther 1: 16–17.

meditate, more and less explicitly, on the state politics of their own time. Quarles uses his poetic 'manner' to sound clarion political notes, particularly in *Hadassa: Or, the History of Qveene Ester*, dedicated to James I and entered in the Stationer's Register in the same month that James recalled Parliament in the political crisis of January 1621.[47] Quarles's nineteen interpolated meditations return again and again to principles of good and just kingship—at times with an arbitrariness which tests our ability to '*keepe the* Taste *of the* History' in mind. For example, when Esther is brought before King Assuerus, who will choose her as his new wife, Quarles enters into a meditation on the importance of wise and mature counsel, beginning:

> The strongest Arcteries that knit and tye
> The members of a mixed Monarchy,
> Are learned Councels, timely Consultations,
> Rip'ned Advice, and sage Deliberations.

Richard II, he declares, was undone by 'greene advisements', and the meditation concludes with a rousing address to 'My sacred Sov'raigne, in whose onely brest, / A wise Assembl' of Privy Councels rest'.[48] In the context of January 1621, when tension flared between James and the Parliament he was forced to recall, these are strong endorsements of the King's ultimate authority in the model of mixed monarchy to which Quarles refers. Quarles's anti-militant royalist sympathies are most explicit in his twenty-ninth and penultimate meditation, where he concludes that moral law 'lyes in Kings', and 'A lawfull King / Is God's Lieu-tenant; in his sacred eare / God whispers oft, and keepes his Presence there'.[49]

Southwell's politicized digressions are more oblique, and most evident in her verses on the third and fourth commandments, which appear in the Folger manuscript and, in extended and variant versions, in the Lansdowne manuscript addressed 'to the King'. Her Folger lines on the fourth commandment echo Quarles in delineating the 'Ethicks', 'polyticks', and 'Economicks' that comprise God's soldier, 'he [who] governe[s] like a heauen on earth' (315–17, 321). Three stanzas follow which clearly describe James VI and I, lauded for 'his books, his woorks, his pyety'. Southwell, like Quarles, may be making an anti-militant comment on events of the early 1620s, as she describes an 'all peacefull king' who 'pulls noe neyboure princese by the ears / but Immytates that threefolde deytye / and governes gratiusly in his own sphears' (328, 334–6). A long passage in the Lansdowne verses on the third precept focuses, as does Quarles in his *Hadassa*, on the role of evil advisers, in what appears to be a particularly pointed reference to a specific political machination. Subjects who are false to 'the Lordes anoynted' are likened to Achitophel and Judas, and Southwell reflects that 'I cannott chuse but smile to see these bladders / grow only bigg wth a pestiferous wind, / like naked Iackdawes tumbling from theyr ladders' (379, 397–9). She concludes these several stanzas with a prayer that 'all Catelines may perish'—a reference to the Roman politician Catiline, whose conspiracy to overthrow the Roman Republic was the subject of Ben Jonson's *Catiline His Conspiracy* (1611)—and that, in contrast, 'our Augustus happily may florish' (413–14).[50] It is unclear whether the Lansdowne manuscript is dedicated to James I

---

[47] Streete, 'Frances Quarles' Early Poetry', 98.   [48] Quarles, *Hadassa*, E2[r–v].

[49] *The Complete Works in Prose and Verse of Francis Quarles*, ed. Alexander B. Grosart (New York: AMS Press, 1967), ii. 66.

[50] *Southwell-Sibthorpe Commonplace Book*, ed. Klene, 136–7.

or Charles I, but it seems likely that the expression of loyalty here is addressed to James as, twelve stanzas later, Southwell makes passing reference to his *Daemonologie* (1597).[51]

It is unlikely that Lucy Hutchinson would have known Anne Southwell's poems of the 1620s and 1630s, occurring as they did only in manuscript; and any direct influence of Quarles upon her is necessarily of a more distant and diffuse kind. Hutchinson may well have looked to Cowley in admiration—Milton did, and Cowley became a great favourite among women poets—and it is entirely likely she shared Cowley's view that 'if any man design to compose a *Sacred Poem*, by onely turning a story of the *Scripture*, like Mr. *Quarls's* ... ; He is so far from elevating of *Poesie*, that he onely *abases Divinity*'.[52] Hutchinson nonetheless adopts the framework of the meditational retelling of sacred history, and the parallels between Southwell's, Quarles's, and Hutchinson's poems are suggestive of continuities as well as evolutions in the biblical poetic modes adopted by women writers through the seventeenth century. Southwell and Hutchinson each engage in a mode of biblical verse paraphrase that distinguishes itself against epic, and that repeatedly steps away from the scriptural story to moralize on the social and 'economic' arrangements of their day, and to draw parallels between sacred and contemporaneous political history. Quarles's advice to his readers to '*keepe the* Taste *of the* [sacred] History, *whilest thou redest the* Meditations' articulates precisely the direct parallels between sacred and contemporary history that the discursive and digressive biblical verse paraphrases of Southwell and Hutchinson work to establish.

In its incomplete, twenty-canto version, *Order and Disorder* takes in a broad sweep of sacred history, and throughout the poem Hutchinson uses meditational digressions to step out of the biblical history and comment on social arrangements such as the relationships between husbands and wives. Eve's creation out of Adam's rib prompts a celebration of the value of marriage as an institution that 'curbs and cures wild passions' and provides solace against the threats of death and solitude (3.433–56). Hutchinson's gender politics are conservative, as commentators have noted; she adheres to a strict hierarchy of male above female.[53] Eve's creation in *Order and Disorder*, however, is neither a prompt for misogynistic moralizing (as for Quarles) nor evidence of Adam's blockishness (as for Southwell); rather, it is an illustration that providence works to do us good even 'When we locked up in stupefaction lie' (3.461). Eve is 'A sweet instructive emblem ... to us' (3.458), formed out of sleeping Adam's side, a description that makes explicit a proximity between the moralizing meditation and the emblem that came to infuse mid-seventeenth-century meditational poetics, not least under the influence of Quarles's *Emblemes* (1635).[54] In the spiritual

---

[51] Elizabeth Clarke explores Southwell's poetic responses to James I's Declaration of Sports (1618), and to the Family of Love, in 'Anne, Lady Southwell: Coteries and Culture', in Johanna Harris and Elizabeth Scott-Baumann (eds), *The Intellectual Culture of Puritan Women* (Basingstoke: Palgrave Macmillan, 2011), 57–70.

[52] Kathryn R. King, 'Cowley among the Women: Or, Poetry in the Contact Zone', in Katherine Binhammer and Jeanne Wood (eds), *Woman and Literary History: 'For There She Was'* (Newark, Del.: University of Delaware Press, 2003), 43–63. Cowley, 'The Preface', *Poems* (1656), ¶9ʳ. For the fortunes of Quarles's reputation in the seventeenth century, see Arthur Nethercot, 'The Literary Legend of Francis Quarles', *Modern Philology*, 20 (1923): 225–40.

[53] Joseph Wittreich, assuming the poem was Sir Allen Apsley's, was able to read it as correcting Milton's transgressional insinuation of equality between Adam and Eve: 'Milton's Transgressive Maneuvers: Receptions (Then and Now) and the Sexual Politics of *Paradise Lost*', in Stephen B. Dobranski and John P. Rumrich (eds), *Milton and Heresy* (Cambridge: Cambridge University Press, 1998), 250–2.

[54] Quarles's *Emblemes* ran to eighteen editions in the next ninety years.

mode exemplified by Quarles, the emblem was closely related to the occasional meditation promulgated by Joseph Hall and adopted by women writers from Jane Cavendish to
Hester Pulter; and it encouraged and codified the typological reading of the Bible as bearing directly on the seventeenth-century world.[55]

Hutchinson, like Southwell, uses the digressive structure of the biblical verse paraphrase
to merge social comment and pointedly political critique, bringing the sacred history to
bear on 'public' as well as 'private' and 'economic' matters. Southwell's Lansdowne poem
on the third commandment rails against the 'peacocks of the court' and those who 'from
tauernes come to heare a preaching'; she describes Lot and Noah as 'drownd in wine' and
she condemns the drunken courtiers who defend them by spinning the scriptures to their
own ends, 'vs[ing] gods worde as wolues doe vse theyr holes'.[56] Southwell's acerbic critique
of court drunkenness parallels in its theme as well as its digressive structure the lengthy
and politicised condemnation of Noah that Hutchinson incorporates into the ninth canto
of her Genesis poem. Noah is 'stupefied with liquor' (9.12), and Hutchinson breaks with the
scriptural narrative to elaborate on the ills of inebriation over 170 lines, before returning at
last to Noah, 'the new world's monarch', who 'here lies drunk' (9.187). Hutchinson's excoria-
tion of social ills here shores up a sharp condemnation of the dissolute English Restoration
king, and the copious structure of the sacred history, interposed with meditations, repeatedly enables her to create space for social, moral, and political commentary of this kind.
God's designation of six days for Adam's use, for example, instigates a particularly pointed
disquisition on the responsibility of kings to maintain their realms 'As guardians, not as
owners of the land', and not to spend their days 'drunk with his sensual pleasures, / ... / As
now his fall'n sons do, that arrogate / His forfeited dominion and high state' (3.635, 628–31).

Hutchinson, then, uses the discursive and emblematic potential of biblical verse paraphrase to pointed political effect, applying the sacred history to the contemporaneous to
reflect upon the political culture of post-Restoration England. Nimrod, a favourite type of
the tyrant in mid-century royalist and republican literature alike, is the subject of one such
emblematic vignette: in Hutchinson's poem, his status as father to 'the first mighty monarchs of the earth' is sullied by his descent from 'Noah's graceless son' Ham (10.10, 19–20).
Nimrod's 'vain arrogance' (10.91) in attempting to reach heaven is thus associated, as it is in
Paradise Lost, with the false pride of earthly monarchs. Significantly, Nimrod's construction of the Tower of Babel also constitutes an emblematic moment in Milton's epic poem.
The vision of Nimrod's vainglorious attempt to claim sovereignty from heaven prompts
Adam to expostulate against his 'execrable son' and Michael to drive home the moral of
the vision: 'Justly thou abhorr'st / That son, who on the quiet state of men / Such trouble
brought, affecting to subdue / Rational liberty' (XII.64, 79–82).

Adam and Michael's dialogic summations articulate the moral to the emblematic scriptural episode, as does their dialogue of this kind throughout books XI and XII of Milton's
poem. Indeed, in books XI and XII, Milton's epic is at its closest to the episodic, discursive,
and emblematic structure that marks the paraphrastic elaboration of scripture; this can
hardly be coincidental, given the close association of the emblem and the biblical verse

---

[55] For the emblem, the devotional lyric, and women writers, see Ross, *Women, Poetry, and Politics*; and
Alice Eardley (ed.), *Lady Hester Pulter: Poems, Emblems, and The Unfortunate Florinda* (Toronto: Centre
for Reformation and Renaissance Studies, 2014).

[56] *Southwell-Sibthorpe Commonplace Book*, ed. Klene, 129–30.

paraphrase with didactic and moralizing poetics, and given that Michael's aim in these books is to teach Adam (and the reader) through the revelation of sacred history.[57] Given also the persistent critical evaluation of emblematics and biblical verse paraphrase as secondary or subliterary modes of writing, it is surely no coincidence that books XI and XII of *Paradise Lost* have been criticized as insufficiently poetic. C. S. Lewis, for example, described them as an 'untransmuted lump'.[58]

Even the pre-eminent biblical epic in the English literary canon, then, is touched by the digressive, moralizing, and emblematic mode of biblical verse paraphrase epitomized by Du Bartas and Quarles and embraced by women writers: generic variegation is itself a feature of Milton's epic poem.[59] Lucy Hutchinson's poem on Genesis, similarly, needs to be read as a nuanced, knowing, and adept engagement with the biblical verse narrative meditation, an engagement that also encompasses aspects of more elite literary modes. Hutchinson is a different poet to Southwell in very many ways: her elite intellectual pedigree—her 'expensive' literary tastes—are evident not only in her Lucretius translation but in her commonplace book, which incorporates translations of Virgil's *Aeneid* by John Denham and Sidney Godolphin, and her own translations on lines of love from Ovid.[60] Emblematic passages in her poem are directly indebted to Virgil and Ovid, as David Norbrook and Edward Paleit have shown: her description of Lot's wife is modelled on the petrification of Niobe in Ovid's *Metamorphoses*; and that of the Babel Tower's construction alludes to Virgil's description of the building of Carthage.[61] Her close interest in Denham's and Godolphin's translations, and in classicizing allusion, underscores a temperamental as well as a temporal distance from Du Bartas and Quarles, favourites of the typical seventeenth-century woman reader; at the same time, it makes all the more striking her choice not to frame her Genesis poem as epic.

Other comparisons are possible. Mary Roper's *The Sacred Historie* (c.1669–70), a biblical verse paraphrase of Genesis roughly contemporaneous to Hutchinson's poem, retells key episodes in bald couplets, and uses the history of Joseph to lament the demise of Charles I and celebrate the restoration of his son. Roper intensifies the emblematic implications of her narrative through cutting and pasting into her manuscript illustrations from Henry Hills's illustrated Bible (1660) and the *Eikon Basilike* (1649); her text offers a less elite, more material, and arguably more feminine illustration of the contemporaneous political work

---

[57] Barbara Kiefer Lewalski notes that 'Michael's lectures on Christian historiography' in books 11 and 12 are among those sections of the poem that 'have not been much studied from the perspective of genre': 'The Genres of *Paradise Lost*', in Dennis Danielson (ed.), *The Cambridge Companion to Milton*, 2nd edn (Cambridge: Cambridge University Press, 1999), 114. Alastair Fowler refers in passing to Milton's reliance in them on the model of 'Bartasian epic': *Kinds of Literature: An Introduction to the Theory of Genres and Modes* (Oxford: Clarendon Press, 1982), 175.

[58] C. S. Lewis, *A Preface to Paradise Lost* (Oxford, 1942), 123; see H. R. MacCallum, 'Milton and Sacred History': Books XI and XII of *Paradise Lost*', in M. MacLure and F. W. Watt (eds), *Essays in English Literature from the Renaissance to the Victorian Age, Presented to A. S. P. Woodhouse* (Toronto: University of Toronto Press, 1964), 149.

[59] See Lewalski, 'Genres of *Paradise Lost*'.

[60] Jerome de Groot, 'John Denham and Lucy Hutchinson's Commonplace Book', *SEL* 48 (2008): 149–50. For Hutchinson's elite status, see Susan Wiseman, *Conspiracy and Virtue: Women, Writing, and Politics in Seventeenth-Century England* (New York: Oxford University Press, 2006), 229–33.

[61] *Order and Disorder*, ed. Norbrook, pp. xxv–xxvi; Edward Paleit, 'Women's Poetry and Classical Authors: Lucy Hutchinson and the Classicisation of Scripture', in Susan Wiseman (ed.), *Early Modern Women and the Poem* (Manchester: Manchester University Press, 2013), 21–41.

that the retelling of sacred history can perform.[62] Roper's and Hutchinson's texts are as dissimilar as they are alike, but neither poem, nor those of Southwell, Quarles, or Du Bartas, claim to be the Christianized epic that is *Davideis* or *Paradise Lost*; all of these texts affiliate with the 'secondary kind of writing' that the biblical verse paraphrase embodies.

Southwell's Decalogue verses and Quarles's *Histories* suggest a rich culture of sub-canonical biblical poetry in seventeenth-century England, one in which women as well as men engaged, and one that provides a context in which to understand Lucy Hutchinson's generic choices, and the discursive qualities so frequently noted in her poem. That Hutchinson's version of Genesis is different in kind from Milton's should not entirely surprise us; to the contrary, the apparent generic anomalies of *Order and Disorder* are a reminder that we need to afford respect to women poets' knowing association of their work with less glamorous genres and to attend to its aesthetic implications—as well as to the very real differences between different women's work. Claiming allegiance to Milton's epic offers one way to read Hutchinson's poem: it bestows upon it the prestige of proximity to canonization and, if nuanced, reveals much about Hutchinson's responses to that epic. Reading it alongside Southwell and Quarles offers another context, one that allows us to identify positively the engagements of Hutchinson's poem in the broader biblical poetic culture of her time, and one that is suggestive of ways in which the biblical poetic engagements of women in seventeenth-century England push against the parameters of literary canon-formation and the hierarchies of genre that they impose.

Further Reading

Harris, Johanna, and Elizabeth Scott-Baumann, eds. *The Intellectual Culture of Puritan Women* (Basingstoke: Palgrave Macmillan, 2011).

Hutchinson, Lucy. *Lucy Hutchinson: Order and Disorder*, ed. David Norbrook (Oxford: Blackwell, 2001).

Mayer, Robert. 'Lucy Hutchinson: A Life of Writing'. *The Seventeenth Century*, 22 (2007): 305–35.

Norbrook, David. 'John Milton, Lucy Hutchinson and the Republican Biblical Epic', in Mark R. Kelley, Michael Lieb, and John T. Shawcross (eds), *Milton and the Grounds of Contention* (Pittsburgh, Pa.: Duquesne University Press, 2003), 37–63.

Paleit, Edward. 'Women's Poetry and Classical Authors: Lucy Hutchinson and the Classicisation of Scripture', in Susan Wiseman (eds), *Early Modern Women and the Poem* (Manchester: Manchester University Press, 2013), 21–41.

Ross, Sarah C. E. *Women, Poetry, and Politics in Seventeenth-Century Britain* (Oxford: Oxford University Press, 2015).

White, Micheline, ed. *English Women, Religion, and Textual Production, 1500–1625* (Farnham: Ashgate, 2011).

Wilcher, Robert. '"Adventurous song" or "presumptuous folly": The Problem of "utterance" in John Milton's *Paradise Lost* and Lucy Hutchinson's *Order and Disorder*'. *The Seventeenth Century*, 21 (2006): 304–14.

---

[62] University of Leeds Library, Brotherton Collection, MS Lt q 2, excerpted in Jill Seal Millman and Gillian Wright (eds), *Early Modern Women's Manuscript Poetry* (Manchester: Manchester University Press, 2005). For discussion, see Ross, *Women, Poetry, and Politics*.

CHAPTER 31

....

SCRIPTURE AND TRAGEDY IN THE REFORMATION

....

RUSS LEO

DURING the first half of the sixteenth century, tragedy emerged as a privileged dramatic genre through which to read scripture and pose theological problems and questions.[1] The recently rediscovered text of Aristotle's *Poetics* and commentaries on the *Poetics* afforded readers ample intellectual resources to understand the meaning of faith in their devotional lives. Moreover, the translation and widespread availability of ancient tragedies by Sophocles, Euripides, and Seneca provided exemplary models for sacred tragedy, a genre on the rise during the tumultuous early years of the Reformation. Thus, decades before the apex of Elizabethan theatre, poets and theologians alike exploited the exegetical capacities of tragedy to understand scripture. Before popular players trod the commercial stage as Hieronimo, Faustus, Lavinia, and Hamlet, the most celebrated *modern* tragedies (thus, excluding the works of the ancients as well as the *Christus patiens* attributed to Gregory Nazianzen) were those with *fabulae* grounded in scriptural *loci* exploring controversial theological conceits. Looking back on this early period in his pedagogical treatise *The Scholemaster*, Roger Ascham touted the excellence of Thomas Watson's *Absalom* and George Buchanan's *Jephthes*.[2] Even at the beginning of the seventeenth century, William Scott, in *The Modell of Poeseye*, continued to locate Buchanan alone among the Latinate tragedians—'The Greekes have Sophocles and Euripides for Tragedy, we have in Latine Seneca and Buchanan'—rare praise given his low estimation of contemporary tragedies.[3]

This chapter examines the rise of sacred tragedy in the early sixteenth century, its debts to antique poetics, and its exceptional capacities to express the most complex theological problems in dynamic and engaging terms. This is particularly true of the Reformers, with whom I begin. The prolific Buchanan translated Euripides' *Medea* and *Alcestis* into Latin and composed two original tragedies: *Jehphtah, or the Vow (Jephthes, sive*

---

[1] For a classic account of biblical genres in early modernity, albeit focused on lyric rather than tragedy, see Barbara Kiefer Lewalski, *Protestant Poetics and the Seventeenth-Century Religious Lyric* (Princeton: Princeton University Press, 1979), 31–110.

[2] See Roger Ascham, *The Scholemaster* (London, 1570), 57ʳ–57ᵛ.

[3] British Library MS 81083, 13ʳ, 20ᵛ.

votum) and *The Baptist, or the Calumny* (*Baptistes, sive calumnia*). But other prominent Reformed theologians composed tragedies or experimented with tragedy in multiple languages—for instance, Théodore de Bèze's *Abraham sacrifiant* (French, 1550), Heinrich Bullinger's *Lucretia und Brutus* (German, 1533), Francesco Negri's *Free Will* (*Libero arbitrio*) (Italian, 1546), Bernardino Ochino's *Tragedy* (Italian, 1549), or Sixt Birck's *Eva*, based on a *fabula* by Philip Melanchthon.

While I affirm the importance of tragedy among the second-generation Reformers—namely, Martin Bucer, Melanchthon, and Buchanan—it is crucial to note that, even c.1550, sacred tragedies and defences of tragedy generally appealed to wide varieties of readers across regions and confessions. Humanists like Desiderius Erasmus (who translated Euripides' *Hecuba* and *Iphigenia in Aulis*) affirmed the importance of tragedy as well as its theological resources, promoting reform but never Reform, and many like-minded scholars followed suit. Understanding this point requires familiarity with a now-obscure archive of sacred drama in Latin, popular works that were read for their pedagogical import, as propaedeutic tools used to school children in grammar and pronunciation, as well as for their theological claims. I attend to this archive here, tracing the importance and ubiquity of these sacred dramas in print to illustrate how poets used tragedy to frame scripture and apply it to their situations. Moreover, I show how poets exploited formal rules and expectations to explore the meaning of faith, that thorny and divisive Reformation concept, as well as to understand attendant issues of salvation and agency, issues that were ostensibly alien to the *Poetics* before the sixteenth century.

I. *De honestis ludis*

In his remarkable work *De regno Christi*, presented to King Edward VI in 1550, Bucer outlines at length a series of measures intended to advance the Reformation in England far beyond its nascent state. Included among these reforms is a defence of *honestis ludis*, or 'honest pastimes'—activities crucial to 'the civil education of youth, the suppression of idleness, and the introduction and increase of honest crafts (*artibus*) and business affairs (*negotiis*)'.[4] A wide variety of games, shows, spectacles, and forms of play—including song, dance, and gymnastics—are licensed and encouraged, provided they are reverent. Honest pastimes incite people to piety, touching their religious spirits (*afficere debeant religiosos animos*) in the same way that the poet and king David was touched in 2 Samuel 6: 12–15, 'dancing before the Ark of the Lord' in a faithful celebration of the goodness of God.[5] Bucer classifies such *ludi* as forms of praise and, following Psalm 33, affirms the degree to which 'Praise becomes the righteous (*rectos decet laus*)'; moreover, insofar as 'we belong to Christ, if he is our life, if eternal salvation is from him and about him, every cause of joy and gladness ought to be ours'.[6] Bucer's is perhaps the most thorough endorsement of *ludi*

---

[4] Martin Bucer, *De regno Christi*, tr. Wilhelm Pauck and Paul Larkin, in *Melanchthon and Bucer*, ed. Wilhelm Pauck (Philadelphia: Westminster Press, 1969), 354 (hereafter cited as PL); Martin Bucer, *De regno Christi libri duo 1550*, in *Martini Buceri Opera Latina*, xv, ed. François Wendel (Paris and Gütersloh: Presses Universitaires de France and C. Bertelsmann Verlag, 1955), 260 (hereafter Bucer).
[5] PL 347.   [6] PL 348; Bucer, 259, 253, 254.

by any Reformer and challenges enduring assumptions about the place of playing in the earliest stages of the English Reformation.

This is especially true of Bucer's comments on drama. The majority of *De honestis ludis* is devoted to comedy and tragedy—both of which are approved, provided that they are composed by 'devout and wise men experienced in the Kingdom of Christ'.[7] Drama is not only 'a useful form of entertainment, honorable and contributing toward an increase of piety'; comedy and tragedy are also lively frames which present 'on the stage the plans, actions, and events of mankind'.[8] Bucer's is primarily a defence of drama on the grounds that comedies and tragedies traffic in the affections and thus might be exploited to the reformation of the pleasures and passions of mankind. Sacred drama has the laudable capacity to instruct and to touch these affections, seizing on the capacity of poetry to delight as well as teach. Composers of sacred drama, comedians and tragedians alike, depict 'the crimes of reprobate men (*perditorum hominum*)' in order to emphasize 'a certain terror of divine judgment and horror of sin'; moreover, 'when pious and good actions are shown (*dum piae et probae exhibentur actiones*)', we see the very definition of faith: 'a happy, secure, and confident sense of divine mercy (*sensus divinae misericordiae laetus, securaque et confidens*), but moderate and diffident as regards the self, and a joyful trust in God and his promises, with holy and spiritual pleasure in doing good (*cum sancta et spirituali in recte faciendo voluptate*)'.[9] Here, in the sacred drama proper to Bucerian *honesti ludi*, the pious affects are expressed most clearly (*affectus pii clarissime exprimantur*).[10]

Bucer's comments on comedy are telling. Given the importance of Aristotle's *Poetics* (which is notoriously silent on comedy) in his account and his explicit censure of the contemporary comedies that 'miss that acumen and wit and pleasantness of speech which people admire in Aristophanes, Terence, and the tales of Plautus', it is unsurprising that Bucer is so exacting in his instructions on the reformation of comedy in *De regno Christi*.[11] He does not describe any real *formal* characteristics of comedy beyond the fact that comedy shows things 'common and ordinary' (*communium et vulgarium*).[12] Thus, the repertoire for comedic *fabulae*—stories of things 'common and ordinary'—is very broad, and 'apt and pious poets can ... produce many such things from other stories and from occurrences in daily life (*vitae cottidianae*)'.[13] He opposes this directly to tragedy, which presents things 'unique and eliciting admiration'. The major events and figures of scripture are the stuff of tragedy. *Personae* like Abraham and Lot 'are heroic figures appropriate to tragedy', but 'the quarrels that arose among their shepherds were common and ordinary'.[14] The doings of servants, shepherds, the unnamed kindred of the patriarchs are comic affairs, just as temptation (*suggestione Satanae*), corruption, disease, and the weaknesses of human nature are appropriately comic topics.

---

[7] PL 349.   [8] PL 349.
[9] PL 351; Bucer, 257. For a comparable and concurrent definition of faith, see John Calvin's *Institutio christianae religionis* (1559), III.ii.
[10] Bucer, 257.   [11] PL 352.   [12] PL 349.   [13] PL 351; Bucer, 256.
[14] PL 349; Bucer, 254.

Bucer duly illustrates how comedies frame and enliven domestic and familial aspects of scripture, from Abraham's humble willingness to resolve a conflict with his nephew Lot (Genesis 13: 5–12) to the marriage of Isaac and Rebekah (Genesis 24: 2–67), to Jacob's service to his uncle Laban (Genesis 28: 10–33: 20). Jacob's story is especially telling, for while Bucer concedes that there is certainly 'a tragic aspect to this story in the apparition of the Lord on the way and the struggle with the angel', such comedies nevertheless express the everyday 'consolations of God' evident in scripture, and common to all believers (*non sunt alienae a quibusuis vere Christianis*)—pleasures derived from modesty, marriage, friendship, and the like.[15] The story of Jacob and Laban is *comic* insofar as Jacob's life was 'enriched … because of the faithful service he performed for his uncle'—a quotidian pleasure available to all believers and, hence, comic.[16]

Tragedy has a more apparent relationship to the major *personae* and events of scripture. According to Bucer,

> The Scriptures everywhere offer an abundant supply of material for tragedies, in almost all the stories of the holy patriarchs, kings, prophets, and apostles, from the time of Adam, the first parent of mankind. For these stories are filled with divine and heroic personages, emotions, customs, actions, and also events which turned out contrary to what was expected, which Aristotle calls reversals (περιπετείας).[17]

These initial comments tell us much about tragedy and its theological applications as well as the place of playing in the devotional lives of Reformed polities. Notably, Bucer's determination of tragedy is Aristotelian. Not only does he understand tragedy as contributing 'toward a correction of morals and a pious orientation in life', he also experiments with technical terms and their religious province (for instance, 'reversal', περιπέτεια (*peripeteia*), and recognition, the Greek ἀναγνώρισις Latinized as *agnitio* or *agnosco*).[18] Tragedy's emergence as a theological resource in the sixteenth century is concurrent with the reintroduction of Aristotle's *Poetics* to early modern Europe. While Aristotle's text was accessible during the Middle Ages in a number of redactions, reliable editions and translations of the Greek text were not available until the end of the fifteenth century.[19] The renowned Aldine edition of the Greek text was published in Venice in 1508, followed by an edition published in Basle in 1531, part of the *Opera Aristotelis* edited by Desiderius Erasmus and Simon Grynaeus. Among the most important early Latin translations were those by Giorgio Valla Placentinus, first printed in 1498; Alessandro de'

---

[15] PL 349–50; Bucer, 255–6.

[16] PL 350.

[17] PL 351; Bucer, 257.

[18] PL 349; Bucer, 255. See Aristotle, *Poetics*, tr. Stephen Halliwell, *Loeb Classical Library* 199 (Cambridge, Mass.: Harvard University Press, 1995), 51–3; and *Aristotelis poetica, per Alexandrum Paccium, patritium Florētinum, in Latinum conversa* ([Paris?], 1542), 11ᵛ.

[19] See Henry Ansgar Kelly, *Ideas and Forms of Tragedy from Aristotle to the Middle Ages* (Cambridge: Cambridge University Press, 1993), esp. 111–25; Kelly, 'Aristotle-Averroes-Alemannus on Tragedy: The Influence of the "Poetics" on the Latin Middle Ages', *Viator*, 10 (1979): 161–209; and Daniel Javitch, 'The Assimilation of Aristotle's *Poetics* in Sixteenth-Century Italy', in Glyn P. Norton (ed.), *The Cambridge History of Literary Criticism*, iii. *The Renaissance* (Cambridge: Cambridge University Press, 1999), 53–65.

Pazzi (Paccius), in 1536; and Pietro Vettori (Victorius), in 1560. Moreover, readers made sense of the *Poetics* by way of Sophocles, Euripides, and Seneca—also relatively new to early modern Europe, and available in both Greek and Latin editions.[20] Among the editors and translators of Euripides' tragedies, for instance, were Erasmus, Melanchthon, and Buchanan.

Bucer transports the informed humanist investigations of antique poetics, as well as his admiration for 'the gravity, cleverness, and elegance of dialogue of Sophocles, Euripides, and Seneca', to scripture.[21] Indeed, he asserts that scripture is in fact *more* appropriate to the project of tragedy than 'the godless fables and stories of the pagans'.[22] Again, there is a distinctly Aristotelian strain in Bucer's treatment of tragedy. Not only does he emphasize fear and horror (although he is silent on pity), as well as a rational awe proper to tragedy and scripture alike, he is duly critical of excessive spectacle and histrionics. Bucer asks that 'nothing shallow, or histrionic is admitted in the acting', building on the Aristotelian dictum: 'spectacle is emotionally potent but falls quite outside the art and is not integral to poetry'.[23] Moreover, in a complex comment on the proper *materia* of representation, Bucer asks that a tragedy reveal, in the examination of sacred things (*sanctis dumtaxat*), 'not so much the actualities and activities of men (*res ipsae et hominum actiones*) and their feelings and troubles (*affectus et perturbationes*), but rather their habits and dispositions (*mores et ingenia*)'.[24]

What is at stake here is the Aristotelian definition of poetry, more philosophical than history in so far as the poet relates universals while the historian narrates particular details. At this point in *De honestis ludis*, Bucer charges sacred tragedy with a similar focus on 'sacred things' as a *genus* rather than individual sacred things, on their own; he emphasizes patterns, habits, and dispositions, stressing continuities and universals across scripture, rather than the affairs, actions, feelings, and troubles of individual men. There is a principle of accommodation at work here: where *personae* and events in scripture are recognizably distant from modern audiences, tragedy bridges that gap. David, for example, a Palestinian (*Palestinus*), was 'of a nation far more emotional and uninhibited (*pathetici atque commobiles*) than our European people'.[25] Bucer's exegetical project is to discover the universal import of scripture—a task to which tragedy is uniquely fit. Aristotelian tragedy enables this in its focus on necessity and probability: 'With character, precisely as in the structure of events, one should always seek necessity and probability—so that for such a person to say or do such things is necessary or probable, and the sequence of events is also necessary and probable'.[26] Following this principle, the poet can frame scriptural characters and events in a way that communicates their applicability to modern audiences. This, together with the theatrical appeal to the affections—that which 'arouses (*excitetur*) the spectators to an eager imitation', which 'strengthens them (*confirmetur*) in their detestation of [sin] and stimulates them (*excitetur*) to a vigilant avoidance of it'—closes the

---

[20] On the relevance of Seneca in the Middle Ages and early modernity, see Kelly, *Ideas and Forms*, 125–43; and Ronald G. Witt, *In the Footsteps of the Ancients: The Origins of Humanism from Lovato to Bruni* (Leiden: Brill, 2000), 124–9.

[21] PL 352.   [22] PL 351; Bucer, 257.

[23] PL 352; Bucer, 258; and Aristotle, *Poetics*, tr. Halliwell, 53–5. See also *Poetics* 1453b.1–10 (75).

[24] PL 352; Bucer, 258. I have amended Pauck and Larkin's translation of *mores et ingenia* from 'morals and characters' to 'habits and dispositions'.

[25] PL 347–8; Bucer, 253.   [26] Aristotle, *Poetics*, tr. Halliwell, 81.

historical and cultural gaps by emphasizing the universal and enduring qualities of saintly life, the meaning of scripture *in toto*.[27]

Bucer's is the clearest articulation of the relationship between scripture and dramatic genre (namely, comedy and tragedy) by any theologian in the sixteenth century. Bucer's précis on genre and pious drama was programmatic, not only for a variety of Protestants but also for reform-minded Catholics writing in the shadow of Erasmus, especially in this crucial age before the ascension of Jesuit drama. His comments offer keen insight into the mid-century world of sacred drama.

II. *DRAMATA SACRA*

Bucer's generic approach to sacred drama suggests familiarity with a wide variety of sixteenth-century Latin plays written with antique poetics in mind. Indeed, his observations on genre in *De honestis ludis* recall two massive collections of sacred drama published in Basel in the 1540s: the *Several Comedies and Tragedies Taken from the Old and New Testament* (*Comoediae ac tragoediae aliquot ex Novo et Vetere Testamento desumptae*) printed by Nicholas Brylinger in 1541, and the *Sacred Drama: Several Comedies and Tragedies Taken from the Old Testament* (*Dramata sacra: Comoediae atque tragoediae aliquot è Veteri Testamento desumptae*), printed by Johannes Oporinus in 1547.[28] The 1541 volume collected ten plays: William Fullonius [Gnapheus]'s *Acolastus*; Cornelius Crook[Crocus]'s *Joseph*; Petrus Papeus's *The Evangelical Samaritan* (*De Samaritano evangelico*); Jacobus Zovitius of Drieschor's *The Lost Sheep* (*Ovis perdita*); *Susanna*, by Sixt Birck (Xystus Betuleius); *Pammachius* by Thomas Kirchmeyer (Naogeorgus); *Christ Victorious by the Cross* (*Christus xilonicus*), by Nicolas Barthélemy de Loches (Lochiensis); and three comedies by Georgius Macropedius—*Hecastus*, *Andrisia*, and *Bassarus*. All are comedies (or, in the case of *Susanna*, tragicomedies) save for *Pammachius* and *Christus xilonicus*. The larger 1547 volume collected sixteen plays based solely on stories from the Hebrew Testament. In addition to reprinting Birck's *Susanna* and Crocus's *Joseph*, Oporinus included Andreas Diether of Augsburg's *Joseph*; Zovitius's *Ruth*; Ioannis Lorichius of Hadamar's *Job, the Example of Patience* (*Jobus, patientiae exemplum*); Kirchmeyer's *Hamanus*; five plays by Hieronymus Ziegler—*The Sacrifice of Isaac* (*Isaaci immolatio*), *Samson*, *Nomothesia*, *Heli, siue paedonothia*, and *Protoplastus, or the Creation of Man* (*Protoplastus, sive de creatione hominis*); and five additional plays by Birck—namely, *The Wisdom of Solomon* (*Sapientia Solomonis*), *Judith*, *Bel and the Story of a Dragon* (*Beel una cum draconis historia*), *Zorobabel* (translated from German into Latin by Ioannis Entomius of Augsburg), and *Eva*, the latter based on a redaction of scripture by Melanchthon. Of these, seven are comedies, five are tragicomedies, and four are tragedies.

Most, if not all, of these plays and playwrights are unknown to modern audiences, and they certainly do not enter into the usual accounts of sixteenth-century drama. This is perhaps due to the fact that Latin works are generally excluded from national

---

[27] PL 352; Bucer, 258.

[28] *Comoediae ac tragoediae aliquot ex novo et vetere Testamento desumptae* (Basel, 1541); and *Dramata sacra: comoediae atque tragoediae aliquot è veteri Testamento desumptae* (Basel, [1547]).

literary histories, preoccupied as they are with the emergence and celebration of vernacular literatures in early modernity. Moreover, both collections offer significant challenges to *confessional* histories of the Reformation. Brylinger and Oporinus include plays from known Lutherans (such as Thomas Kirchmeyer) as well as traditionalists interested in preserving the constitution of the Roman Church (such as Hieronymus Ziegler), even while promoting pedagogical reforms and local amendments to spiritual and scholarly life. In his preface, Brylinger pitches his volume as a pedagogical resource for students, supplementing the pagan canon of antique plays with Christian plays 'for public theatres and Christian schools', to meet the needs of pious students 'who desire to drink in the rudiments of the Latin language'.[29] Both editors court a scholarly audience interested in using these plays in grammar schools; indeed, this is particularly evident in the comedies across the two volumes, in their attempts to express scriptural *loci* in terms of the follies of youth and in a Latin suitable for didactic purposes.

The Latin volumes seized an economic opportunity by collecting previously printed plays in one convenient place. They circulated widely, regardless of confessional boundaries. Oporinus's volume was read and praised in Italy, even after the initial convention of the Council of Trent in 1545. In *Two Dialogues on Modern Poets* (*Dialogi duo de poetis nostrorum temporum*) (1551), for instance, in the comments attributed to Andreas Grunther celebrating German poetry, Lilio Gregorio Giraldi basically reproduces the table of contents of the 1547 *Dramata sacra* in an effort to list the best examples of German drama (albeit in Latin).[30] Only fifteen years later, in a very different confessional climate, despite Giraldi's early praise of the poets involved, the 1547 collection was included in the 1559 *Index librorum prohibitorum*.[31]

Most of the works in the 1541 and 1547 collections of *Dramata sacra* bear the influence of the revised or amended versions of medieval plays that survived local Reformations, in print and performance—plays that would have been accessible to Bucer, Brylinger, Oporinus, and their contemporaries.[32] This, again, is especially true of the comedies. Macropedius's *Hecastus* is an adaptation of the medieval *Everyman*, just as Fullonius's risqué Plautine version of the parable of the Prodigal Son, *Acolastus*, is consonant with the language, concepts, and didactic purchase of the morality plays. Where the comedies and tragicomedies evince continuities with late medieval genres and practices, however, this is far less true of the tragedies. The poets themselves recognize this, and address it in their works. They exploit recently acquired formal resources—for instance, Aristotle's observations on tragedy in the *Poetics*—for exegetical purposes. They also use tragedy to frame scripture in ways that pose theological problems in exacting and dynamic terms. For instance, the address to the pious reader preceding the Brylinger text of *Christus xilonicus* confirms Debora Shuger's assertion that 'Prior to the Renaissance, the Crucifixion was virtually never described as a tragedy', nor was 'The "tragic" nature of Christ's sacrifice

---

[29] *Comoediae ac tragoediae*, a2ʳ.

[30] See *Lilio Gregorio Giraldi: Modern Poets*, tr. John N. Grant (Cambridge, Mass.: Harvard University Press, 2011), 150–3. Grant offers valuable biographical notes on many of the obscure authors of the *Dramata sacra*.

[31] *Index auctorum et librorum prohibitorum* (Rome, Feb. 1559).

[32] For the survival of late medieval biblical drama in England, see Paul Whitfield White, *Drama and Religion in English Provincial Society, 1485–1660* (Cambridge: Cambridge University Press, 2008), esp. 1–42, 66–101.

... a theological topos'.[33] According to the writer of the preface (probably not Nicolas Barthélemy de Loches himself), Barthélemy's determination of the passion and crucifixion as a tragedy is an intervention in the history of sacred poetry:

> The tragedies of the ancients used to celebrate the disastrous deeds of their leading heroes in very obscure words, often mingling with the historical truth (which is the vanity of heathen antiquity) either false fictions or the fables of empty superstition. But this play we show you, good reader, in this our typographical theatre as a tragedy, brings into the theatre none of these mortal heroes but that everlasting King of all Kings, prince of princes, lord of lords, the son of the everlasting God, the Messiah, Christ, and brings him into the theatre so truly, simply, without any deceit and without anything that is unbecoming to evangelical history, that you will miss nothing here (except perhaps the curious superstitions of the past).[34]

The preface recognizes Barthélemy's contribution to an emerging tradition of sacred drama, citing only the work of Johannes Franciscus Quintianus Stoa (Gianfrancesco Quinziano Stoa)—namely, his *Tragedia de passione domini nostri Iesu Christi*, or *Theoandrathanatos* (1508)—as an exemplar. According to its preface, however, the *Christus xilonicus* far surpasses *Theoandrathanatos*: 'Quintianus Stoa previously wrote a tragedy on the same story but in no way came as near the target of faith as this writer'.[35] Stoa's tragedy, much beholden to Seneca, is an exercise in contrasts; what James Parente has called 'Christ's Stoic forbearance of his persecution' is set determinately against the uncontrolled passion of Mary.[36] Barthélemy distinguishes himself from Quintianus Stoa by exploiting and experimenting with the formal rules of tragedy. *Christus xilonicus* follows *Theoandrathanatos* in so far as both works end with Christ's interment, eschewing the resurrection. Where *Theoandrathanatos* spans five acts, however, Barthélemy's work ends suddenly with Act 4.[37]

Christus xilonicus, the oldest tragedy in either the Brylinger or the Oporinus collection, emerges from an encounter with a variety of antique poetics. Barthélemy's Christ employs a term from Aristotle's *Poetics* in calling the faithful 'in these dark realms ... [to] recognize their own misery (*miseriam agnoscunt suam*), judge themselves, pray for remission of future punishments by tears, and redeem themselves by weeping'.[38] Both the verb

[33] Debora Kuller Shuger, *The Renaissance Bible: Scholarship, Sacrifice, and Subjectivity* (Berkeley, Calif.: University of California Press, 1994), 133–4. On the authorship of the 1541 preface as well as the earlier editions of *Christus xilonicus* see Raymond Lebègue, *La tragédie religieuse en France: Les débuts (1514–1573)* (Paris: Librairie Ancienne Honoré Champion, 1929), 169–84.

[34] C. C. Love (tr.), *Five Sixteenth-Century Latin Plays: From the Collection of Comedies and Tragedies edited by Nicholas Brylinger, Basle, 1540* (Toronto: Amor Christoferi Press, 1995), 181 (hereafter cited as Love); for the Latin, see *Comoediae ac tragoediae*, 450.

[35] *Comoediae ac tragoediae*, 450–1; Love, 181.

[36] James A. Parente, Jr., 'The Development of Religious Tragedy: The Humanist Reception of the *Christos Paschon* in the Renaissance', *Sixteenth Century Journal*, 16 (1985): 366.

[37] Tellingly, neither Barthélemy nor the author of the preface invoke the Euripidean *Christus patiens* attributed to Gregory Nazianzen. *Christus xilonicus*, available print in since 1529, predates the initial edition of the Greek text of *Christus patiens* printed in Rome by Antonius Bladus in 1542, followed by influential Latin translations by Gabriele Garcia Tarraconensi, printed in Paris in 1549, and the physician Franciscus Fabricius Ruremundanus, in Antwerp in 1550. *Christus patiens* established not only an ancient but more importantly a patristic precedent for sacred tragedy. See Parente, 'Development of Religious Tragedy', 351–68.

[38] *Comoediae ac tragoediae*, 455; Love, 184.

agnosco and the attendant noun *agnitio* occur frequently in classical Latin as well as in patristic writing and the Vulgate. They are hardly exclusive to the translations and redactions of Aristotelian texts. As scholars translated the Greek text of the *Poetics* into Latin, however, both verb and noun took on new technical meanings with reference to tragedy. In the most influential Latin translation of the sixteenth century, for instance, Paccius renders Aristotelian 'recognition' as *agnitio*, a powerful formal device, one of 'tragedy's most potent means of emotional effect' (*quibus maxime mortaliū animos Tragoedia delectat*).[39] Here, in *Christus xilonicus*, *agnitio* figures prominently and serves a similar affective function. Faith is inextricable from this *agnitio*, this recognition of one's own misery and depravity in contrast to Christ's humble glory. Christ asks the Chorus and Judas 'impotentiam non agnoscitis?' ('Do you not recognize your own impotence?') as they accost him in the Garden of Gethsemene.[40] It is a key moment where Christ calls for recognition in the tragedy, employing the ancient formal device to move the Chorus and audience alike. The importance of *agnitio* in *Christus xilonicus* suggests a technical use, informed by an encounter with the *Poetics*. In *agnitio* Barthélemy adapts tragic recognition to express the knowledge proper to faith, retrofitting the terms of Aristotelian tragedy to address pressing issues of evidence and belief.

Barthélemy also demonstrates a preoccupation with plot, or constitution. The preface to *Christus xilonicus* begs:

> Do not be disturbed in any way, best reader, that this tragedy has only four acts, though both the tragedies and the comedies of the ancients are seen to consist of five acts. Perhaps the author did not have the luck to finish it or was unwilling that an account of Christian liberty should be bound by those troublesome rules of the heathens (*aut Christianae libertatis rationem anxiis illis aethnicorum legibus astrictam esse noluit*).[41]

This comment looks forward to Bucer's direction in *De honestis ludis*, where 'It is better here to take something away from poetic fitness (*decoro poetico*) rather than from the concern for edifying the piety of the spectators'—where, in other words, the cultivation of a reverent audience trumps integrity to ancient formal principles.[42] But the preface to *Christus xilonicus* invokes Christian liberty—hardly an uncomplicated concept in the early years of the Reformation—to account for the 'unfinished' project. Moreover, the conceit of the unfinished tragedy is not unique to *Christus xilonicus*. In fact, neither of the two tragedies included in the 1541 *Comoediae ac tragoediae* is 'complete'. *Pammachius* does not include a fifth act; moreover, its most famous imitation, John Foxe's *Christus triumphans*, seems to address this in its own declaredly comic catastrophe. I am thus inclined to see these as deliberate formal experiments rather than generic shortcomings or capricious departures from antique rules. What is at stake is the temporality of scripture as well as our human capacities to experience the Word through a privileged medium: sacred tragedy.

---

[39] Aristotle, *Poetics*, ed. Halliwell, 51–3; and *Aristotelis poetica*, 11ᵛ. Giorgio Valla translates *Poetics* 1450a.30–5 in a markedly different way: '& cū his ingētia: q[ui]b[us] animat[em] tragedia: fabule sunt p[ar] tes insolētie & recognitiones'. See *Aristoteles de poetica interprete Georgio Valla Placentino* (Venice, 1515), 3ʳ.

[40] *Comoediae ac tragoediae*, 479; Love, 199. I emend the translation.

[41] *Comoediae ac tragoediae*, 451; Love, 182.

[42] PL 351; Bucer, 257.

To understand this claim, it is first necessary to look carefully at the formal features of a tragic plot c.1529 (when *Christus xilonicus* began to circulate, in an unfinished form). Using terms established by the Roman grammarian Aelius Donatus in his commentaries on Terence, it was not uncommon for readers to transport the four parts or divisions of comedy—*prologus*, πρότασις (*protasis*), ἐπίτασις (*epitasis*), and καταστροφή (*catastrophe*)—to tragedy.[43] The *prologus* is that which precedes the actual composition of the story (*antecedens veram fabulae compositionem*); the *protasis* is the introduction or first act of the story; the *epitasis*, where the argument of the story is complicated (*involutio argumenti*); and the *catastrophe*, 'the unfolding of the story, through which its ending is proven true' (*explicatio fabulae, per quam eventus eius approbatur*).[44] These terms do not correspond to the structure of acts but, rather, describe the arc of the story or the composition of the plot at a slightly more abstract level.[45]

The most telling evidence that Donatus derived these terms from Terence is his unmistakably comic determination of catastrophe, his use of the verb *approbo* that commonly carries with it some sense of approval or commendation. Thus it is not difficult to fit this to Aristotelian tragedy even if, strictly speaking, καταστροφή is not a prominent term in Aristotle's *Poetics*; Donatus's *approbatur* felicitously captures the sense of *Poetics* 1454a.32–7, bringing an appropriate end to a sequence of events: 'With character, precisely as in the structure of events, one should always seek necessity and probability—so that for such a person to say or do such things is necessary or probable, and the sequence of events is also necessary and probable'.[46] The *catastrophe* confirms the truth of the resolution and serves as an adequate translation of λύσις (generally translated as denouement) in 1455b.23–5: 'Every tragedy has both a complication (δέσις, or in Paccius: *connexione*) and denouement (λύσις or, in Paccius: *solutione*): the complication comprises events outside the play, and often some of those within it; the remainder is the denouement'.[47]

Both Donatus and Aristotle, in their comments on *catastrophe* and plot (μῦθος or, in Paccius: *fabula*), respectively, claim that the best and most elegant works emphasize design, consistency, and probability. In this sense, importing 'catastrophe' to describe Aristotelian denouement poses no problem—particularly in the best kinds of *tragic* plots, free of fortune, chance, and divine machines. If 'catastrophe' is a dramatic term meant to inspire awe and confirm that events, characters, actions, and affects in a sequence are united under one design, it is 'because even among chance events we find most awesome those which seem to have happened by design (*illa quidem maximam admirationem prae se ferunt*)'.[48]

Christus xilonicus begins with a protracted sermon, Christ's speech to his *amici* the Apostles at Gethsemene. Much of his initial address is an attempt to manage their fear. Yet Christ does not call for them to dispense with fear; on the contrary, Barthélemy's Christ

---

[43] On the use of the *Poetics* to understand comedy, see Angelo Poliziano, *La commedia antica e L'Andria di Terenzio* [*Angeli Politiani Andria Terenti*], ed. Rosetta Lattanzi Roselli (Florence: Sansoni, 1973), esp. 12–15.

[44] Aelius Donatus, *Aeli Donati commentum Terenti, accedunt eugraphi commentum et scholia Bembina*, ed. Paulus Wessner (Stuttgart: B. G. Tevbner, 1962), i. 27–8.

[45] On the development of five-act structure, as well as the synthesis of Donatus and Aristotle, see T. W. Baldwin, *Shakespere's Five-Act Structure: Shakespeare's Early Plays on the Background of Renaissance Theories of Five-Act Structure From 1470* (Urbana, Ill.: University of Illinois Press, 1947), 252–311.

[46] Aristotle, *Poetics*, ed. Halliwell, 81; *Aristotelis poetica*, 18ᵛ.

[47] Aristotle, *Poetics*, ed. Halliwell, 90–1; *Aristotelis poetica*, 20ᵛ.

[48] Aristotle, *Poetics*, ed. Halliwell, 63; *Aristotelis poetica*, 14ʳ–14ᵛ.

works to utilize and transform their fear in a manner that locates *Christus xilonicus* firmly within the tradition of sacred drama praised by Bucer. He exhorts the faithful to 'Cease to be stirred by danger or fear (*Periculo aut metu moveri absistite*). Only fear him, who by his nod makes heaven tremble and who can sink forever body and soul into bitter death'.[49] But the tragedy is also preoccupied with God's design, so much so that Christ refers to the God of *Christus xilonicus* explicitly as *tyrannus mundi*.[50] This is a God (specifically the Father) that, 'with no one ... opposing him, easily brought the world under his command (*facile orbem presserat / Imperio*): in me he moves, in this place he has set up his standards (*in me movit, loco signa extulit*)'.[51] It is to this *tyrannus*, this absolute monarch, that the Apostles and the faithful owe their allegiance, and it is under a tyrant's severe law that they suffer.

Christ instructs the (sleeping) Apostles that 'The sum of the law (*summa legis*) turns on this double hinge: first, fear God (*veneremini in primis deum*) and yet accept him with all your heart and never cast him out of your breast'.[52] Christ follows his invocation of the law with an apt description of what it means to follow the law: 'Yet say that you are useless slaves (*servos ... inutiles*); do not count the cost of the reward from this (*nec feceritis praemij hinc dispendium*): do not spread to the winds what I have written, who have written only the beginning and the end of all these things'.[53] There is little if any evidence of God's benevolence. Here at Gethsemene even Christ is riddled with anxiety in the face of the Father as Barthélemy glosses the agony and bloody sweat of Luke 22: 43–4: 'Alas, what great dread and what great uneasiness come over me (*Heu quantus horror, quanta me molestia / Invadit*)! ... O the dread of death, harder than any death. O the shame, heavier than any death'.[54]

After Christ's initial sermon, the play unfolds predictably, following the events in the Gospels. We witness the judgement of Christ before the Sanhedrin, Herod, and Pilate as well as the crucifixion and immediate aftermath. Christ dies on the cross in 3.14, and Act 4 is comprised entirely of a conversation between Joseph of Arimathea, Nicodemus, and the Centurion concerning the burial of his body. Nicodemus speaks the final line: 'Let's first protect the tomb with this bolt and next let's roll up this boulder against the opening'.[55] Thus, in a tragedy titled *Christus xilonicus*, named after 'Christ ἐν ξύλῳ, that is, on the wooden cross (*in ligno*), gained the νίκη, this is, victory (*victoria*)', readers never encounter the risen Christ, *Christus triumphans*.[56] There is no Act 5. The crucifixion, not the hell of the *descensus ad inferos* nor the resurrection, is the site of Christ's human victory, *Christus patiens*.

In a tragedy that is fundamentally preoccupied with the 'tyranny' of the law, Barthélemy's avoidance of the resurrection stresses an exegetical point. There is no freedom from the law, even as the preface, addressing the four-act structure, calls *Christus xilonicus* 'an account of Christian liberty' (*Christianae libertatis rationem*).[57] Barthélemy's

---

[49] *Comoediae ac tragoediae*, 457–8; Love, 186.
[50] *Tyrannus* might be used in the most general, and generous sense, to name a monarch or absolute ruler, but it is rare to read the term used without some suggestion of cruelty or severity.
[51] *Comoediae ac tragoediae*, 454; Love, 183.
[52] *Comoediae ac tragoediae*, 472–3; Love, 195.
[53] *Comoediae ac tragoediae*, 473; Love, 195–6.
[54] *Comoediae ac tragoediae*, 476; Love, 197–8.
[55] *Comoediae ac tragoediae*, 532; Love, 237.
[56] *Comoediae ac tragoediae*, 451; Love, 182.
[57] *Comoediae ac tragoediae*, 451; Love, 182.

Christ exhorts characters and readers alike to recognize their misery and depravity, and the constitution of the tragic plot—indeed, of the *fabula* of the Gospels—leads to one necessary and probable conclusion: humanity is damned. As it stands, Barthélemy's is a tragedy without a catastrophe. Even the suffering Christ of *Christus xilonicus* is terrifying, unbridled, and violent:

> Descending here from Heaven, I have come to loose fire on the world (*ignem in orbem immittere / Veni*). I only want that which will burn and carry all things lightly with it up to the height, that which will make more men dry and fiery, harden them for bearing misfortune, cleanse all the gulfs of the human heart (*lustret omneis cordis humani sinus*), loose the hidden vents of the breast through which the untameable heat of the high Heaven may penetrate, and not attack the more open veins lest it receive the water of this savage and raging sea.[58]

Christus xilonicus frames the Gospels in a manner that obscures love and salvation. Christ speaks the requisite lines from the cross, following the *materia* of the Gospels—'My God, my God, why hast thou forsaken me?' (*Eloi, eloi lamazabatani*); 'into thine hands I commend my spirit' (*in manus illum tuas / Mandabo*)—but his final address to God emphasizes an element of mercy that is lacking throughout the tragedy: 'King of men and of gods, my Father, let my holy spirit, entirely free from sin, ascend from this place to you; into your hands I shall commend my spirit. May you be good to me (*sis mihi bonus*)'.[59]

The four acts of *Christus xilonicus* drive home a devastating point: if Christ, the man without sin, can suffer under the law, the deserved suffering of a sinful mankind is inevitable. In this sense Barthélemy's tragedy emerges in conversation with the most pointed and brutal treatments of Christ's passion in the early sixteenth century—not only Quintianus Stoa's *Theoandrathanatos* but also Erasmus's *Disputatiuncula de taedio, pavore, tristitia Jesu* (part of the 1503 *Lucubratiunculae*).[60] Barthélemy's tragedy also looks forward to Jean Calvin's important revision of the doctrine of the *descensus ad inferos*, where Christ experiences the undiluted weight of the law, the gravity of which drives even the man-God without sin to feel lost and abandoned, a figural descent into hell on earth.[61] Moreover, where the preface to *Christus xilonicus* invokes Christian liberty to account for the truncated form of the four-act tragedy, readers are drawn into the epoch-making debate between Luther and Erasmus on precisely this point: the freedom of the Christian.

Erasmus's *A Diatribe or Discourse on the Freedom of the Will* (*De libero arbitrio diatribe sive collatio*) (1524), together with Luther's response, *The Bondage of the Will* (*De servo arbitrio*) (1525), foregrounded the degree to which the true freedom lay in Christ's resurrection, in the Christian's faith in God's benevolence. The controversy is perhaps best summarized in Luther's 1520 tract *The Freedom of a Christian* (*Von der Freiheit eines Christenmenschen*), where 'One thing, and only one thing, is necessary for Christian life, righteousness, and freedom. That one thing is the most holy Word of God, the gospel of Christ, as Christ says,

---

[58] *Comoediae ac tragoediae*, 467; Love, 192.
[59] *Comoediae ac tragoediae*, 525–6; Love, 232–3.
[60] See Shuger, *Renaissance Bible*, 89–127.
[61] See Calvin's 1559 *Institutio religionis Christianae*, 2.15–17.

John 11[: 25], "I am the resurrection and the life; he who believes in me, though he die, yet he shall live"; and John 8[: 36], "So if the Son makes you free, you will be free indeed" '.[62] Barthélemy's four-act tragedy suspends readers between the Erasmian and Lutheran positions. Christian liberty is not only the reason that there is no Act 5, but also the inevitable subject matter of Act 5: Christ's resurrection. *Christus xilonicus* exploits the tragic emphasis on plot and design to show, first, that Christ's human passion is the probable and necessary outcome of sin and death, and that the crucifixion is its endgame. It withholds the catastrophe. Moreover, the tragedy's preoccupation with Christ's humanity in duress, under the weight of the law, shows that the missing Act 5 would have to add something new and different to human affairs, to interrupt a sinful human sequence of events. This is the *deus ex machina* of the resurrection—the events of which disrupt the composition of a human tragedy as per the Aristotelian emphasis on plot but which ultimately must occur for salvation.

Christus xilonicus poses this impossibility, the resurrection, as a formal problem. In this way it foregrounds the very object of faith it obscures, Christ's mediation on behalf of humanity and the faith in God's benevolence that he merits. But this is not only a subtle theological turn; Barthélemy's tragedy, in the 1541 collection, avoids controversy by eschewing any explicitly Lutheran or Erasmian comments on salvation or the will. *Christus xilonicus* had circulated in various forms since 1529 without opposition and Barthélemy, a celebrated poet and Benedictine monk, hardly invoked suspicion among the majority of readers. *Christus xilonicus* reveals a common concern among a variety of religious persuasions—the meaning of faith—in a tragic idiom rather than in the didactic or controversial prose appropriate to period sermons and tracts. For both Barthélemy and Brylinger, tragedy proved to be a more fruitful, experimental, and even ecumenical medium than disputation.

III. CATASTROPHE

The claim that the 1541 and 1547 volumes of *Dramata sacra* appealed to readers and students across confessions and religious persuasions does not hold for Thomas Kirchmeyer, or Naogeorgus. His *Haman* is the only play in Oporinus's 1547 collection that Giraldi does *not* praise and his name (Thomas Naogeorgus) appears on the 1559 *Index librorum prohibitorum*. Moreover, *Pammachius* (which had been available since 1538, with dedicatory addresses to the Archbishop of Canterbury Thomas Cranmer as well as to Luther) became notorious after a 1545 performance at Christ's College, Cambridge, erupted into a minor riot.[63] At least, this was Bishop Stephen Gardiner's account of the event; writing as Chancellor of Cambridge University, Gardiner protested to the Vice-Chancellor Matthew Parker that 'parte of which tragedie is soo pestiferous as wer intollerable' and that the

---

[62] Martin Luther, 'The Freedom of a Christian', tr. W. A. Lambert and Harold J. Grimm, *Three Treatises*, 2nd rev. edn (Philadelphia: Fortress Press, 1970), 279.

[63] Paul Whitfield White, 'The *Pammachius* Affair at Christ's College, Cambridge, in 1545', in Peter Happé and Wim Hüsken (eds), *Interludes and Early Modern Society: Studies in Gender, Power and Theatricality* (Amsterdam and New York: Rodopi, 2007), 261–90.

student audience, 'after they deservedly hissed the bishop of Rome from the stage ... forced off all the doctors with the same authority by jeering'.[64]

Whether or not Gardiner's account is reliable, *Pammachius* is indeed a potent piece of antipapal drama, exploiting spectacle as well as key generic aspects of tragedy. Kirchmeyer defines tragedy itself as that 'which the controversy over doctrine has produced for the world (*Quam orbi doctrinae peperit controuersia*)'; tragedy, in turn, depicts the unfolding of evil events according to God's design, as Satan is loosed upon the world. Christ, speaking to the Apostles Peter and Paul, affirms that 'Now at last you will have a great opponent whom it will not be possible for anyone, unless he be endowed with divine virtue, to recognize, to guard against, to resist—an opponent whom the hand of God shall preserve'.[65] This opponent is the servant of Satan, Pope Pammachius, who, with the help of his adviser Porphyrius, corrupts the visible church and brings the Holy Roman Empire under heel. Christ directs Truth (*Veritas*) and Free Speech (*Parrhesia*) into exile; only then can Satan claim that 'in my kingdom there is the greatest liberty, and it is the extreme sin to speak the truth (*libertas apud me maxima est. / Et verum dicere extremum est piaculum*)'.[66] Satan, with his 'tragic look' (*Vultu tragico*), and Pammachius corrupt the church and cultivate its depravity; Pammachius prays, 'O powerful fortune, bring this tragedy to pass (*O fortuna potens hanc effice tragoediam*)'.[67] Thus the tragedy is the unbridled exploitation of the visible church by the papacy.

Moreover, Kirchmeyer (after Lorenzo Valla) depicts the fallacious Donation of Constantine, through which the papacy wrests control of the secular world from the Emperor Julian. Readers follow as the curate Porphyrius corrupts the laws and customs of the church in real time, complete with marginal annotations connecting the events in the play to existing documents and decrees. The papacy and rites of the Roman Church are revealed as irredeemable, their strategies sinister, and their sacraments fraudulent and opportunistic. According to Porphyrius, 'Nothing troublesome ever emerges, which the mass cannot remove (*non missa queat tollere*)', and, of auricular confession, 'If money is given, the wicked man is soon absolved of his guilt'.[68] *Pammachius* spans the duration of the Middle Ages, until Satan's power and the papacy are checked by Christ:

> I shall also see to it that they do not proceed further than it has been decreed (*constitutum est*) and that evil shall not prevail forever, on account of my followers, any of whom is dearer to me than all the Pammachiuses and than all the tribes of Satan. Fear not, that the wicked shall destroy the just or remove them from my grace (*à mea faciunt alienos gratia*).[69]

Hence, after the gratuitous climax of the tragedy, as Satan and his demons feast on the corpses of misguided medieval Catholics, they are roused from lazy slumber by an announcement concerning the German Reformation. Satan is informed that 'not only the Saxons, but also almost all the Germans are casting off your yoke', but also that 'They teach that mass is not needed because by his exertions Christ wins for the living and the dead

---

[64] Quoted in Love, 170, 178–9.
[65] *Comoediae ac tragoediae*, 325, 326–7; Love, 76, 77.
[66] *Comoediae ac tragoediae*, 376; Love, 113.
[67] *Comoediae ac tragoediae*, 372, 381; Love, 110, 118.
[68] *Comoediae ac tragoediae*, 405, 408; Love, 136, 138.
[69] *Comoediae ac tragoediae*, 438; Love, 161.

forgiveness of sins and that another form of worship is not rightly withdrawn from the people'.[70]

The tragedy ends in 4.5, with Satan's threat: 'That man, the leader of the enemy, will now meet me and I will sate myself to nausea with his blood'.[71] These are the last lines in the drama, directed at an unnamed leader of the German Reformation (most likely, Luther), followed only by an epilogue:

> Do not expect now, good spectators, that a fifth act is to be added to this play. Christ will act that one day at his own time (*suo quem Christus olim est acturus die*). Meanwhile the plots of the fourth act move our affairs to and fro as is well seen at the present time. The whole business of Satan is now making a loud noise. The Papacy is defended and so is the worship of what is wicked. There is strenuous opposition to the glory of Christ .... The Turks rage fiercely against us; we rage no less strongly against our own selves, so that it is troublesome for Christians to live and see perpetually the tragedies of Satan (*spectare jugiter satanae tragoedias*). Now must we hope that in human affairs things will be better, unless God shall put an end to that tragedy by the arrival of his son who shall carry off from the world his own, as gold out of dung, and shall hand over the wicked to the everlasting fires, this will be the denouement of this play (*fabulae totius erit* καταστροφή).[72]

The καταστροφή (catastrophe), then, is Christ's return, the imminent Second Coming. Like Barthélemy in *Christus xilonicus*, Kirchmeyer draws the reader's attention to the scope and unfinished plot of the tragedy, to the design and the formal demand for a resolution.

Nevertheless, where the 'tragedy' in *Pammachius* is literally a description of Satan's impact on human events, Kirchmeyer illustrates that this tragedy cannot be resolved by human means alone. *Pammachius*, rather, requires Christ's intervention. In terms of temporality, the action in the tragedy ends with the Reformation, as Satan and Pammachius precipitate 'the plots of the fourth act [that] move our affairs to and fro as is well seen at the present time'. Kirchmeyer uses the tragic emphases on probability and necessity to connect the wars and upheavals of the sixteenth century, to locate their common origin in the policies of an irredeemably satanic papacy. Moreover, the human affairs of the play are brought firmly into a divine economy or constitution of events, to be completed and made perfect in the coming Act 5. Tragedy, more philosophical than history, helps explain the causal connections between events as well as account for history by way of divine providence. The project of *Pammachius* is not merely to render history intelligible as Christ's design but also to frame the role of human action in this history. At the end of the play, ours is only a 'hope that in human affairs things will be better'. God's plot is complete; our human task, revealed in the form of the tragedy, is to wait and hope.

In *Christus triumphans, comoedia apocalyptica*, first printed by Oporinus in Basel in 1556 and performed at Trinity College, Cambridge, in 1562–3, Foxe revisits the last scene and absent catastrophe of *Pammachius*. Here, in a final Chorus of Virgins, we find that 'Nothing remains except the bridegroom himself, who will bring the final catastrophe

---

[70]   *Comoediae ac tragoediae*, 442, 443; Love, 164, 165.
[71]   *Comoediae ac tragoediae*, 448; Love, 169.
[72]   *Comoediae ac tragoediae*, 448–9; Love, 169.

(*catastrophen*) to our stage'.[73] Moreover, we learn 'When that will happen none will say for sure. The poet has shown what he could'.[74] While Foxe named *Christus triumphans* an 'Apocalyptic Comedy' it is almost certainly indebted to Kirchmeyer's experiments in tragedy; Foxe's project is notably different in so far as the *personae* of *Christus triumphans* encounter human history directly through the book of Revelation, rather than via a history of the Reformation (as in *Pammachius*). In terms of models from antiquity, Foxe seems to follow the catastrophes in Seneca's tragedies which, according to Parente, 'did not necessarily evoke a pessimistic reaction; rather, Christian readers were induced to reaffirm their faith by reflecting anew on the eternal life which awaited them beyond the grave'.[75] In *Christus triumphans*, this extends to a life waiting for them beyond human history, in a larger providential plan confirmed by Revelation.

In this sense, Foxe's is a more ambitious project, with a greater emphasis on typological figures taken directly from scripture. Where Kirchmeyer depicts the papacy through Pammachius and Porphyrius, Foxe dramatizes the conflict between Ecclesia, the Church, and the figures of Revelation: Pornapolis, the Whore of Babylon, and Pseudamnus, the Antichrist. 'Satan's tragedies' in *Pammachius* give way to Christ's Comedy, his messianic promise realized in the Second Coming. Nevertheless, *Pammachius* and *Christus triumphans* are alike in so far as they attempt to map tragic forms and emphases on design and constitution onto scripture. These are precisely the experiments in tragedy which would influence later exegetical projects—most importantly, the Calvinist David Pareus's inventive *Commentary upon the Divine Revelation of the Apostle and Evangelist John* (1618) in which he discovers the scriptural work itself is written according to the poetic and philosophical rules of tragedy.

IV. Jephthah and Consistency

George Buchanan's *Jephthes* is perhaps the most celebrated Latin tragedy of the sixteenth century. It is also the pre-eminent sacred play of the age, the tragedy against which many later seventeenth-century works would be measured. Together with *Baptistes*, Buchanan most likely wrote *Jephthes* during his tenure at the Collège de Guyenne in Bordeaux, between 1539 and 1543.[76] Thus, like the plays collected by Brylinger and Oporinus, *Jephthes* was intended for academic performance by students at the Collège, and no less a figure than the young Michel de Montaigne participated in the earliest productions.[77] It is,

---

[73] John Foxe, *Two Latin Comedies by John Foxe the Martyrologist: 'Titus et Gesippus', 'Christus Triumphans'*, ed. and tr. John Hazel Smith (Ithaca, NY: Cornell University Press, 1973), 370–1. Notably, *Christus triumphans* was also translated into French by the Genevan Jean Bienvenu in 1561.

[74] Foxe, *Two Latin Comedies*, 370–1.

[75] James A. Parente, Jr., *Religious Drama and the Humanist Tradition: Christian Theater in Germany and in the Netherlands, 1500–1680* (Leiden: Brill, 1987), 22.

[76] George Buchanan, *George Buchanan Tragedies*, ed. P. Sharratt and P. G. Walsh (Edinburgh: Scottish Academic Press, 1983), 2–6 (hereafter cited as Sharratt and Walsh); and I. D. McFarlane, *Buchanan* (London: Duckworth, 1981), 78–121.

[77] J. R. C. Martyn, 'Montaigne and George Buchanan', *Humanistica Lovaniensia: Journal of Neo-Latin Studies*, 36 (1977): 132–42.

however, more than a pedagogical exercise, and Buchanan's tragedy certainly enters into conversation with period approaches to tragedy in an effort to make sense of difficult *fabulae*—namely, the violent stories from the book of Judges.[78] Judges is a difficult scriptural work, especially given the foreboding ending: 'In those dayes there was no King in Israél, *but* everie man did that which was good in his eyes' (20: 25). It is a litany of impulsive and cruel acts that defy any easy New Testament typologies, punctuated by a periodic 'falling away' from the Lord, lapses into wickedness and idolatry. This is evident in the story of Jephthah, judge over the Israelites, and his daughter (Judges 11). In the heat of battle against the Ammonites, Jephthah swore a vow to God to offer as a sacrifice the first thing to pass through the door of his house upon his victorious return. After the Lord delivered the victory to him, he returned home and was first met by his only daughter; according to his vow, Jephthah sacrificed his daughter after a period of two months, during which she bewailed her virginity in the wilderness.

The scriptural account does not register any conflict, save for the fact that Jephthah seems to regret his vow. He tears his clothes, and laments, but ultimately affirms 'I have opened my mouth unto the LORD, and I cannot goe backe' (Judges 11: 35). His daughter patiently acquiesces. For Buchanan, however, there is substantial debate among the parties concerned over whether or not Jephthah is bound to honour a rash vow—a promise that ultimately requires him to break God's law (against murder) and ignore his natural affection for his daughter. In some of the most compelling lines of the tragedy, the attendant Priest (*Sacerdos*) cautions Jephthah to forsake his hasty vow:

> It lies in your own hand whether you're wretched or otherwise. It is open to you to choose whether you sacrifice your daughter or not; or to speak more truthfully, it is not an open choice unless one wishes to be wretched voluntarily. How is it open to you to carry through what our sacred mother nature forbids, what our love of kin struggles against, and what God loathes? Nature has implanted in our emotions the love of children first and foremost (*primum amare liberos / Natura nostris inservit affectibus*) ... For the perennial providence (*aeterna providentia*) of the heavenly Father has instilled into the minds of men (*animis indidit mortalium*) this force useful for rearing children, for controlling the general harmony of the world, and for ever renewing a fresh line of offspring. And so that he might implant this title more intimately in our minds, he desired to be called and to be a father.[79]

The Priest, arguing with Jephthah, invokes eternal providence in a plea for consistency. God does not change his laws or demands based on the actions of humans. A vow such as Jephthah's undermines and obscures the very consistency of God's design, instilled not only in the model of the family but also in the minds of men, at the level of our natural and involuntary love for our offspring. The Priest emphasizes, repeatedly, that God is not subject to change, nor are his laws flexible based on contingencies and human affairs; Jephthah may not kill his daughter and thus break the law in order to keep his vow. According to the Priest, 'God's voice is the single, simple, self-consistent truth. What he has once ordained

---

[78] The Jephthah story (as well as other key sections of Judges, including Samson and Judith) figures among the most popular scriptural *loci* for sacred drama in the sixteenth and seventeenth centuries. See Wilbur Owen Sypherd, *Jephthah and his Daughter: A Study in Comparative Literature* (Newark, Del.: University of Delaware, 1948), 12–43; and esp. Shuger, *Renaissance Bible*, 128–66.

[79] Sharratt and Walsh, 81–2; and George Buchanan, *Jephthes sive votum tragoedia, authore Georgio Buchanano Scoto* (Paris, [1554]) (hereafter *Jephthes*), 31–2.

continues fixed and implanted on its unchangeable course, and cannot diverge in the slightest degree left or right'.[80] Jephthah, in opposition, asserts that 'Whatever is performed with a sincere mind is welcome to God, and he always puts to our credit the gifts which issue from a pure heart', and that 'It is not gold but the spirit of the giver which the deity approves'.[81]

In radical contrast to Buchanan's *Jepthes*, John Christopherson's ΪΕΦΘΑΕ, or *Iephte*, initially written in Greek and translated into Latin by the author between 1543 and 1547, presents Jephthah's vow as obligatory.[82] Jephthah is bound by his oath and concedes, 'Against my will I do it, for I must … My vow compels: my daughter I must slay'.[83] Where Buchanan locates necessity in God, and sees the fulfilment of Jephthah's rash vow as negligent act, a misrecognition of God's providence at work in law and nature, Christopherson's Jephthah sees providence at work in his act, even if it proves painful: 'The prudent man (σοφòν) / Pays to the full amount his vow to God; / My stubborn heart will hardly give assent / To pay the vow. Yet must the deed be done; / Such is the mandate of necessity (ἀνάγκη δ' ὡς κέλει), / And I must yield, not to my own desire, / But rather to the Lord'.[84] His is a study of the will and its consequences, where Jephthah, like his enemy Ammon, is 'free to choose' (πάρεστιν αἵρεσις / ποιεῖν τὸ δ' ἢ μή) (*Datur nunc optio / solida agenti*) and the action and catastrophe of the tragedy follows from this choice.[85] The Chorus affirms Jephthah's decision—if not in full approval, then at the very least condoning his vow in the absence of any firm knowledge of God's providence. According to the Chorus, 'reason cannot know (*animus varie mihi distrahitur*) / Whether our captain did aright / Then when he opened first his mouth / Unto the Lord in vow'; nevertheless, the Chorus is bound to honour and even celebrate Jephthah's decision: 'Hardly may we withhold our praise, / Knowing that, ere the battle brake, / On him God's spirit fell' (πρὸ μάχης, Κυρίου κάππεσε πνεῦμα) (*Spiritus irruit ante duellum*).[86] The final Chorus, which closes the play, is even less ambiguous:

> Amen! And in the time to come should all,
> Guided by prudence (σοφῶς) when they make their vows,
>   The future with unerring forethought scan;
> A vow once made may not be set aside. (*vota soluere non licet, / Quae facta sunt*)
>   Thy vision of the future must be clear
>   If thou art gladly to fulfill thy vow
>   Unto the Lord; a vow at random made
>   Oft ends in ruin. Here full proof is found.
>   Vows unto God must e'er be wisely made
>   And paid in full; this is the righteous act.[87]

While Buchanan eventually identified with Calvinism, and Christopherson was an English bishop who remained loyal to Rome, even after his imprisonment (by Elizabeth), neither of

---

[80] Sharratt and Walsh, 83–4; *Jephthes*, 34.

[81] Sharratt and Walsh, 85; *Jephthes*, 37.

[82] John Christopherson, *Jephte*, in *John Christopherson, 'Iephte', William Goldingham, 'Herodes'*, ed. Christopher Upton, Renaissance Latin Drama in England, 2nd ser. 7 (Hildesheim: Georg Olms, 1988), 3 (hereafter Upton).

[83] John Christopherson, *Jephthah*, ed. and tr. Francis Howard Forbes (Newark, Del.: University of Delaware Press, 1928), 118–21 (hereafter Forbes); Upton, 147ᵛ.

[84] Forbes, 124–5.   [85] Forbes, 86–7; Upton, 142ᵛ–143ʳ.   [86] Forbes, 134–5; Upton, 150ʳ.

[87] Forbes, 156–7; Upton, 153ʳ.

their plays exhibit any easy confessional approach to God's providence or the human will. Both use tragedy to emphasize God's consistency in an effort to explain an otherwise disturbing scriptural locus. Both are, foremost, tragedies about an action: Jephthah's vow. In this sense, Buchanan and Christopherson exploit the very definitions of tragedy and plot in the *Poetics*, where:

> Tragedy is mimesis of action, and it is chiefly for the sake of the action that it represents the agents … the plot, since it is mimesis of an action, should be of a unitary and indeed whole action; and the component events should be so structured that if any is displaced or removed, the sense of the whole is disturbed or dislocated.[88]

Though they fundamentally disagree on the meaning of Jephthah's vow, and his obligation to or, in Buchanan's case, *not* to see it through, tragedy enables each poet to bring the act into focus. Thus this important passage in Judges becomes less an episode in a winding and errant scriptural history than an opportunity to use poetry—and, specifically, tragedy—to give contemporary evangelical meaning to an ancient act done under the law.

While Christopherson's *Jephte* may complicate our understanding of confessional poetry during the first half of the sixteenth century, the man himself did not endorse the particular version of sacred drama endorsed by Bucer in *De regno Christi*. Indeed, even after Bucer's death in 1551, Christopherson, the 'elected byshop of Chychester', joined two other inquisitors—Cuthbert Scot, Bishop of Westchester, and Thomas Watson 'elected bishop of Lincolne'—in a 1556/7 investigation of Bucer's legacy and influence on Cambridge.[89] Christopherson's behaviour is memorable. After a thorough admonition of the university officials for their 'heretical' opinions, Watson delivered a Candlemas sermon, during which Christopherson famously fell into a 'sodaine swound' where he 'babled manye thinges unadvisedly, and as though he had bene out of his wittes'.[90] Soon after, on 6 February 1557 commissioners exhumed the bodies of Bucer and Paul Fagius; Watson delivered another sermon as the corpses were burned.

A later (anonymous) chronicle characterized the inquisition at Cambridge and the posthumous execution as an 'enterlude' ultimately unsuccessful in restoring traditional religion to the university: 'that impanate God whom Bucers Carcase had chased from thence, was not yet retourned thither again'.[91] It is perhaps little more than a coincidence that two of the three inquisitors presiding over the burning were themselves tragic poets: Christopherson and Thomas Watson, the writer of the *Absolom* celebrated by Ascham. Nevertheless, the posthumous execution by tragedians is a fitting emblem for the coming age when, as Reformation and Counter-Reformation debates intensified

[88] Aristotle, *Poetics*, ed. Halliwell, 53, 59; Giacomo Cardinali, 'George Buchanan's Tragedies and Contemporary Dramatic Theory', in Philip Ford and Roger P. H. Green (eds), *George Buchanan: Poet and Dramatist* (Swansea: Classical Press of Wales, 2009), 163–82, esp. 165.

[89] *A Briefe Treatise concerning the Burnynge of Bucer and Phagius*, tr. Arthur Golding (London, 1562), A4ʳ.

[90] *A Briefe Treatise*, G8ᵛ.   [91] *A Briefe Treatise*, H4ʳ.

and spread, a variety of confessional and controversial plays would ultimately replace the sacred dramas of the early sixteenth century.

Further Reading

Cartwright, Kent. *Theatre and Humanism: English Drama in the Sixteenth Century* (Cambridge: Cambridge University Press, 1999).

Eden, Kathy. *Poetic and Legal Fiction in the Aristotelian Tradition* (Princeton: Princeton University Press, 1986).

Foxe, John. *Two Latin Comedies by John Foxe the Martyrologist: 'Titus et Gesippus', 'Christus triumphans'*, ed. and tr. John Hazel Smith (Ithaca, NY: Cornell University Press, 1973).

Giebels, Henk, and Frans Slits. *Georgius Macropedius, 1487–1558: Leven en Werken van een Brabantse Humanist* (Tilburg: Stichting Zuidelijk Historisch Contact, 2005).

Grimald, Nicholas. *The Life and Poems of Nicholas Grimald*, ed. L. R. Merrill (New Haven: Yale University Press, 1925).

Kelly, Henry Ansgar. *Ideas and Forms of Tragedy from Aristotle to the Middle Ages* (Cambridge: Cambridge University Press, 1993).

Lake, Peter, and Michael Questier. *The Antichrist's Lewd Hat: Protestants, Papists and Players in Post-Reformation England* (New Haven: Yale University Press, 2002).

McFarlane, I. D. *Buchanan* (London: Duckworth, 1981).

Parker, John. *The Aesthetics of Antichrist: From Christian Drama to Christopher Marlowe* (Ithaca, NY: Cornell University Press, 2007).

Shuger, Debora Kuller. *The Renaissance Bible: Scholarship, Sacrifice, and Subjectivity* (Berkeley, Calif.: University of California Press, 1994).

Streete, Adrian. *Protestantism and Drama in Early Modern England* (Cambridge: Cambridge University Press, 2009).

Waldron, Jennifer. *Reformations of the Body: Idolatry, Sacrifice, and Early Modern Theatre* (New York: Palgrave Macmillan, 2013).

Watson, Thomas. *A Humanist's 'Trew Imitation': Thomas Watson's 'Absalom'*, ed. and tr. John Hazel Smith (Urbana, Ill.: University of Illinois Press, 1964).

White, Paul Whitfield. *Drama and Religion in English Provincial Society, 1485–1660* (Cambridge: Cambridge University Press, 2008).

Whitfield White, Paul. *Theatre and Reformation: Protestantism, Patronage, and Playing in Tudor England* (Cambridge: Cambridge University Press, 1992).

CHAPTER 32

'THIS VERSE MARKS THAT': GEORGE HERBERT'S *THE TEMPLE* AND SCRIPTURE IN CONTEXT

ALISON KNIGHT

> They that insist upon single Texts, without considering the main Designe, can derive no thing from them cleerly; but rather by casting atomes of Scripture, as dust before mens eyes, make every thing more obscure than it is.
>
> (Thomas Hobbes, *Leviathan*[1])

IN a 1545 sermon on Matthew 26, Martin Luther recapitulates his arguments for *tota scriptura*, or scripture's inherent unity, with a textile metaphor. He argues that 'Holy Scripture is the garment that our Lord Christ has put on and in which he lets himself be seen and found. This garment is so woven and so wrought together into one, that it may neither be cut nor parted'.[2] The metaphor was commonplace; in early modern England, descriptions of the Bible as a seamless, unbreakable weave abound. Peter Hay and Anthony Burgess, for example, repeat this Christ's garment metaphor; and John Bale praises the 'very complet summe and whole knitting up' of the 'unyversall verities of the Bible'.[3] Conversely, heretics are described not as misinterpreting scripture, but as rending or tearing it through isolated quotation that deliberately abuses its unity. William Tyndale asserts that Roman Catholics 'rent and teare the scriptures with

---

[1] Hobbes, *Leviathan; or, The Matter, Forme, and Power of a Common Wealth, Ecclesiasticall and Civil* (London, 1651), 331.

[2] 'Die heylige Schrifft ist das fleyd, das unser Herr Christus angezogen hat und sich drinn sehen und finden lest, Solches fleyd ist durchauss gewurcket und in einander dermassen gefasset, das mans nicht schneyden noch teylen kan'. *D. Martin Luthers Werke: Kritische Gesammtausgabe*, lii (Weimar: H. Böhlaus Nachfolger, 1968), 802, ll. 1–4.

[3] Peter Hay, *A Vision of Balaams Asse* (London, 1616), 242; Anthony Burgess, *An Expository Comment, Doctrinal, Controversal [sic], and Practical upon the Whole First Chapter to the Second Epistle of St. Paul to the Corinthians* (London, 1661), 528; John Bale, *The Image of Both Churches* ([London, 1548]), A2ᵛ.

theyr distinctions and expound them violently, contrary to the meanyng of the texte, and to the circumstances that go before and after'.[4] Similarly, George Lightbody accuses the Catholic Mass book of omitting full readings in preference for 'rent and clipped pieces of Scriptures' that, when seen in isolation, support their doctrines.[5] Daniel Featley accuses heretics of 'cutt[ing]' and 'mak[ing] a rent in the Scripture, by taking a part by it selfe to serve [their] turne, contrary to … the whole'.[6] And it is not merely heretics who are described as tearing, or in some way violating, the unity of the Bible; in *Essays in Divinity,* John Donne accuses himself of it, merely for devoting disproportionate attention to the title of Genesis, asking, 'since our merciful God hath afforded us the whole and intire book, why should wee tear it into rags, or rent the seamless garment?'[7] In *The Priest to the Temple,* George Herbert criticizes preachers who excessively subdivide their texts, which he terms 'text-crumbling', arguing that they should expound 'the whole text, as it lyes entire, and unbroken in the Scripture it self'.[8]

Concepts of scripture's unity are fundamental to the Protestant *sola scriptura* approach; scripture is only self-sufficient in so far as it is self-interpreting (that is, its single divine authorship allows disparate parts to interpret one another), and early modern emphases on scripture's seamless unity, with its attendant sense that isolated quotation violates the text, has enormous implications for early modern devotional writing.[9] Current criticism emphasizes early modern devotional writers' tendency to incorporate individual scriptural phrases, even single words, into their language. This is particularly true of Herbert's *The Temple*; his tendency to accumulate references to scripture is the focus of Chana Bloch's *Spelling the Word,* which considers his 'borrowings from scripture at the level of word or phrase'.[10] Stanley Stewart similarly emphasizes Herbert's 'cut-and-paste' biblical references,[11] and Joseph Summers outlines how poems like 'The Altar' are composites of biblical phrases.[12] This seeming contradiction—that devotional writers like Herbert criticize the piecemeal use of scriptural texts, and yet critics have noticed their tendency to pepper their language with scriptural words, often taken very much out of context—suggests new ways of approaching devotional writers' understanding of scriptural unity, and how they understood scriptural language to work within their own.

---

[4] William Tyndale, *The Parable of the Wycked Mammon* (London, 1547), A6^{r-v}.

[5] George Lightbody, *Against the Apple of the Left Eye of Antichrist* ([Holland], 1638), A2^r.

[6] Daniel Featley, *A Second Parallel* (London, 1626), 54.

[7] John Donne, *Essays in Divinity: Being Several Disquisitions Interwoven with Meditations and Prayers,* ed. Anthony Raspa (Montreal: McGill-Queen's University Press, 2001), 16.

[8] George Herbert, *The Works of George Herbert,* ed. F. E. Hutchinson (Oxford: Clarendon Press, 1941), 235.

[9] On which, see Patrick Collinson's 'The Coherence of the Text: How it Hangeth Together: The Bible in Reformation England', in W. P. Stephens (ed.), *The Bible, the Reformation and the Church: Essays in Honour of James Anderson,* Journal for the Study of the New Testament, supplement series 105 (1995): 84–108. Collinson address aspects of biblical unity, but the article is, for the most part, a broad exploration of early modern Protestant biblicism.

[10] Chana Bloch, *Spelling the Word: George Herbert and the Bible* (Berkeley, Calif.: University of California Press, 1985), 4.

[11] Stanley Stewart, *George Herbert* (Boston: Twayne, 1986), 65.

[12] Joseph H. Summers, *George Herbert: His Religion and Art* (London: Chatto & Windus, 1954), 142.

Full comprehension of early modern writers' use of scriptural phrases depends on two related terms, now obsolete (at least in their contemporary sense): *coherence* and *contexture*. The word *coherence* remains so common that inattention to one of its primary early modern meanings is understandable; the *OED* barely registers it as a concrete noun meaning, 'the immediately connected parts of a discourse'. The example the *OED* provides signals the term's scriptural application; it gives William Pemble's statement in his exposition of Zechariah that 'the division of the Chapters here make the cohaerence somewhat difficult'.[13] Pemble uses the term in one of its most common early modern senses: the connection of a verse to its surrounding verses, such that a passage produces a harmonious whole. To borrow the early modern textile metaphor, identifying the coherence of a verse was equivalent to identifying how an individual thread was interwoven with others to produce a pattern.

This meaning of the term describes a fundamental early modern approach to scripture. In sermons, the expectation that preachers would outline the coherence of their texts—that is, clarify how the verses preached on worked with surrounding verses, thereby assuring audiences that their interpretations reflected the true intent of a passage—was so basic to the structure of a sermon, it was one of two fundamentals allowed in James I's 1622 *Directions Concerning Preachers*, which strictly limited 'tak[ing] occasion by the expounding of any text of Scripture whatsoever, to fall into any set discourse or Common-place (otherwise then by opening the coherence and division of his Text)'.[14]

Outside preaching, the concept of a scriptural coherence was more loosely defined; it described not only the contextualized meaning of a verse, but also 'how [scripture] hangeth together: and the agreement that one place hath with another, that thereby that which seemeth darke in one, is made easie in another'.[15] A coherence, then, situates individual pieces of scripture within scripture's overall unity; this could operate on the level of 'the wordes going immediately before … and the wordes folowing',[16] such that writers like Nicholas Byfield could cite sections of scripture by shorthand, as '*Job* 33.25,26. with the coherence',[17] to a widespread 'comparing like places of scripture with like',[18] often termed collation or 'the conference of places'.

Coherence bears considerable similarity to another contemporary term used to describe the internal connections of scripture: *contexture*. Neil Fraistat has resurrected this term to describe the unity of poetic collections, arguing for the literary connotations of the term in early modern usage; he notes the *OED*'s definition, 'the construction or composition of a writing as consisting of connected and coherent members'.[19] Fraistat offers the term as a tool for discussing the 'formal and thematic repetitions, contrasts, and progressions' in a

---

[13] William Pemble, *A Short and Sweete Exposition upon the First Nine Chapters of Zachary* (London, 1629), 160.

[14] George Abbot (Archbishop of Canterbury), *The Coppie of a Letter* ([Oxford, 1622]), 2.

[15] Richard Rogers, *Seven Treatises* (London, 1603), 290.

[16] Gregory Martin, *The Holie Bible Faithfully Translated into English* (Douai, 1609), 435–6.

[17] Nicholas Byfield, *Sermons upon the Ten First Verses of the Third Chapter of the First Epistle of S. Peter* (London, 1626), 229.

[18] John Hales, *A Sermon Preached at St Maries in Oxford upon Tuesday in Easter Weeke* (Oxford, 1617), 36.

[19] Neil Fraistat, 'Introduction: The Place of the Book and the Book as Place', in Fraistat (ed.), *Poems in their Place: The Intertextuality and Order of Poetic Collections* (Chapel Hill, NC: University of North Carolina Press, 1986), 14 n. 2.

volume of poetry;[20] however, the term offers more ways of describing the internal connections of texts than Fraistat takes advantage of, particularly regarding scripture. The word derives from the Latin *con* and *texere*, literally 'to weave together'; in the early modern period, the term was applied to textiles, human tissue, and architecture, as well as more abstract concepts like history or logic. One of its primary uses, however, related to that other derivative of *texere*: texts—very often, scriptural text.

The meaning of scriptural contexture was often synonymous with coherence, albeit a synonym that borrowed from the other applications of the term: scripture was a seamless weave, and reading verses out of context was equivalent to tearing fabric or mutilating human tissue. In *Death's Duel*, Donne explores the material applications of the term in his statement that 'The naturall frame and contexture [of Psalms 68: 20] … the *contignation* and knitting of this building, [is] that hee that is *our God* is the *God of all salvations*'.[21] Donne associates the contexture of the verse with the *contignation* ('the joining or framing together of beams or boards') and the 'knitting together' of the 'building' that is the full meaning of his text. Thomas Jackson argues that while some verses might not seem particularly weighty, they nevertheless contribute to scripture's overarching discourse, for 'how weake or slender soever they bee … in themselves, yet the combination or contexture of them must needs be strong, because it is woven by the finger of God'.[22] Similarly, Samuel Rutherford praises scripture's tendency towards 'a contexture of contraries, as black and white, sweet and sowre woven through other, as day-light and night in a morning twy-light'.[23]

Rutherford here outlines the primary difference between the otherwise synonymous coherence and contexture. While the coherence of a text presupposes harmony—the ways in which portions of a text are woven together to form a meaningful unit—contexture describes the weave of a particular passage, whether it is coherent or not. For Rutherford, this can mean a passage in which 'there is white, and black, good and evil, crooked and straight interwoven'.[24] Jeremy Taylor observes that one might face 'a contexture where one part does not alwayes depend upon another, Where things of differing natures intervene and interrupt'.[25] As parliamentarian George Abbot (1604–46) notes, 'some places require much peasing … else hee may erre in *benè divisis ad malè conjuncta* [well-dividing to the point of ill-conjoining], and cause a falling out of the text either with its coherence and scope, or else of one text with another'.[26] Scriptural verses are inextricably linked to their surrounding text, constantly adjusting each other's potential for meaning; even seemingly disjointed passages cannot merely be parsed or considered in pieces. To take an isolated

---

[20] Fraistat, 'Introduction', 8. Joshua Eckhardt explores the importance of contexture as Fraistat describes it in early modern manuscript miscellanies in *Manuscript Verse Collectors and the Politics of Anti-Courtly Love Poetry* (Oxford: Oxford University Press, 2009); Lara M. Crowley argues for the usefulness of contexture for practices of textual editing in 'Manuscript Context and Literary Interpretation: John Donne's Poetry in Seventeenth-Century England' (Ph.D. thesis, University of Maryland, 2007).

[21] John Donne, *Deaths Duell* (London, 1632), 3–4.

[22] Thomas Jackson, *A Treatise of the Divine Essence and Attributes* (London, 1628), 322.

[23] Samuel Rutherford, *A Sermon Preached to the Honourable House of Commons* (Edinburgh, 1644), 57–8.

[24] Rutherford, *The Tryal & Triumph of Faith* (London, 1652), 105.

[25] Jeremy Taylor, *Treatises of 1. The Liberty of Prophesying, 2. Prayer ex tempore, 3. Episcopacie* (London, 1648), 74.

[26] George Abbot, *The Whole Book of Job Paraphrased* (London, 1640), 3–4.

view of a section of text without 'peasing', or reconciling, its contexture—to well-divide it at the expense of well-conjoining—has a knock-on effect; like a Newton's cradle, it will produce 'a falling out' of a text with its surrounding verses.

This aspect of Protestant approaches to scriptural unity—that individual pieces of scripture cannot be understood in isolation—deeply informs devotional writers' incorporation of scriptural words and phrases into their own language. It is perhaps intuitive to say that when early modern devotional writers quote scriptural words or phrases, they do so with the expectation that readers will understand those words' and phrases' full biblical resonance and particularities. Yet for writers like Donne, Henry Vaughan, or (most representative) Herbert, the invocation of scripture's coherences and contextures is fundamental to their understanding of, and means of effecting, a sense of unity between scripture's language and their own. It is no coincidence that Herbert provides some of the period's most resonant arguments for the impossibility of isolating pieces of scripture from the whole, and yet his poetic language is saturated with scriptural phraseology. Herbert's incorporation of verses deliberately invokes scripture's coherences and contextures in a process of 'weaving himself into the sense' of scripture.

I. Scriptural Unity in *The Temple*: 'The Words Apart are not Scripture'

In 'The H. Scriptures. II.', Herbert makes what Helen Wilcox describes as 'a classic statement of post-Reformation biblical collation'.[27] Because 'the entire Bible was seen as interconnected', Herbert exclaims,

> Oh that I knew how all thy lights combine,
>   And the configurations of their glorie!
>   Seeing not onely how each verse doth shine
> But all the constellations of the storie.
>   This verse marks that, and both do make a motion
> Unto a third, that ten leaves off doth lie. (ll. 1–6)

Wilcox notes the similarity between the collating approach of 'The H. Scriptures. II.' and Herbert's description of optimum approaches to scripture in *A Priest to the Temple*, in which he argues that 'all truth being consonant to it self, and all being penn'd by one and the self-same Spirit, it cannot be, but that an industrious, and judicious comparing of place with place must be a singular help for the right understanding of the Scriptures'.[28] These statements underpin Bloch's *Spelling the Word*, which investigates how scriptural images and words develop meaning as they echo through the Bible, and outlines how 'the marriage of two texts almost invariably generates new meanings'.[29] As such, collation

[27] *The English Poems of George Herbert*, ed. Helen Wilcox (Cambridge: Cambridge University Press, 2007), 211. All quotations from *The Temple* are taken from this edition.
[28] Herbert, *Works*, 229; *English Poems*, ed. Wilcox, 211.   [29] Bloch, *Spelling the Word*, 63.

(also termed 'the conference of places') is rightly acknowledged to be a key concern in *The Temple*.

However, what Wilcox and Bloch describe is only one aspect of Herbert's invocation of biblical unity. Simply, collation is a process that identifies and analyses cross-biblical coherences; as such, it is a component of, and dependent on, coherence. Herbert's engagement with the unity of scriptural words rarely stops there. Although she does not describe it as such, Bloch's approach assumes that individual uses of a word across the Bible must be understood in terms of surrounding text; otherwise, the accumulations and adjustments of meaning that she describes would not occur. While Bloch does not make this requirement explicit, Herbert does; he argues that meaning depends on

> the whole text, as it lyes entire, and unbroken in Scripture it self [... this is] naturall, and sweet, and grave. Whereas ... crumbling a text into small parts ... hath neither in it sweetnesse, not gravity, nor variety, since the words apart are not Scripture, but a dictionary, and may be considered alike in all the Scripture.[30]

Bloch's approach depends on constant attention to words as they stand within their contexts, and not 'the words apart'; collation must be paired with coherent readings for it to offer anything more than a concordance.

Herbert's understanding of biblical unity entirely shapes his incorporation of scripture into his poetic language. Herbert's description of biblical unity in 'The H. Scriptures. II.' concludes by writing himself into that unity:

> Such are thy secrets, which my life makes good,
>   And comments on thee: for in ev'ry thing
>   Thy words do find me out, & parallels bring,
> And in another make me understood. (ll. 9–12)

Richard Strier claims that in this poem, Herbert is 'surely telling us how to read his own volume',[31] arguing for a method that Stewart describes as accessing the 'composite expression' and interrelated meaning of the Bible itself.[32] However, this must not be understood merely as an aspect of the Bible's composition that Herbert seeks to showcase in *The Temple*, but rather something that the scriptural text is able to extend to, and effect in, his work. In 'The H. Scriptures. II.', it is no accident that scripture is the agent of the lines; scripture incorporates him into its own unity, as though he were a verse himself.[33]

In 'Jordan (II)', Herbert describes scripture's incorporation of himself and his language in terms of the textile metaphors common to early modern descriptions of

---

[30] Herbert, *Works*, 235.

[31] Richard Strier, *Love Known: Theology and Experience in George Herbert's Poetry* (Chicago: University of Chicago Press, 1983), 34.

[32] Stewart, *George Herbert*, 67.

[33] This agency of scripture is reminiscent of Stanley Fish and Strier's debate concerning Herbert's poetic agency in Fish, *Self-Consuming Artifacts: The Experience of Seventeenth-Century Literature* (Berkeley, Calif.: University of California Press, 1972), and Strier, *Love Known*. Fish argues that Herbert's poetry 'requires ... the relinquishing of the claims of authorship' in the face of God's authorial control (158); Strier counter-argues that such requirements must be understood as a stance. I do not make an argument for who maintains authority, only that Herbert does not believe that the Bible's modes of making meaning are separate from his poetry, once biblical verses are incorporated into his verse.

coherence and contexture. He claims that his poetry was, in the past, concerned with 'decking the sense' (l. 6)—that is, clothing—the 'heav'nly joyes' (l. 1) he sought to describe, on the basis that 'nothing could seem too rich to clothe the sunne' (l. 11). Herbert claims he was attempting through his words to weave Christ's seamless garment. The attempt, which Wilcox describes as 'inappropriate and born of pride',[34] is not entirely ineffective; he suggests that

> As flames do work and winde, when they ascend,
> So did I weave my self into the sense.
> But while I bustled, I might heare a friend
> Whisper, *How wide is all this long pretence!*
> *There is in love a sweetnesse readie penn'd:*
> *Copie out onely that, and save expense.* (ll. 13–18)

However, Herbert's efforts to produce 'quaint' and 'invent[ive]' (l. 3) poetic garments for Christ are not so much prideful as they are backward and unnecessary. Critics generally approach 'Jordan (II)' as a renunciation of overly ornamental or metaphysical poetry,[35] but this is not the point; Herbert's poetic efforts are not termed sinful, merely superfluous 'bustle' that approaches the Bible from the wrong angle. Herbert attempts to weave a poetic garment for Christ, yet just as flames interweave the higher they ascend, the closer he approaches the genuine seamless garment, the more he discovers that he 'did weave [him]self into the sense'. His emphasis is changed from attempting to weave meaningful commentaries about Christ to recognizing that biblical words generate meaningful words for him.

The contextural metaphor implicit in 'weaving himself into the sense' is key to understanding Herbert's assertion that 'There is in love a sweetnesse readie penn'd: / Copie out onely that, and save expense'. Critics struggle to understand these lines; Barbara Leah Harman observes that what it means to poetically copy out a 'sweetnesse readie penn'd' is not explained.[36] Although most critics agree with Cedric Brown and Maureen Boyd that, in keeping with assertions in 'The Thanksgiving' and 'The Flower', Herbert argues for transcribing the Bible, the problem remains that such transcription is 'hardly a poem'.[37] In fact, these lines continue the contextural metaphor developed throughout 'Jordan (II)'. Returning to Herbert's criticism of 'text-crumbling', it seems that the 'sweetness' he strives for is the same type of 'sweetness' inherent in a scriptural coherence. Because scripture's sweetness, or coherent complexity, is 'readie penn'd', by copying that—that is, by incorporating scriptural words into his poetry—he finds that, rather

---

[34] *English Poems*, ed. Wilcox, 369.

[35] See Herbert, *Works*, ed. Hutchinson, 495, Philip McGuire, 'Herbert's Jordan II and the Plain Style', *Michigan Academian*, 1 (1969): 69–74, and Frances Cruikshank, *Verse and Poetics in George Herbert and John Donne* (Farnham: Ashgate, 2010), 21. Note that Frank Manley, 'Toward a Definition of the Plain Style in the Poetry of George Herbert', in Maynard Mack and George de Forest Lord (eds), *Poetic Traditions of the English Renaissance* (New Haven: Yale University Press, 1982), 209, Arnold Stein, *George Herbert's Lyrics* (Baltimore, Md.: Johns Hopkins University Press, 1968), 22, and Summers, *George Herbert*, 110, caution that such a rejection of complex poetry is not without irony.

[36] Barbara Leah Harman, *Costly Monuments: Representations of the Self in George Herbert's Poetry* (Cambridge, Mass.: Harvard University Press, 1982), 48.

[37] Cedric C. Brown and Maureen Boyd, 'The Homely Sense of Herbert's "Jordan"', *Studies in Philology*, 79 (1982): 150.

than needing to worry about weaving intricately wrought poems to suit Christ, Christ (through the Bible) gives richer, more intricate meanings to his verse. If Strier is correct in his belief that in 'The H. Scriptures. II.' Herbert instructs his reader in how to read *The Temple*, then in 'Jordan (II)', Herbert instructs the reader that the scriptural words and phrases he incorporates are not to be read in isolation. In essence, he understands the Bible to be part of the 'sweetnesse' of *The Temple*; his poems only yield their full meaning when the reader refers back to a verse 'as it lyes entire, and unbroken in the scripture it self'.[38]

As Herbert's self-effacement (or at least his self-subordination to the Bible) might indicate, the scriptural coherences that Herbert invokes generally work to correct or call into question the aims and conclusions of his verse. This type of contextural correction is at the core of 'The Odour, 2 Cor. 2'. From the title, it is clear that the poem cannot be read without reference to scripture. However, how it is to be read in relation to 2 Corinthians 2 is not immediately clear. Critics agree that the poem hinges on Herbert's play upon the idea of a 'sweet savour', taken from 2 Corinthians 2: 15 ('For we are unto God a sweet savour of Christ'). The importance of 2 Corinthians 2: 15 in 'The Odour, 2 Cor. 2' leads critics to single out that verse as the sole element of 2 Corinthians 2 that contributes to the poem; Herbert's title becomes citational imprecision. Wilcox, for example, states that 'the title source is 2 Corinthians ii 15', and in his edition of *The Temple*, Hutchinson goes so far as to correct the title to 'The Odour. 2 Cor 2.15', even though he admits the adjustment has no textual basis.[39] Yet the reader must consider the chapter as a whole before determining that 2 Corinthians 2: 15 is what Herbert intends. In doing so, it becomes clear that, while 2 Corinthians 2: 15 speaks loudest through Herbert's lines, it is the verse in context that is invoked:

> Now thankes bee unto God, which alwayes causeth us to triumph in Christ, and maketh manifest the savour of his knowledge by us in every place.
> For wee are unto God, a sweet savour of Christ, in them that are saved, and in them that perish.
> To the one *wee are* the savour of death unto death; and to the other, the savour of life unto life: and who is sufficient for these things?
> For wee are not as many which corrupt the word of God: but as of sinceritie, but as of God, in the sight of God speake we in Christ. (2 Corinthians 2: 14–17)

2 Corinthians 2 provides not the subject of Herbert's lines, but the solution: Herbert searches for a way to become a sweet savour to God, of reciprocating the sweetness he receives. He argues that by mutual call and response between Christ and himself, he will be able to participate in Christ's sweetness.

Herbert declares that

> This breathing would with gains by sweetning me
> (As sweet things traffick when they meet)
> Return to thee.
> And so this new commerce and sweet
> Should all my life employ, and busie me. (ll. 26–30)

---

[38] Herbert, *Works*, 235.   [39] See *English Poems*, 603; and *Works*, 174.

2 Corinthians 2 allows a solution that Herbert's words, in themselves, do not achieve. Herbert strives to be a sweet savour *to* Christ; in 2 Corinthians 2, an individual can only be a sweet savour *of* Christ, 'in them that are saved'. St Paul praises the fact that God, through Christians, 'maketh manifest the savour of his knowledge by us in every place'. The sweet savour of Christ is the savour of his word sincerely preached and sincerely heard; this is the genuine 'sweet traffic' that should 'employ, and busie' Herbert (especially as preacher at Bremerton) all his life. 2 Corinthians 2: 15 informs the question; when read in context, its entire coherent meaning provides a solution that the poem otherwise misses.

One of *The Temple*'s most resonant examples of the Bible's contextural correction of a poem's meaning is 'The Altar'. Achsah Guibbory correctly suggests that 'The Altar' 'calls into question human invention in ways that echo Puritan iconoclasm'.[40] However, it is not the poem itself, but rather the biblical verses that Herbert incorporates into the poem, read in context, that undermine human poetic invention. As already mentioned, Summers notes that 'there is hardly a phrase in "The Altar" that is not taken from a specific biblical passage';[41] these biblical source materials become the stones that 'The Altar' is constructed from. As such, the parts of 'The Altar' are indeed 'as [God's] hand did frame' (l. 3), establishing a fourth altar in the poem (beyond a stone altar, an altar of the heart, and the altar that is the poem): the altar of scripture. It is on this scriptural altar that Herbert's 'sacrifice of praise' is finally located.

Wilcox identifies Herbert's primary source texts as Deuteronomy 27: 5 ('and there shalt thou build an Altar unto the Lord thy God, an altar of stones') and Psalms 51: 17 ('The sacrifyce of God is a troubled sprete, a broken and contrite hert (O God) shalt thou not despyse').[42] These verses appear within chapters that are concerned with the breakdown of human devotional invention. Read as a whole, Psalm 51 emphasizes the brokenness of human utterance—the speaker claims to be 'shapen in wyckednesse' (Psalms 51: 5) and requests that God will

> Delyver me from bloud gyltynesse (O God) thou that art the God of my health, and my tonge shall syng of thy ryghteousnesse.
> O Lord, open thou my lips; and my mouthe shall shewe furth thy praise.
> For thou desyrest no sacrifice; else wolde I geve it thee: but thou delytest not in burnt-offerynge.
> The sacrifyce of God is a troubled sprete, a broken and contrite hert (O God) shalt thou not despyse. (Psalms 51: 14–17)[43]

Because the speaker is broken and contrite, he requests that God will provide him with words of praise—that God will both 'open his lips' and provide 'his praise', which the speaker will only 'shew forth'. It is these words, which God causes to issue from a broken and contrite heart, that provide the replacement for the sacrifice of a burnt offering.

---

[40] Achsah Guibbory, *Ceremony and Community from Herbert to Milton: Literature, Religion, and Cultural Conflict in Seventeenth-Century England* (Cambridge: Cambridge University Press, 1998), 47.

[41] Summers, *George Herbert*, 142.

[42] *English Poems*, 92.

[43] Verse 15 is given in the version provided in the order for Morning Prayer from the 1559 Prayer Book, as it is the form in which this verse was most commonly encountered. I have, however, returned 'our lips' and 'our mouth' to the form that appears in all English Bibles. See Brian Cummings, *The Book of Common Prayer: The Texts of 1549, 1559, and 1662* (Oxford: Oxford University Press, 2011), 104.

Similarly, the true altar on which this sacrifice of praise can be made emerges in Deuteronomy 27. The full instructions concerning the construction of the altar read

> and there shalt thou build an Altar unto the Lord thy God, an altar of stones: thou shalt not lift any iron *toole* upon them.
> Thou shalt build the Altar of the LORD thy God of whole stones: and thou shalt offer burnt offerings theron unto the LORD thy God.
> And thou shalt offer peace offerings, and shalt eate there, and rejoyce before the LORD thy God.
> And thou shalt write upon the stones all the words of this Law very plainely. (Deuteronomy 27: 5–8)

The altar stones, which according to Deuteronomy 27: 5 cannot be polluted with the 'workman's tool', are also stones upon which the Israelites must write 'all the words of this Law very plainely'. This perplexing biblical command presents a devotional conundrum. It is clear that God requires an altar built with scriptural stones, but how can Herbert or the Israelites be expected to carve the words of the law upon stones that they are forbidden to touch with tools? The answer is obvious: they cannot. At least, not in a traditional sense: instead, this verse subtly demands an altar of the word, which Herbert and the Israelites must assemble, but not author.

This perplexing request is explained through collation with 2 Corinthians 3: 3, which explains that the believer will become 'the Epistle of Christ ... written not with inke, but with the Spirit of the living God, not in tables of stone, but in fleshy tables of the heart'. Wilcox suggests an additional biblical source for line 6, 'The heart alone is such a stone', in Ezekiel 11: 19 ('I will take the stonie heart out of their flesh, and will give them an heart of flesh').[44] Importantly, what makes hearts 'stony', and thus prevents God from inscribing them with internalized scripture, is the human tendency to idolize their own creations; God provides and writes on hearts of flesh so that humans

> may walke in [his] statutes, and keepe [his] ordinances, and doe them ...
> But *as for them* whose heart walketh after the heart of their detestable things, and their abominations, [he] wil recompense their way upon their owne heads. (Ezekiel 11: 20–1)

Essentially, 'workmen'—those who are more interested in creating their own 'abominations' than following God's 'statutes' (scriptures)—are devotionally stony and unable to receive the inscribing of the Word onto the softened heart. As such, these verses in their coherences and contextures speak through Herbert's text to deconstruct the perfectly formed workmanship of his 'altar of words', replacing it with an altar of the Word.

Herbert's poetic reliance on the corrective action of scripture's coherences and contextures is similarly the focus of 'The Flower', in which Herbert's speaker both refers to, and essentially misses the point of, Job 14. Wilcox suggests that the poem invokes several biblical verses concerned with human ephemerality, particularly Job 14: 2 ('Hee commeth forth like a flower, and is cut downe') and Psalms 103: 15 ('The dayes of Man are but as grasse, for he florisheth as a floure of the felde').[45] Wilcox is correct to emphasize the connections

---

[44] *English Poems*, 93.   [45] *English Poems*, 566.

Herbert draws between the natural world's cycles of death and rebirth, and his inclusion of himself in that natural cycle, which he links to the rising and falling of his own poetic efficacy. However, Wilcox does not note how heavily the poem is derived from various passages of Job, particularly the entire chapter of Job 14, nor how extensively Herbert invokes Job's articulations of the cycle of the natural order through death and rebirth, as well as humanity's dependence on God through it.

The connections between Job 14 and death and resurrection were well established in the period; Job 14: 1–2 was included in the Book of Common Prayer's 'Order for Buriall', and was one of nine passages from Job included in the medieval Sarum liturgy's *Dirige*, or 'dirge';[46] both works similarly include Job 19: 25–6, which reads

> I knowe that my redemer lyveth, and that I shal rise out of the earth in the last daye, and shalbe covered agayne with my skinne, and shall se God in my flesh: yea, and I my selfe shall beholde hym, not with other, by with these same eyes.

However, Job 14: 1–2 reads, 'Man that is borne of a woman, hathe but a short tyme to lyve, and is full of miserye: he commeth up, and is cut doune lyke a floure, he flyeth as it were a shadow, and never continueth in one staye'.[47] These verses do not appear to hold the promise of resurrection that Herbert (and indeed the Book of Common Prayer) locates in them; rather, they seem to serve as an expression of unavoidable mortality. However, the chapter proceeds to say,

> For there is hope of a tree, if it be cut downe, that it will sprout againe, and that the tender branch thereof will not cease.
> Though the roote thereof waxe old in the earth, and the stocke thereof die in the ground:
> *Yet* through the sent of water it will bud, and bring forth boughes like a plant.
> But man dyeth, and wasteth away: yea, man giveth up the ghost, and where is hee?
> As the waters faile from the sea, and the floud decayeth and dryeth up:
> So man lyeth downe, and riseth not: till the heavens be no more, they shall not awake; nor bee raised out of their sleepe.
> O that thou wouldest hide mee in the grave, that thou wouldest keepe me secret, untill thy wrath bee past, that thou wouldest appoint me a set time, and remember me.
> If a man die, shall he live againe? All the dayes of my appointed time will I waite, till my change come.
> (Job 14: 7–14)

While Job 14: 1–2 likens the human lifespan to a mown flower, the remainder of the passage maintains emphasis on the fundamental differences between the human lifespan and death in the natural world. Cycles of rising and falling are only discernible in plants, not humans. Job complains about the finality and singularity of human death; the natural world demonstrates resurrection in sprouting branches, budding roots, and rising rivers, whereas the powerless human body 'lyeth down, and riseth not'—at least until the last day. However, if

---

[46] This association was upheld in English vernacular primers; see Charles C. Butterworth, *The English Primers (1529–1545): Their Publication and Connection with the English Bible and the Reformation in England* (Philadelphia: University of Pennsylvania Press, 1953), 100–2, 115–16.

[47] *Book of Common Prayer*, ed. Cummings, 171. The 'Order for Buriall' contains numerous other statements and scriptural passages (esp. 1 Cor. 15) that emphasize bodily resurrection.

human resurrection is excluded from the natural cycle and dreadful in the face of the grave, it in fact possesses more promise; nature eventually will perish in the last day, and man alone will be resurrected by God. Job 14: 1–2 represents the first, despairing half of what, read in full, becomes a balanced whole. Yet in 'The Flower', Herbert composes a poem that ignores this fundamental argument of Job 14 and advances a completely opposite devotional position.

The second stanza recapitulates Job 14: 8–9's description of plants returning to the ground in a prelude to resurrection and rebudding, as well as the human ability to hide in the ground from the destruction of the apocalypse in Job 14: 12–13:

Who would have thought my shrivel'd heart
Could have recover'd greennesse? It was gone
Quite under ground; as flowers depart
To see their mother-root, when they have blown;
Where they together
All the hard weather,
Dead to the world, keep house unknown.

Herbert here invokes Job 1: 21 ('Naked came I out of my mothers wombe, and naked shall I returne thither'), another component of the 'Order for Buriall', in his description of 'returning' to a mother in the ground; he ignores the deep distinctions that are made in Job 14 between the retreat of plants to the ground, and human burial, and explicitly presents himself as participating in a natural cycle of death and rebirth. Herbert returns to Job 14: 14 ('If a man die, shall he live againe? All the dayes of my appointed time will I waite, till my change come') through his request, 'O that I once past changing were, / Fast in thy Paradise, where no flower can wither!' (l. 22).

This line offers Herbert's first indication of dissatisfaction with or separation from the natural world's cycle through death and renewal. It becomes clear that Herbert's frustration with natural life's vagaries is not physical, but literary; Herbert taps into the Joban nexus of the natural world's regenerative cycle in terms of poetic capacity and the ephemeral flowering of his poesy/posy. Herbert parallels the rebudding of the mother-root when it 'scents the water' (Job 14: 9) in that

now in age I bud again,
After so many deaths I live and write;
I once more smell the dew and rain,
And relish versing. (ll. 36–9)

Humans are to him 'flowers that glide' (l. 44) insofar as they experience God's favour and compositional blessing intermittently; Herbert claims that to expect constant linguistic blessing, or to 'grow in a straight line, / Still upwards bent, as if heav'n were mine own' (ll. 29–30) would incur God's wrath, in a manner equivalent to God's anger at the presumption and verbal capacities of the builders of the Tower of Babel. Herbert generates through his use of the language of Job a nuanced and highly meaningful devotional poem; if, however, it is read in terms of the original context of the verses he alludes to, it is clear that the reading derived from Job does not correspond with the point of the passage. Herbert invokes Job 14's language of cyclical natural renewal as if it confirms and describes his participation in that cycle and his experience of God's action in his life, but God's compositional action in Herbert's life cannot be explained in terms of cyclical nature—at least with

Job as proof-text. It is rather what pulls him out of such variation and establishes spiritual constancy.

Herbert offers a similar misreading of Job in 'The Pearl. *Matth. 13*'. Roberts W. French and Wilcox have noted the reference to Job 6: 12 ('*Is* my strength the strength of stones? or *is* my flesh of brasse?') in line 27 of the poem, 'my stuffe is flesh, not brasse; my senses live'.[48] Yet by not considering the verse in context, critics have missed the full intensity of the turn provided to Herbert's devotional stance in the poem (that is, that the speaker's description of renouncing the world is, in fact, arrogant). Many do not notice the turn at all; Wilcox categorizes it as a 'poem of renunciation' and feels that it is 'summed up by [Helen] Vendler as a "fine repudiary poem" which "casts off the world while yet recognising its appeal to the full"'.[49] Certainly, the poem does amply describe wordly temptations and renounces them with full knowledge. Yet Strier notes a slight qualification to that renunciation in the way that it focuses on 'the way to the kingdom of heaven' rather than 'the value of the kingdom' (87).

French provides a stronger reading of the turn involved in the poem; he suggests that 'the movement of "The Pearl" is through error toward a concluding restoration of perspective' (330), which is that 'the delights of learning, honour, and pleasure that the speaker values are, by comparison to the kingdom of heaven, negligible' (330). The contribution of Job, he argues, is to contrast Job's heroic patience with the speaker's 'pampered' laments (330). While French touches on a contextural reading, in that his interpretation depends on a shift in the meaning of the phrase 'my flesh is brass' based on the differences between Job's situation and the speaker's, his reading does not make available the full correction of the speaker's approach that is made via a coherent reading of Job 6: 12. In response to criticism from his friends for his complaints against God, Job protests,

> Oh that my griefe were throughly weighed, and my calamitie layd in the balances together.
> For now it would be heavier then the sand of the sea, therefore my words are swallowed up.
> For the arrowes of the Almightie are within me, the poyson whereof drinketh up my spirit: the terrors of God doe set themselves in aray against mee.
> Doeth the wilde asse bray when he hath grasse? or loweth the oxe over his fodder?
> Can that which is unsavery, bee eaten without salt? or is there any taste in the white of an egge?
> The things *that* my soule refused to touch, are as my sorrowfull meat.
> Oh that I might have my request! and that God would graunt mee the thing that I long for!
> Even that it would please God to destroy mee; that he would let loose his hand, and cut me off.
> Then should I yet have comfort, yea I would harden my self in sorrow; let him not spare, for I have not concealed the words of the holy One.
> What *is* my strength, that I should hope? and what *is* mine ende, that I should prolong my life?
> *Is* my strength the strength of stones? or *is* my flesh of brasse? (Job 6: 2–12)

---

[48] Roberts W. French, '"My Stuffe is Flesh": An Allusion to Job in George Herbert's "The Pearl"', *Notes and Queries*, 27 (1980): 329; *English Poems*, ed. Wilcox, 325.

[49] *English Poems*, ed. Wilcox, 321; Helen Vendler, *The Poetry of George Herbert* (Cambridge, Mass.: Harvard University Press, 1975), 182.

Job cries out in response to the suffering that flesh is heir to; his question, 'is my flesh of brass?', is intended to argue that, being mere flesh, he does not have the strength to withstand the afflictions that assault him. It is intended to justify his repeated requests to leave the world. The speaker, however, uses the phrase to describe his susceptibility to pleasure, and as such he uses the verse out of context and without understanding it. If he did, then, as Strier and French suggest, like Job he would recognize that the sufferings of this world far outweigh its pleasures, and like Job, he would approach Matthew 13 as a gift rather than a sacrifice.

'The Flower' and 'The Pearl. *Matth. 13*' beg the question of how deliberate these misreadings and contextural corrections are intended to be: is Herbert actually taking his texts out of context and misapplying them as a result, or is he staging such a process, thereby undermining his own proficiency as a reader and erasing a false boundary between his poems and the Bible? To a certain degree, it is entirely impossible to determine—there are no knowing winks in *The Temple*. Yet it seems highly improbable that Herbert would have been unaware of the ways in which his uses of scripture depart from the original. In the case of Job 14 in particular, a different set of conclusions than those of 'The Flower' would have been reinforced at every burial he attended. We can only assume, based on Herbert's general familiarity with scripture and his own comments about how to read it, that these misreadings are intended to express something about how scripture and his poetry work together.

It should not come as a surprise to critics of Herbert that he might employ his own erroneous application and mistaken understanding of scripture as a means by which to point to the more powerful capacity to weave meanings offered by full, unbroken reading of scripture. Tuve, Strier, and Sophie Read discuss Herbert's use of the rhetorical device of *metanoia*, or *correctio*; that is, as Read describes, his tendency to 'say something and then think better of it'.[50] Yet, while Tuve argues that familiar biblical figures are '*within not outside* the poem' due to their commonplace nature,[51] and while Earl Miner discusses Herbert's shifts of perspective between the poems of *The Temple*, from Christ to Christian, or passion to eucharist,[52] critics have not considered the ways in which Herbert's use of *correctio* and perspective depend on fundamental Protestant theories of how scripture's language works. Herbert does not only correct himself or shift perspectives within his poems; he depends on an essential continuity between his words and the Bible's, such that a shift in perspective to the Bible will correct misreadings or misapplications of texts.

Herbert demonstrates that the incorporation of scripture into his own devotional language cannot be considered a 'cut-and-paste' approach—the ties that individual verses had to the Bible were by no means cut. Rather, he provides a particularly saturated exemplar of a technique for approaching the language of the Bible that was fundamental to the Reformation, espoused by Luther, Tyndale, Featley, Perkins, and countless others: the

---

[50] Sophie Read, 'Rhetoric of Real Presence in the Seventeenth Century' (Ph.D. thesis, University of Cambridge, 2007), 63; see Strier, *Love Known*, 240; Rosemond Tuve, *A Reading of George Herbert* (Chicago: University of Chicago Press, 1952), 124.

[51] Tuve, *Reading*, 29.

[52] Earl Miner, 'Some Issues for Study of Integrated Collections', in Neil Fraistat (ed.), *Poems in their Place: The Intertextuality and Order of Poetic Collections* (Chapel Hill, NC: University of North Carolina Press, 1986), 34.

Bible is a unified whole, with every part affecting the others, and with every part having endless effect on human words.

FURTHER READING

Bloch, Chana. *Spelling the Word: George Herbert and the Bible* (Berkeley, Calif.: University of California Press, 1985).

Cruikshank, Frances. *Verse and Poetics in George Herbert and John Donne* (Farnham: Ashgate, 2010).

Eckhardt, Joshua. *Manuscript Verse Collectors and the Politics of Anti-Courtly Love Poetry* (Oxford: Oxford University Press, 2009).

Fish, Stanley. *Self-Consuming Artifacts: The Experience of Seventeenth-Century Literature* (Berkeley, Calif.: University of California Press, 1972).

Guibbory, Achsah. *Ceremony and Community from Herbert to Milton: Literature, Religion, and Cultural Conflict in Seventeenth-Century England* (Cambridge: Cambridge University Press, 1998).

Stein, Arnold. *George Herbert's Lyrics* (Baltimore, Md.: Johns Hopkins University Press, 1968).

Strier, Richard. *Love Known: Theology and Experience in George Herbert's Poetry* (Chicago: University of Chicago Press, 1983).

Summers, Joseph H. *George Herbert: His Religion and Art* (London: Chatto & Windus, 1954).

Vendler, Helen. *The Poetry of George Herbert* (Cambridge, Mass.: Harvard University Press, 1975).

CHAPTER 33

'BLESSED JOSEPH! I WOULD THOU HADST MORE FELLOWS': JOHN BUNYAN'S JOSEPH

NANCY ROSENFELD

JOHN Bunyan's famous Apology, the rhymed introduction to *The Pilgrim's Progress* in which the author describes how he 'Fell suddenly into an Allegory', serves as a convenient introduction to the preacher's use of biblical characters as a means both to understand his own life and to create fictional characters. The Apology is devoted to a justification of the metaphors upon which the story of Christian's and Christiana's journey is based:

> Solidity, indeed becomes the Pen
> Of him that writeth things divine to men:
> But must I needs want solidness, because
> By Metaphors I speak; Was not God's Laws,
> His Gospel-Laws, in older time held forth
> By Types, Shadows and Metaphors? ...
> [The sober man] rather stoops,
> And seeks to find out what by pins and loops,
> By Calves, and Sheep, by Heifers, and by Rams;
> By Birds, and Herbs, and by the blood of Lambs,
> God speaketh to him.[1]

As U. Milo Kaufmann points out: 'There is a conspicuous tension between the didactic and literalist methods widespread in Puritanism and the imaginative methods native to the grand tradition in literature'.[2] Kevin Killeen, however, notes that:

> Literal interpretation in early-modern thought permitted phenomenal latitude. For all
> that the central Protestant dictum, *sola scriptura*, the sufficiency of the Bible alone, might

---

[1] John Bunyan, *The Pilgrim's Progress*, ed. James Blanton Wharey, 2nd edn, rev. Roger Sharrock (Oxford: Clarendon Press, 1960), 1, 4.

[2] U. Milo Kaufmann, *The Pilgrim's Progress and Traditions in Puritan Meditation* (New Haven: Yale University Press, 1966), 5.

be thought to imply a lack of engagement with non-scriptural learning, the interpretative habits of the commentary tradition are underpinned very much by their receptivity to non-theological material to explicate the scriptures. *Sola Scriptura*, in the mid-seventeenth century, at least, did not imply the Bible's insularity as much as its primacy.[3]

John Bunyan did not need such latitude. His use of biblical characters, both in his sermons and in his imaginative writing, served less to interpret the holy text than to interpret his own life: his overall approach to the Bible was indeed literal. In Killeen's terms, Bunyan reversed the interpretative paradigm; in his practice of commentary, scriptural material was used to explicate non-theological material. In this sense Bunyan did not lay himself open to charges—or, perhaps more important, to self-recrimination—for overuse of allegory. When Bunyan implies or draws a comparison between himself and Joseph the falsely accused prisoner, or Joseph who pays a heavy price for speaking the truth, he relates to the biblical character as detailed in the literal words of the text.

This chapter opens with an overview of Bunyan's reading practice vis-à-vis the Bible; the Joseph character of Genesis is then discussed; finally examples of Bunyan's use of the character in three representative texts are touched upon: *The Life and Death of Mr. Badman*, an allegory which details how the Christian should conduct his or her daily affairs as merchant, friend, parent, spouse; *The Acceptable Sacrifice*: a sermon-tract; and *Grace Abounding to the Chief of Sinners*, Bunyan's highly popular spiritual diary.

By the beginning of the seventeenth century there was general acceptance of the legitimacy of translations of the Bible into English. There remained, however, an undertone of discomfort with the very accessibility of the English text, to which Patrick Cary (c.1624–57) gave expression:

> Our church still flourishing w'had seene
> If th'holy-writt had ever beene
> Kept out of lay-men's reach;
> But, when 'twas English'd, men halfe-witted,
> Nay women too, would be permitted
> T'expound all texts, and preach.
> Then what confusion did arise!
> Coblers, devines gan to dispise,
> Soe that they could but spell:
> This, ministers to scorne did bring;
> Preaching was held an easy thing,
> Each-one might doe't as well.[4]

The availability of the holy texts in English was especially important to John Bunyan, whose literacy differed from that of a majority of English-speaking clergymen of the time; Bunyan could have been the artisan-turned-preacher whom Cary had in mind. While most seventeenth-century clergymen, whether owing allegiance to the established church or to dissenting frameworks, could be assumed proficient in Latin, to some extent in Greek, and possibly in Hebrew, Bunyan, as far as is known, could not read any

[3] Kevin Killeen, *Biblical Scholarship, Science and Politics in Early Modern England: Thomas Browne and the Thorny Place of Knowledge* (Farnham: Ashgate, 2009), 66–7.

[4] Patrick Cary (Carey), *Trivial Poems, and Triolets: Written in Obedience to Mrs. Tomkin's Commands* (1651; London: John Murray, 1820), 15–16.

of the classical languages. He does not, however, apologize for this ignorance. Indeed he notes—one assumes with the proverbial tongue in cheek—that 'Christ's little ones ... are not gentlemen; they cannot with Pontius Pilate speak Hebrew, Greek and Latin'.[5]

According to Christopher Hill:

> By the seventeenth century the Bible was accepted as central to all spheres of intellectual life: it was not merely a 'religious' book in our narrow modern sense of the word religion. Church and state in Tudor England were one; the Bible was, or should be, the foundation of all aspects of English culture. On this principle most Protestants were agreed.[6]

John Bunyan was persecuted for being unwilling to accept that, in Hill's words, the institutions of 'Church and state were one'; he refused to refrain from preaching, even when ordered to do so by local lay magistrates committed to enforcing the strictures of the restored Church of England.[7] As part of one's overall approach to life in this world and the next, however, Bunyan would not have understood the possibility of a boundary between what is now termed 'the religious' and 'the secular'. Scripture, after all, does not generally differentiate between religious and extra-religious spheres. The God of the Hebrew Bible—the Old Testament—is a hands-on deity: he is involved in issues of daily life, whether of direct religious significance (male circumcision; construction of altars; animal sacrifice[8]) or seemingly extra-religious, even intimate family and sexual questions: dietary issues; a woman's inability to become pregnant; how to treat one's servant-girl; accidentally viewing one's father's nakedness.[9]

The degree to which what came to be known as the secular was not differentiated from the religious may be seen in an almost randomly chosen example: chapter 12 of Leviticus. In this one chapter the deity speaks to Moses, ordering him to pass on instructions to the people as to actions behooving a woman who has recently given birth. A boy-child is to be circumcised on his eighth day. There is medical advice: the mother is considered unclean, and should be separated for a period of time dependent on whether the child is male or female. At the end of the period of bleeding following the birth, the mother is to bring an offering to the door of the tabernacle of the congregation. If the family is of limited means, turtledoves or pigeons—more easily available to the poor—should be substituted for a lamb. Religious, medical, and economic practices are interwoven; the reader hardly notices where one ends and the next begins.

For Bunyan, the Bible was thus not only central to all spheres of religious and intellectual life; it was a book to live by, or in Hill's words, 'for most men and women the Bible was their point of reference in all their thinking ... the Bible was the source of virtually all ideas; it supplied the idiom in which men and women discussed them'.[10] Bunyan looked to

---

[5] John Bunyan, *Miscellaneous Works*, gen. ed. Roger Sharrock (Oxford: Clarendon Press, 1976–94), i. 304.

[6] Christopher Hill, *The English Bible and the Seventeenth-century Revolution* (London: Penguin Books, 1994), 7.

[7] The situation of dissenters in Bedford may be contrasted with that of their fellows in e.g. Dorchester. As David Underdown notes, Dorchester in the 1660s 'was a haven for dissenters, protected by magistrates who had no interest in enforcing the punitive Clarendon Code, as Cavalier justices in the county were doing. The town's JPs deliberately avoided disturbing the nonconformist conventicles that met both in and outside the Gaol'. David Underdown, *Fire from Heaven: Life in an English Town in the Seventeenth Century* (London: HarperCollins, 1992), 239.

[8] See e.g. Lev. 11; Gen. 17; extensive sections of Leviticus, Numbers.

[9] See e.g. Gen. 9, 16, 21.   [10] Hill, *English Bible*, 34.

the sacred text for enlightenment both as to the world to come and as to this world. In his daily reading and meditating on biblical texts he sought hints of his own future: was he numbered among the elect or the reprobate? Meditating on Esau (one who is duped into selling his birthright and then cheated out of his father's blessing) increased the preacher's almost unbearable fear as to his own salvation. He simultaneously found in the various biblical literary genres—poetry, tales, dialogues, historiography, wisdom collections, word-play—illuminating depictions of human life, both in terms of past history and as to how one should conduct daily interactions with others. The shopkeeper deciding whether to extend credit to the poor widow could look to scripture for guidance just as surely as should the preacher searching for a topic for the coming Sunday's sermons.

It is generally accepted that one of the defining aspects of the Protestant Reformation was the emphasis placed on the believer's unmediated connection with the sacred texts of his creed. Generations of Protestant Christians were thus raised on the stories told in the Old Testament, and especially on the tales of the patriarchs in Genesis and the life of Moses and his family in Exodus. Bunyan would arguably have agreed with Leveller leader William Walwyn's unmediated approach to the holy texts: 'there is no place in Scripture too hard for us: shew us the mysteries we cannot reveale: the Parables that wee cannot clearly open'. Addressing those believers who lacked a university education, Walwyn argues: 'why may not one that understands English onely, both understand and declare the true meaning of [the text] as well as an English Hebrician, or Grecian, or Roman whatsoever?'[11]

Bunyan, of course, did not function in an intellectual or religious vacuum, and while he hesitated to allegorize biblical texts, he did belong to a community of interpreters. As Maxine Hancock notes, he had been 'initiated by sermon-hearing and intense discussion into the Calvinistic community of nonconforming English puritanism as his interpretive community'.[12] For Bunyan, preaching was his own road to salvation:

> I was made to see that the Holy Ghost never intended that men who have Gifts and Abilities should bury them in the earth, but rather did command and stir up such to the Exercise of their Gift, and also did commend those that were apt and ready to do so, *They have addicted themselves to the ministry of the saints.*[13]

Bunyan's nonconformist preaching was said to be talented, articulate, convincing, and therefore dangerous to the newly restored monarchy and its established church. The local Bedfordshire gentry regarded him as a troublemaker, a rabble-rouser who must, in today's terms, either shut up or be shut up.

Steeped as he was in scripture, Bunyan was intimately familiar with the leading characters of the Genesis-Exodus family romance: figures such as Jacob and Esau served him as models of the believer's attitude towards election or reprobation. Simultaneously these figures could be taken as role-models: when faced with a moral dilemma, one could learn from the choices made by a biblical figure. Yet metaphorizing a biblical narrative could

---

[11] William Walwyn, *The Power of Love* (London, 1643), 9, 46. On Leveller approaches to the Bible, see the chapter by Andrew Bradstock in this volume.

[12] Maxine Hancock, 'Bunyan as Reader: The Record of *Grace Abounding*', *Bunyan Studies*, 5 (1994): 74.

[13] John Bunyan, *Grace Abounding to the Chief of Sinners*, ed. Roger Sharrock (Oxford: Clarendon Press, 1962). Citations of *Grace Abounding* (GA) are to paragraph number: para. 270. Quote in Bunyan's italics is from Foxe's *Acts and Monuments*. (In Bunyan's day *addict* meant *disciple* or *adherent*.)

easily be seen as distancing oneself from the literal text. Thus Bunyan trod a fine line between respect for the literal text, while dramatizing tales or figures, and uses of the biblical characters which might seem unacceptably metaphorical.[14] He succeeded in treading this line by using the literal, the uninterpreted, text to interpret an individual life. A construction of Bunyan's imaginary is beyond the scope of this chapter; but it may be argued that his use of a biblical character to better understand the nature of a living, historical, or literary character is what enabled Bunyan to produce living, breathing, imaginary creations. Bunyan's use of the Joseph figure of Genesis illustrates the problematics of cleaving to the biblical text, while making imaginative use of one of the major characters of the Old Testament as a means to understand and interpret one's own choices. If John Bunyan was, as is generally agreed, one of the forefathers of the novel, the latter achievement results in no small part from his response to biblical figures.

In any discussion of responses to written texts believed to be sacred, it is difficult to avoid a certain amount of specification as to what is meant by *reading*. Recent scholarship has begun, albeit tentatively, to question what Philip Benedict terms 'the hoariest of all generalizations about the long-term consequences of the Reformation, namely, that the establishment of Protestantism encouraged Bible reading and thus literacy'.[15] For Bunyan, however, as for most of his literate co-religionists, whether Church of England or dissenting, reading was central to daily religious practice. The latter consisted of reading portions of the holy text silently and aloud, both in the privacy of one's 'closet' and with family, household, and congregation members; meditating on individual words, verses and stories; regular, even daily, writing of spiritual diaries whose content was in large measure based on one's reading of the Bible; sharing of those diaries with one's clergyman and fellow congregants.

Diarmaid MacCulloch suggests that: 'For someone who really delighted in reading, religion might retreat out of the sphere of public ritual into the world of the mind and the imagination'.[16] And as Monica Furlong points out, for Bunyan, as for many of his contemporaries, the Bible was 'the world of books, plays, poetry, learning, which his poverty and lack of education denied him'.[17] John R. Knott, Jr. notes the importance of Bunyan's comparative lack of formal education in any attempt to analyse his work. Bunyan, in Knott's words,

> approached the Bible as only a relatively uneducated person of the seventeenth century could, with an acute sense of the power of the Word to terrify or comfort one who wrestled with it ... His torment is that of an unlearned man who must search the Scripture with the conviction that any one verse can save or damn him.[18]

Yet while the preacher's commitment to *sola scriptura* was total, claims that he was unfamiliar with extra-scriptural texts should be taken with the proverbial grain of salt. Bunyan is known to have read certain of Martin Luther's works of biblical exegesis, and his extra-scriptural reading was arguably broader and more sophisticated than is traditionally

---

[14] On the literal sense of scripture, see the chapter by Debora Shuger in this volume.

[15] Philip Benedict, *Christ's Churches Purely Reformed: A Social History of Calvinism* (New Haven: Yale University Press, 2002), 431.

[16] Diarmaid MacCulloch, *The Reformation: A History* (New York: Penguin, 2003), 75.

[17] Monica Furlong, *Puritan's Progress* (New York: Coward, McCann & Geoghegan, 1975), 31.

[18] John R. Knott, Jr., *The Sword of the Spirit* (Chicago: University of Chicago Press, 1980), 130, 132.

acknowledged. Arthur Dent's *The Plaine Man's Pathway to Heaven*, with which Bunyan was familiar, contains references to a wide range of classical authors, whether religious or secular: Homer, Sophocles, Hesiod, Demosthenes, Euripides, to name but a few.[19] According to the practice of the time, the margins of each page were dotted not only with sources of citations from the Old and New Testaments, but with references to other authors and texts, many of which had been rendered into English by the seventeenth century. It would not have been difficult for Bunyan to borrow such texts from those of his colleagues and admirers who possessed well-stocked libraries, and the more one's familiarity with Bunyan's writing increases, the more one is aware that the author was well-read in terms of what was available to him in English.

Bunyan's sensitivity to the problems inherent in interpreting sacred texts (problems that centred upon assigning meaning to the specific text above—or below—its so-called literal meaning) directed his practice as a reader. His meditation on the holy text enabled him to use the characters and situations depicted in the Bible to interpret events in his own life and in the lives of others. Kaufmann suggests that the Puritan tradition of heavenly meditation, in which Bunyan was immersed, was founded on the 'assumption that for the individual to improve his conceptions of things above, he must compare them with things below'. According to Kaufmann, when Bunyan says that:

> 'My dark and cloudy words they do but hold / The Truth, as Cabinets inclose the Gold', his conception of the relationship between truth and words is conventionally Puritan: truth was 'contained' in words, ready to be emptied into the mind in the simple process of reading; but little allowance was made for the possibility that it might be incommensurate with its containers, that the event might perhaps be a slightly more commodious vessel than the word.[20]

Meditation on the lives of biblical characters was especially important to Bunyan, since he did not expect God's ways to be immediately comprehensible via cognition. This flows from his basic Calvinist approach according to which the individual cannot know for sure that he is one of the fortunate elect, neither by way of sensing that he is saved, nor by performing good works, which would be a sign of election. In Calvin's words:

> It is asked, how it happens that of two, between whom there is no difference of merit, God in his election adopts the one, and passes by the other? I, in my turn, ask, Is there any thing in him who is adopted to incline God towards him? If it must be confessed that there is nothing, it will follow, that God looks not to the man, but is influenced entirely by his own goodness to do him good. Therefore, when God elects one and rejects another, it is owing not to any respect to the individual, but entirely to his own mercy which is free to display and exert itself when and where he pleases.[21]

According to Bunyan's autobiographical descriptions in *Grace Abounding*, while meditating upon a particular biblical verse or short passage he often sensed that a specific word or phrase was forcing itself into his mind. Bunyan felt this to be a process over which he had little, if any, control. He took these attacks seriously, seeing in them sacred messages;

[19] Arthur Dent, *The Plaine Man's Path-way to Heaven* (London, 1629).
[20] Kaufmann, *Pilgrim's Progress*, 171, 11.
[21] John Calvin, *Institutes of the Christian Religion*, tr. Henry Beveridge (Grand Rapids: Eerdmans Publishing, 1997), III.23.9.

he was tortured by his inability to interpret these messages, almost telegraphic in their terseness.[22] Scholars have long pondered the nature of what for Bunyan were terrifying attacks. Richard L. Greaves suggests, albeit cautiously, that during the 1650s and early 1660s Bunyan suffered at least two bouts of what is now known as clinical depression. For Greaves, the specific words and phrases which Bunyan perceived as forcing themselves upon his consciousness are symptoms, while the process of their sudden appearance and disappearance outlines a pathology and its cure.[23] Although *Grace Abounding* may convincingly serve as a psychiatric case study, Bunyan's spiritual autobiography can—and generally is—read as the record of the progress of the pilgrim's union with his saviour, a union which is not necessarily permanent, but is repeatedly sought. In his discussion of *Grace Abounding*, Brainerd P. Stranahan emphasizes the significance of the 'dramatic appearance of biblical passages in [Bunyan's] mind: the sudden arrivals of these texts are among the most important happenings in the narrative ... we cannot tell when a new text will ambush the hero and produce either intense joy or despair'.[24]

Bunyan's practice may be usefully compared to an earlier, non-Christian interpretative tradition. Joseph Heinemann notes that since the sages who created the *aggadot* (the post-biblical Hebrew legends)

> assumed that the meaning of Scripture was manifold, they felt it was necessary to try to extract the full range of implications not only from the contents of the biblical text but from every apparently superfluous word as well. The assumption that 'one biblical statement may carry many meanings' (B. Sanhedrin 34a) led to their interpretation of every locution in the biblical text, often in disregard of its meaning in context ... They were of the opinion that the Bible intended to impart moral and religious instruction, to teach us how to live, rather than to supply dry factual information of a geographical or genealogical nature, for example.[25]

Bunyan would probably not have agreed that 'the meaning of Scripture was manifold'. He would have agreed, however, that no word in the holy text could be superfluous; and while his experience of being, as it were, attacked by individual words or phrases could be seen as removing the word or phrase from its original context, he might not have seen the validity of differentiating between the meaning of a word within and without its context.

The Joseph of Genesis (chapters 37–50) served Bunyan as a moral exemplar in his willingness to speak truth, even when the act of speaking exacted a heavy personal price. Joseph's willingness to speak truth to power is seen in his response to sexual temptation and false accusation on the part of his master's wife, as well as in his response to undeserved imprisonment. His refusal to lie with his master's wife is, perhaps surprisingly, not

---

[22] See *GA*, para. 91: 'These words [MY LOVE] came again into my thoughts, and I well remember as they came in, I said thus in my heart, What shall I get by thinking on these two words? ... that sentence fell in upon me'; para. 93: 'I was much followed by this scripture, *Simon, Simon, behold, Satan hath desired to have you*'; para. 94: 'it [the sound of the latter] would sound so loud within me, yea, and as it were call so strongly after me'.

[23] Richard L. Greaves, *Glimpses of Glory: John Bunyan and English Dissent* (Stanford, Calif.: Stanford University Press, 2002), 7–8.

[24] Brainerd P. Stranahan, 'Bunyan's Special Talent: Biblical Texts as "Events" in *Grace Abounding* and *The Pilgrim's Progress*', *English Literary Renaissance*, 11 (1981): 329, 331.

[25] Joseph Heinemann, 'The Nature of the Aggadah', in Geoffrey H. Hartman and Sanford Budick (eds), *Midrash and Literature* (New Haven: Yale University Press, 1986), 48.

presented by the biblical narrator as an example of the overcoming of sexual desire (the reader knows that Joseph was young and handsome, but is given no information as to the attractions of Potiphar's wife). Rather the young man's rejection of his mistress's advances is shown as another example of his willingness to speak honestly to those in positions of power, even at the price of lengthy imprisonment.

The Joseph character of Genesis might now be called a man of multiple meanings: a talented economist and manager both on the local and national level, his ability to interpret dreams indicates psychoanalytic brilliance. For those interested in family roles and their literary expression—whether in ancient mythology or the more recent *bildungsroman*—he is an archetype of the motherless younger son, favoured by his father but thoroughly disliked by his siblings, sent away from home, forced into servitude, to face a series of challenges which will test him and enable him to grow into his intended role of responsible adult. In his discussion of the tales of the patriarchs from Genesis, Thomas H. Luxon points out that:

> [R]eading out of these stories a clear case for true identity as a redemption/ transformation experience requires that many of their details be ignored or allegorized, but the Joseph story presents even harder problems. Taken as a whole, it is too willing to meditate on the contradictions, ironies, and contingencies of identity and the self's relation to God. Perhaps this is why Protestantism never adopts it as a model for the redeemed self as it did the others. Joseph, at so many points, is both self and other—Hebrew patriarch and Egyptian master, a son of Abraham and adoptively a son of Ishmael, both a Jacob (an ambitious younger son) and an Esau (excluded from the messianic line).[26]

Because of clear parallels between their life-experiences, Bunyan found in Joseph 'a model for the redeemed self' in two of Joseph's *personae*: the unfairly accused sexual harasser and the prisoner. In Joseph's lengthy incarceration the two overlapped; he was imprisoned for allegedly assaulting his master's wife. For John Bunyan the two were not connected: after the Restoration of the monarchy and the re-establishment of the Church of England he spent some twelve years in prison for refusing to promise to refrain from preaching. At other stages in his career as a dissenting minister, whose London sermons were sometimes attended by hundreds of eager listeners, the preacher faced slander when a rumour circulated that he was seen in the company of loose women; although these rumours infuriated Bunyan, they were apparently not taken seriously, and did not damage his career or reputation.

The Genesis narrative tells of two periods in which Joseph was incarcerated. At the age of 17 he unwisely strengthens his brothers' already strong dislike: having been sent out to help tend the flocks of his half-brothers, the sons of the serving maids Bilhah and Zilpah, on his return he 'brought unto his father their ill report' (Genesis 37: 2).[27] The reader is not surprised when the brothers, away from parental supervision, cast Joseph into a pit, thus enabling a group of Midianite traders to sell the youth to a caravan of Ishmaelites on their

---

[26] Thomas H. Luxon, *Literal Figures: Puritan Allegory and the Reformation Crisis in Representation* (Chicago: University of Chicago Press, 1995), 119.

[27] References to the Bible are to *The Holy Bible, containing the Old and New Testaments, Translated Out of the Original Tongues and with the Former Translations Diligently Compared and Revised by His Majesty's Special Command A.D. 1611* (London: British and Foreign Bible Society, 1967).

way to Egypt (Genesis 37). It is, however, only chapters and years later, when the brothers come to Egypt and recall their earlier behaviour, that we learn of Joseph's screams and pleading while he lay in the pit: 'And they said one to another, We are verily guilty concerning our brother, in that we saw the anguish of his soul, when he besought us, and we would not hear' (Genesis 42: 21).

The young Joseph's anguish and pleas contrast with his stoical behaviour years later when he languishes in prison on an unjust accusation; we are not told of screams and pleading on his part. Joseph's imprisonment in Egypt, of course, is lengthier than the hours, or at most days, which he had spent in the pit near Dothan. Moreover in the dungeon Joseph's abilities are recognized and he is put in charge of the whole prison household. Eventually his patience is rewarded but until pharaoh's chief butler remembers him, he is seemingly content to wait.

In his view of Joseph, Bunyan may be said to cleave to the Genesis depiction of the hero's character and motivation. Joseph is shown to be patient, certainly a loving son, a responsible servant, and one who understands his role as a tool of the Deity. He does not lack a sense of pride, however, and willingly accepts both the responsibilities placed upon him and the concomitant status symbols: the coat of many colours which his father, perhaps unwisely, bestows on his adored son; years later, pharaoh's ring, the use of a chariot, the daughter of a high-ranking Egyptian as wife. In his role of leader he does not project humility: once revealed to his brothers he is kind and forgiving, but maintains his pride and dignity.

This may be contrasted with the character as depicted by Rene de Cerisiers (1609–62) in *The Innocent Lord, or, the Divine Providence. Being The incomparable History of Joseph* (available to Bunyan in an English translation by William Lowre, though there is no evidence that he was familiar with it). De Cerisiers's young Joseph is little less than perfect: 'he had all the vertues of his father, and the beauty of his mother. So many graces perfectionated his body … Oftentimes the neighbors would come unto the house of Laban, to see onely his visage'. Moreover:

> To see him on his knees, his hands joyned, his eyes halfe shut, one would have thought that it was a statue of marble, if those lips had not given some motion to his prayer, or an Angel, if he had not sighed sometimes. I speak not of the reverence with which he honoured his parents; the belief thereof is easie through the sweetness that rendred him pleasing to all the world.[28]

Bunyan might not have been disturbed by de Cerisiers's anachronisms, had he encountered them: Hebrews did not pray on their knees, and as a rule did not address the Deity silently. He would, however, have noticed contradictions with the biblical text: Joseph angered his father on more than one occasion; he was surely not 'pleasing to all the world'; and of all possible descriptives, 'sweet' is arguably not one of the first to come to mind. For Bunyan, unlike for de Cerisiers, the biblical text was not a jumping-off point from which one could develop a character via additions whose source was in the writer's imagination. In other words, Bunyan did not engage in wishful thinking: he accepted the biblical tale in its literal version, even when the behaviour depicted was not what he would have wanted it to be.

[28]   Rene de Cerisiers, *The Innocent Lord, or the Divine Providence*, tr. William Lowre (London, 1654) 3, 5.

Bunyan's *Life and Death of Mr Badman* is an allegory couched in the framework of a dialogue: a conversation between Mr Wiseman and Mr Attentive, neighbours in an English market town, who fall in together while out on a walk and have a long, comfortable gossip about their neighbour Mr Badman, lately deceased. Although much of the text critiques the protagonist's financial behaviour, many of the most vivid sections of the dialogue detail Badman's marriages and relationships with women other than his wife. While canvassing Badman's penchant to fall into 'the deep pit' of the flattering mouth of a strange woman, and conversely to tempt maids 'to commit uncleanness with him', Attentive and Wiseman compare such men to Joseph: *'But how far off are these men from that Spirit and Grace that dwelt in* Joseph'.[29]

Wiseman and Attentive at first speak disparagingly of Joseph's mistress, even calling her unclean, a whore, culminating in Attentive's apostrophe *'Blessed* Joseph! *I would thou hadst more fellows!'*[30] This lack of generosity, of Christian charity, is mitigated by Wiseman's next comment:

> Mr. *Badman* has more fellows than *Joseph*, else there would not be so many Whores as there are: For though I doubt not but that *that* Sex is bad enough this way, yet I verily believe that many of them are made Whores at first by the flatteries of *Badmans* fellows. Alas! there is many a woman plunged into this sin at first even by promises of Marriage.[31]

Joseph is here depicted by Bunyan as concerned both with his duty to his master and with his own salvation; at the same time he appears to bear a didactic duty towards his mistress. In his appeal to the latter Joseph speaks first on the social/ legal level, and then appeals to religion. There is an unspoken contract between the handsome young Israelite and his Egyptian master: Joseph has been granted the run of the house, and of course the running of the household, on condition that he has no sexual involvement with his mistress. When this argument does not convince the lady, Joseph asks 'how then can I do this great wickedness, and sin against God?' (Genesis 39: 9). As a composer of sermons, and as a counsellor to his parishioners, Bunyan knew that it could be useful to raise more than one argument in order to convince: some listeners might be convinced by a presentation of a social contract, while others might be convinced by a statement of the Deity's pleasure or displeasure at a certain act. In his envisioning of Joseph in *Mr Badman*, Bunyan does not add to or interpret the biblical text. Those elements of Joseph's narrative which apply to Bunyan's own life story—his role as honest servant and teacher, his acceptance of imprisonment, his determination to act according to religious strictures—are emphasized.

Bunyan's 'The Acceptable Sacrifice: or the Excellency of a Broken Heart: shewing the Nature, Signs and Proper Effects of a Contrite Spirit' was probably one of his last writings, and indeed was in press at the time of his death in 1688. 'The Acceptable Sacrifice' might be termed a *midrash* on Psalm 51, also known as the Penitential Psalm or the Miserere, after its Latin opening 'Miserere mei Deus'. A written sermon some eighty pages in length, 'The Acceptable Sacrifice' focuses on verse 17: 'The sacrifices of God are a broken spirit: a broken and a contrite heart, O God, thou wilt not despise'. As is clear from the text's subtitle, Bunyan meditates upon and explicates the nature, signs, and effects of a broken heart and

---

[29] John Bunyan, *The Life and Death of Mr. Badman*, ed. James F. Forrest and Roger Sharrock (Oxford: Clarendon, 1988), 54, 55.

[30] Bunyan, *Badman*, 55.   [31] Bunyan, *Badman*, 55.

spirit. If the pre-eminent sacrifice of all time was that offered by Jesus Christ via his suffering on the cross, the suffering, the mental anguish figured by the 'broken heart' is the believer's way of partaking of Christ's sacrifice. Bunyan refers to Joseph's predicament as part of his depiction of the signs of a broken heart: 'When *Joseph's* Mistress tempted him to lie with her, he was afraid of the *Word* of God; *How shall I do this great Wickedness*, said he, *and sin against God*? He stood in awe of *God's Word*, durst not do it, because he kept in Remembrance, what a dreadful thing 'twas to Rebel against *God's Word*'.[32]

As was the case in *Badman*, Bunyan's description of Joseph's thoughts, as the latter, alone in his master's villa with his eager mistress, decides on his course of action, does not include any reference to overcoming sexual desire. It may be that the biblical text's lack of reference to the possibility of romantic interest in his mistress on Joseph's part was convenient for Bunyan, in the sense that by cleaving to his source he avoided what might have been an uncomfortable issue. In Bunyan's view, Joseph apparently hoped that an appeal to a religious authority would be more convincing than an appeal to the wife's presumed loyalty to her husband. As a religious leader and public preacher, Bunyan was aware that a warning of divine retribution might be effective in convincing a sinner to refrain from committing his or her 'darling sin'.[33] In 'Acceptable Sacrifice' he points to Joseph's use of a religious argument in his attempt to avoid his mistress's attentions. In Joseph's case, this argument was not successful; he might have learned from his boyhood conflicts with his brothers and parents that preaching, occupying the moral high ground, is not always helpful in making one's point. Bunyan, however, who believed in the ultimate efficacy of preaching, and was willing to pay a heavy personal price in his struggle against those who would deny him a pulpit, was aware of the efficacy of appealing to his interlocutor on more than one level.

Grace Abounding to the Chief of Sinners, first published in 1666, is Bunyan's spiritual autobiography, chief representative of the genre of diaries in which the believer records his or her spiritual struggles while working toward a sense of salvation. *Grace Abounding* and 'A Relation of the Imprisonment of Mr. John Bunyan', which since 1765 has been published in tandem with *Grace Abounding*, includes sections detailing Bunyan's hardships—physical, familial, and spiritual—while in jail. Bunyan details his pain at being separated from his wife and children, as well as his fears for their well-being, and especially that of his beloved blind daughter. Although Joseph is not mentioned by name in *Grace Abounding*, Bunyan may be said to have taken a page from the book of the young Joseph in the pit near Dothan who gave loud, anguished expression to his anger and pain. For Bunyan, the adult Joseph's quiet acceptance of his patently unjust imprisonment in Egypt may have served as an example possibly to be admired, though not followed.

Sid Sondergard has suggested that the prison metaphors occurring throughout Bunyan's work are intentional and didactic. They establish and authenticate his spiritual authority. Such authentication may have been necessitated by Bunyan's physical separation from his congregation; moreover according to Sondergard the preacher's lack of 'formal rhetorical training may explain why his use of images of violence and imprisonment seems designed

---

[32] John Bunyan, 'The Acceptable Sacrifice, Last Sermon, et al'., *The Miscellaneous Works of John Bunyan*, xii, ed. W.R. Owens (Oxford: Clarendon Press, 1994), 41.

[33] Gordon S. Wakefield defines the 'darling sin' as 'that particular sin to which we are constitutionally prone'. '"To Be a Pilgrim": Bunyan and the Christian Life', in N. H. Keeble (ed.), *John Bunyan: Conventicle and Parnassus: Tercentenary Essays* (Oxford: Clarendon Press, 1988), 121.

to address its audiences at the level of human empathy and experience'.[34] Although lengthy imprisonment can enhance one's reputation as a leader, its effect on the individual may be long-term and unexpected. As Sondergard suggests, the idea that 'the experience of imprisonment precludes the possibility of ever being truly free again' is specifically asserted in *The Life and Death of Mr Badman*.[35] For Bunyan, sin was a prison from which one could never be completely free: as Mr Wiseman states, '[t]he Prisoner that is to dye at the Gallows for his wickedness, must first have his Irons knock't off his legs; so he seems to goe most at liberty, when indeed he is to be executed for his transgressions'.[36] But if Bedford Gaol served as a figure for sin in the sense that neither could be escaped from, Bunyan's suffering and that of his family, as depicted in *Grace Abounding*, was literal. It can therefore be argued that Joseph's first imprisonment—in the pit in the wilderness near Dothan—from which his cries could be heard clearly, served Bunyan as a predictor of his own reaction to lengthy imprisonment.

Bunyan's descriptions of his and his family's suffering may be compared to a scene described by Edmund Calamy in a biblical paraphrase. Calamy (who had been imprisoned for three months in 1662 for preaching a sermon, although 'by reason of his inconformity' he was 'disabled to preach or read any Lecture or Sermon') describes Eli (1 Samuel 4: 13–18) as the latter sat watching a battle in which his two sons took part:

> now let us consider what old *Eli* was doing all the while the battel was fighting. The good old man was 98. years old, he was not able to go to the battel; but he got upon a seat by the way side, near the battel where it was fought, and there he sits watching what will become of the Ark: *And lo Eli sat upon a seat by the way side, watching; for his heart trembled for fear of the Ark of God*: For fear lest the Ark of God should be taken. He was not troubled what would become of his two Sons, he was not troubled what should become of the people of Israel; but all his trouble was for the Ark of God; he sat by the way side watching, for his heart trembled for the Ark of God.[37]

A look at the biblical text reveals that Eli collapsed and died after learning of the capturing of the Ark and of the death of his sons. One wonders what Bunyan would have made of Calamy's suggestion that Eli was not troubled by what should befall his sons; the latter claim has no textual basis. Just as the biblical redactor did not hide Joseph's suffering, Bunyan did not delegitimize his own pain as a father.

As did Joseph in his Egyptian imprisonment, Bunyan utilized his years in jail both to raise his own status and to help others. By reading and writing he was able to remain in touch with his followers, encouraged by the hope that his 'Brief and Faithful relation of the Exceeding Mercy of God in Christ to his poor Servant ... would help in the support of the weak and tempted people of God'.[38] In this sense the details of his sufferings which fill *Grace Abounding* need not be seen as whining: the preacher was sharing them with his parishioners in order to show them that they could overcome their own struggles.

[34] Sid Sondergard, '"This Giant Has Wounded Me as Well as Thee": Reading Bunyan's Violence and/ as Authority', in K. Z. Keller and G. J. Schiffhorst (eds), *The Witness of Times: Manifestations of Ideology in Seventeenth Century England* (Pittsburgh, Pa.: Duquesne University Press, 1993), 220, 218.
[35] Sondergard, 'This Giant', 223.   [36] Bunyan, *Badman*, 165.
[37] Edward Calamy, *Eli Trembling for Fear of the Ark: A Sermon Preached at St. Mary Aldermanbury, Decemb. 28. 1662. / by Edmund Calamy; upon the Preaching of Which He Was Committed Prisoner to the Gaol of Newgate, Jan 6. 1662* [i.e. 1663] (Oxford, 1663), 2.
[38] Bunyan, *Grace Abounding*, frontispiece.

In conclusion, John Bunyan's references to Joseph are best seen in the light of his sense that the Bible, its characters, and stories constituted the world outside his own home and congregation. Bunyan's use of Joseph is less allegorical than dramatic: he assumes that his readers and listeners are familiar with the biblical tales of the patriarchs and draws a comparison or contrast between Joseph in a certain situation, or vis-à-vis a specific trait, and himself, or a literary character of his creation, who is faced with a similar situation. Bunyan's use of Joseph, the prisoner, the unfairly accused, as a point of reference in his constant examination of his own conduct, helped him to assign meaning to events in his own life—lengthy imprisonment, unfair accusations of misconduct—which he might otherwise have found difficult to accept and interpret. His examination of Joseph's life also enabled him to use Joseph in his own life's work of convincing his parishioners and readers via preaching and imaginary writing. Finally, his use of the character is reflected in the images of the less-than-perfect pilgrim who served as a model for the rounded, human characters of what would become the novel.

FURTHER READING

Benedict, Philip. *Christ's Churches Purely Reformed: A Social History of Calvinism* (New Haven: Yale University Press, 2002).

Bunyan, John. *The Pilgrim's Progress*, ed. James Blanton Wharey, 2nd edn, rev. Roger Sharrock (Oxford: Clarendon Press, 1960).

Bunyan, John. *Grace Abounding to the Chief of Sinners*, ed. Roger Sharrock (Oxford: Clarendon Press, 1962).

Bunyan, John. *The Life and Death of Mr. Badman*, ed. James F. Forrest and Roger Sharrock (Oxford: Clarendon Press, 1988).

Bunyan, John. *The Acceptable Sacrifice, Last Sermon, etc.*, ed. W. R. Owens (Oxford: Clarendon Press, 1994).

Furlong, Monica. *Puritan's Progress* (New York: Coward, McCann & Geoghegan, 1975).

Greaves, Richard L. *Glimpses of Glory: John Bunyan and English Dissent* (Stanford, Calif.: Stanford University Press, 2002).

Hill, Christopher. *The English Bible and the Seventeenth-Century Revolution* (London: Allen Lane, 1993).

Kaufmann, U. Milo. *The Pilgrim's Progress and Traditions in Puritan Meditation* (New Haven: Yale University Press, 1966).

Killeen, Kevin. *Biblical Scholarship, Science and Politics in Early Modern England: Thomas Browne and the Thorny Place of Knowledge* (Farnham: Ashgate, 2009).

Knott, John R., Jr. *The Sword of the Spirit* (Chicago: University of Chicago Press, 1980).

Luxon, Thomas H. *Literal Figures: Puritan Allegory and the Reformation Crisis in Representation* (Chicago: University of Chicago Press, 1995).

MacCulloch, Diarmaid. *The Reformation: A History* (New York: Penguin, 2003).

Rosenfeld, Nancy. *The Human Satan in Seventeenth-Century English Literature: From Milton to Rochester* (Aldershot: Ashgate, 2008).

Underdown, David. *Fire from Heaven: Life in an English Town in the Seventeenth Century* (London: HarperCollins, 1992).

CHAPTER 34

....

PARADISE LOST, THE BIBLE, AND BIBLICAL EPIC

....

BARBARA K. LEWALSKI

IN the opening lines of *Paradise Lost*, Milton proposes to soar above Olympus and also echoes Ariosto's claim in his romantic epic *Orlando Furioso* to have produced a work 'unattempted yet in Prose or Rhyme'.[1] But as a biblical epic Milton's poem is not unique. From the time of Juvencus, Dracontius, and other fourth- and fifth-century patristic poets until Milton published *Paradise Lost* (1667/74), probably more than a hundred poets wrote biblical poems making some claims to epic status, in Latin, German, Old English, French, Italian, and English.[2] Most, though not quite all, are eminently forgettable, and have been forgotten. But, beyond the implication that he has succeeded where most have failed, Milton means something more: that he has met successfully the challenges both of classical epic form and biblical truth. And he has done so in a Protestant culture marked by a newly intense focus on—and anxieties about altering—the biblical text, anxieties prompted in part by the vernacular translations.

Previous biblical epics, some of which Milton knew, had taken various formats: long panoramic poems dealing with the entire Bible, or the Gospel story, or some grouping of events from Genesis or Exodus or the life of Christ;[3] and shorter poems (three to six books) focused on a single book of the Bible, or the Apocrypha or a single (often martial) hero—Judith, David, Moses, Job, Esther, Joseph, Christ, Susanna.[4] Most begin *ab ovo* (at

---

[1] 1.16. All quotations are from *John Milton: Paradise Lost*, ed. Barbara Lewalski (Oxford: Blackwell, 2007). Cf. Lodovico Ariosto, *Orlando Furioso* (Ferrara, 1516), tr. John Harington (London, 1591), book 1, canto 2, line 2.

[2] For an account of many of these, see Barbara K. Lewalski, *Milton's Brief Epic* (London: Methuen, 1966), chs 3 and 4.

[3] For example, Juvencus, *Evangeliorum* (c.350); Avitus, *De spiritalis historiae gestis* (c.494); the Anglo-Saxon *Genesis A* (c.700) and *Genesis B* (ninth century); Guillaume de Salluste Du Bartas, *La sepmaine* (Paris, 1578) and *La seconde sepmaine* (Paris, 1584, unfinished); Abraham Cowley, *Davideis* (London, 1656, unfinished).

[4] For example, Jacopo Sannazaro, *De partu virginis* (Naples, 1526); Marco Girolamo (Marcus Hieronymus) Vida, *Christiad* (Cremona, 1535); Du Bartas, *Judit* (Bordeaux, 1574); Giovanni Battista Marino, *La Strage de gl'innocenti* (Venice, [1620?]).

the beginning) and proceed *seriatim* (in chronological order), though they often incorporate episodes from other parts of the Bible, to convey a sense of scope or typological reference.

Their claims to epic status varied: the wonders of the biblical stories (better Samson's exploits than those of Hercules, better Noah's Flood than Deucalion's); the sheer scope and scale of this 'true' history; the heroism of the biblical figures in their martial exploits or their exemplary sanctity; the fact that some parts of the Bible (notably Exodus and Job) were themselves often identified as epic. The patristic poets and many Italian humanist poets like Jacopo Sannazaro and Marco Girolamo Vida aligned themselves with epic tradition by using Latin hexameters, Virgilian diction, and epic thematic statements. The Old English Genesis and Exodus used the four-beat alliterative line, epic formulas, sea similes, epithets, and heroic institutions from Germanic and Old English secular epic. Several Neo-Latin humanist poems of the Quattro- and Cinquecento (notably Vida's influential *Christiad*) took over familiar classical epic topics: thematic statements, councils in hell and heaven, an Allecto passage, a heavenly messenger passage, recitals, and prophecies. These earlier poems show little anxiety about dramatizing or elaborating biblical episodes, though they sometimes voiced uneasiness about using the classical supernatural and the muses even as allegory, or about portraying the Christian supernatural worthily—especially God.

During the sixteenth and seventeenth centuries, the new translations of the Bible in the vernacular prompted philological attention to biblical imagery, metaphor, and simile as well as to matters of genre and form in the various books of the Hebrew Bible and the New Testament. It became commonplace to designate certain parts of scripture as poetic, labelled as such in some Bibles, including the Coverdale Bible (1535), and sometimes published separately, like prayer books, in duodecimo volumes. Sir Philip Sidney in his *Defence of Poesy* (c.1580, published 1595) gave an influential restatement of this long tradition, designating the usual biblical books and also referring, as was common, to other songs and hymns throughout scripture. His summary also invited recognition of the Bible as incorporating many kinds of poetry:

> The chiefe [poets] both in antiquitie and excellencie, were they that did imitate the inconceivable excellencies of God. Such were *David* in his Psalmes, *Salomon* in his song of songs, in his Ecclesiastes and Proverbs, *Moses* and *Debora* in theyr Hymnes, and the writer of *Job*: which beside other, the learned *Emanuell Tremelius*, and *F. Junius* doo entitle the Poeticall part of the scripture. (C1ᵛ–C2ʳ)

This emphasis upon the poetics of the Bible prompted an upsurge of new Psalm translations, paraphrases, and poetic versions, as well as paraphrases and meditations on other biblical books, and also a flowering of personal religious lyric: in England by John Donne (*Poems*, 1633, 1635), George Herbert (*The Temple*, 1633), Henry Vaughan (*Silex Scintillans*, 1650, 1655) and many others.[5] It also encouraged attempts to write biblical epic, giving rise to questions as to how to do so.

---

[5] For some others, see Barbara K. Lewalski, *Protestant Poetics and the Seventeenth-Century Religious Lyric* (Princeton: Princeton University Press, 1979), esp. ch. 7.

These questions revolved around what kind of subject to choose (martial or otherwise), what format to use, whether it was allowable to alter or significantly add to the text, whether to make any use of classical or supernatural features (gods, muses, fate, Fama), and whether use of the Christian supernatural (angels and devils and especially God) might risk blasphemy. These problems were exacerbated in some reformist quarters, and especially among Puritans in England, by biblical literalism. An example is William Ames's comment in his influential *Marrow of Sacred Divinity* (1643):

> In all those things which were made known by supernaturall inspiration, (whether they were matters of right, or fact) [God] did inspire not onely the things themselves, but did dictate and suggest all the words in which they should be written ... [T]here is onely one sence of one place of Scripture: because otherwise the sence of the Scripture should be not onely not cleere and certaine, but none at all: for that which doth not signifie one thing, signifieth certainly nothing.[6]

One prominent response to these issues was provided by the poems of Guilliame Salluste, Sieur Du Bartas, in the original French and in many English translations.[7] 'Uranie' (1574) a short dream-vision poem translated by King James in 1585 and Joshuah Sylvester in 1605, urged the case for biblical poetry, including epic, and provided a new muse for that poetry by baptizing the Muse of Astronomy, Urania.[8] The poem records that Urania visited Du Bartas (as she would several later poets) urging him to reclaim poetry, which had been perverted by Satan from its divine origin in the Bible. Her biblical examples are David, Moses, Job, Jeremiah, and, as martial epic subjects, '*Debora* and *Judith*, in the Campe' (stanza 50). Du Bartas wrote a biblical epic on one of those topics, *Judit* (1574), translated into English by Thomas Hudson (1584) and Sylvester (1614). In the preface, Du Bartas claimed to be the first in France to wed biblical truth to classical form and diction, and he also asserted poetic licence to depart from the biblical text: 'I have not so much aimed to follow the phrase or text of the byble, as I have preased, (without wandring from the veritie of the Historie) to imitate *Homer* in his *Iliades*, and *Virgil* in his *Æneidos*'.[9] This is a brief epic (six books, 2,000 hexameters) with a unified martial subject, the siege and deliverance of Bethulia, but with other scenes and stories from the Bible incorporated through recitals, prophecies, and iconographical representations. It also displays the full classical apparatus: epic proposition and invocation, an *in medias res* beginning, councils, martial trappings, classical epithets, and supernatural agents, both classical and Christian.

Far more influential was Du Bartas's massive, panoramic *Sepmaine* (1578, seven books, c.6,500 hexameters) on the seven days of Creation, together with his unfinished *Seconde sepmaine* (1584–1608, four books) treating episodes of biblical history. Sylvester translated and published parts of the work at various times, and relatively complete editions in 1605, 1608, 1611, 1613, 1621, and subsequently. Though the several books contain a

---

[6] William Ames, The *Marrow of Sacred Divinity* (London, 1642), 168–71. On the literal sense of scripture, see the chapter by Debora Shuger in this volume.

[7] On the importance of Du Bartas to women writers, see the chapter by Sarah Ross in this volume.

[8] Du Bartas, 'L'Uranie', *La muse Chrestiene* (Bordeaux, 1574); 'The Uranie, or Heavenly Muse', tr. James VI, *The Essayes of a Prentise, in the Divine Art of Poesie* (Edinburgh, 1584), D1ʳ–G1ʳ; 'Urania', in *Bartas: His Devine Weekes and Workes*, tr. Joshuah Sylvester (London, 1605), 528–42.

[9] *The Historie of Judith*, tr. Thomas Hudson (Edinburgh, 1584), A5ʳ.

classical proposition and invocation, and many epic devices, episodes, diction, and epithets, the loose and irregular structure departs from epic norms. Du Bartas defended his approach on the grounds that the novelty of the subject demanded 'a new and unaccustomed method'.[10] He readily incorporates expansive descriptions, recondite lore, didactic sermonizing, and meditations on the biblical texts. For example, he expands the general categories in the Genesis account by describing each individual fish, bird, and animal. However, he also voices anxiety about going beyond the text. In describing Eden he declines to be 'too curious' and 'over bold' in speculating about how Adam and Eve lived in Eden, whether they had sex, whether they would or would not have propagated as men do now ('Eden', ll. 625–708), all matters Milton dealt with without hesitation.

Much sixteenth-century Italian literary theory based on Aristotle insisted on neoclassical structure for all epics, and also on the choice of the probable or verisimilar rather than true history as subject, to allow room for poetic invention. On that principle Lucan's *Pharsalia* was sometimes excluded from the epic category, as adhering too closely to the historical facts of the Roman Civil Wars between Pompey and Caesar. This principle called into question the very possibility of biblical epic: in his influential treatise *Discorsi dell poema heroica* (1594), Tasso argued that a Christian poet should not choose a biblical subject for epic because it cannot be altered by poetic invention, and should instead portray a Christian national hero from times distant enough that poetic changes will not be recognized—precepts he exemplified in his important epic, *Gerusalemme liberata* (1581).

In England these issues were raised continuously throughout the seventeenth century. Michael Drayton in the preface to *Moyses in a Map of His Miracles* (1604) claimed to have found appropriate scope for poetic invention in that work by adding poetic figures, allegories, descriptions, and new episodes as 'Jems and exterior ornaments' which did not affect the substance of the true biblical account. On the other hand William Davanent and Thomas Hobbes forcefully reiterated the claim that invention is not possible with true and sacrosanct biblical materials, offering Davenant's incomplete poem *Gondibert* (1651) as an example of what the new heroic poem should be: secular, completely fictional, eliminating all supernatural powers (classical or Christian), and eschewing all claims of inspiration as assuming a 'saucie' or blasphemous familiarity with God.[11]

In the preface to his *Davideis* (1656) Abraham Cowley explained his intention to be the first writer in English to create a biblical heroic poem in twelve books according to neoclassical standards, with a martial subject, all the expected epic topics, and Virgilian diction, while making use also of the full Christian supernatural. Echoing Du Bartas and others, he denied that fiction is essential to poetry and claimed that the biblical stories are superior to their classical counterparts not only for their truth but also for their heroic character, their martial actions, and their wonders: 'All the *Books* of the *Bible* are either already most admirable, and exalted pieces of *Poesie*, or the best *Materials* in the world for it'.[12] His twelve-book format was chosen, he explained, 'not for the *Tribes* sake but after the

[10] 'The Advertisement of William of Salust, Lord of Bartas, upon the first and second Weeke', in Simon Goulart, *A Learned Summary upon the Famous Poeme of William of Saluste Lord of Bartas*, tr. Thomas Lodge (London: George Purslowe for John Grismond, 1621), [A6r].

[11] William Davenant, *Gondibert, an Heroick Poeme* (London, 1651), 24; Thomas Hobbes, 'The Answer of Mr. Hobbes to Sir Wil. Davenant's Preface before Gondibert', *Gondibert*, 52–64.

[12] Abraham Cowley, *Davideis, or, A Sacred Poem of the Troubles of David* (London, 1656), (b)3r. The *Davideis* is included in Cowley's 1656 *Poems*, but has a separate dated title-page, pagination, and register.

Patern of our Master *Virgil'* ((b)2ᵛ) and he proposed to incorporate through recitals and prophecies other 'illustrious' Old Testament and secular stories. But he completed only four books, pointing to the difficulty of achieving the 'fertility of *Invention*', the 'luster and vigor of *Elocution*', and the 'modesty and majesty of *Number*' that his enterprise needed. He ended by voicing the hope that his imperfect poem might prompt such an enterprise by 'some other persons, who may be better able to perform it thoroughly and successfully' ((b)ʳ⁻ᵛ). Milton, who certainly knew Cowley's works, might have taken this as an invitation or a challenge.

In his commendatory poem to *Paradise Lost* (1674) Milton's friend and fellow poet Andrew Marvell speaks to possible readerly anxieties about the poem's use of biblical materials. He voices his initial fears that Milton would 'ruine (for I saw him strong) / The sacred Truths to Fable and old Song', then reports his discovery that Milton has preserved the divine matter 'inviolate', and has soared so far 'above humane flight' that he must have been inspired.[13] But Milton did not preserve the literal biblical text inviolate: he treated his biblical text with remarkable freedom, departing readily from orthodox understandings of texts and doctrine in the service of a compelling vision of the human condition. He devised scenes and situations with no biblical basis. He created memorable characters in Satan, Adam, and Eve, barely described in scripture (for example, the tempter in Genesis 3: 1–5 is identified as the serpent, not Satan, whose most extended appearance in scripture is as the tempter of Job (Job 1: 1–6)). He did so by drawing on psychological insights, political observation, and human experience. And he portrayed the Christian supernatural—including heaven, angels, and God himself—as well as unfallen Eden, at great length and without apology or hesitation.

Milton's study and writing for more than two decades prepared him for this challenge. Like his English contemporaries, in his polemic treatises he cited biblical texts thought to bear on the issues in question and read them in ways that supported his then radical positions on the abolition of bishops, divorce for incompatibility, a free press and intellectual freedom, regicide, republicanism, religious liberty, church disestablishment, and more. He also wrote, over many years, a theological treatise in Latin, *De doctrina Christiana*, explaining in the 'Epistle' that he did so to 'puzzle out a religious creed for myself' based only on scripture and relying on no outside authority—not ecclesiastical officers, church councils, or theologians, the usual arbiters of orthodoxy.[14] He did not depend on English translations, but regularly cited the Hebrew Bible and the Greek New Testament, as well as the Junius-Tremellius Protestant Latin Bible and others.[15] The scholarship that marked the King James Bible, as well as the absence of the heavy marginalia that dictated interpretation in the Geneva Bible, made it also an important reference point for him. The principles of biblical interpretation he worked out in these treatises liberated his poetic imagination in writing his biblical epic.

From the time of his divorce tracts (1643–5) Milton repudiated biblical literalism, scornfully denouncing the 'crabbed textuists' (YP 2.235) who cited Matthew 19: 3–9 as prohibiting divorce save for adultery, for resting 'in the meere element of the Text' with an

---

[13] In *Paradise Lost*, ed. Lewalski, ll. 7–8, 34, 44.
[14] *De doctrina Christiana*, ed. Maurice Kelley, *The Complete Prose Works of John Milton*, gen. ed. Don M. Wolfe (New Haven: Yale University Press, 1953–82), 6. 118. Hereafter YP.
[15] For more on Milton's biblical scholarship, see the chapter by Neil Forsyth in this volume.

'obstinate literality' and an 'alphabeticall servility' (YP 2.236, 279–80). He came to believe, and reaffirmed in *De doctrina Christiana,* that the illumination of the indwelling spirit in every believer is not only necessary to the right interpretation of scripture but even takes priority over the literal text in authorizing faith and revealing truth: 'We have, particularly under the gospel, a double scripture. There is the external scripture of the written word, and the internal scripture of the Holy Spirit …. The pre-eminent and supreme authority, however, is the authority of the Spirit, which is internal, and the individual possession of each man' (YP 6.587). In *Of Civil Power in Ecclesiastical Causes* (1659), Milton affirmed that scripture is 'not possible to be understood without this divine illumination' which reveals truths 'warrantable only to our selves and to such whose consciences we can so persuade'. And since 'no man can know [this illumination] at all times to be in himself, much less to be at any time for certain in any other' (YP 7.242), no person or institution can mandate a creed for others. He does not expect (like the Quakers or Ranters) that the internal pro-phetic Spirit will promote enthusiastic testimony, but rather, as his comment states, that it will prompt reasoned argument that might carry conviction to others. In *Areopagitica,* Milton insists that openness to emergent truth is the precondition for the advancement of knowledge in religion as in other matters: 'The light which we have gain'd, was given us, not to be ever staring on, but by it to discover onward things more remote from our knowl-edge' (YP 2.550–80).

In *Paradise Lost,* Milton as poet proclaimed his need for the Spirit's illumination in the proems to books I and III, where he calls on the Spirit of God and the Celestial Light, as fig-ures for inspiration, to help him understand the essence of the biblical story. In the proem to book VII he seeks assistance from the Christianized heavenly muse Urania (creating a new mythic origin for her, based on Proverbs 8, in which she delights God himself with her 'Celestial Song' (VII.11–12). And in the proem to book IX he declares with confidence that his poem is founded upon the dream-like imaginative experiences she fosters nightly, as she 'dictates to me slumbring, or inspires / Easie my unpremeditated Verse' (IX.21–4). She evidently fosters an imaginative vision of what the Spirit reveals—the essential meaning rather than the literal details of the biblical story—freeing Milton to invent what his epic poem requires.

Milton's interpretation of scripture was also guided by reason. While he allowed that theological doctrines derived from scripture are above reason he insisted that God's rev-elation will not flatly contradict reason and that in moral and political matters reason, the law of nature, and revelation will agree: 'The hidden wayes of his providence we adore & search not; but the law is his reveled will … herein he … gives himself to be understood by men, judges and is judg'd, measures and is commensurat to right reason' (YP 2.292). This insistence upon the accord between reason and revelation informs Milton's political and polemical writing. God cannot contradict himself in his two covenants. Since the Hebrew Bible permits divorce, the Gospel cannot mean to forbid it: 'God hath not two wills but one will, much lesse two contrary'. Moreover, 'the teachings of the Gospel accord with reason and with the laws of nations' (YP 4.l.383) in affording warrant for revolution, popular sov-ereignty, and republican government.

In *De doctrina Christiana* Milton's insistence that revealed theological doctrines do not contradict or violate reason undergirds several heterodox doctrines that also contribute significantly to the literary success of the epic: monism (the concept that all creation is of one substance, denying usual dualist differentiation into matter and spirit); creation *ex Deo* (the concept that God created all things out of some material aspect of himself, not *ex nihilo*, out of nothing, as orthodoxy held); Arminianism (a doctrine which made some place for free will, opposing Calvinist predestination by God which did not); and near-Arianism (a doctrine that makes the Son a creature, much inferior to the Father, not one with and equal to him as orthodox trinitarians held). He defends that last position vigorously and at length, arguing both the lack of biblical support for trinitarianism and the idea that God himself cannot defy the laws of logic, obfuscating the reasonable and usual meaning of oneness:

> The numerical significance of 'one' and of 'two' must be unalterable and the same for God as for man ... If you were to ascribe two subsistences or two persons to one essence, it would be a contradiction in terms ... If my opponents had paid attention to God's own words ... they would not have found it necessary to fly in the face of reason or, indeed, of so much glaring scriptural evidence. (YP 6.212–13)

Milton's near-Arianism allows him to portray the Son of God in the epic as the first creature of God, not omniscient or eternal or omnipotent but only sharing divine attributes when and as God devolves them upon him. He can thereby be portrayed as making heroic choices from limited knowledge: the Son does not know in book III what God's pronouncements regarding man's Fall may mean or his own role in man's redemption, until he works that out in dialogue with God. Nor does he know how the battle in heaven will end until God commissions and empowers him to end it.

Another principle is accommodation, the common exegetical concept that God is always described not as he really is but in such a way as will make him conceivable to us. But Milton interprets this concept in radical terms, making the Bible's accounts of God's nature and works into a vast metaphor for what is unknowable. Since God 'as he really is' is utterly beyond a creature's conception or imagination (YP 6.133), all biblical representations of him are necessarily metaphoric. Nor does the qualification that 'we ought to form just such a mental image of him [God] as he, in bringing himself within the limits of our understanding, wishes us to form' (YP 6.133) lead back to literalism. Rather, Milton's insistence that interpreters should not explain away biblical passages that seem 'unworthy' of God or that describe him anthropomorphically—for example, references to his wrath, regret, or other passions (YP 6.133–5)—frees Milton as epic poet to make imaginative use of the multiple and sometimes conflicting representations of God and his works throughout the scriptures. This helped him resolve the worrisome problem of how properly to use the Christian supernatural in epic.

Milton's poem honours God's transcendence by insisting on the necessarily fragmentary and metaphoric nature of all representations of God and his works, since God can only be perceived and represented metaphorically in some of his aspects. So God is described in an angelic hymn as a mystical figure whose skirts are 'dark with excessive bright' (III.380), as a Socratic educator in Adam's report of their conversation to Raphael, and in various other guises in Raphael's narratives to Adam: a monarch seated on a glorious throne presiding over heavenly festivities but also delivering arbitrary commands carrying fearsome penalties; a general directing the battle in heaven; and a potent male creative force inseminating great Mother Earth, thereby beginning a vibrant and ongoing creative process.

On such principles, Milton in book VII makes use of the Genesis account of a six-day Creation, but prevents a literal interpretation of it. The angel Raphael cites God's creating words from chapter 1 almost exactly as they appear in the King James Bible, but he prefaces that account with a caveat about his own insufficiencies as narrator of this subject, and Adam's deficiencies as human auditor: 'to recount Almightie works / What words or tongue of Seraph can suffice, / Or heart of man suffice to comprehend?' (VII.112–14). Moreover, he states explicitly that his account is metaphoric, an accommodation to human understanding:

> Immediate are the Acts of God, more swift
> Then time or motion, but to human ears
> Cannot without process of speech be told.
> So told as earthly notion can receive. (VII.176–9)

Another creation account in the poem underscores the limitations of even angelic reporters who can describe God's works only as they partially perceive them. Uriel, the angel in the sun, describes the Creation to Satan disguised as a 'stripling Cherube' (III.636), but first points to the limitations in understanding he shares with all creatures: 'But what created mind can comprehend / Thir number, or the wisdom infinite / That brought them forth, but hid thir causes deep' (III.705–7). Then he reports what he himself witnessed from his vantage point in the heavens—creation of the cosmos, the stars, and the planets—saying nothing whatever about creation on earth.

These principles also allow Milton to deal with the cosmos in ways that avoid biblical literalism and remain open to the science of his present. Epic traditionally locates its stories in a vast historical and geographical terrain, and Milton's chosen subject required representation of the universe itself: hell, heaven, chaos, the planets, earth. But, although the cosmological theories of Copernicus and Galileo were by now accepted by advanced thinkers, they still met widespread resistance, as contradicting the biblical text. Du Bartas had ridiculed Copernicus in his *Semaine* and Luther had famously fulminated, 'Holy writ declares, it was the sun and not the Earth which Joshua commanded to stand still'.[16] Later clerics repeated that example and cited other biblical texts, marshalling them against Galileo; many such texts were gathered by Alexander Ross to support the thesis he set forth in the long title of a book he published in 1646:

> *The New Planet No Planet: or, the Earth No Wandring Star except in the Wandring Heads of Galileans. Here out of the Principles of Divinity, Philosophy, Astronomy, Reason, and Sense, the Earth's Immobility is Asserted, the True Sense of Scripture in this Point, Cleared; the Fathers and Philosophers Vindicated; Divers Theologicall and Philosophicall Points Handled, and Copernicus His Opinion, as Erroneous, Ridiculous, and Impious, Fully Refuted.*

Milton, who had a lifelong interest in science and mathematics, and in his *Areopagitica* described a meeting with Galileo in Florence, confronts this issue directly in book VIII of his epic. Adam assumes that the planetary system indeed operates as the naked eye and Ptolemy perceive it to do, but concludes that a cosmos so ordered is irrational and absurd, thereby casting unintended aspersions on its maker. He appeals urgently to Raphael to resolve this matter, as something 'onely thy solution can resolve' (VIII.14). Raphael however

[16] Du Bartas, *Bartas: His Devine Weekes*, tr. Sylvester, K4ᵛ–K5ʳ. Luther is cited in Thomas S. Kuhn, *The Copernican Revolution* (Cambridge, Mass.: Harvard University Press, 1977), 190, see Jos. 10: 12–13.

does not resolve it but instead—alluding, perhaps, to Galileo's *Dialogue concerning the Two Chief World Systems* ('Dialogo sopra i due massimi sistemi del mondo', 1632)—he enacts a dialogue of one, playing both the Ptolemaic and Copernican roles, though his conception of the cosmos is as clearly Copernican as was Galileo's. In a tone 'Benevolent and facil' Raphael first honours Adam's desire to read the Book of Nature—'To ask or search I blame thee not, for Heav'n / Is as the Book of God before thee set'—then argues the Ptolemaic case, in order to critique Adam's faulty values in assuming folly and disproportion in a geocentric universe. He recites some of the usual arguments: the greatness and brightness of the other planets do not make them superior to the fruitful earth. Those noble planets do not serve earth as such but man who is more noble still. And their speed would testify to their Maker's 'high Magnificence'. But unlike Galileo's Simplicio and many other Ptolemaic apologists, Raphael does not place man at the centre of such a cosmos: he lodges only 'in a small partition, and the rest /Ordained for uses to his Lord best known' (VIII.104–6).

Then Raphael takes on the Copernican role, stating explicitly that his Ptolemaic argument was intended only as a corrective to Adam's dubious assumptions, underscoring the point that the cosmic system one credits depends on one's vantage point:

> But this I urge,
> Admitting Motion in the Heav'ns, to shew
> Invalid that which thee to doubt it mov'd;
> Not that I so affirm, though so it seem
> To thee who hast thy dwelling here on Earth. (VIII.114–18)

To angels who move among the planets, the cosmos evidently invites Copernican and even more radical cosmic speculations, which Raphael lays out in a series of provocative suggestions that Adam had not begun to imagine. The sun may be a stationary centre to the world; the seemingly steadfast earth might move 'Insensibly three different Motions' (VIII.130) fetching day and night by her travels; the spots on the moon might be atmospheric clouds providing food for moon-dwellers; there may be life on other planets; and (as a last dizzying suggestion) a vast universe may contain unknown galaxies with other suns and moons and inhabited planets. Raphael concludes by reiterating that Adam need not resolve whether the sun rises on the earth, or earth on the sun, to admire God's order in the cosmos. Then he warns Adam against probing into 'matters hid'—identifying those not as all speculation about the cosmos but specifically, twice, as speculations about other creatures elsewhere in the universe:

> Sollicit not thy thoughts with matters hid,
> Leave them to God above, him serve and feare;
> Of other Creatures, as him pleases best,
> Wherever plac't, let him dispose. Joy thou
> In what he gives to thee, this Paradise
> And thy faire *Eve*: Heaven is for thee too high
> To know what passes there; be lowlie wise:
> Think onely what concernes thee and thy being;
> Dream not of other Worlds, what Creatures there
> Live, in what state, condition, or degree. (VIII.167–76)

By having Raphael refuse to 'reveal' planetary motion to Adam on his angelic authority, Milton removes astronomy from the domain of revelation—the literal text of the

Bible—leaving it squarely in the domain of science. Moreover by making the issue of life on other planets a 'matter hid'—God's business not man's—he places out of bounds one major theological objection to the new cosmological theories: the difficulty of incorporating possible beings from other worlds into the revealed story of the Fall and Redemption of Adam and his progeny. Also, by causing Raphael to advance a plethora of radical cosmological theories, Milton avoids fixing cosmological knowledge where it is in his own day by giving it a heavenly stamp of approval, instead inviting recognition that the scientific orthodoxy of one moment cannot explain the entire order of things for all time. Finally, Raphael indicates that Adam's primary attention, care, and joy should be directed to human things: 'thy being', 'this Paradise / And thy fair Eve'.

Two other principles informing Milton's interpretation of the Bible allowed him to advance his stated purpose in *Paradise Lost* (I.26)—to 'justifie the wayes of God to men'—in terms that go well beyond the case for theodicy based on free will that he has God argue in his dialogue with the Son in heaven. One such major interpretative principle is charity. With Jesus and Augustine, Milton insists that charity is the sum of the law and the prophets, but for him that principle essentially undergirds the assumption that God intends and acts to accomplish the good of his creatures: 'the divine and softening breath of charity ... turns and windes the dictat of every positive command and shapes it to the good of mankind' (YP 2.604–5). We must, he insists, make 'charitie the interpreter and guide of our faith', rather than 'resting in the meere element of the Text' (YP 2.236) when that patently causes harm, as with Christ's apparent categorical prohibition of divorce in Matthew 19: 3–9:

> Who so preferrs either Matrimony, or other Ordinance before the good of man and the plain exigence of Charity, let him profess Papist, or Protestant, or what he will, he is no better then a Pharise, and understands not the Gospel ... Charity is the high governesse of our belief, and ... wee cannot safely assent to any precept but as charity commends it to us. (YP 2.340)

Still another principle is experience. Though not always reliable, experience can indicate what serves human good and what accords with human nature. It may encompass the experience of a people codified in history and cultural tradition, testifying to the evils of monarchy as cited in *The Readie and Easie Way* (YP 7.448). It can also imply personal and common psychological experience, as when Milton's divorce tracts appeal continually and poignantly to what 'lamented experience daily teaches' about the loneliness and desperate unhappiness of being linked without recourse to a mate who is not a soulmate and companion. Such unions threaten health, faith, and even life itself, producing that 'melancholy despair which we see in many wedded persons' (YP 2.254), and bringing on 'a daily trouble and paine of losse to some degree like that which Reprobates feel' (YP 2.312).

In *Paradise Lost* Milton creates several scenes in which characters respond to God's words not by an unthinking obedience but by interpreting them in terms of charity and experience—a belief in God's beneficence based on prior experience. In the dialogue in heaven (3.56–343), the subordinate Son probes the ambiguities in the Father's first speech that seems to decree the damnation and destruction of humankind for wilful sin, beginning from his own experience of God's goodness, which leads him to conclude that God cannot intend the destruction of humankind which his words might seem to imply: 'That be from the farr'. The Son goes so far as to suggest that to do this would make defense of that goodness impossible: 'So should thy goodness and thy greatness both / Be questiond and blasphem'd without defence' (III.150–66). This dialogue challenges the Son to discover that his own sacrifice must be the means by which humans can obtain grace, and to choose freely to implement the divine purpose—always working from the assumption that God intends good to his creatures.

In his dialogue with God over his request for a mate, Adam works from the same principles. After expressing his gratitude for God's goodness in presenting him with the garden and all its creatures to rule over, he declares that he cannot enjoy all this alone. God, however, directs him to the creatures for society, and Adam thought that God 'seem'd / So ordering' (VIII.376–7). But he persists in arguing his case on rational grounds, confident both of the needs of his own nature—his 'single imperfection'—and of God's beneficent intent toward him, winning at length God's approval of his 'Good reason' (VIII.443). Declaring that he always intended to meet Adam's need, knowing it 'not good for Man to be alone', God promises Adam 'Thy likeness, thy fit help, thy other self, / Thy wish exactly to thy hearts desire' (VIII.444–51). This scene dramatizes Milton's conviction (based on Genesis 2: 18) that companionship was the primary purpose for which God instituted marriage, with procreation only a secondary purpose.

Milton also devised scenes in which characters respond variously to God's arbitrary commands that serve to test their understanding and obedience. For the angels that test is God's proclamation of the Son as their king on a day of joyous festival, replete with song, dance, parades, feasting, courtly ceremonies, and pastoral delights. While the literal text of his dictum is perfectly clear, its deeper meaning and implications are ambiguous: the angels do not yet know why the Son is suddenly elevated, or what his elevation will mean for their lives and their society. So, Milton devises a dramatic debate in book V, unique among literary treatments of the war in heaven, in which Satan provokes his legions to revolt by arguing that the Son's elevation must cause their demotion, and that monarchy violates their right 'to govern not to serve', since they are substantially equal and perfectly good without law (V.794–802). Here, misapplied, are time-honoured republican arguments concerning the natural law rights of a free citizenry, which were also Milton's arguments about the bases of human government and political liberty in his *Tenure of Kings and Magistrates*.

The angel Abdiel counters by correcting Satan's political theory in the light of heaven's special circumstances (V.809–48). He agrees that the antimonarchical principle pertains to equals, but insists that angels, as creatures, cannot be equal to God their Creator or to his Son, the agent of that creation. Then he speaks directly to Satan's assumption that this monarchy will degrade the angels by appealing to their past experience of God's beneficence to them:

> Yet by experience taught we know how good,
> And of our good, and of our dignitie
> How provident he is, how farr from thought
> To make us less, bent rather to exalt
> Our happie state. (V.826–30)

From that ground he interprets the Son's new role as a kind of 'incarnation' honouring the angels in that the Son is 'reduc't' to one of their number. Satan then denies the angels' nature as creatures, arguing that since they cannot remember their moment of origin they

were 'self-begot, self-raised / by our own quick'ning power' (V.856–61). This specious argument calls for empirical evidence where none can exist, since no one can remember his or
her conception. Still less can this inevitable ignorance be a basis to argue for self-creation,
to deny all derivation. This scene provides Satan's troops, Adam and Eve (the audience for
Raphael's narrative), and Milton's readers an example of sound and erroneous uses of reason, experience, and charity in interpreting a divine text.

Milton imagines for Eve a comparable test in the satanic challenge to misconstrue
God's arbitrary pronouncement against eating of the Tree of Knowledge of Good and
Evil. Led unawares to the forbidden tree she paraphrases the command precisely, showing that she understands its literal meaning and also that it is a direct command of God—
'Sole Daughter of his voice' (IX.653)—distinct from the law of reason that governs all
other prelapsarian behaviour. That clear understanding might have allowed her to withstand the barrage of rational arguments Satan adduces. But Satan suggests that the prohibition is intended to keep humans low by denying them access to the special knowledge
and powers implied in the tree's name, concluding that Eve need not obey such an unjust
God. His most effective argument is a false report of personal experience, voicing for the
serpent a story of gaining speech and reason by eating apples from the forbidden tree
and concluding that Eve might reasonably expect a proportional elevation in the scale
of being, becoming like God. Here Eve, like Abdiel, is called upon to construe the as yet
unknown implications of a divine command in the light of her own experience of the
joy and happiness of her present life. Her Fall arises in part from her readiness to accept
the supposed snake's reported experience and the satanic claim of harm to humans in
God's prohibition, rather than to judge with charity by her own past experience, after
Abdiel's model. She might also have recalled Raphael's projection of their gradual transformation (in this monist universe) to something like angelic state. But to judge rightly by
experience is difficult and Eve fails the test, as Adam will later. So they discover the true
meaning of the text of prohibition as they experience evil in its manifold physical, psychological, and spiritual forms.

Milton's biblical epic succeeds where so many failed because he created a poetic universe based not on the letter of scripture but on his conception of its spirit. His principles of reason, charity, accommodation, and the right use of experience in interpreting
scripture, along with the several heterodoxies emerging from them, provide a humane
basis for the theodicy he identifies as one purpose for his epic, justifying God's ways. His
monist philosophy leads him to present all the places and persons in his poetic universe
in process, not stasis—neither heaven nor prelapsarian Eden are fixed in static perfection, but are shown to be advancing toward greater perfection. Adam and Eve's ideal
human life in innocence involves continual cultivation and pruning, both of their burgeoning garden that would otherwise revert to wild, and of their own sometimes way-
ward impulses and passions. They must work out their relationship to God and to each
other, meeting ever new challenges: the emotions attending love and sex, the intellectual
curiosity which is both assuaged and stimulated by the lengthy education Raphael supplies, the problems arising from gender hierarchy within companionate marriage, the
tension between interdependence and independent moral responsibility, and the subtle temptations to wrong interpretations presented by Satan. Milton's poem suggests
that God's ways can be justified especially because they encourage liberty, intellectual
growth, challenging moral choices, and love, heavenly and human. Those goods are held

forth again in the poem's moving and evocative final lines describing Adam and Eve's departure from Eden:

> The World was all before them, where to choose
> Their place of rest, and Providence thir guide:
> They hand in hand with wandering steps and slow,
> Through Eden took thir solitarie way. (XII.646–9)

FURTHER READING

Campbell, Lily B. *Divine Poetry and Drama in Sixteenth Century England* (Cambridge: Cambridge University Press, 1959).

Du Bartas, Guilliaume Salluste. *La Judit [par] G. Salluse Du Bartas*, ed. André Baïche (Toulouse: Faculté des lettres et sciences humaines, 1971).

Du Bartas, Guilliaume Salluste. *The Divine Weeks and Works of Guillaume de Saluste, Sieur du Bartas*, tr. Joshuah Sylvester, ed. Susan Snyder, 2 vols (Oxford: Clarendon Press, 1979).

Evans, J. M. *'Paradise Lost' and the Genesis Tradition* (Oxford: Clarendon Press, 1968).

King, John N. *English Reformation Literature: The Tudor Origins of the Protestant Tradition* (Princeton: Princeton University Press, 1982).

Kirkconnell, Watson. *The Celestial Cycle: The Theme of 'Paradise Lost' in World Literature with Translations of the Major Analogues* (Toronto: University of Toronto Press, 1952).

Kuhn, Thomas S. *The Copernican Revolution: Planetary Astronomy in the Development of Western Thought* (Cambridge, Mass.: Harvard University Press, 1957).

Lewalski, Barbara K. *Milton's Brief Epic: The Genre, Meaning, and Art of Paradise Regained* (London: Methuen, 1966).

Lewalski, Barbara K. *Protestant Poetics and the Seventeenth-Century Religious Lyric* (Princeton: Princeton University Press, 1979).

Lewalski, Barbara K. *The Life of John Milton: A Critical Biography*, rev. edn (Oxford: Blackwell, 2003).

Milton, John. *The Complete Prose Works of John Milton*, gen. ed. Don M. Wolfe, 8 vols (New Haven: Yale University Press, 1953–82).

Milton, John. *Paradise Lost*, ed. Barbara Lewalski (Oxford: Blackwell, 2007).

Radzinowicz, Mary Ann. *Milton's Epics and the Book of Psalms* (Princeton: Princeton University Press, 1989).

Rosenblatt, Jason P. *Torah and Law in 'Paradise Lost'* (Princeton: Princeton University Press, 1994).

Sayce, R. A. *The French Biblical Epic in the Seventeenth Century* (Oxford, 1955).

Sidney, Philip. *The Defence of Poesie* (London, 1595).

Sims, James H. *The Bible in Milton's Epics* (Gainesville, Fla.: University of Florida Press, 1962).

PART VI

RECEPTION
HISTORIES

Introduction to Part VI

RECEPTION history has been influential in biblical, literary, and historical scholarship, as well as the history of art. Rooted in Hans-Georg Gadamer's distinction between *Rezeptionsgeschichte* (reception history), which emphasizes the agency involved in appropriating and applying a biblical text, and *Wirkungsgeschichte* (the history of use), which explores the shaping force of the text on society and culture, work in this capacious field asks how people took hold of and reworked texts, ideas, and artefacts to a variety of ends.[1] The chapters in this section consider the appropriation and reworking of the Bible. The first three chapters offer case studies in early modern reception, ranging from what we might term John Donne's 'virtual Bible', his compilation of interpretative and biblical resources, through the peculiarly Machiavellian Bible of John Saltmarsh, to the range of Bible stories that did so much to define post-Reformation Protestant visual culture. The final three chapters, in contrast, tackle questions of interiority, atheism, and critique, tracing shifting interpretations of the Bible in post-Reformation England, and demonstrating how scripture itself provided the interpretative resources which structured and inspired its changing uses.

Throughout his sermons, John Donne showcases a remarkable ability to track a single image across multiple books of the Bible. Emma Rhatigan notes that Donne rarely seems concerned to establish which of the available translations is most accurate; through the detailed analysis of a single sermon, delivered at Lincoln's Inn, Rhatigan demonstrates that many of Donne's quotations appear to come from memory or extra-biblical resources

---

[1] Hans-Georg Gadamer, *Truth and Method*, tr. Joel Weinsheimer and Donald G Marshall, 2nd edn (London: Continuum, 2004; 1st German edn 1960). On the impact of reception theory on biblical study, see Michael Lieb, Emma Mason, and Jonathan Roberts (eds), *The Oxford Handbook of the Reception History of the Bible* (Oxford: Oxford University Press, 2011).

rather than any individual Bible. Her chapter considers the relationship between Donne's biblical scholarship and the rhetorical and didactic demands of the sermon. The evidence of Donne's most favoured Bible translation, the heavily glossed Vulgate, requires us, Rhatigan argues, to re-evaluate the distinction between 'original' and 'secondary' sources and to take into account the widespread use of commentaries and glosses as an essential intra-biblical resource.

Andrew Morrall's chapter on domestic decoration also ties together the issues of dissemination addressed in Part III of this handbook ('Spreading the Word'), and the question of how early modern men and women appropriated and interpreted a rich biblical culture. Though the Reformation has long been understood as iconoclastic and even iconophobic,[2] recent scholarship has done much to recover a rich visual culture surrounding Protestant worship. Morrall explores the variety of Bible stories that constituted part of the visual experience of northern European householders, from windows to jugs, and fireplace tiles to moulded plasterwork. Biblical stories and scenes, Morrall argues, formed the basis for a common ethical education, promoted by leading humanists and Reformers. Catholic saints were replaced with a fund of exemplary biblical figures offering instruction in the paths of righteous living.

In contrast, Kevin Killeen explores the idiosyncratic readings produced by one individual, John Saltmarsh, who read biblical stories not as models of exemplary Christian behaviour, but for the Machiavellian social and economic strategies that could be derived from them. While the scriptures were usually understood to provide a resource to address morally complex problems, Saltmarsh discovered in them a biblical realpolitik. Interpreters were, however, faced with the problem of biblical characters who lie, cheat, and sin. Killeen explores the hermeneutic techniques used to mitigate these moments, including, most influentially, Augustine's typological and figurative readings of the Old Testament. Saltmarsh scarcely fits this model, however, as he attempts instead to animate the Bible as a guide to political manoeuvre and economic advantage. Yet, Killeen demonstrates, Saltmarsh was scarcely an irreligious cynic; his approach to the Bible reveals shifting early modern understandings of the Bible, which distinguished between local narrative instances and the overall purpose of the word of God.

The final three chapters in this section get to grips with two of the major narratives of Western history: the 'secularization thesis' and the idea of inwardness. Erica Longfellow engages with debates surrounding the extent to which the early modern period gave birth to a new sense of individual identity and interiority.[3] Longfellow approaches this question from a novel angle, charting the ways in which the Bible itself played with and produced effects of inwardness. Emphasizing the degree to which inwardness was already present in Christian discourse and in scripture, Longfellow explores how Protestant English translations of the New Testament worked to construct, but also to deny or criticize, the inward

---

[2] See, most influentially, Patrick Collinson, *From Iconoclasm to Iconophobia: The Cultural Impact of the Second English Reformation*, Stenton Lecture 1985 (Reading: University of Reading, 1986).

[3] See esp. Jacob Burckhardt, *The Civilization of the Renaissance in Italy*, tr. S. G. C. Middlemore, with a foreword by L. Goldscheider (London: Phaidon, 1944; 1st publ. as *Die Kultur der Renaissance in Italien*, 1860; Middlemore's translation 1st publ. 1878). Burckhardt's thesis has been widely critiqued, particularly by new historicist scholars. See e.g. Margreta de Grazia, Maureen Quilligan, and Peter Stallybrass, 'Introduction' to de Grazia et al. (eds), *Subject and Object in Renaissance Culture* (Cambridge: Cambridge University Press, 1996), 1–14.

self. With the advent of Protestantism, Longfellow argues, the existing medieval tendency to conceive of the passions (emotions) as both physically and metaphorically inward was transformed into a paradigm of inward faith. This changing understanding of inwardness defined the relationship of the self to God and to other people. In the margins of the scriptures, Longfellow argues, Bible translators began a crucial debate about the limits of the hidden self in a visible world.

Roger Pooley's chapter prompts readers to engage with another dominant historical and critical narrative: the 'secularization thesis', which holds that the early modern period witnessed a shift from a predominantly religious social order, in which the church and practices of belief dominated social and political life, to a rational and secular society founded on the distinction between church and state.[4] Because of the legal as well as social impossibility of openly declaring one's atheism, the evidence for atheism in this period comes mostly from a burgeoning anti-atheist literature. Pooley's chapter first explores the misquotation or rejection of the Bible in drama and other literary forms, in which scepticism and irreligion can safely be attributed to characters, rather than to their author. Moving on to examine how atheism is voiced in the anti-atheist literature, Pooley demonstrates that, in many cases, writers against atheism avoid direct references to the scriptures, preferring to argue from nature or philosophy. Where they do occur, appeals to the Bible cluster around key texts, especially Psalm 14 and Romans 1: 18–22, which resonate across a range of literary and theological writings.

Where Pooley explores the possibilities and limits of atheism, Yvonne Sherwood approaches the secularization thesis from a different standpoint, bringing it into dialogue with questions of hermeneutics and critique. Like Killeen, Sherwood acknowledges the numerous inconsistencies, narrative doublings, and repetitions of the Bible. Sherwood examines treatments of King David between the Reformation and Pierre Bayle's *Dictionnaire historique et critique* (first edition, 1697, translated into English in 1709) to dismantle the critical notion of early modernity as a watershed between theist pre-modernity and secular modernity. Exploring the inner-biblical tropes used to understand and negotiate the Bible's own complexity, Sherwood takes issue with a Foucauldian concept of critique as encroaching on the biblical from the outside. Paying attention to the ways in which these texts were appropriated in the early modern period, the chapter shows how the era expanded the centuries-old interpretative machinery of 'accommodation' and traditional doctrines of divine judgement and original sin. Taken together, these chapters remind us of the variety of sometimes conflicting resources offered by scripture, and show the ways in which the scriptures' very copiousness and inconsistency made possible new ways of thinking—including new ways of thinking about the Bible.

[4] For a summary of recent debates, see Pippa Norris and Ronald Inglehart, 'The Secularization Debate', in Norris and Inglehart (eds), *Sacred and Secular: Religion and Politics Worldwide* (Cambridge: Cambridge University Press, 2004), 3–32.

CHAPTER 35

DONNE'S BIBLICAL
ENCOUNTERS

EMMA RHATIGAN

DON Cameron Allen's exhaustive, and surely exhausting, survey of over one thousand scriptural references in the 1640 folio of Donne's sermons concludes with a rather disparaging account of Donne's use of the Bible. He tells us the results of his analysis are 'hardly a credit to Donne's scholarship ... [Donne] knew some Hebrew and apparently some Greek, but he consults the original text only when the mood is on him'.[1] Allen continues: '[Donne] was, after all, a poet who became a preacher; and though he was perhaps well-read for a poet and highly gifted for a clergyman, he was never the prize-winning schoolboy, who becomes, by biological fixation, a professor'.[2] Allen's reading of Donne is telling in terms of what it reveals about his understanding of the place of the Bible in sermon composition in the period; namely, that conscientious preaching is predicated on direct access to the Bible, ideally in the most 'original' form possible, in order to obtain an accurate translation, what Allen terms the 'best reading' of the text.

By contrast, whilst at all times maintaining the importance of scripture, there are moments when Donne himself seems more sanguine about biblical scholarship. Thus, excusing Augustine for a misreading of Psalm 38: 4, Donne explains that he 'truly had either never true copy of the Bible, or else cited sometimes, as the words were in his memory, and not as they were in the Text'.[3] Never mind consulting the 'original text', Augustine, according to Donne, is not even using a physical copy of the Bible. As Katrin Ettenhuber has recently argued, such moments are part of Donne's celebration of Augustine as a reader. For Donne, such is Augustine's knowledge and, indeed, spiritual empathy for the biblical text, that a local misreading in fact points to a fruitful interpretation.[4] Clearly

---

[1] Don Cameron Allen, 'Dean Donne Sets his Text', *English Literary History*, 10 (1943): 227. I am grateful to Mary Morrissey who read and commented on this chapter prior to publication

[2] Allen, 'Dean Donne', 229.

[3] *The Sermons of John Donne*, ed. George Potter and Evelyn Simpson (Berkeley, Calif.: University of California Press, 1953–62), ii. 109–10.

[4] Katrin Ettenhuber, *Donne's Augustine: Renaissance Cultures of Interpretation* (Oxford: Oxford University Press, 2011), 9.

Donne was not advocating that preachers dispensed with the Bible as they prepared their sermons; he stresses that 'S. *Augustine's* is an useful mistaking, but it is a mistaking'. However, while the point of Donne's example is that Augustine is an exception, textual accuracy, as Allen notes, does not seem to have been a priority in Donne's use of the Bible. His interest rarely seems to be in ascertaining which is the most accurate translation and more often than not his quotations appear to draw on no particular English Bible. Indeed, in one sense Donne's Bible too is absent, or rather displaced, since rather than straining after the 'original text' Donne frequently does the reverse, gaining his biblical knowledge through a variety of commentaries and glosses, what we might call 'secondary texts'. Donne's understanding of how a preacher might use the Bible appears, then, to have been very different to the ideal endorsed by Allen.

In this chapter I want to shed further light on these issues and the ways Donne drew on the Bible when preparing his sermons through a close reading of a Lincoln's Inn sermon on Psalm 38: 2 ('For thine arrowes stick fast in me, and thy hand presseth me sore').[5] Weaving its way through a myriad of allusions to scriptural arrows, Donne's sermon is a biblical *tour-de-force*, and thus an ideal text with which to explore both how Donne gained his biblical knowledge and selected his scriptural examples, and how he negotiated various biblical translations. Throughout I consider the relationship between Donne's biblical scholarship and his commitment to a particular rhetorical and didactic occasion, arguing that studies of preachers' biblical encounters need to take account of both 'original texts' and paratexts.

I. DONNE'S BIBLICAL EXEGESIS

Donne structures his sermon on Psalm 38: 2 around two exegetical approaches to the psalm. The first of these is focused on an analysis of the psalm as a series of reasons and arguments presented to God by David; he tells us 'This whole Psalm is a *Prayer* ... grounded upon Reasons'.[6] The second is the highly conventional model of exegesis in which the psalm is read literally with reference to David, then morally as it concerns mankind, and finally typologically as it can be applied to Christ.[7] These two approaches to the psalm operate in tandem. Thus Donne first considers in what way a man might attempt to reason with or oppose God (part 1), before turning to the specific reasons in his text

---

[5] The sermon is no. 2 in vol. ii in *Sermons*, ed. Potter and Simpson. It was most likely preached in the summer of 1618; see *Sermons*, ed. Potter and Simpson, ii. 13–14.

[6] *Sermons*, ed. Potter and Simpson, ii. 50. All subsequent references to the sermon will be to this edition, incorporated into the text.

[7] On the patristic and medieval origins of this model of exegesis, see Henri de Lubac, *Medieval Exegesis: The Four Senses of Scripture*, tr. Mark Sebanc and E. M. Macierowski (Grand Rapids, Mich.: William B. Eermans; Edinburgh: T. & T. Clark, 1998–2009); and Beryl Smalley, *The Study of the Bible in the Middle Ages*, 3rd edn (Oxford: Basil Blackwell, 1983). On the changes of emphasis introduced by Protestant exegetes, see Richard A. Muller, 'Biblical Interpretation in the Era of the Reformation: The View from the Middle Ages', in Richard A. Muller and John L. Thompson (eds), *Biblical Interpretation in the Era of the Reformation* (Grand Rapids, Mich., and Cambridge: William B. Eerdmans, 1996), 3–22; and David C. Steinmetz, 'Divided by a Common Past: The Reshaping of the Christian Exegetical Tradition in the Sixteenth Century', *Journal of Medieval and Early Modern Studies*, 27 (1997): 245–64.

(part 2). However, in moving into this second part he simultaneously moves from an interpretation of his text in terms of David's personal history as recounted in 2 Samuel, to a reading of the psalm as a text which speaks to all men, telling his congregation 'these *Psalmes* were made, not onely to vent *David's* present holy passion, but to serve the Church of God' (ii. 55). This second part is subdivided into a consideration of five reasons presented by the text; that God's arrows are tribulations, that they are many, that they stick, that they stick fast, and that they stick fast in us. Within this, the first subdivision on the arrows as temptation is further divided into a consideration of the arrows as they are shot from others, swift in coming, and hard to see. Next, in a third part, Donne turns to the second half of his text, God's hand, which 'follows the blow, and presses it' (ii. 66), inviting his congregation to meditate on how God's arrows always hit the mark, how they are sent as temptations, but also how they are sent to instruct and ultimately reclaim man. Then, to finish, he reads the psalm in terms of Christ, concluding the sermon with a reading of the crucifixion in which Christ takes on the sinful arrows of mankind.

Running throughout the sermon, in counterpoint to this exegetical structure, is the image of the arrow, Donne's central metaphor for the tribulations and temptations which assail mankind. The sermon offers a virtuoso survey of biblical arrows, including the arrows God ordains against persecutors in Psalm 7: 13, the arrows with which the wicked persecute the upright in heart in Psalm 11: 2, 'the arrow that flieth by day' in Psalm 91: 5, God's arrows 'drunk with blood' in Deuteronomy 32: 42, the arrow Elisha instructs Joash to shoot out of the window in 2 Kings 13: 17, the arrow which shoots Jehoram in 2 Kings 9: 24, the arrow Jonathan shoots behind himself in 1 Samuel 20, and the image of God's arrows and glittering spear in Habbakuk 3: 11, to list just a few. As the sermon progresses, Donne extends these Old Testament arrows into the New Testament. Thus David's arrows are aligned with the 'fiery darts' of the wicked described in Paul's letter to the Ephesians (Ephesians 6: 16) and later with the 'thorn in the flesh' he describes in his letter to the Corinthians (2 Corinthians 12: 7); Donne tells his congregation 'One of these arrows was shot into Saint *Paul* himselfe, and it stuck, and stuck fast' (ii. 64). Ultimately, in the final typological reading of the text, the arrows are reconceived as the nails and thorns which torture Christ in the crucifixion. Thus Donne in a direct address to Christ claims 'these arrows were in *thee*, in *all* thee: from thy *Head* torn with thorns, to thy *feet* pierced with nayls' (ii. 71).

Such an array of biblical arrows must have been no less impressive for Donne's Lincoln's Inn congregation than it is for his modern readers. Even by the standards of seventeenth-century biblical literacy, his ability to trace a single image across multiple books of the Bible is striking, and a perfect example of the type of rhetorically ornate and often ostentatiously learned preaching Donne was perfecting in elite pulpits such as the Inns of Court. But presumably Donne was not able to identify all his biblical examples unaided; such a feat would seem to demand an almost impossibly encyclopedic knowledge of the Bible and it is hard to believe Donne wrote the sermon without drawing on a series of scholarly aids. The question, then, is what sort of secondary texts guided Donne in his reading of the Bible. One type of biblical finding-aid has been identified by Winfried Schleiner who has suggested that Donne could have been using a text along the lines of the Pseudo-Melito *Clavis*.[8] The *Clavis*, a medieval work once thought to be by Melito of Sardes,

---

[8] Winfried Schleiner, *The Imagery of Donne's Sermons* (Providence, RI: Brown University Press,

is a symbolic key to the Bible offering a series of allegorical interpretations. Organized by topic, it includes a chapter 'De metallis' (on metals), within which there is a section on arrows, offering the reader a summary of their properties and spiritual meanings and referencing key biblical texts.[9]

It is immediately evident how Donne could have been exploiting a text such as the *Clavis*. At the most basic level it would have helped him navigate the image of the arrow in the Bible. The *Clavis* provides the precise reference for half of the biblical arrows Donne refers to and points him to the right book, chapter, or biblical figure for all but three of the remainder. In fact, it also provides references to a further nine biblical arrows which Donne does not use. Faced with such a finding-aid Donne would have been spoilt for choice. Drawing his attention to further biblical examples would not, however, have been the only way a guide such as the *Clavis* would have shaped Donne's reading of his text. In a list of the properties of an arrow the *Clavis* identifies a number of the qualities that Donne uses to structure his exegesis. For example, it specifically details the swiftness of an arrow ('velocitas experditio'), its power to wound deeply ('subito percutit et profunde'), and its relative invisibility, which means it can signify both hidden temptations ('tentatio occulta') and open temptations ('tentatio manifesta'). All of these feature in Donne's subdivisions to the second part of his sermon, in which he analyses the properties of the arrows which assail mankind.

Moreover, the *Clavis* also identifies the arrow as signifying both man's sins of the flesh ('impetus carnis'), which Donne elaborates on when he conceives of the arrows as temptations such as '*chambering* and *wantonnesse*' (ii. 62), and the sufferings inflicted on Christ in the passion ('Facta Judaeorum in passione Christi'), which is the focus of the final section of the sermon, drawing the congregation to a consideration of 'the weight of [Christ's] torments in the crucifixion' (ii. 71). This particular *Clavis* would not have been available to Donne in print, nor is there any evidence that he would have had access to it in manuscript, consequently any attempt to identify it as a 'source' must remain tentative. The apparent echoes between his exegesis of the arrow and that offered in the *Clavis* does, however, suggest that he was influenced by a text in this tradition and, moreover, that such a work not only guided him to particular biblical texts, but shaped how he read them and how he incorporated them into his sermon.

One of the most important advantages of a biblical key such as the *Clavis* would have been its topical organization, which meant Donne could go straight to the biblical image he wanted to interrogate. Commentaries organized by biblical text would also, though, have been useful and there is compelling evidence to suggest that Donne was drawing on one in particular, Joannes Lorinus's (Jean Lorin) *Commentaria in librum Psalmorum*.[10] In

1970), 172–3. The *Clavis* is edited by J. B. Pitra, included in *Spicilegium solesmense* (Paris, 1812–89), ii. Recent scholarship, rejecting Melito's authorship, dates the *Clavis* to the eight century; see R. E. Kaske, Arthur Groos, and Michael W. Twomey, *Medieval Christian Literary Imagery: A Guide to Interpretation* (Toronto: University of Toronto Press, 1988), 42; and Smalley, *Study of the Bible*, 246–8. I am extremely grateful to David Colclough who first pointed me towards these references.

[9] Pitra, *Spicilegium solesmense*, ii. 307–9.

[10] Joannes Lorinus, *Commentaria in librum Psalmorum* (Lyon, 1611–16). The discussion of Ps. 38: 2 (Ps. 37: 3 in the Vulgate numbering) is in vol. i, NNN3^v–NNN4^r. On Donne's reading of patristic texts and the finding-aids through which he navigated them, see Ettenhuber, *Donne's Augustine*. Ettenhuber discusses Donne's reference to the image of the arrow in Augustine at p. 81.

terms of providing further examples of biblical arrows, Lorinus is not nearly as useful as the *Clavis*; Donne could only have found three of his biblical references there. However, Lorinus could have been Donne's source for the refiguring of the arrows as the fiery darts in Ephesians 6: 16; he, like Donne, draws a clear analogy between the two texts. Moreover, he could also have provided Donne with a valuable patristic text on the figure of the arrow in his sermon, Augustine's discussion of the arrow of God's love in the *Confessions*. Lorinus points his readers to *Confessions* 9.2 and this is precisely the text cited by Donne when he tells his congregation, 'There is a *probatum est* in S. *Aug. Sagittaveras cor meum*, Thou hast shot at my heart' (ii. 68). Finally, in what constitutes some of the most compelling evidence that Donne was using Lorinus, the commentary would have taken him to two historical allusions.

Not content with dazzling his congregation with an array of arrows from the Bible, Donne also provides them with two extra-biblical examples. The first is an allusion to the Persian king Darius. Emphasising that the arrows of his text are the more deadly because they are shot from others, Donne illustrates his point by explaining that the arrow 'was the Embleme, and Inscription, which *Darius* took for his coin, *Insculpere sagittarium*, to shew his greatnesse that he could wound afar off, as an Archer does' (ii. 56).[11] Then later in the sermon he alludes to Leonidas, king of Sparta, telling his congregation 'You may have read, or heard that answer of a *Generall*, who was threatned with that danger, that his enemies arrows were so many, as that they would cover the Sun from him' (ii. 68–9). Both these specific examples are given by Lorinus, who also provides references to Piero Valeriano's *Hieroglyphica* for an account of Darius's coin and Valerius Maximus, *Factorum et dictorum memorabilium*, for the story of Leonidas.[12] Tellingly, however, Donne's text is so close to Lorinus's there is no evidence that he went any further than the commentary.

There is compelling evidence, then, that Donne used biblical commentaries and finding-aids as he constructed his sermon. However, these texts could only ever be said to provide Donne with some of his raw materials, and the sermon itself is far more than a concordance of arrows and their allegorical meanings. Rather, the arrow and its metaphorical transformations become the central expression of the sermon's transition from an analysis of temptation to a promise of salvation. This is expressed most directly in the movement from Old Testament to the New, when the arrows of God's punishment are refigured as the nails and thorns which pierce Christ. Here, the metaphorical transformation of the arrow epitomizes the threefold exegetical model Donne established at the start of his sermon when he explained how his biblical text held within it both a historical and a typological meaning.

This transition is, however, anticipated throughout the sermon in the ways in which the biblical arrows reflect onto and echo each other. For example, the hand of God pressing the arrow into David in Donne's scriptural text ('thy hand presseth me sore') mirrors the hand of Elisha guiding Joash as he shoots in 2 Kings 13: 16–17. Donne explains, 'The Prophet bade

[11] The Persian king Darius (522–486 BC) was credited with instituting the gold coin known as the Daric which depicted the king holding a bow or spear.
[12] See Lorinus, *Commentarium*, i, NNN3ᵛ: 'Denique Symbolum imperii sagittarius erat, quem idcirco nummis insculpsit Darius, quia eminus feriunt sagittæ', and NNN4ʳ: '& cum alio respondere, sagittarum multitudinem tantam, quæ solem obscurare posse videantur, strenuè certantibus esse pro vmbra vs pugnare tutò, & cum victoria valeant'.

the King shoot, but *Elisha* laid his hand upon the Kings hand; So from what instrument of Satan soever, thy affliction comes, Gods hand is upon *their hand* that shoot it' (ii. 67). The echo between the biblical passages means the story of Joash can be used to prompt the listener to reconsider the psalm; what might at first reading have appeared to be an image of God's punishment is reinterpreted as an instance of God using affliction to bring man to repentance. On another occasion, when Donne is seeking to identify comfort in Christian suffering, the threatening cloud of arrows facing Leonidas is metamorphosed into the shadow of God's wings, a recurring image of divine protection in the psalms; Donne reassures his congregation that 'though the clouds of these arrows may hide all suns of worldly comforts from thee, yet thou are still *under the shadow of his wings*' (ii. 69).

The references provided by Donne's sources are, then, transformed into a finely crafted rhetorical structure. Indeed, it seems highly appropriate that at the start of the sermon Donne specifically identified the psalms as 'poetry', a form which 'is both curious and requires diligence in the making' (ii. 50). Donne uses the adjective 'curious' here in the sense of 'made with care or art, skilfully, elaborately or beautifully wrought' (*OED*, 7.a) and it is precisely this sense of being skilfully wrought which captures his own play with the image of the arrow. The sermon's biblical exegesis is indistinguishable from its rhetorical construction, and for a modern scholar the process of tracing Donne's scholarship becomes a highly rewarding exercise in close reading. It is ironic, of course, that this is precisely the criticism that Allen makes, that Donne's sermons are the 'work of a poet rather than a scholar'. Analysing the way Donne reads and responds to the Bible in this sermon suggests, rather, that this rhetorical work of the 'poet' is precisely what sheds clearest light on how Donne was interpreting his biblical text.

II. DONNE'S BIBLICAL TEXT

Biblical scholarship is not, however, limited to knowledge of the contents of the Bible and, as Allen's article demonstrates, some of the central charges against Donne as a scholar are linguistic; that he has only limited understanding of Hebrew and Greek, that he consults the 'original text' only occasionally, 'when the mood is on him', and that he has relatively little interest in comparing different translations.[13] On the surface, the sermon on Psalm 38: 2 would seem to support such criticisms. A survey of Donne's biblical quotations reveals that his preferred translation of the Bible is the Vulgate and that when citing in English he moves freely between the King James Bible and the Geneva, with a slight preference for the former.[14] There is just one occasion when Donne quotes from what must have been either the Bishops' or Douay-Rheims translation. This pattern of citation corresponds to the initial findings of the *Oxford Edition of the Sermons of John Donne* (gen. ed. Peter McCullough) which suggest that in his first years in the pulpit Donne had a preference for the Geneva, but that by the early 1620s he had shifted to the King James Bible.

---

[13] On the variety of biblical translations available to Donne, see Allen, 'Dean Donne', 209–12.

[14] There are eleven citations from the King James Bible and eight from the Geneva. There are, of course, numerous other instances when there is no difference between the two translations and so it is impossible to know which Donne is using, or when Donne is paraphrasing, rather than quoting.

Instances in this sermon of Donne going beyond these translations to engage with 'original texts' are limited to just two references to the Hebrew and two to the Chaldee paraphrase and there is no evidence in these cases that he was consulting these 'originals' directly.[15] For example, Donne's discussion of the Hebrew originals might seem to imply that he is ranging independently across the Hebrew, Vulgate, and King James Bible. He states with confidence of Lamentations 3: 13 ('He hath caused the arrows of his quiver to enter into my reins', King James Bible) that 'The Roman Translation reads that *filias, The daughters of his quiver* ... But the Original hath it *filios*, the sons of his quiver' (ii. 62). However, this linguistic example would have been easily available to Donne in a text such as Pagninus's interlinear translation of the Books of Solomon which translates the Hebrew, as Donne says, into the masculine 'filio'.[16]

Later, Donne offers what appears to be a more complicated foray into Hebrew grammar. Analysing his biblical text, he tells his congregation: 'for that word, in which the Prophet here expresses this sticking, and this fast sticking of these arrows, which is *Nachath*, is here, (as the Grammarians in that language call it) in *Niphal, figere factæ*, they were made to stick' (ii. 67). 'Niphal' is one of the seven major verb stems in biblical Hebrew and usually denotes the passive or reflexive voice, hence Donne's translation of 'they were meant to stick'. Such analysis would appear to suggest Donne had some understanding of the Hebrew language, but, while this may be the case, in this instance all the main points of Donne's grammatical excursus are to be found in Lorinus's commentary, providing yet more suggestive evidence that Donne drew on this text to guide his biblical scholarship. Lorinus provides not only the Latin transliteration 'nachath', but also the explanation that the verb is 'in niphal'; he writes 'Verbum Hebræum in niphal, est ... *nichathu*, vel legerunt Lxx. & Hieronymus à ... *chatath*'.[17] A similar pattern emerges with regard to Donne's two references to the Chaldee paraphrase. Donne first refers to the Chaldee when commenting on Psalm 91: 5 ('Thou shalt not be afraid for the terror by night; nor for the arrow that flieth by day'), telling his congregation 'the Chalde paraphrase calls it there expresly, *Sagitta mortis*, The arrow of death' (2: 61). A quick look at Lorinus's commentary on this verse reveals that he provides a translation of the Chaldee, 'Chaldaicè, *à sagitta angeli mortu*', which could have prompted Donne to his more concise version.[18] Then later, glossing the second half of his biblical text, Donne explains 'the Chalde paraphrase carries it farther then, to *Mansit super me vulnus manus tuæ*; Thy hand hath wounded mee, and that hand keeps the wound open' (ii. 66). And, once again, we find Donne had no need to go further than Lorinus who states: 'Chald. *mansit super me vulnus manu tua*'.[19]

---

[15] On Donne's use of the Hebrew Bible and Chaldee paraphrase, see Allen, 'Dean Donne', 212–19; and Chanita Goodblatt, *The Christian Hebraism of John Donne* (Pittsburgh, Pa.: Duquesne University Press, 2010). On the study of Hebrew more widely in the period, see Mordechai Feingold, 'Oriental Studies', in Nicholas Tyacke (ed.), *The History of the University of Oxford*, iv. *Seventeenth-Century Oxford* (Oxford: Clarendon Press, 1997), 449–503; and G. Lloyd Jones, *The Discovery of Hebrew in Tudor England: A Third Language* (Manchester: Manchester University Press, 1983).

[16] Xanthus Pagninus [Xantes Pagnino], *Proverbia Salominis Hebraice: Cum interlineari versione* (Leiden, 1608), Z6[r].

[17] Lorinus, *Commentariorum*, i, NNN3[v]. By 'LXX' Lorinus is referring to the Septuagint, the Greek translation of the Hebrew Old Testament.

[18] Lorinus, *Commentariorum*, ii, HHhh3[v].

[19] Lorinus, *Commentariorum*, i, NNN4[r]. The cumulative evidence suggests Lorinus is Donne's source here, but it is worth noting that a Latin translation of both Chaldee paraphrases would also have been easily available to him in the Antwerp Polyglot. See *Biblia sacra Hebraice, Chaldaice, Graece, et Latine*, ed. Arias

This sermon at least does not provide evidence that Donne had a detailed knowledge of either Hebrew or Aramaic. Certainly he was engaged in scholarship, but in scholarship of what we might term 'secondary', rather than 'original', texts. However, to return to Allen's criticisms of Donne, we find that he is not only concerned with the limits of Donne's linguistic knowledge, but with the fact that Donne's choice of translation appears 'whimsical' and 'capricious'.[20] Yet an analysis of the moments when Donne introduces his linguistic excurses suggests something very different. As the discussion so far demonstrates, Donne's references to the Hebrew and Chaldee paraphrase are, while admittedly giving at least some sense of ostentatiously paraded linguistic knowledge, always carefully incorporated into part of a larger exegetical argument. To take just one example, Donne's insistence that the Hebrew in Lamentations 3: 13 should be translated as 'sons', rather than 'daughters', could appear to be a rather arbitrary distinction, nothing more than an excuse to draw attention to his biblical scholarship. However, closer analysis of the passage reveals that Donne uses the crux as a means to guide his congregation through the division of his sermon.

Having set out his linguistic analysis Donne tells his auditory: 'If it were but so, *daughters*, we might limit these arrows in the signification of *tentations*, by the many occasions of tentation, arising from *that sex*. But the Originall hath it *filios*, the sons of his quiver, and therefore we consider these arrows in a stronger signification, *tribulations*, as well as *tentations*' (ii. 62). The grammatical move from feminine to masculine becomes a means of drawing listeners' attention to his transition from an analysis of the arrows as temptations to a reading of them as tribulations. Moreover, much of Donne's analysis of temptation thus far has emphasized sins of licentiousness, warning against 'arrows of *gaming*, or *chambering*, and *wantonnesse*' (ii. 62).[21] Such a focus seems appropriate if we consider that Donne was preaching to an Inns of Court congregation which consisted in large part of young gentleman students regularly criticized for indulging in precisely these sorts of vices, but it also reveals how this emphasis on the masculinity of the arrows assailing Jeremiah provides Donne with a timely opportunity to lead his auditory away from the easy and comfortable assumption that vice and temptations can be displaced onto women.[22] In other words, read within a broader didactic and pastoral context, Donne's allusion to the Hebrew text appears not so much arbitrary, as central to his attempt to craft his sermon to engage the particular congregation before him.

A similarly judicious approach is evident on the occasion when Donne chooses not to follow either the King James Bible or the Geneva, but instead to use the wording of either the Bishops' or the Douai-Rheims translation. The moment comes in Donne's *exordium* when, having celebrated God's care in speaking to man in poetry and psalms, he insists that man's speech to God must be equally carefully crafted: 'Let all our speech to [God], be

---

Montanus (Antwerp, 1567–73), 3.2P2^r: 'Non timebis à timore demonum qui ambulant in nocte, à sagitta angeli mortis, qua[m] emittit interdiu', and 3.2F6r: 'Quoniam sagittæ tuæ irruerunt in me, & mansit super me vulnus tuæ'.

[20] Allen, 'Dean Donne', 227, 228.

[21] This warning invokes the verse from Paul that Augustine claimed as the prompt to his conversion; for its use as a 'conversion-scripture', see the chapter by Helen Smith in this volume.

[22] On the constitution of the Lincoln's Inn congregation, see Emma Rhatigan, 'Donne's Readership at Lincoln's Inn', in Jeanne Shami, M. Thomas Hester, and Dennis Flynne (eds), *The Oxford Handbook of John Donne* (Oxford: Oxford University Press, 2011), 576–88.

weighed, and measured in the weights of the *Sanctuary*' (ii. 50). The 'weight of the sanctuary' is a term only used in the Bishops' and Douai-Rheims translations; the King James Bible and Geneva Bible translate the phrase as 'the shekel of the Sanctuary'.[23] Donne's choice of 'weight' rather than 'shekel' makes perfect sense given the immediate context of his argument that prayer to God should be carefully considered; weighed and measured. It also develops his opening identification of the psalms as poetry and thus prayers in which 'all the words are numbered and measured, and weighed' (ii. 250). Moreover, the semantic echo between the weight of the temple and the weighed words of prayer allows for the analogy between the offerings to God made in the Temple in the Old Testament and the offerings of prayer made by Donne's congregation in the church. But 'weight' is also an important word in terms of Donne's text. As his reading of Lorinus would already have told him, the 'pressing' of God's hand in Psalm 38: 2 was commonly understood as a weight. Lorinus writes that '*confirmatio* grauem impressionē denotar ac oppressionem, quasi grauissimo impositio onere' and Donne follows this closely explaining that in addition to the arrows 'there is another weight upon us, in the Text, there is still a *Hand* that follows the blow, and presses it' (ii. 66). Weighed words are developed into a meditation on the 'weight' of God's hand.

Donne's argument is, however, not only that man's words should be 'weighed' in the 'weight' of the Sanctuary, but that they should be 'measured', and in the first part of the sermon in which he discusses how a man might reason with God, he picks up on this, describing how: '*David* presents onely to God the sense of his corrections, and implies in *that*, that since the cure is wrought, ... God would now be pleased to remember all his other gracious promises too; and to admit such a zealous prayer as he doth from *Esay* after, *Be not angry, O Lord, above measure*' (ii. 54). Donne's quotation from Isaiah 64: 9 comes from the Geneva Bible; the King James Bible reads instead 'Be not wroth very sore, O Lord'. And it is not difficult to see why Donne has chosen this particular translation given how clearly it echoes and recalls his *exordium*. Indeed, Donne presses home the semantic reverberations in his qualification 'that is, above the measure of thy *promises* to repentant souls, or the measure of the *strength* of our bodies' (ii. 54). Just as God speaks to man in 'measured' words (and, of course, demands equally carefully 'weighed and measured' words in return from man) so God's anger will be in 'measure', in proportion to man's sins.

Clearly it is not always possible to identify such a clear rhetorical rationale in Donne's choice of biblical translation. On many occasions it seems he chooses one translation over another simply because that is the one which comes first to mind. On still more occasions, his wording reflects no single Bible. The instances discussed suggest, however, that we should not be too quick to dismiss his commitment to reading across different translations. Nor should the possibility he gleaned his translations of the Hebrew and Aramaic from secondary sources blind us to their importance in a sermon's construction. Once again, it becomes necessary to re-evaluate the distinction between poetry and scholarship. In the 'weighed words' of Donne's sermon, the grammatical and linguistic insights offered by the work of translation are exploited as part of a larger commitment to the persuasive purpose of the sermon as a whole. Crucially, the question of how much Hebrew Donne knew must not be allowed to obscure the question of how he used it within the sermons. Nor should

[23] See e.g. Exod. 30: 24.

too narrow a focus on 'original texts' cause us to shy away from exploring Donne's use of mediating sources. Indeed, a consideration of Donne's persistently most favoured translation, the Vulgate, requires a re-evaluation of this very distinction between 'original' and 'secondary' source.

III. Rethinking 'Original Texts'

Donne quotes from the Vulgate twenty-one times in his sermon on Psalm 38: 2. This is approximately twice as often as any other Bible translation. Moreover, although he takes his text from the King James Bible, the majority of his *divisio* subheadings look to the Latin syntax of the Vulgate; for example, *Sagittae, Infixa sunt, Infixae mihi*, and *Manus*. Use of the Vulgate was by no means unusual in preaching of this period, especially not in elite pulpits such as the Inns of Court. However the extent to which Donne uses it would certainly have been distinctive, and it is at least possible that his reliance on it stemmed from his upbringing as a Catholic. The Vulgate would have been the first Bible he encountered and the text in which he was educated and it is not therefore surprising that it was also the Bible which dominated his imagination and came most easily to mind after his conversion. Perhaps, as he described Augustine, he was citing 'as the words were in his memory'.

While the reasons for Donne's use of the Vulgate can only remain the subject of speculation, there is more compelling evidence about the particular version of the Vulgate on which he was drawing. Initial work annotating Donne's sermons for the forthcoming *Oxford Edition of the Sermons of John Donne* suggests that he was using the Vulgate with *Glossa*, in the edition which he was later to give to Lincoln's Inn as a leaving gift.[24] In such editions the Vulgate text is surrounded by the *Glossa ordinaria*, glosses on the text drawn, for the most part, from patristic authorities.[25] Beneath this are the *Postilla* of Nicholas of Lyra, a further commentary on the biblical text.[26] Then, at the end of each chapter, are the 'Additiones Burgensis in postillam Nicholai de Lyra', a response to Lyra by Paul of Saint Marie, Bishop of Burgos, and the 'Tractatus magistiri Matthiæ Doring', a critique, in turn, of Paul of Burgos's work by Matthias Doring, a German Franciscan. In other words, this is a Bible in which the biblical text is framed by, and mediated through, generations of biblical commentary.

A reading of Donne's sermon on Psalm 38: 2 against this edition of the Vulgate suggests Donne's exegesis of his text was influenced both by the *Glossa* and Lyra's *Postilla*. In particular, a reading of his second section on the nature of the arrows shows him moving between the various sections of text on the page before him, interweaving readings of the psalm prompted by patristic sources in the *Glossa* and the commentary

---

[24] *Biblia sacra cum glossa ordinaria* (Venice, 1606).

[25] On the *Glossa ordinaria*, see Smalley, *Study of the Bible*, esp. 46–66; and Lesley Smith, *The Glossa Ordinaria: The Making of a Medieval Bible Commentary* (Leiden and Boston: Brill, 2009). On the printing of the *Glossa ordinaria* and its influence in the sixteenth century, see Karlfried Froehlich, 'The Fate of the *Glossa ordinaria* in the Sixteenth Century', in David C. Steinmetz (ed.), *Die Patristik in der Bibelexegese des 16. Jahrhunderts* (Wiesbaden: Harrassowitz, 1999), 19–47.

[26] On Lyra's *Postilla*, see Philip D. W. Krey and Lesley Smith (eds), *Nicholas of Lyra: The Sense of Scripture* (Leiden: Brill, 2000).

offered by Lyra. Donne opens this second branch of the sermon by offering his congregation a reading of the psalm as David's prayer to God to forbear punishing him further. He explains '*David* in a rectified conscience findes that he may be admitted to present *reasons* against farther correction, And that this may be received as a reason, *That Gods Arrows are upon him*' (ii. 54). A glance at the *Glossa* situated immediately to the left of the verse suggests a likely source for this reading. Keyed by lemma to the start of the verse, 'Quoniam sagittæ', the *Glossa* provides a reference to Augustine and the note 'Quoniam sagittae. Numerat quae patitur, vt quia multa sunt, satis sint Deo ne peiora patiatur'.[27] This note is a summary of part of Augustine's commentary on the Psalm. Augustine writes:

> But why implore not to be rebuked in indignation or chastised in wrath? It is as though the Psalmist were saying to God: 'Since the evils I endure are so many, so grievous, let them suffice I beg of thee'. And he begins to enumerate them, offering to God as a satisfaction all he now suffers, in order to suffer nothing worse, *For thy arrows are fastened in me, and thy hand hath been strong upon me*.[28]

This interpretation of David's listing of his miseries as part of a request to God to refrain from further punishment would seem to be an obvious prompt for Donne's reading of the arrows as a series of 'reasons', with the very arrangement of the page taking him to Augustine.

Having identified the arrows as the sufferings David is presenting to God, Donne proceeds to analyse the nature of these miseries in more detail. He tells his congregation:

> In this place, some understand by these Arrows, foul and infectious *diseases*, in his body, derived by his *incontinence*. Others, the sting of *Conscience*, and that fearfull choice, which the Prophet offered him, *war, famine*, and *pestilence*. Others, his passionate *sorrow* in the *death* of *Bethsheba's first childe*; or in the *Incest of Amnon* upon his sister, or in the *murder* upon *Amnon* by *Absolon*; or in the *death of Absolon* by *Joab*; or in many other occasions of sorrow, that surrounded *David* and his family, more, perchance, then any such family in the body of story. (ii. 55)

Donne seems keen to indicate that these various interpretations are supported by a weight of exegetical tradition, but he holds back from informing his congregation of the identity of the 'some' who interpret the arrows these ways. However, if you look below the Vulgate text to the postilla of Lyra printed on the same page, a source for Donne's claim of exegetical authority emerges into view. Lyra reads Psalm 38 in terms of David's life as it is recounted in 2 Samuel. For example, his postil on verse 2, again linked by lemma to the first words of Donne's text, reads

---

[27] *Biblia sacra cum glossa*, 3. Z1ᵛ.

[28] 'Quare autem petit iste ne in indignatione arguatur, neque in ira emendetur? Tanquam dicens Deo, Quoniam jam ista quae patior multa sunt, magna sunt, quaeso ut sufficiant. Et incipit illa enumerare satisfaciens Deo, offerens illa quae patitur, ne pejora patiatur: *Quoniam sagittae tuae infixae sunt mihi, et confirmasti super me manum tuam*'. Augustine, *Ennarationes in Psalmos*, 'In Psalmum XXXVII', *Patrologia Latina*, 36.397. *St Augustine on the Psalms*, tr. Scholastica Hebgin and Felicitas Corrigan, *Ancient Christian Writers*, 30 (London: Longmans, Green & Co., 1961), ii. 332–3.

Quoniam sagitte, &c. *idest, pęnæ mihi denuntiatæ ex part uta per Nathan prophetam dicentem*: Hæc dicit d[ic]ens aut septem annis veniat tibi fames in terra tua, aut trib[us] mensibus fugies aduersarios tuos, aut tribus dieb[us] erit tibi pestilentia in terra.[29]

This interpretation of the arrows in terms of 2 Samuel 24: 13, when David is given a choice between famine 'fames in terra', fleeing before his enemies 'fugies adversarios', and pestilence 'pestilentia', would be an obvious source for Donne's reference to the authority who reads the arrows in terms of David's choice of war, famine, or pestilence. Moreover, Lyra's postils on other verses of the psalm could have provided Donne with his other authorities. Thus the postil on verse 7 'Et non est santitas in carne mea. *quia ex infirmitate carnis procedit luxuria*' suggests the reading of the arrows as 'foul and infectious diseases' derived from 'incontinence'; the postil on verse 3 'A facie peccatorum meorum. *idest propter peccata mea: per hoc insinuans, quod multo plus dolebat de culpa quam de pœna, ideo subditur*' points to the reading of the arrow as the 'sting of Conscience'; and the postil on verse 6 describes David's fasting for Bathsheba's child.[30] Clearly Lyra is not offering a series of interpretations of the arrows here, but his postils colour the psalm with the narratives of 2 Samuel, proving a useful source for Donne as he sets out his 'historical' reading of the text.

At this point Donne's exegetical structure requires him to move from a reading of the psalm with reference to David, to a reading of it as it speaks to the condition of all mankind. Thus he exhorts his congregation to 'Extend this *Man*, to all *Mankind*; carry *Davids* History up to *Adams* History, and consider us in that state, which wee inherit from *him*' (ii. 33) and proceeds to develop a 'moral' reading of the arrows as original sin and the sufferings which man must endure as a result of the Fall. He tells his congregation that since 'wee were all shot in Adam ... these arrows which are lamented here, are all those miseries, which sinne hath cast upon us; *Labor*, and the childe of that, *Sicknesse*, and the off-spring of that, *Death*' (ii. 55). This reading is the very next one suggested by the *Glossa*. The second half of the note on Donne's text which I quoted earlier states 'Portant enim corpus mortale tot miseriis subditum'. This again refers to Augustine's commentary on the psalm where he writes of the psalmist 'He has now entered upon the recital of his present woes, woes however which are the outcome of the Lord's wrath, because the outcome of the lord's vengeance. What vengeance? The vengeance He wreaked upon Adam', and then goes on to state explicitly 'What has caused the arrows to transpierce him? The penalty, the vengeance we have spoken of, perhaps also the pains of both mind and body that must be endured in this life—these are what he terms arrows'.[31] The *Glossa* would have provided Donne with a useful shortcut to Augustine's commentary on the psalm. But more than that, as Donne moves between the historical and moral readings of his text, so too is he reading across the multiple layers of interpretation provided by the Vulgate with *Glossa*. The arrows emerge from his sermon as a focus for a range of different readings, just as on the page before him they are framed by a collective exegesis.

---

[29] *Biblia sacra cum glossa*, 3.z1ᵛ.   [30] *Biblia sacra cum glossa*, 3.z1ᵛ.

[31] 'Jam haec dicebat hic patiebatur: et tamen hoc jam de ira Domini, quia et de vindicta Domini. De qua vindicta? Quam excepit de Adam'; 'Unde ergo sagittae infixae? Ipsam poenam, ipsam vindictam, et forte dolores quos hic necesse est pati, et animi et corporis, ipsas dicit sagittas'. Augustine, *Ennarationes in Psalmos*, 36.397–8. *St Augustine*, tr. Hebgin and Corrigan, ii. 332–3.

At the start of this chapter I quoted Donne excusing Augustine for working without a Bible in front of him and suggested that, while Donne is making no such case for himself, his sermons too suggest that the Bible might be, if not absent, then a text which could apparently be displaced by the use of commentaries and biblical 'keys'. The Vulgate with *Glossa*, though, as a Bible which breaks down the distinction between text and scholarship, offers a useful reminder that working with 'secondary' material need not involve turning away from the 'original text'. Indeed, when reading this Bible, access to the 'original' Greek, Hebrew, and Aramaic is available through the various 'secondary' glosses, postils, and commentaries. And this is precisely what made it such an attractive source for preachers such as Donne for whom linguistic insights were only useful if accompanied by an understanding of how the different senses of the words fed into the exegetical tradition. The Vulgate with *Glossa*, then, exemplifies Donne's process of sermon composition whereby mediating sources are not replacements for the biblical text, but a series of lenses through which it can be encountered. After all, Donne does not simply lift material from biblical commentaries and place it within his sermon. Rather, the grammatical, linguistic, historical, and exegetical ideas he encounters in his reading become the raw materials for sustained and rhetorically sophisticated interrogations and reinterrogations of his scriptural text.

FURTHER READING

Allen, Don Cameron. 'Dean Donne Sets his Text'. *English Literary History*, 10 (1943): 208–29.

Ettenhuber, Katrin. *Donne's Augustine: Renaissance Cultures of Interpretation* (Oxford: Oxford University Press, 2011).

Goodblatt, Chanita. *The Christian Hebraism of John Donne* (Pittsburgh, Pa.: Duquesne University Press, 2010).

Jones, G. Lloyd. *The Discovery of Hebrew in Tudor England: A Third Language* (Manchester: Manchester University Press, 1983).

Muller, Richard A., and John L. Thompson, eds. *Biblical Interpretation in the Era of the Reformation* (Grand Rapids, Mich., and Cambridge: William B. Eerdmans, 1996).

Schleiner, Winfried. *The Imagery of Donne's Sermons* (Providence, RI: Brown University Press, 1970).

Shami, Jeanne, M. Thomas Hester, and Dennis Flynne, eds. *The Oxford Handbook of John Donne* (Oxford: Oxford University Press, 2011).

Smith, Lesley. *The Glossa ordinaria: The Making of a Medieval Bible Commentary* (Leiden and Boston: Brill, 2009).

Steinmetz, David C. 'Divided by a Common Past: The Reshaping of the Christian Exegetical Tradition in the Sixteenth Century'. *Journal of Medieval and Early Modern Studies*, 27 (1997): 245–64.

CHAPTER 36

....

DOMESTIC DECORATION AND THE BIBLE IN THE EARLY MODERN HOME

....

ANDREW MORRALL

It is a paradox of the Reformation that a religious movement that placed such emphasis upon the Word should have inspired a richly visual domestic culture. Across social and confessional divides and with substantial local variations, on painted glass, woodwork, textiles, plasterwork, and ceramics, the stories of the Bible became a normative part of the visual experience of northern European householders.[1] Such decorations were profoundly influenced by vernacular printed and illustrated Bibles and were developed within the context of new habits of domestic Bible reading. In recent years, scholars have begun to investigate what an attention to such forms of material culture can tell us about the habits of everyday life and embodied practice. In the field of religious studies, in particular, the turn to material culture has opened up new questions concerning practical devotion, and, crucially, the ways in which doctrinal and theological positions were received and trans-formed across different levels of society.[2] In keeping with this approach, this chapter will consider some of the registers of religious domestic imagery and offer evidence as to their various sources, functions, and usage in order to suggest how they served to extend the culture of the Bible within the home. Ranging widely across northern Europe, the chapter investigates the attitude of the major Reformers and educationalists to the promulgation of images, and the variety of forms in which biblical texts were encountered, particularly in early modern England.

---

[1] For the Netherlands, see T. G. Koote (ed.), *De bijbel in huis: Bijbelse verhalen op huisraad en meubilair inde zeventiende en acttiende eeu*w (Utrecht: Musuem Het Catherijnenconvent, 1992); for Britain, Tara Hamling, *Decorating the 'Godly' Household: Religious Art in Post Reformation Britain* (New Haven: Yale University Press, 2010).

[2] See, e.g., Caroline Walker Bynum, *Christian Materiality: An Essay on Religion in Late Medieval Europe* (Brooklyn: Zone Books, 2011); David Morgan (ed.), *Religion and Material Culture: The Matter of Belief* (London: Routledge, 2009); and, more generally, Tara Hamling and Catherine Richardson (eds), *Everyday Objects: Medieval and Early Modern Material Culture and its Meanings* (Aldershot: Ashgate, 2010).

From the earliest years of the Reformation, the idea of presenting stories from the scriptures in visual form within the home was sanctioned by all the major Reformers, who, while hostile or at best lukewarm to the presence of images in churches, favoured their judicious use in non-liturgical contexts. For Martin Luther, it 'would be Christian work' for 'the whole Bible to be painted on houses, on the outside and inside, so that all can see it'.[3] John Calvin, while less sympathetic than Luther to most religious imagery, allowed that biblical scenes, shown in their historical function, could be of 'use in teaching or admonition'.[4] Huldrych Zwingli and his successor Heinrich Bullinger in Zürich also justified the use of images in houses for purposes of moral example, teaching, and as household decoration. Such attitudes to domestic images were part of a longer term shift in lay religious culture for Catholics and Protestants alike, that resulted in the home, as much as the church, becoming an important locus of spiritual and moral instruction. The origins of this rise in lay spirituality all over northern Europe had begun earlier, in the fifteenth century, under the impulse of the reforming ideals of the *devotio moderna* in the Netherlands; it was given renewed momentum by the reforming ideals of Erasmian morality of the early sixteenth century and gathered pointed ideological force with the Protestant Reformation's rejection of the cult of saints. As a consequence, many of the impulses that had fed monumental church decoration left the altars and found new expression in domestic settings, albeit now, for Protestants, stripped of their devotional purpose. This is made explicit in Bullinger's insistence that images 'should be removed from the churches but be tolerated in the streets, in houses, in windows, where, without the offices ("dienst") or worship offered to them, they can serve as decoration, and thus not be open to misuse'.[5]

Bullinger's explicit recommendation of 'windows' as a suitable locus for biblical imagery is a reference to domestic silver-stain glass painting, a medium that emerged in the later fifteenth century as an increasingly popular form of household decoration in urban centres such as Zürich, Augsburg, Nuremberg, and Antwerp and enjoyed an extraordinary flourishing until the last quarter of the sixteenth century.[6] The relatively brief flowering of this particular art form is a useful marker of both economic and spiritual responses to the Reformation, that is, of the sudden decline in church patronage and a concomitant intensification of lay demand for edifying domestic decoration. An underlying stimulus for its development was undoubtedly the increasing disposable income of the merchant classes of the burgeoning urban centres, who adopted the glass medium as a fashionable form of decoration, in which they could have illustrated a wide array of themes, profane as well as religious. Yet it is equally clear that a number of painters, when the Reformation seriously

[3] Quoted in Ernest B. Gilman, *Iconoclasm and Poetry in the English Reformation* (Chicago: University of Chicago Press, 1986), 35.

[4] Jean Calvin, *Calvin: Institutes of the Christian Religion*, ed. John T. McNeill, tr. Ford Lewis Battles (Philadelphia: Westminster, 1960), I.11.12.

[5] Heinrich Bullinger, *Summa christlicher religion / durch Heinrychen Bullingern* (Zurich: Christoffel Froschower, 1597), 53ᵛ, 54ʳ: 'Und deren keines soellend wir waeder gottes noch der heiligen / oder goetteren bildtnussen bewysen: ka zuo soelichem bruch und zuo vereerung soellend wir gar ueberal keine bilder haben. Gmaelde vssert den kilchen / uff den gassen / in hueseren / in fensteren/ und one dienst und vererung moegend zur zierd gebrucht/ und so sy keinen missbruch zogen / geduldet warden'.

[6] See Barbara Butts and Lee Hendrix (eds), *Painting on Light: Drawings and Stained Glass in the Age of Dürer and Holbein* (Oxford: Oxford University Press, 2001).

affected their usual market for religious paintings and altarpieces, turned to other secular media, including designs for painted glass, to supplement their incomes.

This is true, for instance, of the Augsburg artist, Jörg Breu the Elder (c.1475–1537), whose glass roundel designs came to sudden prominence in Augsburg in the 1520s, precisely during the period of greatest popular unrest and iconoclastic outbursts as the Reformation took hold there. A series of glass roundels that Breu designed in the later 1520s on the theme of 'The Works of Mercy' can be seen as a direct response to the biblical literalism of the new evangelical teaching, of which Breu was himself a passionate proponent (Figure 36.1).[7] The subject is drawn from Matthew 25: 34–46, in which Christ on the Day of Judgement turns to those on his right side and bids them enter the kingdom of heaven: 'For I was hungry and you gave me to eat; I was thirsty and you gave me to drink ...'. In each of the six surviving panels and preparatory designs, well-to-do burghers dispense charity while a prominent figure of Christ looks on, making an exhortatory gesture. Breu's images, around which Christ's commands are writ large in German vernacular, possess the quality of a visual sermon: their character is directly didactic, as if driving home the necessity to perform the works of mercy, to literally live the biblical text.

Breu's series, drawing on the New Testament, is rare in showing an artist's response in a new medium to new doctrines even as they were being formed and contains within it a polemical element born of contemporary debates not yet resolved. As the Reformation took hold, however, the great majority of religious subjects in domestic glass painting as in other media tended to be drawn from the Old Testament. This was in keeping with a Protestant and humanist ethos that, ever since Martin Luther's 1522 September Testament, regarded the stories of the Bible as both historical truth and as 'a fixed code of laws'. From them, as Jacob van Liesveldt wrote in the preface to his 1526 Dutch translation of the Bible that closely followed Luther's, men and women could learn to distinguish good from evil.[8] This didactic emphasis represented a departure from the traditional medieval manner of regarding stories of the Old Testament typologically, as precursors of the events of the New Testament, although this older tradition never fully disappeared. Moralizing readings of the Old Testament stood in some measure as a substitute for the Catholic veneration of saints and the cultic practices that Reformers sought to eradicate: in Reformed households the heroes and heroines of the Bible replaced the images of saints and house altars that had functioned as devotional aids.

From the 1520s onwards, Old Testament stories became the basis of a common ethical education throughout northern Europe, providing a fund of exemplary figures from whom one might learn the paths of righteous living, and within this broad Bible-centred culture, the prism through which contemporaries understood their moral world. Popular themes such as the Life of Joseph involved intense sibling rivalries, betrayal, hardships

[7] See Andrew Morrall, *Jörg Breu the Elder: Art, Culture and Belief in Reformation Augsburg* (Aldershot: Ashgate, 2002), 142–50.

[8] The first Reformed Bible in the Netherlands, van Liesveldt's 1st edition contained illustrations only for the books of the Old Testament. See Walter S. Melion, 'Bible Illustration in the Sixteenth-Century Low Countries', in James Clifton and Walter S. Melion (eds), *Scripture for the Eyes: Bible Illustrations in Netherlandish Prints of the Sixteenth Century* (New York and London: Museum of Biblical Art/D. Giles Ltd, 2009), 15–17. Ilyja M. Veldman, 'Characteristics of Iconography in the Lowlands during the Period of Humanism and the Reformation: 1480–1560', in Timothy Husband (ed.), *The Luminous Image: Painted Glass Roundels in the Lowlands, 1480–1560* (New York: Metropolitan Musueum of Art, 1995), 20.

FIGURE 36.1 Jörg Breu the Elder, 'Giving Drink to the Thirsty', Design for yellow stained-glass roundel, pen and brush with black ink, with some red tone, 18.3 cm diam. Staatliche Museen, Kupferstichkabinett, Berlin.

endured, and the eventual restoration of family unity and honour. The story of Abraham who was forced to repudiate Hagar and Ishmael, his firstborn son, and to offer his other son, Isaac, as a sacrifice, was an exemplary tale of the trials of faith, of patriarchal duty, and of filial obedience. The ordeal and eventual vindication of Susanna, who withstood the Elders' attempted seduction and blackmail, made her a paragon of chastity and marital fidelity. These stories spoke directly to contemporary questions of family relations, of duties and obligations between husband and wife, parents and children, and to the equal subjection of men and women to God's will. Disseminated through a range of didactic literature and prints, these Old Testament heroes and heroines came to serve as exemplars in the education of the young and a source of moral guidance in the home.[9]

From this mentality emerged a tradition of domestic pictorial decoration that employed the same pious themes. A glass panel of Susanna and the Elders, originally one of four panels that recounted the story of Susanna's attempted seduction, false accusation, trial,

[9] See P. van der Coelen, *De Schrift verbeeld: Oudtestamentische prenten uit renaissance en barok* (Nijmegen: Uitgeverij KU Nijmegen, 1998); Ilyja M. Veldman, *Images for the Eye and Soul: Function and Meaning in Netherlandish Prints (1450–1650)* (Leiden: Primavera Pers, 2006).

FIGURE 36.2 Circle of the Pseudo-Ortkens Group, *Susanna and the Elders*, yellow stained-glass roundel, c.1520–5, diam. 9½ in (24.1 cm) with border 13 in (33 cm). New York, Metropolitan Museum of Art, Cloisters Collection, inv. no. 199.119.1.

and vindication, exemplifies this mode. It is attributed to the so-called Pseudo-Ortkens, a painter active in the southern Netherlands between c.1520 and 1540 (Figure 36.2).[10] The sober and decorous portrayal of Susanna withstanding attempts at seduction and blackmail, aptly expresses the image's purpose as a warning against both adultery and false accusation, one reinforced by the surrounding inscription, a truncated version of the biblical text from Daniel 13: 7–9.

Such habits of decoration developed in parallel with the increasing demand for printed vernacular editions of the Bible as well as the popular genre of the picture Bible.[11] These latter consisted of compilations of biblical illustrations, usually with accompanying rhyming summaries of the relevant biblical text. Read as a continuous sequence of images, they inculcated a sense of the Bible as easily remembered exemplary story and as historical truth. To follow their influence upon domestic decoration is to illustrate the avenues by

---

[10] See Husband, *Luminous Image*, 139–41.
[11] See M. Engammare, 'Les figures de la Bible: Le destin oublié d'un genre littéraire en image (XVIe–XVIIe s.)', *Mélanges de l'École Française de Rome*, 106 (1994): 549–91.

which the culture of vernacular Bible reading entered into the broader mentality and everyday visual experience of the age.

This influence is very clearly to be seen in the ceramic wares of the Rhineland. Since the fifteenth century, the producers of stoneware jugs and drinking vessels had decorated their wares with moulded relief designs of a steadily increasing variety and sophistication. As David Gaimster has argued, in the course of the sixteenth century, the coming together of the print revolution and improved methods of mass-producing moulded relief decoration significantly raised the status and social desirability of the stoneware medium and the range of decoration.[12] Very soon after their initial publication the woodcut images of such series as Sebald Beham's *Biblische Figuren*, first published by Christian Egenollf in Frankfurt in 1533, and Hans Holbein the Younger's *Historiarum Veteris instrumenti icones* (*Historical Images of the Old Testament*) of 1538 were reproduced as relief medallions by the potters of Siegburg. Even more heavily used was Sigmund Feyerabend's *Biblische Figuren des Alten und Neuen Testaments* (Frankfurt, 1560) that contained 147 woodcuts by Virgil Solis, together with the 1564 Feyerabend version of the Luther Bible, illustrated by Jost Amman. Subjects from these sources can all be traced in the surface decorations of an array of ceramic wares, from simple drinking vessels to elaborately decorated tiled stoves, showing the ready and popular market for such themes. They include the Garden of Eden, the Temptation, the Expulsion, the History of Joseph, Daniel in the Lion's Den, Joshua, David and Bathsheba, Samson and Delilah; and, from the New Testament, the Prodigal Son, the Marriage at Cana, and the Last Supper, among others.[13]

What purpose might such religious imagery have served? What meanings might they have acquired through this ornamental and decorative context? In the first place, a directly instructional and homiletic function is suggested by their frequent presence as decoration on ceramic tiled stoves in the alpine regions of South Germany and Switzerland or on fireplace surrounds in England and the Netherlands. As the central source of heat, the hearth and stove were the natural loci around which families would gather and a place for communal Bible reading and spiritual instruction. Documentary evidence of such uses is sparse, and one has to go to England at the very end of the period covered by this volume to find explicit examples. John Collett Ryland (1723–92), a Baptist minister and schoolmaster from Warwick and Northampton, educated his son John Ryland (1753–1825) in techniques for learning from the Bible, including the compiling of commonplaces and the memorization of passages of scripture.[14] Yet it was with his mother in earliest infancy that he first encountered the Bible. According to his biographer: 'The story is told of him ... that the parlour fireplace was fitted with Dutch tiles representing Bible characters and events, and in the tiles the mother found a picture-book for her child in which a grand procession of patriarchs and prophets, heroes and kings, confessions and martyrs, passed before the imagination and appealed to the heart

[12] David Gaimster, *German Stoneware 1500–1900: Archaeology and Cultural History* (London: British Museum, 1997), 143.

[13] For a full discussion, see Gaimster, *German Stoneware*, 145–6, and cat. nos. 5–7, 170–3. Also B. Lippeheide, *Das Rheinische Steinzeug und die Graphik der Renaissance* (Berlin: Verlag Gebr. Mann, 1961), 22–3, 27.

[14] Scott Mandelbrote, 'The Bible and Didactic Literature in Early Modern England', in Natasha Glaisyer and Sara Pennell (eds), *Didactic Literature in England 1500–1800* (Aldershot: Ashgate, 2003), 20.

of the boy'.[15] In the very first years of the eighteenth century, the mother of another Congregationalist minister, Philip Doddridge (1702–51), had 'taught him the history of the Old and the New Testament before he could read, by the assistance of some Dutch tiles in the chimney of the room, where they commonly sat'. Doddridge 'frequently recommended' this way of teaching to parents, recalling that it had been 'the means of making some good impressions upon his heart, which never wore out'.[16]

These testimonies to the affective appeal of images constitute a continuation of the ideas of early sixteenth-century Reformers for whom moral instruction should begin early and at home, both through Bible reading and through images. Doddridge's words echo the convictions of the sixteenth-century book printer and publisher, Jean de Tournes about the workings of the image upon the sensibilities of his contemporaries. At the beginning of his widely influential picture-Bible, the *Quadrins historiques de la Bible* (first published 1553), he advised his readers, that

> should you not have the leisure to read and to enjoy the Word as you might wish, you may at least adorn the chambers of your memory with these said images, and more worthily, as we think, than if you covered those same rooms and halls with genre histories ('histoires eth-niques'), which are less appropriate to the faithful.[17]

In these quotations, separated by some 150 years, we see how images—whether printed woodcuts or painted tiles—might work upon both heart and mind; first, as stories to be learned and memorized, but second, more profoundly, by the lasting 'impression' of the image upon the heart, and by the adornment of the chambers of memory, thus to form the very essence of the individual's moral identity.[18]

The habit of placing images strategically on personal possessions and household furnishings was due in large part to the educational agenda of humanists and reformers across the confessional divide, who encouraged the practice on didactic and pedagogical grounds. In his instructions on the education of the young prince, Erasmus of Rotterdam

---

[15] James Culross, *The Three Rylands: A Hundred Years of Various Christian Service* (London: Elliot Stock, 1897), 70. Cited by Mandelbrote, 'The Bible and Didactic Literature', 20.

[16] Job Orton, *Memoirs of the Life, Character, & Writings, of the Late Rev. Philip Doddridge, D.D.* (Edinburgh: Waugh and Innes, 1825; 1st edn 1765), 38–9. Cited by Mandelbrote, 'The Bible and Didactic Literature', 20.

[17] Tr. from Claude Paradin, *Quadrins historiques de la Bible par Claude Paradin; revuz, & augmentez d'un grand nombre de figures* (Lyon, 1555; 1st edn 1553). In his 1553 English translation, which demonstrates the problems attending foreign-language printing, Peter Derendel translated this passage: 'if tow [thou] maiest not enjoi the letter so frelie, as thow wodlest thisdf [list?], thow maiest tapisse [sic] sure the chambres of thi minde and remembraunce with the figures therof, and mor honestlie, after us, then thou doest the chanbres [sic], and halles of thi house with ethnike stories, thus evill becoming the faithfull'. *The True and Lyvely Historyke Purtreatures of the Woll Bible* (Lyon, 1553), A6ᵛ.

[18] In a different spirit, Benjamin Franklin in a letter to Peter Burdett, dated 3 Nov. 1773, pointed out the relative abundance of imported scripture tiles in the colonies during the eighteenth century, and the conventionalized and slapdash quality of their production. 'As the Dutch Delphware tiles were much used in America, which are only or chiefly Scriptural Histories, wretchedly scrawled, I wished to have those moral prints (which were originally taken from Horace's Poetical Figures) introduced on Tiles, which being about our Chimneys, and constantly in the Eyes of Children when by the Fire-side, might give Parents an Opportunity, in explaining them, to impress moral sentiments ...'. Cited in *The Papers of Benjamin Franklin*, xx, ed. William Willcox (New Haven: Yale University Press, 1976), 459. (I would like to thank Leslie Kerhauser for this reference.)

urged just such a judicious use of images, inscriptions, and material objects (and it is interesting to note how he regards them as ontologically indistinguishable) to inculcate awareness of the virtues in the young child:

> They must be fixed in his mind, pressed in, and rammed home. And they must be kept fresh
> in the memory in all sorts of ways: sometimes in a moral maxim, sometimes in a parable,
> sometimes by an analogy, sometimes by a live example, an epigram, or a proverb; they must
> be carved on rings, painted in pictures, inscribed on prizes, and presented in any other way
> that a child of his age enjoys, so that they are always before his mind even when he is doing
> something else.[19]

Erasmus was to give the idea exemplary literary form in his *Convivium religiosum* (*The
Godly Feast*) of 1522. This popular dialogue describes a luncheon party of humanist friends
who congregate at the country house of their host Eusebius.[20] The house's decoration is
described, inside and out, in elaborate detail: in every room on doorways and walls, in gal-
leries and garden flowerbeds and on fountains, speaking inscriptions and images engage
the guests, so that, as one of them comments, there is 'nothing inactive, nothing that's not
saying, or doing something'.[21] The guests read the mottoes, take note of the images and
emblems and draw moral lessons from them. The inscriptions are biblical; the emblems
likewise orient the guests towards things spiritual: the garden fountain points to the
Fountain of Life; a polluted stream symbolizes the dangers of corrupting the pure source
of scripture; real and *trompe-l'œil* plants and animals are used to evoke the goodness of
God through nature and art.[22]

As Terence Cave has shown, Erasmus was employing an elaborate form of *enargeia*,
the rhetorical evocation of place.[23] Nonetheless, the notion of a speaking environment, as
something almost living and breathing, did not exist solely as a humanist literary creation but was carried into actual houses. In a letter of February 1523, Erasmus called the
house of Johann von Botzheim, canon of Constance, an abode of the Muses, neat, elegant, and expressive. Botzheim's house contained an abundance of pictures and figures,
which, according to Erasmus, drew and held the viewer.[24] The country retreat of Erasmus's
English friend John Colet in Sheen outside London, is also recorded as featuring painted
images on the walls.[25] In certain cases where images or inscriptions were a fixed form of
wall decoration in a living or reception chamber, library, or gallery, the rooms became in
effect a kind of ideal physical realization of the owner's mind.[26] Surviving wall decorations

[19] *Erasmus: The Education of A Christian Prince with the Panegyric for Archduke Philip of Austria*, ed.
Lisa Jardine, tr. Neil M. Cheshire and Michael J. Heath (Cambridge: Cambridge University Press, 1997), 8.
[20] Desiderius Erasmus, 'Convivium religiosum' in *The Colloquies of Erasmus*, tr. Craig R. Thompson
(Chicago: Chicago University Press, 1965), 46–78.
[21] Erasmus, 'Convivium religiosum', 53.
[22] Erasmus, 'Convivium religiosum', 52.
[23] Terence Cave, '*Enargeia*: Erasmus and the Rhetoric of Presence in the Sixteenth Century', *L'Esprit
Createur*, 16 (1976): 5–19.
[24] Erasmus, *Opus epistolarum Des. Erasmi Roterodami, v. 1522-4*, ed. P. S. Allen and H. M. Allen
(Oxford: Clarendon Press, 1924), 212.336–54.
[25] Erasmus, *Colloquies*, 46–7.
[26] As for instance Montaigne's famous library with its fifty-four sayings painted on the rafters, or the
series of *sententiae* painted in Nicholas Bacon's Long Gallery at Gorhambury Park. See William N. West,
'Reading Rooms: Architecture and Agency in the Houses of Michel de Montaigne and Nicholas Bacon',
Comparative Literature, 56 (2004): 111–29. 'Sir Anthony's Study' in Norbury Manor, near Ashbourne,

of the sixteenth-century solarium of a merchant's house at 35 Upper High Street, Thame, Oxforshire, give some sense of their appearance. Elaborate cartouches frame inscriptions including a quotation from St Paul, as well two others, attributed to Pythagoras and Aristotle. These latter two have been taken from William Baldwin's *The Sayings of the Wise* of 1547, a compendium of useful and edifying sayings. The ready market for such books and that they could act as sourcebook for such decorative schemes indicates the popularity of inscriptional and commonplace wisdom across different registers of domestic life.[27]

Yet how, precisely, were such inscriptions apprehended and used? The English humanist, Thomas Elyot, gave a very explicit sense of the different ways such images and written inscriptions might act upon the beholder. In *The Booke Named the Governor* he closely echoed Erasmus, advising the wise householder to paint 'some monument of virtue' on his walls:

> wherby other men in beholdynge may be instructed, or at the lest wayes to vertue persuaded. In like wise his plate and vessaile wolde be ingraved with histories, fables, or quicke and wise sentences, comprehending good doctrine or counsailes: whereby one of these commodities may happen, either that they which do eate or drinke havying those wisedoms ever in sighte, shall happen with the meate to receive some of them: or by purposinge them at the table, may sussitate some disputation or reasonynge: whereby some parte of tyme shall be saved, whiche els by superflouse eating and drinkyng wolde be idely consumed.[28]

Beyond the issue of straightforward visual instruction, therefore, as in the case of the hearth and stove tiles, the 'speaking' presence of decorated dishes might have two further desired consequences: they might create an atmosphere of sober piety such as to inculcate virtue even as one ate; and secondly, they could be props to stimulate pious conversation.

An example of this first usage is found in the English poet-divine, George Herbert's description of a country parson's house, wherein 'Even the walls are not idle, but something is written or painted there which may excite the reader to a thought of piety; especially the 101 psalm, which is expressed in a fair table, as being the rule of the family'.[29] The presence of Psalm 101, particularly the second verse: 'I will behave in a perfect way. O when wilt though come unto me? I will walk within my house with a perfect heart', is both prescriptive and invocatory, serving an almost liturgical purpose: to evoke the sense of Christ's actual presence within the room. This is to echo the spirit of Erasmus's *Convivium religiosum*, where the written sentences on walls and on wine glasses are combined at the beginning of the meal with the reading of a passage from scripture to ensure, as the host,

---

Derbyshire, the house of the Recusant Fitzherbert family, features inscriptions on almost every part of the panelled room, thought to have been placed there by Sir Anthony Fitzherbert in 1612. All the inscribed quotations are from the Vulgate and render the room a sort of *locus meditationis*. See Peter Davidson, 'The Inscribed House', in Michael Bath, Pedro F. Campa, and Daniel S. Russell (eds), *Emblem Studies in Honor of Peter M. Daly* (Baden Baden: Verlag Valentin Koerner, 2002), 41–62.

[27] The wall decorations are now installed in Thame Museum. The quotation from St Paul is from 1 Rom. 11: 33–6; of the other quotations, 'Desire nothing of God save what is profitable' Baldwin attributes to Pythagoras (I4ʳ); 'Science is got by diligence; but Discretion and Wisdom cometh of God' to Aristotle (I4ᵛ), and, later, to Socrates (N1ᵛ). *A Treatise of Morall Phylosophie contaynyng the sayings of the wyse* (London, 1547).

[28] Thomas Elyot, *The Boke Named the Governour* (London, 1531), O4ʳ.

[29] George Herbert, *A Priest to the Temple, or, the Country Parson, His Character or Rule of Holy Life* (London, 1652), D9ᵛ.

Eusebius, says, that 'we make ourselves the readier for so great a guest ... that Christ may mingle with all our food and drink, so that everything may taste of him, but most of all may he penetrate our hearts!'[30]

Evidence for such a desired sacramental presence amidst the everyday is garnered from a number of family portraits in which family members are shown at table. The painting of the family of the Basel goldsmith Hans Rudolf Faesch, painted in 1559 by Hans Hug Kluber, showing the family at table, summons up the unseen presence of Christ in their midst by an empty place-setting in the foreground, luxuriously laid out, with an expensive set of knife, fork, and spoon.[31] An (old-fashioned) fifteenth-century silver wine decanter, reserved, as Hanspeter Lanz has suggested, for the guest of honour, together with a loaf of bread to the right, make unmistakable reference to the Last Supper and evoke the familiar saying of Matthew 18: 20 'Where two or three are gathered together in my name, I am there in the midst of them'.[32]

A seventeenth-century group portrait of the family of Hans Conrad Bodmer, Bürgermeister of Zürich and Landvogt von Greifensee, of 1643, attributed to Heinrich Sulzer (Figure 36.3),[33] shows a decorative wall tablet behind the tiled stove, containing an inscription, today in a considerably rubbed state of preservation. It reads:

> Im heyssen Ofen / Der truebsal ..../ Probiert Gott sin / Kinder a [...]/ O Jesu Christ Dein tueres [Blut?] / Bewar uns vor / Der hellen [Gluot].
> In the hot stove of our afflictions, God tests his children .../ O Jesus Christ, protect us from the fires of hell with your hard won blood.

The saying, based on such biblical foundations as Isaiah 48: 10: 'Behold I have refined thee, but not with silver; I have chosen thee in the furnace of affliction', plays with the experience of heat and sweating and specifically evokes the fear of hell.[34] Regarded in the light of Sir Thomas Elyot's prescriptions or of the experience of the guests in Erasmus's *Convivium religiosum*, one can begin to understand how such a biblical metaphor would have hovered over and mingled with the heat of the physical environment, infusing it with a sense of holy immanence and charging the atmosphere with the force of holy injunction.

Beyond their ability to instruct or to evoke divine presence, a further, more proactive use is suggested by Thomas Elyot's assertion that inscriptions 'may sussitate some disputation or reasonynge'. How might 'quicke and wise sentences' of this sort have stimulated virtuous conversation? And what form might such conversations have taken? We can turn again to Erasmus's guests in his *Convivium religiosum* for insight into the mechanics of just such a conversation. As one of the assembled guests says: 'So far from silent is your house that not only the walls but the cup too says something ...'. Another guest says of his cup: 'Mine

---

[30]   Erasmus, *Colloquies*, 56.

[31]   Tempera on canvas, 127.5 × 207.5 cm, Basel, Öffentliche Kunstsammlung, Kunstmuseum.

[32]   Hanspeter Lanz, '"Komm Herr Jesus, sei unser Gast"', *Zeitschrift für Schweizerische Archäologie und Kunstgeschichte*, 61 (2004): 221–5.

[33]   Oil on canvas, 73 × 93 cm. Zürich, Schweizerisches Landesmuseum. (On loan from a private collection.)

[34]   See Dietrich W. H. Schwartz, *Sachgüter und Lebensformen: Einführung in die materielle Kulturgeschichte des Mittelalters und der Neuzeit* (Berlin: Schmidt, 1970), 19; Dione Flühler-Kreis, 'Die Stube als sakraler Raum. Das Familienporträt des Zürcher Landvogts von Greifensee, Hans Conrad Bodmer', *Zeitschrift für Schweizerische Archäologie und Kunstgeschichte*, 61 (2004): 215–16.

FIGURE 36.3 Heinrich Sulzer (attrib.), Portrait of the Family of Hans Conrad Bodmer, Landvogt von Greifensee, 1643. Oil on canvas, 73 × 93 cm. Zürich, Schweizerisches Landesmuseum, inv. no. DEP-3721 (on loan from a private collection).

speaks Greek: "In wine there's truth"'. Eusebius replies with an explanation of the general moral admonition it contains (counselling discretion). Another guest follows this with an *exemplum* in the form of historical anecdote (concerning Egyptian priests), and Eusebius, the host, generalizes the point by posing a topical question: 'Everyone is allowed to drink wine nowadays. Whether or not this is wise, I don't know'.[35] This leads to a broad discussion centred on the passage, 1 Corinthians 6: 'All things are lawful unto me, but all things are not expedient: all things are lawful for me, but I will not be brought under the power of any'. In this manner, from the wine cups' simple inscriptions, there develops an extended exchange of deliberations, which includes further passages in Proverbs, Corinthians, and Matthew, from which a general theme emerges: the true nature of Christian liberty: inner, spiritual freedom as contrasted with convention and ecclesiastical or political constraints.

Erasmus's conversation is a polished exercise that exemplifies a humanist method of instruction in rhetorical method that was widely adopted in the Latin schools in the sixteenth century. From the very first schoolboy exercises, this emphasized the memorization and collection of fragments of elegant, useful. and ethically oriented phrases, drawn from the student's reading and compiled within a commonplace book. Here they were ordered under headings that were usually concerned with moral topics such as prudence, justice, temperance, fortitude, and their cognates (mirrored in William Baldwin's printed compendium). The saying, *sententia*, or aphorism was then later reused in more advanced rhetorical exercises, which, as Peter Mack has shown, involved subjecting it to a series of opposite or varied points of view and holding up to scrutiny its ethical implications.[36] While serving as a useful training in language and rhetorical amplification, such exercises also by their nature necessitated thinking around the chosen commonplace and successfully constructing a moral argument, as Erasmus's guests demonstrate. Training in rhetorical method therefore carried within it the possibility of advancing ethical thinking by establishing a form of dialectical reasoning around the opposite or varying views of different authorities. More generally, it encouraged rhetorical habits of thought and reasoning centred upon the commonplace that carried on into adult life.[37]

One can discover traces of such table talk still frozen within the forms of certain dining accoutrements. A set of twelve wooden fruit trenchers, dating from the late sixteenth or early seventeenth century, provides a case in point.[38] In early modern England, fruit trenchers were used at the dessert course of a meal, that is to say, the recreational part, to hold fruit or sweetmeats. These were typically thin wooden roundels or rectangular-shaped platters, painted with proverbs or sayings drawn from all kinds of sources—vernacular,

---

[35] Erasmus, 'Convivium religiosum', 62–3.

[36] Peter Mack, 'Rhetoric, Ethics and Reading in the Renaissance', *Renaissance Studies*, 19 (2005): 1–21.

[37] See Anthony Grafton and Lisa Jardine, *From Humanism to the Humanities* (Cambridge, Mass.: Harvard University Press, 1986); Mary Thomas Crane, *Framing Authority: Sayings, Self and Society in Sixteenth-Century England* (Princeton: Princeton University Press, 1993); Peter Mack, 'Renaissance Habits of Reading', in S. Chaudhuri (ed.), *Renaissance Essays for Kitty Scoular Datta* (Calcutta: Oxford University Press, 1995), 1–25; E. R. Kintgen, *Reading in Tudor England* (Pittsburgh, Pa.: University of Pittsburgh Press, 1995); Ann Moss, *Printed Commonplace Books and the Structuring of Renaissance Thought* (Oxford: Clarendon Press, 1996).

[38] Metropolitan Museum of Art, New York, inv. Nos. 64.101.1579–1591a, b. They were discovered in 1825 in Elmley Castle, Worcestershire, and exhibited at the Winchester meeting of the Archeological Institute in 1845. See A. H. Church, 'Old English Fruit Trenchers', in A. H. Church et al., *Some Minor Arts as Practised in England* (London: Seely & Co., 1894), 53.

classical, or biblical. They were often filled with humorous folk wisdom: rhyming verses about the battle of the sexes or the pleasures and pains of married life. Unusually, each of this set of twelve trenchers is replete with biblical quotations from the Old and New Testament and the Apocrypha; and each of the trenchers addresses a different area of moral life. They include: self knowledge and the need for repentance; the need to guard against covetousness, against greed, lust, bad language, anger, and hatred; and the need to be charitable to the poor. In one example (Figure 36.4), the quotations are collectively centred upon the fact of human mortality, each one prompting a slightly different direction of thought. The central inscriptions read: 'Set an order in thy house, for thou shalt dye and not lyve. (Esaie. 38). For the truth stryve unto death, and god shall fight for thee against thyne enemies (Eccl. 4). Be faythfull unto they which dye in the Lorde (Apocal.14)'. Around the four edges are further inscriptions. In the left border: 'Do goode or thou dye. (Eccl. 14.)'. In the top border, 'Remember the ende and thou shalt never do amysse (Ecc. 7)'. In the right border: 'Our tyme is but shorte and tedious (Sap. 3)'. And in the lower border: 'Death is better then a wretched lyfe or contynuall syckeness (Eccl. 30)'.

The trencher's structure reflects the form of the typical commonplace book in its compilation of pithy texts relating to a common theme. And indeed, the conceit is intentional, for the collection of trenchers is kept in a container formed as a book, so that the contents literally reflect the culled and collated 'flowers of wisdom' of the commonplace method. What

FIGURE 36.4 Fruit Trencher, English, early seventeenth century, Gouache on wood, New York, Metropolitan Museum of Art, inv. no. 64.101.1582.

makes the trenchers significant is their functional character. Because the inscriptions were intended for use in some kind of social context as stimuli to discussion or rumination, they form a concrete bridge between the commonplace book and the lost habits of Elizabethan conversation. Though their use at table is unclear, it is evident from their form that each quotation would allow elaboration in a slightly different direction around a central theme, perhaps, like Erasmus's wine cups, to provoke discursive discussion. The seriousness of theme is certainly unusual among the surviving sets of fruit trenchers.[39] It likely reflects a highly educated and theologically literate milieu, perhaps not too distant from that of the Baptist minister and schoolmaster, John Collett Ryland, who included making commonplaces and committing suitable passages of scripture to memory among the techniques in the education of his son. One can imagine the trenchers' role in such mnemonic and broadly rhetorical training.

For young women, whose upbringing and education was intended primarily to prepare them for marriage and the effective running of a household, and for whom expectations of literacy were more limited, one of the chief ways biblical knowledge and domestic virtue were inculcated was through the practice of needlework. Contemporary moralists, in texts that strictly defined women's roles, made needlework chief among activities considered suitable in the upbringing and education of young girls. By the seventeenth century, the activity of fine embroidering—as opposed to straightforward sewing—was considered 'good work' and an active sign of female virtue; it kept women in the home, away from idle pursuits, and focused on pious devotions.[40] As a result, biblical images—the great majority drawn from the Old Testament—came to be applied to a whole range of embroidered household furnishings that included valances, cushion covers, table carpets, the surfaces of caskets, book covers, and even items of clothing. This was particularly true of England in the late sixteenth and seventeenth centuries, where domestic embroidery underwent an extraordinary flowering. From about 1630 onwards, a fashion arose for embroidered biblical pictures made apparently with no specific practical function in mind.

The embroidered biblical images are distinctive in that the majority of their themes specifically address women: they show the pious and heroic actions of exemplary females and presented them visually in a manner that makes the moral underpinning of the story explicit. Above all, they express the specific domestic moral qualities expected of women of the day. Susanna, the paragon of chastity and marital fidelity, remained very popular in this medium; the tale of David and Bathsheba warned against adultery; while Abigail's gift of provisions to King David exemplified prudent good sense and foresight expected in a wife (Figure 36.5). Other tales, such as the Judgement of Solomon, Hagar and Ishmael, or the Story of Samuel, involved themes of maternal love and childbearing; Solomon and the Queen of Sheba and Esther and Ahasuerus provided ideal married types.[41]

---

[39] Church cites 'thirty to forty' surviving sets: 'Old English Fruit Trenchers', 50.

[40] See for instance, Juan Luis Vives, *Institutione feminae christianae: Liber primus*, ed. C. Fantazzi and C. Matheeussen, tr. C. Fantazzi (New York and Cologne: Brill Acade, 1996); repr. as *The Education of a Christian Woman*, ed. and tr. C. Fantazzi (Chicago: University of Chicago Press, 2000). See also Ruth Geuter, 'Embroidered Biblical Narratives and their Social Contexts', in Melinda Watt and Andrew Morrall (eds), *English Embroidery in the Metropolitan Museum of Art, 1580–1700 'Twixt Art and Nature'* (New Haven: Yale University Press, 2008), 57–77.

[41] Watt and Morrall, *English Embroidery*, 225–55.

FIGURE 36.5 'David and Abigail', English, third quarter seventeenth century, canvas worked with silk thread, 37 × 44.7 cm. Gift of Irwin Untermeyer 1964, New York, Metropolitan Museum of Art, inv. no. 64.101.1310.

Such meanings, specifically aimed at propagating female domestic virtue, were popularized by sixteenth-century continental reformers and humanists and spread via prints and an array of printed conduct books intended to teach women the household virtues that would make them good wives and mothers.[42] Trained to spend long hours embroidering images of biblical heroines, young girls literally had these heroic exemplars inured into their being through the act of making; and once completed and put to use, the finished works became part of the habitus of the pious household in which embroidery and religious devotion were integral and related parts of a daily routine.

Because of their quotidian and functional character, works of embroidery can in certain cases bring us close to their owners' attitudes and habits of personal Bible reading. An embroidered Bible cover today in the Pierpont Morgan Library adorns a 1639 reprint of the Geneva Bible, published by Robert Barker. It portrays an image of Adam and Eve that is derived in part from the Bible's woodcut frontispiece of the same subject contained inside (Figures 36.6, 36.7,).[43] The purpose of such a frontispiece was to proclaim scripture's purpose: to show man his redemptive destiny and to indicate how it may be achieved. The presence of Adam and Eve, progenitors of the human race, was thus natural at the opening scene of what was regarded as the great drama of redemption.

The iconography of the woodcut makes explicit this message of scripture's redemptive purpose. Both Adam and Eve hold fruit, suggesting their mutual culpability in the Fall; the banderoles they hold state: 'desire to knowe hath wrought ovr woe. By tasting this th'exile of blisse'. Yet their other scrolls express their hope of future salvation: 'By promise made restord we be to pleasures of eternitye'. Around them stands the whole of creation that is primordially good, symbolized by the Tree of Knowledge with its inscription: 'Created good and faire, by breach of lawe a snare'. As Diane McColley has pointed out, the teeming creation and the equal share of man and woman in both fall and recovery were preferred themes for illustrations of Genesis in the vernacular Bibles of the Reformation, and therefore part of a wide culture of lay theological understanding.[44]

Inscriptions written on the inside of the Bible's front cover read: 'Tessie Wynn Freer from her Mother'; and a further couplet: 'Anne Cornwalys Wrought me / now she is called Anne Leigh'. Although ambiguous, the inscriptions provide evidence of an embroidered cover probably made around 1640 by a private, amateur embroiderer. That a mother handed it down to her daughter, and that she or her daughter felt it sufficiently important a gift to record it as such, points to the personal significance such objects could possess between family members. The inscription speaks to a personal object whose significance lay as much in the hand-wrought cover, the product of the mother's pious industry, as in the Bible itself as a coveted and well-used personal possession. In both aspects, it constitutes a symbol and a token of the mother's spiritual life, to be cherished as such by her daughter.

[42] See Yvonne Bleyerveld, 'Chast, Obedient and Devout: Biblical Women as Patterns of Female Virtue in Netherlandish and German Graphic Art, ca 1500–1750', *Simiolus*, 28 (2000–1): 219–50.

[43] The connection was noted by Nancy Graves Cabot, 'Pattern Sources of Scriptural Subjects in Tudor and Stuart Embroideries', *Bulletin of the Needle and Bobbin Club*, 20 (1946): 17–21.

[44] Diane Kelsey McColley, *A Gust for Paradise, Milton's Eden and the Visual Arts* (Urbana, Ill.: University of Illinois Press, 1993), 58–60.

FIGURE 36.6 Frontispiece to Genesis, *Geneva Bible* (London, Robert Barker, 1607), woodcut, New York, Metropolitan Museum of Art, inv. no. 64.101.1291.

FIGURE 36.7 Anne Cornwalys, embroidered Bible cover with Adam and Eve (front) and the resurrected Christ (back). English, c.1641. New York, Pierpont Morgan Library, inv. no. PM17197.

Anne Cornwallis's own highly idiosyncratic design closely follows the spirit of the Robert Barker frontispiece. She transferred from the print the poses of Adam and Eve, each holding an apple, thereby retaining the emphasis upon a mutual fall, a convention based on John Calvin's commentary that 'not the sinne came by the woman, but by Adam by Him selfe'.[45] This provided the basis of the gloss on Genesis 3: 6 found in the Geneva Bible, the same edition for which Anne Cornwallis made her cover. This states that Adam ate 'Not so much to please his wife, as moved by ambition at her persuasion'. Calvin was countering the popular view that Adam was seduced by Eve's 'alluring entisements' rather than by Satan. Adam did not 'transgresse the lawe which was given unto him onely to obey his wife: but being also drawne by her pestilent ambition ... he did give more credit to the flattering speeches of the devell, then to the holy word of God'.[46] Cornwallis's imagery thus fits within a tradition of a mutual culpability, which was one aspect of a peculiarly Calvinist interpretation of the Fall.

Within an otherwise original composition, Anne Cornwallis's cover, like the Barker frontispiece, also encapsulates the Bible's central message of human redemption, albeit in a completely original way. The back cover is embroidered with the New Testament anti-type of the Fall, an image of the resurrected Christ, the second Adam, appearing to Mary Magdalene in the Garden, with blazing halo and holding a flowering rod, symbol of resurrection and spiritual renewal. The sun and moon stand over him, just as they do over Adam and Eve in the first days of Creation on the front cover. The surrounding border moreover contains symbols of the passion and crucifixion in an interesting survival of imagery drawn from a much earlier meditational handbook tradition. It is easy to imagine too, a sense of personal identification between the female maker and the penitent Magdalene. Taken in combination therefore, the front and back covers show how Cornwallis created a wholly original and deeply personal design around a coherent typological theme that is imbued with an understanding of scripture's larger redemptive purpose. It brings us close to a subjective pattern of female piety, which appears to combine an informed reading of the Bible with the continuation of an older form of personal meditational practice.

The redemptive theme that placed Adam and Eve at the beginning of the vernacular Bibles is also found as a subject of domestic decoration. It is present in typological form, for instance, in the series of four glass panels set into the windows of the family *Stube* in the Bodmer family portrait (Figure 36.3). Represented from left to right are: the Fall, Cain Killing Abel, Abraham's Sacrifice of Isaac, and Jacob's Dream of the Ladder of Angels ascending and descending from heaven. These scenes are to be understood as essentially regenerative: man by his actions at the Fall (Adam and Eve) became subject to sin and loss (Cain Killing Abel); but through faith and obedience to God's will (Abraham's Sacrifice of Isaac), he can regain Eden in Paradise (Jacob's Dream of the Ladder of Angels). In temporal terms too, the series runs symbolically from the beginning to the end of time, offering a condensed form of providential history, from Eden to the time when heaven and earth meet. Jacob's dream (Genesis 28: 12) points typologically towards Christ who also reunites heaven and earth in the Gospel of St John 1: 51: 'And he said to him, "Truly, truly, I say to

---

[45] John Calvin, *A Commentarie of John Calvine, upon the First Booke of Moses Called Genesis*, tr. Thomas Tymme (London, 1578), 92.

[46] Calvin, *Commentarie*, 92. For a wider discussion of his point, see McColley, *A Gust for Paradise*, 56.

you, you will see heaven opened, and the angels of God ascending and descending on the Son of Man" '.[47]

Beneath the biblical scenes, incorporated into each of these glass panels, are coats-of-arms of earlier family forebears. From this earlier generation, to the parents at the head of the table, and finally to the younger generation, extending back into time and on into the future, the Bodmer family thus stands literally beneath the arc of providence, their own family history tied by visual association to their Old Testament progenitors, their demonstration of collective piety at table the righteous expression of their presumed state of election.

In both content and compositional form the Bodmer family portrait brings together many of the uses and meanings of domestic decoration examined here. The family has chosen to commemorate itself in an act of communal piety, saying grace at table, a compositional device that is in fact based closely on the tradition of the *Tischzucht*, the popular printed guides to good manners and comportment.[48] Even at this structural level, therefore, the painting bodied forth a didactic principle that equated orderly comportment with moral virtue. More generally, the array of decorated household objects speak directly to the family's religious and ethical values: the grand *Kachelofen*, decorated with the cardinal and theological virtues, points to the family's ethical code of conduct; the inscribed roof beams in the kitchen are suggestive of useful and ethically oriented texts, directed even to the household's servants; while the inscribed tablet behind the stove and the painted glass panels in the window might have summoned up the holy in somatic and symbolic terms. Each had its own set of specific meanings and, as we have seen, would have encouraged varying kinds of address, from the prescriptive and didactic to the invocatory and discursive. In its details, the portrait, itself an object of commemoration and a mirror and lesson in virtuous living, perfectly illustrates the ways in which biblical imagery and inscription in the home were deeply bound up with a reformist cultural ideal that sought to remould human nature through the ordination of civility, moral education, and piety, by continuously reinforcing the religious significance that attached to the activities of everyday life.

FURTHER READING

Bleyerveld, Yvonne. 'Chaste, Obedient and Devout: Biblical Women as Patterns of Female Virtue in Netherlandish and German Graphic Art, ca. 1500–1750'. *Simiolus*, 28 (2000–1): 219–50.

Dyrness, William A. *Reformed Theology and Visual Culture: The Protestant Imagination from Calvin to Edwards* (Cambridge: Cambridge Univeristy Press, 2004).

---

[47] Comparable typological schemes can be found in Bible frontispieces and title-pages. See Morrall, 'Representations of Nature in Seventeenth-Century English Embroideries', in Watt and Morrall, *English Embroidery*, 79–97.

[48] The earliest printed example is by Georg Pencz, with text by Hans Sachs, printed in Nuremberg; for later Swiss, French, and Dutch examples in this tradition, which often include painted typological schemes on the walls, see Wayne E. Franits, *Paragons of Virtue: Women and Domesticity in Seventeenth-Century Dutch Art* (Cambridge: Cambridge University Press, 1993), 142–51. An example from Zürich by Conrad Meyer, dated 1645, stands in a very close relationship with the Bodmer portrait.

Gaimster, David. *German Stoneware 1500–1900: Archaeology and Cultural History* (London: British Museum, 1997).

Gaimster, David, and Roberta Gilchrist, eds. *The Archaeology of Reformation, 1480–1580*, Societies for Medieval and Post-Medieval Archaeology (Leeds: Maney Publishing, 2003).

Hamling, Tara. *Decorating the 'Godly' Household: Religious Art in Post-Reformation Britain* (New Haven: Yale University Press, 2010).

Husband, Timothy. *The Luminous Image: Painted Glass Roundels in the Lowlands, 1480–1560* (New York: Metropolitan Museum of Art, 1995).

Koote, T. G., ed. *De bijbel in huis: Bijbelse verhalen op huisraad en meubilair inde zeventiende en acttiende eeuw* (Utrecht: Musuem Het Catherijnenconvent, 1992).

Mack, Peter. 'Rhetoric, Ethics and Reading in the Renaissance'. *Renaissance Studies*, 19 (2005): 1–21.

Moss, Ann. *Printed Commonplace Books and the Structuring of Renaissance Thought* (Oxford: Clarendon Press, 1996).

Todd, Margo. 'Humanists, Puritans and the Spiritualised Household'. *Church History*, 49 (1980): 18–34.

Watt, Melinda, and Andrew Morrall, eds. *English Embroidery in the Metropolitan Museum of Art, 1580–1700: 'Twixt Art and Nature'* (New Haven: Yale University Press, 2008).

Wells-Cole, Anthony. *Art and Decoration in Elizabethan and Jacobean England: The Influence of Continental Prints, 1558–1625* (New Haven: Yale University Press, 1997).

CHAPTER 37

'MY EXQUISITE COPIES FOR ACTION': JOHN SALTMARSH AND THE MACHIAVELLIAN BIBLE

KEVIN KILLEEN

THE ethical parameters of the Bible in the seventeenth century—what it enjoined or what it implied about behaviour—were not the most pressing questions asked of the scriptures. Myriad aspects of doctrine, theology, and its political imperatives dominated attention. But when behaviour was subject to scrutiny, it was, of course, an important document. Some of the edicts derived from it could address in quite straightforward fashion the social problems that communities saw in their midst: drunkenness, profanity, and fornication might be chastized via its pages. The scriptures served equally as the site on which moral complexity could be tested. Long-standing theological interest in 'cases of conscience' sought to assess any moral conundrum against biblical models of behaviour. The difficulty in this, however, was that instances abound in which biblical characters lie, cheat, and are underhand. And though, sometimes, comment on these might be dismissed as a scoffing irreligiosity, there also existed a rich arsenal of interpretative techniques to mitigate or explain them: whether the Augustinian rule of charity, by which any aspect of the Bible should be made to cohere with the overall texture, or the designation of events as being typological in meaning, or contextual-historical explanation of action.[1] What was almost universally agreed was that the Bible was there to edify.

Almost universally agreed, but not quite. John Saltmarsh, writing his impressively scandalous work of advice, *The Practice of Policie in a Christian Life, Taught from the Scriptures* (1639) undertakes to do for the Bible what Machiavelli did for Livy, animating it as a guide to political manoeuvre. He advises dipping one's cup in the well of scripture to fetch out aphoristic nuggets, which he describes as: 'my exquisite copies for action':

---

[1] Augustine, *De doctrina Christiana* 1.35.39–1.36.41.

I observed too, that the famous Politician brought his vessell to this holy cisterne and drew some sacred Aphorismes, though too few for action, rather devoting his penne to the Romane *Livie* for copy and imitation than hither.[2]

The kind of 'action' upon the 'sacred aphorisms' that Saltmarsh intends is not sacred in any modern or indeed early modern sense, nor is it exemplary, in any straightforward fashion.[3] Saltmarsh's dark readings of scripture describe a series of political lessons, together with a biblical instance from which each might be derived. So, on the basis of the apparently offhand phrase, 'This thing is of the Lord', by which Laban responds to the providence of Abraham's servant meeting them at a well, Saltmarsh advises the judicious reader not that they ought to remain on the look-out for the signs of divine will, the ostensible meaning of the text, but rather that they should play and wheedle with the religious inclinations of any relatively gullible auditors, who might be swayed by lines like 'this thing is of the Lord':

> When you have favours to request of any, that are inclined religiously, and with whom you have credit, you may advance and further your Designe, with relating how farre you have observed Gods hand, in moving to it … hee that wooes thus, makes GOD his Spokesman, and is sure to speed well with the religiously affected.[4]

Saltmarsh construes the text to suggest not that Laban's expostulation itself hides darker designs—there is little at this moment in Genesis to suggest so—but that deployed with apparent spontaneity, the biblical phrase will serve to throw any who are liable to believe such things off guard. The 'religiously affected', he suggests, can be manipulated by punctuating one's talk with pieties. Saltmarsh explores such matters across some three hundred pages of policy maxims, ordered in so far as they follow the Bible from Genesis through to the New Testament.

Much of the text addresses how one should maintain the political upper hand, although there is frequently only an oblique connection between the biblical text and the 'lesson' it illustrates. In Acts 9: 39, Peter is brought to the house where Tabitha (Dorcas) died, her body laid out and surrounded by weeping widows, who show him the tunics and garments that she had worn and made when she was alive. Peter, moved by the sight, takes pity on the widows' pain and restores the woman to life. This is the apostolic assumption of that quintessential Christological power, the miraculous adjudication on life and death, but it prompts Saltmarsh to the tangential reflection that, since the sight of the garments is at the root of this sudden outpouring of emotion, it is expedient, politically speaking, to destroy every object and sign whose memory might prompt recall of anything liable to stir the passions:

> If you would have any eminent act forgotten … rase out all memorials and tokens which belonged to it … for so long as they are extant, and to be seene, they refresh and keepe wake the memory.[5]

---

[2] John Saltmarsh, *The Practice of Policie in a Christian Life: Taught from the Scriptures* (1639), A7ᵛ, A5ʳ⁻ᵛ.

[3] Lisa Jardine and Anthony Grafton, '"Studied for Action": How Gabriel Harvey Read his Livy', *Past and Present*, 129 (1990): 30–78.

[4] Saltmarsh, *Practice of Policie*, 22 (Gen. 24: 48–52).

[5] Saltmarsh, *Practice of Policie*, 204 (Acts 9: 39).

What kind of exemplarity is this that so misrepresents the ethical grain of the moment—its presentation of the apostolic infusion of spirit and the preternatural pity of the apostles—so that for Saltmarsh, seeing and reacting to grief prompts thought on the political need to expunge all traces of one's enemies? *The Practice of Policy* spends a good deal of time upon biblical wiliness as a model for emulation, but also enjoins what appears to be creative misreading and cunning upon the text, even to the point of deception. This apparently cynical abandon is not how we suppose early modern England treated its scriptures.

It is worth noting at the outset the equally discordant fact that Saltmarsh's purposes are almost certainly not sceptical ones, to 'scandalise' the scriptures, as the early modern lexicon of insults would term any maligning of the Bible. Saltmarsh is usually accounted one of the early modern godly: his early works were a volume of sacred poems, and another of emblematics, although his theological positions become increasingly radical on the controversial matter of free grace and antinomianism over the course of the 1640s, a point to which I will return.

Accounts of Saltmarsh have not, to my knowledge, ever addressed the aberration of his 1639 work, *The Practice of Policie*, though Nicholas McDowell has demonstrated a set of counterintuitive similarities with the Catholic poet, Richard Crashaw, a stylistic and theological allegiance very much at odds with the political landscape of radicalism. This incongruity is further amplified in the idiosyncracy of *The Practice*.[6] It is a work that prompts not only its own improvident questions about Saltmarsh, but a wider set of issues about early modern biblical interpretation. What kind of reading practices and protocols are at work in a text that derives lessons on imposture and guile from the holy page? Can a text whose purposes are divine teach secular lessons in, for example, how conspiracy is to be handled? And did it, in some fashion, debase the scriptures to do so? No such meta-questions are addressed in the text itself, in so far as Saltmarsh does not dwell on the propriety of what he is doing.

The early modern understanding of the Bible included an intrinsic presumption that it was a political text, not just because theology was politicized, but in the stronger sense that it was very much a book about polity and government. More or less every political commentator in seventeenth-century England makes use of the Bible. No Sallust, nor Cicero, nor Machiavelli attracted anything like the volume or variety of political thought that surrounded the scriptures. There is, then, nothing strange in Saltmarsh's treating the Bible as a work of politics, nor even that he is so uncircumspect about its flexible and dark moralities. Nobody who reads the Bible with the thoroughness that early modern readers did could fail to notice how frequently strategy and deception are a part of its political landscape.

---

[6] Nicholas McDowell, 'The Beauty of Holiness and the Poetics of Antinomianism: Richard Crashaw, John Saltmarsh and the Language of Religious Radicalism in the 1640s', in Ariel Hessayon and David Finnegan (eds), *Varieties of Seventeenth- and Early Eighteenth-Century English Radicalism in Context* (Burlington, Vt.: Ashgate, 2011), 31–50; Roger Pooley's *DNB* article on Saltmarsh presents a very good synoptic account of Saltmarsh: 'Saltmarsh, John (*d.* 1647)', *ODNB*, 2004 <http://www.oxforddnb.com/view/article/24578>; see also Leo F. Solt, 'John Saltmarsh: New Model Army Chaplain', *Journal of Ecclesiastical History*, 2 (1951): 69–80; Douglas Gwyn, 'John Saltmarsh: Quaker Forerunner', *The Journal of the Friends' Historical Society*, 60 (2003): 3–24; W. K. Jordan, 'Sectarian Thought and its Relation to the Development of Religious Toleration, 1640–1660: Part II: The Individualists', *Huntington Library Quarterly*, 3 (1940): 289–314.

Even its prophets lie to strategic purpose.[7] What Saltmarsh produces, however, pushes further than a political reading of the sacred text. His is a book about misreading, about lying with the Bible, a primer on deception.

Any such claim, however, rests upon a set of presumptions about *how* early modern readers held the Bible to be true and this is a complex and amorphous question. Though it is evidently the case that they did, with very little dissent, consider the Bible to be 'true' in a manner that other books could not be, qualifying and expanding upon this with a range of literal and deuteroscopic caveats, this only tells us so much. The nature of biblical truth ran from the theological (on salvation or the sacrificial economics of sin and its expiation) to the moral and didactic, but equally to a complex set of political, natural, and ethical-philosophical matters. Most readers presumed a complexity to the Bible, not least in the interpretative ricochet by which the Old Testament reverberated in the New. Early modern readers demanded a thicker texture of truth than the straightforwardly literal and one was reading wrongly if one lighted on the mere axiom, outside of the wider fabric of biblical truths. Saltmarsh's strategies of reading the sacred aphorism, though by such criteria skewed, reveal a great deal about both the politics and parameters of hermeneutics in early modern England.

I. The History of Biblical Deceit

That the Bible might be put to manipulative and Machiavellian uses was evident and much commented upon, whether by Shakespeare's Richard Gloucester who jokes how impressively he can 'clothe my naked villainy / With odd old ends stol'n forth of Holy Writ', or Thomas Nashe's atheist: 'A holie looke he will put on when he meaneth to do mischiefe, and have Scripture in his mouth, even whiles hee is in cutting his neighbours throate'.[8] What greater depravity, the suggestion goes, than to wrest and pervert scripture to profane ends.[9] But there is a difference between wielding the Bible with egregious intent and supposing that the Bible endorses or rewards deception, a difference between those who know they are bending the text out of shape, and those who suppose the Bible's liars—from Jacob in Genesis to Peter in Galatians—are imitable figures.[10] Saltmarsh treads a fine line on how to take advantage of circumstances and yet to stop short of outright deceit. He is, in this, part of a long and sometimes fierce debate on what lying was in late Renaissance culture.

In *Ways of Lying* (1990), Perez Zagorin explored how early modern culture 'discovered' or reanimated interest in an arsenal of strategies of moderate deceit: equivocation, mental reservation, casuistry, and, never far from the surface, the era's magnetic attraction to Machiavelli.[11] He traces an outpouring of interest in dissimulation, from the camouflage

---

[7] 2 Kings 6: 19 on which Jeremy Taylor reports: 'Thus *Elisha* told a lie to the *Syrian* army which came to apprehend him'. *Ductor dubitantium, or, the Rule of Conscience in All Her Generall Measures Serving as a Great Instrument for the Determination of Cases of Conscience* (1660), 1.93.

[8] William Shakespeare, *Richard III*, 1.3.334–8; Thomas Nashe, *Christs Teares over Jerusalem: Whereunto is Annexed a Comparative Admonition to London* (1593), 59.

[9] 2 Peter 3: 16.   [10] Gen. 25–7; Gal. 2: 12.

[11] Perez Zagorin, *Ways of Lying: Dissimulation, Persecution and Conformity in Early Modern Europe* (Cambridge, Mass.: Harvard University Press, 1990), 1; Machiavelli's use of the Bible is explored in Graham Hammill, *The Mosaic Constitution: Political Theology and Imagination from Machiavelli to Milton*

and mimicry of animals, plants, and flowers, which offered models of acceptable guile, through to the scandal of recusants who, for many, subverted the truth with half-truths and equivocal answers. The English stage is relentless in its presentation of deceit; guile, bad conscience, and Machiavellianism are accusations thrown by almost every denomination of Christian against others.[12] Few accepted that deceit was licit, without caveat, but many 'cases of conscience' as they were called, were all about caveats.

Early modern readers were wholly attuned to how the scripture provided models of those who deceived and lied outright and yet remained the vessels of providence and whose acts were baptized as a kind of holy mendacity. Jeremy Taylor's *Ductor dubitantium, or, The rule of Conscience* (1660), a work of 'practical divinity' (as distinct from the full case law of casuistry), comments on St Gregory's possibility of 'pious cosenage'.[13] Taylor suggests both a non-negotiable moral line on the issue of lying or deception and a vast moral grey area:

> *Whether it can in any case be lawful to tell a lie.* To this I answer, that the Holy Scriptures of the Old & New Testament doe indefinitely and severely forbid lying … But then lying is to be understood to be something said or written to the hurt of our neighbour, which cannot be understood otherwise then to differ from the mind of him that speaks.[14]

This coexistence of apparently incompatible positions is typical of the manoeuvres of early modern thought on the matter. There are certain audiences to whom lying is entirely acceptable: 'It is lawful to tell a lie to children or to mad-men, because they having no powers of judging, have no right to truth'; 'To tell a lie for charity, to save a mans life, the life of a friend, of a husband, of a Prince, of an useful and a publick person, hath not onely been done in all times, but commended by great and wise and good men'.[15]

Taylor's list of those to whom a 'charitable lie' might be told is large. Good intention is the yardstick—so a physician can lie to 'hypochondriacal and disordered persons' and maintain his integrity.[16] Taylor cites many and detailed classical instances and, like Saltmarsh, notes Lipsius's *Politics* as a rich model of deception to political and military ends.[17] But the crux of the matter tends to devolve upon biblical instances, the holy and heroic mendacity

(Chicago: Chicago University Press, 2012), 31–66; Christopher Lynch, 'Machiavelli on Reading the Bible Judiciously', in Gordon Schochet, Fania Oz-Salzberger, and Meirav Jones (eds), *Political Hebraism: Judaic Sources in Early Modern Political Thought* (Jerusalem: Shalem Press, 2008), 29–54.

[12] See e.g. Tobias B. Hug, *Impostures in Early Modern England: Representations and Perceptions of Fraudulent Identities* (Manchester: Manchester University Press, 2010); Kate Loveman, *Reading Fictions, 1660–1740: Deception in English Literary and Political Culture* (Aldershot: Ashgate, 2008).

[13] Taylor, *Ductor dubitantium*, 2.99. On casuistry and cases of conscience, see Edmund Leites (ed.), *Conscience and Casuistry in Early Modern Europe* (Cambridge: Cambridge University Press, 1988); Edward Vallance and Harald Braun (eds), *Contexts of Conscience in Early Modern Europe, 1500–1700* (Houndmills: Palgrave Macmillan, 2004); Thomas Wood, *English Casuistical Divinity during the Seventeenth Century: With Special Reference to Jeremy Taylor* (London: SPCK, 1952).

[14] Taylor, *Ductor dubitantium*, 1.82.

[15] Taylor, *Ductor dubitantium*, 2.84–5. On the distinctions between casuistry and practical divinity, and the transposition between Catholic and Protestant forms of moral thought, see James F. Keenan, 'Was William Perkins' *Whole Treatise of Cases of Consciences* Casuistry? Hermeneutics and British Practical Divinity', in Vallance and Braun, *Contexts of Conscience*, 17–31.

[16] Taylor, *Ductor dubitantium*, 1.84.

[17] Taylor, *Ductor dubitantium*, 1.96, Saltmarsh, *Policie*, A5[v]. Justus Lipsius, *Politicorum sive civilis doctrinae libri sex* (1582), tr. William Jones as *Six Bookes of Politickes or Civil Doctrine* (1594), 5.17.

of the Bible—the deceptions of Ehud, Esther, Judith, and with a greater moral ambiguity Abraham, Dinah's brothers, Tamar, Rahab, or David:

> all those examples recorded in Scripture of great persons telling a lye in the time of the danger of themselves or others is no warrant, no argument of the lawfulness of it; for they were under a looser law, but we under a more perfect and more excellent.[18]

Taylor notes for instance that, at Pharaoh's instruction to kill the male children on the birthstool, 'the *Egyptian* midwives are commended because by their lie they sav'd the Israelitish infants'.[19] However, the moral ambiguity of the Bible remains, and Taylor comments somewhat harshly on a number of instances where deception occurs: Tamar (ancestor of Christ in the genealogy of Matthew) deceived her father-in-law into sex and pregnancy, by disguising herself as a prostitute on the roadside. Being part of Christ's genealogy, her actions were necessarily transmuted to their future ends, 'but she plai'd the harlot in deed as well as in words'. Dinah's brothers, in revenge for her rape, tricked the enemy king and soldiers into circumcising themselves, on the promise that they might marry her, only to be attacked when they were sore and unable to fight, but, Taylor comments, though their stratagem succeeded, they 'troubled the house of Israel by it'.[20]

The nature of deception was a matter of long-running Christian commentary and dispute, the *locus classicus* being Augustine's *Contra mendacium* (*Against Lying*), along with his *De mendacio*, the former of which was written against Priscillian, who in response to persecution, held that lying or withholding the full truth might in some circumstances be justified. Augustine's response is generally seen as an uncompromising denunciation of any such equivocating, and in many ways it is just that, but it is so only via a hermeneutic of near sublimity, a biblical landscape of lies in whose presence one must see near-incomprehensible mystery.

Augustine, who, we might say, taught Western culture to read in the way it does, provides moral clarity only at the weighty cost of hermeneutic complexity (a point I will explore in relation to Saltmarsh). In *Contra mendacium,* he takes on what may be the most problematic instance of biblical deception, Jacob's cozening of his father, Isaac, at his mother's bidding, in Genesis 27. This episode was difficult first because it was so outright a lie, so unadorned and enormous, and secondly because it was so successful with God who founds his covenant with Israel on the basis of a stolen patrimony. This is the second instance in which Jacob has cozened his brother, the long rivalry between the twins beginning with their wrestling in the womb, and Jacob's catching at the heel of his firstborn brother, Esau, who grows up to be an 'an hairy man'. When their old and blind father, Isaac, is about to give his blessing to Esau, and sends him to the field to get venison, Rebecca, Jacob's mother, seizes the moment and cooks up a goat, dressing Jacob in the skin, so that he can mimic the hairiness of Esau, to his father's touch. Then, in the largest and most unequivocal lie in the Bible, Jacob steals Esau's blessing, even at the point where a suspicious Isaac asks directly and for the second time 'Art thou my very son Esau? And he said, I am'.

---

[18] Taylor, *Ductor dubitantium*, 1.88.
[19] Taylor, *Ductor dubitantium*, 1.85, Exod. 1: 16–19.
[20] Taylor, *Ductor dubitantium*, 1.106; Tamar, Gen. 38; Dinah, Gen. 34, Saltmarsh, *Policie*, 41.

Augustine argues that Jacob's action 'is not a lie, but a mystery', in which we are not entitled to suppose ordinary psychological motivation or personal gain prompted the charade.[21] His acts occur within a scheme of divine reference, almost a divine poetics, which he himself is unaware of. So when Jacob says to his father, 'I am Esau thy firstborn', according to Augustine:

> If we seek the proximate cause, we shall think that it was to lie, for he did this in order that he might be thought to be someone he was not. But if this deed is referred to that signification for which it was in fact done, by goat skins are signified sins and by him who covered himself with goat skins is signified one who carried not his own sins but those of others.[22]

Augustine circumvents any question of moral propriety by referring the matter to a divine sign-theory that occurs outside of human time and Old Testament time. Rebecca and Jacob may suppose their actions to be a matter of out-manoeuvring Esau, in a proto-Machiavellian contrivance. But this is because they are not in a position to know the real referent of their actions, which is Christological, the vicarious taking on of sin and death, figured forth mysteriously as the donning of a goat-skin. One early modern correlate of this is Donne's Holy Sonnet, 'Spit in my face you Jews' which has Christ's human flesh figured as being symbolically goaty: 'And Jacob came clothed in vile harsh attire / But to supplant and with gainful intent'. Jacob's 'gainful intent' is for Augustine a failure of reference. The text does not refer to a lie, but to a truth.

Making the case that lying is utterly and always wrong, with no get-out clause, Augustine produces his spectacular sophistry: 'If this is referred to those two sons, it will seem a lie. But if it is referred to that signification for which those deeds were done and those words written, He is here to be understood in His body, which is His Church, who spoke of this matter'.[23] We might note here Augustine's distance from Jeremy Taylor, who repeatedly refers the question of probity to the intention of the speaker—whether the lie is underwritten by an honest motive—while for Augustine, the case is almost the opposite. The intention of Jacob and Rebecca is entirely irrelevant, because the action's meaning occurs elsewhere.

The point here is not quite the same as Augustine's better known argument on sign-theory in *De doctrina Christiana*, although the outlines of it are repeated here: in order to understand the literal meaning of a text, we have to discern its figurative language in a non-literal manner. He notes that we would not call a parable or a figure of speech a lie, when somebody says 'the grain fields wave' or 'the eyes sparkle'. Nor do we have to take

---

[21] Augustine, *Contra mendacium* (*Against Lying*), tr. Harold B. Jaffee, in *Treatises on Various Subjects*, ed. Roy J. Deferrari, The Fathers of the Church 16 (Washington, DC: Catholic University of America Press, 1952), 121–79 (152–3).

[22] Augustine, *Contra mendacium*, 154–5: 'si causam proximam requiramus, mentitum putabimus; hoc enim fecit, ut putaretur esse qui non erat; si autem hoc factum ad illud propter quod significandum reuera factum est referatur, per haedinas pelles peccata, per eum uero, qui eis se operuit, ille significatus est, qui non sua, sed aliena peccata portauit. Verax ergo significatio nullo modo mendacium recte dici potest'. From *Contra mendacium*, PL 40.517–48, ch. 10, para 24. Gen. 27: 19.

[23] Augustine, *Contra mendacium*, 154–5: 'Hoc si referatur ad duos illos geminos, mendacium uidebitur; si autem ad illud, propter quod significandum ista gesta, dicta, conscripta sunt, ille est hic intellegendus in corpore suo, quod est eius ecclesia, qui de hac re loquens ait'. Augustine refers this to Luke 13: 28–30, Jacob's being taken to heaven, as an instance of 'things clarified by subsequent events'.

figuration literally, and imagine in the phrase 'Christ the rock' a basalt Jesus. However, the point in *Contra mendacium* is somewhat different in that it relates to the referent of actions, rather than phrasing. Jacob's deeds 'are veiled in figures, in garments as it were'; he acts metaphorically.[24] This providential calculus, the Old Testament as prefigurative of the New is the standard Augustinian, though also early modern, get-out clause for coping with moral ambiguities in the scriptures: at moments of reprehensible behaviour by blessed figures, we should read not with the tools of exemplarity but with a transpositional hermeneutics.

II. SALTMARSH AND READING ASLANT

To return the focus, then, to *The Practice of Policie* and give a fuller sense of its scope and wiles: Saltmarsh ranges across the political field that an aspiring courtier might tread—the orchestrating of faction, the use of spies, and the heading off of rebellion. Faction, the practice of divide and rule, emerges repeatedly as a theme that any prince should understand, and Saltmarsh suggests that this can be patterned upon hexameral sub-principles: God's dividing the chaos, the 'confused masse of creation', teaches us to 'in perplexed businesses divide and disperse'. Babel, by its example, similarly teaches that 'division is the mother of confusion', so in dangerous circumstances, 'your course is to plot a division' among potential conspirators.[25] Saltmarsh addresses a number of aphorisms to the management of political discontent, how to quell 'the great complaints and murmurings of People by reason of grievances'. The continual task that Moses faces, for instance, is how to 'becalm a mutiny'. Addressing 'How to make subjects feare their king', Saltmarsh notes the benefit of occasional exemplary demonstrations of violence and he elucidates with an account of Saul's hacking and hewing a yoke of oxen in pieces.[26] He includes strategy on military subterfuge, and how to infiltrate an enemy king's army, as with King Jehu's pretending to be a Baal worshipper, even though kings pretending to worship one way in public and practising another in private was a fraught subject in Caroline England at the end of the 1630s: Saltmarsh concludes that 'if you would discover or be acquainted with the secret affections and inclinations of any, you may pretend to affect what you think you are disposed to, and make their affections yours'.[27] He also considers the expedient use of bribes, such as King Asa's shameless buying off of the Syrian King, Benhadad.[28]

Saltmarsh deals extensively with the use of intelligence. Jonathan and David, with their code of arrows by which the other might know the moods of Saul, are the precedent for the 'private intelligence' of code-language, showing how one should 'invent some thing which may signifie so to your selves by your secret confederacy'.[29] Indeed, Saltmarsh finds the Bible abounding in such strategy. Noah's dove, for example, is his 'winged intelligencer'.[30]

---

[24] Augustine, *Contra mendacium*, 154.
[25] *Practice of Policie*, 4 (Gen. 1: 4), 11 (Babel, Gen. 11: 6–8).
[26] *Practice of Policie*, 55 (Exod. 15: 25), 116–17 (Saul, in 1 Sam. 11: 7).
[27] *Practice of Policie*, 157 (2 Kings 10: 18–26).
[28] *Practice of Policie*, 170 (Benhadad, Chron. 16: 2–3).
[29] *Practice of Policie*, 133 (1 Sam. 20: 39).
[30] *Practice of Policie*, 10 (Noah, Gen. 8: 11).

He discusses 'how to have intelligences and spies abroad' in cases 'where you feare prac-tise and conspiracies, use the subtlety to mingle instruments of intelligence' by which 'you may be well informed in the others complots'. The latter piece of advice is part of the most elaborate case of plot and counterplot: Absalom's rebellion against his father, spurred by Achitophel.

This range of explicitly political advice—not at the level of constitutional generality, but a politics of gritty quotidian management—figures the work as a book of counsel, addressing itself to the service of princes, that genre by which one might demonstrate one's capacity for guile, dealing with or advising on plots at court or among the populace. It is dedicated to Lord Henry Rich, Earl of Holland, whose long-running wrangles at court and in Privy Council, and ability to make long-lasting enemies throughout the 1620s and 1630s, suggest a figure who might be alert to lessons on intrigue. The dedication does not sug-gest that Saltmarsh was necessarily in Holland's political orbit, but there is evident aspi-ration in his titling the work as a book of 'policie', a term, which like 'politician' in early modern usage, implied one's grasp of wily strategy.[31] Saltmarsh's strategy, even flagged as Florentine, would hardly constitute scandalous advice and is only slightly counterintuitive in its moral logic. However, in its counterintuitive *exegesis* it is unique, making the Bible yield meanings which run athwart the original meaning and context.

Most startlingly, the morals Saltmarsh draws take almost no account of their place in the narrative dynamics of the Bible. Delilah, deceptive and darkly idolatrous though she may be, nevertheless usefully demonstrates 'how to behave your selfe to obtain your desire'. In step-by-step dissimulation, first one must observe when your 'friend is disposed to your hand', and then drop into the conversation how neglected you have been feeling, 'observe to insinuate and let fall by the way, the want of affection which you shall have cause to suspect in the deniall'. In this manner, Delilah discovered the answer to Samson's riddle, and shows also how you can 'dally with them by circulatory speeches, runne them into a ring and delude them merrily'.[32] In any early modern understanding, Samson is the provi-dential pulse and purpose of the story and Delilah the ungodly snare: to focus on the sheer efficacy of her guile, without attention to its frustrating of God's plan, goes against every exegetical fibre of a culture that saw the unity of the scriptures as central. For Saltmarsh, it seems, a model remains valuable even when it works obliquely and counter to the whole.

Thus Saul, consorting to the Witch of Endor in the most diabolic of consultations, can be praised for the expedient use of disguise: 'Saul did wisely though his business was wicked'.[33] Saltmarsh seems conspicuously unconcerned that his aphorisms and advice are out of harmony with their source-story. Ishmael, the son of Hagar, was foolish in allowing Sarah, whose bondswoman his mother was, to catch sight of their mocking, but the lesson of this is not that one ought to avoid such scurrilous behaviour—early modern responses to the scriptures tend to see scoffing and mocking as particularly heinous—but that it is 'wisdome to conceale ones hatred'.[34] When Gideon, that most upright of Judges refuses the

---

[31] R. Malcolm Smuts, 'Rich, Henry, First Earl of Holland (*bap.* 1590, *d.* 1649)', *ODNB*, 2004; online edition, May 2009, <http://www.oxforddnb.com/view/article/23484>; Jacqueline Rose, 'Kingship and Counsel in Early Modern England', *Historical Journal*, 54 (2011): 47–71.

[32] *Practice of Policie*, 97–8 (Judges 14: 16 and Judges 16).

[33] *Practice of Policie*, 128 (1 Sam. 28: 8). On the variety of early modern responses to Saul, see the chapter by Anne Lake Prescott in this volume.

[34] *Practice of Policie*, 18 (Gen. 21: 9–10).

crown (Gideon was frequently presented as the quintessential republican and, a decade later, the model of Cromwellian reticence towards taking the crown), Saltmarsh praises it as teaching the successful use of mock modesty and pretended devoutness.[35] While King David might seem to be the narrative and ethical hub of the book of Samuel, it is his enemies, the Philistines, who demonstrate the moral wisdom 'not to trust a reconciled enemy' in refusing to trust him in their temporary alliance.[36]

Saltmarsh is also disconcertingly frank in his assertions that economic as well as political wiles can be learned from the Bible. Commenting on the enigmatic scene in Genesis of Leah's picking the mandrakes that Rachel then attempts to beg from her ('Leah would not part with her Mandrakes to Rachel, but thus, Jacob shall lie with thee to night'), Saltmarsh detects a harsh economics of scarcity and advantage: 'hee is a cunning Tradesman that knows how to raise his rate in a quicke Market'.[37] The scriptures, it seems, constitute a boundless set of advice on managing disadvantage. One of the important classical models of early modern thought on deception was an example from Cicero's *De officiis* on how far concealing information constitutes dishonesty. A merchant carrying grain to a famine-hit people in Rhodes, where food is selling at 'fabulous prices' is aware that behind him there are plentiful stocks arriving from Alexandria. Is he entitled to conceal this information and sell at a higher price?[38] Cicero gives a range of responses to this by the Stoic philosopher Diogenes of Babylonia and his pupil Antipater, addressing the various moral vectors of the case. Saltmarsh answers similar circumstances with reference to Jacob's bargaining with his starving brother Esau, demanding that, in exchange for food, he surrender his birthright. This, Saltmarsh has it, is good economics, 'opposing the supply', and anyway, God may want you to have the best of the bargain: 'yet these you deale thus with would bee Esaus such whom their wicked and desperate improvidence hastens to the bargaine, and then it is no neglecting, God may intend to make their Birthright yours'.[39] Saltmarsh proposes the ruthless manipulation of circumstances on the off-chance that God may intend your cheating to succeed. While it was understood that the scriptures contained many examples of guile, there were numerous exegetical strategies for reading such moments, so as not to rend the moral fabric of the Bible: Jacob, as the origin of the Jewish covenant might, after the Augustinian model, be referred to this. Saltmarsh simply and repeatedly fails to deploy the most straightforward of hermeneutical get-out clauses. His Jacob has no providential meaning, but teaches quite effectively how to cheat the poor and starving.

There are, then, various dynamics at play in *The Practice of Policie* that render it unique. It addresses itself to political manoeuvring but it does so via conspicuously skewed exegetical practices, its readings being so wrenched from their context as to have no parallel. As examples multiply through the text, we might suppose ourselves to be in the presence of a sublime cynic, a figure who cuts through platitude and sanctity to expose the

---

[35] *Practice of Policie*, 92–3 (Judges 8: 22–3).   [36] *Practice of Policie*, 130 (2 Sam. 29: 4).

[37] *Practice of Policie*, 33 (Gen. 30: 13–14).

[38] Cicero, *De officiis* 3.12.50; Cicero's test-case of deceit and disclosure is discussed by Toon van Houdt, 'Word Histories and Beyond: Fraud and Deceit in Early Modern Times', in van Houdt, Jan L. de Jong, Zoran Kwak, Marijke Spies, and Marc van Vaeck (eds), *On the Edge of Truth and Honesty: Principles and Strategies of Fraud and Deceit in the Early Modern Period* (Leiden: Brill, 2002), 1–32.

[39] *Practice of Policie*, 26 (Gen. 25: 31).

dirty realpolitik either of the Bible or of life in early-modern England. But in regard to Saltmarsh, and everything we know of him, it would seem quite out of character to suppose that cynicism underlies his work. I have delayed any detailed account of his biography and his other writings until now for precisely this reason; that the work has been left out of every critical account of Saltmarsh to date is perhaps not coincidental.

In the late 1630s Saltmarsh was producing devotional poetry in *Poemata sacra* (1636) and a work of devout emblematics, the meditative *Holy Discoveries and Flames* (1640), dedicated to King Charles, works which, it has been said, have the aesthetic mannerisms of a Herbert or Crashaw.[40] He left Magdalene College, Cambridge, in the year of his *Practice of Policie* (1639). As the 1640s rolled on, however, he became increasingly radical and positioned himself as one of the early modern 'godly', refusing any tithed income or parish support. A dispute with Thomas Fuller, across a series of works in 1643–4, led to Saltmarsh being named in Parliament for disparaging and dangerous comments on monarchy, in which he was defended vigorously by the republican Henry Martin, the dispute leading to Martin's brief imprisonment in the Tower.[41]

In the mid-1640s, Saltmarsh engaged in lengthy disputes on Presbyterianism, tithes, and antinomianism with Samuel Rutherford, Thomas Gataker, and John Ley, among others.[42] Increasingly drawn into the military conflict, he took the role of parliamentary army chaplain to Sir Thomas Fairfax and was reported by Richard Baxter to be one of the two best preachers in the army (together with the radical William Dell).[43] Thomas Edwards chastizes him in *Gangræna* for a host of things in his 'many trashie Pamphlets', including allowing a woman to preach.[44] A posthumous work transposes his name anagrammatically from Saltmarsh to 'Smartlash'.[45] However, the most serious and radical of Saltmarsh's heresies, indeed the 'predominant Infection' in the army according to Baxter, was antinomianism, according to which the Old Law had been abolished by Christ. Antinomianism threatened an almost anarchic liberty from the moral weight of the Old

[40] McDowell, 'Beauty of Holiness', 31–50; Pooley, 'Saltmarsh'.

[41] Saltmarsh, *Examinations, or, a Discovery of Some Dangerous Positions* (1643); Thomas Fuller, *Truth Maintained* (Oxford, 1643); Saltmarsh, *Dawnings of Light* (1645); Fuller gives a generous account of Saltmarsh in his *Worthies of England* (1662), 3.212.

[42] Among the works in which Saltmarsh is the major subject of attack, see Samuel Rutherford, *Christ Dying and Drawing Sinners to Himselfe* (1647), A3ʳ, A4ᵛ–B1ʳ; Samuel Rutherford, *A Survey of the Spirituall Antichrist* (1648); John Ley, *An After-Reckoning with Mr Saltmarsh* (1646); John Ley, *Light for Smoke* (1646); John Ley, *The New Quere, and Determination upon It, by Mr. Saltmarsh Lately Published* (1645); Thomas Gataker, *Shadowes without Substance, … in Way of Rejoynder unto Mr John Saltmarsh* (1646); Thomas Gataker, *A mistake, or Misconstruction, … between the Antinomians and Us* (1646); also Hanserd Knollys, *The Shining of a Flaming-Fire in Zion* (1646).

[43] Richard Baxter, *Reliquiae Baxterianae*, (1696), i. 56. See T. Cooper, *Fear and Polemic in Seventeenth-Century England: Richard Baxter and Antinomianism* (Aldershot: Ashgate, 2001); Baxter addresses Saltmarsh's response to the Westminster Assembly in *A Plea for Congregationall Government* (1646).

[44] Thomas Edward attacks Saltmarsh on antinomianism. *The Second Part of Gangræna* (1646), 19–20; *The Third Part of Gangræna* (1646), 113.

[45] Samuel Gorton, *An Antidote against the Common Plague of the World, or, an Answer to a Small Treatise (as in Water, Face Answereth to Face) Intituled Saltmarsh Returned from the Dead and by Transplacing the Letters of His Name, This Is Smartlash* (1657); on the Civil War fashion for anagrammatic games with names, see Lois Potter, *Secret Rites and Secret Writing: Royalist Literature, 1641–1660* (Cambridge: Cambridge University Press, 1989), 50–1.

Testament.[46] This is the aspect of Saltmarsh's reputation that has endured, and the critical writings on Saltmarsh treat him, quite correctly, as a consummate Civil War radical.[47]

What then, to make of *The Practice of Policy*? What do we do when a writer has a text so discordant with the remainder of their work? Nothing about Saltmarsh's career and earnest engagement in theological quarrel indicate a figure who would suppose the Bible simply a pliable and playable tool. This may have something to say about the dangerous and slippery pigeonholes of biography. It is also quite possible that Saltmarsh, like many a radical, could only look back to the 1630s with a slight embarrassment at the unprincipled jostling for place they had engaged in. Perhaps it was youthful indiscretion. But nor does this fit entirely. In the many responses to Saltmarsh's later radicalism none of his antagonists refer back to his 'Book of Policie' as something that might cast doubt on his devout motives. John Ley, begins one of his texts, in a series of disputes with Saltmarsh, by reporting on his opponent's grave and serious demeanour, but is aghast at his raising publicly the question of separation, marvelling 'that he, who hath written a whole booke of *policy*, should be so *unpoliticke* as to thinke it *seasonable*, to set forth such a *Quere*'.[48] Why, we might wonder, does Ley look this polemical gift-horse in the mouth? Neither he nor Rutherford nor Edwards nor Fuller describes it as the scandal upon religious probity that it evidently seems, unless that is, it did not seem so.

Another possibility might be that Saltmarsh's Machiavellian Bible was possible *because* of his antinomianism. If the Old Testament law and force has been abolished in the New, then perhaps the Old Testament had become, in effect, a secular work, open to machination and description as a work of policy, given that the spiritual was confined to the New Testament. All the theology one needed might be from the Gospels. And yet not only is there no indication of antinomianism in his writings before the early to mid-1640s, Saltmarsh derives almost as many maxims of policy from the New Testament.

Considering, for instance, how 'the scribes and elders consult to take Jesus, but not on the Feast day, least there bee an uproar among the people', Saltmarsh affects to learn 'how to observe the time and persons in the action of a thing', though the strategies of those about to send Christ to his death might not seem the best to imitate.[49] Again, the strategy he derives from the scriptures by no means follows the ethical grain of the text itself. On the contrary it is frequently the wiles of the scribes and Pharisees, or the Sanhedrin's plotting against Jesus that provides the pattern for policy. When the Jews object to Pilate about the phrase 'The King of the Jews' on the cross, Saltmarsh can see their point and argues that in any such case of 'pretence and imposture, doe not allow the imposture by way of any ironicall indulgence'.[50] Returning to the theme of how to deal with faction and conspiracy, Saltmarsh considers the verses in John on the raising of Lazarus 'When the Pharisees saw the people goe after Christ when he had raised Lazarus, they consulted to put Lazarus to death'. This swift action is, apparently, a thing to learn from: 'If you see a faction much

---

[46] Baxter, *Reliquiae Baxterianae*, (1696), i. 111.

[47] Joan S. Bennett, *Reviving Liberty: Radical Christian Humanism in Milton's Great Poems* (Cambridge, Mass.: Harvard University Press, 1989), 97–103, on Milton and Saltmarsh; Leo Solt, *Saints in Arms: Puritanism and Democracy in Cromwell's Army* (Stanford, Calif.: Stanford University Press, 1959), 29–72.

[48] Ley, *The New Quere*, 4.   [49] *Practice of Policie*, 180 (Matt. 26: 4–5).

[50] *Practice of Policie*, 185–6 (John 19: 21).

swaied and transported with any one occasion, study the remove and extinction of the cause'.[51] It is not only the scribes and Pharisee from whom one might derive policy: Jesus himself is the supreme intelligencer, from whom we might learn how to deflect or stone-wall questions during interrogation, 'when you are questioned strictly and severely, and have no desire to resolve the question', as he showed with Pilate.[52] The New Testament provides a not very different set of scurrilous lessons, and Saltmarsh's antinomianism, even if we could trace it back to 1639, does not make sense of this biographical discontinuity.

The resolution of this dilemma, may, in fact, have less to do with Saltmarsh and the state of his Machiavellian soul, and more to do with how early modern readers understood their Bible. Robert Boyle, in his *Considerations touching the Style of the Holy Scriptures* (1661) takes to task those whose captious objections to Bible fail to take into account its rhetorical complexity and insists 'That we should carefully distinguish betwixt what the Scripture it self sayes, and what is only said in the Scripture'.[53] Aimed at those who would decontextualize or fail to disentangle the biblical narrative from its spiritual referent, Boyle's distinction is one that the era was increasingly conscious of. An isolated aphorism or an instance of biblical skulduggery could not be equated with the purpose of the word of God. More or less every reader would concede the distinction, but this was not the same as supposing no didactic use could be made of a local narrative instance—be it the Sanhedrin's decision-making, or Jacob's strategies of lying—even when that was at odds with the wider texture of the Bible.

Indeed, it was not entirely unusual that, in the course of commonplacing, readers would take notice of such things. John Brinsley, the Yarmouth minister, preaching on the art of preaching, praised the Assyrian general, Rabshakeh, who was almost universally reviled as a loutish blasphemer, for the clear voice with which he bellowed to the Jews that they would have to eat their dung and drink their own piss, noting that 'we may make use of the actions of wicked men, as our Saviour doth of the unrighteous Judge in the parable'.[54] Noam Reisner suggests that, as a rhetorical and humanist practice, this was the deeply embedded presumption that allowed the classics to be so readily enfolded into Christian discourse, and that when in homilies we encounter what may seem discordant usage: 'a preacher's disregard for the original context of a profane quotation is not a calculated evangelical gesture, but a symptom of the literary culture of the time more generally. Grammar-school boys were encouraged to disregard the original context of classical texts' in favour of creative plundering, 'a fondness for arbitrary and eclectic collection'.[55] Saltmarsh's *Practice of Policie* might be seen as this procedure in reverse, the assemblage of sacred *florilegia* for a profane context, exemplary behaviour for a politician and potential courtier, for whom chicanery, subterfuge, and machination might be wholly necessary. That he creates a set of lessons discordant with the text is evident, and that his work skates on thin spiritual ice is also clear, but the early modern Bible tended not to be locked in a

---

[51] *Practice of Policie*, 197 (John 12: 9).   [52] *Practice of Policie*, 179.

[53] Robert Boyle, *Some Considerations Touching the Style of the H. Scriptures* (1661), 16; Rabshakeh at 2 Kings 18: 27.

[54] John Brinsley, *The Preachers Charge, and Peoples Duty about Preaching and Hearing of the Word* (1631), 6.

[55] Noam Reisner, 'The Preacher and Profane Learning', in Peter McCullough, Hugh Adlington, and Emma Rhatigan (eds), *The Oxford Handbook of the Early Modern Sermon* (Oxford: Oxford University Press, 2011), 80.

box for religious moments, but was rather the everyday tool of reference, imbricated in every thought.

Saltmarsh's career-moment in the dark arts of quasi-Machiavellian advice was brief, and his increasing theological and political radicalism took him into very different modes of public engagement. However, he was to offer one final piece of advice to princes, albeit not strictly monarchical. A posthumous work opens with an account of his death, telling how Saltmarsh, esteemed in both army and parish because 'He medled not with the present times', had a vision in which he was commanded 'to go presently to the Army', to warn them against their suppression of the Levellers. On the journey, from Essex towards 'this side of Windsor', he stopped first in a London inn, where he began to explain his visions to the landlord and lady, who 'gave no credit to what he said', and later, lost in a forest, he called up to a house, whose owner would not come down, but 'gave him directions of his way; and Mr. Saltmarsh gave him instructions in the way to heaven'. Coming then to the army's camp to see, first, Fairfax, whose Chaplain he was: 'he went to the Generall, (but did not move his hat,) saying, That he had not command from God to honour him now at all' and then Cromwell himself, again refusing to remove his hat, as he told him that 'the Lord was very angry with him, for causing those godly men to be imprisoned, sleighted, and abused … the Armies falling off from their former principles'. Saltmarsh is credited with effecting a reconciliation, his reputation humbling all sides and bringing them at least temporarily together. He left cheerfully and two days later he 'complained that his head did ake, desiring to lie down upon his bed' and died.[56]

FURTHER READING

Como, David R. *Blown by the Spirit: Puritanism and the Emergence of an Antinomian Underground in Pre-Civil War England* (Stanford, Calif.: Stanford University Press, 2004).

Cooper, T. *Fear and Polemic in Seventeenth-Century England: Richard Baxter and Antinomianism* (Aldershot: Ashgate, 2001).

Hammill, Graham. *The Mosaic Constitution: Political Theology and Imagination from Machiavelli to Milton* (Chicago: Chicago University Press, 2012).

Hug, Tobias B. *Impostures in Early Modern England: Representations and Perceptions of Fraudulent Identities* (Manchester: Manchester University Press, 2010).

Keenan, James F. 'Was William Perkins' *Whole Treatise of Cases of Consciences* Casuistry? Hermeneutics and British Practical Divinity', in Edward Vallance and Harald Braun (eds), *Contexts of Conscience in Early Modern Europe, 1500–1700* (Houndmills: Palgrave Macmillan, 2004), 17–31.

Leites, Edmund, ed. *Conscience and Casuistry in Early Modern Europe* (Cambridge: Cambridge University Press, 1988).

Loveman, Kate. *Reading Fictions, 1660–1740: Deception in English Literary and Political Culture* (Aldershot: Ashgate, 2008).

---

[56] John Saltmarsh, *Wonderfull Predictions Declared in a Message, as from the Lord, to His Excellency Sr. Thomas Fairfax and the Councell of His Army* (1648), 2–6. See also the defence of Saltmarsh for refusing to doff his hat in *Clarke Papers*, ed. C. H. Firth (London: Royal Historical Society, 1992), ii. 249 (appendix, letter from Thomas Margetts).

Lynch, Christopher. 'Machiavelli on Reading the Bible Judiciously', in Gordon Schochet, Fania Oz-Salzberger, and Meirav Jones (eds), *Political Hebraism: Judaic Sources in Early Modern Political Thought* (Jerusalem: Shalem Press, 2008), 29–54.

McDowell, Nicholas, 'The Beauty of Holiness and the Poetics of Antinomianism: Richard Crashaw, John Saltmarsh and the Language of Religious Radicalism in the 1640s', in Ariel Hessayon and David Finnegan (eds), *Varieties of Seventeenth- and Early Eighteenth-Century English Radicalism in Context* (Burlington, Vt.: Ashgate, 2011), 31–49.

Solt, Leo. 'John Saltmarsh: New Model Army Chaplain'. *Journal of Ecclesiastical History*, 2 (1951): 69–80.

Solt, Leo. *Saints in Arms: Puritanism and Democracy in Cromwell's Army* (Stanford, Calif.: Stanford University Press, 1959).

Van Houdt, Toon. 'Word Histories and Beyond: Fraud and Deceit in Early Modern Times', in Toon Van Houdt, Jan L. de Jong, Zoran Kwak, Marijke Spies, and Marc van Vaeck (eds), *On the Edge of Truth and Honesty: Principles and Strategies of Fraud and Deceit in the Early Modern Period* (Leiden: Brill, 2002), 1–32.

Wood, Thomas. *English Casuistical Divinity during the Seventeenth Century: With Special Reference to Jeremy Taylor* (London: SPCK, 1952).

Zagorin, Perez. *Ways of Lying: Dissimulation, Persecution and Conformity in Early Modern Europe* (Cambridge, Mass.: Harvard University Press, 1990).

CHAPTER 38

....

UNBELIEF AND THE BIBLE

....

ROGER POOLEY

Is it worth quoting scripture to atheists? In his *Atheomastix* (1622) Martin Fotherby, the former Bishop of Salisbury, argues that there have been plenty of writers and preachers who have
proved the existence of God from scripture, but very few (as he is about to do) who have proved
it from the evidence of the creation: in other words, 'to inforce, by strength of Argument, both
Infidels, and *Epicures,* and *Atheists,* who will not beleeve God in his word; yet to beleeve him
without his word'.[1] Later, he aims to prove to 'atheists and infidels' that the Bible is the word of
that God whose existence he has proved. It is not as though Fotherby is abandoning scripture,
simply suggesting that it does not function for those who don't accept its authority.

In the anti-atheist literature of the seventeenth century there is quite often a reluctance to
argue directly from the Bible, because the argument from nature or natural reason is deemed
adequate. So, for example, J.M.'s *The Atheist Silenced* (1672) announces on its title-page
'The Existence of a Deity, His Creation and Government of the World. Demonstrated from
Reason, and the Light of Nature only. In a plain and *Mathematical Method By AXIOMS and
THEOREMS*'. The argument from mathematics is worth noting because several early modern philosophers argued that God was the first mathematician. As Jean-Luc Marion explains
it in the context of a chapter on definitions of God in the time of Descartes, 'humans can
interpret the physical world in mathematical language because God first conceived the world
that was to be created in accordance with mathematical rationality'.[2]

Others would disagree with Fotherby. In a dialogue between Euphues and Atheos in John
Lyly's *Euphues and his England* (first published 1580), Euphues tells his fictional opponent:

> Thou seest, Atheos, how the Scriptures come from the mouth of God and are written by the
> finger of the Holy Ghost in the consciences of all the faithful. But if thou be so curious to ask
> other questions, or so quarrelous to strive against the truth, I must answer thee as an old
> father answered a young fool.[3]

---

[1] Martin Fotherby, *Atheomastix: Clearing Foure Truths, against Atheists and Infidels* (London,
1622), A6ʳ.

[2] Jean-Luc Marion, *On the Ego and on God: Further Cartesian Questions,* tr. Christina M. Gschwandtner
(New York: Fordham University Press, 2007), 182–3.

[3] John Lyly, '*Euphues: The Anatomy of Wit*' and '*Euphues and his England*', ed. Leah Scragg (Manchester:
Manchester University Press, 2003), 130.

Later, Sir Charles Wolseley, in his *The Unreasonableness of Atheism* (1669) alludes to scripture's 'innate worth, and the evidence it carries within it of its own divine authority';[4] though his arguments are almost all from reason, and he hardly ever quotes from the Bible. Wolseley and many of his contemporaries do express ideas found in the Bible, but the appeal to reason is a matter of tactics. As Michael J. Buckley notes, what is really remarkable is that Jesus Christ is rarely, if ever, cited in seventeenth-century anti-atheist arguments.[5]

Who were those atheists? David Berman's *History of Atheism in Britain* starts with Hobbes in the mid-seventeenth century. Other historians of atheism in the European context, such as Michael J. Buckley and Gavin Hyman, note that the term was in existence long before the recognizably modern version of asserting that God does not exist.[6] The term 'atheist' had a wider range of meaning and usage in the early modern period than it has now. It was used as an accusation in religious polemic; so a Protestant might call a Catholic atheist and vice versa as part of the dispute. 'Atheist' was sometimes just another word for 'heretic'. *The Unmasking of the Politike Atheist* by John Hull, published in 1602, points with heavy irony to the 'benefits thou shalt receive by entertaining Papistry, namely heresie, pollicie, superstition, Atheisme, and all ungodlinesse'.[7] Atheism, as so often in this period, occurs here as one bad quality in a list. That great master of the list, Robert Burton, classifies atheism as a consequence of religious melancholy in defect: '*Parties affected, Epicures, Atheists, Hypocrities, Worldly Secure, Carnalists, all Impious Persons, Impenitent Sinners, etc.*'[8] Does this mean that atheism is a precise term among many others for various species of unbelief? Or that it is one of many vague, accusatory terms lobbed over the walls of orthodox Christianity in the direction of its opponents?

The early modern definition of atheism is rather more capacious (or, if you prefer, voracious) than our contemporary one. The modern atheist is defined as someone who does not believe in a supreme being (and an agnostic, a term not coined until the nineteenth century, as someone who believes there is no compelling evidence for theism or atheism).[9] In the early modern period an 'atheist' was someone who might well have some belief in God, but did not believe that God intervenes in his creation any more; someone who denied the providence of God, or the Last Judgement and all that goes with it, like heaven and hell, was likely to be labelled an atheist.[10] So Dr John Dove, in his 1605 *A Confutation of Atheisme*, links 'Pagans, Infidels and Idolaters', who may be 'very devout, religious, and

---

[4] Charles Wolseley, *The Unreasonableness of Atheism Made Manifest* (London, 1669), B5^r.

[5] Michael J. Buckley, *At the Origins of Modern Atheism* (New Haven: Yale University Press, 1987), 40.

[6] Buckley focuses largely on French material; Gavin Hyman, *A Short History of Atheism* (London: I. B. Tauris: 2010), esp. chs 1–3.

[7] John Hull, *The Unmasking of the Politique Atheist* (London, 1602), A4^v.

[8] Robert Burton, *The Anatomy of Melancholy*, ed. Holbrook Jackson (London: J. M. Dent & Sons, 1972), iii. 379.

[9] Michael Martin, 'General Introduction', in Martin (ed.), *The Cambridge Companion to Atheism* (Cambridge: Cambridge University Press, 2007), 1–8.

[10] The best discussion remains Michael Hunter and David Wootton (eds), *Atheism from the Reformation to the Enlightenment* (Oxford: Clarendon Press, 1992), to be read alongside Hunter's essay, 'The Problem of "Atheism" in Early Modern England', *Transactions of the Royal Historical Society*, 5th ser. 35 (1985): 135–57; and, more recently, Michael Bryson, *The Atheist Milton* (Farnham: Ashgate, 2012), esp. 17–63. The pioneering work of Don Cameron Allen, *Doubt's Boundless Sea: Skepticism and Faith in the Renaissance*

godly' in their own way, but do not acknowledge the true God.[11] He finds instances of atheism in the old philosophers like Epicurus and Lucretius (and the epicurean line of atheism is a distinctive and growing one in this period; Lucretius had insisted that the happiness of the gods consisted in their being indifferent to human affairs); and there are atheists even in the Bible, like Holofernes, and particularly Pharoah in the Exodus story, who refused to let God's people go because 'I know not the Lord' (A4ʳ). However, Dove seems most worried by the Machiavels, 'the English Italians', who:

> Dispute against the Bible, reckon up Genealogyes more auncient than *Adam*, alleadge arguments to prove that the story of *Noah* his Arke and the Deluge were fables: Finally, they holde that the Scriptures were devised by men, onely for policys sake, to maintaine peace in states and Kingdomes, to keep subjects in obedience to lawes, and loyalties to Magistrates, by thus terrifying them from enormities when their consciences are possessed with an opinion of hell fire, and alluring them to subjection by hope of eternall life, that so Princes may enjoy outward peace and temporall prosperitie. (A4ᵛ–B1ʳ)

Dove's eloquence here expresses the alarm of many writers against atheism, that it is able to undermine the foundations of civil obedience. Ironically, he voices the terms of atheism in a way that would be impossible to do in print without the orthodox framing offered by his condemnation.

There are various distinctions within the term 'atheist'. So, for example, Edward Leigh asserts, 'There are few Atheists in opinion, more in affection, and most of all in life and conversation'.[12] This contrast, between philosophical atheism and 'practical atheism', between believing that God doesn't exist, and acting as if he doesn't exist, in rebelliousness or debauchery, for example, was widespread. Of course, the various regimes of censorship and anti-blasphemy laws made it almost impossible to express open philosophic (or 'speculative') atheism in print. Because of the legal impossibility of openly declaring one's atheism, the evidence for atheism in this period comes mostly from a burgeoning anti-atheist literature. In that way, early modern atheism is a bit like those early Christian heresies that only survive in their refutations by the church fathers.

Such views were, however, also framed and explored in literature. There are atheist figures in the drama, where they can be safely killed, made to look foolish, or repent for the views they have so heinously expressed. This chapter first explores the misquotation or denying of the Bible in the drama, and other literary forms where such a position is deniable as an expression of the author's own beliefs. The argument then moves on to the way that atheism is voiced in the anti-atheist literature. In many cases, as we have noted, this studiously avoids the Bible for arguments from nature or philosophy, but where they occur the appeals to the Bible are interesting; in particular, they appear to cluster around certain key texts, especially Psalm 14 and Romans 1: 18–22.

In the opening scene of Marlowe's *Dr Faustus*, Faustus works his way through the fields of knowledge represented by the books in his study. He jettisons learning: philosophy

---

(Baltimore, Md.: Johns Hopkins Press, 1964) remains valuable; despite its title, it is mostly about European atheism.

[11] John Dove, *A Confutation of Atheisme* (London, 1605), A3ʳ.

[12] Edward Leigh, *A Systeme or Body of Divinity* (London, 1654), S2ʳ.

(represented by Aristotle), medicine (the figure of Galen), and law (Justinian) before turning to Jerome's Bible (the Vulgate). This is how he does it:

> Jerome's Bible, Faustus; view it well.
> *Stipendium peccati mors est.* Ha! *Stipendium, &c.*
> The reward of sin is death? That's hard.
> *Si peccasse negamus, fallimur, et nulla est in nobis veritas;*
> If we say that we have no sin,
> We deceive ourselves, and there's no truth in us.
> Why, then, belike we must sin,
> And so consequently die.
> Ay, we must die, an everlasting death.
> What doctrine call you this? *Che sara, sara,*
> What will be, shall be? Divinity, adieu![13]

Faustus, as many commentators have pointed out, is quoting 1 John 1: 8, but not the second half of the sentence in 1 John 1: 9, where the 'hard' saying, 'If we say we have no sin, we deceive ourselves' is complemented with 'If we acknowledge our sins, he is faithful and just, to forgive our sins, and to cleanse us from all unrighteousness' (Geneva Bible). We might see Faustus's omitting to read on as a wilful rejection of this offer of forgiveness; although verse 8 without verse 9 is quoted at the beginning of Morning Prayer in the 1559 Book of Common Prayer, as one of the sentences calling the congregation to confession. The omission is made good in the 1662 Prayer Book.[14] A bit late for Marlowe, one might say frivolously, though one might also say that he knew what he was doing. It is possible that this part of the speech was triggered by hearing the sentence on its own, without its conclusion, in one of the services that, at some times in his life, he was compelled to attend.

Marlowe is an unusual example of an author who, like his roommate and fellow dramatist Thomas Kyd, was actually accused of atheism. This is distinct from more general attacks on the drama by Puritans who had other reasons for regarding it as sinful. Kyd got off the accusation of having written the atheist papers in their rooms by saying they were Marlowe's (possibly under torture), even though they were actually copies of part of a book by the Arian John Assheton.[15] *Dr Faustus,* in the versions that we have, printed long after Marlowe's death, ends with Faustus being seized by the Devil. The farewell to divinity results in divine punishment.

In its conclusion Kyd's great, innovative revenge play, *The Spanish Tragedy* (first printed 1592, though written in the late 1580s), has no equivalent scene of divine justice. It feels more like an atheist play, not just a play with an atheist in it. Like *Dr Faustus,* it also has a character who quotes scripture in Latin. At the beginning of Act 3, scene 13, Hieronimo enters with a book in his hand, which turns out to be an edition of Seneca's plays. But his opening phrase, '*Vindicta mihi*' is not from Seneca, but from Romans 12: 19: 'Dearly beloved, avenge

---

[13] Christopher Marlowe, *Christopher Marlowe's Dr Faustus: A 1604 Edition*, ed Michael Keefer (Peterborough, ON: Broadview Press, 1991), 1.1.38–49.

[14] *The Book of Common Prayer: The Texts of 1549, 1559, and 1662*, ed. Brian Cummings (Oxford: Oxford University Press, 2011), 103 and 240.

[15] For Marlowe's atheism, see Nicholas Davidson, 'Christopher Marlowe and Atheism', in Darryll Grantley and Peter Roberts (eds), *Christopher Marlowe and English Renaissance Culture* (Aldershot: Ashgate, 1996), 129–47; for the story of Kyd and Marlowe's arrests, see Charles Nicholl, *The Reckoning* (London: Jonathan Cape, 1992), ch. 5.

not yourselves, but rather give place unto wrath: for it is written, Vengeance is mine; I will repay, saith the Lord'. To begin with, Hieronimo appears to agree:

> Ay, heaven will be revenged of every ill,
> Nor will they suffer murder unrepaid.
> Then stay, Hieronimo, attend their will,
> For mortal men may not appoint their time.[16]

But Hieronimo then proceeds to open his Seneca and comes immediately to an opposite conclusion: '*Per scelus semper tutum est sceleribus iter*'. He freely translates this tag from Seneca's *Agamemnon* in the next line: 'Strike, and strike home, where wrong is offered thee'. He thus turns from being a wronged father to an avenging father. In portraying this 'conversion' Kyd inaugurates the genre of the English revenge tragedy. Hieronimo, like Faustus, dies at the end of the play. Faustus is carried off by a devil; Hieronimo commits suicide. They both die unredeemed. Whatever Kyd's own faith or lack of it he is clearly dramatizing a rejection of the Bible, and thus the biblical teaching about leaving revenge to God, in these lines.

The hypocritical pretence of using the Bible to fool people is perhaps less likely to undermine the Christian position because it can be comfortably placed alongside the example of the Devil quoting scripture in the temptation of Christ in the wilderness (Matthew 4: 1–11). So, in Shakespeare's play, Richard III's stratagem of quoting scripture to hide his villainy from the credulous is simply part of the play's demonizing of him:

> But then I sigh, and with a piece of scripture
> Tell them that God bids us do good for evil;
> And thus I clothe my naked villainy
> With odd old ends, stol'n forth of Holy Writ,
> And seem a saint, when most I play the devil.[17]

A rather more complex misuse of the Bible can be found in Cyril Tourneur's play *The Atheist's Tragedy* (1611). The eponymous hero, D'Amville (there is a double wordplay in his name on 'damned' and the French meaning 'of a vile soul') begins the play with an argument that there is little difference between man and beast: 'Observ'st thou not the very self-same course / Of revolution both in man and beast?' 'Revolution' is used here not in the modern sense of violent change, but the early modern sense of cyclical change, birth, and death.

His friend Borachio (meaning 'drunkard') agrees, though he suggests that man has a 'better composition'. But, D'Amville suggests,

> … where that favour of his nature is
> Not full and free you see a man becomes
> A fool, as little-knowing as a beast.
> *Borachio:* That shows there's nothing in a man above
> His nature: if there were, consid'ring 'tis
> His being's excellency, 'twould not yield

---

[16] Thomas Kyd, *The Spanish Tragedy*, ed. Andrew Gurr and J. R. Mulryne (London: Methuen, 2009), 3.13.2–5.

[17] Shakespeare, *Richard III*, in *The Norton Shakespeare: Based on the Oxford Edition*, ed. Stephen Greenblatt et al. (New York: W. W. Norton & Co., 1997), 1.3.332–6.

> To nature's weakness.
> *D'Amville:* Then if death casts up
> Our total sum of joy and happiness
> Let me have all my senses feasted in
> Th'abundant fullness of delight at once,
> And with a sweet insensible increase
> Of pleasing surfeit melt into my dust.[18]

There are two scripture references here. The word 'fool' invokes Psalm 14: 1, 'the fool says in his heart there is no God'; and, rather more obviously for the last speech, the parable of the rich fool in Luke 12, who builds his barn, fills it, and then says, 'Soul, thou hast much goods laid up for many years; take thine ease, eat, drink, *and* be merry'. But then God says to him 'Thou fool, this night thy soul shall be required of thee'. In this opening scene Tourneur is framing D'Amville within two discourses of atheism, or, more strictly, anti-atheism. The first is the argument from humanity as the apex of nature; the second is biblical. D'Amville's extraordinary final soliloquy, after he has accidentally knocked his brains out, reminds us of the word 'fool', but it is also a rejection of nature without providence: 'nature is a fool: there is a power above her that hath overthrown the pride of all my projects and posterity' (5.2.252–5).

Attention to nature remained the focus of much anti-atheist argument throughout the seventeenth century; but that did not mean that scripture was necessarily sidelined. The title-page of the Cambridge Platonist Ralph Cudworth's massive *True Intellectual System of the Universe* (1678), proclaims in the first volume, 'Wherein, all the reason and philosophy of atheism is confuted; and its impossibility demonstrated'. Much of it is devoted to the distinction between the Platonist strand in ancient philosophy, which allows for the existence of a deity, and the atheist strand (which he labels 'Democritick' or atomistic), which doesn't. Having argued this at considerable length and with wide-ranging multilingual scholarship, he goes on to rabbinical and Old Testament material, and finally, on p. 471, to chapter 1 of the Epistle to the Romans, which he quotes in Greek before making his own translation.

In the following passage the first sentence in italics is from Romans 1: 19:

> Again the same Apostle there affirmeth … *That which may be Known of God, was manifest within them, God himself having shewed it unto them.* There is something of God *Unknowable* and *Incomprehensible* by all Mortals, but that of God *which is knowable, his Eternal Power and Godhead,* with the Attributes belonging thereunto, is made manifest to all mankind, from his works. *The invisible things of him, from the Creation of the World, being clearly seen and understood by the things that are made.* Moreover this Apostle expressly declareth, the Pagans to have known God.[19]

For Cudworth, his comprehensive investigation of ancient philosophy supports Paul's argument, that it is possible to discover the main attributes of God from attention to natural phenomena. At the same time, he recognizes that there were ancient philosophers who drew the opposite conclusion, in the same way that D'Amville does, from

---

[18] Cyril Tourneur, *The Plays of Cyril Tourneur*, ed. George Parfitt (Cambridge: Cambridge University Press, 1978), 1.1.12–24.

[19] Ralph Cudworth, *The True Intellectual System of the Universe* (London, 1678), facsimile edn (New York and London: Garland Publishing, 1978), i. 471.

the same evidence. The question is, did they do it honestly? The biblical case against the atheists is that they are dishonest doubters, according to most seventeenth-century commentators. Cudworth regards atheism as a sign of degeneracy: 'since Human Nature is so Mutable and Depravable, as that notwithstanding the *Connate Idea* and *Prolepsis* of God into the Minds of Men, some unquestionably do degenerate and lapse into atheism' (i. 631).

John Bunyan, as one might expect, is the most trenchant in his biblical skewering of the explicit atheist. The appeal to nature, so prominent in more learned apologetics, is absent. In the first part of *The Pilgrim's Progress*, Christian and Hopeful meet Atheist, who is travelling in precisely the opposite direction to the true pilgrims. Already bruised from their recent encounter with the Flatterer, they are suspicious. Atheist laughs at their announcing that they are going to Mount Zion: 'There is no such place as you dream of in all the World'. And when they say that it is to be found in the life to come, he reveals that he was once a believer, or at least a seeker, but is now disillusioned:

> When I was at home in mine own Country, I heard as you now affirm, and from that hearing went out to see, and have been seeking this City these twenty years, but find no more of it than I did the first day I set out.[20]

There are two biblical references in the margin here: Jeremiah 22: 13, 'Woe unto him that buildeth his house by unrighteousness, and his chambers by wrong; that useth his neighbour's service without wages, and giveth him not for his work', and Ecclesiastes 10: 15, 'The labour of the foolish wearieth every one of them, because he knoweth not how to go to the city'. The second verse is easy enough: the 'fool' is a common term in the Wisdom literature for the atheist, so it is no wonder that he cannot find his way to the Celestial City. The first, I would argue, is also an argument that Atheist is not converted (or elected), so he has not received imputed righteousness from Christ, and certainly does not act righteously when he exploits his neighbour. Christian asserts that Atheist is 'blinded by the God of this World', and the pilgrims move on. It is a sign that they have learned from previous encounters; Atheist does not trouble them in the way that other opponents or false pilgrims do.

The original sequel to *The Pilgrim's Progress* was not the second part, where Christiana travels to the Celestial City, but *The Life and Death of Mr Badman* (1680). This is where Bunyan confronts atheism in a more sustained way, though the emphasis is on practical rather than speculative atheism, atheistical deeds rather than thoughts. In the course of Mr Badman's journey to perdition, he actually becomes an atheist, at least as far as the dialogic narrators and commentators Wiseman and Attentive see it. Attentive, who is the keener and less experienced of the two, is quick off the mark:

> I think he was an Atheist: For no man but an Atheist can do this. I say, it cannot be, but that the man that is such as this Mr. *Badman*, must be a rank and stinking Atheist; for he that believes that theer is either God or Devil, or Death and Judgment after, cannot doe as Mr. *Badman* did; I mean, if he could do these things without reluctancy and check of Conscience; yea, if he had not sorrow and remorse for such abominable sins as these.[21]

---

[20] John Bunyan, *The Pilgrim's Progress*, ed. Roger Pooley (London: Penguin Books, 2008), 138.
[21] John Bunyan, *The Life and Death of Mr. Badman*, ed. James F. Forrest and Roger Sharrock (Oxford: Clarendon Press, 1988), 84.

Wiseman has to restrain Attentive's enthusiasm a little later on, when he decides that Badman is a devil rather than atheist. Atheist is the right term, suggests Wiseman. His response is interesting in two ways. First, he is reluctant to admit 'there be such a thing as an Atheist in the world', and then a few sentences later 'there is abundance of such as he' (83).

For both Wiseman and Attentive (and, we would have to conclude, for Bunyan himself), the issue is conscience. Is an atheist without a conscience, or has he just got used to suppressing it? 'I believe that at times God did let down fire from Heaven into his Conscience', says Wiseman, with a reference to Job 21: 17 in the margin: 'How oft is the candle of the wicked put out! and [sic] how oft cometh their destruction upon them! God distributeth sorrows in his anger'. It is a puzzling reference, because it is not about conscience, simply about God's anger with the wicked. Conscience is not an Old Testament word at all, although it is very common in Paul's writing in particular in the New Testament. But it does seem to be an integral part of the early modern worry about atheism, because it was thought to be a part of the human nature that God gave humanity to recognize his existence and to know right from wrong: the 'umpire conscience' as Milton calls it in *Paradise Lost*, III.195. If one part appears not to be functioning—or is being ignored—then the other is in trouble, and the consequences for civil society are dire.

The fear of atheism is often the fear of anarchy, often linked with other fears, like that of the political threat associated with 'Papists'. An anonymous pamphlet of 1641, *Seven Arguments Plainly Proving That Papists are Trayterous Subjects,* asserts that:

> They that receive, entertaine, reade and recommend such lying libels and heart-stealing pamphlets, as whereby his Majesties right is impeached, his regiment reviled, his title of supremacy defaced, his fame defamed, Christian religion nourished by him, called heretical, devilish and damnable, and the professours thereof worse than nullifidians and infidelious Atheists, can be no good subjects.[22]

These are religious, if not exactly biblical arguments. There are some anti-atheist writers, however, who take the reverse of that view, and suggest that atheists think that religion is only there as a prop for the powerful. Thomas Hobbes, who was often accused of atheism, scandalously proposed in *Leviathan* (1651) that what really causes men to bind together in societies is not, first of all, the fear of God, but the fear of anarchy. In an alternative myth of the origin of society, the famous chapter 13, he argues that 'during the time men live without a common Power to keep them in awe, they are in that condition which is called Warre; and such a warre, as is of every man, against every man'.[23] Consequently, they have to enter into a contract with each other to avoid it. That is not all that Hobbes says about the origin and practice of sovereign authority; but it is in contrast to the alternatives, such as the derivation of power from Adam as a parent in Filmer's *Patriarcha* (written in the 1630s, but not published until 1680, during the Exclusion Crisis). Hobbes's text was written in a Europe that had just emerged from the hugely destructive Thirty Years War, as well as the English Civil War. He was also writing within the court in exile, where the (for the moment) powerless Laudian Anglicans were not to his taste.

[22] *Seven Arguments Plainly Proving that Papists Are Trayterous Subjects to All True Christian Princes* (London, 1641), A3ʳ.
[23] Thomas Hobbes, *Leviathan*, ed. Richard Tuck (Cambridge: Cambridge University Press, 1991), 88.

As Richard Tuck argues, Hobbes retained a belief in God as the originator and supreme power of the universe, but in *Leviathan*: 'Christianity became in effect the civil religion of modern England, with no other meaning to its doctrines than the performative ones attached to any worship ... it was Hobbes' ecclesiology which made him into an atheist'.[24] Hobbes continues to argue from the Bible, though, particularly in books 3 and 4 of *Leviathan*, less attended to by modern readers more concerned with political theory. For example, he uses the example of the healing of Naaman the Syrian in 2 Kings 5 to support his contention that 'Beleef, and Unbeleef never follow mens Commands. Faith is a gift of God, which Man can neither give, nor take away by promise of rewards, or menaces of torture' (343). In the fascinating chapter 44, 'Of Spiritual Darkness from Misinterpretation of Scripture', he argues against mainly Catholic tenets, such as purgatory, from scripture, like any good Protestant. However, combine the argument for freedom of conscience in religion with arguments from human nature for civil obedience, and we can see how Hobbes might be thought to be atheistical by his contemporaries, because the penalty for disobedience is no longer God's final judgement:

> I ground the Civill Right of Soveraigns, and both the Duty and Liberty of Subjects, upon the known naturall Inclinations of Mankind, and upon the Articles of the Law of Nature; of which no man, that pretends to reason enough to govern his private family, ought to be ignorant. And for the Power Ecclesiastical of the same Soveraigns, I ground it on such Texts, as are both evident in themselves, and consonant to the Scope of the whole Scripture. (489)

Hobbes remained content to argue from scripture, while effectively shrinking its scope.

One common figure of the atheist in the period—or, at least, someone who is their way to becoming an atheist—is the scoffer. Contemporary accounts of Marlowe picture him in that mode. There is a danger in thinking that, because Marlowe was such a spectacular figure, there were few like him. He appears to have been more flamboyant than many, but there are occasional glimpses of other 'scoffers', particularly in the Restoration. Pepys tells the story of Sir Charles Sedley in his diary for 1663, who exposed himself from a balcony of the Cock Tavern in Bow Street:

> acting all the postures of lust and buggery that could be imagined, and abusing of scripture and as it were, preaching a Mountebank sermon from that pulpit, saying that he hath to sell such a powder as should make all the cunts in town run after him.[25]

Scoffing at scripture while drunk, along with sexual innuendo: Sedley is the textbook Restoration rakehell. But the tradition of scoffing had a longer history, as the case of Marlowe confirms. One of the causes of atheism according to Bacon's essay 'Of Atheism' (1612) is the 'custom of profane scoffing in holy matters, which doth by little and little deface the reverence of religion'.[26] 'Abusing of scripture' is part of the mockery of the scoffer in the chapter on 'The Atheist' in Thomas Fuller's *The Profane State* (1642), his analysis of contemporary and historical examples of those who live a life of unbelief. 'He scoffs and makes

---

[24] Richard Tuck, 'Hobbes' Christian Atheism', in Hunter and Wootton, *Atheism*, 129–30.

[25] Samuel Pepys, *The Diary of Samuel Pepys*, ed. Robert Latham and William Matthews (Berkeley-Los Angeles, Calif.: University of California Press, 1970–83), iv. 209.

[26] Francis Bacon, *The Essays*, ed. John Pitcher (Harmondsworth: Penguin Books, 1985), 110. The essay was first published in the 1612 edition.

sport at sacred things' and thence 'proceeds to take exception at Gods word'. Fuller regards an attack on scripture as a dangerous part of the atheist's armoury:

> He keeps a register of many difficult parts of Scripture, not that he desires satisfaction therein, but delights to puzzle Divines therewith; and counts it a great conquest when he hath posed them. Unnecessary questions out of the Bible are his most necessary study … his principal delight is to sound the alarm, and set several places of Scripture to fight one against another.[27]

From the point of view of the Bible's apologists, the scoffer is the descendant of 'the fool' in Psalm 14: 1 who 'hath said in his heart, there is no God'. Consequently we should look to sermons on and expositions of this text to find the early modern believer's response to the atheist threat. One line of exposition goes back to Calvin. In England, his commentaries were translated in 1571, and his analysis of the verse puts a double emphasis on the fools as ungodly in their actions as well as their feelings:

> they have bereft themselves of all feeling of godlynesse, namely, because they have perverted all order, so as there remained no difference of right or wrong, no regard of honestie, no love of humanitie … and he sayth that they speke in their hart: bycause they spew not this cursed blasphemie out of their mouths; yet the unbridled loosenesse of their lyfe cryeth out.[28]

Calvin thus underlines one characteristic early modern fear of atheism in his exposition: that it will result in civil disobedience, though his emphasis is on the personal rather than the political; immorality and dishonesty more than outright rebellion; and on feelings rather than intellectual conviction. He characterizes the atheist 'fool' as someone who chokes the knowledge of the right that God 'droppeth into them', linking up with the Pauline conviction that revelation is clear, making atheism a wilful act of ignorance. But not everyone writing about this verse agrees. George Abbot, in his popular commentary on the Psalms, has a much gloomier version of human capacity: 'Man by his fall hath lost, and naturally is void of the right understanding of God'.[29]

The most extensive and subtle approach to Psalm 14: 1 in this period is probably that of the nonconformist divine Stephen Charnock in his *Several Discourses upon the Existence and Attributes of God*. Charnock is in the Calvinist tradition: like Calvin, he characterizes the atheist as being unwilling to express blasphemy, even though he lives it. But he takes the thought further, by suggesting that most people have a tendency to secret atheism; rather than it being a startling, scandalously exceptional aberration from the Christian norm, atheism is something we all have bit of, believers or not. It is not like pregnancy, in the popular sense that you can't be a little bit pregnant. Almost everyone is at least a little bit atheist:

> There is something of a secret Atheisme in all which is the fountain of evil practices in their lives, not an utter disowning of the Being of a God, but a denial or doubting of some of the

---

[27] Thomas Fuller, *The Holy State* (Cambridge, 1642), Ccc2^{r-v}. *The Profane State*, included in this volume, has a separate title-page, but register and pagination are continuous.

[28] *The Psalmes of David and Others: With M. John Calvins Commentaries* (London, 1571), F2^v.

[29] George Abbot, *Brief Notes upon the Whole Book of Psalms* (London, 1651), F4^r.

UNBELIEF AND THE BIBLE 623

rights of his nature. When men deny the God of purity they must needs be polluted in Soul and Body and become brutish in their actions.[30]

Later he puts it more concisely: 'All sin is founded in a secret atheism' (H1ᵛ). In the moments when we sin intentionally, we are, briefly, atheist.

In his exposition of Psalm 14, Charnock draws on another biblical opposition, of folly and wisdom, that is a constant theme of Proverbs. 'He that trusteth in his own heart is a fool: but whoso walketh wisely, he shall be delivered' (e.g. Proverbs 28: 26). He is also quite in line with the usual opinion that atheism is a threat to social order: 'A City of Atheists would be a heap of confusion' (F4ʳ). But he is interested in imagining a moral atheist set against a nominal or hypocritical Christian:

> suppose you knew an absolute Atheist, who denied the being of a God, yet had a life free from any notorious spot or defilement; would you in reason count him so bad as the other that owns a God in being, yet lays, by his course of action, such a black imputation of folly an impurity upon the God he professeth to own? (H2ᵛ)

There is certainly some biblical thinking behind this, on the practical evidence for faith: 'by their fruits ye shall know them' (Matthew 7: 20).

Far less elastic in his approach is Richard Bentley in his Boyle lectures, *The Folly of Atheism*, delivered and published in 1692; again he starts from Psalm 14: 1, and moves on to confute atheism from the faculties of the Soul (Acts 17: 27), from the origin of human bodies (Acts 17: 27), and from the frame of the world (Acts 14: 15). These are all, in essence, arguments from design for the existence of God; and they also, explicitly, confront the new challenge of Deism, which is identified as no more than a variant of atheism. Running alongside this new challenge was a much older one, deriving from the Latin poet Lucretius, himself the interpreter of the Greek philosopher Epicurus. While Lucretius was read by many English writers—he was drawn on by Spenser, for example in the Garden of Adonis in *The Faerie Queene*, and much quoted in Burton's *Anatomy of Melancholy* and (via Florio's translation) Montaigne's *Essays*—sustained efforts at translation really begin in the mid-seventeenth century, with John Evelyn, Thomas Creech, and Lucy Hutchinson.[31] Aphra Behn responded to Creech's translation with an acknowledgement of what she saw as its clear-sighted atheism:

> It Pierces, Conquers and Compels,
> Beyond poor Feeble Faith's dull Oracles.
> Faith the despairing Souls content,
> Faith the Last Shift of Routed Argument.[32]

[30] Stephen Charnock, *Several Discourses upon the Existence and Attributes of God* (London, 1682), B1ᵛ. The first chapter is 'A Discourse on the Existence of God', with Ps. 14: 1 as its text. For Charnock's career, see Richard L. Greaves, 'Charnock, Stephen (1628–1680)', *ODNB*, 2004; online edition, Jan. 2008 <http://www.oxforddnb.com/view/article/5172>.

[31] See Stuart Gillespie, 'Lucretius in the English Renaissance'; David Hopkins, 'The English Voices of Lucretius from Lucy Hutchinson to John Mason Good', in Gillespie and Philip Hardie (eds), *The Cambridge Companion to Lucretius* (Cambridge: Cambridge University Press, 2007), 242–53, 254–7; and the last two chapters of Stephen Greenblatt, *The Swerve: How the Renaissance Began* (London: Bodley Head, 2011).

[32] Aphra Behn, *Poems upon Several Occasions: With a Voyage to the Island of Love* (London, 1684), E3ʳ.

Creech was not happy, and in the enlarged version of his translation in 1683 silently emended these lines to:

> It Pierces, Conquers and Compells
> As strong as Faiths resistless Oracles,
>   Faith the Religious Souls content,
> Faith the secure Retreat of Routed Argument.[33]

Hutchinson's translation of Lucretius is a remarkable effort, with a clarity and concise-ness that arguably makes it superior to the versions that found their way into print. It sur-vives in a presentation manuscript, addressed to the Earl of Anglesey; the dedicatory letter makes it clear that she regards its contents as dangerous, though she managed to survive her own encounter with faith intact.

> When I, in the mirrour of opposed truth and holinesse and blessedness, saw the ugly deformitie, in the desperate tendency of corrupted nature, in its greatest pretences, and hav-ing by rich grace scapd the shipwreck of my soule among those vaine Philosophers, who by wisdom knew not God [a reference to 1 Corinthians 1: 21], I could not but in charity sett up this seamarke, to warn incautious travelers.[34]

The manuscript also contains a few marginal glosses, pointing out Lucretius's 'usual atheism'.[35] It would appear that part of Hutchinson's motive in composing the biblical verse epic *Order and Disorder*, first published anonymously and in part in 1679, was to 'vindicate myself from those heathenish authors I have been conversant in'.[36] In the same preface she laments that the young are led, 'before their faith be fixed, to exercise themselves in the study of vain, atheistical poesy'.

Order and Disorder is based on the early chapters of Genesis, and in the manuscript version goes as far as Genesis 30, though the biblical references in the margins range far and wide through the scriptures. In that way, it is interestingly comparable to *Paradise Lost*. If Milton's poem attempts to 'justify the ways of God to man', one explicit aim of Hutchinson's poem seems to be to justify the ways of God to atheists. For her, the way to do it is to rework the biblical story of creation. For many of her contemporaries, the solution was to assert the old truths of natural theology within the framework of the new science, with the Bible as a starting point—what is sometimes described as 'physio-theology'.[37] The

---

[33] Titus Carus Lucretius, *T. Lucretius Carus, the Epicurean Philosopher, His Six Books De natura* (Oxford, 1683), D4^r. Creech's 1st edition of 1682 did not include the mass of commendatory verses which accompany the 2nd edition.

[34] *Lucy Hutchinson's Translation of Lucretius: De rerum natura*, ed. Hugh de Quehen (Ann Arbor, Mich.: University of Michigan Press, 1996), 26.

[35] The editors of the most recent edition of Hutchinson's translation observe a synthesis of Epicurean and Christian doctrine in her translation, though whether this represents a Christanizing of Lucretius remains unclear. See *The Works of Lucy Hutchinson*, i. *The Translation of Lucretius* ed. Reid Barbour and David Norbrook, with Latin text by Maria Christina Zerbino (Oxford: Oxford University Press, 2012), pp. lxv–lxxi.

[36] Lucy Hutchinson, *Order and Disorder*, ed. David Norbrook (Oxford: Blackwell, 2001), 4. On *Order and Disorder*, and Hutchinson's relationship to traditions of biblical paraphrase, see the chapter by Sarah Ross in this volume.

[37] For 'physico-theology' (a term coined by Walter Charleton in the 1650s: sometimes 'physio-theology'), see Jonathan Israel, *Radical Enlightenment: Philosophy and the Making of Modernity 1650–1750* (Oxford: Oxford University Press, 2001), 456–64, and Richard W. F. Kroll, *The Material Word: Literate Culture in the Restoration and Early Eighteenth Century* (Baltimore, Md.: Johns Hopkins University Press, 1991), 151–2.

terms of argument remain those set by the Bible, with the atheist framed as the mocker or denier of the truth of scripture. Scripture remains important, however, because it is not just unbelief that is at issue in the early modern discourse of atheism, but wrong belief.

As we observe the Bible being quoted by anti-atheists and (usually fictional) atheists in early modern England, we can see that it tracks many of the changes of emphasis in ideas of what the Bible can and cannot do during the period. So, for example, the argument from design for the existence of God takes on the clothing of the new experimental science as well as the standard arguments from Cicero and Aquinas, but rarely abandons arguments from the Bible entirely. A rather subtler sense of Christianity as the foundation of civil obedience begins to emerge, as does the concept of the virtuous atheist. 'Atheist' remains an accusation, or part of a list of accusations. For most writers throughout the period, it is an extreme and almost unthinkable position, but there is an increasing amount of it about, and there is a whiff of panic about this reaction. Easier, perhaps, to regard one's opponent as a witty scoffer or rakehell on the road to perdition than to argue on equal terms and agreed bases; or to write to the converted to confirm them in their views of those outside the flock. But, as the seventeenth century progressed, it became increasingly clear that there was a serious argument to be had, and the role of the Bible in that argument was beginning to be open to question.

FURTHER READING

Bryson, Michael. *The Atheist Milton* (Farnham: Ashgate, 2012).

Buckley, Michael J. *At the Origins of Modern Atheism* (New Haven: Yale University Press, 1987).

Davidson, Nicholas. 'Christopher Marlowe and Atheism', in Darryll Grantley and Peter Roberts (eds), *Christopher Marlowe and English Renaissance Culture* (Aldershot: Ashgate, 1996), 129–47.

Hunter, Michael. 'The Problem of "Atheism" in Early Modern England'. *Transactions of the Royal Historical Society*, 5th ser. 35 (1985): 135–57.

Hunter, Michael, and David Wootton, eds. *Atheism from the Reformation to the Enlightenment* (Oxford: Clarendon Press, 1992).

Hyman, Gavin. *A Short History of Atheism* (London: I. B. Tauris, 2010).

Israel, Jonathan. *Radical Enlightenment: Philosophy and the Making of Modernity, 1650–1750* (Oxford: Oxford University Press, 2001).

Martin, Michael, ed. *The Cambridge Companion to Atheism* (Cambridge: Cambridge University Press, 2007).

CHAPTER 39

....

INWARDNESS AND ENGLISH BIBLE TRANSLATIONS

....

ERICA LONGFELLOW

THE idea that our selves are somehow inside our bodies has become such a part of Anglophone culture that we do not tend to notice the particular significance of inwardness in early modern English literature and culture. Christian writers have long been influenced by the biblical trope of an outward show of cleanliness or godliness that could conceal an inward corruption, as in Christ's warning that the Pharisees 'make cleane the outside of the cup, and of the platter, but within they are full of extortion and excesse' (Matthew 23: 25, KJB).[1] In medieval English literature it was a commonplace that a person's thoughts and emotions were inside or inward, and might be quite different from their outward, observable actions and words. Sir Thomas Malory, for example, describes Launcelot failing in the grail quest because 'in his prevy thoughtes and in his myndes' he was 'so sette inwardly to the quene as he was in semyng outward to God'.[2] *Inward* came to designate a person's real emotions, as opposed to what he showed to others or, sometimes, to himself.

Although inward motives in scripture are often corrupt, in English *inward* could also be used for what we would now call 'spiritual'. Julian of Norwich, for example, uses *outward* and *inward* to characterize the difference between sinful flesh and grace-filled spirit:

---

[1] See also Matt. 7: 15, 23: 26–8, Luke 11: 39–41, and 1 Peter 3: 3. Unless otherwise noted, quotations from the Bible in this chapter are from the following editions:

Vulgate: *Biblia sacra iuxta vulgatam versionem*, ed. Robert Weber, Roger Gryson, et al., 5th edn (Stuttgart: Deutsche Bibelgesellschaft, 2007). Greek New Testament: *Novum Testamentum Graece*, 28th edn (Stuttgart: Deutsche Bibelgesellschaft, 2013). Tyndale: *Tyndale's New Testament*, ed. David Daniell (New Haven: Yale University Press, 1989).

Geneva translation: *The Geneva Bible: A Facsimile of the 1560 Edition* (Peabody, Mass.: Hendrickson, 2007). King James translation (KJB): *The Holy Bible Quartercentenary Edition*, ed. Gordon Campbell (Oxford: Oxford University Press, 2010). Luther: *Luthers Werke im WWW, Bibel. 7. Band, Deutsche Bibel 1522/46* (Cambridge: Pro-Quest, 2000-13). <http://luther.chadwyck.co.uk/english/frames/home/home>.

[2] *Caxton's Malory: A New Edition of Sir Thomas Malory's 'Le Morte Darthur' Based on the Pierpoint Morgan Copy of William Caxton's Edition of 1485*, ed. James W. Spisak and William Matthews (Berkeley, Calif.: University of California Press, 1983), i. 506.

And tho be two partes: that on outward, that other inwarde. The outwarde party is our dedely flesh, which is now in paine and now in wo ... And that party was that repented. The inward party is a high and a blisseful life, which is alle in peece and in love, and this is more prively felte. And this party is in which mightly, wisely, and wilfully, I chose Jhesu to my heven .... the inward party draweth the outward party, by grace, and both shalle be oned in blisse without ende by the vertu of Christ[.][3]

Julian, typically, develops this metaphor into her own distinct theology of sanctification, a mystical interpretation of Paul's epistle to the Romans that allows for 'a high and a blisseful life' of the spirit after repentance, even as the flesh continues to suffer the painful consequences of sin. The early fifteenth-century poet John Lydgate uses the term more simply when he imagines the Virgin as 'Thorough light of vertu, Inwardely Iocounde', praying for 'paciens and inwarde myldenesse'; grace enables her 'inwarde' soul to be pure. But as well as spiritual purity, *inward* continued to indicate real (unfeigned) passions of a less noble kind. When Lydgate's Joseph hears the news that his 'faythfull and trwe' maiden is pregnant, 'it satte so Inwardely' that eventually 'for distresee, this Joseph fer in age / Of Inwarde thought, caught was in a rage'. Joseph's mental struggle with the 'Inwarde smerte' of jealousy is as internal as Mary's spiritual purity.[4]

The idea that emotions of all kinds were inside the body was more than just a convenient metaphor. Early modern physiology taught that the passions originated physically within the body, and this physiological theory of emotion combined with the biblical metaphor to have a significant effect on the English language before the Reformation.[5] By the sixteenth century *inward* had become almost redundant when it was used in phrases such as 'inward compassion' and 'inward hate', even when there was no hint of hypocrisy. With the advent of Protestantism, however, this cultural tendency to conceive of the passions as both metaphorically and physically inward was transformed into a paradigm of inward faith that radiated metaphors throughout the language. Theologians, lay devotional writers, and religious poets reimagined inwardness, drawing promiscuously on Protestant theology, physiologies of the passions, Augustine's journey through his memory in the *Confessions*, and Ovid's lush tales of secret erotic encounters.[6]

Together these texts charted a new inner landscape of faith: not Julian of Norwich's 'high and blisseful life', but rather a place of tangled paths and dangerous temptations. The entirety of *The Faerie Queene*, for example, could be said to be one long inward journey in which the knights, and the reader, learn to understand and control the passions. Spenser's language reminds us repeatedly that, whatever the monsters they encounter, the real battles of his knights and ladies

[3] *The Writings of Julian of Norwich: A Vision Showed to a Devout Woman and A Revelation of Love*, ed. Nicholas Watson and Jacqueline Jenkins (University Park, Pa.: Pennsylvania State University Press, 2006), 189.

[4] *A Critical Edition of John Lydgate's 'Life of Our Lady'*, ed. Joseph A. Lauritis, Ralph A. Klinefelter, and Vernon F. Gallagher (Pittsburgh, Pa.: Dusquesne University Press, 1961), 274, 280, 389, 392, 401. Compare *OED*, 'inward', A.2.a, b, and c.

[5] On Renaissance theories of the physiology of the passions see Michael C. Schoenfeldt, *Bodies and Selves in Early Modern England: Physiology and Inwardness in Spenser, Shakespeare, Herbert, and Milton* (Cambridge: Cambridge University Press, 1999), 1–39.

[6] Phillip Cary, *Augustine's Invention of the Inner Self: The Legacy of a Christian Platonist* (Oxford: Oxford University Press, 2000); Theresa M. Krier, *Gazing on Secret Sights: Spenser, Classical Imitation, and the Decorums of Vision* (Ithaca, NY: Cornell University Press, 1990), esp. 121–3, 151–3.

are against 'inward tyne' (sorrow), 'privy paine', 'secret envie', and 'inward griefe', and when they are 'inly swelt' by impatience or 'Privily pricked' by lust.[7] In book I Redcrosse Knight is repeatedly lost in his own disordered inner world: the 'wandring wood' of Error, its many wide paths 'leading inward farr'; the 'secret part' where he witnesses false Una embracing the false knight.[8] Only when he reaches the House of Holiness and the Virtues teach him to order his inner life is Redcrosse capable of sustained virtuous action. Disordered inwardness is also a theme of George Herbert's poems, as the speaker pleads anxiously with God for release from the closets and chests of his sinful inner self, where 'thy Architecture meets with sinne; / For all thy frame and fabrick is within'.[9] It was not until Milton's archangel escorted Adam and Eve out of Eden with the promise of a 'paradise within thee, happier farr', that it became possible for a Protestant writer to conceive of sustained ordered inwardness (through grace) after the Fall.[10] For these and many other writers, the changing English understanding of inwardness defined the relationship of the self to God and to other people as it evolved in this volatile period.

This is, of course, not a new observation; the pervasiveness of inwardness in early modern Protestant literature has been the subject of much study. Anne Ferry, Katherine Maus, and Michael Schoenfeldt have investigated secular sources of the metaphor, including legal standards of evidence and physiological understandings of the passions.[11] A generation ago scholars of Protestant poetry, intent on excavating the origins of Protestant authorship and influenced by narratives of the rise of the modern individualist self, seized on the growing dominance of inwardness as a metaphor for the self. Such scholars did valuable work identifying Protestant tropes, but at times overstated the modernness of the early modern inward self, and similarly understated the degree to which inwardness was already present in Christian discourse, in the Bible, and particularly in Augustine.[12] There is much room for exploring what is particularly Protestant about this metaphor, and why it came to pervade English literature and the English language of the self from the late sixteenth-century onwards. This chapter approaches the subject by considering how Protestant English translations of the New Testament construct the inward self.

The idea that there is a distinction between the 'inner man', as Paul terms it in Ephesians 3: 16, and an outward, material person is sprinkled throughout the Greek New Testament, using four distinct Greek phrases. The three Synoptic Gospels use ἔσωθεν, 'inside' or 'inwardly', in warnings against hypocrisy and valuing adherence to the ceremonial law

---

[7] Edmund Spenser, *The Faerie Queene*, ed. A. C. Hamilton, Hiroshi Yamashita, and Toshiyuki Suzuki, rev. 2nd edn (Harlow: Pearson Longman, 2007), VI.v.24.1.5; IV.ii.7.8; III.ix.30.2; III.xi.27.1; I.xi.27.1; IV.x.45.7.

[8] Spenser, *Faerie Queene*, I.i.13.6; I.i.7.8; I.ii.5.3.

[9] *The English Poems of George Herbert*, ed. Helen Wilcox (Cambridge: Cambridge University Press, 2007), 'Sion', 382, ll. 11–12.

[10] John Milton, *Paradise Lost*, ed. Alastair Fowler (Harlow: Pearson Longman, 2007), XII.587.

[11] Anne Ferry, *The 'Inward' Language: Sonnets of Wyatt, Sidney, Shakespeare, Donne* (Chicago: University of Chicago Press, 1983); Katharine Eisaman Maus, *Inwardness and Theater in the English Renaissance* (Chicago: University of Chicago Press, 1995); Schoenfeldt, *Bodies and Selves*.

[12] Barbara Kiefer Lewalski, *Protestant Poetics and the Seventeenth-Century Religious Lyric* (Princeton: Princeton University Press, 1979); Richard Strier, *Love Known: Theology and Experience in George Herbert's Poetry* (Chicago: University of Chicago Press, 1983); Cecile M. Jagodzinski, *Privacy and Print: Reading and Writing in Seventeenth-Century England* (Charlottesville, Va.: University Press of Virginia, 1999).

over virtue, such as 'Beware of false prophets which come to you in sheepes clothing, but inwardly they are ravening wolves' (Matthew 7: 15, KJB).[13] The Pauline epistles introduce the phrase 'the inner man' or 'our inner man' (ὁ ἔσω ἄνθρωπος (ἡμῶν)) to distinguish between physical and spiritual well-being. 2 Corinthians 4: 16 ('though our outward man perish, yet the inward man is renewed day by day', KJB) sets the sufferings of the physical life against the gains of the spiritual life; Ephesians 3: 16 is a prayer for spiritual fortitude, 'to bee strengthened with might, by his Spirit in the inner man' (KJB).

Romans 7: 22 ('For I delight in the Lawe of God, after the inward man', KJB) is superficially similar, but in the context of the whole epistle these verses relate to the distinction Paul sketches there between the flesh, the world, and the law—all outward, in early modern terms—and the Holy Spirit and grace, in a complex series of interlinked metaphors that would take on overriding importance for the theologians of the Reformation, and which will be discussed in greater detail in this chapter. Romans 2: 28–9 ('For hee is not a Jew, which is one outwardly, neither is that Circumcision, which is outward in the flesh: But he is a Jew which is one inwardly, and Circumcision is, that of the heart, in the spirit, and not in the letter', KJB) is part of this developing argument, but the Greek words are not ἔξωθεν ('outwardly') and ἔσωθεν ('inwardly') but the phrases ἐν τῷ φανερῷ, 'apparent' and ἐν τῷ κρυπτῷ, 'in secret'. 1 Peter 3: 3–4 uses the same word κρυπτός to contrast women's 'outward *adorning* of plaiting the haire, and of wearing of gold, or of putting on of apparell' with 'the hidden man of the heart, in that which is not corruptible, *even the ornament* of a meeke and quiet spirit' (KJB).

The final passage that refers to the inner person is Luke 17: 20b–21: 'The kingdome of God cometh not with observation. Neither shall they say, Loe here, or loe there: for behold, the kingdome of God is within you' (KJB) (ἰδοὺ γὰρ ἡ βασιλεία τοῦ θεοῦ ἐντὸς ὑμῶν ἐστιν). These verses are more ambiguous than they might seem. ἐντὸς does usually mean 'within' but the second person pronoun (ὑμῶν) is plural, so that the phrase could mean 'among you [disciples]'. The ambiguity is of course more apparent in early modern translations that use distinct singular and plural forms of the second person pronoun (*thou* and *ye*) than it is in modern English. Nevertheless, the 1611 translators added one of their rare marginal notes to 17: 21b, to indicate that the phrase might also mean 'among you'.

What unites all of these verses is the designation of the inward as that which is hidden or secret because it cannot be detected by the senses, a concept reflected in the use of the Greek word for 'hidden' in Romans 2: 28–9 and 1 Peter 3: 3. In English translations, however, this concept of inwardness occasionally becomes muddled with the ancient idea that emotion originated in the bowels. By New Testament times using 'bowels' (σπλάγχνα) for emotions, and particularly compassion, appears to have been a dead metaphor, much as we might have a gut feeling, even though we no longer believe that conviction is created in our intestines. In Reformation times the physiological theories that linked bowels and emotions were still known, but the metonymy was rare.[14] As a result, the literal-minded King James translators rendered Philippians 2: 1 as, 'If *there bee* therefore any consolation in Christ, if any comfort of love, if any fellowship of the Spirit, if any bowels & mercies', as if Paul thought the Philippians' good digestive habits would spur them to compassion. (They also had Paul tell the Corinthians, 'yee are straitned in your owne bowels': 2 Corinthians 6:

---

[13] Also Matt. 23: 25–8, Mark 7: 21, and Luke 11: 39–41.
[14] See Schoenfeldt, *Bodies and Selves*, 12–15.

12.) More frequently, the translators substituted their own common metaphor, inwardness, as in 2 Corinthians 7: 15 ('And his inward affection is more aboundant toward you', KJB), although the King James translators added in a note that the Greek was 'bowels'.[15]

Initially, this may seem like a large sample, evidence that inwardness is an important biblical metaphor. But in fact the idea of the self as hidden inside the person only appears in isolated passages in the Synoptic Gospels and four epistles, in each case with slightly different nuance. Inwardness is notably absent from the highly metaphorical Gospel of John, where the metaphor of 'in'-ness refers not to the self but to connections between people, such as Jesus's frequent tongue-twisting declarations that those who abide in him, he will abide in them.[16] Nor is the metaphor of the inward self given more than a passing reference in any book of the New Testament other than Romans. One modern commentator on Ephesians, for example, insists that Paul did not understand 'the inner person' in Ephesians 3: 16 'in a naturalistic or dualistic way of the spiritual essence of a human being, but rather of the believer in Christ turned towards and waiting expectantly for the life of the age to come'.[17] The idea of a hidden interior self distinct from an external body was available to the writers of the New Testament, but it was not yet the dominant metaphor that it would become in Reformation England.

The story of inwardness in the Reformation begins with Luther's *Preface to St Paul's Letter to the Romans*, written for his own translation of the Bible into German in 1522, and revised in 1546.[18] The *Preface* was one of the founding documents of the Reformation, in which Luther set out, in brief, the doctrine of *sola gratia* and justification by faith as established in this 'rechte hewbtstuckt des newen testaments, und das aller lauterst Evangelion' ('really the chief part of the New Testament, and is truly the purest gospel').[19] In the first half of the *Preface* Luther explains the novel way that Paul uses key theological terms, including *law, sin, grace, gift*, and *faith*. To tease out Paul's use of these terms, Luther draws on the metaphor of hiddenness and inwardness that appears twice in Romans.

As we have seen, Romans 7: 22, 'For I delight in the Lawe of God, after the inward man' (KJB) (συνήδομαι γὰρ τῷ νόμῳ τοῦ θεοῦ κατὰ τὸν ἔσω ἄνθρωπον), is unambiguous. The Greek adverb ἔσω is used spatially in the Gospels and Acts, but here and in two other verses in the epistles it is used to indicate the hidden part of the self.[20] English translators of Romans 7: 22 consistently use 'inner man' (Wycliffite, Tyndale, Matthew, Geneva) or 'inward man' (Coverdale, Great Bible, Bishops' Bible, Douai-Rheims, KJB).[21] In 2: 28–29a, however, the writer of Romans employs the contrast between visibility and hiddenness:

οὐ γὰρ ὁ ἐν τῷ φανερῷ Ἰουδαῖός ἐστιν, οὐδὲ ἡ ἐν τῷ φανερῷ ἐν σαρκὶ περιτομή: ἀλλ᾽ ὁ ἐν τῷ κρυπτῷ Ἰουδαῖος, καὶ περιτομὴ καρδίας ἐν πνεύματι οὐ γράμματι[.]

---

[15] See also Luke 1: 78 (KJB) and note.

[16] See e.g. John 6: 56, 10: 38, 14: 20, 15: 4–10, 17: 21.

[17] John Muddiman, *A Commentary on the Epistle to the Ephesians* (London: Continuum, 2001), 167.

[18] 'Vorrede auf die Epistel S. Pauli an die Römer', *Luthers Werke im WWW, Bibel. 7. Band, Deutsche Bibel: Episteln und Offenbarung 1522/46* (Cambridge: Pro-Quest, 2000–13), <http://luther.chadwyck.co.uk/english/frames/home/home>.

[19] 'Vorrede auf die Epistel S. Pauli an die Römer', 2. English translation from *The Works of Martin Luther*, xxxv, ed. E. Theodore Bachmann (Philadelphia: Fortress Press, 1960), 365.

[20] Matt. 26: 58; Mark 14: 54, 15: 16; John 20: 26; Acts 5: 23; Eph. 3: 16.

[21] From *The Bible in English Database*, version 1.0 (Cambridge: Pro-Quest, 1996).

For he is not a Jew that is one in appearance, nor is circumcision that which is apparent in the flesh; but [a Jew is] the one that is in hiddenness a Jew, and circumcision is of the heart in spirit, not in the letter[.][22]

The conviction that truth is seen by God but hidden from human beings is a key biblical concept, and more common than the idea of an inner self. The Vulgate preserves the metaphor by translating ἐν τῷ φανερῷ as 'in manifesto' and ἐν τῷ κρυπτῷ as 'in abscondito', and this is reflected in the earliest English translation's 'in opyn' and 'in hidd'.[23] By the Reformation, however, there had been a shift. All of the Reformation English translations render ἐν τῷ φανερῷ as 'outward' or 'outwardly' and ἐν τῷ κρυπτῷ as 'hid within' (Tyndale, Coverdale, the Great Bible, the Matthew Bible) or, later, 'inwardly' (Bishops' Bible, KJB) or 'within' (Geneva).[24] Luther employs the similar German adverbs 'außwendig' and 'inwendig'. The Douai-Rheims, unsurprisingly, reverts to the more literal 'in open shew' and 'in secret'.[25] The visible and the hidden now had a specific location, outside and inside the person.

Luther uses this dichotomy between inward and outward to clarify Paul's use of key terms in the first half of Romans. *Law*, for example, should not be understood in the ordinary human way of a code of what can and cannot be done. For Paul (according to Luther), the *law* cannot be fulfilled by outward works alone—he is not a Jew that is one in appearance. The law can be broken even when there are outward good works ('ausswendig viel gutter werck') if there is no will from the depths of the heart ('des hertzen grund') to do good. Likewise, *sin* for Paul is not only outward works ('nicht alleyne das euserliche werck'), but everything that moves the person to do those outward works, that is, the depth of the heart with all of its powers ('sondern alle das gescheffte, das sich mit reget und wegt zu dem euserlichen werck, nemlich des hertzen grund mit allen krefften'). Because one can keep the law outwardly but yet sin inwardly, *grace* is when God pours into us the Holy Spirit and its gifts ('den Geist mit seinen gaben inn uns zu gissen'), and *faith* is 'ein gotlich werck inn uns', 'a divine work in us'. Luther does not, however, strongly emphasize the internal quality of faith; he is far more concerned to emphasize that faith is the work of God, not human effort.[26]

Luther was aware of the dangerous dualism inherent in dividing the person between outward actions and inward motives. He is careful to explain that the Pauline categories of *flesh* and *spirit* are not coterminous with outward and inward:

Fleisch und geist mustu hie nicht also verstehen, das fleisch allein sei, was die unkeuscheit betreffe, und geist, was das innerliche im hertzen betreffe, sondern fleisch heist Paulus, wie Christus Johan. 3 alles was aus fleisch geporn ist, den gantzen menschen, mit leib und seele, mit vernunfft und allen synnen …. Widderumb, auch den geistlich heissist, der mit den aller euserlichsten wercken umbgehet, als Christus, da er der junger fuss wusch, und Petrus da er das schiff furet und fischet. Also, das fleisch sei ein mensch, der innwendig und ausswendig lebt und wirckt, das zu des fleischs nutz und zeitlichem leben dienet, Geist sei, der innwendig und ausswendig lebt und wirckt, das zu dem geist und zukunfftigem leben dienet.[27]

---

[22] Author's own translation.
[23] Wycliffe (Early), c.1384, from *The Bible in English Database*.
[24] From *The Bible in English Database*.   [25] From *The Bible in English Database*.
[26] 'Vorrede auf die Epistel S. Pauli an die Römer', 4, 6, 8, 10; *Works of Luther*, xxxv. 370.
[27] 'Vorrede auf die Epistel S. Pauli an die Römer', 12; *Works of Luther*, xxxv. 371, 372.

> Flesh and spirit you must not understand as though flesh is only that which has to do with
> unchastity and spirit is only that which has to do with what is inwardly in the heart. Rather, like
> Christ in John 3[: 6], Paul calls everything 'flesh' that is born of the flesh—the whole man, with
> body and soul, mind and senses—because everything about him longs for the flesh .... On the
> contrary, you should call him 'spiritual' who is occupied with the most external kind of works,
> as Christ was when he washed the disciples' feet [John 13: 1–14], and Peter when he steered his
> boat and fished. Thus 'the flesh' is a man who lives and works, inwardly and outwardly, in the
> service of the flesh's gain and of this temporal life. 'The spirit' is the man who lives and works,
> inwardly and outwardly, in the service of the Spirit and of the future life. (371, 372)

If the disjunction between outward works and inner disposition was so important, this
passage seems rather odd: spirit is, Luther asserts, both inward and outward. Luther was
attempting to elucidate the nuance of the Pauline original; for Paul *flesh* and *spirit* are not
body and soul but opposing wills. 'I know, that in me (that is, in my flesh,) dwelleth no
good thing', he admits. 'For to will is present with me: but *how* to perform that which is
good, I find not' (Romans 7: 18, KJB) (οἶδα γὰρ ὅτι οὐκ οἰκεῖ ἐν ἐμοί, τοῦτ' ἔστιν ἐν τῇ
σαρκί μου, ἀγαθόν· τὸ γὰρ θέλειν παράκειταί μοι, τὸ δὲ κατεργάζεσθαι τὸ καλὸν οὔ·). In
very simple terms, *flesh* is the will to sin, and *spirit* is the will to do good. What is in the
flesh 'dwells in me' (οἰκεῖ ἐν ἐμοί) as much as the good that is in the mind: 'For I delight
in the Lawe of God, after the inward man', Paul concludes. 'But I see another Lawe in my
members, warring against the Lawe of my minde, and bringing me into captivity to the
Law of sinne, which is in my members' (Romans 7: 23, KJB) (βλέπω δὲ ἕτερον νόμον ἐν
τοῖς μέλεσίν μου ἀντιστρατευόμενον τῷ νόμῳ τοῦ νοός μου καὶ αἰχμαλωτίζοντά με ἐν τῷ
νόμῳ τῆς ἁμαρτίας τῷ ὄντι ἐν τοῖς μέλεσίν μου.) The inward man of the spirit is opposed
by another man of the flesh who is also 'in' Paul, not an external force.

Luther knew that if this nuance was lost it could appear that he was promoting an inner
spiritual purity that has no regard for external good works, the inverse of the legalism he
sought to overturn. Understanding these words correctly was key to understanding not
only the whole of Romans, but the whole of scripture ('On solchen verstand diser wortter,
wirstu dise Epistel sanct Pauli, noch kein buch der heiligen schrifft nimer verstehen').[28] In
spite of this careful warning about not conflating the inward self with all that is spiritual,
however, Luther's *Preface* nevertheless cemented a link between inwardness and the key
Reformation doctrine of justification by faith.

William Tyndale borrowed Luther's link and embellished it in a paraphrase of Luther's
Preface to St Paul's Letter to the Romans printed separately in 1526 and included in
Tyndale's 1534 English New Testament.[29] Tyndale employs the metaphor of inwardness
sparingly in his translation of the New Testament, using the word 'inward' or 'inwardly'
only six times.[30] In his paraphrase of Luther's *Preface*, however, Tyndale repeatedly adds
inwardness to Luther's careful distinction between the heart and outward works. Where
Luther wrote of the redeemed Christian doing everything 'aus freiem herzten'—from a

---

[28] 'Vorrede auf die Epistel S. Pauli an die Römer', 12.

[29] *A Compendious Introduccion, Prologe or Preface un to the Pistle off Paul to the Romayns* (probably Worms, 1526); *Tyndale's New Testament.*

[30] In Matt. 7: 15, Luke 11: 39, 2 Cor. 4: 16 and 7: 5 Tyndale is translating straightforwardly from the Greek. In Luke 22: 15 he translates the emphatic Greek construction Ἐπιθυμίᾳ ἐπεθύμησα' as 'I have inwardly desired'; the KJB has 'With desire I have desired'. In 2 Cor. 7: 15 Tyndale uses 'his inward affection' for the bowels metaphor.

free heart—Tyndale freely translated, 'of a free heart, and of inward lust'. Where Luther had the law fulfilled when its works are done 'mit lust und liebe', Tyndale added 'love, lust and inward affection and delectation'. In several cases where Luther spoke of what was 'im Herzen' or came 'von Herzens Grund'—in the heart or from the bottom of the heart—Tyndale added 'inwardly' to clarify, and in one case he explained the concept of a free heart as one that will 'lust inwardly of [its] own accord'. '[L]iebe' became 'inwarde love', 'freud' became 'inward joy'.[31]

In addition to this seasoning of Luther's text with inwardness, Tyndale also interpolated several long lists of examples into Luther's *Preface*, turning Luther's theology into something more practical and polemical. Some of these revert Luther's (and Paul's) careful nuancing of *flesh* and *spirit* back towards the simpler distinction between outward show and inward truth. For example, to Luther's clarification of *flesh* and *spirit* Tyndale adds that a man is of the flesh if he is unredeemed in 'the very motions of his heart and mind, his learning, doctrine and contemplation of high things, his preaching, teaching and study in scripture, building of churches, founding of abbeys, giving of alms, mass, matins and whatsoever he doeth, though it seem spiritual and after the law of God'. Tyndale is bolder and clearer than Luther in his attack on specific deeds the church considered virtuous. He goes on to add that 'all the deeds of matrimony are pure spiritual, if they proceed of faith, and whatsoever is done within the laws of God, though it be wrought by the body, as the very wiping of shoes and such like, howsoever gross they appear outward'. Graphically, he includes the most bodily actions imaginable, sexual intercourse and menial physical labour, among things of the spirit 'if they proceed of faith' and are lawful. Tyndale's paraphrase thus has the effect of broadening the targets for reformation: not merely the church's teaching about faith and works, but the nature of what is considered sin and the structures of the church that enforced those teachings. In giving his own, radical examples of what is flesh and what is spirit, however, Tyndale shifts the focus from grace and faith to hypocrisy, the potential disjunction between inward purity and outward appearance. Sex and shoe polishing are of the spirit 'howsoever gross they appear outward', but 'contemplation of high things' may not be as spiritual as it seems.[32]

Tyndale reinforces this point when he adds to Luther's explanation of why it is impossible for a fallen human being to fulfil the law without grace. 'To abstain from adultery as concerning the deed can I do of mine own strength', Tyndale concedes, 'but not to desire in mine heart is as unpossible unto me as is to chose whether I will hunger or thirst, and yet so the law requireth'.[33] We have willpower over the 'uttewarde dede[s]' we commit, but not over the desires in our hearts, any more than we can control our need for food or drink.[34] Tyndale's example is almost the opposite of Paul's assertion that he does not have control over his members 'warring against the Lawe of my minde, and bringing me into captivity to the Law of sinne' (Romans 7: 23, KJB). Paul *cannot* stop his body committing sin

---

[31] 'Vorrede auf die Epistel S. Pauli an die Römer', 4, 6, 14, 16, 18; see also 'hymlichen zorn', 24; *Tyndale's New Testament*, 209, 215, 218, 217. The assertion that the law 'can not be fulfylled and satisfied / but with in warde love and affeccio[n] / so greately it can not be fulfilled with outeward dedes and werkes only' in 1526 becomes 'unfeigned love and affection' in 1534. *A Compendious Introduccion / prologe or preface*, a3[v].

[32] *Tyndale's New Testament*, 214.   [33] *Tyndale's New Testament*, 220.

[34] *A Compendious Introduccion*, B6[r].

even as he wills himself not to; Tyndale has control over his body but not over the desires of his mind. But this inversion nevertheless reflects the subtle distinction between flesh and spirit, outward and inward: Tyndale's mind is inward but of the flesh understood as the will to sin. His phrasing, however, links the passage to warnings against hypocritical difference between 'uttewarde dede' and inward motive, subtly shifting the focus from Paul's concern about conflicting human wills because he needs to assert that 'a man may do many things outwardly clean against his heart'.[35]

Tyndale was not making a distinctly new theological point by interpolating so much inwardness into his *Prologue to Romans*. He retained, in beautifully clear phrasing, Luther's warning against assuming that 'flesh were only that which pertaineth unto unchastity, and the spirit that which inwardly pertaineth to the heart: but Paul calleth flesh here … the whole man with life, soul, body, wit, will, reason and whatsoever he is or doth within and without'. None of Tyndale's additions of inwardness contradict this interpretation; nowhere does he suggest that inwardness is wholly good or of the spirit, and he notes that sinners 'hate the law inwardly', 'grudging inwardly against God'.[36] In some cases Tyndale added inwardness to Luther's *Preface* to evoke the Gospel passages on hypocrisy, but in most cases he was simply employing his gift for putting complex theologies into everyday language, and using a word that indicated emotions before the term existed. But Tyndale's translations were so influential that phrases that he picked up from the everyday language of his own time, such as 'pondered', became much more widespread and enduring than they might have been without his assistance.[37] In the *Prologue* to the Romans, the overwhelming influence of Luther's interpretation of Romans combined with Tyndale's equally pervasive influence on the English language to cement the link between inwardness and key doctrines of Reformation theology.

This developing link is most clearly evident in the marginal annotations to the Geneva New Testament, particularly if we compare different editions. The annotations to the 1560 Geneva New Testament tend to be fairly simple clarifications, often of a particular word or phrase rather than a whole verse. These notes only occasionally invoked inwardness when it was not part of the original text, usually in reference to hypocrisy, which was linked to inwardness in the verses from the Synoptic Gospels already discussed. For example the editors glossed 1 Thessalonians 2: 1, 'For ye your selves knowe, brethren, that our entrance in unto you was not in vaine', as 'Not in outwarde shew and in pompe, but in travel & in the feare of God'. The Greek κενὴ, 'empty', might refer to the purpose or result of the Apostles' visit, as well as its manner, but the 1560 Geneva note pushes the meaning towards hypocritical show. Similarly, the description of the unrighteous as 'welles without water, *and* cloudes caryed about with a tempest' in 2 Peter 2: 17 (Οὗτοί εἰσιν πηγαὶ ἄνυδροι καὶ ὀμίχλαι ὑπὸ λαίλαπος ἐλαυνόμεναι) is explained as clouds 'That have some appeara[n]ce outwarde, but within they are drie and barren, or at moste they cause but a tempest'. The gloss adds inwardness to the metaphor of a cloud being blown about without producing good rain. The next verse does condemn sinners for the hypocrisy of 'speaking swelling wordes of

---

[35] *Tyndale's New Testament*, 220.   [36] *Tyndale's New Testament*, 213–14, 215.
[37] David Daniell, *The Bible in English: Its History and Influence* (New Haven: Yale University Press, 2003), 136–9.

vanitie', but the Greek text of verse 17 does not suggest that the promising appearance of the clouds hides an inner emptiness, but rather that the force of the wind prevents the clouds from dropping their rain.[38]

In the 1560 Geneva Bible these instances are relatively uncommon. In the notes from Laurence Tomson's 1576 revision of the Geneva New Testament, however, the early modern paradigm of inwardness begins to subsume other biblical metaphors for the self.[39] Tomson penned his own annotations, mostly accessible interpretations of key passages, and included many more references to inwardness than in 1560. But Tomson also translated the annotations of Theodore Beza to his Latin New Testament of 1565, and printed these alongside his own.[40] Beza's notes summarize or interpret whole verses in pithy little statements of Reformation doctrine, and it is in these notes that inwardness appears again and again, to explain a wide range of theological concepts.

1 Corinthians 8: 7 should suffice as an example of these three different ways of annotating scripture. The text in 1560 is 'But everie man hathe not knowledge: for some having co[n]science of the idole, until this houre, eat as a thi[n]g sacrificed unto the idole, and so their conscience being weake, is defiled' (Ἀλλ᾽ οὐκ ἐν πᾶσιν ἡ γνῶσις· τινὲς δὲ τῇ συνηθείᾳ ἕως ἄρτι τοῦ εἰδώλου ὡς εἰδωλόθυτον ἐσθίουσιν, καὶ ἡ συνείδησις αὐτῶν ἀσθενὴς οὖσα μολύνεται). In part the need for the notes arises from what modern New Testament scholars think is probably an instance of eye-skip by early transcribers. In some manuscripts the first half of the verse uses συνηθείᾳ, 'custom', not συνειδήσει, 'conscience'. The most reliable modern English translation reads 'It is not everyone, however, who has this knowledge. Since some have become so accustomed to idols until now, they still think of the food they eat as food offered to an idol; and their conscience, being weak, is defiled'.[41] On the page, the 1560 Geneva notes for chapter 8 do not quite fill the margin, and the annotation for this verse is a typically concise and straightforward explanation of the very compact Greek: 'In that they thought yᵉ meat offerd up to the image, not to be pure, and therefore colde not eat it with a good co[n]science'. The note, like the Greek text, makes no mention of inwardness.

In comparison, Tomson's and Beza's notes to this chapter are so extensive that they take up more space on the page than the biblical text. Tomson's annotation paraphrases and clarifies the 1560 note, but glosses 'conscience of the idol' as 'the secret judgment' 'within' a person, even though the knowability or otherwise of conscience is not relevant to this verse. Tomson was drawing on Beza, who interprets the passage in two parts. The first note explains the confusing phrase, 'But everie man hathe not knowledge':

> The reason why that foloweth not is this: because there are many men which doe not knowe that which you knowe: Now the judgments of outward things depend not only upon your

---

[38] The accepted reading for this verse is now 'ὁμίχλαι', 'mists', not 'νεφέλαι', 'clouds'. The most reliable New Testament manuscripts have the former, but some manuscripts imported the latter reading from 1 Jude 12. In the sixteenth century 'νεφέλαι' was the accepted reading for 2 Peter 2: 17.

[39] *The New Testament of our Lord Jesus Christ, Translated out of Greeke by Theod. Beza*, tr. Laurence Thomson (London, 1577).

[40] Daniell, *The Bible in English*, 352–7.

[41] *New Revised Standard Version of the Bible*, National Council of the Churches of Christ (New York: Harper Collins, 2014).

conscience, but upon the consciences of them that behold you, and therefore your actions must be applied not only to your knowledge, but also to the ignoraunce of your brethren.

Beza explains the limitations of conscience in 'the judgments of outward things', a key point of Reformation doctrine that related to all manner of ceremonial actions, and came to underpin later understandings of freedom of conscience. Beza here favours a conservative interpretation: the fact that believers have varying degrees of knowledge does not justify each believer acting as he or she feels fit, but rather demands that a believer consider others' limitations as well as his or her own conscience.

In the second note, Beza continues his warning against elevating one's own conscience above the 'wavering conscience' of fellow believers:

> There are many which can not eate of things offered to Idols, but with a wavering conscience, because they thinke them to be uncleane: therefore if by thy example they enterprise to doe that which inwardly they thinke displeaseth God, their conscience is defiled with this eating, and thou hast bene the occasion of this mischiefe.

A believer might appear to act righteously, his outward actions in accordance with his conscience, but still cause a weaker believer to act hypocritically, against her inward judgement. None of these interpretations stray very far from the original or are especially polemical, but they do impose the early modern distinction between inward and outward on a Bible verse that frames the issue in terms of an interplay between conscience and food.

All of these annotators applied the principle of the analogy of faith, by which one passage of scripture could be used to interpret any other. Because Luther's interpretation of Romans was so key to Reformation doctrines, Romans was often used to interpret the entire New Testament, sometimes with startling results. Consider 1 Corinthians 10: 2, Paul's reminder to the Corinthians that their Jewish ancestors 'were all baptized unto Moses, in the cloude, and in the sea'. 1560 sets out the different interpretations of this difficult verse as concisely as possible: 'Moses being their guide, or minister, or as some read, the J[ews] were baptized unto Moses Lawe, others, by Moses'. Tomson offers a more strictly Calvinist interpretation: 'Al of them were baptized with the outward signe, but not in deede, wherewith god can not be charged, but they them selves'. Similarly, Jesus's prayer for his disciples in John 17: 19, 'And for their sakes sanctifie I my self, that they also may be sanctified thorugh the trueth', is paraphrased in the 1560 note as 'Which thi[n]g declareth that Christs holines is ours'. Tomson's note again introduces a narrower interpretation: 'The true and substantiall sanctification of Christ, is set against the outward [pu]rifyings'. In each case, Tomson applies the Protestant definition of a sacrament as an outward seal of an inward grace, drawn in part from Paul's distinction between inward and outward circumcision in Romans 2, to verses that that have nothing to do with inwardness or, in the case of John 17: 19, with sacraments.[42]

Beza applies another key doctrine from Romans, the Pauline concept of the law, to 1 Timothy 1: 9: 'the Law is not given unto a righteous man, but unto the lawless and disobedient'. In many ways this verse seems to say the opposite of Romans 7: 12: 'the Law *is* holie, and the commandement *is* holie, and just, & good'. The 1560 notes cross-reference these

---

[42] On sacraments, see Richard Hooker, *Of the Lawes of Ecclesiasticall Politie: The Fift Booke* (London, 1597), 128.

verses, and the annotation to 1 Timothy 1: 9 makes it clear that Paul is not saying one thing to the Romans and another to Timothy. The godly would be guided by the Spirit 'to do y^t willi[n]gly w^c the Law requireth, so y^t their godlie affection is to them a Law without further co[n]straint'. Beza's annotation is far more subtle. Like the Geneva editors, he warns that the righteous man 'giveth himself with all his heart to observe' the law, but he glosses the unrighteous as one concerned with debating trifles, 'a vaine babling of outward and curious matters'. The phrasing suggests Jesus's arguments with the Pharisees, such as in Luke 11, that employed a metaphorical distinction between inward and outward. But in trying to bring this verse in line with those passages and with Romans, Beza effectively makes this verse mean nearly the opposite of what it says, for it and the next verse go on to include a long list of sins, including stealing, manslaughter, and patricide, that are far from 'outward and curious matters'.

Beza's gloss to 1 John 3: 22 is equally distorting. The original implies that good works will ensure God's blessing on the believer: 'whatsover we aske', the writer promises, 'we receive of [God], because we kepe his com[m]andements, and do those things which are pleasing in his sight'. Beza explains this seeming contradiction by restating the subordination of works to God-given faith. 'The conclusion', he asserts, is 'that Faith in Christ and love, one towardes an other are things joyned together, and therefore the outward testimonies of sanctification must and do answere that inward testimonie of the Spirit given unto us'. Doing those things which are pleasing unto God is a sign that the believer has been saved by grace; if the inward and outward do not conform, there is no salvation, but inward faith must come first. In annotating this verse and 1 Timothy 1: 9 Beza uses the distinction between inward and outward to wrestle the scripture text into line with Reformation doctrine.

These are just a few of the many, many uses of the inward paradigm in the Geneva Bible annotations, but even these few examples should suffice to demonstrate that, from being a rare, and slightly obscure, metaphor in a handful of New Testament passages, inwardness became increasingly linked with nearly all of the New Testament and most of the key doctrines of the Reformation, including the Pauline distinction between the flesh and the world, Christian freedom in things indifferent, sacramental theology, the law and grace, and salvation by faith rather than works. In other words, inwardness as a metaphor came to bear increasingly heavy doctrinal weight, and became integral to so many different doctrines that it took on many subtle variations of meaning. And because the Geneva Bible was so widely read and so influential, those many and varied understandings of inwardness took root in a wide variety of writers, not only theologians but also devotional poets and prose writers of all kinds.

What does this proliferation of Protestant inwardness mean for scholars reading the early modern English Bible and literary texts that invoke the metaphor of inwardness? First, it means we need to be very, very careful of assuming that inwardness is the same as introspection, or that it indicates a development of interest in the self. Inwardness could be both positive and negative, turned towards God or turned towards sin. As a metaphor it encouraged self-denial as much as self-knowledge, a self-critical fear of hypocrisy as much as a self-involved desire to explore one's inner landscape. We can glimpse the limits of inwardness in interpretations of Luke 17: 20b–21, 'The kingdome of God cometh not with observation. Neither shall they say, Loe here, or loe there: for behold, the kingdome of God is within you' (KJB). The annotators, even in the usually reserved King James, are all quick to gloss παρατηρήσεως ('observation', used only in this verse in the New Testament) as 'outwarde shew, or majestie' (1560) and ἐντὸς ὑμῶν as 'among you', since the 'you' is plural, although the Greek ἐντὸς elsewhere means 'within'. In addition, Tyndale, the 1560 Geneva, and Tomson all elaborate on exactly what is within you, lest a reader mistakenly assume that God is immanent in every believer.[43] 1560 offers two interpretations: 'Either by reason of the worde of God, wᶜ is received by faith, or that yᵉ Messias whome thei soght, as absent, is now present, eve[n] within their owne dores, and yet they knowe hi[m] not, John 1.11'. The first is an acceptable Reformed understanding of the kingdom within a believer, the Word received by faith; the second the more literal sense of Jesus physically among his disciples. Tomson opts conservatively for this second interpretation: the Messiah is not absent, but 'is amongest you, in the middes of you'. Tyndale sees the verse not as a stumbling block, but as an opportunity for a profound little statement of Reformed doctrine: 'The kingdom of God is to love God with all thine heart, and to put thy whole trust in him according to the covenant, made in Christ: and for Christ's sake to love thy neighbour as Christ loved thee. And all this is within thee'. What is within the Christian is not God Godsself, but the ability to turn to God, through grace. For post-Reformation English writers, this inner turning to God is also a turning away from the disordered inner landscape of the fallen self.

Secondly, as scholarly readers we need to take careful note of the range of subtle variations of meaning invoked when early modern people wrote of inwardness. What unites all of these variations is that that which is inward 'is most secret & hidden', as Beza puts it in his note to 1 Peter 2: 9, and cannot be known to any but God. This distinction is subtly present in some of the key Bible passages, such as 1 Peter 3: 3, or Matthew 7: 15, but it was particularly live in sixteenth-century Europe, when Reformation scholars scrambled to discern how they should act in the face of religious persecution. Did outward—visible—worship matter if what was inward, or hidden, was correct? Reformation commentaries on the book of Daniel, for example, explored this matter at length, and of course Elizabeth was said to have declared that she did not wish to make windows into men's souls.[44] The inverse of this fear of persecution was the Reformers' outrage at the hypocrisy of worship and deeds that were, as Tyndale put it, 'outwardly clean' but done 'against [the] heart'.

In England this context of persecution and corruption came to intersect with a number of other cultural trends, such as a suspicion of secrecy and solitude, in the metaphor of inwardness. As a result, we can best read inwardness as an empty signifier, a term which points towards the limits of signification by signifying a lack within the system of signification itself. In other words, an empty signifier is a word, such as love or freedom, that people use in a variety of subtle and even contradictory ways, all the while believing they agree on its general meaning.[45] It is the nature of empty signifiers to disguise their emptiness as universality: for every scholar or poet who points up the ambiguity of love, community, freedom—or, in early modern times, inwardness—there are many who believe that a shared awareness of these concepts is inherent in their culture, or even in humankind as a

---

[43] Luke Timothy Johnson, *The Gospel of Luke* (Collegeville, Minn.: Liturgical Press, 1991), 263 note to verse 21. Johnson agrees that 'ἐντὸς' should mean 'among' when coupled with the plural 'ὑμῶν'.

[44] George Joye, *The Exposicion of Daniel the Prophete* ([Antwerp], 1545), 84ᵛ; Jean Calvin, *Commentaries of that Divine John Calvine, upon the Prophet Daniell*, tr. Anthony Gilby (London, 1570), 98ʳ–99ᵛ; Andrew Willet, *Hexapla in Danielem* (London, 1610), 180–1.

[45] Ernesto Laclau, *Emancipations* (London: Verso, 1996), 36–46.

whole. Inwardness operates as such an empty signifier in Reformation discourse, allowing theologians, poets, and lay writers to appear to agree on a uniform interpretation of scripture drawn from Luther's interpretation of Romans. In the very margins of that scripture text these early translators of the Bible into English began a crucial debate about the limits of the hidden, unknowable self in a material world that can be seen and therefore controlled by authority.

FURTHER READING

Betteridge, Maurice. 'The Bitter Notes: The Geneva Bible and its Annotations'. *Sixteenth Century Journal*, 14 (1983): 41–62.

Daniell, David. *The Bible in English: Its History and Influence* (New Haven: Yale University Press, 2003).

Hamel, Christopher de. *The Book: A History of the Bible* (London: Phaidon Press, 2005).

Gribben, Crawford. 'Deconstructing the Geneva Bible: The Search for a Puritan Poetic'. *Literature and Theology*, 14 (2000): 1–16.

CHAPTER 40

....

EARLY MODERN DAVIDS: FROM SIN TO CRITIQUE

....

YVONNE SHERWOOD

It is commonly believed that his adultery with Bathsheba, the murder of Uriah, and the numbering of the people, are the only faults with which [David] can be charged: but this is a great mistake; for there are many other things in his life which deserve censure ...

(Pierre Bayle, 'David', *Dictionnaire historique et critique*[1])

Let us say that critique is historically biblical.

(Michel Foucault, 'What is Critique?'[2])

In the past decade, scholars in the humanities have set about interrogating the two things that, previously, could be taken as given—indeed as the very foundations of our academic labours. There has been a burst of work examining the anthropology and genealogy of what is called, loosely, 'the secular' and, relatedly, 'critique'.[3] These enquiries have often led to the Bible and the seventeenth century. They have led us to this particular moment in what is called, revealingly, 'early (nascent?) modernity', because the English seventeenth century has played a crucial role in the conceptual and historical formation of 'the secular'.

---

[1] Bayle, 'David', in *A General Dictionary, Historical and Critical* (London, 1734–41), iv. 537.

[2] Michel Foucault, 'What is Critique', in James Schmidt (ed.), *What is Enlightenment? Eighteenth Century Answers and Twentieth Century Questions* (Berkeley, Calif.: University of California Press, 1996), 385.

[3] See e.g. Vincent P. Pecora, *Secularization and Cultural Criticism* (Chicago: University of Chicago Press, 2006), and Talal Asad, Wendy Brown, Judith Butler, and Saba Mahmood, *Is Critique Secular? Blasphemy, Injury and Free Speech* (Berkeley, Calif.: Townsend Center for the Humanities/University of California Press, 2009).

This century has supplied various watersheds 'between theist pre-modernity and secular modernity' from the Civil War to the Restoration to the Glorious Revolution of 1688.[4] In an automatic reflex pointed out, and repented of, by historians such as Tim Harris, Paul Seward, and Mark Goldie, the century has traditionally been sliced into two (near) halves: the excessively *religious* first half up to the Restoration, followed by the clearly *secular* recoil from the excesses of Puritan godly politics.[5] Traditionally, the narrative of progressive secularization has been bound up with the political story of 'divine right' becoming extinct, like the dodo. (Sensing that it could contribute an apposite chronological metaphor, the dodo obligingly chose the 1680s to kick up its feet, or flippers, or whatever dodos used to have on the end of their legs.) Much hinges, traditionally, on the death of divine right and the birth of the ostensibly 'secular' politics of Lockean constitutionalism. The making-secular of the political world is connected to the traditional reading of the 1688 Revolution as a cautionary tale of 'How Divine Right Went Wrong'.[6]

The theoretical problematization of secularization has led inexorably to the Bible and religion, because secularization is the other of religion, forever haunted by its ghosts. As Hans Blumenberg puts it, intrinsic to the logic of the secular is the notion that 'Something was absent, which is supposed to have been present before' and were that something to disappear entirely 'one would cease to understand the term "secularization"'—or indeed critique.[7] Offering a provocative preliminary definition of critique as 'the art of not being governed so much', Foucault explores how critique, which always 'exists in relation to something other than itself', could only emerge in contrast to a state of submission to authority: iconically, religious authority.[8] The natural prologues to critique are Christian confession—the state of letting oneself be 'governed … directed towards his salvation, by someone to whom he is bound in a total, and at the same time meticulous and detailed, relation of obedience' (384)—and all that is implied, for Kant, in the verb *leiten*: a verb that belongs, primarily, to the field of theology and that means 'to govern, rule, guide, or lead' (386).

Histories of critique lead us to the Bible, and through the Bible. Functioning like the axiomatic BC and AD, 'befores' and 'afters' describing different modes of relation to the Bible are used to define the essence of critique. Foucault writes:

> At a time when the governing of men was essentially a spiritual art or an essentially religious practice linked to the authority of a church, to the magisterium of Scripture, not wanting to be governed in that way was essentially seeking in Scripture a relationship other than the one that was linked to the operating function of God's teaching. To not want to be

---

[4] See Karl Polanyi, *The Great Transformation* (New York: Farrar & Rhinehart, 1944); J. C. D. Clark, *English Society 1688–1832: Ideology, Social Structure and Political Practice during the Ancien Regime* (Cambridge: Cambridge University Press, 1985), 14.

[5] Tim Harris, 'Revising the Restoration', in Tim Harris, Paul Seaward, and Mark Goldie (eds), *The Politics of Religion in Restoration England* (Oxford: Basil Blackwell, 1990), 1–28; Mark Goldie, 'The Civil Religion of James Harrington', in Anthony Pagden (ed.), *The Languages of Political Theory in Early Modern Europe* (Cambridge: Cambridge University Press, 1987), 198.

[6] Gerald Straka, 'The Final Phase of Divine Right Theory in England, 1688–1702', *English Historical Review*, 77 (1962): 639.

[7] Hans Blumenberg, *The Legitimacy of the Modern Age*, tr. Robert M. Wallace (Cambridge, Mass.: MIT Press, 1985), 4.

[8] Foucault, 'What is Critique?', 384, 383.

governed was a certain way of refusing, challenging, limiting … the ecclesiastic magisterium. It was a return to Scripture, it was a question of what is authentic in Scripture, of what was actually written in Scripture, it was a question concerning the kind of truth Scripture tells, how to have access to this truth of Scripture in Scripture and perhaps despite what is written, until one arrives at the ultimately very simple question: Was Scripture true? In short, from Wycliffe to Pierre Bayle, I believe that critique was developed in an important, but of course not exclusive, part in relation to Scripture. *Let us say that critique is historically biblical.* (385)

As an academic pilgrim following in the footsteps of scholars such as Debora Shuger and Jonathan Sheehan, I am less interested in versions of the Bible than in the changing shapes, forms, and limits of 'the biblical'. I am interested in the cultural and political *edges* of the Bible: the sense of what is inside and what is outside Christian scriptures. I am interested in the mobile limits of the thinkable in relation to what a Bible might, and *must*, mean. Moving beyond the old models of 'Revelation' engaged in a death struggle with 'Reason' (with Reason moving in on Religion from a putative space outside Religion), this chapter explores how *effects of secularization* arise from strategic rearrangements in the Bible and changing modes of engagement with biblical texts.

In previous work, I have described a Bible that became something of a public commonplace in the late seventeenth century: a Bible that I have called, by way of shorthand, the Liberal or Lockean Bible.[9] This Bible proclaims that the true Christian Bible and its God are fundamentally allergic to theocracy, divine right, or dictatorial literalism. It insists that the Christian scriptures have never existed in an exceptional relationship to human institutions, such as government and law. I use the present tense deliberately. This three-hundred-year-old version of the Christian Bible, equated with the very essence of 'the biblical', is still very much in evidence today. The whole purpose of the Liberal Bible was to show that the Christian Bible was not surprised by new constitutional arrangements. Rather it sponsored them, and even generated them. In Locke's response to Sir Robert Filmer, the first words in Genesis became, effectively: 'And God said "Let there be *rights*" and there were rights'. This announcement by a hands-off deity was followed by a kenotic self-sacrifice of scripture. The Bible withdrew from the scene of politics and facilitated, *from within the biblical*, the separation of 'religion' and 'politics' as independent domains.

The Liberal Bible is not a version, nor a translation, nor even a text. It is more an abdication from the Bible as text. Just like the Christ who, though 'in the form of God' did not 'count equality a thing to be grasped, but emptied himself, taking the form of a servant' (Philippians 2: 6, 7), this Bible shows how the Bible and its God habitually humble themselves and graciously devolve power. Locke's *First Treatise* is the perfect illustration of Foucault's brief sketch of the genealogy of critique. In it, the Christian Bible models forms of 'refusing', 'challenging', and 'limiting' dominion, but as a movement from within the Bible and as an expression of the Bible's own desire. The Bible itself tutors us in the 'art of not being governed so much'.

---

[9] See Sherwood, 'The God of Abraham and Exceptional States: The Early Modern Rise of the Whig/Liberal Bible', *Journal of the American Academy of Religion*, 76 (2008): 312–43; and *Biblical Blaspheming: Trials of the Sacred for a Secular Age* (Cambridge: Cambridge University Press, 2012), 303–32.

I. Inner-Biblical and Traditional Resources for 'Critique'

I want to begin to flesh out Foucault's wager: 'Let us say that critique is historically biblical'. My argument is this: rather than encroaching on the biblical from the outside, *effects of critique* were produced by putting new spin on well-worn inner- and extra-biblical devices for managing the Bible's own complexity. In a moment, I will explore how an early modern critique of King David was created as authors extended traditional expositions, and biblical confessions, of David's sin. But first, I want to contextualize this move within other pre-modern devices—some biblical, some extra-biblical—that were in place to relativize and 'criticize' parts of the Bible long before the modern invention of critique.

There are good reasons why these myriad devices have rarely been discussed or named. Because we want to maintain a clear contrast with 'secular', 'modern' times when the Bible became famously divided and problematic, we are prone to exaggerate how easily the Bible was consumed by authors and readers in more pious eras.[10] And due to the segregation of the humanities (biblical scholars in one corner, early modern scholars in the other) those who work on early modern Bibles rarely access, or even imagine, the difficulties experienced on the *inside* of the Bible by the original authors, compilers, and annotators of the text.

The Bible is a composite archive: a 'box containing heterogeneous materials'.[11] It was not written by 'authors' commissioned by Oxford University Press for a (handbook?) project called 'The Bible', or (as Robert Alter quips) 'the Iron Age Equivalents of Flaubert or Henry James'.[12] The largest portion of the Bible that we know as the Old Testament was written in the Babylonian, Persian, and Hellenistic periods (c.600–200 BC), prior to the invention of 'book', 'author', or 'character' as organizational devices. The writers were artisans rather than authors: a trained administrative class. At times, the Bible is acutely aware of itself as an unsteady syncretistic adventure. Though there are clear hallmarks of shaping ideological agendas—for example in the revision of Kings in 2 Chronicles—there is also clear evidence of competing traditions coexisting, awkwardly, 'cheek by jowl'.[13] Chronicles' radical rewriting of Kings suggests a desire to creatively rework Kings and then discard the earlier work: entirely acceptable practice in a context where the work of textual reproduction involved transcription, compilation, integration, expansion, and supplementation. But, surprisingly, the two versions still coexist, allowing us to glimpse an inner-biblical example of an 'original' and a 'reproduction' (from which we could never have deduced much about the original, had it not survived). The two versions persist in the biblical corpus, as do

---

[10] For important counterpoints to these tendencies, see Debora K. Shuger, *The Renaissance Bible: Scholarship, Sacrifice and Subjectivity* (Berkeley, Calif.: University of California Press, 1994); and Brian Cummings, *The Literary Culture of the Reformation: Grammar and Grace* (Oxford: Oxford University Press, 2002).

[11] Karel van der Toorn, *Scribal Culture and the Making of the Hebrew Bible* (Cambridge, Mass.: Harvard University Press, 2007), 15. Several of the observations in this chapter are indebted to Toorn.

[12] Robert Alter, cover notes on Toorn, *Scribal Culture*.

[13] Morton Smith, *Palestinian Parties and the Politics that Shaped the Old Testament* (London: SCM, 1988), 77.

doublets, or triplets, of the same base narrative, competing religious-political visions, and conflicting legal codes. Particularly surprising is the tendency to keep, rather than delete, the memory of the other older brothers/tribes, displaced by Israel/Judah but remembered in the archive.[14] Evidence for and even celebration of intermarriage mixes awkwardly with campaigns for purity. Rites of sacrifice, *and* their repudiation or revision, collide.

As Jan Assmann points out, a written archive creates a host of problems unknown to oral cultures: 'conscious variation in the sense of a controlled deviation can only be found in a written culture, where a text can be compared with an original version'. The storehouse of writing soon 'encompasses *the age-old, out-of-the-way, and discarded*. In contrast to the collective, bonding memory, it includes the *noninstrumentalizable, heretical, subversive and disowned*'.[15] These truths are manifest on the surface of the Bible. Moreover—and this is a fact hardly ever remembered in relation to the Bible—the 'book' that we now know as the Bible already incorporates elements that some of its contributors felt to be well past their use-by date. When the author of Daniel attempted to interpret the old, already 'scriptural', prophet Jeremiah, 'failure and incomprehension' was the result.[16] The corpus clearly includes texts that were illegible to other biblical authors as well as elements that they would have liked to have discarded, and maybe would have, had they been able to avail themselves of the resources of censorship or had there been a controlling 'they' presiding over the production of the 'book'.

Late moderns tend to exaggerate the ability of the authors, editors, and pre-modern interpreters of the Bible to live with, harmonize, or be oblivious to difference. Pre-modern interpreters lived in the eternal time of typology, we assume. Authors and editors were unperturbed about allowing conflicting accounts of the law or variants of the same base narrative to coexist. We tend to imagine 'the Bible' and 'the pre-modern Bible' in particular as confident structures with no idea of the distinctly modern explosions that are coming. Gathering the epiphany of difference, time, and history into the epiphany of 'the secular', we imagine that differentiation began with the rise of historical criticism; the distinction between the Jesus of the Gospels and the 'historical Jesus'; and the shattering of Mosaic authorship into the alphabetized shards 'J', 'E', 'D', and 'P'.

In fact it is hard to imagine *any* act of reading that does not enlist the thoroughly traditional idea of two Bibles: an ideal Bible and a bible incarnate, or a Bible upper and lower case. Developing an ancient and thoroughly traditional split between the ideal 'Torah' and Torah incarnate, sixteenth-century writers regularly imagined actual bibles in tension with, and presided over by, an ideal Bible. These distinctions are mirrored within the Bible. This sprawling corpus has in-built devices for remembering and forgetting, contextualizing, distinguishing between times, and amending and reinterpreting texts that one would rather disown, qualify, forget, or mark as 'age-old' or 'out-of-the-way': belonging to a different time and space.

---

[14] Cf. Sherwood, 'The Perverse Commitment to Overcrowding and Doubling in Genesis: Implications for Ethics and Politics', in Catherine Dell and Paul Joyce (eds), *Biblical Interpretation and Method: Essays in Honour of Professor John Barton* (Oxford: Oxford University Press, 2012), 311–28.

[15] Jan Assmann, *Religion and Cultural Memory*, tr. Rodney Livingstone (Stanford, Calif.: Stanford University Press, 2006), 114, 27 (my italics).

[16] Hugh Pyper, 'Reading in the Dark: Zechariah, Daniel and the Difficulty of Scripture', *Journal for the Study of the Old Testament*, 29 (2005): 492.

In Matthew 19: 8–9, Jesus explains that 'Moses allowed you to divorce your wives, but from the beginning it was not so'. He explains divorce by setting up a distinction between times: the time of original truth; the time of concession to human weakness; and the time of truth's restoration. Jeremiah's God stridently corrects an alternative inner-biblical tradition centred on the temple/tabernacle and sacrifice. When he brought the people out of the land of Egypt, he 'did *not* speak to them or command them concerning burnt offerings and sacrifices', God maintains. He only gave a general and conveniently open command to 'obey' and 'listen to [his] voice' (Jeremiah 7: 22, 23). Alternative biblical traditions, giving more detailed content to God's speech, are the result of a mishearing—or worse. Jeremiah does not blanch at accusing rival groups of falsification. Seemingly denouncing the 'rediscovered' book of Deuteronomy as a forgery, his pen locks swords with the 'lying pen of the scribes' (Jeremiah 8: 8).

These examples show what later interpreters did with elements of the tradition they would have liked to disown—or that disowned them. (The most frequently corrected passages are those that sealed off any hope of redemption.) They were not deleted. Rather, they were *relegated or exported to other times and spaces that remain inside the biblical text.*

It is fascinating to watch this mobile corpus revise and redistribute itself, while trying to maintain a sense of truth, *more or less* (in all senses of the phrase). Some statements, traditions, and practices are located close to here and now. Some are pushed away into the 'there' (foreign influence, or a truth that does not apply to Israel), or 'then'. Truth—or rather core truth—moves. In the redistribution some elements become *more* than truth: superfluous. Some things become *less* than truth, waiting for the better truth to come. But it is all roughly the same truth. The process of redistribution is not controlled by one all-surveying managerial eye. The fact of canonization holds the whole together as a 'rule': an implied overarching principle that 'This is all truth, more or less'.

Post-biblical interpretation extrapolated these devices. It developed a panoply of resources for preserving—by revising—sense. When the biblical God annotated earlier speeches, or put them in the past tense, he anticipated the typological manipulation of time; the principle that, as Augustine put it '*symbols (figurae) … may change with time much as the form of a verb may change according to its tense*'.[17] Like a living language, the book of God contains old words that have fallen out of common usage, but that still remain 'in' the language: useful only if rightly (re)read. In the syncopated times of typology, truth is distributed to different levels of intensity and different tenses. Some texts and practices are in the past preterite. They are over and done with. Others extend, intensely, into the future and the present.

Already, inside the Bible, we find the idea that God spoke things, and biblical authors wrote things, for reasons other than truth as such. This develops into the principle of accommodation or *sygkatabasis*/condescension, based on the principle: *scriptura*

[17] Stephen D. Benin, 'Sacrifice as Education in Augustine and Chrysostom', *Church History: Studies in Christianity and Culture*, 52 (1983): 12. Benin is glossing Augustine, *Contra Faustus*. 19.16–17 (CSEL 25.1.512–14).

humane loquitur ('The scriptures speak the language of man'). Understood as a 'loving gesture of divine considerateness' modelled on the incarnation, accommodation presumed that 'holy scripture frames itself to our manner of conceiving and speaking'.[18] It allowed certain problematic texts to be read as concessions to context, foreign influence, weakness, or sin. In its thoroughly traditional, orthodox forms, it allowed Calvin to demur from 'Moses's homely and uncultivated style' or to judge that, were it not for the miracles, the Flood narrative would be 'cold, and trifling, and ridiculous'.[19] Accommodation has always been a convenient mechanism for managing disappointment with scripture by calling on devices like the 'puerility of [the] audience', God/scripture's self-sacrificing withdrawal for the sake of human comprehension, or the truism that the Bible only ever aspired to perfection in the 'things of salvation', never aspiring to truth in 'philosophy, cosmography, geometry and similar arts'.[20]

Long before the advent of historical criticism, accommodation opened scripture to the vagaries of time and context. It permitted the sources of biblical letters to be pluralized so that origins could be other than divine. Accommodation allowed certain parts of the tradition to be confined, closer to the 'then' and 'there' than the 'here' and 'now'. Thus parochialized, and localized, these truths were seen as overshooting truth (as 'more than truth'), or falling short of truth (as 'less than truth'). But they could still function (vaguely) as 'truth, more or less'. Ways of thinking the relation between the testaments extended practices already in operation in the Old Testament. In a complex model of time and space management, the Old Testament—no less than three-quarters of the canon—became continuous, even synonymous, with the New, while at the same time being localized and parochialized as something 'past'. According to the New logic, the Old Testament must be Christian through and through, *but also of a time before the Christian and also something else.* In the attempt to give radical new spin to the Old traditions, Paul patented two flexible devices that gave immense poetic license to future generations: the living 'spirit' versus the dead 'letter'; and the 'natural law' in a potentially ambiguous relation to the letter of the text (Romans 2: 14–15; 2: 29; 2 Corinthians 3: 1–7).

Built into the biblical corpus were devices for exceeding and 'critiquing', or qualifying, its own letters. In the period that we know as early modernity, writers began to manipulate these resources so as to create what we can think of as *effects of 'Reason'*, or effects of critique. These appeared to emerge from the book of Revelation, sponsored and supported by it. A critical, 'modern' demystification of scripture as an all-too-human production was not presented as an alien invader, so much as an extension of biblical tropes and thoroughly orthodox interpretative machines.

---

[18] Amos Funkenstein, *Theology and the Scientific Imagination from the Middle Ages to the Seventeenth Century* (Princeton: Princeton University Press, 1989), 213; Robert C. Hill, *Reading the Old Testament in Antioch* (Leiden: Brill, 2005), 36–7, 85.

[19] John Calvin, *Commentaries on the first book of Moses called Genesis*, tr. John King (Edinburgh: Edinburgh Printing Co., 1847), 86, 257.

[20] Bartolomé de Las Casas, *In Defense of the Indians*, ed. and tr. Stafford Poole (DeKalb, Ill.: Northern Illinois University Press, 1992), 146.

II. Reformation Davids (The David of Samuel Safely Subordinated to Psalms)

At the heart of these transitions was King David, the man after God's own heart (1 Samuel 13: 14; Acts 13: 22).[21] As Foucault points out, the question of critique is intimately related to politics; critique is 'the art of not being governed so much'. The early modern fates of David amply demonstrate this tight relation, since the King is the focus for renegotiating the Bible's relation to politics and critique. In the Civil War period, the biblical king became the focus for a mutiny against divine right sovereignty staged strategically (and relatively diplomatically) from within the Bible. David's double election by God and people in 2 Samuel 5: 1–5 became a proof-text for asserting that sovereigns are appointed by, and in some sense accountable to, the people (rather than being enclosed in a mystical holy trinity comprising God, the Law, and themselves). In *Killing Noe Murder* (1657) Edward Sexby (masquerading as 'William Allen') strategically manipulated the fact that 'David was appointed king by [Samuel], but was afterwards, after Saul's death, confirmed by the people of Judah, and seven years after by the Elders of Israel, the people's deputies' to insist that God leaves the 'confirmation and ratification of the choice to the people themselves'.[22] Later in the 1680s the Whig lawyers who were so active in creating and enforcing the (gentle) Liberal Bible, used the same text to establish a compromise agreement between *vox populi* and *vox dei*. 'David was made King by God's immediate appointment, yet he himself called all Israel together at Hebron, and there they made a covenant with him', insisted Sir Robert Atkyns, attempting to curb the kingly abuse of the dispensing power in the case of Godden versus Hales.[23]

A study of the fates of David allows us to explore the intimate relationship between governance, critique, and the biblical that Foucault gestures to, but does not develop. The effect of critique emerged as interpreters tinkered with the traditional balance between the David of the book of Samuel and the David of the Psalms, and manipulated the traditional device of accommodation and doctrines of original sin. More specifically, it emerged as readers (now nascent 'critics') renegotiated the traditional relationship between two key moments: David's Bathsheba-Gate (2 Samuel 11) where the king is caught red-handed offending against no less than two core commandments (adultery and murder); and the psalm that Christians traditionally read as the scene of his repentance and rehabilitation: Psalm 51.

As is well known, the Reformation located the palpitating heart of the Old Testament in the book of Psalms, understood as 'the very hidden treasure of [the] heart's feelings',

---

[21] On competing interpretations of David and Saul, see the chapters by Kim Ian Parker and Anne Lake Prescott in this volume.

[22] William Allen (i.e. Edward Sexby), *Killing Noe Murder: Briefly Discourst in Three Quaestions* (1657), in David Wootton (ed.), *Divine Right and Democracy: An Anthology of Political Writing in Stuart England* (Indianapolis: Hackett, 2003), 365.

[23] Sir Robert Atkyns, 'An Enquiry into the Power of Dispensing with the Penal Statutes', in T. B. Howell (ed.), *A Complete Collection of State Trials and Proceedings for High Treason and Other Crimes and Misdemeanours, from the Earliest Period to the Year 1783* (London: Hansard, 1816–28), xi, case 350, cols 1200–47 (col. 1213). For the case of Godden versus Hales, see Sherwood, 'The God of Abraham'.

indeed, the recording of the voice, soul, and spirit of David.[24] The increased emphasis on authorship and antiquity in the Hellenistic period had long since turned the psalms into the Psalms of David. The already vivified sense of persona was given a new intensity in the Reformation through the aesthetics and theology of print. As Manfred Schneider argues, the Reformation invested print with the 'absolute visual spirituality of scripture' and the belief that one could see through the 'blackness of the printed letters' to the 'psycho-gram in the beyond of letters'.[25] Like the Pauline letters, the Psalms offered a rare and pre-cious instance of the first person, inside the Bible. They could be read as the equivalent of Protestant emblem books, such as Daniel Cramer's *Emblemata sacra* of 1617. As biblical 'heart' texts such as Jeremiah 31: 33 ('I will put my law in their inward parts and write it in their hearts') and Ezekiel 36: 26 ('A new heart I will give you, and a new spirit will I put within you, and I will take away the stony heart out of your flesh, and I will give you a heart of flesh'),[26] formed the basis of a heart-shaped Protestant emblematics (Figure 40.1), so the words of David promised a seductive cardiographics of the 'man after God's own heart'.

As Luther gushed, the Psalms 'give you not only the outward David, but, more expres-sively still, the inner David; and that more descriptively than he could do it himself, if he were to talk with you face to face'.[27] By contrast, 'In other scriptures and histories ... the works and bodily exercises only of the saints are described: you have very few histories which give you the words, expressions, and sighs of the saints, which are the indexes of the state of their minds'. Luther's target is overtly extra-scriptural (the Catholic *Lives*) but perhaps covertly inner-scriptural. 'Other scriptures and histories' may refer to other scriptures and histories outside the Bible or other corners of scripture far less 'instru-mentalizable' than the Psalms. The taciturn Old Testament is infamously parsimonious with the first person and problematically sparing with the precious quality of speech. And for Luther, drawing on Galen and Aristotle, speech was what 'differentiate[d] man from other animals', so much so that a 'dumb man', is like a 'lifeless post' or a 'brute beast' (6). Thus Luther exclaims: 'I had much rather hear David or any such eminent saint *speak* than merely see the works or exercises of his body; so much rather would I know the inmost thoughts of David's heart, and the inward conflicts and struggles of his faith' (8). It is hard to imagine that he is not casting a sideways glance at the David of the books of Samuel and Chronicles: a patchwork composite of (often conflicting) narratives, presented in the third person. Whereas the David of 1 Chronicles is a whitewashed pietist, the David of Samuel is more mixed, and compromised. Though chosen, he worships other gods and he has, at the most conservative estimate, ten concubines and eight wives.[28]

In Reformation tactics of biblical resource management, the Psalms served as a space for subsuming, transforming, and mediating other parts of the Old Testament that

---

[24] Martin Luther, *A Manual of the Book of Psalms: Or, the Subject-Content of All the Psalms by Martin Luther*, tr. Henry Cole (London: Seeley & Burnside, 1837), 6. (Henceforth, Luther, *Psalms*.)

[25] Cf. Manfred Schneider, 'Luther with McLuhan', in Hent de Vries and Samuel Weber (eds), *Religion and Media* (Stanford, Calif.: Stanford University Press, 2001), 198–215, esp. 210–11 and 213.

[26] See Barbara Kiefer Lewalski, *Protestant Poetics and the Seventeenth Century English Lyric* (Princeton: Princeton University Press, 1979), 102, 179–212. Compare Michael Bath's discussion of 'biblical emblematics' in *Speaking Pictures: English Emblem Books and Renaissance Culture* (London: Longman, 1994), 160–95.

[27] Luther, *Psalms*, 6.

[28] 2 Sam. 3: 2–5 and 5: 13–15. The catalogue of wives in 2 Sam. 3: 2–5 misses Michal and Bathsheba.

EMBLEMAT. SACR. 24

XXIV. EMBLEM.

Elegi te in camino paupertatis.

. *Eſa.* 48. 10.

Jch wil dich außerwehlet machen im Ofen deß Elendes.

PROBOR

X XIV.

Vrit & exercet Dominus nos igne camini:
Sis probus & conſtans, atque probandus eris.

XXV. EM-

FIGURE 40.1 'Probor', in Daniel Cramer, *Societas Jesu et Roseae crucis vera: Hoc est, Decades quator emblematum sacrorum ex sacra Scriptura, de dulcissimo nomine et cruce Jesu Christi* (Frankfurt: Nicolai Hoffmann, 1617).

'transcend[ed] the horizon of a knowledge of the past that [could] be put to immediate use', and that one suspects that the Reformers would have rather liked to 'disown' or 'discard'.[29] Calvin famously used David as a 'glass' for his own spiritual biography.[30] He never quite got round to publishing sermons on Samuel, but of course wrote copiously on Psalms. This strategically lop-sided relationship between Psalms and the historical books

---

[29] Assmann, *Religion and Cultural Memory*, 27; my italics.
[30] See John Calvin, *A Commentary on the Psalms of David* (Oxford: A. Talboys, 1840), i, pp. viii–xii.

was repeated, in microcosm, around the pageant of David's sin. Psalm 51 was used to subsume, transcend, and forgive the unexpected (and unwanted) testimony of 2 Samuel 11. Through a careful application of the balm of psalm, the horrific double sin against the Ten Commandments could be 'purged with hyssop' and 'wash[ed] … whiter than snow' (Psalm 51: 4). The mechanisms of 'faith versus works' and 'spirit versus letter' clicked in, relegating David's actions to the external letter. These could then be subsumed, cleansed, and forgiven by the greater and more intimate truth of David's soul and David's speech.

Conveniently, Psalm 51 lent itself to adoption as a virtual Protestant creed. Verse 5—'Behold I was brought forth in iniquity, and in sin did my mother conceive me'—was seized on as a refutation of Pelagianism and a 'striking testimony in proof of original sin entailed by Adam upon the whole human family'.[31] Verses 16–17 could be nudged to assert the inefficacy of *all* sacrifices and masses. For Calvin, David's 'Deliver me from bloods' (51: 14) no longer referred to the particular (and criminal) act of spilling Uriah's blood. It signalled the universal bloodguilt on us all, crucifiers of Christ through sin.

The psalm was made to serve as a surrogate print confessional, stripped of priestly mediation. It became a secret textual chamber, to which only God, David, and the reader had access, and a demonstration of how 'we may lawfully and freely lay bare before [God and reader] the infirmities which a sense of shame prevents our confessing to men'.[32] As in Cramer's emblems, the heart was laid bare, in words and code. The reader was invited to enter into, and decipher, David's heart. In a compelling performance of the equality of all believers, the most lowly of readers could be privy to the blush of the king.

But, at the same time, hierarchies were firmly maintained. The fact that the populace was permitted to read this at all was interpreted as a manifestation of divine and kingly *grace*. As the French Reformer, Theodore Beza, gushed:

> What a rare example is this of so great a king and so worthy a Prophet, that laying aside all humane respect, either of his royall Majesty or private reputation, did not onely suffer the story of that his crime to be put in writing, but even he him selfe wrote a perpetuall testimony of his acknowledging of the fact, thereby to satisfie the whole church.[33]

Beza, like Knox, supported active resistance against the tyrannical or heretical (that is, un-Reformed) monarch, provided such resistance was confined to the nobles or magistrates. But he left the Bible's divine and human king in the traditional position: beyond law and beyond compulsion. The fact that King David submitted his crimes to public scrutiny was an act of *grace*. And his psalm (which he allowed to be recorded) stands as a permanent witness to his laudable desire to leave a lasting transcript of the workings of grace.

Three centuries later, the standard Reform position had undergone a revealing change. *'[David] escaped being tried before an earthly tribunal*; but his conscience told him that he stood at the bar of Heaven, laden with the guilt of murder' writes the editor to an English translation of Calvin's *Psalms* published in 1846.[34] The clear implication is that

---

[31] John Calvin, *A Commentary on the Book of Psalms*, tr. James Anderson (Edinburgh: Calvin Translation Society, 1846), ii. 290–1. (Henceforth Calvin, *Psalms*.)

[32] Calvin, *Psalms*, i, p.viii.

[33] Theodore Beza, *The Psalms of David, Truly Opened and Explaned by Paraphrasis, According to the Right Sense of Every Psalme*, tr. Anthonie Gilby (London, 1580), 127.

[34] See the editorial comments by James Anderson in Calvin, *Psalms*, ii. 302; my italics.

David *should not have escaped*. The difference starkly illustrates the changing shapes of truth, faith, and piety in relation to questions of governance and critique. For Beza it was unthinkable to demand that the biblical king appear before the law. For the nineteenth-century commentator, it is equally unthinkable that he should not put clear critical-political space between himself and the murderer-king. The relationship between kings, laws, bibles, and judgement has been radically rearranged, and the reorganization of these relations goes to the heart of what we call critique. For critique is essentially a performance of judgement and freedom, the enactment of a certain distance from which to judge. The more critical stance of the later commentator reflects the ascendancy of the Liberal Bible, which insists that true gods and kings should submit to law in order to qualify as such. Under the benign regime of the Liberal Bible, the murderer-king becomes an inner-biblical liability. For the Liberal Bible (gently) dictates that any scriptures and deities wanting to be recognized as truly Christian and truly 'modern' must abandon voluntarism and bring themselves into the open, even to the point of agreeing to be tried before the law.

III. Lapses in Character and Written Characters: Bayle's David between Sin and Critique

These pressures on King David begin in the late seventeenth century, with the deeply controversial David entry in Pierre Bayle's *Dictionnaire historique et critique*.[35] Bayle (1647–1706), a Huguenot living in Rotterdam, was one of the most well-known figures in the European republic of letters. His dictionary (first published 1697; expanded second edition 1702) circulated in English and German, and went through eight French editions in fifty years. The uncensored version of his entry on David opens with an excruciatingly carefully crafted sentence: 'DAVID, king of the Jews, was one of the greatest men in the world, though we should not consider him as a Royal Prophet, who was a man after God's own heart'.[36] The cunningly stockpiled subordinate clauses leave the reader stranded, unsure as to how far the force of negation extends. The author abdicates all authority. He issues no commands; gives no clear direction. In the same spirit, the dictionary deprivileges 'David (king)'. 'King' is in parentheses, almost as a common noun, and David is just one 'D' among many extra-biblical D's such as John Daurat.

The biblical is relegated and dispersed in what is effectively an 'exemplary print-era hypertext'[37] and a very different print object to Reformation editions of the Psalms. Bayle was an innovator, and proliferator, of the footnote. According to the editors of the famous

---

[35] For the controversy generated by this article, see Walter Rex, 'Pierre Bayle: The Theology and Politics of the Article on David', *Bibliothèque d'Humanisme et Renaissance*, 24 (1962), 168–89.

[36] Pierre Bayle, 'David', 532. The French is similarly double-handed: 'David, roi des Juifs, a été un des plus grands hommes du monde, quand même on ne le considérerait pas comme un roi prophète, qui était selon le coeur de Dieu' (accessed via <http://artfl-project.uchicago.edu/node/79>).

[37] Daniel Rosenberg, 'Electronic Memory', in Rosenberg and Susan Harding (eds), *Histories of the Future* (Durham, NC: Duke University Press, 2005), 128.

Encyclopédie, Diderot and D'Alembert, Bayle was so enamoured of footnotes that he multiplied them to the point of virtually squeezing out his primary text.[38] Decades before Jean Astruc's *Conjectures* on Genesis (1753), and well over a century before Julius Wellhausen's *Prolegomena* (1878/1883), the biblical is cut up, dispersed, and tagged to alphabetic (footnote) markers. Pieces of Bible appear as one element of many in a sea of footnotes. Floating atop this massive edifice of footnotes we find not direct citation of the biblical, but Bayle's own life of David reported in historically distanced third person. Densely packed with annotation, the crowded page performs the thick impenetrable layers of mediation that block easy access to David's 'heart'. As an effect of print format and page layout, this 'David' is the very antithesis of the David of Reformation editions of the Psalms.[39] He is closer to the David of the Bible, insofar as we see many Davids or many potential 'David' networks that can be tracked through the composite text.

Bayle's article inverts the traditional relationship between the David of Samuel and the king of interiority of the Psalms. After a brief, pious disclaimer ('David's piety is so conspicuous in the Psalms, and in several of his actions, that it cannot be sufficiently admired'), the entry continues:

> There is one thing which is no less admirable in his conduct; to wit that he could so happily reconcile so much piety with the loose maxims of the art of reigning. It is commonly believed that his adultery with Bathsheba, the murder of Uriah, and the numbering of the people, are the only faults with which he can be charged: but this is a great mistake; for there are many other things in his life which deserve censure. (535-7)

The Bible openly concedes that David sins. Repackaged and represented by Bayle, 'the Bible' becomes a hypertext itemizing and enumerating David's sins, in the same style as the *Dictionnaire*. According to what is now being read as an inner-biblical dictionary entry, David's sins are (a) adultery, (b) murder, and (c) the census: a sin of *counting, or the numbering of the people*. The Bible numbers three sins including the sin of counting. Bayle counts considerably more. He totals thirteen, and lists them in thirteen footnotes 'A' to 'M'. Many of these then break down further into various subpoints, ricocheting across the page.

Biblical texts are reduced to supporting cross-references, collocations of letters and numbers such as '1 Samuel 27'. Fragments of biblical texts are then brought together in a network coordinated around the key term: David's sin. Bayle's much expanded inventory of the sins of David includes polygamy; his 'criminal action' in relation to Nabal; his readiness to gain power by treachery against Saul's son Ishbosheth, the lawful king, in 2 Samuel 2–4 (impressive in terms of 'policy' but less 'agreeable' to 'severe morals' and the 'strict laws of equity', Bayle comments); his deception of Achish, king of Gath, in 1 Samuel 27 ('Has a private man, as he was, a fugitive, who finds shelter in the territories of a neighbouring Prince, a right to commit hostilities for his own account, and without a commission from the Sovereign of the country? Had David any such commission? ... It is certain that if a private person, let his birth be ever so great, should behave at this day as David did on this occasion, he would unavoidably have no very honourable names given

---

[38] Jean le Rond d'Alembert, 'Dictionnaire', in Denis Diderot and Jean Le Rond d'Alembert (eds), *Encyclopédie ou dictionnaire raisonné des sciences, des arts et des métiers* (Paris, 1751–72), iv. 967.

[39] Bayle, 'David', 538.

him'); and the breaking of his oath not to kill Shimei. Bayle is also at pains to point out that David regularly committed war-crimes and acts of torture that would have appalled even 'the Tartars' and 'the Turks'. This is a scandal for the more dominant negotiation between Christianity and modernities expressed in the Liberal Bible. For Liberal interpreters Christianity comes out top, as the most naturally critical and self-giving religion, fundamentally different to the others. As Gil Anidjar argues, by patenting the categories of the 'religious' and the 'secular' (also 'critical'), Christian Europe displaced the atavistic and violent dimensions of 'religion' onto other religions—chiefly the 'Jew', 'Moor', and 'Turk'.[40]

Bayle and some of his contemporaries have not yet learnt this trick of displacement, which is also a trick of turning the Bible into a foundation, or symbol, rather than a text. Intransigently, he forces us into close reading, and deliberately sets up collisions between contemporary visions of political justice and the letter of the text. For example, he cautions that just war theorists declaiming against our modern princes must be careful. If they insist that the only permissible war is defensive war, then their criticism will rebound, inadvertently, on David and the scriptures that he represents. Scripture 'often represents [David] as the aggressor' (536). As in his opening sentence, Bayle gives us no solid ground to stand on. He leaves us trapped between rival forms of piety and justice forcing us to sacrifice one or the other. If we start from the assumption that we must condone David because he is a sovereign and a hero of scripture, then, logically, we are forced to condone conquest and sacrifice just war. Alternatively, if we press for just war, we will have to sacrifice David to justice, and allow the 'great Prophet' to become a casualty of the overriding principle.

By emphasizing that for much of his career the king was a *private man*, even a *fugitive*, Bayle dethrones David. By implication, he questions the lordship of scripture. He creates openings, on an equal footing, for other private persons. (Compare the leverage gained by appealing to the involvement of the people and Elders in electing David king.[41]) He starkly performs the intimate relation between governance, politics, and critique. As Bayle puts it, in a decorous soft-shoe shuffle: 'It is very allowable for private persons, such as my self, to judge of facts contained in Scripture, when they are not expressly qualified by the Holy Ghost' (537). This carefully poised statement of the relationship between human and divine judgement proposes two different modes of piety rather than a stark and easy contrast between piety and impiety. In one, piety defers to any directive statements from 'the Holy Ghost'. In the other, human judgement mirrors divine judgement so zealously that it extends it—*even to the point where it questions the Bible and criticises the sins of the man after God's own heart.*

Bayle gives us several examples of what might follow from this hyper-critical, pious zeal. Shimei's curse on David as a 'man of blood' (cf. 2 Samuel 16: 17) is read as a clue to an alternative extra-canonical David story that has been obscured beneath the *partial* and *partisan* letters before us. How many others would have wanted to call David the 'man of blood', or similar names? Whereas the Bible presents Shimei's statement as 'slander', Bayle reads it as a 'small specimen' of a very different David tradition which could have been written by the court and family of Saul.[42] The move seems strikingly proto-modern;

---

[40] Gil Anidjar, 'Secularism', *Critical Inquiry*, 33 (2006): 62–3.

[41] Cf. the discussion on p. XXX.

[42] 'History has preserved a small specimen of the abuses to which David was exposed among the friends of Saul'. Bayle, 'David', 537.

an example of what biblical scholars might call an 'ideological' reading, or 'reading against the grain'. How would the archive of the Bible look, Bayle asks, obliquely, if other 'slanders' had survived? He also invites us to imagine the *libels* that would have been written by more neutral, impartial, observers. 'If the people of Syria had been as great Writers of Libels, as the Europeans are at this day, they would have strangely disfigured David's glory'.

Bayle creates a new, diffuse 'biblical' scene, where the Bible is splintered into fragments and (competing) factions. King David is effectively presented with a subpoena by Uriah, and all the other 'Uriahs' (Nabal, Ishbosheth, Achish, Shimei), not to mention the people of Syria and all the nations against whom he wages wars of conquest. This is a graphic illustration of the changing relationship between kings, laws, bibles, and private persons. It starkly demonstrates the increasing pressure on kings and scriptures to abandon hyper-sovereignty and prove a fundamental alliance with law, even to the point where law and kingship (human and divine) are effectively the same. Crucially, Bayle coordinates this major readjustment using scriptural figures and that constant biblical commonplace: human sin. The Bible only presents Uriah's case, but others are implied. Bayle is being more biblical than the Bible, he suggests, by so rigorously extending the inner-biblical principle of David's sin now read as David's crime.

We are now in a position to develop and nuance Foucault's condensed statement: 'from Wycliffe to Pierre Bayle, I believe that critique was developed in an important, but of course not exclusive, part in relation to Scripture'. Bayle's David reveals a new genealogy of 'the critical'. *Criticism, from krino ('to separate', 'to decide', 'to judge', 'to accuse') can arise from extrapolating God's quasi-legal judgement of the human and the doctrine of original sin.* Once it is uncovered, this genealogy seems obvious. But it has been buried because our histories and mythologies of the modern tend to be constructed around the axiomatic contrast between the cry of *Sapere Aude* and the exit from 'thraldom', and that most potent sign of 'thraldom' and abjection: original sin. But if one of the sources of the 'modern' is an 'anthropological transfer of the prerogatives of God',[43] as Charles Taylor neatly puts it, then a crucial element of the transferred package is the prerogative—indeed the obligation—to denounce and correct sin.

Deftly attempting to sidestep expected outrage from the Catholic Consistory, Bayle insists that only a mathematical, technical difference separates the heterodox from the orthodox. As he puts it, the 'difference between us' (between the guardians of piety and his own piety, which might be misread as impiety) is merely 'in regard to the number of faults' (537). They are all on the same page, and the same page as the Bible, insofar as they all concur that David sinned. Strategically Bayle gathers his critique of David under the principle of the Fall. He makes it appear as if the doctrine of the Fall inevitably spawns critique. Everything spiralling out from the biblical in this controversial hypertext flows, or falls out from, the thoroughly orthodox truism that '[David] was subject to the alternatives of passion and grace: a fatality adhering to our nature ever since the time of Adam'. And what flows, or follows, is a massive flowchart or performance of 'critique'.

---

[43] Charles Taylor, *Sources of the Self: The Making of the Modern Identity* (Cambridge: Cambridge University Press, 1992), 82.

The uncontroversial fact of 'David's sins' is expanded in two senses. David now stands accused of many sins. And, crucially, *imperfection expands to include the text, its author, and the words on the page*. The sins of David come to include not just lapses in David's character, but sins of miswriting, *lapses in the written characters*. Gathered into the paradigm of Fall and the traditional device of accommodation, the text and its author also become imperfect: all-too-human. In Bayle's terms they are too *partial* in two senses. They are too partial to particular groups and individuals. And they are too prone to stray into the wild lands of the idiosyncratic and exceptional. In a word, they are too *'particulier'*. *Particulier* was a loaded word in French theology and politics. In a move analogous to, but not the same as, the development of the Liberal Bible in English, the transformation of the divine into the civic was based on God's growing identification with the *volonté générale* rather than the *volonté particulière*.[44]

As I have argued elsewhere, the late modern machine of biblical studies spawned many methodologies centred around *history* in order to overcome the *moral* questioning of the Bible that was the strongest component of early modern biblical critique.[45] For writers like Pierre Bayle and the third Earl of Shaftesbury, Anthony Ashley Cooper, the primary concern was the Bible's (im)morality and, relatedly, its social standing and political effects. The interrogation of biblical *characters* (in the double sense of *personae* and letters) was bound to a consideration of the Bible's 'character' and 'manners', and its role as political and social exemplar. With their obsession with sources, modern biblical scholars isolated the question of textual 'integrity' in a purely formal sense. But in the seventeenth and eighteenth century this question was, at most, only a subset of the more pressing question of *moral integrity* and good character. The Bible and its characters and kings were exposed to tests of character. The traditional—and indeed orthodox—acknowledgement of the limit of the letter was extended beyond the written characters into human *character*. The Bible was examined as if it were a person, a social and political agent (as indeed it was in the seventeenth and eighteenth centuries). It was scrutinized in relation to principles of etiquette and gentlemanly politesse.

For Bayle, textual discrepancies are interesting, but incidental. He notes *in passing* how Saul seems to suddenly suffer from a bout of amnesia in the Goliath story and forget that he has already met David (1 Samuel 17: 58), adding ironically that

> If such a relation were found in Thucydides or Livy, all the critics would unanimously conclude that the transcribers had transposed the pages, forgotten something in one place, repeated something in another, or inserted additional passages in the Author's Work. But we must not entertain such suspicions with regard to the Bible. (533)

---

[44] See Patrick Riley, *The General Will Before Rousseau: The Transformation of the Divine into the Civic* (Princeton: Princeton University Press, 1986).

[45] See Stephen D. Moore and Yvonne Sherwood, *The Invention of the Biblical Scholar: A Critical Manifesto* (Minneapolis: Fortress, 2011); and Ward Blanton and Yvonne Sherwood, 'Bible/Religion/Critique', in Richard King (ed.), *Theory/Religion/Critique* (New York: Columbia University Press, 2012), xx–xx.

But the primary critical issue is what Kant would later crystallize as the problem of *moral unbelief*.[46] It all comes down to characters and, strategically, David, a character who takes us to the palpitating heart and character of scripture, since he is allegedly joined to God through the heart. Zealously extrapolating a steely Calvinism that condemns the dangerous softness of 'cavillators' who pander to biblical characters simply because they are in the Bible, Bayle refuses to sacrifice the 'general interests of morality' to 'the reputation of a particular person [*un particulier*]'.[47]

IV. David the *Particulier* and Commoner: Class and Critique

Bayle's critique of partial letters expands the thoroughly traditional machinery of accommodation: the principle that 'Scripture speaks according to our way of imagining and speaking'.[48] The frameworks of accommodation and original sin are pushed even further in the third Earl of Shaftesbury's *Characteristics of Men, Manners, Opinions, Times* (1711). In a mock-apologia, the gentleman-reader laments that he cannot enter the biblical text because he is all too human/humane.

> There is a certain perverse humanity in us which inwardly resists the divine commission, though never so plainly revealed. The wit of the best poet is not sufficient to reconcile us to the campaign of a Joshua or the retreat of a Moses by the assistance of an Egyptian loan. *Nor will it be possible, by the Muses's art, to make that royal hero appear amiable in human eyes who found such favour in the eye of Heaven.* Such are mere human hearts that they can hardly find the least sympathy with that only one which had the character of being after the pattern of the Almighty's.[49]

'Incomprehensible in philosophy … above the pitch of the mere human historian, the politician, or the moralist … too sacred to be submitted to the poet's fancy', the Bible is isolated in the particular-deviant sphere of the *particulier*. This idiosyncratic zone is alien to history, politics, morality, or poetry. In that same way that separation from 'religion' creates the category of 'politics' (and defines the latter, by contrast, as one of general access), so contrast with the peculiar biblical helps to establish history, morality, and poetry as independent, general, critical domains. In the same gesture, the Bible becomes particularly atavistic and arcane: the property of the 'divines'.[50]

Shaftesbury presents himself as standing before the gate of the letter, like Kafka's man before the law. But Shaftesbury is not a 'man from the country', but from the city. It is his

---

[46] See Sherwood, 'Reflections on "Modern" Biblical Studies, or Why Philip Davies is (Just a Little Bit) like Immanuel Kant', in Duncan Burns and John Rogerson (eds), *Far from Minimal: Celebrating the Work and Influence of Philip R. Davies* (London: Bloomsbury, 2012), 386–409.

[47] Bayle, articles on 'Abraham' and 'Sarah' in *A General Dictionary*.

[48] José de Acosta, *The Natural and Moral History of the Indies* (1590), ed. Jane E. Mangan, intro. and commentary Walter D. Mignolo, tr. Frances López-Morillas (Durham, NC: Duke University Press, 2002), 21.

[49] Anthony, Earl of Shaftesbury, *Characteristics of Men, Manners, Opinions, Times*, ed. John M. Robertson, intro. Stanley Grean (Indianapolis: Bobs-Merill Co., 1964), 229–30.

[50] Shaftesbury, *Characteristics*, 229–30.

civility that denies him access. And Shaftesbury's figure of an impenetrable text which cannot be entered is made through a strategic rearrangement of the inner-biblical trope of the spirit versus the letter, the soul versus the flesh. No longer a container yielding to the 'absolute visual spirituality of scripture', the letter is now purely itself, its own character, subdivided into footnotes, splitting and ricocheting across the page. If Reformation aesthetics and piety centre on seeing through print to the 'psychogram in the beyond of letters', Bayle and Shaftesbury feel acutely the 'blackness of the printed letters'. The letters are haunted by black, morally dark, elements. And they fold back on themselves.

What is controversial is not making the Bible human but making it a particular kind of human: sinful and lower class. Highly pertinent here is Steven Shapin's discussion of the intrinsic connection between truth, integrity, and 'gentle identity'. In England in the seventeenth century, truth was bound to performances of 'epistemological decorum'.[51] The ability, or *power*, to be a reliable witness was linked to independent means. The giddy Enlightenment cry of release from intellectual thraldom into self-possession was more than metaphorically related to property. There was a direct correlation between being intellectually and economically free.

While boldly announcing the critical freedom of the 'private man' (with the intellectual and economic means to engage other 'private persons' on equal footing in scripture), Bayle and Shaftesbury separate themselves from much-feared readers lower down the social pecking order, with a fetishistic and credulous relationship to scripture. Shaftesbury savages those who believe that biblical characters (in both senses) are 'angelically and divinely-wrought by a supernatural hand and sacred pencil' or made by a 'hand like Raphael's', and therefore sealed off from any questions of quality or 'justness and proportion'. There is something simultaneously aesthetic, social, and moral about the tests of 'quality' and 'proportion' to be applied by more enquiring minds. Corroborating the lofty cultural status of the King James Bible—the high cultural version that has always been most amenable to translation into history, politics, morality, or poetry—Shaftesbury judges that it is the Anglicans who are least likely to 'rest their religion on the common aspect or obvious form of their *vulgar Bible*, as it presents itself in the printed copy or modern version'.[52] This conscious separation from the vulgar Bible (and its dark characters, in both senses) is what distinguishes Anglicans from 'Mahometan clergy', 'Eastern religionists', and Catholics.[53]

Figures like Shaftesbury and Bayle appear to us as 'critical' or 'proto-secular' not simply because they see the Bible as the product of human hands, but because they insinuate that there is dirt under the fingernails of those hands. Critique is ultimately a question of class and style. Judicious Anglican divines maintain that the 'holy authors' have 'written according to their best faculties and the strength of their natural genius' or, what is effectively the same thing, their social standing: 'a shepherd like a shepherd', 'a prince like a prince', 'a man of reading, and advanced in letters, like a proficient in the kind', and 'a man of meaner capacity and reading, like one of the ordinary sort, in his own common idiom and imperfect manner of narration' (302). Bayle, similarly, makes a point of the fact that David was a mere *berger*. Coming at the king obliquely—a king he has already

---

[51] Steven Shapin, *A Social History of Truth: Civility and Science in Seventeenth Century England* (Chicago: University of Chicago Press, 1994), pp. xxix, 42.

[52] Shaftesbury, *Characteristics*, 300.   [53] Shaftesbury, *Characteristics*, 297–8, 300–1.

described as a private person—he decorously hazards that a more neutral (less partial or particular) observer might have used 'infamous names and titles' to describe the 'troop of Adventurers who went to join [David] after he had retired from Saul's Court' (537).

The controversial point is not that David is outside the law. God and scripture and Nathan the prophet say that, at least in relation to the isolated cases of the census and Bathsheba. The controversial point is that Bayle makes an inference about *social standing* from this state-of-being-outside-the-law. David is an outlaw, a fugitive, with an entourage of low-life thugs. This is a particularly stark fulfilment of the threat of the vernacular Bible, torn between addressing 'publicans, fishers, and shepherds' (according to Cranmer's Preface to the Great Bible) and fearing the subversion of authority by publicans and shepherds. The worst comes to pass, it seems, in the spectacle of the dethroned biblical king, expelled from the palace and the gentleman's table and associating himself with adventurers in the wilds beyond the law. Bayle and Shaftesbury obey the rules that, as one seventeenth-century writer puts it, 'If one has to say *no* in contradiction to some person of quality, you must not say bluntly or positively, *no*, but by way of circumlocution'.[54] But at the same time they imply a 'no' that is robustly uttered to one who is of lower social standing. It is this social lowering, I suggest, that is essence of the critical, and the threat and promise of the critical. For ultimately, criticism releases the spectre of anarchy or revolution among the lower classes, who may also find a taste for 'not being governed so much'.

FURTHER READING

Assmann, Jan. *Religion and Cultural Memory*, tr. Rodney Livingstone (Stanford, Calif.: Stanford University Press, 2006).

Cummings, Brian. *The Literary Culture of the Reformation: Grammar and Grace* (Oxford: Oxford University Press, 2002).

Foucault, Michel. 'What is Critique', in James Schmidt (ed.), *What is Enlightenment? Eighteenth Century Answers and Twentieth Century Questions* (Berkeley, Calif.: University of California Press, 1996), 382–98.

Sherwood, Yvonne. *Biblical Blaspheming: Trials of the Sacred for a Secular Age* (Cambridge: Cambridge University Press, 2012).

Shuger, Debora K. *The Renaissance Bible: Scholarship, Sacrifice and Subjectivity* (Berkeley, Calif.: University of California Press, 1994).

Toorn, Karel van der. *Scribal Culture and the Making of the Hebrew Bible* (Cambridge, Mass.: Harvard University Press, 2007).

---

[54] Shapin, *A Social History of Truth*, 115, citing Antoine De Courtin, *The Rules of Civility: Or, Certain Ways of Deportment Observed amongst All Persons of Quality* (London, 1685; 1st edn 1671), 17–18, 29, 40, 42.

CHRONOLOGY

GIVEN the vast intellectual resources ploughed into biblical scholarship, and the reach of religion into every quarter of political and cultural life, the following is a necessarily partial account of key events.

Date	Political and Ecclesiastical Context	The Bible and its Translations	Scholarship and Commentary	Cultural developments
1511	Henry VIII joins the Holy League			Desiderius Erasmus, *Praise of Folly*
1512	Fifth Council of Lateran begins			Erasmus, *De copia* (first edn)
1513	James IV of Scotland defeated at the Battle of Flodden Field			Machiavelli, *Il Principe*
	James V succeeds James IV of Scotland			Thomas More, *History of Richard III*
1514	Wolsey made Archbishop of York			
	Peace with France			
1515	Wolsey made Cardinal			
1516	Erasmus, humanist scholar, makes last visit to England, at the invitation of Henry VIII	Erasmus translates New Testament into Latin with Greek Parallels	Targum (and translation), plus Hebrew–Chaldee lexicon, with Complutensian Polyglot	Thomas More, *Utopia*
				Ludovico Ariosto, *Orlando furioso*
1517	Fifth Council of Lateran ends	1517 Bomberg Rabbinic Bible	Erasmus, *Vetus Testamentum multiplici lingua nu[n]c primo impressum* (1514–17)	
	Luther's Ninety Five Theses circulated in Wittenberg; Protestant Reformation begins in Germany			
1518	Melanchthon teaching at Wittenberg	Aldine Bible (1518–19)	Johannes Reuchlin, *De accentibus et orthographia linguae hebraicae*	Luther, *Heidelberg Disputation*
	Treaty of Universal Peace			
1519	Leipzig Disputation between Luther and Eck		Martin Luther, *Operationes in Psalmos* (1519–21)	Magellan begins his voyage around the world
	Charles V of Hapsburg crowned Holy Roman Emperor			

Year			
1520		Complutensian Polyglot, 1513–17 (including Hebrew, Aramaic, Greek OT, and Latin), publ. 1520	Apologia Edouardi Leei contra quorundam Calumnias and Annotationes Edouardi Leei in Annotationes noui testamenti Desiderii Erasmi (Paris: Egidii Gourmont)	Thomas Wyatt's poems circulate in MS
			Cyprian, *Opera* (Basel), ed. Erasmus	
			Philip Melanchthon, *Loci communes rerum theologicarum*	
1521	Luther is excommunicated. Diet of Worms condemns his teaching		
	Henry VIII is given title of Defender of the Faith by Pope Leo X for opposing Luther		
	Zwingli active in Zurich		
1522		Luther's translation of the Bible into German (Wittenberg)		Ignatius begins to write his Spiritual Exercises
1523	Thomas More becomes Speaker of the House of Commons		
1524	Tyndale settles on continent, refused support by Tunstall, Bishop of London	Zürich Bible (1524–9)	
		Greek Septuagint, ed. Johannes Lonicerus (Strasburg, 1524–6)	
1526		Dutch Bible, publ. Jacob van Liesveldt (Antwerp, 1526)	Jerome, *Opera* (Basel), ed. Erasmus	Hans Holbein the Younger active in England
		Biblia Rabbinica (Venice, 1525–6)	Jacopo Sannazaro, *De partu Virginis* (Naples)	
		William Tyndale's New Testament (Worms, 1526)		

(Continued.)

Date	Political and Ecclesiastical Context	The Bible and its Translations	Scholarship and Commentary	Cultural developments
1527	Treaty of Westminster forms an alliance between France and England			
	Archbishop William Warham secretly holds an inquiry into the legality of Henry VIII's marriage to Katherine of Aragon			
1528	The blocking of Henry VIII's divorce from Katherine of Aragon by a papacy influenced by her nephew, Charles V		Thomas More, *Supplication of Souls*	William Tyndale, *The Obedience of a Christian Man*
			William Tyndale, *That Faith the Mother of all Good Works Justifieth Us* (Antwerp)	Thomas More, *A Dialogue of Heresies*
				Castiglione, *Il cortegiano*
1529	Zwingli and Luther debate at Marburg Colloquy		Guillaume Budé's *Commentarii linguae Graecae* (Paris)	
	Fall of Cardinal Wolsey		Augustine, *Opera omnia* (Basel, 1528–9), ed. Erasmus	
	Thomas More made Lord Chancellor			
1530	Augsburg Confession, of Lutheran Faith	Tyndale translates the Pentateuch	Robert Barnes, *A Supplication*	Agrippa, *The Vanity and Uncertainty of the Arts and Sciences*
			Tyndale, *Answer to More*	Martin Luther, *Eine predigt, das man Kinder zur Schulen halten solle*
1531		Tyndale completes his translation of the first fourteen books of the Old Testament		Thomas Elyot, *The Boke Named the Governour*
		Zwingli's *Zürcher Bible*		

Year			
1532	More is imprisoned; Thomas Cromwell is made Lord Chancellor	Thomas More, *The Confutation of Tyndale's Answer* (1532–3)	Leonard Cox, *The Arte or Crafte of Rhetoryke*
1533	Henry VIII marries Ann Boleyn and by Act of Parliament becomes Supreme Head of the Church of England	Martin Luther, *Prefaces to the Apocrypha* (1533–4)	Rabelais, *Gargantua et Pantagruel* (1532–4)
	Pope Paul III elected		
1534	Luther's German Bible, *Biblia, das ist, die gantze Heilige Schrifft*	More, *Dialogue of Comfort*	
1535	Execution of More and Fisher	Coverdale's *Concordance of the New Testament*, first English concordance	
	John Calvin arrives in Geneva	Eugubinus, *Cosmopoeia, vel de mundano opificio*	
	Coverdale Bible	Miles Coverdale, *Goostly Psalmes and Spirituall Songes*	
	La Bible (Neuchâtel) Huguenot translation, by Pierre-Robert Olivétan		
1536	Dissolution of the smaller monasteries leads to the northern rebellion (Pilgrimage of Grace)	Origen, *Opera omnia* (Basel), ed. Erasmus	
	Ten Articles of Religion	John Calvin, *Institutio Christianæ religionis*	
	William Tyndale burned		
1537	**The Matthew Bible**, derived from Tyndale, Vulgate, Luther, and Coverdale's OT		
	Calvin's theocracy is established in Geneva		

(Continued.)

Date	Political and Ecclesiastical Context	The Bible and its Translations	Scholarship and Commentary	Cultural developments
1538	Cromwell authorizes Bible in English, leading to Great Bible, available in every parish	*The Newe Testament both in Latine and Englyshe Eche Correspondente to the Other After the Vulgare Texte, Communely Called S. Jeromes. Faythfullye Translated by Johan Hollybushe [sic]* (Southwark)		John Bale, *Kynge Johan*; Thomas Elyot, *Dictionary*
1539	1539 Dissolution of greater monasteries	**The Great Bible**, based upon the Coverdale Bible **Taverner's Bible**, a revised edition of Matthew's	Calvin's Commentary on Romans Tommaso de Vio, Cardinal Cajetan, *Opera omnia* *A Paraphrasis upon all the Psalmes of David, Made by Johannes Campensis, Reader of the Hebrue Lecture in the Universite of Louvane, and Translated out of Latine into Englisshe* (London)	
1540	Jesuits founded by Ignatius of Loyola Fall and execution of Thomas Cromwell		The Great Bible is reissued with a preface by Archbishop Thomas Cranmer	Thomas Elyot, *Defence of Good Women*
1541	Henry VIII assumes the title of King of Ireland and makes himself supreme head of the Church in Ireland		John Calvin, *Institutio Christianæ Religionis* translated into French	
1542	Roman Inquisition founded James V of Scotland dies and is succeeded to the throne by Mary who is six days old		Paulus Fagius, *Exegesis sive expositio dictionum Hebraicorum literalis*	
1543	Act for the Advancement of True Religion restricts Bible reading		John Bale, *Yet a Course at the Romyshe Foxe* (Antwerp)	Copernicus, *De revolutionibus*, with preface by Andreas Osiander

Year	Events			
1544			Epiphanius, *Contra octoaginta haereses opus* (Paris), tr. Cornarius	Sebastian Münster, *Cosmographia*
1545	Council of Trent. Start of the Counter-Reformation			John Bale, *The Image of Both Churches*
	1545 King's primer regularizes liturgical material in English			
1546	Death of Luther	Stephanus Bible (Paris 1546), Textus Receptus	Peter Becker, *De prima rerum origine*	Bale, *Acts of English Votaries; First Examination of Anne Askew*
1547	Dissolution of Chantre			Cranmer, *Certain Sermons or Homilies*
	Edward VI, king of England (1547–53)			
1548	Trent declares the Deutero–Canonical OT Books, formerly regarded as Apocrypha, to be fully scriptural. Catholic Bible in English an eventual by-product		*Certayne Psalmes Chosen out of the Psalter of David, and Drawen Into Englishe Metre by Thomas Sternhold Grome of ye Kynges Maiesties Roobes* (London)	
			Nicholas Udall, *The Paraphrase of Erasmus upon the New Testament*	
1549	Anti-enclosure riots	Coverdale's biblical translations are used in the first Book of Common Prayer and later editions		
	Kett's Rebellion			
1550	Pope Julius III elected		Martin Bucer, *De regno Christi libri duo*	Vasari, *Lives of the Painters*
1551	Anti-enclosure riots end			
1552	Forty-Two Articles			
	Revised Prayer Book			
	Württemberg Confession of Faith			

(Continued.)

Date	Political and Ecclesiastical Context	The Bible and its Translations	Scholarship and Commentary	Cultural developments
1553	Mary Tudor Queen of England (1553–8). Marries Philip II of Spain to cement Catholic Ascendancy			Mary's burning of Protestants sends many of their leaders into exile on the continent
1554	Lady Jane Grey executed (1537–54) Peace of Augsburg			
1555	Hugh Latimer and Nicholas Ridley burned	*La Bible nouvellement translatée* (1555), by Sébastien Châteillon		*Myrroure for Magistrates* (first ed.)
1555	Peace of Augsburg and Calvinist prosecutions			
1556	Thomas Cranmer burned Reginald Pole appointed Archbishop of Canterbury			
1557	Benedictine monks return to Westminster Abbey	Whittingham publishes NT at Geneva in 1557	Giulio Cesare Paschali translates Calvin, *Institutio Christanæ religionis* into Italian	Robert Recorde, *The Whetstone of Witte*
1558	1558 The French recapture Calais from the English Mary dies. Elizabeth I, Queen of England (1558–1603). New Act of Settlement makes her Supreme Governor of the Church of England.			John Knox, *First Blast of the Trumpet Against the Monstrous Regiment of Women*

Year			
1559	Pope Pius IV elected		
	Act of Supremacy		
	Matthew Parker Archbishop of Canterbury		
1560	Scottish Reformation Parliament	Geneva Bible published, also known as Breeches Bible, so named from its translation of Genesis 3:7	
	Proclamation prohibiting the Destruction of Church Monuments		
1561	Mary Queen of Scots returns home. Her Masses at court lead to tension with, and lectures from, the Presbyterian divine, John Knox.	Thomas Norton translates Calvin's *Institutes of Christian Religion* into English	Thomas Norton and Thomas Sackville, *Gorboduc*
1562	French Wars of Religion start	Marot-Beza Psalter	Codex Bezae discovered at Lyons by Theodore Beza	Latimer, *27 Sermons*
		Sternhold and Hopkins, *Whole Book of Psalms*		
1563	Thirty-Nine Articles			Foxe's *Acts and Monuments* (Book of Martyrs) published. Placed in many Protestant churches alongside the Bible.
	Act requires Welsh services in three years			
	Council of Trent closes			
1564	Theodore Beza succeeds Calvin in Geneva.		
1565		**Beza's Greek NT with Vulgate and own Latin translation**	
1566		Sixtus of Siena, *Bibliotheca sancta ex præcipuis Catholicæ Ecclesiæ auctoribus collecta*	

(Continued.)

Date	Political and Ecclesiastical Context	The Bible and its Translations	Scholarship and Commentary	Cultural developments
1567	Mary Queen of Scots forced to abdicate. Her baby son succeeds to the Scottish throne as James VI.	William Salesbury works on **NT in Welsh**, with archaic Latinate English orthography for English clergy. It is unacceptable to Welsh speakers who prefer their own properly phonetic Welsh spelling.	Matthias Flacius Illyricus, *Clavis Scripturae* Immanuel Temellius, trans. of Targum of Jonathan	
1568	Mary Queen of Scots escapes imprisonment, flees to England after military defeat.	*The Whole Psalter*, translated by Matthew Parker The **Bishops' Bible** published with the initials of each translator at the end of every chapter for which he was responsible.		
1569	Revolt of Northern Earls	1569–79: New Latin translation of Bible, N.T. by Theodore Beza Antwerp Polyglot, *Biblia sacra Hebraice, Chaldaice, Graece, Latine* (1569–73), reproduced as *Biblia Regia* including Peshito, Syriac lexicon and grammar.	Immanuel Tremellius, *Grammatica Chaldaea et Syra* Peter Martyr (Vermigli), *In primum librum Mosis*	
1570	Pope Pius V excommunicates Elizabeth I		Irenaeus, *Adversus portentosas haereses* (Geneva)	John Dee, Euclid's *Elements* Homily against Disobedience Foxe, *Ecclesiastical History*
1571	Treason Act	*The Psalms of David and Others, as Rendered into English by Arthur Golding, his Translation of Calvin's Latin Version Extracted from Commentaries on the Psalms* (London)		

1572	St Bartholomew's Day massacre of Huguenots Admonition to the Parliament		Edward Coke, Reports (circulated in ms)
1573		Thomas Cooper, A Brief Exposition of Such Chapters of the Olde Testament as Usually are Redde in the Church at Common Praier on the Sondayes	George Gascoigne, A Hundreth Sundrie Flowres
1574		Guillaume de Salluste Du Bartas, 'L'Uranie', La Muse Chrestiene (Bordeaux); Judit	
1575	Edmund Grindal appointed Archbishop of Canterbury	Tremellius and Junius, OT Latin (1575–9)	
1576	Priests from Douai arrive in England	Revision of Geneva NT by Laurence Tomson based on Theodore Beza's work of 1565 Augustine, Opera d. Aurelii Augustini (Antwerp, 1576–7), Louvain divines.	El Greco at Toledo. Titian's Pietà. William Byrd and Thomas Tallis granted monopoly to print music paper and musical notation by Elizabeth I The Theatre opens; it is the first purpose-built playhouse in London Bodin, Les six livres de la République
1577	Lutheran confession regularized in Germany	Eusebius of Caesarea, The Auncient Ecclesiasticall Histories (London), tr. Meredith Hanmer	Holinshed, Chronicles
1578		Guillaume de Salluste Du Bartas, La sepmaine, ou création du monde	John Lyly, Euphues, the Anatomy of Wit

(Continued.)

Date	Political and Ecclesiastical Context	The Bible and its Translations	Scholarship and Commentary	Cultural developments
1579	The Union of Utrecht unites Protestant Dutch; English Jesuit College at Rome founded			Edmund Spenser, *The Shepheardes Calendar*; Buchanan, *De jure regni*; Michel de Montaigne, *Essais*; John Stow, *Chronicle*
1580	Jesuit mission in England begins	Franciscus Junius and Immauael Tremellius translate the Bible into Latin, *Testament veteris Biblia Sacra*		Tasso, *Gerusalemme Liberata*
1581	Execution of Edmund Campion; 'Act to retain the Queen's Majesty's Subjects in their due Obedience', enforcing attendance at Anglican church worship, fining recusants and making it treasonable to convert subjects to Catholicism			
1582		**Douai-Rheims Bible** [Roman Catholic version of NT in English]	Gregory Martin. *A Discoverie of the Manifold Corruptions of the Scriptures*	University of Edinburgh founded

1583	John Whitgift, Archbishop of Canterbury. Irish rebellion suppressed	William Rainolds, *A Refutation of Sundry Reprehensions, Cavils, and False Sleightes, by which M. Whitaker Laboureth to Deface the Late English Translation, and Catholike Annotations of the New Testament* (Paris) William Fulke, *A Defence of the Translations of the Holy Scriptures* Jacobus Brocardus, *Mystica et prophetica libri Genesis interpretatio* Tertullian, *Opera* (Paris), ed. Jacques de Pamèle	Joseph Justus Scaliger, *Opus de emendatione temporum*
1584	William of Orange assassinated		Walter Ralegh attempts (and fails) to colonize Virginia
1585	Treaty of Nonsuch commits England to support the Spanish Netherlands in a revolt against the Habsburgs	Biblia Polyglotta Vatabli or Polyglotta Sanctandreana (Heidelberg, 1586–99)	Robert Greene, *Planetomachia*
1586		Rome Septuagint (Greek), based on Codex Vaticanus, under Pope Sixtus V.	
1587	Mary Queen of Scots' involvement in plots against Elizabeth culminates in the Babington Plot, for which she is executed. Cardinal William Allen founds three Catholic Colleges for Mission to England.		Christopher Marlowe, *Tamburlaine*

(Continued.)

Date	Political and Ecclesiastical Context	The Bible and its Translations	Scholarship and Commentary	Cultural developments
1588	Philip II of Spain sends an Armada against England	**Y Beibl Cymraeg** [Welsh Bible] translated and seen through the printers at Westminster by William Morgan	William Whitaker, *Disputatio de Sacra Scriptura*	William Byrd, *Psalms, Sonnets and Songs*
	Marprelate controversy begins		George Wither, *A View of the Marginal Notes of the Popish Testament, Translated into English by the English Fugitive Papists Resident at Rhemes in France*	
			Faustus Socinus, *De Sacrae Scripturae auctoritate*	
1589			William Fulke, *The Text of the New Testament of Jesus Christ, Translated out of the Vulgar Latine by the Papists*	George Puttenham, *Arte of English Poesie*
			Benedictus Pererius, *Commentariorum et disputationum in Genesim* (1589–98)	
1590	Death of Francis Walsingham	Sixtine Bible, under Pope Sixtus V		Edmund Spenser, *The Faerie Queene*, Books I–III
				Philip Sidney, *Arcadia* printed
1591	Recusancy laws become more severe		Hieronymus Zanchius, *De operibus Dei*	Philip Sidney, *Astrophel and Stella* printed
1592		Clementine Bible, under Clement VIII	William Perkins, *Prophetica, sive, de sacra et unica ratione concionandi tractatus*, trans. *Arte of Prophecying*	
			Andrew Willet, *Synopsis Papismi*	
1593	1593 Henry IV accepts Catholicism in France		Richard Hooker, *Of the Lawes of Ecclesiasticall Politie*, books I–IV	Thomas Nashe, *Christ's Tears Over Jerusalem*
	Series of poor harvests (1593–7)			

Year	Events			
1595			Andrew Maunsell, *The First Part of the Catalogue of English Printed Bookes: Which Concerneth Such Matters of Divinitie, as Have Bin Either Written in our Owne Tongue, or Translated out of Anie Other Language*	Walter Ralegh, voyage to Guiana Sidney's *Defence of Poesie* appears in print
1596	Poor harvests lead to riots Lambeth Articles stating English Calvinist orthodoxy Essex attacks Cadiz	Hamburg Polyglot		Edmund Spenser, *The Faerie Queene*, books IV–VI Johannes Kepler, *Mysterium Cosmographicum*
1597	Campaign in Low Countries		Richard Hooker, *Of the Lawes of Ecclesiasticall Politie*, book V	Francis Bacon *Essayes or Counsels* (1597, enlarged, 1612, 1625)
1598	Edicts of Nantes offers toleration of Huguenots, marking an end of the French Wars of Religion		Antonio Brucioli, *A Commentary upon the Canticle of Canticles.*	James VI of Scotland (later James I of England), *The Trew Law of Free Monarchies* Christopher Marlowe, *Dr Faustus*
1599		Nürnburg Polyglot (1599–1602)	Johannes Drusius, *Quaestionum Ebraicarum*	Richard Hakluyt, *Principall Navigations* (1598–1600) Globe Theatre opens
1600	East India Company granted royal charter			James VI and I, *Basilikon Doron* William Gilbert, *De Magnete* Mary Sidney completes the Sidney psalter
1601	Essex rebellion			William Shakespeare, *Twelfth Night* (c.1601–2)

(Continued.)

Date	Political and Ecclesiastical Context	The Bible and its Translations	Scholarship and Commentary	Cultural developments
1602		Gaelic Bible published in Dublin		Bodleian Library founded
				William Shakespeare, *Troilus and Cressida*
1603	Elizabeth I dies. Succeeded by James VI of Scotland, becoming James I of England (1603–25)			William Shakespeare, *Hamlet*
	Millenary Petition to James			
	London plague			
1604	James calls the Hampton Court Conference and accepts the wish of the Puritans for a new translation of the Bible		William Barlow, *The Sum of the Conference at Hampton Court*	William Shakespeare, *All's Well that Ends Well; Measure for Measure; Othello*
	Richard Bancroft – Archbishop of Canterbury.		Richard Bancroft, *The Rules to be Observed in Translating the Bible*	
	Anglo-Spanish peace treaty			
1605	Guy Fawkes conspiracy–attempt to blow up King & Parliament on 5 November fails		Johannes Buxtorf, *Praeceptiones grammaticae de lingua Hebraea*	Francis Bacon, *Advancement of Learning*
			Andrew Willet, *Hexapla in Genesin*	William Shakespeare, *King Lear*
1606	Oath of Allegiance controversy begins		Gregory of Nyssa, *Opera omnia* (Paris)	William Shakespeare, *Macbeth*
				Ben Jonson, *Volpone*
1607			Johannes Buxtorf, *Lexicon Hebraicum et Chaldaicum*	

Year				
1608	Union with Scotland rejected by Parliament		Andrew Willet, *Hexapla in exodum*	William Perkins, *Works*
1609	James persuades the Church of Scotland to accept episcopacy.	Douai-Rheims Bible's OT (1609–10) published	Martin del Rio, *Pharus Sacrae sapientiae*; David Pareus, *In Genesin Mosis commentarius*	
1610	John Donne, *Pseudo Martyr*		Augustine, *Of the Citie Of God*, tr. Vives.	
1611	George Abbott, Archbishop of Canterbury; Ulster is colonised	King James Bible [Authorized Version] published	John Rainolds, *Censura librorum Apocryphorum veteris Testamenti* (Oppenheim)	Aemilia Lanyer, *Salve Deus Rex Judaeorum*
1612			Hugh Broughton, *A Censure of the Late Translation for our Churches*; Henry Ainsworth, *Annotations on the Pentateuch, the Psalms of David, and the Song of Solomon, The Book of Psalmes*	
1613	Marriage of Princess Elizabeth Stuart and Frederick, Elector of Palatine. Prince Henry dies.		John Chrysostom, *Opera Graecè*, 8 vols (Eton), ed. Henry Savile	
1614	Addled Parliament	John Taylor the Water Poet's *Thumb Bible*	Cornelius a Lapide, *Commentaria in omnes divi Pauli Epistolas*	Walter Ralegh, *History of the World*
1615			Justin Martyr, *Opera* (Paris)	Joseph Swetnam, *Arraignment of Lewd Idle and Froward Women*

(Continued.)

Date	Political and Ecclesiastical Context	The Bible and its Translations	Scholarship and Commentary	Cultural developments
1616	Ejection of Christian missionaries from Japan		Johannes Drusius, *Ad voces Ebraeas NT commentarius duplex*	
1617			Cornelius a Lapide, *Commentaria in vetus et Novum Testamentum* William Fulke, *A Defense of the Sincere and True Translation of the Holy Scriptures into the English Tongue* Johannes Drusius, *Ad loca difficiliora Pentateuchi*	Rachel Speght, *A Mouzell for Melastomus*
1618	Thirty Years War begins Synod of Dort opens		Johann Buxtorf, *Biblia sacra Hebraica* (1618–19) Benedictus Fernandez, *Commentariorum atque observationes moralium in Genesim* (1618–27)	Declaration of Sports
1619	Synod of Dort closes		George Wither, *A Preparation to the Psalter*	
1620	English Parliament agitates to intervene in Thirty Years War Pilgrim Fathers land at Plymouth, Mass.	Definitive version of William Morgan's Welsh Bible	Juan de Mariana, *Scholia in vetus et Novum Testamentum*	Francis Bacon, *Novum organum*
1621	John Donne is made Dean of St Paul's, a position he holds until 1629.			Robert Burton, *The Anatomy of Melancholy*
1622	Directions for Preachers			

Year			
1623	Charles pursues Spanish match, sailing secretly to Madrid.		
1624	Renewed war between Britain and Spain	William Ames, *Medulla theologica* Marin Mersenne, *Questiones celeberrimae in Genesim* Salomon Glassius, *Philologia Sacra* Louis Cappel, *Arcanum punctationis revelatum*	Herbert of Cherbury, *De veritate*
1625	Death of James 1 Charles I (1625–49) Three parliaments in conflict with Charles over financial and foreign policy disputes		Hugo Grotius, *De jure belli ac pacis*
1627		Andreas Rivetus, *Isagoge, seu introductio generalis ad Scripturam sacram veteris et Novi Testamenti*	Hugo Grotius, *De veritate* Lucan, *Pharsalia*, tr Thomas May
1628	The Duke of Buckingham bans the teaching of predestination at Cambridge	Edition of Septuagint, *Vetus Testamentum, secundum LXX* (Paris), ed. Jean Morin (1591–1659)	Coke's *Institutes*—first volume of foundational law writings William Harvey publishes work on circulation of the heart Rubens and Van Dyck are employed by the King and the royal collection is built up
1629	Personal rule of Charles I begins	Paris Polyglot (1629–1645), including Samaritan Pentateuch and Arabic OT First Cambridge edition of KJB	
1630		Project for Gaelic Old testament	

(Continued.)

Date	Political and Ecclesiastical Context	The Bible and its Translations	Scholarship and Commentary	Cultural developments
1631		'Wicked Bible' (re Exodus 20: 14)	John Brinsley, *The Preachers Charge, and Peoples Duty about Preaching and Hearing of the Word* (London)	
1632				Galileo Galilei, *Dialogo sopra i due massimi sistemi del mondo*
1633	William Laud, Archbishop of Canterbury, intensifies Caroline anti-Calvinism.	First Scottish KJB (Edinburgh)		George Herbert, *The Temple*
1634	Laudian bishops' visitations			John Milton, *Comus*
	Ship money levied, in the face of stiff opposition			
1636	Book of Canons imposed on Scotland			
1637	Charles I faces crisis over unpopular imposition of a new liturgy (Book of Common Prayer) on Scotland	Dutch Bible (Amsterdam)		John Milton, *Lycidas*
1638			William Chillingworth, *The Religion of Protestants*	
1639	First Bishops' War against Scots		Johannes Buxtorf, *Lexicon Chaldaicum Talmudicum et Rabbinicum*	
1640	11 Years of Personal Government by Charles ends with Short, then Long Parliament	Bay Psalm Book (Massachusetts)		
	Second Bishops' War			
	The Root and Branch Petition (against episcopacy)			

1641	The Grand Remonstrance		Hugo Grotius, *Annotationes in libros evangeliorum* (Amsterdam)
	Thomas Wentworth found guilty of treason and executed		John Milton, *Of Reformation Touching Church Discipline in England*
	Censorship breaks down		Richard Baker, *An Apologie for Lay-Mens Writing in Divinity*
1642	Outbreak of Civil War in England, Ireland, Scotland, and Wales		Thomas Browne, *Religio medici*
	Suspension of episcopacy		John Milton, *Apology for Smectymnuus*
			Playhouses are closed at the outbreak of Civil War
1643	Solemn League and Covenant	*The Souldiers Pocket Bible*	Jean Diodati, *Pious and Learned Annotations*
	Westminster Assembly of Divines		
	Licensing order attempts to impose press censorship		
1644	Trial of Archbishop Laud begins		Hugo Grotius, *Annotata ad vetus Testamentum*
			Westminster Annotations
			John Milton, *Areopagitica*
1645	Laud found guilty of treason and executed		
	New Model Army formed		
	Ordinance of Worship and Presbyterian Church Government		
1646	First Civil War ends		Edward Leigh, *A Treatise of Divinity*	Thomas Edwards, *Gangraena*
	Episcopacy abolished		John Gregory, *Notes and Observations Upon Some Passages of Scripture*	Thomas Browne, *Pseudodoxia epidemica*
			Richard Baxter, *A Plea for Congregational Government*

(Continued.)

Date	Political and Ecclesiastical Context	The Bible and its Translations	Scholarship and Commentary	Cultural developments
1647	An Agreement of the People, series of tracts, printed between 1647 and 1649 Putney Debates		John Lightfoot, *The Harmony, Chronicle, and Order of the Old Testament*	
1648	Second Civil War begins *Articles of Christian Religion* Pride's Purge, leaving Rump Parliament		Gerrard Winstanley, *The Mysterie of God Concerning the Whole Creation*	Robert Herrick, *Hesperides and Noble Numbers*
1649	Trial and execution of Charles I; England declared a commonwealth Leveller mutinies and suppression Cromwell's Siege of Drogheda leads to massacre of Irish Peace of Westphalia, ending Thirty Years War			Charles I (attrib.), *Eikon Basilike* John Milton, *Eikonoklastes* Gerrard Winstanley, *The New Law of Righteousnes Budding Forth*
1650	Anglican Book of Common Prayer abolished Diggers suppressed Brutal campaign in Ireland culminates in the Battle of Dunbar, and crushes Irish resistance		Louis Cappel, *Critica Sacra*	
1651	Navigation Act: war between England and the Netherlands Prince Charles acknowledged as King of Scotland Royalist defeat at Battle of Worcester			Thomas Hobbes, *Leviathan* William Davenant, *Gondibert*
1652	Engagement Controversy ends		James Ussher, *De textus hebraici veteris Testamenti variantibus lectionibus ad Ludovicum Cappellum Epistola*	

Year			
1653	Rump Parliament dissolved Barebones Parliament Cromwell becomes Lord Protector	'Quakers' Bible', printed by Giles Calvert	James Shirley's masque *Cupid and Death* performed before the Ambassador of Portugal.
1654	War against Dutch ends	Edward Leigh, *A System or Body of Divinity*	
1655	England takes Jamaica from Spain	John Lightfoot, *Harmony, Chronicall and Order of the NT* Thomas Fuller, *The Church History of Britain*	Isaac de La Peyrère, *Praeadamitae*
1656		John Bunyan, *Some Gospel–Truths Opened*	Abraham Cowley, *Davideis; Or, A Sacred Poem of the Troubles of David*
1657	Oliver Cromwell refuses the crown and establishes the second Protectorate	*Biblia Sacra London Polyglotta*, ed. Brian Walton, including Codex Alexandrinus, Peshitto, Ethiopic psalms and NT, Persian Pentateuch and Gospels, targums. Also textual-critical collations and annotations. Theodore Haak's Bible with Dutch Annotations	Edward Sexby, *Killing Noe Murder*
1658	Cromwell dies. His son, Richard becomes Lord Protector. Savoy Declaration of Independent Churches		

(Continued.)

Date	Political and Ecclesiastical Context	The Bible and its Translations	Scholarship and Commentary	Cultural developments
1659	Richard Cromwell abdicates; the Rump Parliament and the republic are restored	New Testament in shorthand (Jeremiah Rich)	Robert Gell, *An Essay toward the Amendment of the last English Translation of the Bible*	John Bunyan, *The Doctrine of the Law and Grace Unfolded*
1660	Colonel George Monck marches on London; Rump Parliament dissolved. Charles II succeeds to the throne of England (r. 1660–85) Act of Free and General Pardon, Indemnity, and Oblivion Cromwell, and other regicides, exhumed, posthumously hanged and decapitated		*Critici Sacri*, ed. John Pearson	Samuel Pepys begins his diary Theatres reopen; William Davenant and Thomas Killigrew appointed managers of the two theatre companies. Royal Society founded
1661	Election of Cavalier Parliament Fifth Monarchist uprising in London The Corporation Act limits the holding of public office to Anglicans		John Owen, *Theologoumena Pantodapa* Robert Boyle, *Considerations Touching the Style of the Holy Scriptures*	
1662	Act of Uniformity. Ejection of Puritans from Anglican livings Licensing of the Press Act			Royal Society granted its first charter
1663		Massachusetts Bible, tr. into Wampanoag Native American		John Bunyan, *Prison Meditations*
1664	Conventicle Act restricts nonconformist meetings			

1665	Anglo–Dutch War begins	
	The Five Mile Act prohibits dissenters from coming within five miles of municipal areas	
	Great Plague of London	
1666	Great Fire of London.	John Bunyan, *Grace Abounding to the Chief of Sinners*
		Margaret Cavendish, *The Blazing World*
		John Milton, *Paradise Lost*
1667	Anglo–Dutch War ends in defeat and humiliation after Dutch ships set fire to the English fleet in the Medway	
1668		John Dryden, *Essay of Dramatick Poesie*
1669		Matthew Poole, *Synopsis criticorum* (1669–74)
1670	Secret Treaty of Dover, where Louis XIV of France gives Charles financial aid upon condition that he converts to Catholicism	Baruch Spinoza, *Tractatus theologico-politicus*
	Second Conventicle Act against nonconformists	
1671		John Milton, *Samson Agonistes*; *Paradise Regained*
1672	Declaration of Indulgence	KJB printed with Geneva Notes
1673	Parliament forces the repeal of the Declaration of Indulgence and introduces the Test Act	Thomas Traherne, *Roman Forgeries*
		Christiaan Huygens, *Horologium Oscillatorium*

(Continued.)

Date	Political and Ecclesiastical Context	The Bible and its Translations	Scholarship and Commentary	Cultural developments
1674				John Milton, *Paradise Lost*, 2nd edn, which redivides the narrative from ten books into twelve
1675	Proclamation for the suppression of Coffee Houses	First Oxford Edition of KJV		Thomas Traherne, *Christian Ethics*
1676				Joseph Glanville, *Essays On Several Important Subjects in Philosophy and Religion* George Etherege, *Man of Mode*
1677	William Sancroft, Archbishop of Canterbury			
1678	Titus Oates's sensational allegations lead to Popish Plot fever		Richard Simon, *Histoire critique du Vieux Testament* (1678–85)	John Bunyan, *Pilgrim's Progress*
1679	New Parliament elected and prorogued by Charles Exclusion Crisis begins; attempting to exclude James from succeeding the throne.			Lucy Hutchinson, first five books of *Order and Disorder* printed
1680		Gaelic New Testament published in London		John Wilmot, Earl of Rochester, reportedly converts to Catholicism on his deathbed
1681	Exclusion Crisis ends when Charles dissolves Parliament Charles rules without Parliament until his death in 1685			John Dryden, *Absalom and Achitophel*

Year			
1682	Anthony Ashley Cooper, first Earl of Shaftesbury, escapes treason charges by fleeing England		Bideford Witch Trial leads to the last known hangings for witchcraft in England
			Gottfried Wilhelm von Leibniz, *Acta eruditorum*
1683	Rye House Plot	Matthew Poole, *Annotations*	
	Algernon Sidney executed		
1685	Charles II dies	Gaelic Old Testament published in London	
	James II succeeds to the crown (r. 1685–8)		
	Monmouth Rebellion		
1687	James's First Declaration of Indulgence		Isaac Newton, *Philosophiae naturalis principia mathematica*
			Aphra Behn, *Oroonoko*
1688	William of Orange lands at Torbay; James abdicates and flees England		
1689	William III and Mary II proclaimed joint constitutional monarchs		John Locke, *Two Treatises of Government*
	Bill of Rights and Toleration Act		
	Start of the Nine Years War/War of Grand Alliance		
1690			John Locke, *An Essay Concerning Human Understanding*
1691	John Tillotson made Archbishop of Canterbury		John Dryden and Henry Purcell, *King Arthur*

(Continued.)

Date	Political and Ecclesiastical Context	The Bible and its Translations	Scholarship and Commentary	Cultural developments
1694	Triennial Act			Bank of England established by royal charter
	Death of Mary II; William III reigns in his own right until his death in 1702. Succeeded by Mary's sister, Anne.			Mary Astell, *A Serious Proposal to the Ladies, for the Advancement of Their True and Greatest Interest*
1696	Unsuccessful Jacobite plot to assassinate William III		Richard Baxter, *Reliquiœ Baxterianœ*	
1697	Treaty of Ryswick ends Nine Year's War/ War of Grand Alliance		John Locke, *A Common-place Book to the Holy Bible*	
1698	Whitehall Palace destroyed by fire			Jeremy Collier, *A Short View of the Immorality and Profaneness of the English Stage*
	Royal African Company monopoly abolished, effectively permitting anyone to enter the slave trade.			
1699	Standing army limited to 7,000 'native born' men by Parliament			John Blow appointed composer to the Chapel Royal.
1700				William Congreve, *The Way of The World*
				Mary Astell, *Some Reflections Upon Marriage*

Bibliography

Manuscripts Cited

The British Library, London

Add. MS 24
Add. MS 4820
Add. MS 4987
Add. MS 6489
Add. MS 81083
Add. MS 15852
Add. MS 28721
Burney 363
Cotton MS Cleopatra. E. V
Egerton 2884
Harley 422
Harley 750
Harley 1328
Lansdowne 740
Sloane 118
Sloane 3827
Sloane 4051
Royal 17.B.XX
Royal 18 B.16

Bodleian Library, Oxford

MS Auct. F. 6. 22
MS Barlow 10
MS Bodley 666
MS Bodley 670
MS D 1.14 Th.Seld.
MS Eng.th.e.14
MS Rawlinson C 849
MS Rawlinson C 850
MS Rawlinson D 280
MS Rawlinson D 1290
MS Smith 73
MS Tanner 278
MS Tanner 437

Cambridge, Corpus Christi College, Parker Library

MS 242
MS 106

Cambridge University Library, Cambridge

MS Add. 3856
MS Add. 7647

Corpus Christi College, Oxford

MS 312

Dublin, Trinity College

MS 125
MS 126
MS 382
MS 388

Edinburgh University Library

MS. La. III 116

Folger Shakespeare Library, Washington DC

MS V.b.198

Gloucester, Gloucestershire Record Office

Lloyd Baker MSS D 3549, box 77

Huntington Library, San Marino, California

Ellesmere MS 1172

University of Leeds Library, Brotherton Collection

MS Lt q 2

Leicester, Leicestershire Record Office

Conant MSS, Barker Correspondence, vol. 2

Leiden University Library

MS VMI 4

London, Lambeth Palace Library

MS 592
Warham's Register, I

London, Royal Society

MS Register Book 15

Maidstone, Kent History and Library Centre

MS 23/1–2
MS 25/1–3
MS U1121/ Z 22

National Library of Ireland, Dublin

MS GO 68

National Records of Scotland

CH2/121/1
CH2/121/2
CH2/271/2
GD1/649/1

Northampton, Northamptonshire Record Office

Finch Hatton MSS 2623-5

Princeton University Library, NjP, Robert Taylor Collection

MS RTCO1

Stanford University Library

SUL, HP 25/2/21B–22A

Trinity College, Cambridge

MS O.10.33

Trowbridge, Wiltshire Record Office

MS 1178/631

Venerable English College Rome

Liber 1394

Warwickshire County Record Office

MS CR 136/A/12

BIBLES

Alter, Robert, tr., *The Wisdom Books: Job, Proverbs, and Ecclesiastes, A Translation with Commentary* (New York and London: W. W. Norton & Co., 2010).

An Biobla naomhtha … noch atá anois chum maitheas coitcheann na nGaóidheail Albanach, áthruighte go haireach as an litir Eíreandha chum na mion-litre shoi-léighidh Romhanta (London: Robert Everingham, 1690).

Biblia sacra Hebraice, Chaldaice, Graece, et Latine, ed. Arias Montanus, 8 vols (Antwerp: Christopher Plantin, 1567–73).

Biblia sacra iuxta vulgatam versionem, ed. Robert Weber, Roger Gryson, et al., 5th edn (Stuttgart: Deutsche Bibelgesellschaft, 2007).

Biblia sacra polyglotta complectentia textus originales, Hebraicum, cum Pentateucho Samaritano, Chaldaicum, Graecum: versionumque antiquarum, Samaritanae, Graecae LXXII interp., Chaldaicae, Syriacae, Arabicae, Æthiopicae, Persicae, Vulg. Lat., quicquid compari poterat, ed. Brian Walton, 6 vols (London: Thomas Roycroft, 1654–7).

Bibliorum sacrorum cum glossa ordinaria, 6 vols (Venice: Giunta, 1603).

Biblia the Bible, That Is, the Holy Scripture of the Olde and New Testament, tr. Miles Coverdale (Cologne: E. Cervicornus & J. Soter?, 1535).

Bissell, Edwin. *The Apocrypha of the Old Testament with Historical Introductions, a Revised Translation, and Notes Critical and Explanatory* (New York: Charles Scribner's Sons, 1880).

Blenkinsopp, Joseph. *Isaiah 1–39: A New Translation with Introduction and Commentary*, The Anchor Bible (New York: Doubleday-Anchor Bible, 2000).

Coogan, Michael, Marc Brettler, Carol Newsom, and Pheme Perkins, eds. *The New Oxford Annotated Bible: New Revised Standard Version with the Apocrypha*, 3rd edn. (New York: Oxford University Press, 2001).

Goostly Psalmes and Spirituall Songes Drawen out of the Holy Scripture, for the Co[m]forte and Consolacyon of Soch as Love to Rejoyse in God and his Worde, compiled by Miles Coverdale ([London]: [J. Rastell] for John Gough, [1535?]).

King James Bible: A Selection, ed. W. H. Stevenson (London: Longman, 1994).

La Bible, qui est toute la saincte escriture du vieil et du nouveau testament (Geneva: [Jérémie des Planches], 1558).

La Bible, qui est toute la saincte escriture, ascavoir le vieil et nouveau Testament (Geneva: Nicolas Barbier & Thomas Courteau, 1559).

La sainte Bible, contenant les saintes escritures, tant du vieil, que du nouveau testament (Lyon: Balthazar Arnoulet, 1550).

Metzger, Bruce M., and Roland E. Murphy, eds. *New Oxford Annotated Bible with the Apocryphal/Deuterocanonical Books* (New York: Oxford University Press, 1991).

New Revised Standard Version of the Bible, National Council of the Churches of Christ (New York: Harper Collins, 2014).

Novum Testamentum Graece, 28th edn, ed. Eberhard Nestle, Erwin Nestle, Barabara Aland, Kurt Aland, and Holger Strutwolf (Stuttgart: Deutsche Bibelgesellschaft, 2013).

Rhodes, Erroll F., and Liana Lupas, eds. *The Translators to the Reader* (New York: American Bible Society, 1997).

Robertson, William. *Safer tehilim usafer eykhah sepher tehilim u-sepher echam: The Hebrew Text of the Psalmes and Lamentations, but Published (for to Encourage and Facilitate Beginners in Their Way) with the Reading Thereof in Known English Letters, excepting only the Letter, Which Because of the Incertainty of Its Genuine Pronunciation is Left Either to Be Read or Not, According as the Reason of the Reader Shall Judge Most Convenient* (London: for the author, 1656).

Testamenti Veteris Biblia sacra sive libri canonici, priscae Iudaeorum ecclesiae a Deo traditi, / Latini recens ex Hebraeo facti, brevibusq[ue] scholiis illustrati ab Immanuele Tremellio & Francisco Junio (London: Henry Middleton, 1585).

Testamenti Veteris Biblia sacra sive libri canonici... Latini recens ex Hebraeo facti, tr. Immanuel Tremellius and Franciscus Junius (London: Henry Middleton [& Thomas Vautrollier] for William Norton, 1593).

The Apocrypha and Pseudepigrapha of the Old Testament in English, ed. R. H. Charles, 2 vols (Oxford: Clarendon Press, 1913; reprinted, 1973).

The Bible: In Englyshe (London: Edward Whitchurch, 1540).

The Bible and Holy Scriptures Conteyned in the Olde and Newe Testament (Geneva: Rowland Hall, 1560).

The Bible and Holy Scriptures Conteined in the Olde and Newe Testament (Edinburgh: Alexander Arbuthnot, 1579).

The Bible: That Is, the Holy Scriptures Conteined in the Old and New Testament (London: Deputies of Christopher Barker, 1599).

The Bible: Authorized King James Version, ed. Robert Carroll and Stephen Prickett (Oxford: Oxford University Press, 1997).

The Book of Psalms, tr. Robert Alter (New York: W. W. Norton & Co., 2007).

The Byble, Which is all the Holy Scripture, trans. Thomas Matthew [pseud. for William Tyndale and Miles Coverdale] (Antwerp: Matthias Crom, 1537).

The First Part of the Psalmes of David in English Meter by T. Sternhold and Others (London: John Day, 1566).

The Geneva Bible: A Facsimile of the 1560 Edition (Madison: University of Wisconsin Press, 1969; repr. Peabody, MA: Hendrickson, 2007).

The Gospel according to Saint Matthew, and Part of the First Chapter of the Gospel according to Saint Mark, Translated into English from the Greek, with Original Notes by Sir John Cheke, ed. James Goodwin (London: Pickering, 1843).

The Holie Bible Faithfully Translated into English... by the English College of Doway (Douai: Laurence Kellam, 1609).

The Holy Bible, Containing the Old and New Testaments, with the Apocryphal Books, in the Earliest English Versions Made from the Latin Vulgate by John Wycliffe and His Followers, ed. Josiah Forshall and Frederic Madden (Oxford: Oxford University Press, 1850).

The Holy Bible, containing the Old Testament and the New. Authorised and Appointed to be Read in Churches (London: Robert Barker, 1602).

The Holy Bible, Conteyning the Old Testament, and the New: Newly Translated out of the Originall Tongues: & with the Former Translations Diligently Compared and Revised (London: Robert Barker, 1611).

The Holy Bible according to the Authorized Version (A.D. 1611). With an Explanatory and Critical Commentary: Apocrypha, ed. Henry Wace (London: John Murray, 1888).

The Holy Bible, containing the Old and New Testaments, Translated Out of the Original Tongues and with the Former Translations Diligently Compared and Revised by His Majesty's Special Command A.D. 1611 (London: British and Foreign Bible Society, 1967).

The Holy Bible: New Revised Standard Version, Anglicized Edition (Oxford: Oxford University Press, 1995).

The Holy Bible Quartercentenary Edition, ed. Gordon Campbell (Oxford: Oxford University Press, 2010).

The New Testament of Jesus Christ, Translated Faithfully into English, tr. Gregory Martin (Rheims: John Fogny, 1582).

The New Testament of our Lord Jesus Christ, Translated out of Greeke by Theod. Beza, tr. Laurence Thomson (London: Christopher Barker, 1576).

The New Testament of our Lord Jesus Christ, translated out of Greeke by Theod. Beza, tr. Laurence Thomson (London: Christopher Barker, 1582).

The Newe Testament Both in Latine and Englyshe Eche Correspondente to the Other after the Vulgare Texte,Communely Called S. Ieromes: Faythfullye Translated by Iohan Hollybushe [sic] (Southwark: James Nicholson, 1538).

The Newe Testament of Our Lord Jesus Christ. Conferred with the Greke, and Best Approued Translations (London: T. V. for Christopher Barker, 1575).

The Newe Testament, Dylygently Corrected and Compared with the Greke by Willyam Tindale (Antwerp: Martin Emperowr, 1534).

The Old Testament Pseudepigrapha, ed. James H. Charlesworth, 2 vols (New York: Doubleday, 1985).

The Pentateuch, tr. William Tyndale (Malborow in the lande of Hesse [i.e. Antwerp]: Hans Luft [i.e. Johan Hoochstraten], 1530).

The Sidney Psalter: The Psalms of Sir Philip and Mary Sidney, ed. Hannibal Hamlin, Michael G. Brennan, Margaret P. Hannay, and Noel J. Kinnamon (Oxford: Oxford University Press, 2009).

The Souldiers Pocket Bible, 2nd edn (London: G. B. for G. C., 1644).

The Volume of the Bokes Called Apocripha (London: John Day & William Seres, 1549).

The Whole Booke of Psalmes with Their Wonted Tunes, as They Are Song in Churches, Composed into Foure Parts (London: Thomas East, 1592).

Tiomna Nuadh (London: Robert Everington, 1681).

Tiomna nuadh ar dtighearna agus ar slanaightheora Iosa Criosd, trans. Uilliam Ó Domhnuill (Dublin: William Kearney & John Franckton, 1602).

Printed Primary sources

PL stands for J. P. Migne et al. (eds), *Patrologiae cursus completus... series latina*, 217 vols (Paris: Imprimerie Catholique, 1844–55), <http://pld.chadwyck.co.uk>.

A Booke of Certaine Canons, concerning Some Parte of the Discipline of the Church of England (London: John Day, 1571).

A Briefe Treatise concerning the Burnynge of Bucer and Phagius, at Cambrydge, in the tyme of Quene Mary, with Theyr Restitution in the Time of our Moste Gracious Soverayne Lady That Nowe Is, tr. Arthur Golding (London: Thomas Marshe, 1562).

A Complete Collection of State Trials and Proceedings for High Treason and Other Crimes and Misdemeanours, from the Earliest Period to the Year 1783, ed. T. B. Howell, 34 vols (London: Hansard, 1816–28).

A Declaration of Certayne Principall Articles of Religion… for the Unitie of Doctrine [Thirty-Nine Articles] (London: Richard Jugge, [1561?]).

A Directory for the Publike Worship of God Throughout the Three Kingdomes of Scotland, England, and Ireland (Edinburgh: Evan Tyler, 1645).

A Discovery of the Rebels by J. V., Prisoner (London: s.n., 1643).

A Dyaloge of Syr Thomas More … Wherin be Treatyd Dyvers Maters, as of the Veneration & Worshyp of Ymages (London: William Rastell, 1529).

A Letter from a Scholler in Oxenford to his Uncle a Merchant in Broad Street (London: s.n., 1643).

A Parallel between the Israelites Desiring of King Saul, and Englands Desiring of a Parliament (London: for Robert Wood, 1643).

A Proclamation Made and Divysed by the Kingis Hyghnes wyth the advise of his Honorable Counsaile, for Dampning of Erroneous Bokes and Heresies, and Prohibitinge of the Havinge of Holy Scripture (London: Thomas Berthelet, 1530).

A Protestant Catechisme for Little Children (London: for Thomas Parkhurst, 1673).

Abbot, George. *The Coppie of a Letter Sent from My Lords Grace of Canterburie Shewing the Grave and Weighty Reasons Which Induced the Kings Majestie to Prescribe those Former Directions for Preachers* ([Oxford: J. Lichfield & J. Short, 1622]).

Abbot, George. *The Whole Book of Job Paraphrased* (London: Edward Griffin for Henry Overton, 1640).

Abbot, George. *Brief Notes upon the Whole Book of Psalms* (London: William Bentley, 1651).

Acosta, José de. *The Naturall and Morall Historie of the East and West Indies*, tr. E.G. (London: Valentine Sims for Edward Blount & William Aspley, 1604).

Acosta, José de. *The Natural and Moral History of the Indies*, ed. Jane E. Mangan, intro. and commentary Walter D. Mignolo, tr. Frances López-Morillas (Durham, NC: Duke University Press, 2002).

Acts and Proceedings of the General Assemblies of the Kirk of Scotland, 3 vols (Edinburgh: Bannatyne Club, 1839–45).

Acts of the General Assembly of the Church of Scotland, M.DC.XXXVIII.–M.DCCC.XLII (Edinburgh: Edinburgh Print and Publishing Co., 1843).

Adtimchiol an chreidimh, ed. R. L. Thomson (Edinburgh: Scottish Gaelic Texts Society, 1962).

Aelfric, Abbot of Eynsham. *A Saxon Treatise concerning the Old and New Testament … Now First Published in Print … by William L'isl of Wilburgham* (London: John Haviland for Henry Seile, 1623).

Aibidil gaoidheilge & caiticiosma: Seaán Ó Cearnaigh's Irish Primer of Religion Published in 1571, ed. Brian Ó Cuív (Dublin: Dublin Institute for Advanced Studies, 1994).

Alabaster, William. *Unpublished Works by William Alabaster (1560–1640)*, ed. Dana F. Sutton, Salzburg Studies in English Literature, 126 (Salzburg: Salzburg Poetry, 1997).

Alexander, Gavin, ed. *Sidney's 'The Defense of Poesy' and Selected Renaissance Literary Criticism* (London: Penguin, 2004).

Allen, Ward, ed. *Translating for King James: Notes Made by a Translator of King James's Bible* (London: Allen Lane, 1970).

Ames, William. *Conscience with the Power and Cases Thereof* (Leiden and London: [W. Christiaens, E. Griffin, J. Dawson], 1639).

Ames, William. The *Marrow of Sacred Divinity, Drawne out of the Holy Scriptures* (London: Edward Griffin for Henry Overton, 1642).

Amico, Bernardino, *Trattato de sacri edificii di Terra Santa* (Rome: ex typographia linguarum externarum, 1609).

An Abridgement of That Booke Which the Ministers of Lincolne Diocese Delivered to his Majestie (Leiden: W. Brewster, 1617).

An Account of the Design of Printing about 3000 Bibles in Irish, with the Psalms of David in Metre, for the Use of the Highlanders (London?: s.n., 1690?).

An Admonition to the Parliament ([Hemel Hempstead?: J. Stroud?, 1572]).

An Almanack and Prognostication for 1544 ([London: John Mayler, 1544]).

An teagasg Criosduighe: as cóir do nuile dhuine dfoghluim, suil cuirfighther fa láimh easbuig é (London: Robert Everingham, 1680).

Andrewes, Lancelot. *Tortura Torti: siue, ad Mattaei Torti librum responsio* (London: Robert Barker, 1609).

Andrewes, Lancelot. *A Sermon Preached Before His Majestie at White-Hall, On the 24 March last, being Easter day* (London: Robert Barker, 1611).

Andrewes, Lancelot. *XCVI. Sermons by the Right Honorable and Reverend Father in God, Lancelot Andrewes, Late Lord Bishop of Winchester* (London: George Miller for Richard Badger, 1629).

Andrewes, Lancelot. *Lancelot Andrewes: Selected Sermons and Lectures*, ed. Peter McCullough (Oxford: Oxford University Press, 2005).

Annotations upon All the Books of the Old and New Testament… By the Joynt-Labour of Certain Learned Divines, thereunto Appointed (London: John Legatt & John Raworth, 1645).

Anon. *Eight Learned Personages Lately Converted* (London: for J. B., 1601).

Aquinas, Thomas. *The Summa theological of St. Thomas Aquinas*, ed. and tr. Fathers of the English Dominican Province, 5 vols (New York: Benziger Bros. edn, 1947; CCEL, 1981).

Ariosto, Lodovico. *Orlando Furioso*, tr. John Harington (London: Richard Field, 1591).

Aristotelis poetica, per Alexandrum Paccium, patritium Florentinum, in Latinum conversa ([Paris?]: Jacobum Bogardum, 1542).

Aristotle. *Aristoteles de poetica interprete Georgio Valla Placentino* (Venice: Georgium Arrivabenum, 1515).

Aristotle. *Poetics*, tr. Stephen Halliwell, *Loeb Classical Library* 199 (Cambridge, Mass.: Harvard University Press, 1995).

Arnold, Matthew, ed. *Isaiah of Jerusalem in the Authorized English Version, with an Introduction, Corrections, and Notes* (London: Macmillan, 1883).

Articles of Christian Religion (London: for Edward Husband, 1648).

Articles to be Enquired of Within the Dioces of London, in the Second Trienniall Visitation (London: Elizabeth Allde, 1631).

Articles to be Enquyred in the Visitacion, in the Fyrste Yeare of the Raygne of our Moost Drad Soueraygne Lady, Elizabeth (London: Richard Jugge & John Cawood, 1559).

Articles Whereupon It Was Agreed by the Archbishoppes and Bishoppes of Both Provinces, and the Whole Cleargie in the Convocation Holden at London in the Yere of Our Lorde God. 1562 (London: Richard Jugge & John Cawood, 1571).

Articles, to be Enquired of Within the Dioces of London, in the Third Generall Visitation of the Reverend Father in God, Richard Bishop of London (London: [William White] for Clement Knight, 1604).

Ascham, Roger. *The Scholemaster, or Plaine and Perfite Way of Teachyng Children, to Understand, Write, and Speake, the Latin Tong* (London: John Daye, 1570).

Augustine. *De civitate Dei* (PL 41).

Augustine. *The Confessions of the Incomparable Doctour S. Augustine*, tr. Tobie Matthew (St Omer: English College Press, 1620).

Augustine. *Saint Augustines Confessions Translated: And With Some Marginall Notes Illustrated*, tr. William Watts (London: John Norton for John Partridge, 1631).

Augustine. *Contra mendacium* (PL 40).

Augustine. *Contra mendacium* (*Against Lying*), tr. Harold B. Jaffee, in *Treatises on Various Subjects*, ed. Roy J. Deferrari, The Fathers of the Church, 16 (Washington, DC: Catholic University of America Press, 1952), 121–79.

Augustine. *De doctrina Christiana*, ed. R. P. H. Green (Oxford: Oxford University Press, 1997).

Augustine. *On Christian Doctrine*, ed. and tr. R. P. H. Green (Oxford: Clarendon Press, 1995).

Augustine. *Ennarationes in Psalmos* (PL 36).

Augustine. *St Augustine on the Psalms*, tr. Scholastica Hebgin and Felicitas Corrigan, *Ancient Christian Writers*, 30 (London: Longmans, Green & Co., 1961).

Augustine. *Epistolae* (PL 33).

Augustine. *De utilitate credendi*, tr. C. Cornish, *Nicence and Post-Nicene Fathers*, 1st ser. 3, ed. Philip Schaff (Buffalo, NY: Christian Literature Publishing Co., 1887).

Augustine. *On the Profit of Believing*, tr. C. Cornish, *Select Library of the Nicene and Post-Nicene Fathers*, 1st ser., ed. Philip Schaff (Grand Rapids, Mich.: William B. Eerdemans, 1887).

Avitus. *The Fall of Man: De spiritalis historiae gestis libri I–III*, ed. Daniel J. Nodes, Toronto Medieval Latin Texts, 16 (Toronto: Pontifical Institute of Medieval Studies, 1985).

Aylesbury, Thomas. *A Sermon Preached at Paules-Crosse* (London: George Eld for Leonard Becket and Robert Wilson, 1623).

Bacon, Francis. *The Twoo Bookes of Francis Bacon: Of the Proficience and Advancement of Learning, Divine and Humane* (London: Thomas Purfoot & Thomas Creede for Henrie Tomes, 1605).

Bacon, Francis. *The Essays*, ed. John Pitcher (Harmondsworth: Penguin Books, 1985).

Baillie, Robert. *A Dissuasive from the Errours of the Time* (London: for Samuel Gellibrand, 1645).

Baillie, Robert. *The Letters and Journals of Robert Baillie*, 3 vols (Edinburgh: Bannatyne Club, 1841–2).

Baker, Richard. *An Apologie for Lay-Mens Writing in Divinity* (London: Edward Griffin for Frances Eglesfield, 1641).

Baker, Richard. *A Chronicle of the Kings of England* (London: R.C. and R.H. for Daniel Frere, 1643).

Baker, Thomas. *Reflections upon Learning* (London: for A. Bosvile, 1699).

Baldwin, William, ed. and tr., *A Treatise of Moral Phylosophie: contaynyng the Sayinges of the Wyse* (London: Edward Whitchurch, 1547).

Bale, John [as John Harryson, *pseud.*]. *Yet a Course at the Romyshe Foxe* (Zurich [i.e. Antwerp]: Oliver Jacobson [i.e. A. Goinus], 1543).

Bale, John. *The Image of Both Churches* ([London: Richard Jugge, 1548?]).

Bancroft, Richard. *Daungerous Positions and Proceedings Published and Practiced within This Iland of Brytaine, Under Pretence of Reformation, and for the Presbiteriall Discipline* (London: John Wolfe, 1593).

Banks, Jonathan. *The Life of the Right Reverend Father in God, Edw. Rainbow, D.D.* (London: Samuel Roycroft for Robert Clavell, 1688).

Barclay, William. [*Contra monarchomachos*] *De regno et regali potestate adversus Buchananum, Brutum, Boucherium, & reliquos monarchomachos, libri sex* (Paris: G. Chaudière, 1600).

Barlow, Thomas. *The Genuine Remains of That Learned Prelate Dr. Thomas Barlow* (London: for John Dunton, 1693).

Barlow, William. *The Summe and Substance of the Conference... at Hampton Court* (London: John Windet for Mathew Law, 1604).

Barlow, William. *An Answer to a Catholike English-Man* (London: Thomas Haviland for Mathew Law, 1609).

Barrow, Henry. *A Brief Discoverie of the False Church* (Dort?: s.n., 1590).

Barrow, Henry. *A Collection of Certaine Sclaunderous Articles Gyven out by the Bishops* (Dordrecht?: s.n., 1590).

Battiferrai degli Ammannati, Laura. *I sette salmi penitentiali profeta Davit tradotti in lingua Toscana* (Florence: Bernardo I Giunta, 1566).

Battiferrai degli Ammannati, Laura. *Laura Battiferra and her Literary Circle: An Anthology*, ed. and tr. Victoria Kirkham (Chicago: University of Chicago Press, 2006).

Baxter, Richard. *A Plea for Congregationall Government* (London: for Thomas Underhill, 1646).

Baxter, Richard. *The Unreasonableness of Infidelity; Manifested in Four Discourses* (London: R. W[hite]. for Thomas Underhill, 1655).

Baxter, Richard. *The True and Only Way of Concord of All the Christian Churches* (London: for John Hancock, 1680).

Baxter, Richard. *Reliquiae Baxterianae* (London: for T. Parkhurst, J. Robinson, J. Lawrence, & J. Dunton, 1696).

Bayle, Pierre. *A General Dictionary, Historical and Critical: In Which a New and Accurate Translation of That of the Celebrated Mr. Bayle Is Included*, 10 vols (London: James Bettenham, 1734–41).

Behm, Martin. *Tragicomödia: Ein schön teutsch Spiel vom Holoferne unnd der Judith* (Wittenberg: n.publ., 1618).

Behn, Aphra. *Poems upon Several Occasions: With a Voyage to the Island of Love* (London: for R. Tonson & J. Tonson, 1684).

Behn, Aphra. *A Congratulatory Poem to His Most Sacred Majesty on the Happy Birth of the Prince of Wales* (London: Will Canning, 1688).

Bernard, Nicholas. *Certain Discourses ... unto Which is Added a Character of Bishop Bedel* (London: for John Crook, 1659).

Beveridge, William. *Institutionum chronologicarum libri II* (London: Thomas Roycroft, 1669).

Beza, Theodore. *The Psalms of David, Truly Opened and Explaned by Paraphrasis, According to the Right Sense of Every Psalme*, tr. Anthonie Gilby (London: John Harison & Henry Middleton, 1580).

Bilson, Thomas. *A Sermon Preached at Westminster before the King and Queenes Majesties, at their Coronations* (London: Valentine Simmes for Clement Knight, 1603).

Boate, Arnold, and Francis Tayler, *Examen praefationis Morini* (Leiden: Joannis Maris, 1636).

Boethius. *Consolatio philosophiae*, ed. and with a commentary by James J. O'Donnell, 3 vols (Bryn Mawr, Pa.: Bryn Mawr Latin Commentaries, 1990).

Bois, John. *Veteris interpretis cum Beza aliisque recentioribus collatio* (London: T. Roycroft for R. Littlebury, 1655).

Bolton, Robert. *Two Sermons Preached at Northampton* (London: George Miller, 1635).

Bomelius, Henricus. *The Summe of the Holye Scripture*, tr. Simon Fish (Antwerp: n.publ., 1529).

Booker, John. *No Mercurius Aquaticus, but a Cable-Rope, Double Twisted for John Tayler* (London: for G. B., 1644).

Boyd, Zachary. *Two Orientall Pearles, Grace and Glory* (Edinburgh: John Wreittoun, 1629).

Boyd, Zachary. *Selected Sermons of Zachary Boyd*, ed. David W. Atkinson (Scottish Text Society, 1989).

Boyle, Robert. *Some Considerations Touching the Style of the H. Scriptures* (London: Henry Herringman, 1661).

Boyle, Robert. *The Lismore Papers (Second Series) viz. Selections from the Private and Public (or State) Correspondence of Sir Richard Boyle, First and Great Earl of Cork*, ed. Alexander B. Grosart, 4 vols (London: Chiswick Press, 1887).

Boyle, Robert. *Robert Boyle by Himself and His Friends*, ed. Michael Hunter (London: William Pickering, 1994).

Boyle, Robert. *The Correspondence of Robert Boyle*, ed. Michael Hunter, Antonio Clericuzio, and Lawrence M. Principe, 6 vols (London: Pickering & Chatto, 2001).

Boys, John. *An Exposition of Al the Principall Scriptures Used in Our English Liturgie* (London: Felix Kingston for Martin Clerk, 1609).

Boys, John. *An Exposition of the Dominical Epistles and Gospels* (London: for William Apsley, 1610).

Boys, John. *An Exposition of the Last Psalme* (London: Felix Kingston for William Apsley, 1613).

Boys, John. *The Workes of John Boys* (London: John Haviland for William Apsley, 1622).

Bramhall, John. *The Serpent Salve, or, a Remedie for the Biting of an Aspe* (s.l.: s.n., 1643).

Bray, William. *Innocency and the Blood of the Slain Souldiers* (London: s.n., 1649).

Bridge, William. *The Truth of the Times Vindicated* (London: T.P. and M.S. for Benjamin Allen, 1643).

Brinsley, John. *The Preachers Charge, and Peoples Duty about Preaching and Hearing of the Word* (London: for Robert Bird, 1631).

Broughton, Hugh. *An Apologie in Briefe Assertions Defending That Our Lord Died in the Time Properly Foretold to Daniel* (London: [T. East, R. Watkins, and E. Allde for] William Kearney, 1592).

Broughton, Hugh. *Daniel His Chaldie Visions and His Ebrew: Both Translated after the Original: and Expounded Both* (London: Richard Field [& Gabriel Simson] for William Young, 1596).

Broughton, Hugh. *An Epistle to the Learned Nobilitie of England: Touching Translating the Bible from the Original, with Ancient Warrant for Everie Worde* (Middleburgh: Richard Schilders, 1597).

Broughton, Hugh. *Principle Positions for Groundes of the Holy Bible* ([Amsterdam]: [Giles Thorp], 1609).

Broughton, Hugh. *A Censure of the Late Translation for Our Churches* ([Middelburg: R. Schilders, 1611?]).

Brown, P. Hume, ed. *Early Travellers in Scotland* (Edinburgh: D. Douglas 1891).

Browne, Thomas. *Thomas Browne: 21st-Century Oxford Authors*, ed. Kevin Killeen (Oxford: Oxford University Press, 2014).

Bucer, Martin. *Martini Bvceri Opera Latina*, xv, ed. François Wendel (Paris and Gütersloh: Presses Universitaires de France and C. Bertelsmann Verlag, 1955).

Bucer, Martin. *De regno Christi*, tr. Wilhelm Pauck and Paul Larkin, in *Melanchthon and Bucer*, ed. Wilhelm Pauck (Philadelphia: Westminster Press, 1969), 174–394.

Buchanan, George. *Jephthes sive votum tragoedia, authore Georgio Buchanano Scoto* (Paris: Guil. Morelium, [1554]).

Buchanan, George. *George Buchanan Tragedies*, ed. P. Sharratt and P. G. Walsh (Edinburgh: Scottish Academic Press, 1983).

Buchanan, George. *A Dialogue on the Law of Kingship among the Scots*, ed. and tr. Roger A. Mason and Martin S. Smith (Aldershot: Ashgate, 2004).

Bulkeley, Edward. *An Answere to Ten Frivolous and Foolish Reasons, Set Downe by the Rhemish Jesuits and Papists in Their Preface before the New Testament by Them Lately Translated into English* (London: George Bishop, 1588).

Bullinger, Heinrich. *The Christian State of Matrimony, Wherein Husbands & Wyves May Learne to Keepe House Together wyth Love*, tr. Miles Coverdale (London: John Awdeley, 1575).

Bullinger, Heinrich. *Summa christlicher religion / durch Heinrychen Bullingern* (Zurich: Christoffel Froschower, 1597).

Bünting, Heinrich. *Itinerarium et chronicon ecclesiasticum totius sacræ scripturæ* (Magdeburg: Kirchner, 1597).

Bunyan, John. *Grace Abounding to the Chief of Sinners* (London: George Larkin, 1666).

Bunyan, John. *Grace Abounding to the Chief of Sinners*, ed. Roger Sharrock (Oxford: Clarendon Press, 1962).

Bunyan, John. *The Pilgrim's Progress*, ed. James Blanton Wharey, 2nd edn, rev. Roger Sharrock (Oxford: Clarendon Press, 1960).

Bunyan, John. *The Pilgrim's Progress*, ed. Roger Pooley (London: Penguin Books, 2008).

Bunyan, John. *Miscellaneous Works*, 13 vols, gen. ed. Roger Sharrock (Oxford: Clarendon Press, 1976-94).

Bunyan, John. *The Life and Death of Mr. Badman*, ed. James F. Forrest and Roger Sharrock (Oxford: Clarendon Press, 1988).

Bunyan, John. *The Acceptable Sacrifice, Last Sermon, etc.*, ed. W. R. Owens (Oxford, Clarendon Press, 1994).

Burchard of Mt. Sion. *Description of the Holy Land*, tr. Aubrey Stewart (London: Palestine Pilgrims' Text Society, 1897 [1896]).

Burgess, Anthony. *An Expository Comment, Doctrinal, Controversal [sic], and Practical upon the Whole First Chapter to the Second Epistle of St. Paul to the Corinthians* (London: A. M. for Abel Roper, 1661).

Burnet, Gilbert. *The Protestant's Companion* (London, for Richard Chiswell, 1685).

Burnet, Gilbert. *An Answer to a Paper Printed with Allowance, Entitled, a New Test of the Church of England's Loyalty* ([Amsterdam?]: s.n., 1687).

Burnet, Gilbert. *Bishop Burnet's History of His Own Time*, i (London: for Thomas Ward, 1724).

Burnet, Thomas. *The Theory Of The Earth* (London: R. Norton for Walter Kettilby, 1684).

Burroughs, Jeremiah. *Sions Joy. A Sermon Preached to the Honourable House of Commons ... September 7. 1641* (London: T.P. and M.S. for R. Dawlman, 1641).

Burroughs, Jeremiah. *The Glorious Name of God, the Lord of Hosts* (London: for R. Dawlman, 1643).

Burton, Henry. *A Replie to a Relation, of the Conference between William Laude and Mr. Fisher the Jesuite* ([Amsterdam: Cloppenburg Press, 1640]).

Burton, Robert. *The Anatomy of Melancholy*, ed. Thomas C. Faulkner, Nicholas K. Kiessling, and Ronda L. Blair, intro. J. B. Bamborough, 3 vols (Oxford: Clarendon Press, 1989–94).

Butler, John. *[Christologia]. Or A Brief (but True) Account of the certain Year, Moneth, Day and Minute of the Birth of Jesus Christ* (London: Joseph Moxon, 1671).

Butler, Richard, ed. *The Annals of Ireland* (Dublin: Irish Archaeological Society, 1849).

Byfield, Nicholas. *Sermons upon the Ten First Verses of the Third Chapter of the First Epistle of S. Peter* (London: H. Lownes for George Latham, 1626).

Byrd, William. *Liber primus sacrarum cantionum quinque vocum* (London: Thomas East, 1589).

Byrd, William. *Graduala: ac cantiones sacrae* (London: Thomas East, [1605]).

Calamy, Edmund. *The Noble-Mans Patterne of True and Reall Thankfulnesse* (London: G. M. for Christopher Meredith, 1643).

Calamy, Edmund. *Eli Trembling for Fear of the Ark. A Sermon Preached at St. Mary Aldermanbury, Decemb. 28. 1662.* (London and Oxford: [s.n.], 1662).

Calamy, Edmund. *The Nonconformist's Memorial*, ed. Samuel Palmer, 3 vols (London: Button & Son, 1802–3).

Calvin, John. *Institutio Christianæ religionis* (Geneva: Robert I Estienne, 1559).

Calvin, John. *Institutes of the Christian Religion*, tr. Henry Beveridge (Grand Rapids, Mich.: Eerdmans, 1953).

Calvin, John. *Calvin: Institutes of the Christian Religion*, ed. John T. McNeill, tr. Ford Lewis Battles, 2 vols, Library of Christian Classics, 20–1 (Philadelphia: Westminster, 1960).

Calvin, John. *Commentaries of that Divine John Calvine, upon the Prophet Daniell*, tr. Anthony Gilby (London: John Daye, 1570).

Calvin, John. *The Psalmes of David and Others: With M. John Calvins Commentaries* (London: Thomas East and Henry Middleton for Lucas Harison & George Bishop, 1571).

Calvin, John. *A Commentarie of John Calvine, upon the First Booke of Moses Called Genesis*, tr. Thomas Tymme (London: [Henry Middleton] for John Harison & George Bishop, 1578).

Calvin, John. *Commentaries on the First Book of Moses called Genesis*, tr. John King (Edinburgh: Edinburgh Printing Co., 1847).

Calvin, John. *A Commentarie upon the Epistle of Saint Paul to the Romanes*, tr. Christopher Rosdell (London: Thomas Dawson for John Harison & George Bishop, 1583).

Calvin, John. *The Sermons of M. Iohn Calvin upon the Fifth Booke of Moses Called Deuteronomie*, tr. Arthur Golding (London: Henry Middleton for George Bishop, 1583).

Calvin, John. *A Commentary on the Psalms of David*, 3 vols (Oxford: A. Talboys, 1840).

Calvin, John. *A Commentary on the Book of Psalms*, tr. James Anderson, 5 vols (Edinburgh: Calvin Translation Society, 1846).

Calvin, John. *Commentary on the Book of the Prophet Isaiah*, tr. William Pringle, 4 vols (Edinburgh: Calvin Translation Society, 1850–3).

Camerarius, Johannes. *Notatio figurarum sermonis in libris quatuor evangeliorum* (Leipzig: Andreas Schneider aus Ortrant & Ernst Vögelin, 1572).

Camerarius, Johannes. *Commentarius in novum foedus* (Cambridge: Roger Daniels, 1642).

Campen, Jan Van. *A Paraphrasis upon All the Psalmes of David, Made by Johannes Campensis, Reader of the Hebrue Lecture in the Universite of Louvane, and Translated out of Latine into Englisshe* (London: Thomas Gybson, 1539).

Canne, John. *A Necessitie of Separation from the Church of England* (Amsterdam: successors of Giles Thorp, 1634).

Cartwright, Thomas. *A Confutation of the Rhemists Translation, Glosses and Annotations on the New Testament* (Leiden: W. Brewster, 1618).

Cary, Patrick. *Trivial Poems, and Triolets: Written in Obedience to Mrs. Tomkin's Commands* (1651) (London: John Murray, 1820).

Cary, Robert. *Palaeologia chronica* (London: J. Darby for Richard Chiswell, 1677).

Caryl, Joseph. *An Exposition with Practicall Observations upon the Three First Chapters of the Book of Job* (London: G. Miller for Henry Overton, Luke Fawne, & John Rothwell, 1643).

Casaubon, Meric. *Generall Learning: A Seventeenth-Century Treatise on the Formation of the General Scholar*, ed. Richard Serjeantson (Cambridge: RTM Publications, 1999).

Catena Graecorum patrum in beatum Iob, collectore Niceta Heracleae metropolita … accessit ad calcem textus Jobi στιχηρως, ed. Patrick Young (London: Ex typographio regio, 1637).

Cerisiers, René de. *The Innocent Lord, or the Divine Providence*, tr. William Lowre (London: S.G. for Charles Adams, 1654).

Chamberlain, John. *The Letters of John Chamberlain*, ed. Norman McClure, 2 vols (Philadelphia: American Philosophical Society, 1939).

Charnock, Stephen. *Several Discourses upon the Existence and Attributes of God* (London: for D. Newman, T. Cockerill, Benj. Griffin, T. Simmons, & Benj. Alsop, 1682).

Cheynell, Francis. *The Rise, Growth, and Danger of Socinianisme* (London: for Samuel Gellibrand, 1643).

Chillingworth, William. *The Religion of Protestants a Safe Way to Salvation* (London: Miles Flesher for John Clark, 1638).

Christopherson, John. *Jephthah*, ed. and tr. Francis Howard Forbes, intro. Wilbur Sypherd (Newark, Del.: University of Delaware Press, 1928).

Christopherson, John. *Jephte*, in *John Christopherson, 'Iephte', William Goldingham, 'Herodes'*, ed. Christopher Upton, Renaissance Latin Drama in England, 2nd ser. 7 (Hildesheim: Georg Olms, 1988).

Chrysostom, John. *S. Ioannis Chrysostomi opera Graecè*, 8 vols (Eton: John Norton, 1613).

Cicero. *De legibus*, tr. C. W. Keyes, Loeb Classical Library (Cambridge, Mass.: Harvard University Press, 1988).

Cicero. *De officiis*, tr. Walter Miller, Loeb Classical Library (Cambridge, Mass.: Harvard University Press, 1989).

Clarke, Samuel. *Englands Covenant Proved Lawfull* (London: for Henry Overton, 1643).

Clarke, William. *The Clarke Papers: Selections from the Papers of William Clarke, Secretary to the Council of the Army, 1647–1649, and to General Monck and the Commanders of the Army in Scotland, 1651–1660*, ed. C. H. Firth, 4 vols (London: Camden Society, 1891–1901).

Claxton [Clarkson], Laurence. *The Lost Sheep Found: or, the Prodigal Returned to His Fathers House* (London: for the author, 1660).

Clement I, Pope. *Clementis ad Corinthios epistola prior*, ed. Patrick Young (Oxford: John Lichfield, 1633).

Clogie, Alexander. *Vox Corvi: or, the Voice of a Raven* (London: W. B., 1694).

Cockburn, John. *Fifteen Sermons Preach'd upon Several Occasions, and on Various Subjects* (London: J. L. for William Keblewhite, 1697).

Cocks, Roger. *Hebdomada sacra: A Weekes Devotion: or, Seven Poeticall Meditations upon the Second Chapter of St. Matthewes Gospel* (London: Felix Kingston for Henry Seile, 1630).

Como, David R. *Blown by the Spirit: Puritanism and the Emergence of an Antinomian Underground in pre-Civil-War England* (Stanford: Stanford University Press, 2004).

Comoediae ac tragoediae aliquot ex novo et vetere Testamento desumptae, quarum catalogū proxima pagella indicabit (Basel: Nikolaus Brylinger, 1540.

Constitutions and Canons Ecclesiastical, Treated upon by the Bishop of London (London: Robert Barker, 1604).

Conway, Anne. *The Conway Letters*, ed. Marjorie Hope Nicolson, rev. Sarah Hutton (Oxford: Clarendon Press, 1992).

Cooper, Thomas. *A Brief Exposition of Such Chapters of the Old Testament as Usually Are Read in the Church at Common Prayer on the Sundays* (London: Henry Denham for Rafe Newbery, 1573).

Cooper, Thomas. *An Admonition to the People of England* (London: Deputies of Christopher Barker, 1589).

Coppe, Abiezer. *Some Sweet Sips of Some Spirituall Wine* (London: for Giles Calvert, 1649).

Coppe, Abiezer. *Abiezer Coppe: Selected Writings*, ed. Andrew Hopton (London: Aporia Press, 1987).

Coryate, Thomas. *Coryats Crudities; Hastily Gobbled up in Five Months Travells* (London: W[illiam] S[tansby for the author], 1611).

Coster, François de. *Enchiridion controversiarum præcipuarum nostri temporis de religione* (Cologne: Arnold Mylius, 1585).

Coulton, Richard. *The Loyalty of the Church of England* (York: J. White, 1685).

Courtin, Antoine de. *The Rules of Civility: Or, Certain Ways of Department Observed in France, amongst All Persons of Quality* (London: for R. Chiswell, T. Sawbridge, G. Wells, & R. Bently, 1685).

Cowley, Abraham. *Poems: viz. I. Miscellanies. II. The Mistress, or, Love Verses. III. Pindarique Odes. And IV. Davideis, or, a Sacred Poem of the Troubles of David* (London: [Thomas Newcombe] for Humphrey Moseley, 1656).

Cranmer, Thomas. *Miscellaneous Writings and Letters of Thomas Cranmer, Archbishop of Canterbury, Martyr, 1556*, ed. John Edmund Cox (Cambridge: Parker Society, 1846).

Crashaw, Richard. *Steps to the Temple. Sacred Poems, with Other Delights of the Muses* (London: T. W. for Humphrey Moseley, 1646).

Critici sacri: sive doctissimorum vivorum in SS. Biblia annotationes, & tractatus, ed. John Pearson et al., 9 vols (London: Jacob Flesher, sold by Cornelius Bee, Richard Royston, William Wells, Samuel Thomson, Thomas Robinson & William Mordern, 1660).

Crossman, Samuel. *The Young Mans Monitor* (London: J. H. for S. Thompson & T. Parkhurst, 1664).

Cruso, Timothy. *The Mighty Wonders of a Merciful Providence* (London: Thomas Cockerill & John Salisbury, 1689).

Cudworth, Ralph. *The True Intellectual System of the Universe* (London, 1678), facsimile edn, 2 vols (Stuttgart-Bad Canstatt: Friedrich Frommann Verlag, 1964).

Cuningham, William. *The Cosmographical Glasse, Conteinyng the Pleasant Principles of Cosmographie, Geographie, Hydrographie, or Nauigation* (London: John Day, 1559).

Dasent, John Roche, ed. *Acts of the Privy Council of England*, NS 15 (AD 1587–1588) (London: Her Majesty's Stationery Office, 1897).

Dasent, John Roche, ed. *Acts of the Privy Council of England*, NS 22 (AD 1591–2) (London: Her Majesty's Stationery Office, 1901).

Davenant, William. *Gondibert, an Heroick Poeme* (London: for John Holden, 1651).

Davids Three Mighties: or Sovereignties Three Champions (Oxford: Leonard Lichfield, 1643).

Davies, John. *The XII Wonders of the World* (London: John Browne, 1611).

Dekker, Thomas, and Thomas Middleton. *The Roaring Girl*, ed. Elizabeth Cook (London: Methuen, 1997).

Dent, Arthur. *The Plaine Man's Path-way to Heaven* (London: H. L[ownes] for George Latham, 1629).

Diderot, Denis, and Jean Le Rond d'Alembert, eds. *Encyclopédie ou dictionnaire raisonné des sciences, des arts et des métiers*, 28 vols (Paris: André le Breton, Michel-Antoine David, Laurent Durand, & Antoine-Claude Briasson, 1751–72).

Diodati, Giovanni. *Pious Annotations, upon the Holy Bible* (London: T. B. for Nicholas Fussell, 1643).

Doble, C. E., et al., eds. *Remarks and Collections of Thomas Hearne*, 11 vols (Oxford: Oxford Historical Society, 1885–1921).

Donatus, Aelius. *Aeli Donati commentvm Terenti, accedunt eugraphi commentum et scholia Bembina*, ed. Paulus Wessner, 3 vols (Stuttgart: B. G. Tevbner, 1962).

Donne, John. *Pseudo-Martyr* (London: William Stansby for Walter Burre, 1610).

Donne, John. *A Sermon upon the XV Verse of the XX Chapter of the Booke of Judges* (London: William Stansby, 1622).

Donne, John. *Devotions upon Emergent Occasions* (London: Augustine Mathewes for Thomas Jones, 1624).

Donne, John. *Deaths Duell* (London: Thomas Harper for Richard Redmer & Benjamin Fisher, 1632).

Donne, John. *The Life and Letters of John Donne*, ed. Edmund Gosse, 2 vols (London: William Heinemann, 1899).

Donne, John. *The Complete English Poems*, ed. C. A. Patrides (London: Dent, 1985).

Donne, John. *John Donne's 1622 Gunpowder Plot Sermon: A Parallel-Text Edition*, ed. Jeanne Shami (Pittsburgh, Pa.: Duquesne University Press, 1996).

Donne, John. *Essays in Divinity: Being Several Disquisitions Interwoven with Meditations and Prayers*, ed. Anthony Raspa (Montreal: McGill-Queen's University Press, 2001).

Donne, John. *The Sermons of John Donne*, ed. George Potter and Evelyn Simpson, 10 vols (Berkeley, Calif.: University of California Press, 1953–62).

Donne, John. *Oxford Sermons of John Donne*, gen. ed. Peter McCullough (Oxford: Oxford University Press, 2014-).

Dove, John. *A Confutation of Atheisme by John Dove Doctor of Divinitie* (London: Edward Allde for Henry Rockett, 1605).

Downham, G. *Rex meus est deus* (London: s.n., 1643).

Dramata sacra: Comoediae atque tragoediae aliquot è Veteri Testamento desumptae (Basel: Johann Oporinus, 1547).

Drusius, Johannes. *Veterum interpretum Graecorum in totum vetus Testamentum fragmenta* (Arnheim: Johannem Janssonium, 1622).

Dryden, John. *Britannia Rediviva: A Poem on the Birth of the Prince* (London: J. Tonson, 1688).

Du Bartas, Guillaume de Salluste. *La muse Chrestiene* (Bordeaux: Simon Millanges, 1574).

Du Bartas, Guillaume de Salluste, *La sepmaine, ou création du Monde* (Paris: Michel Gadoulleau, 1578).

Du Bartas, Guillaume de Salluste, *The Historie of Judith*, tr. Thomas Hudson (Edinburgh: Thomas Vautrollier, 1584).

Du Bartas, Guillaume de Salluste. *La Judit [par] G. Salluse Du Bartas*, ed. André Baïche (Toulouse: Faculté des lettres et sciences humaines, 1971).

Du Bartas, Guillaume de Salluste. *Bartas: His Devine Weekes and Workes*, tr. Joshuah Sylvester (London: Humfrey Lownes, 1605).

Du Bartas, Guillaume de Salluste. *The Divine Weeks and Works of Guillaume De Saluste Sieur Du Bartas, Translated by Josuah Sylvester*, ed. Susan Snyder, 2 vols (Oxford: Clarendon Press, 1979).

Durham, James. *The Parliaments Commission* (London: R. Austin & A. Coe, 1643).

Ebn Izra, Abraham. *The Commentary of Ibn Ezra on Isaiah*, tr. and ed. M. Friedlaender, 2 vols (London, 1873).

Eck, Johann. *Enchiridion locorum communium adversus Lutheranos* (London: Michael Hillenius for Henry Pepwel, 1531).

Edwards, Thomas. *The First and Second Part of Gangræna: Or A Catalogue and Discovery of Many of the Errors, Heresies, Blasphemies and Pernicious Practices of the Sectaries of This Time* (London: T[homas] R[atcliffe] and E[dward] M[ottershed] for Ralph Smith, 1646).

Edwards, Thomas. *The Second Part of Gangræna, or, a Fresh and Further Discovery of the Errors, Heresies, Blasphemies, and Dangerous Proceedings of the Sectaries of this Time* (London: T.R. and E.M. for Ralph Smith, 1646).

Edwards, Thomas. *The Third Part of Gangræna or, a New and Higher Discovery of the Errors, Heresies, Blasphemies, and Insolent Proceedings of the Sectaries of These Times* (London: for Ralph Smith, 1646).

Eliot, John. *A Brief Narrative of the Progress of the Gospel amongst the Indians in New-England* (London: for John Allen, 1671).

Eliot, John. *Indian Dialogues for their Instruction in that Great Service of Christ* (Cambridge: [s.n.], 1671).

Eliot, John. *The Logick Primer* (Cambridge, Mass.: Marmaduke Johnson, 1672).

Ellis, John. *The Sole Path to a Sound Peace* (London: John Raworth, for George Latham & John Rothwell, 1643).

Elyot, Thomas, Sir. *The Boke Named the Governour* (London: Thomas Berthelet, 1531).

Englands Second Alarm to War, against the Beast (London: for Thomas Underhill, 1643).

Englands Third Alarm to Warre (London: for Thomas Underhill, 1643).

Erasmus, Desiderius. *An Exhortation to the Diligent Studye of Scripture* (Antwerp: Hans Luft [i.e. Hoochstraten, [1529]).

Erasmus, Desiderius. *The first Tome or Volume of the Paraphrase of Erasmus upon the Newe Testament*, ed. Nicholas Udall (London: Edward Whitchurch, 1548).

Erasmus, Desiderius. *Opus epistolarum Des. Erasmi Roterodami*, ed. P. S. Allen, H. M. Allen, and H. W. Garrod, 12 vols (Oxford: Clarendon Press, 1906–58).

Erasmus, Desiderius. *The Colloquies of Erasmus*, tr. Craig R. Thompson (Chicago: Chicago University Press, 1965).

Erasmus, Desiderius. *Collected Works of Erasmus*, 86 vols to date (Toronto: University of Toronto Press, 1974–).

Erasmus, Desiderius. *Christian Humanism and the Reformation: Selected Writings of Erasmus*, ed. and tr. John C. Olin (New York: Fordham University Press, 1987).

Erasmus, Desiderius. *Erasmus: The Education of A Christian Prince with the Panegyric for Archduke Philip of Austria*, ed. Lisa Jardine, tr. Neil M. Cheshire and Michael J. Heath (Cambridge: Cambridge University Press, 1997).

Espagne, Jean d'. *Shibboleth, or The Reformation of Severall Places in the Translations of the French and of the English Bible*, tr. Robert Codrington (London: T. W. for Anthony Williamson, 1655).

Estienne, Robert. *Hebraea & Chaldaea nomina virorum, mulierum, populorum, idoloru[m],…, quae in Bibliis leguntur* (Paris: R. Estienne, 1549).

Eusebius. *Palestine in the Fourth Century A.D.: The 'Onomasticon' by Eusebius of Caesarea*, ed. Joan E. Taylor, tr. G. S. P. Freeman-Grenville (Jerusalem: Carta, 2003).

Evelyn, John. *Diary of John Evelyn*, ed. Henry B. Wheatley, 4 vols (London: Bickers & Son, 1906).

Evelyn, John. *The Diary of John Evelyn*, ed. John Bowle (Oxford: Oxford University Press, 1985).

Everard, John. *The Arriereban a Sermon Preached to the Company of the Military Yarde* (London: Edward Griffin for Thomas Walkley, 1618).

Extracts from the Council Register of the Burgh of Aberdeen, 1625–1642 (Edinburgh: Scottish Burgh Records Society, 1871).

Featley, Daniel. *A Second Parallel* (London: [J. Haviland] for Robert Milbourne, 1626).

Featley, Daniel. *Clavis Mystica* (London: R[obert] Y[oung] for Nicolas Bourne, 1636).

Fell, Margaret. *For Manasseth Ben Israel: The Call of the Jewes out of Babylon* (London: Giles Calvert, 1656).

Fenner, William. *The Soules Looking-Glasse, Lively Representing its Estate before God* (Cambridge: Roger Daniel, 1643).

Fenner, William. *A Divine Message to the Elect Soule* (London: T.R. and E.M. for John Stafford, 1647).

Fergusson, David. *Ane Sermon Preichit befoir the Regent and Nobilitie, Upon a Part of the Third Chapter of the Prophet Malachi* (St Andrews: Robert Lekprevik, 1572).

Ferne, Henry. *The Camp at Gilgal. Or, a View of the Kings Army, and Spirituall Provision Made for It* (Oxford: Leonard Lichfield, 1643).

Ferne, Henry. *Conscience Satisfied* (Oxford: Leonard Lichfield [i.e. London], 1643).

Ferne, Henry. *A Reply unto Severall Treatises* (Oxford: Leonard Lichfield, 1643).

Ferne, Henry. *The Resolving of Conscience upon this Question* (Oxford: for W. Webb, 1643).

Feyerabend, Sigmund. *Reyssbuch des heyligen Lands* (Franckfurt am Main: J. Feyerabendt for Sigmundt Feyerabendts, 1584).

Filmer, Robert. *Patriarcha and Other Writings*, ed. J. P. Sommerville (Cambridge: Cambridge University Press, 1991).

Fincham, Kenneth, ed. *Visitation Articles and Injunctions of the Early Stuart Church*, 2 vols (Woodbridge: Boydell Press, 1994–8).

Fish, Simon. *A Supplicacyon for the Beggers* ([Antwerp? J. Grapheus? 1529?]).

Fisher, Samuel. *Rusticus ad academicos* (London: for Robert Wilson, 1660).

Fisher, Samuel. *Something concerning Agbarus, Prince of the Edesseans; With his Epistle to Christ and Christ's Epistle in Answer Thereto* (London: n.publ., 1663?).

Fisher, Samuel. *The Testimony of Truth Exalted*, ed. William Penn (London, 1679).

Flavel, John. *Navigation Spiritualized: Or, A New Compass for Sea-Men* (London: J. C. for Thomas Fabian, 1677).

Foirm na n-urrnuidheadh: John Carswell's Gaelic Translation of the Book of Common Order, ed. R. L. Thomson (Edinburgh: Scottish Gaelic Texts Society, 1970).

Forester, James. *The Marrow and Juice of Two Hundred and Sixtie Scriptures* (London: Simon Waterson, 1611).

Fotherby, Martin. *Atheomastix Clearing Foure Truths, against Atheists and Infidels* (London: Nicholas Okes, 1622).

Foxe, John. *The Gospels of the Fower Evangelistes Translated in the Olde Saxons Tyme Out of Latin into the Vulgare Toung of the Saxons, Newly Collected Out of Auncient Monumentes of the Sayd Saxons, and Now Published for Testimonie of the Same* (London: John Day, 1571).

Foxe, John. *Actes and Monuments of Matters most Speciall and Memorable, Happenyng in the Church* (London: John Day, 1583).

Foxe, John. *Acts and Monuments*, ed. George Townsend, 8 vols (London: R. B. Seeley & W. Burnside, 1843–9).

Foxe, John. *Foxe's Book of Martyrs: Select Narratives*, ed. John N. King (Oxford: Oxford University Press, 2009).

Foxe, John. *The Unabridged Acts and Monuments Online* (Sheffield: HRI Online Publications, 2011), <http//www.johnfoxe.org>.

Foxe, John. *Two Latin Comedies by John Foxe the Martyrologist: 'Titus et Gesippus', 'Christus Triumphans'*, ed. and tr. John Hazel Smith (Ithaca, NY, and London: Cornell University Press, 1973).

Franklin, Benjamin. *The Papers of Benjamin Franklin*, gen. ed. Ellen R. Cohn, 41 vols to date (New Haven: Yale University Press, 1959–).

Frere, W. H., and W. M. Kennedy, eds. *Visitation Articles and Injunctions of the Period of the Reformation*, 2 vols, Alcuin Club Collections, 15 (London: Longmans, Green & Co., 1910).

Frith, John. *A Pistle to the Christen Reader: The Revelation of Antichrist* ([Antwerp: Johannes Hoochstraten, 1529]).

Fulke, William. *A Defense of the Sincere and True Translations of the Holie Scriptures into the English Tong* (London: Henry Bynneman, 1583).

Fulke, William. *A Defence of the Sincere and True Translations of the Holy Scriptures into the English Tongue*, ed. Charles H. Hartshorne (Cambridge: Cambridge University Press, 1843).

Fulke, William. *The Text of the New Testament of Jesus Christ, Translated out of the Vulgar Latine by the Papists* (London: Deputies of Christopher Barker, 1589).

Fuller, Thomas. *The Holy State* (Cambridge: R. D. for John Williams, 1642).

Fuller, Thomas. *A Sermon of Reformation* (London: s.n., 1643).

Fuller, Thomas. *Truth Maintained, or Positions Delivered in a Sermon at the Savoy* (Oxford [actually London]: s.n., 1643).

Fuller, Thomas. *A Pisgah-sight of Palestine and the Confines Thereof* (London: M. F. for John Williams, 1650).

Fuller, Thomas. *Two Sermons the First, Comfort in Calamitie* (London: for G. and H. Eversden, 1654).

Fuller, Thomas. *The Church-History of Britain* (London: for John Williams, 1655).

Fuller, Thomas. *The History of the Worthies of England* (London: J. G[rismond], W. L[eybourne], and W. G[odbid] for Thomas Williams, 1662).

Funck, Johann. *Chronologia hoc est* (Nürnberg: Georg Wachter & Cyriacus Jacob, 1545).

Galileo, Galilei. *Dialogo di Galileo Galilei linceo matematico sopraordinario dello studio di Pisa... sopra i due massimi sistemi del mondo Tolemaico, e Copernicano* (Florence: Giovanni Batista Landini, 1632).

Gardiner, Stephen. *The Letters of Stephen Gardiner*, ed. James Arthur Muller (Cambridge: Cambridge University Press, 1933).

Gascoigne, George. *The Droomme of Doomes Day* (London: Thomas East for Gabriell Cawood, 1576).

Gataker, Thomas. *A Mistake, or Misconstruction Removed. (Whereby Little Difference is Pretended to Have Been Acknowledged between the Antinomians and Us.)* (London: Edward Griffin for F. Clifton, 1646).

Gataker, Thomas. *Shadowes without Substance, or Pretended New Lights* (London: for Robert Bostock, 1646).

Gell, Robert. *Aggelokratia theon. Or a Sermon Touching Gods Government of the World by Angels* (London: John Legatt for Nathaniel Brooks, 1650).

Gell, Robert. *An Essay toward the Amendment of the Last English-Translation of the Bible* (London: R. Norton for Andrew Crook, 1659).

Gell, Robert. *Eirenikon: or, a Treatise of Peace between the Two Visible Divided Parties* (London: T. J. for Nathaniel Brooks, 1660).

Gell, Robert. *Gell's Remains: or, Several Select Scriptures of the New Testament Opened and Explained* (London: for Nathaniel Brooke, 1676).

Gell, Robert. *Ein Versuch, Muster oder Probe zur Verbesserung der letzten Englischen Ubersetzung der Bibel: oder eine ... Exempel ... dass die letzte Ubersetzung der Bibel ins Englische möge verbessert werden; die erste Theil in Pentateuchum ...* (Berleburg: n.publ., 1723).

Gerard, John. *John Gerard: The Autobiography of an Elizabethan*, tr. Philip Caraman, intro. Graham Greene (London: Longmans, 1951).

Gibbon, Edward. *The History of the Decline and Fall of the Roman Empire*, i (London: William Strahan & Thomas Cadell, 1776).

Gibbon, Edward. *The History of the Decline and Fall of the Roman Empire*, ed. J. B. Bury, 7 vols (London: Methuen, 1896–1902).

Giraldi, Lilio Gregorio. *Lilio Gregorio Giraldi: Modern Poets*, tr. John N. Grant (Cambridge, Mass.: Harvard University Press, 2011).

Glanvill, Joseph. *Essays On Several Important Subjects in Philosophy and Religion* (London: J. D[arby] for John Baker & Henry Mortlock, 1676).

Godwyn, Morgan. *Trade Preferr'd before Religion and Christ Made to Give Place to Mammon Represented in a Sermon Relating to the Plantations* (London: for B. Took & Isaac Cleave, 1685).

Goffe, Thomas. *Deliverance from the Grave* (London: G. Purslowe for Ralph Mab, 1627).

Goodwin, John. *The Divine Authority of the Scriptures Asserted, or, The Great Charter of the Worlds Blessedness Vindicated* (London: A. M[iller]. for Henry Overton, 1648).

Gorton, Samuel. *An Antidote against the Common Plague of the World* (London: J. M. for A. Crook, 1657).

Gouge, William, ed. *Strength out of Weakness. Or a Glorious Manifestation of the Further Progresse of the Gospel amongst the Indians in New-England* (London: M. Simmons for John Blague & Samuel Howes, 1652).

Goulart, Simon. *A Learned Summary upon the Famous Poeme of William of Saluste Lord of Bartas*, tr. Thomas Lodge (London: George Purslowe for John Grismond, 1621).

Grace Book B II: Containing the Accounts of the Proctors of the University of Cambridge. ed. Mary Bateson (Cambridge: Cambridge University Press, 2009).

Greenhill, William. *Axinē pros tēn rhizan. The Axe at the Root* (London: R.O. and G.D. for Benjamin Allen, 1643).

Gregory, John. *Notes and Observations upon Some Passages of Scripture* (Oxford: H. Hall for Ed. Forrest Junior, 1646).

Gregory, John. *Gregorii posthuma: or, Certain Learned Tracts*, ed. John Gurganie (London: William Dugard for Laurence Sadler, 1649).

Grimald, Nicholas. *The Life and Poems of Nicholas Grimald*, ed. L. R. Merrill (New Haven: Yale University Press, 1925).

Grotius, Hugo. *Annotationes in libros evangeliorum* (Amsterdam: Johannus & Cornelius Blaeu, 1641).

Hales, John. *A Sermon Preached at St Maries in Oxford upon Tuesday in Easter Weeke* (Oxford: John Lichfield & William Wrench, 1617).

Hall, Edward. *The Union of the Two Noble and Illustre Famelies of Lancastre [and] Yorke* (London: Richard Grafton, 1548).

Hall, Peter, ed. *Harmony of the Protestant Confessions* (London: J. F. Shaw, 1842).

Haller, William and Godfrey Davies, eds. *The Leveller Tracts, 1647–1653* (New York: Columbia University Press, 1944).

Hamilton, Hans Claude, ed. *Calendar of the State Papers Relating to Ireland, of the Reign of Elizabeth, 1586–1588, July* (London: Her Majesty's Public Record Office, 1877).

Hamilton, Hans Claude, ed. *Calendar of the State Papers, Relating to Ireland, of the Reign of Elizabeth, 1592, October–1596, June* (London: Her Majesty's Stationery Office, 1890).

Harrison, William. *The Description of England by William Harrison*, ed. G. Edelen (Washington, DC: Folger Shakespeare Library, 1994).

Hay, Peter. *A Vision of Balaams Asse* (London: [Eliot's Court Press] for John Bill, 1616).

Hebbel, Friedrich. *Judith*, afterword by Helmut Bachmaier (Stuttgart: Verlag 1986).

Heigham, John. *The Gagge of the Reformed Gospell* (St Omer: widow of C. Boscard, 1623).

Hemmingsen, Niels. *A Postill, or Exposition of the Gospels* (London: Henry Bynneman, for Lucas Harrison & George Bishop, 1569).

Henry, William, Prince of Orange. *The Prince of Orange His Declaration: Shewing the Reasons Why he Invades England* (London: Randal Taylor, 1688).

Herbert, George. *A Priest to the Temple, or, the Country Parson His Character and Rule of Holy Life* (London: T. Maxey for T. Garthwait, 1652).

Herbert, George. *The Works of George Herbert*, ed. F. E. Hutchinson (Oxford: Clarendon Press, 1941).

Herbert, George. *The English Poems of George Herbert*, ed. Helen Wilcox (Cambridge: Cambridge University Press, 2007).

Herbert, William. *Croftus sive de Hibernia liber*, ed. Arthur Keaveney and John A. Madden (Dublin: Irish Manuscripts Commission, 1992).

Herle, Charles. *Davids Song of Three Parts* (London: T. Brudenell for N. A., 1643).

Hermetica: the Greek 'Corpus Hermeticum' and the Latin 'Asclepius', ed. and tr. Brian P. Copenhaver (Cambridge: Cambridge University Press, 1992).

Heylyn, Peter. *The Rebells Catechism* (Oxford, s.n., 1643).

Heylyn, Peter. *Aerius redivivus, the History of the Presbyterians* (Oxford: for Jo. Crosley, 1670).

Hicks, William. *Apokalypsis apokalypseos, or, The Revelation Revealed Being a Practical Exposition on the Revelation of St. John* (London: J. Macock, for Daniel White, 1659).

Hieron, Samuel. *A Defence of the Ministers Reasons* (Amsterdam?: [J. Hondius], 1607).

Hinton, Edward. *The Vanity of Self-Boasters* (London: R. Bishop for S. Gellibrand, 1643).

Hobbes, Thomas. *Leviathan; or, the Matter, Forme, and Power of a Common Wealth, Ecclesiasticall and Civil* (London: Andrew Crooke, 1651).

Hobbes, Thomas. *Leviathan*, ed. Richard Tuck (Cambridge: Cambridge University Press, 1991).

Holbrooke, William. *Loves Complaint, for Want of Entertainement* (London: [John Windet] for Nathaniel Butter, 1610[?]).

Holder, William. *A Discourse concerning Time* (London: J. Heptinstall for L. Meredith, 1694).

Homer. *The Iliads of Homer Prince of Poets*, tr. George Chapman (London: Nathaniel Butter, 1611).

Homer. *The Iliad of Homer*, tr. Richmond Lattimore, intro. and notes Richard Martin (Chicago: University of Chicago Press, 2011).

Hooker, Richard. *Of the Lawes of Ecclesiasticall Politie Eyght Bookes [Books 1–4]* (London: John Windet, [1593]).

Hooker, Richard. *Of the Lawes of Ecclesiasticall Politie: The Fift Booke* (London: John Windet, 1597).

Hooker, Richard. *Of the Lawes of Ecclesiasticall Politie* (London: Richard Bishop for John Crook, 1648).

Hooker, Richard. *Of the Laws of Ecclesiastical Polity*, ed. Christopher Morris, 2 vols (London: J. M. Dent, 1963).

Hooker, Richard. *The Answere of Mr. Richard Hooker to a Supplication Preferred by Mr Walter Travers to the HH. Lords of the Privie Counsell* (Oxford: Joseph Barnes, 1612).

Hooker, Richard. *The Works of Mr. Richard Hooker*, ed. John Gauden (London: J. Best, for Andrew Crook, 1662).

Hooker, Richard. *The Folger Library Edition of the Works of Richard Hooker*, 5 vols (Cambridge, Mass., and London: Belknap Press of Harvard University Press, 1977–90).

Hopton, Andrew, ed. *Digger Tracts 1649–50* (London: Aporia Press, 1989).

Hoskins, Edgar, ed. *'Horae Beatae Virginis' or Sarum and York Primers* (London: Longmans, 1901).

Hoskins, John. *Sermons Preached at Pauls Crosse and Elsewhere* (London: William Stansby for Nathaniel Butter, 1615).

How, Samuel. *The Sufficience of the Spirits Teaching, without Humane Learning* ([Amsterdam]: [at the Cloppenburg Press, 1640]).

Howie, John, ed. *A Collection of Lectures and Sermons, Preached upon Several Subjects, Mostly in the Time of the Late Persecution* (Glasgow: J. Brice, 1779).

Hubbard, William. *A Narrative of the Troubles with the Indians in New-England* (Boston: John Foster, 1677).

Hudson, Anne, ed. *Selections from English Wycliffite Writings* (Cambridge: Cambridge University Press, 1978).

Hull, John. *The Unmasking of the Politike Atheist* (London: Felix Kingston for Ralph Howell, 1602).

Humble Proposals concerning the Printing of the Bible (London, s.n., 1650?).

Hume, David. *The History of the Houses of Douglas and Angus* (Edinburgh: Evan Tyler, 1644).

Hunton, Philip. *A Treatise of Monarchie* (London: for John Bellamy & Ralph Smith, 1643).

Hutchinson, Lucy. *Lucy Hutchinson: Order and Disorder*, ed. David Norbrook (Oxford: Blackwell, 2001).

Hutchinson, Lucy. *Lucy Hutchinson's Translation of Lucretius: De rerum natura*, ed. Hugh de Quehen (Ann Arbor, Mich.: University of Michigan Press, 1996).

Hutchinson, Lucy. *The Works of Lucy Hutchinson*, i. *The Translation of Lucretius*, ed. Reid Barbour and David Norbrook, with Latin text by Maria Christina Zerbino (Oxford: Oxford University Press, 2012).

Hyde, Edward, Earl of Clarendon. *Animadversions upon a Book Intituled, Fanaticism Fanatically Imputed to the Catholick Church, by Dr. Stillingfleet* (London: for Richard Royston, 1673).

Index auctorum et librorum prohibitorum, qui ab Officio Sanctae Romanae Inquisitionis caveri ab omnibus caveri ab omnibus & singulis in universa Christiana Republica mandantur (Rome: Ex Officina Salviana, 1559).

Injunctions Geven by the Quenes Majestie (London: Richard Jugge and John Cawood, 1559).

Isaacson, Henry. *Saturni ephemerides sive Tabula historic-chronologica* ([London]: B[ernard] A[lsop] and T[homas] F[awecet] for Henry Seile & Humphrey Robinson, 1633).

Isidore of Seville. *Etymologies*, ed. Stephen A. Barney et al. (Cambridge: Cambridge University Press, 2006).

J., W. *Obedience Active and Passive due to the Supream Power* (Oxford [actually London]: s.n., 1643).

Jackson, Arthur. *A Help for the Understanding of the Holy Scripture* (Cambridge: Roger Daniel, 1643).

Jackson, Thomas. *A Treatise of the Divine Essence and Attributes* (London: M[iles] F[letcher] for John Clarke, 1628).

James I and VI. *The Essayes of a Prentise, in the Divine Art of Poesie* (Edinburgh: Thomas Vautroullier, 1584).

James I and VI. *Ane Fruitfull Meditatioun* (Edinburgh: Henry Charteris, 1588).

James I and VI. *Ane Meditatioun upon the First Buke of the Chronicles of the Kingis* (Edinburgh: Henry Charteris, 1589).

James I and VI. *The True Lawe of Free Monarchies* (Edinburgh: Robert Waldegrave, 1598).

James I and VI. *Triplici nodo, triplex cuneus. Or an Apologie for the Oath of Allegiance* (London: Robert Barker, 1607).

James I and VI. *His Majesties Declaration concerning his Proceedings … in the Cause of D. Conradus Vorstius* (London: Robert Barker, 1612).

James I and VI. *The Workes of the Most High and Mighty Prince, James* (London: Robert Barker & John Bill, 1616).

James I and VI. *The Kings Majesties Declaration to his Subjects, concerning Lawfull Sports to be Used* (London: Bonham Norton & John Bill, 1618).

James I and VI. *A Meditation upon the Lords Prayer* (London: Bonham Norton & John Bill, 1619).

James I and VI. *A Meditation upon St. Matthew: Or a Paterne for a Kings Inauguration* (London: John Bill, 1620).

James I and VI. *His Majesties Declaration, Touching his Proceedings in the Late Assemblie and Convention of Parliament* (London: Bonham Norton & John Bill, 1621 [1622]).

James I and VI. *The Poems of James VI of Scotland*, ed. James Craigie, 2 vols (Edinburgh and London: William Blackwood & Sons, 1955–8).

James I and VI. *The Political Works of James I*, ed. C. H. McIlwain (New York: Russell & Russell, 1965).

James I and VI. *Minor Prose Works of King James VI and I*, ed. James Craigie (Edinburgh: William Blackwood & Sons, 1982).

Jennens, Charles, and Georg Friedrich Handel. *Messiah: An Oratorio* (Dublin: James Hoey, 1745).

Jerome. *S Eusebii Hieronymi stridonensis presbyteri commentariorum in Isaiam Prophetam libri duodeviginti* (PL 24).

Jerome. *Praefatio in pentateuchum* (PL 28).

Jerome. *Praefatio in quatuor evangelia* (PL 29).

Jerome. 'Prologus Galeatus', tr. W. H. Fremantle as 'Preface to the Books of Samuel and Kings', in Philip Schaff and Henry Wace (eds), *Select Library of the Nicene and Post-Nicene Fathers*, 2nd ser. 6 (Grand Rapids, Mich., and Edinburgh: William B. Eerdmans and T. & T. Clark, 1893).

Jerome. *De optimo genere interpretandi*, in *Lettres*, ed. and tr. Jérôme Labourt, 8 vols (Paris: Société d'Edition 'Les Belles Lettres', 1958).

Jewell, John. *An Apologie or Answere in Defence of the Churche of Englande* (London: Reginald Wolfe, 1564).

Johnson, Richard. *The Most Famous History of the Seaven Champions of Christendome* (London: [J. Danter] for Cuthbert Burby, 1596).

Jones, Henry. *A Sermon of Antichrist, Preached at Christ-Church, Dublin, Novemb. 12. 1676* (London: Randal Taylor, 1686).

Jonson, Ben. *Ben Jonson*, ed. C. H. Herford, Percy and Evelyn Simpson, 11 vols (Oxford: Clarendon Press, 1925–52).

Jordan, Thomas. *Piety, and Poesy* (London: Robert Wood, 1643).

Joye, George. *The Exposicion of Daniel the Prophete* ([Antwerp]: successor of A Goinus, 1545).

Julian of Norwich. *The Writings of Julian of Norwich: A Vision Showed to a Devout Woman and A Revelation of Love*, ed. Nicholas Watson and Jacqueline Jenkins (University Park, Pa.: Pennsylvania State University Press, 2006).

Juventus, Caius Vettius Aquilinus. *Libri evangeliorum IIII*, ed. Karl Marold (Leipzig: B. G. Teubner, 1886).

Karlstadt, Andreas Bodenstein von. *De canonicis scripturis libellus* (Wittenburg: Johann Rhau-Grunenbeg, 1520).

Killigrew, Henry. *A Sermon Preached before the Kings Most Excellent Majesty* (Oxford: for W. Web, 1643).

Kingdon, Robert M., and Jean-François Bergier, eds. *Registres de la Compagnie des pasteurs de Genève au temps de Calvin*, 2 vols (Geneva: Droz, 1962).

Knollys, Hanserd. *The Shining of a Flaming-Fire in Zion* (London: Jane Coe, 1646).

Kyd, Thomas. *The Spanish Tragedy*, ed. Andrew Gurr and J. R. Mulryne (London: Methuen, 2009).

La Peyrère, Isaac de. *Men before Adam: Or A Discourse upon the Twelfth, Thirteenth, and Fourteenth Verses of the Fifth Chapter of the Epistle of the Apostle Paul to the Romans* (London: s.n., 1656).

Lamb, John. *A Collection of Letters, Statutes, and Other Documents, from the MS. Library of Corp. Christ. Coll., Illustrative of the History of the University of Cambridge, during the Period of the Reformation* (London: John W. Parker, 1838).

Langhorne, Lancelot. *Mary Sitting at Christs Feet: A Sermon preached at the Funerall of M^ris Mary Swaine* (London: Arthur Johnson, 1611).

Lapide, Cornelius à. *Commentaria in scripturam sacram*, ed. Augustinus Crapon, 23 vols (Paris: Vivès, 1881).

Larke, Nicholas. *The Practice of Thankefulnesse: Or Davids Choyse Directions How to Prayse God* (London: G. P[urslowe]. for Roger Jackson, 1622).

Las Casas, Bartolomé de. *In Defense of the Indians*, ed. and tr. Stafford Poole (DeKalb, Ill.: Northern Illinois University Press, 1992).

Latimer, Hugh. *Sermons and Remains*, ed. George Elwes Corrie, Parker Society (Cambridge: Cambridge University Press, 1845).

Laud, William. *A Relation of the Conference Betweene William Lawd, Then, Lrd. Bishop of St. Davids; Now, Lord Arch-Bishop of Canterbury: And Mr. Fisher the Jesuite* (London: Richard Badger, 1639).

Laud, William. *The works of William Laud*, 7 vols (Oxford: J. H. Parker, 1847–60).

Leabhuir na Seintiomna ar na ttarruing go Gaidhlig tre chúram 7 dhúthracht an doctúir Uilliam Bedel, roimhe so easbug Chille móire a néirinn, agus anois ar na ccur a ccló chum maithios puiblidhe na Tíresin (London: s.n., 1685).

Lawlor, Hugh Jackson, ed. *The Fasti of St Patrick's, Dublin* (Dundalk: W. Tempest, 1930).

Lee, Edward. *Annotationes Edouardi Leei in annotationes noui Testamenti Desiderii Erasmi* (Paris: Egidii Gourmont 1520).

Lee, Edward. *Apologia Edouardi Leei contra quorundum calumnias* (Paris: Egidii Gourmont, 1520).

Leigh, Edward. *A Treatise of Divinity* (London: E. Griffin for William Lee, 1646).

Leigh, Edward. *A System or Body of Divinity: Consisting of Ten Books* (London: A[braham]. M[iller]. for William Lee, 1654).

Ley, John. *The New Quere, and Determination upon It, by Mr. Saltmarsh Lately Published* (London: for C. Meredith, 1646 [i.e. 1645]).

Ley, John. *An After-Reckoning with Mr Saltmarsh* (London: for Christopher Meredith, 1646).

Ley, John. *Light for Smoke* (London: I. L. for Christopher Meredith, 1646).

Lightbody, George. *Against the Apple of the Left Eye of Antichrist* ([Holland: s.n.], 1638).

Lightfoot, John. *Erubhin or Miscellanies Christian and Judaicall, and Others* (London: G. Miller for Robert Swayne & William Adderton, 1629).

Lightfoot, John. *Elias Redivivus* (London: R. Cotes for Andrew Crooke, 1643).

Lipsius, Justus. *Politicorum sive civilis doctrinae libri sex* (Lyon: ex officinal Hugues de la Porte apud frères Gabiano, 1582).

Lipsius, Justus. *Six Bookes of Politickes or Civil Doctrine*, tr. William Jones (London: Richard Field for William Ponsonby, 1594).

Liturgical Services ... Set Forth in the Reign of Queen Elizabeth, ed. W. K. Clay (Cambridge: Parker Society, 1847).

Lloyd, William. *An Historical Account of Church-Government as It Was in Great-Britain and Ireland, When They First Received the Christian Religion* (London: Charles Brome, 1684).

Lloyd, William. *Papists no Catholicks, and Popery no True Christianity* (London: for the author, 1677; repr. London: s.n., 1686).

Lloyd, William. *A Sermon Preach'd before their Majesties at Whitehall, on the Fifth Day of November, 1689* (London: R. Clavell, 1689).

Lloyd, William. *An Exposition of the Prophecy of Seventy Weeks, Which God Sent to Daniel by the Angel Gabriel* ([London?]: s.n., 1690).

Loches, Nicolas Barthélemy de. *Christus xilonicus* (Paris: Guillaume de Bossozel, 1529).

Locke, John. *Two Treatises of Government* (London: for Awnsham Churchill, 1690).

Loe, William. *Songs of Sion for the Joy of Gods Deere Ones, Who Sitt Here by the Brookes of this Worlds Babel, & Weepe When They Thinke on Jerusalem Which Is on Highe* ([Hamburg: s.n., 1620]).

Lollards of Coventry 1486–1522, ed. and tr. Shannon McSheffrey and Norman Tanner, Camden 5th ser. 22 (Cambridge: Cambridge University Press, 2003).

Lorinus, Joannes. *Commentaria in librum Psalmorum*, 3 vols (Lyon: Horatii Cordon, 1611–16).

Love, C. C., tr., *Five Sixteenth-Century Latin Plays: From the Collection of Comedies and Tragedies edited by Nicholas Brylinger, Basle, 1540* (Toronto: Amor Christoferi Press, 1995).

Love, Christopher. *A Treatise of Effectual Calling and Election* (London: for John Rothwell, 1653).

Lucretius, Titus Carius. *T. Lucretius Carus, the Epicurean Philosopher, His Six Books De Natura* (Oxford: L. Lichfield for Anthony Stephens, 1683).

Luther, Martin. *A Manual of the Book of Psalms: Or, the Subject-Content of All the Psalms by Martin Luther*, tr. Henry Cole (London: Seeley & Burnside, 1837).

Luther, Martin. *D. Martin Luthers Werke: kritische Gesammtausgabe*, 121 vols (Weimar: Herman Böhlaus Nachfolger, 1883–2009).

Luther, Martin. *Luther's Works*, gen. eds Jaroslav Pelikan and Helmut Lehmann, 55 vols (Philadelphia: Fortress Press; and St Louis: Concordia Publishing House, 1955–86).

Luther, Martin. *Martin Luther. Selections from his Writings*, ed. John Dillenberger (New York: Anchor Books, 1962).

Luther, Martin. *Three Treatises*, tr. W. A. Lambert and Harold J. Grimm, 2nd rev. edn (Philadelphia: Fortress Press, 1970).

Luther, Martin. *Luthers Werke im WWW, Bibel*, vii. *Deutsche Bibel 1522/46* (Cambridge: Pro-Quest, 2000–13), <http://luther.chadwyck.co.uk/english/frames/home/home>.

Lydgate, John. *A Critical Edition of John Lydgate's 'Life of Our Lady'*, ed. Joseph A. Lauritis, Ralph A. Klinefelter, and Vernon F. Gallagher (Pittsburgh, Pa.: Duquesne University Press, 1961).

Lydiat, Thomas. *Tractatus de variis annorum formis* (London: [Eliot's Court Press], 1605).

Lydiat, Thomas. *Defensio tractatus de variis annorum formis* (London: Felix Kingston, 1607).

Lydiat, Thomas. *Thomae Lydiat canones chronologici* (Oxford: at the Sheldonian Theatre, 1675).

Lyly, John. *'Euphues: The Anatomy of Wit' and 'Euphues and His England'*, ed. Leah Scragg (Manchester: Manchester University Press, 2003).

Lynch, John. *The Portrait of a Pious Bishop; or, the Life and Death of the Most Reverend Francis Kirwan, Bishop of Killala*, tr. C. P. Meehan (Dublin: James Duffy, 1848).

Malory, Thomas. *Caxton's Malory: A New Edition of Sir Thomas Malory's 'Le Morte Darthur' Based on the Pierpoint Morgan Copy of William Caxton's Edition of 1485*, ed. James W. Spisak and William Matthews, 2 vols (Berkeley, Calif.: University of California Press, 1983).

Marino, Giovanni Battista. *La strage de gl'innocenti* (Venice: Baba, [1620?]).

Marlowe, Christopher. *Christopher Marlowe's Dr Faustus: a 1604 edition*, ed. Michael Keefer (Peterborough, Ontario: Broadview Press, 1991).

Marshall, Benjamin. *A Chronological Treatise upon the Seventy Weeks of Daniel* (London: for James Knapton, 1725).

Marshall, Benjamin. *Chronological Tables* ([Oxford]: at the Sheldonian Theatre, 1712–13).

Marshall, Stephen. *A Sermon Preached Before the Honourable House of Commons … November 17. 1640* (London: J. Okes for Samuel Man, 1641).

Marshall, Stephen. *A Plea for Defensive Armes* (London: for Samuel Gellibrand, 1643).

Marsham, John. *Diatriba chronologica* (London: Jacob Flesher, 1649).

Marsham, John. *Chronicus canon Ægyptiacus Ebraicus Græcus et disquisitions D. Johannis Marshami* (London: Thomas Roycroft for William Wells & Robert Scott, 1672).

Martin, Gregory. *A Discoverie of the Manifold Corruptions of the Holy Scriptures by the Heretikes of Our Daies, Specially the English Sectaries* (Rheims: John Fogny, 1582).

Martini, Martino. *Sinicae historiae decas prima* (Munich: Lucae Strabii, for Joannis Wagneri, 1658).

Mather, Increase. *A Brief History of the War with the Indians in New-England* (Boston: John Foster, 1676).

Maunsell, Andrew. *The First Part of the Catalogue of English Printed Bookes: Which concerneth Such Matters of Divinitie, As Have Bin Either Written in Our Owne Tongue, or Translated Out of Anie Other Language* (London: John Windet [and James Roberts] for Andrew Maunsell, 1595).

Maunsell, Andrew. *The Seconde Parte of the Catalogue … Which concerneth the Sciences* (London: James Roberts for Andrew Maunsell, 1595).

Maxwell, John. *Sacro-sancta regum majestas: or, The Sacred and Royall Prerogative of Christian Kings* (Oxford: [Henry Hall], 1644).

Mede, Joseph. *Clavis apocalyptica* (Cambridge: [T. and J. Buck] for the author, 1627).

Mede, Joseph. *The Works Of The Pious and Profoundly-Learned Joseph Mede, B. D.*, ed. John Worthington (London: James Flesher for Richard Royston, 1664).

Mercurius Aulicus, 32nd week (Oxford: Henry Hall for William Webb, 12 Aug. 1643).

Millman, Jill Seal, and Gillian Wright, eds. *Early Modern Women's Manuscript Poetry* (Manchester: Manchester University Press, 2005).

Milner, John. *A Defence of Arch-Bishop Usher against Dr Cary and Dr Isaac Vossius* (Cambridge: J. Hayes for Benjamin Tooke, 1694).

Milton, John. *The Works of John Milton*, gen. ed. Frank Allen Patterson, 18 vols (New York: Columbia University Press, 1931-1940).

Milton, John. *The Complete Prose Works of John Milton*, gen. ed. Don M. Wolfe, 8 vols (New Haven: Yale University Press, 1953–82).

Milton, John. *The Riverside Milton*, ed. Roy Flannagan (Boston: Houghton Mifflin, 1998).

Milton, John. *Paradise Lost*, ed. Alastair Fowler (Harlow: Pearson Longman, 2007).

Milton, John. *Paradise Lost*, ed. Barbara Lewalski (Oxford: Blackwell, 2007).

Monro, Alexander. *Sermons Preached upon Several Occasions* (London: for Joseph Hindmarsh, 1693).

Montagu, Richard. *A Gagg for the New Gospell? No: a New Gagg for an Old Goose* (London: Thomas Snodham for Matthew Lownes & William Barret, 1624).

Montaigne, Michel de. *The Essayes or Morall, Politike and Millitarie Discourses of Lo: Michaell de Montaigne*, tr. John Florio (London: Valentine Sims for Edward Blount, 1603).

Montano, Benito Arias. *Antiquitates Judaicae* (Leiden: Raphelengius, 1593).

More, Henry. *Conjectura cabbalistica: or, a Conjectural Essay of Interpreting the Minde of Moses, according to a Threefold Cabbala: viz. Literal, Philosophical, Mystical, or, Divinely Moral* (London: James Flesher, 1653).

More, Thomas. *The Supplycacyon of Soulys* (London: William Rastell, 1529).

More, Thomas. *The Confutacyon of Tyndales Answere Made by Syr Thomas More Knight Lorde Chauncellour of Englonde* (London: William Rastell, 1532).

More, Thomas. *A Letter of Syr Tho. More Knight Impugnyge the Erronyouse Writing of John Fryth against the Blessed Sacrament of the Aultare* (London: William Rastell, 1533).

More, Thomas. *The Correspondence of Sir Thomas More*, ed. Elizabeth Frances Rogers (Princeton: Princeton University Press, 1947).

More, Thomas. *Responsio ad Lutherum*, ed. John M. Hadley (New Haven: Yale University Press, 1969).

More, Thomas. *The Complete Works of St. Thomas More*, 15 vols (New Haven: Yale University Press, 1963–97).

Morin, Jean. *Exercitationes biblicae* (Paris: Vitray, 1633).

Morin, Jean. *Antiquitates ecclesiae orientalis* (London: George Wells, 1682).

Morton, A. L., ed. *Freedom in Arms: A Selection of Leveller Writings* (London: Lawrence & Wishart, 1985).

Muis, Siméon de. *Assertio veritatis hebraicae adversus exercitationes ecclesiasticas in utrumque Samaritanorum Pentateuchum Hoannis Morini* (Paris: J. Libert, 1631).

Münster, Sebastian. *Geographiae Claudij Ptolemæi Alexandrini* (Basel: H. Petri, 1552).

Nadal, Gerónimo. *Annotations and Meditations on the Gospels*, ed. and tr. Frederick A. Homann, with an introductory study by Walter S. Melion, 3 vols (Philadelphia: St Joseph's University Press, 2003–5).

Nalson, John. *An Impartial Collection of the Great Affairs of State from the Scotch Rebellion in the Year MDCXXXIX to the Murther of Charles I* (London: for S. Mearne, T. Dring, B. Tooke, T. Sawbridge, & C. Mearne, 1682).

Nashe, Thomas. *Christs Teares over Jerusalem* (London: James Roberts, sold by Andrew Wise, 1593).

Nazianzenus, Gregorius. *Tragodia, Christs paschon* (Rome: Anthony Bladen, 1542).

Neale, John M., tr. *Mediæval Hymns and Sequences* (London: Joseph Masters, 1851).

Newton, Isaac. *Unpublished Scientific Papers of Isaac Newton*, ed. A. R. Hall and Marie Boas Hall (Cambridge: Cambridge University Press, 1962).

Nicholls, K.W. *The Irish Fiants of the Tudor Sovereigns* (Dublin: Éamonn de Búrca for Edmund Burke Publisher, 1994).

Nichols, John Gough, ed. *Narratives of the Days of the Reformation* (London: Camden Society, 77, 1859).

Nichols, John, ed. *The Progresses and Public Processions of Queen Elizabeth*, 3 vols (London: John Nichols, 1823).

Nicoll, John. *A Diary of Public Transactions and Other Occurrences, Chiefly in Scotland, from January 1650 to June 1667* (Edinburgh: Bannatyne Club, 1836).

Nye, Stephen. *The Trinitarian Scheme of Religion concerning Almighty God; and Mankind Considered Both before and after the (Pretended) Fall* (London: s.n., 1692).

Ó Cuinn, Cosslett, ed. *Scéalta as an Apocrypha* (Dublin: Oifig an tSoláthair, 1971).

Orton, Job. *Memoirs of the Life, Character, and Writings, of the Late Rev. Philip Doddridge, D.D.* (Edinburgh: Waugh & Innes, 1825; 1st edn 1765).

Otes, Samuel. *An Explanation of the Generall Epistle of Saint Jude* (London: Elizabeth Purslow for Nicholas Bourne, 1633).

Owen, David. *Puritano-Jesuitismus* (London: for William Sheares, 1643).

Owen, John. *Of the Divine Originall, Authority, Self-Evidencing Light, and Power of the Scriptures* (Oxford: Henry Hall [and A. Lichfield] for Thomas Robinson, 1659).

Owen, John. *The Works of John Owen*, ed. William H. Goold, 24 vols (Edinburgh: Johnstone and Hunter, 1850–3).

Oxford University Statutes, tr. G. R. M. Ward, 2 vols (London: William Pickering, 1845–51).

Page, Samuel. *Nine Sermons upon Sun[drie] Texts of Scripture* (London: Nicholas Okes for Simon Waterson, 1616).

Pagitt, Ephraim. *Heresiography: Or, a Description of the Hereticks and Sectaries of These Latter Times* (London: M. Okes, 1645).

Pagninus, Xanthus. *Proverbia Salominis, Job, Canticum Canticorum, Ruth, Lamentationes Jeremiæ, Ecclesiastes, & Esther, Hebraicè: cum interlineari versione Xantis Pagnini* (Leiden: Officina Plantiniana Raphelengii, 1608).

Palmer, Herbert. *Scripture and Reason Pleaded for Defensive Armes* (London: John Bellamy & Ralph Smith, 1643).

Paradin, Claude. *Quadrins historiques de la Bible par Claude Paradin; revuz, & augmentez d'un grand nombre de figures* (Lyon: Jean de Tournes, 1555; 1st edn 1553).

Paradin, Claude. *The True and Lyvely Historyke Purtreatures of the Woll Bible* (Lyon: Jean of Tournes, 1553).

Parker, Henry. *Accommodation Cordially Desired, and Really Intended* (London: n.publ., 1643).

Parr, Richard, ed. *The Life of the Most Reverend Father in God, James Usher* (London: for Nathanael Ranew, 1686).

Parsons, Robert. *A Briefe Discourse Containing Certaine Reasons, Why Catholikes Refuse to Goe to Church* (Doway [i.e. England: English secret press,] 1601).

Parsons, Robert. *The First Booke of the Christian Exercise Appertayning to Resolution* ([Rouen: Fr Parsons' Press], 1582).

Pemble, William. *A Short and Sweete Exposition upon the First Nine Chapters of Zachary* (London: R. Young for John Bartlet, 1629).

Pepys, Samuel. *The Diary of Samuel Pepys*, ed. Robert Latham and William Matthews, 11 vols (Berkeley-Los Angeles, Calif.: University of California Press, 1970–83).

Perkins, William. *A Reformed Catholike, or, a Declaration Shewing How Neere We May Come to the Present Church of Rome in Sundrie Points of Religion* ([Cambridge]: John Legat, 1597).

Perkins, William. *The Whole Works of That Famous and Worthy Minister of Christ in the Universitie of Cambridge, M. William Perkins, in Three Volumes* (London: [vols i and iii, John Legatt; vol. ii, John Haviland], sold by James Boler, George Lathum, John Grismond, Robert Milbourne, and John Bellamie, 1631).

Peucer, Kaspar. *De dimensione terrae* (Wittenberg: Johann I Krafft, 1554).

Peyrère, Isaac La. *A Theological Systeme upon That Presupposition, That Men Were before Adam* (London: s.n., 1655).

Pitra, J. B. *Spicilegium solesmense*, 4 vols (Paris: Firmin Didot, 1812–89).

Plato. *The Collected Dialogues of Plato*, ed. Edith Hamilton and Huntington Cairns (Princeton: Princeton University Press, 1961).

Poliziano, Angelo. *La commedia antica e L'Andria di Terenzio [Angeli Politiani Andria Terenti]*, ed. Rosetta Lattanzi Roselli (Florence: Sansoni, 1973).

Pont, Robert. *Against Sacrilege, Three Sermons Preached by Maister Robert Pont* (Edinburgh: Robert Waldegrave, 1599).

Powell, Vavasour. *Spirituall Experiences, of Sundry Beleevers* (London: Robert Ibbitson, 1653).

Pratt, Samuel Jackson. *The Sublime and Beautiful of Scripture*, 2 vols (London: for J. Murray, 1777).

Prideaux, Humphrey. *The Old and New Testament Connected*, 2 vols (London: for R. Knaplock, 1716–18).

Prideaux, Humphrey, ed. *Marmor Oxoniensia* (Oxford: at the Sheldonian Theatre, 1676).

Proceedings in Parliament, 1610, 2 vols, ed. Elizabeth Read Foster (New Haven: Yale University Press, 1966).

Proclus. *Elements of Theology*, tr. E. R. Dodds (Oxford: Oxford University Press, 1963).

Prynne, William. *The Third Part of the Soveraigne Power of Parliaments and Kingdomes* (London: for Michael Sparke, Sr., 1643).

Prynne, William. *The Fourth Part of the Soveraigne Power of Parliaments and Kingdomes* (London: for Michael Sparke, Sr., 1643).

Psalmes of David in Englishe Metre, by T. Sterneholde and Others (London: [J. Day,] 1560).

Ptolemy. *Claudii Ptolemaei Alexandrini geographicae enarrationis libri octo* (Lyon: Melchior & Gaspar Trechsel, 1535).

Purchas, Samuel. *Purchas his Pilgrimes in Five Bookes* (London: for Henry Fetherston, 1625).

Quaresmius, Franciscus. *Historica theologica et moralis Terræ Sanctæ elucidatio* (Antwerp: Balthasar Moretus, 1639).

Quarles, Francis. *A Feast for Wormes. Set Forth in a Poeme of the History of Jonah* (London: Felix Kingston for Richard Moore, 1620).

Quarles, Francis. *Hadassa: Or the History of Queene Ester* (London: [Felix Kingston] for Richard Moore, 1621).

Quarles, Francis. *Job Militant: With Meditations Divine and Morall* (London: Felix Kingston for George Winder, 1624).

Quarles, Francis. *The Complete Works in Prose and Verse of Francis Quarles*, ed. Alexander B. Grosart, 3 vols (New York: AMS Press, 1967).

Rainbowe, Edward. *A Sermon Preached at the Funeral of the Right Honorable Anne Countess of Pembroke* (London: for R. Royston, 1677).

Rainolds, John. *The Summe of the Conference betwene John Rainoldes and John Hart: Touching the Head and the Faith of the Church* (London: [John Wolfe] for George Bishop, 1584).

Rainolds, William. *A Refutation of Sundry Reprehensions, Cavils, and False Sleightes, by Which M. Whitaker Laboureth to Deface the Late English Translation, and Catholike Annotations of the New Testament, and the Booke of Discovery of Heretical Corruptions* (Paris: [for Richard Verstegan?], 1583).

Raleigh, Walter. *The History of the World* (London: [William Stansby] for Walter Burre, 1614).

Rauwolf, Leonhart, et al. *A Collection of Curious Travels & Voyages*, 2 vols (London: for S. Smith & B. Walford, 1693).

Ray, John. *The Ornithology of Francis Willughby* (London: A[ndrew] C[larke] for John Martyn, 1678).

Reading, John. *Anabaptism Routed... With a Particular Answer to All That is Alledged in Favour of the Anabaptists, by Dr. Jer. Taylor, in his Book, Called, The Liberty of Prophesying* (London: for Thomas Johnson, 1655).

Records of the Parliaments of Scotland to 1707, ed. Keith M. Brown et al. <http://www.rps.ac.uk>.

Register of the Diocesan Synod of Dunblane, 1662–1688, ed. John Wilson (Edinburgh: William Blackwood & Sons, 1877).

Richard Bernard, *Rhemes against Rome* (London: Felix Kingston for Robert Milbourne [variant issue for Edward Blackmore], 1626).

Richardson, John. *Choice Observations and Explanations upon the Old Testament* (London: T.R. & E.M., 1655).

Rider, John. *A Friendly Caveat to Irelands Catholickes* (Dublin: John Franckton, 1602).

Rogers, Nehemiah. *A Strange Vineyard in Palaestina* (London: John Haviland for Edward Brewster, 1623).

Rogers, John. *A Godly & Fruitful Exposition upon All the First Epistle of Peter* (London: John Field, 1650).

Rogers, John. *'Ohel Ohel or Beth-shemesh* (London: for R. I. and G. and H. Eversden, 1653).

Rogers, Richard. *Seven Treatises, containing Such Direction as is Gathered Out of the Holie Scriptures, Leading and Guiding to True Happines* (London: Felix Kingston for Thomas Man & Robert Dexter, 1603).

Ross, Alexander. *The New Planet No Planet: or, the Earth No Wandring Star; except in the Wandring Heads of Galileans* (London: J. Young, 1646).

Row, William. *The Life of Mr Robert Blair, Minister of St Andrews*, ed. Thomas M'Crie (Edinburgh: Wodrow Society, 1848).

Russell, C. W., and John P. Prendergast, eds. *Calendar of the State Papers, Relating to Ireland, of the Reign of James I. 1603–1606* (London: Her Majesty's Public Record Office, 1872).

Rutherford, Samuel. *Lex, Rex: The Law and the Prince* (London: for John Field, 1644).

Rutherford, Samuel. *A Sermon Preached to the Honourable House of Commons* (Edinburgh: Evan Tyler, 1644).

Rutherford, Samuel. *Christ Dying and Drawing Sinners to Himselfe* (London: J[ohn] D[awson] for Andrew Crooke, 1647).

Rutherford, Samuel. *A Survey of the Spirituall Antichrist* (London: J[ohn] D[awson] and R[obert] I[bbitson] for Andrew Crooke, 1648).

Rutherford, Samuel. *The Tryal & Triumph of Faith* (London: John Field, 1652).

Sall, Andrew. *A Sermon Preached at Christ-Church in Dublin, before the Lord Lieutenant and Council, the Fifth Day of July, 1674* (Dublin: Benjamin Tooke, 1674).

Saltmarsh, John. *The Practice of Policie in a Christian Life: Taught from the Scriptures* (London: E[dward] G[riffin] for Samuel Endarby, 1639).

Saltmarsh, John. *Examinations, or, a Discovery of Some Dangerous Positions Delivered in a Sermon of Reformation Preached... by Tho. Fuller, B. D. and Since Printed* (London: for Lawrence Blaiklock, 1643).

Saltmarsh, John. *A Solemn Discourse upon the Grand Covenant* (London: for Laurence Blaicklock, 1643).

Saltmarsh, John. *Dawnings of Light* (London: for R. W., 1644).

Saltmarsh, John. *Wonderfull Predictions Declared in a Message, as from the Lord, to His Excellency Sr. Thomas Fairfax and the Councell of His Army* (London: Robert Ibbitson, 1648).

Sancroft, William. *The Articles Recommended by the Arch-Bishop of Canterbury to All the Bishops within His Metropolitan Jurisdiction, the 16th of July, 1688* ([London?]: s.n., 1688).

Sannazaro, Jacopo. *De partu virginis* (Naples: Antonio Frezza, 1526).

Scalamonti, Francesco. *Vita viri clarissimi et famosissimi Kyriaci Anconitani*, ed. Charles Mitchell and Edward W. Bodnar, Transactions of the American Philosophical Society, 86/4 (Philadelphia, Pa.: American Philosophical Society, 1996).

Scaliger, Josephus Justius. *Thesaurus temporum* (Leiden: Thomas Basson, 1606; 2nd edn, 2 vols, Amsterdam: Joannis Janssen, 1658).

Schonaues, Cornelius. *Sacrae comoediae sex: Nempe, Tobaeus, Nehemias, Saulus, Naaman, Josephus, Juditha* (Haarlem: Gillis Rooman, 1592).

Scot, Reginald. *The Discoverie of Witchcraft, wherein the Lewde Dealing of Witches and Witchmongers is Notablie Detected* (London: [Henry Denham for] William Brome, 1584).

Scots Confession, 1560 (Confessio Scoticana) and Negative Confession, 1581 (Confessio negativa), ed. G. D. Henderson (Edinburgh: Church of Scotland, Committee on Publications, 1937).

Selden, John. *Ioannis Seldeni De synedriis & præfecturis juridicis veterum Ebræorum*, 3 vols (London: Jacob Flesher for Cornelius Bee, 1650–5).

Selden, John. [Theanthropos]: Or, God made Man. A Tract Proving the Nativity Of Our Saviour to be on the 25. of December (London: J[ohn]. G[rismond]. for Nathaniel Brooks, 1661).

Selden, John. *The Table-Talk of John Selden*, ed. Samuel Weller Singer (London: Reeves & Turner, 1890).

Selections from the Records of the Kirk Session, Presbytery, and Synod of Aberdeen (Aberdeen: Spalding Club, 1846).

Seven Arguments Plainly Proving that Papists Are Trayterous Subjects to All True Christian Princes ([London: s.n.], 1641).

Shaftesbury, Anthony Ashley Cooper, Earl of. *Characteristics of Men, Manners, Opinions, Times*, ed. John M. Robertson, intro. Stanley Grean (Indianapolis: Bobbs-Merill Company, 1964).

Shakespeare, William. *The Norton Shakespeare: Based on the Oxford Edition*, ed. Stephen Greenblatt et al. (New York: W. W. Norton & Co., 1997).

Shakespeare, William. *The Arden Shakespeare Complete Works*, gen. ed. Richard Proudfoot (Walton-on-Thames: Nelson, 1998).

Shakespeare, William. *The Complete Works of Shakespeare*, gen. ed. David Bevington, 5th edn (New York: Pearson, 2004).

Sharp, Andrew, ed. *The English Levellers* (Cambridge: Cambridge University Press, 1998).

Shawe, John. *Britannia Rediviva: Or the Proper and Sovereign Remedy for the Healing and Recovering of These Three Distracted Nations* (London: Robert White, 1649).

Sherlock, William. *A Sermon Preached at St Margarets Westminster, May 29, 1685. Before the Honourable House of Commons* (London: J. Amery & A. Swalle, 1685).

Sherry, Richard. *A Treatise of Schemes and Tropes: And His Translation of The Education of Children by Desiderius Erasmus*, ed. Herbert W. Hilderbrandt (Gainesville, Fla.: Scholar's Facsimiles and Reprints, 1961).

Shuckburgh, E. S., ed. *Two Biographies of William Bedell* (Cambridge: Cambridge University Press, 1902).

Shuger, Debora, ed. *Documents of Anglophone Christianity: Early Stuart England* (Waco, Tex.: Baylor University Press, 2012).

Shurtleff, Nathaniel B., ed. *Records of the Governor and Company of the Massachusetts Bay in New England*, 5 vols (Boston: William White, 1853–4).

Sibelius, Caspar. *Of the Conversion of Five Thousand and Nine Hundred East-Indians* (London: John Hammond, 1650).

Sibthorpe, Robert. *A Counter-Plea to an Apostataes [sic] Pardon* (London: Bernard Alsop for George Fairbeard, 1618).

Sidney, Algernon. *Court Maxims*, ed. H. Blom, Eco Haitsma-Mulier, and Ronald Janse (Cambridge: Cambridge University Press, 1996).

Sidney, Algernon. *Discourses concerning Government*, ed. Thomas G. West (New York: Liberty Fund, 1996).

Sidney, Philip. *The Defence of Poesie* (London: [Thomas Creede] for William Ponsonby, 1595).

Simpson, Edward. *Chronicon historiam catholicam complectens, ab exordio mundi ad nativitatem D.N. Iesv Christi* (Oxford: L[eonard] L[ichfield] & H[enry] H[all], 1652).

Slatyer, William. *The Compleat Christian, and Compleat Armour and Armoury of a Christian* (London: for the author, 1643).

Sleidan, Johann. *De quatuor summis imperiis* (Strasbourg: Josias Rihel & Theodosius Rihel, 1556).

Sleidan, Johann. *A briefe Chronicle of the Foure Principall Empyres*, tr. Stephan Wythers (London: Rowland Hall, 1563).

Sleidan, Johann. *De quatuor summis imperiis* (London: Robert Waldegrave for Thomas Woodcock, 1584).

Sleidan, Johann. *The Key of Historie: Or, A Most Methodicall Abridgement of the Foure Chiefe Monarchies* (London: Miles Flesher, for William Sheeres, 1627).

Smith, Henry. *The Preachers Proclamacion* (London: [E. Allde? for] William Kearney, 1591).

Smith, Miles. *Sermons of the Right Reverend Father in God Miles Smith, Late Lord Bishop of Gloucester* (London: Elizabeth Allde for Robert Allot, 1632).

Smith, Nigel, ed. *A Collection of Ranter Writings from the 17th Century* (London: Junction Books, 1983).

Spelman, John. *The Case of our Affaires, in Law, Religion, and Other Circumstances Briefly Examined and Presented to the Conscience* (Oxford: H. H. for W. W., 1643 [i.e. 1644]).

Spencer, John. *Votivae Angliæ* (London: H[enry] Dudley, 1643).

Spenser, Edmund. *Spenser: The Faerie Queene*, ed. A. C. Hamilton; text ed. Hiroshi Yamashita and Toshiyuki Suzuki, 2nd edn (Harlow: Pearson Longman, 2007).

Statutes of the Realm: Printed by Command of His Majesty King George the Third, 9 vols (London: George Eyre & Andrew Strahan, 1810–25).

Stillingfleet, Edward. *Origines Sacrae, or A Rational Account of the Grounds of Christian Faith* (London: R[obert]. W[hite]. for Henry Mortlock, 1663).

Stillingfleet, Edward. *A Rational Account of the Grounds of Protestant Religion Being a Vindication of the Lord Archbishop of Canterbury's Relation of a Conference, &c., from the Pretended Answer by T.C.* (London: Rob. White for Henry Mortlock, 1665).

Stillingfleet, Edward. *Origines Britannicæ, or, the Antiquities of the British Churches* (London: M. Flesher for Henry Mortlock, 1685).

Stillingfleet, Edward. *Scripture and Tradition Compared in a Sermon Preached at Guild Hall Chapel, November 27th, 1687* (London: for Henry Mortlock, 1688).

Stirling Presbytery Records, 1581–1587, ed. James Kirk (Edinburgh: Scottish History Society, 1981).

Stow, John. *A Survey of London by John Stow*, ed. Charles Lethbridge Kingsford, 2 vols (Oxford: Clarendon Press, 1908).

Strunk, Oliver, ed. *Strunk's Source Readings in Music History*, ed. Leo Trietler, rev. edn (New York and London: Norton, 1978).

Strype, John. *Annals of the Reformation and Establishment of Religion* (London: for John Wyat, 1709; new edn, 4 vols, Oxford: Clarendon Press, 1824).

Stubbes, Phillip. *A Christal Glasse for Christian Women* ([s.l.: R. Jhones, 1591]).

Tasso, Torquato. *Discorsi del poema heroica* (Naples: Nicola Antonio Stigliola for Paolo Venturino, [1594?]).

Taylor, Jeremy. *Of the Sacred Order, and Offices of Episcopacy, by Divine Institution, Apostolicall Tradition, & Catholike Practice* (Oxford: Leonard Lichfield, 1642).

Taylor, Jeremy. *Theologia 'eklektikē: A Discourse of the Liberty of Prophesying* (London: for R. Royston, 1647).

Taylor, Jeremy. *Treatises of 1. The Liberty of Prophesying, 2. Prayer ex tempore, 3. Episcopacie* (London: R. Royston, 1648).

Taylor, Jeremy. *The Rule and Exercises of Holy Living* (London: for Richard Royston, 1650).

Taylor, Jeremy. *The Golden Grove, or, a Manuall of Daily Prayers and Letanies, Fitted to the Dayes of the Week* (London: J. F[lesher]. for R. Royston, 1655 [i.e. 1654]).

Taylor, Jeremy. *Symbolon ēthiko-polemikon: Or a Collection of Polemical and Moral Discourses Wherein the Church of England in Its Worst as Well as More Flourishing Condition is Defended in Many Material Points* (London: for R. Royston, 1657).

Taylor, Jeremy. *Ductor dubitantium, or, the Rule of Conscience in All Her Generall Measures Serving as a Great Instrument for the Determination of Cases of Conscience* (London: James Flesher for Richard Royston, 1660).

Taylor, Thomas. *The Pilgrims Profession. Or a Sermon Preached at the Funerall of Mris Mary Gunter* (London: J. D. for John Bartlet, 1622).

Thaddaeus, Joannes. *The Reconciler of the Bible* (London: for Simon Miller, 1655).

The Anglican Canons, 1529–1947, ed. Gerald Bray (Woodbridge: Boydell & Brewer, 1998).

The Booke of Common Praier, and Administration of the Sacramentes (London: Richard Jugge & John Cawood, 1559).

The Book of Common Prayer 1559, ed. J. F. Booty (Charlottesville, Va.: University Press of Virginia, 1976).

The Book of Common Prayer: The Texts of 1549, 1559, and 1662, ed. Brian Cummings (Oxford: Oxford University Press, 2011).

The Confession of Faith and Catechisms (London: for Robert Bostock, 1649).

The Dying Speeches, Letters and Prayers, & c. of those Eminent Protestants who Suffered… under the Cruel Sentence of the Late Lord Chancellour (London: for John Dunton, 1689).

The First Book of Discipline, ed. James K. Cameron (Edinburgh: St Andrew Press, 1972).

The Holy Harmony: Or, a Plea for the Abolishing of Organs and Other Musick out of the Protestant Churches of Great Britain (London: R. Austin & A. Coe, 1643).

The Humble Advice of the Assembly of Divines, Now By Authority of Parliament Sitting at Westminster, concerning a Confession of Faith (London: for the Company of Stationers, 1647).

The Judgment and Decree of the University of Oxford Past in Their Convocation, July 21. 1683, against Certain Pernicious Books, and Damnable Doctrines (Oxford: at the Sheldonian Theatre, 1683)

The Life of the Reverend Humphrey Prideaux (London: for J. & P. Knapton, 1748).

The McCulloch Examinations of the Cambuslang Revival (1742), ed. Keith Edward Beebe, 2 vols (Scottish History Society, 2011).

The Perth Kirk Session Books, 1577–1590, ed. Margo Todd (Woodbridge: Scottish History Society, 2012).

The Praise of Musicke: Wherein besides the Antiquitie, Dignitie, Delectation, & Use Thereof in Civill Matters, is also Declared the Sober and Lawfull Use of the Same in the Congregation and Church of God (Oxford: Joseph Barnes, 1586).

The Register of the Privy Council of Scotland, 1st ser., ed. John H. Burton, 14 vols (Edinburgh: H. M. General Register, 1877–98).

The Register of the Synod of Galloway, from October 1664 to April 1671 (Kirkcudbright: J. Nicholson, 1856).

The Responsa Scholarum of the English College, Rome, ed. and tr. Anthony Kenny, 2 vols (London: Catholic Record Society, 1962–3).

The Saxon Genesis: An Edition of the West Saxon 'Genesis B' and the Old Saxon Vatican 'Genesis', ed. Alger N. Doane (Madison, Wis.: University of Wisconsin Press, 1991).

The Second Book of Discipline, ed. James Kirk (Edinburgh: St Andrew Press, 1980).

The Southwell-Sibthorpe Commonplace Book: Folger MS V.b.198, ed. Jean Klene, Renaissance English Text Society, 7th ser. 20 (Tempe, Ariz.: Medieval & Renaissance Texts & Studies, 1997).

The Two Books of Homilies Appointed to be Read in Churches, ed. J. Griffiths (Oxford: Oxford University Press, 1859).

The Un-Deceiver (London: for Samuel Gellibrand, 1643).

Thevet, André. *Cosmographie de Levant* (Geneva: Droz, 1985).

Thomson, T., and C. Innes, eds. *The Acts of the Parliaments of Scotland*, 12 vols (Edinburgh, 1814–44).

Thorold, Thomas. *Labyrinthus Cantuariensis, or, Doctor Lawd's Labyrinth* (Paris: John Billaine, 1658).

Todd, Henry John. *Memoirs of the Life and Writings of the Right Rev. Brian Walton*, 2 vols (London: for F. C. & J. Beverington, 1821).

Toland, John. *John Toland's 'Nazarenus' (1718)*, ed. J. A. I. Champion (Oxford: Voltaire Foundation, 1999).

Tombes, John. *Jehova Iireh: Or, Gods Providence in Delivering the Godly* (London: Richard Cotes, 1643).

Topsell, Edward. *The Historie of Foure-Footed Beastes* (London: William Jaggard, 1607).

Tourneur, Cyril. *The Plays of Cyril Tourneur*, ed. George Parfitt (Cambridge: Cambridge University Press, 1978).

Travers, Walter. *A Supplication Made to the Privy Counsel by Mr Walter Travers* (Oxford: Joseph Barnes, 1612).

Tudor Royal Proclamations, ed. Paul L. Hughes and James F. Larkin, 3 vols (New Haven: Yale University Press, 1964).

Turnbull, H. W., et al., eds. *The Correspondence of Isaac Newton*, 7 vols (Cambridge: Cambridge University Press, 1959–77).

Tyndale, William. *Compendious Introduccion, Prologe or Preface un to the Pistle off Paul to the Romayns* ([Worms: P. Schoeffer, 1526]).

Tyndale, William. *That Faith the Mother of All Good Works Justifieth Us (The Parable of the Wicked Mammon)* ([Antwerp: J. Hoochstraten, 1528]).

Tyndale, William. *The Obedience of a Christen man and How Christen Rulers Ought to Governe* ([Antwerp: J. Hoochstraten, 1528]).

Tyndale, William. *The Parable of the Wycked Mammon* (London: John Day, 1547).

Tyndale, William. *Expositions and Notes on Sundry Portions of Holy Scriptures*, ed. Henry Walker (Cambridge: Parker Society, 1849).

Tyndale, William. *The Work of William Tyndale*, ed. G. E. Duffield (Philadelphia: Fortress Press, 1965).

Tyndale, William. *Tyndale's New Testament*, ed. David Daniell (New Haven and London: Yale University Press, 1989).

Tyrrell, James. *Patriarcha non monarcha. The Patriarch Unmonarch'd: Being Observations on a Late Treatise and Divers Other Miscellanies* (London: for Richard Janeway, 1681).

Ussher, James. *Annales veteris testament, a prima mundi origine deducti*, 2 vols (London: J. Flesher, [1650]).

Ussher, James. *De textus Hebraici Veteris Testament variantibus lectionibus ad Ludovicum Capellum epistola* (London: J. Flesher for J. Crook & J. Baker, 1652).

Ussher, James. *De graecâ septuaginta, interpretum versione syntagma* (London: for John Crook, 1655).

Ussher, James. *The Annals of the World* (London: E. Tyler for J. Crook, 1658).

Vaughan, Henry. *Henry Vaughan: The Complete Poems*, ed. Alan Rudrum (Harmondsworth: Penguin, 1976).

Vergil. *The Aeneid*, tr. Sarah Ruden (New Haven: Yale University Press, 2008).

Vicars, John. *Unholsome Henbane between Two Fragrant Roses* (London: for John Rothwell, 1645).

Vida, Marco Girolamo. *Christiad*, tr. James Gardner, ed. James Hankins, The I Tatti Renaissance Library, 39 (Cambridge, Mass.: Harvard University Press, 2009).

Vives, Juan Luis. *Institutione feminae christianae: Liber primus*, ed. C. Fantazzi and C. Matheeussen, tr. C. Fantazzi (New York and Cologne: Brill Acade, 1996).

Vives, Juan Luis. *The Education of a Christian Woman: A Sixteenth-Century Manual*, ed. and tr. C. Fantazzi (Chicago: University of Chicago Press, 2000).

Voltaire. *Dictionnaire philosophique portatif* (Geneva: [Gabriel Grasset], 1764).

Vossius, G. J. *Dissertatio gemina* (Amsterdam: J. Blaue, 1643).

Vossius, G. J. *Chronologiae sacrae isagoge*, ed. I Vossius (The Hague: A. Vlacq, 1659).

Vossius, Isaac. *De septuaginta interpretibus eorumque tralatione & chronologia dissertationes* (The Hague: A. Vlacq, 1661).

Vossius, Isaac. *Dissertatio de vera aetate mundi* (The Hague: A. Vlacq, 1659).

Walker, Anthony. *Eureka, Eureka: The Virtuous Woman Found Her Loss Bewailed, and Character Exemplified in a Sermon Preached… At the Funeral of That Most Excellent Lady the Right Honourable and Eminently Religious and Charitable Mary, Countess Dowager of Warwick* (London: for Nathanael Ranew, 1678).

Walton, Izaak. *The Life of Mr. Rich. Hooker, the Author of those Learned Books of the Laws of Ecclesiastical Polity* (London: J. G[rismond]. for Rich. Marriott, 1665).

Walwyn, William. *The Power of Love* (London: R.C. for John Sweeting, 1643).

Walwyn, William. *A Whisper in the Eare of Mr Thomas Edwards, Minister* (London: Thomas Paine for William Ley, 1646).

Walwyn, William. *The Writings of William Walwyn*, ed. Jack McMichael and Barbara Taft (Athens, Ga.: University of Georgia Press, 1989).

Watson, Thomas. *A Humanist's 'Trew Imitation': Thomas Watson's 'Absalom'*, ed. and tr. John Hazel Smith (Urbana, Ill.: University of Illinois Press, 1964).

Weever, John. *An Agnus Dei* (London: V. Sims for Nicholas Ling, 1601).

Welsh, John. *A Preface, Lecture, and a Sermon* ([Holland?]: s.n., 1686).

Wesley, Susanna. *Susanna Wesley: The Complete Writings*, ed. Charles Wallace, Jr. (Oxford: Oxford University Press, 1997).

Wheare, Degory. *The Method and Order Of Reading Both Civil and Ecclesiastical Histories*, tr. Edmund Bohun (London: M. Flesher, for Charles Brome, 1685).

Whiston, William. *A New Theory of the Earth, from its Original, to the Consummation of All Things* (London: R. Roberts for Benjamin Tooke, 1696).

Whitaker, William. *Ad Nicolai Sanderi demonstrationes quadraginta* (London: Thomas Vautrollier for Thomas Chard, 1583).

Whitaker, William. *An Answere to a Certeine Booke, Written by M. William Rainolds Student of Divinitie in the English Colledge at Rhemes, and Entituled, a Refutation of Sundrie Reprehensions, Cavils, &c* (London: [Eliot's Court Press], 1585).

Whitgift, John. *The Defense of the Aunswere to the Admonition* (London: Henry Binneman, for Humphrey Toye, 1574).

Whittingham, William (attrib.). *A Brief Discourse of the Troubles at Frankfort, 1554–1558*, ed. Edward Arber (London: Elliot Stock, 1908).

Wickens, Robert. *A Compleat & Perfect Concordance of the English Bible Composed after a New, and Most Compendious Method, Whereby May be Readily Found Any Place of Canonicall Scripture* (Oxford: H. Hall for Th. Robinson, 1655).

Wilkins, David. *Concilia magnae Britanniae et Hibernia*, 4 vols (London: for R. Gosling, F. Gyles, T. Woodward, & C. Davis, 1733–7).

Wilkins, John. *Of the Principles and Duties of Natural Religion: Two Books* (London: A. Maxwell for T. Basset, H. Brome & R. Chiswell, 1675).

Willet, Andrew. *Synopsis Papismi, That Is, a Generall Viewe of Papistry... Now This Second Time Perused and Published* (London: widow Orwin for Thomas Man, 1594).

Willet, Andrew. *Hexapla in Danielem* (Cambridge: Leonard Greene, 1610).

William III or Lloyd, William. *Utrum Horum; Or, God's Ways of Disposing of Kingdoms* (London: Richard Baldwin, 1691).

Wilson, Thomas. *Jerichoes Down-Fall* (London: for John Bartlet, 1643).

Winstanley, Gerrard. *The Mysterie of God* ([London?]: s.n., 1648).

Winstanley, Gerrard. *The New Law of Righteousnes Budding Forth* (London: for Giles Calvert, 1649).

Winstanley, Gerrard. *The Works of Gerrard Winstanley*, ed. George H. Sabine (New York: Cornell University Press, 1941).

Winstanley, Gerrard. *The Complete Works of Gerrard Winstanley*, ed. Thomas N. Corns, Ann Hughes and David Loewenstein, 2 vols (Oxford: Oxford University Press, 2009).

Wither, George. *A View of the Marginal Notes of the Popish Testament, Translated into English by the English fugitiue Papists Resiant [sic] at Rhemes in France* (London: Edmund Bollifant for Thomas Woodcocke, 1588).

Wither, George. *A Preparation to the Psalter* (London: Nicholas Okes, 1619).

Wither, George. *Campo-Musae: or The field-Musings of Captain George Wither* (London: by R. Austin, 1643).

Wodrow, Robert. *Analecta: or, Materials for a History of Remarkable Providences*, 4 vols (Glasgow: Maitland Club, 1842–3).

Wolfe, Don M., ed. *Leveller Manifestoes of the Puritan Revolution* (New York: Thomas Nelson, 1944).

Wolseley, Charles. *The Unreasonableness of Atheism Made Manifest* (London: for Nathanel Ponder, 1669).

Woodhouse, A. S. P., ed. *Puritanism and Liberty: Being the Army Debates (1647–49) from the Clarke Manuscripts* (London: J. M. Dent, 1938).

Wootton, David, ed. *Divine Right and Democracy: An Anthology of Political Writing in Stuart England* (Harmondsworth: Penguin, 1986; repr. Indianapolis: Hackett, 2003).

Worse & Worse: Or, a Description of their Desperate Condition Who Shall Presume to Take the New Oath or Covenant ([London: s.n.], 1643).

Wright, William Ball. *The Ussher Memoirs; or Genealogical Memoirs of the Ussher Families in Ireland* (Dublin: Sealy, Bryers & Walker, 1889).

Writer, Clement. *Fides divina: The Ground of True faith Asserted* (London: for the author, 1657).

Ziegler, Jacob, and Wolfgang Wissenburg. *Terrae Sanctae, quam Palaestinam nominant,… description* (Strasburg: Rihel, 1536).

Zuallart, Jean. *Le tresdeuot voyage de Jerusalem* (Antwerp: Arnold Conincx, 1608).

Secondary sources

Abbott, T. K. 'On the History of the Irish Bible'. *Hermathena*, 17 (1913): 29–50.

Adams, David, and Adrian Armstrong, eds. *Print and Power in France and England, 1500–1800* (Aldershot: Ashgate, 2006).

Allen, Don Cameron. 'Dean Donne Sets his Text'. *English Literary History*, 10 (1943): 208–29.

Allen, Don Cameron. *The Legend of Noah: Renaissance Rationalism in Art, Science, and Letters* (Urbana, Ill.: University of Illinois Press, 1949).

Allen, Don Cameron. *Doubt's Boundless Sea: Skepticism and Faith in the Renaissance* (Baltimore, Md.: Johns Hopkins Press: 1964).

Allen, W. S., and E. C. Jacobs. *The Coming of the King James Gospels* (Fayetteville, Ark.: University of Arkansas Press, 1995).

Almond, Philip C. *Adam and Eve in Seventeenth-Century Thought* (Cambridge: Cambridge University Press, 1999).

Almond, Philip C. 'Adam, Pre-Adamites, and Extra-Terrestrial Beings in Early Modern Europe'. *Journal of Religious History*, 30 (2006): 163–74.

Alter, Robert. *Pen of Iron: American Prose and the King James Bible* (Princeton: Princeton University Press, 2010).

Amory, Hugh. 'The Trout and the Milk: An Ethnobibliographical Talk'. *Harvard Library Bulletin*, NS 7 (1996): 50–65.

Andersen, Jennifer, and Elizabeth Sauer, eds. *Books and Readers in Early Modern England: Material Studies* (Philadelphia: University of Pennsylvania Press, 2002).

Anderson, Christopher. *Historical Sketches of the Native Irish and their Descendants* (Edinburgh: Oliver & Boyd, 1828).

Anidjar, Gil. 'Secularism'. *Critical Inquiry*, 33 (2006): 52–77.

Arber, Edward. *A Transcript of the Registers of the Company of Stationers of London, 1554–1640 A.D.*, 4 vols (London, 1875–94; repr. New York: Peter Smith, 1950).

Arias, Santa. 'Rethinking Space: An Outsider's View of the Spatial Turn'. *GeoJournal*, 75 (2010): 29–41.

Asad, Talal, Wendy Brown, Judith Butler, and Saba Mahmood. *Is Critique Secular? Blasphemy, Injury and Free Speech* (Berkeley, Calif.: Townsend Center for the Humanities/University of California Press, 2009).

Asselt, Willem J. van, and Eef Dekker, eds. *Reformation and Scholasticism: An Ecumenical Enterprise* (Grand Rapids, Mich.: Baker Academic, 2001).

Assmann, Jan. *Religion and Cultural Memory*, tr. Rodney Livingstone (Stanford, Calif.: Stanford University Press, 2006).

Aston, Margaret. *England's Iconoclasts*, i. *Laws Against Images* (Oxford: Oxford University Press, 1988).

Aston, Margaret. 'Lap Books and Lectern Books: The Revelatory Book in the Reformation', in R. N. Swanson (ed.), *The Church and the Book, Studies in Church History*, 38 (2004): 163–89.

Atkinson, Ernest George, ed. *Calendar of State Papers, Relating to Ireland, of the Reign of Elizabeth, 1596, July–1597, December* (London: Her Majesty's Stationery Office, 1893).

Atkinson, Ernest George, ed. *Calendar of the State Papers, Relating to Ireland, of the Reign of Elizabeth, 1599, April–1600, February* (London: Her Majesty's Stationery Office, 1899).

Atkinson, Nigel. *Richard Hooker and the Authority of Scripture, Tradition and Reason: Reformed Theologian of the Church of England?* (Carlisle: Paternoster Press, 1997).

Austern, Linda Phyllis, Kari Boyd McBride, and David L. Orvis, eds. *Psalms in the Early Modern World* (Farnham: Ashgate, 2011).

Auvray, Paul. 'Jean Morin (1591–1659)'. *Revue biblique*, 66 (1959): 397–414.

Backus, Irena. 'Laurence Tomson (1539–1608) and Elizabethan Puritanism'. *The Journal of Ecclesiastical History*, 28 (1977): 17–27.

Backus, Irena. *The Reformed Roots of the English New Testament: The Influence of Theodore Beza on the English New Testament* (Pittsburgh, Pa.: Pickwick Press, 1980).

Backus, Irena. *Historical Method and Confessional Identity in the Era of the Reformation (1378–1615)* (Leiden: Brill, 2003).

Baer, Yitzhak. 'Rashi and the Historical Reality of his Time'. *Tarbiz*, 20 (1950): 320–32.

Bainton, Roland H. *Hunted Heretic: The Life and Death of Michael Servetus, 1511–1553* (Boston: Beacon Press, 1960).

Baldwin, T. W. *Shakespere's Five-Act Structure: Shakespere's Early Plays on the Background of Renaissance Theories of Five-Act Structure from 1470* (Urbana, Ill.: University of Illinois Press, 1947).

Bamji, Alexandra, Geert J. Janssen, and Mary Laven, eds. *The Ashgate Research Companion to the Counter-Reformation* (Aldershot: Ashgate, 2013).

Barber, Charles. *Early Modern English*, rev. edn (Edinburgh: Edinburgh University Press, 1997).

Barber, Charles, Joan C. Beal, and Philip A. Shaw, eds. *The English Language: A Historical Introduction*, 2nd edn (Cambridge: Cambridge University Press, 2009).

Barker, Sara K., and Brenda M. Hosington, eds. *Renaissance Cultural Crossroads: Translation, Print and Culture in Britain, 1473–1640* (Leiden: Brill, 2013).

Baroway, Israel. 'The Bible as Poetry in the English Renaissance: An Introduction'. *Journal of English and Germanic Philology*, 32 (1933): 447–80.

Barr, James. 'Why the World was Created in 4004 B.C: Archbishop Ussher and Biblical Chronology'. *Bulletin of the John Rylands University Library of Manchester*, 67 (1984–5):575–608.

Barton, John, and John Muddiman, eds. *Oxford Bible Commentary* (Oxford: Oxford University Press, 2001).

Barton, John. *Isaiah 1–39: Old Testament Guides* (Sheffield: Sheffield Academic Press, 1995).

Bath, Michael. *Speaking Pictures: English Emblem Books and Renaissance Culture* (London: Longman, 1994).

Bauckham, Richard, Jr. 'The Career and Thought of Dr. William Fulke (1537–1589)' (Ph.D. thesis, University of Cambridge, 1973).

Baukman, Richard. *The Theology of the Book of Revelation* (Cambridge: Cambridge University Press, 1993).

Baxter, Jamie Reid. 'Thomas Wode, Christopher Goodman and the Curious Death of Scottish Music'. *Scotlands*, 4 (1997): 1–20.

Baxter, Jamie Reid. 'Metrical Psalmody and the Bannatyne Manuscript: Robert Pont's Psalm 83'. *Renaissance and Reformation*, 30 (2007): 41–62.

Baxter, Jamie Reid. 'Mr Andrew Boyd (1567–1636): A Neo-Stoic Bishop of Argyll and his Writings', in Julian Goodare and Alasdair A. MacDonald (eds), *Sixteenth-Century Scotland: Essays in Honour of Michael Lynch* (Leiden: Brill, 2008), 395–426.

Bell, William, and N. D. Emerson, eds. *The Church of Ireland, A.D. 432–1932* (Dublin: Church of Ireland Printing and Publishing Co., 1932).

Ben Amos, Dan. 'Talmudic Tall Tales', in Linda Dégh, Henry Glassie, and Felix J. Oinas (eds), *Folklore Today: A Festschrift for Richard M. Dorson* (Bloomington, Ind.: Research Center for Language and Semiotic Studies, Indiana University, 1976), 25–43.

Benedict, Philip. *Christ's Churches Purely Reformed: A Social History of Calvinism* (New Haven: Yale University Press, 2002).

Benin, Stephen D. 'Sacrifice as Education in Augustine and Chrysostom'. *Church History: Studies in Christianity and Culture*, 52 (1983): 7–20.

Bennett, Jim, and Scott Mandelbrote. *The Garden, the Ark, the Tower, the Temple* (Oxford: Bodleian Library, 1998).

Bennett, Joan S. *Reviving Liberty: Radical Christian Humanism in Milton's Great Poems* (Cambridge, Mass.: Harvard University Press, 1989).

Berg, Johannes van den. *Religious Currents and Cross-Currents*, ed. Jan de Bruijn, Pieter Holtrop, and Ernestine van der Wall (Leiden: Brill, 1999).

Berger, David. 'The Jewish–Christian Debate in the High Middle Ages', in Jeremy Cohen (ed.), *Essential Papers on Judaism and Christianity in Conflict* (New York: NYU Press, 1991), 484–513.

Bernard, George. *The King's Reformation: Henry VIII and the Remaking of the English Church* (New Haven: Yale University Press, 2005).

Besse, Jean-Marc. 'Quelle géographie pour le prince chrétien? Premières remarques sur Antonio Possevino'. *Laboratoire italien ('Géographie et politique au début de l'âge moderne')*, 8 (2008): 123–43.

Betteridge, Maurice. 'The Bitter Notes: The Geneva Bible and its Annotations'. *The Sixteenth Century Journal*, 14 (1983): 41–62.

Bhaldraithe, Tomás de. 'Leabhar Charswell in Éirinn'. *Éigse*, 9 (1958): 61–7.

Black, David. *Mission Culture in the Upper Amazon: Native Tradition, Jesuit Enterprise and Secular Policy in Moxos, 1660–1880* (Lincoln, Neb.: University of Nebraska Press, 1994).

Black, Ronald. 'Gaelic Religious Publishing 1567–1800', in Colm Ó Baoill and Nancy R. McGuire (eds), *Caindel Alban: Fèill-sgrìobhainn do Dhòmhnall E. Meek* (Aberdeen: University of Aberdeen, 2008), 73–85.

Blair, Ann. 'Mosaic Physics and the Search for a Pious Natural Philosophy in the Late Renaissance'. *Isis*, 91 (2000): 32–58.

Blank, Paula. *Broken English: Dialects and the Politics of Language in Renaissance Writings* (London: Routledge, 1996).

Blanton, Ward, and Yvonne Sherwood, 'Bible/Religion/Critique', in Richard King (ed.), *Theory/Religion/Critique* (New York: Columbia University Press, forthcoming).

Blayney, Peter W. M. *The Stationers' Company and the Printers of London, 1501–1557*, 2 vols (Cambridge: Cambridge University Press, 2013).

Bleyerveld, Yvonne. 'Chaste, Obedient and Devout: Biblical Women as Patterns of Female Virtue in Netherlandish and German Graphic Art, ca. 1500–1750'. *Simiolus*, 28 (2000–1): 219–50.

Bloch, Chana. *Spelling the Word: George Herbert and the Bible* (Berkeley, Calif.: University of California Press, 1985).

Bloom, Harold. *The Shadow of a Great Rock: A Literary Appreciation of the King James Bible* (New Haven and London: Yale University Press, 2011).

Blumenberg, Hans. *The Legitimacy of the Modern Age*, tr. Robert M. Wallace (Cambridge, Mass.: MIT Press, 1985).

Boer, E. A. de. *John Calvin on the Visions of Ezekiel* (Leiden: Brill, 2004).

Borot, Luc. 'The Bible and Protestant Inculturation in the *Homilies* of the Church of England', in Richard Griffiths (ed.), *The Bible in the Renaissance* (Aldershot: Ashgate, 2001), 150–75.

Bose, M. C. A., and J. P. Hornback II, eds. *Wycliffite Controversies* (Turnhout: Brepols, 2011).

Boulton, J. P. 'The Limits of Formal Religion: The Administration of Holy Communion in Late Elizabethan and Early Stuart London'. *London Journal*, 10 (1984): 135–54.

Bracht, Katharina, and David S. du Toit, eds. *Die Geschichte der Daniel-Auslegung in Judentum, Christentum und Islam* (Berlin: De Gruyter, 2007).

Bradstock, Andrew. *Faith in the Revolution: The Political Theologies of Müntzer and Winstanley* (London: SPCK, 1997).

Bradstock, Andrew. *Radical Religion in Cromwell's England: A Concise History From the English Civil War to the End of the Commonwealth* (London: I. B. Tauris, 2011).

Bragg, Melvyn. *The Book of Books: The Radical Impact of the King James Bible 1611–2011* (Berkeley, Calif.: Counterpoint, 2011).

Brailsford, H. N. *The Levellers and the English Revolution* (Nottingham: Spokesman Books, 1976).

Brecht, Martin. 'Die Berleburger Bibel: Hinwiese zu ihrem Verständnis'. *Pietismus und Neuzeit*, 8 (1982): 162–200.

Bredenhof, W. 'Guy de Brès and the Apocrypha'. *Westminster Theological Journal*, 74 (2012): 305–21.

Breeze, Andrew. 'Andrew Sall (†1682), Andrew Sall (†1686), and the Irish Bible'. *Éigse*, 28 (1994–5): 100–2.

Brewer, J. S., and William Bullen, eds. *Calendar of the Carew Manuscripts, Preserved in the Archiepiscopal Library at Lambeth. 1589–1600* (London: Longmans, Green, & Co., 1869).

Brightman, F. E. *The English Rite: Being a Synopsis of the Sources and Revisions of the Book of Common Prayer*, 2 vols (London: Rivingtons, 1915–22).

Brinkley, R. Florence. 'Coleridge's Criticism of Jeremy Taylor'. *Huntington Library Quarterly*, 13 (1950): 313–23.

Brown, Cedric C., and Maureen Boyd. 'The Homely Sense of Herbert's "Jordan"'. *Studies in Philology*, 79 (1982): 147–61.

Brown, Laura Feitzinger. 'Brawling in Church: Noise and the Rhetoric of Lay Behavior in Early Modern England'. *The Sixteenth Century Journal*, 34 (2003): 955–72.

Brown, Matthew P. *The Pilgrim and the Bee: Reading Rituals and Book Culture in Early New England* (Philadelphia: University of Pennsylvania Press, 2007).

Bruce, F. F. *The English Bible: A History of Translations from the Earliest English Version to the New English Bible*, rev. edn (London: Lutterworth Press, 1970).

Bruce, John, ed. *Calendar of State Papers Domestic: Charles I, 1634–35* (London: Longman, 1864).

Brún, Pádraig de. *Scriptural Instruction in the Vernacular: The Irish Society and its Teachers 1818–1827* (Dublin: Dublin Institute for Advanced Studies, 2009).

Brún, Pádraig de, and Máire Herbert. *Catalogue of Irish Manuscripts in Cambridge Libraries* (Cambridge: Cambridge University Press, 1986).

Bryson, Michael. *The Atheist Milton* (Farnham: Ashgate, 2012).

Buchwald, Jed Z., and Mordechai Feingold. *Newton and the Origin of Civilization* (Princeton: Princeton University Press, 2013).

Buckley, Michael J. *At the Origins of Modern Atheism* (New Haven: Yale University Press, 1987).

Burckhardt, Jacob. *The Civilization of the Renaissance in Italy*, tr. S. G. C. Middlemore, with a foreword by L. Goldscheider (London: Phaidon, 1944).

Burke, Peter. *Popular Culture in Early Modern Europe* (1978; 3rd edn, Aldershot: Ashgate, 2009).

Burke, Victoria E. '"My poor Returns": Devotional Manuscripts by Seventeenth-Century Women', in Sarah C. E. Ross (ed.), 'Early Modern Women and the Apparatus of Authorship', *Parergon*, 29/2 (2012): 47–68.

Burnett, Stephen G. *From Christian Hebraism to Jewish Studies: Johannes Buxtorf (1564–1629) and Hebrew Learning in the Seventeenth Century* (Leiden: Brill, 1996).

Burns, Norman T. *Christian Mortalism from Tyndale to Milton* (Cambridge, Mass.: Harvard University Press, 1972).

Burrow, J. A. 'Allegory: The Literal Level', in J. A. Burrow (ed.), *Essays on Medieval Literature* (Oxford: Clarendon Press, 1984), 192–212.

Burrows, Donald. *Handel: Messiah* (Cambridge: Cambridge University Press, 1991).

Bush, Sargent, and Carl J. Rasmussen. *The Library of Emmanuel College, Cambridge, 1584–1637* (Cambridge: Cambridge University Press, 1986).

Butterworth, Charles C. *The English Primers (1529–1545): Their Publication and Connection with the English Bible and the Reformation in England* (Philadelphia: University of Pennsylvania Press, 1953).

Büttner, Manfred. 'The Significance of the Reformation for the Reorientation of Geography in Lutheran Germany'. *History of Science*, 17 (1979): 151–69.

Butts, Barbara, and Lee Hendrix, eds. *Painting on Light: Drawings and Stained Glass in the Age of Dürer and Holbein* (Oxford: Oxford University Press, 2001).

Bynum, Caroline Walker. *Christian Materiality: An Essay on Religion in Late Medieval Europe* (Brooklyn: Zone Books, 2011).

Caball, Marc. *Poets and Politics: Reaction and Continuity in Irish Poetry, 1558–1625* (Cork: Cork University Press, 1998).

Caball, Marc. 'Gaelic and Protestant: A Case Study in Early Modern Self-Fashioning, 1567–1608'. *Proceedings of the Royal Irish Academy*, 110 (2010): 191–215.

Caball, Marc. '"Solid divine and worthy scholar": William Bedell, Venice and Gaelic Culture', in James Kelly and Ciarán Mac Murchaidh (eds), *Irish and English: Essays on the Irish Linguistic and Cultural Frontier, 1600–1900* (Dublin: Four Courts Press, 2012), 43–57.

Cabot, Nancy Graves. 'Pattern Sources of Scriptural Subjects in Tudor and Stuart Embroideries'. *Bulletin of the Needle and Bobbin Club*, 20 (1946): 17–21.

Cadbury, H. J. 'Early Quakerism and Uncanonical Lore'. *Harvard Theological Review*, 40 (1947): 177–205.

Calderwood, David. *The History of the Kirk of Scotland*, 8 vols (Edinburgh: for the Wodrow Society, 1842).

Calhoun, Joshua. 'The Word Made Flax: Cheap Bibles, Textual Corruption, and the Poetics of Paper'. *PMLA* 126 (2011): 327–44.

Cambers, Andrew. 'Demonic Possession, Literacy and "Superstition" in Early Modern England'. *Past and Present*, 202 (2009), 3–35.

Cambers, Andrew. *Godly Reading: Print, Manuscript and Puritanism in England, 1580–1720* (Cambridge: Cambridge University Press, 2011).

Cameron, Euan. *The European Reformation* (Oxford: Oxford University Press, 1994).

Campbell, Gordon. *Bible: The Story of the King James Version 1611–2011* (Oxford: Oxford University Press, 2010).

Campbell, Gordon, and Thomas Corns. *John Milton: Life, Work, and Thought* (Oxford: Oxford University Press, 2008).

Campbell, Lily B. *Divine Poetry and Drama in Sixteenth Century England* (Cambridge: Cambridge University Press, 1959).

Canny, Nicholas. 'Why the Reformation Failed in Ireland: Une question mal posée'. *The Journal of Ecclesiastical History*, 30 (1979): 423–50.

Capp, Bernard. *Astrology and the Popular Press: English Almanacs 1500–1800* (London: Faber, 1979).

Capp, Bernard. 'The Political Dimension of Apocalyptic Thought', in C. A. Patrides and Joseph Wittreich (eds), *The Apocalypse in English Renaissance Thought and Literature: Patterns, Antecedents, Repercussions* (Manchester: Manchester University Press, 1984), 93–124.

Cardinali, Giacomo. 'George Buchanan's Tragedies and Contemporary Dramatic Theory', in Philip Ford and Roger P. H. Green (eds), *George Buchanan: Poet and Dramatist* (Swansea: Classical Press of Wales, 2009), 163–82.

Carleton, James G. *The Part of Rheims in the Making of the English Bible* (Oxford: Clarendon, 1902).

Cartwright, Kent. *Theatre and Humanism: English Drama in the Sixteenth Century* (Cambridge and New York: Cambridge University Press, 1999).

Cary, Phillip. *Augustine's Invention of the Inner Self: The Legacy of a Christian Platonist* (Oxford: Oxford University Press, 2000).

Cave, Terence. '*Enargeia*: Erasmus and the Rhetoric of Presence in the Sixteenth Century'. *L'Esprit Createur*, 16 (1976): 5–19.

Chadwick, Owen. *The Reformation* (Harmondsworth: Penguin, 1964).

Chalmers, Hero. *Royalist Women Writers 1650–1689* (Oxford: Oxford University Press, 2004).

Champion, J. A. I. 'Apocrypha, Canon and Criticism from Samuel Fisher to John Toland 1650–1718', in A. P. Coudert, Sarah Hutton, R. H. Popkin, and G. M. Weiner (eds), *Judaeo-Christian Intellectual Culture in the Seventeenth Century: A Celebration of the Library of Narcissus Marsh (1638–1713)* (Dordrecht: Kluwer, 1999), 91–117.

Charlton, Kenneth. *Women, Religion and Education in Early Modern England* (London: Routledge, 1999).

Chassagnette, Axelle. 'La géométrie appliquée à la sphère terrestre: Le *De Dimensione Terrae* (1550) de Caspar Peucer'. *Histoire et Mesure*, 21 (2006): 7–28.

Chernaik, Warren. 'Biblical Republicanism'. *Prose Studies*, 23 (2000): 147–60.

Chester, Allan G. *Hugh Latimer: Apostle to the English* (Philadelphia: University of Pennsylvania Press, 1954).

Church, A. H. 'Old English Fruit Trenchers', in A. H. Church et al., *Some Minor Arts as Practised in England* (London: Seely & Co., 1894), 47–54.

Clark, J. C. D. *English Society 1688–1832: Ideology, Social Structure and Political Practice during the Ancien Regime* (Cambridge: Cambridge University Press, 1985).

Clarke, Aidan. 'Varieties of Uniformity: The First Century of the Church of Ireland', in W. J. Sheils and Diana Wood (eds), *The Churches, Ireland and the Irish* (Oxford: Basil Blackwell, 1989), 105–22.

Clarke, Danielle. *The Politics of Early Modern Women's Writing* (Harlow: Longman, 2001).

Clarke, Elizabeth. *Politics, Religion and the Song of Songs in Seventeenth-Century England* (Basingstoke: Palgrave Macmillan, 2011).

Claydon, Tony. *William III and the Godly Revolution* (Cambridge: Cambridge University Press, 1996).

Coelen, Peter van der. *De Schrift verbeeld: Oudtestamentische prenten uit renaissance en barok* (Nijmegen: Uitgeverij KU Nijmegen, 1998).

Coffey, John. *Politics, Religion and the British Revolutions: The Mind of Samuel Rutherford* (Cambridge: Cambridge University Press, 1997).

Coffey, John. *John Goodwin and the Puritan Revolution* (Woodbridge: Boydell & Brewer, 2006).

Coffey, John. 'Quentin Skinner and the Religious Dimension of Early Modern Political Thought', in Alister Chapman, John Coffey, and Brad S. Gregory (eds), *Seeing Things their Way: Intellectual History and the Return of Religion* (Notre Dame, Ind.: University of Notre Dame Press 2009), 46–74.

Coffey, John. *Exodus and Liberation: Deliverance Politics from John Calvin to Martin Luther King Jr* (Oxford: Oxford University Press, 2014).

Coggins, John. 'Isaiah', in John Barton and John Muddiman (eds), *Oxford Bible Commentary* (Oxford: Oxford University Press, 2001), 433–86.

Cogswell, Thomas. *The Blessed Revolution: English Politics and the Coming of War, 1621–1624* (Cambridge: Cambridge University Press, 1989).

Cohn, Norman. *The Pursuit of the Millennium: Revolutionary Millenarians and Mystical Anarchists of the Middle Ages*, rev. edn (London: Paladin, 1970).

Coles, Kimberly Anne. *Religion, Reform, and Women's Writing in Early Modern England* (Cambridge: Cambridge University Press, 2008).

Collins, Victor. *Attempt at a Catalogue of the Library of Late Prince Louis-Lucien Bonaparte*, 2 vols (London: Henry Sotheran & Co., 1894).

Collinson, Patrick. 'The English Conventicle', in W. J. Sheils and Diana Woods (eds), *Voluntary Religion, Studies in Church History*, 23 (1986): 229–59.

Collinson, Patrick. *The Elizabethan Puritan Movement* (London: Jonathan Cape, 1967).

Collinson, Patrick. *The Religion of Protestants: The Church in English Society 1559–1625* (Oxford: Clarendon Press, 1982).

Collinson, Patrick. *From Iconoclasm to Iconophobia: The Cultural Impact of the Second English Reformation*, Stenton Lecture 1985 (Reading: University of Reading, 1986).

Collinson, Patrick. 'The Coherence of the Text: How it Hangeth Together: The Bible in Reformation England', in W. P. Stephens (ed.), *The Bible, the Reformation and the Church: Essays in Honour of James Anderson*, Journal for the Study of the New Testament, Supplement Series, 105 (1995): 84–108.

Collinson, Patrick. 'The Bible, the Reformation and the English Language', in *Douglas Southall Freeman Historical Review* (University of Richmond, Va., 1999), 4–41.

Collinson, Patrick. *From Cranmer to Sancroft* (London: Hambledon Continuum, 2006).

Collinson, Patrick , and Polly Ha, eds. *The Reception of Continental Reformation in Britain*, Proceedings of the British Academy, 164 (Oxford: Oxford University Press/British Academy, 2010).

Como, David R. *Blown by the Spirit: Puritanism and the Emergence of an Antinomian Underground in Pre-Civil War England* (Stanford, Calif.: Stanford University Press, 2004).

Cooper, T. *Fear and Polemic in Seventeenth-Century England: Richard Baxter and Antinomianism* (Aldershot: Ashgate, 2001).

Copeland, Rita, and Peter T. Struck, eds. *The Cambridge Companion to Allegory* (Cambridge: Cambridge University Press, 2010).

Cormack, Lesley B. *Charting an Empire: Geography at the English Universities, 1580–1620* (Chicago: University of Chicago Press, 1997).

Corns, Thomas N. *Uncloistered Virtue: English Political Literature 1640–1660* (Oxford: Oxford University Press, 1992).

Cornwall, Robert D. *Visible and Apostolic: The Constitution of the Church in High Church Anglican and Non-Juror Thought* (Newark, Del.: University of Delaware Press, 1993).

Coster, Will, and Andrew Spicer, eds. *Sacred Space in Early Modern Europe* (Cambridge: Cambridge University Press, 2005).

Cotton, Henry. *Rhemes and Doway: An Attempt to Shew What Has Been Done by Roman Catholics for the Diffusion of the Holy Scriptures in English* (Oxford: Oxford University Press, 1855).

Craik, Katharine A. *Reading Sensations in Early Modern England* (Basingstoke: Palgrave Macmillan, 2007).

Crane, Mary Thomas. *Framing Authority: Sayings, Self and Society in Sixteenth-Century England* (Princeton: Princeton University Press, 1993).

Cressy, David. 'Purification, Thanskgiving and the Churching of Women in Post-Reformation England'. *Past and Present*, 141 (1993): 106–46.

Cressy, David. *Birth, Marriage and Death: Ritual, Religion, and the Life-Cycle in Tudor and Stuart England* (Oxford: Oxford University Press, 1997).

Cressy, David. *Bonfires and Bells: National Memory and the Protestant Calendar in Elizabethan and Stuart England* (Stroud: Sutton, 2004).

Crocker, Robert. 'Henry More: A Biographical Essay', in Sarah Hutton (ed.), *Henry More (1614–1687): Tercentenary Studies* (Dordrecht, Kluwer Academic Pubishers, 1990), 1–18.

Crowley, Lara M. 'Manuscript Context and Literary Interpretation: John Donne's Poetry in Seventeenth-Century England' (Ph.D. thesis, University of Maryland, 2007).

Cruikshank, Frances. *Verse and Poetics in George Herbert and John Donne* (Farnham: Ashgate, 2010).

Crystal, David. *Begat: The King James Bible and the English Language* (Oxford: Oxford University Press, 2010).

Culross, James. *The Three Rylands: A Hundred Years of Various Christian Service* (London: Elliot Stock, 1897).

Cuming, G. J. *A History of Anglican Liturgy* (London: Macmillan, 1969).

Cuming, G. J. *The Godly Order: Texts and Studies Relating to the Book of Common Prayer* (London: Alcuin Club, 1983).

Cummings, Brian. *The Literary Culture of the Reformation: Grammar and Grace* (Oxford: Oxford University Press, 2002).

Dainville, François de. *La géographie des humanistes* (Paris: Beauchesne, 1940).

Dainville, François de. *Cartes anciennes de l'église de France: Historique—répertoire—guide d'usage* (Paris: J. Vrin, 1956).

Daniell, David. *William Tyndale: A Biography* (New Haven: Yale University Press, 1994).

Daniell, David. *The Bible in English: Its History and Influence* (New Haven: Yale University Press, 2003).

Dannenfeldt, Karl H. *Leonhard Rauwolf: Sixteenth-Century Physician, Botanist, and Traveler* (Cambridge, Mass.: Harvard University Press, 1968).

Darlow, T. H., and H. F. Moule. *Historical Catalogue of Printed Editions of the English Bible 1525–1961*, rev. and expanded by A. S. Herbert (London: British and Foreign Bible Society, 1968).

Daston, Lorraine, and Katharine Park. *Wonders and the Order of Nature, 1150–1750* (New York: Zone Books, 1998).

Daubney, William. *The Use of the Apocrypha in the Christian Church* (London: C. J. Clay & Sons, 1900).

Davidson, Nicholas. 'Christopher Marlowe and Atheism', in Darryll Grantley and Peter Roberts (eds), *Christopher Marlowe and English Renaissance Culture* (Aldershot: Ashgate, 1996), 129–47.

Davidson, Peter. 'The Inscribed House', in Michael Bath, Pedro F. Campa, and Daniel S. Russell (eds), *Emblem Studies in Honor of Peter M. Daly*, Saecla Spiritualia, 41 (Baden Baden: Verlag Valentin Koerner, 2002), 41–62.

Davies, C. S. L. 'The Youth and Education of Christopher Wren'. *English Historical Review,* 123 (2008): 300–27.

Davis, J. C. 'The Levellers and Christianity', in Brian Manning (ed.), *Politics, Religion and the English Civil War* (London: Edward Arnold, 1973), 225–50.

Dawson, Jane E. A. *Scotland Re-formed, 1488–1587* (Edinburgh: Edinburgh University Press, 2007).

Dawson, Jane E. A. 'Patterns of Worship in Reformation Scotland', in Duncan B. Forrester and Doug Gray (eds), *Worship and Liturgy in Context: Studies and Case Studies in Theology and Practice* (London: SCM Press, 2009), 136–51.

de Grazia, Margreta, Maureen Quilligan, and Peter Stallybrass, eds. *Subject and Object in Renaissance Culture* (Cambridge: Cambridge University Press, 1996).

de Groot, Jerome. 'John Denham and Lucy Hutchinson's Commonplace Book'. *Studies in English Literature,* 48 (2008): 147–63.

DeCoursey, Matthew. 'The Thomas More/William Tyndale Polemic'. *Early Modern Literary Studies,* Texts Series, 3 (2010), <http://purl.org/emls/moretyndale.pdf>.

Devereux, James A. 'Reformed Doctrine in the Collects of the First *Book of Common Prayer'*. *Harvard Theological Review,* 58 (1965): 48–68.

Dimmock, Matthew. *Mythologies of the Prophet Muhammad in Early Modern English Culture* (Cambridge: Cambridge University Press, 2013).

Dinsmore, Charles Allen. *The English Bible as Literature* (London: Allen & Unwin, 1931).

Ditchfield, Simon. *Liturgy, Sanctity and History in Tridentine Italy: Pietro Maria Campi and the Preservation of the Particular* (Cambridge: Cambridge University Press, 1995).

Ditchfield, Simon. 'Text before Trowel: Antonio Bosio's *Roma sotterranea* Revisited', in R. N. Swanson (ed.), *The Church Retrospective, Studies in Church History,* 33 (1997): 343–60.

Dix, E. R. McC. 'William Kearney, the Second Earliest Known Printer in Dublin'. *Proceedings of the Royal Irish Academy,* 28 (1910): 157–61.

Dix, E. R. McC. *Printing in Dublin Prior to 1601* (Dublin: At the Sign of the Three Candles, 1932).

Dobson, William T. *History of the Bassandyne Bible, the First Printed in Scotland* (Edinburgh: William Blackwood, 1887).

Doelman, James. *King James I and the Religious Culture of England* (Woodbridge: D. S. Brewer, 2000).

Dolan, Frances E. *Whores of Babylon: Catholicism, Gender and Seventeenth-Century Print Culture* (Notre Dame, Ind.: University of Notre Dame Press, 1999).

Donaldson, Gordon. 'Covenant to Revolution', in Duncan B. Forrester and Douglas M. Murray (eds), *Studies in the History of Worship in Scotland,* 2nd edn (Edinburgh: T. & T. Clark, 1996), 52–64.

Dove, Mary. *The First English Bible: The Text and Context of the Wycliffite Versions* (Cambridge: Cambridge University Press, 2007).

Dowling, Maria. 'Anne Boleyn and Reform'. *The Journal of Ecclesiastical History,* 35 (1984): 30–46.

Dyrness, William A. *Reformed Theology and Visual Culture: The Protestant Imagination from Calvin to Edwards* (Cambridge: Cambridge Univeristy Press, 2004).

Duffy, Eamon. *The Stripping of the Altars: Traditional Religion in England, 1400–1580* (New Haven: Yale University Press, 1992).

Duffy, Eamon. *Marking the Hours: English People and their Prayers 1240–1570* (New Haven: Yale University Press, 2006).

Duffy, Eamon. *Saints, Sacrilege and Sedition: Religion and Conflict in the Tudor Reformations* (London: Continuum, 2012).

Dunbar, Linda J. *Reforming the Scottish Church: John Winram (c. 1492–1582) and the Example of Fife* (Aldershot: Ashgate, 2002).

Dunkelgrün, Theodor W. 'The Multiplicity of Scripture: The Confluence of Textual Traditions in the Making of the Antwerp Polyglot Bible (1568–1573)' (Ph.D. thesis, University of Chicago, 2012).

Dunkelgrün, Theodor. 'The Hebrew Library of a Renaissance Humanist: Andreas Masius and the Bibliography to his *Iosuae Imperatoris Historia* (1574), with a Latin Edition and an Annotated English Translation'. *Studia Rosenthaliana*. 42–3 (2010–11): 197–252.

Durkacz, Victor Edward. *The Decline of the Celtic Languages* (Edinburgh: John Donald, 1983).

Durston, Christopher, and Judith Maltby, eds. *Religion in Revolutionary England* (Manchester: Manchester University Press, 2006).

Eckhardt, Joshua. *Manuscript Verse Collectors and the Politics of Anti-Courtly Love Poetry* (Oxford: Oxford University Press, 2009).

Eden, Kathy. *Poetic and Legal Fiction in the Aristotelian Tradition* (Princeton: Princeton University Press, 1986).

Edmonson, Stephen. *Calvin's Christology* (Cambridge: Cambridge University Press, 2004).

Edson, Evelyn. *Mapping Time and Space: How Medieval Mapmakers Viewed their World* (London: British Library, 1997).

Edwards, Karen L. *Milton and the Natural World* (Cambridge: Cambridge University Press, 1999).

Edwards, Richard M. *Scriptual Perspicuity in the Early English Reformation in Historical Theology* (New York: Peter Lang, 2009).

Eliot, Thomas Stearns. *Selected Prose of T. S. Eliot*, ed. Frank Kermode (London: Faber & Faber, 1975).

Empson, William. *Milton's God* (London: Chatto & Windus, 1961; rev. edn, 1965).

Engammare, M. 'Les figures de la Bible: Le destin oublié d'un genre littéraire en image (XVIe–XVIIe s.)'. *Mélanges de l'École française de Rome*, 106 (1994): 549–91.

Ettenhuber, Katrin. *Donne's Augustine: Renaissance Cultures of Interpretation* (Oxford: Oxford University Press, 2011).

Ettenhuber, Katrin. '"Take up and read the Scriptures": Patristic Interpretation and the Poetics of Abundance in "The Translators to the Reader" (1611)', *Huntington Library Quarterly*, 75 (2012): 213–32.

Evans, G. R. *Problems of Authority in the Reformation Debates* (Cambridge: Cambridge University Press, 1992).

Evans, J. M. *'Paradise Lost' and the Genesis Tradition* (Oxford: Clarendon Press, 1968).

Farrar, Frederic. *History of Interpretation: Eight Lectures Preached before the University of Oxford in the Year MDCCCLXXXV* (London: Macmillan, 1886).

Ferguson, Jamie. 'Faith in the Language: Biblical Authority and the Meaning of English in the More-Tyndale Polemics'. *The Sixteenth Century Journal*, 43 (2012): 989–1011.

Ferrell, Lori Anne. *Government by Polemic* (Stanford, Calif.: Stanford University Press, 1998).

Ferrell, Lori Anne. *The Bible and the People* (New Haven: Yale University Press, 2008).

Ferrell, Lori Anne. 'The King James Bible in Early Modern Political Context', in David G. Burke, John F. Kutsko, and Philip H. Towner (eds), *The King James Version at 400: Asserting its Genius as Bible Translation and its Literary Influence* (Atlanta, Ga.: Society of Biblical Literature, 2013), 31–42.

Ferrell, Lori Anne, and Peter E. McCullough, eds. *The English Sermon Revised: Religion, Literature and History 1600–1750* (Manchester: Manchester University Press, 2000).

Ferry, Anne. *The 'Inward' Language: Sonnets of Wyatt, Sidney, Shakespeare, Donne* (Chicago: University of Chicago Press, 1983).

Figgis, John N. *The Divine Right of Kings* (Gloucester, Mass.: Peter Smith, 1970); first published as *The Theory of the Divine Right of Kings* (Cambridge: Cambridge University Press, 1896).

Fincham, Kenneth. 'The Restoration of Altars in the 1630s'. *The Historical Journal*, 44 (2001): 919–40.

Fincham, Kenneth. *Prelate as Pastor: The Episcopate of James I* (Oxford: Clarendon Press, 1990).

Fiorani, Francesca. *The Marvel of Maps: Art, Cartography and Politics in Renaissance Italy* (New Haven: Yale University Press, 2005).

Firth, Katharine R. *The Apocalyptic Tradition in Reformation Britain, 1530–1645* (Oxford: Oxford University Press, 1979).

Fischlin, Daniel, and Mark Fortier, eds. *Royal Subjects: Essays on the Writings of James VI and I* (Detroit, Mich.: Wayne State University Press, 2002).

Fish, Stanley. *Surprised by Sin: The Reader in Paradise Lost* (London: Macmillan, 1967; 2nd edn, Cambridge, Mass.: Harvard University Press, 1997).

Fish, Stanley. *Self-Consuming Artifacts: The Experience of Seventeenth-Century Literature* (Berkeley, Calif.: University of California Press, 1972).

Fissell, Mary. 'The Politics of Reproduction in the English Reformation'. *Representations*, 87 (2004): 43–81.

Fitzsimon, Betsey Taylor. 'Conversion, the Bible and the Irish Language: The Correspondence of Lady Ranelagh and Bishop Dopping', in Michael Brown, Charles Ivar McGrath, and Thomas P. Power (eds), *Converts and Conversion in Ireland, 1650–1850* (Dublin: Four Courts Press, 2005), 157–82.

Fletcher, Harris Francis. *The Use of The Bible in Milton's Prose* (New York: Haskell House, 1929).

Flinn, Richard. 'Samuel Rutherford and Puritan Political Theory'. *Journal of Christian Reconstruction*, 5 (1978–9): 65–96.

Flühler-Kreis, Dione. 'Die Stube als sakraler Raum: Das Familienporträt des Zürcher Landvogts von Greifensee, Hans Conrad Bodmer'. *Zeitschrift für Schweizerische Archäologie und Kunstgeschichte*, 61 (2004): 211–20.

Ford, Alan. *The Protestant Reformation in Ireland, 1590–1641* (Dublin: Four Courts Press, 1997).

Ford, Alan. 'James Ussher and the Godly Prince in Early Seventeenth-Century Ireland', in Hiram Morgan (ed.), *Political Ideology in Ireland, 1541–1641* (Dublin: Four Courts, 1999), 203–28.

Ford, Alan. *James Ussher* (Oxford: Oxford University Press, 2007).

Forsyth, Neil. '*Paradise Lost* and the Origin of Evil'. *International Journal for the Classical Tradition*, 6 (2000): 516–48.

Forsyth, Neil. *The Satanic Epic* (Princeton: Princeton University Press, 2003).

Forsyth, Neil. *John Milton: A Biography* (Oxford: Lion, 2008).

Foucault, Michel. *The Order of Things: An Archaeology of the Human Sciences*, tr. A. M. Sheridan Smith (London: Tavistock, 1970).

Foucault, Michel. 'What is Critique', in James Schmidt (ed.), *What is Enlightenment? Eighteenth Century Answers and Twentieth Century Questions* (Berkeley, Calif.: University of California Press, 1996), 382–98.

Fowler, Alistair. *Kinds of Literature: An Introduction to the Theory of Genres and Modes* (Oxford: Clarendon Press, 1982).

Fox, Adam. *Oral and Literate Culture in England, 1500–1700* (Oxford: Oxford University Press, 2000).

Fraistat, Neil, ed. *Poems in their Place: The Intertextuality and Order of Poetic Collections* (Chapel Hill, NC: University of North Carolina Press, 1986).

Franits, Wayne E. *Paragons of Virtue: Women and Domesticity in Seventeenth-Century Dutch Art* (Cambridge: Cambridge University Press, 1993).

Frank, Georgia. *The Memory of the Eyes: Pilgrims to Living Saints in Christian Late Antiquity* (Berkeley, Calif.: University of California Press, 2000).

Freedman, David et al., eds. *Anchor Bible Dictionary* (New York: Doubleday, 1992).

Frei, Hans. *The Eclipse of Biblical Narrative* (New Haven: Yale University Press, 1974).

French, Roberts W. '"My Stuffe is Flesh": An Allusion to Job in George Herbert's "The Pearl"'. *Notes and Queries*, 27 (1980): 329–31.

Fresch, Cheryl. 'Milton's Eve and the Problem of the Additions to the Command'. *Milton Quarterly*, 12 (1978): 83–91.

Froehlich, Karlfried. 'The Fate of the *Glossa Ordinaria* in the Sixteenth Century', in David C. Steinmetz (ed.), *Die Patristik in der Bibelexegese des 16. Jahrhunderts* (Wiesbaden: Harrassowitz, 1999), 19–47.

Fry, Francis. *A Description of the Great Bible... also of the Editions, in Large Folio, of the Authorized Version of the Holy Scriptures* (London: Willis & Sotheran, 1865).

Funkenstein, Amos. *Theology and the Scientific Imagination from the Middle Ages to the Seventeenth Century* (Princeton: Princeton University Press, 1989).

Furlong, Monica. *Puritan's Progress* (New York: Coward, McCann & Geoghegan, 1975).

Furniss, Tom. 'Reading the Geneva Bible: Notes towards an English Revolution?' *Prose Studies*, 31 (2009): 1–21.

Gadamer, Hans-Georg. *Truth and Method*, tr. Joel Weinsheimer and Donald G. Marshall, 2nd edn (London: Continuum, 2004).

Gaimster, David. *German Stoneware 1500–1900: Archaeology and Cultural History* (London: British Museum, 1997).

Gaimster, David, and Roberta Gilchrist, eds. *The Archaeology of Reformation, 1480–1580*, Societies for Medieval and Post-Medieval Archaeology (Leeds: Maney Publishing, 2003).

Gallagher, E. L. 'The Old Testament "Apocrypha" in Jerome's Canonical Theory'. *Journal of Early Christian Studies*, 20 (2012): 213–33.

Gardiner, Anne Barbeau. 'Dryden's "Britannia Rediviva": Interpreting the Signs of the Times in June 1688'. *Huntington Library Quarterly*, 48 (1985): 257–84.

Garner, Mark. 'Preaching as a Communicative Event: A Discourse Analysis of Sermons by Robert Rollock (1555–1599)'. *Reformation and Renaissance Review*, 9 (2007): 45–70.

Garrett, Christina. *Marian Exiles: A Study in the Origins of Elizabethan Puritanism* (Cambridge: Cambridge University Press, 1938, repr. 2010).

Genette, Gérard. *Paratexts: Thresholds of Interpretation*, tr. Jane E. Lewis (Cambridge: Cambridge University Press, 1997).

George, Timothy. *Reading Scripture with the Reformers* (Downers Grove, Ill.: Intervarsity Press, 2011).

Gibbs, Lee W. 'Biblical Interpretation in Medieval England and the English Reformation', in Alan J. Hauser and Duane F. Watson (eds), *A History of Biblical Interpretation*, 2 vols (Grand Rapids: Eerdmans, 2009), ii. 372–402.

Gibson, William. *James II and the Trial of the Seven Bishops* (Basingstoke: Palgrave Macmillan, 2009).

Giebels, Henk, and Frans Slits. *Georgius Macropedius, 1487–1558: Leven en Werken van een Brabantse Humanist* (Tilburg: Stichting Zuidelijk Historisch Contact, 2005).

Gillespie, Raymond. 'Reading the Bible in Seventeenth-Century Ireland', in Bernadette Cunningham and Máire Kennedy (eds), *The Experience of Reading: Irish Historical Perspectives* (Dublin: Rare Books Group of the Library Association of Ireland, 1999), 10–38.

Gillespie, Raymond. *Seventeenth-Century Dubliners and their Books* (Dublin: Dublin City Public Libraries, 2005).

Gillespie, Stuart, and Philip Hardie, eds. *The Cambridge Companion to Lucretius* (Cambridge: Cambridge University Press, 2007).

Gilman, Ernest B. *Iconoclasm and Poetry in the English Reformation* (Chicago: University of Chicago Press, 1986).

Gilmont, Jean-François. 'Protestant Reformations and Reading', in Guglielmo Cavallo and Roger Chartier (eds), *A History of Reading in the West*, tr. Lydia G. Cochrane (Cambridge: Polity Press, 1999), 213–37.

Gliozzi, Guiliano. *Adamo e il nuovo mondo* (Florence: La nuova Italia editrice, 1977).

Goldie, Mark. 'The Civil Religion of James Harrington', in Anthony Pagden (ed.), *The Languages of Political Theory in Early Modern Europe* (Cambridge: Cambridge University Press, 1987), 197–224.

Goldie, Mark. 'The Political Thought of the Anglican Revolution', in Robert Beddard (ed.), *The Revolutions of 1688* (Oxford: Oxford University Press, 1991), 102–36.

Gomez-Géraud, Marie-Christine. *Le crépuscule du Grand Voyage: Les récits des pèlerins à Jérusalem (1458–1612)* (Paris: Honoré Champion, 1999).

Goodblatt, Chanita. *The Christian Hebraism of John Donne* (Pittsburgh, Pa.: Duquesne University Press, 2010).

Goodman, Martin, John Barton, and John Muddiman, eds. *The Apocrypha (Oxford Bible Commentary)* (Oxford: Oxford University Press, 2012).

Gordon, Bruce, ed. *Protestant History and Identity in Sixteenth Century Europe*, 2 vols (Aldershot: Scholars Press, 1996).

Grafton, Anthony. *Joseph Scaliger: A Study in the History of Classical Scholarship*, 2 vols (Oxford: Clarendon Press, 1983–93).

Grafton, Anthony. *What was History? The Art of History in Early Modern Europe* (Cambridge: Cambridge University Press, 2007).

Grafton, Anthony, and Lisa Jardine. *From Humanism to the Humanities* (Cambridge, Mass.: Harvard University Press, 1986).

Grafton, Anthony, and Keith Mills, eds. *Conversion: Old Worlds and New* (Suffolk: Boydell & Brewer, 2003).

Grafton, Anthony, and Joanna Weinberg. *'I Have Always Loved the Holy Tongue': Isaac Casaubon, the Jews, and a Forgotten Chapter in Renaissance Scholarship* (Cambridge, Mass.: Harvard University Press, 2010).

Greaves, Richard L. *Glimpses of Glory: John Bunyan and English Dissent* (Stanford, Calif.: Stanford University Press, 2002).

Greaves, Richard L., and R. Zaler, eds. *A Biographical Dictionary of British Radicals in the Seventeenth Century* (Brighton: Harvester Press, 1982–4).

Green, Ian. *The Christian's ABC: Catechisms and Catechizing in England c.1530–1740* (Oxford: Clarendon Press, 1996).

Green, Ian. *Print and Protestantism in Early Modern England* (Oxford: Oxford University Press, 2000).

Green, Ian. *Continuity and Change in Protestant Preaching in Early Modern England* (London: Dr Williams's Trust, 2009).

Green, Ian. *Humanism and Protestantism in Early Modern English Education* (Farnham: Ashgate, 2009).

Green, Ian. 'L'utilisation protestante des psaumes en Angleterre (1530–1740)'. *Bulletin de la Societe de l'Histoire du Protestantisme Français*, 158 (2012): 351–72.

Greenblatt, Stephen. *The Swerve: How the Renaissance Began* (London: Bodley Head, 2011).

Greenslade, S. L., ed. *The Cambridge History of the Bible*, iii. *The West from the Reformation to the Present Day* (Cambridge: Cambridge University Press, 1963).

Greg, W. W. *A Companion to Arber, Being a Calendar of Documents in Edward Arber's Transcript of the Registers of the Company of Stationers of London 1554–1640* (Oxford: Oxford University Press, 1967).

Gregg, Pauline. *King Charles I* (Berkeley, Calif.: University of California Press, 1984).

Gribben, Crawford. 'Deconstructing the Geneva Bible: The Search for a Puritan Poetic'. *Literature and Theology*, 14 (2000): 1–16.

Gribben, Crawford. *The Puritan Millennium: Literature and Theology 1550–1682* (Dublin: Four Courts, 2000).

Gribben, Crawford. 'Samuel Rutherford and Liberty of Conscience'. *Westminster Theological Journal*, 71 (2009): 355–73.

Gribben, Crawford. 'Reading the Bible in the Puritan Revolution', in Robert Armstrong and Tadhg O'Hannrachain (eds), *Early Modern Bibles*, St Andrews Studies in Reformation History (Farnham: Ashgate, forthcoming).

Griffiths, Antony. *The Print in Stuart Britain 1603–1689* (London: British Museum Press, 1998).

Guibbory, Achsah. *Ceremony and Community from Herbert to Milton: Literature, Religion, and Cultural Conflict in Seventeenth-Century England* (Cambridge: Cambridge University Press, 1998).

Guibbory, Achsah. 'Bible, Religion, Spirituality in *Paradise Lost*', in Angelica Duran (ed.), *A Concise Companion to Milton* (Oxford: Blackwell, 2007), 128–43.

Gurney, John. *Gerrard Winstanley: The Digger's Life and Legacy* (London: Pluto Press, 2013).

Gwyn, Douglas. 'John Saltmarsh: Quaker Forerunner'. *Journal of the Friends' Historical Society*, 60 (2003): 3–24.

Hackel, Heidi Brayman. *Reading Material in Early Modern England* (Cambridge: Cambridge University Press, 2005).

Haigh, Christopher. *The English Reformation Revised* (Cambridge: Cambridge University Press, 1987).

Haigh, Christopher. *English Reformations: Religion, Politics, and Society under the Tudors* (Oxford: Clarendon Press, 1993).

Hamel, Christopher de. *The Book: A History of the Bible* (London: Phaidon Press, 2005).

Hamilton, Alastair. *The Apocryphal Apocalypse: the Reception of the Second Book of Esdras (4 Ezra) from the Renaissance to the Enlightenment* (Oxford: Clarendon Press, 1999).

Hamilton, Alastair. *The Family of Love* (Cambridge: James Clarke & Co., 1981).

Hamilton, Hans Claude, ed. *Calendar of the State Papers Relating to Ireland, of the Reigns of Henry VIII., Edward VI., Mary, and Elizabeth: 1509–1573* (London: Her Majesty's Public Record Office, 1860).

Hamilton, Hans Claude, ed. *Calendar of the State Papers Relating to Ireland, of the Reign of Elizabeth, 1586–1588, July* (London: Her Majesty's Public Record Office, 1877).

Hamilton, Hans Claude, ed. *Calendar of the State Papers, Relating to Ireland, of the Reign of Elizabeth, 1592, October–1596, June* (London: Her Majesty's Stationery Office, 1890).

Hamlin, Hannibal. *Psalm Culture and Early Modern English Literature* (Cambridge: Cambridge University Press, 2004).

Hamlin, Hannibal, and Norman W. Jones, eds. *The King James Bible After 400 Years: Literary, Linguistic, and Cultural Influences* (Cambridge: Cambridge University Press, 2010).

Hamling, Tara. *Decorating the 'Godly' Household: Religious Art in Post-Reformation Britain* (New Haven: Yale University Press, 2010).

Hamling, Tara, and Catherine Richardson, eds. *Everyday Objects: Medieval and Early Modern Material Culture and its Meanings* (Farnham: Ashgate, 2010).

Hammill, Graham. *The Mosaic Constitution: Political Theology and Imagination from Machiavelli to Milton* (Chicago: Chicago University Press, 2012).

Hammond, Gerald. *The Making of the English Bible* (Manchester: Carcanet, 1982).

Hammond, Gerald. 'The Sore and Strong Prose of the English Bible', in Neil Rhodes (ed.), *English Renaissance Prose: History, Language, and Politics* (Tempe, Ariz.: Medieval & Renaissance Texts & Studies, 1997), 19–34.

Hancock, Maxine. 'Bunyan as Reader: The Record of *Grace Abounding*'. *Bunyan Studies*, 5 (1994): 68–84.

Hankey, Wayne. 'Augustinian Immediacy and Dionysian Mediation in John Colet, Edmund Spenser, Richard Hooker and the Cardinal de Bérulle', in Dominique Courcelles (ed.), *Augustinus in der Neuzeit: Colloque de las Herzog August Bibliothek de Wolfenbüttel* (Turnhout: Brepols, 1998), 125–60.

Hardy, Nicholas. 'The *ars critica* in Early Modern England' (D.Phil. thesis, Oxford University, 2012).

Harman, Barbara Leah. *Costly Monuments: Representations of the Self in George Herbert's Poetry* (Cambridge, Mass.: Harvard University Press, 1982).

Harris, Jason. 'The Religious Position of Abraham Ortelius', in Arie-Jan Gelderblom, Jan L. de Jong, and M. van Vaeck (eds), *The Low Countries as a Crossroads of Religious Beliefs* (Leiden: Brill, 2004), 89–139.

Harris, Johanna, and Elizabeth Scott-Baumann, eds. *The Intellectual Culture of Puritan Women* (Basingstoke: Palgrave Macmillan, 2011).

Harris, Tim. 'Revising the Restoration', in Tim Harris, Paul Seaward, and Mark Goldie (eds), *The Politics of Religion in Restoration England* (Oxford: Basil Blackwell, 1990), 1–28.

Harris, Tim. *Revolution: The Great Crisis of the British Monarchy, 1685–1720* (Harmondsworth: Penguin, 2007).

Harris, Tim, and Stephen Taylor, eds. *The Final Crisis of the Stuart Monarchy: The Revolutions of 1688–91 in their British, Atlantic and European Contexts* (Woodbridge: Boydell Press, 2013).

Harrison, Peter. *The Bible, Protestantism and the Rise of Natural Science* (Cambridge: Cambridge University Press, 1998).

Hart, A. Tindal. *William Lloyd, 1627–1717* (London: SPCK, 1952).

Haskin, Dayton. *Milton's Burden of Interpretation* (Philadelphia: University of Pennsylvania Press, 1994).

Haugen, Kristine Louise. 'Thomas Lydiat's Scholarship in Prison: Discovery and Disaster in the Seventeenth Century'. *Bodleian Library Record*, 25 (2012): 183–216.

Headley, John M. 'Geography and Empire in the Late Renaissance: Botero's Assignment, Western Universalism, and the Civilization Process'. *Renaissance Quarterly*, 53 (2000): 1119–55.

Heal, Felicity. 'Appropriating History: Catholic and Protestant Polemics and the National Past'. *Huntington Library Quarterly*, 68 (2005): 109–32.

Heal, Felicity. 'Mediating the Word: Language and Dialects in the British and Irish Reformations'. *Journal of Eccleciastical History*, 56 (2005): 261–86.

Hefling, Charles, and Cynthia Shattuck, eds. *The Oxford Guide to the Book of Common Prayer: A Worldwide Survey* (Oxford: Oxford University Press, 2006).

Heinemann, Joseph. 'The Nature of the Aggadah', tr. Marc Bregman, in Geoffrey H. Hartman and Sanford Budick (eds), *Midrash and Literature* (New Haven: Yale University Press, 1986), 41–55.

Henderson, G. D. *Religious Life in Seventeenth-Century Scotland* (Cambridge: Cambridge University Press, 1937).

Hessayon, Ariel. *'Gold Tried in the Fire': The Prophet TheaurauJohn Tany and the English Revolution* (Aldershot: Ashgate, 2007).

Hessayon, Ariel. 'The Making of Abiezer Coppe'. *The Journal of Ecclesiastical History*, 62 (2011): 38–58.

Hessayon, Ariel, and Nicholas Keene, eds. *Scripture and Scholarship in Early Modern England* (Farnham: Ashgate, 2006).

Hessayon, Ariel, and David Finnegan, eds. *Varieties of Seventeenth- and Early Eighteenth-Century English Radicalism in Context* (Burlington, Vt.: Ashgate, 2011).

Hesselink, I. John. 'Calvin's Theology', in Donald K. McKim (ed.), *The Cambridge Companion to John Calvin* (Cambridge: Cambridge University Press, 2004).

Hill, Christopher. *The World Turned Upside Down: Radical Ideas during the English Revolution* (Harmondsworth: Penguin, 1972; repr. 1991).

Hill, Christopher. *Milton and the English Revolution* (London: Faber & Faber, 1977).

Hill, Christopher. *The Religion of Gerrard Winstanley*, Past and Present, suppl. 5 (Oxford: Past and Present Society, 1978).

Hill, Christopher. *A Nation of Change and Novelty: Radical Politics, Religion and Literature in Seventeenth-Century England* (London: Routledge, 1990).

Hill, Christopher. *The English Bible and the Seventeenth-Century Revolution* (London: Allen Lane, 1993).

Hill, Robert C. *Reading the Old Testament in Antioch* (Leiden: Brill, 2005).

Hinds, Hilary. *God's Englishwomen: Seventeenth-Century Radical Sectarian Writing and Feminist Criticism* (Manchester: Manchester University Press, 1996).

Hirsch, E. D. *The Aims of Textuality* (Chicago: University of Chicago Press, 1976).

Hirschfeld, Heather. *Joint Enterprises: Collaborative Drama and the Institutionalization of the English Renaissance Theater* (Amherst, Mass.: University of Massachusetts Press, 2004).

Hobbs, R. Gerald. 'How Firm a Foundation: Martin Bucer's Historical Exegesis of the Psalms'. *Church History*, 53 (1984): 484–6.

Hoogvliet, Margriet. *Pictura et scriptura: Textes, images et herméneutique des 'mappae mundi' (XIIIe–XVIe siècles)* (Turnhout: Brepols, 2007).

Houlbrooke, Ralph, ed. *James VI and I: Ideas, Authority, and Government* (Aldershot: Ashgate, 2006).

Houston, Alan Craig. *Algernon Sidney and the Republican Heritage in England and America* (Princeton: Princeton University Press, 1991).

Houston, R. A. *Scottish Literacy and the Scottish Identity: Illiteracy and Society in Scotland and Northern England, 1600–1800* (Cambridge: Cambridge University Press, 1985).

Howorth, H. H. 'The Origin and Authority of the Biblical Canon in the Anglican Church'. *Journal of Theological Studies*, os 8 (1906): 1–40.

Howorth, H. H. 'The Origin and Authority of the Biblical Canon According to the Continental Reformers: I. Luther and Karlstadt'. *Journal of Theological Studies*, os 8 (1907): 321–65.

Howorth, H. H. 'The Origin and Authority of the Biblical Canon According to the Continental Reformers: II. Luther, Zwingli, Lefèvre, and Calvin'. *Journal of Theological Studies*, os 9 (1908): 188–232.

Howorth, H. H. 'The Canon of the Bible among the Later Reformers'. *Journal of Theological Studies*, os 10 (1909): 183–232.

Hudson, Anne. *The Lollards and their Books* (London: Hambledon Press, 1985).

Hug, Tobias B. *Impostures in Early Modern England: Representations and Perceptions of Fraudulent Identities* (Manchester: Manchester University Press, 2010).

Hunt, Arnold. 'The Lord's Supper in Early Modern England'. *Past and Present,* 161 (1998): 39–83.

Hunt, Arnold. *The Art of Hearing: English Preachers and their Audiences, 1590–1640* (Cambridge: Cambridge University Press, 2010).

Hunter, Michael. 'The Problem of "Atheism" in Early Modern England'. *Transactions of the Royal Historical Society,* 5th ser. 35 (1985): 135–57.

Hunter, Michael. 'Robert Boyle, Narcissus Marsh and the Anglo-Irish Intellectual Scene in the Late Seventeenth Century', in Muriel McCarthy and Ann Simmons (eds), *The Making of Marsh's Library: Learning, Politics and Religion in Ireland, 1650–1750* (Dublin: Four Courts Press, 2004), 51–75.

Hunter, Michael. 'Robert Boyle and the Uses of Print', in Danielle Westerhof (ed.), *The Alchemy of Medicine and Print: The Edward Worth Library, Dublin* (Dublin: Four Courts Press, 2010), 110–24.

Hunter, Michael, and David Wootton, eds. *Atheism from the Reformation to the Enlightenment* (Oxford: Clarendon Press, 1992).

Hunter, William B., et al., eds. *A Milton Encyclopedia,* 9 vols (Lewisburg: Bucknell University Press, 1978–83).

Huntley, Frank Livingstone. *Bishop Joseph Hall and Protestant Meditation in Seventeenth-Century England* (Binghampton, NY: Medieval & Renaissance Texts & Studies, 1981).

Husband, Timothy. *The Luminous Image: Painted Glass Roundels in the Lowlands, 1480–1560* (New York: Metropolitan Museum of Art, 1995).

Hyman, Gavin. *A Short History of Atheism* (London: I. B. Tauris, 2010).

Ingalls, Ranall. 'Richard Hooker on the Scriptures: Saint Augustine's Trinitarianism and the Interpretation of Sola Scriptura' (PhD thesis, University of Wales Lampeter, 2004).

Israel, Jonathan. *Radical Enlightenment: Philosophy and the Making of Modernity 1650–1750* (Oxford: Oxford University Press, 2001).

Ives, Eric. *Anne Boleyn* (Oxford: Blackwell, 1986).

Jackson, Ken, and Arthur Marotti. 'The Turn to Religion in Early Modern English Studies'. *Criticism,* 46 (2004): 167–90.

Jacobs, A. S. 'The Disorder of Books: Priscillian's Canonical Defense of Apocrypha'. *Harvard Theological Review,* 93 (2000): 135–59.

Jacobs, E. C. 'Two Stages of Old Testament Translation for the King James Bible'. *The Library,* 6th ser. 11 (1980): 16–39.

Jagodzinski, Cecile M. *Privacy and Print: Reading and Writing in Seventeenth-Century England* (Charlottesville, Va.: University Press of Virginia, 1999).

Jardine, Lisa, and Anthony Grafton. '"Studied for Action": How Gabriel Harvey Read his Livy'. *Past and Present,* 129 (1990): 30–78.

Javitch, Daniel. 'The Assimilation of Aristotle's *Poetics* in Sixteenth-Century Italy', in Glyn P. Norton (ed.), *The Cambridge History of Literary Criticism,* iii. *The Renaissance* (Cambridge: Cambridge University Press, 1999), 53–65.

Jeffrey, David. *A Dictionary of Biblical Tradition in English Literature* (Grand Rapids, Mich.: Eerdmans, 1992).

Jensen, Michael. '"Simply" Reading the Geneva Bible: The Geneva Bible and its Readers'. *Literature and Theology,* 9 (1995): 30–45.

Johns, Adrian. *The Nature of the Book: Print and Knowledge in the Making* (Chicago: University of Chicago Press, 1998).

Johnson, David. *Music and Society in Lowland Scotland in the Eighteenth Century* (London: Oxford University Press, 1972).

Johnson, Luke Timothy. *The Gospel of Luke* (Collegeville, Minn.: Liturgical Press, 1991).

Johnston, George P. 'Notices of a Collection of MSS. Relating to the Circulation of the Irish Bibles of 1685 and 1690 in the Highlands and the Association of the Rev. James Kirkwood Therewith'. *Papers of the Edinburgh Bibliographical Society*, 6 (1901–4): 1–18.

Johnston, Warren. *Revelation Restored: the Apocalypse in Later Seventeenth-Century England* (Woodbridge: Boydell, 2011).

Jones, G. Lloyd. *The Discovery of Hebrew in Tudor England: A Third Language* (Manchester: Manchester University Press, 1983).

Jones, Norman. *The English Reformation: Religion and Cultural Adaptation* (Oxford: Blackwell, 2002).

Jones, R. F. *The Triumph of English: A Survey of Opinions concerning the Vernacular from the Introduction of Printing to the Restoration* (Stanford, Calif.: Stanford University Press, 1953).

Jordan, W. K. 'Sectarian Thought and its Relation to the Development of Religious Toleration, 1640–1660: Part II. "The Individualists"'. *Huntington Library Quarterly*, 3 (1940): 289–314.

Jorink, Eric, and Dirk van Miert, eds. *Isaac Vossius (1618–1689) between Science and Scholarship* (Leiden: Brill, 2012).

Jue, Jeffrey K. *Heaven upon Earth: Joseph Mede (1586–1638) and the Legacy of Millenarianism* (Dordrecht: Springer, 2006).

Kalter, Barrett. *Modern Antiques: The Material Past in England, 1660–1780* (Lewisburg: Bucknell University Press, 2012).

Kamesar, Adam. *Jerome, Greek Scholarship, and the Hebrew Bible: A Study of the 'Quaestiones Hebraicae in Genesim'* (Oxford: Clarendon Press, 1995).

Kampen, Kimberly van, and Paul Saenger, eds. *The Bible as Book: The First Printed Editions* (London and Newcastle: British Library and Oak Knoll Press, 1999).

Karrow, Robert W., Jr. *Mapmakers of the Sixteenth Century and their Maps: Bio-Bibliographies of the Cartographers of Abraham Ortelius, 1570* (Chicago: Speculum Orbis Press, 1993).

Kaske, R. E., Arthur Groos, and Michael W. Twomey. *Medieval Christian Literary Imagery: A Guide to Interpretation* (Toronto: University of Toronto Press, 1988).

Katz, David S. *Philo-Semitism and the Readmission of the Jews to England, 1603–1655* (Oxford: Clarendon Press, 1982).

Katz, David S. 'Isaac Vossius and the English Biblical Critics, 1670–1689', in R. H. Popkin and A. J. Vanderjagt (eds), *Scepticism and Irreligion in the Seventeenth and Eighteenth Centuries* (Leiden: Brill, 1993), 142–84.

Katz, David S. *God's Last Words: Reading the English Bible from the Reformation to Fundamentalism* (New Haven: Yale University Press, 2004).

Kaufmann, U. Milo. *The Pilgrim's Progress and Traditions in Puritan Meditation* (New Haven: Yale University Press, 1966).

Kaye, Bruce N. 'Authority and Interpretation of Scripture in Hooker's *Of the Laws of Ecclesiastical Polity*'. *Journal of Religious History*, 21 (1997), 80–109.

Kearney, James. *The Incarnate Text: Imagining the Book in Reformation England* (Philadelphia: University of Pennsylvania Press, 2009).

Keeble N. H., ed. *John Bunyan: Conventicle and Parnassus: Tercentenary Essays* (Oxford: Clarendon Press, 1988).

Keeble N. H., ed. *The Cambridge Companion to Writing of the English Revolution* (Cambridge: Cambridge University Press, 2001).

Kellar, Clare. *Scotland, England, and the Reformation, 1534–1561* (Oxford: Oxford University Press, 2003).

Kelly, Henry Ansgar. 'Aristotle-Averroes-Alemannus on Tragedy: The Influence of the "Poetics" on the Latin Middle Ages'. *Viator*, 10 (1979): 161–209.

Kelly, Henry Ansgar. *Ideas and Forms of Tragedy from Aristotle to the Middle Ages* (Cambridge: Cambridge University Press, 1993).

Kemke, Johannes, ed. *Patricius Junius* (Leipzig: M. Spirgatis, 1898).

Kerrigan, William. *Prophetic Milton* (Charlottesville, Va.: University of Virginia Press, 1974).

Kess, Alexandra. *Johann Sleidan and the Protestant Vision of History* (Aldershot: Ashgate, 2008).

Kesson, Andy, and Emma Smith, eds. *The Elizabethan Top Ten: Defining Print Popularity in Early Modern England* (Farnham: Ashgate, 2013).

Killeen, Kevin. *Biblical Scholarship, Science and Politics in Early Modern England: Thomas Browne and the Thorny Place of Knowledge* (Farnham: Ashgate, 2009).

Killeen, Kevin. 'Chastising with Scorpions: Reading the Old Testament in Early Modern England', in Jennifer Richards and Fred Schurink (eds), 'The Textuality of Reading in Early Modern England'. *Huntington Library Quarterly*, 73 (2010): 491–506.

Killeen, Kevin. 'Hanging up Kings: The Political Bible in Early Modern England'. *Journal of the History of Ideas*, 72 (2011): 549–70.

King, John N. *English Reformation Literature: The Tudor Origins of the Protestant Tradition* (Princeton: Princeton University Press, 1982).

King, Kathryn R. 'Cowley among the Women: or, Poetry in the Contact Zone', in Katherine Binhammer and Jeanne Wood (eds), *Woman and Literary History: 'For There She Was'* (Newark, Del.: University of Delaware Press, 2003), 43–63.

Kintgen, E. R. *Reading in Tudor England* (Pittsburgh, Pa.: University of Pittsburgh Press, 1995).

Kirby, Torrance. 'Richard Hooker's Theory of Natural Law in the Context of Reformation Theology'. *The Sixteenth Century Journal*, 30 (1999): 681–703.

Kirby, Torrance. *Richard Hooker, Reformer and Platonist* (Aldershot: Ashgate, 2005).

Kirby, Torrance, ed. *A Companion to Richard Hooker* (Leiden: Brill, 2008).

Kirk, James. *Patterns of Reform: Continuity and Change in the Reformation Kirk* (Edinburgh: T. & T. Clark, 1989).

Kirkconnell, Watson. *The Celestial Cycle: The Theme of 'Paradise Lost' in World Literature with Translations of the Major Analogues* (Toronto: University of Toronto Press, 1952).

Knight, Alison. 'Pen of Iron: Scriptural Text and the Book of Job in Early Modern English Literature' (Ph.D. thesis, University of Cambridge, 2012).

Knoppers, Laura Lunger, ed. *The Oxford Handbook of Literature and the English Revolution* (Oxford: Oxford University Press, 2012).

Knott, John R. *The Sword of the Spirit: Puritan Responses to the Bible* (Chicago: University of Chicago Press, 1980).

Koote, T. G., ed. *De bijbel in huis: Bijbelse verhalen op huisraad en meubilair inde zeventiende en acttiende eeuw*, exh.cat. (Utrecht: Musuem Het Catherijnenconvent, 1992).

Krey, Philip W. D., and Lesley Smith, eds. *Nicholas of Lyra: The Sense of Scripture* (Leiden: Brill, 2000).

Krier, Theresa M. *Gazing on Secret Sights: Spenser, Classical Imitation, and the Decorums of Vision* (Ithaca, NY: Cornell University Press, 1990).

Kroll, Richard W. F. *The Material Word: Literate Culture in the Restoration and Early Eighteenth Century* (Baltimore, Md.: Johns Hopkins University Press, 1991).

Krontiris, Tina. *Oppositional Voices: Women as Writers and Translators of Literature in the English Renaissance* (London: Routledge, 1992).

Kugel, James. *The Idea of Biblical Poetry: Parallelism and its History* (New Haven and London: Yale University Press, 1981).

Kuhn, Thomas S. *The Copernican Revolution: Planetary Astronomy in the Development of Western Thought* (Cambridge, Mass.: Harvard University Press, 1957).

Laclau, Ernesto. *Emancipations* (London: Verso, 1996).

Lake, Peter. *Anglicans and Puritans? Presbyterianism and English Conformist Thought from Whitgift to Hooker* (London: Unwin Hyman, 1988).

Lake, Peter, and Michael Questier. *The Antichrist's Lewd Hat: Protestants, Papists and Players in Post-Reformation England* (New Haven: Yale University Press, 2002).

Lakowski, R. I. 'The Dialogue concerning Heresies'. *Interactive Early Modern Literary Studies* (1995), <http://extra.shu.ac.uk/emls/iemls/work/chapters/heresy1.html#BT4>.

Lamont, William M. *Richard Baxter and the Millennium* (London: Croom Helm, 1979).

Lampe, G. W. H. ed. *The Cambridge History of the Bible*, ii. *The West from the Fathers to the Reformation* (Cambridge: Cambridge University Press, 1969).

Lane, Anthony. 'Sola Scriptura? Making Sense of a Post-Reformation Slogan', in P. E. Satterthwaite and D. F. Wright (eds), *A Pathway into the Holy Scripture* (Grand Rapids, Mich.: Eerdmans, 1994), 297–327.

Langley, Christopher R. 'Times of Trouble and Deliverance: Worship in the Kirk of Scotland, 1645–1658' (Ph.D. thesis, University of Aberdeen, 2012).

Lanz, Hanspeter '"Komm Herr Jesus, sei unser Gast"'. *Zeitschrift für Schweizerische Archäologie und Kunstgeschichte*, 61 (2004): 221–25.

Laplanche, François. *L'écriture, le sacré et l'histoire: Érudits et politiques protestants devant la Bible en France au XVIIe siècle* (Amsterdam: APA-Holand University Press, 1986).

Laplanche, François. *La Bible en France entre mythe et critique (XVIe–XIXe siècle)* (Paris: Albin Michel, 1994).

Lasker, Daniel. 'Jewish–Christian Polemics at the Turning Point'. *Harvard Theological Review*, 89 (1996): 161–73.

Leaver, Robin R. *'Goostly Psalms and Spirituall Songes': English and Dutch Metrical Psalms from Coverdale to Utenhove, 1535–1566* (Oxford: Oxford University Press, 1991).

Lebègue, Raymond. *La tragédie religieuse en France: Les débuts (1514–1573)* (Paris: Librairie Ancienne Honoré Champion, 1929).

Legaspi, Michael C. *The Death of Scripture and the Rise of Biblical Studies* (Oxford: Oxford University Press, 2010).

Legg, J. Wickham. *English Church Life from the Restoration to the Tractarian Movement* (London: Longmans, 1914).

Leites, Edmund, ed. *Conscience and Casuistry in Early Modern Europe* (Cambridge: Cambridge University Press, 1988).

Lennon, Colm. *The Lords of Dublin in the Age of Reformation* (Blackrock, Co. Dublin: Irish Academic Press, 1989).

Lennon, Colm, and Ciaran Diamond. 'The Ministry of the Church of Ireland, 1536–1636', in T. C. Barnard and W. G. Neely (eds), *The Clergy of the Church of Ireland 1000–2000: Messengers, Watchmen and Stewards* (Dublin: Four Courts Press, 2006), 44–58.

Lentricchia, Frank. *After the New Criticism* (Chicago: University of Chicago Press, 1980).

Lepore, Jill. *The Name of War: King Philip's War and the Origins of American Identity* (New York: Vintage Books, 1999).

Letis, Theodore. *The Ecclesiastical Text: Text Criticism, Biblical Authority and the Popular Mind* (Philadelphia: Institute for Renaissance and Reformation Biblical Studies, 1997).

Levitin, Dmitri. 'From Sacred History to the History of Religion: Paganism, Judaism, and Christianity in European Historiography from Reformation to "Enlightenment"'. *The Historical Journal*, 55 (2012): 1117–60.

Levitin, Dmitri. 'John Spencer's *De Legibus Hebraeorum* (1683–85) and "Enlightened" Sacred History: A New Interpretation'. *Journal of the Warburg and Courtauld Institutes*, 76 (2013): 49–92.

Lewalski, Barbara K. *Milton's Brief Epic* (London: Methuen, 1966).

Lewalski, Barbara K. *Protestant Poetics and the Seventeenth-Century Religious Lyric* (Princeton: Princeton University Press, 1979).

Lewalski, Barbara K. 'Milton, the Bible and Human Experience'. *Topoi*, 7 (1988): 221–9.

Lewalski, Barbara K. 'The Genres of *Paradise Lost*', in Dennis Danielson (ed.), *The Cambridge Companion to Milton*, 2nd edn (Cambridge: Cambridge University Press, 1999), 113–29.

Lewalski, Barbara K. *The Life of John Milton: A Critical Biography*, rev. edn (Oxford: Blackwell, 2003).

Lewis, C. S. *A Preface to Paradise Lost* (Oxford: Oxford University Press, 1942).

Lewis, C. S. *The Literary Impact of the Authorized Version* (Philadelphia: Fortress Press, 1963).

Lewis, Marilyn A. '"The Messiah Promised in the Sacred Scripture Came a Long Time Ago": The Cambridge Platonists' Attitudes towards the Readmission of the Jews, 1655–56'. *Jewish Historical Studies: Transactions of the Jewish Historical Society of England*, 45 (2013): 41–61.

Lieb, Michael, Emma Mason, and Jonathan Roberts, eds. *The Oxford Handbook of the Reception History of the Bible* (Oxford: Oxford University Press, 2011).

Liere, Katherine van, Simon Ditchfield and Howard Louthan, eds. *Sacred History: Uses of the Christian Past in the Renaissance World* (Oxford: Oxford University Press, 2012).

Lindsay, Maurice. *History of Scottish Literature* (London: Hale, 1977).

Lippeheide, B. *Das Rheinische Steinzeug und die Graphik der Renaissance* (Berlin: Verlag Gebr. Mann, 1961).

Livingstone, David. 'Science, Magic, and Religion: A Contextual Reassessment of Geography in the Sixteenth and Seventeenth Centuries'. *History of Science*, 26 (1988): 269–94.

Lloyd Jones, G. *The Discovery of Hebrew in Tudor England* (Manchester: Manchester University Press, 1983).

Longfellow, Erica. *Women and Religious Writing in Early Modern England* (Cambridge: Cambridge University Press, 2004).

Loveman, Kate. *Reading Fictions, 1660–1740: Deception in English Literary and Political Culture* (Aldershot: Ashgate, 2008).

Lowes, John Livingston. 'The Noblest Monument of English Prose', *Essays in Appreciation* (Boston and New York: Houghton Mifflin Co., 1936), 3–31.

Lowth, Robert. *De Sacra Poesi Hebraeorum Praelectiones* (Oxford: Clarendon Press, 1753).

Lowth, Robert. *Lectures on the Sacred Poetry of the Hebrews*, tr. George Gregory, 2 vols (London: for J. Johnson, 1787).

Lubac, Henri de. *Exégèse medievale*, 4 vols (Paris: Aubier, 1959–64).

Lubac, Henri de. *Medieval Exegesis: The Four Senses of Scripture*, tr. Mark Sebanc and E. M. Macierowski, 3 vols (Grand Rapids, Mich.: William B. Eerdmans; Edinburgh: T. & T. Clark, 1998–2009).

Lund, Roger D., ed. *The Margins of Orthodoxy: Heterodox Writing and Cultural Response, 1660–1750* (Cambridge: Cambridge University Press, 1995).

Luxon, Thomas H. 'Calvin and Bunyan on Word and Image: Is there a Text in Interpreter's House?' *English Literary Renaissance*, 18 (1988): 438–59.

Luxon, Thomas H. *Literal Figures: Puritan Allegory and the Reformation Crisis in Representation* (Chicago: University of Chicago Press, 1995).

Lynch, Christopher. 'Machiavelli on Reading the Bible Judiciously', in Gordon Schochet, Fania Oz-Salzberger, and Meirav Jones (eds), *Political Hebraism: Judaic Sources in Early Modern Political Thought* (Jerusalem: Shalem Press, 2008), 29–54.

Lynch, Kathleen. *Protestant Autobiography in the Seventeenth-Century Anglophone World* (Oxford: Oxford University Press, 2012).

Lynch, Michael. 'Preaching to the Converted? Perspectives on the Scottish Reformation', in A. A. MacDonald, Michael Lynch and Ian B. Cowan (eds), *The Renaissance in Scotland: Studies in Literature, Religion, History and Culture Offered to John Durkan* (Leiden: Brill, 1994), 301–43.

McAdoo, H. R. *The Spirit of Anglicanism: A Survey of Anglican Theological Method in the Seventeenth Century* (London: A. & C. Black, 1965).

MacCallum, H. R. 'Milton and Sacred History: Books XI and XII of *Paradise Lost*', in M. MacLure and F. W. Watt (eds), *Essays in English Literature from the Renaissance to the Victorian Age, Presented to A. S. P. Woodhouse* (Toronto: University of Toronto Press, 1964), 149–68.

McCallum, John. *Reforming the Scottish Parish: The Reformation in Fife, 1560–1640* (Farnham: Ashgate, 2010).

McCaughey, Terence. *Dr. Bedell and Mr. King: The Making of the Irish Bible* (Dublin: Dublin Institute for Advanced Studies, 2001).

McCaughey, Terence. 'Andrew Sall (1624–82): Textual Editor and Facilitator of the Irish Translation of the Old Testament', in Cathal G. Ó Háinle and Donald E. Meek (eds), *Léann na Tríonóide Trinity Irish Studies* (Dublin: School of Irish, Trinity College, 2004), 153–71.

McClure, Alexander. *The Translators Revived* (New York: Scribner, 1853).

McColley, Diane. *Milton's Eve* (Urbana, Ill.: University of Illinois Press, 1983).

McColley, Diane. *A Gust for Paradise, Milton's Eden and the Visual Arts* (Urbana, Ill.: University of Illinois Press, 1993).

MacCulloch, Diarmaid. *Thomas Cranmer: A Life* (New Haven: Yale University Press, 1996).

MacCulloch, Diarmaid. *The Reformation: A History* (New York: Penguin, 2003).

MacCulloch, Diarmaid. *Reformation: Europe's House Divided* (London: Penguin, 2004).

McCullough, Peter. *Sermons at Court: Politics and Religion in Elizabethan and Jacobean Preaching* (Cambridge: Cambridge University Press, 1998).

McCullough, Peter. 'Donne as Preacher', in Achsah Guibbory (ed.), *The Cambridge Companion to John Donne* (Cambridge: Cambridge University Press, 2006), 167–81.

McCullough, Peter, Hugh Adlington, and Emma Rhatigan, eds. *The Oxford Handbook of the Early Modern Sermon* (Oxford: Oxford University Press, 2011).

MacDonald, Alan R. *The Jacobean Kirk, 1567–1625: Sovereignty, Polity and Liturgy* (Aldershot: Ashgate, 1998).

McDowell, Nicholas. 'Jeremy Taylor', in Garrett Sullivan, Jr., et al. (eds), *The Encyclopedia of English Renaissance Literature*, 3 vols (Oxford: Blackwell, 2012), iii. 947–8.

McDowell, Nicholas. *The English Radical Imagination: Culture, Religion, and Revolution, 1630–1660* (Oxford: Oxford University Press, 2003).

McFarlane, I. D. *Buchanan* (London: Duckworth, 1981).

McGrade, Arthur Stephen, ed. *Richard Hooker and the Construction of Christian Community* (Tempe, Ariz.: Medieval & Renaissance Texts & Studies, 1997).

McGrath, Alister. *In the Beginning: The Story of the King James Bible* (London: Hodder & Stoughton, 2001).

McGregor, J. F., and Barry Reay, eds. *Radical Religion in the English Revolution* (Oxford: Oxford University Press, 1984).

McGuinne, Dermot. *Irish Type Design: A History of Printing Types in the Irish Character* (Blackrock, Co. Dublin: Irish Academic Press, 1992).

McGuire, James, and James Quinn, eds. *Dictionary of Irish Biography*, 9 vols (Cambridge: Cambridge University Press, 2009).

McGuire, Philip. 'Herbert's Jordan II and the Plain Style'. *Michigan Academian*, 1 (1969): 69–74.

Mack, Peter. 'Renaissance Habits of Reading', in S. Chaudhuri (ed.), *Renaissance Essays for Kitty Scoular Datta* (Calcutta: Oxford University Press, 1995), 1–25.

Mack, Peter. 'Rhetoric, Ethics and Reading in the Renaissance'. *Renaissance Studies*, 19 (2005): 1–21.

MacKenzie, Cameron A. *The Battle for the Bible in England, 1557–1582* (New York: Peter Lang, 2002).

McKim, Donald. *Dictionary of Major Biblical Interpreters* (Downers Grove, Ill.: InterVarsity Press, 2007).

MacKinnon, Donald. *The Gaelic Bible and Psalter* (Dingwall: Ross-shire Printing and Publishing Co. Ltd, 1930).

Maclean, Donald. 'The Life and Literary Labours of the Rev. Robert Kirk, of Aberfoyle'. *Transactions of the Gaelic Society of Inverness*, 31 (1922–4): 328–66.

MacLean, Gerald, and Nabil Matar. *Britain and the Islamic World* (Oxford: Oxford University Press, 2011).

McLean, Matthew. *The Cosmographia of Sebastian Münster: Describing the World in the Reformation* (Aldershot: Ashgate, 2007).

McMillan, William. *The Worship of the Scottish Reformed Church, 1550–1638* (London: James Clarke, 1931).

McNeill, Charles, ed. 'Fitzwilliam Manuscripts at Milton, England'. *Analecta Hibernica*, 4 (1932): 287–326.

Maddison, R. E. W. 'Robert Boyle and the Irish Bible'. *Bulletin of the John Rylands University Library of Manchester*, 41 (1958): 81–101.

Major, Emma. *Madam Britannia: Women, Church, and Nation, 1712–1812* (Oxford: Oxford University Press, 2012).

Malcolm, Noel. *Aspects of Hobbes* (Oxford: Oxford University Press, 2002).

Malcolmson, R. W. *Popular Recreations in English Society 1700–1850* (Cambridge: Cambridge University Press, 1973).

Maltby, Judith. *Prayer Book and People in Elizabethan and Early Stuart England* (Cambridge: Cambridge University Press, 1998).

Mandelbrote, Scott. 'The Bible and Didactic Literature in Early Modern England', in Natasha Glaisyer and Sara Pennell (eds), *Didactic Literature in England 1500–1800* (Aldershot: Ashgate, 2003), 19–40.

Mandelbrote, Scott. 'The Authority of the Word: Manuscript, Print and the Text of the Bible in Seventeenth-Century England', in Julia Crick and Alexandra Walsham (eds), *The Uses of Script and Print, 1300–1700* (Cambridge: Cambridge University Press, 2004), 135–53.

Mandelbrote, Scott. 'Origen against Jerome in Early Modern Europe', in Silke-Petra Bergjan and Karla Pollmann (eds), *Patristic Tradition and Intellectual Paradigms in the Seventeenth Century* (Tübingen: Mohr Siebeck, 2010), 105–35.

Mandelbrote, Scott, and Michael Ledger-Lomas, eds. *Dissent and the Bible in Britain, c.1650–1950* (Oxford: Oxford University Press, 2013).

Mangani, Giorgio. 'Abraham Ortelius and the Hermetic Meaning of the Cordiform Projection'. *Imago Mundi*, 50 (1998): 59–83.

Manley, Frank. 'Toward a Definition of the Plain Style in the Poetry of George Herbert', in Maynard Mack and George de Forest Lord (eds), *Poetic Traditions of the English Renaissance* (New Haven: Yale University Press, 1982), 203–17.

Mann, Alastair J. *The Scottish Book Trade, 1500–1720: Print Commerce and Print Control in Early Modern Scotland* (East Linton: Tuckwell Press, 2000).

Manuel, Frank E. *Isaac Newton: Historian* (Cambridge: Cambridge University Press, 1963).

Manuel, Frank E. *The Broken Staff: Judaism through Christian Eyes* (Cambridge, Mass.: Harvard University Press, 1992).

Marion, Jean-Luc. *On the Ego and on God: Further Cartesian Questions,* tr. Christian M. Gschwandtner (New York: Fordham University Press, 2007).

Marsh, Christopher. *Popular Religion in Sixteenth-Century England* (Basingstoke: Macmillan, 1998).

Marsh, Christopher. *The Family of Love in English Society, 1550–1630* (Cambridge: Cambridge University Press, 1994).

Marsh, Christopher. *Music and Society in Early Modern England* (Cambridge: Cambridge University Press, 2010).

Marshall, Peter. *The Reformation: A Very Short Introduction* (Oxford: Oxford University Press, 2009).

Marshall, Peter. '(Re)Defining the English Reformation', *Journal of British Studies,* 48 (2009): 564–86.

Marshall, Peter, and Alec Ryrie, eds. *The Beginnings of English Protestantism* (Cambridge: Cambridge University Press, 2002).

Martin, Charles. *Les protestants anglais refugiés à Geneve au temps de Calvin 1555–1560* (Geneva: Jullien, 1915).

Martin, Jessica, and Alec Ryrie, eds. *Private and Domestic Devotion in Early Modern Britain* (Farnham: Ashgate, 2012).

Martin, Michael, ed. *The Cambridge Companion to Atheism* (Cambridge: Cambridge University Press, 2007).

Martyn, J. R. C. 'Montaigne and George Buchanan'. *Humanistica Lovaniensia: Journal of Neo-Latin Studies,* 36 (1977): 132–42.

Mason, Colin. 'Political Theology and the Levellers: A Discussion of the Theological Sources of the Political Thought of the Levellers and of Some Implications for Modern Understandings of Political Liberalism' (Ph.D. thesis, University of Durham, 2009).

Massimi, Jean-Robert. 'Montrer et démontrer: Autour du Traité de la situation du Paradis terrestre de P. D. Huet (1691)', in Alain Desreumaux and Francis Schmidt (eds), *Moïse géographe: Recherches sur les représentations juives et chrétiennes de l'espace* (Paris: J. Vrin, 1988), 203–25.

Matar, Nabil. *Islam in Britain 1558–1685* (Cambridge: Cambridge University Press, 2008).

Mather, F. C. 'Georgian Churchmanship Reconsidered: Some Variations in Anglican Public Worship 1714–1830'. *The Journal of Ecclesiastical History,* 36 (1985): 269–75.

Maus, Katharine Eisaman. *Inwardness and Theater in the English Renaissance* (Chicago: University of Chicago Press, 1995).

Maxwell, William D. *A History of Worship in the Church of Scotland* (London: Oxford University Press, 1955).

Mayer, Robert. 'Lucy Hutchinson: A Life of Writing'. *Seventeenth Century,* 22 (2007): 305–35.

Meek, Donald. 'The Gaelic Bible', in David F. Wright (ed.), *The Bible in Scottish Life and Literature* (Edinburgh: St Andrew Press, 1988), 9–23.

Meek, Donald. 'The Reformation and Gaelic Culture: Perspectives on Patronage, Language and Literature in John Carswell's Translation of "The Book of Common Order"', in James Kirk (ed.), *The Church in the Highlands* (Edinburgh: Scottish Church History Society, 1998), 37–62.

Meek, Donald. 'The Pulpit and the Pen: Clergy, Orality and Print in the Scottish Gaelic World', in Adam Fox and Daniel Woolf (eds), *The Spoken World: Oral Culture in Britain, 1500–1850* (Manchester: Manchester University Press, 2002), 84–118.

Meganck, Tine L. 'Erudite Eyes: Artists and Antiquarians in the Circle of Abraham Ortelius' (Ph.D. thesis, Princeton University, 2003).

Melion, Walter S. '*Ad ductum itineris et dispositionem mansionum ostendendam*: Meditation, Vocation, and Sacred History in Abraham Ortelius's "Parergon"'. *The Journal of the Walters Art Gallery,* 57 (1999): 49–72.

Melion, Walter S. 'Bible Illustration in the Sixteenth-Century Low Countries', in James Clifton and Walter S. Melion (eds), *Scripture for the Eyes: Bible Illustrations in Netherlandish Prints of the Sixteenth Century* (New York and London: Museum of Biblical Art/D. Giles Ltd, 2009), 14–106.

Mencken, H. L. *Treatise on the Gods* (New York: Alfred A. Knopf, 1930, repr. 1946).

Metzger, Bruce. *An Introduction to the Apocrypha* (Oxford: Oxford University Press, 1957).

Meyendorff, John. 'Wisdom-Sophia: Contrasting Approaches to a Complex Theme', *Dumbarton Oaks Papers,* 41, Studies in Art and Archaeology in Honor of Ernst Kitzinger on his Seventy-Fifth Birthday (1987), 391–401.

Miller, Perry. *Errand into the Wilderness* (Cambridge, Mass.: Belknap Press, 1956).

Miller, Peter N. 'Making the Paris Polyglot Bible: Humanism and Orientalism in the Early Seventeenth Century', in Herbert Jaumann (ed.), *Die Europäische Gelehrtenrepublik im Zeitalter des Konfessionalismus* (Wiesbaden: Harrassowitz, 2001), 59–85.

Miller, Peter N. 'The "Antiquarianization" of Biblical Scholarship and the London Polyglot Bible'. *Journal of the History of Ideas,* 62 (2001): 463–82.

Milner, Matthew. *The Senses and the English Reformation* (Farnham: Ashgate, 2011).

Milton, Anthony. *Catholic and Reformed: The Roman and Protestant Churches in English Protestant Thought, 1600–1640* (Cambridge: Cambridge University Press, 1995).

Milton, Anthony, ed. *The British Delegation and the Synod of Dort (1618–1619)* (Woodbridge: Boydell Press, 2005).

Miscall, Peter D. *Isaiah 34–35: A Nightmare/A Dream, Journal for the Study of the Old Testament,* supplement series, 281 (Sheffield: Sheffield Academic Press, 1999).

Molekamp, Femke. 'Using a Collection to Discover Reading Practices: The British Library Geneva Bibles and a History of their Early Modern Readers'. *Electronic British Library Journal,* art. 10 (2006): 1–13, <http://www.bl.uk/eblj/2006articles/pdf/article10.pdf>.

Molekamp, Femke. '"Of the Incomparable treasure of the Holy Scriptures": The Geneva Bible in the Early Modern Household', in Matthew Dimmock and Andrew Hadfield (eds), *Literature and Popular Culture in Early Modern England* (Farnham: Ashgate, 2009), 121–37.

Molekamp, Femke. *Women and the Bible in Early Modern England: Religious Reading and Writing* (Oxford: Oxford University Press, 2013).

Momigliano, Arnaldo. 'Ancient History and the Antiquarian'. *Journal of the Warburg and Courtauld Institutes,* 13 (1950): 285–315.

Monod, Paul Kléber. *Jacobitism and the English People, 1688–1788* (Cambridge: Cambridge University Press, 1989; repr. 1993).

Moore, C. A. 'Miltoniana (1679–1741)'. *Modern Philology,* 24 (1927): 321–39.

Moore, Helen, and Julian Reid, eds. *Manifold Greatness: The Making of the King James Bible* (Oxford: Bodleian Library, 2011).

Moore, Stephen D., and Yvonne Sherwood, *The Invention of the Biblical Scholar: A Critical Manifesto* (Minneapolis, Minn.: Fortress, 2011).

Morrall, Andrew. *Jörg Breu the Elder: Art, Culture and Belief in Reformation Augsburg* (Aldershot: Ashgate, 2002).

Morrill, John. *Oliver Cromwell* (Oxford: Oxford University Press, 2007).

Morgan, David, ed. *Religion and Material Culture: The Matter of Belief* (London: Routledge, 2009).

Morrin, James, ed. *Calendar of the Patent and Close Rolls of Chancery in Ireland*, 2 (Dublin and London: Her Majesty's Stationery Office, 1862).

Morrissey, Mary. 'Scripture, Style and Persuasion in Seventeenth-Century English Theories of Preaching'. *The Journal of Ecclesiastical History*, 53 (2002): 686–706.

Morrissey, Mary. *Politics and the Paul's Cross Sermons, 1558–1642* (Oxford: Oxford University Press, 2011).

Morrow, Jeffrey L. 'Pre-Adamites, Politics and Criticism: Isaac La Peyrère's Contribution to Modern Biblical Studies'. *Journal of the Orthodox Center for the Advancement of Biblical Studies*, 4 (2011): 1–23.

Mortimer, Sarah. *Reason and Religion in the English Revolution: The Challenge of Socinianism* (Cambridge: Cambridge University Press, 2010).

Morton, Timothy, and Nigel Smith, eds. *Radicalism in British Literary Culture, 1650–1830* (Cambridge: Cambridge University Press, 2002).

Moss, Ann. *Printed Commonplace Books and the Structuring of Renaissance Thought* (Oxford: Clarendon Press, 1996).

Mosshammer, Alden A. *The 'Chronicle' of Eusebius and Greek Chronographic Tradition* (Lewisburg: Bucknell University Press, 1979).

Mozley, J. F. *William Tyndale* (London: SPCK, 1937).

Muddiman, John. *A Commentary on the Epistle to the Ephesians* (London: Continuum, 2001).

Muilenburg, James. 'The Literary Character of Isaiah 34'. *Journal of Biblical Literature*, 59 (1940): 339–65.

Mukherji, Subha, ed. *Thinking on Thresholds: The Poetics of Transitive Spaces* (London: Anthem Press, 2011).

Mullan, David George. *Episcopacy in Scotland: The History of an Idea, 1560–1638* (Edinburgh: John Donald Publishers, 1986).

Mullan, David George. *Scottish Puritanism, 1590–1638* (Oxford: Oxford University Press, 2000).

Mullan, David George. *Narratives of the Religious Self in Early-Modern Scotland* (Farnham: Ashgate, 2010).

Muller, Richard A. *Christ and the Decree: Christology and Predestination in Reformed Theology from Calvin to Perkins* (Grand Rapids, Mich.: Baker Academic, 1988).

Muller, Richard A. 'The Hermeneutics of Promise and Fulfillment in Calvin's Exegesis of the Old Testament Prophecies of the Kingdom', in David C. Steinmetz (ed.), *The Bible in the Sixteenth Century* (Durham, NC: Duke University Press, 1990), 68–82.

Muller, Richard A. *Post-Reformation Reformed Dogmatics: The Rise and Development of Reformed Orthodoxy, ca. 1520 to ca. 1725*, 2nd edn, 4 vols (Grand Rapids, Mich.: Baker Academic, 2003).

Muller, Richard A. 'John Calvin and later Calvinism', in David Bagchi and David Steinmetz (eds), *The Cambridge Companion to Reformed Theology* (Cambridge: Cambridge University Press, 2006).

Muller, Richard A., and John L. Thompson, eds. *Biblical Interpretation in the Era of the Reformation* (Grand Rapids, Mich.: Eerdmans, 1996).

Murray, Molly. *The Poetics of Conversion in Early Modern English Literature: Verse and Change from Donne to Dryden* (Cambridge: Cambridge University Press, 2009).

Narveson, Kate. *Bible Readers and Lay Writers in Early Modern England* (Farnham: Ashgate, 2012).

Nelson, Eric. *The Hebrew Republic: Jewish Sources and the Transformation of European Political Thought* (Cambridge, Mass.: Harvard University Press, 2010).

Nethercot, Arthur. 'The Literary Legend of Francis Quarles'. *Modern Philology*, 20 (1923): 225–40.

Neuman, Kalman. 'Political Hebraism and the Early Modern "*Respublica Hebraeorum*": On Defining the Field'. *Hebraic Political Studies*, 1 (2005): 57–70.

Nevalinen, Terttu. 'Early Modern English Lexis and Semantics', in Roger Lass (ed.), *The Cambridge History of the English Language*, iii. *1476–1776* (Cambridge: Cambridge University Press, 1999).

Nevitt, Marcus. *Women and the Pamphlet Culture of Revolutionary England* (Farnham: Ashgate, 2006).

Nice, Jason A. '"The Peculiar Place of God": Early Modern Representations of England and France'. *English Historical Review*, 121/493 (2006): 1002–18.

Nicholl, Charles. *The Reckoning* (London: Jonathan Cape, 1992).

Nicolson, Adam. *God's Secretaries: the Making of the King James Bible* (New York: Harper Collins, 2003).

Nicolson, Adam. *Power and Glory: Jacobean England and the Making of the King James Bible* (London: Harper Collins, 2003).

Nicolson, Adam. *When God Spoke English: The Making of the King James Bible* (London: HarperPress, 2011).

Nida, Eugene. *Toward a Science of Translating, with Special Reference to Principles and Procedures Involved in Bible Translating* (Leiden: Brill, 1964).

Noonan, Thomas F. *The Road to Jerusalem: Pilgrimage and Travel in the Age of Discovery* (Philadelphia: University of Pennsylvania Press, 2007).

Norbrook, David. 'A Devine Originall: Lucy Hutchinson and the "Woman's Version"'. *TLS* (19 Mar. 1999): 13–15.

Norbrook, David. *Poetry and Politics in the English Renaissance*, rev. edn (Oxford: Oxford University Press, 2002).

Norbrook, David. 'John Milton, Lucy Hutchinson and the Republican Biblical Epic', in Mark R. Kelley, Michael Lieb, and John T. Shawcross (eds), *Milton and the Grounds of Contention* (Pittsburgh, Pa.: Duquesne University Press, 2003), 37–63.

Norris, Pippa, and Ronald Inglehart. 'The Secularization Debate', in Norris and Inglehart (eds), *Sacred and Secular: Religion and Politics Worldwide* (Cambridge: Cambridge University Press, 2004), 3–32.

Norton, David. *A History of the Bible as Literature* (Cambridge: Cambridge University Press, 1993; rev. edn, *A History of the English Bible as Literature*, 2000).

Norton, David. 'John Bois's Notes on the Revision of the King James Bible New Testament: A New Manuscript'. *The Library*, 6th ser. 18 (1996): 328–46.

Norton, David. *A Textual History of the King James Bible* (Cambridge: Cambridge University Press, 2005).

Norton, David. *The King James Bible: A Short History from Tyndale to Today* (Cambridge: Cambridge University Press, 2011).

Nothaft, Carl Philipp Emanuel. 'From Sukkot to Saturnalia: The Attack on Christmas in Sixteenth-Century Chronological Scholarship'. *Journal of the History of Ideas*, 72 (2011): 503–22.

Nothaft, Carl Philipp Emanuel. *Dating the Passion* (Leiden: Brill, 2012).

Nutall, G. F., and N. H. Keeble, eds. *Calendar of the Correspondence of Richard Baxter: 1638–1660*, 2 vols (Oxford: Oxford University Press, 1991).

Nuttall, G. F. *James Nayler: A Fresh Approach* (London: Friends Historical Society, 1954).

Ó Ciosáin, Niall. 'Print and Irish, 1570–1900: An Exception among the Celtic Languages?' *Radharc: A Journal of Irish and Irish-American Studies*, 5–7 (2004–6): 73–106.

Ó Cuív, Brian. *Irish Dialects and Irish-Speaking Districts* (Dublin: Dublin Institute for Advanced Studies, 1971).

Ó Fearghail, Fearghus. 'The Irish New Testament of 1602 in its European Context'. *Proceedings of the Irish Biblical Association*, 31 (2008): 77–107.

Ó Fearghail, Fearghus. 'Uilliam Ó Domhnaill's Irish Version of the *Book of Common Prayer* (1608) and his Old Testament Translations into Irish'. *Proceedings of the Irish Biblical Association*, 32 (2009): 99–130.

Ó Fiaich, Tomás. 'Pól Ó hUiginn'. *Maynooth Review*, 2 (1976): 42–51.

Ó Macháin, Pádraig. 'Two Nugent Manuscripts: The Nugent *duanaire* and Queen Elizabeth's Primer'. *Ríocht na Midhe*, 23 (2012): 121–42.

Ogborn, Miles. *Indian Ink: Script and Print in the Making of the English East India Company* (Chicago: University of Chicago Press, 2007).

Osherow, Michele. *Biblical Women's Voices in Early Modern England* (Farnham: Ashgate, 2009).

O'Sullivan, Orlaith, ed., and Ellen N. Herron, assistant ed., *The Bible as Book: The Reformation* (London and Newcastle: British Library and Oak Knoll Press, 2000).

Owen, John. *The Works of John Owen*, ed. William H. Goold, 24 vols (Edinburgh: Johnstone and Hunter, 1850–3).

Owens, W. R. 'Sequential Bible Reading in Early Modern England'. *Bunyan Studies*, 15 (2011): 64–74.

Oz-Salzberger, Fania. 'The Political Thought of John Locke and the Significance of Political Hebraism'. *Hebraic Political Studies*, 1 (2006): 569–70.

Pagels, Elaine. *Revelations: Visions, Prophecies, and Politics in the Book of Revelation* (Harmondsworth: Penguin, 2012).

Pak, Sujin G. *The Judaizing Calvin* (Oxford: Oxford University Press, 2010).

Paleit, Edward. 'Women's Poetry and Classical Authors: Lucy Hutchinson and the Classicisation of Scripture', in Susan Wiseman (ed.), *Early Modern Women and the Poem* (Manchester: Manchester University Press, 2013), 21–41.

Parente, James A., Jr. 'The Development of Religious Tragedy: The Humanist Reception of the *Christos Paschon* in the Renaissance'. *The Sixteenth Century Journal*, 16 (1985): 351–68.

Parente, James A., Jr. *Religious Drama and the Humanist Tradition: Christian Theater in Germany and in the Netherlands, 1500–1680* (Leiden: Brill, 1987).

Parker, John. *The Aesthetics of Antichrist: From Christian Drama to Christopher Marlowe* (Ithaca, NY: Cornell University Press, 2007).

Parker, Kim Ian. *The Biblical Politics of John Locke* (Waterloo, ON: Wilfrid Laurier University Press, 2004).

Parker, T. H. L. *Calvin's Preaching* (Edinburgh: Clark, 1992).

Paster, Gail Kern. *Humoring the Body: Emotions and the Shakespearean Stage* (Chicago: University of Chicago Press, 2004).

Patrick, Millar. *Four Centuries of Scottish Psalmody* (Oxford: Oxford University Press, 1949).

Patterson, Annabel, and Martin Dzelzainis. 'Marvell and the Earl of Anglesey: A Chapter in the History of Reading'. *The Historical Journal*, 44 (2001): 703–26.

Patterson, W. B. *King James VI and I and the Reunion of Christendom* (Cambridge: Cambridge University Press, 1997).

Pattison, Mark. *Isaac Casaubon* (London: Longmans, Green, & Co., 1875).

Pauw, Amy. 'Becoming a Part of Israel', in Claire McGinnis and Patricia Tull (eds), '*As Those Who Are Taught': The Interpretation of Isaiah from the LXX to the SBL* (Atlanta, Ga.: Society of Biblical Literature, 2006), 201–21.

Pecora, Vincent P. *Secularization and Cultural Criticism* (Chicago: University of Chicago Press, 2006).

Pender, Patricia. *Early Modern Women's Writing and the Rhetoric of Modesty* (Basingstoke: Palgrave Macmillan, 2012).

Perl-Rosenthal, Nathan R. 'The "Divine Right of Republics": Hebraic Republicanism and the Debate over Kingless Government in Revolutionary America'. *The William and Mary Quarterly*, 66 (2009): 535–64.

Pettegree, Andrew. *Marian Protestantism: Six Studies* (Aldershot: Scolar Press, 1996).

Pettegree, Andrew. *The Book in the Renaissance* (New Haven: Yale University Press, 2010).

Picciotto, Joanna. *Labors of Innocence in Early Modern England* (Cambridge, Mass.: Harvard University Press, 2010).

Pietsch, Andreas. *Isaac La Peyrère. Bibelkritik, Philosemitismus und Patronage in der Gelehrtenrepublik des 17. Jahrhunderts* (Berlin: De Gruyter, 2012).

Pincus, Steve. *1688: The First Modern Revolution* (New Haven: Yale University Press, 2011).

Pocock, J. G. A. 'Post-Puritan England and the Problem of Enlightenment', in Perez Zagorin (ed.), *Culture and Politics: From Puritanism to the Enlightenment* (Berkeley, Calif.: University of California Press, 1980), 91–111.

Polanyi, Karl. *The Great Transformation* (New York: Farrar & Rhinehart, 1944).

Pollard, Alfred W., ed. *Records of the English Bible: The Documents Relating to the Translation and Publication of the Bible in English, 1525–1611* (London: Oxford University Press, 1911; repr. Mansfield Centre, Conn.: Martino, 1974).

Pollard, M. *Dublin's Trade in Books 1550–1800* (Oxford: Clarendon Press, 1989).

Poole, Robert. *Time's Alteration: Calendar Reform in Early Modern England* (London: UCL Press, 1998).

Poole, William. *Milton and the Idea of the Fall* (Oxford: Oxford University Press, 2005).

Poole, William. *The World Makers* (Oxford: Peter Lang, 2010).

Porter, J. R., and W. M. S. Russell, eds. *Animals in Folklore* (Cambridge: Brewer, 1978).

Porter, James. '"Blessed spirits, sing with me!" Psalm-Singing in Context and Practice', in James Porter (ed.), *Defining Strains: The Musical Life of Scots in the Seventeenth Century* (Oxford: Peter Lang, 2007), 299–322.

Potter, Lois. *Secret Rites and Secret Writing: Royalist Literature, 1641–1660* (Cambridge: Cambridge University Press, 1989).

Prescott, Anne Lake. 'The Reception of Du Bartas in England'. *Studies in the Renaissance*, 15 (1968): 144–73.

Prescott, Anne Lake. 'Evil Tongues at the Court of Saul'. *Journal of Medieval and Renaissance Studies*, 12 (1991): 163–86.

Prescott, Anne Lake. '"Formes of Joy and Art": Donne, David, and the Power of Music'. *John Donne Journal*, 25 (2006): 3–36.

Preston, C. D., and P. H. Oswald. 'James Duport's Rules for his Tutorial Pupils: A Comparison of Two Surviving Manuscripts'. *Transactions of the Cambridge Bibliographical Society*, 14 (2011): 317–62.

Preston, Thomas R. 'Biblical Criticism, Literature, and the Eighteenth-Century Reader', in Isabel Rivers (ed.), *Books and their Readers in Eighteenth-Century England* (Leicester: Leicester University Press, 1982), 97–126.

Preus, J. Samuel. *Spinoza and the Irrelevance of Biblical Authority* (Cambridge: Cambridge University Press, 2001).

Procter, F., and W. H. Frere. *A New History of the Book of Common Prayer* (London: Macmillan, 1925).

Pulsiano, Phillip. 'William L'Isle and the Editing of Old English', in Timothy Graham (ed.), *The Recovery of Old English: Anglo-Saxon Studies in the Sixteenth and Seventeenth Centuries* (Kalamazoo, Mich.: Medieval Inst., 2000).

Pyper, Hugh. 'Reading in the Dark: Zechariah, Daniel and the Difficulty of Scripture'. *Journal for the Study of the Old Testament*, 29 (2005): 485–504.

Quantin, Jean-Louis. 'Du Chrysostome latin au Chrysostome grec: Une histoire européenne (1588–1613)', in Martin Wallraff and Rudolf Brändle (eds), *Chrysostomosbilder in 1600 Jahren: Facetten der Wirkungsgeschichte eines Kirchenvaters* (Berlin: De Gruyter, 2008), 267–346.

Quantin, Jean-Louis. *The Church of England and Christian Antiquity: The Construction of a Confessional Identity in the Seventeenth Century* (Oxford: Oxford University Press, 2009).

Questier, Michael. *Conversion, Politics and Religion in England, 1580–1625* (Cambridge: Cambridge University Press, 1996).

Quin, Cosslett. 'Nicholas Walsh and his Friends: A Forgotten Chapter in the Irish Reformation'. *Journal of the Butler Society*, 2 (1984): 294–8.

Quinn, D. B. 'John Denton Desires William Kearney to Print Books for Use in Down, *circa* 1588: A Sidelight on Printing in Ireland'. *Irish Booklore*, 3 (1977): 87–90.

Quitslund, Beth. *The Reformation in Rhyme* (Aldershot: Ashgate, 2008).

Radzinowicz, Mary Ann. *Milton's Epics and the Book of Psalms* (Princeton: Princeton University Press, 1989).

Raffe, Alasdair. 'Presbyterians and Episcopalians: The Formation of Confessional Cultures in Scotland, 1660–1715'. *English Historical Review*, 125 (2010): 570–98.

Raffe, Alasdair. *The Culture of Controversy: Religious Arguments in Scotland, 1660–1714* (Woodbridge: Boydell Press, 2012).

Rappaport, Rhoda. *When Geologists were Historians, 1665–1750* (Ithaca, NY: Cornell University Press, 1997).

Read, Sophie. 'Rhetoric of Real Presence in the Seventeenth Century' (Ph.D. thesis, University of Cambridge, 2007).

Rees, Graham, and Maria Wakely. *Publishing, Politics and Culture: The King's Printers in the Reign of James I and VI* (Oxford: Oxford University Press, 2009).

Reid, Steven J., and Emma A. Wilson, eds. *Ramus, Pedagogy, and the Liberal Arts: Ramism in Britain and the Wider World* (Farnham: Ashgate, 2011).

Rembaum, Joel. 'The Development of a Jewish Exegetical Tradition Regarding Isaiah 53'. *Harvard Theological Review*, 75 (1982): 289–311.

Reuss, Eduard. *History of the Canon of the Holy Scriptures in the Christian Church*, tr. David Hunter, 2nd edn (Edinburgh: James Gemmell, 1884).

Reventlow, Henning Graf. 'The Saints of the Most High und die Rätsel der Chronologie—Danielrezeption in England im 17. und 18. Jahrhundert', in Mariano Delgado, Klaus Koch, and Edgar Marsch (eds), *Europa, Tausendjähriges Reich und Neue Welt* (Stuttgart: Kohlhammer, 2003), 306–25.

Rex, Richard. *Henry VIII and the English Reformation* (Basingstoke: Palgrave Macmillan, 1993).

Rex, Walter. 'Pierre Bayle: The Theology and Politics of the Article on David'. *Bibliothèque d'Humanisme et Renaissance*, 24 (1962), 168–89.

Rice, Eugene. *Saint Jerome in the Renaissance* (Baltimore, Md.: Johns Hopkins University Press, 1985).

Richey, Esther Gilman. *The Politics of Revelation in the English Renaissance* (Columbia, Mo.: University of Missouri Press, 1998).

Rickard, Jane. *Authorship and Authority: The Writings of James VI and I* (Manchester: Manchester University Press, 2007).

Ricks, Christopher. *Milton's Grand Style* (Oxford: Clarendon Press, 1963).

Riley, Patrick. *The General Will Before Rousseau: The Transformation of the Divine into the Civic* (Princeton: Princeton University Press, 1986).

Rissanen, Matti. "'Strange and inkhorne termes'. Loan-Words as Style Markers in the Prose of Edward Hall, Thomas Elyot, Thomas More and Roger Ascham', in Håkan Ringbom (ed.), *Style and Text: Studies Presented to Nils Erik Enkvist* (Stockholm: Skriptor, 1975), 250–62.

Rivers, Isabel. *Reason, Grace, and Sentiment: A Study of the Language of Religion and Ethics in England, 1660–1780*, i. *Whichcote to Wesley* (Cambridge: Cambridge University Press, 1991).

Romm, James. 'Biblical History and the Americas: The Legend of Solomon's Ophir, 1492–1591', in Paolo Bernardini and Norman Fiering (eds), *The Jews and the Expansion of Europe to the West, 1450 to 1800* (New York: Berghahn Books, 2001), 27–46.

Rose, Jacqueline. *Godly Kingship in Restoration England: The Politics of the Royal Supremacy, 1660–1688* (Cambridge: Cambridge University Press, 2011).

Rose, Jacqueline. 'Kingship and Counsel in Early Modern England'. *The Historical Journal*, 54 (2011): 47–71.

Rosenberg, Daniel. 'Electronic Memory', in Rosenberg and Susan Harding (eds), *Histories of the Future* (Durham, NC: Duke University Press, 2005), 123–52.

Rosenberg, Daniel, and Anthony Grafton. *Cartographies of Time: A History of the Timeline* (New York: Princeton Architectural Press, 2010).

Rosenblatt, Jason P. *Torah and Law in 'Paradise Lost'* (Princeton: Princeton University Press, 1994).

Rosenfeld, Nancy. *The Human Satan in Seventeenth-Century English Literature: From Milton to Rochester* (Aldershot: Ashgate, 2008).

Rowland, Christopher. *Blake and the Bible* (New Haven: Yale University Press, 2010).

Rowley, H. H. *Darius the Mede and the Four World Empires* (Cardiff: University of Wales Press, 1935).

Rubel, Veré L. *Poetic Diction in the English Renaissance from Skelton through Spenser* (New York: Modern Language Association, 1941).

Rubiés, Joan-Pau. 'Instructions for Travellers: Teaching the Eye to See'. *History and Anthropology*, 9 (1996): 139–90.

Rubin, Rehav. *Image and Reality: Jerusalem in Maps and Views* (Jerusalem: Hebrew University Magnes Press, 1999).

Russell, Conrad. 'Divine Rights in the Early Seventeenth Century', in John Morrill, Paul Slack, and Daniel Woolf (eds), *Public Duty and Private Conscience in Seventeenth-Century England: Essays Presented to G. E. Aylmer* (Oxford: Oxford University Press, 1993), 101–20.

Russell, Frederick V. 'Augustine: Conversion by the Book', in James Muldoon (ed.), *Varieties of Religious Conversion in the Middle Ages* (Gainesville, Fla.: University Press of Florida, 1997), 13–30.

Ryrie, Alec. *The Origins of the Scottish Reformation* (Manchester: Manchester University Press, 2006).

Ryrie, Alec. 'The Psalms and Confrontation in English and Scottish Protestantism'. *Archiv für Reformationsgeschichte*, 101 (2010): 114–37.

Sæbø, Magne, ed. *Hebrew Bible/Old Testament: The History of its Appropriation*, i/2. *The Middle Ages* (Göttingen: Vanderhoeck & Ruprecht, 2000).

Sæbø, Magne, ed. *Hebrew Bible, Old Testament: The History of its Interpretation*, ii. *From the Renaissance to the Enlightenment* (Göttingen: Vandenhoeck & Ruprecht, 2008).

Saintsbury, George. *A History of English Prose Rhythm* (London: Macmillan & Co., 1912).

Sawyer, J. F. A. *The Fifth Gospel: Isaiah in the History of Christianity* (Cambridge: Cambridge University Press, 1996).

Sayce, R. A. *The French Biblical Epic in the Seventeenth Century* (Oxford: Clarendon Press, 1955).

Scafi, Alessandro. *Mapping Paradise: A History of Heaven on Earth* (Chicago: University of Chicago Press, 2006).

Scarisbrick, J. J. *Henry VIII* (Berkeley, Calif.: University of California Press, 1968).

Scarisbrick, J. J. *The Reformation and the English People* (Oxford: Blackwell, 1997).

Schleiner, Winfried. *The Imagery of Donne's Sermons* (Providence, RI: Brown University Press, 1970).

Schneider, Manfred. 'Luther with McLuhan', in Hent de Vries and Samuel Weber (eds), *Religion and Media* (Stanford, Calif.: Stanford University Press, 2001), 198–215.

Schoenfeldt, Michael C. *Bodies and Selves in Early Modern England: Physiology and Inwardness in Spenser, Shakespeare, Herbert, and Milton* (Cambridge: Cambridge University Press, 1999).

Schüssler Fiorenza, Elisabeth. 'The Words of Prophecy: Reading the Apocalypse Theologically', in Stephen Moyise (ed.), *Studies in the Book of Revelation* (London: T. & T. Clark, 2001), 9–19.

Schwartz, Dietrich W. H. *Sachgüter und Lebensformen: Einführung in die materielle Kulturgeschichte des Mittelalters und der Neuzeit* (Berlin: Schmidt, 1970).

Schwartz, Regina M. 'Milton on the Bible', in Thomas N. Corns (ed.), *A Companion to Milton* (Oxford: Blackwell, 2001), 37–54.

Scott, Brendan. 'Accusations against Murtagh King, 1638'. *Archivium Hibernicum*, 65 (2012): 76–81.

Scott, Jonathan. *Algernon Sidney and the English Republic, 1623–1677* (Cambridge: Cambridge University Press, 1988).

Scott, Jonathan. *Algernon Sidney and the Restoration Crisis* (Cambridge: Cambridge University Press, 1991).

Scott-Baumann, Elizabeth. *Forms of Engagement: Women, Poetry, and Culture 1640–1680* (Oxford: Oxford University Press, 2013).

Scribner, Bob. 'Heterodoxy, Literacy and Print in the Early German Reformation', in Peter Biller and Anne Hudson (eds), *Heresy and Literacy, 1000–1530* (Cambridge: Cambridge University Press, 1994), 255–78.

Scrivener, F. H. A. *The Authorized Edition of the English Bible (1611): Its Subsequent Reprints and Modern Representatives* (Cambridge: Cambridge University Press, 1884).

Seifert, Arno. *Der Rückzug der biblischen Prophetie von der neueren Geschichte* (Cologne: Böhlau, 1990).

Shagan, Ethan. *Popular Politics and the English Reformation* (Cambridge: Cambridge University Press, 2002).

Shakespeare, Joy, and Maria Dowling. 'Religion and Politics in Mid-Tudor England through the Eyes of a Protestant English Woman: The Recollections of Rose Throckmorton'. *Bulletin of the Institute of Historical Research*, 55 (1982): 94–102.

Shalev, Zur. 'Measurer of All Things: John Greaves (1602–1652), the Great Pyramid and Early Modern Metrology'. *Journal of the History of Ideas*, 63 (2002): 555–75.

Shalev, Zur. *Sacred Words and Worlds: Geography, Religion, and Scholarship, 1550–1700* (Leiden: Brill, 2012).

Shalev, Zur, and Charles Burnett, eds. *Ptolemy's 'Geography' in the Renaissance* (London: Warburg Institute, 2011).

Shami, Jeanne M. 'Donne on Discretion'. *ELH* 47 (1980): 48–66.

Shami, Jeanne M. *John Donne and Conformity in Crisis in the Late Jacobean Pulpit* (Cambridge: D. S. Brewer, 2003).

Shami, Jeanne M., M. Thomas Hester, and Dennis Flynne, eds. *The Oxford Handbook of John Donne* (Oxford: Oxford University Press, 2011).

Shapin, Steven. *A Social History of Truth: Civility and Science in Seventeenth Century England* (Chicago: University of Chicago Press, 1994).

Sheehan, Jonathan. *The Enlightenment Bible: Translation, Scholarship, Culture* (Princeton: Princeton University Press, 2005).

Sherman, William H. *Used Books: Marking Readers in Renaissance England* (Philadelphia: University of Pennsylvania Press, 2007).

Sherwood, Yvonne. 'The God of Abraham and Exceptional States: The Early Modern Rise of the Whig/Liberal Bible'. *Journal of the American Academy of Religion*, 76 (2008): 312–43.

Sherwood, Yvonne. *Biblical Blaspheming: Trials of the Sacred for a Secular Age* (Cambridge: Cambridge University Press, 2012).

Sherwood, Yvonne. 'The Perverse Commitment to Overcrowding and Doubling in Genesis: Implications for Ethics and Politics', in Catherine Dell and Paul Joyce (eds), *Biblical Interpretation and Method: Essays in Honour of Professor John Barton* (Oxford: Oxford University Press, 2012), 311–28.

Sherwood, Yvonne. 'Reflections on "Modern" Biblical Studies, or Why Philip Davies is (Just a Little Bit) like Immanuel Kant', in Duncan Burns and John Rogerson (eds), *Far from Minimal: Celebrating the Work and Influence of Philip R. Davies* (London: Bloomsbury, 2012), 386–409.

Shoaf, R. A. *Milton, Poet of Duality: A Study of Semiosis in the Poetry and the Prose*, 2nd edn (Gainsville, Fla.: University of Florida Press, 1993).

Shuger, Debora K. *Sacred Rhetoric: The Christian Grand Style in the English Renaissance* (Princeton: Princeton University Press, 1988).

Shuger, Debora K. *Habits of Thought in the English Renaissance: Religion, Politics, and the Dominant Culture* (Berkeley, Calif.: University of California Press, 1990).

Shuger, Debora K. *The Renaissance Bible: Scholarship, Sacrifice, and Subjectivity* (Berkeley, Calif.: University of California Press, 1994).

Shumaker, Wayne. *The Occult Sciences in the Renaissance: A Study in Intellectual Patterns* (Berkeley, Calif.: University of California Press, 1972).

Signori, Gabriela, ed. *Dying for the Faith, Killing for the Faith: Old Testament Faith-Warriors (1 and 2 Maccabees) in Historical Perspective* (Leiden: Brill, 2012).

Simpson, James. *Burning to Read: English Fundamentalism and its Reformation Opponents* (Cambridge, Mass.: Harvard University Press, 2007).

Sims, James H. *The Bible in Milton's Epics* (Gainesville, Fla.: University of Florida Press, 1962).

Sinfield, Alan. 'Sidney and Du Bartas'. *Comparative Literature*, 27 (1975): 8–20.

Sinneme, Donald. 'Beza's View of Predestination in Historical Perspective', in Irena Backus (ed.), *Theodore de Beze (1519–1605)* (Geneva: Librarie Droz, 2007), 219–41.

Sledd, James. 'A Footnote on the Inkhorn Controversy'. *University of Texas Studies in English*, 28 (1949): 49–56.

Slights, William W. E. '"Marginal Notes that Spoile the Text": Scriptural Annotation in the English Renaissance'. *Huntington Library Quarterly*, 55/2 (1992): 255–78.

Smalley, Beryl. *The Study of the Bible in the Middle Ages*, 3rd edn (Oxford: Basil Blackwell, 1983).

Smith, Barbara, and Ursula Appelt, eds. *Write or Be Written: Early Modern Women Poets and Cultural Constraints* (Aldershot: Ashgate, 2001).

Smith, Bruce. 'Hearing Green', in Gail Kern Paster, Katherine Rowe, and Mary Floyd-Wilson (eds), *Reading the Early Modern Passions: Essays in the Cultural History of Emotion* (Philadelphia: University of Pennsylvania Press, 2004), 147–68.

Smith, Catherine Delano, and Elizabeth M. Ingram. *Maps in Bibles, 1500–1600: An Illustrated Catalogue* (Genève: Droz, 1991).

Smith, Helen. '"More swete vnto the eare / than holsome for ye mynde": Embodying Early Modern Women's Reading'. *Huntington Library Quarterly*, 73 (2010): 413–32.

Smith, Helen. '"The needle may convert more than the pen": Women and the Work of Conversion in Early Modern England', in Simon Ditchfield and Helen Smith (eds), *Conversions: Gender and Religious Change in Early Modern Europe* (Manchester: Manchester University Press, forthcoming, 2015).

Smith, Helen, and Louise Wilson, eds. *Renaissance Paratexts* (Cambridge: Cambridge University Press, 2011).

Smith, Jeremy L. *Thomas East and Music Publishing in Renaissance England* (Oxford: Oxford University Press, 2003).

Smith, Jeremy L. 'Turning a New Leaf: William Byrd, the East Music-Publishing Firm and the Jacobean Succession', in Robin Myers, Michael Harris, and Giles Mandelbrote (eds), *Music and the Book Trade from the Sixteenth to the Twentieth Century* (Newcastle and London: Oak Knoll Press and British Library, 2008), 25–43.

Smith, Lesley. *The Glossa ordinaria: The Making of a Medieval Bible Commentary* (Leiden: Brill, 2009).

Smith, Morton. *Palestinian Parties and the Politics that Shaped the Old Testament* (London: SCM, 1988).

Smith, Nigel. *Perfection Proclaimed: Language and Literature in English Radical Religion, 1640–1660* (Oxford: Oxford University Press, 1989).

Smith, Nigel. 'The Uses of Hebrew in the English Revolution', in Peter Burke and Roy Porter (eds), *Language, Self and Society: A Social History of Language* (Cambridge: Polity Press, 1991), 51–71.

Smith, Nigel. *Literature and Revolution in England, 1640–1660* (New Haven: Yale University Press, 1994).

Smith, Nigel. 'Hidden Things Brought to Light: Enthusiasm and Quaker Discourse'. *Prose Studies*, 18 (1995): 57–69.

Smith, Nigel. *Andrew Marvell: The Chameleon* (New Haven: Yale University Press, 2010).

Smith, Ruth. *Handel's Oratorios and Eighteenth-Century Thought* (Cambridge: Cambridge University Press, 1995).

Smyth, Adam. '"Shreds of holinesse": George Herbert, Little Gidding, and Cutting up Texts in Early Modern England'. *English Literary Renaissance*, 42 (2012): 452–81.

Smout, T. C. 'Born Again at Cambuslang: New Evidence on Popular Religion and Literacy in Eighteenth-Century Scotland'. *Past and Present*, 97 (1982): 114–27.

Solt, Leo. 'John Saltmarsh: New Model Army Chaplain'. *The Journal of Ecclesiastical History*, 2 (1951): 69–80.

Solt, Leo. *Saints in Arms: Puritanism and Democracy in Cromwell's Army* (Stanford, Calif.: Stanford University Press, 1959).

Sondergard, Sid. '"This Giant Has Wounded Me as Well as Thee": Reading Bunyan's Violence and/as Authority', in K. Z. Keller and G. J. Schiffhorst (eds), *The Witness of Times: Manifestations of Ideology in Seventeenth Century England* (Pittsburgh, Pa.: Duquesne University Press, 1993), 218–37.

Sowerby, Scott. *Making Toleration: The Repealers and the Glorious Revolution* (Cambridge, Mass.: Harvard University Press, 2013).

Spalding, John. *The History of the Troubles and Memorable Transactions in Scotland and England, from M.DC.XXVI. to M.DC.XLV*, 2 vols (Edinburgh: Bannatyne Club, 1828–9).

Spellman, W. M. *The Latitudinarians and the Church of England, 1660–1700* (Athens, Ga.: University of Georgia Press, 1993).

Spence, R. T. *Lady Anne Clifford* (Stroud: Sutton, 1997).

Spicer, Andrew, and Sarah Hamilton, eds. *Defining the Holy: Sacred Space in Medieval and Early Modern Europe* (Aldershot: Ashgate, 2005).

Spiller, Elizabeth. *Reading and the History of Race in the Renaissance* (Cambridge: Cambridge University Press, 2011).

Spinka, Matthew. 'Acquisition of the Codex Alexandrinus by England'. *Journal of Religion*, 16 (1936): 10–29.

Spranks, C. J. *The Life and Writings of Jeremy Taylor* (London: SPCK, 1952).

Spurr, John. '"A special kindness for dead bishops": The Church, History, and Testimony in Seventeenth-Century Protestantism'. *Huntington Library Quarterly*, 68 (2005): 313–34.

Spurr, John. '"Rational Religion" in Restoration England'. *Journal of the History of Ideas*, 49 (1988): 563–85.

Stallybrass, Peter. 'Books and Scrolls: Navigating the Bible', in Jennifer Andersen and Elizabeth Sauer (eds), *Books and Readers in Early Modern England: Material Studies* (Philadelphia: University of Pennsylvania Press, 2002), 42–79.

Starke, Sue. '"The Eternal Now": Virgilian Echoes and Miltonic Premonitions in Cowley's "Davideis"'. *Christianity and Literature*, 55 (2006): 195–219.

Steckley, John L. 'The Warrior and the Lineage: Jesuit Use of Iroquoian Images to Communicate Christianity'. *Ethnohistory*, 39 (1992): 478–509.

Stein, Arnold. *George Herbert's Lyrics* (Baltimore, Md.: Johns Hopkins University Press, 1968).

Steinmetz, David C. 'The Superiority of Pre-Critical Exegesis'. *Theology Today*, 37 (1980): 27–38.

Steinmetz, David C. 'Divided by a Common Past: The Reshaping of the Christian Exegetical Tradition in the Sixteenth Century'. *Journal of Medieval and Early Modern Studies*, 27 (1997): 245–64.

Steinmetz, David C. *Calvin in Context* (Oxford: Oxford University Press, 2010).

Steven, William. *The History of the Scottish Church, Rotterdam* (Edinburgh: Waugh & Innes, 1833).

Stevenson, David. 'The Radical Party in the Kirk, 1637–45'. *The Journal of Ecclesiastical History*, 26 (1974): 135–65.

Stewart, Laura A. M. *Urban Politics and the British Civil Wars: Edinburgh, 1617–53* (Leiden: Brill, 2006).

Stewart, Stanley. *George Herbert* (Boston: Twayne, 1986).

Stilma, Astrid J. 'King James VI and I as a Religious Writer', in Crawford Gribben and David George Mullan (eds), *Literature and the Scottish Reformation* (Aldershot: Ashgate, 2009), 127–41.

Stilma, Astrid J. '"As Warriouris in Ane Camp": The Image of King James VI as a Protestant Crusader', in Kevin J. McGinley and Nicola Royan (eds), *The Apparelling of Truth: Literature and Literary Culture in the Reign of James VI* (Cambridge: Cambridge Scholars Publishing, 2010), 241–51.

Stolzenberg, Daniel. 'John Spencer and the Perils of Sacred Philology'. *Past and Present*, 214 (2012): 129–63.

Straka, Gerald. 'The Final Phase of Divine Right Theory in England, 1688–1702'. *English Historical Review*, 77 (1962): 638–58.

Stranahan, Brainerd P. 'Bunyan's Special Talent: Biblical Texts as "Events" in *Grace Abounding* and *The Pilgrim's Progress'. English Literary Renaissance*, 11 (1981): 329–43.

Strauss, Gerald. *Sixteenth-Century Germany: Its Topography and Topographers* (Madison, Wis.: University of Wisconsin Press, 1959).

Streete, Adrian. *Protestantism and Drama in Early Modern England* (Cambridge: Cambridge University Press, 2009).

Streete, Adrian. 'Frances Quarles' Early Poetry and the Discourses of Jacobean Spenserianism'. *Journal of the Northern Renaissance*, 1 (2009): 88–108.

Strier, Richard. *Love Known: Theology and Experience in George Herbert's Poetry* (Chicago: University of Chicago Press, 1983).

Summers, Joseph H. *George Herbert: His Religion and Art* (London: Chatto & Windus, 1954).

Sutcliffe, Adam. *Judaism and Enlightenment* (Cambridge: Cambridge University Press, 2003).

Sypherd, Wilbur Owen. *Jephthah and his Daughter: A Study in Comparative Literature* (Newark, Del.: University of Delaware, 1948).

Tadmor, Naomi. *The Social Universe of the English Bible: Scripture, Society, and Culture in Early Modern England* (Cambridge: Cambridge University Press, 2010).

Talmage, Frank. *Apples of Gold*, ed. Barry Dov Walfish (Toronto: Pontifical Institute of Medieval Studies, 1999).

Targoff, Ramie. *Common Prayer: The Language of Public Devotion in Early Modern England* (Chicago: University of Chicago Press, 2001).

Tavard, George H. *The Seventeenth Century Tradition: A Study in Recusant Thought* (Leiden: Brill, 1978).

Taylor, Charles. *Sources of the Self: The Making of the Modern Identity* (Cambridge: Cambridge University Press, 1992).

Temperley, Nicholas. *The Music of the English Parish Church* (Cambridge: Cambridge University Press, 1979).

Tillyard, E. M. W. *The Elizabethan World Picture* (Cambridge: Cambridge University Press, 1943).

Todd, Margo. 'Humanists, Puritans and the Spiritualised Household'. *Church History*, 49 (1980): 18–34.

Todd, Margo. *The Culture of Protestantism in Early Modern Scotland* (New Haven: Yale University Press, 2002).

Toomer, G. J. *Eastern Wisedome and Learning: The Study of Arabic in Seventeenth-Century England* (Oxford: Clarendon Press, 1995).

Toomer, G. J. *John Selden: A Life in Scholarship*, 2 vols (Oxford: Oxford University Press, 2009).

Toorn, Karel van der. *Scribal Culture and the Making of the Hebrew Bible* (Cambridge, Mass.: Harvard University Press, 2007).

Toorn, Karel van der, Bob Becking, and Pieter W. van der Horst, eds. *Dictionary of Deities and Demons in the Bible*, 2nd edn (Leiden: Brill, 1999).

Trench, Richard Chevenix. *On the Authorized Version of the New Testament* (New York: Redfield, 1858).

Tribble, Evelyn B. *Margins and Marginality: The Printed Page in Early Modern England* (Charlottesville, Va.: University Press of Virginia, 1993).

Turner, H. L. 'Some Small Tapestries of Judith with the Head of Holofernes: Should they be called Sheldon?' *Textile History*, 41 (2010): 161–81.

Tuttle, Elizabeth. 'Biblical Reference in the Political Pamphlets of the Levellers and Milton, 1638–1654', in David Armitage, Armand Himy, and Quentin Skinner (eds), *Milton and Republicanism* (Cambridge: Cambridge University Press, 1995), 63–81.

Tuve, Rosemond. *A Reading of George Herbert* (Chicago: University of Chicago Press, 1952).

Tyacke, Nicholas, ed. *The History of the University of Oxford*, iv. *Seventeenth-Century Oxford* (Oxford: Clarendon Press, 1997).

Underdown, David. *Fire from Heaven: Life in an English Town in the Seventeenth Century* (London: HarperCollins, 1992).

Underwood, Lucy. 'Youth, Religious Identity, and Autobiography at the English Colleges in Rome and Valladolid, 1592–1685'. *The Historical Journal*, 55 (2012): 349–74.

Vallance, Edward, and Harald Braun, eds. *Contexts of Conscience in Early Modern Europe, 1500–1700* (Houndmills: Palgrave Macmillan, 2004).

Van Houdt, Toon. 'Word Histories and Beyond: Fraud and Deceit in Earl Modern Times', in Van Houdt, Jan L. de Jong, Zoran Kwak, Marijke Spies, and Marc van Vaeck (eds), *On the Edge of Truth and Honesty: Principles and Strategies of Fraud and Deceit in the Early Modern Period* (Leiden: Brill, 2002), 1–32.

Veldman, Ilyja M. *Images for the Eye and Soul: Function and Meaning in Netherlandish Prints (1450–1650)* (Leiden: Primavera Pers, 2006).

Vendler, Helen. *The Poetry of George Herbert* (Cambridge, Mass.: Harvard University Press, 1975).

Verschuur, Mary. *Politics or Religion? The Reformation in Perth, 1540–1570* (Edinburgh: Dunedin Academic Press, 2006).

Vicars, Arthur, ed. *Index to the Prerogative Wills of Ireland, 1536–1810* (Dublin: Edward Ponsonby, 1897).

Visser, Arnoud. *Reading Augustine in the Reformation: The Flexibility of Intellectual Authority in Europe 1500–1620* (Oxford: Oxford University Press, 2011).

Voak, Nigel. 'Richard Hooker and the Principle of *Sola Scriptura*'. *Journal of Theological Studies*, 59 (2008): 96–139.

Vos, Alvin. 'Humanistic Standards of Diction in the Inkhorn Controversy'. *Studies in Philology*, 73 (1976): 376–96.

Wabuda, Susan. 'Bishop John Longland's Mandate to his Clergy, 1535'. *The Library*, 6th ser. 13 (1991): 255–61.

Wabuda, Susan. 'Bishops and the Provision of Homilies, 1520 to 1547'. *The Sixteenth Century Journal*, 25 (1994): 551–66.

Wabuda, Susan. 'The Woman with the Rock: The Controversy on Women and Bible Reading', in Susan Wabuda and Caroline Litzenberger (eds), *Belief and Practice in Reformation England: A Tribute to Patrick Collinson from his Students* (Aldershot: Ashgate, 1998), 40–59.

Wabuda, Susan. *Preaching during the English Reformation* (Cambridge: Cambridge University Press, 2002).

Wabuda, Susan. 'Triple-Deckers and Eagle Lecterns: Church Furniture for the Book in Late Medieval and Early Modern England', in R. N. Swanson (ed.), *The Church and the Book, Studies in Church History*, 38 (2004): 143–52.

Wabuda, Susan. 'The Reformation of the English Church under Henry VIII', in Arthur L. Schwarz (ed.), *Vivat Rex! An Exhibition Commemorating the 500th Anniversary of the Accession of Henry VIII* (New York: Grolier Club, 2009), 30–44.

Waldron, Jennifer. *Reformations of the Body: Idolatry, Sacrifice, and Early Modern Theater* (New York: Palgrave Macmillan, 2013).

Walsham, Alexandra. '"Frantick Hacket": Prophecy, Insanity and the Elizabethan Puritan Movement'. *The Historical Journal*, 41 (1998): 27–66.

Walsham, Alexandra. *Providence in Early Modern England* (Oxford: Oxford University Press, 1999).

Walsham, Alexandra. 'Unclasping the Book? Post-Reformation English Catholicism and the Vernacular Bible'. *Journal of British Studies*, 42 (2003): 141–66.

Walsham, Alexandra. 'Angels and Idols in England's Long Reformation', in Peter Marshall and Alexandra Walsham (eds), *Angels in the Early Modern World* (Cambridge: Cambridge University Press, 2006), 134–67.

Walsham, Alexandra. 'Beads, Books and Bare Ruined Choirs: Transmutations of Catholic Ritual Life in Protestant England', in Benjamin J. Kaplan, Bob Moore, Henk van Nierop, and Judith Pollmann (eds), *Catholic Communities in Protestant States: Britain and the Netherlands c.1570–1720* (Manchester: Manchester University Press, 2009), 103–22.

Watt, Melinda, and Andrew Morrall, eds. *English Embroidery in the Metropolitan Museum of Art, 1580–1700: 'Twixt Art and Nature'* (New Haven: Yale University Press, 2008).

Watt, Tessa. *Cheap Print and Popular Piety* (Cambridge: Cambridge University Press, 1993).

Watts, John. *Scalan: The Forbidden College, 1716–1799* (East Linton: Tuckwell, 1999).

Watts, Michael. *The Dissenters: From the Reformation to the French Revolution* (Oxford: Oxford University Press, 1985).

Watts, Pauline Moffitt. 'The European Religious Worldview and its Influence on Mapping', in David Woodward (ed.), *The History of Cartography*, iii. *Cartography in the European Renaissance* (Chicago: University of Chicago Press, 2007), 382–400.

Weber-Möckl, Annette. *Das Recht des Königs, der über euch herrschen soll: Studien zu I Samuel, 11ff. in der Literatur des frühen Neuzeit* (Berlin: Duncker & Humblot, 1986).

Weil, Rachel J. 'The Politics of Legitimacy: Women and the Warming-Pan Scandal', in Lois G. Schwoerer (ed.), *The Revolution of 1688–9: Changing Perspectives* (Cambridge: Cambridge University Press, 1992), 65–82.

Weinberg, Joanna. 'Invention and Convention: Jewish and Christian Critique of the Jewish Fixed Calendar'. *Jewish History*, 14 (2000): 317–30.

Wells-Cole, Anthony. *Art and Decoration in Elizabethan and Jacobean England: The Influence of Continental Prints, 1558–1625* (New Haven: Yale University Press, 1997).

West, William N. 'Reading Rooms: Architecture and Agency in the Houses of Michel de Montaigne and Nicholas Bacon'. *Comparative Literature*, 56 (2004): 111–29.

Westcott, Brooke Foss. *The Bible in the Church: A Popular Account of the Collection and Reception of the Holy Scriptures in the Christian Churches* (London and Cambridge: Macmillan & Co., 1866).

Wheatley, Chloe. *Epic, Epitome, and the Early Modern Historical Imagination* (Farnham: Ashgate, 2011).

White, Micheline, ed. *English Women, Religion, and Textual Production, 1500–1625* (Farnham: Ashgate, 2011).

White, Peter. *Predestination, Policy and Polemic: Conflict and Consensus in the English Civil War* (Cambridge: Cambridge University Press, 2002).

White, Paul Whitfield. *Theatre and Reformation: Protestantism, Patronage, and Playing in Tudor England* (Cambridge: Cambridge University Press, 1992).

White, Paul Whitfield. 'The *Pammachius* Affair at Christ's College, Cambridge, in 1545', in Peter Happé and Wim Hüsken (eds), *Interludes and Early Modern Society: Studies in Gender, Power and Theatricality* (Amsterdam: Rodopi, 2007), 261–90.

White, Paul Whitfield. *Drama and Religion in English Provincial Society, 1485–1660* (Cambridge: Cambridge University Press, 2008).

Wilcher, Robert. '"Adventurous song" or "presumptuous folly": The Problem of "utterance" in John Milton's *Paradise Lost* and Lucy Hutchinson's *Order and Disorder'. Seventeenth Century*, 21 (2006): 304–14.

Wilcher, Robert. 'Lucy Hutchinson and Genesis: Paraphrase, Epic, Romance'. *English*, 59 (2010): 25–42.

Wilcox, Helen. *1611: Authority, Gender and the Word in Early Modern England* (Oxford: Wiley Blackwell, 2014).

Williams, George H. *Wilderness and Paradise in Christian Thought* (New York: Harper, 1962).

Williams, N. P. *The Ideas of the Fall and of Original Sin* (London: Longman, 1927).

Williams, Nicholas. *I bprionta i leabhar: na protastúin agus prós na Gaeilge 1567–1724* (Dublin: An Clóchomhar, 1986).

Williams, Wes. *Pilgrimage and Narrative in the French Renaissance: 'The Undiscovered Country'* (Oxford: Clarendon Press, 1998).

Williamson, H. G. M. *The Book Called Isaiah: Deutero-Isaiah's Role in Composition and Redaction* (Oxford: Clarendon Press, 1994).

Willis, Jonathan. *Church Music and Protestantism in Post-Reformation England: Discourses, Sites and Identities* (Farnham: Ashgate, 2010).

Wilson, Ruth Mack. *Anglican Chant and Chanting in England, Scotland and America, 1660 to 1820* (Oxford: Clarendon Press, 1996).

Wiseman, Susan. *Conspiracy and Virtue: Women, Writing, and Politics in Seventeenth-Century England* (New York: Oxford University Press, 2006).

Wistreich, Richard. 'Musical Materials and Cultural Spaces'. *Renaissance Studies*, 26 (2012): 1–12.

Withers, Charles W. J. 'Place and the "Spatial Turn" in Geography and in History'. *Journal of the History of Ideas*, 70 (2009): 637–58.

Witt, Ronald G. *In the Footsteps of the Ancients: The Origins of Humanism from Lovato to Bruni* (Leiden: Brill, 2000).

Wittreich, Joseph. 'Milton's Transgressive Maneuvers: Receptions (Then and Now) and the Sexual Politics of *Paradise Lost*', in Stephen B. Dobranski and John P. Rumrich (eds), *Milton and Heresy* (Cambridge: Cambridge University Press, 1998), 244–66.

Wodrow, Robert. *Analecta: or Materials for a History of Remarkable Providences, Mostly Relating to Scotch Ministers and Christians*, ed. Matthew Leishman, 4 vols (Glasgow: Maitland Club, 1842–3).

Wood, *Athenae Oxonienses*, ed. Philip Bliss, 4 vols (Oxford: J. H. Parker, 1813–20).

Wood, Thomas. *English Casuistical Divinity during the Seventeenth Century: With Special Reference to Jeremy Taylor* (London, SPCK, 1952).

Wooding, Lucy. *Rethinking Catholicism in Reformation England* (Oxford: Clarendon Press, 2000).

Wooding, Lucy. *Henry VIII* (London: Routledge, 2009).

Wormald, Jenny. 'Reformed and Godly Scotland?', in T. M. Devine and Jenny Wormald (eds), *The Oxford Handbook of Modern Scottish History* (Oxford: Oxford University Press, 2012), 204–19.

Yeoman, Louise A. 'Heart-Work: Emotion, Empowerment and Authority in Covenanting Times' (Ph.D. thesis, University of St Andrews, 1991).

Young, John. 'The Covenanters and the Scottish Parliament, 1639–51: The Rule of the Godly and the "Second Scottish Reformation"', in Elizabethanne Boran and Crawford Gribben (eds), *Enforcing Reformation in Ireland and Scotland, 1550–1700* (Aldershot: Ashgate, 2006), 131–58.

Zagorin, Perez. *Ways of Lying: Dissimulation, Persecution and Conformity in Early Modern Europe* (Cambridge, Mass.: Harvard University Press, 1990).

Zeitlin, S. 'Jewish Apocryphal Literature'. *Jewish Quarterly Review*, NS 40 (1950): 223–50.

Zim, Rivkah. *English Metrical Psalms: Poetry as Praise and Prayer, 1535–1601* (Cambridge: Cambridge University Press, 1987).

Zook, Melinda S. *Protestantism, Politics, and Women in Britain, 1660–1714* (Basingstoke: Palgrave Macmillan, 2013).

INDEX

Abbot, George (Archbishop of
    Canterbury) 143, 262 n. 5, 305, 376,
    380, 521, 622
Abarbanel, Isaac (Abravanel) 395
Acosta, José de, *Naturall and moral historie of
    the East and West Indies* 361–2
Act of Supremacy (1559) 166, 170
Act of Uniformity (1559) 166, 170
Acts of the Apostles 35, 281, 345, 358, 361
    n. 59, 410, 630
Adam and Eve 6, 62, 74, 107, 155, 202, 210, 214,
    218–22, 279, 313, 391, 393, 402–4, 463,
    484, 486, 489, 491–2, 494–6, 549–50,
    553–8, 575, 592, 595, 620, 628, 650
Adams, Bernard (Bishop of Limerick) 491
Admonition to the Parliament (1572) 280
Admonition Controversy 167
Adrichomius, Christianus, *Theatrum terrae
    sanctae* 12
Act for the Advancement of True Religion
    (1543) 4, 36
Africa 361
Africanus, Julius 184
Aggadot 539
Agnosticism 614
Alabaster, William 356–7
Alcuin 134
Alexander the Great 181
Allen, William (cardinal) 5, 355
Allin, Richard 189–90
Ambrose, St 221
Ames, William (Puritan) 310
    Marrow of Sacred Divinity 548
Amico, Bernardino (Franciscan) 198–9
Amman, Jost 582
Anabaptists 147, 238, 241, 245–6, 398 n. 8
Andrewes, Lancelot 120, 150, 151–2, 155,
    161–2, 186, 376, 461
    Tortura torti 377

Anglicans and Anglicanism 115, 239–40,
    244–6, 249, 251–2, 325, 345, 358,
    367–8, 398, 434–6, 439, 443, 445, 447,
    620, 657
Anne of Denmark 462–3
Annesley, Arthur, 1st Earl of
    Anglesey 486, 624
Antiquarianism 1, 198, 200–1
Antinomianism 408–9, 600, 608–10
anti-trinitarianism 194, 249
Antony, St 351–2, 356
apocalypse 51, 1467, 276, 443, 529,
Apocrypha 102, 114, 119–20, 122, 131–47,
    243, 249, 215, 276–7, 281, 321, 343,
    346, 358 n. 44, 546, 589
apostles 56, 58–9, 60–1, 64, 78, 93, 100, 142–3,
    169, 174, 199, 207, 209, 211, 313, 404,
    406, 431–2, 434–6, 501, 507–8, 511, 600,
    618, 634; *see also individual entries*
Apostles' Creed 247–9, 329
Apsley, Sir Allen 485
Aquila of Sinope 124
Aquinas, Thomas 164 n. 1, 165 n. 7, 174
    n. 60, 625
Arianism 59, 238, 552
Ariosto, *Orlando furioso* 546
Aristophanes 500
Aristotle 165, 488, 500, 549, 585, 616, 648
    Poetics 453, 498, 500–1, 504–7, 516
Arminians and Arminianism 103, 216, 238,
    249, 368, 552
Arndt, Johann, *Wahres Christenthum* 106
Arnold, Matthew 469
Articles of Faith 314, 335
Articles of Inquiry (Visitation
    Articles) 257–8, 262–4, 266–7, 269
Articles of Religion
    Forty-two Articles of Religion (1552) 139
    Ten Articles of Religion (1536) 139

Articles of Religion (*cont.*)
  Thirty-nine Articles of Religion (1571) 133,
      139–40, 142, 144, 277, 437, 439
  Thirty-one Articles of Religion (1648) 144
Arundel, Thomas (Archbishop of
      Canterbury) 3
Ascham, Roger, *The Scholemaster* 498
Ashley, Thomas 34
Askew, Anne 484
Assheton, John 616
Astell, Mary 484
astrology 8, 103, 106, 180 n. 19
Astruc, Jean, *Conjectures* 652
Athanasius of Athens 133
atheism 108, 238, 350, 406, 420, 561, 563,
      601, 613–25
Atkyns, Sir Robert 647
Augustine, St 60, 66, 68, 74, 77, 117, 134,
      152–3, 214, 216, 291–2, 296, 308,
      351–3, 356–7, 555, 562, 564–5, 573–6,
      628, 645
  City of God 67
  Confessions 351–2, 568, 627
  Contra cresconium 59, 61
  Contra mendacium 603–5
  De doctrina Christiana 154, 550, 604–5
  De mendacio 603
  De utilitate credendi 152, 155
Augustinians (monastic order) 199
Aylett, Robert 488
Aylmer, John 146
Aylsebury, Thomas (preacher) 310–11

Bacon, Francis 247
  The Advancement of Learning 375–6
  Of Atheism 621
Bacon, Nicholas 584 n. 26
Bacon, Robert 99, 104
Badius, Conrad (printer) 41–2
Baillie, Robert (Scottish minister) 326–7
Bainbridge, John 178
Baker, Sir Richard 12
  Chronicle of the Kings of England 416
Baker, Thomas 191
  Reflections upon Learning 191–2
Baldung, Hans (artist) 146
Baldwin, William, *The Sayings of the
      Wise* 585, 588

Bale, John 50
  Yet a Course at the Romyshe Foxe 85
Bancroft, Richard (Archbishop of
      Canterbury) 5, 263, 266, 268, 378,
      459 n. 9
  Dangerous Positions and Proceedings 241
baptism 40 n. 11, 57, 59 n. 16, 61, 100, 206,
      262, 267, 279, 283, 358, 361, 405, 435
Baptists 235, 238, 246, 249–50, 406, 408
Barbier, Nicholas (printer) 42–3, 46–8
Barclay, William 385, 395
  Contra monarchomachos 391
Barker, Christopher (printer) 228
Barker, Robert (printer) 6, 592, 594
Barlowe, Ralph (preacher) 305–7, 311–12, 314
Barlow, Thomas 179
Barlow, William (bishop) 71, 140,
      268, 376–7
  Answer to a Catholicke English-man 377
Barnes, Robert (Augustinian prior) 352
Barrow, Henry 142, 241
Barthélemy de Loches, Nicolas 505
  Christus xilonicus 503–10, 512
Battiferra, Laura 288 n. 7
Baxter, Richard 103–4, 145, 358, 608
  The Unreasonableness of Infidelity 250
Bayle, Pierre 251, 642, 651, 653–8
  *Dictionnaire historique et
      critique* 563, 651–2
Beaumont, Francis (playwright) 467
Becke, Edmund 133, 139
Bede 134, 355
Bedell, William 332–3, 343–4, 346–8
Bedford, Arthur 194
  Animadversions 194
  *Scripture Chronology Demonstrated by
      Astronomical Calculations* 194
Beham, Sebald, *Biblische figuren* 582
Behm, Martin 145 n. 43
Behn, Aphra 438, 444, 623
Belgic Confession (1561) 139
Bellarmine, Robert (Jesuit) 11, 121 n. 20,
      138–9, 143, 388–9
Bentley Bibles 231
Bentley, Richard 119
  The Folly of Atheism 623
Bernard, Edward 179
Béroalde, Matthieu 180

Beza, Theodore 39, 41, 48–50, 89, 211, 341
　　n. 36, 650–1, 635–8
Abraham sacrifant 499
Bible
　circulation of the 3–6, 8, 15, 19, 38, 50–1,
　　115, 227, 230, 233, 257–9, 261, 263, 266,
　　272, 274, 283–4, 285, 288–9, 318–20,
　　330, 335, 347–8, 361–3, 367, 383
　interpretation of the 2–3, 5–6, 8, 10–14,
　　20–1, 28, 39, 41–2, 44–6, 48–9, 55–6,
　　59–60, 71–2, 74, 83, 92–3, 101, 113–15,
　　120, 136, 149, 151–62, 197–8, 200–1,
　　203, 212, 218, 228, 240–2, 244, 247,
　　249–50, 259, 268, 273, 285, 289, 303,
　　307–12, 319, 367–9, 371–2, 374, 378,
　　380, 382–5, 393, 399, 415, 426, 437,
　　453, 461–3, 468, 473, 484, 502, 519–20,
　　533, 536–9, 542, 550, 552, 555, 557,
　　561–2, 564–7, 569, 573–6, 595, 598,
　　606–7, 634, 636, 644–6
　languages of the 15, 26, 344, 363, 470
　manuscript copies of the 3, 19, 25–6,
　　117–18, 121–5, 127–9, 133, 184, 210,
　　233–4, 344, 349
　marginalia 43
　misinterpretation and mistranslation of
　　the 21, 31, 99–102, 106–7, 142, 211,
　　213, 244, 249–50, 253, 470
　paratextual features of the 10, 14, 39, 41–9,
　　52, 55–7, 62, 115, 123, 203, 228, 355,
　　463, 565
　　chronologies 11, 51, 115, 176–81, 183–6,
　　　189–94, 227
　　cross-references 42–3, 52, 59
　　genealogies 44, 55, 62, 64, 69
　　glosses and glossaries 21, 42, 45, 52, 58,
　　　72–4, 81, 91–2, 121–2, 157, 227, 229
　　Glossa ordinaria 78, 573–6
　　illustrations and diagrams 41–4, 62, 64,
　　　71, 135, 137, 140, 227, 229
　　indexes and concordances 42, 55, 69,
　　　140, 228–9, 284
　　maps and charts 41, 43–4, 50–1, 55,
　　　69, 71, 114, 140, 197–9, 203, 207, 227,
　　　229, 284
　　marginal notes 41–6, 48, 50, 52, 55, 57–8,
　　　68, 69, 71–2, 80–2, 86, 101, 107, 139–42,
　　　227–30, 233, 268, 284, 355, 377–8, 473

reading the 2, 5, 8, 10, 12–13, 24, 27, 32,
　　35–6, 39, 42–3, 45–6, 52, 55, 68–9,
　　69 n. 29, 72, 80–1, 95, 102, 114, 144,
　　212–13, 218, 224–5, 229–30, 233,
　　235, 258, 263–6, 269–70, 272–82,
　　284–5, 287, 289–90, 293, 301, 321,
　　323, 326–30, 351, 354–9, 363–4, 398,
　　452, 461–2, 472, 483–5, 495, 537, 577,
　　595, 650
　private 3–4, 24–5, 27–8, 36, 38, 41, 46,
　　132, 241, 246, 259, 264–5, 268, 270,
　　319, 350, 352–3, 592
　public 36, 81, 142, 145, 258–9, 264–5,
　　268, 270, 319, 326–8, 466, 481, 582
reception of the 15, 39, 51, 147, 224, 226,
　　261, 263, 452, 470–2
translators and translation of the 2–4, 6,
　　15, 19–21, 25, 27–8, 30, 31–5, 37, 40–6,
　　49, 52, 54–6, 59–60, 62, 64, 66–8,
　　71, 74, 76–81, 88–91, 93–6, 98–102,
　　107–9, 113–15, 120–9, 137–8, 141,
　　210, 217, 224–30, 232–3, 235, 243–4,
　　249, 257, 259, 261, 263–4, 268, 272,
　　284, 288, 310, 319–21, 332–4, 337, 351,
　　355, 358–9, 361–3, 367, 371, 377–8,
　　383, 435, 452, 456–9, 461–2, 464, 466,
　　468, 470–3, 475, 477–80, 482, 534,
　　546–7, 550, 561–3, 565, 569, 571–2,
　　628–31, 639
versions of the American Standard
　　Version 475
　Bassandyne 228
　Bishops' 5–6, 37, 51–2, 72, 90, 94–5,
　　140–1, 227, 267–8, 284, 459, 473,
　　475–6, 480–1, 569, 571–2, 630–1
　Bomberg Rabbinic 148
　Breeches 6
　Bug 6
　Clementine 139, 141
　Coverdale 4, 20, 95, 136–7, 476, 480,
　　482, 547, 630–1
　Douay-Rheims 5–6, 21, 46, 52, 54–62,
　　66–9, 85–6, 88–9, 91–6, 133, 141,
　　243–4, 355–6, 358, 459, 473, 481, 569,
　　571–2, 630–1
　Dutch 135, 144, 579
　English Revised Version 475
　French (Neuchâtel) 136

Bible (*cont.*)

Gaelic 259, 320, 332–4, 337, 339–9, 363

Geneva 5–6, 20–1, 38–52, 56, 71–4,
78–82, 89–90, 99, 140–5, 161–2, 225,
227–30, 233, 267–8, 284, 291, 319–21,
341 n. 36, 353, 377–8, 399, 410, 413,
459, 471–3, 477–8 n. 37, 480, 482,
550, 569, 571–2, 592, 595, 630–1,
634–5, 637

Good News 479

Great 4, 21, 23, 25, 35–7, 39, 41, 46, 72,
85–6, 90, 100, 137, 140, 227–8, 273–4,
279, 282, 473, 630–1, 658

Gutenburg 3

King James 4, 6, 21, 24, 37–8, 52, 54–7,
59, 60–2, 64, 66–9, 72–4, 76, 80–2,
98–102, 106–7, 109, 118–9, 128–9, 133,
140–1, 143, 150, 162, 209, 212, 214–16,
221, 224–7, 229–31, 245, 268, 270,
284, 291, 320–1, 343, 346, 351, 358,
371–2, 378, 399, 413–14, 429, 433, 435,
437, 445, 447, 452, 455–82, 550, 553,
569–73, 629–31, 637–8, 657

Judas 6

Lithuanian 363

Luther 4, 135, 582

Massachusetts 363

Matthew 4, 21, 35, 45, 137, 228,
473, 630–1

New International Version 475

New Living Translation 475

Printers' 6

Sixtine 139, 185

Taverner's 137, 139

Thumb 257

Tigurine 106

Turkish 344, 363

Tyndale 4, 19, 28, 33–4, 37, 39, 45, 136,
227, 291, 630–4, 638

Vulgate 3, 19–20, 26–7, 41, 54, 57, 59,
66–7, 76–7, 82, 84, 86, 88, 90–2, 94,
113, 117–18, 123, 133, 136–9, 141, 221,
224–5, 272, 274, 385, 506, 562, 569–70,
573–6, 616, 631

Wicked 6, 209

Wycliffe 24–5, 76–8, 95 n. 34, 134, 291,
472, 478, 630

Zurich 135–6

see also Apocrypha; biblical imagery; biblical
paraphrase; Christology; Gospels;
Hermeneutics; Parables; Pentateuch;
Polyglot; Psalters; Septuagint; *sola
scriptura. For books and persons of the
Bible, see individual entries.*

biblical exegesis, *see* Bible, Interpretation of

biblical imagery 3, 10, 43–4, 577–96

biblical paraphrase 20, 83, 141, 146, 212,
264, 273, 275, 283, 285, 287–8, 293,
306, 373–4, 378–9, 382, 388, 394, 438,
451–3, 484–6, 489–92, 494–7, 544,
547, 633

Bill, John (printer) 6

Bilson, Thomas 375–6, 378

Bingham, Sir Richard 341

Birck, Sixt 499, 503

Bishops' book 273

Bladus, Antonius 505 n. 37

Blake, William 478

Bloody Assizes 438

Bochart, Samuel 198
  Geographiae sacrae 12

Bodin, Jean 180

Bodley, John 38

Boethius 168

Böhme, Jakob 105, 109

Bois, John 118–22, 125–6, 128–9, 141
  Collatio 120–1

Bolton, Robert (Puritan) 379

Booker, John, *No mercurius aquaticus* 416

The Book of Certaine Canons (1571,
  1604) 265–7

Book of Common Prayer 40, 114, 139–40,
  142, 145, 147, 166, 168, 263, 267–9,
  274–5, 277, 280–5, 287–8, 293, 295,
  326, 336–7, 447, 528, 616
  Gaelic 259, 337, 341–2, 344–5, 347–8

Book of Sports 79

Books of Hours 26–7

Boleyn, Anne 34, 433

Bomelius, Henricus, *The Summe of the Holye
  Scripture* 31

Bonfrère, Jacques 200 n. 17

Boyd, Zachery (Scottish minister) 324–5

Boyle, Robert 251, 259, 332, 340, 344–7, 363
  *Some Considerations Touching the Style of
  the H. Scriptures* 237, 610

Boys, John 305
 *Exposition of Al the Principal Scriptures .
    . .* 283
 *Exposition of the Dominical Epistles and
    Gospels* 281
 An Exposition of the Last Psalme 312, 471
Brady, Hugh (bishop) 334
Bramhall, John, *Serpent salve* 423
Branthwaite, William 141
Bray, William 405
Brès, Guy de (martyr) 139
Breu, Jörg (the Elder) 579
Breviaries 275
Bridge, William
 Truth of the Times Vindicated 420–1
Bridges, John 167
*A Briefe Discourse Containing Certaine
    Reasons Why Catholicks Refuse to Goe
    to Church* (1601) 294
Bright, John 478
Brinsley, John 610
Brisson, Barnabé 121
Broughton, Hugh 6, 131, 180–1, 341 n. 43,
    473, 477, 482
 *A Censure of the Late Translation for our
    Churches* 6, 470
 *Epistle to the Learned Nobilitie of
    England* 470
Browne, Sir Thomas 151, 218, 221, 478
Brownism 326–7
Brylinger, Nicholas 504, 510, 513
 *Several Comedies and Tragedies Taken from
    the Old and New Testament* 503–6
Bucer, Martin 499–504, 506, 508, 516
Buchanan, George 373, 383, 499, 502
 Baptistes, sive calumnia 499, 513
 Jephthes, sive votum 498, 513–16
 De Jure Regni apud Scotos 372–3, 375
Buckmaster, William 30
Budé, Guillaume 121
Bulkeley, Edward 86
Bullinger, Heinrich 8, 48, 172, 293, 578
 Lucretia und Brutus 499
Bunny, Edmund 356
Bunyan, John 146, 230, 354 n. 21, 400, 453,
    478, 482, 533–45, 619
 The Acceptable Sacrifice 534, 542–3

 *Grace Abounding to the Chief of
    Sinners* 534, 538–9, 543–4
 The Life and Death of Mr. Badman 534,
    542–4, 619–20
 The Pilgrim's Progress 533, 619
Burchard of Mt. Sion 201–2
Burgess, Anthony 518
Burke, Edmund 415
Burnet, Gilbert 432, 434–6, 438, 445
 *Bishop Burnet's History of His Own
    Time* 429, 432
 The Protestant's Companion 432–3, 436
Burnet, Thomas 192
 Archaeologiae philosophiae 190–1
 Telluris theoria sacra 190
Burroughs, Jeremiah 234
 The Glorious Name of God 419
Burton, Henry (minister) 143
Burton, Robert 478, 614
 Anatomy of Melancholy 623
Butler, Samuel
 Hudibras 418–19
Buxtorf, Johannes (the elder) 11, 121
Byfield, Nicholas 520
Byrd, William 296, 298–9

Cajetan, Tommaso (cardinal) 135
Calamy, Edmund 544
 *The Noble-Mans Patterne Of True and Reall
    Thankfulnesse* 418, 425
Calfhill, James (clergyman) 145
Calvin, John 5, 12, 38, 40–1, 44, 46–9, 51,
    58–9, 136, 156, 158, 160–2, 167, 172,
    203, 216, 218, 227, 291–2, 296, 347,
    422, 471, 646, 649–50, 509, 538, 578,
    595, 622
 Commentary upon Romans 47
 Commentaries on Isaiah 51, 156–8,
    160, 161
 Institutes of the Christian Religion 8,
    47, 172
 Sermons on Deuteronomy 205–6
Calvinists and Calvinism 20, 49, 52, 59, 131,
    140, 142, 147, 160, 179, 198, 243, 250,
    252, 265, 268, 318, 329, 336, 368, 405,
    464, 515, 536, 538, 552, 622, 636
Calvinus judizans 157

Cambridge, University of 6, 29–30, 102–3, 108–9, 118–19, 141, 178–9, 190–2, 245, 333–4, 336, 339, 341, 510, 512, 515
Camden, William 178–9
Camerarius, Johannes 49
Cameron, Richard (preacher) 329
Campbell, Archibald, Earl of Argyll 335
Canini, Angelo 121
Canne, John 143
Cant, Andrew (Scottish minister) 326
Cappel, Jacques 179
Carew, Sir Nicholas 352–3
Carion, Johann 179 n. 16
Carswell, John 335–6, 347, 349
Cartwright, Thomas 5 n. 16, 89, 91, 93, 142, 166–7, 241
    Answere to the Preface of the Rhemish Testament 88
    A Confutation of the Rhemists Translation 88
Cary, Lucius, Viscount Falkland 242
Cary, Patrick 534
Cary, Robert (antiquary) 176–7, 181, 183–5, 189, 194
Caryl, Joseph, *An Exposition . . . upon the Three First Chapters of the Book of Job* 418, 424–5
Casaubon, Isaac 120–1, 249
Casaubon, Meric 249
Case, John, *The Praise of Musicke* (1586) 295
Castellio, Sebastian 104, 107
catechism 12, 115, 230, 257, 274, 283, 318, 336–7, 339, 344–5, 347–8, 361–4
cathedrals 24, 36, 193, 262, 265, 277, 280, 282, 304, 336, 339–40
Catholics and Catholicism 2, 10, 12–13, 20–1, 50, 54, 57–61, 64, 66, 68–9, 79, 84–6, 88–93, 95–7, 114–15, 118, 122, 125, 127, 129, 131, 133, 134, 136–8, 141–2, 147, 151, 157, 162, 181, 197, 199, 200, 207, 209, 239–40, 242–4, 246, 249, 252–3, 259, 261, 288, 292, 294–6, 299, 301, 318, 323, 330, 333, 354–8, 361–2, 367, 369, 371, 374, 378–9, 385, 388, 406, 415, 420, 425, 429–39, 442–3, 452, 503, 511, 518, 562, 573, 578–9, 614, 621, 654, 657

Catiline 493
Cavendish, Jane 484, 495
Cavendish, Margaret 484
Cecil, Robert, 1st Earl of Salisbury 340
Cecil, William, Lord Burghley 340
Chaderton, Laurence 333
Chaldee Paraphrase 570–1
chapels 25, 31, 103, 273, 277, 280, 444–5
Chapman, George 457–8
Charles I 103, 118, 122, 245, 258, 261, 270, 321, 326, 359, 379, 396, 398–400, 412–16, 418–24, 426–7, 435, 494, 496, 608
    Eikon Basilike 496
Charles II 184, 329, 344, 389, 391, 426, 495–6
Charnock, Stephen, *Several Discourses upon the Existence and Attributes of God* 622–3
Charteris, Henry (bookseller) 320
Cheke, Sir John 84
Chemnitz, Martin 121
Cheynell, Francis (Presbyterian) 244
Chillingworth, William 115, 242–8, 252, 161
    The Religion of Protestants a Safe Way to Salvation 243
China 177, 185, 361
Cholinus, Petrus 122
Christology 11–12, 41, 48–9, 152, 156, 159–61, 169–70, 599, 604
Christopherson, John, *Iephte* 515–16
Chrysostom, St John 36, 57, 120
churches 3–6, 14, 24, 36, 41, 51, 81, 90, 100, 137, 257–8, 262–5, 268, 270, 272–7, 280–5, 287–8, 291–6, 301, 320–2, 324, 327, 329–30, 373, 442, 462, 466, 470, 578, 633
Church of England 30, 34, 73, 86, 109, 118, 134, 147, 167, 238–9, 240–2, 244–7, 251–2, 258, 261–4, 266–70, 362, 372, 379, 430–7, 439, 442–3, 535, 537, 540
    Convocation 28, 277
    see also Anglicans and Anglicanism
Church of Scotland 319, 321, 372, 374
    Book of Common Order 322, 335–7, 377 n. 23
    First Book of Discipline (1560) 319, 321, 323
    Second Book of Discipline (1578) 321, 328

Cicero, Marcus Tullius 88, 91, 168, 474, 478, 600, 625
De officiis 607
Cisneros, Ximénez de (cardinal) 26, 134
Clarendon Code 535 n. 7
Clarke, Samuel, *Englands Covenant Proved Lawfull* 420, 425
Clarkson, Lawrence 409–10
Clarius, Isidore 160
Clement of Alexandria 132
Clement I (pope) 122, 125, 128, 434
Epistle to the Corinthians, *see* Codex Alexandrinus
Clement VII (pope) 275
Clement VIII (pope) 66, 139
Clifford, Lady Anne 285
Clogie, Alexander, *Vox corvi: Or, the Voice of a Raven* 353–4
Codex Alexandrinus 120, 122–5, 127, 129
Codex Vatinicus 125, 129
Codrington, Robert 230
Coker, Matthew 108
Colet, John 584
Collier, Thomas 406
Collins, An 484
Collyer, David (clergyman) 285
Columbus, Christopher 198
Comestor, Peter 134
Compton, Henry 442
Constantine, Donation of 511
conversion, religious 11, 13, 44, 104, 124, 147, 259, 326, 330, 350–9, 361–4, 573
Conway, Anne, Lady Conway 99, 104–5, 108–9
Cooper, Anthony Ashley, 1st Earl of Shaftesbury 391
Cooper, Anthony Ashley, 3rd Earl of Shaftesbury 655, 657–8
Characteristics of Men, Manners, Opinions, Times 656
Cooper, Thomas, *A Brief Exposition of Such Chapters of the Old Testament . . .* 278
Copernicus 553
Coppe, Abiezer 109, 409–10
A Fiery Flying Roll 407–8
Coppin, Richard, *Divine Teachings* 407–8
Corporation Act (1661) 436
Coryate, Thomas, *Coryates Crudities* 464–5

Coulton, Richard 436, 438
Council of Florence 135, 138
Council of Trent 121 n. 17, 123 n. 22, 138, 142, 224, 385, 504
Counter-Reformation 10–11, 361, 516
Courteau, Thomas (printer) 42–3, 46–8
Covenanters 226, 234, 259, 319, 321, 326, 328–30
Coverdale, Miles 4, 20, 35, 83, 90, 95, 136–7, 227–8, 292–4, 296, 352, 447, 459, 473, 475
Cowley, Abraham 485, 488, 494
Davideis 489, 497, 549–50
Cox, Roger 491–2
Hebdomada sacra 492
Cramer, Daniel, *Emblemata sacra* 648, 650
Cranach, Lucas 135, 146
Cranmer, Thomas (Archbishop of Canterbury) 4, 23, 25, 30, 34–7, 46, 72, 137, 139, 269, 272, 274–6, 282, 293, 510, 658
Crashaw, Richard (poet) 600, 608
creation of the world 1, 184–6, 189–90, 193–4, 210, 213, 218, 402–3, 410, 485–6, 489–92, 494, 548, 551–3, 595, 605, 618, 624
Creech, Thomas 623–4
Crespin, Jean (printer) 41–2
Cressy, Hugh Serenus 13
Crom, Matthew (printer) 137
Cromwell, Oliver 399–400, 402, 406, 410, 426, 611
Cromwell, Thomas 4, 35, 137–8, 272
Crook, Cornelius 503
Crossman, Samuel (minister) 353–4
Cruso, Timothy 438
Crusius, Paulus 179 n. 16
Cudworth, Ralph 181
The True Intellectual System of the Universe 618–19
Cuningham, William
Cosmographical Glasse 197
Cyprian, St 61, 357
Cyrus the Persian 161, 181, 216

Damasus (pope) 132
Daniel (biblical figure) 146, 476, 582, 644

768 INDEX

Daniel, Book of 135, 138, 180, 184, 189, 193, 382, 400–1, 404, 470, 477, 638
Davenant, William, *Gondibert* 549
David (biblical king) 150, 158–9, 289–90, 293, 297, 308, 310, 368, 373–4, 412–15, 417–26, 429, 499, 502, 546–8, 563, 565–6, 568, 572, 574–5, 582, 590, 603, 605, 607, 649, 643, 647–55, 657–8
Davids Three Mighties 422, 425
Davies, John, *The XII Wonders of the World* 467
Declaration of Indulgence 430, 436, 442
De Cerisiers, René, *The Innocent Lord* 541
De Costere, Frans, *Enchiridion controversiarum praecipuarum nostri temporis de religione* 355
Dee, John 178
Defoe, Daniel 318
deists and deism 239, 253, 410, 623
Dekker, Thomas, *The Roaring Girl* 467
Dell, William 608
demons 75–9
Demosthenes 538
Denham, John 496
Dent, Arthur, *The Plaine Man's Pathway to Heaven* 538
Descartes, René 613
Des Gallars, Nicholas 42, 45–6
D'Espagne, Jean, *Shibboleth, or the Reformation of . . . the French and of the English Bible* 230
Deucalion 547
Deuteronomy, Book of 115, 205–6, 211, 213, 278–9, 386–96, 471, 645
Diether, Andreas 503
Diggers 146, 397, 400–3, 407, 410
Diodati, Giovanni 343
  Pious Annotations 424
Diogenes of Babylonia 607
Dives and Pauper 3
Doddridge, Philip (clergyman) 285, 583
Donatus, Aelius 507
Donatists 59 n. 16, 61
Donne, John 151, 312, 372, 380–3, 464, 472, 478, 522, 547, 561, 564, 573, 576
  'The Anatomy of the World' (The first anniversary) 459–60

Death's Duel 521
Essays in Divinity 519
Gunpowder Plot sermon 311, 380–3
Holy sonnets 451, 604
Lincoln's Inn sermon 310, 561–2, 565–76
Pseudo-martyr 377
Doring, Matthias 573
Dove, Dr John, *A Confutation of Atheisme* 614–15
Downes, Andrew 119, 141
Downham, G., *Rex meus est deus* 418, 422
Dowriche, Anne, *The French History* 451–2
Dracontius 546
Drayton, Michael 488
  Moyses in a Map of his Miracles 549
Drayton, Thomas 104
Drusius, Johannes 121, 126–8
Drury, Elizabeth 459
Dryden, John 444
Du Bartas, Guillaume de Salluste 485, 487–91, 496–7, 548–9, 600
  La seconde semaine 488–90, 548–9, 553
  La semaine ou création du monde 487–90, 548–9, 553
  L'Uranie 487–8, 548
Duport, John 141
Durham, James, *The Parliaments Commission* 419

Easter 24, 150, 155, 162, 180, 193, 274–5, 279, 282, 303–4, 313, 429, 461
East, Thomas 298–9, 301
Ecclesiastes, Book of 1, 137, 145, 278, 281, 376, 470, 547
Ecclesiology 12, 54, 56, 58, 60, 64, 68, 115, 226, 232–3, 235, 319, 368, 621
Eck, Johann 134–5
  Enchiridion 28
Edward I 146
Edward VI 5–6, 36–7, 90, 139, 263, 273–4, 277, 282, 293, 499
Edwards, Thomas 609
  Gangraena 210, 237–8, 608
Egenollf, Christian 582
Egypt and Egyptians, ancient 181, 189–91, 200, 386, 401, 445, 475, 540–4, 588, 603, 645, 656

Eliot, John 362–3
Elizabeth I 5, 37, 46, 51–2, 90, 139, 146,
　　227–8, 257, 261, 263–7, 269, 273–4,
　　277–8, 282, 290, 304, 333–4, 339, 340,
　　359, 412, 416, 425, 432–3, 444, 458,
　　515, 638
Ellis, John, *Sole Path to a Sound Peace* 416–17
Elsheimer, Adam 146
Elyot, Thomas 84
　The Booke Named the Governor 585–6
England
　Civil Wars in 13, 115, 146, 176, 229, 234,
　　238–9, 245–6, 303, 368–9, 385, 389,
　　396, 400, 410, 412–13, 427, 429–30,
　　432–3, 437, 439, 442, 444–5, 447, 484,
　　486, 620, 641, 647
　Enlightenment in 239–40, 657
　Exclusion Crisis 369, 385, 391, 396, 620
　Glorious Revolution 147, 193, 330, 396,
　　429, 641
　Interregnum 115, 269–70, 400
　Long Parliament (1640) 262
　Post-Reformation in 72, 258, 261, 266,
　　452–3, 455, 472, 522, 561, 638
　Reformation in 2, 20, 39–40, 52, 147, 262,
　　499–500, 630
　Restoration in 81–2, 103, 109, 145, 233,
　　239, 246, 250, 252, 282, 325, 369, 389,
　　427, 484, 486, 495, 540, 621, 641
　see also Church of England
Englands Second Alarm to War 418, 420
Englands Third Alarm to Warre 418
Epicurus 152, 615, 623
epiphany 57, 274, 278–9
Episcopalians 318, 324–6
Erasmus 26–7, 30, 91 n. 24, 121, 135, 137, 211,
　　359, 499, 501–3, 583–4
　Commentaries on Jerome 27
　Convivium religiosum 584–6, 588, 590
　*A Diatribe or Discourse on the Freedom of
　　the Will* 509
　Disputatiuncula de taedio 509
　De duplici copia rerum ac verborum 84
　Novum instrumentum 3, 27, 39, 333
　Paraclesis 26, 35
　Paraphrases upon the New Testament 20,
　　264, 273

Esther, Book of 133, 135, 138, 278
Estienne, Robert (printer) 39, 41, 42
eucharist 24, 531
Euripides 498, 502, 538
　Alcestis 498
　Hecuba 499
　Iphegenia in aulis 499
　Medea 498
Eusebius 177, 185, 251, 584, 586, 588
　Onomasticon 197
evangelists 56, 143; *see also individual entries*
Evelyn, John 246, 432, 442, 444–5, 623
Everard, John (preacher) 15
Everingham, Robert 345–7
Exodus, Book of 279, 429, 536, 546–7, 615
exorcism 10
Ezekiel (prophet) 196

Fagius, Paul 516
Fairfax, Sir Thomas 608, 611
Family of Love and Familists 103–4, 109, 147,
　　398 n. 8
Farmer, Anthony 431
Featley, Daniel (preacher) 306–7, 313–14, 519, 531
　Clavis mystica 305
　*The Spouse, her Precious
　　Borders* 305–6, 312
Fell, Margaret (Quaker) 359
Fenner, William (preacher) 350–1
　*Soules Looking-Glasse . . . with a Treatise of
　　Conscience* 417, 422, 425
Fenton, Roger (preacher) 305
Fergusson, David (preacher) 324
Ferne, Henry 416, 420–1
　Camp at Gilgal 419
　Conscience Satisfied 415, 420
　Reply unto Severall Treatises 414–15
　Resolving of Conscience 414
Ferrabosco, Alfonso (composer) 467
Ferrar, Nicholas 8
Feyerabend, Sigmund, *Biblische figuren des
　　Alten und Neuen Testaments* 582
Fifth Monarchists 226, 234, 400
Figgis, John, *The Divine Right of Kings* 387
Filmer, Sir Robert 385, 391, 641
　Patriarcha 391–5, 620
Fisher, John (bishop) 26, 28, 34–5, 242

Fisher, Samuel 146–7, 210, 246, 250–2, 359
  Rusticus ad academicos 250–1
  *Something Concerning Agbarus, Prince of
    Edesseans* 251
Fish, Simon 33
  Supplicacyon for the Beggars 31
Fitzralph, Richard (Archbishop of
    Armagh) 334
Fletcher, John (playwright) 467
Florio, John 623
Forester, James, *The Marrow and Juice of Two
    Hundred and Sixtie Scriptures* 461
Forret, Thomas 352
Fotherby, Martin, *Atheomastix* 613
Fowler, Constance Aston 484
Fox, George 105, 210
Foxe, John 3, 40, 50, 437
  Acts and Monuments 264–5
  Christus triumphans 506, 512–13
  The Gospels of the Fower Evangelistes 96
Franciscans 199, 202, 275, 345
Frank, Mark (preacher) 281
Franklin, Benjamin 583 n. 18
Frankton, John 339
Frith, John 27
  Revelation of Antichrist 31
Frith, Mary 467
Fulke, William 5–6, 60–1, 67, 89, 91–2, 95
  *A Defence of the Sincere and True
    Translations of the Holy
    Scriptures* 60, 84–6
  *The Text of the New Testament of Jesus
    Christ* 5, 86
Fuller, John (Chancellor of Ely) 357
Fuller, Thomas 196, 284, 608–9
  A Pisgah-Sight of Palestine 12, 203
  The Profane State 621
Fullonius, William [Gnapheus] 503–4
Funck, Johann 181

Galen 616, 648
Galileo, Galilei 553
  *Dialogue Concerning the Two Chief World
    Systems* 554
Galloway, Patrick (Scottish
    minister) 374, 376
Gardiner, Stephen 31, 35–7, 85–6, 95, 510–11
Garraway, Henry 421

The Loyal Citizen Revived 421
Gascoigne, George 353
Gataker, Thomas 119, 608
Gaunt, Elizabeth 437–9
Gell, Robert 102–5, 109
  Aggelokratia theon 106, 108
  *An Essay Toward the Amendment of
    the Last English Translation of the
    Bible* 21, 98–102, 106–9, 230
  Remains 104–5
Genesis, Book of 14, 102, 106–8, 149, 211,
    214–15, 217–22, 278–9, 285, 346, 353,
    391, 403, 410, 484–5, 491–2, 495–7,
    519, 534, 536–7, 539–41, 546–7, 549,
    552, 592, 599, 601, 607, 624, 641, 652
Gerrard, Father John 355
Gibbon, Edward 200, 207, 214
Gilby, Anthony (Bible translator) 40, 49
Giraldi, Lilio Gregorio 504, 510
Gnostics 132
God 26, 29, 34, 44–5, 47–50, 56–7, 62, 64,
    66–7, 72–6, 81, 88, 99, 100–1, 106–8,
    139, 154–7, 160–1, 165–6, 168–75, 186,
    196, 200, 202–3, 205, 209–10, 213–18,
    220–2, 233–4, 242, 246–7, 249–50,
    258, 266, 275, 278–9, 281, 291, 294–9,
    307–9, 313, 322, 326, 341, 355–6, 358,
    371, 375–6, 378, 380–1, 384, 386–7,
    388–90, 392–5, 397–400, 404–5,
    408–10, 412–13, 416–18, 420–5, 430,
    432, 434–9, 445, 462, 472, 476, 478,
    481, 486–90, 495, 499–500, 505,
    508–12, 514–16, 518, 521, 525–30, 535,
    538, 540, 542, 544, 547–8, 550–7, 563,
    565–6, 568–9, 571–2, 574–5, 580, 584,
    595–6, 599, 603, 605–7, 611, 613–15,
    617–25, 628–31, 633–4, 636–8, 641–2,
    645–8, 650–1, 653–6, 658
  Word of 1, 3, 11, 15, 20–1, 23–4, 33–4, 36,
    55–6, 67, 80, 96, 131, 142, 171–2, 210,
    222, 241, 247, 249–51, 258–9, 264–5,
    267, 270, 274–5, 278, 287, 301, 312,
    319, 321, 323, 330, 334, 354, 363, 372,
    374–6, 383, 386, 395, 399–400, 406–7,
    433, 435–6, 445, 452, 456–7, 506, 509,
    527, 537, 545, 562, 577, 583, 595, 610,
    622, 638
Godefroy, Jacques 199

Godolphin, Sidney 496
Godwyn, Morgan 361–2
Goffe, Thomas (preacher) 305 n. 11
Goodman, Christopher 40, 227
  How Superior Powers Oght to be Obeyd of Their Subjectes 51
Goodwin, John 115
  Divine Authority of the Scriptures Asserted 210
  Hagiomastix or the Scourge of the Saints 210
Gospels 8, 24, 26–7, 56, 184, 233, 246, 273–4, 279–81, 285, 307, 313, 345, 351, 359, 361, 361 n. 59, 397–8, 407, 434, 437, 508–9, 630
  St John's 35, 341, 350, 472, 609, 630
  St Luke's 35, 159, 341, 447
  St Mark's 248–9
  St Matthew's 57, 84, 143, 159, 210–11 n. 10, 361, 481, 588
Goudimel, Claude 296
Grafton, Richard (publisher) 137
Greaves, John 189
Greece and Greeks, Ancient 2, 11, 77, 180, 190
Greenhill, William, *The Axe at the Root* 416
Greenwood, John 241
Gregory XV (pope) 361
Gregory, John 1, 13–14, 141, 178
Gregory, St 36, 134, 311, 602
Greston, Matthew 34
Gribelin, Simon 443
Grindal, Edmund (Archbishop of Canterbury) 276
Grotius, Hugo 119 n. 11, 128 n. 42, 181, 253 n. 40, 394
  De veritate religionis Christianae 363
Grynaeus, Simon 501
Grunther, Andreas 504
Gunter, Marie 13
Gutenburg, Johannes 228–9

Hackett, William 241
Hagiographa 133, 137
Hall, John (surgeon) 145
Hall, Joseph (preacher) 305, 490, 495
Hall, Rowland (printer) 38

Hamelin, Philbert (printer) 42
Hammond, Henry 253 n. 40
Hampton Court Conference 6, 71, 140, 142, 267–8, 270, 376, 455, 457
Handel, George Frederic 445
Harington, John 471
Harrington, James 385, 395, 399
Harrison, William 277, 280, 282
Hastings, Henry, 3rd Earl of Huntington 49
Hay, Peter 518
Hearne, Thomas (antiquarian) 194
Hebbel, Friedrich 145 n. 43
Heinsius, Daniel 121
Helmont, Francis Mercurius van 109
Helwig, Christoph 178, 179 n. 16
Hemmingsen, Neils, *A Postill, of Exposition of the Gospells* 281
Henry VII 425
Henry VIII 4, 6, 19–20, 24, 28–36, 90, 136–8, 263, 272–3, 433, 452
Henry, Matthew (clergyman) 285
Herbert, George 151, 453, 522–31, 547, 585, 608, 628
  The Priest to the Temple 519, 522
  The Temple 519, 523, 525–6, 531
    'The Altar' 526–7
    'The Flower' 524, 527–31
    'The H. Scriptures. II' 522–3, 525
    'Jordan (II)' 523–5
    'The Odour, 2 Cor. 2' 525–6
    'The Pearl. Matth. 13' 530–1
    'The Thanksgiving' 524
Herbert, Philip, 5th Earl of Pembroke 104, 105
Herbert, Sir William 335
Hercules 547
Herle, Charles 416
hermeneutics 21, 41, 45–6, 54–5, 69, 109, 113–15, 151–5, 160–1, 248–9, 324, 605
Herodotus 141
Herrey, Robert, Concordance to the Geneva Bible 284
Hesiod 538
Heylyn, Peter
  Mercurius aulicus 424
  Rebells catechism 420
Hickes, John 439

Higgin, Anthony (preacher) 281
Hills, Henry 496
Hinton, Edward, *Vanity of Self-Boasters* 419–20
Hobbes, Thomas 115, 239–40, 385, 390, 399, 549, 614
  Leviathan 211, 620–1
Hobart, Lady Francis 285
Hogarth, William 146
Holbein, Hans (the younger), *Historiarum veteris instrumenti icones* 582
Holbrooke, William, *Loves Complaint, for Want of Entertainment* 310
Hollar, Wenceslaus 146
Holy Communion 24, 269, 279–81, 283, 435
Holy Ghost 57, 59, 94, 100–1, 138, 141, 145, 149, 153–5, 169, 210, 212, 214, 241, 249, 279, 308–10, 312, 314–15, 325–6, 362, 369, 443, 536, 551, 613, 629, 631, 653
Holy Harmony: Or, a Plea for the Abolishing of Organs . . . Out of the Protestant Churches of Great Britain 417
Homer 217, 488, 538
  Iliad 168, 457–8, 548
homilies 24, 36, 139–40, 273–4, 281, 283, 610
Hooker, Richard 12, 115, 165–6, 239, 243–5, 247, 251–2, 392
  Of the Lawes of Ecclesiasticall Politie 114, 164–74, 240–2
Hopkins, John 293–4
  The Whole Booke of Psalms 284, 293–5, 298–9
Horace 471, 488, 583 n. 18
Hoskins, John (preacher) 305, 313–15
Host 24, 26
How, Samuel 248
Howard, Henry (poet) 289
Howard, Thomas, 3rd Duke of Norfolk 29
Hudson, Thomas 548
Huggins, William 146
Hugh of Saint-Cher 134
Hugh of St Victor 134
Hull, John, *The Unmasking of the Politike Athiest* 614
humanists and humanism 3, 39–40, 113, 118, 121–3, 131, 133, 162, 168, 180, 197, 200, 252, 263, 272, 310, 385, 456–8, 502, 562, 579, 584, 588, 592, 610

Humble Proposals Concerning the Printing of the Bible 224–6
Hume, David, *History of the Houses of Douglas and Angus* 422
Humfrey, Laurence 49, 334–5
Hunton, Philip 423
  Treatise of Monarchie 415
Hurt, Robert 104
Hutchinson, Lucy 485–6, 488, 490, 494–5, 497, 623–4
  Order and Disorder 452, 484–8, 494–7, 624
Hyde, Edward, 1st Earl of Clarendon 13

Ibn Ezra 158, 160
Illyricus, Matthias Flacius 153–7, 162
  Clavis scripturae sacrae 151–2
Independents 237–8, 245–6, 248
Ireland 3, 52, 231, 234, 246, 258, 320, 332–49, 359, 415, 444
  Reformation in 259, 332, 335–6, 342, 348
Isaacson, Henry, *Saturni ephemerides* 186
Isaiah, Book of 72–81, 89, 125, 150–2, 154–62, 215–17, 276, 278–9, 357–8, 429, 447, 471, 474, 480
Isaiah (prophet) 73, 150, 152, 156–7, 159–61, 202, 480
Isham, Elizabeth 297
Isidore of Seville 77 n. 28
Islam and Muslims 1, 11, 359, 406
Israel and Israelites 56, 72–3, 114, 147, 150, 158, 160, 181, 190, 197, 200–3, 205–7, 279, 306, 308, 373–4, 381, 386–9, 391–5, 399, 404–5, 410, 412–15, 417, 421, 425–6, 437–9, 514, 527, 540, 542, 604, 645–6
Jerusalem 57, 143, 159, 184, 197–9, 201–2, 306, 410, 438, 480

Jackson, Arthur, *Help for the Understanding of the Holy Scripture* 416, 419
Jackson, Thomas (preacher) 281
James VI and I 6, 51, 52, 71–4, 118, 140, 142, 180 n. 19, 228, 257, 261, 266–8, 270, 290, 298, 319, 321, 339–40, 342, 358, 368, 371–83, 385–6, 388, 395, 422–3, 432, 455, 457, 458, 461–4, 473, 487–8, 493–4, 548
  An Apologie for the Oath of Allegiance 377–8

Basilikon doron 375

Daemonologie 423, 494

Directions for Preachers 376, 379–80, 520

The Essayes of a Prentise, in the Divine Art of Poesie 373, 487

An Fruitfull Meditatioun 373–6, 378

His Majesties Declaration, Touching his Proceedings in the Late Assemblie 381–2

An Meditatioun 374–6, 378

A Meditation upon the Lords Prayer 379

A Meditation upon St. Matthew 379

Paraphrase upon the Revelation 373–4, 378–9

The True Lawe of Free Monarchies 375, 380–2, 385

The Workes of the Most High and Mighty Prince, James 376, 378–9

James II 369, 391, 429–33, 435–9, 442–5

James Stuart, Prince of Wales 443–4

James, St, Epistle of 114, 135, 249, 410

Jennes, Charles 445, 447

Jeremiah (prophet) 137–8, 644–5

Jerome, St 3, 19, 27, 66, 74, 77–9, 91, 102, 117, 131–9, 143, 277, 426, 471, 616

Jesus 26, 41, 47–8, 57–8, 61–2, 72, 84, 89, 93, 100, 105, 107, 114, 140, 143, 150–7, 159, 161–2, 169–70, 180–1, 184, 186, 193, 198, 201, 209, 211–13, 233, 248–51, 274, 276, 280, 282–3, 306, 308–11, 313–14, 351, 353–4, 358–9, 375, 379, 382, 400–2, 404, 406, 408–9, 412, 426, 434–6, 438, 461–2, 471–2, 474, 481, 499, 505–13, 518, 524–7, 531, 535, 543, 546, 552, 555–6, 565–8, 579, 585–6, 595, 603, 605, 608–10, 614, 626–7, 630, 632, 636–8, 642, 644, 650

Jesuits 11, 179, 199, 243, 245, 345, 355, 361, 368, 429, 435, 438, 503

Jewel, John (bishop) 139, 281, 357

Apology of the Church of England 277

Jews and Judaism 11, 15, 48, 61, 73, 77, 91, 93, 98, 108, 114, 117, 119, 121, 131–3, 135, 137, 140, 142, 144, 146–7, 153, 156–62, 176–7, 180–1, 184, 197, 203, 210, 216, 218, 232–3, 248, 276, 278–9, 314, 359, 384, 386, 392, 395, 404, 406, 417, 474, 607, 609–10, 629, 631, 636, 651, 653

J.M., *The Atheist Silenced* 613

Job (biblical figure) 528–31, 546, 548, 550

Job, Book of 124, 165, 278, 424, 470–2, 528, 547

John of Leiden 241

John of Salisbury 134

John, St 50, 93, 212, 374–5, 400, 474

Johnson, Robert (composer) 467

Jones, Henry (dean) 344–6

Jones, Inigo 465, 467

Jones, Katherine, Viscountess Ranelagh 345

Jonson, Ben 464, 467

    Catiline his Conspiracy 493

    Oberon, the Faery Prince 465–7

Jordan, Thomas, *Piety, and Poesy* 424

Josephus, Flavius 133, 141, 179, 184, 189, 198, 392, 394–5, 471

    Antiquities 184

Joshua, Book of 125

Joshua (biblical figure) 553, 582, 656

Jud, Leo 39, 136

Judas 6, 211, 402, 493, 506

Judges, Book of 514, 516

Julian (emperor) 511

Julian of Norwich 626–7

Junius, Franciscus 50, 51, 92–3, 122, 141, 211, 215, 227, 350, 357, 547, 550

    Apocalypsis, a Brief and Learned Commentarie 50

Junius, Robert (missionary) 362

Justinian 616

Justin Martyr 248

Juvencus 546

kabbalah and kabbalists 103, 105, 108

Kant, Emmanuel 641, 656

Karlstadt, Andreas Bodenstein von 134

    De Canonicis Scripturis Libellus 134

Katherine of Aragon 29

Kearney, William 337–9, 341, 348

Keble, John 244

Keyser, Martin de (printer) 136

Killigrew, Henry 416

Kimhi, David 158–9

King, Dr John (preacher) 305–6

King, Martin Luther 478

King Philip's War (Metacom's Rebellion) 362–3

King's book 273

Kings, Books of 132
Kirchmeyer, Thomas 504, 513
   Hamanus 503, 510
   Pammachius 503, 506, 510–13
Kirk, Robert 347
Kirkwood, James 347
Kluber, Hans Hug 586
Knott, Edward (Jesuit) 243
Knox, John 10, 40, 650
   *The First Blast of the Trumpet against the
      Monstrous Regiment of Women* 51
   Liturgy 335
Kyd, Thomas 616
   The Spanish Tragedy 616–17

Lamb, Thomas 249
Langhorne, Lancelot 461–2
Lanyer, Aemelia 452, 484
   Salve deus rex judaeorum 462–3
La Peyrère, Isaac 177 n. 3, 210
Lapide, Cornelius à 11, 153–7, 162
   Commentaria in pentateuchum 221 n. 45
   *Commentaria in quatuor prophetas
      maiores* 151, 152
Larke, Nicholas, *The Practice of
      Thankfulnesse* 471
Latimer, Hugh 29–31, 34–5, 281
Latimer, William 31
latitudinarians and latitudinarianism 115,
     239–40, 246, 248, 252–3, 436, 439, 443
Laud, William (Archbishop of
     Canterbury) 5, 51, 71 n. 4, 99, 103,
     242, 245, 252, 262 n. 5, 269–70, 280
   *A Relation of the Conference between William
      Laud . . . and Mr. Fisher the Jesuit* 242
Laudians and Laudianism 103, 143–4, 232–3,
     243–4, 248, 304, 312, 620
lectionaries 139, 142, 145, 147, 269, 323
Lee, Edward 27, 30
Lefèvre d'Étaples, Jacques 136
Leibniz, Gottfried Wilhelm von 109
Leigh, Edward 144, 209–10, 615
   *A Treatise of Divinity Consisting of Three
     Books* 210
Leighton, Robert (bishop) 329–30
Leo X (pope) 28
Levant, The 11, 202

Levellers 12, 250, 369, 397–8, 400, 402–8,
   410, 611
Levi Ben Gersom (rabbi) 391
Leviticus, Book of 278, 474
Lewis, C. S. 479, 481, 496
Ley, John 608–9
Liesveldt, Jacob van 135
Lightbody, George 519
Lightfoot, John (Hebraist) 143–4
Lilburne, John (Leveller) 402, 406
   The Free Man's Freedom Vindicated 405
Lipsius, Justus, *Politics* 602
Lisle, William, *A Saxon Treatise Concerning
     the Old and New Testament* 96–7
Lively, Edward 179, 181
Livy 598, 655
Lloyd, William 192–3, 429, 434, 436, 445
   *Papists no Catholicks, and Popery no True
     Christianity* 436
Lock, Anne 484
Locke, John 385, 395, 642
   Two Treatises on Government 391, 393, 642
Loe, William (chaplain) 290
Loftus, Adam (Archbishop of Armagh) 334
L'Oiseleur, Pierre (Huguenot) 49
Lollards 24–5, 28, 398 n. 8
Longland, John (bishop) 28
Lonicerus, Johannes 135
Lorichius, Ioannis 503
Lorinus, Joannes, *Commentaria in librum
     psalmorum* 567–8, 570, 572
Love, Christopher 353, 357–8
Lowth, Robert (bishop) 472
Loyola, Ignatius 361
Lucan, *Pharsalia* 549
Lucaris, Cyril 122
Lucas, Martin (printer) 6
Lucretius 615, 623–4
   De rerum natura 486, 496
Lufft, Hans (printer) 135
Luther, Martin 4, 12, 28, 30–1, 58–9, 101, 105,
     107, 117, 121, 134–7, 139, 143, 149, 157,
     161, 172, 214, 358, 385, 405, 422, 426,
     471, 510, 512, 518, 531, 537, 553, 578–9,
     630–4, 636, 639, 648
   The Bondage of the Will 509
   The Freedom of a Christian 509

Lutherans and Lutheranism 19, 28, 105, 109, 114, 131, 135, 138, 147, 157, 179, 249, 274, 281, 504, 510
Lydgate, John 627
Lydiat, Thomas 178, 180–1
Lyly, John, *Euphues and his England* 613

Macaulay, Thomas Babington 469
Mac Bruaideadha, Maoilín Óg 341, 342
Maccabees 114, 139, 142, 146
Machiavelli, Niccolò 598, 600–2
Macropedius, Georgius 503–4
Maimonides, Moses 394–5
Malory, Sir Thomas 626
Manetho 189
Manichaeism 248
Marbeck, John 8
Mark, St 474
Marlowe, Christopher 621
    Dr Faustus 615–17
Marprelate, Martin 143, 167
Marsh, Narcissus 332, 345–6
Marshall, Benjamin (chaplain) 193
Marshall, Stephen 234
    Plea for Defensive Armes 415
Marsham, Sir John 189, 191
    Diatriba chronologica 189
Martin, Gregory 5, 57, 59–61, 67, 69, 89, 92, 95, 355
    A Discovery of the Manifold Corruptions of the Holy Scriptures 60, 86, 88
    The New Testament Faithfully Translated into English 21
Martin, Henry 608
Martyr, Peter 8, 121
Marvell, Andrew (poet) 103, 550
Mary I 5, 20, 38, 40, 90, 146, 226, 263, 293
Mary II 429, 442, 445
Mary of Guise 146, 317
Mary of Modena 429, 442
Mary, Queen of Scots 372, 416, 425
Mary, Virgin 134, 410, 505
Masius, Andreas 121, 125
Masoretic Text 80
Mass, Catholic 24–5, 36, 263, 294, 519
Matthew, Thomas, *see* Rogers, John (Bible translator)
Matthew, Toby (Archbishop of York) 281

Matthew, Tobie 352
Maunsell, Andrew 8, 257
Maxwell, John 385, 395
    Sacro-sancta regnum majestas 388–92, 393
Mede, Joseph (biblical scholar) 102, 108, 180–1
Melanchthon, Philip 121, 134–5, 179, 179 n. 16, 308, 499, 502–3
Melville, Elizabeth 484
Melville, Herman 478
Melville, James 486
Menasseh ben Israel (rabbi) 359
Middleton, Elizabeth 484
Middleton, Thomas, *The Roaring Girl* 467
Mildmay, Grace 284
Mildmay, Sir Walter 333
millenarianism 103, 115, 177, 180–1, 185, 404, 443
Millenary Petition 6
Milton, John 73, 102, 103, 108, 115, 145, 209–22, 227, 385, 395, 400, 453, 471–2, 482, 484–9, 549–52
    Areopagitica 551, 553
    Of Civil Power in Ecclesiastical Causes 551
    De doctrina christiana 115, 211, 213, 216–17, 550–2
    Doctrine and Discipline of Divorce 212–13, 550, 555
    Lycidas 155
    Paradise Lost 107, 115, 212–22, 453, 484–9, 495–7, 546, 550–8, 620, 624, 628
    Paradise Regained 212
    The Readie and Easie Way 555
    Samson Agonistes 212, 487
    Tenure of Kings and Magistrates 556
    Tetrachordon 212 n. 25
Modena, Leon 343
monasteries, dissolution of the 25
monism 551, 557
Monmouth's Rebellion 432, 437
Montaigne, Michel de 513, 584 n. 26
    Essays 623
Montano, Benito Arias 102, 107, 198, 203
Montague, James 376, 378–9
More, Henry 99, 103, 105, 108–9
    Conjectura cabbalistica 108
More, Sir Thomas 20, 27, 30–2, 35, 89–92, 95, 209, 426
    Dyaloge 31

Morice, Ralph 35
Morin, Jean 123–9
Moses 155–6, 190–2, 200, 202, 205, 211–13,
    278–9, 305, 386–7, 389, 394, 406, 410,
    535–6, 546–8, 605, 636, 645–6, 656
Moxon, Joseph 345
Muis, Siméon de 125 n. 29
Munday, Anthony (playwright) 145
Münster, Sebastian 102, 137, 160–1, 206
    Cosmography 207
Musculus, Wolfgang 8
mystery plays 453

Nadal, Jeronimo, *The Annotations and
    Meditations on the Gospels* 361
Nalson, John, *An Impartial Collection of the
    Great Affairs of State . . .* 427
Nangle, James 343
Nashe, Thomas 601
Nayler, James 146
Nazianzen, St Gregory 36, 498
Negri, Francesco, *Free Will* 498
Neoplatonists 165, 173
Newdigate, Richard 305–6
Newman, John Henry (cardinal) 244, 469
Newton, Isaac 178–9, 189, 192–4
New World 52, 198, 259, 263, 270, 344, 348,
    351, 359, 361–4, 395
Nicetas 124
Nicholas of Lyra 134, 160–1
    Postilla 157, 573–5
Niclaes, Hendrik 104, 109
Nicoll, John (diarist) 327
Nicolson, James (printer) 136
Nimrod 495
Nixe, Richard (bishop) 29
non-conformists 13
Norton, Bonham (printer) 6
Nugent, Christopher 334
Nuttall, Geoffrey 104
Nye, Stephen 210
Nyndge, Alexander 10

Oath of Allegiance 376–8
*Obedience Active and Passive Due to the
    Supream Power* 424
Ochino, Bernadino, *Tragedy* 499

Ockham, William 134
Ó Cearnaigh, Seaán 336–7, 339, 341
    Aibidil 336–7, 339
Ó Cionga, Muircheartach 343
Ó Domhnalláin, Fearganainm 336,
    339, 341–2
Ó Domhnuill, Uilliam 333, 336, 339–42,
    344, 346
Ó Duinnín, Uilliam 346
Ó hUIginn, Domhnall Óg 342
Ó hUIginn, Philib Bocht 337
Ó hUIginn, Pól 346
O'Reilly, Hugh 345–6
O'Neill, Hugh 348
Olivetan, Pierre (Bible translator) 41,
    136–7, 140
Oporinus, Johannes 504, 512–13
    *Sacred Drama: Several Comedies and
        Tragedies Taken from the Old
        Testament* 503–5, 510
Origen 123–7, 132, 216, 471
Ortelius, Abraham 199
Ottoman Empire 147, 350, 359
Overton, Richard (Leveller) 405
    *The Appeale from the Degenerate
        Representative Body* 405
Ovid 627
    Metamorphoses 496
Owen, Dr David
    Puritano-Jesuitismus 415
Owen, John 226–7, 232–3, 251
Oxford, University of 6, 25, 49, 140, 143,
    178–9, 232, 245–6, 345, 431
    *Judgment and Decree of the University of
        Oxford . . . Against Certain Pernicious
        Books* 389
Oxford Movement 244–5

pagans and paganism 77, 79, 114, 121, 180
Page, Samuel, *Nine Sermons upon Sun[drie]
    Texts of Scripture* 471
Pagitt, Ephraim, *Heresiography* 238
Pagnino, Santes [Pagninus] 39, 102, 106,
    135–6, 570
Palestine 11, 114, 181, 200–2, 205
Palmer, Herbert 416
Papeus, Petrus 503

parables 84, 280, 308, 471, 504, 536, 584, 604, 610, 618
Paracelsus 106
Parallel between the Israelites . . ., A 420
Pareus, David, *Commentary upon the Divine Revelation* 513
parishes and parishioners 4, 24–5, 36, 51, 103, 227, 257, 262, 264–9, 272–4, 277, 280–2, 287, 322–3, 325–8, 330, 333, 346, 367, 542, 544–5, 608, 611
Paris, University of 3
Parker, Henry, *Accommodation Cordially Desired* 415
Parker, Matthew (Archbishop of Canterbury) 38, 90, 140, 276, 510–11
Parker, William 104
Parkhurst, John (bishop) 140
Parr, Katherine 20, 484
Patrick, Simon (clergyman) 285
Paul, St 44, 46, 92, 135, 146, 216, 291, 309, 356, 359, 409, 429, 434–5, 474, 481, 511, 526, 585, 620, 646, 648
    Epistles to the Corinthians 120, 291, 566, 588, 629, 636
    Epistles to the Romans 46–7, 166, 280, 352–3, 618, 627, 630–4, 636–7, 639
    Epistle to the Ephesians 166, 566, 628–30
Paul of Saint Marie (Bishop of Burgos) 573
Paul II (Pope) 68–9
Paul the Apostle 352
Pazzi, Alessandro de' [Paccius] 501–2, 506–7
Pemble, William 520
Penry, John 143, 241; *see also* Marprelate, Martin
Pentateuch 4, 66, 133, 183, 211, 276, 475
Pepys, Samuel 621
Pererius, Benedict 11
perfectionism 104–5
Perkins, William (theologian) 12, 50, 142, 531
    Commentary on Galatians 309
Perrot, John 105
Persons, Robert, *A Book of Christian Exercise, Appertaining to Resolution* 355–6
Petau, Denis 177, 179, 179 n. 16, 185
Peter of Cluny 134
Peter, St 61, 93, 379, 382, 436, 470, 511, 599, 601, 632

Petrarch 352
Petre, Charles 445
Petre, Father Edward 435
Petty, Sir William 344
Peucer, Casper 179 n. 16, 201 n. 23
Philip (apostle) 358
Philip, Father Robert 125 n. 30
Philip II 203
Philips, Katherine 484
Philo 395
Pietists 21, 98–9, 109, 648
Pindar 471, 488
Pistles and Gospels 273
Placentinus, Giorgio Valla 501
Plantagenet, Arthur, 1st Viscount Lisle 36
Plantin, Christophe 102, 203
Plato 92, 101, 165, 168
    Republic 217
Platonists and Platonism 98, 108, 618
Plautus 500
Pliny 141, 198
Pococke, Edward 11, 363
Polyglot Bibles 113, 115, 118, 141
    Antwerp 102, 123, 203
    Complutensian 26, 122, 134, 141
    London 113, 118, 127, 129, 141, 200 n. 17, 231–3, 245, 251
    Paris 123, 232
Pont, Robert (preacher) 324
Poole, Matthew (Presbyterian) 103–4, 106–7
Popish Plot 434
Postel, Guillaume 198
Powell, Humphrey 337
Pratt, Samuel Jackson 470
    The Sublime and Beautiful of Scripture 469
prayers and praying 26, 43, 142, 258, 264, 267, 269, 275, 280, 282, 291, 296, 321–2, 326–7, 336, 342, 353, 462, 483, 547, 572–3
    Lord's Prayer 14, 257, 273, 283, 326, 329, 335, 379
    Prayers for Intercession 40 n. 11
predestination 46–50, 108, 213, 243, 552
Presbyterians and Presbyterianism 103, 142, 226, 237–8, 241, 244–8, 318, 321, 324–6, 328–30, 347, 368, 436, 438, 608
Price, Richard 439
Price, Thomas 345

Prideaux, Humphrey 193
Priestly, Joseph 439
Priscillian 603
Proclus 174
Procopius of Gaza 125–6
Promised Land 200–3, 205–7
prophecies 41, 48, 72, 77, 81, 143, 150, 152–6,
    158–9, 161, 176–7, 180–1, 184, 186, 189,
    193, 278, 282, 289, 313, 443, 476–7,
    480, 547–8, 550
Prophets (part of Hebrew Bible) 133
Protestants and Protestantism 2, 5, 10,
    12–13, 20–1, 38–40, 44–5, 50–1,
    54, 56, 59–61, 64, 68, 71, 79, 84–5,
    88–93, 95–7, 114–15, 117–20, 122,
    125, 129, 131, 133, 138–40, 142, 143,
    145, 149, 151, 153, 157, 162, 171, 181,
    197, 199–200, 207, 210, 212, 226–7,
    243–5, 248, 259, 261, 263–6, 275–6,
    279, 281, 283–4, 287, 292–6, 299, 301,
    317–19, 323, 332–3, 335–6, 341, 343,
    348, 353–9, 361, 369, 374, 385–6, 415,
    425–6, 429–31, 433–6, 438–9, 442–3,
    445, 453, 461, 503, 519, 522, 533,
    536–7, 540, 546, 561–3, 578–9, 614,
    621, 627–8, 636–7, 648, 650
Protestant Settlement (1559) 166–8, 170–1,
    262–3, 303
Proverbs, Book of 137, 145, 165, 278–9, 281,
    547, 588, 623
Prynne, William, The Soveraigne Power of
    Parliament 421–2, 425
Psalms, Book of 26, 48, 231, 248, 258, 269,
    273–5, 278, 282–3, 285, 287–99, 301,
    308–9, 313, 321–2, 326–8, 343, 346,
    352, 361, 361 n. 59, 363, 373–4, 413,
    429, 447, 483–4, 547, 565–6, 569,
    571–5, 585, 622, 647–52
Psalters 52, 83, 90, 229, 269, 292, 320, 373
  Gaelic Psalter 347
  Paris Psalter 288
  Scottish Psalter 322
  Sidney Psalter 289–90
  Sternhold and Hopkins, The Whole booke
    of Psalms 284, 288, 293–5, 298–9
Pseudo-Melito, Clavis 566–8
Pseudo-Ortkens 580

Ptolemy 198, 553
  Geography 203, 205–6
Puckering, Sir John 298
Pulleyne, John 145
pulpit crosses 24, 304
Pulter, Hester 495
Pulton, Thomas (alias Brooke) 355–6
Purchas, Samuel 351
purgatory 89, 114, 135, 621
Puritans and Puritanism 6, 21, 48–51, 81, 98,
    131, 141–3, 145, 151, 166–7, 170, 213,
    228, 233–4, 240–3, 245, 251, 259, 264,
    266–8, 319, 333, 342, 367, 376, 379,
    388–9, 395, 415, 419, 464, 526, 533,
    536, 538, 548, 616, 641
Purvey, John 134
Puttenham, George 471
Pythagoras 585

Quadriga 114, 152–3, 369
Quakers and Quakerism 13, 103, 105, 146–7,
    250, 253, 551
Quarles, Francis 485, 488, 490–1, 494, 496–7
  Emblemes 491, 494–5
  A Feast for Wormes 490
  Hadassa 490, 492–3
  The Historie of Samson 490
  Job Militant 490
Quentell, Peter 4
Quiñones, Francesco de (cardinal) 275

rabbinism 102, 113
Radcliffe, Jeremiah 141
Rainolds, John 5 n. 16, 6, 84, 140, 142–3,
    267–8, 455, 480
  Censura librorum apocryphorum veteris
    testamenti 143
Rainolds, William 88, 91 n. 27, 93, 356–7
  A Refutation of Sundry Reprehensions,
    Cavils, and False Sleightes 85, 86, 94
Ralegh, Sir Walter 178–9, 392
  History of the World 177–8
Ramism 325
Ramsay, James (bishop) 320
Ramus, Petrus 166
Ranters 109, 146, 400–1, 407–10, 551
Rashi (rabbi) 158–60, 162, 221

Rauwolf, Dr Leonhard 202–3
Ray, John (naturalist) 80 n. 35, 329 n. 81
Reading, John 246, 248, 250
   Anabaptism Routed 246
Reformation 2, 3, 10–11, 15, 19–20, 23–4,
   38, 44, 73, 90, 114, 133–4, 149–50,
   153, 162, 165, 167, 199, 213, 225, 231,
   258–9, 288, 294, 350, 352, 369, 384–5,
   387, 436, 453, 456, 484, 498–9, 504,
   506, 513, 516, 531, 536–7, 562–3,
   577–9, 592, 627, 629, 631–2, 634–9,
   647–8, 511, 512, 651–2, 657; *see also*
   England, Reformation in; Scotland,
   Reformation in
Reitz, Johann Heinrich 109
Rembrandt 146
Republic of Letters 113, 200
Reuchlin, Johannes 134
Revelation, Book of 50–1, 119, 135, 180,
   227, 276, 373–4, 378–9, 400–1, 404,
   408, 429–30, 439, 442–3, 447, 476–7,
   513, 646
Richard II 493
Richard III 425
Richardson, John 183
Richardson, Thomas 185
Rich, Henry, 1st Earl of Holland 606
Rich, Mary, Countess of Warwick 357
Rich, Robert (Quaker) 105
Robertson, William, *Safer tehilim usafer*
   eykhah sepher tehilim u-sepher
   echam 232
Rogers, John (Bible translator) 4, 35,
   136–7, 473
Rogers, John (Fifth Monarchist) 143
   Ohel ohel or Beth-shemesh 232
Rogers, Nehemiah (preacher) 15
Rollock, Robert (preacher) 325
Rome and Romans, Ancient 11, 77, 79
Roper, Mary, *The Sacred Historie* 496–7
Rosier, James (Jesuit) 355
Ross, Alexander, *The New Planet No*
   Planet 553
Rowe, Elizabeth Singer 484
Royal Injunctions (1538) 36, 272–3
Royal Injunctions (1547) 274
Royal Injunctions (1559) 264, 266–7

Roye, William 359
Ruremundanus, Franciscus
   Fabricius 505 n. 37
Ruskin, John 469
Rutherford, Samuel 226, 385, 395, 521, 608–9
   Lex, rex 389–91
Ruyl, Albert Cornelius 361
Rye House Plot 389–90
Ryland, John Collett 582, 590
Ryland, John 582

Sall, Andrew 345–6
Saltmarsh, John 561–2, 608–9
   Holy Discoveries and Flames 608
   Poemata sacra 608
   The Practice of Policie in a Christian
   Life 598–602, 605–11
   Solemn Discourse upon the Grand
   Covenant 424
Samaritans 61, 183, 190
Sampson, Richard 31, 304
Sampson, Thomas (Bible translator/
   preacher) 40
Samuel, Books of 132, 368, 380, 382, 389,
   412, 607, 647–8, 652
Samuel (prophet) 373, 375, 381, 387, 389, 392,
   394, 412–14, 416–17, 421, 423–4, 590,
   647, 649
Sancroft, William (Archbishop of
   Canterbury) 432–3, 435, 442
Sander, Nicholas, *De visibili monarchia*
   ecclesiae 85
Sannazaro, Jacopo 547
Sarcerius, Erasmus 8
Sarum Missal 279, 528
Satan 79, 100, 151–2, 155, 161, 206, 210, 212,
   216, 218–22, 511–13, 548, 550, 556–7,
   569, 595, 619
Saul (biblical king) 368, 387, 389, 392, 394,
   412–26, 605–6, 652–3, 655
Savage, Sarah 284
Savile, Sir Henry 120
Savoy Conference 145, 277
Scaliger, Joseph 11, 121, 177–9, 181, 183,
   185–6, 189, 192–3
   De emendatione temporum 11
Schonaeus, Corneilus 145 n. 43

Scot, Cuthbert (bishop) 516
Scot, Reginald, *Discoverie of Witchcraft* 423
Scott, Sir Walter 443
Scott, William, *The Modell of Poesy* 498
Scotland 3–5, 51–2, 71 n. 1, 227, 231, 234–5,
    258–9, 275, 317–30, 334–5, 347, 359,
    372, 374, 377, 383–4, 391, 418, 444, 487
  Black Acts 373
  Cambuslang revival 330
  Enlightenment in 239
  National Covenant 326
  Post-Reformation in 322
  Reformation in 259, 317–20, 322, 324
  Restoration in 324, 329–30
see also Church of Scotland
Scots Confession (1560) 233–4
Second Helvetic Confession (1564) 234
Sedley, Sir Charles 621
Selden, John 119 n. 11, 178, 231, 385, 478
  De Diis syris 11
  Tabletalk 477
Seneca 478, 498, 502, 505, 513, 616–17
Septuagint 55, 64, 74, 108, 113, 117–29,
    132–3, 136, 141, 147, 177, 183–5,
    217, 343
  Aldine Septuagint 122, 141
  Greek Septuagint 91 n. 24, 135
  Hexpla 123, 125, 127
  Rome Septuagint 119, 122–4, 128, 141
sermons 2, 14–15, 24–5, 32, 36, 106, 114,
    144, 146, 150–1, 155, 166, 193, 203,
    205, 234, 257–8, 266, 275, 278, 281,
    285, 303–7, 309–15, 318, 321–30, 350,
    353–4, 357–8, 372, 375–9, 395, 416,
    418–18, 429–31, 433, 445, 461–2, 466,
    471, 483, 507–8, 516, 520, 534, 536,
    540, 542, 544, 561–2, 565, 621–2, 649
  Lincoln's Inn sermon 310, 561–2, 565–76
  Gunpowder Plot sermon 380–3
  Sermon on the Mount 406, 481
*Seven Arguments Plainly Proving that Papists
    are Trayterous Subjects* (anon.) 620
Servetus, Michel 203, 205–7
Sexby, Edward, *Killing noe Murder* 647
Shakespeare, William 145
  Love's Labour's Lost 84–5, 97
  Merchant of Venice 145–6

Richard III 601, 617
The Tempest 460, 467
Troilus and Cressida 422
The Winter's Tale 458, 467
Shawe, John, *Britannia rediviva* 430
Sheldon, Gilbert (Archbishop of
    Canterbury) 103
Sherlock, William (chaplain) 429–30
Sherry, Richard 84
  Treatise of Schemes and Tropes 83
Sibelius, Casper 362
Sibthorpe, Richard (preacher) 310
Sidney, Algernon 385
  Court maxims 395
  Discourses Concerning Government 393–5
Sidney, Sir Henry 337
Sidney, Mary 289–90, 452, 484
Sidney, Sir Philip 290, 471, 488 n. 19
  Defense of Poesy 289, 472, 547
Simon, Richard 251
Simpson, Edward 179, 179 n. 16, 181
Sixtus V (pope) 66, 123, 139
Sixtus of Siena, *Biblioteca sancta ex praecipius
    Catholicae ecclesiae auctoribus
    collecta* 138
Slayter, William, *Compleat Christian* 425
Sleidan, Johann 178–80
Smith, Henry (preacher) 15, 341 n. 43
Smith, Miles 21, 55, 60–2, 64, 66–9, 73–4, 80,
    378, 456, 458–9, 461, 467, 472, 480
Socinianism 244
Socrates 101, 217
sola scriptura 11, 20, 114, 134, 164, 167,
    172, 175, 209–10, 212, 243, 245, 262,
    266–8, 287, 292, 301, 384–5, 453, 519,
    533–4, 537
Solis, Virgil 582
Solomon (biblical king) 137, 189, 393, 547, 590
Song of Songs 26, 137, 139, 274–6, 278, 283,
    307–9, 410, 474, 484, 547
Sophocles 498, 502, 538
Soteriology 11, 166, 250
Souldiers Pocket Bible, The 146, 231
Southwell, Anne 452, 485, 488–97
Spanish Armada 374, 418, 432, 451–2
Speght, Rachel 484
Spelman, Sir John, *Case of Our Affaires* 422

Spencer, John, *Votive Angliae* 417–18

Spenser, Edmund, *The Fairie Queene* 451, 623, 627–8

Spinoza, Baruch 251

Stapleton, Thomas 355

Sternhold, Thomas 293–4
   The Whole Booke of Psalms 284, 293–5, 298–9

Stillingfleet, Edward 177, 249, 252, 434
   A Rational Account of the Grounds of Protestant Religion 252
   Scripture and Tradition Compared 435

Stoa, Johannes Franciscus Quintianus, *Theoandrathanatos* 505, 509

Stoics 165

Stokesley, John (bishop) 35

Stow, John 304–5

Strype, John 304

Stubbes, Katherine 452

Stubbs, John 359

Stukeley, William 192

Suarez, Francisco (Jesuit) 388–9

Sulzer, Heinrich 586

Sylvester, Joshuah 487–9, 548

Symmachus 124

Syncellus 177

Synod of Dort 144, 305

Tallis, Thomas 298

Talmud 144, 385

Tany, TheaurauJohn 232

Tarraconensi, Gabriele Garcia 505 n. 37

Tasso
   Discorsi del poema heroica 549
   Gerusalemme liberata 549

Taverner, Richard 137

Taylor, Jeremy 104, 115, 151, 240, 245–50, 253, 521, 604
   Discourse of the Liberty of Prophesying 246–51
   Ductor dubitantium, or, the Rule of Conscience 602–3
   The Golden Grove, or, a Manual of Daily Prayers and Litanies 245–6
   Of the Sacred Order, and Offices of Episcopacy 245
   Polemical and Moral Discourses 245, 247

The Rule and Exercises of Holy Living 245

Ten Commandments 140, 273–4, 279–80, 283, 335, 426, 489–91, 497, 650

Terence 500, 507

Tertullian, *De praescriptionibus adversus haereticos* 58–9

Test Acts (1673 and 1678) 436

Thaddaeus, Joannes, *The Reconciler of the Bible* 230

Theodotion 123–4, 126

Thorold, Thomas (Jesuit) 143, 242

Throckmorton, Job 143; *see also* Marprelate, Martin

Throckmorton, Rose 4

Thucydides 655

Titian 146

Toland, John 147, 251

Tombes, John, *Jehova iireh* 422–3

Tomson, Laurence 48–50, 89, 227, 635–6, 638

Topsell, Edward, *Historie of Foure-Footed Beastes* 475

Tostado, Alonso 134

tota scriptura 518

Tournes, Jean de, *Quadrins historiques de la Bible* 583

Tourneur, Cyril, *The Athiest's Tragedy* 617–18

Transubstantiation 97

Travers, Walter 166–7
   A Supplication Made to the Privie Counsell 166

Tremelius, Immanuel 92–3, 122, 162, 211–12, 215, 472, 547, 550

Trench, Richard Chenevrix (Archbishop of Dublin) 474

Trinitarians 100, 552

Trismegistus, Mercurius 168

Tunstall, Cuthbert (Bishop of London) 4, 31

Tyndale, William 3–4, 19–20, 24, 27–8, 31, 33–6, 44–5, 89–92, 95, 136, 209, 264, 342, 422, 437, 459, 470, 473, 475, 477, 481–2, 518, 531, 632

Tyrrell, James 395
   Patriacha non monarcha 393

Udall, Nicholas, *The First Tome or Volume of the Paraphrase of Erasmus upon the Newe Testamente* 20, 83

Un-Deceiver, The 415
Universalists 105
Urban VIII (pope) 361
Ussher, James 178, 179 n. 16, 181, 183–5, 189,
    192–4, 231, 336
    Historia dogmatica 192
Ussher, John 339
Ussher, Sir William 339, 341

Valeriano, Piero, Hieroglyphica 568
Valerius Maximus, Factorum et dictorum
    memorabilium 568
Valla, Lorenzo 511
Van Campen, Jan 83
Van Liesveldt, Jacob 579
Vatable, François 162, 471
Vaughan, Henry 14, 522, 547
Vaughan, Richard, 2nd Earl of Carbery 245
Vicars, John
    Discovery of the Rebels by J. V.,
        Prisoner 418
    Unholsome Henbane between Two Fragrant
        Roses 144
Vida, Marco Girolamo 547
    Christiad 547
Viret, Pierre (Bible translator) 41
Virgil 152, 215, 488, 550
    Aeneid 489, 496, 548
Visitation Articles, see Articles of Inquiry
Vettori, Pietro [Victorius] 502
Voltaire 200
Von Botzheim, Johann 584
Vossius, Gerardus 183–184
Vossius, Isaac 181, 183–6, 189, 191
    Dissertatio de vera aetate mundi 184
    De septuaginta interpretibus 184

Wagner, Fredericus 103
Wakefield, Robert 478
Wales 3, 200, 245, 444
Walker, Anthony 357
Wallington, Nehemiah 284
Walsh, Nicholas 336–7, 340
Walsingham, Sir Francis 5 n. 16, 49
Walton, Brian 226, 231–3, 251
Walton, Izaak 240
Walwyn, William (Leveller) 210, 397–8, 402,
    405, 407, 536

The Still and Soft Voice from the
    Scriptures 406
A Whisper in the Eare of Mr Thomas
    Edwards, Minister 406
Ward, Robert 141
Ward, Samuel 141
Warham, William (Archbishop of
    Canterbury) 28, 30–4
Warton, Thomas (clergyman) 145
Watkyns, Richard 34
Watson, John 30
Watson, Thomas 516
    Absalom 498, 516
Weever, John, An Agnus Dei 257
Wellhausen, Julius, Prolegomena 652
Welsh, John (preacher) 329
Wesley, John 151
Wesley, Susanna 14
Westminster Assembly of Divines 144–5,
    230–1, 326–7
Westminster Confession of Faith
    (1647) 144–5, 230, 234, 324
Westminster Directory for Public Worship
    (1645) 145, 325, 327–30
Wharton, Henry 192
Wheare, Degory 178
Whigs 239, 391, 429, 438
Whiston, William 189–90, 193
Whitaker, William 5 n. 16, 88, 91 n. 27,
    121, 356
    Ad Nicolai Sanderi demonstrationes
        quadraginta 85–6
    An Answere to a Certeine Booke, Written
        by M. William Rainolds 85, 93–4
Whitchurch, Edward (publisher) 137
Whitefield, George 318
White, Francis (preacher) 305 n. 11
Whitehall, Robert (poet) 145
Whitgift, John (Archbishop of
    Canterbury) 46, 142–3, 167, 352
Whitman, Walt 478
Whittingham, William (Bible translator) 40,
    90 n. 22, 227
Wickens, Robert, A Compleat and Perfect
    Concordance of the English Bible 230
Wickram, Georg 145 n. 43
Wildman, John (Leveller) 406
    Truths Triumph 406–7

William III 145, 369, 429–30, 433–5, 438, 442, 444–5
Wilson, Nicholas 31
Wilson, Thomas, *Jerichoes Down-Fall* 419
Winstanley, Gerrard (Digger) 12–13, 210, 397–8, 400–4, 407–10
Wisdom, Book of 132–5, 137–9, 141, 146, 165, 170, 278
Wither, George 86, 296–8
   Campo-musae 416
   Hymnes and Songs of the Church 298
Wode, Thomas 322
Wodrow, Robert (historian) 194, 327–8
Wolman, Richard 31
Wolseley, Charles 8
   The Unreasonableness of Atheism 614
Wolsey, Thomas (cardinal) 28, 30, 34
Woodward, John 191–2
Worse and Worse 425
worship
   private 2, 282, 294, 301

public 2, 28, 132, 231, 258–9, 275, 282, 291–6, 301, 319, 321–2, 326–7, 329
Wotton, Sir Henry 343
Writer, Clement 210, 238, 248–51
   Fides divina 248, 251
Wren, Christopher 178 n. 7
Württemburg Confession of Faith (1552) 139
Wyatt, Thomas (poet) 289
Wycliffe, John 20, 24, 31, 642, 654
Wycliffism 3, 24–5

Xenophon 92

Young, Patrick 118, 120, 122–9
   Catena 124–5, 129

Ziegler, Hieronymous 503
Zoroastrianism 216
Zovitius, Jacobus 503
Zuallart, Jean 202–3
Zwingli, Huldrych 58, 135, 292, 578

Lightning Source UK Ltd.
Milton Keynes UK
UKHW03f0629251018
331171UK00002B/4/P